MODERN
BUSINESS
LAW

MODERN BUSINESS LAW

Thomas W. Dunfee
University of Pennsylvania,
The Wharton School

Frank F. Gibson
Ohio State University

John D. Blackburn
Ohio State University

Douglas Whitman
University of Kansas

F. William McCarty
Western Michigan University

Bartley A. Brennan
Bowling Green State University

 RANDOM HOUSE BUSINESS DIVISION / NEW YORK

ipso facto
bifurcated
euthanasia

*To our students
from whom we have learned so much.*

First Edition
987654
Copyright © 1984 by Thomas W. Dunfee, Frank F. Gibson, John D.
Blackburn, Douglas Whitman, F. William McCarty, Bartley A.
Brennan

Library of Congress Cataloging in Publication Data
Main entry under title:

Modern business law.

  Includes index.
  1. Commercial law—United States. I. Dunfee, Thomas W.
KF889.M6 1984   346.73′07   83-24539
ISBN 0-394-32888-4   347.3067

Design by Jennie Nichols/Levavi & Levavi

Manufactured in the United States of America

Preface

Modern Business Law is designed for the business law courses of the 1980s. Emphasizing current developments, it surveys the major areas of the law that have an impact on the operation of business firms. These areas include the legal environment, contracts, commercial transactions, business organizations, property, and government regulation.

Based on our combined experience as classroom teachers, active practitioners, and business consultants, *Modern Business Law* features in every chapter major issues relevant to prospective business managers, including issues in such emerging fields as checks and electronic transfer, bankruptcy, securities, the FTC and consumer protection, and social responsibility and business ethics. Throughout the text, excerpts of court opinions from important cases are used to demonstrate the application of various rules of law to business problems.

Court opinions, in each chapter, are integrated directly into the text discussion, so that important corresponding legal issues can be analyzed and examined as they are introduced. Cases have been selected for the text on the basis of three criteria: (1) readability, (2) relevance to a major point or issue in the text, and (3) business context, or capacity to demonstrate the business application of a legal question. We have made an effort throughout the text to choose case excerpts that are neither too short—and therefore meaningless—nor too long—and therefore tedious for the student. The excerpting of the *Modern Business Law* cases to a manageable length, preserves their context, tone, and meaning while reducing them to appropriate proportions. In addition, case introductions to the cases, in a separate section and in a second color, are provided by the authors in order to help the student understand the background and impact of the cases.

AACSB curriculum standards affecting the direction of changes in the business law curriculum have been given careful attention in the development of *Modern Business Law*. These standards require that courses include:

> . . . a background of the economic and legal environment as it pertains to profit and/or nonprofit organizations, along with ethical considerations and social and political influences as they affect such organizations.

In an effort to be responsive to the main theme of this AACSB standard, *Modern Business Law* has included, in Part I, two separate chapters which discuss the legal system as a major societal institution, and two additional chapters covering business torts and crimes. In addition, there is also a separate chapter on corporate social responsibility, and four chapters, in Part IV, on various aspects of business regulation.

The primary emphasis of the text, however,

is on the traditional business law topics. *Modern Business Law* extensively covers Contracts, Chapters 5–14; Commercial Transactions, Chapters 15–24; Business Organizations, Chapters 25–32; and Property Law, Chapters 33–36. Within these areas of the law, materials were selected for their relevance to business practitioners. Underlying policy issues are highlighted, and chapter review problems based on actual cases to which the student is referred by specific citations, are provided at the end of each chapter as a means of stimulating class discussions.

In the design of the text and its supplements, attention was also given to pedagogical features helpful to both the professor and the student. For example, each case is not only integrated into the text discussion, but also introduced to the student in a separate section, and set off in a distinct typeface and second color, so that there is no confusion between the excerpt and the comments from the authors. A complete glossary of legal terms, a table of cases, and a detailed appendix are also included. The appendix provides students and faculty with such important information as the Uniform Commercial Code, the Uniform Partnership Act, the Uniform Limited Partnership Act, the 1983 Revised Model Business Corporation Act, and a Cross-Reference Table correlating this new act with the former MBCA.

We have also worked together to produce a thorough set of supplementary resource materials, which include a detailed instructor's manual, testbank, and updates on case opinions that have an impact on the text material. These are scheduled to be published on a regular and continuing basis to keep *Modern Business Law* as current as possible. In addition, a study guide prepared by Ray Catanzano of Nassau Community College, is also available with the text.

Many persons assisted in the preparation of this text. We are grateful to John E. Adamson, Southwest Missouri State University; Glenn E. Droegemueller, University of Northern Colorado; Susan Grady, University of Massachusetts; Beverly Hunt, Thomas M. Cooley Law School; James Jackman, Oklahoma State University; Elliott Klayman, Ohio State University; Glen E. Laughlin, Oklahoma State University; Michael A. Mass, American University; Nicholas Ordway, University of Texas at Arlington; Lawrence W. Ross, University of Oregon; and Edwin W. Tucker, University of Connecticut–Storrs, who provided many helpful comments and suggestions. We would like to thank Elliot Goldstein, Esq., chairman of the Committee on Corporate Laws for his assistance in obtaining permission to reprint excerpts of the Revised Model Business Corporations Act.

We also wish to thank Barbara Gladman, Helen Horn, Patricia Leas, and Beverly Schoenberg for their able assistance in preparing the manuscript. We are grateful to Paul Donnelly for his support of the project, and to the incredibly competent staff at Random House: Molly Frances, our Developmental Editor; Anne Mahoney, the Developmental Editor who helped us put together the supplements; Susan Israel, our Manuscript Editor, and their associates at Random House, who were a delight to work with. We also wish to acknowledge the support of Sandy and of the Irish Mafia: Kelly, Sean, and Shannon Elizabeth.

Thomas W. Dunfee
Frank F. Gibson
John D. Blackburn
Douglas Whitman
F. William McCarty
Bartley A. Brennan

Contents in Brief

Contents

PART I
LEGAL ENVIRONMENT OF BUSINESS

Nature and Functions of Law and Legal Systems

T his chapter is about law and legal systems. Think for a moment about the meaning of these two terms. They are very significant terms; yet they are hard to define precisely. In fact, we could give a number of quite different definitions for each term, and each definition might be correct in a given context. One reason for the seemingly ambiguous nature of the words *law* and *legal systems* is that each encompasses a wide variety of ideas and activities. This chapter discusses a few of these many ideas and activities and describes some of the immediate sources of law.

LEGAL SYSTEMS

Most of us would agree that human beings are social creatures and that we depend upon each other in countless ways. This interdependence is the result of both biological and psychological needs; it is also the key to survival in a world in which nature only grudgingly provides the requirements for subsistence. Difficult problems, however, arise from interdependence and community living—especially among organisms that think and aspire. Over the centuries, appreciable amounts of mankind's effort have gone into providing solutions for these problems. A universally adopted approach to the problems of social organization is the development of a legal system.

A legal system makes possible the peaceful solution of some of society's serious problems by establishing processes that govern and regulate the conduct of the society's members. These processes and the structure in which they operate are characterized by orderliness and formality. Within the legal system are numerous subsystems. These include the courts, the legislative bodies, the law enforcement agencies, and the practicing bar, as well as various types of administrative boards, commissions, and departments. The component processes and structures that make up the legal system will be discussed in Chapter 2.

Because of the many variations in conduct resulting from differences in the environments in which they live, people experience a wide variety of problems. *Matter of Quinlan,* the case that follows, illustrates a legal effort to solve a particularly difficult problem that has arisen in our technological society—that is, the use of life-sustaining apparatus for individuals who are no longer sentient.

Matter of Quinlan
Supreme Court of New Jersey
355 A.2d 647 (1976)

On the night of April 15, 1975, Karen Ann Quinlan, for unknown reasons, ceased breathing for at least two fifteen-minute periods. After some ineffectual mouth-to-mouth resuscitation, she was taken to a hospital in a coma. For many weeks Karen remained comatose, surviving with the support of life-sustaining mechanisms. Medical consensus was that she existed at a primitive reflex level with no awareness of anything or anyone around her and that she had no chance of emerging from this condition.

Due to Karen's condition, Joseph Quinlan, her father, asked the court to declare her incompetent and to appoint him as guardian of her person and property. He also asked for the power to authorize the discontinuance of extraordinary procedures allegedly sustaining her life, since no hope existed of eventual recovery.

Mr. Quinlan's requests were opposed by Karen's doctors, the hospital, the county prosecutor, and the state of New Jersey. The lower court granted him guardianship of her property; however, guardianship over her person and authorization to remove the life-sustaining apparatus were denied. Mr. Quinlan appealed.

Hughes, C. J.

1. Was the trial court correct in denying the specific relief requested by plaintiff, that is, authorization to terminate the life-supporting apparatus, on the case presented to him?
2. Was the court correct in withholding letters of guardianship from the plaintiff?

The Right of Privacy

It is the issue of the constitutional right of privacy that has given us most concern, in the exceptional circumstances of this case. Here a loving parent, *qua* parent and raising the rights of his incompetent and profoundly damaged daughter, probably irreversibly doomed to no more than a biologically vegetative remnant of life, is before the court. He seeks authorization to abandon specialized technological procedures which can only maintain for a time a body having no potential for resumption or continuance of other than a "vegetative" existence.

The claimed interests of the State in this case are essentially the preservation and sanctity of human life and defense of the right of the physician to administer medical treatment according to his best judgment. In this case the doctors say that removing Karen from the respirator will conflict with their professional judgment. The plaintiff answers that Karen's present treatment serves only a maintenance function; that the respirator cannot cure or improve her condition, but at best can only prolong her inevitable slow deterioration and death; and that the interests of the patient, as seen by her surrogate, or guardian, must be evaluated by the court as predominant. . . . Plaintiff's distinction is significant. . . . We think that the State's interest . . . weakens and the individual's right to privacy grows as the degree of bodily invasion increases and the prognosis dims. Ultimately there comes a point at which the individual's rights overcome the State interest. It is for that reason that we believe Karen's choice, if she were competent to make it, would be vindicated by the law. Her prognosis is extremely poor,—she will never resume cognitive life. And the bodily invasion is very great,—she requires 24-hour intensive nursing care, antibiotics, the assistance of a respirator, a catheter and feeding tube.

. . . [W]e have concluded that Karen's right of privacy may be asserted on her behalf by her guardian under the peculiar circumstances here present.

The Medical Factor

Having declared the substantive legal basis upon which plaintiff's rights as representative of Karen must be deemed predicated, we face . . . the assertion on behalf of defendants that our premise unwarrantably offends prevailing medical standards. . . .

> The nature, extent and duration of care by societal standards is the responsibility of a physician. The morality and conscience of our society places this responsibility in the hands of the physician. What justification is there to remove it from the control of the medical profession and place it in the hands of the courts?

Such notions as to the distribution of responsibility, heretofore generally entertained, should however neither impede this Court in deciding matters clearly justiciable nor preclude a re-examination by the Court as to underlying human values and rights. Determinations as to these must, in the ultimate, be responsive not only to the concepts of medicine but also to the common moral judgment of the community at large. In the later respect the Court has a nondelegable judicial responsibility.

Put in another way, the law, equity and justice must not themselves quail and be helpless in the face of modern technological marvels presenting questions hitherto unthought of. Where a Karen Quinlan, or a parent, or a doctor, or a hospital, or a State seeks the process and response of a court, it must answer with its most informed conception of justice in the previously unexplored circumstances presented to it. That is its obligation and we are here fulfilling it, for the actors and those having an interest in the matter should not go without remedy.

In regard to the foregoing it is pertinent that we consider the impact on the standards both of the civil and criminal law as to medical liability and the new technological means of sustaining life irreversibly damaged.

The modern proliferation of substantial malpractice litigation and the less frequent but even more unnerving possibility of criminal sanctions would seem, for it is beyond human nature to suppose otherwise, to have bearing on the practice and standards as they exist. . . .

. . . [T]here must be a way to free physicians, in the pursuit of their healing vocation, from possible contamination by self-interest or self-protection concerns which would inhibit their independent medical judgments for the well-being of their dying patients. We would hope that this opinion might be serviceable to some degree in ameliorating the professional problems under discussion.

[The court at this point suggests that the medical profession consider the creation of Ethics Committees to aid attending physicians by sharing the responsibility for making ethical decisions in cases comparable to that of Karen Quinlan.]

Alleged Criminal Liability

Having concluded that there is a right of privacy that might permit termination of treatment in the circumstances of this case, we turn to consider the relationship of the exercise of that right to the criminal law. . . . We conclude that there would be no criminal homicide in the circumstances of this case. We believe, first, that the ensuing death would not be homicide but rather expiration from existing natural causes. Secondly, even if it were to be regarded as homicide, it would not be unlawful.

These conclusions rest upon definitional and constitutional bases. The termination of treatment pursuant to the right of privacy is, within the limitations of this case, *ipso facto* lawful. . . . There is a real and in this case determinative distinction between the unlawful taking of the life of another and the ending of artificial life-support systems as a matter of self-determination.

The Guardianship of the Person

The trial judge bifurcated the guardianship, as we have noted, refusing to appoint Joseph Quinlan to be guardian of the person and limiting his guardianship to that of the property of his daughter.

. . . The court felt . . . that the obligation to concur in the medical care and treatment of his daughter would be a source of anguish to him and would distort his "decision-making processes." We disagree, for we sense from the whole record before us that while Mr. Quinlan feels a natural grief, and understandably sorrows because of the tragedy which has befallen his daughter, his strength of purpose and character far out-weighs these sentiments and qualifies him eminently for guardianship of the person as well as the property of his daughter. . . .

DECLARATORY RELIEF

We thus arrive at the formulation of the declaratory relief which we have concluded is appropriate to this case. . . . [W]e are transferring to the plaintiff as guardian the choice of the attending physician. . . . [W]e herewith declare the following affirmative relief. . . . Upon the concurrence of the guardian and family of Karen, should the responsible attending physicians conclude that there is no reasonable possibility of Karen's ever emerging from her present comatose condition to a cognitive, sapient state . . . , they shall consult with the hospital "Ethics Committee" . . . of the institution in which Karen is then hospitalized. If that consultative body agrees, . . . the present life-support system may be withdrawn and said action shall be without any civil or criminal liability therefore on the part of any participant, whether guardian, physician, hospital or others. . . .

Modified and remanded.

CASE NOTES

1. Karen Quinlan confounded medical experts by surviving after the removal of the life-sustaining mechanism. As of this writing she was still alive; however, she had not emerged from her comatose condition and no indications existed that she would.

2. Publicity related to the Quinlan case and similar situations sparked appreciable interest in euthanasia and the "living will." Although numerous bills dealing with euthanasia have been introduced in state legislatures since the 1930s, few have been seriously considered. The majority of the proposals would permit passive euthanasia, the omission of a life-extending act. An example would be a decision not to put a patient on a respirator. All of these proposed bills require that a written request be made by the patient. In almost none is there a requirement that the patient's request be honored. The final decision is made by the attending physician. Also, as any request must be signed by the patient, a decision for a person in Karen Quinlan's condition would be precluded unless made prior to becoming comatose. The living will attempts to solve this problem.

   A living will is a document directing one's physician not to take heroic or artificial means to keep the signer alive if there comes a time when no reasonable expectation of recovery from physical or mental disability exists. Although these documents are not legally binding upon physicians, they have been signed by thousands of people. Most living wills are drafted in a manner that contemplates a decision by both physician and family if the person is physically or mentally unable to decide.

   In 1976 California became the first state to enact specific legislation recognizing the right of a person to make a living will. The legislation, however, does not require a physician to honor the directive.

   At present the legal status of a physician who withholds treatment at the request of the patient is not clear. Legal experts believe that the probability of successful criminal or civil action against a physician for withholding treatment is reduced if the physician has followed the requests contained in a living will. In addition to legal questions, ethical, philosophical, and religious considerations complicate decisions involving euthanasia and a living will.

SPECIFIC TASKS OF LEGAL SYSTEMS

Early in our study, we need to consider in detail some of the specific tasks of the legal system as it helps resolve some of the hard questions that society faces. At the same time we must remember that other social institutions play important roles in solving some of these same problems. In spite of this, at least in the Western world, organized societies appear to rely most heavily upon legal systems to work out solutions to these problems.

Maintain Order

Probably the most important function of the legal system, certainly the most frequently articulated, is the maintenance of order within the community. Laws define the ramifications of relationships within a society so that people can live together with a minimum of friction and a maximum of opportunity to attain their physiological and psychological needs. The absence of order requires individuals to spend inordinate amounts of time and energy dealing with issues that might disrupt the community or groups within it. A means for orderly solution of social issues is especially important in an era such as the present when technology causes rapid and extensive changes in people's lives. *Matter of Quinlan* illustrates this need.

Provide a Forum for Settling Disputes

An important means by which society maintains order is by providing a forum in which individuals can settle their disputes. Without such a forum the quarrels of individuals become family, clan, or tribal problems. Frequently a group takes some form of violent action that calls forth a violent counterresponse from the individual attacked and his or her supporters. Violence continues, and in many instances no final settlement is reached until the parties and their supporters are exhausted. A principal role of the legal system even in very primitive cultures is to provide some authoritative institutional process for settling disputes.

Protect Expectations

Another task of the legal system is to ensure a measure of predictability in societal relations. For life to have meaning—in fact, for people just to survive—they must know that the agreed-upon or anticipated consequences of acting in a particular manner will generally be as expected. For example, when tenants sign a twelve-month lease for an apartment, their expectations of a place to live for at least a year are reinforced by knowledge that the legal system will provide a remedy if the owner— or anyone else—interferes with their occupancy. At the same time, the owner's expectation of a certain income for the year is supported by the existence of a functioning legal system. When a consumer buys a ladder, the legal system reinforces an expectation that the user will not suffer injury because the ladder was made defectively. Of course, no law can guarantee that a person will not be injured. But the law provides compensation for injury caused by a defect and thus indirectly encourages the producer to be careful in the manufacturing process.

Maintain Established Political Authority

In almost all societies another clearly discernible function of the legal system is to maintain the dominant political authority. Laws punishing members of the society for treason are among those that have as their purpose perpetuating the established order. Authorities use to advantage the many sanctions that the legal system provides for controlling behavior. Although sanctions operate within most group relationships, the organized sanctions of the legal system, supported by political authority, are the most extensive and effective. The most potent sanctions—such as the taking of life—frequently are used to protect the existing political structure.

Bring About Social Change

Although maintaining order, providing a forum for resolving disputes, ensuring a degree of predictability, and preserving the existing political order have been important functions of even relatively primitive legal systems, legal systems also have been used to fulfill other societal needs and to help the community attain other objectives. As an important agent for accomplishing change, the legal system is effective because of the many sanctions that it can employ and because its elements ("the courts" and "the law of the land") are impersonal but respected powers that have public support. Antitrust, civil rights, and environmental protection statutes are examples of the legal system operating to accomplish social change.

NATURE OF LAW

Although the influence of law on society varies according to time and place, legal institutions have played an important role in most cultures. Through the ages, men and women have attempted to explain the nature of law and the legal order. These explanations have attempted to answer questions about matters such as the sources of law, the extent of the individual's legal obligations, the justice and adequacy of the legal system, and the social and economic costs of operating the system.

For many reasons, no single explanation has been generally accepted. A familiarity with each explanation that has been offered is important for understanding the legal environment. Ideas inherent in each theory are part of a community's value structure, and in each there appears to be some validity. For example, the belief that all people have certain rights and that the fundamental task of law is to strive to attain these rights might influence an administrator to behave positively when faced with a decision involving the civil rights of an employee. On the other hand, an administrator convinced that the essence of law is pure political power might well react differently when faced with the same civil rights problem.

At the present time opinions in Western society about the nature of law can be divided into two basic approaches. One school of thought considers law to be ordained by nature and in some sense independent of human disposition. The other approach analyzes law and legal institutions as these actually exist—created by and regulating members of the community. The first concept postulates a core of ideas that stem from a reality over and above the material world. These higher ideas exist independently of human experience. The term that generally has been used to designate this concept is *natural law.* The alternative line of thought denies any reality except that experienced through the senses and argues that existence can be comprehended only upon the basis of observable facts. In legal philosophy this empirical approach is referred to generally as *positivism.*

Following the Byrn case (below), which illustrates natural law and legal positivism, the text discusses two additional philosophies of law—sociological jurisprudence and legal realism. Both are empirical in nature since they are based upon observation of human experience. Like those who expound natural law and positivism, those who promulgate the ideas and concepts of sociological jurisprudence and legal realism are striving to understand and improve the legal system.

Natural Law

To understand the natural law philosophy as it relates to modern society, rules of law must be classified. First, there are laws of convenience. These are rules that are adopted merely because it is convenient for society to have some position. For these laws justice is in no way involved until the rule is adopted. A good example would be laws that require vehicles to travel on a particular side of the road. On the other hand, there are many laws that deal with conditions and situations universal among men relating to fundamental rights and behavior. These are the concerns of natural law. Examples would be laws that protect human freedom and dignity.

Many variations of the natural law theme have existed throughout the ages, but underlying each is the idea that certain higher principles of right and justice exist for all people independent of both culture and time. Examples of these principles would be the rights of "life, liberty, and the pursuit of happiness," which the Declaration of Independence states are man's inalienable rights. Men and women as moral and rational creatures must strive to discover these principles and, through law and legal institutions, attempt to secure them for mankind. Because of this emphasis upon the existence of a body of higher law that man-made law must attempt to emulate and by which man-made laws are judged, this body of thought about the essential nature of law has often been described as the "ought-to-be" or "ought" school.

Natural law concepts are fundamental to the result in the Quinlan Case. In its opinion, the court weighs the state's interest in preserving life against Karen's right to order the termination of the life-sustaining equipment. The court concludes that, as bodily invasion increases and prognosis for recovery dims, the individual's right to privacy outweighs any statutory directive promulgated by the state to sustain life. In so concluding, the court recognizes a higher law than that of the state.

Legal Positivism

When attempting to explain the essence of legal order, many people contend that any sensible explanation must be based upon what actually exists, not what ought to be. These people deliberately divorce their investigations of law and legal institutions from intuitive moral and ethical postulates. Their methods, based upon observation, are scientific and empirical as contrasted with the intuitive and metaphysical approach of natural law analysis.

The legal scholars who developed this type of analysis in the late eighteenth century regarded as law only those rules adopted by the state that obligated citizens generally to do or refrain from doing particular acts. Laws were a species of commands emanating from the sovereign. Justice consisted of the unbiased application of the laws. Society had a duty to institute a legal system clearly and formally developed on logical principles.

Because of their focus on the analysis of existing laws and institutions to improve the operation of the legal system, advocates of this approach have been referred to as the *analytical* school. Others have named them the *imperative* school because they emphasized law as the command of the sovereign.

Today, there continue to be many who contend that law and legal institutions are nothing more than operative rules backed by the political power of the state. At the same time, the analysis of legal systems based upon observation of what exists has become the basis for a variety of new theories about legal systems. In the case that follows, the alternative concepts of analytical positivism and natural law are the bases for majority and dissenting opinions.

Byrn v. New York City Health & Hospitals Corporation
Court of Appeals of New York
31 N.Y. 2d 194 (1972)

Byrn (plaintiff-appellant), as guardian ad litem for unborn children, sought a judgment declaring the 1970 New York abortion "liberalization" statute unconstitutional. Plaintiff obtained a temporary injunction to restrain New York City Hospital (defendant-appellee) from "performing any abortional acts" except where the mother's life was endangered. The appellate court vacated the injunction and remanded the case to the trial court to enter a declaratory judgment sustaining the validity of the statute. Plaintiff appealed.

Breitel, Judge

The issue, a novel one in the courts of law, is whether children in embryo are and must be recognized as legal persons or entities entitled under the State and Federal Constitutions to a right to life. . . .

The . . . debate . . . turns on whether a human entity, conceived but not yet born, is and must be recognized as a person in the law. If so, it is argued that the person is immediately subsumed under the class entitled to constitutional protection, it being assumed that an entity if treated anywhere in the law as a person must be so treated —for all purposes. . . . Conceptually, whether in philosophy or in religious doctrine, and the doctrine is not confined to any one religion, a conceived child may be regarded as a person, albeit at a fetal stage. It is not true, however, that the legal order necessarily corresponds to the natural order. That it should or ought is a fair argument, but the argument does not make its conclusion the law. It does not make it the law anymore than that the law by recognizing a corporation or a partnership as persons, or according property rights to unconceived children, make these "natural" nonentities facts in the natural order.

When the proposition is reduced to this simple form, the difficulty of the problem is lessened. What is a legal person is for the law, including, of course, the Constitution, to say, which simply means that upon according legal personality to a thing the law affords it the rights and privileges of a legal person. . . . Whether the law should accord legal personality is a policy question which in most instances devolves on the Legislature, subject again of course to the Constitution as it has been "legally" rendered. That the legislative action may be wise or unwise, even unjust and violative of principles. beyond the law, does not change the legal issue or how it is to be resolved. The point is that it is a policy determination whether legal personality should attach and not a question of biological or "natural" correspondence. . . .

There are, then, real issues in this litigation, but they are not legal or justiciable. They are issues outside the law unless the Legislature should provide otherwise. The Constitution does not confer or require legal personality for the unborn; the Legislature may, or it may do something less, as it does in limited abortion statutes, and provide some protection far short of conferring legal personality.

Accordingly, the order of the Appellate Division should be affirmed without costs.

Burke, Judge *(dissenting)*

The majority opinion states the issue as: "whether the law should accord legal personality is a policy question which in most instances devolves on the Legislature, subject again of course to the Constitution as it has been 'legally' rendered."

This argument was not only made by Nazi lawyers and judges at Nuremberg, but also is advanced today by the Soviets in Eastern Europe. It was and is rejected by most western world lawyers and judges because it conflicts with natural justice and is, in essence, irrational. To equate the judicial deference to the wiseness of a Legislature in a local zoning case with the case of the destruction of a child in embryo which is conceded to be "human" and "is unquestionably alive" is an acceptance of the thesis that the "State is supreme," and that "live human beings" have no inalienable rights in this country. . . . The late Chief Judge Lehman once wrote of these rights: "The Constitution is misread by those who say that these rights are created by the Constitution. The men who wrote the Constitution did not doubt that these rights existed before the nation was created and are dedicated by God's word. By the Constitution, these rights were placed beyond the power of Government to destroy." . . . Human beings are not merely creatures of the State, and by reason of that fact, our laws should protect the unborn from those who would take his life for purposes of comfort, convenience, property or peace of mind rather than sanction his demise. . . .

The Attorney-General argues that the legislative determination in choosing between the competing values involved herein is a *value judgment* committed to the legislative process of government, not to the discretion of the judiciary. Furthermore, it is argued that there is a legitimate State interest in a woman's right of privacy and in the undesirable effect of unwanted children upon society. Upon scrutiny, these arguments are not persuasive, and the legislation cannot stand for two reasons—it is irrational and unconstitutional.

The more telling fact than the present legislation's irrationality is its unconstitutionality. The unconstitutionality stems from its inherent conflict with the Declaration of Independence, the basic instrument which gave birth to our democracy. The Declaration has the force of law and the constitutions of the United States and of the various States must harmonize with its tenets. The Declaration when it proclaimed "We hold these truths to be self-evident, that all men are created equal, that they are endowed by their Creator with certain unalienable Rights, that among these are Life, Liberty and the pursuit of Happiness" restated the natural law. It was intended to serve as a perpetual reminder that rules, legislators, and Judges were without power to deprive human beings of their rights. . . .

We began our legal life as a Nation and a State with the guarantee that these were inalienable rights that come not from the State but from an external source of authority superior to the State which authority regulated our inalienable liberties and with which our laws and Constitutions must now conform. That authority alone establishes the norms which test the validity of State legislation. It also tests the Constitutions and the United Nations Convention against genocide which forbids any Nation or State to classify any group of living human beings as fit subjects for annihilation. In sum, there is *THE* law which forbids such expediency. It is the inalienable right to life in the nature of the child embryo who is "a human" and is "a living being." Inalienable means that it is incapable of being surrendered. Thus, the butchering of a foetus under the present law is inherently wrong, as it is an illegal interference with the life of a human being of nature. . . .

The Appellate Division arrived at the obvious contradiction that even though the foetus is a human being with "a separate life from the moment of conception," it need not be considered a person under the Fifth Amendment. Again the Appellate Division adopted the theory that the State is supreme and free to degrade the inalienable rights of human beings which were not given to them by the State and cannot be diminished nor taken away by the State. . . .

To sum up, conception can be legally avoided—adoption opportunities are enormous—abortion legislation except in rare medical cases is neither necessary, humanly acceptable, legal nor constitutional.

Accordingly the order of the Appellate Division should be reversed and Chapter 127 of Laws of 1970 be declared unconstitutional.

[The dissenting opinion of Judge Scileppi is omitted.]

CASE NOTE

The leading case dealing with abortion is Roe v. Wade, 401 U.S. 113 (1973). In this case the U.S. Supreme Court determined that a Texas statute making abortion a crime was unconstitutional. In its opinion the Court recognized the existence of a constitutional right to privacy broad enough to encompass a woman's decision to terminate her pregnancy. On the other hand, the Court maintained that the state has a legitimate interest in protecting potential human life. At some point in pregnancy the state's interest becomes sufficiently compelling to sustain regulation of the abortion decision. In Akron Center for Reproductive Health v. City of Akron 51 L.W. 4767 (June 15, 1983), the point was determined to be the second trimester.

Sociological Jurisprudence

The sociological theory is the principal twentieth-century effort to explain the nature of law and analyze its underlying principles. This theory is based on the concept that the legal system is but one element of the social structure, albeit an important one. The sources of law are found in the activities of society. Economic, political, and social pressures determine what the legal system does and how it operates. For example, industrialization in Western Europe and the United States during the late nineteenth century resulted in appreciable social turmoil. Society in both Europe and the United States reacted to this turmoil by using laws and legal institutions to provide remedies for many social needs. Social security, workmen's compensation, and unemployment insurance, as well as innovative forms of governmental organization such as the administrative agency, provided at least partial cures for some of the problems.

Because the legal system is closely integrated with the social structure, it is important to clearly understand the nuances of this relationship. This can best be accomplished by empirical observation of actual laws in operation in society, which is the real source of law. The twentieth-century empiricists were interested only peripherally in analyzing rules of law. They rejected as unimportant relationships between law and logic and saw little truth in the natural law doctrine of absolute principles of universal validity.

Several important concepts that appreciably influence twentieth-century legal thought result from the focus that sociological legal theorists placed upon interactions between law and society. They recognized that society is dynamic—changing for better or worse with a variety of interests that exist in continually differing patterns. So, too, they accepted the idea that the legal structure changes to reflect what is taking place in the society at large.

At the same time they recognized that the legal system as a part of the social system influences the entire social fabric. This led to the belief that the many conflicting interests—public and private, group and individual—can be balanced through properly functioning legal institutions. Thus the legal system can be used to channel behavior in a manner that will secure the maximum of human wants with a minimum of friction. The potential existing within the legal system for this adjustment of human wants by balancing interests is often referred to as *social engineering.*

Roscoe Pound, who for many years was the principal American exponent of social engineering, advocated the identification of various social interests that potentially are to be secured and protected by law. As these interests are often in conflict, the task of legislators and judges in carrying out their legal roles is to weigh and balance the interests in a manner that will secure the maximum benefit for soci-

ety. In order to accomplish this effectively, in-depth studies of social problems are necessary background for legislation and litigation.

Social Control

Social engineering and much of the resultant legislation of the last half century take advantage of the effectiveness of the legal system as a means of social control. In fact, many authorities look upon social control as the chief function of any legal system.

When the law is discussed as a means of social control, the term is not used in the sense of regimentation. It is used to indicate methods of influencing individual behavior. Society employs numerous methods to influence behavior. They may be asserted consciously or unconsciously, and they include both force and ideas. The ideas are frequently represented by symbols such as flags, songs, or documents. Pressures may be asserted by organizations such as schools, churches, labor unions, or families.

Political and legal institutions are among society's most effective means of asserting social control. The legal system backed by government has available the most formidable coercive pressures. It can deprive a person of property, liberty, even life itself. At the same time government and the legal system are often closely allied with highly respected—even revered—ideas such as "love of country" and, in much of the Western world, the "rule of law."

Legal Realism

Legal realism is an offshoot of the sociological school. Both see the law and legal institutions as reflections of economic, political, and social influences operating in an organized society, and both are concerned with the functions of law. The major difference appears to be that most of the legal realists are more concerned with how the legal system operates than with the relationships between law and society.

The legal realist argues that law is determined by the actual behavior of judges and lawyers as well as officials such as sheriffs, police officers, and others involved in the operation of the system. Realists are skeptical and cynical about the value or even the existence of a unified legal structure, the basis of which is the formal rule of law. Rules are unsatisfactory because society is always in a state of flux. Reality lies in the manner in which legal officials act.

Although legal realism has no unified program, one objective of many realists is to expand knowledge of the operative legal system by observation of what actually occurs. They believe that it is only with this expanded knowledge applied to improve legal techniques that a successful assault upon the problems of the system is possible. For example, some realists have paid particular attention in their examination of the judicial system to factors that influence the decisions of appellate judges; others have been concerned with the uncertainties that exist in the trial courts because of difficulties involved in determining the actual facts in a controversy. By these observations the realists hope to guide lawyers and litigants in predicting the outcome of legal problems and trends taking place within society.

SOURCES OF LAW

In trying to understand the legal environment, people need to know some of the ideas that exist about the nature of law and legal systems. Most people, however, appear more interested in determining what particular laws are and where law can be found. One of the prevailing myths accepted by many is that all laws are found in nicely indexed, officially published books of statutes. All a person has to do to learn about a law is to find the correct page in the right book, and the law will be there in clear black letters. The following sections dispel this misconception and introduce the various sources of law.

The sources of law discussed here are not the underlying sources of law such as the Judeo-Christian religious heritage or the mores and traditions of ethnic groups often reflected in the laws of a particular legal system. Instead, the sources that the individual must consult to determine what the law is are presented together with the application of these sources in particular cases.

JUDICIAL LAW

A distinguishing feature of Anglo-American law is its reliance upon previously decided cases as a primary source of law. For many centuries judges and lawyers have looked for past similar cases to determine what the law is in a particular situation. Reliance upon judicial decisions, known as case law or common law, is based in part on the concept of stare decisis. Stare decisis, which is Latin for "to abide by or to adhere to decided cases," reflects the policy that, once a court applies a particular principle of law to a certain set of facts, that same legal principle will govern all future cases in which the facts are substantially the same.

Stare Decisis

The major problem in applying the doctrine of stare decisis arises because there are often conflicting precedents that can be analogized to the case under consideration. Opposing attorneys will argue that the facts of the present case are similar to those of cases in which different results were reached.

For example, consider a tort case involving a suit by a paying spectator at a recreation league hockey game in a municipal rink who is injured by a hockey stick flying into the stands after a player swings at a puck. Let's assume the state is one in which the statutory or common law decisions indicate that a city, as an agency of the sovereign state, is immune from suit if it is engaged in a governmental function but is not immune and can be held liable if it is engaged in a proprietary or businesslike function. The attorney for the spectator will research previous cases. He or she may find a case in which another city's operation of a municipal football stadium was found to be a businesslike operation, and thus the city could be sued and held liable for negligent operation of the stadium. On the other hand, the city attorney may find a previous case in which a city's operation of a municipal park system, including baseball diamonds, was held to be a part of the recreation program of the city, for the benefit of its citizens, and not a businesslike operation.

Which of those precedent cases would apply to the operation of a hockey rink? Would it make a difference who could use the rink? Does it matter if the city charged admission or made a profit on the operation of the rink? Is it relevant if there are privately owned rinks in or near the city? What basis for comparison or contrast would you find important?

Factual Distinction. Even if a statement in a prior case is considered to be precedent for subsequent cases, the facts of a later case may be different from those of the prior case. Even if a similar set of facts is presented in two cases, the legal issues of one case may differ from those previously considered. Thus the problem of determining whether a hockey rink owned and operated by the city is being run as a "governmental function" or as a "business enterprise" presents different facts from the problem of determining the same question for a city baseball field, park, or football area. While the legal issues in the two cases are the same, significant future distinctions regarding the sport or recreational activity certainly could exist. For example, there might be differences in the degree of supervision exercised by the city over those using the facilities or in the existence of alternative and competing private enterprises engaged in the same activity.

When major factual distinctions exist between a case under consideration and a supposed precedent, the cases are said to be distinguished. Stare decisis does not apply to cases that can be distinguished from the relevant precedents.

Changed Conditions. On occasion courts do refuse to follow previous decisions, even though such decisions are based on similar facts, because conditions have changed significantly. The changes may involve new technology or novel economic, social, or political circumstances. An example of a change of conditions is illustrated by the case of *Flagiello v. Pennsylvania Hospital*. Note the comments of both the majority and the dissenting opinion as to the effect of stare decisis on their decisions. As you read the case, look for the various reasons influencing the majority decision.

Flagiello v. Pennsylvania Hospital

Supreme Court of Pennsylvania

208 A.2d 193 (1965)

While Mary Flagiello (plaintiff-appellant) was a patient in Pennsylvania Hospital (defendant-appellee), she fell because of the negligence of two hospital employees. In falling she fractured her right ankle. This injury was entirely unrelated to the ailment which brought her into the hospital.

The broken ankle necessitated further hospital and medical care. As a result, Mary Flagiello and her husband brought suit against the hospital for the additional medical expense, pain, and suffering as well as impairment of earning power.

The hospital moved that their action be dismissed, asserting that under Pennsylvania law a charitable hospital was not responsible for the negligent acts of its employees. The lower court granted the motion and plaintiffs appealed.

Musmanno, Judge

The hospital has not denied that its negligence caused Mrs. Flagiello's injuries. It merely announces that it is an eleemosynary institution, and, therefore, owed no duty of care to its patient. It declares in effect that it can do wrong and still not be liable in damages to the person it has wronged. It thus urges a momentous exception to the generic proposition that in law there is no wrong without a remedy.

On what basis then may a hospital, which expects and receives compensation for its services, demand of the law that it be excused from responding in damages for injuries tortiously inflicted by its employees on paying patients? The hospital . . . replies to that question with various answers, some of which are: it is an ancient rule that charitable hospitals have never been required to recompense patients who have been injured through negligence of their employees; the rule of *stare decisis* forbids that charitable hospitals be held liable . . . ; if the rule of charitable immunity is to be discarded, this must be done by the State Legislature. . . .

We have seen how originally charitable hospitals devoted all their energies, resources, and time to caring for indigent patients. Today this has changed almost completely. In 1963, the fees received from patients in the still designated charitable hospitals throughout Pennsylvania constituted 90.9% of the total income of the hospitals.

But conceding that it could not operate without its paying patients the defendant hospital still objects to being categorized with business establishments because, it says, the law of charitable immunity is so deeply imbedded in our law and is of such ancient origin that it can only be extirpated by legislative enactment.

Each court which has upheld the immunity rule has relied for its authority on a previous decision or decisions, scarcely ever placing the subject for study on the table of self-asserting justice. . . .

In the early part of the twentieth century, however, some cracks began to show in the . . . edifice, and then, in 1942, Judge Rutledge (later Justice of the Supreme Court of the United States) of the United States Court of Appeals for the District of Columbia revealed in perhaps the most searching, analytical, and penetrating opinion on the subject up to that time, that the charity immunity doctrine was built on a foundation of sand. As one reads and reflects on that opinion (*Georgetown College* v. *Hughes*), he is forced to the irresistible conclusion that the immunity doctrine began in error, lifted its head in fallacy and climbed to its shaky heights only because few dared to question whether charity was really charity.

England, which is supposed to have launched the doctrine, abandoned it before it ever really set out on an authoritative voyage, and does not accept it today. Nor do Australia, Canada and New Zealand. In the United States, at least twenty-four states have wholly discarded the rule and fourteen other states have modified its application. . . .

If havoc and financial chaos were inevitably to follow the abrogation of the immunity doctrine, as the advocates for its retention insist, this would certainly have become apparent in the states where that doctrine is no longer a defense. But neither the defendant hospital nor the Hospital Association of Pennsylvania has submitted any evidence of catastrophe in the states where charitable hospitals are tortiously liable.

The appellee and the *amicus curiae* insist that if the charity immunity doctrine is to undergo mutation, the only surgeon capable of performing the operation is the Legislature. We have seen, however, that the controverted rule is not the creation of the Legislature. This court fashioned it, and, what it put together, it can dismantle. . . .

Of course, the precedents here recalled do not justify a light and casual treatment of the doctrine of *stare decisis* but they proclaim unequivocally that where justice demands, reason dictates, equality enjoins, and fair play decrees a change in judge-made law, courts will not lack in determination to establish that change. . . .

The judgments of the Court below are reversed.

Chief Justice Bell (*dissenting*)

I am very greatly disturbed by the virtual extirpation of the principle of stare decisis, on which the House of Law was built. In the last six years the Supreme Court of Pennsylvania has overruled cases in over forty different areas of the law which had been, prior thereto, firmly established. Today no one knows from week to week, or Court session to Court session, whenever the Supreme Court of the United States or the Supreme Court of Pennsylvania meets, what the law will be tomorrow, or what are one's rights, privileges, responsibilities and duties.

In a constitutional republican form of government such as ours, which is based upon law and order, *Certainty* and *Stability* are *essential*. . . . This has been the beacon light for Anglo-American Courts, for text authorities, and for law-abiding Americans ever since the foundation of our Country. In the realm of the law it is usually expressed in the principle known as Stare Decisis. Stare Decisis is one of the bed-rocks upon which the House of Law has been erected and maintained.

Dicta. Not all the statements of the court in a previous case must be followed in subsequent cases. Those statements or expressions that are required by the facts and directly relate to the result in the case before the prior court are *precedent* to which the doctrine of stare decisis is applicable. Other statements which are not necessary to determine the decision in the case are referred to as *dicta* and need not be followed in subsequent court decisions.

Scope of Precedent

Each state has its own sources of law, its own constitution, legislative enactments, administrative rulings, and judge-made precedent. As the *Flagiello* opinion notes, the courts of one state do not have to follow decisions of other states. Of course, external decisions may be consulted for reference, particularly where there are no previous decisions on the point in question in the state where a case is being heard or where, as in *Flagiello*, the reasons for adoption of new policies by another state's court may be considered applicable in the state in which the case is being heard.

Courts in each jurisdiction—federal or state —are grouped in a particular hierarchy. In this hierarchy appellate courts are generally referred to as higher courts, trial courts as lower courts. Every federal or state trial court is "under" an appellate court. Precedent flows down the hierarchy from higher to lower courts.

All courts are bound by a U.S. Supreme Court decision. In each state the lower trial and appellate courts must abide by precedent established by the highest court of the state. Courts that are on the same level of the hierarchy are not bound to follow an opinion of a coequal court. Trial courts only need follow precedent from the appellate court covering their jurisdiction. Thus the U.S. District Court for the Southern District of New York—a federal trial court—is not bound by a decision of the Ninth Circuit Court of Appeals, whose geographic control is limited to the West Coast.

The doctrine of stare decisis furthers the predictability of the law. If a previous case has been based upon a certain principle, that principle will be used in a subsequent case although different parties are involved in the latter case. By the principle of stare decisis, judicial decisions thus affect not only the parties to the lawsuit but also persons who are involved in a later case that is found to be similar to prior cases. People thus anticipate the legal result of their actions from a consideration of the legal results of similar actions in previous decisions. Courts are legitimately hesitant to renounce or reverse their prior decisions, preferring instead to allow any desired change to be made by the legislature.

STATUTES

Although for many years cases were the chief source of Anglo-American law, statutes were also important as a source both in England and the United States. For many reasons, during the past 150 years statutory law has increased in importance. In addition, much of the judge-made law of previous centuries has been enacted by legislative bodies into statute. This process is called *codification*. Today, a person trying to determine the law in a particular field probably would first look for a statute covering the question. The term *statutory law* as used here encompasses not only the enactments of state and federal legislatures but also municipal ordinances, administrative rules and regulations, executive decrees, and treaties.

Distinction Between Statutory and Judicial Law

Statutory law in contrast to judicial law is usually more directly responsive to political, social, and economic considerations. While judges are clearly cognizant of societal forces that affect and are affected by their case interpretations, their written decisions are usually replete with express references to prior cases and only implicit references to the relative merits of the underlying forces involved in the case.

Statutory enactments are general and prospective, whereas judicial decisions are usually specific and retrospective. A legislative provision, for example, is usually enacted to address the problems of large numbers of people. On the other hand, the common law of judicial decisions is limited to the specific facts and legal dispute in controversy between the litigating parties. Nevertheless, a court decision not only terminates legally the dispute of the parties but, as we have seen, also has the effect of establishing principles of law that will be followed in similar situations in subsequent cases.

Conversely, statutes are prospective in nature, changing or adding to the existing law from the effective date of the statute and thus affecting actions yet to occur as opposed to preexisting disputes. There are exceptions to these distinctions between statutory law and the common law of judicial decisions. Some statutes are so specifically drafted that only one or a small number of individuals or firms are affected by their provisions. Other judicial decisions affect many who are not parties to the particular judicial controversy.

Statutory Interpretation

The increasing use of statutes to provide solutions for social problems has not appreciably reduced the importance of cases as a source of law. Most statutes are broadly written, indicating only the outlines of legislative policy. Before the meaning of a statute is established, it often has to be interpreted or, as lawyers say, construed by the courts. Thus in many situations, when a person needs to know what the law is, he or she looks first at the statutory provision and then at cases in which it has been applied. These cases indicate what the statute actually means.

Logically, the process of judicial interpretation at first seems questionable because in effect the courts are explaining what the legislature actually meant. Upon further examination the process makes good sense, for it allows the meaning of the law to be filled in by the courts. They are better equipped than the legislature to respond to specific problems and less affected by the political pressures of the moment. Although having the courts interpret statutes is not without risk, courts in the United States have consistently stated that, in interpreting statutes, their primary function is to determine and give effect to the intention of the legislature.

As legislative bodies seldom, if ever, have specific intents, statutory interpretation is, at best, an imperfect science. To add some certainty to the process, courts have developed a number of principles, or canons of statutory interpretation, that they apply to determine legislative intent.

In applying these principles, a court must take into consideration the general purpose of the legislation. This purpose is determined from the entire act in light of its historical background, the evils at which the statute is directed, and its evident objectives. The canons of construction, which include looking at the plain meaning of terms, contextual analysis, and examination of the statute's legislative history, must yield if they conflict with clear evidence of the legislative will.

Plain Meaning. There may be words or phrases in a statute that can be interpreted in a variety of ways. A basic first step in all statutory interpretations is to look to the plain meaning of the words used to determine what the statute means. As a general rule, the words of a statute will be given their common meaning. Courts presume that the legislature intended to use them as they are used in everyday communication. In many instances, the plain meaning is obvious and no further interpretative analysis is required.

On occasion, the same word may be used in different contexts by the legislature to mean different things. In some statutes *person* includes a corporation while in others, a rape statute for example, *person* would not include a corporation. A doctor's or lawyer's practice may be a *business* for some purposes and not for others. For such words a simple dictionary definition will not suffice. Instead, the courts must consider the context in which the words are used and they must attempt to identify any relevant legislative purpose. It must be noted, however, that not all words are ambiguous. In fact, reasonable people would agree on the meanings of most words in most statutes. For example, the Uniform Partnership Act defines a partnership as "an association of two or more persons." Section 2 of the Act defines *person* as including "individuals, partnerships, corporations, and other associations." Thus, no one could reasonably argue that *under the provisions of the U. P. A. a* corporation could not be a partner in a partnership.

Contextual Analysis. Some legislative enactments are really segments of a larger statutory scheme. In interpreting language that is part of a larger body of legislative provisions, the courts analyze how the specific provision fits into the context of the entire legislative package. Several examples will illustrate.

In 1981 Congress passed a series of legislative enactments designed to solve pressing national economic problems. The enactments included an across-the-board reduction in personal tax rates, accelerated depreciation credits for business investment, and numerous provisions to encourage individuals to save. In interpreting a specific section of this legislation, the courts might feel constrained to analyze a provision in the context of the entire package that became law.

Similarly, one part of the Internal Revenue Code usually cannot be interpreted without reference to other sections of the Code. Thus Section 1221 of the Internal Revenue Code defines a capital asset as "property held by the taxpayer (whether or not connected with his trade or business) . . ." and then details those items which are not capital assets, . . .

  (2) property used in his trade or business, of a character which is subject to the allowance for depreciation provided in section 167 . . .
  (4) accounts or notes receivable acquired in the ordinary course of trade or business for services rendered or from the sale of property described in paragraph (1).

The Code's definition of capital asset is the basis for determining the tax rate to be assessed on income derived from the sale or exchange of property. If the property is not a capital asset, the gain derived is taxed at ordinary income rates instead of at capital-gains rates. Thus the definition of a capital asset in the Internal Revenue Code would be a part of all other Code sections that directly or indirectly refer to either capital gain (or loss) or to ordinary gain (or loss) derived from the sale or exchange of property.

In reaching a decision that will reflect accurately the intent of the legislative branch, the courts seek to analyze the context in which a particular section of the Code is to be placed. Thus, the U.S. Supreme Court notes:

It would do violence to the rules of statutory construction or interpretation to single out and divorce a single phrase in a section without reference to the other portions of the Act and without reference to the manifest purpose of Congress. The legislative interest is to be determined not by taking the word or clause in question from its setting and viewing it apart, but by considering it in connection with the context, the general purposes of the statute in which it is found, the occasion and circumstance of its use, and other appropriate tests for the ascertainment of the legislative will. [Helvering v. Stockholms Enskida Bank, 293 U.S. 84 (1934)]

Legislative History. In seeking to interpret the meaning of statutory provisions, courts sometimes refer to committee reports, hearings, speeches from the floor of the legislature, prior drafts of the statute, failed amendments, and other aspects of the statute's legislative history. These various components of the statute's history shed light on what the legislature intended.

Dangers, however, exist when a court relies upon legislative history to determine legislative intent. Quite often, legislative history is ambiguous. Legislators vote for a statute for different reasons. A statement by one senator in a committee hearing may not represent the majority view. In addition, lawmakers, aware that courts use legislative history to interpret statutes, may be tempted to make statements supporting their own views of what the legislative policy should be although they know that this is not the position of the statute's drafters. A further problem with legislative history is that many state legislatures keep few records of the deliberations and discussions upon which a statute is enacted. This problem is enlarged as often, even when they do exist,

these records are not readily available to the legal profession.

In the case that follows, the court applies some of the techniques just mentioned to determine what Congress intended in enacting a section of the Consumer Product Safety Act.

Consumer Product Safety Commission et al. v. GTE Sylvania, Inc. et al.

U.S. Supreme Court
447 U.S. 102 (1980)

The Consumer Product Safety Commission (Commission) obtained various accident reports from GTE Sylvania. After receiving Freedom of Information Act (FOIA) requests from two consumer groups, the Commission decided to release these reports.

GTE Sylvania (plaintiff-appellee) sued to enjoin the Commission (defendant-appellant) from making these disclosures. GTE Sylvania's request was based upon Sec. 6(b)(1) of the Consumer Product Safety Act (CPSA), which regulates the "public disclosure" of information by the Commission. The Commission contended that Sec. 6(b)(1) applies only when the Commission affirmatively undertakes to disclose information to the public, not when it merely complies with a request for information under the FOIA.

The district court held that Sec. 6(b)(1) is applicable to disclosures in response to FOIA requests. It also found that the Commission had failed to comply with Sec. 6(b)(1) procedures. Thus it concluded that the release of the accident reports would be contrary to the CPSA, and the injunction was granted. Upon appeal by the Commission, the court of appeals affirmed.

The Supreme Court granted certiorari.

Justice Rehnquist

The question presented is whether Section 6(b)(1) of the Consumer Product Safety Act, governs the disclosure of records by the Consumer Product Safety Commission pursuant to a request under the Freedom of Information Act. . . .

I

In 1972, Congress enacted the Consumer Product Safety Act (CPSA). . . . The Act created the Consumer Product Safety Commission . . . to carry out the statutory purposes. . . .

Section 6(b)(1) . . . requires the Commission, at least 30 days before the public disclosure of information pertaining to a consumer product, to notify the manufacturer and to provide it with a summary of the information to be disclosed. . . . The manufacturer must be given a reasonable opportunity to submit comments regarding the information. And the Commission must take reasonable steps to assure that such information is accurate and that disclosure is "fair in the circumstances and reasonably related to effectuating the purposes" of the Act. If the Commission subsequently finds that it has made public disclosure of inaccurate or misleading information that adversely reflects on a manufacturer's products or practices, the Commission must "publish a retraction. . . ."

II

We begin with the familiar canon of statutory construction that the starting point for interpreting a statute is the language of the statute itself. Absent a clearly expressed legislative intention to the contrary, that language must ordinarily be regarded as conclusive.

Section 6(b)(1) by its terms applies to the "public disclosure of *any* information" obtained by the Commission . . . and to any information "to be disclosed to the public in connection therewith." Nothing in the language of that section, or in any other provision of the CPSA, supports petitioners' claim that Section 6(b)(1) is limited to disclosures initiated by the Commission. And as a matter of common usage the term "public" is properly understood as including persons who are FOIA requesters. A disclosure pursuant to the FOIA would thus seem to be most accurately characterized as a "public disclosure" within the plain meaning of Section 6(b)(1).

Section 6(b)(2) of the CPSA . . . contains specific exceptions to the requirements of Section 6(b)(1). But the list of exceptions does not include the disclosure of information in response to an FOIA request. If Congress had intended to exclude FOIA disclosures from Section 6(b)(1) it could easily have done so explicitly in this section as it did in respect to the other listed exceptions. . . . We are consequently reluctant to conclude that Congress' failure to include FOIA requests within the exceptions to Section 6(b)(1) listed in Section 6(b)(2) was unintentional.

III

Petitioners next argue that the legislative history of the CPSA requires the conclusion that Section 6(b)(1) is inapplicable to FOIA requests. In making their argument, petitioners concede that "the preenactment history of the legislation does not directly address the precise issue of statutory construction involved in this case." . . . More importantly, a full examination of the legislative history of the CPSA prior to its enactment indicates that for purposes of Section 6(b)(1) no distinction was made between information affirmatively disclosed by the Commission and information released pursuant to the FOIA.

. . . The House Report on the CPSA states:

> "If the Commission is to act responsibly and with adequate basis, it must have complete and full access to information relevant to its statutory responsibilities. . . . [T]he committee has built into this bill broad information-gathering powers. . . . Accordingly, the committee has written into Section 6 of the bill detailed requirements and limitations relating to the Commission's authority

to disclose information which it acquires in the conduct of its responsibilities under this act."

The House Report does not provide any indication that the safeguards for the release of CPSA information are inapplicable when the Commission discloses information in response to an FOIA request. . . . Nor does the Conference Report contain any suggestion that Section 6(b)(1) does not apply to FOIA requests. As observed by the Court of Appeals, the "conferees' description of section 6(b)(1) is instructive in that the accuracy and fairness requirements for 'publicly disclosed information' are mentioned in almost the same breath as the description of section 6(a)(1), stating that no information need be 'publicly disclosed' by the Commission if it is exempt from disclosure under the FOIA."

Further support for this construction of Section 6(b)(1) can be found in examining comments made with respect to earlier versions of the House bill. In commenting on the disclosure provisions of the Administration bill, Representative Moss, Chairman of the Subcommittee on Commerce and Finance, which was considering the House bills, stated "I am sure the subcommittee will want to examine carefully this proposed change in the Freedom of Information Act." . . .

Section 4(c) and the provision that was finally enacted as Section 6(b) by their terms include both affirmative disclosures by the Commission and information released pursuant to the FOIA. And the Department of Health, Education, and Welfare, the agency that drafted H.R. 8110, stated in its section by section analysis . . .

> "Section 4(c) would protect the Secretary's refusal to disclose information not required to be released by the (FOIA), and would expressly prohibit his disclosure of commercial secrets, or of illness or injury data revealing [the] identity of the victim. . . ."

The legislative history of Section 6(b)(1) thus fails to establish that petitioners' proposed distinction should be read into the section.

Affirmed.

The application of the conventional tools of statutory interpretation can leave a court in doubt as to the meaning of a statute. When this occurs, numerous other techniques for determining the legislature's intention are available. A court may look at the interpretation given to the legislation by the administrative agencies responsible for enforcing it. Sometimes reference is made to earlier laws on the same subject; however, if this is done, the court must be certain that the legislature did not intend to change the law. When a statute affirms judge-made or common law, the intention of the legislature may be determined by looking at the cases that developed the common law principle. Other clues to legislative intent are statements by those who proposed the legislation and the manner in which the Congress or legislative bodies have viewed similar legislation. All of these techniques, as well as many others, have proved helpful in the search for legislative intention.

CONSTITUTIONS

Constitutions are fundamental sources of law. They establish the basic framework within which governments, both state and federal, must operate. The authority of a constitution is absolute regarding all points that it covers. In these areas, the constitution is controlling unless changed by the authority that established it. Constitutions have three major functions: (1) they guarantee individuals certain basic rights; (2) they allocate power among the legislative, judicial, and executive branches of government; and (3) they allocate power among political subdivisions.

Each state and the federal government has its own constitution. Constitutions derive their authority from the people. In the Constitution of the United States, the people, acting through state governments, grant certain powers to the federal government. In spheres where the federal government has power, its actions are supreme. On the other hand, federal action, such as a congressional enactment, is invalid unless supported by a specific constitutional provision. The Constitution also restricts actions that Congress, the President, or the federal judiciary can take. For example, Congress cannot pass a law penalizing a person for an action that was legal when committed nor can a federal agency take a person's property without providing compensation. In addition to limiting actions of government officials, the Constitution also ensures that they will not violate the rights and liberties of individuals.

State constitutions distribute the powers of government within the three branches of state government. They also provide for the distribution of power to political subdivisions. A number of state constitutions have "home rule" provisions. A provision of this nature allows municipalities the right of self-government in local affairs. Like the federal Constitution, most state constitutions declare basic rights and liberties to which people are entitled.

In the legal system operating in the United States, the courts have the task of nullifying legislative or executive actions that violate a constitutional provision. In 1934 the U.S. Supreme Court declared unconstitutional the National Recovery Act, which was the cornerstone of President Roosevelt's program to end the Great Depression. When President Truman attempted to seize the steel mills in 1952 in order to end a strike that interfered with the Korean War effort, the Supreme Court determined that he did not have constitutional authority to do so.

In determining that legislative or executive actions are unconstitutional, courts have to interpret the document. Constitutional and statutory interpretation are similar, but differences do exist. Since a constitution declares fundamental principles and is intended to last for a long time, its language may be given a broader interpretation than statutory language. Chapter 2 includes some cases in which the U.S. Supreme Court has interpreted provisions of the U.S. Constitution especially relevant to business.

ADMINISTRATIVE RULES AND ORDERS

One of the major changes that has occurred in American political life during the past hundred years is the increasing use of administrative agencies to carry out some of the tasks of government. Agencies play important roles in local, state, and national affairs. Many but not all of them have the authority to adopt rules and regulations that have the force of law. Frequently business managers as well as private citizens must be aware of these rules when making decisions.

One example of a business in which an agency's rules and regulations are significant is the sale of securities. In 1934 Congress passed the Securities Exchange Act to insure fairness in securities transactions. This act established the Securities and Exchange Commission (SEC). On the basis of authority granted to it, the SEC has adopted numerous rules that regulate issuing and trading securities. Although the rules are not made by a legislative body, a person or firm violating them is subject to penalties such as the revocation or suspension of the privilege to market a new security or possible criminal prosecution. Other important administrative agencies with rule-making authority are the Federal Trade Commission (FTC), the National Labor Relations Board (NLRB), and the Environmental Protection Agency (EPA).

In addition to the authority to promulgate rules, administrative agencies often have the authority to hear cases and issue orders. This is referred to as administrative adjudication. When hearing cases, the agency frequently must interpret a statute that is involved. Although these agency interpretations are subject to limited review by the courts, the interpretations are an important indication of the law. The reason is that generally courts accord great deference to an agency's interpretation of the statute that it administers. Presumably the administrators have the specialized knowledge and technical skill in their area of expertise that judges do not have.

Since administrative rule-making and adjudication are undoubtedly as significant to the business manager as what courts do, the work of administrative agencies is discussed in depth in Chapter 37.

REVIEW PROBLEMS

1. Ludenia Howard was charged with violating the Federal Black Bass Act. The Act made unlawful "transportation . . . from any State . . . any black bass . . . if (1) such transportation is contrary to the law of the State . . . from which fish . . . is transported. . . ." The Florida Fish and Game Commission had a rule prohibiting the transportation of black bass out of the state. The commission was a body authorized by the state constitution. Its members were appointed by the governor.

   Howard's attorney argued that the federal act did not apply since the commission's rule was not a "law of the State." Discuss the validity of this defense. What are the characteristics of a law? (United States v. Howard, 352 U.S. 212 [1956])

2. Butler and a number of other people organized a corporation ostensibly to assist small business firms to secure loans. They were to be compensated by a finder's fee. The firms for whom loans were to be located had to pay an initial membership charge. The firms were solicited by mail. If a firm indicated an interest, it was visited by a salesperson. The entire scheme was a fraud. The corporation retained the membership fees and did nothing to secure loans.

   The corporation, Butler, and twenty-nine others were prosecuted in a single action for mail fraud. Several of the defendants asked to have their cases severed and tried separately as combining this number of defendants in a single case was unfair. Discuss the validity of a government argument based on stare decisis and citing a number of cases in which large numbers of defendants had been tried in a single case. Is the trial court bound by these cases? (Butler v. United States, 317 F2d 249 [1963])

3. Section 301(a) of the Federal Food, Drug, and Cosmetics Act prohibits the introduction into interstate commerce of any drug that is misbranded. According to Section 502(a), a product is misbranded if its "labeling is false or misleading" unless the labeling bears "adequate directions for use."

The term "labeling" is defined to mean "all labels and other written, printed, or graphic matter (1) upon any article or any of its containers or (2) accompanying such article." Violation of the act is a crime.

Kordel sells health-food products that are compounds of vitamins, minerals, and herbs. These items are sold to stores. In addition to supplying the product, Kordel separately furnishes pamphlets describing the products. Much of the literature is shipped separately from the drugs and at different times—both before and after drug shipments. Kordel is charged with violating the Food and Drug Act. Based upon the above facts, outline a defense available to him. Explain how the prosecution might overcome this defense. (Kordel v. United States, 335 U.S. 345 [1948])

Legal Systems

T his chapter examines the structure of the legal system and some of the important processes by which the system seeks to accomplish the tasks discussed in Chapter 1. Initially, the chapter discusses briefly the relationship between the different branches of government, each of which plays a significant role in the operation of the system. Next the chapter considers the interplay between state and federal legal systems, especially as this influences the business community. Finally, the chapter deals with the judicial process and some of the general characteristics of legal dispute resolution.

RELATIONSHIP OF BRANCHES OF GOVERNMENT

Government and law are not the same, but they are closely related. As a result, some of the basic principles of government appreciably influence the manner in which the legal system functions. Conversely, many legal maxims affect the operation of government.

One example is the principle that government officials at all levels must act within limits prescribed by law. This principle, which is vital to the continuance of American democracy, is often referred to as the "rule of law" or "supremacy of law." Simultaneously, many of these same officials whose actions are circumscribed by law often play major roles in the development of law and in the administration of the legal system. The following material discusses actions of officials in different branches of government as these actions influence the legal system. The rule of law is reflected in the accompanying cases.

Separation of Powers

The separation-of-powers doctrine involves the division of the authority of government among legislative, judicial, and executive branches and contemplates that none of the three shall exercise any of the powers belonging to the others. Chief Justice John Marshall described the end result of the doctrine as follows: "The difference between the departments undoubtedly is, that the legislature makes, the executive executes, and the judiciary construes the law."[1]

Making, executing, and interpreting the law do not have to be independent of each other for a legal system to function effectively. These three services might well be performed by a single entity. However, since the adoption of the Constitution, a cardinal principle of American political life has been to separate the three branches of government. Separation is intended to prevent the domination of one branch by another and to protect the liberties of the people by preventing the accumulation of power in a single source.

Early in the 1950s, the U.S. Supreme Court applied the separation-of-powers principle when President Truman attempted to avert a nationwide strike of steelworkers. The President believed that this strike would jeopardize the national defense, so he issued an executive order directing the Secretary of Commerce to seize and operate the steel mills. No specific constitutional or legislative authority existed for the seizure, but President Truman argued that his action was supported by "inherent powers" implied from the aggregate of presidential power under the Constitution. He relied especially upon the power vested in him as Commander in Chief of the Armed Forces and his responsibility as President to see that "the laws be faithfully executed." The mill owners contended that the President's order amounted to lawmaking, a function that the Constitution expressly confined to Congress. Holding that the President did not have the authority to seize the mills, the Supreme Court in *Youngstown Sheet and Tube* v. *Sawyer*[2] made the following observation.

Even though "theater of war" be an expanding concept, we cannot with faithfulness to our constitutional system hold that the Commander in Chief of the Armed Forces has the ultimate power as such to take possession of private property in order to keep labor disputes from stopping production. This is a job for the Nation's lawmakers, not for its military authorities.

Nor can the seizure order be sustained because of the several constitutional provisions that grant executive power to the President. In the framework of our Constitution, the President's power to see that the laws are faithfully executed refutes the idea that he is to be a lawmaker. The Constitution limits his functions in the lawmaking process to the recommending of laws he thinks wise and the vetoing of laws he thinks bad. And the Constitution is neither silent nor equivocal about who shall make laws which the President is to execute. The first section of the first article says that "All legislative Powers herein granted shall be vested in a Congress of the United States. . . ."[3]

In spite of the statements in *Youngstown Sheet and Tube,* the business or public administrator viewing the legal environment might readily decide that the separation-of-powers principle is more honored in the breach than in the observance. It is certainly true that the American legal system has never embodied complete separation of powers. This would be inefficient even if it were possible. In fact, the checks-and-balances system, which is integral to the federal Constitution and those of most states, is based upon the concept that each of the three constituent elements of government has a substantial influence on the others. There is enough influence to ensure that power to some extent will be balanced. Although nothing requires state governments to adhere to the separation-of-powers principle, most state constitutions follow the federal pattern. Even when not especially provided for by a state constitution, the concept is usually maintained in practice or required by judicial decision.

Numerous illustrations of the intermixture of functions can be cited. Congress, if it does not violate constitutional mandates, can modify much of the jurisdiction of federal courts. Congress can restrict the power of the President to remove certain federal officials, investigate the executive departments, and remove the President from office. The judiciary can determine if legislative enactments are constitutional, and the President can veto bills passed by Congress.

During the early 1970s, the separation-of-powers principle was the subject of considerable national discussion and concern. Much of the legal controversy surrounding the Watergate investigation revolved around the power of the President to ignore requests of congressional committees for information and orders from federal courts that he produce certain tapes that were in his possession. The case that follows is the culmination of that controversy.

United States v. Nixon
U.S. Supreme Court
418 U.S. 683 (1974)

On March 1, 1974, a federal grand jury indicted several members of the White House staff and political supporters of President Nixon for various offenses, including conspiracy to defraud the United States and to obstruct justice. In order to obtain evidence to be presented at their trials, Special Prosecutor Jaworski filed a motion in the district court for a subpoena *duces tecum* requiring the President to produce certain tapes and documents relating to precisely identified conversations and meetings between the President and others. The President, claiming absolute executive privilege, moved to quash the subpoena. After treating the subpoenaed material as presumptively privileged, the district court concluded that the Special Prosecutor had made a sufficient showing to overcome the privilege, denied the motion, and ordered an *in camera* examination of the material. The President appealed to the Court of Appeals. This proceeding was stayed pending a special review by the U.S. Supreme Court, requested by both parties.

Chief Justice Burger

THE CLAIM OF PRIVILEGE

A

Having determined that the requirements of Rule 17(c) were satisfied, we turn to the claim that the subpoena should be quashed because it demands "confidential conversations between a President and his close advisors that it would be inconsistent with the public interest to produce." The first contention is a broad claim that the separation of powers doctrine precludes judicial review of a President's claim of privilege.

Notwithstanding the deference each branch must accord the others, the "judicial Power of the United States" vested in the federal courts by Art. III, Sec. 1, of the Constitution can no more be shared with the Executive Branch than the Chief Executive, for example, can share with the Judiciary the veto power, or the Congress share with the Judiciary the power to override a Presidential veto. Any other conclusion would be contrary to the basic concept of separation of powers and the checks and balances that flow from the scheme of a tripartite government. We therefore reaffirm that it is the province and duty of this Court "to say what the law is" with respect to the claim of privilege presented in this case.

B

The second ground asserted by the President's counsel in support of the claim of absolute privilege rests on the doctrine of separation of powers. Here it is argued that the independence of the Executive Branch within its own sphere, insulates a President from a judicial subpoena in an ongoing criminal prosecution, and thereby protects confidential Presidential communications.

However, neither the doctrine of separation of powers, nor the need for confidentiality of high-level communications, without more, can sustain an absolute, unqualified Presidential privilege of immunity from judicial process under all circumstances. Absent a claim of need to protect military, diplomatic, or sensitive national security secrets, we find it difficult to accept the argument that even the very important interest in confidentiality of Presidential communications is significantly diminished by production of such material for *in camera* inspection with all the protection that a district court will be obliged to provide.

The impediment that an absolute, unqualified privilege would place in the way of the primary constitutional duty of the Judicial Branch to do justice in criminal prosecutions would plainly conflict with the function of the courts under Art. III. In designing the structure of our Government and dividing and allocating the sovereign power among three co-equal branches, the Framers of the Constitution sought to provide a comprehensive system, but the separate powers were not intended to operate with absolute independence. . . .

C

Since we conclude that the legitimate needs of the judicial process may outweigh Presidential privilege, it is necessary to resolve those competing interests in a manner that preserves the essential functions of each branch. The right and indeed the duty to resolve that question does not free the Judiciary from according high respect to the representations made on behalf of the President. . . .

The right to production of all evidence at a criminal trial similarly has constitutional dimensions. The Sixth Amendment explicitly confers upon every defendant in a criminal trial the right "to be confronted with the witnesses against him" and "to have compulsory process for obtaining witnesses in his favor." Moreover, the Fifth Amendment also guarantees that no person shall be deprived of liberty without due process of law. It is the manifest duty of the courts to vindicate those guarantees, and to accomplish that it is essential that all relevant and admissible evidence be produced.

In this case we must weigh the importance of the general privilege of confidentiality of Presidential communications in performance of the President's responsibilities against the inroads of such a privilege on the fair administration of criminal justice. The interest in preserving confidentiality is weighty indeed and entitled to great respect.

On the other hand, the allowance of the privilege to withhold evidence that is demonstrably relevant in a criminal trial would cut deeply into the guarantee of due process of law and gravely impair the basic function of the courts. A President's acknowledged need for confidentiality in the communications of his office is general in nature, whereas the constitutional need for production of relevant evidence in a criminal proceeding is specific and central to the fair adjudication of a particular criminal case in the administration of justice. Without access to specific facts a criminal prosecution may be totally frustrated. The President's broad interest in confidentiality of communications will not be vitiated by disclosure of a limited number of conversations preliminarily shown to have some bearing on the pending criminal cases.

We conclude that when the ground for asserting privilege as to subpoenaed materials sought for use in a criminal trial is based only on the generalized interest in confidentiality, it cannot prevail over the fundamental demands of due process of law in the fair administration of criminal justice.

Affirmed.

RELATIONSHIP BETWEEN FEDERAL AND STATE LEGAL SYSTEMS

Business administrators today are often concerned and frequently puzzled by the mass of rules, regulations, directives, forms, and reports emanating from both state and federal governments. The cost to business of meeting the demands from these systems is staggering. A single 1974 data-gathering program of the Federal Trade Commission had an average cost of $56,000 for each firm required to report. One firm's reporting costs were over $1.2 million.[4] A 1979 Business Roundtable study of forty-eight companies found that in 1977 regulatory costs equaled 16 percent of the firms' after-tax profits, and in 1980 government officials estimated that business paid $100 billion a year to comply with federal regulations.

In addition to bewilderment caused by the

sheer mass of government requirements, additional confusion results because federal and state laws attempting to achieve different objectives sometimes conflict. Consider the plight of firms faced with the following dilemma:

In 1980 the federal Equal Employment Opportunity Commission adopted a rule prohibiting insurers from using mortality tables differentiating between males and females. At about the same time, California and New York adopted rules requiring insurers to use mortality tables that differentiated between males and females buying annuity and life insurance contracts. What tables should the firms use?

In spite of the dissatisfaction that sometimes arises from being forced to cope with two major governmental units, the business administrator must remember that this system does have some benefits. Many matters are more effectively carried out by local authorities familiar with problems peculiar to their region. At the same time, the diffusion of power between the states and the federal government reduces the authority of each. By extending the centers of power, an enduring majority becomes less possible and minority interests have some protection.

The dual nature of government in the United States is attributable to *federalism*. Although the term is not mentioned in the Constitution and has seldom been defined by the judiciary, the concept is basic to understanding the American political and legal systems. In essence, American federalism is a system that allocates the powers of sovereignty between the state and federal governments.

The genesis of the American federal system is the Constitution, which is actually a compact between the individual states and the federal government. As a result of this compact, each of the states—a sovereign entity in its own right—has delegated certain powers to the federal government. When the federal government acts within the framework of these delegated powers, its actions are su-

preme. Similarly, the actions of each state are supreme when the state acts on the basis of a retained power. At the same time there are some powers that are concurrent in the sense that they can be asserted by both state and federal governments. The power to tax is an example. Both state and federal governments have this authority.

THE DUAL COURT STRUCTURE

As a result of the federal system, a dual structure of courts prevails in the United States. Each person is not only subject to the laws of a particular state, which generally are interpreted by the courts of that state, but each is also subject to the laws of the United States, which are generally interpreted by the federal courts. Before examining some of the effects of the dual nature of government in the United States, a brief survey of the general structure and jurisdiction of American courts is in order.

In view of the fifty-one independent court systems that operate within the United States, this might seem an impossible task. The task, however, is simplified by a common structural pattern that exists for most states. This structure can be understood if each state system and the federal system are envisioned as pyramids with two or sometimes three levels.

Trial Courts

Federal Trial Courts. At the base of this pyramid are the trial courts. In the federal system these are called U.S. District Courts. The nation is divided into ninety-one districts, and each has a single district court. The district courts are courts of original jurisdiction and are the courts in which most federal cases are initiated. They might also be described as courts of general jurisdiction because they have the power to hear all types of federal cases except those assigned by Congress to special courts, such as the U.S. Court of Customs.

State Trial Courts. In the states, the trial-court base of the structural pyramid is complicated by the existence of both courts of general and courts of limited jurisdiction. Each state has trial courts of general jurisdiction throughout the state. In Ohio they are called courts of common pleas; New York refers to them as supreme courts. Probably the most common designation is county court.

Although the titles differ from state to state, these general trial courts have some common characteristics. Usually they are organized on a county basis. They have the power to hear a wide variety of cases, both criminal and civil, and there are ordinarily no upper limits on their monetary jurisdiction. Their remedial powers usually include traditional remedies such as specific performance, which is a court order requiring a defendant to perform a particular act, or the injunction, which is a court order prohibiting a person from performing a particular act. It is often only in these courts that parties have a right to jury trials in civil cases. Especially in heavily populated areas, many courts of general jurisdiction have specialized divisions to hear cases that involve domestic relations, juveniles, and decedent estates. In some states an independent probate or surrogate court handles decedent estate matters. In a number of states the specialized courts are set up independently of the state-wide trial courts. It is also a common practice to separate the courts with criminal jurisdiction from those that hear civil cases.

All states have a number of trial courts of limited jurisdiction. These courts can decide only those cases in which the plaintiff is seeking monetary damages of a limited amount. Frequently they have no power to issue injunctions or to order specific performance, and their criminal jurisdiction is limited to petty offenses and minor misdemeanors. It is impossible to make general statements about these courts because of the wide variety of tasks that have been assigned to them in different states. In some areas these lower trial courts have extensive monetary jurisdiction and are manned by a number of full-time, legally trained judges with large staffs. These courts often play significant roles in the administration of justice. In other places these courts hear only the most trivial cases and are presided over by part-time judges, sometimes with no legal training. Courts of this latter kind often exist only because state legislatures have failed to modernize local judicial administration.

Intermediate Appellate Courts

Federal Appellate Courts. If we consider judicial structure as a pyramid built of several levels, both the federal system and those of the heavily populated states have a second layer—the intermediate appellate courts. The federal intermediate appellate courts are called U.S. Courts of Appeals. The United States is currently divided into thirteen geographic circuits with a court of appeals for each. These courts hear appeals from the federal district courts and from actions taken by many federal administrative agencies.

State Intermediate Appellate Courts. State intermediate appellate courts are found only in the heavily populated states. In half the states no intermediate level of review exists. Often this is because the highest court of the state can handle all cases that are appealed. In some states a need for an intermediate level of review exists, but neither the state constitution nor the legislature has authorized the creation of this court.

The purpose of intermediate appellate courts is to improve the administration of justice by reducing the burden on the state's court of last resort. This both speeds up the

judicial process and allows the high court to concentrate on important cases.

State intermediate appellate courts have broad appellate jurisdiction. They hear appeals from trial courts of general jurisdiction and, frequently, from trial courts of limited jurisdiction and/or specialized courts. In many states the intermediate appellate courts also hear appeals from administrative agency determinations. Like the trial courts, these courts have a variety of names. A number of states call them courts of appeals; superior court is also a common designation. In New York these courts are the appellate division of the supreme court.

Although these courts are not the highest appellate court, for most appeals they are the court of last resort. There are two principal reasons for this. First, an appeal is a very expensive process. Most litigants cannot afford even an initial review, much less the cost of the two appeals necessary to argue their case before the highest appellate court. Second, in most states with an intermediate level of review the highest court has the discretion to review only those cases that it considers important. A person appealing from the intermediate level must petition the high court. Ordinarily, these petitions are rejected because the high court is satisfied that justice has been accorded by the intermediate appellate court's review.

Courts of Last Resort

The apex of the pyramid in each of the fifty state judicial systems and the federal system is occupied by a court that makes the final determination for almost all cases appealed within the jurisdiction. This court is most frequently called the supreme court as in the federal system, but in New York and Kentucky the highest court is called the court of appeals. Ordinarily a party whose case is heard at this level in a state system can appeal the case no further. In some few instances, however, a case appealed to the highest court of a state can be reviewed by the U.S. Supreme Court. This is true only if the case involves a substantial federal question, such as the interpretation of the U.S. Constitution or of a federal statute, and if the U.S. Supreme Court agrees to consider the state court judgment.

Only a few cases are appealable to the U.S. Supreme Court as a matter of right. In all other circumstances the party unhappy with the federal circuit court decision must first ask the Supreme Court to hear the case by petitioning for an order of *certiorari*. If the Supreme Court wants to hear the case, it will grant the petition. Most petitions for certiorari are denied.

FEDERAL COURT JURISDICTION

The dual nature of American federalism impels citizens to take into account both state and federal legal systems. Because of the nature of powers retained by the states, most criminal and civil litigation is decided in state courts. Matters such as domestic relations and the administration of decedents' estates as well as matters of contract and tort law are also largely concerns of state courts. Although many more cases are tried in the state courts than in the federal, the jurisdiction of federal courts is significant to the business community because many important business regulatory statutes are federal.

Federal Questions

In order for a case to be tried in the federal system, the controversy must involve a matter over which the federal courts have jurisdiction. Jurisdiction is a term designating the power of a court to hear a case. Federal courts have jurisdiction when the decision depends upon the interpretation of the Constitution of the United States, a federal statute, or a treaty. These cases are said to involve a *federal ques-*

tion. A large percentage of federal litigation consists of federal question cases. These cases include those based upon statutes such as the Sherman Act, the Securities Exchange Act, and the National Labor Relations Act.

Diversity of Citizenship

A second important source of litigation in the federal courts arises from the constitutional provision permitting Congress to grant jurisdiction to the federal courts in "controversies between citizens of different states." In the original Judiciary Act adopted in 1789, Congress granted the federal courts original jurisdiction in these kinds of cases. Although some of the conditions have changed, federal courts have had diversity jurisdiction since that time.

In order to limit the number of diversity cases that the federal courts have to decide, legislation requires that the amount in controversy must exceed $10,000. Additional limitations require that each plaintiff's claim in a multiple-party action exceed $10,000 and that no plaintiff or defendant be a citizen of the same state. In 1958 Congress, to further limit diversity cases, adopted legislation declaring a corporation to be a citizen both of the state of incorporation and of the state in which it has its principal place of business.

The original purpose of diversity jurisdiction was to protect a citizen of one state from possible bias in favor of a party whose case was being heard in his or her home state. Today, almost no one believes that the courts of a citizen's state would favor that person over the citizen of another state. As a result, many people are critical of diversity jurisdiction. They argue that it unduly complicates litigation, increases the cost of the federal judicial system, and forces the federal courts to hear cases that might more effectively be decided by state courts since the cases involve state law.

INTERSTATE COMMERCE

The Commerce Clause. One of the powers that the states delegated to the federal government was the power "to regulate commerce with foreign nations, and among the several states. . . ." Over the years "the commerce clause," as this grant of authority is called, has been subject to varying interpretations by the U.S. Supreme Court. Today it is largely through the use of this power that the federal government regulates many aspects of American economic life.

The different interpretations of the commerce clause over nearly 200 years of constitutional history provide an example of the manner in which the legal system responds to economic, political, and social change. In *Gibbons* v. *Ogden,*[5] the most famous of the early cases interpreting the clause, both *commerce* and *regulate* were given broad meanings. These insured that the national government and not the states would have authority to control navigation on public waterways, even those wholly within a state. The decision thus met the needs of expanding national economic interests for an efficient means of moving goods that could not be restricted by local pressures. At the same time the decision reflected the rise of national spirit in much of the nation at that time.

The Commerce Clause Redefined. As the nation expanded geographically and economically, there appeared to be little need for either government assistance or control. Public energies were directed primarily to the business of creating material wealth. Laissez faire based upon rugged individualism was the prevailing economic philosophy. Factors such as these led to changes in legal attitudes that were reflected in new interpretations of the commerce clause.

Decisions of the U.S. Supreme Court up to 1840 construed the commerce clause broadly and laid the groundwork for the extension of congressional power over the economy. But by 1870 the commerce clause had been reinterpreted in a manner that empowered the states to regulate many aspects of interstate commerce along with the federal government. This was accomplished when the Court permitted state regulation of local aspects of interstate commerce if no conflicting federal legislation existed. Later federal regulation was further curtailed by a series of Supreme Court decisions that limited congressional power by defining commerce very narrowly. The Court redefined commerce as transportation among the states. In this manner it excluded from federal regulation all types of manufacturing and refining as well as businesses such as insurance and advertising that were conducted within a single state.

Although this narrow interpretation of the commerce clause was modified gradually over the years, federal dominance in economic regulation was not reestablished until the 1930s.

Reassertion of Federal Dominance. Conditions brought about by the Great Depression resulted in a new approach to regulation by the federal government. In the 1930s, with the increase of unemployment, the collapse of industrial production, and the fall of national income, it became apparent that only solutions on a nationwide basis could solve the problems plaguing the United States. Legislation based upon the commerce clause was passed by Congress and with some reluctance accepted by the courts. The case that follows indicates the manner in which the courts expanded the scope of the term "commerce" and the meaning of trade among the states.

United States v. South-Eastern Underwriters Association

U.S. Supreme Court

322 U.S. 533 (1943)

South-Eastern Underwriters Association (defendant-appellee), its membership of nearly 200 private stock fire insurance companies, and twenty-seven individuals were charged by the United States (plaintiff-appellant) with numerous violations of the Sherman Antitrust Act.

The U.S. District Court felt compelled by previous cases to dismiss the indictment against them for the sole reason that "the entire 'business of insurance' (not merely the part of the business in which contracts are physically executed) can never under any possible circumstances be 'commerce,' and that, therefore, even though an insurance company conducts a substantial part of its business transactions across state lines, it is not engaged in 'commerce among the States' within the meaning of either the Commerce Clause or the Sherman Antitrust Act." Under the Criminal Appeals Act, plaintiffs appealed directly to the U.S. Supreme Court.

Justice Black

I.

Ordinarily courts do not construe words used in the Constitution so as to give them a meaning more narrow than one which they had in the common parlance of the times in which the Constitution was written. To hold that the word "commerce" as used in the Commerce Clause does not include a business such as insurance would do just that. Whatever other meanings "commerce" may have included in 1787, the dictionaries, encyclopedias, and other books of the period show that it included trade: business in which persons bought and sold, bargained and contracted. And this meaning has persisted to modern times. Surely, therefore, a heavy burden is on him who asserts that the plenary power which the Commerce Clause grants to Congress to regulate "Commerce among the several States" does not include the power to regulate trading in insurance to the same extent that it includes power to regulate other trades or businesses conducted across state lines. . . .

In 1869 this Court held, in sustaining a statute of Virginia which regulated foreign insurance companies, that the statute did not offend the Commerce Clause because "issuing a policy of insurance is not a transaction of commerce." *Paul* v. *Virginia,* 8 Wall 168, 183. Since then, in similar cases, this statement has been repeated, and has been broadened.

Today, however, we are asked to apply this reasoning, not to uphold another state law, but to strike down an Act of Congress which was intended to regulate certain aspects of the methods by which interstate insurance companies do business; and, in so doing, to narrow the scope of the federal power to regulate the activities of a great business carried on back and forth across state lines. But past decisions of this Court emphasize that legal formulae devised to uphold state power cannot uncritically be accepted as trustworthy guides to determine Congressional power under the Commerce Clause.

One reason advanced for the rule in the *Paul* case has been that insurance policies "are not commodities to be shipped or forwarded from one State to another." But both before and since *Paul* v. *Virginia* this Court has held that Congress can regulate traffic though it consist of intangibles. Another reason much stressed has been that insurance policies are mere personal contracts subject to the laws of the state where executed. But this reason rests upon a distinction between what has been called "local" and what "interstate," a type of mechanical criterion which this Court has not deemed controlling in the measurement of federal power. We may grant that a contract of insurance, considered as a thing apart from negotiation and execution, does not itself constitute interstate commerce. But it does not follow from this that the Court is powerless to examine the entire transaction, of which that contract is but a part, in order to determine whether there may be a chain of events which becomes interstate commerce. In short, a nationwide business is not deprived of its interstate character merely because it is built upon sales contracts which are local in nature.

Another reason advanced to support the result of the cases which follow *Paul* v. *Virginia* has been that, if any aspects of the business of insurance be treated as interstate commerce, "then all control over it is taken from the States and the legislative regulations which this Court has heretofore sustained must be declared invalid." Accepted without qualification, that broad statement is inconsistent with many decisions of this Court. It is settled that, for Constitutional purposes, certain activities of a business may be intrastate and therefore subject to state control, while other activities of the same business may be interstate and therefore subject to federal regulation. . . .

The power confined to Congress by the Commerce Clause is declared in The Federalist to be for the purpose of securing the "maintenance of harmony and proper intercourse among the States." It is the power to legislate concerning transactions which, reaching across state boundaries, affect the people of more states than one; —to govern affairs which the individual states, with their limited territorial jurisdictions, are not fully capable of governing. This federal power to determine the rules of intercourse across state lines was essential to weld a loose confederacy into a single, indivisible Nation; its continued existence is equally essential to the welfare of the Nation. . . .

[Note: In the concluding portion of the opinion the Court held that the Sherman Antitrust Act applied to insurance.]

Reversed.

CASE NOTE

The 1943 *South-Eastern Underwriters* decision caused much controversy and uncertainty in the insurance business. As a result of the early case of *Paul* v. *Virginia,* federal law had not been applicable to insurance, and regulation had been carried out by the states. The immediate effect of *South-Eastern Underwriters* was to make insurance companies subject to the federal antitrust laws. Insurance companies and state insurance departments were greatly concerned because the prospective effect of federal regulation was unknown. As a result, they lobbied in Congress for legislation that would exempt the companies from federal regulation.

In 1945 Congress enacted the McCarran-Ferguson Act. This act declared that the continued regulation and taxation by the states of the business of insurance was in the public interest. The states were authorized to continue to regulate insurance, and the companies were exempted from the federal antitrust laws to the extent that the states regulated insurance company practices. This has led to the enactment of a large body of state regulation. In general, the federal government has become involved only when the states have failed to regulate effectively.

The Commerce Clause Today. Since the 1920s the U.S. Supreme Court has gradually broadened the interpretation of the commerce clause, as illustrated by the *South-Eastern Underwriters* opinion. By midcentury the Court's position was that any intrastate activity that was part of the "flow of commerce" across state lines was subject to federal control. For example, a federal statute is applicable to a contract between local sugar-beet growers and local sugar refiners as long as sugar is shipped out of state. Federal authority based upon the commerce clause also has been extended to wholly local intrastate activities that in a substantial manner affect interstate commerce. Based upon this view of the commerce clause, federal regulation is permissible even though the subject of the regulation never enters the stream of interstate commerce.

As economic, political, and social problems placed demands upon government that many felt could be solved only on a national basis, congressional legislation, supported by the expanded concept of interstate commerce, has increased markedly. Although other powers of the federal government such as the power to tax have been used to expand national authority over business, the commerce power is used most frequently. As the federal authority expands, the power of the states to regulate for the purpose of promoting the health, safety, and welfare of their citizens must give way. This residual power of the states, known as the police power, and federal actions based upon the commerce clause have over the years been recurring sources of conflict, as the following case indicates.

City of Philadelphia v. New Jersey
U.S. Supreme Court
437 U.S. 617 (1978)

Chapter 363 of 1973 New Jersey Laws prohibited bringing most types of solid waste into the state. This statute prevented performance of contracts for waste disposal between operators of private landfills in New Jersey and cities in other states. These cities, led by Philadelphia (plaintiff-appellant), joined in a suit against New Jersey in the courts of that state. The plaintiffs argued that Chapter 363 was unconstitutional because it discriminated against interstate commerce. The trial court accepted this contention and awarded plaintiff cities summary judgment. Upon appeal by the state, the New Jersey Supreme Court reversed the trial court, and plaintiffs appealed to the U.S. Supreme Court.

Justice Stewart

The purpose of ch. 363 is set out in the statute itself as follows:

> "The Legislature finds and determines that . . . the volume of solid and liquid waste continues to rapidly increase, that the treatment and disposal of these wastes continues to pose an even greater threat to the quality of the environment of New Jersey, that the available and appropriate land fill sites within the State are being diminished, that the environment continues to be threatened by the treatment and disposal of waste which originated or was collected outside the State, and that the public health, safety and welfare require that the treatment and disposal within this State of all wastes generated outside of the State be prohibited."

The New Jersey Supreme Court accepted this statement of the state legislature's purpose. The state court additionally found that New Jersey's existing landfill sites will be exhausted within a few years; that to go on using these sites or to develop new ones will take a heavy environmental toll, both from pollution and from loss of scarce open lands; that new techniques to divert waste from landfills to other methods of disposal and resource recovery processes are under development, but that these changes will require time; and finally, that "the extension of the lifespan of existing landfills, resulting from the exclusion of out-of-state waste, may be of crucial importance in preventing further virgin wetlands or other undeveloped lands from being devoted to landfill purposes." Based on these findings, the court concluded that ch. 363 was designed to protect, not the State's economy, but its environment, and that its substantial benefits outweigh its "slight" burden on interstate commerce.

The appellants strenuously contend that ch. 363, "while outwardly cloaked in the currently fashionable garb of environmental protection, . . . is actually no more than a legislative effort to suppress competition and stabilize the cost of solid waste disposal for New Jersey residents. . . ." They cite passages of legislative history suggesting that the problem addressed by ch. 363 is primarily financial: Stemming the flow of out-of-state waste into certain landfill sites will extend their lives, thus delaying the day when New Jersey cities must transport their waste to more distant and expensive sites. . . .

This dispute about ultimate legislative purpose need not be resolved, because its resolution would not be relevant to the constitutional issue to be decided in this case. Contrary to the evident assumption of the state court and the parties, the evil of protectionism can reside in legislative means as well as legislative ends. Thus, it does not matter whether the ultimate aim of ch. 363 is to reduce the waste disposal costs of New Jersey residents or to save remaining open lands from pollution, for we assume New Jersey has every right to protect its residents' pocketbooks as well as their environment. And it may be assumed as well that New Jersey may pursue those ends by slowing the flow of *all* waste into the State's remaining landfills, even though interstate commerce may incidentally be affected. But whatever New Jersey's ultimate purpose, it may not be accomplished by discriminating against articles of commerce coming from outside the State unless there is some reason, apart from their origin, to treat them differently. Both on its face and in its plain effect, ch. 363 violates this principle of nondiscrimination.

The Court has consistently found parochial legislation of this kind to be constitutionally invalid, whether the ultimate aim of the legislation was to assure a steady supply of milk by erecting barriers to allegedly ruinous outside competition; or to create jobs by keeping industry within the State; or to preserve the State's financial resources from depletion by fencing out indigent immigrants. In each of these cases, a presumably legitimate goal was sought to be achieved by the illegitimate means of isolating the State from the national economy.

Also relevant here are the Court's decisions holding that a State may not accord its own inhabitants a preferred right of access over consumers in other States to natural resources located within its borders. These cases stand for the basic principle that a "State is without power to prevent privately owned articles of trade from being shipped and sold in interstate commerce on the ground that they are required to satisfy local demands or because they are needed by the people of the State."

The New Jersey law at issue in this case falls squarely within the area that the Commerce Clause puts off limits to state regulation. On its face, it imposes on out-of-state commercial interests the full burden of conserving the State's remaining landfill space. What is crucial is the attempt by one State to isolate itself from a problem common to many by erecting a barrier against the movement of interstate trade.

Today, cities in Pennsylvania and New York find it expedient or necessary to send their waste into New Jersey for disposal, and New Jersey claims the right to close its borders to such traffic. Tomorrow, cities in New Jersey may find it expedient or necessary to send their waste into Pennsylvania or New York for disposal, and those States might then claim the right to close their borders. The Commerce Clause will protect New Jersey in the future, just as it protects her neighbors now, from efforts by one State to isolate itself in the stream of interstate commerce from a problem shared by all. The judgment is

Reversed.

The instrusion of federal power into every conceivable aspect of American life has not gone unchallenged on the national political scene. Many commentators assert that the 1980 election of Ronald Reagan was a grass-roots expression of dissatisfaction with pervasive federal regulation. Whether or not this dissatisfaction will be reflected in judicial reevaluation of the commerce clause is a question that probably will be answered during the 1980s.

STATE COURT JURISDICTION

Although the commerce clause provides the federal government with considerable influence over business, laws adopted by the states are just as important. As each state retains the powers not delegated to the federal government, conflicting state laws and policies could cause much confusion. Imagine the problems that people in the United States would face if the judgments, public acts, and public records of each of the states could be ignored by the courts and other official bodies in another state. A business firm that won a contract case in one state might have to fight the same battle in each of the other states in which it was necessary to enforce the judgment. A person validly married in Ohio might not be recognized as married in New York. A divorce granted in California might not be recognized in any other state. The problems both to business and to the community at large would be endless and frustrating. The framers of the Constitution fortunately anticipated these difficulties and included in the Constitution several sections designed to reduce the impact of state sovereignty.

The Full Faith and Credit Clause

Article IV, Section 1, of the Constitution states as follows: "Full Faith and Credit shall be given in each state to the public Acts, Records and judicial Proceedings of every other State." The intention of this sentence was to prevent states from refusing to recognize the judgments, public acts, and records of a sister state. In adopting the Constitution each of the states surrendered this portion of its sovereign power.

The full faith and credit clause permits a litigant who wins a judgment in one state to take this judgment into the courts of another state, which must accept it as binding. Of course, a litigant who loses a case in the courts of one state is also denied an opportunity to bring it in another state.

As a result of the full faith and credit clause, a business firm winning a judgment for damages in Ohio can have this judgment enforced in any of the other states. This is true even though the cause of action is not recognized in the other state, the Ohio judgment is the result of legal error, or the Ohio judgment contravenes the public policy of the second state. The full faith and credit clause does not, however, require the courts of the second state to recognize a judgment rendered by a court that does not have jurisdiction. Nor does the enforcing state have to recognize a judgment obtained in violation of due process.

The full faith and credit clause is not applicable to criminal cases. A state does not have to enforce the criminal law of sister states. The criminal defendant is entitled to be tried by the courts in the state where the crime was committed. Defendants who flee to another state can be extradited and returned for trial to the state where the crime was committed.

The Privileges and Immunities Clause

The privileges and immunities clause of Article IV also has had an important influence on economic activity throughout the nation. The clause bars state statutes discriminating against citizens of other states where there is no substantial reason for discrimination except the fact that they are citizens of another state. This clause guarantees that a business firm operating in a state even though chartered elsewhere will be treated in the same manner as firms of the home state. Disparate treatment, however, is not barred when based upon valid reasons. In one case, a Virginia statute denied out-of-state firms the right to harvest oysters in Virginia waters. The statute was held valid on the grounds that oyster beds were common property held in trust by the state for its citizens and that the state was merely trying to conserve this natural resource.

Conflict of Laws

Today, business and most other significant human activities cut across state boundaries. Conversely, these same state boundaries are important to the structure of the American legal system. As we have seen, each state makes and enforces its own laws within its boundaries. There is no indication at this time that the legal importance of state boundaries will decrease, but it is clear that technological advances in communication and transportation will further reduce the importance of these boundaries in most other areas of American life.

The dichotomy between the limited importance of state boundaries in human activity generally and its continued importance in legal administration creates numerous problems for the business community. The following is a minute sample of the many important legal questions that the business administrator should consider if business is carried on in more than one state:

1. Are the provisions of all legal documents such as contracts, promissory notes, and bills of exchange valid in each state where used?
2. Do the same time limitations for bringing suit exist in other states where the firm is doing business?
3. If employees based in one state are assigned temporarily to jobs in another, which state's workmen's compensation laws apply?
4. Is income taxable in the state where earned also taxable in the firm's home state?
5. How does the firm's responsibility for defective merchandise vary in the states where its products are marketed?

The fact that much activity, both commercial and otherwise, ignores state lines also creates a major problem for judicial administration. In many instances state courts will be called upon to settle disputes with a substantial out-of-state dimension. In these situations, a question that frequently must be answered is: What state law applies?

Although we would expect that a state court would apply its own state's law in all litigation, it doesn't always do so. Many instances exist in which state courts apply the laws of a sister state instead of its own state's laws. Public-policy considerations underlie this choice. Both statutes and cases recognize that in a legal dispute the controlling law should be that which the parties reasonably would expect it to be. Results in litigation should not depend upon fortuitous circumstances that determine the forum. In addition, the U.S. Supreme Court has held that due process is violated if a state court applies its own laws to transactions that have more substantial contacts with other states. As even small businesses often operate across state lines, the business administrator must be aware of the law that applies to actions taken not only at home but in other states as well.

THE LITIGATION PROCESS

A number of different processes furnish the means by which the legal system seeks to accomplish the tasks discussed in Chapter 1. The following material examines some of these processes and, in addition, points out some general characteristics of legal dispute resolution.

A casual glance at the legal system indicates several distinct processes in operation. One is the legislative process. Another is litigation, which can be broken down by level into a trial or appellate process and by subject matter into criminal or civil litigation. The administrative process and arbitration, methods of private dispute settlement recognized by the courts, are also parts of the legal system. Sometimes the major objectives of a process are fairly clear, but in other instances a process

designed to accomplish a particular objective does much more than that. For instance, compare legislation with litigation. The legislative process is a systematic series of actions to make laws for the community. Litigation is a process in which the primary objective is to settle disputes, but in doing this the actions taken also create laws.

All of the mentioned processes have common characteristics that identify them in a broad sense as legal. When compared with nonlegal efforts directed at solving the same and similar problems, the legal solution generally is more formal and systematic. The legal solution ordinarily takes longer to reach a decision, and the result is subject to a much greater degree of public accountability than is the result from other processes that work within the community.

One result of the greater degree of accountability is that many judicial decisions are explained in a publicly available opinion. The appellate opinions included in this text are indicative of the type of explanation that legal decision makers provide.

CRIMINAL AND CIVIL LITIGATION

Although the distinction between criminal and civil litigation is not always clear, criminal cases are brought by a public official against a defendant who has offended society at large by violating a statute that typically was enacted for the protection of other individuals or property. Criminal statutes provide that the defendant be punished in some way, usually by a fine or imprisonment. Civil cases are actions between private parties trying to resolve a question of private right or actions instituted by government in which the relief sought is not criminal—for example, an injunction prohibiting certain types of behavior.

Both civil and criminal litigation are pursued at trial and appellate levels. Initially, a trial court tries to resolve the dispute. If either or both of the parties think that the trial court has committed some type of legal error, an appeal can be taken to a higher court. Because the objectives of trial and appellate courts differ, the trial and appellate processes have different rules and procedures. In some jurisdictions the government's right to appeal in criminal cases is restricted.

THE ADVERSARY PRINCIPLE

In the United States, civil and criminal litigation are characterized by the *adversary principle.* This principle places the responsibility for developing and proving cases upon the parties rather than upon some designated legal official, with the court serving primarily as a referee. Because of the complexities of litigation, ordinarily the parties hire lawyers to represent them and to argue for them.

The rationale for the adversary principle is that truth and justice will be most effectively attained by making each litigant responsible for his or her case. Those directly involved have more incentive than outsiders to see the evidence, the legal arguments, and other factors in their favor presented in the best light.

For a number of reasons, the adversary principle has been subject to considerable criticism, especially in criminal cases. Some argue that in an adversary system winning or losing often depends upon the skill of the attorneys instead of the merits of the case. Others claim that in a criminal case the resources of the state are so much greater than those of the defendant that the defendant is placed at a disadvantage. Another objection is that, because each party's primary interest is to win, each has an incentive to distort or hide facts unfavorable to his or her position.

During the past fifty years the impact of the adversary principle has been lessened as a result of several developments. The legal system has adopted a number of procedural reforms that help the individual search out information to support his or her case. Courts have become more willing to bring in witnesses and to rely upon experts. Litigants with limited resources are being furnished legal aid. And finally, new processes are being developed to substitute for traditional courtroom litigation.

BASIC CONDITIONS OF DISPUTE RESOLUTION

For the effective legal resolution of a dispute between individuals, four problems must be solved:

1. There must be machinery to enable the tribunal to find out what differences exist between the parties and to separate these from areas of agreement.
2. A means must be provided for determining what the actual facts, events, and circumstances were in the particular case. In some instances questions of this kind are the only differences between the parties.
3. As the parties often disagree about the law, some means for determining the applicable law must be provided. In litigation, disputes about events and circumstances are called "issues of fact," and disputes that involve law are called "issues of law."
4. If the legal system is to survive, its procedures must meet standards of fairness acceptable to the community.

PRETRIAL PROCEDURES

The mechanisms that have evolved to meet these conditions provide the framework for civil litigation. Although civil and criminal litigation are similar, major differences exist in procedures, especially in the pretrial stages.

Jurisdiction over the Person

An initial problem confronting an attorney in a civil action is to determine a court that can acquire personal jurisdiction over the defendant. Traditionally, personal jurisdiction is acquired by a court through physical control of the defendant. In a civil case this does not mean that the defendant has to be held, only that he or she be served with the proper papers within the state in which the court sits. Thus a state court ordinarily acquires personal jurisdiction over a resident or nonresident defendant served within the state. Although the concept of control must be stretched somewhat, a court also retains jurisdiction over residents who are not in the state. As long as procedures for service are designed to give the absent resident notice of the action, he or she will be subject to the state's courts.

Long-Arm Jurisdiction. During the past sixty years the development of the automobile and the expansion of business enterprises into national markets have led to rules that extend the jurisdiction of state courts beyond state boundaries. These rules are a good example of the manner in which the legal system adapts to a changing environment. In view of the traditional requirement that the defendant be served personally, consider the difficulties of the plaintiff in each of the following situations:

1. Plaintiff is an Ohio resident injured in Ohio by a Missouri driver who returns home immediately after the accident.
2. Plaintiff is a California resident injured in California by a defective lathe manufactured by a New York firm.

In both instances the plaintiff might bring suit in the court of the state in which defendant resides or, under certain conditions, in the federal courts. Although these possibilities exist, very likely they would be both inconvenient and expensive, and plaintiff ordinarily would prefer to sue in his or her home state.

To permit injured plaintiffs to bring suit against nonresident drivers causing injury, a number of states in the 1920s adopted legislation that gave the local courts jurisdiction over nonresidents driving within the state based upon the fictitious appointment by the nonresident of some designated state official to receive process in defendant's behalf. This procedure, although challenged as a violation of due process, was held constitutional by the U.S. Supreme Court.[6] During the 1930s this "long arm" theory was extended to cover not only nonresidents driving on the state's highways but also various business-related activities carried on within the state. In 1945 the Supreme Court ruled that, as long as the defendant has certain minimal contacts with a state that make it fair for plaintiff to sue in that state, due process is not violated and the courts of plaintiff's state have jurisdiction.[7]

Pleadings

The first stage in a civil case is called the *pleadings*. In this stage the parties exchange legal documents in which they outline the bases of their claims and defenses. The basic pleadings are the *petition* or *complaint* and the *answer*. Copies of each document of the pleadings are filed with the court.

The Summons. A lawsuit actually begins when the defendant is served with a *summons*. The summons informs the defendant that action is being brought and that a judgment against the defendant will be entered by default if no appropriate response is made. The summons tells the defendant little or nothing about the nature of plaintiff's claim. Traditionally, the law has required that the summons be handed to the defendant, but most states today allow service by a variety of methods, including publication, mailing, or delivery to the defendant's residence.

The Complaint. The complaint, which is the initial pleading, spells out in some detail the nature of the claim. In practice, in many jurisdictions the summons and the complaint are served together. The statements in the complaint as well as the other pleadings are statements of fact. The procedural rules of one state direct that the statements be "plain and concise" and "sufficiently particular to give the court and parties notice of the transactions, occurrences . . . intended to be proved. . . ."

The Answer. Probably the most frequent answer is that all or at least some of the allegations in the complaint are just not true. This is called a *denial*. Another possible response is that there are facts not mentioned in the complaint that constitute a defense. For example, the defendant might allege in response to a complaint for money owed that payment has been made. An answer of this kind is called an *affirmative defense*. The defendant may also counterclaim. A *counterclaim* is an assertion by the defendant that he has a claim against the plaintiff that could be the basis for an independent action. A sample complaint and answer are shown in Figures 2-1 and 2-2.

FIGURE 2-1

IN THE COURT OF COMMON PLEAS, FRANKLIN COUNTY, OHIO CIVIL DIVISION

Joan Smith
59 S. High Street
Columbus, Ohio
   Plaintiff

-vs-

                                 Case No. 75CV-05-4236

Tom Jones
32 W. 11th Ave.
Columbus, Ohio
   Defendant

COMPLAINT

COUNT I

1. On or about the 23rd day of February, 1980, on Cleveland Avenue at Ottawa Drive, Columbus, Franklin County, State of Ohio, defendant Tom Jones negligently drove a motor vehicle into a vehicle owned and occupied by plaintiff, Joan Smith.

2. As a result, plaintiff Joan Smith sustained injuries to her head, face and jaw. She has incurred medical expenses to date in the sum of Eight Hundred Dollars ($800.00), and expects additional medical expenses in the future.

3. Plaintiff Joan Smith has incurred permanent injuries, pain and suffering and expects to incur further pain and suffering.

4. Further, as a result of defendant's negligence, plaintiff Joan Smith's automobile was damaged in the amount of approximately Fifteen Hundred Dollars ($1,500.00).

COUNT II

5. On or about the 23rd day of February, 1980, on Cleveland Avenue at Ottawa Drive, City of Columbus, County of Franklin, State of Ohio, defendant Tom Jones willfully and wantonly drove a motor vehicle into a vehicle owned and occupied by plaintiff Joan Smith.

6. Plaintiff Joan Smith realleges paragraphs 2, 3, and 4 of the complaint.

WHEREFORE, Plaintiff Joan Smith prays for damages in the sum of Eight Thousand Dollars ($8,000.00), punitive damages in the sum of Nine Thousand Dollars ($9,000.00), special damages in the sum of Three Thousand Dollars ($3,000.00), costs and attorney fees.

> MARY DOE
> Attorney for Plaintiff
> 75 E. Rich Street
> Columbus, Ohio

JURY DEMAND

Plaintiff requests trial of these causes by a jury of eight (8).

> MARY DOE
> Attorney for Plaintiff

FIGURE 2-2

IN THE COURT OF COMMON PLEAS, FRANKLIN COUNTY, OHIO CIVIL DIVISION

Joan Smith
59 S. High Street
Columbus, Ohio
          Plaintiff

-vs-
                                            Case No. 75CV-05-4236

Tom Jones
32 W. 11th Avenue
Columbus, Ohio
          Defendant

ANSWER

FIRST DEFENSE

1. Defendant admits that on or about February 23, 1980 a collision occurred between his vehicle and a vehicle operated by plaintiff on Cleveland Avenue at Ottawa Drive, Franklin County, State of Ohio.

2. Defendant denies each and every allegation not heretofore admitted to be true.

3. Defendant denies he was negligent.

SECOND DEFENSE

4. If defendant is found to be negligent, which he expressly denies, plaintiff was contributorily negligent, proximately resulting in her alleged injuries.

BETH JONES
Attorney for Defendant
65 S. Front Street
Columbus, Ohio

<u>JURY DEMAND</u>

Now comes the defendant and requests that the within cause be tried by a jury of eight (8).

BETH JONES
Attorney for Defendant

Motions. Other important responses that the defendant might make are motions. Simply stated, a *motion* is an application to the court for an order of some kind. A wide variety of motions can be made. They are important at every stage of litigation. During the trial, motions are generally made orally in open court. Motions made before or after trial, however, are generally made in writing. In most instances, a party making a motion must give notice to his or her adversary, and the court provides an opportunity for each to argue for or against the motion.

During the pleading stage many motions are made. The majority of these are designed to correct defects in the pleadings. However, the *motion to dismiss* on the grounds that the complaint does not state a cause of action is of major importance to the continuation of the suit. The motion to dismiss is based upon the defendant's contention that, even if all the facts are as the plaintiff alleges, no legal recourse is available to the plaintiff. For example, the ABC Company, a small business, contracts to buy a tract of land in order to construct a plant. After the contract is signed, the firm states that it might be interested in buying the adjoining tract, which the seller also owns. The seller indicates that the company can have thirty days to decide if it wants the adjoining parcel. Within the thirty-day period, however, the seller contracts to sell to another party. In a suit brought by the ABC Company, seller's attorney would move to dismiss, for even if all the facts are true the ABC Company would not win since no contract for the adjoining land was ever made. The motion to dismiss challenges the legal sufficiency of the plaintiff's claim. If the motion is granted, the plaintiff's case is dismissed. If the motion is denied, the plaintiff has the right to go on with the case.

Functions of Pleadings. The pleadings serve different purposes. They provide notice to the parties of the opposition's claims. In many jurisdictions this is their chief purpose. Where notice is the function of the pleadings, their purpose is to provide for fairness in the litigation. A second purpose of the pleadings is to determine what differences exist between the parties as each sees the facts and understands the law. In answering, if the defendant does not deny a statement that the plaintiff has made in the complaint, the court assumes that no dispute exists regarding that particular fact. If the defendant does deny an allegation made in the complaint, an issue of fact exists that must be resolved in some manner. Similarly, if the defendant makes a motion to dismiss on the ground of legal insufficiency, then an issue of law—a dispute as to what the law is—exists that also must be resolved.

From Pleadings to Trial

After each of the parties has responded to the claims of fact and law made by the other, the pleadings terminate. If the only difference between the parties is a legal issue, the trial court judge will resolve it. If one of the differences is a dispute as to the facts, the case must proceed to trial. From the end of the pleadings to the trial, a number of significant actions take place. These actions, like the pleadings, are designed to solve some of the basic problems of legal dispute settlement. Three of the important procedures that are often used at this stage of litigation are summary judgment, discovery, and the pretrial conference.

Summary Judgment. Either of the parties can make a motion for *summary judgment.* The party who makes the motion is contending that there really is no genuine issue of fact so litigation need proceed no further. Ordinarily, a motion for summary judgment will be based upon one party's affidavits and documentary evidence that show that the other party's factual claims have no merit. Once the motion is made, the opposing party may present his or her proof and argue against the motion. If the court is convinced that in reality no factual issue exists, it will grant the motion and the litigation terminates. The purpose of summary judgment is to terminate litigation where no genuine dispute exists. Even when a court is unable to grant summary judgment, the supporting documents often indicate that the actual dispute regarding the facts is not so extensive as the parties believed. The procedure thus serves to narrow the factual controversy.

Discovery. The devices that the parties use to obtain further information about the case are called *discovery procedures.* Additional information tends to further reduce the facts upon which the parties disagree. Discovery procedures also tend to reduce the possibility of surprise during the trial. The use of discovery thus helps to add fairness to the litigation process. By proper use of discovery procedures either party can obtain further particulars about the opposition's case, sworn state-

ments from hostile or friendly witnesses, and information about the prospective testimony of a particular witness. Books, papers, and items relevant to the litigation can be examined, and under certain circumstances either of the parties can be required to submit to physical or mental examination.

Pretrial Conference. Most courts throughout the United States use *pretrial conferences* to expedite litigation. The format of these conferences varies from one jurisdiction to another. In some courts the pretrial conference is a formal affair; in others, there is considerable informality. Often the parties themselves attend the conference, but in some jurisdictions only the opposing counsel and the conferring judge meet. In large metropolitan courts, one or two judges will be assigned to supervise the pretrial calendar, but in rural areas the judge assigned the case will usually direct the conference.

At the conference an effort is made to narrow and simplify the factual and legal issues. If possible, admissions of fact and of documents that will avoid unnecessary proof are obtained. The parties may consider other items such as the number of expert witnesses who will testify, the need to amend the pleadings, and the date for the trial.

Exploring the issues at a pretrial conference helps to eliminate surprise at the trial. Thus the outcome is more likely to reflect a fair resolution of the issues between the parties. In many instances the pretrial conference is used to consider the possibilities of settling the case. If the parties are not too far apart, the conferring judge may try to persuade them to reach a settlement. Under no circumstances, however, should the parties be forced to settle, since a forced settlement denies them their right to trial. In some areas the pretrial conference has been criticized as a device used by the court to force settlements in order to reduce the number of cases pending on the court dockets.

THE TRIAL

In many instances litigation results because the parties are unable to agree about what actually happened—what the facts are. The purpose of the trial is to process the information that will be used to determine the facts. For most civil litigation, the American legal system uses the *petit jury*—a group of lay persons—to decide these important questions. Parties, however, may waive their right to have a jury determine the facts. If the right is waived or the case is one in which the parties do not have the right to a jury trial, the trial judge decides the facts.

The Jury System

Although the jury system has many critics, it continues to be important in American law because of strong historic support. For many decades Americans have looked upon the jury as a bulwark of democracy. It is an institution in which citizens participate directly, and it is often seen as a protection against the power of government. These sentiments stem primarily from the use of juries in criminal cases, but parties in civil cases generally feel more satisfied when their claims are determined by juries rather than judges. Today the history and tradition of trial by jury are so ingrained in our legal system that many would raise strong objections to proposals to further limit the right to trial by jury.

Traditionally, the civil jury consisted of twelve persons. Over the past twenty-five years there has been a trend toward smaller trial juries, and many jurisdictions now allow juries of fewer than twelve in most civil cases. Historically, the civil jury's verdict was required to be unanimous, but here again change has taken place, and in more than half the states unanimous verdicts are no longer required. These changes have been made primarily to shorten trials and make it possible for the courts to try more cases with less delay.

One of the first steps in the jury trial is the selection of the jurors. Lists of prospective jurors are made from various sources depending upon the jurisdiction. The names should be chosen at random from these sources, and the lists should represent a fair cross section of the community.

In spite of the fact that random selection of jurors is attempted, many people chosen for jury duty will have obvious biases. These biases might influence their decisions. To insure a greater degree of fairness, the parties are given the right to exclude certain jurors by *challenge.* Each side has a limited number of *peremptory challenges* that allow a party to exclude a prospective juror without giving any reason whatsoever. In addition, any prospective juror may be challenged and excluded *for cause.*

Trial Stages

After the jury has been selected, the principal steps in the trial are the attorneys' opening statements, the presentation of evidence, the attorneys' closing statements or summations, the judge's charge or instructions to the jury, the verdict, and the judgment. The extent and manner of use of these steps is characterized by numerous procedures to insure fairness and due process of law. Parties have the right to object to any deviation from the accepted pattern of procedures that might result in an unfair determination of the issues. For example, most evidence is presented by oral testimony of witnesses in response to questions asked by attorneys. Matters such as who can be asked what or the type, form, and content of questions are governed by the rules of evidence, and parties have a right to object to questions that do not come within the framework of these rules.

After the plaintiff's witnesses have testified, the defendant frequently moves to dismiss on the grounds that the plaintiff has failed to prove all the facts necessary to establish a case.

If the court agrees, it can terminate the case at this point. A similar motion is often made by one or both of the parties after all the evidence has been presented. This motion in many jurisdictions is referred to as a *motion for a directed verdict*. If granted, the case is in effect taken from the jury and determined by the judge.

Instructions to the Jury. After all the evidence has been submitted and counsel have summed up their cases, the judge explains to the jury the law that applies to the case. This process, which is called *instructing* or *charging* the jury, presents the jury with information about the essential facts that each party must prove to support its position as well as the relationships between the evidence presented and the legal issues involved.

Instructions given by the court are ordinarily based upon requests made by opposing counsel. The instructions are read to the jury in open court, and in many jurisdictions they are furnished to the jury in writing as well.

Basically, the instructions present alternatives indicating the legal result of each possible factual finding the jury might make. Suppose that in litigation involving Joe, a defendant, and Mary, a plaintiff, the single contested fact is whether Joe made a statement to Mary with the intention of deceiving her. Legally, if he did intend to deceive he will be liable; if he did not, the case against him will be dismissed. The judge might charge the jury as follows: "If you determine that the defendant made the statement with the intention of deceiving the plaintiff, you must find for the plaintiff. If, however, you determine that the defendant's statement was made with no intention of deceiving the plaintiff, you must find for the defendant."

Another important function of the judge's instructions is to explain to the jury the complex legal rules regarding which side has the burden of proof on each issue in the case. This is an especially important task, since in many situations the decision about which side has the burden of proof will determine the outcome of the case. In civil cases, for example, the plaintiff usually must prove each element of the case by a preponderance of the evidence. There may, however, be situations where the defendant will bear the burden of proof.

Although the basic concept underlying the charge to the jury is quite simple, in most cases there are numerous factual differences that can influence the outcome of the case. The result is that instructions, unless carefully drafted, can confuse the jury. In addition, determining proper instructions in many cases is a complicated, argumentative process that delays litigation and frequently results in appeal. Because of these problems, a number of jurisdictions now either encourage or require the use of standard or patterned instructions. These instructions are developed by bar associations and courts to adequately and simply explain the law to the jury.

The Verdict. A trial is usually concluded when the jury brings in a *verdict,* an answer to the questions that the court has submitted to it. In a civil action, the verdict will be either general or special. A *general verdict* is one in which the jurors comprehensively determine the issues for either the plaintiff or the defendant. If the jury finds for the plaintiff, the amount of damages will also be stated. In a *special verdict* the jury will provide written answers to specific questions of fact that the court submitted to it. The court, using these answers, then applies the law and resolves the issues in dispute between the parties.

Judgment and Execution. The judgment establishes the relief to which the parties are entitled. If the jury finds for the defendant, the judgment will dismiss plaintiff's suit. If the plaintiff wins the case, ordinarily the judgment will award him or her a sum of money. When a monetary award does not furnish the plaintiff adequate relief, the court may order relief of another sort.

If the plaintiff has won a monetary judgment, the court provides machinery for locating the defendant's assets, for preventing defendant from disposing of these assets, and finally for selling the assets with proceeds of the sale being used to satisfy the judgment. The defendant is often referred to as a *judgment debtor*. The final step is accomplished by a sheriff who seizes and then sells the assets. If the judgment debtor's assets are in the hands of a third party, the court can order the third party to turn the property over to the plaintiff. This procedure, referred to as *garnishment*, is sometimes used to require an employer to turn over to a creditor a portion of the wages of an employee who is a judgment debtor.

Sometimes a judgment debtor has assets that are income producing. Under these circumstances the court can appoint a receiver who will operate the property and pay the proceeds to the creditor after deducting operating expenses. Often the receiver will be empowered to negotiate the sale of the property and apply the net proceeds to the debt instead of having the property seized by the sheriff and auctioned off at what might be an inopportune time.

THE APPELLATE PROCESS

The function of an appellate court is to review the legal rulings that one or both of the parties think the trial court judge made incorrectly. This is a different function from that of the trial court, which is charged primarily with deciding differences between the parties about the facts. Because of this difference in function, the appellate process differs substantially from the trial process.

In an appeal, a determination of facts is un-necessary since all factual issues have already been decided at the trial. Because the oral testimony of witnesses and other types of evidence are not needed, the direct and cross examination of witnesses and the rules of evidence, which are designed to help the finders of fact make a correct determination, are eliminated. Interim procedures such as discovery and motions for summary judgment also have no place in an appellate court, since these procedures exist to help resolve factual issues.

When deciding if a legal error has been committed, the appellate court gets considerable information. This includes a record of the trial. Additional input is supplied by the parties, who, in our adversary system, are responsible for either pointing out the errors or supporting the rulings of the lower court. In fact, if one or both of the parties does not argue that some substantial legal error has been made, the appellate court has no power to review the trial.

The input from the parties generally consists of oral arguments before the court supported by written presentations called *briefs*. The appellate court judges, especially in the higher courts, make their decisions based upon the oral arguments of the parties, the briefs, and their own research and group discussion. For many cases, the appellate court decision then is supported by a published written opinion.

Another difference between the trial and appellate process is the number of judges involved. Appeals are heard by a number of judges whereas in a trial a single judge presides. This difference, too, is related to function.

In a trial the judge is not the important decision maker, unless the parties have waived a jury or are not entitled to one. Although the judge makes legal decisions, these are made within the context of his or her primary job, which is to see that the trial is conducted properly and with reasonable speed. A single judge can more efficiently carry out these tasks.

Appellate courts are made up of a number of judges. They are the primary decision makers, and they deal only with legal questions. As their answers to these legal questions influence the entire system, it is reasonable to have several experts deliberate and decide upon the correct decision.

In spite of fundamental differences between the appellate and trial processes, important similarities exist. These similarities give an additional inkling of some of the common characteristics of legal dispute resolution referred to earlier in the chapter.

Both trial and appellate litigation are characterized by formal, clearly articulated procedures designed to insure a solution that not only is just but appears just. Both are characterized by time-consuming deliberation with significant input from the parties, and the results of each are open to public scrutiny.

THEORY AND REALITY

A wide disparity often exists between the manner in which legal institutions are supposed to operate and the way in which they actually do. The differences between theory and reality must be recognized by business and public administrators who are trying to understand the legal system. As potential litigants, they must take these differences into account when dealing with federal and state administrative agencies, when considering proposed legislation, and when confronting a myriad of other situations in connection with the legal system.

One reality often overlooked by the layperson is the extent to which the human element often influences the system's outputs. The legal system is operated by people. Most are honest, dedicated, and hardworking, but some are not. Some are greedy, some are vain, and some are arbitrary. Some are authoritarian, while others are permissive. While many are intelligent, a fair share are not. All make mistakes. Some lie. Many work long hours and believe in what they are doing; a few do not. These, then, are the legislators, judges, lawyers, prosecutors, bailiffs, clerks, arbitrators, and mediators who play important, often critical, roles in operating the legal system. Everyone who comes into contact with the system must recognize that it is administered by ordinary people and plan accordingly.

Like the people who operate the legal system, the system's processes and procedures vary in effectiveness. Some make sense and clearly accomplish their objectives. Others are clearly a waste of time and effort.

As we look at the steps in the typical civil case, it is easy to be impressed by their orderliness and by the manner in which they appear to be directed toward solving the problems inherent in dispute settlement. For a contrasting view, ask the plaintiff who has waited three years for a case to come to trial, the executive who has lost a suit because an attorney forgot to file an important document, or the business person who has been hurt by the action of a judge who was biased, overworked, or just did not care. In spite of such problems, civil dispute resolution has long provided an effective means for resolving important differences between members of the community. It plays an integral part in limiting violence and self-help and in maintaining the rule of law.

REVIEW PROBLEMS

1. The Agricultural Adjustment Act of 1938 attempted to reduce the production of certain crops by limiting the acreage that farmers could plant. Filburn received an acreage allotment of 11.1 acres for wheat. He sowed, however, 23 acres and har-

vested from his excess acreage 239 bushels, for which he was penalized $117.11. Filburn sought to enjoin enforcement of this penalty on grounds that the Agricultural Adjustment Act did not apply to him since the wheat raised on the excess acreage was not sold but used on the farm. Filburn also argued that the law was unconstitutional as applied to him because the wheat grown on the excess acreage was not part of interstate commerce. Argue against Filburn's position. What result should the court reach? (Wickard v. Filburn, 317 U.S. 111 [1942])

2. Maryland has approximately 3,800 retail service stations selling over twenty different brands of gasoline. About 5 percent of these stations are owned by refiners, although no petroleum products are produced or refined within the state. Three of the refiners operate solely through company-operated stations. In 1974 Maryland adopted legislation prohibiting refiners of petroleum products from operating retail service stations within the state.

Shortly before the effective date of the statute, Exxon filed a declaratory judgment action challenging the statute on grounds that it violated the commerce clause. Should the declaratory judgment be granted? Discuss. (Exxon Corp. of America v. Maryland, 437 U.S. 117 [1977])

3. McLain filed a class action under Sec. 1 of the Sherman Act, alleging that real-estate brokers, members of the Real Estate Board of New Orleans, were guilty of fixing the rate of commissions. The defendant brokers argued that the Sherman Act did not apply to them since they were not involved in interstate commerce. Considering that the function of a real-estate broker is to bring buyers and sellers together, what arguments could McLain advance to support federal jurisdiction? (McLain v. Real Estate Board of New Orleans, 444 U.S. 232 [1980])

4. Robinson purchased a new Audi from Seaway Volkswagen, Inc. (Seaway) in Massena, N.Y. The following year Robinson was injured in an automobile accident while driving through Oklahoma to a new home in Arizona. The injury was caused when the Audi caught fire after being struck in the rear. Robinson claimed that her injuries resulted from defective design of the Audi's gas tank. She sued Seaway; World-Wide Volkswagen, the regional distributor in New York; and the importer, Volkswagen of America, in the Oklahoma courts. Neither Seaway nor World-Wide Volkswagen conducted business in Oklahoma. Robinson argued that it was foreseeable that an automobile purchased in New York would travel to Oklahoma and thus that the Oklahoma courts had jurisdiction. Discuss the validity of this claim from a legal and public-policy standpoint. (World-Wide Volkswagen v. Woodson, 444 U.S. 286 [1980])

5. Ollie's Barbecue is a family-owned restaurant in Birmingham, Ala. It is located on a state highway eleven blocks from an interstate and a somewhat greater distance from railroad and bus stations. The restaurant employs thirty-six persons, two-thirds of whom are Blacks. The restaurant purchases locally approximately $150,000 worth of food, 46 percent of which is meat bought from a local supplier who has procured it from out of state. Ollie's does not buy directly from out of state. The restaurant has a policy of not serving Blacks. In view of these facts, do the federal courts have jurisdiction to hear a case brought by the U.S. Department of Justice charging a violation of federal civil rights statutes? Discuss. (Katzenbach v. McClung, 379 U.S. 294 [1964])

FOOTNOTES

[1]Wayman v. Southard, 10 Weat. 1 (1825).
[2]343 U.S. 579 (1951).
[3]343 U.S. 579 at 588.
[4]Bureau of National Affairs, *Antitrust & Trade Regulation Report,* 1975, No. 721, p. A-11.
[5]9 Wheat. 1 (1824).
[6]Hess v. Pawolski, 274 U.S. 352 (1927).
[7]International Shoe v. Washington, 326 U.S. 310 (1945).

CHAPTER 3

White Collar Crime and Intentional Torts

WHITE COLLAR CRIME

White collar crime is a catch-all phrase to describe crime committed in a commercial context, often by members of the managerial or professional class. Specific examples include embezzlement, employee theft, shoplifting, antitrust violations, income tax evasion, securities fraud, and cheating on Medicaid.

White collar crime costs the economy billions of dollars every year, yet often it seems less evil than "traditional" crime. This attitude can be attributed to the fact that white collar crime is often impersonal, with no specific victim. Instead, the only identifiable victim is an abstract agency such as the government or a large institution. White collar criminals rationalize their actions by claiming they "didn't hurt anyone," they "just beat the system."

In fact, everyone pays for white collar crime in higher prices. In addition, the widespread existence of white collar crime damages the ability of our industrial system to produce goods, to grow, to cope with changing conditions in the international sphere, and to provide a fairer distribution of wealth. Similarly, the various types of fraud committed against government agencies add substantially to the cost of running the government. They increase the probability that less desirable systems will evolve—systems selected for their ability to control abuse rather than for their ability to serve the public interest. For example, an income tax may be the equitable method of raising revenue. But an income tax is ineffective if not backed by a significant

57

level of voluntary compliance. A payroll tax is much easier to enforce, but by its nature it is likely to be more regressive.

Most white collar crimes are considered crimes *malum prohibitum* as opposed to *malum in se*. Crimes *malum in se* are those like murder and rape that are considered by all reasonable people to be "naturally wrong." Business people are not expected to differ from the general public in agreeing that the letter and spirit of laws proscribing such crimes should be strictly complied with. Crimes *malum in se* require *mens rea* (a guilty mind), or criminal intent. Crimes *malum prohibitum* are considered wrong only because a statute declares them to be so. Crimes *malum prohibitum* do not require *mens rea*. They are strict liability offenses, their commission being criminal even in the absence of criminal intent. Driving on the left side of the road or selling furniture on Sunday may be criminal acts under *malum prohibitum* statutes.

Antitrust and environmental pollution laws are examples of laws that managers are likely to hold in lower esteem than does the general public. Most managers seek to obey the letter of such laws but may be less concerned about their spirit. They often use a "claimed difficulty of understanding" justification for engaging in activities of borderline legality under these laws.

White collar crimes are difficult to punish. Arguably the most effective sanction that could be imposed upon a corporate manager is imprisonment. No reasonable business person wants to serve a jail term. Yet jail terms are rarely imposed upon corporate managers, even in instances where violations of safety laws have resulted in deaths or in millions of dollars in damages. Why is this? There are a number of reasons, which, taken together, have a significant impact on the criminal justice system. First, in most cases of corporate criminal activity the requisite criminal intent is hard to prove. Corporations often take actions that none of its managers would take as individuals. This is a common result of consensus and/or organizational decision making. Thus an "organizational mind" rather than an individual mind seems responsible. Second, corporate executives are likely to be represented in criminal matters by exceptionally experienced and able counsel. Finally, business people are often respected community leaders, and the consequences of their alleged criminal actions are likely to seem uncertain and remote to other members of the community. All of these factors militate against jail sentences being imposed.

Corporations are generally viewed as profit maximizers. Many corporate executives want financial security and an expensive life style. Logically, then, it would seem to follow that financial sanctions imposed for violations of law would be very effective. But the fines actually assessed are rarely of relative significance to large business firms. The Sherman Act now provides for a fine of $1 million per count. The maximum fine under a three-count indictment would be of little significance to General Motors. The fines available under many of the criminal laws related to protecting the environment or worker safety are much smaller than those available under the Sherman Act.

The impact of a fine on the corporation or manager is not likely to be truly significant. But even if fines were increased significantly, there is still the fundamental question of whether such a threat would be likely to influence corporate behavior—that is, whether large corporations are purely profit maximizers. If firms were not profit maximizers, they would be less likely to be concerned about incurring additional costs by engaging in actions that could result in fines or judgments of liability. Christopher Stone argues that there is a tendency to exaggerate the extent to which large companies are profit maximizers.[1] His thesis is that, once basic needs such as survival and an established market niche are satisfied, corporate managers become concerned with other goals (peer recognition, keeping up with the corporate Joneses). The profit goal becomes one of maintaining a reasonable level of income. In fact, exceedingly high profits may be bad public relations. Stone argues that managers are likely to view fines or civil judgments as strokes of ill luck that are not nearly as bad as losses from poor management decisions.

The threat of a fine is also diminished by the fact that ignoring a pollution-control or worker-safety law may save millions of dollars of capital costs. Engaging in price fixing may generate substantial sales and profits. Thus we come to the disturbing conclusion that it may often be economically advantageous for a large corporation to violate the law intentionally.

What are corporate attitudes about this issue? Experience indicates that some corporate management teams are law-abiding while others are not. The extensive upper-management involvment in the Equity Funding scandal involving bogus insurance policies is an extreme example of pervasive willful disrespect for and violation of the law. Stone details how the Holland Furnace Company continued using unethical and fraudulent sales techniques for twenty-five years in the face of a host of lawsuits and administrative actions. Finally, the company's chief executive officer was imprisoned—for a six-month term. On the other side, many corporations have strong internal control procedures designed to ensure strict compliance throughout the corporation with all applicable laws.

Some critics have argued that managers in general "customarily feel and express contempt for law, for government, and for governmental personnel."[2] Sutherland contended that corporate criminality was a persistent phenomenon and that managers who violated regulatory provisions did not lose status among their peers.[3]

Discussion of specific elements of the various white collar crimes would fill volumes.

However, some of the crimes—bribery, antitrust crimes, securities fraud, and violations of the federal Food, Drug, and Cosmetic Act—are briefly described below.

The corrupt giving, offering, or promising of anything of value to public officials for the purpose of diverting them from the proper performance of their jobs is a felony under federal law. Similarly, a public official who corruptly solicits, receives, or agrees to receive a bribe commits a felony. A person convicted under the statute may be imprisoned for not more than fifteen years, may be disqualified from holding any office, and will be fined not more than $20,000 or three times the monetary equivalent of the thing of value, whichever is greater.

The Foreign Corrupt Practices Act of 1977 makes it a federal crime to give anything of value to any foreign official for the purpose of influencing a foreign government. Violations are punishable by fines of up to $1 million for companies and by fines of up to $10,000 and imprisonment for not more than fifty-five years for individuals.

Federal antitrust violations are punishable under the Sherman Antitrust Act, which prohibits monopolization, conspiracies, and attempts to monopolize, as well as the entering into any contract, combination, or conspiracy in restraint of trade. Violation of the Sherman Act is a felony and may result in imprisonment for up to three years. Although the imposition of jail terms in Sherman Act proceedings has received considerable publicity when it has occurred, the number of instances in which jail terms have actually been imposed on defendant business people is relatively small. The Sherman Act also provides for fines of $100,000 per count for individuals and $1,-000,000 per count for corporations. Antitrust law is discussed in more detail in Chapter 38.

The federal securities acts of 1933 and 1934 regulate the issuance and trading of securities. It is a crime to willfully make an untrue statement about a material fact or omit to state any material fact in connection with the offering of a security. Convictions may carry fines of up to $10,000 or five years' imprisonment or both. The securities laws are discussed in detail in Chapter 31.

The federal Food, Drug, and Cosmetic Act is a public health statute. Among its many prohibitions are: misbranding or adulterating a food, drug, mechanical device, or cosmetic; failure by a drug producer to register with the Food and Drug Administration (FDA); and refusing to permit an inspection. An example of the operation of this act's criminal provisions is the case of *United States* v. *Park* reported in Chapter 25.

TORT LAW: PURPOSE AND NATURE

A tort is a civil wrong, other than a breach of contract, for which a court will provide a remedy. The term "tort" is a French word meaning injury or wrong; it comes from the Latin *tortus,* which means "twisted," as in conduct that is twisted, or not straight.

Tort law is the legal system's recognition of those injuries for which the injured party can seek compensation in a noncriminal or civil court. Its basic purposes are to compensate the injured party at minimal cost to the government and to deter undesirable behavior. The law of torts reflects social decisions on what injuries should be compensated, what interests should be protected, and what conduct should be deterred. Because new forms of social behavior are constantly introduced in an evolving society, new torts are constantly being recognized. In considering whether to recognize a new tort, the courts weigh the interest of the injured party (the plaintiff), the social desirability of the defendant's conduct, the unreasonableness of the defendant's intent, whether the defendant has departed from a standard of reasonable conduct, and the social consequences that will follow from recognizing a right to civil redress in the form

of a tort claim versus recognizing the right of the defendant to engage in certain conduct. Statutes now play an increasing role in the development of tort law, but much of tort law is still common law.

Although tort law regulates the behavior of people in general, it is especially relevant to individuals in the business world. Whether liability will follow from a particular act is often an important consideration in business planning. For example, in the field of product liability alone in recent years there have been hundreds of appellate court cases and new and sometimes controversial legislative developments.

In reading about particular torts, note that some tortious acts are also acts the criminal law punishes. In fact, a single act may be a tort, compensable in civil court, and at the same time a crime, punishable by a fine or incarceration. This situation does not expose the defendant to unconstitutional or unfair double jeopardy since the sources of tort law and criminal law are different. Tort law and criminal law address separate and distinct injuries and serve different social functions. The injury caused by a tort is to a particular person, the victim who suffers the loss. The injury caused by a crime, however, is considered to be inflicted on the state and the social interests it represents. Obviously, some acts are tortious but not criminal and vice versa. Basically, tort law provides a system of private compensation to victims of private wrongs, while criminal law proscribes acts that society either is unable to or chooses not to tolerate.

Torts fall into three categories: intentional torts, negligence, and strict liability. Intentional torts are characterized by voluntary intent on the part of the defendant to engage in conduct that interferes with the socially protected interest of the plaintiff. Negligence does not involve the presence of wrongful intent but rather the failure of the defendant to conform to a standard of reasonable conduct. Strict liability assesses liability without regard to either the unreasonableness of the defendant's intent or the unreasonableness of his conduct; it is liability without fault. The rest of this chapter focuses on intentional torts; Chapter 4 discusses negligence and strict liability.

INTENTIONAL TORTS

Intentional torts are distinguished from other torts by the presence of voluntary intent to bring about results that the law does not sanction. The required element of intention does not necessarily mean an evil motive or desire to harm, for an actor may be liable for the consequences of a practical joke or for the consequences of an act he or she did not believe would cause injury. Rather, the actor does something knowingly, and his or her responsibility extends not only to desired consequences, such as a bloody nose from a punch in the face, but also to those that the actor believes or should believe are likely to follow. Courts apply the "substantial certainty test" for determining whether the defendant possessed the requisite intent for purposes of committing an intentional tort. This test may be expressed as follows: Where a reasonable person in the defendant's position would believe that a particular result was substantially certain to follow, he or she will be considered to have intended it. The likely result must appear as a substantial certainty. Mere knowledge of the likelihood of harm is not the same as intent. The distinction between knowledge and intent is a fine one. It is the difference between merely knowing the risk and being substantially certain of it.

Several intentional torts are discussed briefly below. For convenience, they are classified into four categories: torts against the person, torts against property interests, competitive torts, and other business torts.

TORTS AGAINST THE PERSON

Several torts protect an individual from intentional interference with his or her body and mind. Starting with the tort of battery, this section discusses the torts that provide redress for the intentional infliction of bodily or mental harm.

Battery

Battery is the intentional touching of another without justification and without consent. Battery also includes the unprivileged touching of another with some substance put in motion by the aggressor. Thus shooting someone constitutes a battery. "Justification," a term of art (a word with a special meaning to a particular profession or trade—in this case, law), is usually the key to whether a battery has been committed. Obviously, minimal or social touching is not considered battery, but justification is not established merely because onlookers approve of the action. Reasonableness is the standard. Generally, courts hold that a person can meet force or the threat of force with similar force without liability. However, if the perceived threat is to a third party or if the threat is to property, the chance of establishing justification is less. Consider the following case.

Katko v. Briney

Supreme Court of Iowa
183 N.W. 2d 657 (1971)

Katko was injured when a spring gun discharged and shot him in the leg while he was trespassing in an unoccupied farm house owned by the Brineys. Katko sued the

Brineys for battery, and the jury returned a verdict for Katko against the Brineys for $20,000 actual damages and $10,000 punitive damages. The trial court denied the Brineys' motion for judgment notwithstanding the verdict and for new trial and entered judgment on the verdict. The Brineys appealed to the Iowa Supreme Court, which affirmed the trial court decision. Katko is the plaintiff; the Brineys are the defendants.

Moore, Chief Justice

The primary issue presented here is whether an owner may protect personal property in an unoccupied boarded-up farm house against trespassers and thieves by a spring gun capable of inflicting death or serious injury.

We are not here concerned with a man's right to protect his home and members of his family. Defendants' home was several miles from the scene of the incident to which we refer infra.

Plaintiff's action is for damages resulting from serious injury caused by a shot from a 20-gauge spring shotgun set by defendants in a bedroom of an old farm house which had been uninhabited for several years. Plaintiff and his companion, Marvin McDonough, had broken and entered the house to find and steal old bottles and dated fruit jars which they considered antiques.

For about ten years, 1957 to 1967, there occurred a series of trespassing and housebreaking events with loss of some household items, the breaking of windows and "messing up of the property in general." The latest occurred June 8, 1967, prior to the event on July 16, 1967, herein involved.

Defendants through the years boarded up the windows and doors in at attempt to stop the intrusions. They had posted "no trespass" signs on the land several years before 1967. The nearest one was thirty-five feet from the house. On June 11, 1967, defendants set a "shotgun trap" in the north bedroom. After Mr. Briney cleaned and oiled his 20-gauge shotgun, the power of which he was well aware, defendants took it to the old house where they secured it to an iron bed with the barrel pointed at the bedroom door. It was rigged with wire from the doorknob to the gun's trigger so it would fire when the door was opened. Briney first pointed the gun so an intruder would be hit in the stomach but at Mrs. Briney's suggestion it was lowered to hit the legs. He admitted he did so "because I was mad and tired of being tormented" but he "did not intend to injure anyone." He gave no explanation of why he used a loaded shell and set it to hit a person already in the house. Tin was nailed over the bedroom window. The spring gun could not be seen from the outside. No warning of its presence was posted.

Plaintiff lived with his wife and worked regularly as a gasoline station attendant in Eddyville, seven miles from the old house. He had observed it for several years while hunting in the area and considered it as being abandoned. He knew it had long been uninhabited. In 1967 the area around the house was covered with high weeds. Prior to July 16, 1967, plaintiff and McDonough had been to the premises and found several old bottles and fruit jars which they took and added to their collection of antiques. On the latter day about 9:30 P.M. they made a second trip to the Briney property. They entered the old house by removing a board from a porch window which was without glass. While McDonough was looking around the kitchen area plaintiff went to another part of the house. As he started to open the north bedroom door the shotgun went off striking him in the right leg above the ankle bone. Much of his leg, including part of the tibia, was blown away. Only by McDonough's assistance was plaintiff able to get out of the house and after crawling some distance was put in his vehicle and rushed to a doctor and then to a hospital. He remained in the hospital forty days.

Plaintiff testified he knew he had no right to break and enter the house with intent to steal bottles and fruit jars therefrom. He further testified he had entered a plea of guilty to larceny in the nighttime of property of less than $20 value from a private building. He stated he had been fined $50 and costs and paroled during good behavior from a sixty-day jail sentence. Other than minor traffic charges this was plaintiff's first brush with the law. On this civil case appeal it is not our prerogative to review the disposition made of the criminal charge against him.

The main thrust of defendants' defense in the trial court and on this appeal is that "the law permits use of a spring gun in a dwelling or warehouse for the purpose of preventing the unlawful entry of a burglar or thief." They repeated this contention in their exceptions to the trial court's instructions 2, 5, and 6.

In the statement of issues the trial court stated plaintiff and his companion committed a felony when they broke and entered defendants' house. In instruction 2 the court referred to the early case history of the use of spring guns and stated under the law their use was prohibited except to prevent the commission of felonies of violence and where human life is in danger. The instruction included a statement that breaking and entering is not a felony of violence.

Instruction 5 stated: "You are hereby instructed that one may use reasonable force in the protection of his property, but such right is subject to the qualification that one may not use such means of force as will take human life or inflict great bodily injury. Such is the rule even though the injured party is a trespasser and is in violation of the law himself."

Instruction 6 stated: "An owner of premises is prohibited from wilfully or intentionally injuring a trespasser by means of force that either takes life or inflicts great bodily injury; and therefore a person owning a premises is prohibited from setting out 'spring guns' and like dangerous devices which will likely take life or inflict great bodily injury, for the purpose of harming trespassers. The fact that the trespasser may be acting in violation of the law does not change the rule. The only time when such conduct of setting a 'spring gun' or a like dangerous device is justified would be when the trespasser was committing a felony of violence or a felony punishable by death, or where the trespasser was endangering human life by his act."

The overwhelming weight of authority, both textbook and case law, supports the trial court's statement of the applicable principles of law. Prosser on Torts, third edition, pages 116–18 states:

> "the law has always placed a higher value upon human safety than upon mere rights in property, it is the accepted rule that there is no privilege to use any force calculated to cause death or serious bodily injury to repeal the threat to land or chattels, unless there is also such a threat to the defendant's personal safety as to justify a self-defense. . . . Spring guns and other man-

killing devices are not justifiable against a mere trespasser, or even a petty thief. They are privileged only against those upon whom the landowner, if he were present in person would be free to inflict injury of the same kind."

Restatement of Torts, section 85, page 180, states:

"The value of human life and limbs, not only to the individual concerned but also to society, so outweighs the interest of a possessor of land in excluding from it those whom he is not willing to admit thereto that a possessor of land has, as is stated in Sec. 79, no privilege to use force intended or likely to cause death or serious harm against another whom the possessor sees about to enter his premises or meddle with his chattel, unless the intrusion threatens death or serious bodily harm to the occupiers or users of the premises. . . . A possessor of land cannot do indirectly and by a mechanical device that which, were he present, he could not do immediately and in person. Therefore, he cannot gain a privilege to install, for the purpose of protecting his land from intrusions harmless to the lives and limbs of the occupiers or users of it, a mechnicial device whose only purpose is to inflict death or serious harm upon such as may intrude, by giving notice of his intention to inflict, by mechanical means and indirectly, harm which he could not, even after request, inflict directly were he present."

The facts in Allison v. Fiscus, 156 Ohio 120, 100 N.E.2d 237, 44 A.L.R.2d 369, decided in 1951, are very similar to the case at bar. There plaintiff's right to damages was recognized for injuries received when he feloniously broke a door latch and started to enter defendant's warehouse with intent to steal. As he entered a trap of two sticks of dynamite buried under the doorway by defendant owner was set off and plaintiff seriously injured. The court held the question whether a particular trap was justified as a use of reasonable and necessary force against a trespasser engaged in the commission of a felony should have been submitted to the jury. The Ohio Supreme Court recognized plaintiff's right to recover punitive or exemplary damages in addition to compensatory damages.

The legal principles stated by the trial court in instructions 2, 5, and 6 are well established and supported by the authorities cited and quoted supra. There is no merit in defendants' objections and exceptions thereto. Defendants' various motions based on the same reasons stated in exceptions to instructions were properly overruled.

Affirmed.

CASE NOTE

There is much symbolism in the above case. The case pits a thief-trespasser against a farm couple who exemplify Grant Wood's painting "American Gothic," which was painted in Iowa and now hangs in the Chicago Art Institute.

Public reactions to *Katko* v. *Briney* were reflected in the letters-to-the-editor column of the *Des Moines Register*. One letter, published February 21, 1971, asked: "What kind of propaganda will this make for Russia? Why are people leaving Iowa? It's self-explanatory, isn't it?" Another letter advised that, in light of this case, the safe thing to do to a prowler in one's home is "Aim between his eyes and shoot." A physician described the decision as the "Most nefarious thing that has happened in the annals of jurisprudence, and how anyone can hold any respect for that type of justice is beyond reason." The *Register* commented: "We are discouraged that so many of the people in this civilized society place property rights over human life."

Letters in support of the case were published a week later. One correspondent wrote, "Apparently Iowans are becoming more barbaric than we'd like to admit, and place little value on human life." Another wrote, "How many adventurous Tom Sawyers and Huck Finns would ever have grown to adulthood if death traps were permitted on all such property?" Still another declared ironically, "To arms, to arms, the prowlers are coming, should be the battle cry of all God-fearing, law-abiding citizens of Iowa." To these the *Register* responded: "Our confidence in the good judgment and fairness of Iowans has been restored."

Support for the Brineys consisted of more than words. The Brineys auctioned off eighty acres to pay the judgment. After the sale, a public fund from sympathizers amounting to $7,000 was given to them. Among the contributors were thirty convicts of an Iowa prison who donated $100.

The particular brand of law and order the Brineys made their own may not be limited to the spring gun. Consider the following story that was published in *Time,* March 22, 1971, at p. 12:

> "Four times in the past year, John Fretwell's air conditioning equipment store in Dallas was broken into and robbed. Fretwell took to renting a Doberman pinscher watchdog for weekend duty, but at $75 a weekend, the protection itself seemed little better than petty larceny.
>
> "Then Fretwell went up to Oklahoma a month or so ago for a snake hunt, and he brought back what may be the ultimate in burglar protection: seven diamondback rattlesnakes. During business hours, he cages the snakes in the window of his business office, labeled with a sign: DANGER: SNAKES BITE. At night, before going home, he frees the 5-ft. rattlers to glide around the premises. In the morning, armed with a hooked stick and a burlap bag, he rounds them up. There were a few uneasy days when one snake disappeared —it turned up later snoozing in a dark corner—but the rattlers seem to be working like a charm against burglars.
>
> "When news of Fretwell's protection service spread, the Dallas fire department served notice that Fretwell's place could burn to the ground before a fireman would step inside, and City Hall eventually found an ordinance against keeping snakes uncaged inside the city limits. None of which bothers Fretwell. He and his partner have even gone out on other snake hunts and brought back about 100 rattlers to protect their business acquaintances. As a matter of fact, says Fretwell, 'I heard about a fellow who's tinkering with a cobra.' Presumably, Dallas burglars should now pack a concealed mongoose instead of a .38."

Assault

Assault is the intentional act of putting someone in immediate apprehension for his or her physical safety. The victim need not necessarily be "frightened"; apprehension is used to mean "expectation." For example, words alone typically do not constitute an assault because they usually are not sufficient to put an ordinary person in apprehension of immediate harm. On the other hand, if the words are coupled with a threat of immediate physical harm—for example, a menacing gesture—an assault could be established.

It is the actor's, rather than the victim's, intention to act and the victim's, rather than the actor's, apprehensive state of mind that are relevant in cases of assault.

False Imprisonment

False imprisonment is the intentional confinement of a nonconsenting individual within boundaries fixed by the defendant for an appreciable time. The tort protects an individual's freedom of movement or liberty. The tort arises in business contexts from attempts to deal with suspected shoplifters or with employees suspected of dishonest behavior. Here the customer's or employee's interest in unrestrained movement conflicts with the storeowner's or employer's interest in protecting his or her property. At common law, a storekeeper is liable in tort for false imprisonment if he or she detains a suspected shoplifter who ultimately is found innocent. This places the storekeeper in a dilemma: if the storekeeper suspects a person of shoplifting, has the individual arrested, and then discovers that the person did not steal anything, the storekeeper is liable for false imprisonment; if the storekeeper does nothing and permits the suspected shoplifter to leave the store, all hope of proof is lost forever. The result is that, in most cases, unless he or she is absolutely sure, the storekeeper will let the suspected shoplifter go and will pass on the loss to the consuming public.

Because shoplifting is a major social problem, costing the consuming public billions of dollars through inflated prices, many legislatures have resolved the conflict between the storekeeper's property interest and the consumer's liberty interest by conferring a limited or qualified privilege upon the storekeeper to reasonably detain those he or she reasonably suspects of shoplifting. By statute, most states now limit the storekeeper's liability to detentions made without reasonable cause or in bad faith. The Ohio statute is typical. It provides: "A merchant who has probable cause to believe that items have been taken by a customer has the right to detain him for a reasonable time. The burden of proof on the issue of probable cause is upon the merchant." This statutory limitation of liability is a privilege granted by the legislature; if it is abused, the storekeeper can be liable. Thus if a storekeeper detains someone he or she has probable cause to believe is a shoplifter, but detains that person for an unreasonable length of time, the privilege will be lost. What starts out as a lawful detention can end up as the tort of false imprisonment.

Another issue often raised in cases of false imprisonment is whether the acquiescence of the alleged shoplifter to remaining in a store to be questioned constitutes consent. On the grounds that such behavior should be encouraged, most courts hold that it is not consent. They reason that persons should not forfeit their causes of action because they were reasonable, did not flee, and did not encourage the storekeeper to commit battery.

The term "false imprisonment" conjures up confinement within walls and iron bars. The tort, however, has a much broader application, as the following case illustrates.

National Bond & Investment Co. v. Whithorn

Court of Appeals of Kentucky
123 S.W. 24 263 (1939)

William Whithorn sued National Bond & Investment Company for false imprisonment. A jury verdict was rendered in his favor for $700 compensatory damages and $900 punitive damages. National Bond Investment appealed that judgment to the Kentucky Court of Appeals, which affirmed the trial court decision. National Bond & Investment Company is the appellant; William Whithorn is the appellee.

Fulton, Justice

The evidence discloses that the appellant had, or at least claimed to have, a conditional sales contract on a car in possession of appellee, and that payments due under this contract had not been made. Appellant desired to repossess the car and assigned its employees, O'Brien and Baer, to this task. Baer appears to have been a highpowered repossessor in the employ of appellant in Chicago and was imported to Louisville for some special work along this line. These employees, after making inquiry from a relative of appellee, and after a little "fast work" connected with this inquiry, learned where appellee lived and by so doing managed to find him driving the car on a street in Louisville. In their car they followed appellee in his car for some distance and hailed him down for the purpose of making a repossession.

There is considerable conflict in the testimony as to what occurred between appellee and these two employees of appellant on the occasion of this repossession, but the jury evidently accepted appellee's version of the melee.

When O'Brien and Baer hailed appellee he thought they were officers and stopped his car, whereupon O'Brien got out of his car, walked up to appellee's car, and invited him to get out and come back and talk to Baer. This appellee refused to do, so finally Baer also came to appellee's car and from that time things began to move rapidly. Appellee was informed that these employees desired to repossess the car and was notified to get out and take his personal belongings. Appellee demanded evidence of their authority, which they assured him they had, but their assurance did not satisfy appellee and the argument as to authority continued for some time. The repossessors became impatient at being balked of their quarry and finally one of them said, "Don't you move this machine, I will have an officer here in about two minutes."

After O'Brien came back he made the statement that "the officers will be here any minute." Shortly after O'Brien returned, a wrecker, which had been called by O'Brien, pulled up and one of the appellant's employees motioned for the wrecker to pull in front of appellee's car to hook on, whereupon appellee started the motor in his car for the purpose of driving off, but O'Brien raised the hood of the car and jerked loose the distributor wire. Appellee, not desiring to see his car put hors du combat, opened the door of his car and started out after him. When appellee opened the door of his car and started out, Baer attempted to reach through the window of the car on the other side and get the car key, but appellee, sensing what was in the wind, beat Baer to the key, and this seemed to "peeve" the repossessors very much. O'Brien then said, "He has acted so smart I will have him put in jail," and got in his machine and left. He came back in a short while and it does not clearly appear whether or not he called the police officers, but at any rate a police officer, pursuant to a telephone call from someone, showed up a while afterwards.

When O'Brien returned from his second departure Baer directed the driver operating the wrecker to hook to appellee's car and pull out with it, but in view of appellee's vehement protests the driver of the wrecker hesitated to act, but after repeated demands by O'Brien finally coupled up with appellee's car and hoisted the front wheels off the ground. Baer then climbed in appellee's car and the wrecker started pulling the car down the street, whereupon appellee put on the emergency brake and threw the car into reverse, thereby managing to stall the wrecker and bring the car to a stop after it had been pulled down the street something like 75 to 100 feet. During the progress down the street, appellee who says he tried to prevent Baer from getting in the car with him, attempted to eject Baer from the car by kicks on the shins, which Baer says in his testimony were rather forcefully administered, but his attempts to dislodge this Chicago repossessor were wholly unavailing.

While all this was occurring numerous cars were passing up and down the street; some of them stopping and looking and then driving on. In other words, the passing public seemed to realize that a good act was being put on and did not miss the opportunity to enjoy at least a portion of it. After appellee had managed to bring the procession to a halt by stalling the wrecker, a policeman came up and inquired as to the meaning of the controversy, and the contestants on the respective sides stated their case. The policeman says that he refused to pass on the merits of the controversy, but he did demand appellee's driver's license, which it appears appellee had but had left at home. Appellee seemed to think the policeman was taking sides with the repossessors and became rather angry, demanding the policeman's badge number and name, whereupon the policeman placed him under arrest. The drama of repossession ended with the policeman departing with appellee in tow and O'Brien and Baer departing with appellee's car in tow, the result being a complete and satisfying repossession, at least satisfying in its results to appellant's employees, O'Brien and Baer, but highly unsatisfactory to appellee.

It appears that nothing was done about the charge against appellee for not having a driver's license. He apologized to the policeman for being angry, and this apparently satisfied the gentleman and appellee was "permitted to go on his own bond."

If appellant had a valid conditional sales contract on appellee's car, and he was behind in the payments, appellant had the right to repossess the car if it could do so peaceably, but, of course, had no right to create a breach of the peace in doing so, or to put appellee under any kind of restraint, or to use any force directed against him in making the repossession.

Appellant contends the transaction above recited did not amount to false imprisonment, its theory being that appellee was in no wise restrained or impeded, and that he was perfectly at liberty at any time to go his way.

We are unable to agree with appellant's contention. A reading of the evidence we have quoted above makes it immediately apparent that appellee, in the present case, was placed under restraint by O'Brien and Baer. They had him in his car under forcible control, being pulled down the street some 75 to 100 feet, against his vehement protest, and we are firmly of the opinion that such conduct on their part was a false imprisonment.

It is true, as appellant argues, that appellee was at liberty to depart and these employees were not preventing him from doing so, but the result of his departure would have been an automatic parting with his automobile, which he did not desire to part with, and which he did not have to part with, and which O'Brien and Baer had no right to take over his protests. While he was in his car he was in a place he had a legal right to be, and in which neither O'Brien nor Baer had a legal right to be, by force, and when these men hooked the wrecker on and hoisted the front wheels in the air, forcibly dragging appellee down the street in his car, this was unquestionably a restraint imposed upon him and a detention of his person, such as constitutes a false imprisonment.

Affirmed.

Defamation

Defamation is the publication of untrue statements about another that injure the victim's reputation or character. The term "publication" is a term of art meaning "communicated"; its meaning is not limited to printed or written communication. For the tort to exist, the defamatory statement must be communicated to a third person, who understands it. This is because the interest protected by the tort is that of reputation.

The tort of defamation comprises the two torts of slander and libel. Slander is oral defamation (slander is said); libel, although often thought of as written, is defamation that is characterized by permanency (e.g., a film, recording, or radio script). The distinction between the two torts historically rested in the requirement that the plaintiff prove special damages in a slander case, whereas damages in a libel case were conclusively presumed and did not need to be specially pleaded and proved. Today that distinction has been erased in a majority of states; both torts require proof of special damages.

Special damages are those supported by specific proof, such as loss of customers, business, or a particular contract. General damages include wounded feelings and humiliation, pain and suffering, and future damage. The reason that the special damage requirement was relaxed for libel was that libel, because of its permanent embodiment in print, was considered by the courts to be a more serious and potentially more damaging form of defamation. The myriad forms of modern communication, and the problem of characterization that has presented to the courts, has resulted in the two torts being placed on equal footing with regard to the requirement of proof of special damages.

An exception exists to the requirement of proof of special damages in a defamation action. A form of defamation known as defamation *per se* is actionable without proof of special damage. This exception evolved out of a recognition that certain utterances are sufficient in themselves to cause pecuniary loss. There are four categories of defamation *per se*. Defamation *per se* exists when the plaintiff alleges that the defendant (1) accused the plaintiff of committing a morally reprehensible crime (e.g., murder); (2) attributed to the plaintiff a loathsome communicable disease (e.g., a venereal disease or leprosy); (3) associated the plaintiff with conduct incompatible with the plaintiff's profession or business (e.g., called a physician a butcher); and (4) when the plaintiff is a woman, imputed unchastity to her.

For either libel or slander, the plaintiff must establish that the defendant's statement was defamatory. Whether a statement is sufficiently derogatory to be injurious to the victim's reputation or character is judged by the audience of the statement. This third-party judgment is the reason for the publication requirement. In other words, because a person's good name exists only in the opinions of others, if the audience does not believe that the remarks are derogatory or if no one hears the remarks there is no injury to the victim's character and thus no defamation. Further, if the statements are true, as established by a preponderance of the evidence, there is no defamation.

Another defense against a charge of defamation is privilege, either qualified or absolute. If defamation occurs in a privileged context, no legal relief is available to the victim of the defamation. An absolute privilege exists for judges, legislators, counsel, parties, and witnesses while acting in their official capacities or in the roles for which the privilege exists. A qualified privilege exists for nonofficials if the statements are made by someone who has a duty to do so and if the statements are communicated only to those who have an immediate interest in receiving them. For example, if a former employer is asked by a prospective employer to comment on the character of a former employee, the former employer enjoys a qualified privilege to do so. The qualified privilege is lost if the plaintiff can establish malice on the part of the speaker.

Although defamation is traditionally classified as an intentional tort, proof of intent is required only in cases involving public figures (discussed below). The general rule is that a defendant is strictly liable for innocent conduct, without proof that he or she intended the consequences or was at all negligent with respect to them. The basis of liability is the publication, not intent or negligence. In some states, a plaintiff must prove negligence. That is, the defendant may avoid liability by establishing that he or she acted carefully by taking reasonable measures to guard against any defamatory statements.

Where the plaintiff is a public figure, intent is a factor in liability. The plaintiff must prove that the libelous or slanderous remarks were not only untrue and published but also that they were made with malice. Thus a qualified privilege exists where the subject of the remarks is a public figure. Liability does not attach to untrue statements about a public figure except where the statement is made with malice.

The privilege in regard to defamatory statements about public figures is based on the Constitution's protection of free speech and press. The U.S. Supreme Court has resolved the conflict between the plaintiff's reputation interest and the defendant's constitutional right to free speech and press by holding that liability for defamation of a public figure exists only where the statement is made "with 'actual malice'—that is, with knowledge that it was false or with reckless disregard of whether it was false or not."[4] This constitutional privilege with regard to public figures is rationalized by the fact that, unlike a private individual, a public figure enjoys greater access to the public forum and can more easily rebut the untrue statements. The Supreme Court has defined a public figure as one who is thrust into the public light.

Invasion of Privacy

A person's dignity and the right to be let alone are protected by the tort of invasion of privacy.

The courts have recognized four types of invasion of privacy: (1) intrusion upon the plaintiff's physical solitude (e.g., illegal searches of persons, eavesdropping, peering into windows); (2) appropriation of the plaintiff's name or likeness (e.g., using the picture of the plaintiff in an advertisement); (3) placement of the plaintiff in a false light in the public eye (e.g., falsely attributing authorship of a poem to a well-known poet); and (4) the public disclosure of private facts (e.g., disclosing an employee's illness to a third party). The 1973 Supreme Court abortion decisions, recognizing under certain circumstances the right to have an abortion, represent a constitutional extension of the right of privacy. Invasion of privacy is distinguished from defamation in that truth is not a defense. The injury is unreasonable and irrelevant exposure to the public. Unreasonable and irrelevant exposure means that the plaintiff's privacy was entitled to protection, that the plaintiff was not a public figure or otherwise in the news, and that disclosure was not in the public interest. Although a privilege exists with regard to disclosures about public figures, such disclosures must be newsworthy. Furthermore, a public figure may recover from gross violators of privacy where the disclosure is an affront to public morals (e.g., a pornographic magazine publishing photos of a former First Lady sunbathing nude on a private beach). Another qualified privilege of the defendant to protect his or her own legitimate interest is also recognized where a potential creditor obtains information relevant to a potential debtor's credit rating.

Intentional Infliction of Emotional Distress

A person's interest in emotional tranquility is protected as a result of a recent trend to recognize intentional infliction of emotional distress as a separate tort. The tort may be defined as the intentional causing of severe mental suffering in another by means of extreme and outrageous conduct. Liability is limited to outrageous acts that cause bona fide emotional injury. The defendant's conduct must be what the average community member would consider extremely outrageous. The plaintiff's emotional distress must in fact exist and it must be severe. Minor offenses, such as name calling, are not actionable though they may wound the feelings of the victim and cause some degree of mental upset. The plaintiff cannot recover merely because of hurt feelings; the law is not concerned with trifles and cannot provide a civil remedy for every personal conflict in a crowded world. Previously, the acts had to result in direct physical injury for there to be recovery for the mental distress. Even the more liberalized modern standard is difficult to sustain in most cases.

TORTS AGAINST PROPERTY INTERESTS

Three torts exist to redress intentional interference with an individual's interest in the possession of property: trespass, conversion, and nuisance.

Trespass

The tort of trespass is really two torts: trespass to land and trespass to personal property.

Trespass to land may be defined as intentionally entering upon another's land or causing an object or a third person to do so. Trespass to land may also occur where a person intentionally remains on another's land or fails to remove from the land an object that he or she is under a duty to remove. Liability exists for trespass to land even where no harm results from the trespass. In this context, land means not only the land and objects attached to it or embedded in it but also the airspace immediately over it.

Trespass to land may result from a momentary invasion, as when one walks across another's field. A person may commit trespass without personally entering onto the land—for example, by throwing a rock against a building.

There are several defenses to trespass to land. The major defenses are: consent, accidental intrusion, and necessity. It is a defense if the landowner consented to the entry. Consent may be express, as where the landowner grants an easement, or it may be implied, as where a landowner observes a trespasser repeatedly walking across his or her property and acquiesces in the practice. Liability does not extend to accidental intrusions, as where a driver suffers a stroke, loses control of his or her car, and drives upon someone's lawn. The defense of accidental intrusion does not extend to intrusions resulting from carrying on an abnormally dangerous activity, such as construction blasting. The defense of necessity exists where in an emergency someone enters upon the land for the purpose of protecting himself or herself, the possessor of land, a third person, or the land or goods of any such persons. An example of necessity is a pilot forced to land a plane on a farmer's field.

Trespass to personal property may be defined as intentionally taking or damaging the personal property of another. An example of trespass to personal property is a creditor, attempting to repossess a car held as collateral for a loan to a debtor, mistakenly taking someone else's car. The defenses of consent, unavoidable accident, and necessity apply also to the tort of trespass to personal property.

Conversion

Conversion is the intentional exercise of control over personal property, thereby seriously interfering with another person's right of possession. The difference between the torts of trespass to personal property and conversion lies in the measure of damages for the torts. The measure of damages for trespass to personal property is the diminished value of the

personal property because of any injury to it. The measure of damages for conversion is the full value of the property at the time it was converted. Because of the larger recovery, conversion is limited to serious interferences with the right of possession that justify requiring the defendant to pay its full value. Thus, in the example above of the creditor who repossesses the wrong car, there is no conversion if the creditor immediately returns the car. He or she would, however, be liable for trespass to personal property and could be required to pay such costs as gasoline and depreciation. If the creditor totally wrecked the car while driving it away, he or she would be liable for the full value of the car to the car's owner for the tort of conversion.

Nuisance

A nuisance is an unlawful interference with a person's use or enjoyment of his or her land. It includes any use of property that gives offense to or endangers life or health—for example, by unreasonably polluting the air. The interference with the landowner's interest must be substantial. The standard is similar to the test for the tort of intentional infliction of emotional distress: a definite and substantial offensiveness, inconvenience, or annoyance to the normal person in the community.

The interference must not only be substantial, it must also be unreasonable. This involves weighing the gravity and probability of harm resulting from the defendant's conduct against its social utility. Thus a defendant may engage in a reasonable use of his or her property at the expense of the neighbors.

Although most nuisance cases are brought as intentional tort claims, the basis of liability is the nature of the interference with the plaintiff's use and enjoyment of property, not the intent of the defendant. Liability may extend to negligent interferences and, where the interference results from an abnormally offensive activity, to strict liability.

COMPETITIVE TORTS

The American economic system relies primarily upon the free market for the allocation of resources. Substantial economic and legal opinion supports the proposition that the market assures the most efficient allocation of goods and services while preserving economic, social, and political freedom. Nevertheless, limited government intervention has been deemed necessary to prevent competition from taking socially undesirable and destructive forms. In order to assure fair and honest competition, the courts have applied common law tort theory to provide redress for unfair trade practices.

The following discussion focuses on some of the ways tort theory has been applied to competitive practices. Special attention is given to the torts of unfair competition, appropriation of trade values, and interference with contractual relations. Several federal statutes that provide redress for the infringement of patents, copyrights, trade names, and trademarks are not discussed because of their specialized nature.

Prima Facie Tort Theory

Most of the torts discussed in this section have evolved from what is called "prima facie tort" theory. Historically, tort liability existed only if the plaintiff could fit his or her case within some specific and established rule of liability. The plaintiff was required to show that the case fit one of the recognized forms of action, which in the law of torts meant one of the recognized torts. During the second half of the nineteenth century there were significant reforms, and the rigors of the earlier rules were relaxed. The development of the prima facie tort doctrine was an important outgrowth of this change.

Prima facie tort theory was an effort to develop a general unifying principle of tort liability from which specific rules could be deduced and applied to new cases. Its most notable accomplishment, however, has been to spawn a myriad of new and often nameless torts. The principle was first formulated in this country by Justice Holmes, who, speaking for the U.S. Supreme Court, stated: "It has been considered that, prima facie, the intentional infliction of temporal damage is a cause of action, which, as a matter of substantive law, whatever may be the form of pleading, requires a justification for the defendant to escape."[5] Prima facie tort theory has been widely applied in the field of business competition, but the principle is not limited to this field. The principle is an expression of a general policy that compensation ought to be awarded for actual damage intentionally caused by conduct that had no moral, social, or economic justification.

Unfair Competition

Because of the high value placed on competition, the law recognizes a qualified privilege to engage in business in good faith. Someone who causes loss of business to another merely by engaging in a business in good faith is not liable for the loss he or she causes. The theory is that, in the long run, competition promotes efficiency and general economic welfare and that to subject a person to liability merely for competing would prevent competition. However, the privilege is lost if a person acts in bad faith and engages in a business primarily for the purpose of causing loss of business to another and with the intention of terminating the business when that purpose is accomplished. Bad faith is usually manifested by the use of predatory business practices. The following case illustrates the use of prima facie tort theory to determine the fairness of conduct of a new market entrant.

Tuttle v. Buck

Supreme Court of Minnesota
119 N. W. 946 (1909)

Tuttle was a barber in a small town in Minnesota. He sued Buck, a banker, alleging that Buck had set up a rival barbershop for the sole purpose of driving Tuttle out of business. The trial court overruled Buck's general demurrer (an antiquated motion in most states today, but one that is essentially the same as a motion to dismiss for failure to state a claim). Buck appealed to the Minnesota Supreme Court, which affirmed the trial court's decision. Buck is the appellant; Tuttle is the appellee.

Elliot, J.

It has been said that the law deals only with externals, and that a lawful act cannot be made the foundation of an action because it was done with an evil motive. In Allen v. Flood, (1898) A.C. 151, Lord Watson said that, except with regard to crimes, the law does not take into account motives as constituting an element of civil wrong. In Mayor v. Pickles, (1895) A.C. 587, Lord Halsbury stated that if the act was lawful, "however ill the motive might be, he had a right to do it." In Raycroft v. Tayntor, 68 Vt. 219, 35 A. 53, 33 L.R.A. 225, 54 Am. St. Rep. 882, the court said that, "where one exercises a legal right only the motive which actuates him is immaterial." In Jenkins v. Fowler, 24 Pa. 318, Mr. Justice Black said that "mischievous motives make a bad case worse, but they cannot make that wrong which in its own essence is lawful." Such generalizations are of little value in determining concrete cases. They may state the truth, but not the whole truth. Each word and phrase used therein may require definition and limitation. Thus, before we can apply Judge Black's language to a particular case, we must determine what act is "in its own essence lawful." What did Lord Halsbury mean by the words "lawful act"? What is meant by "exercising a legal right"? It is not at all correct to say that the motive with which an act is done is always immaterial, providing the act itself is not unlawful. Numerous illustrations of the contrary will be found in the civil as well as the criminal law.

We do not intend to enter upon an elaborate discussion of the subject, or become entangled in the subtleties connected with the words "malice" and "malicious." We are not able to accept without limitations the doctrine above referred to, but at this time content ourselves with a brief reference to some general principles. It must be remembered that the common law is the result of growth, and that its development has been determined by the social needs of the community which it governs. It is the resultant of conflicting social forces, and those forces which are for the time dominant leave their impress upon the law. It is of judicial origin, and seeks to establish doctrines and rules for the determination, protection, and enforcement of legal rights. Manifestly it must change as society changes and new rights are recognized. To be an efficient instrument, and not a mere abstraction, it must gradually adapt itself to changed conditions. Necessarily its form and substance has been greatly affected by prevalent economic theories. For generations there has been a practical agreement upon the proposition that competition in trade and business is desirable, and this idea has found expression in the decisions of the courts as well as in statutes. But it has led to grievous and manifold wrongs to individuals, and many courts have manifested an earnest desire to protect the individuals from the evils which result from unrestrained business competition. The problem has been to so adjust matters as to preserve the principle of competition and yet guard against its abuse to the unnecessary injury to the individual. So the principle that a man may use his own property according to his own needs and desires, while true in the abstract, is subject to many limitations in the concrete. Men cannot always, in civilized society, be allowed to use their own property as their interests or desires may dictate without reference to the fact that they have neighbors whose rights are as sacred as their own. The existence and well-being of society requires that each and every person shall conduct himself consistently with the fact that he is a social and reasonable person.

Many of the restrictions which should be recognized and enforced result from a tacit recognition of principles which are not often stated in the decisions in express terms. Sir Frederick Pollock notes that not many years ago it was difficult to find any definite authority for stating as a general proposition of English law that it is wrong to do a willful wrong to one's neighbor without lawful justification or excuse. But neither is there any express authority for the general proposition that men must perform their contracts. Both principles, in this generality of form and conception, are modern and there was a time when neither was true. After developing the idea that law begins, not with authentic general principles, but with the enumeration of particular remedies, the learned writer continues: "If there exists, then, a positive duty to avoid harm, much more, then, exists the negative duty of not doing willful harm, subject, as all general duties must be subject, to the necessary exceptions. The three main heads of duty with which the law of torts is concerned, namely, to abstain from willful injury, to respect the property of others, and to use due diligence to avoid causing harm to others, are all alike of a comprehensive nature." Pollock, Torts, (8th Ed.) p. 21. He then quotes with approval the statement of Lord Bowen that "at common law there was a cause of action whenever one person did damage to another, willfully and intentionally, without just cause and excuse." In Plant v. Woods, 176 Mass. 492, 57 N.E. 1011, 51 L.R.A. 339, 79 Am. St. Rep. 330, Mr. Justice Hammond said: "It is said, also, that where one has the lawful right to do a thing, the motive by which he is actuated is immaterial. One form of this statement appears in the first headnote in Allen v. Flood, as reported in (1898) A.C. 1, as follows: 'An act lawful in itself is not converted by a malicious or bad motive into an unlawful act, so as to make the doer of the act liable to a civil action.' If the meaning of this and similar expressions is that, where a person has the lawful right to do a thing irrespective of his motive, his motive is immaterial, the proposition is a mere truism. If, however, the meaning is that where a person, if actuated by one kind of a motive, has a lawful right to do a thing, the act is lawful when done under any conceivable motive, or that an act lawful under one set of circumstances is therefore lawful under every conceivable set of circumstances, the proposition does not commend itself to us as either logically or legally accurate."

It is freely conceded that there are many decisions contrary to this view; but, when carried to the extent contended for by the appellant, we think they are unsafe, unsound, and illy adapted to modern conditions. To divert to one's self the customers of a business rival by the offer of goods at lower prices is in general a legitimate mode of serving one's own interest, and justifiable as fair competition. But when a man starts an opposition place of business, not for the sake of profit to himself, but regardless of loss to himself, and for the sole purpose of driving his competitor out of business, and with the intention of himself retiring upon the accomplishment of his malevolent purpose, he is guilty of a wanton wrong and an actionable tort. In such a case he would not be exercising his legal right, or doing an act which can be judged separately from the motive which actuated him. To call such conduct competition is a perversion of terms. It is simply the application of force without legal justification, which in its moral quality may be no better than highway robbery.

Nevertheless, in the opinion of the writer this complaint is insufficient. It is not claimed that it states a cause of action for slander. No question of conspiracy or combination is involved. Stripped of the adjectives and the statement that what was done was for the sole purpose of injuring the plaintiff, and not for the purpose of serving a legitimate purpose of the defendant, the complaint states facts which in themselves amount only to an ordinary everyday business transaction. There is no allegation that the defendant was intentionally running the business at a financial loss to himself, or that after driving the plaintiff out of business the defendant closed up or intended to close up his shop. From all that appears from the complaint he may have opened the barber shop, energetically sought business from his acquaintances and the customers of the plaintiff, and as a result of his enterprise and command of capital obtained it, with the result that the plaintiff, from want of capital, acquaintance, or enterprise, was unable to stand the competition and was thus driven out of business. The facts thus alleged do not, in my opinion, in themselves, without reference to the way in which they are characterized by the pleader, tend to show a malicious and wanton wrong to the plaintiff.

A majority of the Justices, however, are of the opinion that, on the principle declared in the foregoing opinion, the complaint states a cause of action, and the order is therefore affirmed.

Affirmed.

Appropriation of Trade Values

The appropriation of trade values may be accomplished in a variety of ways. For example, an inventor's idea may be stolen by someone the inventor shares the idea with, or a competitor may "palm off" another's product as his own or steal another's trade secret. When this occurs, tort law provides remedies in the torts of misappropriation, palming off, and wrongfully obtaining a trade secret.

Misappropriation. Corporations continually receive unsolicited ideas from the general public concerning possible inventions, product innovations, or suggested advertising schemes. Difficulties arise if the corporation's own research has paralleled the suggested idea. When the company later comes out with a product similar to the suggested product or with an advertising scheme similar to the one proposed, people who sent the unsolicited ideas may become aware of the corporation's product or advertisement and bring suit for the misappropriation of their ideas. Misappropriation is the unlawful taking of the product or idea of another and making use of it as though it belonged to the party taking it. A plaintiff suing for misappropriation of unsolicited ideas will have a difficult time establishing a case, because he or she must prove: (1) that the information was presented to the company with the clear expectation that he or she was to be compensated for its use; (2) that he or she has a protected property interest in the idea described; and (3) that the company's use of the idea was wrongful vis-à-vis the plaintiff's protected property interest.

Palming Off. The tort of palming off involves an attempt by one producer to pass off its product as that of another manufacturer who has built up considerable good will. Thus one manufacturer might make its product look similar to the well-advertised product of its competitor, hoping to confuse some of the buying public as to the source of the product. This allows the party palming off to take a "free ride" on its competitor's advertising. In order for such activities to constitute the tort of palming off, the courts require (1) that the original product have acquired a secondary meaning and (2) that the original product be so similar to the copied product as to cause confusion in the marketplace regarding the source of the copied product. "Secondary meaning" attaches to a product that, through long production by a particular manufacturer, has come to be recognized as its product. The consumer thus associates the product with a particular firm and draws a secondary conclusion as to the quality of the product.

Appropriation of Trade Secrets. Someone who discloses or uses another's trade secret, without a privilege to do so, may be liable to the owner of such information for the damages caused. The information obtained must qualify as a trade secret—that is, it must be information not generally known in the industry. Absolute secrecy is not required. A license may be granted allowing another firm to use trade-secret information, and the licensor will be protected as long as the information is given in strict confidence.

In addition to being not generally known, the information must have been obtained or used in a wrongful manner. The wrongful obtaining of confidential information includes the practice of industrial espionage, whereby one corporation hires an agent to spy upon and discover the commercial secrets of a competitor. Consider the following case.

E.I. duPont deNemours & Co., Inc. v. Christopher
United States Court of Appeals, Fifth Circuit
431 F.2d 1012 (1970)

E. I. duPont deNemours & Co., Inc. (DuPont) sued Rolfe and Gary Christopher for damages and an injunction, alleging that the Christophers had disclosed trade secrets to an unnamed third party. The trial court granted DuPont's motion to compel disclosure of the third party's identity and denied the Christophers' motion to dismiss. The Christophers filed an interlocutory appeal (an immediate appeal while legal proceedings are pending) to the Fifth Circuit Court of Appeals, which affirmed the district court decision. The Christophers are the defendants-appellants; DuPont is the plaintiff-appellee.

Goldberg, Circuit Judge

This is a case of industrial espionage in which an airplane is the cloak and a camera the dagger. The defendants-appellants, Rolfe and Gary Christopher, are photographers in Beaumont, Texas. The Christophers were hired by an unknown third party to take aerial photographs of new construction at the Beaumont plant of E. I. duPont deNemours & Company, Inc. Sixteen photographs of the DuPont facility were taken from the air on March 19, 1969, and these photographs were later developed and delivered to the third party.

DuPont employees apparently noticed the airplane on March 19 and immediately began an investigation to determine why the craft was circling over the plant. By that afternoon the investigation had disclosed that the craft was involved in a photographic expedition and that the Christophers were the photographers. DuPont contacted the Christophers that same afternoon and asked them to reveal the name of the person or corporation requesting the photographs. The Christophers refused to disclose this information, giving as their reason the client's desire to remain anonymous.

Having reached a dead end in the investigation, DuPont subsequently filed suit against the Christophers, alleging that the Christophers had wrongfully obtained photographs revealing DuPont's trade secrets which they then sold to the undisclosed third party. DuPont contended that it had developed a highly secret but unpatented process for producing methanol, a process which gave DuPont a competitive advantage over other producers. This process, DuPont alleged, was a trade secret developed after much expensive and time-consuming research, and a secret which the company had taken special precautions to safeguard. The area photographed by the Christophers was the plant designed to produce methanol by this secret process, and because the plant was still under construction parts of the process were exposed to view from directly above the construction area. Photographs of that area, DuPont alleged, would enable a skilled person to deduce the secret process for making methanol. DuPont thus contended that the Christophers had wrongfully appropriated DuPont trade secrets by taking the photographs and delivering them to the undisclosed third party.

This is a case of first impression, for the Texas courts have not faced this precise factual issue, and . . . we must . . . divine what the Texas courts would do if such a situation were presented to them. The only question involved in this interlocutory appeal is whether DuPont has asserted a claim upon which relief can be granted. The Christophers argued both at trial and before this court that they committed no "actionable wrong" in photographing the DuPont facility and passing these photographs on to their client because they conducted all of their activities in public airspace, violated no government aviation standard, did not breach any confidential relation, and did not engage in any fraudulent or illegal conduct. In short, the Christophers argue that for an appropriation of trade secrets to be wrongful there must be a trespass, other illegal conduct, or breach of a confidential relationship. We disagree.

It is true, as the Christophers assert, that the previous trade secret cases have contained one or more of these elements. However, we do not think that the Texas courts would limit the trade secret protection exclusively to these elements. On the contrary, in Hyde Corporation v. Huffines, 1958, 158 Tex. 566, 314 S.W.2d 763, the Texas Supreme Court specifically adopted the rule found in the Restatement of Torts which provides:

"One who discloses or uses another's trade secret, without a privilege to do so, is liable to the other if
    (a) he discovered the secret by improper means, or
    (b) his disclosure or use constitutes a breach of confidence reposed in him by the other in disclosing the secret to him . . ."
Restatement of Torts Sec. 757 (1939)

Thus, although the previous cases have dealt with a breach of a confidential relationship, a trespass, or other illegal conduct, the rule is much broader than the cases heretofore encountered. Not limiting itself to specific wrongs, Texas adopted subsection (a) of the Restatement which recognizes a cause of action for the discovery of a trade secret by any "improper" means.

If breach of confidence were meant to encompass the entire panoply of commercial improprieties, subsection (a) of the Restatement would be either surplusage or persiflage, an interpretation abhorrent to the traditional precision of the Restatement. We therefore find meaning in subsection (a) and think that the Texas Supreme Court clearly indicated by its adoption that there is a cause of action for the discovery of a trade secret by any "improper means."

The question remaining, therefore, is whether aerial photography of plant construction is an improper means of obtaining another's trade secret. We conclude that it is and that the Texas courts would so hold. The Supreme Court of that state has declared that "the undoubted tendency of the law has been to recognize and enforce higher standards of commercial morality in the business world." *Hyde Corporation* v. *Huffines,* supra. That court has quoted with approval articles indicating that the proper means of gaining possession of a competitor's secret process is "through inspection and analysis" of the product in order to create a duplicate.

We think, therefore, that the Texas rule is clear. One may use his competitor's secret process if he discovers the process by reverse engineering applied to the finished product, one may use a competitor's process if he discovers it by his own independent research, but one may not avoid these labors by taking the process from the discoverer without his permission at a time when he is taking reasonable precautions to maintain its secrecy. To obtain knowledge of a process without spending the time and money to discover it independently is improper unless the holder voluntarily discloses it or fails to take reasonable precautions to ensure its secrecy.

In the instant case the Christophers deliberately flew over the DuPont plant to get pictures of a process which DuPont had attempted to keep secret. The Christophers delivered their pictures to a third party who was certainly aware of the means by which they had been acquired and who may be planning to use the information contained therein to manufacture methanol by the DuPont process. The third party has a right to use this process only if he obtains this knowledge through his own research efforts, but thus far all information indicates that the third party has gained his knowledge solely by taking it from DuPont at a time when DuPont was making reasonable efforts to preserve its secrecy. In such a situation DuPont has a valid cause of action to prohibit the Christophers from improperly discovering its trade secret and to prohibit the undisclosed third party from using the improperly obtained information.

We note that this view is in perfect accord with the position taken by the authors of the Restatement. In commenting on improper means of discovery the authors of the Restatement said:

f. Improper means of discovery. The discovery of another's trade secret by improper means subjects the actor to liability independently of the harm to the interest in the secret. Thus, if one uses physical force to take a secret formula from another's pocket, or breaks into another's office to steal the formula, his conduct is wrongful and subjects him to liability apart from the rule stated in this Section. Such conduct is also an improper means of procuring the secret under this rule. But means may be improper under this rule even though they do not cause any other harm than that to the interest in the trade secret. Examples of such means are fraudulent misrepresentation to induce disclosure, tapping of telephone wires, eavesdropping or other espionage. A complete catalogue of improper means is not possible. In general they are means which fall below the generally accepted standards of commercial morality and reasonable conduct. Restatement of Torts Sec. 757, comment f at 10 (1939).

In taking this position we realize that industrial espionage of the sort here perpetrated has become a popular sport in some segments of our industrial community. However, our devotion to free wheeling industrial competition must not force us into accepting the law of the jungle as the standard of morality expected in our commercial relations. Our tolerance of the espionage game must cease when the protections required to prevent another's spying cost so much that the spirit of inventiveness is dampened. Commercial privacy must be protected from espionage which could not have been reasonably anticipated or prevented. We do not mean to imply, however, that everything not in plain view is within the protected vale, nor that all information obtained through every extra optical extension is forbidden. Indeed, for our industrial competition to remain healthy there must be breathing room for observing a competing industrialist. A competitor can and must shop his competition for pricing and examine his products for quality, components, and methods of manufacture. Perhaps ordinary fences and roofs must be built to shut out incursive eyes, but we need not require the discoverer of a trade secret to guard against the unanticipated, the undetectable, or the unpreventable methods of espionage now available.

In the instant case DuPont was in the midst of constructing a plant. Although after construction the finished plant would have protected much of the process from view, during the period of construction the trade secret was exposed to view from the air. To require DuPont to put a roof over the unfinished plant to guard its secret would impose an enormous expense to prevent nothing more than a school boy's trick. We introduce here no new or radical ethic since our ethos has never given moral sanction to piracy. The market place must not deviate far from our mores. We should not require a person or corporation to take unreasonable precautions to prevent another from doing that which he ought not do in the first place. Reasonable precautions against predatory eyes we may require, but an impenetrable fortress is an unreasonable requirement, and we are not disposed to burden industrial inventors with such a duty in order to protect the fruits of their efforts. "Improper" will always be a word determined by time, place and circumstances. We therefore need not proclaim a catalogue of commercial improprieties. Clearly, however, one of its commandments does say "thou shall not appropriate a trade secret through deviousness under circumstances in which countervailing defenses are not reasonably available."

Regardless of whether the flight was legal or illegal in that sense, the espionage was an improper means of discovering DuPont's trade secret.

The decision of the trial court is affirmed and the case remanded to that court for proceedings on the merits.

Interference with Contractual Relations. One who intentionally and without justification causes a third person not to perform a contract with another is liable for the resulting harm. The traditional elements of the tort of inducing breach of contract are: (1) an existing contract between the plaintiff and a third party; (2) the defendant's knowledge of this contract; (3) an intentional unjustified inducement to breach the contract; (4) a subsequent breach by the third party; and (5) resulting damage to the plaintiff. In recent years, the requirement of an existing contract has been relaxed, and liability has extended to wrongful interference with a reasonable expectancy of a commercial relation. Thus liability for inducing breach of contract is now regarded as but one instance, rather than the limit, of protection against unjustified interference in business relations. The chief justification is competition. It is no tort to beat a business rival to a prospective customer. However, where the competitor is not engaging in bona fide competition but commits any of the acts previously discussed (e.g., predatory trade practices, palming off) liability may exist for this tort as well.

OTHER BUSINESS TORTS

Malicious Prosecution and Abuse of Process

Malicious prosecution and abuse of process are tort actions brought in response to alleged misuse of the judicial process. The former follows a criminal case and the latter follows a civil case where the present plaintiff was the defendant. These torts exist to resolve an in-herent conflict in the law. On one hand, the law looks for certainty and the quick resolution of disputes. The law does not usually allow, therefore, a second cause of action to challenge the appropriateness of the first cause of action. On the other hand, because the judicial process can be engaged at rather minimal cost and subjected to misuse, it may be used to harass a defendant. The torts of malicious prosecution and abuse of process resolve this conflict by setting the following standard: If there was reasonable cause in the first instance to file the cause of action, there is no liability under malicious prosecution or abuse of process. If the present plaintiff prevailed in the first case and can show there was no reasonable cause for that suit to have been filed, then damages may be recovered.

The Emerging Tort of Abusive Discharge

As mentioned at the beginning of this chapter, tort law is not stagnant. New torts are continually being recognized by the courts. The advent of prima facie tort theory made possible the recognition of new causes of action. The tort of abusive discharge is such a frontier-area tort. The development of this cause of action by the courts reflects the development of law in response to particular interests and concerns of today's society and demonstrates that tort law continues to display much ferment and change.

In states where the tort of abusive discharge is recognized, a fired employee may recover against his or her former employer where the employer terminates the employee in bad faith and against public policy. That is, the employee must prove that the termination was motivated by a reason unrelated to the workplace and that it is in the public interest to protect the employee from termination. For example, it has been held to constitute the tort of abusive discharge for an employer to terminate an employee for serving on a jury, because to allow such a termination would undermine the jury system.

In states that do not recognize the tort of abusive discharge, an employment relation of indefinite duration is considered to be terminable by either the employer or the employee at will, unless there exists a contract or a statute to the contrary. An example of such a contract would be a collective bargaining contract that contains a clause prohibiting discharges except for cause. An example of a statute would be Title VII of the Civil Rights Act, which forbids discharges based on the employee's race, sex, religion, or national origin. Where no contract or statute exists to provide a different rule, an employer may discharge an employee for cause or no cause, in good faith or maliciously, for reason or no reason.

In the following case, the court recognizes the tort of abusive discharge.

Tameny v. Atlantic Richfield Co.

Supreme Court of California
164 Cal. Rptr. 839 (1980)

Gordon Tameny sued his former employer, Atlantic Richfield Company (Arco), alleging that Arco had discharged him after fifteen years of service because he refused to participate in a scheme to fix retail gasoline prices. Tameny contended that Arco's conduct in discharging him for refusing to commit a criminal act was tortious and subjected the employer to liability for compensatory and punitive damages under normal tort principles. Arco demurred to the complaint, contending that Tameny's allegations, even if true, did not state a cause of action in tort. The trial court accepted Arco's argument and sustained a general demurrer to Tameny's tort action. Tameny appealed to the California Supreme Court, which reversed the trial court decision. Tameny is the plaintiff-appellant; Arco is the defendant-appellee.

Tobriner, Justice

Under the traditional common law rule, codified in Labor Code section 2922, an employment contract of indefinite duration is in general terminable at "the will" of either party. Over the past several decades, however, judicial authorities in California and throughout the United States have established the rule that under both common law and the statute an employer does not enjoy an absolute or totally unfettered right to discharge even an at-will employee. In a series of cases arising out of a variety of factual settings in which a discharge clearly violated an express statutory objective or undermined a firmly established principle of public policy, courts have recognized that an employer's traditional broad authority to discharge an at-will employee "may be limited by statute . . . or by considerations of public policy."

In light of the foregoing authorities, we conclude that an employee's action for wrongful discharge subjects an employer to tort liability.

California courts have not been alone in recognizing the propriety of a tort remedy when an employer's discharge of an employee contravenes the dictates of public policy. In Nees v. Hocks (1975), 272 Or. 210, 536 P.2d 512, for example, the Oregon Supreme Court upheld an employee's recovery of compensatory damages in tort for the emotional distress suffered when her employer discharged her for serving on a jury. Similarly, in Harless v. First Nat. Bank in Fairmont (W. Va. 1978) 246 S.E.2d 270, the Supreme Court of West Virginia upheld a wrongful discharge action by a bank employee who was terminated after attempting to persuade his employer to comply with consumer protection laws, reasoning that "where the employer's motivation for [a] discharge contravenes some substantial public policy principle, then the employer may be liable to the employee for damages occasioned by the discharge," and concluding that the employee's cause of action "is one in tort and it therefore follows that rules relating to tort damages would be applicable." (Id, at p. 275, fn. 5.)

Indeed, the *Nees* and *Harless* decisions are merely illustrative of a rapidly growing number of cases throughout the country that in recent years have recognized a common law tort action for wrongful discharge in cases in which the termination contravenes public policy.

These recent decisions demonstrate a continuing judicial recognition of the fact, enunciated by this court more than 35 years ago, that "[t]he days when a servant was practically the slave of his master have long since passed." Greene v. Hawaiian Dredging Co. (1945) 26 Cal.2d 245, 251, 157 P.2d 367, 370. In the last half century the rights of employees have not only been proclaimed by a mass of legislation touching upon almost every aspect of the employer-employee relationship, but the courts have likewise evolved certain additional protections at common law. The courts have been sensitive to the need to protect the individual employee from discriminatory exclusion from the opportunity of employment whether it be by the all-powerful union or employer. This development at common law shows that the employer is not so absolute a sovereign of the job that there are not limits to his prerogative. One such limit at least is the present case. The employer cannot condition employment upon required participation in unlawful conduct by the employee.

We hold that an employer's authority over its employee does not include the right to demand that the employee commit a criminal act to further its interest, and an employer may not coerce compliance with such unlawful directions by discharging an employee who refuses to follow such an order. An employer engaging in such conduct violates a basic duty imposed by law upon all employers, and thus an employee of such discharge may maintain a tort action for wrongful discharge against the employer.

Accordingly, we conclude that the trial court erred in sustaining the demurrer to plaintiff's tort action for wrongful discharge.

The judgment is reversed and the case is remanded to the trial court for further proceedings consistent with this opinion.

REVIEW PROBLEMS

1. Mrs. Marion Bonkowski, accompanied by her husband, left Arlan's Department Store in Saginaw, Michigan, about 10:00 A.M. on December 18, 1962 after making several purchases. Earl Reinhardt, a private policeman on duty that night in Arlan's, called to her to stop as she was walking to her car about thirty feet away in the adjacent parking lot. Reinhardt motioned to Mrs. Bonkowski to return toward the store, and when she had done so Reinhardt said that someone in the store had told him Mrs. Bonkowski had put three pieces of jewelry into her purse without having paid for them. Mrs. Bonkowski denied she had taken anything unlawfully, but Reinhardt told her he wanted to see the contents of her purse. On a cement step in front of the store, Mrs. Bonkowski emptied the contents of her purse into her husband's hands. Mr. Bonkowski produced sales slips for the items she had purchased, and Reinhardt, satisfied that she had not committed larceny, returned to the store. Mrs. Bonkowski brought suit against Earl Reinhardt and Arlan's Department Store, claiming that, as a result of defendants' tortious acts, she suffered numerous psychosomatic symptoms, including headaches, nervousness, and depression. Who wins? Explain. Bonkowski v. Arlan's Department Store, 162 N.W.2d 347 (1968).

2. On leaving a restaurant, X by mistake takes Y's hat from the rack, believing it to be his own. When he reaches the sidewalk, X puts on the hat, discovers his mistake, and immediately reenters the restaurant and returns the hat to the rack. Has X committed either trespass to personal property or conversion? Blackinton v. Pillsbury, 165 N.E. 895 (1927).

3. H obtained a credit card in his name only from Slick Oil Company and used it in making purchases at Slick gas stations. W, a secretary at Cow College, handled family finances. W informed H (but not Slick) that she would not make further payments on the account, and the account became delinquent in the amount of $200. Slick sent a letter to the personnel director at Cow College seeking assistance. The letter claimed W was Slick's customer and had incurred expenses, and it requested Cow College's assistance in interviewing W. Did Slick commit any intentional torts? Signal Oil & Gas Company v. Conway, 191 S.E. 2d 624 (Ct. App. Ga. 1972).

4. A, a wholesaler of gasoline and motor oil who does not operate and does not intend to operate any retail stations, demands that B, the proprietor of a retail gasoline station, carry A's oil exclusively. B refuses. A thereupon determines to drive B out of business. A leases a vacant lot next to B's station for six months and daily sends a gasoline truck to park on the lot and sell gasoline directly from the truck. Is A liable to B under any tort theory? Restatement of Torts Sec. 709, Illustration 3 (1928).

5. Morgan owned a tract of nine acres of land on which he had his dwelling, a restaurant, and accommodations for thirty-two trailers. High Penn Oil Co. owned an adjacent tract on which it operated an oil refinery, at a distance of 1,000 feet from Morgan's dwelling. Morgan sued High Penn to recover damages for a nuisance and to abate such nuisance by injunction. Morgan's evidence was that for some hours on two or three different days each week the refinery emitted nauseating gases and odors in great quantities, which invaded Morgan's land and other tracts of land. High Penn failed to put an end to this atmospheric pollution after receiving notice and demand from Morgan to abate it. High Penn's evidence

was that the oil refinery was a modern plant of the type approved, known, and in general use for renovating used lubricating oils; that it was not so constructed or operated as to give out noxious gases or odors in annoying quantities; and that it had not annoyed Morgan or other persons save on a single occasion when it suffered a brief mechanical breakdown. Who should win? Explain. Morgan v. High Penn Oil Co., 77 S.E.2d 682 (N.C. 1953).

6. Brents, an exasperated creditor, put a placard in the show window of his garage, on the public street, which stated that "Dr. W. R. Morgan owes an account here for $49.67. This account will be advertised as long as it remains unpaid." Morgan sued Brents for the tort of invasion of privacy. Who wins? Explain. Could Brents hold the authors of this text liable for invasion of privacy by reason of their publishing the incident in this text? Explain. Brents v. Morgan 299 S.W. 967 (Ky. 1927).

FOOTNOTES

[1]Stone, WHERE THE LAW Ends (New York: Harper & Row, 1975), p. 38.

[2] Sutherland, WHITE COLLAR CRIME (Bloomington, Ind.: Indiana University Press, 1944).

[3]Id.

[4]New York Times Co. v. Sullivan, 376 U.S. 254 (1964).

[5]Aikens v. Wisconsin, 195 U.S. 194, 204 (1904).

CHAPTER 4

Negligence and Strict Liability

NEGLIGENCE————————————————————————

STRICT LIABILITY————————————————————

T his chapter considers the two remaining classifications of tort law, both of which are concerned with civil redress for unintentional injuries: (1) negligence and (2) strict liability. Early tort law was based on a theory of strict, or no-fault, liability. A person was held liable for the harm he or she inflicted upon others. Liability extended even to purely accidental injuries. Thus, in the eighteenth century, a person was the insurer of his or her own conduct.

Starting in the nineteenth century, tort liability for unintended injuries focused on the fault or blameworthiness of the defendant. In order for a plaintiff to obtain relief from a defendant, the plaintiff had to show that the defendant's conduct was below a standard of conduct expected of a good citizen in the community. Liability was based on the defendant's negligence.

The fault standard, which held the defendant liable only if the defendant was negligent, coincided with the nineteenth-century Industrial Revolution. During this time, Anglo-American society was undergoing transformation from an agricultural to a manufacturing society. Industrialization became a social goal. The introduction of liability based on negligence meant that the emerging industries were relieved of the risk of injury to consumers and workers as long as industry acted carefully—that is, did not act negligently.

During the late nineteenth and early twentieth centuries it became increasingly clear that injuries were an inevitable concomitant of industry, even when the manufacturer took all reasonable precautions to prevent injuries from occurring. In certain dangerous occupations, such as blasting, injuries were highly probable even where negligence was not present. During the twentieth century there has been a return to a general acceptance of the strict liability standard. Although earlier limited to ultrahazardous activities, strict liability theory now extends to injuries resulting from defectively manufactured products. Critics have decried the return to strict liability as causing a "liability explosion."

Although the shift has been toward strict liability, the tort of negligence continues to account for most tort claims. Plaintiffs frequently plead their claims under both theories of recovery. By pleading negligence along with strict liability, a plaintiff may later introduce evidence of the defendant's negligent conduct and thus seek to gain the jury's sympathy. Because of the "liability explosion" of recent years, and the pressure the increased litigation has exerted on judicial dockets, certain types of cases—for example, automobile accidents and worker injuries—have been increasingly removed from the court system and assigned to an administratively operated compensation system funded through insurance. Many states now have compulsory automobile insurance systems that remove accident cases from the litigation process and treat them administratively under a no-fault standard.

This chapter first examines negligence theory, then considers strict liability and the related concepts of vicarious liability and no-fault insurance.

NEGLIGENCE

Negligence is conduct that creates an unreasonable risk of harm to another. Where such conduct injures someone, the injured person may seek redress in court by bringing a civil action for the tort of negligence. The great majority of tort cases fall into the category of negligence.

Unlike intentional torts, negligence is not based on the tortfeasor's motive but on the unreasonableness of the tortfeasor's conduct. For example, the dim-witted tortfeasor may not intend to injure anyone when leaving a garden rake lying prongs up on the lawn. Nevertheless, the conduct may be considered unreasonable, and the tortfeasor would be liable to a guest who, without reason to know of the rake's position, is injured when stepping on the prongs.

Liability for the tort of negligence is based on fault—that is, the blameworthiness of the defendant for the plaintiff's injury. Where the plaintiff's injury is caused by conduct of the defendant that created an unreasonable risk of harm to the plaintiff, the defendant is liable to the plaintiff for the tort of negligence. As a general rule, the successful plaintiff may recover only compensatory damages from the defendant. These may take the form of monetary recompense for medical expenses, property damage, personal injuries, pain and suffering, loss of services, and other economic losses.

Punitive damages are normally not available for tort liability based on ordinary negligence. Some jurisdictions award punitive damages for a category of negligence called gross or aggravated negligence, which is sometimes defined as reckless disregard for the known probable consequences of one's misconduct. For example, a driver who, after drinking intoxicating beverages, drives an automobile at an excessive speed on a rainy night down a highway that the driver knows is slippery when it is wet, may be liable in some states for gross negligence. Knowing the condition of the highway as well as the effects of intoxication, the driver may be said to have knowingly disregarded the probable consequences of such conduct, and an innocent injured victim would, in some states, be entitled to recover punitive damages in addition to compensatory damages.

Elements of Negligence

In order to establish a prima facie case of negligence, the plaintiff must establish five elements. These are:

1. That the defendant owed a *duty of care* to the plaintiff. The plaintiff must establish that the law recognized an obligation of the defendant to conform to a certain standard of conduct for the protection of the plaintiff against an unreasonable risk of harm. Under the law of negligence, an actor is liable when he or she causes injury by breaching a duty of care owed to the injured party. Determining the precise limits of this duty of care is a significant problem in negligence cases.

2. That the defendant *breached this duty*. The plaintiff must prove that the defendant failed to conform to the standard required by law.

3. That the plaintiff sustained an *injury*.

4. That a causal relationship exists between the defendant's conduct and the plaintiff's injury. The plaintiff must show that the defendant caused the plaintiff's injury and that therefore the defendant is the proper person from whom to seek redress. This is known as *cause in fact* or *actual cause.*

5. That the defendant's conduct was the *proximate or legal cause* of the plaintiff's injury. That is, the plaintiff must show a reasonably close causal connection between the defendant's conduct and the resulting injury to the plaintiff. Not every injury actually caused by the defendant is compensable, only those that are foreseeable and probable consequences of the defendant's conduct. Thus, in addition to showing that the defendant actually caused the plaintiff's injury, the plaintiff must establish that the injury was a foreseeable consequence of the defendant's conduct.

Each of these elements necessary to a prima facie case of negligence will be examined in more detail in the discussion that follows. A plaintiff who fails to present evidence establishing all of these elements will have failed to establish negligence. The result will be a directed verdict in favor of the defendant at the close of the plaintiff's case in chief. Where the plaintiff succeeds in establishing all five elements, the plaintiff bears the further burden of persuading the trier of fact (usually the jury) by a preponderance of the evidence that the plaintiff is entitled to a recovery.

Duty of Care. The first element of a plaintiff's prima facie case of negligence is the existence of a duty on the part of the defendant to protect the plaintiff from injury resulting from the defendant's conduct. It is not enough for the plaintiff to show that he or she was injured by the defendant's conduct. The plaintiff must show that the law imposed a duty on the defendant to protect the plaintiff from the consequences of the defendant's conduct.

The determination of whether a duty of care is to be imposed upon the defendant is a question of law that is decided by the judge. The judge must determine whether there is any "law" that would require the defendant to bear the risk or whether the plaintiff must bear his or her own loss.

If tort law is viewed as society's judgment as to which victims of social activity are to be compensated, the determination of the duty element in a negligence case is society's way of expressing its choice through the judicial system. The law does not require compensation to be paid for every injury, no matter how slight or remote. If everyone were the insurer of his or her conduct, with unlimited liability for every injury caused, society would stagnate. There would be no social intercourse, no industrial development, no experimentation with new products, because the risks would be too great. On the other hand, a legal system that refuses to compensate some injured victims underwrites its social and industrial development with the lives and limbs of those who are injured and further encourages dangerous conduct.

Tort law is an investigation of the duties persons owe each other. Thus the initial element in the tort of negligence is the existence of a duty upon the defendant to protect the plaintiff from his or her unreasonable conduct. If the law does not recognize a duty, the defendant is free to engage in behavior that may cause injury to the plaintiff.

There are no hard and fast rules as to when a duty exists. A duty will exist when society wants it to exist. As such, the determination of the existence of a duty is a question of law—and ultimately of policy—for the court to resolve.

Usually the issue of duty is raised by the defendant through a motion to dismiss. The defendant thereby asks the court to rule that the plaintiff cannot ground a claim of negligence on the defendant's conduct because the defendant was under no duty to protect the plaintiff. Essentially the defendant is saying to the court, "Although I may have injured the plaintiff, the law does not impose a duty on me to protect the plaintiff; thus I cannot be liable for negligence." By ruling on the issue, the court decides if the first element in a tort of negligence exists.

Several factors may influence the court's decision. Although each case will be determined according to its circumstances, the following quotation from *Raymond* v. *Paradise Unified School District of Butte County*[1] is a particularly good statement of the factors affecting the determination of duty:

... An affirmative declaration of duty simply amounts to a statement that two parties stand in such relationship that the law will impose on one a responsibility for the exercise of care toward the other. Inherent in this simple description are various and sometimes delicate policy judgments. The social utility of the activity out of which the injury arises, compared with the risks involved in its conduct; the kind of person with whom the actor is dealing; the workability of rule of care, especially in terms of the parties' relative ability to adopt practical means of preventing injury; the relative ability of the parties to bear the financial burden of injury and the availability of means by which the loss may be shifted or spread; the body of statutes and judicial precedents which color the parties' relationship; the prophylactic effect of a rule of liability; in the case of a public agency defendant, the extent of its powers, the role imposed upon it by law and the limitations imposed upon it by budget; and finally, the moral imperatives which judges share with their fellow citizens—such are the factors which play a role in the determination of duty.

The following case illustrates the analysis of these factors in determining the existence of a duty.

Dreisonstok v. Volkswagen of America

United States Court of Appeals, Fourth Circuit

489 F.2d 1066 (1974)

Terry Dreisonstok, along with her mother, sued Volkswagen of America, a car manufacturer, for "enhanced" injuries sustained by her when the Volkswagen microbus in which she was riding crashed into a telephone pole. Terry was seated in the center of the seat, next to the driver, with her left leg under her. As a result of the impact, her right leg was caught between the back of the seat and the dashboard of the van and she was apparently thrown forward. She sustained severe injuries to her ankle and femur. She sought to recover for her injuries, and her mother sought to recover for medical expenses, from Volkswagen, contending that Volkswagen was guilty of negligent design because of the lack of crashworthiness of its vehicle. The action was tried without a jury. The District Court concluded that Volkswagen had been guilty of negligence in failing to use due care in the design of its vehicle by providing "sufficient energy-absorbing materials or devices or 'crash space,' if you will, so that at 40 miles an hour the integrity of the passenger compartment would not be violated," and that, as a result, the injuries of the plaintiff were enhanced "over and above those injuries which the plaintiff must have incurred." From judgment entered on the basis of that conclusion in favor of Terry and her mother, Volkswagen appealed. The Circuit Court of Appeals reversed. Volkswagen is the appellant; Terry Dreisonstok and her mother are the appellees.

Russell, Circuit Judge

The correctness of the finding by the District Court that the defendant manufacturer was guilty of negligent design in this case depends on the determination of what extent a car manufacturer owes the duty to design and market a "crashworthy" vehicle, which, in the event of a collision, resulting accidentally or negligently from the act of another and not from any defect or malfunction in the vehicle itself, protects against unreasonable risk of injury to the occupants. The existence and nature of such a duty is a legal issue, for resolution as a matter of law. In arguing in favor of liability, the appellees stress the foreseeability in this mechanical age of automobile collisions, as affirmed in numerous authorities, and would seemingly deduce from this a duty on the car manufacturer to design its vehicle so as to guard against injury from involvement of its vehicle in any such anticipated collisions. The mere fact, however, that automobile collisions are frequent enough to be foreseeable is not sufficient in and of itself to create a duty on the part of the manufacturer to design its car to withstand such collisions under any circumstances. Foreseeability, it has been many times repeated, is not to be equated with duty; it is, after all, but one factor, albeit an important one, to be weighed in determining the issue of duty. Were foreseeability of collision the absolute litmus test for establishing a duty on the part of the car manufacturer, the obligation of the manufacturer to design a crash-proof car would be absolute. . . .

It would patently be unreasonable "to require the manufacturer to provide for every conceivable use or unuse of a car." Nader & Page, Automobile Design and the Judicial Process, 55 Cal.L.Rev. 645, 646. Liability for negligent design thus is imposed only when an unreasonable danger is created. Whether or not this has occurred should be determined by general negligence principles, which involve a balancing of the likelihood of harm, and the gravity of harm if it happens against the burden of the precautions which would be effective to avoid the harm. In short, against the likelihood and gravity of harm must be balanced in every case the utility of the type of conduct in question. The likelihood of harm is tied in with the obviousness of the danger, whether latent or patent, since it is frequently stated that a design is not unreasonably dangerous because the risk is one which anyone immediately would recognize and avoid. The purposes and intended use of the article is an even more important factor to be considered. After all, it is a commonplace that utility of design and attractiveness of the style of the car are elements which car manufacturers seek after and by which buyers are influenced in their selections. In every case, the utility and purpose of the particular type of vehicle will govern in varying degree the standards of safety to be observed in its design. Price is, also, a factor to be considered, for, if a change in design would appreciably add to cost, add little to safety, and take an article out of the price range of the market to which it was intended to appeal, it may be unreasonable as well as impractical for the courts to require the manufacturer to adopt such change. Of course, if an article can be made safer and the hazard of harm may be mitigated by an alternate design or device at no substantial increase in price, then the manufacturer has a duty to adopt such a design but a Cadillac may be expected to include more in the way of both conveniences and "crashworthiness" than the economy car. Moreover, in a "crashworthy" case it is necessary to consider the circumstances of the accident itself. In summary, every case such as this involves a delicate balancing of many factors in order to determine whether the manufacturer has used ordinary care in designing a car, which, giving consideration to the market purposes and utility of the vehicle, did not involve unreasonable risk of injury to occupants within the range of its intended use.

Applying the foregoing principles to the facts of this particular case, it is clear that there was no violation by the defendant of its duty of ordinary care in the design of its vehicle. The defendant's vehicle, described as "a van type multipurpose vehicle," was of a special type and particular design. This design was uniquely developed in order to provide the owner with the maximum amount of either cargo or passenger space in a vehicle inexpensively priced and of such dimensions as to make possible easy maneuverability. To achieve this, it advanced the driver's seat forward, bringing such seat in close proximity to the front of the vehicle, thereby adding to the cargo or passenger space. This, of course, reduced considerably the space between the exact front of the vehicle and the driver's compartment. All of this was readily discernible to anyone using the vehicle; in fact, it was, as we have said, the unique feature of the vehicle. The usefulness of the design is vouchsafed by the popularity of the type. It was of special utility as a van for the transportation of light cargo, as a family camper, as a station wagon and for use by passenger groups too large for the average passenger car. It was a design that had been adopted by other manufacturers, including American. It was a design duplicated in the construction of the large trucking tractors, where there was the same purpose of extending the cargo space without unduly lengthening the tractor-trailer coupling. There was no evidence in the record that there was any practical way of improving the "crashability" of the vehicle that would have been consistent with the peculiar purposes of its design. The plaintiff's theory of negligent design . . . was that, to meet the test of ordinary care in design so as to avoid "unreasonable risk" of injury, the vehicle of the defendant had to conform with the configuration of the standard American passenger car, . . . i.e., its motor must be in front, not in the rear; its passenger compartment must be "in the middle"; and the space in front of the passenger compartment must be approximately the same as that in a "standard American passenger car." Under this standard, any rear engine car would be "inherently dangerous"; any microbus or front-end tractor —both in wide use in 1968 and now—would be declared "inherently dangerous." To avoid liability for negligent design, no manufacturer could introduce any innovative or unique design, even though calculated to provide some special advantage such as greater roominess. Such a strait-jacket on design is not imposed. . . . It is entirely impermissible to predicate a conclusion of negligent design simply because a vehicle, having a distinctive purpose, such as the microbus, does not conform to the design of another type of vehicle, such as a standard passenger car, having a different nature and utility.

The District Court, however, seems to have accepted plaintiffs' theory, though expressing it somewhat differently from the standard stated by the plaintiffs in their brief. It stated the standard of ordinary care in design to require that a vehicle be able to withstand a "head-on" collision at 40 miles an hour without a violation of "the integrity of the passenger compartment" and held that the defendant had "violated" its duty in failing to meet their standard. Accepting the principle that a manufacturer must anticipate that its product will likely at some point in its use be involved in a collision, does ordinary care demand that, in taking precautions, it must provide against impacts at a speed of 40 miles per hour? Is this the "reasonable risk," as it has been defined in the authorities . . . against which the manufacturer must provide protection? and why "40 miles an hour" as the standard anyway? This standard was adopted, it seems clear from the District Court's order, because the plaintiffs contended that a "standard American passenger car" had sufficient "crash space" that its passenger compartment would not have been invaded in a 40 mile impact. Both the plaintiffs and the District Court employed an improper standard in determining whether the defendant had been guilty of negligent design.

Reversed and remanded with directions to the District Court to enter judgment in favor of the appellants-defendants.

Breach of Duty. The plaintiff must satisfy the judge or the jury that the defendant breached his or her duty to exercise due care. The courts have established a standard of behavior to determine breach of duty. The standard is that of the hypothetical "reasonable and prudent person under the same or similar circumstances." The judge or jury compares the defendant's conduct with the presumed conduct of the reasonably prudent person under the same or similar circumstances. If the defendant's conduct does not conform to this ideal standard of conduct, the defendant will be deemed to have breached his or her duty to exercise due care.

The attributes of the reasonable and prudent person will vary in each case. In physical characteristics, the reasonable person is identical to the defendant. For example, the conduct of a handicapped person must be reasonable in light of his or her knowledge of the infirmity, which is treated as one of the circumstances. Thus someone who is subject to epileptic seizures may be required to refrain from driving a vehicle unless under proper medication.

If the defendant possesses superior knowledge or skill, the standard of care by which the jury will judge the defendant's conduct will be commensurate with that expertise. Thus an ordinary physician will be evaluated by what a reasonable and prudent physician would have done under the same or similar circumstances; a specialist will be evaluated by what a reasonable and prudent specialist would have done. On the other hand, the standard of care will not be lowered to take into account the defendant's lack of knowledge or skill. Thus the neophyte physician will be evaluated by what the ordinary physician would have done, not by what might be expected of a beginner. In this way society establishes a minimum level of acceptable conduct based upon what is common to the community.

The reasonable-and-prudent-person standard will vary from community to community. For example, what might be considered reasonable and prudent conduct for a physician in a remote rural area may be considered unreasonable in a metropolitan community where the physician has access to the latest technology. Different juries may return different verdicts. While this may appear to some as an inconsistency in the law, in reality it introduces needed flexibility into the legal process. Thus there is no universal definition of reasonable care. As circumstances vary, so may the decision in an individual case.

The following case presents the reasonable and prudent person in some very unusual circumstances.

Cordas v. Peerless Transportation Co.

City Court of New York, New York County
27 N.Y.S.2d 198. (1941)

Cordas, her husband, and her two children sued Peerless Transportation Co. for injuries sustained by Cordas and her children when they were run over by a Peerless taxi. The trial court granted the defendant's motion to dismiss. The Cordas family are the plaintiffs; Peerless Transportation Co. is the defendant.

Carlin, Justice

This case presents the ordinary man—that problem child of the law—in a most bizarre setting. As a lonely chauffeur in defendant's employ he became in a trice the protagonist in breath-bating drama with a denouement almost tragic. It appears that a man, whose identity it would be indelicate to divulge, was feloniously relieved of his portage goods by two nondescript highwaymen in an alley near 26th Street and Third Avenue, Manhattan; they induced him to relinquish his possessions by a strong argument ad hominem couched in the convincing cant of the criminal and pressed at the point of a most persuasive pistol. Laden with their loot, but not thereby impeded, they took an abrupt departure, and he, shuffling off the coil of that discretion which enmeshed him in the alley, quickly gave chase through 26th Street toward 2d Avenue, toward which they were resorting "with expedition swift as thought" for most obvious reasons. Somewhere on that thoroughfare of escape they indulged the stratagem of separation ostensibly to disconcert their pursuer and allay the ardor of his pursuit. He then centered on for capture the man with the pistol, whom he saw board the defendant's taxicab, which quickly veered south toward 25th Street on 2d Avenue, where he saw the chauffeur jump out while the cab, still in motion, continued toward 24th Street; after the chauffeur relieved himself of the cumbersome burden of his fare the latter also is said to have similarly departed from the cab before it reached 24th Street.

The chauffeur's story is substantially the same except that he states that his uninvited guest boarded the cab at 25th Street while it was at a standstill waiting for a less colorful fare; that his "passenger" immediately advised him "to stand not upon the order of his going but go at once," and added finality to his command by an appropriate gesture with a pistol addressed to his sacroiliac. The chauffeur in reluctant acquiescence proceeded about fifteen feet, when his hair, like unto the quills of the fretful porcupine, was made to stand on end by the hue and cry of the man despoiled, accompanied by a clamorous concourse of the law-abiding who paced him as he ran; the concatenation of "stop thief," to which the patter of persistent feet did maddingly beat time, rang in his ears as the pursuing posse all the while gained on the receding cab with its quarry therein contained. The holdup man sensing his insecurity suggested to the chauffeur that in the event there was the slightest lapse in obedience to his curt command that he, the chauffeur, would suffer the loss of his brains, a prospect as horrible to an humble chauffeur as it undoubtedly would be to one of the intelligentsia.

The chauffeur, apprehensive of certain dissolution from either Scylla, the pursuers, or Charybdis, the pursued, quickly threw his car out of first speed in which he was proceeding, pulled on the emergency, jammed on his brakes and, although he thinks the motor was still running, swung open the door to his left and jumped out of his car. He confesses that the only act that smacked of intelligence was that by which he jammed the brakes in order to throw off balance the hold-up man, who was half-standing and half-sitting with his pistol menacingly poised. Thus abandoning his car and passenger the chauffeur sped toward 26th Street and then turned to look; he saw the cab proceeding south toward 24th Street, where it mounted the sidewalk. The plaintiff-mother and her two infant children were there injured by the car, which at the time, appeared to be also minus its passenger, who, it appears, was apprehended in the cellar of a local hospital where he was pointed out to a police officer by a remnant of the posse, hereinbefore mentioned. He did not appear at the trial. The three aforesaid plaintiffs and the husband-father sued the defendant for damages, predicating their respective causes of action upon the contention that the chauffeur was negligent in abandoning the cab under the aforesaid circumstances. Fortunately the injuries sustained were comparatively slight. . . .

Negligence has been variously defined but the common legal acceptation is the failure to exercise that care and caution which a reasonable and prudent person ordinarily would exercise under like conditions or circumstances. . . . Negligence is, "not absolute or intrinsic," but "is always relevant to some circumstances of time, place or person." In slight paraphrase of the world's first bard it may be truly observed that the expedition of the chauffeur's violent love of his own security outran the pauser, reason, when he was suddenly confronted with unusual emergency which "took his reason prisoner." The learned attorney for the plaintiffs concedes that the chauffeur acted in an emergency, but claims a right to recovery upon the following proposition taken verbatim from his brief: "It is respectfully submitted that the value of the interest of the public at large to be immune from being injured by a dangerous instrumentality such as a car unattended while in motion is very superior to the right of a driver to abandon same while it is in motion, even when acting under the belief that his life is in danger and by abandoning same he will save his life."

To hold this under the facts adduced herein would be tantamount to a repeal by implication of the primal law of nature written in indelible characters upon the fleshy tablets of sentient creation by the Almighty Law-giver, "the supernal Judge who sits on high." There are those who stem the turbulent current for bubble fame, or who bridge the yawning chasm with a leap for the leap's sake, or who "outstare the sternest eyes that look, outbrave the heart most daring on the earth, pluck the young sucking cubs from the she-bear, yea, mock the lion when he roars for prey" to win a fair lady, and these are the admiration of the generality of men; but they are made of sterner stuff than the ordinary man upon whom the law places no duty of emulation. The law would indeed be fond if it imposed upon the ordinary man the obligation to so demean himself when suddenly confronted with a danger, not of his creation, disregarding the likelihood that such a contingency may darken the intellect and palsy the will of the common legion of the earth, the fraternity of the ordinary man—whose acts or omissions under certain conditions make the yardstick by which the law measures culpability or innocence, negligence or care. . . .

Returning to our chauffeur. If the philosophic Horatio and the martial companions of his watch were "distilled almost to jelly with the act of fear" when they beheld "in the dead vast and middle of the night" the disembodied spirit of Hamlet's father stalk majestically by "with a countenance more in sorrow than in anger," was not the chauffeur, though unacquainted with the example of these eminent men-at-arms, more amply justified in his fearsome reactions when he was more palpably confronted by a thing of flesh and blood bearing in its hand an engine of destruction which depended for its lethal purpose upon the quiver of a hair? When Macbeth was cross-examined by Macduff as to any reason he could advance for his sudden despatch of Duncan's grooms he said in plausible answer, "Who can be wise, amazed, temperate and furious, loyal and neutral in a moment? No man." . . .

Kolanka v. Erie Railroad Co., 215 App. Div. 82, 86, 212 N.Y.S. 714, 717, says, "The law in this state does not hold one in an emergency to the exercise of that mature judgment required of him under circumstances where he has an opportunity for deliberate action. He is not required to exercise unerring judgment, which would be expected of him, were he not confronted with an emergency requiring prompt action." The circumstances provide the foil by which the act is brought into relief to determine whether it is or is not negligent. If under normal circumstances an act is done which might be considered negligent, it does not follow as a corollary that a similar act is negligent if performed by a person acting under an emergency, not of his own making, in which he suddenly is faced with a patent danger with a moment left to adopt a means of extrication.

The chauffeur—the ordinary man in this case—acted in a split second in a most harrowing experience. To call him negligent would be to brand him coward; the court does not do so in spite of what those swaggering heroes, "whose valor plucks dead lions by the beard," may bluster to the contrary. The court is loath to see the plaintiffs go without recovery even though their damages were slight, but cannot hold the defendant liable upon the facts adduced at the trial. Motions, upon which decision was reserved, to dismiss the complaint are granted, with exceptions to plaintiffs. Judgment for defendant against plaintiffs dismissing their complaint upon the merits.

Injury. The plaintiff must establish that he or she sustained an injury, typically a physical one, as a result of the defendant's act. Although a person may be acting in an unreasonably dangerous manner, if there is no injury there is no tort. A person who drives seventy miles per hour through a school zone during recess commits no tort unless someone is injured. There is no such thing as negligence in the abstract. Injury is usually easy to establish, but damages sufficient to compensate the plaintiff for his or her loss may be difficult to calculate in money terms.

The injury incurred by the plaintiff is typically a physical injury to the plaintiff's person or property. The courts are reluctant to allow liability to extend to mental injuries because they are difficult to establish. In most states, the plaintiff may recover damages for negligent infliction of mental distress only if the defendant causes immediate physical injury to the plaintiff or causes mental distress that is followed by physical harm. The requirement that the mental injury be manifested by a physical injury is known as the *trauma rule*. It is designed to guarantee that the claimed mental injury is not spurious.

Actual Cause. The plaintiff must establish a causal relationship between the injury and the defendant's act. Usually this *cause in fact* connection is relatively easy to establish by use of the "but for" test or the "substantial factor" test. Under the "but for" test the plaintiff must prove that, but for the defendant's action, the plaintiff would not have been injured. For example, a plaintiff-pedestrian might establish that, but for the defendant's losing control of his or her car, the plaintiff would not have been struck by it.

There is one type of situation where the "but for" test is not satisfactory. If two causes concur to bring about an event, and either one of them, operating alone, would have been sufficient to cause the identical result, some other test is needed. In these situations, the "substantial factor" test is used. Under this test, the defendant's conduct is a cause of the event if it was a material element and a substantial factor in bringing it about. If the defendant's conduct was a substantial factor in causing the plaintiff's injury, the defendant will not be absolved from liability merely because other causes contributed to the result.

Proximate Cause. Probably the most confusing element to comprehend in the prima facie case of negligence is the element of proximate cause. This is because the terms *proximate* and *cause* when used in this context are mis-

nomers, and because the element is often discussed by courts in connection with other elements of negligence, such as duty.

Although the term cause is used in the label of the doctrine, it is important to separate the issue of proximate cause from the determination of actual cause or cause in fact. The determination of actual cause truly focuses on the cause-and-effect relationship between the defendant's conduct and the plaintiff's injury. However, assuming such a causal connection can be shown, the doctrine of proximate cause is a policy determination of whether the defendant's legal responsibility extends to all the events that actually occurred.

The issue of proximate cause arises in situations where the defendant's original negligence, either by happenstance or intervening acts, leads to unforeseen consequences. Because one act of negligence should not subject a defendant to unlimited liability for all the consequences that could possibly result, tort law has developed the doctrine of proximate cause to limit the defendant's liability to only those events that are reasonably foreseeable. Under the doctrine of proximate cause, a defendant is liable only for the natural, probable, foreseeable, and thus avoidable consequences of his or her conduct, not for all consequences, however remote. The need for the doctrine arises because it is theoretically possible to trace the causal effects of some events through a number of ever-more-distant occurrences. In such situations, it may be theoretically possible to say that the defendant actually caused the injury by setting forth a chain of events that resulted in injury to the plaintiff. However, it is another thing to say that the defendant should be liable for the plaintiff's loss where the likelihood of injury was not foreseeable. Underlying the proximate cause requirement is recognition of the fact that a particular wrong may set off a chain of events so completely unforeseeable, and resulting in an injury so remotely related to the wrong itself, that common sense suggests that the defendant should not be liable for it. Thus the doctrine of proximate cause should be viewed as a principle of law and policy that limits liability to foreseeable injuries. Some courts and commentators see the doctrine of proximate cause as a variant of the duty question.

Procedural Doctrines

The plaintiff has the burden of persuading the trier of fact that he or she is entitled to a recovery. This burden of proving the defendant's negligence is placed upon the plaintiff because it is the plaintiff who is asking the court for relief. In certain cases, the plaintiff may have the burden of proof lightened by two procedural doctrines: *negligence per se* and *res ipsa loquitur.*

Negligence per se. Under the doctrine of negligence per se, a plaintiff may use the defendant's violation of a criminal statute to establish the defendant's negligence. Thus a criminal statute may become a measure of civil liability. If a statute proscribes certain behavior and the defendant violates the statute, most states hold that the violation of the statute is negligence itself. That is, the violation of the statute creates a conclusive presumption that the defendant was negligent. In a few states, the court admits the information of the defendant's violation of the statute as evidence of negligence.

In order for the doctrine of negligence per se to apply, the statute must be relevant to the case; that is, the court must determine that the statute was intended to apply as a standard of civil liability. Thus the court must examine the legislative purpose in enacting the statute. Since most state statutes do not contain any expression of the legislative purpose, this must be surmised by the court. Courts determine whether a statute was intended to apply in the case at hand by determining whether the plaintiff falls within the class of individuals that the statute was intended to protect and whether the injury sustained by the plaintiff was of the type that the statute was intended to prevent. If these two factors are present, the plaintiff may invoke the doctrine of negligence per se.

Res ipsa loquitur. The doctrine of res ipsa loquitur ("the thing speaks for itself") uses circumstantial evidence to establish a prima facie case of negligence. In situations where the plaintiff can establish (1) that his or her injury is a type that does not ordinarily occur without negligence and (2) that the defendant was in exclusive control of the instrumentality that caused the injury, the plaintiff has established a prima facie case of negligence. Such proof is sufficient to support a jury verdict for the plaintiff. Because this prima facie case is based on inferences, however, the defendant has the opportunity to come forward with some explanation of the situation other than negligence. The res ipsa loquitur doctrine is used frequently in cases of product liability, surgical malpractice, and negligent construction of buildings. It should be remembered that res ipsa loquitur is a doctrine of limited applicability and is not used to resolve conflicting testimony. Rather, it is designed for cases where the plaintiff cannot know the exact negligent act.

Defenses

There are two basic defenses to a negligence action: *contributory negligence* and *assumption of risk.* The burden of pleading and proving these defenses is on the defendant. Current trends with regard to these defenses have undercut their utility.

Contributory Negligence. Contributory negligence is conduct by the plaintiff that contributes as a legal cause to the harm he or she has suffered and that falls below the standard to which the plaintiff is required to conform for his or her own protection. In other words, the plaintiff's failure to exercise due care for his or her own safety constitutes a contributing cause to his or her injury. Contributory negligence, raised by the defendant, alleges that, although the defendant may have been negligent, the plaintiff was also negligent in some way directly related to the plaintiff's injury. The existence of contributory negligence is an issue of fact, governed by the same tests and rules as the negligence of the defendant. The plaintiff is required to conform to the standard of conduct of the reasonable prudent person under the same or similar circumstances.

Since the tort of negligence bases liability upon fault, proof of contributory negligence was formerly an absolute bar to recovery by the plaintiff. The rationale for this result was that, because both parties were at fault in the eyes of the law, the defense established the plaintiff's disability rather than the defendant's innocence.

Because of the harshness of this rule, two mitigating theories were developed: the *last clear chance* doctrine and the concept of *comparative negligence.*

An exception to the absolute bar to recovery in cases of contributory negligence is the last clear chance doctrine. This doctrine allows a negligent plaintiff to recover from a defendant under very strictly defined circumstances. It applies in situations where the negligent plaintiff is helpless or inattentive and where the defendant knows of the danger and has time to avoid it without risk.

For example, suppose plaintiff was run over by a train while inattentively walking on the tracks. The railroad company could normally argue that the plaintiff was contributorily negligent in walking on the tracks and thus avoid liability. However, if it could be shown that the train's engineer saw plaintiff and had an opportunity to brake the train to a stop, the engineer would be deemed to have had the last clear chance of avoiding plaintiff's injury. In this situation, the last clear chance doctrine would circumvent the contributory negligence defense.

In a few states, the defendant has the further responsibility to avoid the harm even though the defendant does not in fact know of it if he or she might have discovered it. In other states, there is the additional requirement that the plaintiff's negligence has ceased.

The last clear chance doctrine, besides reducing the harshness of the contributory negligence complete bar rule, encourages people to avoid injuring others if at all possible.

Comparative negligence is an alternative to contributory negligence now followed in a majority of states. This defense weighs the relative negligence of the parties and either reduces the amount of recovery in proportion to the plaintiff's negligence or bars recovery only if the plaintiff's negligence was greater than the defendant's. The proof required for comparative negligence is the same as for contributory negligence. Several states have adopted the comparative negligence standard by statute, and others have adopted it by case law. In the following case, the Supreme Court of California adopted comparative negligence.

Li v. Yellow Cab Company of California

Supreme Court of California

532 P. 2d 1226 (1975)

Nga Li, a motorist, brought an action against the Yellow Cab Company of California and its driver for personal injuries sustained by her in an intersectional collision with a taxicab. The jury found that Li was contributorily negligent, and the Superior Court entered judgment for Yellow Cab. Li appealed the judgment. The Supreme Court of California reversed. Nga Li is the plaintiff; Yellow Cab Company of California is the defendant.

Sullivan, Judge

> Contributory negligence is conduct on the part of the plaintiff which falls below the standard to which he should conform for his own protection, and which is a legally contributing cause cooperating with the negligence of the defendant in bringing about the plaintiff's harm. (Rest. 2d Torts § 463.)

Thus the American Law Institute, in its second restatement of the law, describes the kind of conduct on the part of one seeking recovery for damage caused by negligence which renders him subject to the doctrine of contributory negligence. What the effect of such conduct will be is left to a further section, which states the doctrine in its clearest essence:

> Except where the defendant has the last clear chance, the plaintiff's contributory negligence bars recovery against a defendant whose negligent conduct would otherwise make him liable to the plaintiff for the harm sustained by him (Rest. 2d Torts, § 467.)

This rule, rooted in the long-standing principle that one should not recover from another for damages brought upon oneself has been the law of this state from its beginning. Although criticized almost from the outset for the harshness of its operation, it has weathered numerous attacks, in both the legislative and the judicial arenas, seeking its amelioration or repudiation. We have undertaken a thorough reexamination of the matter, giving particular attention to the common law and statutory sources of the subject doctrine in this state. As we have indicated, this reexamination leads us to the conclusion that the "all-or-nothing" rule of contributory negligence can be and ought to be superseded by a rule which assesses liability in proportion to fault.

It is unnecessary for us to catalogue the enormous amount of critical comment that has been directed over the years against the "all-or-nothing" approach of the doctrine of contributory negligence. The essence of that criticism has been constant and clear: the doctrine is inequitable in its operation because it fails to distribute responsibility in proportion to fault.

It is in view of these theoretical and practical considerations that to this date, 25 states have abrogated the "all or nothing" rule of contributory negligence and have enacted in its place general apportionment statutes calculated in one manner or another to assess liability in proportion to fault. In 1973 these states were joined by Florida, which effected the same result by judicial decision. We are likewise persuaded that logic, practical experience, and fundamental justice counsel against the retention of the doctrine rendering contributory negligence a complete bar to recovery —and that it should be replaced in this state by a system under which liability for damage will be borne by those whose negligence caused it in direct proportion to their respective fault. . . .

We are thus brought to the second group of arguments which have been advanced by defendants and the amici curiae supporting their position. Generally speaking, such arguments expose considerations of a practical nature which, it is urged, counsel against the adoption of a rule of comparative negligence in this state even if such adoption is possible by judicial means.

The most serious of these considerations are those attendant upon the administration of a rule of comparative negligence in cases involving multiple parties. One such problem may arise when all responsible parties are not brought before the court: it may be difficult for the jury to evaluate relative negligence in such circumstances. And to compound this difficulty such an evaluation would not be res judicata in a subsequent suit against the absent wrongdoer. Problems of contribution and indemnity among joint tort feasors lurk in the background.

A second and related major area of concern involves the administration of the actual process of fact-finding in a comparative negligence system. The assigning of a specific percentage factor to the amount of negligence attributable to a particular party, while in theory a matter of little difficulty, can become a matter of perplexity in the face of hard facts. The temptation for the jury to resort to a quotient verdict in such circumstances can be great. These inherent difficulties are not, however, insurmountable. Guidelines might be provided the jury which will assist it in keeping focused upon the true inquiry and the utilization of special verdict or jury interrogatories can be of invaluable assistance in assuring that the jury has approached its sensitive and often complex task with proper standards and appropriate reverence.

The third area of concern, the status of the doctrines of last clear chance and assumption of risk, involves less the practical problems of administering a particular form of comparative negligence than it does a definition of the theoretical outline of the specific form to be adopted. Although several states which apply comparative negligence concepts retain the last clear chance doctrine, the better reasoned position seems to be that when true comparative negligence is adopted, the need for last clear chance as a palliative of the hardships of the "all-or-nothing" rule disappears and its retention results only in a windfall to the plaintiff in direct contravention of the principle of liability in proportion to fault. As for assumption of risk, we have recognized in this state that this defense overlaps that of contributory negligence to some extent and in fact is made up of at least two distinct defenses.

To simplify greatly, it has been observed . . . that in one kind of situation, to wit, where a plaintiff reasonably undertakes to encounter a specific known risk imposed by a defendant's negligence, plaintiff's conduct, although he may encounter that risk in a prudent manner, is in reality a form of contributory negligence. . . . Other kinds of situations within the doctrine of assumption of risk are those, for example, where plaintiff is held to agree to relieve defendant of an obligation of reasonable conduct toward him. Such a situation would not involve contributory negligence, but rather a reduction of defendant's duty of care.

We think it clear that the adoption of a system of comparative negligence should entail the merger of the defense of assumption of risk into the general scheme of assessment of liability in proportion to fault in those particular cases in which the form of assumption of risk involved is no more than a variant of contributory negligence. . . .

It remains to identify the precise form of comparative negligence which we now adopt for application in this state. Although there are many variants, only the two basic forms need be considered here. The first of these, the so-called "pure" form of comparative negligence, apportions liability in direct proportion to fault in all cases. This was the form adopted by the Supreme Court of Florida in Hoffman v. Jones, supra, and it applies by statute in Mississippi, Rhode Island, and Washington. Moreover it is the form favored by most scholars and commentators. . . . The second basic form of comparative negligence, of which there are several variants, applies apportionment based on fault up to the point at which the plaintiff's negligence is equal to or greater than that of the defendant—when that point is reached, plaintiff is barred from recovery. Nineteen states have adopted this form or one of its variants by statute. The principal argument advanced in its favor is moral in nature: that it is not morally right to permit one at fault in an accident to recover from one less at fault. Other arguments assert the probability of increased insurance, administrative, and judicial costs if a "pure" rather than a "50 percent" system is adopted, but this has been seriously questioned. . . .

We have concluded that the "pure" form of comparative negligence is that which should be adopted in this state. In our review the "50 percent" system simply shifts the lottery aspect of the contributory negligence rule to a different ground. . . .

For all the foregoing reasons we conclude that the "all-or-nothing" rule of contributory negligence as it presently exists in this state should be and is herewith superseded by a system of "pure" comparative negligence, the fundamental purpose of which shall be to assign responsibility and liability for damage in direct proportion to the amount of negligence of each of the parties. . . .

Reversed.

Assumption of Risk. The defense of assumption of risk discussed above in *Yellow Cab* is also based upon the notion of fault. It exists when the plaintiff actually had or should have had knowledge of the risk and voluntarily exposed himself or herself to it. In such a situation the defendant, although negligent, is not responsible for the resulting injury. This is analogous to consent to an intentional tort, which also denies recovery.

There are two types of assumption of risk: express assumption of risk and implied assumption of risk. In express assumption of risk, the plaintiff expressly agrees in advance that the defendant is under no obligation to care for the plaintiff and shall not be liable for the consequences of conduct that would otherwise be negligent. As a result of this consent, the defendant is relieved of the legal duty of due care to the plaintiff, and no recovery is allowed against the defendant. Express assumption of risk is covered in Restatement (Second) of Torts § 496(b) (1965) which states: "A plaintiff who by contract or otherwise expressly agrees to accept a risk of harm arising from the defendant's negligent or reckless conduct cannot recover for such harm, unless the agreement is invalid or contrary to public policy."

Implied assumption of risk is epitomized by

Restatement (Second) of Torts § 496 (C) (1965):

A plaintiff who fully understands a risk of harm to himself or his things caused by the defendant's conduct or by the condition of the defendant's land or chattels, and who nevertheless voluntarily chooses to enter or to remain within the area of that risk, under circumstances that manifest his willingness to accept it, is not entitled to recover for harm within that risk.

Implied assumption of risk requires the presence of the following elements:

1. There must be a risk of harm to the plaintiff caused by the defendant's conduct or the condition of the defendant's land or chattels.
2. The plaintiff must have actual knowledge of the particular risk and appreciate its magnitude.
3. The plaintiff must voluntarily choose to enter or remain within the area of that risk under circumstances that manifest the willingness to accept the particular risk.

As with express assumption of risk, the touchstone of implied assumption of risk is consent. Contributory negligence arises when the plaintiff fails to exercise due care. Assumption of risk arises regardless of the due care used. It is based, fundamentally, on consent. Contributory negligence is not. In implied assumption of risk, the consent is manifested by the plaintiff's actions after he or she has been informed of the nature and magnitude of the specific danger involved. Therefore, when the plaintiff voluntarily enters into some relationship with the defendant, with knowledge that the defendant will not protect him or her against the risk, the plaintiff is regarded as tacitly or impliedly consenting to the possible negligence and agreeing to take a chance. For example, the plaintiff may accept employment knowing that he or she is expected to work in a danger-

ous area; or ride in a car with knowledge that the brakes are defective; or enter a baseball park, sit in an unscreened seat, and thereby consent that the players proceed with the game without taking any precautions to protect the plaintiff from being hit by the ball. In effect, the defendant is simply relieved of the duty that would otherwise exist.

STRICT LIABILITY

As was mentioned earlier in this chapter, the early law of torts was not concerned with fault but was based on a concept of strict liability. In the nineteenth century, the fault standard emerged. Liability existed only where the defendant's conduct failed to conform to the standard of care expected of good citizens in the community. In this century, the trend has been toward holding the defendant strictly liable even where the defendant has not acted unreasonably.

Application of Strict Liability

The strict liability standard has been applied in situations where the defendant's conduct creates an unusually high risk of harm even if due care is exercised. In such situations injury is highly probable, and to require the plaintiff to prove negligence is to require him or her to bear the risk inherent in the defendant's dangerous conduct. Although the law could simply prohibit such conduct on the part of the defendant, there is some hazardous conduct that is socially beneficial, such as blasting done during the construction of buildings. The strict liability standard reflects a social policy that the defendant may engage in the activity but must bear the inherent risk of loss. The result of the strict liability standard is that the injured plaintiff is compensated for his or her injury by the party who caused it, who in turn must consider such liability as a cost of undertaking that type of activity.

Strict liability was early applied to the keepers of dangerous animals. A dangerous animal is one that is known by its keeper to be likely to inflict injury, such as a lion, a tiger, or a poisonous snake. For strict liability to apply, the keeper must know or have reason to know of the animal's dangerous propensities.

Strict liability was later applied to ultrahazardous activities. Common examples are blasting operations, public fireworks, and storing gasoline in dangerous proximity to nearby property.

Although strict liability is often called absolute liability, there are limits to the extent of strict liability. The defendant must be aware of the abnormally dangerous activity and voluntarily engage in it. Further, liability is limited to the reasonably expected consequences of such ultrahazardous conduct. For example, liability would not extend to damage done by a rock hurled an unusual distance as a result of a blasting operation. This limitation is similar to the concept of proximate cause in negligence.

Although contributory negligence is no defense to strict liability, a defendant is not liable to a plaintiff who voluntarily and unreasonably encounters a known danger. For example, strict liability would not be available to a plaintiff who agrees to work with animals that the plaintiff knows are dangerous. This is similar to the assumption of risk defense to negligence.

During the past twenty years, strict liability theory has been applied in product liability cases. The rule is stated in Restatement of Torts (Second) § 402A as follows:

1. One who sells any product in a defective condition unreasonably dangerous to the user or consumer or to his property is subject to liability for physical harm thereby caused to the ultimate user or consumer or to his property, if
   a. the seller is engaged in the business of selling such a product, and
   b. it is expected to and does reach the user or consumer without substantial change in the condition in which it is sold.
2. The rule stated in subsection 1 applies although
   a. the seller has exercised all possible care in the preparation and sale of his product, and
   b. the user or consumer has not bought the product from or entered into any contractual relation with the seller.

Strict product liability has been applied to buyers, users, and bystanders. It does not extend to injuries arising from an unintended, abnormal, and unforeseeable use of the products. Assumption of risk is a defense to strict product liability, although contributory negligence is not.

The developing law of product liability is discussed in Chapter 18. The following case involves application of strict product liability and also involves an issue of proof of causation.

Sindell v. Abbott Laboratories

Supreme Court of California
607 P.2d 924 (1980)

Judith Sindell sued eleven drug companies, including Abbott Laboratories, that were engaged in the business of distributing diethylstibestrol (DES), a drug prescribed for use by Sindell's mother to prevent miscarriages. Sindell alleged that she had developed a cancerous tumor and suffered from adenosis (precancerous vaginal and cervical growths) as a result of her mother's ingestion of DES. Sindell predicated her complaint upon various theories of recovery, including strict liability. She was unable to identify which company manufactured the precise drug that caused the injury. Consequently, the trial court dismissed the action against the defendants. The Supreme Court of California reversed. Sindell is the plaintiff; Abbott Laboratories is the defendant.

Mosk, Justice

We begin with the proposition that, as a general rule, the imposition of liability depends upon a showing by the plaintiff that his or her injuries were caused by the act of the defendant or by an instrumentality under the defendant's control. . . .

There are, however, exceptions to this rule. Plaintiff's complaint suggests several bases upon which defendants may be held liable for her injuries even though she cannot demonstrate the name of the manufacturer which produced the DES actually taken by her mother.

Plaintiff places primary reliance upon cases which hold that if a party cannot identify which of two or more defendants causes an injury, the burden of proof may shift to the defendants to show that they were not responsible for the harm. This principle is sometimes referred to as the "alternative liability" theory.

The celebrated case of Summers v. Tice, a unanimous opinion of this court, best exemplifies the rule. In *Summers,* the plaintiff was injured when two hunters negligently shot in his direction. It could not be determined which of them had fired the shot which actually caused the injury to the plaintiff's eye, but both defendants were nevertheless held jointly and severally liable for the whole of the damages. We reasoned that both were wrongdoers, both were negligent toward the plaintiff, and that it would be unfair to require plaintiff to isolate the defendant responsible, because if the one pointed out were to escape liability, the other might also, and the plaintiff-victim would be shorn of any remedy. In these circumstances, we held, the burden of proof shifted to the defendants, "each to absolve himself if he can."

We stated that under these or similar circumstances a defendant is ordinarily in a "far better position" to offer evidence to determine whether he or another defendant caused the injury.

Nevertheless, plaintiff may not prevail in her claim that the *Summers* rationale should be employed to fix the whole liability for her injuries upon defendants, at least as those principles have previously been applied. There is an important difference between the situation involved in *Summers* and the present case. There, all the parties who were or could have been responsible for the harm to the plaintiff were joined as defendants. Here, by contrast, there are approximately 200 drug companies which made DES, any of which might have manufactured the injury-producing drug.

In our contemporary complex industrialized society, advances in science and technology create fungible goods which may harm consumers and which cannot be traced to any specific producer. The response of the courts can be either to adhere rigidly to prior doctrine, denying recovery to those injured by such products, or to fashion remedies to meet these changing needs. Justice Traynor in his landmark concurring opinion in Escola v. Coca Cola Bottling Company recognized that in an era of mass production and complex marketing methods the traditional standard of negligence was insufficient to govern the obligations of manufacturer to consumer. . . .

From a broader policy standpoint, defendants are better able to bear the cost of injury resulting from the manufacture of a defective product. As was said by Justice Traynor in *Escola,* "The cost of any injury and the loss of time or health may be an overwhelming misfortune to the person injured, and a needless one, for the risk of injury can be insured by the manufacturer and distributed among the public as a cost of doing business." The manufacturer is in the best position to discover and guard against defects in its products and to warn of harmful effects; thus, holding it liable for defects and failure to warn of harmful effects will provide an incentive to product safety. These considerations are particularly significant where medication is involved, for the consumer is virtually helpless to protect himself from serious, sometimes permanent, sometimes fatal, injuries caused by deleterious drugs.

But we approach the issue of causation from a different perspective: we hold it to be reasonable in the present context to measure the likelihood that any of the defendants supplied the product which allegedly injured plaintiff by the percentage which the DES sold by each of them for the purpose of preventing miscarriage bears to the entire production of the drug sold by all for that purpose.

The presence in the action of a substantial share of the appropriate market also provides a ready means to apportion damages among the defendants. Each defendant will be held liable for the proportion of the judgment represented by its share of that market unless it demonstrates that it could not have made the product which caused plaintiff's injuries.

We are not unmindful of the practical problems involved in defining the market and determining market share, but these are largely matters of proof which properly cannot be determined at the pleading stage of these proceedings. Under the rule we adopt, each manufacturer's liability for an injury would be approximately equivalent to the damages caused by the DES it manufactured. Reversed and remanded.

Vicarious Liability

Under the doctrine of vicarious liability, an employer is liable for the negligence committed by an employee within the scope of his or her employment. The doctrine is also known as *imputed neglience* or *respondeat superior* ("let the superior respond"). It is an application of strict liability theory, meaning that for policy reasons liability is imposed regardless of the employer's fault or blame. However, unlike other applications of strict liability, the employer's liability is based upon some fault of the employee.

Justification. It seems odd that courts recognize a rule imposing liability upon an otherwise innocent employer for the employee's wrongdoing. Liability could be limited only to instances where the employer knowingly hires a careless agent or commands the agent's tortious conduct. Expressing his own bewilderment at the rule of respondeat superior, Justice Holmes offered this explanation for its existence:

I assume that common sense is opposed to making one man pay for another man's wrong, . . . unless . . . he has induced the immediate wrongdoer to do acts of which the wrong . . . was the natural consequence. . . . I therefore assume that common sense is opposed to the fundamental theory of agency, although I have no doubt that the possible explanations of its various rules . . . together with the fact that the most flagrant of them presents itself as a seemingly wholesome check on the indifference and negligence of great corporations, have done much to reconcile men's minds to that theory.[2]

The "possible explanations" for the doctrine's existence mentioned by Holmes show why the rule had been a legal axiom for centuries. There are many other rationales for respondeat superior as well. A review of them presents the thoughts of several scholars on the subject and shows why, as one of them put it, "We make men pay for faults they have not committed."[3]

The earliest rationale for the doctrine was offered by the courts in the form of a Latin maxim: *Qui facit per alium facit per se* ("he who acts through another, acts himself"). The courts thus created a legal fiction that the employer and employee were one, much in the same way the courts resolved that when two people married they became one person for legal purposes. This fictitious identification of the employee with the employer became a convenient way for courts to reach their desired result. Citing the survival of the identification fiction from ancient times, Holmes maintained that the modern rule depends upon a fiction for its present existence. Later he concluded: "I look forward to a time when the part played by history in the explanation of dogma shall be very small . . . and instead . . . we shall . . . study . . . the ends sought to be attained and the reasons for desiring them."[4]

Following Holmes's prodding, other scholars began exploring the policy justifications for respondeat superior. John Wigmore philosophized:

If . . . I employ knowingly a careless servant, here at least I should be liable, just as for imprudently keeping a dog known to be ferocious. But even this may on practical grounds be too lenient a rule, for I may still find means of evading due responsibility under that test. Public convenience then may demand that I should be liable up to still a further point, even though I select agents carefully; in other words we may say I employ a substitute more or less at my peril.[5]

Wigmore recognized a policy reason for respondeat superior that may be called the evidence theory: the difficulty of proving whether an employer exercised care in hiring the employee or knew of the employee's activities requires holding the employer liable. As another scholar succinctly stated: "It is difficult to prove exactly who directed the damage, but you can tell whose servant did it."[6]

Another justification for the doctrine is the entrepreneur or enterprise theory, which is a financial explanation based upon the best way to distribute loss. Under this theory, the risk of liability is viewed as simply a cost the employer bears for the privilege of doing business. Imposing this cost upon the employer is not viewed as unfair because the employer benefits from the employee's activities and thus acquires the means to pay for the employee's torts. Furthermore, it is maintained that the employer is in a better position to bear the risk of loss, since the employer can pass the loss on to consumers in the form of higher prices. Viewed this way, respondeat superior is seen as a form of risk spreading, with the loss ultimately falling upon the community. The leading proponent of the entrepreneur theory, Young B. Smith, gave the following example as an illustration of its operation:

A taxicab negligently runs into a pedestrian. If the injured person's sole remedy is against the negligent chauffeur, in most cases the loss will fall on the pedestrian. On the other hand, if the person carrying on the taxicab business is held responsible, the loss will not fall on him alone. . . . [I]t is feasible for him (through the medium of insurance) to spread the loss among others carrying on a similar business, and he can pass his proportionate part of slightly higher charges to the hundreds and thousands of persons who use his cabs and thus "the shock of the accident may be borne by the community."[7]

The entrepreneur theory conforms to reality. It is a financial fact of life that while many business people insure their businesses against liability, few people bother to adequately provide protection against accidental harm to themselves.

Respondeat superior need not be seen simply as the application of a financial theory. It may be viewed as serving a managerial as well as a financial function. An employer who is responsible for the consequences of the employee's conduct is more apt to take precautions to prevent the injurious consequences from arising. The employer will be more careful to hire safety-conscious employees, supervise their conduct, and discipline their carelessness. Thus respondeat superior has a preventive, or deterrent effect. As C. Robert Morris stated: "[N]ot only could the manager insure and spread the risk, but he could also seek to minimize the loss or prevent it altogether."[8] Although the availability of insurance reduces the economic impact, to the employer faced with premium increases and possible cancellation of coverage these managerial aspects of the doctrine take on added significance.

Respondeat superior was also seen by one scholar as a reflection of a fundamental change in legal thinking. Recognizing the doctrine's managerial functions, Harold Laski interpreted its emergence as a shift away from the legal protection of individualism toward a theory of social responsibility:

It is becoming more and more clear that we may not be content with an individualistic commercial law. Just as that individualism was the natural reaction from the too strict and local paternalism of medieval policy—perhaps aided by the self-centeredness of Puritan thought—so we are compelled to turn away from every conception of the business relation which does not see the public as an effective, if silent, partner in every enterprise. . . . It is simply a legal attempt to see the individual in his social context. That at which we industrially aim is the maximum public good as we see it. In that respect the employer is himself no more than a public servant, to whom, for special purposes, a certain additional freedom of action, and therefore a greater measure of responsibility has been vouchsafed. If that employer is compelled to bear the burden of his servant's torts even when he is himself personally without fault, it is because in a social distribution of profit and loss, the balance of least disturbance seems thereby best to be obtained. . . . If we allow the master to be careless of his servant's torts we lose hold upon the most valuable check in the conduct of social life.[9]

Others have been less lofty in their rationalizations of respondeat superior. These cynics see the doctrine as a method of making the person with the money pay the price, and their theory is appropriately called the deep-pocket theory. As Thomas Baty, the originator of the idea, put it, "Servants are an impecunious race. Should we nowadays hold masters answerable for the uncommanded torts of their servants if servants were able to pay for the damages they do? In hard fact, the reason for employers' liability is . . . the damages are taken from the deep pocket."[10]

One theme is central to all of these theories: Between two innocent persons, the employer and the injured person, it is the employer who should pay for the employee's torts because, for various policy reasons, the employer is in the better position to bear this burden.

Scope of Employment Limitation. While respondeat superior is recognized because society believes it desirable and expedient to make the employer responsible for injuries inflicted by the employee, the employer is not made responsible for each and every tort the employee commits. Only when the employee commits a tort in the scope of employment—that is, when the injury is caused by the employee's wrongdoing incidental to the employment purposes—is the employer liable under respondeat superior. To make the employer responsible for acts that are in no way connected with employment goals would be unfair. The employer can be expected to bear only those costs that are closely associated with the business.

This limit on the employer's liability is easier to state than to apply. Determining if the employee is acting within the scope of employment often is difficult because the employee may temporarily be performing a personal errand, or doing the employer's work while also serving a personal purpose, or performing the employer's work in a forbidden manner. No precise formula exists to solve the problem whether at a particular moment a particular employee is engaged in the employer's business. Whether the employee is inside or outside the scope of employment often is a matter of degree. Since the scope of employment test determines whether respondeat superior applies as a guide in close cases, reference should be made to the larger policy purposes respondeat superior is supposed to serve.

No Fault Insurance Systems

In two areas, state-mandated insurance compensation systems have replaced the traditional tort litigation system as a means of loss allocation. These are the areas of workers' compensation and no-fault automobile insurance.

Workers' Compensation. The defenses of contributory negligence and assumption of risk, along with the fellow-servant rule (which provided that an employer was not liable for a worker's injury where the injury resulted from the negligence of a fellow worker), made it extremely unlikely that an employee could hold the employer liable for on-the-job injuries. In response to the growing number of job-related injuries and the political pressure generated by labor groups, state legislatures in the early twentieth century enacted workers' compensation statutes. By 1949, every state had some form of workers' compensation system. Although the laws vary, they have certain common features.

Workers' compensation statutes substitute a strict liability standard for negligence with regard to job-related injuries. Fault is immaterial. Employees are entitled to benefits whether or not they were negligent and whether or not their employer was free from fault.

Injuries that arise out of and during the course of employment are compensable under workers' compensation statutes. This standard is similar to the scope-of-employment test of the respondeat superior doctrine discussed previously.

Under workers' compensation, employers are required to contribute either to a state-administered workers' compensation fund or, as in most states, procure workers' compensation insurance from private insurers.

Claims for workers' compensation benefits are administered by a state agency, usually called the Industrial Commission or Workers' Compensation Bureau. If the employer contests the claim, the agency holds a hearing and determines if the injury is compensable under the statute. Because an employer's contribution to the state fund or the employer's insurance premiums depend upon the employer's experience rating, there is an economic incentive for employers to contest doubtful claims.

Workers' compensation benefits are computed according to a schedule of compensation. The schedule establishes the financial amount an injured employee is entitled to according to the type of injury or disability that the employee suffered.

No-Fault Automobile Insurance. Many negligence cases involve automobile accidents. Because of the amount of time courts devote to these cases, states have enacted statutes that, to varying degrees, remove recovery for automobile accident injuries from the courts to administrative agencies. The purpose of these statutes is to provide an injured party with an automatic but minimal amount of recovery rather than a day in court with its potential for a greater recovery. The laws differ from state to state. Basically, they provide that the injured party need not prove negligence in the traditional way but only that the no-fault insurance statute is applicable to the case. As long as the amount claimed by the injured party is below a prescribed maximum, his or her own insurance pays the claim without regard to fault. This process is analogous to the change from the use of negligence to workers' compensation insurance for recovery by injured employees.

REVIEW PROBLEMS

1. Breisig operated an automobile repair shop. Roberts took his car to Breisig's shop for repairs. When Roberts asked when the car would be ready, Breisig said that he hoped the repairs would be completed by the end of the day. If they were, Breisig said, he would park the car in his shop's parking lot so Roberts could pick it up that evening. About 7 P.M. Breisig finished the work and parked the car in the lot, leaving the keys in the ignition. Soon thereafter two teenage boys stole the car and drove it around town. They picked up two friends and left the car on a street overnight. The next day one of the friends, Williams, returned to the car and, while driving negligently, struck George, who suffered serious injuries. George sued Breisig, claiming that leaving the keys in an unattended car was negligence, particularly since Breisig's shop was located in a deteriorating neighborhood. Breisig denied liability. Who wins? Explain. George v. Breisig, 477 P.2d 983 (Kan. 1970).

2. A passenger was running to catch one of the Long Island Railroad Company's trains. A railroad employee, trying to assist the passenger to board the train, dislodged a package from his arms, and it fell upon the rails. The package contained fireworks, which exploded with some violence. The concussion overturned some scales, many feet away on the platform, and they fell upon Palsgraf and injured her. Palsgraf sued the Long Island Railroad Company, claiming that it was liable for her injuries as a result of its employee's negligence. Long Island Railroad disclaimed any liability. Who wins? Explain. Palsgraf v. Long Island Railroad Co., 162 N.E. 99 (N.Y.1928).

3. A driver for the Coca Cola Bottling Company delivered several cases of Coca Cola to the restaurant where Escola worked as a waitress. She placed the cases on the floor, one on top of the other, under and behind the counter, where they remained for over thirty-six hours. Escola picked up the top case and set it upon a nearby ice-cream cabinet in front of and about three feet from the refrigerator. She then proceeded to take the bottles from the case with her right hand, one at a time, and put them into the refrigerator. After she had placed three bottles in the refrigerator and had moved the fourth bottle about eighteen inches from the case, it exploded in her hand. The bottle broke into two jagged pieces and inflicted a deep five-inch cut, severing blood vessels, nerves, and muscles of the thumb

and palm of her hand. Escola sued Coca Cola, relying on the doctrines of res ipsa loquitur and strict product liability theory. Will Escola succeed under these theories? Explain. Escola v. Coca Cola Bottling Co. of Fresno, 150 P.2d 436 (Calif. 1944).

4. A dead mouse is found baked inside a loaf of bread from the Continental Baking Co., and Doyle is injured by eating the bread. Continental introduces evidence of many witnesses who testify that all possible care was used in the bakery, and that such precautions were taken that it was impossible for mice to get into the product. Continental makes a motion for a directed verdict in its favor. Will the court grant the motion? Doyle v. Continental Baking Co., 160 N.E. 325 (1928).

5. On a stormy night the owner of a tractor truck left it parked without lights in the middle of the road. The driver of a car in which Hill was a passenger saw it in time to turn and avoid hitting it, but negligently failed to do so. Hill is injured. Who is liable to her? Hill v. Edmonds, 270 N.Y.S.2d 1020 (1966).

6. A fireman developed lung cancer after some years of inhaling smoke while fighting fires and also smoking cigarettes. The fireman filed a claim for workers' compensation benefits. Will the fireman recover benefits? McAllister v. Workmen's Compensation Appeals Board, 445 P.2d 313 (1968).

7. The Kosmos Portland Cement Co. failed to clean petroleum residue out of an oil barge, which was tied to a dock. Lightning struck the barge, the vapor with which it was filled exploded, and workers on the dock were injured. Is Kosmos liable to the workers for their injuries? Johnson v. Kosmos Portland Cement Co. 64 F.2d 193 (6th Cir. 1933).

8. Anthony and Jeannette Luth were driving south on the Seward Highway in Alaska when their car collided with another driven by Wayne Jack. The accident occurred when Jack attempted to pass another vehicle going north. On the day of the accident and for the previous six weeks, Jack was employed by Rogers and Babler Construction Company as a flagman on a road construction project. At the time of the accident, he was returning home to Anchorage from his job site, having completed a 7-A.M.-to-5:30-P.M. workday. Since he did not live near the job site, Jack commuted approximately twenty-five miles to work by car every day. The Master Union Agreement under which Jack worked provided for additional remuneration of $8.50 a day since the job site was located a considerable distance from Anchorage. However, all of the firm's employees on this particular construction project received the $8.50 additional remuneration whether they commuted from Anchorage or lived near the job site. The Luths sued Rogers and Babler Construction, claiming that the company was responsible under the doctrine of respondeat superior for their injuries. Is the company liable? Explain. Luth v. Rogers and Babler Const. Co., 507 P.2d (761 Alaska 1973).

FOOTNOTES

[1] 28 Cal. App.2d 1, 31 Cal. Rptr. 847 (Calif. App. Ct. 1963).

[2] Holmes, *The History of Agency*, 5 HARV. L.REV. 1, 14 (1891).

[3] Laski, *The Basis of Vicarious Liability*, 26 YALE L.J. 105, 111 (1916).

[4] Holmes, *The Path of the Law*, 10 HARV. L.REV. 457, 474 (1897).

[5] Wigmore, *Responsibility for Tortious Acts: Its History*, 7 HARV. L.REV. 383, 404–405 1 (1894).

[6]Baty, Vicarious Liability 147 (1916).

[7]Smith, *Frolic and Detour,* 23 Colum. L. Rev. 444, 458 (1923).

[8]Morris, *Enterprise Liability and the Actuarial Process—The Insignificance of Foresight,* 70 Yale L.J. 554 (1961).

[9]Laski, *The Basis of Vicarious Liability,* 26 Yale L.J. 105, 112 and 114 (1916).

[10]Baty, Vicarious Liability 154 (1916).

PART II

CONTRACTS

CHAPTER 5

Introduction to the Law of Contracts

THE UTILITY OF CONTRACTS _____

CONTRACT DEFINED _____

SOURCE OF CONTRACT LAW _____

CLASSIFICATION OF CONTRACTS _____

A s we shall see in the following chapters, contracts are all-pervasive in our daily lives. For instance, the law of contracts governs a boarding agreement with the university, renting an apartment, buying books at the bookstore, agreeing to lend a roommate money, and buying beer at the local store.

THE UTILITY OF CONTRACTS

Contract law can be viewed in several ways. Some see the freedom of individuals and organizations to contract as fundamental to our basic free-enterprise system.[1] Viewed in this manner, the law of supply and demand learned in economics is implemented every day by innumerable contracts between sellers and buyers. Contract law facilitates exchanges between the parties by protecting both seller and buyer against the possible bad-faith conduct of the other. Without this protection, the parties could breach contracts at will. If the law of contracts did not provide a remedy for the breach of an agreement, sellers would be forced to require deposits, or entire purchase prices, before they would sell and ship goods. This would increase transaction costs and significantly affect the flow of goods in our economy.[2]

Another view of a contract is that it is a tool by which people—often, but not always, assisted by their lawyers—establish a private set of rules to govern a particular business or personal relationship. From a lawyer's perspective, a contract is a device by which a situation may be defined and controlled. The expectations of the contracting parties are made known and serve as guides for future behavior.

For example, by use of a real-estate purchase contract, a seller promises to sell a house and lot to a buyer. In the contract, a number of the parties' expectations are spelled out. Such expectations include: (1) when the buyer may take possession; (2) what kind of document of title the seller is to provide the buyer; (3) what articles the seller may remove from the house and yard; (4) how the taxes owing are to be split among the parties; (5) how the risk of loss is to be allocated among the parties, and so on.

By virtue of this contractual agreement, the buyer and seller have created their own set of rules to govern the house-sale transaction. In a sense, their agreement embodies a private legal system. Not surprisingly, many of the questions that arise concerning the operation of a governmental legal system also come up in the context of private agreements. For example, what is to be done if the parties in the agreement just described fail to provide for responsibility in case of loss and the house is destroyed by a meteor after the contract is signed but before the buyer takes possession? Or what happens if one of the parties blatantly disregards one of the clearly established private rules—for example, by refusing to provide the required evidence of title?

In the first case (loss of a house struck by a meteor) the basic expectations of at least one of the parties cannot be met. Either the buyer will be required to purchase damaged property or the seller will be required to give up a sale he or she thought was closed and final. How can this issue be resolved when the parties have not dealt with the problem themselves and insurance does not cover the loss? For commonly occurring situations of this sort, the courts and legislatures have established guidelines. In addition, general legal principles have been promulgated determining how contractual provisions should be interpreted when issues such as this arise.

The second case (refusing to provide required evidence of title) goes to the heart of contract law. From a public-policy perspective, it would not be desirable for the parties to attempt to enforce their contract by private means. Our legal system does not tolerate the use of threats or force to induce faithful observance of the terms of private agreements. (An ironic use of the term contract is to speak of "putting out a contract" on someone when describing the criminal procurement of violence against a designated victim.) Instead, it allows the parties to a contract to enforce its terms through civil suits.

A number of questions are immediately posed by the intervention of the legal system when private parties disagree. Should all private agreements be enforced—for example, an agreement by two bank robbers to split the proceeds of a holdup 55 percent/45 percent? What type of relief should be provided for the party injured as a result of the other's failure to observe the terms of the agreement? Could a university obtain a court order compelling a professor who has just won a millionaire lottery to teach the last academic year of a three-year teaching contract? Should the legal system enforce only "fair" contracts? If so, what constitutes a fair contract? Should unwritten contracts be enforceable?

Because the case below involved actor Lee Marvin and received extensive media coverage, it provides an interesting introduction to the law of contracts. The reader should try to determine what policy issues the court considered in determining whether a private agreement should be enforced.

Marvin v. Marvin

Supreme Court of California
555 P.2d 106 (1976)

Michelle Triola Marvin (plaintiff) lived with actor Lee Marvin (defendant) from October 1964 to May 1970, when he compelled her to leave. She sued Mr. Marvin, claiming that they had entered into an oral contract in 1964 in which both parties agreed they would share equally their earnings and property no matter who earned them. She claimed that they agreed to represent themselves as husband and wife and that she would be a homemaker and companion, giving up her career as an entertainer and singer. Mr. Marvin in his defense claimed that this was not an enforceable contract because it was made between nonmarital partners, involved in an illicit relationship, and thus was contrary to public policy. A lower court ruled in favor of Mr. Marvin, leaving all property accumulated by the couple with him. Ms. Marvin appealed. Held. Reversed and remanded for new trial.

Tobriner, Justice

During the past 15 years, there has been a substantial increase in the number of couples living together without marrying. Such nonmarital relationships lead to legal controversy when one partner dies or the couple separates.

We conclude: (1) The provisions of the Family Law Act do not govern the distribution of property acquired during a nonmarital relationship, such a relationship remains subject solely to judicial decision; (2) The courts should enforce express contracts between nonmarital partners except to the extent that the contract is explicitly founded on the consideration of meretricious sexual services.

Defendant first and principally relies on the contention that the alleged contract is so closely related to the supposed "immoral" character of the relationship between plaintiff and himself that the enforcement of the contract would violate public policy. He points to cases asserting that a contract between nonmarital partners is unenforceable if it is "involved in" an illicit relationship . . . or made in "contemplation" of such a relationship. A review of the numerous California decisions concerning contracts between nonmarital partners, however, reveals that the courts have not employed such broad and uncertain standards to strike down contracts. The decisions instead disclose a narrower and more precise standard: a contract between nonmarital partners is unenforceable *only to the extent* that it *explicitly* rests upon the immoral and illicit consideration of meretricious sexual services.

In Bridges v. Bridges (1954) 125 Cal. App.2d 359, both parties were in the process of obtaining divorces from their erstwhile respective spouses. The two parties agreed to live together, to share equally in property acquired, and to marry when their divorces became final. The man worked as a salesman and used his savings to purchase properties. The woman kept house, cared for seven children, three from each former marriage and one from the nonmarital relationship, and helped construct improvements on the properties. When they separated, without marrying, the court awarded the woman one-half the value of the property. Rejecting the man's contention that the contract was illegal, the court stated that: "Nowhere is it expressly testified to by anyone that there was anything in the agreement for the pooling of assets and the sharing of accumulations that contemplated meretricious relations as any part of the consideration or as any object of the agreement."

Defendant secondly relies upon the ground suggested by the trial court: that the 1964 contract violated public policy because it impaired the community property rights of Betty Marvin, defendant's lawful wife. Defendant points out that his earnings while living apart from his wife before rendition of the interlocutory decree were community property . . . and that defendant's agreement with plaintiff purported to transfer to her a half interest in that community property. But whether or not defendant's contract with plaintiff exceeded his authority as manager of the community property, defendant's argument fails for the reason that an improper transfer of community property is not void *ab initio,* but merely voidable at the instance of the aggrieved spouse. In the present case Betty Marvin, the aggrieved spouse, had the opportunity to assert her community property rights in the divorce action. The interlocutory and final decrees in that action fix and limit her interest. Enforcement of the contract between plaintiff and defendant against property awarded to defendant by the divorce decree will not impair any right of Betty's, and thus is not on that account violative of public policy.

 Defendant's third contention is noteworthy for the lack of authority advanced in its support. He contends that enforcement of the oral agreement between plaintiff and himself is barred by Civil Code section 5134, which provides that "All contracts for marriage settlements must be in writing. . . ." A marriage settlement, however, is an agreement in contemplation of marriage in which each party agrees to release or modify the property rights which would otherwise arise from the marriage. The contract at issue here does not conceivably fall within that definition, and thus is beyond compass of section 5134.

Defendant finally argues that enforcement of the contract is barred by Civil Code section 43.5, subdivision (d), which provides that "No cause of action arises for . . . [b]reach of a promise of marriage." This rather strained contention proceeds from the premise that a promise of marriage impliedly includes a promise to support and to pool property acquired after marriage to the conclusion that pooling and support agreements not part of or accompanied by promise of marriage are barred by the section. We conclude that section 43.5 is not reasonably susceptible to the interpretation advanced by defendant, a conclusion demonstrated by the fact that since section 43.5 was enacted in 1939, numerous cases have enforced pooling agreements between nonmarital partners, and in none did court or counsel refer to section 43.5.

In summary, we base our opinion on the principle that adults who voluntarily live together and engage in sexual relations are nonetheless as competent as any other persons to contract respecting their earnings and property rights. Of course, they cannot lawfully contract to pay for the performance of sexual services, for such a contract is, in essence, an agreement for prostitution and unlawful for that reason. But they may agree to pool their earnings and to hold all property acquired during the relationship in accord with the law governing community property; conversely they may agree that each partner's earnings and the property acquired from those earnings remains the separate property of the earnings partner. So long as the agreement does not rest upon illicit meretricious consideration, the parties may order their economic affairs as they choose, and no policy precludes the courts from enforcing such agreements.

In the present instance, plaintiff alleges that the parties agreed to pool their earnings, that they contracted to share equally in all property acquired, and that defendant agreed to support plaintiff. The terms of the contract as alleged do not rest upon any unlawful consideration. We therefore conclude that the complaint furnishes a suitable

basis upon which the trial court can render declaratory relief. The trial court consequently erred in granting defendant's motion for judgment on the pleadings.

Held. Reversed and remanded for new trial.

CASE NOTE

The trial court, upon remand, found that the evidence did not show that Ms. Marvin
gave up her career at Mr. Marvin's request or for his benefit. Further, the court found
that the couple's words and conduct showed neither an express nor implied contract
to share property. The court found that performance of "homemaking" services for
a paramour does not of itself imply a contract to share property since such things are
frequently done for other reasons, such as shared affection. Such acts do not in and
of themselves show an "accumulation of property by mutual effort" under California
law. Having found no expressed or implied contract, the court, in equity, awarded
$104,000 to Ms. Marvin for rehabilitation purposes. It noted that this amount would
be approximately equal to the highest scale she ever earned as a singer, $1,000 per
week, for two years. (See Case No. C-23303, Memorandum Opinion, Superior Court
of the State of California, County of Los Angeles, April 18, 1979, reprinted in 5FLR
3077, 3083–3085 [1979].)

Mr. Marvin appealed this decision, and the California Court of Appeals reversed the
trial court, stating that there was no basis in equity or in law for awarding Ms. Marvin
$104,000 to rehabilitate herself (122 Cal. App. 3d.871 [1981]).

CONTRACT DEFINED

The issues posed earlier in this chapter will be
discussed in the following chapters as the basic
outline of the law of contracts is presented.
For now, we need to define a *contract*. The
simplest, most accurate definition is: *A contract is an agreement that the courts will recognize and enforce.* What do the courts require before an agreement will be recognized
and enforced? The following list represents
the elements of enforceability for most types
of contracts in most jurisdictions.[3] In paren-
theses the reader will find the chapter in this
text that discusses each element.

1. A valid offer (Chapter 6)
2. A proper acceptance (Chapter 7)
3. Sufficiency of consideration (Chapter 8)

4. Absence of fraud, force, or legally significant mistake (Chapter 9)
5. Legal capacity of parties (Chapter 10)
6. Consistency with general public policy
   (Chapter 11)
7. Observance of proper legal form (Chapter
   12)
8. Consistency with special rules governing
   the type of agreement involved (Chapter
   13)

Several basic points regarding the true nature of contracts must now be made. First,
almost all contracts are voluntarily carried out
by the parties to their mutual satisfaction, so
the judicial system never becomes involved.
Second, the mere fact that one has a legal right
to sue for breach of contract does not mean
that it is a sound business decision to do so.
Before suit is filed, factors such as likelihood of

again doing business with the other party, industry attitudes about litigious businesses, relative economic strength of the parties, and alternative private means of resolving the dispute should be considered. Third, although we will be discussing basic rules pertaining to contracts in general, there are many specific categories of contracts that have certain individualized rules of law pertaining to them.[4]

SOURCE OF CONTRACT LAW

General contract law has a common law basis. This means that the principles of contract law are to be found in judicial decisions of cases involving contractual disputes. Under the doctrine of precedent, or stare decisis, courts will follow their earlier decisions involving similar situations. This principle of consistency in judicial decision making produces fields of judicially made law, such as contracts, torts, and agency. With the exception of Louisiana, no state has a comprehensive statute promulgating contract law.

There are, however, a number of statutes that spell out special rules for certain types of contracts. For example, state statutes regulate the use of insurance contracts. The most important of the state statutes affecting contract law is the Uniform Commercial Code (UCC). The UCC, which has been adopted at least in part by the legislatures of all fifty states, established a series of rules dealing with all aspects of sales transactions. One part of the UCC, Article 2, contains rules governing sales contracts. (Article 2 of the UCC is included in full in the Appendix.) If the UCC does not provide a rule covering an aspect of a sales contract, the general common law of contracts controls. If there is a UCC rule, it governs sales contracts even when the common law rule is to the contrary. This relationship is spelled out in Figure 5-1.

FIGURE 5-1

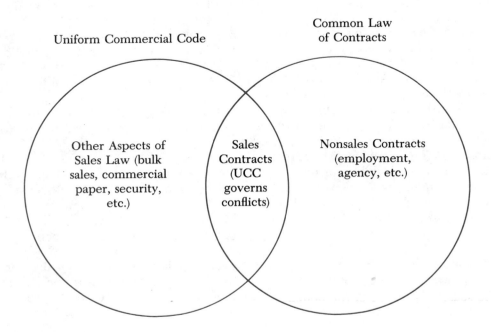

Uniform Commercial Code

Common Law
of Contracts

Other Aspects of Sales Law (bulk sales, commercial paper, security, etc.)

Sales Contracts (UCC governs conflicts)

Nonsales Contracts (employment, agency, etc.)

CLASSIFICATION OF CONTRACTS

The following classification of contracts seeks to aid the reader in analyzing problems related to contracts as they are covered in subsequent chapters. It will be assumed there that the reader is familiar with these categories of contracts and the terminology involved.

Express, Implied, and Quasi Contracts

An *express contract* is one formed by the words of the parties, either oral or written. A *contract implied-in-fact* is derived from the actions of the parties. Going to a doctor, describing symptoms, and accepting treatment establishes a contract implied-in-fact. The test is whether a reasonable person would intend to contract by engaging in such actions.

A *quasi contract*, also known as a *contract implied-in-law*, differs from express and implied-in-fact contracts in that the parties did not intend to make a contract. In creating the legal fiction of a quasi contract, the courts are not trying to fathom the intentions of the parties; they are simply trying to be fair. Suppose, for example, that a doctor performed expensive and valuable services upon a patient who had suddenly become unconscious in the doctor's waiting room. There is clearly no express contract. Further, many courts would refuse to recognize a contract implied-in-fact because no intention could be inferred regarding any actions of the patient. A quasi contract could be posited, however, that would require the patient to pay the reasonable value of the services rendered.

In order for the courts to recognize a quasi contract, there must be (1) a benefit or unjust enrichment retained by the benefited party and (2) no other legal recourse for the "victim" of the benefit. The victim is entitled to recover only the reasonable value of the benefit—not what would have been a likely contract price.

Executed and Executory Contracts

An *executed* contract is one in which all required performances have been rendered. A goes to B's garage, picks up a new tire, and pays B. The contract has been fully performed. Nothing remains to be done by either party. An *executory* contract is one in which some of the required performance remains to be done. A and B enter an agreement whereby B agrees to repair A's car in two weeks and A agrees to pay B $100 upon completion. Since neither party has performed his part of the agreement, it is executory in nature. This distinction is significant, because the courts will be influenced by the performance status of an executory contract in determining the relief to be given to the victim of a breach of contract. Remedies are discussed in Chapter 14.

Valid, Void, and Voidable Contracts

A *valid* contract is one that is perfectly good and that may be enforced by all parties to it. A *void* contract, on the other hand, is not good; it is not enforceable by anyone. A void contract is a contradiction in terms in that it is not really a contract under our definition. For example, if A contracts with B to kill C, who is A's wife, the failure of B to perform will not be grounds for a suit by A because a legally enforceable contract never existed. A *voidable* contract has an in-between status. It is currently valid, but one or more of the parties has the power to render the contract unenforceable. A, a minor, contracts with B, who is of legal age, to paint B's house. The contract is voidable by A. As explained in Chapter 10, A has the right to disaffirm the agreement anytime before reaching majority and shortly thereafter.

Bilateral and Unilateral Contracts

A contract may involve an exchange of promises in which two parties agree that each will perform in a certain way in the future. Player promises to abide by the team rules and be available to play baseball for the coming season. Team promise to pay Player $85,000 for the year. At the moment the contract is signed, neither party starts performing. Instead, the agreed-upon performance will take place in the future. The exchange of a promise for a promise is known as a *bilateral contract.*

Suppose Team promises to pay Player $2,000 for every home run over thirty during the season. Player has not promised to hit more than thirty home runs and will not be in breach of contract for failing to do so. Instead, Team has made a promise that performance will be forthcoming in exchange for an act. This is an offer of a *unilateral contract* that can be accepted only by performance of the act. Most commercial contracts are bilateral. The case that follows illustrates the importance of being able to distinguish between unilateral and bilateral contracts.

Cook v. Johnson
Supreme Court of Washington
221 P. 2d 525 (1950)

Cook (appellant) sued Johnson (respondent) to recover $1,790 for work performed by Cook in cleaning out and extending a drainage ditch located on Johnson's ranch. On December 20, 1947 Johnson wrote offering to pay Cook to clean a drainage ditch and do any work he thought needed to be done. In a letter of December 23, 1947, Cook accepted, noting that he would be finished by January 20, 1948, assuming there were no extreme weather conditions. Unknown to Cook, at the time Johnson wrote the December 20th letter he was negotiating with one Fink for the sale of the ranch. The deal was consummated and the ranch was sold to Fink under a conditional sales contract on January 22, 1948. Cook was never notified of the sale. Shortly thereafter Cook learned of the sale and the fact that Fink was in possession. He did not contact Johnson because he did not know where Johnson was. After Fink and Johnson agreed that Cook should do the work, Cook began, finishing the work in April. An unusually heavy frost had prevented him from completing the work in January. Cook billed Johnson for the work. Johnson refused to pay and Cook brought suit. The lower court ruled in favor of the defendant, concluding that the December 20 and December 23 letters failed to show a meeting of the minds. Plaintiff, Cook, appealed. Held. Reversed and remanded.

Schwellenbach, Justice

The law recognizes, as a matter of classification, two kinds of contracts—bilateral and unilateral. A bilateral contract is one in which there are reciprocal promises; the promise by one party is consideration for the promise by the other. Each party is bound by his promise to the other. A unilateral contract is a promise by one party—an offer by him to do a certain thing in the event the other party performs a certain act. The performance by the other party constitutes an acceptance of the offer and the contract then becomes executed. Until acceptance by performance, the offer may be revoked either by communication to the offeree or by acts inconsistent with the offer, knowledge of which has been conveyed to the offeree. An example of this class of contract is the offer of a reward.

The letters between the parties indicate that they had negotiated for some time with reference to appellant (Cook) cleaning out and extending the ditches. These negotiations culminated in an offer by respondent to pay upon performance by appellant and upon appellant's submission of the bill to him. Up to that point appellant was not obligated to perform. He could have accepted the offer by performance. But he went further than that and promised to do the work. The promises of the two men thereby became reciprocal and binding, each upon the other. The two letters constitute a binding reciprocal agreement between the parties. There was a definite proposal by respondent which was unconditionally accepted by appellant. The minds of the parties met.

Respondent (Johnson) contends that it became appellant's duty, after learning of the conditional sale to Fink, coupled with Fink's possession of the property, to contact respondent before performing—that, under the circumstances, he proceeded with the work at his peril. That might have been true if the contract were unilateral. However, we are here considering the reciprocal promises of the parties, each to the other— a bilateral contract. It was respondent's duty, if he wished to be relieved of his obligation to pay for the work, to contact appellant and attempt to have him agree to a rescission. Furthermore, although the testimony as to what transpired at the meeting in Spokane between respondent and Fink is so conflicting as to make it impossible to determine what was said, respondent then knew that appellant was on the ranch ready to perform and that he had not performed up to that time. He did nothing to stop performance or to protect any rights which he might have claimed under the contract.

Here the appellant (Cook) discharged his obligation by performance in accordance with the terms of the agreement between the parties.

Held. Reversed and remanded.

NOTE TO THE READER

As mentioned earlier, Chapters 6–12 elaborate on the elements of enforceability for most types of contracts in most jurisdictions. Then Chapter 13 covers rights that third parties may have in a contract entered into by others.

Chapter 14 is about the kind of performance or excuse necessary to legally satisfy one's obligations under an enforceable contract. Chapter 14 also includes a discussion of the type of relief the courts will give to the victim of a breach of contract.

REVIEW PROBLEMS

1. What elements must be present before the courts will enforce a contract?

2. What is meant by the statement that contracts is a "common law field"?

3. What contracts are governed by the UCC?
4. How does a contract implied-in-law differ from one implied-in-fact?
5. Cone has a house in a development that looks very similar to his neighbor's house. The neighbor orders landscaping done. The landscaper arrives and starts working on Cone's house. Cone sees the landscaper and does nothing until the lawn has been leveled and several attractive bushes have been planted. Landscaper sues Cone. Result?
6. Suppose that Cone had been gone all day and that Cone did not like the work done. Would that change the outcome in the case?
7. A seller "lists" a house for sale with a real estate broker, thereby promising to pay a 7 percent commission if the broker finds a buyer ready, willing, and able to buy for $75,000. What kind of contract is this?
8. John Doe requests that Jack Maverick paint his house, promising that he will pay him $1,200 when Maverick finishes. Maverick paints the house. What type of contract is this?

FOOTNOTES

[1]See Lawrence Freedman, CONTRACT LAW IN AMERICA (1965) pp. 20–24.

[2]See Richard Posner, ECONOMIC ANALYSIS OF LAW, 2nd ed. (1977), p. 42.

[3]There is no universally accepted, written-in-stone list of the elements of enforceability. Textbooks vary greatly in how these elements boil down to their simplest, most basic levels of enforceability.

[4]See Grant Gilmore, THE DEATH OF CONTRACT (Columbus, Ohio State University Press, 1974) for an interesting analysis concluding that doctrinal contract law has been extinguished and blended into tort law with emphasis upon factual existentialistic decision making.

The Offer

I t is important for parties negotiating an agreement to know if that agreement will be enforced by the legal system. Usually, neither party envisions the need to resort to legal action to enforce their agreement (or to recover monetary damages if the other party has not performed as agreed). Yet each party wants the assurance that, if it becomes necessary, he or she can reasonably expect the law and its institutions to stand behind the agreement.

The law of contracts defines and determines which agreements will be recognized and enforced. Since contract law requires a valid offer to have been made in order for an agreement to be recognized as an enforceable contract, we begin our study of contract law with this requirement.

REQUIREMENTS FOR AN OFFER

In order for a valid offer to exist, contract law requires the offer to:

1. Manifest the intent to enter into a contract
2. Be definite and certain regarding the essential terms of the proposed contract
3. Be communicated to the party (known as the offeree) for whom the offer is intended.

Each of these requirements is discussed in detail in this chapter.

Once the existence of an offer has been determined, the question of whether the offer still exists at the time of its acceptance may arise. Has the offer terminated? How long do offers last before they expire? What brings about the termination of an offer? Questions related to the termination of an offer are discussed at the end of this chapter.

Intent to Contract

Determining Intent. How should a person's intent be determined? Consider the following situations. Suppose you are at a used-car dealer's lot. The price of a car you like is listed as $3,995. You ask the salesperson what he'd take for the car; he doesn't answer you, but responds by asking you what you would offer. If you then say, "I wouldn't pay the list price, but I might pay $3,000 if I could finance it," have you made an offer? Did you intend by that statement to commit to a contract?

An auctioneer selling home furnishings announces at the start of the auction that anyone who wants to bid on an item should simply raise his or her hand when he asks for a certain price. If you, in gesturing to a friend with whom you are talking, raise your hand while the auctioneer is asking for a $500 bid for a couch, have you offered to buy it? Are you intending to contract?

Suppose you receive an advertisement in the mail listing the prices of hundreds of items the local department store wants to sell. Have you received an offer? Did the store intend to make an offer to any person receiving or reading its advertisement?

In order to answer the questions posted in these situations, we must first consider how a person's intent could be ascertained.

Is intent determined by examining what a person was thinking when he or she said something? Does the law look into a person's mind to determine his or her thoughts? Do we simply ask the person what his or her intentions were? A person's actual intentions are very difficult to determine. In fact, a person's subjective state is not susceptible to discovery or verification.

Instead, the law seeks to determine intent entirely by objective standards. What would a reasonable person observing the actions and hearing the statements of the offeror conclude about the offeror's intentions of entering into a contract? The evidence of the offeror's intent is determined not by examining that person's inner feelings, but by reviewing the offeror's actions and words as perceived by a reasonable person.

Social Invitation, Excitement, or Jest. The law presumes that there is no objective manifestation of intent to contract in situations involving social invitations. Thus an invitation to a wedding, even one requesting an RSVP, would not be considered an offer to contract. Similarly, an invitation to attend the movies or to come for dinner is not an offer to contract. Therefore, an acceptance does not impose a contractual obligation on the inviter.

Suppose someone makes a statement in the midst of an exciting event. Our favorite basketball team is in the playoffs and we are watching one of the semifinal games. The opposing team has just taken the lead. In a fit of excitement and anger, I announce to you and to everyone else who can hear me, "I am disgusted with this team. For two cents, I'd sell my tickets to the finals." If our team wins the game after all, and you want to use my tickets, should the law treat my statement to you regarding the use of my tickets as an offer that invites your acceptance?

If it was apparent to you that I was upset and you should have known that I did not really intend to contract, there will not be the requisite manifestation of intent. Factors to be considered in determining whether I manifested contractual intent include the correlation between the "offer" price and the value of the object, the witnessing of the precipitating incident (here, the temporary taking of the lead by the opposing basketball team), whether from an objective viewpoint I appeared excited and upset, and whether we had discussed the sale of the tickets at some previous time.

Sometimes, a statement will be made in jest; there is no manifestation of the intent to contract because the offeror was only kidding. Informal bets often fall into this category: "I'll bet you a hundred dollars you can't throw the ball through the hoop." Similarly, the prankster who says, "I'd pay a thousand dollars to anyone who gives my boss an exploding cigar," cannot be taken seriously. Yet the jester must be careful if the joke relates to a situation where the other party might take the joke seriously. The *Zehmer* case demonstrates the seriousness with which some jocular offers are taken.

Lucy v. Zehmer

Supreme Court of Appeals of Virginia

84 S.E. 2d 516 (1954)

This suit was instituted by W. O. Lucy and J. C. Lucy, plaintiffs, against A. H. Zehmer and Ida S. Zehmer, his wife, defendants, to have specific performance of a contract by which it was alleged the Zehmers had sold to W. O. Lucy a tract of land owned by A. H. Zehmer in Dinwiddie County containing 471.6 acres, more or less, known as the Ferguson farm, for $50,000. Defendants responded that they had considered Plaintiff's offer to have been made in jest and that their signature to the written document was not intended by them to result in a contract. The instrument sought to be enforced was written by A. H. Zehmer on December 20, 1952, in these words: "We hereby agree to sell to W. O. Lucy the Ferguson Farm complete for $50,000.00, title satisfactory to buyer," and signed by both the defendants.

The lower court held that the plaintiffs' complaint failed to establish their right to specific performance and dismissed the case. Plaintiffs appealed the trial court's dismissal to this appellate court. The appeals court reversed the trial court and held that a contract was entered into by the parties and that plaintiffs were entitled to have it specifically performed.

Buchanan, Justice

W. O. Lucy, a lumberman and farmer, testified that he had known Zehmer for fifteen or twenty years and had been familiar with the Ferguson farm for ten years. Seven or eight years ago, he had offered Zehmer $20,000 for the farm which Zehmer had accepted, but the agreement was verbal and Zehmer backed out. On the night of December 20, 1952, around eight o'clock, he took an employee to McKenney, where Zehmer lived and operated a restaurant, filling station and motor court. While there he decided to see Zehmer and again try to buy the Ferguson farm. He entered the restaurant and talked to Mrs. Zehmer until Zehmer came in. On this Saturday night before Christmas, it looked like everybody and his brother came by there to have a drink. When Zehmer entered the restaurant around eight-thirty, Lucy was there and he could see that he was "pretty high." He said to Lucy, "Boy, you got some good liquor drinking, ain't you?" Lucy then offered him a drink. "I was already high as a Georgia pine, and didn't have any more better sense than to pour another great big slug out and gulp it down, and he took one too."

After they had talked awhile, Lucy asked whether he still had the Ferguson farm. He replied that he had not sold it and Lucy said, "I bet you wouldn't take $50,000 for it." Zehmer asked him if he would give $50,000 and Lucy said yes. Zehmer replied, "You haven't got $50,000 in cash." Lucy said he did and Zehmer replied that he did not believe it. They argued "pro and con for a long time," mainly about "whether he had $50,000 in cash that he could put up right then and buy that farm."

Finally, said Zehmer, Lucy told him if he didn't believe he had $50,000, "you sign that piece of paper here and say you will take $50,000 for the farm." He, Zehmer, "just grabbed the back off of a guest check there" and wrote on the back of it, "I do hereby agree to sell to W. O. Lucy the Ferguson Farm for $50,000 complete." Lucy told him he had better change it to "We" because Mrs. Zehmer would have to sign it too. Zehmer then tore up what he had written, wrote the agreement quoted above and asked Mrs. Zehmer, who was at the other end of the counter ten or twelve feet away, to sign it. She at first refused to sign, but did so after he told her that he "was just needling him (Lucy), and didn't mean a thing in the world, that I was not selling the farm." Zehmer then "took it back over there and I was still looking at the dern thing. I had the drink right there by my hand, and I reached over to get a drink, and he said, 'Let me see it.' He reached and picked it up, and when I looked back again he had it in his pocket and he dropped a five dollar bill over there, and he said, 'Here is five dollars payment on it.' I said, 'Hell no, that is beer and liquor talking. I am not going to sell you the farm. I have told you that too many times before.' "

December 20 was on Saturday. On Monday, Lucy engaged an attorney to examine the title. The attorney reported favorably on December 31 and on January 2, Lucy wrote Zehmer stating that the title was satisfactory, that he was ready to pay the purchase price in cash and asking when Zehmer would be ready to close the deal. Zehmer replied by letter, mailed on January 13, asserting that he had never agreed or intended to sell.

Zehmer testified that he bought this farm more than ten years ago for $11,000. He had had twenty-five offers, more or less, to buy it, including several from Lucy, who had never offered any specific sum of money. He had given them all the same answer, that he was not interested in selling it.

The discussion leading to the signing of the agreement, said Lucy, lasted thirty or forty minutes, during which Zehmer seemed to doubt that Lucy could raise $50,000. Lucy suggested the provision for having the title examined and Zehmer made the suggestion that he would sell it "complete, everything there," and stated that all he had on the farm was three heifers.

The defendants insist that the evidence was ample to support their contention that the writing sought to be enforced was prepared as a bluff or dare to force Lucy to admit that he did not have $50,000; that the whole matter was a joke; that the writing was not delivered to Lucy and no binding contract was ever made between the parties.

It is an unusual, if not bizarre, defense. When made to the writing admittedly prepared by one of the defendants and signed by both, clear evidence is required to sustain it.

In his testimony, Zehmer claimed that he "was high as a Georgia pine," and that the transaction "was just a bunch of two doggoned drunks bluffing to see who could talk the biggest and say the most." That claim is inconsistent with his attempt to testify in great detail as to what was said and what was done. It is contradicted by other evidence as to the condition of both parties, and rendered of no weight by the testimony of his wife that when Lucy left the restaurant she suggested that Zehmer drive him home. The record is convincing that Zehmer was not intoxicated to the extent of being unable to comprehend the nature and consequences of the instrument he executed, and hence that instrument is not to be invalidated on that ground.

The appearance of the contract, the fact that it was under discussion for forty minutes or more before it was signed; Lucy's objection to the first draft because it was written in the singular, and he wanted Mrs. Zehmer to sign it also; the rewriting to meet that objection and the signing by Mrs. Zehmer; the discussion of what was to be included in the sale, the provision for the examination of the title, the completeness of the instrument that was executed, the taking possession of it by Lucy with no request or suggestion by either of the defendants that he give it back, are facts which furnish persuasive evidence that the execution of the contract was a serious business transaction rather than a casual jesting matter as defendants now contend.

If it be assumed, contrary to what we think the evidence shows, that Zehmer was jesting about selling his farm to Lucy and that the transaction was intended by him to be a joke, nevertheless the evidence shows that Lucy did not so understand it but considered it to be a serious business transaction and the contract to be binding on the Zehmers as well as on himself. The very next day, he arranged with his brother to put up half the money and take a half interest in the land. The day after that he employed an attorney to examine the title. The next night, Tuesday, he was back at Zehmer's place, and there Zehmer told him for the first time, Lucy said, that he wasn't going to sell and he told Zehmer, "You know you sold that place fair and square." After receiving the report from his attorney that the title was good, he wrote to Zehmer that he was ready to close the deal.

Not only did Lucy actually believe, but the evidence shows he was warranted in believing, that the contract represented a serious business transaction and a good faith sale and purchase of the farm.

In the field of contracts, as generally elsewhere, we must look to the outward expression of a person as manifesting his intention rather than to his secret and unexpressed intention. The law imputes to a person an intention corresponding to the reasonable meaning of his words and acts.

The mental assent of the parties is not requisite for the formation of a contract. If the words or other acts of one of the parties have but one reasonable meaning, his undisclosed intention is immaterial except when an unreasonable meaning which he attaches to his manifestations is known to the other party. An agreement or mutual assent is, of course, essential to a valid contract, but the law imputes to a person an intention corresponding to the reasonable meaning of his words and acts. If his words and acts, judged by a reasonable standard, manifest an intention to agree, it is immaterial what may be the real but unexpressed state of his mind.

So a person cannot set up that he was merely jesting when his conduct and words would warrant a reasonable person in believing that he intended a real agreement. Whether the writing signed by the defendants and now sought to be enforced by the plaintiffs was the result of a serious offer by Lucy and a serious acceptance by the defendants, or was a serious offer by Lucy and an acceptance in secret jest by the defendants, in either event it constituted a binding contract of sale between the parties.

The plaintiffs are entitled to have specific performance of the contract sued on. The decree appealed from is therefore reversed and the cause is remanded for the entry of a proper decree requiring the defendants to perform the contract.

Advertisement of Goods for Sale. Do advertisements in the newspaper constitute offers? If they do, the reader can go into the store and say "I accept" and thereby create a contractual obligation for the store. If five people or fifty or five thousand accept, the store would have to fulfill all acceptances or else be liable for breach of contract.

Courts have interpreted the law as not imposing such an unfair burden on each business advertiser. Thus, as a general principle, advertisements do not constitute offers. However, if the advertiser uses language in the advertisement that, to the reasonable reader, expresses a commitment to contract, the courts will enforce a contract resulting from the offeree's acceptance of the seller's advertisement. While the *Lefkowitz* case is thus an illustration of the application of the exception to the general rule of law, it has become a classic involving the possible interpretation of advertisements as offers.

Lefkowitz v. Great Minneapolis Surplus Store

Supreme Court of Minnesota
86 N.W. 2d 689 (1957)

Plaintiff Lefkowitz brought suit against the defendant store to enforce a contract he had made to purchase a fur offered for sale by defendant in a newspaper advertisement. Defendant responded that its advertisement was not an offer and therefore no contract had been made between it and the plaintiff. The trial court found that a contract did exist and ordered a judgment for the plaintiff in the amount of $138.50 as damages due for defendant's breach of contract. The defendant's request to the trial court for a new trial was denied and defendant then appealed for review by the supreme court.

The supreme court of Minnesota affirmed the trial court's decision and held that the newspaper advertisement was a clear, definite, and explicit offer of sale by defendant and that plaintiff, who was the first to appear at defendant's place of business to be served, was entitled to have the defendant perform the contract or to receive damages from the defendant.

Murphy, Justice

This case grows out of the alleged refusal of the defendant to sell to the plaintiff a certain fur piece which it had offered for sale in a newspaper advertisement. It appears from the record that on April 6, 1956, the defendant published the following advertisement in a Minneapolis newspaper:

Saturday 9 A.M. Sharp
3 Brand New
Fur
Coats

Worth to $100.00
First Come
First Served
$1
Each

On April 13, the defendant again published an advertisement in the same newspaper as follows:

Saturday 9 A.M.
2 Brand New Pastel
Mink 3-Skin Scarfs
Selling for $89.50
Out they go
Saturday. Each. . . . $1.00
1 Black Lapin Stole
Beautiful
Worth $139.50. . . . $1.00
First Come
First Served

The record supports the findings of the court that on each of the Saturdays following the publication of the above-described ads the plaintiff was the first to present himself at the appropriate counter in the defendant's store and on each occasion demanded the coat and the stole so advertised and indicated his readiness to pay the sale price of $1. On both occasions, the defendant refused to sell the merchandise to the plaintiff, stating on the first occasion that by a "house rule" the offer was intended for women only and sales would not be made to men, and on the second visit that plaintiff knew defendant's house rules.

The trial court properly disallowed plaintiff's claim for the value of the fur coats since the value of these articles was speculative and uncertain. The only evidence of value was the advertisement itself to the effect that the coats were "Worth to $100.00," how much less being speculative especially in view of the price for which they were offered for sale. With reference to the offer of the defendant on April 13, 1956, to sell the "1 Black Lapin Stole * * * worth $139.50 * * *" the trial court held that the value of this article was established and granted judgment in favor of the plaintiff for that amount less the $1 quoted purchase price.

The defendant contends that a newspaper advertisement offering items of merchandise for sale at a named price is a "unilateral offer" which may be withdrawn without notice. He relies upon authorities which hold that, where an advertiser publishes in a newspaper that he has a certain quantity or quality of goods which he wants to dispose of at certain prices and on certain terms, such advertisements are not offers which become contracts as soon as any person to whose notice they may come signifies his acceptance by notifying the other that he will take a certain quantity of them. Such advertisements instead have been construed as an invitation for an offer of sale on the terms stated, which offer, when received, may be accepted or rejected by the seller and which therefore does not become a contract of sale until such acceptance. Thus, until a contract has been so made, the seller may modify or revoke such prices or terms as it has advertised.

However, there are numerous authorities which hold that a particular advertisement in a newspaper or circular letter relating to a sale of articles may be construed by the court as constituting an offer, the acceptance of which would complete a contract. The test of whether a binding obligation may originate in advertisements addressed to the general public is whether the facts show that some performance was promised in positive terms in return for something requested. . . .

Whether in any individual instance a newspaper advertisement is an offer rather than an invitation to make an offer depends on the legal intention of the parties and the surrounding circumstances. We are of the view on the facts before us that the offer by the defendant of the sale of the Lapin fur was clear, definite, and explicit, and left nothing open for negotiation. The plaintiff having successfully managed to be the first one to appear at the seller's place of business to be served, as requested by the advertisement, and having offered the stated purchase price of the article, he was entitled to performance on the part of the defendant. We think the trial court was correct in holding that there was in the conduct of the parties a sufficient mutuality of obligation to constitute a contract of sale.

The defendant contends that the offer was modified by a "house rule" to the effect that only women were qualified to receive the bargains advertised. The advertisement contained no such restriction. This objection may be disposed of briefly by stating that, while an advertiser has the right at any time before acceptance to modify his offer, he does not have the right, after acceptance, to impose new or arbitrary conditions not contained in the published offer.

Affirmed.

Definite and Certain Terms

The second requirement of an offer is that it be definite and certain regarding the essential terms of the proposed contract. As the court in the *Lefkowitz* case concluded, where the offeror's statement is clear, definite, and explicit and leaves nothing open for negotiation, an offer (not merely an invitation to make an offer) has been made. What terms must be expressed in order for a statement to be construed as an offer?

If I offer to sell you my 1982 Ford Fiesta and you agree, do we have a contract? In this example, the obvious problem is that we have omitted the most basic element of an agreement—the price. Would a court seek to complete our agreement for us? How would it do

so? Reference to a standard used-car price or a trade price such as is found in a Blue Book wouldn't be of much help. My car could have been driven 5,000 miles or 50,000 miles. It could have been well cared for or poorly cared for. Thus there is no ready reference point that a court could use to enforce this agreement. Since a court does not wish to make a contract where the parties themselves have failed to do so, it would conclude that no offer was made by me when I proposed to sell you my car. Therefore, your agreement in response was not an acceptance of an offer. Obviously, no contract resulted from our expressions.

The general legal principle requires that an offer define the essential terms of performance by both the offeror and the offeree. One of the essential terms that an offer must contain is the subject matter of the proposed transaction. Is the offeror going to sell a car? What car? Does the sale of the car include the sale of the ski rack on top of the car? The spare tire in the trunk? The offer must reasonably identify the subject matter.

A second essential term that an offer must include is the quantity of items being offered. A farmer proposing to sell wheat to a bakery must specify how much wheat he wants to sell. A furniture dealer's agreement to sell you "bedroom furniture" for $500 would be too vague unless it specified how many items were included in the offer.

Finally, as the first example regarding the used-car sale illustrates, the price of the item offered for sale must be specified. The price is specified if it is either fixed or easily determinable. My offer to lend you $1,000 at the prime interest rate in effect at Continental Illinois National Bank is specific. While the offer doesn't state exactly what that rate of interest actually is, the rate is determinable.

The case that follows, *Smith v. House of Kenton Corporation*, illustrates the need for definite terms in a contract. The case involves an agreement to lease space in premises owned by the plaintiff. Note that the agreement that the plaintiff seeks to enforce as a contract is not a document labeled by the parties a "contract." Although the court in this case found that the letters at issue did not constitute a contract, letters can in fact be contracts. So can oral expressions and conversations between the parties. Agreements do not have to be embodied in formal documents prepared by attorneys to be enforced as contracts. As long as the required elements—including the definite terms—of an offer are found to exist, a contract between the parties may result.

Smith v. House of Kenton Corporation

Court of Appeals of North Carolina
209 S.E. 2d 398 (1974)

This is an action for damages for breach of contract. The parties waived jury trial and the evidence tended to show that on and before May 9, 1970, plaintiff owned certain real property located at 1601 Montford Drive in the City of Charlotte. The property was equipped for use as a beauty salon, and at that time defendant operated a beauty salon at another location in Charlotte. On that date, plaintiff employed Davant Realty Company (Davant) to find a tenant to lease the real estate and purchase certain equipment located thereon. Thereafter, Davant had several conversations with Mrs. Shelton, president of defendant, and Mrs. McCormac, an employee of defendant, with respect to defendant leasing the premises and purchasing the equipment. Following those conversations, Davant wrote and sent to Mrs. Shelton a letter dated July 15 stating the terms discussed by the parties for leasing the premise. The letter concluded with the following paragraph: "A lease is being drawn and will be forwarded to you soon. Please execute the copy of this letter as your agreement to these terms and conditions and return to us so we can take the space off the market and hold same for you."

Mrs. Shelton signed an acceptance on the bottom of the letter and returned it to Mr. Davant on July 16. On July 31, Mr. Davant wrote a second letter to Mrs. Shelton and enclosed a lease agreement, prepared by Smith's attorney, with the letter. Subsequent differences between the parties then surfaced. The lease agreement was never signed or returned by Mrs. Shelton. Plaintiff tried to rent the premises to others but was unsuccessful for three years. Plaintiff then brought this suit for breach of contract, claiming as damages the lost rent. Plaintiff alleged that the letter which the defendant's agent, Mrs. Shelton, signed and returned on July 16, 1970, was a contract to execute a lease and was enforceable to the same extent as if the lease agreement had been signed. The trial court found for the plaintiff, and the defendant appealed to the Court of Appeals of North Carolina. The Court of Appeals reversed the decision of the trial court.

Britt, Judge

The theory of plaintiff's action is that the defendant breached a contract to execute a lease. That the judgment was predicated on that theory is indicated by the following conclusion of law:

> "3. That the written offer of the plaintiff dated July 15, 1970, when accepted by the defendant corporation on July 16, 1970, became a contract to execute a lease and as such is enforceable to the same extent as if the parties had entered into a written lease agreement containing the terms of the said contract to execute a lease."

The question then arises, was the letter dated 15 July 1970 sufficient to constitute a binding contract to execute a lease? We answer in the negative.

Our research fails to disclose any precedent in this jurisdiction which is directly in point; however, we find in opinions of our Supreme Court numerous statements of principles which we think are applicable to the case at bar.

In Young v. Sweet, 266 N.C. 623, 625, 146 S.E.2d 669 (1966), we find: "An offer to enter into a contract in the future must, to be binding, specify all of the essential and material terms and leave nothing to be agreed upon as a result of future negotiations."

In Dodds v. Trust Co., 205 N.C. 153, 156, 170 S.E. 652 (1933), the court said:

> "In the formation of a contract an offer and an acceptance are essential elements; they constitute the agreement of the parties. The offer must be communicated, must be complete, and must be accepted in its exact terms. . . . In order to constitute a binding agreement to execute a lease, such agreement must be certain as to the terms of the future lease. A few points of mutual agreement are essential to a valid agreement to lease: First, the minds of the parties must have met as to the property to be included in the lease; second, the terms of the lease should be agreed upon; third, the parties should agree upon the rental; and fourth, the time and manner of payment of rent should be stated. . . ."

In the case at bar, the agreement relied on by plaintiff did not specify all of the essential and material terms of the lease to be executed and left much to be agreed upon by future negotiations. The offer was not complete and the minds of the parties did not meet as to all essential terms. The agreement failed to provide for one of the specifics . . . the time and manner of payment of rent. The necessity for this provision with respect to rent is obvious. Whether the rent was payable monthly, quarterly, semi-annually, annually, or all at one time, and whether it was payable in advance, at the end of a period or otherwise, presented a major question that finds no answer in the agreement. It might be argued that the provision of "$400.00 per month" sufficiently implied that a monthly payment of rent was contemplated by the parties. The question then arises, was the rent payable in advance, in the middle of the month, or at the end of the month? A clear indication that the minds of the parties did not meet on this question is the provision in the formal lease proposed by plaintiff that defendant pay the first and last months' rent at the beginning of the five-year period.

We think there is a further reason why plaintiff was not entitled to recover. Assuming, arguendo, that the 15 July 1970 letter was sufficient to constitute a binding contract to execute a lease, plaintiff failed to show that he tendered a lease conforming to the contract. . . .

The formal lease submitted by plaintiff to defendant in the case at bar reveals a number of provisions not mentioned in the letter; we point out several of them. In addition to requiring payment of the last month's rent at the beginning of the term, it limits the lessee's right to sublet or assign without written consent of the lessor. It requires that lessee shall ". . . maintain and keep in good order and repair all heating, air conditioning, electrical and plumbing equipment located in the demised premises. . . ." It further provides that lessee will purchase and maintain, at its expense, a public liability insurance policy in the amount of $50,000 coverage for any one accident and $100,000 for any one accident involving more than one person, which policy or policies of insurance will show as named assured the lessee and the lessor as their interests may appear.

For the reasons stated, the judgment appealed from is Reversed.

The UCC and Definite Terms. The Uniform Commercial Code has liberalized the definite-and-certain-terms requirement as it applies to the sale of goods. Most contracts covered by the UCC involve business transactions between experienced parties. The business world has many established reference points for value, such as organized trading exchanges and arms-length private sales transactions involving goods identical to the ones in question.

In recognition of these facts Section 2-204(3) of the UCC provides that a sales contract is valid even though it leaves open essential terms if (1) the parties nevertheless intended to make a contract *and* (2) there is a "reasonably certain basis for giving an appropriate remedy." Further, Section 2-305 provides that purposefully leaving open the price term is not fatal and that in such cases the price is to be a reasonable price. Note that under Section 2-305 we would have made a contract for the sale of my used car *if* we had intended to leave the price open while binding ourselves to a contract. Sections 2-308 and 309 also specify how the terms are to be filled in if nothing is said as to place of delivery or time for delivery.

Communication of the Offer

General Rule. The third requirement that must be met for a valid offer to exist is that the offer be communicated to the party for whom the offer is intended. The communication may be expressed or implied. For example, if the offeree learns of an offer from a third person who is not the offeror and the offer is a general offer susceptible of acceptance by anyone who learns of it, the offeree would have the power to accept the communicated offer. Communication is usually not a problem with offers. Two recurring situations, however, present legal problems regarding the effect to be given to the communication of an offer.

The Reward Offer. The first of these is the case of a reward. A reward is an offer for a unilateral contract. It is not unusual for someone to perform the act bargained for in the reward offer without knowing about the reward. If that occurs, then under the technical rules of contract law the party performing the act is not entitled to the reward. But that does not represent sound policy when viewed in the context of the reasonable expectations of our society. Most people expect that rewards will be paid if their terms are met. As a consequence, many states statutorily provide that rewards will be enforceable regardless of whether the person performing the act called for in the offer first received a communication of the offer of a reward.

The Fine-Print Offer. The second situation involves what might be called the fine-print problem. Consumers may often be asked to sign contracts that contain a myriad of fine-print provisions, many of which are quite harsh. For example, a price-adjustment clause may increase the price of a car over the contract price before delivery, or a waiver clause may surrender the consumer's rights to resist the entering of a legal judgment against him upon default of an installment payment. Most consumers signing such contracts are unaware of the existence of and/or the legal effect of such clauses. Some courts have refused to enforce them on the theory that they were not really communicated to the consumer. Consider the following case concerned with the communication of an offer.

Green's Executors v. Smith

Special Court of Appeals of Virginia
131 S.E. 846 (1926)

Plaintiff Howard Smith sued defendant Mrs. A. D. Green to recover damages he had been compelled to pay one John L. Moore in compensation for injuries inflicted on Moore by one of Smith's employees while the employee was driving defendant's automobile through the streets of Richmond.

The plaintiff owned a garage where defendant stored her car. The defendant and plaintiff contracted for the storage of defendant's car and for the delivery of the car by plaintiff's employees to the defendant's residence and the car's return to the garage thereafter when requested by defendant. After having delivered the defendant's car to her, the plaintiff's employee was in the process of returning her car to the plaintiff's garage when he collided with Mr. Moore. Plaintiff alleged the contract he had with the defendant absolved him of liability for negligence which occurred while returning defendant's car to the garage. Defendant responded that the parties had no such contract.

Upon the trial of the case, the jury rendered a verdict in plaintiff's favor for $2,735, for which judgment was entered by the court. Mrs. Green having died, the cause was brought to the Court of Appeals by her executors. The Court of Appeals reversed the decision of the trial court.

Chinn, Justice

The material facts of the case may be fairly stated to be as follows:

Defendant's automobile was first placed at plaintiff's garage some time in the early part of the year 1918 by another garage keeper who had previously kept it, and who was about to discontinue business. Mrs. Green at the time was an old lady, and her daughter, Mrs. B. R. Dunn, who resided with her at her residence on South Third Street, looked after her affairs. There was no formal contract between the parties, but plaintiff advised Mrs. Dunn of the terms and regulations then in effect at his garage for the regular monthly storage of automobiles, which were accepted by the defendant by leaving the car in his custody. According to the terms thus agreed to, in addition to certain other specified services, plaintiff contracted to deliver the car at the owner's residence and take it back to the garage once each day when requested by the owner, with the further understanding that plaintiff should not be responsible for any damage which might occur to the car while in the hands of his employees during such movements. In consideration of these services, plaintiff was to receive the sum of $37 per month, which amount was thereafter paid by Mrs. Green upon receipt of his bill. In October of that year defendant's car was damaged by a collision on the street when being driven to the garage by one of plaintiff's employees, and defendant paid the expense of the repairs without protest. In January, 1920, plaintiff had printed what he called a "folder," which bore on the title page this inscription:

"Service Rates of the Richmond Electric Garage."
"Howard M. Smith, Proprietor, 2035 W. Broad Street, Richmond, Va."
"Effective on and after January 1, 1920."

The center or inside pages of the folder contained a schedule of charges for diverse specified services performed by the garage and other printed matter, which, so far as pertinent, read as follows:

Rates by the Month.
Regular storage, lead battery, $37.
Regular storage includes car storage, delivering, cleaning, polishing, charging, and flushing battery, and oiling with oil can wherever possible upon notice from the owner.

Delivery Service.
Delivering and calling for car once each way daily (see note).
An extra charge of 25 cents each way will be made for extra trips (see note).

Note: The owner agrees to accept our employee as his his or her agent and to absolve this garage from any liability whatsoever arising while his or her car is in the hands of said employee at the request of and as agent of the owner.

The back of the folder contained only a schedule of rates and terms relating to work and services in connection with automobile batteries.

The folder was mailed to all the patrons of the garage, including Mrs. Green, with the bills sent out in the early part of January, which action was repeated the following month; and copies were also placed by the employees of the garage, on several occasions, in defendant's car, as well as all other cars kept at the garage on regular storage. It also appears that the above-mentioned folder was the only document of the kind that plaintiff ever had printed and sent out to his customers. As has been noted, plaintiff seeks to recover in this action upon an alleged contract by which, it is claimed in his declaration, defendant agreed to accept plaintiff's garage employees as her agents, and to indemnify and save him harmless from any and all liability whatsoever arising from the acts of any of said employees while moving her car to and from said garage. In the absence of agreement, the defendant is in no sense liable to the plaintiff for the injuries inflicted upon Mr. Moore under the circumstances disclosed by the record. The plaintiff alone had the right to select and engage the employees of his garage, the power to discharge and control them, and he alone was responsible for the payment of their wages. The real question is, therefore, Was there a valid and subsisting contract between the plaintiff and Mrs. Green, at the time Mr. Moore received his injuries, by which the defendant bound herself to indemnify the plaintiff against the consequences of all such acts of negligence on the part of his employees?

It is elementary that mutuality of assent—the meeting of the minds of the parties —is an essential element of all contracts and, in order that this mutuality may exist, it is necessary that there be a proposal of offer on the part of one party, and an acceptance on the part of the other. It is manifest, however, that, before one can be held to have accepted the offer of another, whether such offer is made by word or act, there must have been some form of communication of the offer; otherwise there could be no assent, and in consequence no contract. In the instant case the plaintiff relies upon the "note" printed in the folder as constituting the terms of the proposed contract, on the fact that said folder was mailed to Mrs. Green on several occasions with her monthly bills and placed in her cars, as a communication of said terms, and on her conduct in continuing to keep her car in his garage as an implied acceptance of the terms specified in said note. The question, therefore, of whether Mrs. Green agreed to, and is bound by, the terms of the "note" in the main depends upon whether the means employed by the plaintiff to communicate such terms were sufficient, under the circumstances, to constitute her act in the premises as implied acceptance of the said terms. The rule as to when the delivery of a paper containing the terms of a proposed contract amounts to an acceptance, is thus stated in 13 Corpus Juris, at page 277:

> "A contract may be formed by accepting a paper containing terms. If an offer is made by delivering to another a paper containing the terms of a proposed contract, and the paper is accepted, the acceptor is bound by its terms; and this is true whether he reads the paper or not. When an offer contains various terms, some of which do not appear on the face of the offer, the question whether the acceptor is bound by the terms depends on the circumstances.

He is not bound as a rule by any terms which are not communicated to him. But he is bound by all the legal terms which are communicated. This question arises when a person accepts a railroad or steamboat ticket, bill of lading, warehouse receipt, or other document containing conditions. He is bound by all the conditions whether he reads them or not, if he knows that the document contains conditions. But he is not bound by conditions of which he is ignorant, even though the ticket or document contains writing, unless he knows that the writing contains terms, or unless he ought to know that it contains terms, by reason of previous dealings, or by reason of the form, size, or character of the document."

There was nothing on the face of the folder, nor in its form or character, to indicate that it contained the terms of the contract which plaintiff has attempted to establish in this case, or any other contract imposing obligations of such a nature upon the defendant. The paper only purported to contain a schedule of rates for services at plaintiff's garage, and defendant had no reason, on account of her previous dealings with the plaintiff or otherwise, to know that plaintiff proposed, by mailing the folder to her along with his monthly bill, and placing a copy of it in her car, to commit her to a new contract of such unusual terms.

Considering the circumstances under which she received the folder, she was justified in assuming it to be only what it purported to be, and, as she already knew the rates prevailing at plaintiff's garage, was justified in paying no attention to it, as she did. There is no evidence that either Mrs. Green or Mrs. Dunn, her agent, ever read the "note" or knew it was printed in the folder. . . . If plaintiff proposed to form a special contract of this kind, he should have, at the least, called Mrs. Green's attention to the terms contained in the folder as he understood to do, upon the advice of counsel, after the accident to Mr. Moore.

Under these circumstances we are of the opinion that the plaintiff has failed to establish the contract alleged in his declaration in the manner that the law requires, and is not, as a matter of law, entitled to recover over from Mrs. Green the damage he was compelled to pay Mr. Moore for the negligence of his employee.

For the foregoing reasons, the judgment complained of will be reversed and judgment entered for the defendant.

Reversed.

TERMINATION OF THE OFFER

If the requirements for an offer have been met, the offeree has a chance to accept and enter into a contract with the offeror. Yet the offer may be terminated prior to its acceptance. The termination of an offer may occur in a variety of ways, as the following sections of this chapter indicate.

Lapse of Time

The offer itself may provide that it will terminate within a specified period. Once that period expires, the offer is terminated. Thus an offer that states "This offer is good until May 30" would terminate after that date. It should be noted that the offeror should take care to be specific regarding the duration of the offer.

Consider the following situation. On March 1, the offeror mails a letter dated February 27 stating that "this offer expires in ten days." The offeree receives the letter on March 4. Does the offer expire ten days from February 27 or from March 4? What policy should the courts follow in interpreting this language? The courts that have considered this problem have reached different decisions. Of course, it must be emphasized that the situation need not occur; careful drafting by the offeror could remove the uncertainty. How would you write the above offer if you were the offeror?

Even if the offeror does not provide for a specific termination date, the offer will lapse after a "reasonable time." How long is a reasonable time? The answer must vary with the circumstances surrounding the offer. An offer to sell real estate such as a home or an office building will probably last for weeks or months. An offer to buy stocks or commodities may be open for acceptance for only minutes.

Further, the definition of reasonable time is affected by the context in which an offer is made. If you seek to buy souvenir pennants to sell outside the Superbowl, your offer to the supplier would probably terminate on the day of the game. The timing of any prior dealings between the offeror and offeree will be relevant in determining what is a reasonable time for an offer to remain open.

Revocation by the Offeror

General Rule. A revocation is a withdrawal of the offer by the offeror. The law requires that, in order to be effective, a revocation, like the original offer, must be communicated to the offeree. Generally, the revocation must be received by the offeree before the offeree has effectively accepted the offer. While an offeror generally has the power to revoke the offer at any time prior to its acceptance, there are several exceptions to this rule.

Even if the offer states that it will remain open for a specified time, the rule allowing the offeror to revoke at any time prior to acceptance usually applies. Thus, in the example given above, the offeror wrote on February 27 that the offer would expire in ten days. Suppose the offeror decides on March 2 that he wants to revoke the offer prior to the end of the ten-day period. Can he do that when he has already committed himself to holding the offer open for ten days? The general answer is "Yes" as long as no acceptance of the offer has been made by the offeree. There are, however, several situations in which the offeror is not permitted to revoke an offer.

Limitations. If an offeree enters into a contract with an offeror to keep an offer open for a certain time, that *option contract* will be enforced and the offer cannot be revoked for the period specified in the contract. For example, a school board offers to sell for $100,000 to Acme Development Company a school that it no longer uses. Acme is thinking of buying the school if it can interest several businesses in renting space there after the building has been remodeled. Acme might agree with the school board to enter into an option contract, by which, in consideration of a payment of $5,000, the school board gives Acme ninety days to accept or reject the offer. During those ninety days, the school board cannot sell to someone else nor can it revoke its offer to Acme.

Second, under Section 2-205 of the Uniform Commercial Code, if an offer to buy or sell goods contains a promise that it will be held open for a specific time, it cannot be revoked by the offeror during that time. This *firm offer* rule of the UCC requires that the offeror must be a merchant in the kind of goods being offered and that the offer must be in writing and signed by the offeror. Finally, the time during which the offer is irrevocable is limited to three months. This UCC provision does not apply to offers that are not made by merchants or that do not involve the sale of goods. Nevertheless, most commercial transactions (other than those for services or for real estate) entered into by business people fall within the terms of the UCC's firm-offer provisions.

Third, if the offer requires an act to be performed in order to accept the offer (i.e., the offer seeks to have the offeree enter into a unilateral contract), the law limits the offeror's power to revoke the offer while the offeree is in the process of performing the requested act of acceptance. While traditionally the offeree's act must be fully completed before an acceptance and a contract result, in recent years the trend of many decisions has been to suspend the offeror's right of revocation until the offeree has had a reasonable time to complete the act called for in the offer.

Finally, in order to avoid unfairness, courts will usually limit an offeror's right to revoke if an offer is made in such a way that the offeree reasonably expects that the offer will not be revoked. This exception to the general rule is known as the doctrine of *promissory estoppel*. It usually requires (1) that the statement of offer is one that the offeror anticipated would be relied on by the offeree, (2) that the offeree in fact does rely on the statement, and (3) that the offeree who has relied on the statement is harmed by that reliance.

Typical of the application of the doctrine of promissory estoppel in limiting the right to revoke an offer is the situation that arises between a general building contractor and various subcontractors. The general contractor requests bids (offers) from potential subcontractors who would do heating, plumbing, electrical, and carpentry work on a building. The general contractor relies on some of these bids in making its own bid to the building owner. Then the general contractor finds that the building owner has accepted its offer to do the required work. Before the general contractor informs the subcontractor that the subcontractor's bid (offer) is accepted, it is revoked by the subcontractor. The following case exemplifies the resolution of such a problem and the court's limitation of the right to revoke an offer.

Drennan v. Star Paving Co.

Supreme Court of California
233 P.2d 757 (1958)

Plaintiff Drennan, a general contractor, was preparing a bid on the "Monte Vista School Job" in the Lancaster school district. After soliciting and receiving bids from various subcontractors, he used a bid from defendant Star Paving Company in computing its own bid to the school, and in that bid it named the defendant as the subcontractor for the paving work.

Plaintiff was then notified that he had been awarded the contract by the school. When he stopped by defendant's office, he was immediately told by defendant's construction engineer that a mistake had been made and that the defendant could not do the work for the bid price given to plaintiff. Plaintiff brought this suit to enforce the contract he says resulted from this transaction. Defendant claims no contract resulted because its bid and offer to plaintiff was revoked before plaintiff accepted. The trial court held for plaintiff and defendant appealed. The Supreme Court of California upheld the judgment of the trial court rendered in plaintiff's favor.

Traynor, Justice

On July 28, 1955, plaintiff, a licensed general contractor, was preparing a bid on the "Monte Vista School Job" in the Lancaster school district. Bids had to be submitted before 8:00 P.M. Plaintiff testified that it was customary in that area for general contractors to receive the bids of subcontractors by telephone on the day set for bidding and to rely on them in computing their own bids. Thus on that day plaintiff's secretary, Mrs. Johnson, received by telephone between fifty and seventy-five subcontractors' bids for various parts of the school job. As each bid came in, she wrote it on a special form, which she brought into plaintiff's office. He then posted it on a master cost sheet setting forth the names and bids of all subcontractors. His own bid had to include the names of subcontractors who were to perform one-half of one per cent or more of the construction work, and he had also to provide a bidder's bond of ten per cent of his total bid of $317,385 as a guarantee that he would perform the contract if awarded the work.

Late in the afternoon, Mrs. Johnson had a telephone conversation with Kenneth R. Hoon, an estimator for defendant. He gave his name and telephone number and stated that he was bidding for defendant for the paving work at the Monte Vista School according to plans and specifications and that his bid was $7,131.60. At Mrs. Johnson's request he repeated his bid. Plaintiff listened to the bid over an extension telephone in his office and posted it on the master sheet after receiving the bid form from Mrs. Johnson. Defendant's was the lowest bid for the paving. Plaintiff computed his own bid accordingly and submitted it with the name of defendant as the subcontractor for the paving. When the bids were opened on July 28th, plaintiff's proved to be the lowest, and he was awarded the contract.

On his way to Los Angeles the next morning plaintiff stopped at defendant's office. The first person he met was defendant's construction engineer, Mr. Oppenheimer. Plaintiff testified:

> I introduced myself and he immediately told me that they had made a mistake in their bid to me the night before, they couldn't do it for the price they had bid, and I told him I would expect him to carry through with their original bid because I had used it in compiling my bid and the job was being awarded them. And I would have to go and do the job according to my bid and I would expect them to do the same.

Defendant refused to do the paving work for less than $15,000. Plaintiff testified that he "got figures from other people" and after trying for several months to get as low a bid as possible engaged L & H Paving Company, a firm in Lancaster, to do the work for $10,948.60.

The trial court found on substantial evidence that defendant made a definite offer to do the paving on the Monte Vista job according to the plans and specifications for $7,131.60, and that plaintiff relied on defendant's bid in computing his own bid for the school job and naming defendant therein as the subcontractor for the paving work. Accordingly, it entered judgment for plaintiff in the amount of $3,817.00 (the difference between defendant's bid and the cost of the paving to plaintiff) plus costs.

Defendant contends that there was no enforceable contract between the parties on the ground that it made a revocable offer and revoked it before plaintiff communicated his acceptance to defendant.

There is no evidence that defendant offered to make its bid irrevocable in exchange for plaintiff's use of its figures in computing his bid. Nor is there evidence that would warrant interpreting plaintiff's use of defendant's bid as the acceptance thereof, binding plaintiff, on condition he received the main contract, to award the subcontract to defendant. In sum, there was neither an option supported by consideration nor a bilateral contract binding on both parties.

Plaintiff contends, however, that he relied to his detriment on defendant's offer and that defendant must therefore answer in damages for its refusal to perform. Thus the question is squarely presented: Did plaintiff's reliance make defendant's offer irrevocable? . . .

We are of the opinion that the defendants in executing the agreement made a promise which they should have reasonably expected would induce the plaintiff to submit a bid based thereon to the Government, that such promise did induce this action, and that injustice can be avoided only by enforcement of the promise. . . .

When plaintiff used defendant's offer in computing his own bid, he bound himself to perform in reliance on defendant's terms. Though defendant did not bargain for this use of its bid neither did defendant make it idly, indifferent to whether it would be used or not. On the contrary it is reasonable to suppose that defendant submitted its bid to obtain the subcontract. It was bound to realize the substantial possibility that its bid would be the lowest, and that it would be included by plaintiff in his bid. It was to its own interest that the contractor be awarded the general contract; the lower the subcontract bid, the lower the general contractor's bid was likely to be and the greater its chance of acceptance and hence the greater defendant's chance of getting the paving subcontract. Defendant had reason not only to expect plaintiff to rely on its bid but to want him to. Clearly defendant had a stake in plaintiff's reliance on its bid. Given this interest and the fact that plaintiff is bound by his own bid, it is only fair that plaintiff should have at least an opportunity to accept defendant's bid after the general contract has been awarded to him.

It bears noting that a general contractor is not free to delay acceptance after he has been awarded the general contract in the hope of getting a better price. Nor can he reopen bargaining with the subcontractor and at the same time claim a continuing right to accept the original offer. . . .

Affirmed.

Rejection by the Offeree

An offer is terminated when it is rejected by the offeree. If the offeree either states that the offer is rejected and will not be accepted or responds with a counteroffer that seeks to change the terms of the offer, the offeree has rejected it. On the other hand, an offeree who merely seeks information about the terms of the offer (Must I pay cash? What credit terms are available? Is that your lowest price?) is making an inquiry that is neither an acceptance nor a rejection of the offer.

It is sometimes difficult to determine how to categorize the response of the offeree to an offer. If the response is an acceptance, the parties have made a contract. If the response is a rejection, the offer is terminated and the parties must begin their negotiations anew. If the response is neither an acceptance nor a rejection, but instead is an inquiry, then the original offer is not terminated but remains for the offeree's review. Note that when the offeree's response is a counteroffer, the original offer is considered to have been terminated. In its place is a new offer (from the original offeree, not from the offeror) that is capable of being accepted and turned into a contract.

Death of a Party

The death of either the offeror or the offeree will terminate an ordinary offer. Assume that the offeree, not knowing about the offeror's death, accepts the offer after the offeror dies but during a reasonable time after the offer has been received. No contract will be formed. There is no requirement that the offeree must have notice of the offeror's death before the offer is considered terminated; the death itself terminates the offer.

An exception to the general rule that the death of either party terminates the offer can occur with the option contract that the parties make to keep the offer irrevocable. In the case of an option contract, there is a contractual obligation to hold an offer open for a set period. The effect of the offeror's death in this case depends upon whether the contractual obligations involved are ordinarily considered to survive the death of the offeror. This issue is discussed in Chapter 14 which deals with the discharge of contractual obligations.

Illegality

Contracts that are contrary to public policy will not be enforced. The concept of illegality

as it affects contracts is discussed in detail in Chapter 11. For present purposes, it is important to note that an offer that is legal when made is terminated if it subsequently becomes illegal; the offer then cannot be accepted. If a state makes illegal the sale of a certain drug as of January 1, an offer to sell it, legally made the prior December 15, terminates on January 1 if it has not been accepted prior to that date.

Destruction of the Subject Matter

Hoper offers to sell his Porsche to Allen, who is familiar with the car. Although neither knew it, five minutes after the offer was made a landslide destroyed Hoper's garage and the car. Such destruction of the subject matter of the offer by an "act of God" will terminate the offer.

Suppose, instead, that Farmer offers to sell 10,000 bushels of apples to Processor and that Farmer's apples are subsequently destroyed by an act of God, such as a tornado. Your immediate reaction is very likely to be that, of course, the offer is terminated because the subject matter of the offer (Farmer's apples) has been destroyed. In fact, that is probably what a court would conclude; it is impossible for the offer to be performed. However, if Processor could prove that Farmer had offered to sell 10,000 bushels of apples in general rather than apples raised specifically from Farmer's property, then the offer would still be valid. In that case, Farmer could purchase the needed apples from someone else; the fact that Farmer's apples were destroyed would not mean that all apples were unavailable. Thus, it is necessary to determine whether the subject matter of Farmer's offer was 10,000 bushels of apples from his particular farm property or merely 10,000 bushels of apples. A tornado destroying Farmer's apples would terminate the offer to sell apples from his farm but would not affect the offer to sell apples in general.

REVIEW PROBLEMS

1. On December 15, Patrick wrote to Kleine about the lot she owned. Patrick's letter said: "If you have not sold, I, of course, am the logical purchaser. . . . I hope I shall have the pleasure of hearing from you soon." On December 16, Kleine responded by letter to Patrick and said: "If you should be interested in my lot, I would be glad to hear from you. The size of the lot is 20 × 100. Price $1,000 (One thousand dollars)." On December 18, Patrick telegraphed Kleine: "Will accept your proposition of one thousand dollars for lot 35 in block 7906. Will get contract and check to you within a day or so." On December 19, Patrick followed with a letter: "Enclosed find contracts in the usual form and also my check for $100 as evidence of good faith. Please sign and return one copy so the title company can institute its search." On December 23, Kleine returned Patrick's $100 check and the contract and stated in her letter that the property had been sold to someone else. Patrick sues to enforce his contract with Kleine. Does he have a valid contract? Patrick v. Kleine, 215 N.Y.S. 305 (App. Div. N.Y. 1926)

2. Rofra, Inc., bid for plumbing work to be done for the Board of Education. The bid was sent in response to a "Solicitation for Connection of Building Sewer to the Public Sewer at Sunatsville Senior High School." Attached to that solicitation notice was a statement of "Contract General Provisions" that included a section reserving to the Board the right "to reject any and all bids, in whole or in part. . . ." Plaintiff Rofra was the second low bidder for the work; the lowest bidder did not have in its employ a "master plumber" as the solicitation terms required. Plaintiff sues to enforce the contract, which it claims exists as a result of the School Board's solicitation offer and its own bid, which was the lowest bid conforming to the offer. Defendant claims no contract exists. Is plaintiff right? Rofra, Inc., v. Board of Education, Prince George's County, Md., 346 A2d 458 (Ct. of Special Appeals, Md. 1975)

3. Sokol made a written offer dated March 10 to purchase a house owned by Hill. At the same time, Sokol delivered to Nash, who was the real estate broker representing Hill, a check for $500 as earnest money. The offer stated that the defendants had three days to accept. Hill signed on March 12. On the same day Sokol called Nash and orally withdrew his offer. Nash deposited the check on March 14. On March 15, Nash hand-delivered the contract form signed by Hill and dated March 12 to Sokol. Sokol sues for the $500. What result? Sokol v. Hill, 310 S.W.2d 19 (Ct. App. Mo. 1958)

4. A subcontractor (Supreme) wrote a general contractor (Blake) with regard to supplying concrete needed in the construction of a school on which the general contractor was bidding. The subcontractor's letter of March 11, 1975, stated that its price for 3,000 psi concrete @ $21.00 per yard net was "a price which will be guaranteed to hold throughout the job." On May 24, 1975, the general contractor was informed it had been awarded the construction job. Its engineering manager testified that he told the subcontractor's salesman that it was to furnish the concrete. "Ben (the subcontractor's salesman) asked me, 'Are we good on that job?' I said, 'Yes, give me a mix design' —like we always do." He said it had notified Supreme on other jobs in the same manner. Subsequently, work was begun by Supreme on the school job. Months later, it sought to raise the price for the concrete being supplied. When it did so, the contractor was forced to purchase concrete from other suppliers at higher prices. It then withheld partial payment from Supreme, claiming that the excess cost should be borne by it

because their contract required Supreme to furnish the necessary concrete at a guaranteed price. Is there a contract by the subcontractor to furnish the goods at the "guaranteed" price? Maryland Supreme Corporation v. Blake Co. 369 A2d 1017 (Court of Appeals of Md., 1977)

5. Employer issued a booklet to employees stating it had been customary for the company to make year-end bonus payments to employees, the amount of payment being dependent on earnings and being discretionary with the Board of Directors. An employee who read the booklet and continued working for the employer contends he has (by working) accepted the offer of the employer to pay him a year-end bonus. Do you agree? Borden v. Skinner Chuck Co., 150 A2d 607 (Superior Court of Conn. 1958)

6. On September 16, 1964, defendant submitted a proposal to plaintiff to repair a pipe-bending machine owned by plaintiff. The price for parts and labor was quoted as $1600 plus freight costs. Defendant's letter also stated that, if the offer was accepted, the rebuilding of the machine would have to be done at a time convenient to both plaintiff and the plant used by defendant. No response was received until January 14, 1965, when plaintiff advised defendant its machine would be shipped that month. Plaintiff claims its response and the subsequent shipment of the machine (received by defendant on January 20, 1965) constituted an acceptance of defendant's offer.

Defendant suggests its offer had expired and the shipment by plaintiff was only an offer, which it later rejected. Is there a contract? Modern Pool Products, Inc. v. Rodel Machinery Co., 294 N.Y.S. 2d 426 (Civ. Ct. of City of New York, 1968)

7. Scheck in writing offered to sell real estate to a specified prospective buyer and agreed to pay a percentage of the sales price as a commission to the broker. The offer fixed a six-day time limit for acceptance. Scheck then revoked the offer. On the morning of the sixth day, the broker received notice of Scheck's revocation. Later that day, the offeree accepted the offer that the broker had given to him. Does the revocation by Scheck to the offeree also revoke the broker's power to act on behalf of Scheck? If the broker had already begun to perform the offer to sell the property to the prospective purchaser, would the offer then be considered irrevocable? Marchiondo v. Scheck, 432 P2d 405 (Supreme Ct. of New Mexico, 1967)

8. Employee brings this action against employer to enforce an alleged contract to pay the employee a bonus and commission. The agreement provided that the amount of bonus and commission would be determined three months later, after marketing operations for a new product had been commenced. However, no later agreement appears to have been made. Is there an offer capable of acceptance by the employee? Sandeman v. Sayres, 314 P2d 428 (Supreme Ct. of Washington, 1957)

The Acceptance

A valid offer that has not been terminated creates a power of acceptance in the offeree. In order to result in a contract, the acceptance of the offer must meet certain criteria. First, like the offer itself, the acceptance must be made with the intent to contract. Second, the acceptance by the offeree must also be communicated to the offeror. Third, the acceptance must usually satisfy all the conditions and terms established by the offer. As was noted in the previous chapter, a change in the terms of an offer usually results not in an acceptance but in a rejection that terminates the offer. This chapter will discuss each of these elements required of an acceptance. Several special situations in which acceptance problems arise, and the cancellation of an acceptance, will also be discussed.

INTENT TO ACCEPT

The courts generally look for the same evidence of intent on the part of the offeree as is required of the offeror. Was the acceptance made with the intent to commit the offeree to enter into a contract? If the offeree replies to an offer by stating "Your offer looks good" or "I will give immediate consideration to your request," there is no manifestation of intent to enter into a contract.

The offeree must show a commitment. "I might accept your offer" leaves open the possibility that the offer will be rejected. Similarly, a response that leaves for the future the commitment of the offeree, "I'll let you know next week if the proposal is satisfactory," does not constitute an acceptance.

As with intent on the part of the offeror, it is the objective manifestation of the offeree's intent, not its subjective basis, that is critical. The law is not concerned with the offeree's state of mind; instead, it asks what the offeree's words or actions would indicate to a reasonable person about his or her intent to accept an offer.

Unless so required by the offer, the acceptance need not be expressed in words. Actions on the part of the offeree can constitute an acceptance. Thus, if a widget manufacturer sends a potential buyer five dozen widgets, with an invoice stating their purchase price, the buyer who says nothing but uses the widgets will have manifested by its action an intent to accept the manufacturer's offer to sell.

147

The *Marrs* case provides an example of a court determining that a person's actions can constitute an acceptance of an offer, even where the offeree argues that he did not "express" any acceptance.

Crouch v. Marrs

Supreme Court of Kansas
430 P.2d 204 (1967)

This is an action brought by plaintiff Crouch who seeks a determination from the Court that an agreement to purchase property that he made with the Purex Corporation resulted in a contract. Purex Corporation claims it made no contract with Crouch, but instead contracted to sell said property to Martin Asche. Martin Asche then responds and states he sold part of the property to Roy Marrs. When Crouch sought to take some of the property which he claims was purchased from Purex Corporation, Marrs prevented Crouch from getting at the property. Crouch then brought this action against Marrs, seeking to prevent Marrs from interfering with the property claimed by Crouch. The other parties involved were then made parties to the suit filed by Crouch. The trial court found against Crouch and in favor of Marrs. Crouch appealed and the Supreme Court of Kansas reversed the trial court judgment.

Hatcher, Commissioner

The facts of the controversy do not appear to be in dispute. Six miles north of Meade, Kansas, was an old silica processing plant which was owned by the Purex Corporation of Lakewood, California. The plant had not been used for many years.

On February 26, 1964, the plaintiff, Crouch, wrote to the Purex Corporation asking for their lowest price if they were interested in selling the building and its contents. The letter read in part:

> I would be interested in buying the old building that housed the plant and what other items that are still left. The items that are still left are: two crushers, furnace and the elevator is about all that is left.

On March 4, 1964, Crouch received a letter of reply from Purex Corporation signed by Frank Knox which stated:

> We will sell this building and the equipment in and about that building for a total of $500.

On March 19, 1964, Crouch wrote to Frank Knox, Purex Corporation, stating that the building was in "pretty bad condition" and asking "would you consider taking $300 for what is left?" This letter was not answered.

Later, on April 16, 1964, Crouch addressed another letter to Frank Knox, Purex Corporation, which read:

> I guess we will try the building for the amount you quoted, $500.
>
> I am sending you a personal check for this amount.
>
> It will be 2 or 3 weeks before we can get started; and I presume that we will be allowed all the time that we need to remove the material.

It is conceded that this letter constituted a new offer and was not a continuation of the previous negotiations.

The record discloses the check signed by Phillip Crouch and made payable to Frank Knox was endorsed by Knox sometime prior to April 23 and then was paid and cancelled by several banks, including the Piqua Bank at which Crouch maintained his checking account.

On April 17, 1964, the Purex Corporation, through Frank Knox, wrote a letter to Martin Asche which stated:

> In answer to your inquiry about our property approximately six miles north of Meade, Kansas.
>
> We will sell for $500 the mine building and whatever machinery and equipment which remains in or about that building. A condition of sale will require that the property purchased be removed from the premises within forty-five days.
>
> If this price is acceptable, we will be pleased to receive a cashier's check to cover.

On April 24, 1964, Asche wrote a letter accepting the offer of April 17, which reads:

> We are enclosing a cashier's check for $500 and the bill of sale of mine buildings with the agreement of option to purchase property.
>
> If the corporation has any other property and machinery in this area for sale, we would be pleased to deal with the corporation. It was our pleasure to deal with the Purex Corporation.

On April 27, 1964, Frank Knox sent Crouch the following telegram:

> Your counter offer received April 23 is unacceptable. Your check mistakenly deposited by Purex will be recovered and returned to you or Purex check will be issued to you if your check cannot be located.

There followed a letter dated May 16, 1964, which read:

> This is a follow-up to our telegram to you of April 27, advising you that your check which we received on April 23 was not acceptable, but that it had been deposited by mistake. Since we were unable to recover your check, we herewith enclose our check for $500 to reimburse you.
>
> We wish to explain, that the reason we could not accept your counter-offer of $500 for the mine building and machinery at Meade, Kansas was because we had received and accepted an offer from another party prior to receipt of yours on April 23.

In the meantime, Martin Asche had entered into a contract to sell the building to Roy Marrs who owned the land surrounding the building site for $500 and had entered into a contract to sell the equipment to the C. & D. Used Truck Parts for $800. Crouch commenced salvage of the building but Roy Marrs put a lock on the gate and would not allow Crouch to enter.

Appellant Crouch contends that on the basis of the prior negotiations the acceptance and endorsing appellant's check by the Purex Corporation constituted the formation of a contract of sale. The question is whether the endorsing and depositing appellant's check constituted an acceptance of his offer to buy? We think it did.

The endorsing and depositing a check constitutes an acceptance of the offer to buy which accompanies it because the act itself indicates acceptance. An offer may be accepted by performing a specified act as well as by an affirmative answer. Also, where the offeree exercised dominion over the thing offered him—in this instance the check—such exercise constitutes an acceptance of the offer. It is elementary that an offer may be accepted by performing or refraining from performing a specified act as well as by an affirmative answer.

We are forced to conclude that the acceptance and endorsement of the check accompanying the offer to purchase the property in controversy constituted an acceptance of the offer.

The judgment is reversed with instructions to the district court to quiet plaintiff's title to the building and equipment in controversy against the defendants and enjoin them from interfering with plaintiff's ingress and egress for the purpose of salvaging the property.

COMMUNICATION OF ACCEPTANCE

An acceptance must be communicated in order to be effective. What action must be taken in order to communicate an acceptance depends on whether the offeror seeks a unilateral or a bilateral contract.

Bilateral or Unilateral Agreement

If the offer is one to enter into a unilateral contract (a promise for an act or an act for a promise), the offeree must either perform the requested act or respond with the requested promise. Thus a promise for an act ("I'll pay you $10 if you type my paper by tomorrow night") requires the offeree to perform the act (type the paper by tomorrow night) in order to accept the offer to pay $10. However, if the offer requires a promise in exchange for an act ("I'll lend you $10 right now if you promise to repay me $11 a week from tomorrow"), the offeree must make the promise to repay (either expressly by stating a promise or impliedly by taking the offered $10) in order to accept the offer. It is also clear that an offeror may seek the offeree's forbearance, an agreement to refrain from doing something that the offeree might otherwise do. Thus the statement "I promise to pay you $100 if you don't smoke cigarettes for a year" is also an offer to enter into a unilateral contract. The offeree is asked to forbear from an act that he or she might otherwise do.

In the case where the offer requires an act

from the offeree ("I'll pay you $10 if you type my paper by tomorrow night"), only the act need be performed in order to accept the offer. The offeree need not first communicate to the offeror that he or she intends to perform the requested act. On the other hand, if the offer requires a promise from the offeree ("I'll lend you $10 now if you *promise* to repay me $11 next Friday") the offeree must of course communicate that promise to the offeror.

Similarly, if the offer is one to enter into a bilateral contract, one in which each party makes a promise ("I'll promise to sell you my 1980 Ford if you promise to pay me $300 cash"), the offeree must also communicate his or her promise in order to accept the offer. In the event of uncertainty as to what the offer requires of an offeree, most courts will interpret an agreement as consisting of bilateral promises, thus requiring a communication from the offeree rather than a requested act of acceptance in exchange for the offeror's promise.

Means of Communication

Usually, any means of communication that gives the offeror notice of the offeree's intent to accept the offer is effective. However, as the third requirement of an acceptance suggests, the offeree must also comply with all the terms of the offer. Thus, if the offer dictates that the acceptance be communicated by certain means or occur at a certain time or place, the offeree generally must comply with those provisions. An acceptance made in a different manner or at a different time or place would be ineffective.

If the offer does not require the offeree to use a specific means of communication, problems can arise concerning the time at which an acceptance by an offeree would be effective. While the time of acceptance is not critical to most contracts, where the offeror has attempted a revocation or where the intended acceptance is delayed or lost, an analysis of the method or time of acceptance is necessary.

Generally, if the means of communication used by the offeree in communicating acceptance is authorized by the offer, the acceptance is effective when delivered by the offeree to the communication agency. The offeror may expressly or impliedly authorize the offeree to use a particular means of communication. Thus, if the offer states, "You may use the mail for your acceptance," the offeree's acceptance is effective at the moment a letter of acceptance is deposited "with the postal service" even if the letter is delayed in reaching the offeror or is lost. The offeree has effectively communicated acceptance by delivering it to the "agent" (post office) authorized by the offeror. Even if the offer does not expressly authorize the use of a particular means of communication, the law holds that an offer made by one means of communication can be accepted by the same means. Thus a mailed offer implies authorization to the offeree to use the mail for acceptance.

In fact, the modern rule in most jurisdictions is that the offeree may use any "reasonable means of communication" in accepting the offer. What constitutes a reasonable means of communication depends on the subject matter of the offer, the custom and usage in a particular trade or business, and the prior conduct or dealings of the parties. If, for example, it is customary in the industry or trade for acceptances to be sent by mail or if the parties in prior transactions had used the mail to enter into contracts, an acceptance would be effective when mailed. An acceptance sent by a means not recognized as an implied or express agent of the offeror will be effective only upon receipt.

The following case demonstrates the application of the rule making an acceptance effective when dispatched by an authorized means of communication.

Pribil v. Ruther

Supreme Court of Nebraska
262 N.W.2d 460 (1978)

Plaintiff Pribil brought this action against defendant Ruther seeking to enforce a contract whereby Pribil agreed to buy real estate owned by Ruther. Defendant claimed she verbally rejected plaintiff's offer to purchase the property before he received her written acceptance of it. The trial court found for plaintiff and defendant appealed. The Supreme Court of Nebraska reversed the trial court's decision.

Boslaugh, Justice

This is an appeal in an action for specific performance of a real estate contract. The defendant Bertha Ruther owns a quarter section of land in Holt County, Nebraska. The defendant listed this property for sale with John Thor, a real estate broker, on January 20, 1976.

On April 12, 1976, the plaintiff Lawrence Pribil executed a written offer to purchase the property for $68,000. The offer to purchase was on a form known as a Uniform Purchase Agreement which included a space for a written acceptance of the offer. The defendant and her husband signed the acceptance on the same day and handed an executed copy of the agreement to Thor for delivery to the plaintiff.

Thor returned to his office in Norfolk, Nebraska, and asked an office employee, Mrs. Kasebaum, to send a copy of the agreement to the plaintiff. Mrs. Kasebaum wrote a letter to the plaintiff, dated April 14, 1976, with a copy of the agreement enclosed, which was sent to the plaintiff by certified mail. The letter was postmarked "April 15, 1976 PM." and was received by the plaintiff on April 16, 1976.

The defendant became dissatisfied with the transaction the day after she had signed the acceptance when she discovered a test well had been drilled on the property at the plaintiff's request and the driller had estimated a well would produce 500 to 800 gallons of water per minute. The defendant testified that she called the plaintiff's home at about 5 P.M. on April 13, 1976, and told the plaintiff's wife that she, the defendant, would not sell the property. The plaintiff's wife testified this conversation did not take place until some ten days later, near the end of April 1976.

The defendant further testified that she called Thor the next morning, April 14, 1976, and said that she was going to "terminate the contract," because Thor had lied to her. According to Thor this conversation took place at 11:42 A.M. on April 15, 1976. Thor testified that immediately after receiving the call from the defendant, he called the plaintiff and told the plaintiff that the defendant was not going to sell the farm.

The principal issue in this case is whether the defendant had effectively rejected the plaintiff's offer and revoked her acceptance of the offer before the acceptance had been communicated to the plaintiff. Since the plaintiff sought to enforce the contract the burden was on the plaintiff to establish that there was a contract. A party who seeks to compel specific performance of a written contract has the burden of proving the contract.

An express contract is proved by evidence of a definite offer and unconditional acceptance. Where the offer requires a promise on the part of the offeree, a communicated acceptance is essential.

The signing of the acceptance on the Uniform Purchase Agreement by the defendant did not make the contract effective. It was necessary that there be some communication of the acceptance to the plaintiff. There must be some irrevocable element such as depositing the acceptance in the mail so that it is placed beyond the power or control of the sender before the acceptance becomes effective and the contract is made. Delivery to the agent of the defendant was not delivery to the plaintiff as it did not put the acceptance beyond the control of the defendant.

The plaintiff contends that the deposit of the acceptance in the mail by Thor satisfied the requirement that the acceptance be communicated. Where transmission by mail is authorized, the deposit of the signed agreement in the mail with the proper address and postage will complete the contract. The difficulty in this case is that there is no evidence that the acceptance was deposited in the mail before Thor called the plaintiff and informed him that the defendant would not sell the property.

The evidence is that Thor handed the purchase agreement to Mrs. Kasebaum with instructions to send a copy to the plaintiff. Mrs. Kasebaum did not testify. Thor testified, "I can't testify when she mailed it, except by reading the postmarks on the envelope and the return receipts." The postmark indicates only that the postage was canceled sometime during the afternoon of April 15, 1976. The telephone call from the defendant was received at 11:42 A.M. on that same date. The call from Thor to the plaintiff was made immediately afterward.

If we assume that transmission by mail was authorized in this case, there is no evidence to show that the acceptance was deposited in the mail before the defendant's call to Thor, and Thor's call to the plaintiff notifying him that the defendant had rejected his offer. The evidence does not show that the acceptance was communicated to the plaintiff and thus became effective before the defendant changed her mind and rejected the offer. Reversed and remanded with directions to dismiss.

SATISFYING TERMS OF THE OFFER

Generally, an acceptance must mirror the terms of the offer. A variation in terms or an addition of new conditions causes the response of the offeree to be considered a rejection instead of an acceptance. There are some situations where the law or facts imply into the offer terms that may not have been expressed. In these cases, the expression of those terms by the offeree in accepting is not considered to add to or vary the terms of the offer.

For example, if you offer to sell me your house for $75,000 and in response I state, "I accept your offer, subject to my attorney checking that you have good title to the property," my response would be considered an acceptance. It is implied by law that the person offering to sell a house guarantees that he or she has a good title to it. My response has not changed the terms of your offer. Similarly, suppose it is customary in an industry (according to trade usage) that an offer to sell goods for a stated price implies that the buyer has "thirty days, same as cash" to pay for them.

The buyer who expresses in an acceptance "I'll accept your offer if the normal credit terms are extended" is not varying the terms of the offer; those credit terms were a part of the original offer, even though not expressed by the offeror.

The general rule that any response that varies the terms of an offer cannot be considered an acceptance has proved unworkable in commercial transactions where each party has form documents that it sends in response to inquiries. The problem of the "battle of the forms" arises because each party desires to be the one whose form controls the transaction.

There are two separate but related situations in which the parties, through their own forms, seek to control the terms of their contracts. The first situation arises when each party wants the other to make an offer. If one party makes an offer, the party who can accept the offer is the one who takes the last action needed to make a contract. That party will be able, at the final moment, to decide whether to accept the offer and create a binding contract or to reject it and terminate the transaction.

Thus the buyer who wants to buy goods from the seller also wants the seller to make the offer. The buyer then sends to the seller a form that says: "If you offered to sell me 500 widgets at $100 each, I'd be likely to accept." Such a statement is too indefinite to be an offer; it merely invites the seller to make the offer. Yet the battle of the forms occurs because the seller responds with a document that in effect states: "If you want to purchase 500 widgets from us at $100 each, sign the enclosed purchase order form. When we receive it from you, we'll review it and respond with our acceptance." Neither party has made an offer; each is merely inviting the other to do so.

The second situation involving the battle of the forms occurs after one party has made an offer. The buyer's form to the seller might say:

"We offer to buy 500 widgets from you at $100 each. The goods are to be shipped to us F.O.B. our plant. They must be packaged in cartons of 50 each. Payment will be due from us 60 days after receipt of the widgets. No variation in the terms of this offer can be made without our written consent." Seller has received a definite offer; he wants to sell the widgets, but on slightly different terms. "We have received your offer and are glad to contract with you. Our goods will be shipped to you F.O.B. your plant. They will be packaged in cartons of 100 each. Payment will be due from you 30 days after receipt of the widgets. Thank you for your order."

Do the parties have a contract? Clearly, there is an offer, but have the terms of the offer been accepted? If the parties simply act as if there's a contract, sending the goods and paying for them without protest, no problems are encountered. But what if one party doesn't perform? Can the buyer seek damages from the seller who doesn't deliver the widgets? Only if there's a contract, and that requires acceptance. Under the common law, if the terms of the offer are not "mirrored" by the terms of the acceptance, no contract results. Under the Uniform Commercial Code, it is clear that in our example situation the parties have agreed to a contract. After reading the next section on "The UCC and Acceptance" determine the terms of the contract our seller of widgets has made with the buyer.

The UCC and Acceptance

The Uniform Commercial Code has sought to deal with problems that arise because of the battle of forms. Section 2-207 provides that, in certain situations, the terms of an acceptance can add to or differ from those proposed in the offer. This provision of the UCC reads as follows:

(1) A definite and seasonable expression of acceptance or a written confirmation which

is sent within a reasonable time operates as an acceptance even though it states terms additional to or different from those offered or agreed upon, unless acceptance is expressly made conditional on assent to the additional or different terms.

(2) The additional terms are to be construed as proposals for addition to the contract. Between merchants such terms become part of the contract unless:

    (a) the offer expressly limits acceptance to the terms of the offer;

    (b) they materially alter it; or

    (c) notification of objection to them has already been given or is given within a reasonable time after notice of them is received.

(3) Conduct by both parties which recognizes the existence of a contract is sufficient to establish a contract for sale although the writings of the parties do not otherwise establish a contract. In such case, the terms of the particular contract consist of those terms on which the writings of the parties agree, together with any supplementary terms incorporated under any other provisions of this Act.

The general approach and structure of Section 2-207 is clear. Subsection (1) determines when a contract is created as a result of an exchange of documents between the parties. In response to the realities of the modern commercial transaction, the rigid requirements of the mirror-image rule have been abolished. Under the provisions of subsection (1), the response is effective as an acceptance, creating a contract "even though it states terms additional to or different from those offered. . . ." While the response need not exactly match the offer, the response containing additional or different terms must meet two requirements to be effective as an acceptance. First, it must be stated in terms of a "definite and seasonable expression of acceptance." Second, it must not be "expressly made conditional on assent to the additional or different terms," which would be the same thing as making a counteroffer at common law. The UCC test of an operative acceptance under Section 2-207 was thus designed to bring about a closer correlation between the controlling legal principles and the commercial understanding of when a "deal" had been closed.

The contract created by the parties' exchange is based—at least insofar as its material terms are concerned—on the terms contained in the offeror's form. Subsection (2) is not concerned with the question of whether a response is in fact an acceptance. This is determined solely under subsection (1). Subsection (2) is intended only to resolve the effect of the additional and/or different terms contained in the response that subsection (1) has already deemed an acceptance. Subsection (2) establishes two separate tracks for handling these variant terms, depending on the characteristics of the parties. If the parties to the contract are not both merchants, the offeree's variant terms are "proposals for addition to the contract." The offeror can either agree to their inclusion or not, as he wishes. If the parties to the contract are both merchants, the variant terms automatically become part of the contract, unless:

1. The offeror has stated in his offer that he will agree only on the basis of his terms; or
2. The variant terms will materially alter the existing contract; or
3. The offeror has already objected or thereafter objects within a reasonable time to the variant terms.

The effect of subsection (2) is to allow changes in the contract, which is based on the offeror's terms, only if the terms are found to be nonmaterial. Even nonmaterial terms will fail to become part of the contract if the offeror objects to them generally, either in advance or after receipt.

The result of the application of subsections (1) and (2) is to form a contract at the time of the exchange between the parties that is based essentially on the offeror's terms. Thus the inequity fostered by the common law rules, which enabled a party to withdraw easily when market conditions changed, presumably has been remedied.

Subsection (3) addresses the typical situation where, despite the fact that no contract has been created by the parties' exchange under the provisions of subsection (1), the parties nevertheless perform. When subsection (3) applies, since performance requires the finding of some contractual relationship, the contract consists of the terms on which the offer and the response agree, "together with any supplementary terms incorporated under any other provisions of [the UCC]." The effect of the application of subsection (3) is to eliminate any preference for the terms of either the offeror or the offeree in a performance situation.

Thus it would seem that the drafters of Section 2-207 attempted to cure the two basic problems that resulted when the common law rules were applied to the exchange of commercial forms. The language of Section 2-207 indicates that the offeror will be protected during the executory stage and that the contract formed on the basis of performance no longer will give a preference to the party making the last response.

Some commentators have proposed that a court should answer the following seven questions in applying Section 2-207 in a specific context:

1. Does the situation involve a response to an offer or a written confirmation? If the latter, a contract has already been formed; skip to step 4.
2. Is the response a definite and seasonable expression of acceptance?
3. Is the acceptance expressly made conditional on assent to the variant terms it contains? If a contract has been formed, continue with step 4. If no contract has been formed,
   a. Has there been conduct by both parties that recognizes the existence of a contract?
   b. Which contract terms appear in the documents of both parties?
   c. What contract terms are missing and what terms would be implied by the Code?
4. Is the transaction between merchants? If yes, then continue. If no, then the terms are those of the offer plus any that the offeror has expressly agreed to.
5. Has the offer expressly limited acceptance to its terms?
6. Do the variant terms materially alter the contract?
7. Has an objection to the variant terms been made by the offeror?

How would you answer these questions when reviewing the Michigan case that follows, and then the Wisconsin case that refers to the Michigan decision?

American Parts Co., Inc. v. American Arbitration Association

Court of Appeals of Michigan
154 N.W.2d 5 (1967)

This action was commenced by the plaintiff-appellant, American Parts Co., Inc. (hereafter referred to as the "purchaser"), against the defendants-appellees, American Arbitration Association and Deering Milliken, Inc. (Deering Milliken being hereafter referred to as the "seller"). The purchaser sought a stay of arbitration proceedings demanded by the seller on July 19, 1966, pursuant to the arbitration provision of an alleged contract on printed forms, called "Confirmation of Order" forms, that were prepared, signed, and mailed by the seller to the purchaser but were never signed by the purchaser.

The trial court found for seller and ordered the arbitration it sought. Purchaser appealed to the Court of Appeals, which reversed the trial order and remanded the case back to the trial court.

Levin, Judge

On May 28, 1965, Gerrish H. Milliken, Jr., and Albert M. Kaufman, officers respectively of the seller and the purchaser, met in New York City to discuss the sale by the seller to the purchaser of a quantity of fabrics to be used in automobile seat covers. The parties agree that some "understanding" was reached, but disagree as to the terms thereof.

Shortly after the meeting, the seller prepared, signed, and mailed to the purchaser confirmation of order No. 8387 (hereafter referred to as "8387") on the seller's printed form, which document Mr. Milliken asserts embodies a "firm agreement" for the sale and purchase of fabrics entered into by Mr. Kaufman and himself at their May 28, 1965, New York City meeting. In contrast, Mr. Kaufman states that "after some discussion [at the New York City meeting], it was suggested that Deering [the seller] prepare a written contract along the lines discussed and submit the same to Detroit Body Products [Division of the purchaser] for its *approval* and execution." (Emphasis added.) Mr. Kaufman further asserts that upon returning to Detroit from an extended trip he found 8387 and immediately responded by a letter dated June 26, 1965, addressed to the seller:

> "After going over this contract, I found everything to be satisfactory with the exception of the Rivoli Pattern. I noted that your figures and your contract call for $1.75 per yard. I cannot recall acknowledging $1.75 on this fabric and my figures show $1.50. This would be the maximum we could go for this particular number.
>
> "If this price meets with your approval and the proper change noted on the contract, it could be signed by us and forwarded to your office immediately."

Mr. Milliken replied in a letter dated June 28, 1965, asserting that 8387 correctly reflects a "firm agreement" entered into by the parties in New York City and requested return of a signed copy of 8387. The purchaser did not reply in writing to the seller's letter of June 28, 1965, but Mr. Kaufman asserts that in further discussions with seller's representatives concerning 8387 he and other representatives of the purchaser continually maintained that the purchaser was not bound by 8387.

On September 10, 1965, Mr. Milliken wrote Mr. Kaufman referring to "your attempts to have the price" for the Rivoli pattern "changed" from $1.75 to $1.50 per yard. Mr. Milliken's letter continued:

"This contract with you was made by Deering Milliken in good faith after all of the styles, yardages and prices had been worked out with you in detail here in New York and *the agreement, as made, was confirmed in writing to you with contract #8387.*" (Emphasis added.)

The purchaser replied by letter dated September 29, 1965, stating that a contract in writing had never been executed "because there was never a complete meeting of the minds" and that the completed deliveries had been "on the basis of specific transactions, and neither you nor we have been under any legal obligation except on specific purchases."

Nevertheless, from July 1965 to February 1966, the seller shipped to the purchaser well over 135,000 yards of fabrics, including quantities of the Rivoli pattern. All such fabrics were accepted and paid for in full by the purchaser, including the invoices covering the Rivoli pattern, which pattern was invoiced to and paid for by the purchaser at the $1.75 price alleged by the seller.

The seller claims that 8387 is a contract and relies heavily on the following language printed immediately above the signature lines on its front page:

"This contract shall be construed and enforced under the laws of the State of New York, *and shall become effective* either (A) *when signed* and delivered by buyer to seller and accepted in writing by seller at its home office, evidenced by the signature of seller's agent below *or* (B) *when buyer accepts delivery* of all or any part of the goods herein described." (Emphasis added [by the court]).

Seller contends that the purchaser's acceptance of the delivery of 135,000 yards (including Rivoli pattern goods) constituted an acceptance of the seller's contract terms including the arbitration provision.

The purchaser responds that the shipments were separate or divisible transactions not governed by 8387 and that it was, therefore, within its rights in advising the seller by letter dated February 22, 1966, to discontinue further shipments.

The parties also disagree concerning the application of section 2207 of the uniform commercial code; and here again the question which emerges is whether 8387 is a written confirmation of a prior oral contract.

Section 2207 provides . . . that an acceptance or a written confirmation operates as an acceptance even though it states terms additional to or different from those previously offered or agreed upon. The additional or different terms do not become a part of the contract unless agreed to by the other contracting party, except that between merchants additional, but not different, terms become part of the contract if they do not materially alter it and the other contracting party does not, within a reasonable time, object to the additional terms.

Section 2207 is intended to validate understandings between parties even though the writings between them do not mesh with the precision traditionally required by the common-law rules of offer and acceptance. Although the principal emphasis is on the situation where there is an exchange of documents containing conflicting provisions, it is clear from both the code and the comments of the National Conference of Commissioners on Uniform State Laws and American Law Institute that the other typical situation sought to be covered is "the written confirmation, where an agreement has been reached either orally or by informal correspondence between the parties and is followed by *one* or both of the parties sending formal memoranda *embodying the terms so far as agreed upon and adding terms not discussed."* (Emphasis added [by the court].)

Section 2207 proceeds on the assumption that businessmen frequently reach firm oral understandings not instantly reduced to writing and signed; that it is commonplace for one or both to confirm such understandings in writing; that not infrequently the writings differ but the parties, nevertheless, commence performance, impelled to do so by the exigencies of the business world. The policy of section 2207 is that the parties should be able to enforce their agreement, whatever it is, despite discrepancies between the oral agreement and the confirmation (or between an offer and acceptance) if enforcement can be granted without requiring either party to be bound to a material term to which he has not agreed.

Applying that policy to this case, if, as the seller contends, there was a firm oral agreement in New York City which was later confirmed by 8387, it is that agreement which should be enforced. However, that pivotal, threshold question cannot be summarily resolved on the basis of the conflicting affidavits submitted. . . .

Mr. Kaufman asserts on affidavit that the oral understandings preceding 8387 contemplated that writings would be submitted by the seller for "approval" by the purchaser. The use in Mr. Kaufman's affidavit of the word "approval" is, of course, somewhat ambiguous. The word "approval" could mean merely a determination by the purchaser whether the written confirmation correctly reflects the "firm agreement" alleged by the seller. On the other hand, "approval" could mean the decision whether to enter into any agreement whatsoever—that the purchaser could withhold approval of the writing to be sent by the seller if it chose to do so; and, if that was the understanding of the parties, then 8387 would not be a writing confirmatory of "terms so far as agreed upon," nothing at all having yet been agreed upon.

If the trial court finds that a firm agreement was reached in New York City, it will then be necessary to determine whether 8387 is a written confirmation of the oral agreement or so far departs therefrom as not to be a "confirmation." In this connection we note that the vitality of a written confirmation is not affected by the inclusion of some "different terms." Thus, if Mr. Kaufman's assertion in his letter of September 29, 1965, that "there was never a complete meeting of the minds" means only that the recollection of the parties as to what they agreed to in New York City does not coincide as to one relatively small item (i. e. the price of the Rivoli pattern), 8387 would, nevertheless, be a written confirmation of any such prior firm oral agreement, even if it is ultimately determined that the price of the Rivoli pattern stated in the written confirmation is a "different term."

If the trial court finds that the parties at the New York City meeting entered upon a firm oral agreement confirmed by 8387, the next inquiry will be whether the arbitration provision is an "additional term." The seller stresses that 8387 was on the same printed form which had on a number of previous occasions been used to reflect contracts for the sale and purchase of fabrics entered into between the parties. The arbitration provision would not be an additional term if the parties had agreed at their New York City meeting that their "understanding" would be confirmed on the seller's standard form of confirmation of order. On the other hand, if the arbitration provision is an additional term it would be deemed (under the provisions of clause (2) of section 2207) a "proposal for addition to the contract." Under section 2207 such proposal would not become part of the contract unless (1) agreed to by the purchaser or (2) the seller and the purchaser are merchants and the arbitration provision is regarded as an immaterial alteration of the prior oral agreement. Whether the parties are merchants and the materiality of the arbitration clause might well depend on facts beyond the documents and affidavits submitted.

Section 2207 seeks to avoid the imposition on businessmen of unagreed terms. Prior to section 2207 terms not agreed upon were often imposed upon one party, generally the purchaser, in consequence of that party's performance of an informal agreement following receipt by such party of a document setting forth additional, often boiler plate, terms.

Under section 2207, a party, except a merchant in the case of an immaterial term, may ignore additional terms, and proceed with performance of the agreement actually negotiated by the parties without fear that such performance will be interpreted by court or jury as acceptance of the other party's additional terms. The fact that, following an oral agreement, one or both of the parties resorts to what some call the battle of forms, does not, under section 2207, change the agreement or prevent the formation of the contract. . . .

Section 2207 recognizes, indeed its genesis is the assumption that businessmen use forms that do not always fit their circumstances and which frequently contain significant modifications of the simple oral agreement of the parties in the form of boiler plate which generally is not read by the other contracting party and perhaps is not expected to be read.

Rather than being opposed to the common law, section 2207 in its flexibility is in the best tradition of the common law. Section 2207 is a mandate upon the courts to discard the concept that an act, verbal or nonverbal, cannot be both an acceptance and a rejection of an offer—an acceptance of that upon which the parties agree and a rejection of that upon which (although verbalized by one party) the parties disagree. The determination of what has or has not been agreed upon will, of course, continue to be made by the trier of fact, but, in making that determination, the fact finder is no longer bound by the last manifestation. Rather all subsisting manifestations are to be considered.

[The court then directed the trial court to determine if the parties reached a firm agreement in New York and if so, whether 8387 is a written confirmation of that agreement. If no agreement was reached, then UCC Section 2207 should be consulted to see if the conduct of the parties established a contract.]

Reversed and remanded.

Air Products & Chem., Inc. v. Fairbanks Morse, Inc.

Supreme Court of Wisconsin
206 N.W.2d 414 (1973)

Plaintiff Air Products, a buyer of large electric motors, brought this action against the manufacturer alleging in effect that the motors, which were manufactured by defendant and sold to plaintiff, contained defective parts that were unreasonably dangerous to parts of other motors and that caused injury to those motors and economic loss to plaintiff. While several issues were posed to and answered by the trial court, the issue of concern to us at this time concerns the effect to be given an acknowledgment form sent by defendant Fairbanks to plaintiff. The trial court said the acknowledgment form could limit plaintiff's right to recover certain damages against defendant. Plaintiff appealed the trial court's decision. The Supreme Court of Wisconsin reversed the trial court.

Hanley, Justice

As an affirmative defense to all the causes of action pleaded by . . . Air Products . . . , Fairbanks set up a provision contained in its "acknowledgments of order" which were sent by Fairbanks to Air Products with Air Products' purchase order which it had executed. The "acknowledgment of order" from Fairbanks to Air Products has the following language printed in reasonably bold face type at the bottom:

> "WE THANK YOU FOR YOUR ORDER AS COPIED HEREON, WHICH WILL RECEIVE PROMPT ATTENTION AND SHALL BE GOVERNED BY THE PROVISIONS ON THE REVERSE SIDE HEREOF UNLESS YOU NOTIFY US TO THE CONTRARY WITHIN 10 DAYS OR BEFORE SHIPMENT WHICHEVER IS EARLIER. BEFORE ACCEPTING GOODS FROM TRANSPORTATION COMPANY SEE THAT EACH ARTICLE IS IN GOOD CONDITION. IF SHORTAGE OR DAMAGE IS APPARENT REFUSE SHIPMENT UNLESS AGENT NOTES DEFECT ON TRANSPORTATION BILL. ACCEPTANCE OF SHIPMENT WITHOUT COMPLYING WITH SUCH CONDITIONS IS AT YOUR OWN RISK.
>
> "THIS IS NOT AN INVOICE. AN INVOICE FOR THIS MATERIAL WILL BE SENT YOU WITHIN A FEW DAYS.
>
> "ACKNOWLEDGMENT OF ORDER"

On the reverse side of the "acknowledgment of order" there are printed six separate provisions which are appropriately numbered and at the very beginning it is stated that:

> "The following provisions form part of the order acknowledged and accepted on the face hereof, as express agreements between Fairbanks, Morse & Co. ("Company") and the Buyer governing the terms and conditions of the sale, subject to modification only in writing signed by the local manager or an executive officer of the Company:"

Provision # 6 which is the subject of the dispute between the parties provides that:

> "6.—The Company nowise assumes any responsibility or liability with respect to use, purpose, or suitability, and shall not be liable for damages of any character, whether direct or consequential, for defect, delay, or otherwise, its sole liability and obligation being confined to the replacement in the manner aforesaid of defectively manufactured guaranteed parts failing within the time stated."

Fairbanks contends that provision # 6 contained on the reverse side of their "acknowledgement of order" became part of the contract between it and Air Products while Air Products contends that its right to rely on the implied warranty of merchantability (U.C.C. 2-314), fitness for particular purposes (U.C.C. 2-315), and consequential damages (U.C.C. 2-714) has in no way been limited by provision #6, since it never was assented to by it, and, therefore, never became part of the contract. Both parties are in agreement that sec. 2-207, of the Uniform Commercial Code is the appropriate standard by which their rights must be determined. . . .

One commentator has aptly stated the threshold questions involved in subsection (1) of 2-207:

> "The second situation covered by this clause concerns confirmatory memoranda which follow an agreement. 'Confirmation' connotes that the parties reached an agreement before exchange of the forms in question. The purpose of Code drafters here must have been to make clear that confirmations need not mirror each other in order to find contract. Simply stated then, under this first clause of section 2-207(1), it is reasonable to assume that the parties have a deal, then there is a contract even though terms of the writings exchanged do not match.
>
> "All of the language following the comma in subsection (1) simply preserves for the offeree his right to make a counter-offer if he does so expressly. This phrase cannot possibly affect the deal between parties that have reached an agreement and then exchanged confirmations. In that situation it is too late for a counter-offer and subsection (2) must be applied to determine what becomes of the non-matching terms of the confirmations. Thus, under subsection (1), there are two instances in which a contract may not have been formed. First, if the offeror could not reasonably treat the response of the offeree as an acceptance there is no contract. Second, if the offeree's acceptance is made expressly conditional on the offeror's assent to variant provisions, the offeree has made a counter-offer. However, under section 2-207(3) either situation may result in contract formation by subsequent conduct of the parties."

Because the reverse side of Fairbanks' Acknowledgment of Order states that the provisions contained there ". . . form part of the order acknowledged and accepted on the face hereof . . ." it would seem that Air Products could have "reasonably" assumed that the parties "had a deal."

Since there is no express provision in the purchase orders making assent to different or additional terms conditioned upon Air Products' assent to them, the second requirement of coming under U.C.C. 2-207 is also met.

Once having satisfied the requirements of subsection (1), any additional matter must fall in subsection (2).

The major impact of sec. 2-207 is that it altered the common law rule which precluded an acceptance from creating a contract if it in any way varied any term of the offer. Subsection (1) expressly provides that there may be a legally binding contract even if the acceptance contains terms "different from" or "additional to" the terms of the offer.

At this point a contract does in fact exist between the parties under (1). Subsection (2) must now be resorted to to see which of the "variant" terms will actually become part of the contract.

At this juncture, Air Products . . . argue[s] that 2-207(2) only applies to "additional terms" while Fairbanks' limitation of liability provisions were "different." To this extent they contend terms are "additional" if they concern a subject matter that is not covered in the offer and "different" if the subject matter, although covered in the offer, was covered in a variant way. . . . Air Products' argument seems to expressly contradict Official U.C.C. Comment #3 which unequivocally states "Whether or not *additional or different* terms will become part of the agreement depends upon the provisions of subsection (2)." (Emphasis added.) One commentator has noted that:

> "On its face, subsection (2) seems only to apply to additional and not conflicting terms, and at least one court has interpreted the language this way. However, this is an unnecessarily limited construction and, as Comment 3 to the section points out, subsection (2) should apply to both additional and different provisions."

In American Parts Co., Inc. v. American Arbitration Association (1967), 8 Mich.App. 156, 154 N.W.2d 5, the court, in explicitly limiting the application of (2) to additional terms, said of the policy behind 2-207:

> "The policy of section 2-207 is that the parties should be able to enforce their agreement, whatever it is, despite discrepancies between the oral agreement and the confirmation (or between an offer and acceptance) *if enforcement can be granted without requiring either party to be bound to a material term to which he has not agreed.*" (Emphasis added)

The implication seems clear. A party cannot be expected to have assented to a "different" term.

The thrust of the "additional-different" dichotomy as averred for by Air Products . . . is that their offer as effectuated by a purchase order includes not only those terms which are expressly stated therein, but also those which are implied by law (e. g. warranty and damage) that will become a part of the contract formed by the seller's acceptance of the offer. Therefore, Fairbanks' limitation of liability terms are different since they are at variance with the implied warranty and damage terms in Air Products' offer. Fairbanks contends that because sec. 2-714(3) provides that "in a proper case" consequential damages may be recovered by an injured buyer they are clearly not implied in all contracts.

Air Products . . . next contend that if the added terms of the "acknowledgment of order" were "additional" terms they still do not become part of the contract because the prerequisite to their becoming a part of the contract which are contained in subsection (2) were not satisfied. Section 2-207(2) required that:

> "The additional terms are to be construed as proposals for addition to the contract. Between merchants such terms become part of the contract unless:
> "(a) the offer expressly limits acceptance to the terms of the offer;
> "(b) they materially alter it; or
> "(c) notification of objection to them has already been given or is given within a reasonable time after notice of them is received."

The language employed by Air Products in its "terms and conditions" was not express enough to bring into play the provisions of either subsection 2-207(a) or (c). The ultimate question to be determined, therefore, is whether the disclaimer contained in Fairbanks' "acknowledgment of order" materially altered the agreement between the parties pursuant to sec. 2-207(2)(b). If they materially alter what would otherwise be firmed by the acceptance of an offer, they will not become terms unless the buyer expressly agrees thereto. "If, however, they are terms which would not so change the bargain they will be incorporated unless notice of objection to them has already been given or is given within a reasonable time."

. . . Air Products contend that the eradication of a multi-million dollar damage exposure is *per se* material. Fairbanks bases its argument on the ground that consequential damages may not be recovered except in "special circumstances" or in a "proper case." 2-714(2), (3).

We agree with plaintiffs . . . Air Products and conclude that the disclaimer for consequential loss was sufficiently material to require express conversation between the parties over its inclusion or exclusion in the contract.

Affirmed in part, reversed in part.

ACCEPTANCE PROBLEMS

At the outset of the chapter, we noted the three requirements that must be met in order for an acceptance to result: there must be an intent to contract, an effective communication, and a response that generally satisfies all the terms and requirements imposed by the offer. It should be noted that, in many situations, it is generally the offeror, not the offeree, who controls the form and manner of the acceptance. This is because of the third requirement—that the acceptance conform to the terms and requirements imposed by the offer. Thus the offeror often has the power to change the general rule applied in many of the situations this chapter has discussed. All the offeror must do is to add to the offer the requirements that it seeks to obtain from the offeree. Several unusual acceptance problems arise because of the offeror's control of the acceptance.

Silence as Acceptance

Generally, the offeree who responds silently to the offer is not considered to be accepting the offer. Mere inaction and silence are usually not regarded as manifestations of intent to agree on a contract. However, some exceptions to this rule occur, usually because of the terms suggested in the offer. Book clubs, record clubs, wine clubs, and gourmet clubs often make agreements under which the person receiving the merchandise being sold will be considered to have accepted the "monthly offer" if that person is silent and does not tell the club that the merchandise is not desired. The exceptions recognized by the law usually occur in one of three situations:

1. If the transactions the parties have entered into in the past show their intent to regard silence as an acceptance, that intent becomes a part of their future transactions. Here, the *course of dealing* between the parties in past transactions is the basis for finding their present intent to have silence constitute acceptance.
2. The *initial agreement* between the parties constitutes the basis for treating silence by the offeree as acceptance. Thus, at the beginning of the transactions, the member of the book, record, or wine club signs a written agreement stating that the member who does not send in the card or notice rejecting the monthly offering agrees to pay for the items received. The member agrees that he or she does not have to affirmatively express his or her acceptance each month; silence on the part of the member is, by virtue of the initial agreement, also a method of accepting the club's monthly offering.
3. If the offeree *uses the goods* and treats them as if he had accepted them, the courts consider the offeree's actions and silence as together constituting the required acceptance. This problem occurs most often with regard to magazines or newspapers mistakenly being sent to people who didn't order them. Courts usually considered that, since the offeror is in business and did not intend a gift, the person who receives them and reads them is assumed to have agreed to pay for them. Most states now have statutes that allow the recipient of unsolicited merchandise, particularly where sent through the mail, to treat such items as gifts. The Postal Reorganization Act provides that mailing unsolicited merchandise is an unfair method of competition unless the product is marked "sample" or is sent by a charity. The Act also provides that the recipient may treat the received merchandise as a gift. Silence and use of such products will not be construed as acceptance of an implied offer to sell.

The Auction

An auction is a sales device whereby members of the public or a designated group come together to compete, by means of bids, for the purchase of goods or realty. Auctions are usually conducted by professional auctioneers or by public officials and may be of two types. In an auction *with reserve*, the object bid for does not have to be sold if the auctioneer is dissatisfied with the level of the bidding. In an auction *without reserve*, the object must be sold to the highest bidder.

Under UCC Section 2-328, an auction is considered to be with reserve unless it is expressly stated to be without reserve. Because at least one court has held that the phrase "will sell to highest bidder" is insufficient to make an auction without reserve, the actual words "without reserve" should be used in an announcement to ensure that the auction is of that type.

In an auction with reserve, each bid is considered an offer. Acceptance is signaled by the fall of the hammer or some other symbolic act customary for the type of auction involved. In an auction without reserve, the announcement is considered the offer and each bid is an acceptance subject to the condition that no higher bid is made.

CANCELLATION OF ACCEPTANCE

We have discussed the problems that occur in determining whether there has been an acceptance of the offer. If an acceptance has been made, the offer can no longer be revoked by the offeror because it has now become part of a contract. Similarly, the offeree who has accepted the offer generally is not free to subsequently reject the offer. Neither party can reverse its original position. While contract law generally follows this interpretation, statutes in many states allow one of the contracting parties to cancel an acceptance (or to

terminate an offer) in certain circumstances.

Typical of these statutes is Michigan's Home Solicitation Sales Act (M.C.L.A. 445.111 et. seq.). The law grants to the buyer of goods or services costing more than $25 who has made an offer or who has accepted an offer the right to revoke the offer or cancel the acceptance within three business days from the date of the transaction. The law applies only to a home solicitation sale made at the residence of the buyer and only the buyer, not the seller, is given the right to revoke the offer or cancel the acceptance. The law is intended to protect the consumer from high-pressured salespeople who force the consumer to act in a way he or she might not if given more time and less pressure. The three-day period is often referred to as a "cooling-off period" since the buyer has this time to reconsider the transaction.

REVIEW PROBLEMS

1. A subcontractor made a contract with a general contractor which allowed the general contractor to use machines of the subcontractor for a specified time period while it was doing construction work on landowner's property. When the time for the use of the subcontractor's machine expired, the subcontractor sent a bill to the landowner for rental due on the machine and an invoice stating the rental rate for the continued use of the machine. The landowner responded to the bill and informed the subcontractor that the equipment needs for future construction work on his property were being examined by the general contractor and that all future rental payments for the use of the subcontractor's machine would be the responsibility of the general contractor. The subcontractor's machines remained on the property of the landowner, but were not used by him or by the

general contractor. Is there a contract between the landowner and the subcontractor for the rental of the subcontractor's machine? Crosby v. Paul Hardeman, Inc., 414 F2d 1 (8th Cir. 1969)

2. Westside & Hurble entered into an option agreement on April 5, 1963, wherein Hurble, for $50, was given a sixty-day option to purchase certain real estate. The option provided that the offer by Westside to sell the real estate at an agreed-upon price was irrevocable. On May 2, 1963, Hurble sent Westside a letter stating that Hurble exercised its option and also noting that "as additional inducement for Hurble to exercise its option, you have agreed that all utilities, gas, water, sewer, and electricity, will be extended to the property prior to the closing date. The contract of sale is hereby amended to provide seller shall extend all utility lines to the property before the clos-

ing date. Please sign this letter to indicate your acceptance of the amendment." On May 14, Hurble sent Westside another letter instructing it to disregard the proposed amendment in the letter of May 2 and that it now was exercising its option without amendment. Has Hurble accepted Westside's offer so as to create a contract? Hurble Oil & Refining Co. v. Westside Invest. Corp. 419 S.W. 2d 448 (Ct. of Civ. App. of Tex., 1967)

3. Systems Engineering offered to sell equipment to Golden Dept. Co. Its proposal stated that a 25 percent down payment must be submitted with any order. It further required the proposal, signed by the purchaser, to be submitted to and accepted by Systems Engineering in order to be effective. Golden Dept. Co. telephoned Systems Engineering and stated that the proposal by Systems to sell its equipment to Golden Dept. was approved and that Systems should begin work. Systems responded, "We'll get on it immediately." Subsequently, a mistake in the quoted price was found by Systems Engineering and it notified Golden Dept. Golden Dept. said it had a contract at the price quoted in the proposal of Systems. Do you agree? Golden Dept. Co., etc. v. Systems Engineering & Mfg. Co., etc. 465 F2d 215 (7th Cir. 1972)

4. Pearce sought to purchase steel products from Dulien Steel Products and on October 22 wrote that he would purchase two cars of 70-pound rail and angle bars for $15 per ton f.o.b. Armstead. Dulien responded on October 23, "We can't sell at $15 per ton, but would accept price on two cars at $17.50 per ton." Pearce then responded on November 9 as follows: "We will purchase from you two carloads of rail at $17.50 per ton, f.o.b. Armstead. Hunt will inspect the rail for our customers and will probably designate rail to be rejected or accepted." On November 12, Dulien responded with a letter which included the following language:

"We do not agree to the matter of Hunt's inspection. We are not selling you subject to Hunt's inspection." Pearce alleges that it is customary in the steel business for the buyer of steel to have the right of inspection and that the offer of Dulien had been accepted by Pearce. Do you agree? Pearce v. Dulien Steel Products, Inc. 127 P2d 271 (Supreme Court of Washington, 1942)

5. An antinuclear protest group, the Clamshell Alliance, sought permission to rent the National Guard armory in Portsmouth, New Hampshire, for the night of April 29, 1978. In response to that request, the Adjutant General on March 31 mailed an offer to rent the armory and specified the terms that had to be met. The offer specified that a signed acceptance be returned to the office of the Adjutant General. Cushing, a member of the Alliance, received the offer on April 3; that same date, he signed the acceptance on behalf of the Alliance and placed the letter in the office's outbox. At 6:30 P.M. on April 4, Cushing received a telephone call from the Adjutant General revoking the offer. Cushing replied that he had already accepted the offer. The procedure followed in the Alliance office indicates that letters placed in the office outbox one day usually are put in the mailbox before 5:00 P.M. on the following day. The letter of acceptance sent by Cushing was received by the Adjutant General's office on April 6; the postmark on the letter was April 5. Was the acceptance effectively communicated before the offer was revoked? Cushing v. Thompson, 386 A2d 805 (Supreme Court of New Hampshire, 1978)

6. Farley solicited a bid from Clark whereby the latter agreed to fabricate 100 trailers at a designated price. Farley considered other bids and decided to award the job to another firm. Farley prepared a check for the other firm and sent it by mistake to Clark. The check was for $18 less per unit than the

offer. Clark deposited the check and began production. Farley sued to recover the proceeds of the check. What result? Farley v. Clark Equipment Co. 484 S.W.2d 142 (Ct. Civ. App. Tex. 1972)

7. In September 1969, Buske, an insurance agent, sent Roberts a renewal of an automobile liability policy that was a renewal of one Robert's father had previously held for him. Roberts accepted that policy and paid the premium. In September 1970, just prior to the expiration date of the policy, Buske again sent a renewal notice to Roberts. The notice stated that if Roberts did not wish to accept it, he must return it or be liable for the premium. Roberts made no response to that notice or to subsequent ones sent to him. Roberts had in fact purchased a policy from another company, but Buske did not learn of that fact until December. The insurance agent says that Roberts's silence constitutes his acceptance of the offer to renew the policy. Do you agree? Roberts v. Buske, 298 N.E. 2d 795 (Appellate Court of Illinois, 1973)

8. Over a series of transactions occurring during a two-year period, plaintiff, Carpet Mart, purchased a variety of carpeting from the defendant, Collins & Aikman. After checking that the terms agreed to in oral conversations were met, defendant sent an acknowledgment form to plaintiff for each of its orders. The following provision was printed on the acknowledgment form:

"The acceptance of your order is subject to all of the terms and conditions on the face and reverse side hereof, including arbitration, all of which are accepted by buyer; it supersedes buyer's order form, if any. It shall become a contract either (a) when signed and delivered by buyer to seller and accepted in writing by seller, or (b) at seller's option, when buyer shall have given to seller specification of assortments, delivery dates, shipping instructions, . . . or instructions to bill and hold as to all or any part of the merchandise herein described, or when buyer has received delivery of the whole or any part thereof, or when buyer has otherwise assented to the terms and conditions hereof. . . ."

Is the arbitration agreement appearing on the back of the acknowledgment form sent to the Carpet Mart by Collins & Aikman a part of the contract between them? Dorton v. Collins & Aikman Corp. 453 F2d 1161 (6th Cir. 1972)

Consideration

LEGAL DETRIMENT_____

BARGAINED EXCHANGE_____

DISSATISFACTION WITH THE REQUIREMENT OF CONSIDERATION:

THE EVOLUTION OF PROMISSORY ESTOPPEL _____

A contract is a promise or a group of promises that a court will enforce. There is no legal system, however, in which all promises are enforced. For example, a promise to undertake a social obligation is not enforced by the courts. The mere fact that one person promises something to another creates no legal duty and makes no remedy available in case of nonperformance. The problem that has confronted the courts is to determine which promises should be enforced and which should not.

The preceding chapters examined the requirements of a valid offer and acceptance as the essential elements of an agreement. Although agreement is essential to the formation of a contract, not all agreements are contracts. This chapter focuses on the additional element that is generally necessary for an agreement to rise to the level of a contract. This element is the consideration. Over the centuries, the courts have been adamant in their requirement that, to be enforceable, a contract must be supported by consideration. Consideration is the exchange element of a contract. It is what induces the parties' agreement. It is what one party must give to another to make the other party legally obligated to perform its promise. If there is no consideration there is no contract, and this is true even if there has been a valid offer and acceptance.

Consideration may be defined as a *legal detriment* that is incurred by a promisee as the *bargained exchange* for a promise. The American Law Institute defines it as something that is bargained for by the promisor and given by the promisee in exchange for a promise. Society benefits from the enforcement of promises where enforcement satisfies the reasonable expectation that a promise will be performed. A society that refused to enforce any promise would place a promisee in a perilous position. A promisor's word would be good only so far as the promisor had developed a reputation for performance. On the other hand, no society can enforce all promises, for in the ordinary course of events some promises are made that no reasonable promisee would rely on, or of which the nonperformance does not harm the promisee.

The judiciary is the institution by which social force is exerted to enforce promises. The chief purpose of exerting social force through the courts to enforce a promise is to prevent disappointment and ensure that there is no loss to the promisee. The courts require specific and convincing evidence that the promisee's expectation of performance and the promisee's reliance were reasonable. The existence of consideration is treated as evidence that the promisee's expectation was reasonable and that nonperformance would injure the community.

169

The following discussion examines in detail the two components of the element of consideration: the *legal detriment* incurred by the promisee as the *bargained exchange* for the promise.

LEGAL DETRIMENT

A legal detriment is incurred when a person voluntarily agrees to assume a duty or to relinquish a right. It is doing or promising to do an act that one was not under a duty to perform, or refraining from doing or promising to refrain from doing an act that one had the right to perform. Thus the promisee must do or promise to do what he or she was not legally obligated to do, or refrain from doing or promise to refrain from doing what he or she has a right to do.

Note the adjective "legal" in the term "legal detriment." A legal detriment is not synonymous with real detriment or loss. In deciding whether a promisee has incurred a legal detriment, the courts focus not on whether the promisee suffered some actual economic or physical loss but on whether the promisee agreed either to assume a *duty* or to relinquish a *right*. In most cases the promisee will incur both a real detriment and a legal detriment, but for purposes of contract-law analysis the courts focus on the legal detriment.

Courts focus on the legal detriment rather than the actual detriment incurred by the promisee out of regard for the limits of judicial expertise. Assume that a promisee sues a promisor to recover for the damage resulting from nonperformance, and the promisor argues that the promise was not supported by consideration because the promisee did not incur a real or economic detriment in exchange for the promise. The courts are ill-suited to determine whether the promisee incurred a real or economic detriment, for that would require judicial scrutiny of the parties' commercial transactions. Courts are better suited to examine the parties' legal relationship. Legal concepts, such as the concepts of "right" and "duty," are the stuff of the law. Thus, in analyzing whether a promisee incurred a legal detriment, the focus of inquiry is on whether the promisee assumed a duty or relinquished a right rather than on whether the promisee did or promised to do anything of value. The analysis of whether the promisee incurred a legal detriment is a legal analysis, not an economic analysis. Hence, the nature of the detriment that is required is a legal detriment, not an economic or physical detriment.

The following case illustrates the distinction between the two kinds of detriments. Note that the promisee, the nephew, engaged in behavior that was physically beneficial to him, yet the court concludes that he suffered a legal detriment.

Hamer v. Sidway

Court of Appeals of New York, Second Division
27 N.E. 256 (1891)

On March 20, 1869, William E. Story, Sr. promised his nephew, William E. Story, 2d, that if the nephew would refrain from drinking, using tobacco, swearing, and playing cards or billiards for money until his twenty-first birthday, the uncle would pay him the sum of $5,000. On January 31, 1875, having reached his twenty-first birthday and having satisfied all of his uncle's conditions, the nephew wrote his uncle claiming that he was entitled to receive the $5,000. On February 6, the uncle replied with the following letter:

> Dear Nephew:
>   Your letter of the 31st ult. came to hand all right, saying that you had lived up to the promise made to me several years ago. I have no doubt but you have, for which you shall have $5,000, as I promised you. I had the money in the bank the day you was 21 years old that I intend for you, and you shall have the money certain. Now, Willie, I don't intend to interfere with this money in any way until I think you are capable of taking care of it, and the sooner the time comes the better it will please me. I would hate very much to have you start out in some adventure that you thought all right, and lose this money in one year. . . . This money you have earned much easier than I did, besides acquiring good habits at the same time; and you are quite welcome to the money. Hope you will make good use of it. . . . W.E. STORY. P.S. You can consider this money on interest.

As a result, the nephew consented to leave the money in his uncle's care in accordance with the terms of the letter.

In 1877, with his uncle's consent and permission, the nephew conveyed his claim to the $5,000 to his wife, who in turn conveyed her interest to the plaintiff. When William E. Story, Sr. died, the plaintiff presented a claim for the $5,000 to the executor of the estate, who denied the claim. Plaintiff recovered at trial, but the judgment was reversed on appeal. The action was brought on appeal from the order for a new trial.

Parker, J.

The question which provoked the most discussion by counsel on this appeal, and which lies at the foundation of plaintiff's asserted right of recovery, is whether by virtue of a contract defendant's testator, William E. Story, became indebted to his nephew, William E. Story, 2d, on his twenty-first birthday in the sum of $5,000. The trial court found as a fact that "on the 20th day of March, 1869, . . . William E. Story agreed to and with William E. Story, 2d, that if he would refrain from drinking liquor, using tobacco, swearing and playing cards or billiards for money until he should become twenty-one years of age, then he, the said William E. Story, would at that time pay him, the said William E. Story, 2d, the sum of $5,000 for such refraining, to which the said William E. Story, 2d, agreed," and that he "in all things fully performed his part of said agreement." The defendant contends that the contract was without consideration to support it, and therefore invalid. He asserts that the promisee, by refraining from the use of liquor and tobacco, was not harmed, but benefited; that that which he did was best for him to do, independently of his uncle's promise—and insists that it follows that, unless the promisor was benefited, the contract was without consideration—a contention which, if well founded, would seem to leave open for controversy in many cases whether that which the promisee did or omitted to do was in fact of such benefit to him as to leave no consideration to support the enforcement of the promisor's agreement. Such a rule could not be tolerated, and is without foundation in the law. The exchequer chamber in 1875 defined "consideration" as follows: "A valuable consideration, in the sense of the law, may consist either in some right, interest, profit or benefit accruing to the one party, or some forbearance, detriment, loss, or responsibility given, suffered, or undertaken by the other." Courts "will not ask whether the thing which forms the consideration does in fact benefit the promisee or a third party, or is of any substantial value to any one. It is enough that something is promised, done, forborne, or suffered by the party to whom the promise is made as consideration for the promise made to him." Anson, Cont. 63. "In general a waiver of any legal right at the request of another party is a sufficient consideration for a promise." Pars. Cont. *444. "Any damage, or suspension, or forbearance of a right will be sufficient to sustain a promise." 2 Kent, Comm. (12th Ed.) *465. Pollock in his work on Contracts, (page 166) after citing the definition given by the exchequer chamber, already quoted, says: "The second branch of this judicial description is really the most important one. 'Consideration' means not so much that one party is profiting as that the other abandons some legal right to the present, or limits his legal freedom of action in the future, as an inducement for the promise of the first." Now, applying this rule to the facts before us, the promisee used tobacco, occasionally drank liquor, and he had a legal right to do so. That right he abandoned for a period of years upon the strength of the promise of the testator that for such forbearance he would give him $5,000. We need not speculate on the effort which may have been required to give up the use of those stimulants. It is sufficient that he restricted his lawful freedom of action within certain prescribed limits upon the faith of his uncle's agreement, and now, having fully performed the conditions imposed, it is of no moment whether such performance actually proved a benefit to the promisor, and the court will not inquire into it; but, were it a proper subject of inquiry, we see nothing in this record that would permit a determination that the uncle was not benefited in a legal sense.

The order appealed from should be reversed, and the judgment of the special term affirmed, with costs payable out of the estate. All concur.

Adequacy vs. Sufficiency of Consideration

When deciding whether a contract is supported by consideration, it is important to distinguish between the *adequacy* of the consideration and the *sufficiency* of the consideration. Although the semantic distinction between these terms is small, the legal distinction between them is significant. So watch your language!

The term "adequacy" refers to the quantity or value of the consideration. Courts do not generally inquire into the adequacy of the consideration; they are concerned only that there is a legally sufficient consideration, meaning that the promisee incurred a legal detriment in exchange for the promise. Thus any legal detriment will constitute valuable consideration no matter how economically inadequate it may be.

For example, suppose that for $1 Penelope gave to Ring Telephone Company the right to install and maintain telephone wire over her land. Later Penelope found that other property owners had received substantially more money for giving the same rights to Ring. Penelope could not later refuse to let Ring on her land by arguing that she had received an inadequate consideration for her promise to Ring. In order for Ring to obtain the enforcement of Penelope's promise, Ring must show that Penelope received sufficient consideration for her promise. Ring would be able to obtain enforcement because, by paying $1 to Penelope, Ring relinquished the right it had to keep its money. Thus Ring incurred a legal detriment in exchange for Penelope's promise. A court would not refuse to enforce Penelope's promise because it appears she made a bad deal; rather, a court would enforce her promise because the economic value of the consideration in relation to the value of the promise given for it is not relevant in determining whether there is a valid consideration.

Courts will not inquire into the adequacy of consideration—that is, the substantial equality or relative value of the items in a bargained-for exchange. The reason for this rule is that the efficient administration of the law of contracts requires that courts should not be required to police the marketplace in an effort to protect people from their own imprudence. The rule represents a policy of judicial self-restraint in dealing with matters of economic consequence. It recognizes the limits of judicial expertise. It is consistent with the common law notion that the courts will not make a contract for the parties, that the parties should be free to make their own contracts. As such, the rule seeks to preserve freedom of contract.

However, the rule that courts will refrain from inquiring into the adequacy of consideration assumes that the parties have freely entered into their agreement. Where this assumption is questioned, the courts *will* take into account the adequacy of consideration. If one of the parties argues that the contract was procured through fraud, misrepresentation, duress, undue influence, or mistake, a court will examine the adequacy of the consideration as evidence of the existence of those factors.

The only other circumstance in which the adequacy of consideration will be examined involves the equal exchange of fungible goods or equal exchanges of money. Goods that are fungible are indistinguishable and interchangeable. One carload of wheat cannot be distinguished from another; the carloads of wheat are thus fungible goods. Under the fungible-goods doctrine, a contract calling for an exchange of equal amounts of wheat would not be supported by consideration. A similar result occurs with equal exchanges of money. As a result, parties who put a clause in their agreement to the effect that each has given the other $1 as consideration for the agreement will find that they have no contract because there is no consideration.

Unlike adequacy of consideration, sufficiency of consideration is readily examined by the courts. If what was given in exchange for a promise is insufficient to constitute consideration, there is no contract. Consideration requires a legal detriment bargained for and given in exchange for a promise. When what is tendered is in fact not a legal detriment newly incurred as a result of the promise, then it is not sufficient to constitute consideration and there is no contract.

Illusory Promises

Any promise that leaves to the discretion of the promisor whether to perform or not to perform is illusory. Thus a person who promises to do something "if I feel like it" has not promised anything at all and has incurred no legal detriment. Even though the language used may be couched in promissory terms, if the promisor is not required to do anything, the promise is illusory. An illusory promise is not sufficient consideration because nothing has been promised.

Although the rule that an illusory promise cannot serve as sufficient consideration is logical, the result of such a rule can be harsh in certain cases. The rule allows a person to avoid an apparent contractual obligation by arguing that his or her own promise was illusory, hence no contract exists. For example, suppose Julius promises to buy all the widgets that he needs from Penelope at $1 per widget. Julius' promise might be considered illusory because he could later claim that he no longer needed any widgets from Penelope. If Penelope later seeks to hold Julius to his promise, Julius could avoid liability by asserting that his own illusory promise cannot constitute a sufficient consideration to support the contract.

Faced with this situation, courts and legislatures have sought ways to circumvent the rule. Three categories of promises illustrate this area of law: cancellation or termination clauses; promises based on unlikely conditions; and output/requirements contracts.

Cancellation or Termination Clauses.

Contracts frequently allow one or both parties to cancel or terminate their obligations under certain circumstances. If the cancellation clause allows a party to avoid the obligation at his or her election, the contract is voidable, meaning that the contract may be terminated at the election of one of the parties. A contract that is voidable upon the election of one of the parties is illusory.

For example, if A and B enter into a contract in which B promises to buy and A promises to sell 500 widgets per month, but B has the right to cancel "at any time without notice," there is no contract, for lack of consideration, because B's promise is illusory. B has the right to terminate the agreement at will—he is not required to perform. B has not actually assumed a duty to buy, hence B has incurred no legal detriment. However, the result would be different if B were required to provide notice to A that B was terminating the contract. Most courts hold that a termination clause requiring notice is sufficient to overcome a claim that the contract is based on an illusory promise, reasoning that, by assuming the duty to notify the promisee in advance of the termination,

the promisor has incurred a legal detriment.

Additionally, Section 2-309(3) of the UCC and many courts have said that when a termination clause contains no notice requirement, the requirement of a reasonable notice of termination will be inferred. This will be done when it is clear that both parties intended to enter into a binding contract. This approach seeks to preserve the intent of the parties and reflects legislative and judicial reluctance to strike down an otherwise valid agreement on the technicality that one of the terms is illusory.

Promises Based on Unlikely Conditions.

Promises based on conditions that have no likelihood of being fulfilled are illusory and not sufficient to support a contract. If A lends $5,000 to B on the condition that B, a 45-year-old ironworker, will repay the loan if he becomes a space-shuttle pilot, there is no contract. The limitation placed on B approaches the vanishing point given the prerequisites for becoming a shuttle pilot, so in essence there is no limitation placed on B. A has made a gift couched in contractual terms, because B will never have to repay the "loan."

Output/Requirements Contracts.

An output contract is an agreement to sell one's entire production of goods to a purchaser. A requirements contract is an agreement whereby one party agrees to purchase all its requirements of a given product from the seller. Such contracts are useful, especially for newer businesses. However, in the past courts frequently held that such agreements were illusory because the contracts provided no standards as to just how much of the product was to be sold or bought. That is, the seller might choose not to produce all of the product that it is capable of producing, and the buyer might choose not to have any requirements for the product.

The UCC has legitimized output/requirements contracts by providing standards required for enforcement. Section 2-306(1) requires the reading of commercial background and intent into the language of any output or requirements contract for supplies. What could have been an illusory promise is now a promise supported by consideration, because Section 2-306 imposes an obligation on the party who will determine the quantity to act in good faith. This good-faith obligation im-posed by the UCC constitutes a sufficient consideration for any output or requirements contract.

The illusory-promise problem is illustrated in the following case. Determine whether the court made the best decision in terms of both the law and what should be good commercial practice. The decision pre-dates the UCC.

Streich v. General Motors Corporation

Appellate Court of Illinois
126 N.E.2d 389 (1955)

Frank Streich alleged that General Motors Corporation had entered into a contract with him in which it promised to buy from him all its requirements of air magnet valves for the period between September 1, 1948 and August 31, 1949. Streich claimed that he had been led to believe that 1,600 or more units of this particular item would be needed, and that in reliance on this he expended a great deal of money, time, and effort to gather the materials for production. Because the valves were a specialty item they could not be taken from Streich's ordinary inventory but instead had to be made to order.

When General Motors ordered only twelve of the valves, Streich sued for breach of contract. The trial court sustained General Motor's motion to dismiss, and Streich appealed. Much of the court's discussion focused on a General Motors Purchase Order, No. 11925, which was said by General Motors to contain the entire agreement between itself and Streich in twenty-five separate clauses, many of which were very detailed and printed in small type.

McCormick, Presiding Justice

It is the contention of the plaintiff, Frank Streich, hereafter referred to as "seller," that the defendant, General Motors Corporation, hereafter referred to as the "buyer," had entered into a binding contract to purchase all the requirements of the buyer from September 1, 1948 through August 31, 1949 from the seller, and that, while the amount of the requirements was not specified, parol evidence might be properly introduced to show what the requirements were.

In order to determine whether or not the seller stated a cause of action in his complaint it is necessary to analyze the agreements between the parties.

There is no question but that under the law a contract properly entered into whereby the buyer agrees to buy all its requirements of a commodity for a certain period, and the seller agrees to sell the same as ordered, is a valid and enforceable contract and is not void for uncertainty and want of mutuality. The contract in the instant case is not such a contract. Reading and construing the two documents together, notwithstanding the detailed provisions contained on the reverse side of the purchase order, the result is an agreement on the part of the seller to sell a certain identified valve at a certain fixed price in such quantities as the buyer may designate, when and if it issues a purchase order for the same.

Here, the buyer proffers purchase order 11925, with its twenty-five or more clauses, to the seller for acceptance. In the instrument it makes no promise to do anything. On the surface it appears to be an attempt to initiate a valid bilateral contract. The seller accepts, and as by a flash of legerdemain the positions of the buyer and the seller shift. The buyer now becomes the promisee and the seller the promisor. The promise of the seller to furnish identified items at a stated price is merely an offer, and cannot become a contract until the buyer issues a release or order for a designated number of items. Until this action is taken the buyer has made no promise to do anything, and either party may withdraw. The promise is illusory, and the chimerical contract vanishes. "An agreement to sell to another such of the seller's goods, wares, and merchandise as the other might from time to time desire to purchase is lacking in mutuality because it does not bind the buyer to purchase any of the goods of the seller, as such matter is left wholly at the option or pleasure of the buyer." Willard Sutherland & Co. v. United States, 262 U.S. 489, 43 S. Ct. 592, 67 L.Ed. 1086.

In Higbie v. Rust, 211 Ill. 333, 71 N.E. 1010, 1011, the court says:

> "Where there is no consideration for the promise of one party to furnish or sell so much of the commodity as the other may want, except the promise of the other to take and pay for so much of the commodity as he may want, and there is no agreement that he shall want any quantity whatever, and no method exists by which it can be determined whether he will want any of the commodity, or, what quantity he will want, the contract is void for lack of mutuality. Hoffman v. Maffioli, 104 Wis. 630, 80 N.W. 1032, 47 L.R.A. 427; Bailey v. Austrian, 19 Minn. 535; National Furnace Co. v. Keystone Mfg. Co., 110 Ill. 427."

See also Williston on Contracts, Rev. Ed., Vol. 1, sec. 49 (p. 138) and sec. 104 (p. 349). In the instant case, when the seller accepted purchase order No. 11925, no contract came into being.

The agreement in question is an adaptation of what was termed an "open end contract," which was used extensively by the federal government during the late war. However, it was used only in cases where the commodities dealt with were staples and either in the possession of or easily accessible to the seller. In this case the use of the contract is shifted and extended to cover commodities which must be manufactured before they are available for sale. According to the admitted statements in the complaint, special tools had to be manufactured in order to produce the item herein involved. The seller here, misled by the many and detailed provisions contained in purchase order No. 11925 and ordinarily applicable to an enforceable bilateral contract, undoubtedly, as he alleged in his complaint, did go to considerable expense in providing tools and machines, only to find that by the accepted agreement the buyer had promised to do absolutely nothing. A statement of expectation creates no duty. Courts are not clothed with the power to make contracts for parties, nor can they, under the guise of interpretation, supply provisions actually lacking or impose obligations not actually assumed.

The seller also argues the fact that he has alleged in his complaint he was advised by the defendant it would release approximately 1,600 units for shipment under the said purchase order. The written purchase order 11925 contains a provision that the terms and conditions thereof are the complete and final agreement between the buyer and the seller.

In the instant case the seller argues that the suit should not be dismissed because if the case were tried he should be permitted to introduce parol evidence for the purpose of showing an agreement on the part of the buyer to purchase approximately 1,600 valves. The formal agreement contained in purchase order 11925 purports to be a final and complete agreement. A provision therein contained so recites. Parol evidence of this character would vary and contradict the terms of the agreement, and such evidence is inadmissible.

The agreement contained in purchase order No. 11925 was artfully prepared. It contains, in print so fine as to be scarcely legible, more than twenty-three clauses, most of which are applicable to bilateral contracts. It has all the indicia of a binding and enforceable contract, but it was not a binding and enforceable contract because the promise was defective. Behind the glittering facade is a void. This agreement was made in the higher echelons of business, overshadowed by the aura of business ethics. To say the least, the agreement was deceptive. In a more subterranean atmosphere and between persons of lower ethical standards it might, without any strain on the language, be denominated by a less deterged appellation.

Nevertheless, as the law is today, on the pleadings in the instant case, the trial court could do nothing but sustain the motion to dismiss the complaint. The judgment of the Circuit Court is affirmed.

Judgment affirmed.

Robson and Schwartz, JJ., concur.

The Preexisting-Duty Rule

The definition of legal detriment as the assumption of a duty or the relinquishment of a right leads to the logical corollary that if the promisee, in exchange for a promise, merely agrees to undertake what he or she is already obligated to do, the promisee has not incurred a legal detriment. This is known as the preexisting-duty rule.

A preexisting duty may be created by law. By law, persons are under a duty not to commit crimes and torts. Thus a promise not to commit a crime or tort cannot serve as consideration for a return promise because the promisee is already under a duty not to engage in those activities. Similarly, public officials cannot collect rewards for the performance of their duty. If A offers a $5,000 reward for the arrest and conviction of the person who burglarized his store, the police officer who diligently pursues and jails the offender will not be able to collect that reward. The officer is already required by law to apprehend criminals and has therefore incurred no new legal detriment that would entitle him or her to enforcement of the promise of reward.

A preexisting duty may be created by contract. Where the promise of one party is merely a repetition of an already-existing promise and there are no additional duties imposed on that party, such a promise cannot constitute consideration of a return promise given by the other party. For example, suppose that Penelope hires Julius, a contractor, to repair her garage door. Julius and Penelope agree that the price of the repair will be $150. However, after starting work, Julius reconsiders his costs and asks Penelope to pay him $200, which she agrees to do. Upon completion of the repair, Julius will be entitled to only $150. Because Julius was already under a contractual duty to repair Penelope's door for $150, he has incurred no legal detriment in exchange for her promise to pay $50 more. Julius has merely agreed to finish the repair, which he was under a contractual duty to do already.

The preexisting-duty rule is often criticized. In the above example, Penelope appears to be able to avoid the enforcement of her promise. The rule seems to stretch logic to its limits and produce an unjust result. The policy rationale for the rule is the concern that enforcement of the second promise would encourage coercion. Most of the cases where the preexisting-duty rule is invoked involve situations in which the second bargain was forced on one party by the other—for example, by a threat to abandon performance of a contract in circumstances that would have left the threatened party with no available or ready replacement. Where the facts do not show coercion, the courts have stretched doctrine to reach a more desired result.

For example, if in consideration for Penelope's promise to pay $50 more, Julius had agreed to do something, however slight, that was not called for in the original contract, Julius would have incurred a legal detriment. A court, searching for a way to enforce Penelope's promise, would seek to discover if Julius had agreed to undertake something not called for in his original contract in exchange for Penelope's promise. The addition of a new duty in exchange for Penelope's promise makes the

promise enforceable without any conflict with the preexisting-duty rule.

Another device for circumventing the preexisting-duty rule is for the parties to enter a mutual agreement to rescind their old contract and make a new one. A contract may be canceled, and a new one made, by mutual consent. The requisite factors are that the rescission be by the uncoerced consent of both parties and that the rescission be expressed. Furthermore, the rescission itself is a contract and must be supported by consideration. This usually takes the form of the parties' agreement to mutually release each other from their obligations. Where the parties rescind their earlier agreement and enter into a new one, there are actually three contracts: the original contract, the rescission contract, and the new contract.

A strong minority of jurisdictions recognizes an exception to the preexisting-duty rule in cases where the second promise results from circumstances of substantial unforeseen difficulties in performance. For example, if a contractor agreed to build a house and a tornado destroyed the construction when the house was half-built, some courts would hold that a subsequent promise by the owner to pay a larger sum to the contractor is binding even though the contractor does not agree to do anything more than was called for by the original contract. Here the suspicion of coercion by the contractor is not present. The criticism might be directed against the owner, who agrees to pay more to induce the contractor to continue but later disavows the promise.

As can be seen, the law in this area has grown contorted by a general rule, based on logic, and the myriad of exceptions to it created by courts seeking to avoid injustices. The various rules may be reconciled by understanding that the courts are seeking to avoid enforcing bargains that are products of coercion. However, there are other legal doctrines, discussed in Chapter 9, that the courts can use to avoid injustice.

The drafters of the UCC cut through the maze of the common law and established a different rule for goods transactions. Section 2-209 states simply: "An agreement modifying a contract within this Article needs no consideration to be binding." For example, suppose that a supplier agrees to deliver goods at $1 a unit. Later, due to market conditions, the supplier calls the buyer and asks if the buyer will agree to pay $2 a unit for the same goods. Under the preexisting duty rule, the buyer's promise to pay the higher price would not be enforceable for lack of consideration. However, under 2-209, if the buyer agrees to pay the higher price, the promise is enforceable because 2-209 dispenses with the requirement of consideration for the modification of an existing goods transaction. Note that the buyer still has to *agree* to pay the higher price; Section 2-209 requires "an agreement." The buyer could refuse to accept the supplier's price change and hold the supplier to the original contract or recover for its breach. However, after having agreed to the modification, neither party can later disavow a subsequent promise with impunity.

Compromise of Debts. Another situation in which the preexisting-duty rule has application is in regard to an agreement between a debtor and a creditor to reach a compromise on the payment of a debt. The delinquent debtor is a perennial problem for creditors. Frequently, the creditor may accept less than the amount owed on the debt, persuaded that a bird in the hand is worth two in the bush. However, sometimes such arrangements are not enforceable for lack of consideration. If the creditor later seeks to recover full payment on the original debt, the debtor may not be able to enforce the creditor's promise to release all claims on the debtor in return for partial payment. The creditor's promise is not supported by consideration, since the debtor has not incurred any new legal detriment.

For example, suppose that D owes C $1,000.

C agrees to accept $300 as full payment. C's promise to release D from all claims is not supported by consideration. Because D was already under a duty to pay $300, plus an additional $700, D has not incurred any additional legal detriment.

The law in this area is based on the English case of *Foakes* v. *Beer* (1884)[1] in which the House of Lords ruled that partial payment of a debt already owed will not, even if accepted by agreement, discharge the debt in the absence of new consideration. As a general proposition, the rule of *Foakes* v. *Beer* is still good law in many jurisdictions. However, because its application can work severe hardship in some cases and discourage honesty and fair dealing in others, the courts have not hesitated to find new consideration of some kind to support the compromise. Thus, when the debtor tenders partial payment on a loan substantially before the loan is due, or when the debtor tenders some combination of money and property as satisfaction of the debt, a court could hold that there had been new consideration to support a modification of the original contract of indebtedness.

The rule of *Foakes* v. *Beer* has also been substantially limited by legislation. Under the bankruptcy laws, once a debtor is declared bankrupt, the debtor is no longer required to pay his or her creditors—the debts are discharged by court order. However, there are certain circumstances in which it would not be advantageous to the bankrupt to cease payments to all former creditors. As a result, even after bankruptcy, the debtor may choose to reaffirm some of the old debts and thereby maintain the former liability. The courts usually hold that the consideration is the refusal of the debtor to use the defense of bankruptcy to avoid the creditor. Debtor and creditor are free to reach a settlement in which the debtor may be allowed to make only partial payment of the debt and yet will be relieved of all further liability.

A slight variation of this device involves

what are called composition agreements. These are used when a debtor is in financial difficulties and fears being unable to pay his or her creditors in full. In order to prevent being forced into bankruptcy, the creditor may call all or some of the creditors together in an effort to convince them to accept something less than what is owed. The expense caused by bankruptcy and the likelihood that some creditors may wind up with nothing may provide the creditors with the necessary incentive to consent to such an agreement. Thus, if Julius thinks that he can pay 40 percent of his total debts, he may seek to enter into a composition agreement with his creditors. In such a case, each creditor agrees to accept 40 percent of the amount due from Julius.

The problem with accepting the enforceability of composition agreements is pinpointing the consideration involved. Fortunately for the debtor, the courts have not hesitated to find ways around the problem. Courts have found consideration in the promises of each of the other creditors to forgo a portion of their claims, forbearance by the debtor to pay the assenting creditors more than equal proportions, the action of the debtor in securing the assent of the other creditors, or the part payment made to other creditors. Regardless of the rationale used, the simple fact is that the courts want to encourage these agreements between creditors and debtors because such arrangements discourage litigation.

Accord and Satisfaction. The rule of *Foakes v. Beer* applies only to contracts involving liquidated debts, that is, cases in which the debtor does not dispute either the existence of the debt or its size. When such a dispute does exist, the claim is unliquidated and the preexisting-duty rule gives way to the doctrine of accord and satisfaction.

An accord and satisfaction is the offer of something different than what was provided for in the original contract (the accord) and an agreement to accept it (the satisfaction). Partial payment of an unliquidated debt, offered as full satisfaction of the obligation, is supported by consideration and will discharge the obligation.

For example, suppose that Julius hires Penelope, a marketing consultant, to provide advice about the location of Julius's business establishment. Penelope performs the service and delivers a bill for $10,000. Julius believes that her fee is much too high for the services rendered. He maintains that a more reasonable fee would be $3,000. Together they settle their dispute by agreeing on a fee of $4,000. Here, the debt is in dispute; the amount owed is uncertain; the debt is unliquidated. By agreeing to pay $4,000, Julius is assuming a duty to pay $1,000 more than he in good faith believes is owed. By agreeing to take $4,000, Penelope is relinquishing her right to collect $6,000 more, which she in good faith believes is owed her. Each party has incurred a legal detriment in exchange for the other's promise; hence, their agreement is supported by consideration.

It should be emphasized that the current trend is that an accord and satisfaction occur with acceptance of partial payment, not delivery. The precise mechanics of the doctrine's application vary among jurisdictions. The most common approach requires, as the first step, that the debtor notify the creditor of the dispute. Then, assuming that the debt is acknowledged but the amount is disputed, the debtor may write a check for the amount the debtor believes is due, indicate on the check itself that it is being tendered as payment in full, and then send it to the creditor along with a note indicating that the amount of liability is disputed. Once the creditor receives the check, the creditor has three options: the creditor can cash the check, in which case the creditor accepts the debtor's offer of settlement and the debt is discharged; the creditor can return the check, refusing the debtor's offer, and proceed as the creditor would in any collection case; or the creditor can cash the check in defiance of the conditions upon which it was tendered, but only after first notifying the debtor that acceptance of the check is under protest. This last option is expressly allowed by Section 1-207 of the UCC. It should be noted that the accord-and-satisfaction doctrine applies only when there is a good-faith dispute. A bad-faith dispute will result in the debt being classified as a liquidated claim, in which case the rule of *Foakes* v. *Beer* will apply.

Forbearance to Pursue a Legal Right. The surrender of, or forbearance to assert, a legal claim is adequate consideration to support a contract, if bargained for. This situation arises most frequently in insurance cases, when an insurance company promises to pay an agreed upon settlement amount in return for a claimant's promise not to file suit to recover for the alleged injury. If the insurance company refuses to make the payment after it has agreed to do so, the claimant is no longer bound by the contract and may file suit. However, the claimant may choose instead to file suit against the insurance company for breach of contract, seeking the promised settlement and any other damages.

The law in this area becomes muddied when the insurance company responds that the claimant did not have a valid claim from the outset. Because one cannot surrender what one does not have a right to in the first place, the insurance company argues that in surrendering, or forbearing to assert, an invalid claim, the claimant has suffered no legal detriment and therefore any promise of settlement made in return by the insurance company is not supported by consideration.

Courts have generally not accepted this argument. Many courts have held that if the claim was made in good faith and a reasonable person could believe that the claim was well founded, surrender or forbearance would provide sufficient consideration. Other courts have held that good faith alone is sufficient. Still other courts have accepted claims when there is objective uncertainty of the validity of the claim. The trend appears to be that if the claim is "neither patently ridiculous nor corruptly asserted," then the court will view surrender or forbearance as adequate consideration.

This area of law is analogous to the doctrine of accord and satisfaction. Agreeing to forbear from pursuing a legal claim constitutes a legal detriment, because the claimant is relinquishing a right to bring suit. Until a court hears the claim and renders a judgment, the claim is disputed, hence the debt is unliquidated. The requirement that the claimant entertain a good-faith belief in the validity of the claim is similar to the requirement of a good-faith dispute for an accord and satisfaction.

The following case illustrates some of the issues involved under the preexisting-duty rule.

---

owner

Levine v. Blumenthal
Supreme Court of New Jersey
186 A. 457 (1936)

On April 16, 1931, William Levine agreed to lease a site in the central business district of Paterson, New Jersey, to Anne Blumenthal and another unnamed person. It was agreed that Blumenthal was to use the store premises as a woman's clothing shop and that the lease was to be for two years with an option to renew for an additional three years. Rent for the first year was to be $2,100, payable in monthly installments of $175 in advance. For the second year the rent was scheduled to increase to $2,400, payable in monthly installments of $200.

In April of 1932, approximately one year into the lease term, Blumenthal told Levine that, due to adverse business conditions generally resulting from the Great Depression, she would be unable to pay the increased rental rate of $200. She asserted that if Levine insisted on the extra $25 a month she would be forced to vacate the premises and perhaps go out of business altogether. Blumenthal later claimed that, as a result, Levine agreed not to demand the increased rent until business improved. Levine, on the other hand, claimed that he agreed to accept the reduced rent "on account." Blumenthal paid rent of $175 for eleven months of the second year of the lease and then vacated the premises without exercising the renewal option.

Levine brought suit to recover the unpaid rent for the last month of the lease and for the unpaid balance of $25 per month for the preceding eleven months. The trial court ruled in favor of Levine, and Blumenthal appealed the judgment.

Heher, Justice

The district court judge found, as a fact, that "a subsequent oral agreement had been made to change and alter the terms of the written lease, with respect to the rent paid," but that it was not supported by "a lawful consideration," and therefore was wholly ineffective.

The insistence is that the current trade depression had disabled the lessees in respect of the payment of the full rent reserved, and a full consideration sufficient to support the secondary agreement arose out of these special circumstances; and that, in any event, the execution of the substituted performance therein provided is a defense of law, notwithstanding the want of consideration. It is said also that, "insofar as the oral agreement has become executed as to the payments which had fallen due and had been paid and accepted in full as per the oral agreement" the remission of the balance of the rent is sustainable on the theory of gift, if not of accord and satisfaction.

The point made by respondent is that the subsequent oral agreement to reduce the rent is nudum pactum, and therefore created no binding obligation.

It is elementary that the subsequent agreement, to impose the obligation of a contract, must rest upon a new and independent consideration. The rule was laid down in very early times that even though a part of a matured liquidated debt or demand has been given and received in full satisfaction thereof, the creditor may yet recover the remainder. The payment of a part was not regarded in law as a satisfaction of the whole, unless it was in virtue of an agreement supported by a consideration. Pinnel's Case, 5 Coke 117, a, 77 Eng. Reprint 237; Foakes v. Beer, 9 App. Cas. 605. The principle is firmly imbedded in our jurisprudence that a promise to do what the promisor is already legally bound to do is an unreal consideration. It has been criticized, at least in some of its special applications, as "mediaeval" and wholly artificial —one that operates to defeat the "reasonable bargains of businessmen." But these strictures are not well grounded. They reject the basic principle that a consideration, to support a contract, consists either of a benefit to the promisor or a detriment to the promisee—a doctrine that has always been fundamental in our conception of consideration. It is a principle, almost universally accepted, that an act or forebearance required by a legal duty owing to the promisor that is neither doubtful nor the subject of honest and reasonable dispute is not a sufficient consideration.

Yet any consideration for the new undertaking, however insignificant, satisfies this rule. Coast National Bank v. Bloom, 113 N.J. Law, 597, 174 A. 576, 578, 95 A.L.R. 528. For instance, an undertaking to pay part of the debt before maturity, or at a place other than where the obligor was legally bound to pay, or to pay in property, regardless of its value, or to effect a composition with creditors by the payment of less than the sum due, has been held to constitute a consideration sufficient in law. The test is whether there is an additional consideration adequate to support an ordinary contract, and consists of something which the debtor was not legally bound to do or give.

And there is authority for the view that, where there is no illegal preference, a payment of part of a debt, "accompanied by an agreement of the debtor to refrain from voluntary bankruptcy," is a sufficient consideration for the creditor's promise to remit the balance of the debt. But the mere fact that the creditor "fears that the debtor will go into bankruptcy, and that the debtor contemplates bankruptcy proceedings," is not enough; that alone does not prove that the creditor requested the debtor to refrain from such proceedings.

The cases to the contrary either create arbitrary exceptions to the rule, or profess to find a consideration in the form of a new undertaking which in essence was not a tangible new obligation or a duty not imposed by the lease, or, in any event, was not the price "bargained for as the exchnge for the promise" (see Coast National Bank v. Bloom, supra), and therefore do violence to the fundamental principle. They exhibit the modern tendency, especially in the matter of rent reductions, to depart from the strictness of the basic common-law rule and give effect to what has been termed a "reasonable" modification of the primary contract.

So tested, the secondary agreement at issue is not supported by a valid consideration; and it therefore created no legal obligation. General economic adversity, however disastrous it may be in its individual consequences, is never a warrant for judicial abrogation of this primary principle of the law of contracts.

It remains to consider the second contention that, in so far as the agreement has been executed by the payment and acceptance of rent at the reduced rate, the substituted performance stands, regardless of the want of consideration. This is likewise untenable. Ordinarily, the actual performance of that which one is legally bound to do stands on the same footing as his promise to do that which he is legally compellable to do. Anson on Contracts (Turck Ed.) p. 234; Williston on Contracts (Rev. Ed.) §§ 130, 130a. This is a corollary of the basic principle. Of course, a different rule prevails where bona fide disputes have arisen respecting the relative rights and duties of the parties to a contract, or the debt or demand is unliquidated, or the contract is wholly executory on both sides. Anson on Contracts (Turck Ed.) pp. 240, 241.

It is settled in this jurisdiction that, as in the case of other contracts, a consideration is essential to the validity of an accord and satisfaction. On reason and principle, it could not be otherwise. This is the general rule. 1 Am. Jur. 235. The cases cited by appellant, are not in point. It results that the issue was correctly determined.

Judgment affirmed with costs.

BARGAINED EXCHANGE

Consideration is a legal detriment incurred as bargained exchange for the promise. A person who receives a promise can incur all kinds of legal detriment, and even much real detriment for good measure, but it will not serve as sufficient consideration unless it is the bargained exchange for the promisor's promise.

Bargain

The requirement that the parties bargain is not so much a requirement that they actually sit down and dicker over the consideration as it is a requirement that the consideration be something that the promisor requested in return for being bound by the promise. An example of an unbargained-for promise is a promise to make a gift. Sometimes a promisor will attach conditions to the making of a gift, things that the promisee must do to accept the gift. A promise to make a gift on condition is not the same as a bargained-for consideration. The critical factor in distinguishing a promise to make a gift on condition from a promise supported by consideration is the motive of the promisor.

Another example of a promise that is not supported by a bargained-for consideration is a promise to do something because of something the promisee has done in the past. Past consideration is no consideration because it was not bargained for in exchange for the promisor's promise. Past consideration cannot be used to support a new promise, because the legal detriment was neither bargained for nor given in exchange for the promise. Because every new contract requires new consideration, past consideration cannot be used to create an enforceable obligation.

The reasoning of the courts in refusing to enforce promises based upon past consideration stems not so much from a lack of legal detriment as from a lack of bargained exchange. The present promise is induced by a past consideration; the past consideration was not given in exchange for the present promise.

Likewise, a promise by one party made to another that is based on only a moral duty generally does not constitute consideration. Technically speaking, if the promisor has received a material benefit that prompts the making of a promise, there is no consideration. For example, if A pulls B from a burning building, saving B's life, and a week later B promises to give A $5,000 "in consideration for saving my life," B's promise is not enforceable because A's conduct was not induced by B's promise.

Many courts have expressed great distaste for this result. Some courts will enforce a promise if there has been a previous material benefit to the promisor that created an extremely compelling moral obligation upon him or her to pay for the benefit received. The few courts that have found liability indicate that the moral obligation to perform the promise supplies the consideration. Consider the following case.

Webb v. McGowin

Court of Appeals of Alabama

168 So. 196 (1935)

In August 1925, Joe Webb was clearing out the upper floor of Mill Number 2 at the W. T. Smith Lumber Company. The ordinary way of clearing the floor was simply to drop materials to the ground below and carry them away. In keeping with this practice, Webb was in the process of dropping a 75-pound pine block from the edge of the upper floor. Just as the block was ready to fall, he noticed J. Greely McGowin on the ground directly beneath the block. Realizing that if the block were to hit McGowin it would probably do him serious harm, or would perhaps kill him, Webb grabbed hold of the block and fell to the ground with it, thereby diverting it from McGowin, who was accordingly uninjured.

Webb, unfortunately, was not so lucky. As a result of the fall he suffered a broken leg, had part of his right heel torn off, and was therefore crippled for life. McGowin, being understandably grateful, promised to care for and maintain Webb at the rate of $15 every two weeks for the rest of Webb's life. McGowin maintained these payments until his own death in 1934, at which time the payments ceased.

Webb brought suit against the executors of McGowin's estate to force reinstatement of the payments. The trial court dismissed the complaint and Webb appealed.

Bricken, Presiding Judge

In other words, the complaint as amended averred in substance: (1) That on August 3, 1925, appellant saved J. Greely McGowin, appellee's testator, from death or grievous bodily harm; (2) that in doing so appellant sustained bodily injury crippling him for life; (3) that in consideration of the services rendered and the injuries received by appellant, McGowin agreed to care for him the remainder of appellant's life, the amount to be paid being $15 every two weeks; (4) that McGowin complied with this agreement until he died on January 1, 1934, and the payments were kept up to January 27, 1934, after which they were discontinued.

The action was for the unpaid installments accruing after January 27, 1934, to the time of the suit.

The averments of the complaint show that appellant saved McGowin from death or grievous bodily harm. This was a material benefit to him of infinitely more value than any financial aid he could have received. Receiving this benefit, McGowin became morally bound to compensate appellant for the services rendered. Recognizing his moral obligation, he expressly agreed to pay appellant as alleged in the complaint and complied with this agreement up to the time of his death; a period of more than 8 years.

Had McGowin been accidentally poisoned and a physician, without his knowledge or request, had administered an antidote, thus saving his life, a subsequent promise by McGowin to pay the physician would have been valid. Likewise, McGowin's agreement as disclosed by the complaint to compensate appellant for saving him from death or grievous bodily injury is valid and enforceable.

Where the promisee cares for, improves, and preserves the property of the promisor, though done without his request, it is sufficient consideration for the promisor's subsequent agreement to pay for the service, because of the material benefit received.

In Boothe v. Fitzpatrick, 36 Vt. 681, the court held that a promise by defendant to pay for the past keeping of a bull which had escaped from defendant's premises and been cared for by plaintiff was valid, although there was no previous request, because the subsequent promise obviated that objection; it being equivalent to a previous request. On the same principle, had the promisee saved the promisor's life or his body from grievous harm, his subsequent promise to pay for the services rendered would have been valid. Such service would have been far more material than caring for his bull. Any holding that saving a man from death or grievous bodily harm is not a material benefit sufficient to uphold a subsequent promise to pay for the service, necessarily rests on the assumption that saving life and preservation of the body from harm have only a sentimental value. The converse of this is true. Life and preservation of the body have material, pecuniary values, measurable in dollars and cents. Because of this, physicians practice their profession charging for services rendered in saving life and curing the body of its ills, and surgeons perform operations. The same is true as to the law of negligence, authorizing the assessment of damages in personal injury cases based upon the extent of the injuries, earnings, and life expectancies of those injured.

In the business of life insurance, the value of a man's life is measured in dollars and cents according to his expectancy, the soundness of his body, and his ability to pay premiums. The same is true as to health and accident insurance.

It follows that if, as alleged in the complaint, appellant saved J. Greely McGowin from death or grievous bodily harm, and McGowin subsequently agreed to pay him for the service rendered, it became a valid and enforceable contract.

It is well settled that a moral obligation is sufficient consideration to support a subsequent promise to pay where the promisor has received a material benefit, although there was no original duty of liability resting on the promisor.

The case at bar is clearly distinguishable from that class of cases where the consideration is a mere moral obligation or conscientious duty unconnected with receipt by promisor of benefits of a material or pecuniary nature. Here the promisor received a material benefit constituting a valid consideration for his promise.

Some authorities hold that, for a moral obligation to support a subsequent promise to pay, there must have existed a prior legal or equitable obligation, which for some reason had become unenforceable, but for which the promisor was still morally bound. This rule, however, is subject to qualification in those cases where the promisor, having received a material benefit from the promisee, is morally bound to compensate him for the services rendered and in consideration of this obligation promises to pay. In such cases the subsequent promise to pay is an affirmance or ratification of the services rendered carrying with it the presumption that a previous request for the service was made.

McGowin's express promise to pay appellant for the services rendered was an affirmance or ratification of what appellant had done raising the presumption that the services had been rendered at McGowin's request.

The averments of the complaint show that in saving McGowin from death or grievous bodily harm, appellant was crippled for life. This was part of the consideration of the contract declared on. McGowin was benefited. Appellant was injured. Benefit to the promisor or injury to the promisee is a sufficient legal consideration for the promisor's agreement to pay.

Under the averments of the complaint the services rendered by appellant were not gratuitous. The agreement of McGowin to pay and the acceptance of payment by appellant conclusively shows the contrary.

Reversed and remanded.

Samford, Judge (concurring)

The questions involved in this case are not free from doubt, and perhaps the strict letter of the rule, as stated by judges, though not always in accord, would bar a recovery by plaintiff, but following the principle announced by Chief Justice Marshall in *Hoffman* v. *Porter,* Fed Cas. No. 6,577, 2 Brock, 156, 159, where he says, "I do not think that law ought to be separated from justice, where it is at most doubtful," I concur in the conclusions reached by the court.

CASE NOTE

Webb is not the prevalent view. Despite its minority status, however, the decision has been adopted by the Restatement (2d) of Contracts. Section 89A of the Restatement (2d) provides:

(1) A promise made in recognition of a benefit previously received by the promisor from the promisee is binding to the extent necessary to prevent injustice.
(2) A promise is not binding under subsection (1)
   (a) if the promisee conferred the benefit as a gift or for other reasons the promisor has not been unjustly enriched; or
   (b) to the extent that its value is disproportionate to the benefit.

The *Webb* decision illustrates a different theory of enforcing promises: the doctrine of moral obligation. Our discussion so far has presented the traditional theory of promise enforcement: the doctrine of consideration, which may be referred to as the *bargain theory of contract* ("a deal is a deal"). The contract as bargain theory holds that to be binding, a promise must be requested. *Webb* cannot be reconciled with the bargain theory. The court's presumption that McGowin's later promise indicated that Webb did the act at McGowin's request is an arbitrary legal fiction. *Webb* brings us face to face with another theory of promise enforcement: the *theory of moral obligation* (succinctly expressed in the child's refrain, "But you promised!").

Should courts enforce a promise simply because the promisor communicated to the promisee an intention to assume an obligation? The *Webb* decision does not go that far. It requires something more than a mere promise. There must be a material benefit to the promisor that prompts the promise. Yet, the case suggests an extension of contract law beyond the bargain theory and suggests an alternative basis for enforcing a promise based on a moral obligation. A contract is viewed not as an obligation arising from a bargain, but as a moral obligation. A justification for the contract as moral obligation theory is that it is normally thought that morality is the arbiter of law, that the law can be justified only if it conforms to morality.

Later in the chapter a third theory of promise enforcement will be presented, the *reliance theory,* which goes under the label of promissory estoppel. Under this theory, promises do not give rise to obligations unless and until they are relied upon.

Exchange

The term "bargained *exchange*" necessarily implies that the legal detriment incurred by the promisee must be induced by the promise and also actually exchanged for the promise. Two parties may sign a written agreement that recites that one party agrees to do something in exchange for the promise of the other party to pay a sum, such as $1 or $10. For example, a promise may be given in exchange for "$1 in hand paid, receipt of which is acknowledged." The statement indicates that the dollar is that which is bargained for and given over in exchange for the promise. Generally, the requirement of consideration is not satisfied by a recital that there is consideration when there is none. If the stated consideration is a pretense, there is no consideration. In most situations, mere recitation that the amount was the bargained-for exchange does not constitute consideration. If there is a nominal consideration, such as the agreement to pay $1 in exchange for a valuable promise, the courts will examine whether that $1 was bargained for and given in exchange for the promise. The dollar must be both (1) bargained for and (2) actually given over in exchange for the promise in order for the promise to be supported by sufficient consideration. A small number of jurisdictions hold that a recital of consideration, if not true, operates as an implied promise to pay the recited sum and that this implied promise satisfies the consideration requirement.

DISSATISFACTION WITH THE REQUIREMENT OF CONSIDERATION: THE EVOLUTION OF PROMISSORY ESTOPPEL

The requirement that a contract must be supported by consideration is part of classic contract law. Up to this point this chapter has attempted to explain the operation and the rationale of the requirement of consideration. However, many courts and scholars have expressed dissatisfaction with the results generated by the requirement of consideration. Legislative dissatisfaction with the consideration doctrine has been expressed in the UCC. As noted in Chapter 6, Section 2-205 provides that a merchant's firm offer cannot be revoked even if consideration is lacking. Furthermore, as discussed earlier in this chapter (p. 179), Section 2-209 eliminates the requirement of consideration for the modification of goods transactions, thereby eliminating problems brought on by the preexisting-duty rule. Finally, in goods transactions, Section 2-306 legitimizes output/requirements agreements that had been suspect as illusory promises. In addition to this legislative reexamination of the consideration requirement, the courts have established a substitute for consideration known as the doctrine of promissory estoppel.

Section 90 of the Restatement (2nd) of Contracts delineates the doctrine of promissory estoppel as follows:

A promise which the promisor should reasonably expect to induce action or forbearance on the part of the promisee or a third person, and which does induce such action or forbearance is binding, if injustice can be avoided only by enforcement of the promise. The remedy granted for breach may be limited as justice requires.

The doctrine permits a remedy based on reliance upon a promise. Under this theory, a promisor will be "estopped" (meaning "made to stop") from denying the existence of the promise where the promisee justifiably relies to his or her detriment upon the promise. Thus a promise that induces detrimental reliance on the part of the promisee may be sufficient to bind the promisor, even though the detriment was not bargained for and given in exchange for the promise, so long as the promisor had reason to expect some act of reliance by the promisee.

Under Section 90, there are four elements that must be established by the promisee. These elements are:

1. A promise. Not just any promise will do. The promise must be the type of promise that the promisor should reasonably expect the promisee will rely upon. The promise must generally be expressed; however, silence may constitute an implied promise where the promisor is under a duty to speak.
2. Justifiable reliance by the promisee upon the promise. The promisee must in fact rely upon the promise. The reliance must be justifiable.
3. Substantial economic detriment. The promisee's reliance must be to the promisee's substantial economic detriment.
4. Injustice can be avoided only by the enforcement of the promise.

As an example of the application of promissory estoppel, consider the case of an employer who promises to pay an employee an annuity for the rest of the employee's life. The employee resigns from a profitable job, as the employer expected the employee would. The employee receives the annuity for several years. In the meantime, the employee becomes disqualified from obtaining employment. Here, the employer's promise would be enforced under the doctrine of promissory estoppel, although it would not constitute a contract supported by consideration. There is no consideration because, although the employer expected that the employee would resign, the employer did not require the employee to resign in exchange for the promised annuity. Now suppose that the employee had been able to regain employment. Under these circumstances the third and fourth elements of promissory estoppel would not be met.

The doctrine of promissory estoppel differs from the requirement of consideration in several ways. First, recovery under promissory estoppel is based upon the reliance of the promisee, even when the reliance is not the bargained exchange for the promise. Second, promissory estoppel requires that the promisee incur substantial *economic* detriment in reliance upon the promise, whereas the requirement of consideration focuses upon the existence of a *legal* detriment. Under the requirement of consideration, courts will not examine generally the economic adequacy of the detriment incurred by the promisee. Under promissory estoppel, however, the promisee must establish that he or she incurred *substantial economic* detriment in reliance upon the promise. Finally, the remedy available to the promisee under promissory estoppel differs from the remedy for breach of a contract supported by consideration. Under promissory estoppel, the promisee is awarded damages only for the amount necessary to compensate the promisee for the economic detriment actually suffered, whereas the promisee who establishes breach of a contract supported by consideration is entitled to the benefit of the bargain. Thus promissory estoppel provides compensation based upon the cost of reliance, whereas the doctrine of consideration provides compensation for a lost expectation.

The following case illustrates the application of promissory estoppel.

Hoffman v. Red Owl Stores

Supreme Court of Wisconsin
133 N.W. 2d 267 (1965)

In 1956, Joseph Hoffman and his wife owned and operated a bakery in Wautoma, Wisconsin. With a desire to expand his operations by establishing a grocery, Hoffman contacted a representative of Red Owl Stores in November 1959 about the possibility of obtaining a Red Owl franchise. As negotiations proceeded over the next two years, Hoffman repeatedly informed Red Owl representatives that he could invest no more than $18,000 in any operation.

To gain experience in grocery store operations, Hoffman bought a small grocery store in Wautoma about Christmas time in 1960. After three months of operations, Red Owl representatives took inventory and examined the books. Finding that the store was being run at a profit, they advised Hoffman to sell the store to his manager and promised him that they would find him a larger store. In reliance on this, Hoffman sold the store, once again reminding Red Owl that he could invest no more than $18,000 in any venture.

In 1961, Red Owl selected a store site for Hoffman in the town of Chilton, and Hoffman made a down payment of $1,000 on the property. In November 1961, Red Owl informed Hoffman that he and his wife would have to sell their bakery before the grocery store deal could be completed, and Hoffman complied with this requirement a short time later. In February 1962, Red Owl presented a balance sheet for the proposed store that showed a capital contribution by Hoffman of $34,000, $13,000 of which was to come from Hoffman's father-in-law as an "absolute gift." Along with various other complaints, Hoffman particularly objected to the requirement that any contribution by his father-in-law be in the form of a gift. At this point negotiations broke down, and Hoffman filed suit seeking to recover as damages the amounts spent by him in reliance on the various promises made by Red Owl representatives.

The trial court entered judgment for the plaintiffs for all but one item of damages. The defendants appealed and plaintiffs cross-appealed.

[The court's discussion of Section 90 of the Restatement of Contracts refers to the first edition of the Restatement. The Restatement was revised in 1979, with minimal change to Section 90.]

Currie, Chief Justice

The instant appeal and cross-appeal present these questions:

(1) Whether this court should recognize causes of action grounded on promissory estoppel as exemplified by sec. 90 of Restatement, 1 Contracts?
(2) Do the facts in this case make out a cause of action for promissory estoppel?
(3) Are the jury's findings with respect to damages sustained by the evidence?

Recognition of a Cause of Action Grounded on Promissory Estoppel
Sec. 90 of Restatement, 1 Contracts, provides (at p. 110):

> "A promise which the promisor should reasonably expect to induce action or forbearance of a definite and substantial character on the part of the promisee and which does induce such action or forbearance is binding if injustice can be avoided only by enforcement of the promise."

Many courts of other jurisdictions have seen fit over the years to adopt the principle of promissory estoppel, and the tendency in that direction continues. As Mr. Justice McFADDIN, speaking in behalf of the Arkansas court, well stated, that the development of the law of promissory estoppel "is an attempt by the courts to keep remedies abreast of increased moral consciousness of honesty and fair representations in all business dealings." Peoples National Bank of Little Rock v. Linebarger Construction Company (1951), 219 Ark. 11, 17, 240 S.W.2d 12, 16.

Because we deem the doctrine of promissory estoppel, as stated in sec. 90 of Restatement, 1 Contracts, is one which supplies a needed tool which courts may employ in a proper case to prevent injustice, we endorse and adopt it.

Applicability of Doctrine to Facts of this Case

The record here discloses a number of promises and assurances given to Hoffman by Lukowitz in behalf of Red Owl upon which plaintiffs relied and acted upon to their detriment.

Foremost were the promises that for the sum of $18,000 Red Owl would establish Hoffman in a store. After Hoffman had sold his grocery store and paid the $1,000 on the Chilton lot, the $18,000 figure was changed to $24,100. Then in November, 1961, Hoffman was assured that if the $24,100 figure were increased by $2,000 the deal would go through. Hoffman was induced to sell his grocery store fixtures and inventory in June, 1961, on the promise that he would be in his new store by fall. In November, plaintiff sold their bakery building on the urging of defendants and on the assurance that this was the last step necessary to have the deal with Red Owl go through.

We determine that there was ample evidence to sustain the answers of the jury to questions of the verdict with respect to the promissory representations made by Red Owl, Hoffman's reliance thereon in the exercise of ordinary care, and his fulfillment of the conditions required of him by the terms of the negotiations had with Red Owl.

There remains for consideration the question of law raised by defendants that agreement was never reached on essential factors necessary to establish a contract between Hoffman and Red Owl. Among these were the size, cost, design, and layout of the store building; and the terms of the lease with respect to rent, maintenance, renewal, and purchase options. This poses the question of whether the promises necessary to sustain a cause of action for promissory estoppel must embrace all essential details of a proposed transaction between promisor and promisee so as to be the equivalent of an offer that would result in a binding contract between the parties if the promisee were to accept the same.

Originally the doctrine of promissory estoppel was invoked as a substitute for consideration rendering a gratuitous promise enforceable as a contract. See Williston, Contracts (1st ed.), p. 307, sec. 139. In other words, the acts of reliance by the promisee to his detriment provided a substitute for consideration. If promissory estoppel were to be limited to only those situations where the promise giving rise to the cause of action must be so definite with respect to all details that a contract would result were the promise supported by consideration, then the defendants' instant promises to Hoffman would not meet this test. However, sec. 90 of Restatement, 1 Contracts, does not impose the requirement that the promise giving rise to the cause of action must be so comprehensive in scope as to meet the requirements of an offer that would ripen into a contract if accepted by the promisee. Rather the conditions imposed are:

(1) Was the promise one which the promisor should reasonably expect to induce action or forbearance of a definite and substantial character on the part of the promisee?

(2) Did the promise induce such action or forbearance?

(3) Can injustice be avoided only by enforcement of the promise?

We deem it would be a mistake to regard an action grounded on promissory estoppel as the equivalent of a breach of contract action. As Dean Boyer points out, it is desirable that fluidity in the application of the concept be maintained. 98 University of Pennsylvania Law Review (1965), 459 at page 497. While the first two of the above listed three requirements of promissory estoppel present issues of fact which ordinarily will be resolved by a jury, the third requirement, that the remedy can only be invoked where necessary to avoid injustice, is one that involves a policy decision by the court. Such a policy decision necessarily embraces an element of discretion.

We conclude that injustice would result here if plaintiffs were not granted some relief because of the failure of defendants to keep their promises which induced plaintiffs to act to their detriment.

DAMAGES

Defendants attack all the items of damages awarded by the jury.

The bakery building at Wautoma was sold at defendants' instigation in order that Hoffman might have the net proceeds available as part of the cash capital he was to invest in the Chilton store venture. The evidence clearly establishes that it was sold at a loss of $2,000. Defendants contend that half of this loss was sustained by Mrs. Hoffman because title stood in joint tenancy. They point out that no dealings took place between her and defendants as all negotiations were had with her husband. Ordinarily only the promisee and not third persons are entitled to enforce the remedy of promissory estoppel against the promisor. However, if the promisor actually foresees, or has reason to foresee, action by a third person in reliance on the promise, it may be quite unjust to refuse to perform the promise. 1A Corbin, Contracts, p. 220, sec. 200. Here not only did defendants foresee that it would be necessary for Mrs. Hoffman to sell her joint interest in the bakery building, but defendants actually requested that this be done. We approve the jury's award of $2,000 damages for the loss incurred by both plaintiffs in this sale.

Defendants attack on two grounds the $1,000 awarded because of Hoffman's payment of that amount on the purchase price of the Chilton lot. The first is that this $1,000 had already been lost at the time the final negotiations with Red Owl fell through in January, 1962, because the remaining $5,000 purchase price had been due on October 15, 1961. The record does not disclose that the lot owner had foreclosed Hoffman's interest in the lot for failure to pay this $5,000. The $1,000 was not paid for the option, but had been paid as part of the purchase price at the time Hoffman elected to exercise the option. This gave him an equity in the lot which could not be legally foreclosed without affording Hoffman an opportunity to pay the balance. The second ground of attack is that the lot may have had a fair market value of $6,000, and Hoffman should have paid the remaining $5,000 of purchase price. We determine that it would be unreasonable to require Hoffman to have invested an additional

$5,000 in order to protect the $1,000 he had paid. Therefore, we find no merit to defendants' attack upon this item of damages.

We also determine it was reasonable for Hoffman to have paid $125 for one month's rent of a home in Chilton after defendants assured him everything would be set when plaintiff sold the bakery building. This was a proper item of damage.

Plaintiffs never moved to Chilton because defendants suggested that Hoffman get some experience by working in a Red Owl store in the Fox River Valley. Plaintiffs, therefore, moved to Neenah instead of Chilton. After moving, Hoffman worked at night in an Appleton bakery but held himself available for work in a Red Owl store. The $140 moving expense would not have been incurred if plaintiff had not sold their bakery building in Wautoma in reliance upon defendants' promises. We consider the $140 moving expense to be a proper item of damage.

We turn now to the damage item with respect to which the trial court granted a new trial, i.e., that arising from the sale of the Wautoma grocery store fixtures and inventory for which the jury awarded $16,735. The trial court ruled that Hoffman could not recover for any loss of future profits for the summer months following the sale on June 6, 1961, but that damages would be limited to the difference between the sales price received and the fair market value of the assets sold, giving consideration to any goodwill attaching thereto by reason of the transfer of a going business. There was no direct evidence presented as to what this fair market value was on June 6, 1961. The evidence did disclose that Hoffman paid $9,000 for the inventory, added $1,500 to it and sold it for $10,000 or a loss of $500. His 1961 federal income tax return showed that the grocery equipment had been purchased for $7,000 and sold for $7,955.96. Plaintiffs introduced evidence of the buyer that during the first eleven weeks of operation of the grocery store his gross sales were $44,000 and his profit was $6,000 or roughly 15 percent. On cross-examination he admitted that this was gross and not net profit. Plaintiffs contend that in a breach of contract action damages may include loss of profits. However, this is not a breach of contract action.

The only relevancy of evidence relating to profits would be with respect to proving the element of goodwill in establishing the fair market value of the grocery inventory and fixtures sold. Therefore, evidence of profits would be admissible to afford a foundation for expert opinion as to fair market value.

Where damages are awarded in promissory estoppel instead of specifically enforcing the promisor's promise, they should be only such as in the opinion of the court are necessary to prevent injustice. Mechanical or rule of thumb approaches to the damage problem should be avoided. In discussing remedies to be applied by courts in promissory estoppel we quote the following on the subject:

> "Enforcement of a promise does not necessarily mean Specific Performance. It does not necessarily mean Damages for breach. Moreover the amount allowed as Damages may be determined by the plaintiff's expenditures or change of position in reliance as well as by the value to him of the promised performance. Restitution is also an 'enforcing' remedy, although it is often said to be based upon some kind of a rescission. In determining what justice requires, the court must remember all of its powers, derived from equity, law merchant, and other sources, as well as the common law. Its decree should be molded accordingly." 1A Corbin, Contracts, p. 221, sec. 200.

"The wrong is not primarily in depriving the plaintiff of the promised reward but in causing the plaintiff to change position to his detriment. It would follow that the damages should not exceed the loss caused by the change of position, which would never be more in amount, but might be less, than the promised reward." Seavey, Reliance on Gratuitous Promises or Other Conduct, 64 Harvard Law Review (1951), 913, 926.

At the time Hoffman bought the equipment and inventory of the small grocery store at Wautoma he did so in order to gain experience in the grocery store business. At that time discussion had already been had with Red Owl representatives that Wautoma might be too small for a Red Owl operation and that a larger city might be more desirable. Thus Hoffman made this purchase more or less as a temporary experiment. Justice does not require that the damages awarded him, because of selling these assets at the behest of defendants, should exceed any actual loss sustained measured by the difference between the sales price and the fair market value.

Since the evidence does not sustain the large award of damages arising from the sale of the Wautoma grocery business, the trial court properly ordered a new trial on this issue.

Order affirmed.

REVIEW PROBLEMS

1. The Boston Redevelopment Authority (BRA), acting under its power of eminent domain, took the buildings owned and operated by the Graphic Arts Finish Company. Graphic's president agreed with BRA that Graphic would receive its "total certified actual moving expenses" from BRA in return for (1) departing the premises peacefully and expeditiously and (2) relocating its business elsewhere and not liquidating. Graphic alleges it performed these promises and demands the $54,069.11 still owed by BRA for moving expenses. Result? Graphic Arts Finish, Inc. v. Boston Redevelopment Authority, 255 N.E. 2d 793 (Sup. Jud. Ct. of Mass. 1970)

2. While Hurley worked for Marine Contractors, he accumulated $12,000 in a retirement trust plan. The plan provided that when an employee left the company for reasons other than disability or retirement at age sixty-five, the employee's share would be held by Marine for five years before distribution to the employee. Marine's president agreed to pay Hurley his $12,000 share immediately if Hurley would not compete with Marine within 100 miles for five years. Hurley agreed and received his money; however, less than a year later Hurley was in active competition with Marine. Was the agreement valid? Marine Contractors Co., Inc. v. Hurley, 310 N.E. 2d 915 (Sup. Jud. Ct. of Mass. 1974)

3. Keen's mother died leaving Keen an interest in property the mother had owned jointly with her husband, Keen's stepfather. Keen agreed not to claim her mother's interest in return for a promise from her stepfather that he would leave the entire property to her upon his death. He died without a will and the state claimed that it was the rightful owner as there had been inadequate consideration in the contract between Keen and her stepfather. Result? Keen v. Larson, 132 N.W.2d 350 (N.D. Sup. Ct. 1964)

4. Sons, Inc., had leased premises from W&T for over three and a half years and wished, contrary to the terms of the lease, to terminate its tenancy. W&T was bound originally by the terms of the lease at least until April 30 of the year following its execution, but it did have the option to terminate after that on ninety days notice to Sons. Sons had no such option, and W&T intended to enforce the lease against it for the full ten-year fixed term. Could Sons terminate? David Roth's Sons, Inc. v. Wright and Taylor, Inc., 343 S.W.2d 389 (Ky. Ct. of App. 1961)

5. The Office of Milk Industry (OMI) of New Jersey established retail milk controls setting minimum prices for gallon and half-gallon containers and prohibiting the giving or lending of anything of value to any customer by a retail establishment. Garden State Farms, a milk dealer, began a program of distributing milk refund certificates to purchasers of milk, authorizing a small refund for each purchase payable "(o)n the day on which retail milk controls . . . are abolished in New Jersey or declared void by the court." Had Garden State violated the regulations? Hoffman v. Garden State Farms, Inc. 184 A.2d 4 (N.J. Sup. Ct. 1962)

6. Gill had performed plumbing work for Black Canyon Construction but had not been paid fully. In October 1971, the stockholders of Black Canyon sold the company and agreed to assume various liabilities the company then had. Gill sued the stockholders in March 1972 for his accumulated debt, but he agreed to dismiss his suit in return for continued work and total payment due.

Gill completed the new work and soon found himself back in court trying to collect his money. The court ruled that he was not a beneficiary of the October sale and could not collect for work done prior to then. Could he enforce the rest of the later agreement? Gill v. Kreutzberg, 537 P.2d 44 (Ariz. Ct. of App. 1975)

7. Carmichael, a shoe store owner, owed International Shoe Company $5,318.92 on open account for shoes sold to him. When his debt had earlier been $12,272.51, Carmichael had agreed to pay International Shoe $8,000 immediately and the balance at $50 a week in return for receipt on account of an additional $2,000 worth of shoes. Carmichael was making payment according to this schedule when suddenly International Shoe Company brought suit for the balance of money owed. Result? International Shoe Company v. Carmichael, 114 So.2d 436 (Fla. D.C. of App. 1959)

8. Stroscio's lease with Jacobs expired on September 1, 1971, but Jacobs gave him an extension of the lease until January 1, 1972, while he negotiated with them for a lease on other property they owned nearby. Following collapse of the negotiations, Jacobs agreed that "in consideration of [p]laintiff's considerable expenditure of time, effort and money, [p]laintiff could remain as tenant at will . . . for such reasonable period of time as [p]laintiff could locate other premises." Stroscio now alleges that Jacobs terminated this lease agreement unreasonably early. Has he any chance of prevailing? Stroscio v. Jacobs, 310 N.E.2d 383 (Mass. App. Ct. 1974)

FOOTNOTE

[1] 9 A.C. 605 (1884).

CHAPTER 9

Genuine Assent

FRAUD _____

DURESS _____

UNDUE INFLUENCE _____

MISTAKE _____

I n the preceding chapters, the elements necessary for the formation of a contract were discussed. Almost all agreements that include those elements will be enforced as contracts. In some situations, however, the elements required for a valid and enforceable contract appear to be present but in reality are not. For example, if a storeowner accepts a gang leader's offer to protect his property from gang violence if he agrees to pay the gang $100 per month, the storeowner is not genuinely assenting to the terms of a contract. Similarly, if a used-car salesperson falsely states that a car has a rebuilt engine and has never been in an accident, the buyer who relies on that information and signs a purchase contract has not genuinely assented. Assent to a contract must be given voluntarily and knowingly by each of the parties; if it is not, there is no genuine assent and thus no contract between them.

This chapter discusses situations involving agreements that lack genuine assent. *Fraud, duress, undue influence,* or even *mistake* may nullify a party's assent to a contract and entitle that party to relief. The relief granted will vary with the circumstances.

FRAUD

A person who has been induced to enter into a contract as a result of fraud will be allowed to cancel or rescind the contract. In addition, since fraud is an intentional tort, the victim of the fraud can sue for damages to compensate for any loss. Punitive damages are also allowed if it can be proved that the intention to commit the fraud was malicious. It is difficult to determine exactly what actions constitute fraud. Literally thousands of acts may be fraudulent. Realizing that it would be impossible to list all possible fraudulent acts, courts have defined fraud in general terms.

The essence of fraud is misrepresentation. One party misrepresents certain facts to the second party, who, relying on the misrepresentations, changes his or her legal position in assenting to enter into a contract. If the party who misrepresents the facts clearly intends the misrepresentation and the resulting deception of the second party, fraud results. On the other hand, a misrepresentation of facts may be unintentional; in that case, there is no fraud. It is important to note, however, that a person who has assented to a contract as a result of a misrepresentation of fact, whether intentional and fraudulent or unintentional and innocent, is allowed to rescind or cancel any contract entered into as a result of the misrepresentation. The difference between the two misrepresentations is that the intentional misrepresentation constituting fraud is also a tort. The victim of such a tort may not only rescind or cancel the contract but can also sue for damages to compensate for any loss incurred. The victim of unintentional misrepresentation has the right only to rescind or cancel the contract; no relief for loss will be granted to that party.

Since fraud requires an intentional misrepresentation of fact, it is difficult to prove. Numerous court rulings have established the elements that must be proven for fraud to exist. Fraud exists where there is:

1. a misrepresentation of a fact
2. that is material
3. that is made with knowledge of its falsity and with intent to deceive the other party
4. who reasonably relies on the misrepresented statement
5. causing injury as a consequence of the reliance

Misrepresentation of Fact

A misrepresentation is active concealment of a material fact or partial disclosure of information represented as the full truth. A misrepresentation may be expressed or implied; it may be made in writing, orally, or through conduct. Silence can constitute a misrepresentation in situations where the law imposes a duty to speak.

Active Concealment of Fact. An active concealment of a fact is the most obvious type of misrepresentation. If the seller of a used car turns back the odometer to conceal the number of miles the car has been driven, fraud has occurred. Of course, an express statement of fact that is a lie also constitutes fraud.

The law holds that the concept of fraud applies to a partially misleading statement as well as to an outright lie. If a company supplies a balance sheet and profit-and-loss statement to a bank from which it seeks to borrow money, and fails to disclose important information about its liabilities or the true nature of its assets, the partial disclosure of the truth constitutes a misrepresentation.

Silence and the Duty to Disclose Information. In order to find a misrepresentation the law generally requires either an affirmative act or an express statement, but on occasion silence may constitute a misrepresentation of fact leading to fraud. In order for silence to be the basis for fraud, the silence must be interpreted as an intentional misrepresentation.

Generally, mere failure to disclose information to the other party does not constitute even an unintentional and innocent misrepresentation because the law does not impose a duty of disclosure.

There are, however, a number of exceptions to this rule. Statutes such as the Truth-in-Lending Act require disclosure regarding finance charges in contracts where money is being lent. Similarly, many jurisdictions recognize an implied warranty, and thus a duty to disclose known defects in the sale of a new house.

Suppose one party knows certain material facts, knows the other party does not know them, and knows that if those facts were known there would be no contract. A prospective seller of land, for example, may know of a hidden defect in the property, one that could not be observed through inspection. If the seller fails to inform the purchaser of the defect, the seller could be held liable for fraud because the silence was intended to mislead the purchaser into assuming there was no defect. The *Sorrell* v. *Young* case exemplifies this type of fraud.

A person in a fiduciary relationship with another must disclose all known information concerning the subject of that special relationship. An agent owes this duty to a principal, a partner owes it to another partner, and an attorney owes it to a client. The disclosure by a physician to a patient of the risk of surgery is a necessary precondition of the patient's ability to consent to the surgery. Silence and nondisclosure in the face of such a duty may be the basis for a finding of fraud.

A Fact Must Be Misrepresented. False statements that are merely opinions cannot be considered the basis for fraud since an opinion is not a fact. Whether a statement is one of fact or opinion is a matter that must be determined in each particular case. In general, an opinion is a statement of one's expectations concerning future events or one's personal beliefs, as indicated in the *Beierle* case. A merchant who sells goods may state that the product will last "a long time" or that the "sale price is reasonable" or that the manufacturer of the goods has "an excellent reputation." Usually, such a statement is known as "puffing" and constitutes a matter of opinion. On the other hand, the car dealer's statement that a used car has been driven only 25,000 miles and was purchased by the present seller from the original owner for $3,000 are statements of fact. Such statements relate to events that either did or did not take place. Their truth or falsity can be proven.

Although statements of opinion are not generally regarded as statements of fact, the opinion of an expert is treated as a statement of fact. When an accountant states that in his or her opinion the books and records of a corporation were kept in a manner consistent with generally accepted accounting procedures he or she speaks as an expert. If there were proof that the accountant actually did not hold that opinion, the statement would constitute a misrepresentation that could be the basis for a finding of fraud.

Materiality

The question of whether a fact is a material fact is determined on a case-to-case basis. The test usually seeks to ascertain whether the person would have entered into a contract if he or she had known of the misrepresentation. The policy of the law is to distinguish between insignificant facts and those that are significant, or material. One cannot simply review a contract with numerous complex clauses, find one minor misrepresentation of fact made by the other party, and then sue for fraud. There is a misrepresentation of a material fact only if the fact in question was one of the important reasons for entering into the contract.

Knowledge of Falsity and Intent to Deceive

The third requirement for fraud is that the misrepresentation of a material fact be made with knowledge of the falsity and with intent to deceive. Knowledge of the falsity and the intent to deceive are often referred to as *scienter*, a Latin word meaning "knowingly." The law does not require proof that the person who committed fraud had an evil or malicious motive. The question is whether that person knew the facts and then misrepresented them. As with other areas of the law in which intent must be determined, a person is deemed to have intended the natural consequences of an action. It is no excuse for the person making a misrepresentation of a material fact to say that he or she did not intend to take advantage of the other party. Nor can a person merely say that he or she did not know the true facts if he or she recklessly disregarded those facts that were available. Knowledge of the facts will be inferred if a person makes a statement with reckless disregard for their truth.

The intent to deceive is found in the intent to create a false impression. Since fraud requires this intent, mere negligence or carelessness cannot constitute fraud. The professional accountant, lawyer, or doctor who fails to disclose certain facts or makes half-true statements is clearly negligent because he or she is not acting as a professional. In order to find fraud, however, the crucial element of scienter also must exist. There must be an active intent to deceive, essentially a cover-up of known facts.

Reliance

The fourth element to be proved in a case of fraud is that the misrepresentation of a material fact that was made knowingly and with intent to deceive was relied upon by the party to whom it was made. A person who does not pay attention to a misrepresented fact, or who conducts his or her own investigation to determine whether a fact is true, is not relying upon what the other party has said or done. In that case, even if there is a misrepresentation of a material fact, since there is no reliance there is no fraud.

Suppose a person acts foolishly in relying on a fraudulent statement. Will the law protect that person? While there is some conflict among court decisions as to what constitutes "unreasonable" reliance, where there is an intentional misrepresentation relief will generally be granted even though the defrauded party was foolish or negligent. In balancing the interests of the foolish person against those of the person intentionally misrepresenting a material fact, the law generally seeks to protect the "victim" of the fraud.

Injury or Damage

The fifth element required to prove fraud is that an injury occurred as a result of the fraud. The party who relied upon a misrepresentation of a material fact that was knowingly and intentionally made must prove that some damage was caused by the fraud. What loss was suffered? If the purchaser of a car relies on a statement that a car has been driven only 30,000 miles and it is later proved to have been driven 60,000 miles, what damage has the purchaser suffered? The basic standard is the difference in value between that which was promised and relied upon and that which in fact was received. If there is no difference, there is no injury; but if there is a difference, the defrauded party will be compensated for the injury suffered. If the fraudulent statement was made maliciously or with extreme carelessness or recklessness, the defrauded party can recover punitive as well as compensatory damages.

Both the cases that follow involve fraud. Analyze which of the required elements of fraud was most closely reviewed in these court decisions. As you examine the cases, consider why it is that each of these elements must be proved. Finally, contemplate other situations in which the court would have to examine the remaining elements needed to prove fraud.

Sorrell v. Young

Court of Appeals of Washington
491 P2d 1312 (1971)

In May 1968, plaintiff Sorrell contracted to buy a lot owned by defendant Young. When he prepared to build a house on the property, Sorrell found that a soil test was needed before he could obtain a building permit. Sorrell's contractor testified that the soil was not stable because a great deal of fill dirt had been added to the lot. The contractor said that it would be necessary to install piling as a foundation for a house and that, even then, there was no certainty that a house could be built. No houses had been built on adjoining property that Young had sold to other purchasers, and at least one other lot owner stated that he had not built on his lot because the cost of soil testing was prohibitive.

Sorrell filed suit against Young seeking to rescind the contract and to recover the money he had already paid to Young, as well as reimbursement for taxes and other expenses. He said Young had misrepresented the property when he told Sorrell "you could build a house on the lot." Furthermore, Young did not tell Sorrell that the lots had been filled.

Young responded that he had purchased the lots in 1960 and that at that time he knew fill dirt had been added to them. He also stated that he added fill dirt himself during the next three years. However, Young did not offer to sell the lots until seven years after he had placed the fill dirt on them, when he considered the lots to be in "good saleable condition." He stated that he could not observe that the land was settling. People who wanted to buy the lots, according to Young, could look at them and then go to the building department and find out if the department considered the land to be in shape to build on.

The trial court found that it was clear that Young had not told Sorrell that the lot had been filled. Further, it was not apparent to Sorrell that the lot had been filled. Finally, the testimony showed that Sorrell had not made any inquiry concerning the existence of the fill dirt and that at the time of purchase he was unaware of it. The trial court found, however, that Sorrell had not met the burden of proving that the contract had been induced by Young's express fraudulent misrepresentation. While there was testimony that Young had stated that "a house could be built on the lot," there was no proof that a house could not in fact be built. Since there was no proof of the "falsity of the misrepresentation" made by Young, the trial court found for the defendant.

The plaintiff appealed to the Court of Appeals, which reversed the trial court's decision.

James, Justice

The plaintiffs contend that the defendants misrepresented the real property in that they contend Mr. Young, the defendant, told them orally that "we could build a house on the lot." The trial court did not find that such a representation was or was not made to the plaintiffs, but found no proof had been offered showing that a house could not be built on said property. Thus, it found the defendants had not misrepresented the property to the plaintiffs.

We are satisfied that the trial judge viewed the evidence too narrowly. A failure to speak when there is a duty to do so may also be fraudulent. The controlling principle is expressed in Restatement of Contracts §472, Comment b (1932):

> A party entering into a bargain is not bound to tell everything he knows to the other party, even if he is aware that the other is ignorant of the facts; and

unilateral mistake, of itself, does not make a transaction voidable (See §503). But if a fact known by one party and not the other is so vital that if the mistake were mutual the contract would be voidable, and the party knowing the fact also knows that the other does not know it, nondisclosure is not privileged and is fraudulent.

The precise question presented here—the right to rescind for nondisclosure of the fact that land was filled—has not confronted a Washington appellate court. Washington's early unqualified adherence to the doctrine of caveat emptor in real estate transactions was relatively short-lived. By the turn of the century, Washington had recognized that "the tendency of the more recent cases has been to restrict rather than extend the doctrine of *caveat emptor."*

We are satisfied that the ruling in Obde v. Schlemeyer, 56 Wash. 2d 449, 353 P2d 672 (1960) has aligned Washington with those jurisdictions which require a seller to disclose the fact that the apartment house he sold was infested with termites. The court noted (1) the infestation was a "manifestly . . . serious and dangerous condition," and (2) the condition was "not readily observable upon reasonable inspection." The court concluded that:

> Under the circumstances, we are satisfied that "justice, equity, and fair dealing," to use Professor Keeton's language, demanded that the Schlemeyers speak—that they inform prospective purchasers, such as the Obdes, of the condition, regardless of the latter's failure to ask any questions relative to the possibility of termites.

Obde's standard for imposing upon a seller a duty to speak—whenever justice, equity, and fair dealing demand it—has been criticized as "possibily difficult of practical application." But the hazards inherent in definitional circumscription were pointed out in American Savings Bank and Trust Co. v. Bremerton Gas Co., 99 Wash. 18, 31, 168, P.775, 780 (1917):

> Fraud is a thing to be described, rather than defined. Deception may find expression in such a variety of ways that most courts have studiously avoided reducing its elements to accurate definition. Human foresight is not sufficiently acute to anticipate the secret and covert methods of the artful and designing or those who endeavor to reap where they have not sown. Once let it be known what the courts consider fraudulent and those engaged in its perpetration will busy themselves in inventing some means of evasion. The courts, therefore, should content themselves with determining from the facts of each case whether fraud does or does not exist. While fraud is not lightly to be inferred, it does not follow that the inference of fraud cannot be gathered from surrounding circumstances, provided they are of sufficient strength and cogency to overcome the presumption of honesty and fair dealing.

We conceive the essential "elements" in proof of fraud by nondisclosure of the existence of a landfill to be: (1) a vendor, knowing that the land has been filled, fails to disclose that fact to the purchaser of the property, and (2) the purchaser is unaware of the existence of the fill because either he has had no opportunity to inspect the property, or the existence of the fill was not apparent or readily ascertainable, and (3) the value of the property is materially affected by the existence of the fill. When these three elements have been proved, a vendor's duty imposed by *Obde*'s general standard of justice, equity, and fair dealing has been violated, and a purchaser of land is entitled to rescind.

Sorrell presented substantial evidence to establish each of the three elements. . . . Young's challenge should have been denied by the trial court and therefore we reverse its decision.

Beierle v. Taylor

Supreme Court of Montana
524 P.2d 783 (1974)

This is an action by the buyers for rescission of a purchase contract on a motel. The complaint alleged fraudulent misrepresentation of the income-producing capability of the motel. The defendant seller suggested that such representations were projections of possible income and thus constituted statements of opinion and not of fact as is required for fraud. The district court of Gallatin county granted summary judgment against the buyers, dismissing their complaint. Buyers appealed to the Supreme Court of Montana, which affirmed the trial court's judgment.

Haswell, Justice

Plaintiffs are Edwin and Agnes Beierle, husband and wife, who bought the Trail-In Motel in West Yellowstone, Montana. Defendants are the sellers, Robert A. Taylor and Wanda K. Taylor, his wife; the real estate agent, United Agencies; and the financing institution, the First National Bank of Bozeman.

Early in 1973, plaintiff Edwin Beierle was contemplating retirement. He was looking for a business he could acquire and make a living. He contacted United, who showed him several business properties.

The Beierles indicated an interest in the Trail-In Motel. United compiled and made available to them a brochure containing a description of the motel; a cost appraisal of the property; an unaudited gross income and expense statement for the years 1969, 1970, and 1971; and an analysis of projected income and expense.

The gross income and expense statements showed net operating losses of approximately $5,000 in 1969; $6,800 in 1970; and $4,600 in 1971.

The analysis of projected income and expense was based on a substantial increase in motel rates, a year-round motel operation by the owners, and an estimated future occupancy rate. The previous motel operation had been essentially a three-month summer operation by an absentee owner.

Several conversations were held between Jack Rosenthal of United and the Beierles. The failure of the motel to make money and the reasons for this were discussed. Rosenthal told Edwin Beierle that he would not be able to make it without outside work for a couple of years until the motel business was built up. The net operating loss statements were not discussed, but were available at the discussion. Copies were not furnished the Beierles.

The Beierles personally inspected the motel property. The asking price was $125,000. Eventually, Beierles purchased the motel property at this price . . . took possession of the motel on May 1, 1973, and have continued to operate it since that time. They have made no monthly installment payments on the note due to the seller.

After the Beierles' default, the entire balance of the note was declared payable. A notice of sale of the motel property was served on the Beierles. Thereafter, Beierles served notice of rescission of the purchase contract followed by a complaint seeking rescission.

The district court granted summary judgment to defendants on the ground that the alleged representations were opinion, not fact. Plaintiff appealed that judgment.

The buyers' principal claim of misrepresentation is found on the projected income figures contained in the brochure. The complaint states:

> ". . . Defendants falsely and fraudulently represented to plaintiffs that said property so exchanged was *capable* of producing an income of Twenty Seven Thousand Six Hundred Forty-eight Dollars . . . ." (Emphasis added).

"Capable" suggests an expression of opinion rather than a statement of fact. Only under unusual circumstances, not present here, can projected future income be considered a fact. Ordinarily future income is but an estimate, subject to the vagaries of the marketplace. It is an opinion, not a guarantee.

A mere expression of opinion, however erroneous, will not warrant rescission of a contract. Although exceptions to this rule exist, none is germane here. Buyers were presented gross income figures for three years which indicated the projected future income was not based on past performance. Buyers were furnished the details of the computation.

Lincoln v. Keane, 51 Wash.2d 171, 316 P.2d 899, 901, states the controlling law here:

> ". . . any statement . . . as to what appellant's future income from the motel would be . . . was a matter of opinion and cannot be the basis of an action for fraud."

The trial court's summary judgment against the buyers is affirmed.

DURESS

A second factor nullifying a party's assent to a contract is duress. Few areas of the law of contracts have undergone such radical changes in the twentieth century as has the law governing duress. Relief from an agreement on the grounds of duress is clearly available if a person is deprived of liberty or property through physical force. Even the threat of physical force, although not carried out, constitutes duress. Yet duress is not limited to these situations.

The essence of duress is lack of free will or

voluntary consent. Any wrongful act or threat that overcomes the free will of the consenting party constitutes duress. Economic coercion, threats to a person's family and loved ones, and other uses of moral or social force to put a person in such fear that his or her act is not voluntary constitute duress.

In determining whether a contract can be avoided on account of duress, it is necessary to ascertain (1) whether the acts or threats were wrongful and (2) whether it was the acts or threats, and not the free will of the party, that induced the required contractual assent.

Duress cannot be limited to the fear that might overcome an ordinary person. If a contracting party, whether brave or timid, is actually coerced into assenting to the contract, duress has occurred. Thus the state of mind of the person who is being threatened must be examined. Did one party involuntarily accept the terms of the other party? Were the circumstances such that there was no practicable alternative? Were those circumstances due to the coercive acts of the other party? Read carefully the *Totem Marine* case, which discusses the requirements of economic duress or business compulsion.

Totem Marine T. & B. v. Alyeska Pipeline, Etc.
584 P.2d 15 (1978)
Supreme Court of Alaska

A contract was made between Totem and Alyeska that required Totem to transport by ship pipeline-construction materials from Texas to a designated port in Alaska. After the contract was made, numerous problems occurred that made it difficult to perform the contract by the required date. Finally, after many difficulties, Alyeska terminated the contract and took the freight off Totem's ship when it was in a California port on its way to Alaska.

Totem then sent Alyeska its invoice for the $260,000–$300,000 in costs and charges it had incurred in its attempt to perform the contract. Totem was in urgent need of cash and was close to bankruptcy. Alyeska delayed making payment and advised Totem it might have to wait months to be paid. Six or seven weeks after Alyeska had terminated the contract, it offered to pay Totem slightly less than $100,000 in exchange for a release by Totem of all claims against Alyeska for further payment.

Totem agreed to the terms, signed the release, and six months later filed suit. It claimed its agreement to accept the partial payment due it and the release of all claims against Alyeska had been made due to the economic duress it was subjected to by Alyeska. Alyeska asserted that, as a matter of law, there was no basis for Totem's claim of economic duress and asked the court to grant a summary judgment in its favor. The trial court agreed with Alyeska and granted its request for a dismissal judgment. Totem appealed to the Alaska Supreme Court. That court reversed the trial court's decision that there was no basis for economic duress asserted by Totem's complaint and remanded the case to the court for trial so that the facts relative to economic duress could be determined.

Burke, Justice

In June of 1975, Totem entered into a contract with Alyeska under which Totem was to transport pipeline construction materials from Houston, Texas, to a designated port in southern Alaska, with the possibility of one or two cargo stops along the way.

By the terms of the contract, Totem was to have completed performance by approximately August 15, 1975. From the start, however, there were numerous problems which impeded Totem's performance of the contract. For example, according to Totem, Alyeska represented that approximately 1,800 to 2,100 tons of regular uncoated pipe were to be loaded in Houston, and that perhaps another 6,000 or 7,000 tons of materials would be put on the barge at later stops along the west coast. Upon the arrival of the tug and barge in Houston, however, Totem found that about 6,700 to 7,200 tons of coated pipe, steel beams and valves, haphazardly and improperly piled, were in the yard to be loaded. This situation called for remodeling of the barge and extra cranes and stevedores, and resulted in the loading taking thirty days rather than the three days which Totem had anticipated it would take to load 2,000 tons. The lengthy loading period was also caused in part by Alyeska's delay in assuring Totem that it would pay for the additional expenses, bad weather and other administrative problems.

The difficulties continued after the tug and barge left Houston. It soon became apparent that the vessels were traveling more slowly than anticipated because of the extra load.

The vessels finally arrived in the vicinity of San Pedro, California, where Totem planned to change crews and refuel. On Alyeska's orders, however, the vessels instead pulled into port at Long Beach, California. At this point, Alyeska's agents commenced off-loading the barge, without Totem's consent, without the necessary load survey, and without a marine survey, the absence of which voided Totem's insurance. After much wrangling and some concessions by Alyeska, the freight was off-loaded. Thereafter, on or about September 14, 1975, Alyeska terminated the contract.

Following termination of the contract, Totem submitted invoices to Alyeska and began pressing the latter for payment. The invoices came to something between $260,000 and $300,000. An official from Alyeska told Totem that they would look over the invoices but that they were not sure when payment would be made—perhaps in a day or perhaps in six to eight months. Totem was in urgent need of cash as the invoices represented debts which the company had incurred on 10–30 day payment schedules. Totem's creditors were demanding payment and without immediate cash, Totem would go bankrupt. Totem then turned over the collection to its attorney, Roy Bell, directing him to advise Alyeska of Totem's financial straits. Thereafter, Bell met with Alyeska officials in Seattle, and after some negotiations, Totem received a settlement offer from Alyeska for $97,500. On November 6, 1975, Totem, through its president Stair, signed an agreement releasing Alyeska from all claims by Totem in exchange for $97,500.

On March 26, 1976, Totem filed a complaint against Alyeska seeking to rescind the settlement and release on the ground of economic duress and to recover the balance allegedly due on the original contract. Alyeska's response asserted that Totem had executed a binding release of all claims against Alyeska and that as a matter of law, Totem could not prevail on its claim of economic duress.

A court's initial task in deciding motions for summary judgment is to determine whether there exist genuine issues of material fact. In order to decide whether such issues exist in this case, we must examine the doctrine allowing avoidance of a release on grounds of economic duress.

This court has not yet decided a claim of economic duress or what is called business compulsion. At early common law, a contract could be avoided on the ground of duress only if a party could show that the agreement was entered into for fear of loss of life or limb, mayhem or imprisonment. The threat had to be such as to overcome the will of a person of ordinary firmness and courage. Subsequently, however, the concept has been broadened to include myriad forms of economic coercion which force a person to involuntarily enter into a particular transaction. The test has come to be whether the will of the person induced by the threat was overcome rather than that of a reasonably firm person.

At the outset, it is helpful to acknowledge the various policy considerations which are involved in cases involving economic duress. Typically, those claiming such coercion are attempting to avoid the consequences of a modification of an original contract or of a settlement and release agreement. On the one hand, courts are reluctant to set aside agreements because of the notion of freedom of contract and because of the desirability of having private dispute resolutions be final. On the other hand, there is an increasing recognition of the law's role in correcting inequitable or unequal exchanges between parties of disproportionate bargaining power and a greater willingness to not enforce agreements which were entered into under coercive circumstances.

Section 492(b) of the *Restatement of Contracts* defines duress as: any wrongful threat of one person by words or other conduct that induces another to enter into a transaction under the influence of such fear as precluded him from exercising free will and judgment, if the threat was intended or should reasonably have been expected to operate as an inducement.

Many courts state the test somewhat differently, eliminating use of the vague term "free will," but retaining the same basic idea. Under this standard, duress exists where: (1) one party involuntarily accepted the terms of another, (2) circumstances permitted no other alternative, and (3) such circumstances were the result of coercive acts of the other party. The third element is further explained as follows:

> In order to substantiate the allegation of economic duress or business compulsion, the plaintiff must go beyond the mere showing of reluctance to accept and of financial embarrassment. There must be a showing of acts on the part of the defendant which produced these two factors. The assertion of duress must be proven by evidence that the duress resulted from defendant's wrongful and oppressive conduct and not by the plaintiff's necessities.

. . . Economic duress does not exist merely because a person has been the victim of a wrongful act; in addition, the victim must have no choice but to agree to the other party's terms or face serious financial hardship. Thus, in order to avoid a contract, a party must also show that he had no reasonable alternative to agreeing to the other party's terms, or as it is often stated, that he had no adequate remedy if the threat were to be carried out. . . . An available alternative or remedy may not be adequate where the delay involved in pursuing that remedy would cause immediate and irreparable loss to one's economic or business interest.

Professor Dalzell, in *Duress by Economic Pressure II,* 20 N. Carolina L. Rev. 340, 370 (1942), notes the following with regard to the adequacy of legal remedies where one party refuses to pay a contract claim:

> Nowadays, a wait of even a few weeks in collecting on a contract claim is sometimes serious or fatal for an enterprise at a crisis in its history. The business of a creditor in financial straits is at the mercy of an unscrupulous debtor, who need only suggest that if the creditor does not care to settle on the debtor's own hard terms, he can sue. This situation, in which promptness in payment is vastly more important than even approximate justice in the settlement terms, is too common in modern business relations to be ignored by society and the courts.

Turning to the instant case, we believe that Totem's allegations, if proved, would support a finding that it executed a release of its contract claims against Alyeska under economic duress. Totem has alleged that Alyeska deliberately withheld payment of an acknowledged debt, knowing that Totem had no choice but to accept an inadequate sum in settlement of that debt; that Totem was faced with impending bankruptcy; that Totem was unable to meet its pressing debts other than by accepting the immediate cash payment offered by Alyeska; and that through necessity, Totem thus involuntarily accepted an inadequate settlement offer from Alyeska and executed a release of all claims under the contract. If the release was in fact executed under these circumstances, we think that under the legal principles discussed above that this would constitute the type of wrongful conduct and lack of alternatives that would render the release voidable by Totem on the ground of economic duress. . . . Therefore, we hold that the superior court erred in granting summary judgment for appellant and remand the case to the superior court for trial in accordance with the legal principles set forth above.

UNDUE INFLUENCE

Undue influence exists when one person exercises mental coercion over another. The cases frequently involve an elderly, sick, and senile person as the coerced victim of another person's undue influence. The essence of undue influence is that the influenced person's own judgment and free will are subjected to those of the dominating person. Thus the assent given by the influenced person is not that person's genuine assent.

In examining a case involving undue influence, the courts usually follow a two-step approach. First, they seek to determine if there has been a dominant-subservient relationship between the two parties. For example, certain fiduciary relationships, such as those between attorney and client, banker and customer, and doctor and patient, involve a high degree of trust by one party in the other. Second, once the relationship is determined to have been one in which one party could by his or her influence dominate the other, the courts shift the presumption of lack of undue influence to a presumption that such undue influence did exist when a contract between the two benefited the dominant party. Unless the dominant party can then prove a lack of undue influence, the subservient party is allowed to avoid the contract. The following case raises questions not only about undue influence but also about fraud and duress. Note that those issues often are interrelated.

Odorizzi v. Bloomfield School District

California Court of Appeals

54 Cal.Rptr. 533 (1966)

Plaintiff Donald Odorizzi was employed during 1964 as an elementary school teacher by defendant Bloomfield School District and was under contract with the district to continue to teach school the following year as a permanent employee. On June 10, he was arrested on criminal charges and on June 11 he signed and delivered to his superiors his written resignation as a teacher, which the district accepted on June 13. In July, the criminal charges against Odorizzi were dismissed and in September he sought to resume his employment with the district. On the district's refusal to reinstate him, he filed suit asserting that his resignation was invalid because he lacked the capacity to make a valid contract.

Odorizzi asserted that his resignation was invalid because it was obtained through duress, fraud, mistake, and undue influence. Specifically, Odorizzi declared that he had been under such severe mental and emotional strain at the time he signed his resignation, having just completed the process of arrest, questioning by the police, booking, and release on bail, and having gone for forty hours without sleep, that he was incapable of rational thought or action.

While he was in this condition and unable to think clearly, the superintendent of the district and the principal of his school came to his apartment. They said that they were trying to help him and had his best interests at heart, that he should take their advice and immediately resign his position with the district, that there was no time to consult an attorney, that if he did not resign immediately the district would suspend and dismiss him from his position and publicize the proceedings, his "aforedescribed arrest," and cause him "to suffer extreme embarrassment and humiliation"; but that if he resigned at once, the incident would not be publicized and would not jeopardize his chances of securing employment as a teacher elsewhere. Odorizzi pleaded that because of his faith and confidence in their representations they were able to substitute their will and judgment for his own and thus obtain his signature to his purported resignation. The trial court dismissed the complaint and Odorizzi appealed. On appeal, the court found the facts were not sufficient to find duress, fraud, or mistake. However, it found the facts sufficient to allow Odorizzi to rescind his contract because of undue influence; accordingly, it reversed the trial court's judgment.

Fleming, Justice

Duress consists in unlawful confinement of another's person, or relatives, or property, which causes him to consent to a transaction through fear. Duress is often used interchangeably with menace, but in California menace is technically a threat of duress or a threat of injury to the person, property, or character of another. We agree with respondent's contention that neither duress nor menace was involved in this case, because the action is not unlawful unless the party making the threat knows the falsity of his claim. The amended complaint shows in substance that the school representatives announced their intention to initiate suspension and dismissal proceedings at a time when the filing of such proceedings was not only their legal right but their positive duty as school officials. Although the filing of such proceedings might be extremely damaging to plaintiff's reputation, the injury would remain incidental so long as the school officials acted in good faith in the performance of their duties. Neither duress nor menace was present as a ground for rescission.

Nor do we find a cause for fraud, either actual or constructive. Actual fraud involves conscious misrepresentation, or concealment, or non-disclosure of a material fact which induces the innocent party to enter the contract. A complaint for fraud must plead misrepresentation, knowledge of falsity, intent to induce reliance, justifiable reliance, and resulting damage. While the amended complaint charged misrepresentation, it failed to assert the elements of knowledge of falsity, intent to induce reliance, justifiable reliance, and resulting damage. A cause of action for actual fraud was therefore not stated.

Constructive fraud arises on a breach of duty by one in a confidential or fiduciary relationship to another which induces justifiable reliance by the latter to his prejudice. Plaintiff has attempted to bring himself within this category. . . . Plaintiff, however, sets forth no facts to support his conclusion of a confidential relationship between the representatives of the school district and himself, other than that the parties bore the relationship of employer and employee to each other. Under prevailing judicial opinion no presumption of a confidential relationship arises from the bare fact that parties to a contract are employer and employee; rather, additional ties must be brought out in order to create the presumption of a confidential relationship between the two. The absence of a confidential relationship between employer and employee is especially apparent where, as here, the parties were negotiating to bring about a termination of their relationship. In such a situation each party is expected to look after his own interests, and a lack of confidentiality is implicit in the subject matter of their dealings. We think the allegations of constructive fraud were inadequate.

However, the pleading does set out a claim that plaintiff's consent to the transaction had been obtained through the use of undue influence.

Undue influence, in the sense we are concerned with here, is a shorthand legal phrase used to describe persuasion which tends to be coercive in nature, persuasion which overcomes the will without convincing the judgment. The hallmark of such persuasion is high pressure, a pressure which works on mental, moral, or emotional weakness to such an extent that it approaches the boundaries of coercion. In this sense, undue influence has been called overpersuasion.

Misrepresentations of law or fact are not essential to the charge, for a person's will may be overborne without misrepresentation. In essence, undue influence involves the use of excessive pressure to persuade one vulnerable to such pressure, pressure applied by a dominant subject to a servient object. In combination, the elements of undue susceptibility in the servient person and excessive pressure by the dominating person makes the latter's influence undue, for it results in the apparent will of the servient person being in fact the will of the dominant person.

Undue susceptibility may consist of total weakness of mind which leaves a person entirely without understanding or, a lesser weakness which destroys the capacity of a person to make a contract even though he is not totally incapacitated; or, the first element in our equation, a still lesser weakness which provides sufficient grounds to rescind a contract for undue influence. . . . The reported cases have usually involved elderly, sick, senile persons alleged to have executed wills or deeds under pressure. In some of its aspects this lesser weakness could perhaps be called weakness of spirit. But whatever name we give it, this first element of undue influence resolves itself into a lessened capacity of the object to make a free contract.

In the present case plaintiff has pleaded that such weakness at the time he signed his resignation prevented him from freely and competently applying his judgment to the problem before him. Plaintiff declares he was under severe mental and emotional strain at the time because he had just completed the process of arrest, questioning, booking, and release on bail and had been without sleep for forty hours. It is possible that exhaustion and emotional turmoil may wholly incapacitate a person from exercising his judgment.

Undue influence in its second aspect involves an application of excessive strength by a dominant subject against a servient object. Judicial consideration of this second element in undue influence has been relatively rare, for there are few cases denying persons who persuade but do not misrepresent the benefit of their bargain. Yet logically, the same legal consequences should apply to the results of excessive strength as to the results of undue weakness. Whether from weakness on one side, or strength on the other, or a combination of the two, undue influence occurs whenever there results that kind of influence or supremacy of one mind over another by which that other is prevented from acting according to his own wish or judgment, and whereby the will of the person is overborne and he is induced to do or forbear to do an act which he would not do, or would do, if left to act freely. Undue influence involves a type of mismatch which our statute calls unfair advantage. Whether a person of subnormal capacities has been subjected to ordinary force or a person of normal capacities subjected to extraordinary force, the match is equally out of balance. If will has been overcome against judgment, consent may be rescinded.

The difficulty, of course, lies in determining when the forces of persuasion have overflowed their normal banks and become oppressive flood waters. There are second thoughts to every bargain, and hindsight is still better than foresight. Undue influence cannot be used as a pretext to avoid bad bargains or escape from bargains which refuse to come up to expectations. A woman who buys a dress on impulse, which on critical inspection by her best friend turns out to be less fashionable than she had thought, is not legally entitled to set aside the sale on the ground that the saleswoman used all her wiles to close the sale. A man who buys a tract of desert land in the expectation that it is in the immediate path of the city's growth and will become another Palm Springs, an expectation cultivated in glowing terms by the seller, cannot rescind his bargain when things turn out differently. If we are temporarily persuaded against our better judgment to do something about which we later have second thoughts, we must abide the consequences of the risks inherent in managing our own affairs.

However, overpersuasion is generally accompanied by certain characteristics which tend to create a pattern. The pattern usually involves several of the following elements: (1) discussion of the transaction at an unusual or inappropriate time, (2) consummation of the transaction in an unusual place, (3) insistent demand that the business be finished at once, (4) extreme emphasis on untoward consequences of delay, (5) the use of multiple persuaders by the dominant side against a single servient party, (6) absence of third-party advisers to the servient party, (7) statements that there is no time to consult financial advisers or attorneys. If a number of these elements are simultaneously present, the persuasion may be characterized as excessive. . . .

The difference between legitimate persuasion and excessive pressure, like the difference between seduction and rape, rests to a considerable extent in the manner in which the parties go about their business. For example, if a day or two after Odorizzi's release on bail the superintendent of the school district had called him into his office during business hours and directed his attention to those provisions of the Education Code compelling his leave of absence and authorizing his suspension on the filing of written charges, had told him that the District contemplated filing written charges against him, had pointed out the alternative of resignation available to him, had informed him he was free to consult counsel or any adviser he wished and to consider the matter overnight and return with his decision the next day, it is extremely unlikely that any complaint about the use of excessive pressure could ever have been made against the school district.

But, according to the allegations of the complaint, this is not the way it happened, and if it had happened that way, plaintiff would never have resigned. Rather, the representatives of the school board undertook to achieve their objective by overpersuasion and imposition to secure plaintiff's signature but not his consent to his resignation through a high-pressure carrot-and-stick technique—under which they assured plaintiff they were trying to assist him, he should rely on their advice, there wasn't time to consult an attorney, if he didn't resign at once the school district would suspend and dismiss him from his position and publicize the proceedings, but if he did resign the incident wouldn't jeopardize his chances of securing a teaching post elsewhere.

Plaintiff has thus pleaded both subjective and objective elements entering the undue influence equation and stated sufficient facts to put in issue the question whether his free will had been overborne by defendant's agents at a time when he was unable to function in a normal manner.

The question cannot be resolved by an analysis of pleading but requires a finding of fact.

We express no opinion on the merits of plaintiff's case, or the propriety of his continuing to teach school, or the timeliness of his rescission. We do hold that his pleading, liberally construed, states a cause of action for rescission of a transaction to which his apparent consent had been obtained through the use of undue influence.

Reversed.

MISTAKE

Mistake is generally defined as a state of mind not in accord with the facts.[1] The term mistake, when used in contract law, refers to a mental attitude coupled with an act having legal significance (such as the execution of a contract).[2] There are many different kinds of mistakes that can be made by parties to a contract. They can make a mistake in the performance or execution of the contract. One party can make a mistake in judgment; another can make a mistaken assumption concerning the subject matter of the contract. Mistakes in typing a written contract can occur, as can mistakes concerning the presumed legality or tax effect of a particular transaction. In most situations in which mistakes are made, the law grants no relief to the mistaken party. If legal relief is to be given when a mistake has occurred, a number of factors must be examined.

The legal significance of any mistake must be determined by answering several questions. Among these are the following:[3]

1. Did one or both parties have a mistaken thought?
2. Did the mistake induce a mutual expression of agreement or merely induce action by one party?
3. Should one or both parties have had reason to know of the mistake?
4. Was the fact as to which a mistake occurred of substantial importance and one that was not part of the risk assumed by either of the parties?

These questions seek to determine not only who made the mistake but also what kind of mistake was made and what effect it had on the contract. Did both parties make a mistake that induced action by only one party, or did one party make a mistake that induced action by both parties? Was it a serious mistake? If a serious mistake was made by one party, does that mean that the other party should have known of the mistake? If a mistake was made by both parties to a contract, it is referred to as a bilateral mistake. If only one of the parties was mistaken, then a unilateral mistake occurred.

Bilateral Mistake

There are several contexts in which contracting parties can make bilateral mistakes. Both parties can make a mistake concerning an important material fact on which the contract is based. Typical cases involving such mistakes are those in which the subject matter of the contract has, unknown to both parties, been destroyed prior to the agreement of the parties. Suppose you agreed to buy my lakefront summer cottage in northern Michigan and I agreed to sell it. We decided to enter into a contract for purchase and sale on our return from the cottage to the city. However, unknown to us, before we got there, a fire destroyed the cottage. Mistakenly believing the cottage was still standing, we contracted for its purchase and sale. Our mistake was a bilateral mistake of an important material fact; we both believed that the cottage still existed. When a bilateral mistake concerning the subject matter of the contract occurs, the courts grant relief to the parties and allow the contract to be rescinded. It was not the fault of either party that their assumptions were mistaken. If the parties actually had known the true facts, they would not have entered into their contract.

Bilateral mistakes may also occur if there is some ambiguity in the terms of the contract and each party interprets the ambiguous terms differently. In the *Volpe* case, presented below, the partners were mistaken concerning one of the provisions of their partnership agreement. The mistake concerned whether their individual franchises were to have been contributed to the partnership as partnership assets. Since the judge found that one of the parties thought the franchises were to have been contributed by each of the parties, while the other party believed the franchises were not to have been contributed to the partnership, the parties really did not agree on the terms for the partnership. While each had a different understanding, each mistakenly assumed that its understanding of the terms for the franchises was also the understanding of the other party.

Volpe v. Schlobohm

614 S.W.2d 615 (1981)
Court of Civil Appeals of Texas

Charles H. and Joneen Lou Schlobohm brought suit against Robert M. Volpe, seeking rescission of a partnership agreement. The partnership was originally composed of the Schlobohms, Volpe, and Edward R. Wright. Wright withdrew from the partnership before the suit was filed and was not a party. Volpe answered and counterclaimed, seeking dissolution, accounting, damages, and other relief.

In a nonjury trial the court ruled in favor of the Schlobohms, finding that the partnership agreement could be rescinded because of mistakes made by the parties. All partnership assets were awarded to the Schlobohms except for $54,083.60 awarded to Volpe as the stipulated value of his 30 percent interest in the partnership in the event rescission was found to be proper. Volpe appealed that judgment. The trial court's decision was affirmed by the appellate court.

Cornelius, Chief Justice

The Schlobohms have been engaged in the food distributing business in Dallas since 1966. Prior to February 1, 1978, they operated a proprietorship which consisted of various distributorships with companies in the prepared food business. Volpe became associated with the Schlobohms as a jobber on June 10 of 1972. On January 28, 1978, the Schlobohms, Volpe and Wright met to discuss the formation of a partnership. Mrs. Schlobohm made notes of the discussions which later formed the basis of a written partnership agreement. The agreement was accepted and agreed to by all parties on February 1, 1978, although it was never signed.

At the commencement of the partnership, Charles Schlobohm was a franchisee of Pepperidge Farms, Volpe was a franchisee of Stella D'Oro, and Wright was a franchisee of Pepperidge Farms. The Schlobohms testified that their Pepperidge Farms franchise was to be excluded from the partnership. Wright also testified that neither of the Pepperidge Farms franchises was to be contributed as a partnership asset. However, the revenues from these franchises were deposited in the partnership account and were divided among the partners according to their percentage interests in the firm. Mr. Volpe testified that he understood that the Pepperidge Farms franchises were to be contributed as partnership assets and that he also understood that he was contributing his Stella D'Oro franchise.

In June of 1978, some four months after the creation of the partnership, Wright withdrew, taking his Pepperidge Farms franchise with him. His interest in the partnership was purchased by the Schlobohms with their own funds. Volpe testified that he was not given the opportunity to purchase his pro rata share of Wright's interest; the Schlobohms asserted that he was given the opportunity but declined to do so because they would not agree to his use of partnership funds to purchase his proportionate interest. Volpe did, however, insist that he was entitled to his proportionate share of Wright's profits and partnership assets; and ultimately this disagreement and the misunderstanding concerning the contribution of the Pepperidge Farms franchises as partnership assets resulted in a deterioration of the relationships between the Schlobohms and Volpe and gave rise to this suit.

At the trial, the Schlobohms asserted that there was a mutual mistake related to the question of whether the Pepperidge Farms franchises were partnership assets, and it was that mistake which should form the basis for the court's grant of rescission. Both sides presented testimony without objection regarding their understandings as to the inclusion of the Pepperidge Farms franchises in the partnership. The trial court's judgment granting a rescission due to the parties' mistake was appealed.

We also conclude that there was sufficient evidence to justify the granting of rescission, although we disagree with the trial court as to the proper legal basis for its action.

A partnership agreement, like any other agreement or relationship, may be rescinded when proper grounds exist. Rescission may be authorized either because of a mutual [bilateral] mistake of the parties, or because of a unilateral mistake if the elements of remediable mistake are present. Although the trial court here based its judgment on remediable mistake, characterizing the misunderstanding about the franchises as a unilateral mistake, the facts found by the trial court actually reveal a mutual mistake of a type which will warrant rescission.

Ordinarily a mutual mistake sufficient to justify rescission exists when both of the parties are laboring under the same misconception as to a common fact, as when the parties know what they have agreed to, but through their common mistake the expression of their contract fails to correctly state that agreement, or when the parties contract on the assumption of a matter material to the contract but not expressed in it, and their common assumption is incorrect. But the mutual mistakes need not be identical. If they relate to the same matter, equitable relief is available even though the mistakes of the parties as to that fact are not the same. Rescission may be granted when there is a mistake of this kind which results in the parties' never having reached a meeting of the minds and thus prevents, ab initio, the formulation of a valid contract.

Examples of this type of mistake are found in cases in which the parties, when attempting to formulate their agreement, were laboring under different conceptions as to the subject matter of the agreement, or as to the identity, character or quantity of a matter or thing with reference to which they were attempting to contract. When one party understands that he is contracting on one set of terms and the other understands that he is contracting on another set of terms, there is no contract unless the circumstances are such as preclude one of the parties from denying that he agreed to the terms set by the other. Of course, this type of mistake will justify relief only if the expression or writing evidencing the purported agreement is uncertain and ambiguous, for if there is no ambiguity with respect to the written or oral expression of the terms neither party will be heard to say that, by his subjective intent, he meant something different from what was actually expressed.

The written partnership agreement involved in this case makes no specific provision concerning whether or not the parties' franchises would be contributed to the firm as partnership assets, and the agreement as a whole is unclear as to whether the franchises were or were not to be included. On the basis of the testimony the trial judge concluded that the franchises were not to be contributed as partnership assets, but he also found that the parties were laboring under opposite understandings with reference to that issue—the Schlobohms thinking that they were not to become partnership assets and Volpe thinking that they were—and that there was no meeting of the minds of the parties on that material issue. Rescission is a proper remedy in such a situation, provided it is possible to restore the contracting parties to their original positions, and provided the rights of innocent third parties have not otherwise intervened.

The trial court rendered judgment in accordance with the parties' stipulation of what their recovery would be in the event rescission was proper. As we have concluded, that rescission was proper.

Affirmed.

Unilateral Mistake

A unilateral mistake is a mistake made by only one of the contracting parties. If one party makes a careless or negligent mistake in negotiating or in performing a contract, the law generally will not grant that party relief from the mistake. There are, however, several exceptions to this rule. Even when a mistake is made by only one party, courts generally grant relief if refusing to do so would impose undue hardship or expense on the mistaken party. In other words, the courts seek to balance the scales of justice. In doing so, the courts examine the relative consequences to both parties of a decision to grant or deny relief for a unilateral mistake. What is the burden that will be imposed on the other party if relief is granted to the mistaken party? What is the hardship suffered by the mistaken party if no relief is granted? Either a slight burden on the innocent party or a great burden on the mistaken party generally will be grounds for granting relief even where only one party has made a mistake.

Knowledge of Mistake

If a mistake was made by only one of the contracting parties, but the other party knew or should have known of the mistake, the courts generally will not allow the other party to take advantage of the mistake by enforcing the contract. Suppose several contractors were asked to submit bids for construction work on a hospital addition and the bid submitted by one of the contractors was significantly lower than all the other bids. If the bid was lower due to the contractor's unilateral mistake in calculation and the error was so great that the hospital to which the bid was submitted had reason to know of the mistake prior to its acceptance of the contractor's bid, the contractor would be granted relief from the obligation. The *McGough* case presented below exemplifies this type of mistake.

Another type of unilateral mistake is one concerning a person's identity. We have seen in the chapters on offer and acceptance that an offer may be accepted only by the person to whom it is made. But what if the offeror receives an acceptance from one whom he mistakenly believes to be the offeree? If offeror A intends to deal only with party B, but party C accepts the offer, there is no contract between C and A even if A mistakenly believes that party C is party B. A's mistake in identifying party C as party B is a unilateral mistake about which party C knew or should have known. Party C never received an offer from A and thus must have known that A was mistaken in identifying C as a person who could accept his offer.

A mistake as to the identity of a person can also be made as a result of fraud. A person can forge identification papers and pass as someone else. Such a situation would be a combination of fraud and mistake. Consequently, there would be double reason to allow the person who was both the victim of fraud and the party who had made a unilateral mistake that was known to the other party to avoid the contract.

However, if a person makes an offer to someone who occupies a certain capacity—for example, the manager of the ABC store—any person who is in that capacity can accept it. If, unknown to the offeror, a new manager has been appointed, the offeror cannot plead mistake because he thought his friend, the former manager, was still there. In this case, the offer is made to any person in the position, not to the individual who was mistakenly thought to be there. There is no mistaken identity in this situation, only a mistaken assumption.

M. J. McGough Company v. Jane Lamb Memorial Hospital
United States District Court S. D. Iowa
302 F.Supp. 482 (1969)

McGough, a contractor, filed a complaint seeking to have its bid declared rescinded and its surety released from liability on bond. The hospital that received the bid filed suit to recover damages for the contractor's refusal to execute the contract and other documents in accordance with the original bid. Upon a consolidated trial of the cases, the District Court held that the contractor was entitled to have its bid rescinded and its surety released from liability on bond, since because of a clerical error, the bid was low by $199,800, or approximately 10 percent of the bid. Accordingly, the Court entered a judgment for the contractor McGough.

Stephenson, Chief Judge

This action arises out of two separate cases filed on April 11, 1968, and consolidated for trial. Jurisdiction exists by reason of diversity and requisite amount in controversy.

The controversy herein arises from the competitive bidding on a hospital improvement proposed by Jane Lamb Memorial Hospital, a nonprofit Iowa corporation. On or about January 1, 1968, the hospital published an invitation for bids on this improvement. M. J. McGough Company, a Minnesota corporation accepted said invitation and submitted a bid along with a bid bond from the Continental Insurance Company. The bid of M. J. McGough was submitted shortly before the opening time of 2:00 P.M., on February 16, 1968. The bids were opened by the Chairman of the Board of Trustees of Jane Lamb Memorial Hospital, Mr. Clark Depue III, at 2:00 P.M., and recorded as follows:

M. J. McGough Co., St. Paul	$1,957,000
Knutson Construction Co., Minneapolis	2,123,643
Steenberg Construction Co., St. Paul	2,185,000
Rinderknecht Construction Co., Cedar Rapids	2,264,000
O. Jorgenson & Sons Construction Co., Clinton	2,322,064
Lovering Construction Co., St. Paul	2,326,380
Universal Construction Co., Kansas City, Mo.	2,500,000
Ringland-Johnson-Crowley Co., Inc., Clinton	2,577,837
Priester Construction Co., Davenport	2,611,000

These figures were relayed to Mr. J. H. McGough, President of M. J. McGough Company, by a representative present at the opening. Mr. McGough was immediately concerned over the ten percent (10%) difference between his low bid and the next lowest bid of Knutson Construction Company. (By his testimony at trial, Mr. McGough explained that Knutson Construction Company was known in the trade as a notoriously low bidder.) Feeling a serious mistake had been made in the compilation of his bid, Mr. McGough called his representative at the opening and instructed him to request that he be allowed to withdraw his bid. This request was transmitted to Mr. Depue at approximately 2:45 P.M., while the Board was still analyzing the bids received. Shortly thereafter, Mr. McGough spoke with Mr. Depue by telephone and Mr. Depue requested a letter explaining the circumstances of the mistake and a written request to withdraw. Mr. McGough and his staff then began checking the papers relating to this bid and discovered an error in the amount of $199,800. The circumstances surrounding the error were set out in a letter dated February 16, 1968, directed to Milton Holmgrain, the hospital administrator. In the letter, McGough offered to "submit to you immediately all of our records relating to this project for verification of this error." In spite of this, the Board of Trustees, without further communication with M. J. McGough Company, at its meeting on February 22, 1968, passed a "Resolution of Intent" to the effect that the Board intended to accept the bid of M. J. McGough Company subject to obtaining the approval of the Division of Hospital Services of the Iowa State Department of Health and the U. S. Public Health Service.

Thereafter, the parties communicated a number of times by telephone, letter and in person on the matter. At all times, M. J. McGough Company sought the withdrawal of its bid and offered to produce its papers to verify the error in its bid. Likewise, the representatives of Jane Lamb Memorial Hospital continuously sought to hold M. J. McGough Company to its original bid. Upon the refusal of M. J. McGough Company to execute the contract and other necessary documents, however, the contract was awarded to the next lowest bidder, Knutson Construction Company.

On April 11, 1968, M. J. McGough Company filed a complaint in this Court seeking to have its bid declared rescinded and the surety, The Continental Insurance Company, be released from liability on the bond. On that same date, Jane Lamb Memorial Hospital filed a complaint in this Court against M. J. McGough Company and the Continental Insurance Company seeking damages in the amount of $190,156.58. (Jane Lamb Memorial Hospital arrived at this amount by adding the difference ($179,393) between the M. J. McGough Company bid and the Knutson Construction

Company bid, plus the amount of increased architect's fees ($10,763.58), which are based on a percentage of the total price.)

The circumstances surrounding the mistake in the bid of M. J. McGough Company are not seriously disputed. The majority of the subcontractor bids used in computing the bid of M. J. McGough Company were received on February 16, 1968, the day of the opening. It is the accepted practice and custom among subcontractors to refrain from submitting their final sub-bids until the day of the opening and, then, only within a matter of hours before the actual opening of bids. The final sub-bids were received by telephone in the offices of M. J. McGough Company in St. Paul, Minnesota, between 10:00 A.M. and 1:00 P.M. on February 16, 1968. The sub-bids were recorded as they were phoned in on a slip of paper. Mr. McGough received the sub-bid of Artcraft Interiors, Inc., during this period of frenzied activity, and although he correctly recorded it on the slip of paper as $222,000, he verbally called it to an employee who recorded it as $22,200. This erroneous figure was, subsequently, transposed by the employee on the recapitulation sheet and used in computing the final bid of M. J. McGough Company. It was not until after the opening of bids, when Mr. McGough sought to check their figures, that the mistake was discovered.

By the overwhelming weight of authority a contractor may be relieved from a unilateral mistake in his bid by rescission under the proper circumstances. The prerequisites for obtaining such relief are: (1) the mistake is of such consequence that enforcement would be unconscionable; (2) the mistake must relate to the substance of the consideration; (3) the mistake must have occurred regardless of the exercise of ordinary care; (4) it must be possible to place the other party in status quo.

Applying the criteria for rescission for a unilateral mistake to the circumstances in this case, it is clear that M. J. McGough Company and his surety, the Continental Insurance Company, are entitled to equitable relief. The notification of mistake was promptly made, and Mr. McGough made every possible effort to explain the circumstances of the mistake to the authorities of Jane Lamb Memorial Hospital. Although Jane Lamb Memorial Hospital argues to the contrary, the Court finds that notification of the mistake was received before acceptance of the bid. The mere opening of the bids did not constitute the acceptance of the lowest bid. Likewise, the acceptance by the Board of Trustees on February 22, 1968, being conditional, was not effective. Furthermore, it is generally held that acceptance prior to notification does not bar the right to equitable relief from a mistake in the bid.

The mistake in this case was an honest error made in good faith. While a mistake in and of itself indicates some degree of lack of care or negligence, under the circumstances here there was not such a lack of care as to bar relief. The mistake here was a simple clerical error. To allow Jane Lamb Memorial Hospital to take advantage of this mistake would be unconscionable. This is especially true in light of the fact that they had actual knowledge of the mistake before the acceptance of the bid.

Nor can it be seriously contended that a $199,800 error, amounting to approximately 10% of the bid, does not relate directly to the substance of the consideration. Furthermore, Jane Lamb Memorial Hospital has suffered no actual damage by the withdrawal of the bid of M. J. McGough Company. The hospital has lost only what it sought to gain by taking advantage of M. J. McGough Company's mistake. Equitable considerations will not allow the recovery of the loss of bargain in this situation.

Under the facts before the Court, therefore, M. J. McGough Company will be allowed to rescind its bid and be relieved from any liability thereon. The Continental Insurance Company, surety on the bid bond, is likewise relieved from liability.

Judgment for McGough.

Mistake of Material Fact

Finally, in determining the legal significance of a mistake, a court seeks to evaluate the performance of the mistake. Was the fact as to which the mistake occurred of substantial importance? Would the party seeking relief from the mistake have entered into the contract even if no mistake had been made? The court must find that it was the mistaken fact that, at least in part, induced the party seeking relief to enter into the contract. The law is reluctant to undo a contract. Only the most significant and important mistakes of fact are grounds for contract rescission.

Related to the determination of the importance of the mistake is the question of the assumption of risk made by the parties. If a mistake of judgment regarding a risk assumed by either of the contracting parties has been made, the court will not grant relief. In many business situations, a contract is made conditional upon an uncertain event. Both parties exchange promises based on their assumptions concerning the likelihood of that event occurring. What is the likelihood of lightning striking your home in the next year? Do you and your insurance company have different assumptions about such an event? What is the value of property located on the outskirts of town? Do seller and purchaser have the same assumptions as to the likelihood of the proposed shopping center locating on or near the property? Certainly, if the parties disagree, one of the parties will be mistaken in its assumption; but no relief will be given if both parties have assumed the risk. The "value" of many items is by nature uncertain because of business custom, prevailing mores, social policy, and existing law. The *Friedman* case exemplifies the court's attitude toward granting relief for the mistaken assumptions of the parties who have entered into a contract.

Friedman v. Grevnin

Supreme Court of Michigan
103 N.W2d 336 (1960)

This action was brought by purchasers of vacant city lots to rescind the purchase contract and for restitution of sums paid on the ground that it had been entered into under mutual mistake of fact. Plaintiffs Grevnin asserted that both parties had been mistaken as to the adequacy of the sewers in the areas of the lot. Defendants Friedman responded that the adequacy of the sewer was not governed by the contract but had been assumed by plaintiffs. The Circuit Court held for plaintiffs, and defendants appealed. The Supreme Court reversed the trial court decision and dismissed plaintiffs' complaint.

Dethmers, Chief Justice

Plaintiffs, purchasers under a land contract, sought its rescission and restitution of sums paid on it on the ground that it had been entered into under a mutual mistake of fact. From decree for plaintiffs, defendants, the sellers, appeal.

Plaintiffs long had been engaged in the business of improvement and development of vacant and platted lands and construction and sale of residences thereon. They were seeking lands for that purpose. They became interested in purchasing 166 vacant, platted, city lots owned by defendants. As early as 1953 one of plaintiffs discussed a purchase of the lots with defendants and made inquiry of the city engineer as to adequacy of the sewers. He was told by the latter that a pump or lifting station would be necessary to accommodate the lots. In October of 1955 plaintiffs approached defendants for the purchase of the lots and negotiations ensued. Plaintiffs informed defendants that they desired that any purchase agreement between them should contain a contingency or condition that the sale was not to be consummated unless a satisfactory agreement could be worked out with the city for sewers and unless Federal Housing Administration and Veterans' Administration approval could be obtained for the lots as building sites, both of which required adequate sewer facilities. Defendants refused to agree to such conditions. Knowing this, plaintiffs, after negotiations had proceeded for three months, presented an offer to purchase, containing no such conditions, and defendants accepted the offer on January 24, 1956. The agreement called for consummation of the sale in 20 days. Nevertheless, plaintiffs delayed execution of a land contract for two months because they were awaiting Veterans' Administration approval of the lots and were making further inquiries concerning adequacy of sewers, feeling that defendants were unreasonable in not permitting a contingency as to adequate sewers to be included in the agreement. As one plaintiff testified, they knew defendants were not willing to guarantee sewers of any kind. Defendants had told them so. Under such circumstances, with defendants' express refusal to permit such condition or guarantee in the contract, a land contract was executed by the parties on April 10, 1956, containing no mention of sewers, because defendants refused to have such condition included. Plaintiffs thereafter made payments on the contract.

In September of 1956 consulting engineers filed a report with the city, advising that the sewers in the area of the lots were overloaded, and recommending certain actions to alleviate the situation. It is that situation with respect to the sewers concerning which plaintiffs claim the parties made a mutual mistake of fact, alleging that, when the agreement and the contract were executed, both sides believed the facilities to be adequate for plaintiffs' contemplated use of the lots. For this reason, rescission is prayed.

For their position plaintiffs' brief quotes as follows:

"... a mistake of one party of such a character that the minds cannot be said to have met, if clearly established, is ground for recission ..." Baas v. Zinke, 218 Mich. 552, 188 N.W. 512.

"Where parties assume to contract, and there is a mistake with reference to any material part of the subject matter, there is no contract, because of the want of mutual assent necessary to create one, ..."

In 3 Corbin on Contracts appears the following:

> "Sec. 598. . . . The same result (denial of rescission) obtains in any case where the risk of the existence of some factor or of the occurrence of an event is consciously considered in agreeing upon terms. There is no mistake; instead, there is awareness of the uncertainty, a conscious ignorance of the future. . . . They were aware of the uncertainty, estimated their chances, and fixed the compensation accordingly."

> "Sec. 605. . . . In these cases (rescission), the decision involves a judgment as to the materiality of the alleged factor, and as to whether the parties made a definite assumption that it existed and made their agreement in the belief that there was no risk with respect to it."

Defendants cite and quote the following:

> "A person is not entitled to rescind a transaction with another if, by way of compromise or otherwise, he agreed with the other to assume, or intended to assume, the risk of a mistake for which otherwise he would be entitled to rescission and consequent restitution." Restatement of the Law of Restitution, Ch. 2, § 11.

> "But if the failure of the article is by reason of a defect as to which the buyer takes the risk, there is no want or failure of consideration, in the legal sense of the rule, even if thereby the article is rendered worthless; as the buyer in such case gets and retains what he bought, that is, the property at his own risk as to such defect." *Bryant* v. *Pember,* 45 Vt. 487.

> "To entitle plaintiffs to reformation of the contract, they must show by clear and convincing proof that by a mutual mistake the provisions of the contract, as written, do not express the true agreement of the parties." *Harris* v. *Axline,* 323 Mich. 585, 36 N.W.2d 154, 155.

There was not here, as in the situations to which plaintiffs' above quotations applied, any want of mutual assent, any lack of meeting of the minds, with respect to the effect that inadequacy of sewers was to have on the contract obligations of the parties. The question of adequacy of the sewers was *"consciously considered"* by the parties. "They (plaintiffs) were aware of the uncertainty, estimated their chances," and made inquiries. They did not make their agreement "in the belief there was no risk with respect to it." Indeed, plaintiffs were sufficiently concerned about the risk involved to request a condition in the contract in that regard. Defendants refused.

Despite all that, plaintiffs entered into the agreement and subsequent contract in which, at defendants' insistence, no condition or guarantee as to sewers was expressed. Under the circumstances it cannot be said that there was mutual mistake. Rather, it was a case of plaintiffs, even though reluctantly, taking their chances. To hold with plaintiffs would be to read, by implication, into the agreement and contract that which defendants expressly refused to have inserted, namely, a provision that if sewers proved to be inadequate the deal was not to go through. This we will not do.

Reversed.

REVIEW PROBLEMS

1. Andersen agreed to sell a portion of his waterfront property to Vermette who had made a visual inspection of it and was satisfied. After settling with Andersen, Vermette drew up plans for the construction of a home on the lot and began to build. The project was halted when a county building inspector found evidence of potential soil slippage. After examining the foundation footings and considering the recent landslide on a nearby lot, the inspector issued an order suspending activities until a soil expert certified the land as being sufficiently stable for the construction of a house. Vermette elected to discharge the contractor and brought an action to rescind the sale. Will he succeed? Vermette v. Andersen, 558 P.2d 258 (Wash. Ct. App. 1976).

2. Greber suffered from a weight problem. After trying a complimentary treatment at the local Slenderella Salon, she immediately agreed to take a weight-reducing course consisting of 150 treatments at a total cost of $300. Greber also had long suffered a back ailment and informed the Slenderella Salon manager of this before signing the agreement. The manager did not discourage Greber from entering into the contract; and, she in fact thought the the treatments would do her back some good. Several days later, prior to engaging in any of the paid treatments, Greber's back hurt so much that she consulted a doctor, who advised her against taking the Slenderella program. Now Slenderella is suing for the money Greber agreed to pay, but she wants to rescind the contract. What result? Slenderella Systems, Inc. v. Greber, 163 A.2d 462 (D.C. Mun. Ct. App. 1960).

3. Oliver, and his transferee Argo, leased property and equipment to Gilreath and Johnson for use as a retail oyster and seafood business. The lease provided in pertinent part: "The lessees agree to make at their own expense, and without expense to the lessor. . . . all of the necessary and needful repairs to said premises. . . ." Soon after agreeing to take the property, Gilreath and Johnson were assured by Oliver that if the equipment needed repairs, he would have Basham fix it at no charge to them. Six months later, various refrigeration equipment broke down, causing other damage and rendering the business inoperable. Gilreath and Johnson called Basham for repairs and he refused to help them. They then vacated the building and claimed Oliver fraudulently induced them to sign the lease. Is their claim justified? Gilreath v. Argo, 219 S.E.2d 461 (Ga. Ct. App. 1975).

4. Usry leased two ice-making machines from Poag, an agent for Granite Management Services (GMS). Prior to the execution of the contract, Poag drew a separate purchase order, signed by Usry, that contained the following: "Customer own[s] equipment at end of lease" and "free service until lease ends." The lease agreement itself contained no such language, but said: "the contract constitutes the entire agreement between the lessor and lessee and . . . no representation or statement made by any representative of lessor or the supplier not stated herein shall be binding. . . ." When the machines failed to perform properly and Usry was refused free service, he discontinued making lease payments. GMS brought suit, but Usry claimed he was induced into signing the agreement by the fraudulent misrepresentation of Poag. Will Usry be able to rescind the contract? Granite Management Services, Inc. v. Usry, 204 S.E.2d 362 (Ga. Ct. App. 1974).

5. Robinson, a young married man, was employed as the assistant manager in one of the Gallaher Drug Company stores. After eighteen months on the job, he was accused of theft and embezzlement. Robinson ad-

mitted his guilt and was discharged from employment. The following day, he was invited to corporate headquarters to discuss restitution of the funds involved. After some discussion, Robinson entered into a written agreement to pay Gallaher Drug the sum of $2,000. He thereafter made payments totaling $741.64 and then refused to continue. The company seeks to enforce the contract, but Robinson says it was procured under duress and is therefore voidable. Is Robinson's defense a good one? Gallaher Drug Company v. Robinson. 232 N.E.2d 668 (Ohio Mun. Ct. 1965).

6. While Avallone was employed as a manager in Elizabeth Arden's Boston beauty salon, she, together with certain other individuals, made plans to open her own salon immediately adjacent to her employer's location. After officers of the Arden corporation discovered Avallone's intentions, they summoned her to the executive headquarters in New York City, ostensibly to discuss new hair dyes. In fact, she was scheduled to attend a conference with several corporate officers who asked her whether the information they had received concerning her future plans was true. Avallone denied any such intentions to open her own salon and upon the officers' request, signed an employment contract that restricted her from competing with the Arden corporation. Upon returning to Boston, she had second thoughts about what she had just done and brought suit to void the agreement due to duress. Result? Avallone v. Elizabeth Arden Sales Corporation, 183 N.E.2d 496 (Mass. Sup. Jud. Ct. 1962).

FOOTNOTES

[1]Second Restatement of Contracts, § 500 (1980)
[2]Williston, Contracts, § 1531, 3rd. Ed. (1959)
[3]Corbin, Contracts, § 597 St. Paul, Minn.: West Publishing Company (1960)

Capacity to Contract

T his chapter reviews a number of situations in which a person's contractual capacity is at issue. The capacity of the person who is allegedly incompetent is examined first. Then contracts made by persons who are minors at the time they agree to contract are discussed. A related concern, that of parental liability for the contracts of minor children, is briefly noted. Finally, contracts made by intoxicated persons are considered.

In the past, married women, convicts, corporations, and unincorporated associations were considered to lack the capacity to make certain contracts, but court decisions and statutory revisions in most states have eliminated their disabilities. Today, the defense of lack of capacity is most often raised by people who claim to have been legally incompetent, under age, or intoxicated at the time of contracting. While the law seeks to protect the person who lacks the capacity to contract, lack of capacity is not presumed. The burden of proof is on the person asserting it. Thus a person who acts senile or who is clearly under age is presumed to be capable of making a valid contract. To void the contract, the protected party must do something to indicate that he or she wants to exercise the option that the law allows.

The test of capacity to make a contract is not whether a person's mind is impaired or unsound, and not whether that person understands all the terms of the contract, but whether that person has the ability to comprehend the nature of the transaction engaged in and to understand its consequences. If a person who lacks the capacity to contract nevertheless enters into a contract, the law will protect that person by letting him or her get out of the contract. The contract of this person is referred to as a voidable contract. It can be upheld as a valid contract, but at the election and choice of the protected party it can be made void.

CONTRACTS OF PERSONS WHO MIGHT BE INCOMPETENT

The law used to be primarily concerned with contracts made by persons who had been found legally to be lunatics or insane. Contracts made by these persons were void. Such agreements could not be enforced even if both parties regarded them as valid. As medical science came to recognize different degrees of mental illness, the courts became concerned with contracts made by persons who might be incompetent. The courts have generally refrained from declaring all contracts made by such persons to be void. The modern rule, as noted in the *Cundick* case that follows, generally treats the contracts made by a person who is suffering from mental illness as voidable instead of void.

Even where the contract is voidable due to possible incompetency, a court generally examines the fairness and equity of allowing one party to avoid his or her contract. If the result of allowing the person to avoid the contract is unfair and inequitable, no right to disaffirm the contract will be granted. Finally, as has been noted, the person who is allegedly incompetent has the burden of proving that at the time of making the contract he or she did not understand the nature and effect of the transaction that resulted in the contract.

Of course, if a person has been legally adjudged to be incompetent after a regular court hearing and a guardian or conservator of that person's property has been appointed by the court, the contracts of that person usually will be regarded as void. Without a separate and independent court determination of legal incompetency, insanity, or inability to manage one's own affairs, however, the presumption of the law is that a person has the legal capacity to enter into contracts.

Cundick v. Broadbent
U. S. Court of Appeals, Tenth Circuit
383 F.2d 157 (1967)

Irma Cundick, guardian ad litem for her husband, Darwin Cundick, brought this diversity suit in Wyoming to set aside an agreement for the sale of (1) livestock and equipment, (2) shares of stock in a development company, and (3) base range land in Wyoming. The alleged grounds for nullification were that at the time of the transaction Cundick was mentally incompetent to execute the agreement; that Broadbent, knowing of such incompetency, fraudulently represented to Cundick that the purchase price for the property described in the agreement was fair and just; and that Cundick relied upon the false representations when he executed the agreement and transferred the property.

The court concluded that Cundick failed to sustain the burden of proving that at the time of the transaction he was mentally incapable of managing his affairs; or that Broadbent knew of any mental deficiency when they entered into the agreement; or that Broadbent knowingly overreached him. The appeal is from a judgment dismissing the action. The Court of Appeals affirmed the judgment.

Murrah, Chief Judge

The contentions on appeal are twofold and stated alternatively: (1) that at the time of the transaction Cundick was totally incompetent to contract; that the agreement between the parties was therefore void ab initio, hence incapable of ratification; and (2) that in any event Cundick was mentally infirm and Broadbent knowingly overreached him; that the contract was therefore voidable, was not ratified—hence rescindable.

At one time, in this country and in England, it was the law that since a lunatic or non compos mentis had no mind with which to make an agreement, his contract was wholly void and incapable of ratification. But, if his mind was merely confused or weak so that he knew what he was doing yet was incapable of fully understanding the terms and effect of his agreement, he could indeed contract, but such contract would be avoidable to his option. But in recent times courts have tended away from the concept of absolutely void contracts toward the notion that even though a contract be said to be void for lack of capacity to make it, it is nevertheless ratifiable at the instance of the incompetent party. The modern rule, and the weight of authority, seems to be . . . "the contractual act by one claiming to be mentally deficient, but not under guardianship, absent fraud, or knowledge of such asserted incapacity by the other contracting party, is not a void act but at most only voidable at the instance of the deficient party; and then only in accordance with certain equitable principles." In recognition of different degrees of mental competency the weight of authority seems to hold that mental capacity to contract depends upon whether the allegedly disabled person possessed sufficient reason to enable him to understand the nature and effect of the act in issue. Even average intelligence is not essential to a valid bargain.

From all this it may be said with reasonable assurance that if Cundick was utterly incapable of knowing the nature and effect of the transaction, the agreement is, without more, invalid, though capable of ratification by his representative or by him during lucid intervals. But, if the degree of disability was such that he was capable of contracting, yet his mental condition rendered him susceptible of being overreached by an unscrupulous superior, his complaint comes under the heading of fraud to be proved as such. The burden is, of course, on the one asserting incompetency and fraud at the crucial time of the making of the challenged agreement.

Cundick was never judicially adjudged incompetent and his guardian ad litem apparently assumes the burden and accepts, as she must, the proposition that if the court's findings are supported by the record, they are conclusively binding here. She meets the issue squarely with the emphatic contention that the findings of the court are utterly without support in the record; that the evidence is all one way to the effect that at the time of the execution of the writings Cundick was mentally incompetent to make a valid contract.

All of the physicians who examined Cundick between 1961 and 1965 testified that in their judgment he was incapable of entering into the contract. When in December, 1960, Cundick first went to his family physician his condition was diagnosed as "depressive psychosis" and he was referred to a psychiatrist in Salt Lake City. When Cundick returned to the family physician more than two years later, he was treated for sore throat and bronchitis. From that time until October, 1965, the family physician saw Cundick about 25 times and treated him for everything from a sore throat to a heart attack suffered in March, 1964, but nothing was said or done about a mental condition. Apparently after this suit was filed and upon order of the court Cundick was examined in March, 1964, by two neurosurgeons in Cheyenne. By extensive tests it was established that Cundick was suffering from an atrophy of the frontal lobes of his brain diagnosed as pre-senile or premature arteriosclerosis. Both physicians used different language to say that from their examination in March, 1964, they were of the opinion that on the date of the transaction, i.e. September 2, 1963, Cundick was a "confused and befuddled man with very poor judgment," and although there were things he could do, he was, in their opinion, unable to handle his affairs at the time of the transaction. A psychologist to whom Cundick was referred in March by the Cheyenne neurosurgeons also testified that in his judgment Cundick was incapable of transacting his important business affairs in September of 1963. There was no medical testimony to the contrary. There was also lay testimony on behalf of Cundick to the effect that he was a quiet, reserved personality changed from one of friendliness to inattentiveness and that during 1963 he was unable to make decisions with respect to the conduct of his ranching business.

This unimpeached testimony may not be disregarded and the trier of the fact is bound to honor it in the absence of countervailing evidence—expert or non-expert —upon which to rest a contrary finding. But, expert evidence does not foreclose lay testimony concerning the same matter which is within the knowledge and compre- hension of the lay witness. A lay witness may tell all he knows about a matter in issue even though it may tend to impugn the conclusions of the expert.

The trial judge who heard and saw the witnesses and felt the pulse beat of the lawsuit is, to be sure, the first and best judge of the weight and value to be given to all of the evidence, both expert and non-expert.

Against the background of medical and lay evidence tending to show Cundick's incompetency on the crucial date, there is positive evidence to the effect that at the time in question he was 59 years old, married and operating a sheep ranch in Wyoming; that in previous years he had sold his lamb crop to Broadbent and on a date prior to this transaction the parties met at a midway point for the purpose of selling the current lamb crop. The meeting resulted in a one page contract signed by both parties in which Cundick agreed to sell all of his ranching properties to Broad- bent. It is undisputed that Cundick and his wife thereafter took his one page contract to their lawyer in Salt Lake City who refined and amplified it into an eleven page contract providing in detail the terms by which the sale was to be consummated. The contract was signed in the lawyer's office by Cundick and Broadbent in the presence of Cundick's wife and the lawyer. The lawyer testified that the contract had been explained in detail and that all parties apparently understood it.

As we have seen Cundick was not treated nor did he consult a physician for his mental condition from the time he returned from Salt Lake City in early 1961, until he was examined apparently by order of the court in March, 1964, after this suit was commenced. The record is conspicuously silent concerning any discussion of his mental condition among his family and friends in the community where he lived and operated his ranch. Certainly, the record is barren of any discussion or comment in Broadbent's presence. It seems incredible that Cundick could have been utterly inca- pable of transacting his business affairs, yet such condition be unknown on this record to his family and friends, especially his wife who lived and worked with him and participated in the months-long transaction which she now contends was fraudulently conceived and perpetrated. All this record silence, together with the affirmative evidence of normal behavior during the period of the transaction speaks loudly in support of the court's finding that Cundick's acts ". . . were the acts, conduct and behavior of a person competent to manage his affairs . . ." As applied to the critical issue of incompetency, this finding leads us to the conclusion reached by the trial judge that when the medical testimony, positive as it may be, is considered in the context of all that was said and done, it does not carry the heavy burden of proving that Cundick was incompetent, i.e. he did not know the extent and condition of his property, how he was disposing of it, to whom and upon what consideration.

Affirmed

CONTRACTS OF MINORS

Overview

The legal capacity to enter into contracts is not the same as the capacity to commit a crime or a tort. The law often holds a minor responsible for criminal or tortious acts, but a minor is not generally liable for contracts. The higher standard applied to contracts is due in part to the fact that contracts generally involve bargaining with another person. A minor contracting with an adult needs to be protected from making unwise or foolish contracts. Similarly, the standard of capacity is also generally higher for contracting than for making a gift or a will. Neither of those methods of disposing of property involves bargaining with other parties, as is the case with contracts.

Historically, the law has provided special protection to minors who enter into contracts. This privileged contractual status has been based on their assumed immaturity and inexperience regarding commercial transactions. Historically the common law has treated people under the age of twenty-one as minors, but since the enactment of the Twenty-sixth Amendment to the U.S. Constitution, which lowered the voting age to eighteen, most states have lowered the age of majority from twenty-one to eighteen. Accordingly, although most of the cases that follow concern individuals who are minors because they are under twenty-one, in most states now only persons under eighteen are considered minors.

The protection extended by the law allows the minor the choice of either carrying out and enforcing the contract or seeking to avoid its provisions. Avoidance of the contract is done by any act that manifests the minor's intent to no longer be bound by the contract. Since most contracts entered into by minors can be avoided, they are generally referred to as voidable contracts. The contracts are valid unless the minor, by disaffirming them, seeks to avoid their provisions. However, there are a number of contracts which a minor is not allowed to disaffirm. Statutes in many states specify that certain contracts are not subject to disaffirmance by a minor. Contracts of this type are considered valid, not voidable. Examples of such contracts are the following:

1. A contract by a minor to enlist in the armed forces
2. A contract by a minor to borrow money from an institutional lender or the government for the purpose of financing some portion of the minor's postsecondary education
3. A contract by a minor consenting to the adoption of a child
4. A contract of a minor to participate in a professional sport
5. A contract of a minor that includes a provision where the minor as an employee or purchaser of a business agrees not to compete with the business of the employer or seller
6. A contract to borrow money from a lender which is served by a mortgage

The contracts that are not voidable by minors vary from state to state. Statutes in each state have to be examined to ascertain exactly which contracts of minors are not subject to disaffirmance.

In addition to enforcing contracts that state statutes declare not subject to disaffirmance, contracts for necessaries are also usually excepted from the general rule allowing minors to avoid their contracts. The law generally holds the minor liable for the reasonable value of the necessaries furnished to him. Thus, if a minor has contracted to pay $100 for necessary and suitable clothes whose reasonable value is only $70, the minor's liability would be $70, not $100.

Although the general presumption is that a minor's contract is subject to disaffirmance, a court deciding whether a minor is liable on his contract must determine the answers to several questions:

1. Do any statutes specify that this particular type of contract should not be subject to disaffirmance?
2. Does the law (statutes or court decisions) consider that the subject of this particular contract constitutes a necessary, so that the minor would not be liable for the contract price but only for the reasonable value of the necessary?
3. If the contract is subject to disaffirmance, has the minor done something that in fact amounts to disaffirmance?

Several other questions that must also be answered to hold a minor liable for his or her contract will be noted later in this chapter.

Fisher v. Cattani

District Court, Nassau County, Third District
278 N.Y.S. 420 (1966)

This was an action brought by an employment agency (Fisher) to recover the amount due on a contract with an infant (Cattani) who sought to disaffirm the contract. The trial court held that the infant Cattani's disaffirmance of the contract was effective since his notice was adequate where it was promptly given and actually occurred during the defendant's minority. Accordingly, the trial court entered a judgment for defendant. (The term "infant" is used by the court in place of the term "minor"; for our purposes, these terms should be considered interchangeable.)

Vitale, District Judge

This action was submitted for decision by the Court, upon an agreed state of facts. In substance they are: The defendant, in September 1962, being then 19 years of age, entered into a contract with the plaintiff, a duly licensed employment agency. The plaintiff obtained employment for the defendant, who found the job unsatisfactory, and resigned after one month. By registered mail notice to the Plaintiff, in November 1962, the defendant disaffirmed the contract of September 1962. The fee due Plaintiff was $146.25. Defendant paid $45. on account. The balance due is $101.25, for which Plaintiff demands judgment.

The law takes cognizance of the infant's lack of business experience and judgment by cloaking him with an inability to contract, except as to express exceptions, created, or recognized by statute. However, infants' contracts are not thereby generally considered void, but merely voidable. The contract being valid until disaffirmed by the infant, it becomes necessary to determine, if notice of disaffirmance was sufficiently given, and if so, whether it effectively terminated the defendant's contractual liability to the Plaintiff.

The notice given to the Plaintiff by the defendant, exceeds the standards usually applied to such acts, in that it was promptly given, was actually received, and was given during the infant's minority. The question of whether or not the disaffirmance was required to be accompanied by a tender of the consideration, received by the infant from the plaintiff, need not be considered. Aside from its intangibility, and the fact that the infant does not seek affirmative relief, the defendant, before disaffirmance, left the position secured for her by the Plaintiff.

The contract between these parties, represented an agreement by the Plaintiff to secure employment for the defendant, and a promise on her part to pay for this service.

A contract of this nature has not been made the subject of a statutory exception, to the right to disaffirm inherent, generally, in infants' contracts. The legislature has seen fit to do so, in other situations wherein it is customary, under present business practices, for infants to contract. For example, an infant, over 16, may not disaffirm, upon the ground of infancy, an agreement extending credit to him for an educational loan. Similarly, he may not, on that ground, and if over 18, avoid a real property mortgage on premises occupied as a home.

Furthermore, an infant may not disaffirm contracts for necessaries. Even here, the phrase necessaries, does not possess a fixed interpretation, but must be measured against both the infant's standard of living, and the ability and willingness of his guardian, if he has one, to supply the needed services or articles. These elements are not present in the facts before the Court, and they may not be presumed.

It well may be that upon a full presentation of the facts, as to the infant's need to work, in order to support himself, and possibly his children, an employment agency contract of this nature, may be regarded as one of the necessaries contemplated by the statutory exception, but such finding cannot be made upon the stipulated facts.

Accordingly it is held that under the submitted facts, the infant properly disaffirmed the contract upon which suit is brought, by reason of his infancy.

Judgment for Defendant.

Disaffirmance of Contracts by Minors

Contracts Subject to Disaffirmance As has been noted, some contracts that minors make are not subject to disaffirmance. Thus the first question that must be answered concerning the minor's act of disaffirmance is whether the contract is one that cannot be disaffirmed. Unless state statutes expressly exempt the particular contract, or its subject matter is considered a necessary, the law generally will treat any contract made by a minor as subject to disaffirmance.

Time of Disaffirmance. Generally a minor may avoid any contract that is subject to disaffirmance during the time of his minority and for a reasonable period of time after attaining the age of majority. The law thus gives the minor a period of time to review and reflect on the contractual agreements made during minority. What constitutes a reasonable time depends on the complexity of the transaction, its subject matter, and the circumstances peculiar to each agreement.

Methods of Disaffirmance. Disaffirmance occurs by the minor manifesting an unwillingness to be bound by the contract. The minor can simply inform the other party (whether an adult or minor) that he intends to disaffirm their contractual agreement. Or the minor can do some other act that clearly indicates that he or she has such an intent. Thus the minor who has agreed to sell goods to one purchaser but instead sells them to a third party has by such an act disaffirmed the contract made with the original purchaser. Similarly, the minor who institutes legal action to avoid responsibility for a contract's obligations manifests an intent to disaffirm the contract.

Disaffirmance and Restitution of Property by the Minor. While the law seeks to protect the minor from unwise or imprudent contracts, there is disagreement among court decisions as to the rights of the parties if a minor cannot return the property he or she received. The majority of decisions hold that the minor may disaffirm a contract and receive back any consideration given even if the minor is unable to return to the other party that which the minor has received. A minority of decisions require the minor to return the consideration received from the other party in order to be able to disaffirm the contract. If the minor is unable to return the property received (or its equivalent value) the minor will not be allowed to disaffirm the contract. Compare the decision of the *Central Bucks Aero* case to that in the *Haydocy Pontiac* case (both cases are given below). Which policy would you follow in similar situations?

Disaffirmance and Misrepresentation of Age. A minor's right to disaffirm a contract can also be influenced by misrepresentations made by the minor. When a minor misrepresents his or her age and such misrepresentation is relied on by the other party, who is then induced to enter into a contract, a conflict between legal policies results.

On the one hand, the law seeks to protect the minor and allow the minor to disaffirm contracts made while he or she was under the age of majority; thus the law wants to ensure that the minor is not victimized by a wiser and more mature adult. On the other hand, if a person is the victim of a fraudulent statement made by another person, the law generally allows the victim of the fraud to rescind or cancel the contract that resulted from the fraud. What should be done if the minor commits the fraud and the adult is the victim? The response to these questions has not been uniform; the court decisions are split.

While all three of the following cases are concerned with the right of the minor to disaffirm a contract, each addresses a distinct problem connected to that right. Can a minor who disaffirms a contract be held liable in tort for damages suffered by the other contracting party? Can the minor who misrepresented her age and is unable to return the consideration she received from the other contracting party disaffirm the contract? Is a minor who appears to be of legal age or who has signed a form that states he is of said age entitled to disaffirm a contract?

Central Bucks Aero, Inc. v. Smith

Superior Court of Pennsylvania

310 A2d 283 (1973)

Central Bucks Aero, Inc., the lessor of an airplane, brought this action against Smith, the minor lessee, to recover for damage to the airplane occurring during landing. The Court of Common Pleas granted the minor lessee's motion for summary judgment on the ground that he had disaffirmed the lease after the accident and the lessor appealed. The Superior Court held that the disaffirmance was effective, and that it barred the suit in tort as well as any direct action on the lease contract. Accordingly, the trial court judgment was affirmed. In the opinion that follows, the airplane lessor (Central) is referred to as the appellant and the minor (Smith) as the appellee.

Spaeth, Judge

This is an appeal from the granting of defendant-appellee's motion for summary judgment. The issue is whether we should overturn the longstanding common law doctrine that a minor by disaffirming a contract can avoid liability under the contract.

Appellee, when twenty years of age, leased an airplane from appellant. In the process of landing, appellee damaged the airplane beyond repair, and also damaged the landing field. After appellant filed suit in trespass, appellee disaffirmed the lease.

When a minor disaffirms a contract, unless the contract is for necessaries the other party cannot recover the value of any item that the minor has obtained pursuant to the contract. The only remedy the other party has is an action in replevin to recover the item itself. If the minor no longer has the item, the other party is remediless.

An action in tort which is the form of action selected by appellant, will not lie. The privilege (to avoid the contract) would be little worth if it might be eluded by fashioning the action into a particular shape. Whenever the substantive ground of an action against an infant is contract, as well where the contract is stated as incident to a supposed tort, as where it is not, the plaintiff cannot recover. In the course of his discussion of the cases in which infants may be sued in tort and those in which they cannot be, Judge Cooley said: "The distinction is this: If the wrong grows out of contract relations, and the real injury consists in the nonperformance of a contract into which the party wronged has entered with an infant, the law will not permit the former to enforce the contract indirectly by counting on the infant's neglect to perform it, or omission of duty under it as a tort. The reason is obvious: To permit this to be done would deprive the infant of that shield of protection which, in matters of contract, the law has wisely placed before him." 1 Cooley on Torts, 3d ed. 181. This principle is followed in most jurisdictions.

It may be granted that upon occasion the courts have decided to remove an immunity from legal responsibility by overruling the cases that created the immunity. In the present case, however, such a decision would be inappropriate.

A businessman may protect himself from loss incident to a minor's disaffirmance of a contract by finding out whether the person with whom he is dealing is a minor. Ordinarily this will present no difficulty. If the person is a minor, or if it is not clear that he is an adult, the businessman may decline to deal with him, or may require that someone he knows is an adult join in the contract. Inasmuch as appellant neglected such precautions, it has only itself to blame for its inability to recover for the damage to its airplane and landing field.

Affirmed.

Haydocy Pontiac, Inc., v. Lee

Court of Appeals of Ohio
250 N.E.2d 898 (1969)

Plaintiff was the seller of an automobile to Lee. At the time of the sale, Lee was 20 years of age and represented to the seller that she was 21. After the sale, Lee gave the car to a friend who had repairs made on it and neither party to this suit can recover possession of the car. Defendant asserted her infancy allows her to avoid the contract and releases her from any obligation to pay anything to plaintiff seller. The trial court agreed and rendered its judgment for the Defendant. Plaintiff seller appealed. The Court of Appeals reversed the trial court's judgment and held defendant Lee liable for the fair value, not to exceed the purchase price, of the automobile she had purchased. (Note that this Court's opinion uses both the terms "infant" and "minor" in referring to the defendant.)

Strausbaugh, Judge

The facts in the case are not in dispute; the defendant Jennifer J. Lee was the only witness at the time of trial. On August 22, 1967, plaintiff sold to the defendant Jennifer J. Lee a 1964 Plymouth Fury automobile; the cash price of the automobile was $1,552, which was paid by the defendant by a "trade-in" automobile of the value of $150; the balance of the purchase price was financed by the defendant executing and delivering to plaintiff a note and chattel mortgage for the unpaid purchase price plus financing charges and insurance charges; the total face amount of the note was $2,016.36. A certificate of title was issued showing that the defendant was owner of the automobile. A note and chattel mortgage were assigned by the plaintiff to a local bank which has reassigned the same back to the plaintiff.

Immediately following delivery of the automobile to the defendant, the defendant permitted one John L. Roberts to take possession of the car; the defendant never at any time thereafter had possession. John L. Roberts, subsequently, delivered the automobile to Consolidated Holdings, Inc., d.b.a. Motorland Do-It-Yourself, for repairs; neither the plaintiff nor the defendant has been able to obtain possession of it. The defendant failed to make any payments on the note and chattel mortgage. The plaintiff commenced this action to recover possession thereof and as an alternative prayer in the amended petition prayed that judgment be granted in its favor for the sum of $2,016.36, the balance due on the note and chattel mortgage, against each of the defendants.

The whereabouts of Roberts is unknown; Consolidated Holdings, Inc., is in receivership and is insolvent. The defendant filed an answer asserting as an affirmative defense to the action that she was a minor of the age of 20 years at the time of purchase, that she has not ratified the agreement to purchase the car, nor has she ratified the note or the mortgage since attaining the age of majority. It is undisputed that defendant was a minor at the time of entering into the contract and at the time of signing the note and mortgage, that the defendant has never returned the car to the plaintiff, and that at the time of the purchase the defendant represented that she was then 21 years of age. The Municipal Court found that at the time of the purchase the defendant was a minor, that she had repudiated her contact and that she, therefore, was not bound thereby, and the court entered judgment in favor of the defendant.

Careful examination of the law in Ohio discloses no case wherein the vendor has recovered from an infant who has repudiated his contract. The cases we have examined in this regard all relate to the question whether the infant can recover from the vendor the purchase price paid and the right of the vendor to counterclaim rather than the facts of this case where the vendor, in the original petition, seeks to recover the property or, in lieu thereof, the balance due on the purchase price. Many of the cases use language to the effect that when the property received by the infant is in his possession, or under his control, to permit him to rescind the contract without requiring him to return or offer to return it would be to permit him to use his privilege as a "sword rather than a shield."

At a time when we see young persons between 18 and 21 years of age demanding and assuming more responsibilities in their daily lives; when we see such persons emancipated, married, and raising families; when we see such persons charged with the responsibility for committing crimes; when we see such persons being sued in tort claims for acts of negligence; when we see such persons subject to military service; when we see such persons engaged in business and acting in almost all other respects as an adult, it seems timely to re-examine the case law pertaining to contractual rights and responsibilities of infants to see if the law as pronounced and applied by the courts should be redefined.

To allow infants to avoid a transaction without being required to restore the consideration received where the infant has used or otherwise disposed of it causes hardship on the other party. We hold that where the consideration received by the infant cannot be returned upon disaffirmance of the contract because it has been disposed of, the infant must account for the value of it, not in excess of the purchase price, where the other party is free from any fraud or bad faith and where the contract has been induced by a false representation of the age of the infant. Under this factual situation the infant is estopped from pleading infancy as a defense where the contract has been induced by a false representation that the infant was of age.

The necessity of returning the consideration as a prerequisite to obtaining equitable relief is still clearer where the infant misrepresents age and perpetrated an actual fraud on the other party. The disaffirmance of an infant's contract is to be determined by equitable principles, whether wrought in a proceeding in equity or a case at law.

The common law has bestowed upon the infant the privilege of disaffirming his contracts in conservation of his rights and interests. Where the infant, 20 years of age, through falsehood and deceit enters into a contract with another who enters therein in honesty and good faith and, thereafter, the infant seeks to disaffirm the contract without tendering back the consideration, no right or interest of the infant exists which needs protection. The privilege given the infant thereupon becomes a weapon of injustice.

Judgment reversed.

Kiefer v. Howe Motors, Inc.

Supreme Court of Wisconsin
158 N.W.2d. 288 (1968)

On August 9, 1965, the plaintiff, Steven Kiefer, entered into a contract with the defendant, Fred Howe Motors, Inc. ("dealer" hereinafter), for the purchase of a 1960 Willys station wagon. Kiefer paid the contract price of $412 and took possession of the car. At the time of the sale Kiefer was twenty years old, married, and the father of one child. Some of the testimony given in the trial court indicated that Kiefer orally stated he was an adult. Furthermore, the purchase contract he signed stated that he represented himself to be twenty-one years of age and that the dealer relied on that representation.

Kiefer had difficulty with the car that he claimed was caused by a cracked block. Kiefer contacted the dealer and asked it to take the car back. Several other attempts to secure some adjustment with the dealer failed and Kiefer contacted Attorney Paul C. Konnor. The attorney wrote a letter to the dealer advising it that Kiefer was under 21 at the time of the sale. The letter declared the contract void, tendered return of the automobile and demanded repayment of the purchase price. There was no response so this action was commenced to recover the $412 purchase price. After a trial to the court, a judgment for the plaintiff was entered and the defendant appealed. The Supreme Court of Wisconsin affirmed the trial court's judgment for plaintiff.

Wilkie, Justice.

Three issues are presented on this appeal. They are:

1. Should an emancipated minor over the age of eighteen be legally responsible for his contracts?
2. Was the contract effectively disaffirmed?
3. Is the plaintiff liable in tort for misrepresentation?

LEGAL RESPONSIBILITY OF EMANCIPATED MINOR.

No one really questions that a line as to age must be drawn somewhere below which a legally defined minor must be able to disaffirm his contracts for nonnecessities. The law over the centuries has considered this age to be twenty-one. Legislatures in other states have lowered the age. We suggest that the appellant might better seek the change it proposes [to lower the age to eighteen] in the legislative halls rather than this court.

Undoubtedly, the infancy doctrine is an obstacle when a major purchase is involved. However, we believe that the reasons for allowing that obstacle to remain viable at this point outweigh those for casting it aside. Minors require some protection from the pitfalls of the market place. Reasonable minds will always differ on the extent of the protection that should be afforded. For this court to adopt a rule that the appellant suggests and remove the contractual disabilities from a minor simply because he becomes emancipated, which in most cases would be the result of marriage, would be to suggest that the married minor is somehow vested with more wisdom and maturity than his single counterpart. However, logic would not seem to dictate this result especially when today a youthful marriage is oftentimes indicative of a lack of wisdom and maturity.

DISAFFIRMANCE.

The appellant questions whether there has been an effective disaffirmance of the contract in this case.

Williston, while discussing how a minor may disaffirm a contract, states:

> "Any act which clearly shows an intent to disaffirm a contract or sale is sufficient for the purpose. Thus a notice by the infant of his purpose to disaffirm a tender or even an offer to return the consideration or its proceeds to the vendor, is sufficient."

The testimony of Steven Kiefer and the letter from his attorney to the dealer clearly establish that there was an effective disaffirmance of the contract.

MISREPRESENTATION.

Appellant's last argument is that the respondent should be held liable in tort for damages because he misrepresented his age. Appellant would use these damages as a setoff against the contract price sought to be reclaimed by respondent.

The 19th-century view was that a minor's lying about his age was inconsequential because a fraudulent representation of capacity was not the equivalent of actual capacity. This rule has been altered by time. There appear to be two possible methods that now can be employed to bind the defrauding minor: He may be estopped from denying his alleged majority, in which case the contract will be enforced or contract damages will be allowed; or he may be allowed to disaffirm his contract but be liable in tort for damages. Wisconsin follows the latter approach.

Having established that there is a remedy against the defrauding minor, the question becomes whether the requisites for a tort action in misrepresentation are present in this case.

The trial produced conflicting testimony regarding whether Steven Kiefer had been asked his age or had replied that he was "twenty-one." Steven and his wife, Jacqueline, said "No," and Frank McHalsky, appellant's salesman, said "Yes." Confronted with this conflict, the question of credibility was for the trial court to decide, which it did by holding that Steven did not orally represent that he was "twenty-one." This finding is not contrary to the great weight and clear preponderance of the evidence and must be affirmed.

Even accepting the trial court's conclusion that Steven Kiefer had not orally represented his age to be over twenty-one, the appellant argues that there was still a misrepresentation. The "motor vehicle purchase contract" signed by Steven Kiefer contained the following language just above the purchaser's signature:

"I represent that I am 21 years of age or over and recognize that the dealer sells the above vehicle upon this representation."

Whether the inclusion of this sentence constitutes a misrepresentation depends on whether elements of the tort have been satisfied. They were not.

We fail to see how the dealer could be justified in the mere reliance on the fact that the plaintiff signed a contract containing a sentence that said he was twenty-one or over. The trial court observed that the plaintiff was sufficiently immature looking to arouse suspicion. The appellant never took any affirmative steps to determine whether the plaintiff was in fact over twenty-one. It never asked to see a draft card, identification card, or the most logical indicium of age under the circumstances, a driver's license. Therefore, because there was no intent to deceive, and no justifiable reliance, the appellant's action for misrepresentation must fail.

Judgment affirmed.

Hallows, Chief Justice (dissenting)

The majority opinion on the issue of whether an emancipated minor legally should be responsible for his contracts "doth protest too much." After giving very cogent reasons why the common-law rule should be abandoned, the opinion refrains from reshaping the rule to meet reality. Minors are emancipated by a valid marriage and also by entering military service. If they are mature enough to become parents and assume the responsibility of raising other minors and if they are mature enough to be drafted or volunteer to bear arms and sacrifice their life for their country, then they are mature enough to make binding contracts in the market place. The magical age limit of 21 years as an indication of contractual maturity no longer has a basis in fact or in public policy.

My second ground of the dissent is that an automobile to this respondent was a necessity and therefore the contract could not be disaffirmed. Here, we have a minor, aged 20 years and 7 months, the father of a child, and working. While the record shows there is some public transportation to his present place of work, it also shows he borrowed his mother's car to go to and from work. Automobiles for parents under 21 years of age to go to and from work in our current society may well be a necessity and I think in this case the record shows it is. An automobile as a means of transportation to earn a living should not be considered a nonnecessity because the owner is 5 months too young. I would reverse.

A Minor's Contract for Necessaries and Parent's Liability for Minor's Contracts

As we have noted, a minor is generally liable for the reasonable value of necessary items for which he has contracted. That liability is limited to the reasonable value of the items, which may be less than their contracted price. What constitutes necessary items varies with the needs of the individual concerned. Generally, food, clothing, and shelter, suitable to the minor's station in life, will be regarded as necessaries. The court looks to see whether the contracted items are essential to the minor's general welfare.

What about the purchase of a stereo set? A car? The contract for the payment of college tuition? Only an analysis of the needs of the individual minor can provide the answer to these questions.

Since the law often protects the minor by allowing contracts to be disaffirmed, those contracting with minors will seek to hold other parties liable for the minor's contracts. With the lowering of the age of majority in most states to eighteen, those who are minors are less likely to be emancipated, self-supporting, or totally independent from their parents or guardians. Business people contracting with sixteen- or seventeen-year-olds are likely to do so only if the parent or another adult is expressly committed to perform the minor's contractual obligations. Banks will require an adult cosignor for any loan made to a minor. Merchants will check to confirm that charge cards are issued in the name of an adult and that the minor child has the express permission of that adult to make purchases. School authorities will require parental permission and approval, as well as the child's consent, prior to participation by the child in extracurricular activities or special programs. Most businesses are aware of the law's desire to protect the minor; they therefore seek to make contracts with adults whose contracts are not subject to disaffirmance.

Even in situations where the merchant does not have an express contract with the parent of a minor, a merchant who furnishes necessary items to a minor may be able to hold one or both of the minor's parents liable. By statute in most states, the law requires a parent to furnish necessary items to his or her minor children. If the merchant can prove that the items the minor agreed to purchase were necessary for the minor, and were not being—but could be—furnished by a parent, the parent can be held liable. The contract between the parent and the merchant is not an express contract, created by the parties; it is implied by the provisions of the law.

Where a merchant furnishes necessary items to a minor, the merchant may hold either the parent or the minor liable for the reasonable value (not the contract price) of those items. If the minor is emancipated and is not dependent for financial support on his or her parents, the merchant can hold the minor liable. A contract for necessaries by a minor is valid; it is not subject to disaffirmance by the minor. If the minor is dependent on one or more parents for financial support and for furnishing his or her necessaries, and if a parent is able to furnish those necessaries, then the merchant can hold the parent liable. In either case, the merchant can recover the reasonable value of necessary items furnished to a minor.

Ratification of Contracts by Minors

In general, a minor can void any contract entered into by exercising the power of disaffirmance. The effective surrender of the power of disaffirmance is known as ratification. Since contracts entered into by a minor are subject to disaffirmance, ratification cannot take place prior to the minor's attainment of the age of majority.

A ratification by a minor can occur in any of three ways. First, the minor may fail to make a timely disaffirmance. Since the minor has the right to disaffirm only for the period of his or her minority, plus a reasonable time after attainment of the age of majority, the minor who does not disaffirm within that time ratifies by such action (or inaction) the contract made during minority. Second, the minor can expressly state, orally or in writing, that he or she intends to ratify the contract. If the express statement is clear and unambiguous and is made after attainment of the age of majority, ratification of the contract has occurred. Once such ratification has occurred, the power and right to disaffirm terminates. Finally, the minor, after attainment of the age of majority, may by conduct manifest an intent to ratify the contract made while a minor. The *Bronx Savings Bank* case illustrates how this concept could be applied.

Bronx Savings Bank v. Conduff

Supreme Court of New Mexico
430 P.2d 374 (1967)

Plaintiff bank brought suit to foreclose a mortgage against defendant Conduff. Conduff claimed that the Daltons had promised to assume the mortgage obligation of Conduff. Dalton defended due to Mr. Dalton's infancy at the time of the sale of the subject property from Conduff to Dalton. The trial court held that since Mr. Dalton made five payments after he had attained the age of majority, he had ratified the contract made with Conduff during Dalton's infancy. Accordingly, the trial court entered a judgment for Conduff. The Supreme Court of New Mexico, finding no ratification, reversed the trial court judgment and directed it to enter judgment for Dalton.

Carmody, Justice

On December 14, 1964, Conduff conveyed the property which is the subject matter of this litigation to the Daltons, at which time Dalton was under twenty-one years of age. Mr. and Mrs. Dalton assumed and agreed to pay the mortgage to which the property was subject. Dalton became twenty-one years of age on June 13, 1965. Thereafter Dalton remained in possession of the property until sometime in September, 1965, making occasional weekly payments during that time. The Daltons made no offer to reconvey the property to Conduff until February 11, 1966, several weeks after this suit was filed.

The court then concluded that Dalton had ratified the purchase of the property by making payments on the mortgage with the intention to ratify the purchase, knowing that such payments would be considered as a ratification, and exercising ownership over the property.

Appellants contend that the quoted findings and the conclusions flowing therefrom are without any support in the evidence, because there is no proof of ratification or intent to ratify on the part of Dalton. Interconnected with this point is the appellants' second point, that a mere partial payment after attainment of majority, without an express promise or intention to ratify, does not constitute a ratification of a contract made while such person was an infant.

There is no substantial evidence to support the findings regarding ratification. We see nothing to indicate that Dalton knew that his payments after June 13, 1965, such as they were, would be considered a ratification of his purchase of the property. Appellee's apparent contention that Dalton's payments after becoming twenty-one years of age constitute a ratification that is supported by the presumption that all men know the law, is not well taken. We disagree with the reasoning expounded therein, and would, in addition, point out that a number of cases have indicated that the presumption that all men know the law, does not necessarily apply in cases such as this. Nor is it shown that Dalton made any payments with the intention of ratifying the purchase. All that has been shown were five partial payments after attainment of majority, and even these payments were only a continuation of pre-majority authorized payroll deductions. The burden of showing a ratification is upon the one who asserts it. This burden has not been met.

In general, a mere partial payment by a person, after coming of age, on a contract made by him during infancy, without an express promise or intention to ratify, does not constitute a ratification of the contract.

The acts of the former infant are not inconsistent with any other purpose than to ratify.

The evidence of payment alone in this case fails to show the requisite intent to ratify. Judgment reversed and remanded.

INTOXICATION AND CAPACITY TO CONTRACT

A person who is intoxicated may be unable to understand the nature and effects of contractual commitments made while in that condition. Generally, the law treats as voidable the contracts made by a person who doesn't know what he is doing or the effects thereof by reason of intoxication. Intoxication thus is usually treated in the same way as incompetency due to mental illness or disease. The same standard is also usually applied to a person who is under the influence of drugs.

Fairness and Fraud

There are, however, several differences in examining the capacity to contract of someone who is under the influence of drugs or alcohol and of someone who is mentally ill. Some states do not allow a person to avoid contracts made while intoxicated or under the influence of drugs unless that party can show that the person with whom his contract was made knew of the person's condition and took advantage of it. If a person is responsible for the intoxication of the other party with whom a contract is made, or if a person takes unfair advantage of the other's intoxication, whether or not responsible for causing it, the courts will often refuse to enforce the contract as a matter of fairness and equity.

Under this method of analysis, the courts are generally concerned not so much with the degree of intoxication affecting one person's capacity to contract as with the conduct of the party with whom that party contracts. In these cases, some degree of intoxication or impairment of judgment, when coupled with fraudulent action by the other contracting party, may allow the intoxicated party to avoid his contract. If one contracting party deceives the intoxicated person with whom he contracts, the court will likely allow the intoxicated person to avoid the contract on the basis of fraud, if not for lack of contracted capacity.

Degree of Intoxication

While fairness and fraud are sometimes reviewed when examining the capacity to contract of the intoxicated person, the law usually is more concerned with the effect of the intoxication on the person's understanding of his contract than on who is responsible for that degree of intoxication. If a person has been legally adjudged to be incompetent because of habitual drunkenness, that person no longer has any capacity to contract; his contracts are considered void, not voidable. In the absence of a legal determination of incompetency due to intoxication, the court must determine if the degree of intoxication is sufficient to allow a person to avoid his contracts by disaffirming them.

Generally, in the absence of fraud or special circumstances, if a person is slightly under the influence of alcohol or is partially intoxicated, contracts made by that person will be considered valid. Intoxication that causes some impairment of a person's judgment or a feeling of exhilaration generally is not sufficient to render contracts voidable. Instead, as the *Olsen* case indicates, there must be intoxication to such a degree that a person is deprived of reason and unable to understand the consequences of his actions.

If a person is so intoxicated as to lack the capacity to contract, he will usually be allowed to disaffirm and avoid its obligations. If, however, the intoxicated person cannot return the consideration he has received, in the absence of fraud by the other party, he will generally not be granted the right to disaffirm the contract. Furthermore, if the contract was for necessaries, the intoxicated person, like the minor, will be held liable for the reasonable value of the furnished items.

Olsen v. Hawkins

Supreme Court of Idaho
408 P.2d 462 (1965)

This case was brought by Olsen to collect proceeds due him from insurance on the life of Turner, who died in 1960. Until 1957, Olsen (Turner's stepson) was Turner's beneficiary. Olsen claimed that the change of beneficiary from himself to Hawkins made by Turner in 1957 occurred while Turner was intoxicated and therefore should not be given effect. The trial court agreed with Olsen and found the contract by which Turner changed his beneficiary to be voidable. Accordingly it entered judgment for Olsen. Hawkins (the appellant) appealed to the Supreme Court, which reversed the trial court's judgment.

Knudson, Justice

We approach this case with full recognition of the long established rule of this court that our province is to examine the record in the light most favorable to the judgment and that when findings of the trial court are supported by competent substantial evidence they are binding and conclusive on appeal.

The only question presented for our determination is whether respondents sustained the burden of proof in support of their charge that Turner was mentally incompetent to execute the change of beneficiary on the policy effective as of March 17, 1960.

Several rules of law are applicable to the case at bar and must be considered during our review of this record. It is a fundamental rule that the law will presume sanity rather than insanity, competency rather than incompetency; that every man is capable of managing his own affairs and responsible for his own acts. Likewise it is presumed that each man is capable of understanding the nature and effect of his contracts.

It may also be stated that as a general rule, all proceedings involving the competency of an individual to execute a valid contract start with the presumption of competency and that this presumption may be relied upon until the contrary is shown.

In the instant case Turner was described by some as being "forgetful and childish." This expression was not further defined. However, a reasonable interpretation of it would be that they did not consider Turner as possessing the mental capacity of the average man of his age. In this connection it should be noted that where a person possesses sufficient mental capacity to understand the nature of the transaction and is left to exercise his own free will, his contract will not be invalidated because he was of a less degree of intelligence than his co-contractor; because he was fearful or worried; because he was eccentric or entertained peculiar beliefs; or because he was aged or both aged and mentally weak. . . .

Clearly, a person's dissipated condition is not in itself a ground for avoiding a contract or deed, since it is well known that while habitual drunkards are, at times, mentally infirm to the same extent as an insane person or an idiot, at other times they are sober and rational. Accordingly, the rule is that in the absence of an adjudication finding a habitual drunkard to be incompetent, in order to avoid his contract or deed on the ground of his incompetency, it must be shown that his mental condition was such, at the time the contract or deed was made, that he lacked the power of reason and was unable to comprehend the nature and consequences of his act in entering into the contract or executing the deed. A deed executed in a sober interval by one who is addicted to the excessive use of liquor, but who has not been adjudicated incompetent and has not suffered a permanent impairment of mind as a result of his excessive indulgence, will stand, at least in the absence of undue influence or fraud.

The evidence submitted in support of respondents' allegations and contentions may be briefly summarized as follows:

Prior to the death of Turner's wife, they, the Turners, lived at Montpelier, Idaho, and they frequently visited respondents, who lived at Pocatello, Idaho. Mrs. Turner died in November 1956. At that time Turner was a retired railroad engineer, receiving two pensions totaling approximately $250.00 a month; that following the death of Mrs. Turner he became a "heavy drinker" and was what may be termed an alcoholic during a substantial portion of the years that followed; that on a number of occasions while he was under the influence of intoxicating liquor he was arrested for various offenses, among which were, being drunk in a public place, driving while drunk and indecent exposure, and was finally committed to the State Hospital South as an alcoholic.

The record shows that following the death of his wife Turner moved to Lava Hot Springs sometime during December 1956 and it was during 1957 when he became involved in most of the arrests hereinbefore mentioned. During May 1957 he voluntarily entered said State Hospital, at which time "he was diagnosed as a case of Chronic Alcoholism," and remained at the hospital about two weeks. Thereafter and on October 24, 1957 he was readmitted to the hospital under a judicial order and the same diagnosis was given him. On May 1, 1958, he was discharged. . . .

Following his discharge from the hospital Turner remained in the city of Blackfoot for three or four months, following which he moved to Ashton, Idaho, where he remained for several months. It was during his stay in Ashton, and on or about March 17, 1960, that the change of beneficiary here involved was accomplished.

This brings us to a consideration of one of the principal issues presented, namely, does the record disclose competent evidence in support of the court's finding that the change of beneficiary was made while Turner was incompetent and unable to transact his business or understand the nature of the transaction. . . . [A] contract by an alcoholic may not be avoided on that ground alone if at the time of its execution he was sober and in the possession of his faculties. Proofs of old age and alcoholic addiction standing alone do not constitute proof of incompetency. The evidence must show that at the time of the act his understanding was clouded or his reason dethroned by intoxication or its effects.

The only evidence regarding Turner's condition during the period of several months both before and after March 17, 1960 was submitted by appellant and three witnesses called by him. Two of said witnesses were employed by the railroad in the capacity of telegrapher-cashiers and the other as a roadmaster clerk. Their testimony may be briefly summarized as follows: They frequently saw and visited with Turner while he lived in Ashton; most of such visits were had at the railroad depot, although one testified that he had had Turner in his home, had visited him in his own apartment and on occasions had gone fishing with him; that he appeared neatly dressed and well-mannered; that he visited and conversed in a normal manner and they were not aware of any addiction he may have had for alcoholic drink. They regarded him as entirely competent; that Turner mentioned to each of them he had changed the beneficiary and to some he stated his reason for so doing. One witness testified that he was requested to and did witness the execution by Turner of the change of beneficiary form and that Turner seemed perfectly normal at that time.

Appellant also testified that at the time the assignment was made he was depot agent for the railroad at Ashton; that he had known Turner for several months prior to March 1960; that he, Turner, would come to the depot office almost each day; on a few occasions he had talked with Turner at Legion meetings and went fishing with him once; that the first time Turner mentioned anything to him about changing the beneficiary on his insurance policy was about the middle of January 1960, which occasion occurred at the depot and was described by appellant as follows:

"Q. All right. Then the two of you were present, and will you tell us as best you recall what was the conversation?

"A. Well, he showed me a letter from the railroad accounting department that said that he was about six months behind on his premiums with his group insurance, and he told me that he had tried to get his stepson to take over this policy and pay the premiums on it, and bury him. He said all he was interested in was to be buried with his wife; she was buried in Pocatello, but he said his stepson, he didn't get along good with him, and he couldn't really trust him and he wouldn't do it for him, and he wanted to know if I would accept the responsibility to pay the premiums in order to collect this insurance."

This testimony of appellant and his witnesses regarding Turner's mental and physical condition at and near the time when the assignment was accomplished is uncontradicted.

Appellant's witnesses also testified that he, Turner, had stated to them that he was not satisfied with respondents' handling of the insurance; that he refused to stop to see respondents while he was in Pocatello and did not speak very highly of them. Whether Turner felt any resentment toward his stepson for causing him to be committed to the hospital is not disclosed; however, there is no contradiction of the foregoing mentioned testimony of appellant's witnesses. It is true that appellant's evidence regarding Turner's demeanor is in contrast to that introduced by respondents. Nevertheless, it is undisputed that Turner moved to Ashton within a comparatively short time after spending approximately seven months in a hospital where no liquor was available to him.

We have not overlooked the fact that respondents also introduced substantial evidence to the effect that commencing with September 1960 and continuing to his death, Turner reverted to his former addiction. In short, we have presented to us by the evidence in this case a man whose conduct prior to and after execution of the instrument here in question, was peculiar to say the least, but the sum and substance of the testimony indicates only that his trouble was caused by intoxication.

Applying the foregoing stated rule to the facts disclosed in this case, appellant's uncontradicted evidence regarding Turner's mental condition at the time the assignment was being considered and accomplished by him cannot be disregarded. We find no substantial evidence in the record to support the finding by the court that Turner was incompetent at the time of making the assignment involved. The judgment is reversed.

REVIEW PROBLEMS

When answering these questions, assume the age of majority is twenty-one.

1. Fellows, a former neighbor, gave seventeen-year-old Cantrell $1,070 to help finance her college education in return for her promise to repay him later. Cantrell had repaid only $40 prior to her twenty-first birthday, and soon thereafter Fellows began requesting more money. At age twenty-six, Cantrell was visited by Fellows, who wanted to discuss the situation. Cantrell then wrote to Fellows: "I have discussed your proposal with close members of my family and an attorney. They seem to feel that [my] future is not secure enough for [me] to sign any kind of a note." Does Fellows have any kind of legal recourse? Fellows v. Cantrell, 352 P.2d 289 (Colo. Sup. Ct. 1960).

2. Pelham, twenty years old, bought a car from Howard Motors for $2,075.60, paying $500 down. In the bill of sale, Pelham certified that he was "twenty-one years of age or older," and he told the salesman he was in fact twenty-two years old. Pelham took the car home but brought it back the next day for repairs. When Howard failed to correct the problems, Pelham had his attorney write the company, repudiating the contract and demanding return of the down payment. Should Pelham prevail? Pelham v. Howard Motors, Inc., 156 N.E.2d 597 (Ill. App. Ct. 1959).

3. Horton, age nineteen, rented three furnished rooms from Johnson. He and his wife occupied the rooms for approximately five months. When Horton moved out, Johnson brought suit for one week's rent, "one week of notice in lieu of intent to terminate tenancy," and damages to certain interior furnishings. Johnson felt certain that Horton would be responsible for the housing ac-

commodations. Do you? Johnson v. Horton, 343 S.W.2d 653 (Mo. Ct. App. 1961)

4. Harrod purchased a watch when he was seventeen years old from Livingston and Company. He paid $3 down and agreed to satisfy the $69.80 balance by paying bimonthly installments of $5. Harrod never made any payments, and he left three months later for a four-year tour of duty with the navy. He lost the watch shortly thereafter. Harrod heard nothing more about the contract until suit to compel payment was instituted almost ten years later. What should the result have been? Harrod v. Kelly Adjustment Co., 179 A.2d 431 (D.C. Man. Ct. App. 1962).

5. Trask undertook to care for Neal, his ninety-seven-year-old father-in-law with whom he lived, after senility had rendered Neal incompetent. Trask and his wife leased their home from Neal in return for performing a variety of tasks, including payment of taxes and insurance on the building and land. This arrangement, however, did not include personal services rendered to Neal. Upon Neal's death, Trask filed a claim in probate court against the executor of Neal's estate for services in nursing and personal care of Neal as an invalid. What result should the court have reached? Trask v. Davis, 297 S.W.2d 792 (Mo. Ct. App. 1957).

6. Stewart and Curry were partners in a paving contracting business. After some marital troubles developed between Curry and his wife, he began to drink heavily and on one occasion was hospitalized for alcoholism. During this time Curry contributed very little to the paving business. For several months Stewart and Curry talked about their business problems. Then an agreement dissolving the partnership was prepared by Stewart and given to Curry. Two weeks later Curry returned the agreement, which he had signed. Stewart also signed the agreement. Several other documents relating to the dissolution of the partnership were subsequently signed by both Stewart and Curry Three months later. Curry filed suit. He claimed he was still recovering from his alcoholism, that he was under the influence of sedatives, and that therefore he is entitled to avoid the dissolution agreement because he lacked the capacity to contract. Do you agree? Curry v. Stewart 368 P 2d 297 (Kan. Sup. Ct. 1962).

7. Bowling, aged 16, purchased a used car from Sperry for several hundred dollars. He paid the full amount in cash. After driving the car for one week he found the main bearing had burned out. He returned the car to Sperry and asked that it be repaired; Sperry said it would cost Bowling $80 to repair it. Bowling said he wouldn't pay that amount and left the car with Sperry. The next week he wrote Sperry and said he wanted to disaffirm his contract of purchase. He also asked for the return of his money. Sperry refused and Bowling sued. Can Bowling disaffirm this contract? How would you decide if this car is a necessary for Bowling? Bowling v. Sperry 184 N E 2d 901 (Ind. Sup. Ct. 1962).

8. A Savings and Loan Association loaned money for a home to Mayer and her husband and took a mortgage on the property. Though Mayer was a minor at the time, she signed in three places an affidavit that stated that she had attained the age of majority. After the loan was made and the home built, Mayer and her husband were divorced. They abandoned the home and no payments were made on the loan after their divorce. The Savings & Loan brought a foreclosure suit on its mortgage and Mayer defended by asserting her lack of capacity. She sought to disaffirm the loan and the mortgage agreement and wanted to recover the payments she had made on the loan and the money she had spent fixing up the property, which would now belong

tion of an uncertain event or a fact in dispute. Bets on a horse race, football game, or roll of the dice are all wagers. The public policy regarding wagering agreements varies from state to state. While most states prohibit many wagering agreements, generally such schemes as raffles, bingo, or the awarding of door prizes are permitted.

A number of states have recognized that substantial revenues can be obtained from gambling and have instituted state-operated lotteries. Similarly, charitable organizations may be licensed under certain conditions to conduct raffles, to give millionaires' parties, or to sponsor bingo games. In a few states, wagering agreements that do not involve substantial amounts are permitted. Thus a friendly bet on the local football game might be permitted in some states while prohibited in others. A poker game among senior citizens in Florida received national attention in 1982 when a local prosecutor decided to enforce the state's gambling laws. Although the enforcement of these laws is usually sporadic, it is wise to check the statutes in your state and to be aware of the possibility (if not the probability) that contracts violating these statutes could not only be unenforceable but also might result in criminal sanctions.

Not all contracts that will reward each party differently depending on a future event are wagers. An insurance policy, for example, is such a contract. Contracts for the sale or purchase of commodities that will be harvested in the future are similarly speculative. These agreements, however, involve items of value that are being sold and purchased. The parties are not merely speculating on the outcome of a future event. The insured has a substantial interest in his life or property, and the commodity purchaser agrees to accept the commodity being bargained for. Since these agreements are not wagers, they are not illegal and unenforceable.

Statutes and Usury Contracts

State statutes often limit the amount of interest that may be charged by a lender.[1] Any contract by which the lender receives more than the permitted interest is illegal. There usually are civil consequences as well as criminal penalties placed upon those who lend money at usurious rates. In most states, the lender is denied the right to collect any interest on a usurious contract. Some states also prohibit the lender from collecting the principal due on the loan as well as the interest. A few states allow the lender to collect the interest permitted by law and prohibit only the excess "illegal" interest. Lenders are usually permitted to recover expenses and fees incurred in preparing loan documents. Similarly, they may be able to assess points as a cost of obtaining a loan. These expenses, fees, or points are not generally considered interest.

There often are many different usury statutes in the same state. Some statutes apply only to small loan associations, while others are aimed at installment loans such as credit-card transactions. Loans made to businesses are often totally exempt from usury statutes. Most states permit interest rates charged by those who issue credit cards to exceed the statutory rate. Similarly, interest charged to finance a home or a car may usually exceed the basic rate. Finally, almost all states permit small loan companies to charge rates up to 36 percent. These rates are permitted so that the borrower who can't go to conventional financial institutions will have a legitimate place from which to borrow.

The primary objective of usury statutes is to protect the borrower from being forced to pay an excessive amount for the use of money. Usury has been illegal since biblical times, and the usurious lender has often been a moral outcast. Yet, frequently, the effect of usury statutes has been to penalize those persons most in need of funds.[2] As inflation pushes the market price for the use of money higher and higher, a usury statute imposing a fixed maximum interest rate forces lenders to stop making unprofitable loans. The effect of such a statute then is to reduce the consumer's options rather than to increase his or her bargaining power with the lender. Indeed, some lenders have refused to make loans in certain states. Others, including some major New York banks, have transferred some of their operations to other states because of the effect of usury laws on their business.

Statutes and Blue Laws

Some states have statutes that forbid "all secular labor and business on the Sabbath." In these states, it would seem that all contracts made on Sunday are illegal and unenforceable, at least as long as they remain executory. Other states prohibit only certain types of transactions or the sale of certain goods on Sunday. Frequently, a state statute or municipal ordinance will prohibit the sale of alcoholic beverages on Sunday. The sale of automobiles or certain other consumer products on Sunday is also prohibited in some communities in order to regulate competition among sellers and to provide a day of rest from commercial activity.

In interpreting these statutes, courts typically seek to avoid the harsh effects that could result if the agreements were totally unenforceable. Instead, if some part of the agreement is made or performed on some day other than Sunday, the contract is usually enforced. Thus a contract that would have been illegal because it was entered into on a Sunday will be legal if the parties later negotiate or in any way approve their earlier illegal agreement. For this reason, blue laws generally have little effect on normal business transactions. However, active enforcement of these laws varies significantly from state to state and even among communities within the same state.

Statutes and Licensing Regulations

Statutes in all states require that licenses, certificates, permits, or registrations be obtained to perform certain acts. For example, the Michigan Department of Licensing and Regulation includes numerous boards and commissions, such as the Board of Accountancy, the Board of Registration for Architects, the Athletic Board of Control, the Board of Barber Examiners, the Builders Residential and Maintenance and Alteration Contractors Board, the Board of Chiropractic Examiners, the Professional Board of Registration for Community Planners, the Board of Dentistry, the Professional Board of Registration for Engineers, the Board of Registration for Foresters, the Board of Horology, the Boards of Regulation for Land Surveyors, etc. Each board and commission is charged with regulating some activity of interest to the state, frequently by issuing licenses or permits to those persons who meet qualifications established for the regulated activity.

In some cases, state statutes merely require a fee to be paid in order to obtain the needed license. These licensing laws are known as revenue statutes since they are primarily concerned with raising revenue, even though there may be some application procedure that also must be completed. Usually, anyone can obtain a fishing license or a minnow and wiggler dealer license.[3] Such licensing laws do not usually subject the licensee to any significant regulation by the state.

On the other hand, the primary purpose of regulatory statutes is to regulate those obtaining a license. The state wants to ensure that its nurses, doctors, real estate brokers, plumbers, lawyers and others who serve the public are competent to engage in the profession or business being licensed. While regulatory statutes are concerned chiefly with the protection of the public, a fee is often assessed to cover administrative costs. There are several consequences for persons who do not comply with the requirements of state licensing statutes. In some cases, the violation of a state licensing law can lead to criminal charges. In other cases, a special panel, board, or professional association may be authorized to take disciplinary action against the person who has not complied with the state's licensing provisions.

Our primary concern in this chapter is not, however, with these criminal or disciplinary consequences to the violator of a state licensing law. Instead, our focus is on the civil law consequences to the parties who have made a contract that does not comply with the licensing requirements. If a state requires you to have a license in order to be an architect, can you contract with someone to provide architectural services if you do not have the required license? Will the state enforce your contract? If you are not paid by the other contracting party, can you bring suit to recover the money you were to be paid? The answer to these questions depends on the wording of the applicable licensing statute.

Frequently, the statute itself will specify that any agreements made by persons who do not comply with its terms will be unenforceable. When the statute is silent concerning the enforceability of such agreements, the courts frequently look to the purpose of the statute. Contracts made without a license in violation of a revenue statute are usually enforceable. Thus a farmer who should but does not have a license to sell his produce at a city market can enforce contracts with those who purchase the products. While the farmer has violated a licensing statute intended to raise revenue for the city, that violation does not affect contracts made by the farmer. If, however, the purpose of the licensing statute is primarily regulatory, the person who performs services or delivers goods without complying with the licensing provisions will be denied the court's aid in enforcing contracts he has made with the purchasers of his goods or services. The *Silver* case exemplifies the approach of the courts to enforcement of contracts that violate these types of licensing statutes.

Silver v. A.O.C. Corporation
Court of Appeals of Michigan
187 N.W.2d 532 (1971)

Plaintiff Silver is a journeyman electrician who had been employed by defendant's predecessor to repair lights at an apartment building in Detroit. He was not licensed as an electrical contractor under state law or city ordinance. Defendant A.O.C. Corporation is an apartment management company that had become the manager of the apartment building in question. When plaintiff met the caretakers at the apartment building, he gave them his card so they could "call him in an emergency if the caretakers could not get ahold of the management company."

In 1967, the caretaker's wife called plaintiff to repair a short circuit in the caretaker's apartment. Subsequently, he was asked by her to fix one or two hallway lights. Plaintiff found the wires in the hallway were burned by oversized bulbs and he undertook to replace and rewire all the defective wiring. His work was accomplished over a four-month period and he submitted a bill to defendant for $893. It was defendant's first notice that the work had been done.

Defendant refused to pay plaintiff and plaintiff sued in the common pleas court. That court found plaintiff's work was a "minor repair" exempt from the licensing statute and awarded judgment for plaintiff. The circuit court affirmed and defendant was granted leave to appeal to the Court of Appeals. The Court of Appeals found plaintiff had violated the state's licensing requirements since his work was not merely minor repairs. Accordingly, it reversed the judgment of the Circuit Court and ordered judgment in favor of defendant.

Per Curiam

This is an appeal by leave granted from a judgment of the Wayne county circuit court which affirmed a judgment for plaintiff entered in common pleas court in a contract action for materials and services rendered.

Plaintiff is a journeyman electrician. At no time pertinent to this action was he licensed as an electrical contractor under either the state electrical administrative act, M.C.L.A. § 338.881 et seq. or the equivalent Detroit ordinance. Defendant is an apartment management company.

In 1966 plaintiff was employed by defendant's predecessor to repair lights at a Second boulevard apartment building in Detroit. At that time he met the caretaker, to whom he gave his card "just in case they had an emergency sometime and they couldn't get ahold of [the management company], they could call me direct."

In 1967 the caretaker's wife called plaintiff to repair a short circuit in the caretaker's apartment. After fixing the short circuit plaintiff was asked by the caretaker's wife to fix one or two hallway lights. Plaintiff discovered that the wires in the hallway fixtures were burned by oversized bulbs. He found that the same condition existed in all the lights in the building and undertook to replace and rewire all the defective wiring. The project was accomplished over a four-month period (July–October, 1967). Plaintiff spent 125 hours on the job and used $143 worth of his own materials. In October, 1967, he submitted a bill for $893 to the defendant. It was defendant's first notice that the work had been done.

Defendant refused payment and plaintiff sued. Judgment for plaintiff was given in common pleas court on findings that the work performed amounted to minor repair work which was exempted from the licensing statute and that the caretaker's wife had actual or apparent authority to contract on behalf of defendant. The circuit court affirmed, finding the characterization of the job as minor repair work not error and the finding of proper agency not against the great weight of the evidence.

Defendant claims the trial courts erred in holding that plaintiff was exempt from the licensing statute because the work done was minor repair work.

The electrical administrative act was an act "to safeguard persons and property" and "to provide for licensing of electricians and electrical contractors and the inspection of electrical wiring." M.C.L.A. § 338.881

The act, in effect, is to insure that persons who do electrical work are duly licensed. Section 7 of the act provides that no person, firm, or corporation shall engage in a business of electrical contracting unless duly licensed as an electrical contractor. An exception to this section is minor repair work, Section 7(a), which is defined as "electrical wiring not in excess of a valuation of $50."

There appears to be little doubt that what plaintiff was doing would be considered to be electrical contracting. Section 1(b) defines electrical contracting as "any person, firm or corporation engaged in the business of erecting, installing, altering, repairing, servicing or maintaining electrical wiring devices, appliances or equipment." One of defendant's witnesses, a senior assistant electrical engineer and supervisor of the Detroit electrical inspection bureau, testified that the type of work done "was required to have been contracted for by a licensed electrical contractor."

Thus, unless the work fell under the "minor repair work" exception it could only be done by a licensed electrical contractor, which plaintiff wasn't.

As stated earlier, "minor repair work" is that which in value is worth $50 or less. Included in this figure must be the material as well as labor necessary to complete the repair and restore the item to good working order. It was stipulated below that the value of the work done was $893. Since this is well in excess of $50, this work would not come under the "minor repair work" exception to the licensing requirement.

Plaintiff was in violation of the licensing act when he did the work. Therefore, his action to recover on the contract should be barred from the courts. When one enters into a contract to perform services or furnish materials in violation of a statute which is enacted to protect the public health, morals, and safety, and which contains a penal provision, as this statute does, he cannot maintain an action to recover thereon.

The judgment of the circuit court affirming the judgment of the common pleas court is reversed and the cause is remanded to the circuit court for entry of a judgment in favor of defendant against the plaintiff in the amount of $1,026.45, the sum recovered by plaintiff through a writ of garnishment while the appeal was pending.

Reversed.

THE COMMON LAW AND ILLEGAL CONTRACTS

There is no clear and distinct rule as to which source, statutory law or common law, is to be referred to when ascertaining the legality of certain contracts. The prudent business person will have both the legislative and judicial sources checked in the event of a possible problem. Since the courts first developed the doctrine of unenforceability regarding most of the illegal agreements indicated in this section, they are noted here as being illegal due to common law or court decisions. However, in some states, statutes have been enacted that make these agreements illegal. This section reviews contracts that are illegal because they restrain trade, relieve one party from some liability to another party, include unconscion-

able provisions, or involve other acts that conflict with public policy.

Agreements in Restraint of Trade

The law disfavors agreements where one person agrees not to compete with another. Such agreements impose too great a restraint on the individual and adversely affect competition within our society. Unless such agreements are incidental to other lawful contracts and are limited to reasonable terms, the courts will not enforce them.

Agreements not to compete are often found in contracts in which a business is being purchased and sold. The purchaser wants to ensure that the seller, who has built up the good will of the business, will not continue to be in competition with the purchased business.

Noncompetitive agreements are also found in employer-employee contracts. An employee may be working in a vital segment of the employer's business. The employer wants to ensure that the employee does not establish a competing business based in part on the valuable information learned from the employer.

A noncompetitive agreement will generally be examined to determine if it is reasonable to the concerned parties and to the public. Agreements that restrain trade by restricting competition between the seller and purchaser of a business are generally viewed in a favorable light by the courts. A court's inquiry will usually focus on whether a contract provision restraining the seller is reasonable in time and space. A provision restricting the seller from being employed in a similar business or opening up a new business that is competitive with the purchaser will be reasonable for several years but not for ten or twenty years. The restraint ordinarily cannot prohibit the seller from opening a similar business in the next state or in a distant community. Instead, the geographic area of the restraint must be the area in which the need for protection by the purchaser is most dominant.

Agreements made between an employer and employee that restrict the employee's right to compete with the employer are usually examined more closely by the courts than are agreements between seller and purchaser. Unlike the purchaser of a business, the employee generally is not in an equal bargaining position with the other contracting party. In the sale of a business, there almost always is a recognized need for the purchaser to be able to protect the good will of the business. Frequently, the good will is the primary asset being purchased, and the purchaser will not be able to protect it if the seller can compete with the business being sold. The employer, on the other hand, does not have as great a need to protect the business' good will against the employee. Usually, an employee is less likely to be able to leave the employer's business and take the employer's good will to his or her own use than is the seller of a business. In these employment cases, the courts will examine not only the need for protection by the employer from the employee but also the relative hardship imposed on the employee. The employee's lack of bargaining power can be a decisive factor in many cases. The public interest, served or defeated by the restraint, also will be examined, particularly when vital services or goods might be withheld from the community if the restraint is enforced.

After the reasonableness of the restraint has been determined, the court must then decide several questions related to the agreement's enforceability. If the parties have made an unreasonable restraint, should the court rewrite the restraint so that it is reasonable and enforce it under those terms or should it leave the one party free from any restraint? Similarly, if a business sale and purchase agreement contains a provision that unreasonably restrains the seller, is that provision one that can be separated from other provisions in the agreement? Is the contract divisible into separate sections? If one part of a contract is illegal and unenforceable, can any part of the remaining contract be enforced?

Knoebel Mercantile Company v. Siders

Supreme Court of Colorado

439 P.2d 355 (1968)

Siders was employed as a salesman with Knoebel. At the time he was hired, he signed an employment contract that included a restrictive covenant providing he would not work for any of Knoebel's competitors for two years after the termination of his employment with Knoebel. Siders worked for Knoebel for several years and then took a position as a salesman with a competing company. Knoebel sued to prevent Siders from working as a salesman with the competing company. The trial court held for Siders. Knoebel appealed that decision. The Supreme Court, finding the agreement unenforceable, affirmed the trial court's judgment in favor of the employee Siders.

Moore, Chief Justice

Knoebel brought the action against Siders, a former employee, seeking to restrain him from working as a salesman for one of its competitors. The injunctive relief sought against Siders was based on a restrictive covenant contained in a written contract of employment entered into between him and Knoebel under date of June 1, 1964. Pertinent portions of the contract are as follows:

> "NOW, THEREFORE, in consideration of Employer's hiring Employee and for other good and valuable consideration, Employee promises and agrees that in the event of the termination of his said employment for any reason whatsoever, for a period of two years from and after the date of such termination he will not, directly or indirectly, either as an owner, officer, employee, agent or otherwise, engage in the institutional food, paper and supply business, bakery supply business, and janitorial supply business, or any part thereof in all or any part of the State of Colorado, Wyoming, Montana, New Mexico, Nebraska, Kansas, So. Dakota, and any other State in which Employer transacts its business at any time up to the date of such employment termination. Employee further promises and agrees that during said two-year period he will not divulge to anyone other than Employer or its officers or authorized employees or agents any of the trade secrets, methods, systems, customer or credit lists, volumes, preferences, purchasing lists and practices, standards and sources, selling and shipping practices and other methods, system records and statistics hereafter disclosed to Employee, reposed in his confidence by Employer or otherwise acquired by Employee in the course of his employment. Failure to perform these promises by the Employee shall give the Employer the right to an injunction to restrain the Employee from further violation, as well as damages. . . ."

Prior to the date of the contract Siders resided in Wyoming and was working as a salesman for a candy and tobacco distributing business. After some preliminary negotiations he was advised on May 14, 1964, that his application for employment was accepted by Knoebel and he reported for work on June 1, 1964. While completing and signing documents relating to insurance, social security, withholding tax and similar matters he was presented for the first time with the restrictive agreement above quoted. He read and then signed the agreement. He was given the customary training course for salesmen, after which Knoebel assigned him to a territory consisting of Colorado Springs, Colorado, and a limited adjacent area in which about 150 customers were located. He was furnished with a price list, prospect cards, some information as to the credit ratings of the customers, their buying habits and other general information. He was also furnished with a car, order books, and other things useful to him as a salesman.

Siders terminated his employment with Knoebel on September 9, 1966, and went to work for John Sexton & Co., a competitor of Knoebel, as a salesman. Though Sexton was in competition with Knoebel there was a considerable difference in the scope of operations in the business of the two companies since it appears from the evidence that Knoebel dealt in 10,000 items of merchandise, all manufactured by others, and Sexton dealt in only 1600 items many of which it manufactured.

The record discloses that although Siders was employed as a salesman, he was assigned to a small territory with only 150 customers, whereas if the restrictive covenant is enforced by injunction as prayed by Knoebel he will be prohibited from operating in all of Colorado, Wyoming, Montana, New Mexico, Nebraska, Kansas, South Dakota, and any other State in which Knoebel was transacting business on the date of termination of his employment.

The undisputed evidence was that Siders intended to and would, unless enjoined therefrom, solicit on behalf of John Sexton & Co. some of the customers he previously solicited on behalf of Knoebel, and the court so found. Lengthy Findings of Fact entered by the trial court included the following:

> "(9) Familiarity between salesman and customer is not of primary importance. Almost all customers buy from several competitors on a continuing basis. Sales in the institutional food industry are based primarily upon product and price with time of delivery being a secondary factor. Defendant Siders is not in a position to control the business of the prior customers as a personal asset. Sales volume may either decrease or increase when the salesman in a territory is changed.
>
> "(10) Siders' services for Plaintiff Knoebel were not unique in character and his place with Plaintiff Knoebel's organization has already been filled.
>
> "(11) The restrictive agreement was designed to restrict Defendant Siders from doing two things. First, it prohibited the disclosure of trade secrets and confidential information acquired by Defendant Siders in the course of his employment. Second, it prohibited Defendant Siders from competing with Plaintiff Knoebel.
>
> "(12) During the course of Defendant Siders' employment by Plaintiff Knoebel, he acquired general information regarding Plaintiff Knoebel's business. The information which Plaintiff Knoebel considered to be secret and confidential is available to Plaintiff Knoebel's competitors and is not confidential and does not involve trade secrets . . .
>
> "(14) A permanent injunction would result in Defendant Siders having to either move from the region in which he has spent most of his adult life or abandon the type of work in which he has most experience.
>
> "(15) The injury to Defendant Siders by enforcement of the agreement outweighs the benefit to Plaintiff Knoebel.
>
> "(16) There is no proof of threatened or actual irreparable damage to Plaintiff Knoebel."

The full record has been read and we find ample evidence to sustain the fact findings of the trial court. We shall not disturb those findings.

It is argued by counsel for Knoebel that the trial court erred as a matter of law in denying Knoebel's claim for injunction and, alternatively, if the restriction was unreasonable as to time and area this court should "reform" the restriction with regard thereto.

. . . The test as to whether a covenant of this kind will be enforced by injunction hinges on a determination of the reasonableness of the restriction under all the facts and circumstances of each case.

. . . If it is unfair and unreasonable in a given set of circumstances, relief by injunction will be denied. The restrictions in contracts not to engage in business in competition with another, to be valid must be reasonable, must not impose undue hardship, must be no wider than necessary to afford the required protection, and each case must stand on its own facts. In the instant case the trial court, after a lengthy and searching inquiry, determined that the restriction here involved was unreasonable under all the pertinent circumstances. We cannot say that the court erred as a matter of law in reaching this conclusion.

The judgment of the trial court is affirmed.

Contracts with Exculpatory Clauses

Exculpatory clauses in a contract relieve or limit the liability of one of the parties in the event that party does not perform his or her part of the contract. Such clauses are viewed with disfavor by the law. The policy of the law is that damages caused by one party's nonperformance of contract terms should be recoverable by the injured party. An exculpatory clause that relieves one party of liability thus may be contrary to legal policy. While it has generally been the courts that have declared such contract provisions to be unenforceable as contrary to public policy, statutes in many states declare some of these clauses to be unenforceable and illegal. For example, in most jurisdictions there are statutes that deny the enforceability of at least some part of exculpatory clauses found in apartment leases prepared by landlords for tenants.

Exculpatory clauses that are unenforceable can be classified under two main headings: (1) those limiting liability of a dealer who sells goods or services to the public and (2) those limiting an employer's liability for negligence that causes injury to an employee. As to clauses of the first type, the law notes that there rarely is equality of bargaining power between the consumer and the dealer. It is in the public interest that those people who serve the public and whose contracts with the public are usually not the subject of bargaining and negotiation not be allowed to relieve themselves of liability for their own negligence. As to clauses of the second type, the policy of the law is to discourage negligence by making wrongdoers pay damages. If an employer or its agent causes injury to anyone, even an employee, the injured party should be able to recover damages. Furthermore, an employee too is generally not in an equal bargaining position with an employer. Thus such clauses are not favored and will not be enforced.

Some exculpatory clauses that limit the liability of one of the contracting parties in the event of nonperformance by that party will be enforced. Some states allow contracting parties the freedom to contract under the broadest possible terms. In these states, freedom of contract outweighs concern over exculpatory clauses. Two factors are particularly important in these instances: the bargaining power of the parties and the degree to which the law otherwise regulates the concerned agreement. If both parties are business firms that have negotiated the terms of their agreement with each other, the courts are more likely to allow one of the parties to limit its liability. Similarly, if one of the businesses is already subject to significant regulatory control by the state, the rules, regulations, and policies of the state regulatory agencies may permit the business to limit its liability in certain contracts.[4]

One of the most common situations in which one of the parties to a contract seeks to limit his or her liability concerns the bailee of property. A bailee is someone who has been given the right to possess property. The restaurant checkroom, the downtown parking lot, the airport baggage counter, the warehouse storing your out-of-season snowmobile are all bailees. These bailees usually have signs on their property, statements on the backs of receipts, or identification tickets that limit their liability, even for their own negligence, in the event your property is lost or damaged.

As the *Akin* case indicates, while such clauses are generally enforceable, in some cases courts will not enforce them because to do so would violate the public policy of the state. While it is impossible to define what constitutes public policy, it is clear that social forces play major roles in shaping this concept. Many courts have refused to enforce such clauses if they involve a transaction exhibiting some or all of the six criteria noted in the *Tunkl* case, which is referred to by the court in *Akin*. Which factors are particularly applicable in the transaction the court is concerned with in the *Akin* case?

Akin v. Business Title Corporation
California Court of Appeals
70 Cal. Rptr. 287 (1968)

Plaintiff Akin was the seller of a bar and restaurant in Orange County, California. Defendant Business Title Corporation, an escrow company, acted as escrow holder in connection with the sale. As part of the purchase price, plaintiff received a note secured by a chattel mortgage on personal property in the bar and restaurant worth about $7,500. Defendant corporation sent the mortgage of chattels to California Land Title Corporation, with whom it had done business for years, for recordation of the mortgage. California Land Title Corporation erroneously recorded the mortgage in Los Angeles County instead of Orange County, where the property was located.

The buyer went bankrupt and plaintiff's mortgage was invalid because it had been erroneously recorded in Los Angeles County instead of Orange County. Plaintiff sued the defendant escrow company for the value of the chattel mortgage plus 7 percent interest. The defendant contended it was not liable because its escrow agreement contained an exculpatory clause that insulated it from its own ordinary negligence. The trial court granted plaintiff a judgment in the amount sued for and defendant appealed to the Court of Appeals. The Court of Appeals found that the exculpatory clause did not relieve the escrow company of liability. Accordingly, it affirmed the trial court's judgment.

Kingsley, Associate Judge

The primary issue presented on this appeal is whether the exculpator
so that defendant would not be liable for its own negligence.

Defendant, Business Title Corporation, relies on the case of Simi
America (1958) 159 Cal.App.2d 566, 323 P.2d 1043. In the *Sin*
defendant bank, the escrow agent, failed to record plaintiff's chatt€
plaintiff sued when the buyer went bankrupt. The escrow agreeme
exculpatory clause similar to the one in the present case. The court up
of the exculpatory clause, stating that contracts relieving individuals from their own
ordinary negligence do not contravene public policy.

Plaintiff Akin relies on the more recent Supreme Court case of Tunkl v. Regents of
the University of California (1963), 60 Cal.2d 92, 383P.2d 441. In *Tunkl,* a patient
was required to sign an exculpatory agreement, relieving UCLA Medical Center from
any type of negligence except certain specific types, before he would be treated at
the hospital. The Supreme Court held the exculpatory clause invalid as against public
policy on the ground that the exculpatory clause in the contract was affected with a
public interest. The *Tunkl* court stated that a contractual provision attempting to
absolve a party from liability for negligence will be held invalid as affecting the public
interest if it involves a transaction which exhibits some or all of the following characteristics:

> "It concerns a business of a type generally thought suitable for public regula-
> tion. The party seeking exculpation is engaged in performing a service of great
> importance to the public, which is often a matter of practical necessity for
> some members of the public. The party holds himself out as willing to perform
> this service for any member of the public who seeks it, or at least for any
> member coming within certain established standards. As a result of the essen-
> tial nature of the service, in the economic setting of the transaction, the party
> invoking exculpation possesses a decisive advantage of bargaining strength
> against any member of the public who seeks his services. In exercising a
> superior bargaining power the party confronts the public with a standardized
> adhesion contract of exculpation, and makes no provision whereby a pur-
> chaser may pay additional reasonable fees and obtain protection against
> negligence. Finally, as a result of the transaction, the person or property of
> the purchaser is placed under the control of the seller, subject to the risk of
> carelessness by the seller or his agents."

*The exculpatory clause reads: "It is understood by the parties hereto that in consideration of
Business Title Corporation acting as an escrow holder, that it shall in no case or event be liable
for the failure of any of the conditions of this escrow, or damage caused by the exercise of
its discretion in any particular manner, or for any other reason, except gross negligence or
wilfull [sic] misconduct with reference to said escrow, and it shall not be liable or responsible
for its failure to ascertain the terms or conditions, or to comply with any of the provisions of
any agreement contract, or other document or written instrument filed herein, or referred to
in the escrow, nor shall it be liable or responsible for or on account of any fraud of any nature
whatsoever, for forgeries of any nature whatsoever, or for false personations."

comparing these six criteria set forth in *Tunkl* to the case at bench we find that the transaction before us is also one that "affects the public interest." The transaction concerns a business of the type generally thought suitable for public regulation, and escrow companies have in fact been regulated to some degree by licensing requirements. . . .

> "[T]he nature of the regulation imposed on a business may still afford a clue as to whether exculpation will be permitted. Regulations creating a duty to serve the public or imposing safety or professional standards for a business indicate public concern, extending beyond the specific regulations, for maintaining a standard of service which exculpation would tend to undermine."

Since Financial Code sections 17200 et seq. set safety standards for escrow businesses, the escrow business is apparently thought to be a business suitable for public concern, satisfying this aspect of the *Tunkl* test.

Continuing our examination of the other standards set forth in *Tunkl*, we also find that the escrow company performs an important public service. Although it is possible for a party involved in a real estate transaction to get another escrow agent, or to not use the standard escrow procedure, it is often a matter of "practical necessity" for some members of the public to use the designated escrow agent. This is particularly true in cases such as the one at bench where the detailed provisions of the bulk sales law were involved. The escrow company holds itself out as willing to perform its service for any member of the public who seeks the service, or at least for any member coming within certain established standards. The escrow company possesses a decisive advantage of bargaining strength against a member of the public who seeks its services. Bargaining power need not be a monopoly, and "the power may simply be the result of a 'monopoly' in judgment, brains and foresight as where one party prepares the contract form which the other signs without considering the possible consequences."

. . . The escrow business also presents to the public a "standardized adhesion contract of exculpation." Additionally, there appears to have been no provision for paying an additional reasonable fee to the escrow company to obtain additional protection against negligence. And, finally, as a result of the transaction, the parties to the transaction are placed under the control of the escrow company and subject to the risk of its carelessness.

While the general rule still is that an exculpatory clause relieving individuals of liability from their own ordinary negligence does not contravene public policy . . . a "contract entered into between two parties of unequal bargaining strength, expressed in the language of a standardized contract, written by the more powerful bargainer to meet its own needs, and offered to the weaker party on a 'take it or leave it' basis carries some consequences that extend beyond orthodox implications." Where the public interest is affected the exculpatory clause will be held invalid. We hold that the exculpatory clause before us cannot relieve the escrow company from liability.

> "[T]oday freedom of contract does not commend itself to us as a social ideal in quite the same way. In the more complicated social conditions of our

industrialized society it wins approval only to the extent that there is reasonable equality of bargaining power between the parties and no injury is done to the economic interests of the community at large. The moral principle that persons should abide by their agreements is today met by the equally cogent principle that one should not take advantage of an unfair contract which one has persuaded another to enter into under economic or social pressure . . ." (Justice C. H. Bright [quotation is an excerpt from a statement by Phillip Jeffry], Controls of Adhesion and Exemption Clauses (November 1967) 41 Australian Law Journal 261, 266.)

The judgment is affirmed.

Unconscionable Contracts

Closely related to the problem of determining whether a contract is illegal and unenforceable because it contains an exculpatory clause and therefore contravenes public policy is the problem of determining whether a particular contract should not be enforced because it is unconscionable. Equity principles dictate that "he who seeks equity must do equity." If a contract is too oppressive or one-sided, the courts will not enforce it. While it is clear that a court has the power to refuse to enforce unconscionable contracts even in the absence of express legislative authority,[5] the basis for most of the litigated cases today is the Uniform Commercial Code. Section 2-302 of the UCC provides:

1. If the court as a matter of law finds the contract or any clause of the contract to have been unconscionable at the time it was made, the court may refuse to enforce the contract, or it may enforce the remainder of the contract without the unconscionable clause, or it may so limit the application of any unconscionable clause as to avoid any unconscionable result.
2. When it is claimed or appears to the court that the contract or any clause thereof may be unconscionable, the parties shall be afforded a reasonable opportunity to present evidence as to its commercial setting, purpose and effect to aid the court in making the determination.

What makes a contract unconscionable is of course for court determination. Several factors seem important. What is the relative bargaining power of the parties? Is one party economically stronger than the other? Does each party have options? Can the seller sell to others or is there only one source of supply from which the buyer can purchase the desired goods? How reasonable are the terms which are claimed to be unconscionable?

Further guidelines are provided by the Official Comment to the UCC. Section 2-302 states:

The basic test is whether, in the light of the general commercial background and the commercial needs of the particular trade or case, the clauses involved are so one-sided as to be unconscionable under the circumstances existing at the time of the making of the contract. Subsection (2) makes it clear that it is proper for the court to hear evidence upon these questions. The principle is one of the prevention of oppression and unfair surprise, and not of disturbance of allocation of risks because of superior bargaining power.

The *Meredith* case that follows concerns several interrelated problems. The "waiver of defense clause" contained in the contract specifies that the purchaser will waive defenses against the seller (perhaps if he's unsatisfied with the quality of the product) and that any of those defenses will also be waived against the seller's assignee (in that case the Personal Finance Company) who has now stepped into the seller's place and stead. Such a clause is similar to the exculpatory clauses just noted since they limit the claims or defenses one party can use against the other party.

The court's analysis of unconscionability thus is often affected by the same factors as would be its analysis of an exculpatory clause. While the Illinois court finds this contract and its waiver of defense clause enforceable, its opinion indicates that other courts have different policies. Again, the state law governing each agreement must be checked to determine whether it is unconscionable and thus unenforceable.

Personal Finance Company v. Meredith
Court of Appeals of Illinois
350 N.E.2d 781 (1976)

Plaintiff-appellee, Personal Finance Company, was the assignee of two retail installment sales contracts under which the defendants, Bennie and Joyce Meredith, purchased a food freezer, notions, staples, and frozen meat from Tri-State Foods Company. One contract provided for the purchase by the defendants of a food freezer at a cash price of $748.00, credit life insurance of $12.91, and a finance charge of $232.69, payable in twenty-four monthly installments of $41.40. The other contract was for "notions, staples, and frozen meat" at a cash price of $552.06, credit life insurance of $1.94, and a finance charge of $43.66, payable in six monthly installments of $99.61. The contracts were assigned to the plaintiff approximately a month after their execution.

Defendants made eight payments totaling $339.63 on the food freezer contract and payments of $493.03 on the other contract. Plaintiff brought suit in Circuit Court to collect the amounts owed on the contracts in the sum of $758.60, plus attorneys fees totaling $253.30 and $1.31 as interest accrued since maturity of the second contract.

The defendants asserted three affirmative defenses to the plaintiff's action: that the contracts were unconscionable, that they failed to comply with the Truth in Lending Act and Regulation Z, and that they failed to comply with the Illinois Retail Installment Sales Act. These defenses were stricken on motion by the trial court as insufficient in law. The trial court awarded judgment to plaintiff for the full amount requested, and defendant appealed to the Court of Appeals.

Karns, Presiding Justice

The record discloses that the defendants were induced to purchase these items by a salesman of Tri-State Foods who appeared at their home one evening while they were preparing to go bowling. They asked him to come back another night, but when he told them he was in town just that day they agreed to listen to him. The defendants testified that they agreed to purchase the food freezer and the frozen meats because the salesman made it sound "like a really good deal." They stated that at that time they did not receive a copy of the contract and the payment terms were not filled in on the contracts. Nor apparently were they furnished with a notice that they had three days to rescind the agreement as required by section 2B of the Consumer Fraud Act. Ill.Rev.Stat.1975, ch. 121½, par. 262B.

The defendants also maintained that the contract price of the food freezer ($748.00) was about $300.00 more than the price quoted them by the salesman and that they thought they were only purchasing the freezer and the meat. The salesman did not testify, as neither the assignee nor the defendants knew his whereabouts. The record discloses that when the contracts were executed defendants were both employed but at the time of the suit they were not.

[The court first determined that the plaintiffs had not violated the Consumer Fraud Act. Then it found that the trial court had erred in not admitting certain evidence related to the rights of the plaintiff as an assignee.]

Notwithstanding this prejudicial error which necessitates vacating the judgment appealed from, we must also determine whether the instant waiver of defense clauses are unconscionable. Defendants argue that the instant contracts are harsh and oppressive; that they did not know that a waiver of defense clause existed since the clause was inconspicuous; that they are persons of little formal education; that they did not "bargain for" these clauses; and, as a matter of public policy, that an assignee is better able to protect itself against losses due to sellers of shoddy merchandise and to prevent such losses. They argue this court to adopt the rationale of decisions in other jurisdictions holding waiver of defense clauses unenforceable in consumer retail installment sales contracts.

Clearly, waiver of defense clauses are not unconscionable per se, being permitted by the Commercial Code, the Retail Installment Sales Act and Illinois case law. The public policy of Illinois thus does not preclude the enforcement of such clauses in consumer transactions. This policy sharply distinguishes this case from those decisions relied upon by the defendants.

However, because these Illinois authorities do not displace the common law principle that an unconscionable contract or clause is unenforceable, that principle is applicable to the instant transaction. Courts will not permit printed, non-negotiated clauses in a seller's contract to waive the buyer's rights and eviscerate the negotiated terms of the transaction, unless the buyer is aware of these terms. Viewed in this light, unconscionability is merely a standard to determine the actual bargain of the parties, or their "agreement." Furthermore, the language of a contract is not controlling as to the parties' "agreement." Other circumstances such as course of dealing, usage of trade or course of performance are also relevant to the inquiry of the parties' bargain in fact. We believe the relevance of these considerations expresses a legislative policy in favor of courts' determining the actual agreement of the parties and against enforcing printed contract terms in a mechanical fashion. Therefore we cannot state that the instant clauses can never be unenforceable on the basis of unconscionability.

An unconscionable contract was unenforceable at common law in Illinois as were individual clauses to the extent they produced an unconscionable result. An unconscionable contract has been described as a one-sided contract or one which no man in his senses and not under delusion would make and no honest and fair man would accept. Other courts have stated that where the aggrieved party reasonably did not know that a certain clause was in the contract or had no meaningful choice but to have that clause included in the contract, that the clause is unconscionable. A clause may also be unconscionable if it purports to eliminate or limit the other party's right to assert and recover for a breach of contract or for a tort arising from the transaction.

A waiver of defense clause is similar in its effect to a disclaimer of liability clause. The latter term bars the opposite party from asserting a claim for breach of contract against the party protected by the clause, just as the former protects an assignee. Another analogous clause is a confession of judgment clause. These clauses are not void but can be useful terms to contracting parties in allocating the burdens and risks of a transaction. However, the use of these provisions can be abused.

We are well aware of the disparity of sophistication and bargaining power that frequently exists in the consumer retail installment sales market and the abuses of the mechanism of judicial enforcement which can result from automatic enforcement of these "agreements." Courts have refused to bind a person who has little education, does not speak or read English, or who has been the victim of deceptive sales techniques, resulting in lack of knowledge or notice of the contract terms. Proof of these objective indications of an aggrieved party's ignorance of the contract are exceptions to the general rule, well-established in Illinois, that a person who signs a contract has manifested his intention to be bound by the terms of that contract and cannot claim he was ignorant of those provisions.

Here the appellants claimed that they did not have an opportunity to read the contracts when they agreed to purchase the freezer and the meat. Nevertheless they signed the contracts and had them in their possession for several months before defaulting. Joyce Meredith testified that they received the contracts when the food and the freezer were delivered while Bennie Meredith stated that the contracts were not received until after that date. By either version, they paid on the contracts for more than four months after the contracts and the merchandise were delivered. While it was alleged that the appellants had little formal education, no proof of this allegation was offered. The record does not indicate that appellants were precluded from examining the contract before they signed. Although their decision to purchase the freezer and food was induced by the salesman's representations, their failure to examine the contract, by their own testimony, was not caused by the salesman's alleged unfair techniques but by their haste to get to their bowling game.

Defendants did not lack a meaningful choice since there is no indication in the record that the items purchased were necessities to defendants or that defendants could not have purchased these same items on credit without these clauses from other sources.

As discussed earlier, the contracts contained an admonition to the defendant-buyers, prominently placed on the face of the contracts above the space for defendants' signatures and in readable type, that unless the defendants notified the person to whom the contracts were assigned within five days of the date they received the merchandise of any claim they had against the seller, they could not assert a claim against the assignee later. Because from the face of the contracts we believe that the defendants should have been aware of the clauses they now challenge and have failed to demonstrate that when they signed the contracts and after they received the contracts they were precluded from reading and understanding their rights under the clause or that they could not discover defects in the merchandise or notify the assignee of their complaints within the five day period, we must conclude that the instant waiver of defense clauses are not unconscionable.

[While the court agreed with the trial court that the terms of the contract were not unconscionable and could be enforced, it reversed and remanded the trial court's decision on other grounds.]

Contracts Against Public Policy

A contract or a provision in a contract may be declared contrary to public policy if it injures the interest of the public or tends to interfere with the public's general welfare, health, safety, or morals. But what constitutes public policy? The term itself is vague and uncertain. Today's public policy may be repudiated by tomorrow's generation. In *Henningsen* v. *Bloomfield Motors*, the New Jersey Supreme Court held that a provision in a printed form contract used by all large automobile companies that disclaimed all warranties express or implied except for one minor warranty in the contract was contrary to public policy. The court stated:

Public Policy is a term not easily defined. Its significance varies as the habits and needs of a people may vary. It is not static and the field of application is an ever increasing one. A contract, or a particular provision therein, valid in one era may be wholly opposed to the public policy of another.[6]

It seems clear that public policy, while being based in constitutions, statutes, and earlier court decisions, stems from political, economic, and historical factors as well. There really is no limit as to what sources a court is permitted to use in determining public policy. An analysis of public-policy court decisions invariably will produce conflicting results among jurisdictions.

In the *Western Cab* case, which follows, the Supreme Court of Nevada examines a contract with a businessman who was to testify at a legal hearing involving the taxicab company to see if such a contract is against public policy.

Western Cab Company v. Kellar

Supreme Court of Nevada
523 P.2d 842 (1974)

Kellar, who owned all the stock of Western Cab Company (Western), agreed to transfer his stock to Crockett. Later, when the Taxicab Authority reviewed the reorganization and change of ownership of Western, Kellar threatened to claim that he never transferred his ownership of the company to Crockett, but instead transferred it to his wife. Western then agreed to pay a sum of money to Kellar if he would testify instead that he had transferred his stock to Crockett. Kellar so testified at the hearing before the taxicab authority but was not paid as agreed. He sued to enforce his agreement. The trial court granted him a judgment enforcing the agreement and Western appealed. The Supreme Court of Nevada, finding his agreement with Western to be contrary to public policy, declined to enforce it and reversed that portion of the trial court's judgment.

Zenoff, Justice

The genesis of the appellant corporation occurred in the early 1950's when Western Enterprises, Inc. was organized to operate the franchise of Western Cab Company. During a subsequent reorganization of Western Enterprises following various financial difficulties, respondent and cross-appellant Charles Kellar obtained an ownership interest in the corporation and assumed responsibility as a corporate officer. Further financial difficulties led to the transfer of all of the corporation's right, title and interest in the franchise to operate the cab company to Kellar. This occurred in July of 1964. In 1966, the corporation's charter was revoked by the state.

Thereafter, appellant Crockett, one of the founders of the business, sought to reactivate the then defunct corporation. In consideration of Crockett's payment of $500.00 and assumption of outstanding obligations of Western Enterprises, Charles Kellar executed an instrument dated May 16, 1968 purporting to convey all of his interest in the business. The agreement, which recited that Kellar was the sole owner of Western Enterprises, was notarized by respondent and cross-appellant, Cornelia Kellar.

Crockett then proceeded to reactivate the company. The corporation's charter was reinstated with the Secretary of State in June of 1968 at which time the corporation's name was changed to Western Cab Company. With the assistance of a substantial cash investment by Herbert Tobman, one of the defendants in the lower court, business was resumed.

Respondents first put forth a claim of ownership in June of 1970 when the defendants filed an application with the Taxicab Authority to change the name listed on the certificates of public convenience and necessity to conform with the new name of the corporation and for authority to issue stock. In July, Kellar appeared at a hearing on the application with the apparent intention of contesting the defendants' ownership of the corporation. That same day, during a luncheon meeting with Tobman, Crockett and Leavitt, it was agreed on behalf of the corporation to pay Kellar $6,000.00 cash and to reimburse him for monies expended on behalf of the corporation between May 16, 1968 and July 16, 1970. In addition, appellant Crockett promised to transfer five hundred of his shares in the corporation to Kellar. In consideration of these promises, Charles Kellar agreed to support the application then pending before the Taxicab Authority and to forbear asserting any claim of ownership in the cab company. In furtherance of this agreement, Kellar appeared before the Authority and gave sworn testimony acknowledging the agreement of May 16, 1968 and receipt of Crockett's $500.00 payment. At that time he represented that on the date of sale he was the sole owner of Western Enterprises, Inc.

The trial court erred however in allowing Kellar to recover on the basis of the July 1970 agreement. In consideration of this agreement the lower court found that Charles Kellar's obligations were two-fold: (1) to support the application then pending before the Taxicab Authority and (2) to forbear asserting any claim of ownership in Western Cab Company. According to Charles Kellar's own memorandum of the agreement, payment was contingent on the successful outcome of the defendants' application then pending before the Taxicab Authority. Kellar testified in open court that in advance of his testimony before the Authority, he had agreed to testify precisely in the manner suggested by the defendants.

A contract to pay a witness for testifying coupled with the condition that the right of the witness to compensation depends upon the result of the suit in which his testimony is to be used, is contrary to public policy and void for the reason that it is the tendency of such a contract to lead to perjury and the perversion of justice. All contracts the purpose of which is to create a situation which tends to operate to the detriment of the public interest are against public policy and void whether in a particular case the purpose of the contract is effectuated. For this reason we reverse that part of the decision in the lower court granting recovery to Charles Kellar and affirm in all other respects.

Thompson, C. J., and Mowbray and Batjer, JJ., concur.

Breen, District Judge

I dissent.

I disagree with that part of the majority opinion which reverses the lower court. I agree with the proposition that a contract made by a witness who testified for a consideration which is contingent upon the outcome of litigation is void as against public policy. However, where that witness is otherwise interested in the result of the litigation; where the witness has a legitimate and otherwise potentially valid claim pertaining to the subject matter of the litigation which he also gives up, there is sufficient consideration to support an enforceable contract.

It is true that Mr. Kellar's testimony was given for a consideration which was, in part, contingent on the outcome of the taxicab proceedings. In addition to that, Mr. Kellar agreed to forebear asserting a claim of right. I do not believe this contract is against public policy because the policy considerations are absent in such a case.

I do not think perjury is promoted any more in this case than testimony which is the result of a compromise of a divorce case or any other compromise litigation between the parties.

When one testifies for a consideration, at least three possibilities arise with respect to that person's status toward the litigation.

If the person has no independent interest in the subject matter, nor the outcome of the proceedings, he is a stranger to the litigation and perhaps the general rule would apply. But one may be an adverse party to the proceedings or one may stand to gain or lose rights as a result of the proceedings and thus be an "interested witness". In these cases, the fact that part of the consideration itself may have illegal aspects won't defeat the agreement. There is ample authority for this proposition of law.

The majority opinion concludes that Kellar's only interest in the outcome of the litigation was created by the July 16 contract, which they say is illegal. Yet they also say that "whatever prior interest Kellar may have had in the outcome of the application before the taxicab authority, it was superseded by the July 16 agreement promising payment in the event of approval." This is confusing to me because it appears to make the agreement both valid and invalid in order to support the conclusion reached. If the July 16 agreement superseded any prior interest, and I agree it did, it must have been supported by good and sufficient consideration otherwise it would not be enforceable.

I would affirm the lower court because its conclusion is supported by substantial evidence in the record and sound legal theory.

EFFECTS OF ILLEGALITY

Not all contracts that are found to be illegal are treated the same. Review the distinctions earlier discussed between contracts violating revenue licensing provisions and those contradicting regulatory licensing requirements. A violation of the former statutes generally will not adversely affect a contract but a violation of the latter will.

The general policy of the law is to refuse to enforce an illegal agreement. But refusing to enforce an agreement is different from saying that no agreement has been made. If a contractual agreement has been made, neither party should keep what the other may have given as consideration. If an agreement that is unenforceable has been made, the party (or parties) who has done something illegal should not be able to enforce the agreement but if one party has not done anything illegal, that party might be able to keep whatever consideration he or she was given. These parties to an illegal but unenforceable agreement have still made a contract even though the courts will usually not aid either of them by enforcing its provisions.

What about an agreement that has both legal and illegal provisions? Can the legal provisions be enforced while still denying enforcement to the illegal portions of the contract? The answer to this question depends on the degree to which the terms of and consideration paid for the contract are separate and divisible. If the essence of the entire contract is illegal, probably none of its provisions can be enforced. On the other hand, if a seller and purchaser agree to sell and buy a business and the contract terms also illegally provide that the seller will not compete with the purchaser in any business in any location for a lengthy period of time, the fact that the restraint on the seller is unreasonable and unenforceable probably would not make illegal and unenforceable the remaining terms for the transfer of the business.

Finally, if the court refuses to enforce some or all of the contractual provisions the parties have agreed to, it must be determined whether either party can seek some other remedy in the courts. Does the unenforceability of the contract extend to other actions that one of the parties might bring against the other? This question is discussed in the *Glyco* case that follows. The lease agreement the parties entered into was found to be unenforceable. Are all the provisions of the lease agreement illegal? Why does the court refuse to allow the landlord to recover unpaid rent? If the landlord cannot recover unpaid rent pursuant to the lease agreement, can she recover any money from the tenant? If the rental agreement is illegal, can the tenant bring a damage suit against the landlord for the landlord's breach of an illegal contract?

Review these questions after reading the *Glyco* case.

Glyco v. Schultz

Municipal Court of Sylvania, Ohio

289 N.E.2d 919 (1972)

Plaintiff Glyco rented a house and thirty acres to Defendants Schultz. The house was not maintained in accordance with the local housing code regulations. After defendants notified plaintiff of the violations and plaintiff did not fix them, defendants stopped paying the rent due plaintiff pursuant to their lease agreement. Plaintiff Glyco sued for the unpaid rent and sought to remove the tenants from possession. The court refused to enforce the lease agreement since it was made in violation of a statutory provision designed to protect the public.

Marvyn R. Lachin, Judge

There is no substantial dispute about the facts in this case. In September of 1970 Plaintiff, Mrs. Jane Glyco, rented a house and thirty acres located at 203 North King Road to defendants. Under the oral month-to-month lease contract the stipulated rent was to be two hundred dollars ($200.00) per month.

The defendants introduced evidence to show that when they moved into the house in September of 1970, there existed serious and substantial violations of the Lucas County Housing Code. The electrical system was in a state of disrepair and woefully underserviced, the furnace was faulty, the steps were deteriorating, and the upstairs floor was weak. These conditions continued throughout the tenancy and resulted in great inconvenience to defendants, loss of personal property and expenditures for repairs. This evidence was not contradicted by plaintiff.

The testimony indicated a constant and continual need to purchase and replace burned out light bulbs and fuses. Two television sets and an electric clock burnt up and were lost, and an electrical fire started due to the condition of the electrical system. The furnace was not properly maintained and on a number of occasions refused to work or emitted smoke and fumes soiling the walls and furniture. Repairs to the furnace were contracted and paid for by defendants. The unmaintained steps collapsed when defendant's mother stepped upon them necessitating their repair. The weak floors rendered it unsafe for the father to go into the children's rooms.

Defendant further stated, and was not contradicted, that the plaintiff landlord was notified by letter on at least three occasions about the condition of the house. Plaintiff refused to repair the defects or to reimburse defendants for their losses or expenses of repair. In fact, plaintiff never inspected or repaired the property during the defendants' tenure, or during the tenure of the former tenants. Instead, plaintiff spent the majority of each year in Florida, leaving no manager or caretaker to maintain the property in her absence.

Defendants testified that damages due to the above conditions amounted to one hundred forty six dollars ($146.00) in repairs and the loss of a one year old color TV set purchased for six hundred fifty dollars ($650.00). These losses do not include the second TV set which was borrowed from defendant's brother, the clock for which no value was given, and is exclusive of the money spent for replacement of light bulbs and fuses.

Throughout these events, even in the face of the conditions of the house and plaintiff's refusals to repair, defendants continued to pay the full rent. In November 1971 defendants began to pay one-half of the rent each month in an effort to secure the necessary repairs. These payments continued through March 1972. The evidence further showed that the former tenants, university students who had rented only the house, paid one hundred twenty dollars ($120.00) per month rent throughout their tenancy.

The uncontroverted testimony of Mr. Donald Brown, Housing Sanitarian, Lucas County District Board of Health and Mr. Donald Werr, Jr., Electrical Inspector, Lucas County Department of Inspection established that the following violations of the Minimum Housing Code and the standards thereunder existed on the property: electrical service substandard (60 amps), insufficient electrical circuits, insufficient electrical outlets, surface wiring of lamp cord (18 gauge), use of surface outlets ("fire hazard" outlets), use of oversized fuses, bathroom outlets not grounded, use of brass light sockets, inoperative porch light socket, failure to maintain furnace, failure to maintain steps, weak floors upstairs, leak in kitchen ceiling, sewage empties on ground, broken floor tile in bathroom, and insufficient ceiling height in upstairs bedrooms.

Both inspectors stated that the condition of the house, especially the substantial electrical violations, constituted a serious danger to the health and safety of the occupants. As a result of these conditions, the house was subsequently condemned as unfit for human habitation.

CONCLUSIONS OF LAW

In brief, the court holds that under Ohio law a lease is a contract and should be interpreted and construed like any other contract. Standards established by any local building, housing, or health codes, in existence at the time and place of the making of a lease contract enter into and become a part of the contract, and where a lessor fails to abide by the provisions of such codes he is liable to the lessee in a suit sounding in contract. Such breach gives rise to the ordinary contract remedies.

In addition where a lease contract is made in violation of a statutory prohibition designed for the protection of health and welfare, such as a housing code, the contract is illegal and void. An illegal contract confers no rights on the wrongdoer.

In Ohio a lease is a contract as well as conveyance and is to be interpreted with reference to contract principles.

The rule is well established in this state, that a contract made in violation of a statutory prohibition designed for police or regulatory purposes is void and confers no rights upon the wrongdoer. . . . And it is clear that the same rule obtains when a lease contract is entered into in violation of a statute.

In the case at bar the evidence was that there existed upon the premises a number of substantial violations of the Lucas County Housing Code at the time of rental and throughout the tenancy. The Housing Code expressly prohibits the rental of a dwelling with such violations.

Having found that at the time the lease contract was entered into, and continuing throughout the tenancy there existed on the premises substantial violations of the Lucas County Housing Code which were known to plaintiffs, the court must consider what rent, if any, plaintiff is entitled to, for defendants' use of demised premises.

Where, as in the present case, a lease contract is entered into in violation of the Housing Code, it is the better view that the lease contract is illegal and void and confers no rights upon the wrongdoer.

Ordinarily, in illegal contract cases, both parties are considered to be equally at fault, or *in pari delicto,* and will be denied recovery of monies paid pursuant to the illegal contract.

equally at fault

However, there is a well recognized exception to the rule of *in pari delicto*—where the statute in question is for the protection of one of the parties and where that party has no real choice but to acquiesce in the illegality, then he will not be held to be *in pari delicto* and denied relief.

In the case at bar, the Housing Code was designed to protect occupants, lessees, and the general public. Defendants' living in a substandard house was certainly not by choice, but from a "constrained acquiescence" in the illegality, and in fact, the lessee continually sought to have the defects cured. In addition, as between the parties the lessee is justified in assuming special knowledge by the lessor of the requirements of law, and therefore may recover any rent monies paid in excess of the reasonable rental value of the property in its defective condition during their tenure.

This court also accepts the view advanced by defendant-lessee that where an owner permits the premises to deteriorate to the extent that a substantial interference with the beneficial enjoyment results, the covenant of quiet enjoyment is again breached. The lack of adequate heat, electrical wiring and structural maintenance certainly interfered with beneficial enjoyment. The defendants did not abandon the house as a result of the breach. However, when the landlord's breach of covenant is raised as an affirmative claim, or counterclaim, there is no requirement of eviction, and the tenant is entitled to damages as will fully and adequately compensate him for the interference with the quiet enjoyment of the premises. The measure of damages for such interference is the difference between the actual rental value of the premises leased and the amount stipulated to be paid under the lease.

The court has determined that the contract was illegal from its inception, and that plaintiff breached the implied warranty of habitability resulting in a failure of consideration. Under each of these theories, as with the breach of covenant of quiet enjoyment, the landlord is only entitled to recover the reasonable rental value of the premises. Therefore, the court must undertake to ascertain that value.

[The court then determined that damages of $1,493 were due to defendant tenants and awarded judgment for them in that amount.]

REVIEW PROBLEMS

1. Tovar, a physician practicing in the state of Kansas, wrote the Paxton Hospital in Illinois to inquire about obtaining a position as a full-time resident. In his letter and in a subsequent personal interview, Tovar fully described the nature and extent of his education, training, and licensing as a physician. The hospital assured him that his professional credentials were satisfactory and hired him. Soon thereafter Tovar, who had relocated to Illinois, was discharged by Paxton Hospital for failure to hold a license to practice medicine in Illinois as required by a state statute. Tovar claimed illegal breach of employment by the hospital. Result? Tovar v. Paxton Comm. Memorial Hospital, 330 N.E.2d 247 (Ill. App. Ct. 1975).

2. Weaver, a high-school dropout, signed a service-station lease with American Oil Company containing a clause in fine print that released the oil company from liability for its negligence and compelled him, as

lessee, to indemnify American for any damage or loss thus incurred. Weaver never read the lease, nor was it ever explained to him. During the course of business, a visiting American Oil employee negligently sprayed gasoline over Weaver and his assistant, causing them to be burned and injured on the leased premises. American disclaimed liability on the basis of the contract clause. Is this correct? Weaver v. American Oil Company, 276 N.E.2d 144 (Ind. Sup. Ct. 1972)

3. Mayfair Fabrics leased commercial premises from Natell upon the condition that Mayfair absolve Natell of all liability for loss or damage to Mayfair's property by fire, explosion, or otherwise. Natell subsequently was negligent in causing a fire that resulted in considerable damage to Mayfair's operations. Mayfair seeks to recover damages on the basis of the landlord's negligence, but Natell urges he is protected under the lease from any liability. Which way would you rule? Mayfair Fabrics v. Henley, 226 A.2d 602 (N.J. Sup. Ct. 1967).

4. Hiyanne worked as a contact lens grinder and fitter for the House of Vision from 1959 until 1964 in branch stores, several in different cities. His employment contract said that upon the termination of his relationship with the employer, he would never engage in the same or similar business anywhere within a thirty-mile radius of any of the branch stores in which he had rendered services. Hiyanne resigned his position in 1964 and began working for a competitor just 150 feet from one of those House of Vision stores. The House of Vision seeks to enforce the restrictive covenant in the original employment contract. What result? House of Vision, Inc. v. Hiyanne, 225 N.E.2d 21 (Ill. Sup. Ct. 1967).

5. The state of Ohio appropriated a portion of Schneider's farm for the relocation and improvement of several highways. The Schneider family received monetary compensation and agreed to the following condition:

> Albert Schneider . . . shall have access to the Hometown Road at all points where (his) property presently abuts Hometown Road, excepting therefrom the right of way for Route 224;

The effect of this clause in the agreement was to give the Schneiders access to U.S. Route 224 from their land. Now the director of highways has filed a second appropriation action against the Schneider land to permit improvements that would make Route 224 a part of the U.S. highway system; but these changes will eliminate the Schneiders' personal access to the road. Schneider is upset and seeks to enforce the earlier agreement. What should the court do? Schneider v. Masheter, 202 N.E.2d 320 (Ohio Ct. App. 1964).

6. Sweazea, a building owner, contracted with Measday for water and gas plumbing work. A local statute provides that a permit be applied for before plumbing work is begun —the intent of the regulation being that work done for which a permit is required is to be inspected for compliance with professional standards. Measday failed to apply for a permit until he had substantially completed the job. Now Sweazea has refused to finish paying him and Measday claims a breach of their contract. Sweazea says the contract cannot be enforced because it is illegal due to the statutory violation. Does the violation make the contract illegal? Measday v. Sweazea, 438 P.2d 525 (N.M. Ct. App. 1968).

FOOTNOTES

[1]In some states, such as Tennessee, the general usury law is found in the constitution rather than in statutes. A recent decision by the Tennessee Supreme Court interpreted the usury provision of that state's constitution as prohibiting the lending of money at an interest rate in excess of 10 percent.

[2]G. J. Wallace, "Uses of Usury: Low Rate Ceilings Reexamined," *Boston University Law Review 56* (1976): 415; Oeltjen, "Usury: Utilitarian or Useless," *Florida State University Law Review 3* (1975): 167; Curolto, "Conflict of Laws and Usury in California: The Impact on Flow of Mortgage Funds," *University of San Francisco Law Review 9* (1975): 441.

[3]Michigan Compiled Laws Annotated § 305.6 (1971).

[4]See Zeidenberg v. Greyhound Lines, Inc., 209 A.2d 697 (Conn. Cir. 1965) and Rosenchein v. Trans World Airlines, Inc., 349 S.W.2d 483 (Mo. 1961) for limitations regarding loss or damage to the passenger's baggage which were held enforceable and not contrary to public policy pursuant to federal legislation.

[5]See Williams v. Walker-Thomas Furniture Co., 350 F.2d 445 (D.C. Cir. 1965).

[6]Henningsen v. Bloomfield Motors, 161 A.2d 69, 95 (Supreme Court of New Jersey 1960).

Legal Form

Many people assume that contracts requiring a future performance must be written in order to be enforceable. In fact, oral contracts are also enforceable. Only a few types of contracts must be written in order to be enforced. This chapter identifies the types of contracts that must be written and then covers what is known as the parol evidence rule and other legal principles relating to the interpretation of contracts.

STATUTE OF FRAUDS

In an illiterate society, "magic words" and symbolic questions must be used to establish legal relationships. Thus during the Middle Ages the seller of real property would literally pick up a clump of earth from the property and before witnesses transfer it to the buyer, intoning appropriate words such as "I enfeoff you and your heirs with livery of seisin." At the same time the buyer would hand over the purchase price. The only "document" of the transaction would be the memory of the witnesses. Suppose, however, that the seller paid the witnesses part of the proceeds of the sale and told them to forget what they had seen. The buyer would be unable to prevent this fraud, because under English law at the time parties to a civil suit were not allowed to testify in their own behalf. Thus the perjured testimony of the witnesses could not be countered in a suit by the buyer to claim the land.

Written Contracts

Determining that fraud through perjured testimony was commonplace, the English Parliament in 1677 enacted a Statute for the Prevention of Frauds and Perjuries. The statute, commonly called the Statute of Frauds (or simply the Statute), attempted to prevent fraudulent allegations regarding the existence or nonexistence of contracts by requiring that certain types of likely-to-be-important contracts be written and signed before they could be enforced. Today all the states in the United States have enacted similar statutes requiring that certain contracts be in writing in order to be enforceable. These contracts, discussed in detail later, include:

1. Contracts involving a promise by an executor to pay the debts of the decedent out of the executor's own funds

2. Contracts involving a promise to pay the debt of another
3. Contracts for the sale of land or an interest in land
4. Contracts not to be performed or performable within one year
5. Contracts for the sale of goods with a contract price of $500 or more
6. Contracts in consideration of marriage

Some states require that certain additional contracts—for example, real estate brokerage agreements—be written to be enforceable.

While the statutes were designed for the broad purpose of preventing fraud and perjury, they serve three more specific purposes. First, requiring a writing is thought to serve an "evidentiary" function. Theoretically, the presence of an actual contract document minimizes the chance that a court and jury will be misled as to the existence or terms of the contract. Second, requiring a writing may have a cautionary effect. People are more likely to think about what they are getting into if they are required to sign something and are therefore less likely to act rashly. Finally, requiring a writing serves as a "channeling" device, distinguishing between those contracts that are enforceable and those that are not.

What type of writing is required? To be enforced, a contract falling within the statute must be evidenced by a memorandum of the contract signed by the party against whom enforcement is sought. In general, the memorandum must identify the parties, the subject matter of the contract, and the basic obligations of the parties. Requirements regarding the memorandum are stricter for a contract for the sale of land than one for the sale of goods. Regarding the latter, the Uniform Commercial Code provides that a memorandum is not insufficient merely because it omits or misstates a term. However, such a contract is not enforceable beyond the quantity of goods shown in the writing.

A legal term, *within*, is used throughout this chapter. If a contract is required to be in writing it is called "within" the Statute; if not required to be in writing, it is called "without" the Statute. Oral contracts within the Statute are considered unenforceable in most states, though they are otherwise valid. Thus, if a party fails to raise the defense of the Statute of Frauds, that party is legally bound by the contract.

Problems with the Rule

In 1954 Parliament repealed the Statute of Frauds except as it related to contracts involving the sale of land or a promise to pay the debt of another. That action is indicative of some underlying problems with the rule. No American state, however, has yet followed suit.[2]

The rule has on occasion worked to the disadvantage of consumers. The experience of one of the author's former students provides a ready example. The student signed a contract for the purchase of a motorcycle for $1,200. The merchant then contacted the student and told him that the dealership could not sell the cycle for less than $1,350. The student produced the contract form. It had never been signed by the merchant. The student could not sue to enforce the agreement.

In similar situations, a contract may be signed by a salesperson who has no agency authority to sign. At best, there are several legal hurdles that must be overcome to enforce such an agreement. At worst, the consumer, thinking that he or she has a "deal," discovers at the end that there is no legal recourse.

Another problem with the Statute can be demonstrated by the example of the student and the motorcycle. The student could not sue the merchant. But could the merchant sue the student? Yes. The student had signed a memorandum evidencing the contract. This problem of one-way enforceability has been a particular thorn regarding the Statute of Frauds and has been partially modified by the UCC in regard to agreements between merchants.[3] Even greater strides have been made with the recent development of consumer protection laws at both state and federal levels. These laws will be discussed later in this chapter.

A final problem arises from the technical application of the rule. The purpose of the statute of frauds is to ensure that there is in fact an underlying contract between the parties. Yet the courts often refuse to enforce oral agreements under the Statute that everyone concedes were made.[4] Court opinions denying enforcement often make casual reference to "the contract" or "the parties' agreement." Thus, when considering the application of the Statute, it is important to recognize that the exceptions are as important as the rule.

CONTRACTS REQUIRED TO BE IN WRITING

Of the six types of contracts required to be in writing listed earlier, two are of little importance today. Contracts in consideration of marriage involve property settlements in exchange for a promise to marry. Such prenuptial agreements are common when two well-to-do persons, both with children of their own, decide to marry late in life. Mutual promises to marry are not within the Statute.[5] While the rule regarding the promises of an executor is similar to the rule regarding promises to pay the debt of another, a discussion of its general provisions is a helpful way of introducing the other statute-of-frauds requirements.

Executor's Promise to Pay the Debts of Decedent

When a person dies, it is almost certain that, along with whatever assets are left behind, there will also be some unpaid bills. It is also a certainty that the creditors will demand payment before the assets are distributed to the heirs and the estate is closed. In order to wind up the deceased's affairs, the executor of the estate will be required to pay the debts. As a general rule, the executor is not personally liable; if the estate is insolvent, the creditors lose. There may be situations, however, in which the executor promises personally to satisfy the obligations of the estate. For example, the executor who is also a family member may want to prevent creditors from seizing and selling family heirlooms, some of great sentimental value, in order to satisfy the debts. To be enforceable, the Statute of Frauds requires such promises to be in writing.

When you consider that bereaved family member who is also serving as an executor can be in an extremely vulnerable emotional state following the death of a loved one, the rationale behind the writing requirement is obvious. In order to protect such people, any contracts entered into by executors acting on behalf of the estate but in their personal capacities must be in writing.

Promise to Pay the Debt of Another

There is some similarity between promises by an executor to be personally liable for debts of an estate and promises by one party to be responsible for the debts of another. The difference is that promises to pay the debts of another are not usually given in states of emotional distress and all the parties are living. In short, we have three parties and two promises, one of which is a promise to satisfy the requirements of the other.

Primary and Secondary Liability. The basic way to determine whether such a promise is within the Statute is to ask whether the third party promisor is primarily liable or secondarily liable. *Primary liability* exists when the creditor can proceed directly against the third-party promisor. *Secondary liability* means that the creditor must look first to the original debtor before proceeding against the third-party promisor. Promises involving secondary liability are within the Statute and must be in writing to be enforced.

Does the distinction between primary and secondary liability make sense? Not really, when viewed theoretically. The subject of the promise in both cases is the debt obligation of another. The reason for the distinction, however, is judicial antagonism toward the statute. By making the distinction, courts reduce the number of contracts within the statute.

Application of the statute of frauds to this area can best be illustrated by the following examples: C is the owner of a local hardware store; B, a recent college graduate, has gone into business for himself as a building contractor. B comes into C's store seeking building supplies because he has just landed his first building contract. C, however, is unwilling to let B have the goods on credit, essentially because B hasn't had time to establish a credit rating. B, prepared for this, has his father, A, a well-known local businessman, call C and guarantee B's credit worthiness. A promises that if B defaults A will cover C's losses. A's promise is covered by the statute of frauds. A has not made an absolute promise to pay B's debts; rather, A has made a *conditional* promise to pay only if B defaults. C must *first* look to B, not to A, for payment. A is secondarily liable. His promise must be in writing.

However, assume that B has won the building contract from A, his father. This time, when A calls C he tells C to give B all the supplies he needs and to send the bill to A. In this case, B has made no promise to pay and thus A is not guaranteeing B's debt. C must look to A for payment. A is primarily liable. His oral promise is enforceable.

Main Purpose Doctrine. In addition to the primary/secondary liability distinction, the courts have developed an additional limiting rule regarding the application of the Statute of Frauds to promises to pay the debt of another

known as the *main purpose doctrine*. Under this doctrine, an oral promise creating secondary liability is nonetheless enforceable if made for the purpose of benefiting the promisor. Assume, for example, that a franchisor of a tool rental business learns that one of his franchisees in a key location is about to be evicted for failure to pay rent on time. Franchisor calls Franchisee's landlord and says, "I'll pay the rent if Franchisee defaults on the current obligation. Don't evict him right now." Such an oral promise would be enforceable because Franchisor's main purpose in making the promise would be self-benefit. The franchise system depends for its success upon a strong distribution system, and the franchisor usually receives direct periodic payments from each operating franchisee. Thus, Franchisor would have a personal motive for making a promise that would have the effect of keeping his or her franchised outlets operating.

Sale of Land or an Interest in Land

For our purposes, land may be considered earth and things permanently affixed thereto. The most common real estate transactions, such as the sale of residential or commercial property, clearly fall under this rule and must be evidenced by a writing. There remains the question, however, of what constitutes an *interest* in land. Assume that I promise to sell to you the right to cross my property for a particular purpose. This is known as an *easement* and it constitutes an interest in land. Thus my promise, if only oral, is not enforceable. An option to buy is considered an interest in land, as is a lien or security interest given against the land.[6] In many states, leases are within the Statute although some states require that only leases for an extended term (for example, more than one year) must be in writing.

A generally recognized exception to the Statute-of-Frauds provision regarding real estate is the doctrine of *part performance*.[7] This doctrine is used in circumstances where one party promises to sell land in return for certain actions by the buyer. For example, Owner of real property may promise to sell part of it to Tenant if Tenant improves the entire property and works it for Owner. After Tenant does the work, Owner refuses to sell and raises the Statute of Frauds as a defense. If the parties have acted as though they had entered into a contract for the sale of certain land and the recognition of an otherwise provable oral agreement is necessary in order to prevent Tenant from being defrauded, the courts will enforce the oral agreement. The part performance must be substantial and in reliance on the oral promise to sell.

Promises Not Performable in One Year

If a contract cannot be performed within a year, it is within the Statute. The easiest example of such a contract is one that expressly states a multiple number of years, such as a five-year-requirements contract or a three-year contract for the services of a professional athlete.

A problem arises with single-year contracts. In order to limit the application of the Statute to such agreements, the courts have adopted a rule of construction in which the fraction of the day on which the contract is made is not counted. Thus if performance begins the day that the contract is made or the next, the promise is outside the Statute because full performance will be completed before *midnight* of the anniversary of that day.

Assume that no date is set in the contract. Instead, the arrangement is to continue until some event occurs or until one of the parties exercises a right to cancel the agreement. Such contracts are not within the Statute if the event could possibly occur within one year or if there is no limitation on the right to cancel during the first year. For example, an agreement to provide service to a person until death is generally held to be without the Statute because death could occur within one year.

One final problem regards contracts involving construction projects. Determining whether such a contract is within the Statute becomes a question of fact. Is there any possibility that if everything goes perfectly (no strikes, good weather) the job could be completed within a year? If so, the contract is without the Statute. Full performance of a contract not performable within a year will take the contract out of the statute and make it enforceable on behalf of the performing party in most states.

The case that follows demonstrates several important facets of Statutes of Frauds, including the manner in which the courts interpret the one-year rule, the applicability of the UCC Statute-of-Frauds section, and the manner in which the testimony of a party inadvertently may decide the outcome of a case.

Buttorff v. United Electronic Laboratories, Inc.

Court of Appeals of Kentucky

459 S.W.2d 581 (1970)

Plaintiff Buttorff charged breach of an oral contract allegedly entered into between himself and defendant United Electronic Laboratories (U.E.L.), a manufacturer of surveillance cameras used by banks and other money-handling institutions. Plaintiff alleged that he was hired to develop a market for the cameras and establish distributorships under his exclusive agency. He was to pay defendant $440 per camera and resell them at $985 plus installation, the difference in the two prices being awarded to him as compensation. Plaintiff testified that this oral agreement was to govern his relationship with U.E.L. until the two parties could negotiate a formal written agreement.

Defendant U.E.L., through its agents, argued that no such exclusive distributorship and agency agreement had ever been reached. In essence, U.E.L. claimed that the parties had never reached an agreement to do anything more than negotiate. U.E.L. further argued that, contrary to plaintiff's allegations that the oral agreement was entered into in February 1961, plaintiff did not begin to sell cameras on behalf of the defendant until May 1961 and that such activity ceased in May 1962.

Reed, Judge

The defendant first argues that there was no enforceable agreement between the parties because a contract between them was never formed. The problem presented is discussed by the late Judge Goodrich with his usual clarity and conciseness:

> If the parties intend not to be bound until a written memorial is executed by each, then they are not bound until that event takes place. On the other hand, although parties may intend to put their agreement in writing, it does not follow that they have not made a contract until the writing is completed and signed. . . . The emphasis of these two eminent writers [Williston and Corbin] is, it seems to us, inclined toward finding the formation of a contract prior to the signing of the document unless the parties pretty clearly show that such signing is a condition precedent to legal obligation. And since contract law has passed the information of elaborate doctrines pertaining to sealed instruments, it seems to us such emphasis is quite natural and quite correct.

The evidence of both parties to the dispute here clearly shows to us that so far as the sale of cameras and the payment of commission were concerned, the signing of an agreement was not a condition precedent. The parties continued in this relationship for over a year.

The plaintiff argues that the general rule pertaining to contracts of employment should be applicable. The general rule is that contracts for employment or other performance that is to begin within a year and is to continue for an indefinite, unspecified period are terminable by either party at any time and are held not to be within the one-year clause of the statute.

Defendant argues that where, from the nature of the contract, it cannot be performed in a year and the parties so contemplated in making it, the statute applies and the contract is unenforceable.

The enforceability of a contract under the one year provision of the statute does not turn on the actual course of subsequent events, nor on the expectations of the parties as to the probabilities. Contracts of uncertain duration are excluded; historically, the statute has been consistently applied only to those contracts where performance cannot possibly be completed within a year. . . .

We agree with the trial judge that the testimony of the plaintiff insofar as concerned the exclusive right-to-sell feature and the unlimited territory in which this exclusive franchise would exist was squarely that performance by him to secure such a comprehensive relationship by establishing a distributor in each major population area was factually impossible to be performed within a year. That was the plaintiff's own testimony. It did not go to expectations or probabilities. It was a plain statement of the impossibility of the performance expected of him within a year. We think that the plaintiff admitted his contract into the operation of the statute. . . . Cameras were sold and commission was paid. We think a contract was formed. The enforceability of it is another matter. . . .

The next argument advanced by the defendant and one on which it appears to place great reliance is that the agreement was unenforceable because of the "sale of goods for the price of $500 or more" section of the statute of frauds which is now incorporated into the Uniform Commercial Code and is embodied as statutory law in Kentucky at KRS 355.2-201. Defendant argues that by the plaintiff's own pleadings the agreement between them was a sale of goods for a price of $500 or more. We are not so persuaded.

Stone v. Krylon, Inc., held that where the agreement was for performance of certain personal services for the defendant corporation and the defendant corporation promised to grant the plaintiff an exclusive agency to sell certain goods, the contract was one for employment and the consideration for the services was not wages or salary but a valuable franchise. There the court refused to declare the agreement unenforceable by reason of U.C.C. 2-201. . . .

We have no hesitation, in view of the proof and considering the pleadings in their entirety, in concluding that this agreement is not a sale of goods as such but is a contract for personal services and, therefore, KRS 355.2-201 does not preclude its enforcement. . . .

The plaintiff asserts that the one-year provision does not apply because the parties agreed to subsequently enter into a written agreement and, according to plaintiff's argument, since it was possible that this written agreement could have been effected within one year, then his present agreement is removed from the operation of the statute. That contention is rejected by Williston. . . .

We believe that the trial judge was correct in concluding that the plaintiff's oral agreement insofar as it undertook to bind the defendant to pay the plaintiff a commission on sales of cameras not effected by plaintiff and to bind the defendant to grant plaintiff an exclusive franchise unlimited as to territory and to receive payment for film sold for use by all cameras whether sold by plaintiff or not was unenforceable under the one-year provision of our statute of frauds. . . .

The real issue now is: May plaintiff recover at the contract rate for the sale of cameras effected by him? We think he can. . . . It is generally held that part-performance not amounting to full performance on one side does not in general take a contract out of the one-year provision. Restitution is available in such cases, and doctrines of estoppel and fraud may be applicable. . . .

The issue here, however, is not restitution, but express contract. Where a part of an oral contract is within the statute of frauds for the reason that it may not be performed within one year and a part is not covered by the statute, if the consideration for both parts is not divisible and apportionable, or if such parts are interdependent, neither part can be enforced. Implicit in that statement is the corollary that if the consideration for both parts is divisible and apportionable and if the parts are independent, then the part not within the statute when fully performed may be enforced at the contract rate. . . . that on performance on one side of each of its successive divisions, the other party becomes indebted for the agreed price of the division. We regard this contract as falling within that category.

. . . [We] hold that the plaintiff is entitled to recover the agreed compensation on the sales of cameras in those instances where the sale was effected by him prior to the termination of the agreement.

Sale of Goods for $500 or More

Section 2-201 of the UCC on the statute of frauds states:

1. Except as otherwise provided in this section a contract for the sale of goods for the price of $500 or more is not enforceable by way of action or defense unless there is some writing sufficient to indicate that a contract for sale has been made between the parties and signed by the party against whom enforcement is sought or by his authorized agent or broker. A writing is not insufficient because it omits or incorrectly states a term agreed upon but the contract is not enforceable under this paragraph beyond the quantity of goods shown in such writing.
2. Between merchants if within a reasonable time a writing in confirmation of the contract and sufficient against the sender is received and the party receiving it has reason to know its contents, it satisfies the requirements of subsection (1) against such party unless written notice of objection to its contents is given within ten days after it is received.
3. A contract which does not satisfy the requirements of subsection (1) but which is valid in other respects is enforceable
   a. if the goods are to be specially manufactured for the buyer and are not suitable for sale to others in the ordinary course of the seller's business and the seller, before notice of repudiation is received and under circumstances which reasonably indicate that the goods are for the buyer, has made either a substantial beginning of their manufacture or commitments for their procurement; or
   b. if the party against whom enforcement is sought admits in his pleading, testimony or otherwise in court that a contract for sale was made, but the contract is not enforceable under the provision beyond the quantity of goods admitted; or
   c. with respect to goods for which payment has been made and accepted or which have been received and accepted.

Subsection 1 establishes the general rule that a contract for the sale of goods for $500 or more must be evidenced by "some writing" in order to be enforceable. The writing must be signed by the party against whom enforcement is sought. The writing requirement may be satisfied by more than one document,[8] and one case held that a signed memo without terms referring to an unsigned document containing terms established an enforceable contract.[9]

The rest of the section places limitations on the general rule. Section 2-201(2) modifies the one-way enforceability result in the case of merchants. Assume that Jones and Smith, both merchants, orally agree to a contract. The next day Jones sends a signed letter to Smith detailing the terms of the agreement. Smith does not respond for ten days. The contract is enforceable against Smith on the basis of Jones's letter.

It is in the context of this subsection that most cases have arisen involving the issue of whether a farmer is a merchant. Typically, a farmer enters into an agreement to sell crops evidenced by a document signed only by the buyer. If the farmer is a merchant, the agreement is enforceable against him or her; if not, the farmer escapes liability.

Court decisions on this issue have gone both ways and have turned upon the circumstances surrounding the creation of the agreement, the business trappings with which the farmer has surrounded himself, the dealings with the particular or similar crop over an extended period of years, the farmer's familiarity with the market problems surrounding his farming operation and the socioeconomic policies of the court regarding those people who have been designated as farmers.[10] Thus courts have held that experienced farmers,[11] particularly those who deal in futures contracts,[12] are merchants, whereas those dealing in one-time sales are not.[13] In essence the courts are trying to determine whether the farmer is a mere tiller of the soil or a shrewd agribusiness person[14] waiting to see how the market goes before committing to the contract.

The three exceptions established in Section 2-201(3) all have a common element: in the situations defined, there is persuasive evidence that a contract has in fact been made. Under (b) there is an outright admission by the defendant that a contract exists. It would be contrary to the basic purpose of the Statute to allow a defense in such a circumstance. Under (c) one can assume that a buyer will not accept goods unless a contract is intended. Note that the contract is enforceable only in regard to the quantity of goods that has been accepted. Similarly, a seller will not accept payment unless a contract is intended. A down payment may satisfy the exception in 2-201(3)(c).[15] This is simply a version of the part-performance exception to the Statute of Frauds, which, until the UCC, applied only to contracts involving an interest in kind. The specially manufactured goods in (a) must be shown to have a reasonable nexus with the buyer. Thus, again, there is extrinsic evidence that a contract has been made.

The case that follows involves the application of the UCC Statute of Frauds.

Southwest Engineering Company v. Martin Tractor Company

Supreme Court of Kansas

473 P.2d 18 (1970)

Plaintiff Southwest Engineering Company was preparing to submit a bid to the U.S. Army Corps of Engineers for construction of runway lighting facilities at McConnel Air Force Base. On April 11, 1966, plaintiff's construction superintendent, R. E. Cloepfil, telephoned the manager of defendant Martin's engine department, Ken Hurt, to inquire about the price of a standby generator and accessory equipment. On April 12, Hurt returned Cloepfil's call and quoted a price of $18,500. This price was reconfirmed by Hurt over the phone on April 13.

In reliance on this figure, Southwest submitted its bid to the government, and this bid was accepted. Cloepfil notified Hurt of this, and the two men agreed to meet in the town of Springfield on April 28. At this meeting, Cloepfil was shocked to learn that

Martin had raised its proposed selling price to $21,500. Nonetheless, the conversation continued and Cloepfil eventually agreed to pay the higher price.

On May 2, Cloepfil wrote to Martin, directing Martin to proceed with shop drawings and submittal documents. However, on May 24, Hurt wrote to Cloepfil, refusing to supply the generator and equipment because of strict government regulations, and withdrawing all verbal price quotations. After receiving this letter Cloepfil telephoned Hurt, who assured Cloepfil that Southwest could obtain the equipment from any other supplier at the same price. However, later investigation proved that this was not true.

Southwest repeatedly attempted to convince Martin to live up to its verbal agreements until September 6. At that time Southwest gave up and eventually secured the required equipment from another supplier at a cost of $27,541.

Southwest filed suit, seeking damages of $6,041 for breach of contract and $9,000 for losses resulting from the delay caused by the breach. The trial court awarded damages of $6,041 for the breach, but failed to award damages for the delay. Martin appealed.

Fontron, Justice

The basic disagreement centers on whether the meeting between Hurt and Cloepfil at Springfield resulted in an agreement which was enforceable under the provisions of the Uniform Commercial Code (sometimes referred to as the Code), which was enacted by the Kansas Legislature at its 1965 session. . . .

Southwest takes the position that the memorandum prepared by Hurt at Springfield supplies the essential elements of a contract required by the foregoing statute, *i.e.*, that it is (1) a writing signed by the party sought to be charged, (2) that it is for the sale of goods and (3) that quantity is shown. In addition, the reader will have noted that the memorandum sets forth the prices of the several items listed. . . .

. . . [D]efendant . . . maintains . . . that the writing in question does not measure up to the stature of a signed memorandum within the purview of the Code; that the instrument simply sets forth verbal quotations for future consideration in continuing negotiations.

But on this point the trial court found there *was* an agreement reached between Hurt and Cloepfil at Springfield; that the formal requirements of K.S.A. 84-2-201 *were* satisfied; and that the memorandum prepared by Hurt contains the three essentials of the statute in that it evidences a sale of goods, was authenticated by Hurt and specifies quantity. . . .

We believe the record supports all the above findings. With particular reference to the preparation and sufficiency of the written memorandum, the following evidence is pertinent:

Mr. Cloepfil testified that he and Hurt sat down at a restaurant table and spread out the plans which Hurt had brought with him; that they went through the specifications item by item and Hurt wrote each item down, together with the price thereof; that while the specifications called for a D353 generator, Hurt thought the D343 model might be an acceptable substitute, so he gave prices on both of them and Southwest could take either one of the two which the Corps of Engineers would approve; that Hurt gave him (Cloepfil) the memorandum "as a record of what he had done, the agreement we had arrived at at our meeting in the restaurant at the airport."

We digress at this point to note Martin's contention that the memorandum is not signed within the meaning of 84-2-201. The sole authentication appears in hand-printed form at the top left-hand corner in these words: "Ken Hurt, Martin Tractor, Topeka, Caterpillar." The court found this sufficient, and we believe correctly so. K.S.A. 84-1-201(39) provides as follows:

> Signed includes any symbol executed or adopted by a party with present intention to authenticate a writing. . . .

It is quite true, as the trial court found, that terms of payment were not agreed upon at the Springfield meeting. Hurt testified that as the memorandum was being made out, he said they wanted 10 percent with the order, 50 percent on delivery and the balance on acceptance, but he did not recall Cloepfil's response. Cloepfil's version was somewhat different. He stated that after the two had shaken hands in the lobby preparing to leave, Hurt said their terms usually were 20 percent down and the balance on delivery; while he (Cloepfil) said the way they generally paid was 90 percent on the tenth of the month following delivery and the balance on final acceptance. It is obvious the parties reached no agreement on this point.

However, a failure on the part of Messrs. Hurt and Cloepfil to agree on terms of payment would not, of itself, defeat an otherwise valid agreement reached by them. K.S.A. 84-2-204(3) reads:

> Even though one or more terms are left open a contract for sale does not fail for indefiniteness if the parties have intended to make a contract and there is a reasonably certain basis for giving an appropriate remedy. . . .

In our view, the language of the two Code provisions is clear and positive. Considered together, we take the two sections to mean that where parties have reached an enforceable agreement for the sale of goods, but omit therefrom the terms of payment, the law will imply, as part of the agreement, that payment is to be made at time of delivery. In this respect the law does not greatly differ from the rule this court laid down years ago. . . .

We do not mean to infer that terms of payment are not of importance under many circumstances, or that parties may not condition an agreement on their being included. However, the facts before us hardly indicate that Hurt and Cloepfil considered the terms of payment to be significant, or of more than passing interest. Hurt testified that while he stated his terms he did not recall Cloepfil's response, while Cloepfil stated that as the two were on the point of leaving, each stated their usual terms and that was as far as it went. The trial court found that only a brief and casual conversation ensued as to payment, and we think that is a valid summation of what took place. . . .

We find no error in this case and the judgment of the trial court is affirmed.

Equitable Estoppel and Promissory Estoppel

The requirements of the Statute of Frauds can be used for the perpetration of fraud. The Statute is often raised by a defendant attempting to avoid being bound by whatever promise he may have made. Courts have become increasingly sensitive to this and have tried to minimize fraudulent results by using the doctrines of equitable estoppel and promissory estoppel.

The use of *equitable estoppel*, a doctrine as old as the Statute of Frauds, occurs in situations where application of the Statute would in itself result in fraud. The part-performance exception to the Statute discussed earlier in this chapter is characterized as nothing more than an application of equitable estoppel. Generally, the doctrine is applied when the instrument of injustice is something other than a promise, usually in the context of a transfer of an interest in land.[16]

Promissory estoppel is a more specific application of the principles of equitable estoppel. As indicated in this chapter promissory estoppel has been used primarily as an exception to the requirement that all contracts be supported by consideration. However, since the turn of the century, the doctrine has been accepted by an increasing number of jurisdictions as a tool for limiting the fraudulent impact that application of the Statute of Frauds can have.

Promissory estoppel is the legal term for the idea that, once having made a promise, a person should not be allowed to avoid the consequences. The basic requirements of the doctrine are found in Section 90 of the *Second Restatement of Contracts.* While the doctrine has been a part of American contract law since the turn of the century, its application to contracts governed by the Statute of Frauds began to take off when Section 217A was added to the *Second Restatement.* Section 217A expressly sanctions the use of the doctrine to avoid the Statute of Frauds. It provides:

A promise which the promisor should reasonably expect to induce action or forbearance on the part of the promisee or a third person and which does induce the action or forbearance is enforceable notwithstanding the Statute of Frauds if injustice can be avoided only by enforcement of the promise. The remedy granted for breach is to be limited as justice requires.[17]

The requirements of Section 90 and Section 217A are very similar. Thus, if the promisor should have known that his promise would induce detrimental reliance by the promisee, and such detrimental reliance took place, the promisor may find that he is obligated to fulfill the contract even if it does not comply with the Statute of Frauds.

Consider how promissory estoppel might apply to a contract governed by the Statute of Frauds. Assume that X is a police captain who will be eligible for retirement in two years. The retirement package includes a pension of full salary, paid medical insurance, life insurance, and other benefits. In addition, the city's contract with the police union provides that no one, union member or not, may be discharged except for cause. Y, chairman of the board of a large corporation, induces X to quit his job as a police officer in exchange for an extremely lucrative ten-year employment contract with Y's company; Y further promises to reduce the contract to writing when he returns from Europe. Unfortunately, Y is killed while traveling and the other board members are reluctant to honor Y's promise of employment to X.

Under traditional Statute of Frauds principles, the contract would be unenforceable. Because it is an offer of employment for ten years, the contract falls within the requirement that contracts not performable within one year be put in writing. X, having already quit his job as a police captain, would be without a remedy and without a job. Fortunately for X, most courts today will not tolerate such an inequitable result. Applying Section 217A(1) of the *Second Restatement,* it is apparent that Y knew and intended that his promise of employment would induce X to quit his current job in reliance on the promise. Because X has been induced to quit his prior job, and because injustice cannot otherwise be avoided, Y's fellow board members are bound by the contract. They are, in essence, estopped from asserting the Statute of Frauds as a defense.

The result would have been different had X not yet quit his current job at the time of Y's death and the refusal of the other board members to honor the contract. All jurisdictions that permit the use of promissory estoppel to avoid the Statute of Frauds have required as a prerequisite that the promisee suffer "unconscionable injury" if the contract is not enforced. In a similar vein, Section 217A(1) requires not only detrimental reliance but also injustice that can be avoided *only* by the enforcement of the promise. Thus, when the contract is wholly executory, or when the promisee's reliance is only minimally detrimental, the Statute of Frauds will be enforced.

When deciding whether to use promissory estoppel as a means for avoiding the Statute of Frauds, it is important to consider the aspect of damages. In an action for breach of contract, a plaintiff can generally recover compensatory damages to the extent that they can be proven. However, this is not true when recovery is based on promissory estoppel. The courts have uniformly held that when promissory estoppel is used as a means of avoiding the Statute of Frauds, only restitutional damages (i.e., out-of-pocket expenses) can be recovered. In these cases, the plaintiff is generally not entitled to the benefit of the bargain; instead, he will only be restored to the position he was in prior to acting in reliance on the defendant's promise. As promissory estoppel gains wider acceptance as a cause of action in its own right, this result is likely to change. To date, however, most courts will limit recovery to restitutional damages.

McIntosh v. Murphy
Supreme Court of Hawaii
469 P.2d 177 1970

In March 1964 defendant Murphy was seeking management personnel for his Chevrolet-Oldsmobile dealerships in Hawaii. In April 1964, plaintiff McIntosh received a call from the general manager of Murphy Motors stating that a job was available. Plaintiff accepted the offer of employment, and notified Murphy by telegram that he would arrive in Honolulu on April 26, 1964. On April 25, Murphy telephoned McIntosh to say that his duties as assistant sales manager would begin on April 27. McIntosh was surprised that the position had changed from sales manager to assistant sales manager, but decided to go to Honolulu anyway.

As a result of his employment with Murphy, McIntosh moved from Los Angeles to Honolulu, transporting or selling his possessions to make the move. He leased an apartment in Honolulu and gave up employment opportunities on the mainland. However, on June 16, 1964, approximately two and one half months after beginning his new job, McIntosh was discharged, allegedly because he could not close deals and was unable to train new salesmen.

At trial the jury returned a verdict in favor of McIntosh in the amount of $12,103.40, and Murphy appealed.

Levinson, Justice

This case involves an oral employment contract which allegedly violates the provision of the Statute of Frauds requiring "any agreement that is not to be performed within one year from the making thereof" to be in writing in order to be enforceable. HRS § 656-1(5). In this action the plaintiff-employee Dick McIntosh seeks to recover damages from his employer, George Murphy and Murphy Motors, Ltd., for the breach of an alleged one-year oral employment contract.

The defendants appeal to this court on four principal grounds, three of which we find to be without merit. The remaining ground of appeal is whether the plaintiff can maintain an action on the alleged oral employment contract in light of the prohibition of the Statute of Frauds making unenforceable an oral contract that is not to be performed within one year. . . .

ENFORCEMENT BY VIRTUE OF ACTION IN RELIANCE ON THE ORAL CONTRACT

In determining whether a rule of law can be fashioned and applied to a situation where an oral contract admittedly violates a strict interpretation of the Statute of Frauds, it is necessary to review the Statute itself together with its historical and modern functions. The Statute of Frauds, which requires that certain contracts be in writing in order to be legally enforceable, had its inception in the days of Charles II of England. Hawaii's version of the Statute is found in HRS § 656-1 and is substantially the same as the original English Statute of Frauds.

The first English Statute was enacted almost 300 years ago to prevent "many fraudulent practices, which are commonly endeavored to be upheld by perjury and subornation of perjury." 29 Car. 2, c. 3 (1677). Certainly, there were compelling reasons in those days for such a law. At the time of enactment in England, the jury system was quite unreliable, rules of evidence were few, and the complaining party was disqualified as a witness so he could neither testify on direct-examination nor, more importantly, be cross-examined. The aforementioned structural and evidentiary limitations on our system of justice no longer exist.

Retention of the Statute today has nevertheless been justified on at least three grounds: (1) the Statute still serves an evidentiary function thereby lessening the danger of perjured testimony (the original rationale); (2) the requirement of a writing has a cautionary effect which causes reflection by the parties on the importance of the agreement; and (3) the writing is an easy way to distinguish enforceable contracts from those which are not, thus chanelling certain transactions into written form.

In spite of whatever utility the Statute of Frauds may still have, its applicability has been drastically limited by judicial construction over the years in order to mitigate the harshness of a mechanical application. Furthermore, learned writers continue to disparage the Statute, regarding it as "a statute for promoting fraud" and a "legal anachronism."

Another method of judicial circumvention of the Statute of Frauds has grown out of the exercise of the equity powers of the courts. Such judicially imposed limitations or exceptions involved the traditional dispensing power of the equity courts to mitigate the "harsh" rule of law. When courts have enforced an oral contract in spite of the Statute, they have utilized the legal labels of "part performance" or "equitable estoppel" in granting relief. Both doctrines are said to be based on the concept of estoppel, which operates to avoid unconscionable injury.

Part performance has long been recognized in Hawaii as an equitable doctrine justifying the enforcement of an oral agreement for the conveyance of an interest in land where there has been substantial reliance by the party seeking to enforce the contract.

It is appropriate for modern courts to cast aside the raiments of conceptualism which cloak the true policies underlying the reasoning behind the many decisions enforcing contracts that violate the Statute of Frauds. There is certainly no need to resort to legal rubrics or meticulous legal formulas when better explanations are available. The policy behind enforcing an oral agreement which violated the Statute of Frauds, as a policy of avoiding unconscionable injury, was well set out by the California Supreme Court. In Monarco v. Lo Greco, a case which involved an action to enforce an oral contract for the conveyance of land on the grounds of 20 years performance by the promisee, the court said:

> The doctrine of estoppel to assert the statute of frauds has been consistently applied by the courts of this state to prevent fraud that would result from refusal to enforce oral contracts in certain circumstances. Such fraud may inhere in the unconscionable injury that would result from denying enforcement of the contract after one party has been induced by the other seriously to change his position in reliance on the contract.

In seeking to frame a workable test which is flexible enough to cover diverse factual situations and also provide some reviewable standards, we find very persuasive section 217A of the Second Restatement of Contracts. That section specifically covers those situations where there has been reliance on an oral contract which falls within the Statute of Frauds. Section 217A states:

> (1) A promise which the promisor should reasonably expect to induce action or forbearance on the part of the promisee or a third person and which does induce the action or forbearance is enforceable notwithstanding the Statute of Frauds if injustice can be avoided only by enforcement of the promise. The remedy granted for breach is to be limited as justice requires.
>   (2) In determining whether injustice can be avoided only by enforcement of the promise, the following circumstances are significant: (a) the availability and adequacy of other remedies, particularly cancellation and restitution; (b) the definite and substantial character of the action or forbearance in relation to the remedy sought; (c) the extent to which the action or forbearance corroborates evidence of the making and terms of the promise, or the making and terms are otherwise established by clear and convincing evidence; (d) the reasonableness of the action or forbearance; (e) the extent to which the action or forbearance was forseeable by the promisor.

We think that the approach taken in the Restatement is the proper method of giving the trial court the necessary latitude to relieve a party of the hardships of the Statute of Frauds. This is to be preferred over having the trial court bend over backwards to take the contract out of the Statute of Frauds. In the present case the trial court admitted just this inclination and forthrightly followed it.

There is no dispute that the action of the plaintiff in moving 2200 miles from Los Angeles to Hawaii was foreseeable by the defendant. In fact, it was required to perform his duties. Injustice can only be avoided by the enforcement of the contract and the granting of money damages. No other remedy is adequate. The plaintiff found himself residing in Hawaii without a job.

It is also clear that a contract of some kind did exist. The plaintiff performed the contract for two and one-half months receiving $3,484.60 for his services. The exact length of the contract, whether terminable at will as urged by the defendant, or for a year from the time when the plaintiff started working, was up to the jury to decide.

In sum, the trial court might have found that enforcement of the contract was warranted by virtue of the plaintiff's reliance on the defendant's promise. Naturally, each case turns on its own facts. Certainly there is considerable discretion for a court to implement the true policy behind the Statute of Frauds, which is to prevent fraud or any other type of unconscionable injury. We therefore affirm the judgment of the trial court on the ground that the plaintiff's reliance was such that injustice could only be avoided by enforcement of the contract.

Affirmed.

THE PAROL EVIDENCE RULE

Even if the parties have to reduce an agreement between them to writing, and even if the writing satisfies all the requirements of the statute of frauds, there are bound to be some disputes over the meaning of the language in the contract, or allegations that the contract has been modified or does not include *all* the terms of the agreement. To solve these problems, it is often helpful to turn to what is known as the parol evidence rule.

Parol evidence has nothing to do with shortening the length of imprisonment of convicted felons. In contract situations, "parol" evidence concerns the intent of the parties that is not contained within the "four corners" of the contract document; it can be either written or oral. The parol evidence rule is similar to the Statute of Frauds in that it imposes a technical, formal requirement regarding writings used by contracting parties. Unfortunately, the parol evidence rule is also similar to the Statute of Frauds in that it often results in harm to consumers and small-business operators.

The parol evidence rule is based upon a simple principle, which when understood makes all of the specific requirements and exceptions of the rule obvious. The simple principle is: When contracting parties draw up a document evidencing their agreement that appears both complete and final on its face, it is appropriate to conclude that the parties have put everything into that document and that the contracting parties should not be able to use evidence regarding prior or concurrent agreements to contradict the written document. The rule can also have the effect of rendering unenforceable promises that were made but not incorporated into the contract document.

Requirements

In order for the parol evidence rule to apply, there must be a writing that is final and complete upon its face. If the writing is obviously incomplete or by its own terms indicates that certain terms are to be filled in later, the rule does not apply. Attorneys have responded to the rule by putting clauses similar to the following in written contracts:

> This contract is the final and complete agreement between the parties. All prior negotiations and/or agreements are merged into this contract and all additions to or alterations or changes in this contract must be in writing and signed by both parties.

Such clauses are known as integration agreements because they are intended to integrate all prior agreements of the parties into the contract document. The hope is that an integration agreement will make it extremely difficult to introduce evidence of extemporaneous prior agreements.

The parol evidence rule does not require that the parties use a writing. Only the various Statutes of Frauds do that. Instead, the parol evidence rule affects the manner in which the contract terms may be established once a final and complete writing has been used.

As noted in the chapters on contract formation, there may be substantial preliminary negotiations prior to determining the final agreement and drafting the final document memorializing the contract. Parol evidence issues typically regard which of the preliminary documents can be considered in interpreting the terms of the agreement. Whether the final document integrates prior documents is in reality a question of fact that must be resolved by considering the particular circumstances of the contract negotiations.

In such a situation the court will first admit the parol evidence solely to prove that the written contract is not fully integrated. If that proof is successful, and the court concludes that the written document is not fully integrated, then the parol evidence will be considered as to the terms of the collateral agreement. Many courts will consider contractual language similar to that used in the earlier example as conclusory that the written document is integrated.[18]

An ambiguous provision of the written agreement may be explained or cleared up by parol evidence. But parol evidence that contradicts the written agreement is inadmissible.

These two issues—whether the document is a final integration, and whether its terms are ambiguous—give the courts leeway to limit the application of the rule. And, as will be demonstrated by the case excerpt that follows, many courts have used this opportunity to make rulings hostile to the rule. Why such hostility? Doesn't the basic principle underlying the parol evidence rule make sense? The answer is that the principle is flawed and that in application the rule often produces an unfair result worthy of judicial hostility.

The parol evidence principle assumes a contract fully negotiated between equals or near equals. But, as we have seen, many written contracts, particularly those entered into by consumers, do not involve arms-length negotiation. Instead, the consumer is handed a form contract to sign that invariably contains a clause indicating that the form represents the final agreement between the parties and that there are no other understandings between them. It is not uncommon for a salesperson to make oral statements such as "We'll extend the warranty thirty extra days," "Of course, we'll provide free servicing for a year," or "Although it's not our usual policy, we will deliver your purchase free of charge." Relying on these statements, the consumer signs the contract and then is prevented by the parol evidence rule from trying to show the "other understandings" that the consumer assumed were part of the deal.

Further, the form contract is drafted for the standard or typical deal. Any customized deal presents a problem with the use of the form. Both the seller's representative (salesperson or office manager) and the consumer will likely be unfamiliar with the legal ramifications of the use of certain language in the form. Thus a parol evidence problem may arise by inadvertence and then be used by the merchant as a shield against liability.

The case that follows shows the manner in which courts have attempted to mitigate the harshness of the parol evidence rule.

Masterson v. Sine
Supreme Court of California
436 P.2d 561 (1968)

Dallas Masterson and his wife Rebecca owned a ranch as tenants in common. On February 25, 1958, they conveyed it to Medora and Lu Sine by a grant deed "reserving unto the grantors herein an option to purchase the above described property on or before February 25, 1968" for the "same consideration as being paid heretofore plus the depreciation value of any improvements grantees may add to the property from and after two and a half years from this date." Medora was Dallas's sister and Lu's wife. After the conveyance, Dallas was adjudicated a bankrupt, and his trustee and Rebecca sued to establish their right to enforce the option. At trial, the court ruled that the option could be exercised, and defendants Medora and Lu Sine appealed.

Traynor, Chief Justice

The trial court determined that the parol evidence rule precluded admission of extrinsic evidence offered by defendants to show that the parties wanted the property kept in the Masterson family and that the option was therefore personal to the grantors and could not be exercised by the trustee in bankruptcy. . . .

Defendants appeal. . . . The trial court properly refused to frustrate the obviously declared intention of the grantors to reserve an option to repurchase by an overly meticulous insistence on completeness and clarity of written expression. . . .

The trial court erred, however, in excluding the extrinsic evidence that the option was personal to the grantors and therefore nonassignable.

When the parties to a written contract have agreed to it as an "integration"—a complete and final embodiment of the terms of an agreement—parol evidence cannot be used to add to or vary its terms. . . . When only part of the agreement is integrated, the same rule applies to that part, but parol evidence may be used to prove elements of the agreement not reduced to writing. . . .

The crucial issue in determining whether there has been an integration is whether the parties intended their writing to serve as the exclusive embodiment of their agreement. The instrument itself may help to resolve that issue. It may state, for example, that "there are no previous understandings or agreements not contained in the writing," and thus express the parties' "intention to nullify antecedent understandings or agreements." Any such collateral agreement itself must be examined, however, to determine whether the parties intended the subjects of negotiation it deals with to be included in, excluded from, or otherwise affected by the writing. Circumstances at the time of the writing may also aid in the determination of such integration. . . .

California cases have stated that whether there was an integration is to be determined solely from the face of the instrument and that the question for the court is whether it "appears to be a complete . . . agreement." . . .

Neither of these strict formulations of the rule, however, has been consistently applied. The requirement that the writing must appear incomplete on its face has been repudiated in many cases where parol evidence was admitted "to prove the existence of a separate oral agreement as to any matter on which the document is silent and which is not inconsistent with its terms"—even though the instrument appeared to state a complete agreement. . . .

In formulating the rule governing parol evidence, several policies must be accommodated. One policy is based on the assumption that written evidence is more accurate than human memory. This policy, however, can be adequately served by excluding parol evidence of agreements that directly contradict the writing. Another policy is based on the fear that fraud or unintentional invention by witnesses interested in the outcome of the litigation will mislead the finder of facts. . . . McCormick has suggested that the party urging the spoken as against the written word is most often the economic underdog, threatened by severe hardship if the writing is enforced. In his view the parol evidence rule arose to allow the court to control the tendency of the jury to find through sympathy and without a dispassionate assessment of the probability of fraud or faulty memory that the parties made an oral agreement collateral to the written contract, or that preliminary tentative agreements were not abandoned when omitted from the writing. He recognizes, however, that if this theory were adopted in disregard of all other considerations, it would lead to the exclusion of testimony concerning oral agreements whenever there is a writing and thereby often defeat the true intent of the parties.

Evidence of oral collateral agreements should be excluded only when the fact finder is likely to be misled. The rule must therefore be based on the credibility of the evidence. One such standard, adopted by section 240(I)(b) of the Restatement of Contracts, permits proof of a collateral agreement if it "is such an agreement as might *naturally* be made as a separate agreement by parties situated as were the parties to the written contract." . . .

The option clause in the deed in the present case does not explicitly provide that it contains the complete agreement, and the deed is silent on the question of assignability. Moreover, the difficulty of accommodating the formalized structure of a deed to the insertion of collateral agreements makes it less likely that all the terms of such an agreement were included. . . . This case is one, therefore, in which it can be said that a collateral agreement such as that alleged "might naturally be made as a separate agreement." *A fortiori,* the case is not one in which the parties "would certainly" have included the collateral agreement in the deed. . . .

It is contended, however, that an option agreement is ordinarily presumed to be assignable if it contains no provisions forbidding its transfer or indicating that its performance involves elements personal to the parties. The fact that there is a written memorandum, however, does not necessarily preclude parol evidence rebutting a term that the law would otherwise presume. . . . In the present case defendants offered evidence that the parties agreed that the option was not assignable in order to keep the property in the Masterson family. The trial court erred in excluding that evidence.

The judgment is reversed.

Burke, Justice (*Dissenting*)

I dissent. The majority opinion:

(1) Undermines the parol evidence rule as we have known it in this state since at least 1872 by declaring that parol evidence should have been admitted by the trial court to show that a written option, absolute and unrestricted in form, was intended to be limited and nonassignable;

(2) Renders suspect instruments of conveyance absolute on their face;

(3) Materially lessens the reliance which may be placed upon written instruments affecting the title to real estate; and

(4) Opens the door, albeit unintentionally, to a new technique for the defrauding of creditors.

The opinion permits defendants to establish by parol testimony that their grant to their brother (and brother-in-law) of a written option, absolute in terms, was nevertheless agreed to be nonassignable by the grantee (now a bankrupt), and that therefore the right to exercise it did not pass, by operation of the bankruptcy laws, to the trustee for the benefit of the grantee's creditors.

And how was this to be shown? By the proffered testimony of the bankrupt optionee himself! Thereby one of his assets (the option to purchase defendants' California ranch) would be withheld from the trustee in bankruptcy and from the bankrupt's creditors. Understandably the trial court, as required by the parol evidence rule, did not allow the bankrupt by parol evidence to so contradict the unqualified language of the written option. . . .

Exceptions

A number of logical exceptions follow directly from the basic premise of the parol evidence rule. The fact that on a particular day two parties sign a formal agreement does not mean that they have intended to bind themselves forever to those particular terms. As a consequence, parol evidence is always admissible to prove a *subsequent modification* of the contract. The major legal problem with modification, as discussed in Chapter 8, is with sufficiency of consideration.

Parol evidence is admissible to clear up an *ambiguity* in the contract terms. It is also admissible to prove fraud, alteration, mistake, illegality, duress, undue influence, or lack of capacity. If any of these things can be shown, then the document does not represent a valid contract. Obviously it would be very poor legal policy to allow the parol evidence rule to operate to protect a defrauding party or to prevent the showing of duress or mistake.

The written document represents a memorial of the parties' contractual deal. Fraud may be perpetrated when one party alters the document or handles the signing of the document in such a manner as to constitute fraud (for example, using a carbon and a second sheet with different terms). Similarly, a mistake may occur as the document is prepared. These occurrences may be proven with the use of parol evidence.

Finally, evidence of agreements concerning *collateral matters* is not barred by the parol evidence rule. If the alleged agreement is not part of the major purpose of the contract but instead concerns some collateral topic, then evidence as to the existence of the agreement may be introduced. The test for determining whether an agreement concerns a matter collateral to the main contract is whether it deals with a subject that is likely to have been included in the contract if the parties had agreed on it. If not, it is a collateral matter and evidence as to its existence may be introduced. Note that any reference at all to the matter in the contract is likely to destroy this exception to the parol evidence rule.

UCC Parol Evidence Rule

Section 2-202 of the UCC has a special parol evidence rule applying to the sale of goods that provides as follows:

Terms with respect to which the confirmatory memoranda of the parties agree or which are otherwise set forth in a writing intended by the parties as a final expression of their agreement with respect to such terms as are included therein may not be contradicted by evidence of any prior agreement or of a contemporaneous oral agreement but may be explained or supplemented
(a) by course of dealing or usage of trade (§ 1-205) or by course of performance (§ 2-208); and
(b) by evidence of consistent additional

terms unless the court finds the writing to have been intended also as a complete and exclusive statement of the terms of the agreement.

This rule is more liberal than the general common law rule. Usage of trade and course of dealing or performance are always admissible whether or not the contract terms are found to be ambiguous. The only way by which such factors would be inadmissible would be by an express contract term to that effect.

Further, unless it is quite clear that the document represents an exclusive statement, noncontradictory *additional* terms may be admitted into evidence. There is no presumption that a writing is considered by the parties as a complete, exclusive statement of their agreement.

The Effect of Consumer Protection Statutes

Consumer protection laws can have an impact on the use of the parol evidence rule. Most states have adopted such laws in the last few years, and they add an interesting twist to the rule. Many such statutes make it illegal for suppliers to *fail* to integrate all prior agreements, oral or otherwise, into the final contract document. Thus, if car salesman A makes a variety of performance and warranty guaranties to car buyer B, but the manufacturer's warranty that comes with the car or the bill of sale does not reflect these guaranties, their salesman A has violated such consumer laws. Further, because of these laws, salesman A will not be able to argue that evidence of such guaranties should not be admitted pursuant to the parol evidence rule. Carrying this even further, once evidence of the agreements is used to prove their existence for purposes of showing violations of the consumer laws, their existence has also been proved for purposes of enforcing the guaranties themselves.

INTERPRETATION OF CONTRACTUAL PROVISIONS

When disputes arise between the parties concerning the meaning of contractual terms, the courts will make use of specific, established rules of interpretation in resolving disagreements. Problems typically arise because:

1. In using already prepared form documents, the parties:
   (a) Add language that contradicts other provisions in the form,
   (b) Do not intend that all of the form provisions apply to their agreement, or
   (c) Add self-contradictory or ambiguous language.
2. In using negotiated, specially prepared documents, the parties:
   (a) Use ambigous language,
   (b) Fail to anticipate a problem later arising during performance, or
   (c) Compromise without coming to precise understandings of certain terms.

In interpreting the particular language used in a written contract, the courts are primarily concerned with correctly ascertaining the intention of the contracting parties. The intentions of the parties cannot be ascertained by simply asking them because, obviously, if they had agreed on such an issue they would not be in court. Consequently, the courts use the following specific rules designed to ascertain the objectively viewed intention of the parties:

1. Words are to be given their plain and ordinary meanings so long as such an interpretation does not result in a clearly unique or strange result.
   (a) The meaning of words may be varied by the prior usage between the parties, i.e., the parties are governed by their course of dealing.
   (b) Technical words and terms are to be given technical meanings unless it is clear that the parties intend some other definition. This rule tends to be important in contracts for the sale of land because of the large number of technical terms used in real property law.
   (c) Trade usage may supply a basis for the interpretation of terms.
2. Writings are to be interpreted as a whole and language is not to be taken out of its appropriate context.
3. Special circumstances under which a contract was made may be used to show the actual understanding of the parties.
4. Legal and reasonable interpretations are preferred over illegal and unreasonable alternatives.
5. Specific provisions control general provisions.
6. Generally, handwritten provisions prevail over typed provisions, and typed provisions prevail over printed provisions. In applying this rule the courts assume that the material most recently added by the parties represents their true intention.
7. In commercial contracts the UCC supplies many implied terms. Usually, the UCC terms are applicable unless the parties provide otherwise in their agreement.

REVIEW PROBLEMS

1. Cohen bought a farm jointly owned by Luca Rienzo and his eight brothers and sisters. After the Cohen purchase, Luca, who had lived there for thirty years, made improvements on the buildings, rented part of the farm, and cultivated the rest. After eleven months Cohen asserted his interest in the property. Luca's wife claims that

there was an oral agreement between her and Cohen that, after Cohen acquired the property, he would reconvey it to her. Decision? Rienzo v. Cohen, 152 A. 394 (Sup. Ct. Conn. 1930).

2. Pope & Cottle sold lumber to Blakely to be used in building a garage for Wheelwright. Blakely failed to pay, and Wheelwright told Pope & Cottle that he would pay Blakeley's debt "from such funds as might be in his hands due the said Blakely." Pope & Cottle then formally released Blakely and demanded payment of the $1,478.63 from Wheelwright, who refused to pay. Pope & Cottle sued Wheelwright on the promise. Decision? Pope & Cottle v. Wheelwright, 133 N.E. 106 (Sup. Jud. Ct. of Mass. 1921).

3. Barney Sorrenson owed Security $1,400. Barney's mother, Ragnhild Sorrenson, wanted to borrow $200 from Security. Security agreed to make the loan if Ragnhild "would secure up the debts of Barney." Security made the loan and the question arose whether Ragnhild's estate was liable for Barney's debts. Is it? Wildung v. Security Mortgage Co. of America, 172 N.W. 692 (Sup. Ct. Minn. 1919).

4. Harris contracted to sell cotton to Hine Cotton Co. and both signed the following document:

This agreement is entered into this date wherein Hine Cotton Company, 103 East Third Street, Rome, Georgia agrees to buy from H. E. Harris and Sons, Route 1, Taylorsville, Georgia all the cotton produced on their 825 acres. The rate of payment shall be as follows:

1) All cotton ginned prior to December 20, 1973 and meeting official U.S.D.A. Class will be paid for at 30¢ per pound. Below Grade Cotton at 24½¢ per pound.

2) All cotton ginned on or after December 20, 1973 will be paid for at the rate of 1,000 over the CCC Loan Rate with Below Grades being paid for at 24½¢ per pound. Settlement will be made on net weights on Commercial Bonded Warehouse Receipts with U.S.D.A. Class cards attached with $1.00 per bale being deducted from the proceeds of each bale.

During the time that the cotton was growing its market value more than doubled and Hine Co. wrote and asked assurance of Harris that he would perform. Harris repudiated by return letter. Hine Co. sued for the $140,000 difference between the contract price and the market price. The trial court denied a motion to dismiss. Harris v. Hine, 205 S.E.2d 847 (Sup. Ct. Ga. 1974).

5. Beanblossom sold 1,000 bushels of soybeans to Lippold at $4.42 per bushel. Lippold then brought suit claiming that the 1,000-bushel transaction was partial performance of an oral contract by which Beanblossom was to sell 7,000 bushels of soybeans at $4.42 per bushel. Beanblossom denies that any oral contract was ever made. Decision? Lippold v. Beanblossom, 319 N.E.2d 548 (App. Div. Ill. 1975).

6. Dragage & Co. contracted with Pacific Gas to remove and replace the cover of a steam turbine. Dragage agreed "to idemnify Pacific against all losses, damage, expense, and liability resulting from . . . injury to property, arising out of or in any way connected with the performance of this contract." During the work the cover fell and injured the turbine. Pacific sued Dragage for the $25,144.51 it spent on repairs. Dragage offered to prove by the testimony of employees of both firms that the parties had understood that the indemnity clause was meant to cover only third parties. Is such proof allowable? Pacific Gas & Electric Co. v. G. W. Thomas Dragage Co., 442 P.2d 641 (Sup. Ct. Calif. 1968).

7. Mitchell agreed by a written contract to purchase a farm from Lath. Mitchell contended that in return for her agreement to

purchase the farm Lath agreed to remove an icehouse that she found objectionable. The icehouse was not removed and Mitchell sued to compel its removal. Decision? Mitchell v. Lath, 160 N.E. 646 (Ct. App. N.Y. 1828).

8. A representative of Mid-South, a plastic supplier, and Fortune Furniture Manufacturing entered into an oral agreement by which Mid-South would provide Fortune with plastic needed in the latter's manufacturing process. As a consequence the following letter was sent and received:

Mr. Sidney Whitlock, President
Fortune Furniture Manufacturers, Inc.
Okolona, Mississippi 38860

Dear Sid:

This is to confirm the agreement entered into this date between myself and Phil Stillpass on behalf of Mid-South Plastic Co. Inc. and you on behalf of Fortune Manufacturing Co. Inc.

We agree to maintain expanded and 21 oz. plastic in the warehouse of Mid-South Furniture Suppliers, Inc. in sufficient amounts to supply all of the plastic for your plant's use, and if for any reason we do not have the necessary plastic you will be at liberty to purchase the plastic from any other source and we will pay the difference in price paid the other source and our current price.

We also agree to pay Fortune 2% rebate on the gross sale price of our plastic as an advertisement aid to your Company which rebate to be paid at your request.

We assure you that all fabrics you need will be in our warehouse at all times and we appreciate your agreeing to buy all of your plastics from us.

Very truly yours,

W. E. Walker, President
(Mid-South)

Mid-South was unable to supply all of Fortune's needs and Fortune had to buy from other suppliers at a higher price. Does Fortune have a cause of action against Mid-South? Fortune Furniture Manufacturing Co., Inc. v. Mid-South Plastic Fabricating Co., 310 So. 2d 725 (Sup. Ct. Miss. 1975).

FOOTNOTES

[1]Note, *Statute of Frauds—the Doctrine of Equitable Estoppel and the Statute of Frauds,* 66 Mich. L. Rev. 170 (1967).

[2]See generally, Russell Decker, "The Repeal of the Statute of Frauds in England," 11 Am. Bus. L. J. 55 (1973).

[3]UCC § 2-201 (2).

[4]This problem, too, has been partially modified by the UCC § 2-201 (3) (b).

[5]Coggins v. Cannon, 112 S.C. 225 (1919).

[6]Laurence P. Simpson, HANDBOOK OF THE LAW OF CONTRACTS, 2d ed. (St. Paul: West Publishing, 1965), p. 153.

[7]Hughes v. Oberholtzer, 162 Ohio St. 330 (1954).

[8]James J. White and Robert S. Summers, UNIFORM COMMERCIAL CODE (St. Paul: West Publishing, 1972), p. 51.

[9]Babdo Sales v. Miller-Wohl Co., 440 F.2d 962 (1971).

[10]Alphonse M. Squillante, "General Provisions, Sales, Bulk Transfers and Documents of Title," 32 Bus. Law. 1067–68 (1977).

[11]Campbell v. Yohel, 20 Ill. App. 3d 702 (1974).

[12]Continental Grain Co. v. Brown, 19 UCC Rep. Serv. 52, 59 (W.D. Wisc. 1976); Sierens v. Clausen, 60 Ill. 2d 585 (1975).

[13]Fear Ranches, Inc. v. Berry, 470 F.2d 905 (1972).

[14]Squillante, note 10, p. 1067.

[15]White & Summers, note 8, p. 58.

[16]Metzger and Phillips, "Promissory Estoppel and the Evolution of Contract Law," 18 Am. Bus. L. J., 139, 179 (1980); Note, "Promisssory Estoppel as a Means of Defeating the Statute of Frauds," 44 Fordham L. Rev. 114, 117–18 (1975).

[17]Restatement (Second) of Contracts, § 217A.

[18]Laurence P. Simpson, HANDBOOK OF THE LAW OF CONTRACTS, p. 235.

Rights of Third Parties

PRIVITY OF CONTRACT

Originally, a plaintiff could maintain a contract action only against the party with whom the contract had been made. Over the years this limiting doctrine, which is generally referred to as privity of contract or privity, has lost most of its importance. Today there are several situations in which a person who is not a party to a contract can use the contract as the basis for suit. The following are some examples:

1. The person suing, often called the third party, has acquired another's contract right by purchase or gift. For example: Smith agrees to sell his house to Jones. Jones decides she does not want the house. She transfers her right to Martin. In most cases Martin would have a right to sue Smith if Smith refused to perform.
2. The original contract was made for the benefit of a noncontracting third party who is the plaintiff. For example: Brown insures his life with Capital Insurance Company. He names Green as beneficiary. If the company refuses to honor the agreement, Green ordinarily has a right to sue.

3. The law by implication creates a right for the third party who is the plaintiff.

The primary focus of this chapter is on the first two situations. The third is treated in the chapter on sales.

Expansion of Third-Party Rights

The expansion of the rights of third parties over the last century and a half is another example of the influence that political, technological, social, and economic developments have on the law. Early common law did not recognize the right of a third party to sue. Contract rights were considered too personal to be placed in hands other than those of the contracting parties. The penalties for debt were so severe that a defaulting debtor was held liable only to the creditor. As the penalties for debt were relaxed, this logic became less important.

Realizing the economic value of contract rights, courts grudgingly began to allow suits by a plaintiff who was not a party to the agreement. Many state legislatures also adopted statutes that further substantiated this principle. As the economy of the United States became more credit-oriented, effective financing could be maintained only if a party to whom a debtor's obligation had been transferred could use it as the basis for suit. Economic need helped to bring about a change in the law.

The expansion of the rights of third parties has also been influenced by technological developments occurring in the United States since the Civil War. Both the Uniform Commercial Code and case law in most American jurisdictions today allow a person who is injured by a defective product to sue the seller even though not a party to the contract of sale. Fifty years ago this was not the case. Implied warranty protection was available only to the plaintiff who had purchased the item. As the number of costly injuries resulting from highly complex products increased, society gradually accepted the idea of enterprise liability. The manufacturer or firm selling a defective product is now legally responsible to the ultimate consumer injured because of the defect. The manufacturer cannot escape this responsibility because it did not deal directly with the injured party. One court, after exhaustive examination, summed up this change in the law as follows:

> The limitations of privity in contracts for the sale of goods developed their place in the law when marketing conditions were simple. . . . With the advent of mass marketing, the manufacturer became remote from the purchaser, sales were accomplished through intermediaries, and the demand for the product was created by advertising media. . . . [W]here the commodities sold are such that if defectively manufactured they will be dangerous to life or limb, then society's interest can only be protected by eliminating the requirement of privity between the maker . . . and the ultimate consumer (in those cases brought on the implied warranty theory).[1]

Current Law

Today, in personal injury suits arising from the failure of a product, most states do not require the plaintiff to establish privity of contract with the defendant. However, some theories of recovery still require proof of this contractual relationship in order for the plaintiff to recover. The question of privity of contract is further discussed in Chapter 18, products liability.

While most plaintiffs do not need to establish privity of contract in suits for personal injuries, in many cases the plaintiff must establish privity of contract with the defendant to recover for economic losses. Suppose a defendant manufacturer delivers machinery to the plaintiff. The plaintiff attempts to use the machinery, but because it is defective, the plaintiff is unable to make it work properly. As a result of this, the plaintiff sustains certain economic losses. If he or she brings suit for breach of warranty, it will probably be necessary to establish a direct contractual relationship with the seller in order to recover.

ASSIGNMENT AND DELEGATION

Assignment

Assignment is the transfer to another of benefits that a person is entitled to under a contract. Contract benefits are generally referred to as rights. A person or firm transferring contract rights is called an *assignor*. The recipient of these rights is the *assignee*. The party responsible for the performance that is the benefit is the *obligor*.

An example emphasizing the basic relationships among parties to a contract often helps to clarify this terminology and some of the legal problems that arise when contract rights are transferred.

Each party to an executory contract acquires rights as a result of the agreement. Each also has obligations or duties that arise because of the agreement. If a farmer promises to sell 1,000 bushels of wheat to a feed mill for $2,200, the farmer has a duty to transfer title to the wheat to the mill. The mill has a right to title. The mill, on the other hand, has a duty to pay the farmer $2,200. The mill's duty is the farmer's right, just as the farmer's duty is the mill's right.

If the farmer chose to transfer his right to the $2,200 to his bank, he could do so by assignment. The farmer would be the assignor; the bank the assignee; the mill the obligor. Of course, the mill could assign its right to the wheat to someone also. The mill would then be the assignor; the recipient of the right the assignee; and the farmer the obligor.

Delegation

In some instances the law allows a person to transfer the duties or obligations that have been assumed by contract. The transfer of contractual duties is called a *delegation*. The farmer in the previous example might be able to delegate his duty to deliver the 1,000 bushels of wheat to someone who had agreed to perform for him.

In business, parties often wish to transfer an entire contract—both rights and obligations. Suppose the mill that purchased the 1,000 bushels of wheat from the farmer sold the contract to a new owner. The contract with the farmer might be transferred to the new owner. Unfortunately, this transfer is referred to as an assignment even though the new owner acquires both rights and duties. Sometimes when business people are negotiating the transfer of an entire contract, they are primarily interested in the rights involved, not the duties. Because they have given little thought to who will perform the duties, their agreement does not cover this responsibility. The problem of whether the assignee who has acquired the rights is also responsible for the duties must be faced at a later time.

Hurst v. West

Court of Appeals of North Carolina
272 S.E.2d 378 (1980)

A client, William F. Hurst (plaintiff), brought an action for breach of contract against his attorneys, West and Groome (defendants). The law firm had entered into a contract with Hurst to represent him on a criminal case. In return, Hurst gave the attorneys an interest in some property he owned. The contract between the parties permitted the attorneys to sell the property and apply the proceeds against their fees. The attorneys succeeded in getting the criminal charges against Hurst dropped. Thereafter, they assigned their interest in the contract to J. D. Hurst and Hurst Distributors, Inc. William Hurst claimed it was a breach of contract for West and Groome to assign the contract. The trial court directed a verdict in favor of the attorneys. The Court of Appeals affirmed the verdict of the trial court.

Harry C. Martin, Judge

The general rule is that contracts may be assigned. The principle is firmly established in this jurisdiction that, unless expressly prohibited by statute or in contravention of some principle of public policy, all ordinary business contracts are assignable, and that a contract for money to become due in the future may be assigned.

The Supreme Court has stated:

> A valid assignment may be made by any contract between the assignor and the assignee which manifests an intention to make the assignee the present owner of the debt. The assignment operates as a binding transfer of the title to the debt as between the assignor and the assignee regardless of whether notice of the transfer is given to the debtor.

Exceptions to the rule that contracts are freely assignable are when the contract expressly provides that it is not assignable, or when performance of some term of the contract involves an element of personal skill or credit. "Whether or not a contractual duty requires personal performance by a specific individual can be determined only by interpreting the words used in the light of experience." 4 A. Corbin, Contracts § 866, 455 (1951).

The contract between William F. Hurst and West and Groome contained no express prohibition against assignment. Although the duty of defendant attorneys to defend plaintiff William Hurst on the charges then pending against him involved an element of personal skill and would not have been assignable to a third party, those obligations were fulfilled and discharged when the criminal charges against Hurst were dismissed. The remaining obligation of defendants under the contract, that they sell the property at a reasonable market value if the option to purchase were not exercised, was not personal in nature, as such a performance can be rendered with equal effectiveness by an assignee of the contract. Thus it is clear that no breach occurred merely by West and Groome's assignment of the contract to J. D. Hurst and Hurst Distributors, Inc.

Traditionally the assignment of a contract did not operate to cast upon the assignee the duties and obligations or the liabilities of the contract if the assignee did not assume such liabilities. But in Rose v. Materials Co., our Supreme Court held that unless a contrary intention is apparent, an assignee under a general assignment of an executory bilateral contract becomes the delegatee of the assignor's duties and impliedly promises to perform them. The Court adopted and reaffirmed as the more reasonable rule:

> "The assignment on its face indicates an intent to do more than simply to transfer the benefits assured by the contract. It purports to transfer the contract as a whole, and since the contract is made up of both benefits and burdens both must be intended to be included. It is true the assignor has power only to delegate and not to transfer the performance of duties as against the other party to the contract assigned, but this does not prevent the assignor and the assignee from shifting the burden of performance as between themselves. Moreover, common sense tells us that the assignor, after making such an assignment, usually regards himself as no longer a party to the contract. He does not and, from the nature of things, cannot easily keep in touch with what is being done in order properly to protect his interests if he alone is to be liable for non-performance. Not infrequently the assignor makes an assignment because he is unable to perform further or because he intends

to disable himself for further performance. The assignee on the other hand understands that he is to carry out the terms of the contract, as is shown by the fact that he usually does. . . .''

In the present case, J. D. Hurst and Hurst Distributors, Inc. expressly agreed to assume all liabilities and responsibilities under the original contract and to hold defendants harmless ''from any liability or responsibility under said contract and particularly from any liability or claim of any kind or description William Hurst may now or hereafter make against the Seller [defendants] for accounting or sale of property.'' J. D. Hurst and Hurst Distributors, Inc., as assignees of the contract, could take by transfer only what rights and interests the assignor had at the time of the assignment, and took subject to any setoffs and defenses available to plaintiffs against the assignor.

Because plaintiff's evidence did not establish the necessary elements of breach of contract, we hold that the directed verdict in favor of defendants was proper.

Affirmed.

Assignment of Monetary Rights

In this credit-oriented society, the contract right most frequently assigned is the right to receive a sum of money. The transfer of rights to receive a monetary payment is an integral part of the American economic system. It is the legal basis for several types of financing. An example would be financing automobile sales. In a large percentage of cases, the buyer of a new automobile purchases on "time." The dealer, however, in order to maintain its inventory and to pay business expenses, must often have cash immediately. In order to obtain this cash the dealer might assign its contract right to the buyer's payment to a financial institution at a small discount. The financial institution, now the owner of the right, would notify the buyer and order the buyer to make payments to it.

Accounts Receivable and Factoring. The assignment is also the basis for accounts-receivable financing and factoring. In accounts-receivable financing, a financial institution advances funds to a business that are secured by the accounts receivable of the business. In factoring, the firm advancing funds makes an absolute purchase of outstanding accounts that are assigned to it. The debtor is instructed to pay the factor directly. If the factor is unable to collect, it ordinarily suffers the loss. In accounts-receivable financing, the debtor usually continues to pay the original creditor who has guaranteed payment of the account to the financing agency.

Because of the economic importance of free transferability of rights to receive money and because the assignment of a monetary obligation does not materially alter the obligor's responsibility, few limitations have been placed upon assignment of money rights. In fact the UCC provides that a contractual term limiting the right to assign a monetary right is ineffective.[2] However, a number of states, for public policy reasons, either prohibit or limit wage assignments.

Wage Assignments. States may regulate and restrict the assignment of wages. Legislatures hope to protect wage earners through such statutes. Some states have prohibited the assignment of future wages. In other states, statutes limit the right to make assignments of future earnings to a specific time period.

In New York, for example, the statute permits the assignment of future earnings; however, it limits the amount collectible in any month to 10 percent of the assignor's future earnings payable during the month. If, when the assignee requests payment from the assignor's employer, any other assignment of future earnings is subject to payment, no amount is collectible while such other assignment is subject to payment.[3]

In the absence of such a statute, the general rule is that future earnings under an existing contract of employment may be assigned. On the other hand, if the assignor is not employed at the time of the assignment, the assignment normally is invalid at law.

Generally, an employee need not obtain the consent of his or her employer before making an assignment of wages under an existing contract of employment.

The following case discusses an assignment of all of a corporation's rights to collect assessments on lots in a subdivision. Note that the court finds the assignee bound by the actions of the assignor.

Chimney Hill Owners Association v. Antignani
Supreme Court of Vermont
392 A.2d 423 (1978)

In 1966, the Chimney Hill Corporation began development of a 900-lot tract in Wilmington, Vermont, for vacation homes known as Chimney Hill. In addition to the lots, there was a 300–500-acre area of common land that contained a clubhouse, pools, tennis courts, roads, and a water system for the community. A standard deed, filed with the local town clerk, provided that each lot was to be assessed an annual charge for the use of the common land and facilities that were maintained by the corporation. The right to collect the annual charge was vested in the corporation, as the grantor of the lots, and its "successors and assigns." The duty to pay the annual charge was imposed upon each lot owner, as the grantee of the lot, and their "heirs . . . successors, and assigns."

In 1968 the Eastern Woodworking Company acquired eleven lots. In addition to the standard sales agreement, which included the covenant to pay the annual charge for the common land, the corporation agreed in writing to charge Eastern only a single assessment on one lot rather than eleven separate assessments.

The corporation conveyed the common land and facilities by quit-claim deed to the Chimney Hill Owners' Association in 1975. The Association collectively represented all property owners in Chimney Hill. The corporation assigned to the Association the right to collect the assessments on each lot for use and maintenance of the common land and facilities. The Association subsequently billed Eastern for a separate assessment on each lot it owned.

The trial court ruled for Eastern. The Supreme Court of Vermont affirmed.

Hill, Justice

A Declaration of Protective Covenants, Restrictions and Reservations pertaining to Chimney Hill was executed by Chimney Hill Corporation and recorded in the Town

Clerk's office in Wilmington. The Declaration was included in each purchase and sales agreement and each deed executed for lots in Chimney Hill. Paragraph 10 of the Declaration is the focus of the dispute in these actions.

Paragraph 10 states that an annual charge shall be assessed against each lot in Chimney Hill and paid "to the grantor, its successors and assigns" for the right to use the common lands, facilities and services maintained and provided by the "grantor, its successors and assigns." The charge is made a debt collectible by suit in a court of competent jurisdiction and a lien on the lot conveyed until paid. Paragraph 10 further provides that acceptance of a deed bound by the Declaration shall be construed to be a covenant by the grantee, his heirs, successors and assigns to pay the charge to the grantor, its successors and assigns. Lastly, Paragraph 10(E) states:

> That this charge shall run with and bind the land hereby conveyed, and shall be binding upon the grantee or grantees, his, her, their, or its heirs, executors, administrators, successors and assigns, until May 31, 1988, unless earlier terminated by written release of the grantor, its successors or assigns.

The plaintiff seeks to recover the assessments, in its own right, under the assignment from Chimney Hill Corporation. In the assignment, the Corporation assigned to the plaintiff the right to collect from each owner in Chimney Hill the annual charge. As assignee, however, the plaintiff takes the right to collect subject to all defenses of the obligor against the assignor that have not been acquired or set up in fraud of the rights of the assignee after notice has been given of their existence.

As to defendant Eastern, the trial court concluded that it possessed a valid release from Chimney Hill Corporation concerning the ten unimproved lots, which was a valid defense to the plaintiff's claim. Paragraph 10(E) of the Declarations reserves to the grantor, Chimney Hill Corporation, its successors and assigns, the right to terminate the annual charge on any of the lots. Eastern's sales agreement, executed by both Eastern and Chimney Hill Corporation, provides that one annual charge only will be assessed on Eastern's eleven lots until one or more have been improved. The sales agreement contains just the release contemplated by Paragraph 10(E).

Eastern's defense based on the release is valid against the plaintiff as assignee of Chimney Hill Corporation.

Defendant Eastern has a valid written release signed by Chimney Hill Corporation, which unequivocally waives the right to annual charges on ten unimproved lots and which is binding on Chimney Hill Corporation. The court found at the time the plaintiff acquired the common lands and facilities it was aware that some multiple lot owners were being charged one assessment. The issue is whether with this knowledge the plaintiff is charged with the duty to inquire further as to when and why such single assessments were made. We think such inquiry should have been made. If such inquiry had been made of the Chimney Hill Corporation, the existence of Eastern's written release would have been revealed.

Affirmed.

Assignment of Nonmonetary Rights

Assignment of monetary rights are almost always enforceable because it really does not make much difference to whom the debtor pays the money.

In determining whether other types of rights are assignable, the guiding principle is whether the transfer materially changes the obligor's duty. The payment of money, the obligation to sell goods, or land, and the obligation to do a job to particular specifications are all freely transferable. If, however, the nature of the assignment or the circumstances are such that the assignment materially changes the obligor's responsibility, an assignment will be ineffective.

Prohibitions of Assignment

Sometimes the parties attempt to prohibit assignment by a contractual provision. A number of courts have refused to recognize restrictions of this nature. Their justification is that a contract right is property, and the owner should be free to transfer it if he or she wishes to do so.

Most jurisdictions in the United States would probably enforce a contractual clause restricting assignment. As one New York court stated,

[W]e think it reasonably clear that, while the courts have striven to uphold freedom of assignability, they have not failed to recognize the concept of freedom to contract. . . . When "clear language" is used, and the "plainest words . . . have been chosen," parties may limit the freedom of alienation of rights and prohibit the assignment.[4]

Rights of the Assignee

Defenses Good Against Assignor and Assignee. Although assignment is an integral element of much business financing, the assignee, ordinarily a financial institution advancing funds, is subject to some legal risk. All that the assignee acquires are the rights possessed by the original assignor. If the obligor has defenses that can be asserted against the assignor, these same defenses can be asserted against the assignee. The axiomatic principle is spelled out clearly in both case law and the UCC.[5] For example, if the original transaction was voidable because of fraud or failure of consideration, the obligor can assert these defenses against the assignee to the same extent that it could have asserted them against the assignor. If the underlying transaction is voidable because the obligor lacked the capacity to contract, this defense can also be asserted by the obligor against the assignee.

Practically, this means that when a financial institution or individual advances funds upon the basis of an assignment, the value of what is acquired is determined by the original transaction. This is true even when the assignee takes in good faith and has no knowledge of what took place in the original transaction. An assignee can protect itself from this risk to a degree by asking the obligor if it has defenses against performance. If the obligor gives assurances that no defenses exist, the obligor may not at a later time assert defenses that are inconsistent with these assurances.

Suppose that First National Bank wishes to purchase a note signed by a homeowner. The homeowner agreed to pay Acme Home Improvement $500 for work done on the home. If the bank, prior to taking the note, asks the homeowner (the obligor on the note) if Acme did the work, and the homeowner says yes, the homeowner may not assert the failure of Acme to do the work as a reason to refuse to pay the bank after it takes the note.

With and Without Recourse. An assignee can also protect itself by extracting from the assignor a commitment to repurchase a claim that is uncollectible. This is usually referred to as a *with recourse* assignment. If the assignee takes *without recourse*, it assumes the risks of collection.

Guarantees Made to Assignee. Even in situations in which an assignment is made "without recourse," the assignor by the very act of assigning makes certain warranties to the assignee. Although collection is not guaranteed, the assignor does guarantee that any document evidencing the right is genuine and that the right is not subject to any undisclosed defenses of which he or she is aware. In addition, the assignor guarantees that he will do nothing to defeat or impair the assignment. If he were to collect the debt himself, he would thus violate this last guarantee.

Notice to the Obligor

Assignment to One Person. For several reasons, the assignee should notify the obligor of the assignment as soon as possible. In most states, after proper notice is given, the obligor can no longer assert counterclaims or defenses against the assignee unless these arise out of the transaction that gave rise to the assignment. Additionally, until the obligor receives notice of the assignment, it may perform its duties to the assignor and thus complete its contractual obligation. Once, however, the obligor has notice of the assignment, it can meet its contractual obligation only by performance to the assignee. If the right assigned is a debt, the debtor is discharged only by payment to the assignee. A debtor who pays the original creditor after notice of assignment would have to make a second payment to the assignee.

Suppose that Mary owes $100 to Betty. Betty then assigns her right to receive $100 from Mary to John. Betty is thus the assignor and John the assignee of a contractual right to receive money. What if John never instructs Mary to pay him rather than Betty? In that situation, because Mary is unaware of the as-signment, she could pay the entire sum to Betty. This would completely discharge Mary of any obligation under the contract. John's only recourse in this situation would be against Betty. John could sue Betty for breach of the implied warranty that she would do nothing to prevent John from obtaining performance from Mary.

Assignment to Two or More Persons. Notice is also important if the assignor fraudulently or mistakenly assigns the same right to two different parties. In a minority of states the assignee who first notifies the obligor is entitled to collect the benefit. In most states the first assignment is valid, the courts reasoning that after the initial assignment the assignor had nothing left to transfer. Even in those states that follow the majority rule, however, immediate notice is important as it exposes the double assignment and thus decreases the possibility of litigation.

In the earlier example in which Mary owes $100 to Betty, Betty could assign her right to receive the $100 to John. If John again fails to notify Mary, this would give Betty the opportunity to assign this same debt to Tom. In most states, because John was the first assignee, he has the right to collect. However, in a state following the minority rule, if Tom notified Mary of the assignment before John did, Tom would be entitled to collect. John's only recourse in that situation would be against Betty.

Form of Assignment

Although an oral assignment ordinarily is valid, for a number of reasons an assignment should be made in a writing signed by the assignor. The principal reason is to provide clear evidence that a transfer of the right has taken place. In addition, many states have statutes that require certain types of assignments to be in writing to be effective. One common example is the wage assignment. The UCC requires that certain assignments must be in writing to be effective. For example, Section 9-203 requires that an assignment given for the purpose of security must be in writing unless the secured party is given possession of the collateral.

The writing should describe the right that is being transferred and identify the party who has the duty to perform. In order to effectuate the giving of notice, the obligor's address should be obtained at the time the assignment is made, if not included in the assignment. A typical assignment of a contract right might be worded as follows:

> The undersigned for value received, receipt of which is hereby acknowledged, does hereby assign to John Smith all her right, title, and interest in a contract between Alice All and Betty Blaine, dated March 31, 1984, to the property described therein and to all the moneys remaining unpaid thereunder.
>
> The undersigned further guarantees payment of all unpaid installments and agrees that if default be made she, Alice All, will pay the full amount to John Smith upon demand.
>
> Dated July 20, 1984
>
> _____
>
> (signed)

Transfer by Negotiation

The principal legal risk of acquiring a contract right by assignment is that the assignee is subject to defenses that the obligor has against the assignor. From very early in its development, the mercantile community has required a means of transferring the right to receive a monetary payment that will free the transferee from defenses that arise out of the agreement that created the right. This need is especially pressing today in an economy in which a large percentage of business is done on credit.

A manufacturing firm that sells $100,000 worth of goods on ninety-day credit has a valuable contract right. If everything goes all right, the firm will receive payment in ninety days. The firm itself, however, often needs immediate cash to meet its own obligations. This might readily be obtained by selling at a slight discount its right to receive the $100,000. A bank or finance company may not be willing to pay much for this right if it has to worry about the risk of nonperformance or improper performance by the firm of the underlying contract. In a transfer by assignment, the financial institution has to take this risk. If assignment were the only method available to transfer contract rights, our credit economy would operate less efficiently.

The mercantile community's need for an easy and safe means of transferring monetary rights gave rise to negotiable instruments and the legal concept of transfer by negotiation. The need was so great that the legal concept developed and was in active use while the law of assignment was in its infancy.

Negotiation involves only rights to receive money. The monetary claim to the right to receive money must be evidenced by particular written instruments known as negotiable instruments. A negotiable instrument with which most people are familiar is the check. Other examples of negotiable instruments are promissory notes and drafts. If these instruments are in the proper form and are transferred properly, the person acquiring them is not subject to many defenses that might exist between the original parties. A person who attains the status of a holder in due course is often in a better legal position than the party who has sold the instrument to him.

The use of a negotiable instrument in a typical business transaction should make this clear. Alice and Ben have entered into a contract in which Ben has promised to sell to Alice 100 molds at $50 per mold. Alice has given Ben in payment a promissory note for $5,000 payable in thirty days. Ben, in need of cash to meet his payroll, has sold this note at a small discount to his bank. If the note is in the proper form and has been transferred properly, the bank has a right to collect the note in thirty days even if Ben has breached the contract by shipping molds that do not meet the specifications of the agreement. If Ben, however, had kept the note, he would not be able to collect the full value because he had breached the contract. The damage to Alice arising from the failure of the molds to meet contract requirements would be set off against the $5,000. If Ben had assigned his claim to a bank instead of using a promissory note, the bank would also not be able to collect the full value of the note as it would be subject to the defense that Alice had against Ben.

As the holder in due course of a negotiable instrument can require the debtor to make payment even when the debtor would not have to pay the original creditor, the law requires negotiable instruments to possess numerous exacting qualities. As an example, the instrument must contain words that in fact amount to an order or promise to pay. A written instrument in which Arthur stated that he owed Sam $5,000 and that he promised to pay it could not be negotiated because Arthur promised to pay Sam only. Arthur has not promised to pay anyone whom Sam orders paid. The instrument lacks the legally required words of negotiability.[6]

Just as there are numerous qualities of form that an instrument must possess to be negotiable, it must also be negotiated properly if the taker is to be a holder in due course. If the bank in the previous example had known of the breach of contract by Ben, the bank would not be a holder in due course because to be in this preferred position the holder must not know of a defense existing between the original parties.

In summary, if a person holds a mere assignment of a contractual right to receive money, he or she "steps into the shoes" of his or her assignor. This means the assignee of a contractual right to receive money is subject to any claims or defenses existing between the original parties to the contract. A holder in due

course of a negotiable instrument validly negotiated to him or her, however, in many cases takes possession free of defenses and claims of the original obligor on an instrument. The holder in due course is thus in a better position than the person from whom he or she took the instrument. In many cases, the holder in due course may enforce the instrument when his or her transferer *could not* enforce the instrument. The problems associated with purchasing and selling negotiable instruments are discussed in depth in Chapters 19–22.

Delegation of Duties

Up to this point we have been looking primarily at situations in which a person who owns a contract right wishes to transfer it. A party to a contract who has an obligation to perform may wish to transfer that obligation to another party. This is permissible as long as those obligations are not personal in nature and transferring them does not violate a public policy. A transfer of contractual duties or obligations is referred to as a *delegation*.

We have seen that when a party to a contract assigns a right, generally no guarantee is given that the new owner of the right will be able to collect. The obligor who transfers his duty makes a different commitment. He or she continues to be liable for performance except in those situations in which the party for whom the obligation must be performed releases the obligor from responsibility. This is called a *novation*. If a novation is carried out properly, the original obligor is released from a duty to perform, and the third party now has the entire obligation.

Delegable Duties. The delegation of a duty is an attempt to extinguish a duty in the assignor and create a similar duty in the assignee. Generally, duties are delegable, although a delegation does not extinguish the duty or relieve the assignor of the duty to perform in the event that the delegate fails to perform. The obligations incurred as a result of most business contracts can be transferred.

Construction contracts are good examples of the type of contract in which the obligor's duties are delegable. Ordinarily the parties understand that the general contractor will not perform all the work. Much will be done by subcontractors, although the prime contractor is responsible for their performance.

Nondelegable Duties. A duty is nondelegable when the performance by the delegate would vary materially from performance by the obligor, or where the original party to the contract has a substantial interest in performance of the duty by the original obligor. Contracts based on a particular artistic skill are not delegable. A contract to be performed by Johnny Cash, for example, could not be performed by Liza Minelli. The two performances are not the same.

Another exception would be those contracts that involve some type of personal service. An employment contract is a clear example of the type of agreement in which the obligor's (employee's) duty would in many cases not be delegable. Even when the employee's duties are of a general nature, the employment relationship is sufficiently personal so that courts will not recognize the employee's attempt to delegate his duties. A contract with one barber to cut a man's hair, or a contract with an attorney or physician, involves unique abilities that make performance by another person unacceptable.

What if, in a contract between Smith and Jones, Jones delegates his duties to Brown, and informs Smith that he will no longer be responsible for the performance of the contract? Smith may treat Jones's action as a breach of contract. If Smith accepts Brown's performance, Jones's obligation to perform is extinguished.

Really, what Jones is trying to do is create a novation. A novation is an agreement between the original parties to a contract and a third party, whereby the third party agrees to perform the duties of one of the original parties to the original contract. The party for whom the third party performs no longer has any obligation under the original contract.

In a situation such as that among Smith, Jones, and Brown, the courts disagree whether Jones can force such an agreement on Smith without Smith's consent. Some courts permit Smith to take Brown's services, and still sue Jones for breach of contract. Other courts treat Smith's acceptance of Brown's services as a consent by Smith to extinguish Jones's liability under the contract.

Assignment under the UCC

Delegating Duties. As you recall, the UCC applies when a person enters into a contract to sell goods. The UCC has its own provisions covering assignments. Section 2-120(2) permits a party to delegate his or her duties of performance absent some contrary provision in the contract—unless the other party has a substantial interest in having the original promisor perform. In any event, merely because a party delegates his or her duties of performance does not relieve that party of any duty to perform or any liability for breach. Suppose that Acme Contracting entered into a contract with Stewart Sand for delivery of sand to Acme's job site. May Stewart delegate its duty to perform to Lignite Sand? Absent a contrary agreement, or unless the other party has a substantial interest in having the original party perform, yes.

It is entirely possible that Acme may not be as satisfied with Lignite. What if Stewart was a very dependable seller, but Lignite was not as trustworthy? The UCC recognizes that the nonassigning original party has a stake in the reliability of the person with whom he or she entered into the original contract. It therefore provides that if a party feels insecure, it may demand assurances of performance from the assignee pursuant to Section 2-609. Thus, in this case, Acme may demand assurances of performance from Lignite. Acme may request such assurances without prejudicing its rights against Stewart.

Assigning Rights. The UCC also provides that, absent a contrary agreement, all rights of the buyer or seller may be assigned. This is true unless the assignment would materially change the duty of the other party, or increase materially the burden or risk imposed on him or her by the contract, or impair materially his or her chance of obtaining a return performance. The UCC thus provides that rights may generally be assigned.

The UCC distinguishes between *rights* and *duties*. Each party to a contract acquires certain rights, but at the same time is obligated to certain duties. Take the sand case. In the original contract, Acme has the *right* to receive a certain amount of sand, but it also has the *duty* to pay for any sand delivered. Likewise, Stewart has a *duty* to deliver the sand pursuant to the contract, but it also has a *right* to receive payment for the sand from Acme. A third party consequently may become a party to a contract in one of two ways: he or she may acquire a right under the contract, called an *assignment,* or he or she may become obligated to perform certain tasks pursuant to the contract, referred to as a *delegation* of duties. A third party may, of course, acquire both rights and duties under a contract.

Clauses Barring Assignment of Rights. Section 2-210(3) indicates that in the absence of a contrary agreement a prohibition of assignment of "the contract" is to be construed as barring only the delegation to the assignee of the assignor's performance. This reflects the UCC's general opposition to clauses that bar the assignment of rights. If the contract between Acme and Stewart stated "there may be no assignment of this contract," the courts must interpret this as meaning that the duty of performance may not be delegated to a third party such as Lignite. On the other hand, what if Stewart wished to assign its right to receive payment under the Acme contract to its bank? May Stewart assign its right to money even in the presence of this antiassignment clause? Yes.

Assigning Rights under a Contract. The UCC lays down a general rule of construction distinguishing between a normal commercial assignment, which substitutes the assignee for the assignor both as to rights and duties, and a financing assignment, in which only the assignor's rights are transferred. Consequently, when someone assigns "the contract" or "all my rights under the contract," this assignment transfers all the rights and delegates all the duties to the assignee, absent a contrary agreement. Acceptance by the assignee constitutes a promise by him or her to perform the duties. In this case the promise is enforceable by either the assignor or the other party to the original contract. If Stewart assigned its contract with Acme to Lignite, and used language such as "all my rights under the contract," Lignite would acquire all of Stewart's rights under the contract (the right to receive money) as well as all of Stewart's duties under the contract (the duty to deliver sand to Acme). Obviously, before a company takes an assignment of a contract, it should understand what its rights and obligations under the contract are. Otherwise, it may end up being obligated to perform certain duties it had not anticipated.

Defenses. In many cases, when the assignee of a contract attempts to collect, the assignee may find the obligor asserting a defense against him or her. What if Stewart assigned its right to receive money from Acme to its bank. When the bank attempts to collect from Acme, Acme might refuse to pay because Stewart has somehow failed to live up to its obligations under the contract. Is there any way the bank can protect itself from the possibility of being confronted by defenses?

One method an assignor might use is to include a waiver-of-defenses clause. In the original contract, the party obligated to pay agrees not to assert any defenses he or she might have against anyone except the party originally obligated to perform. Thus the original contract between Stewart and Acme might state that Acme agrees not to assert any defenses it might have against Stewart against anyone to whom the contract is assigned. Section 9-206 of the UCC covers waiver-of-defenses clauses. Generally, the UCC permits the parties to use such clauses—unless another statute or decision establishes a different rule for buyers or lessees of *consumer* goods. A number of statutes, such as the Uniform Consumer Credit Code and the Truth-in-Lending Act, in fact restrict the use of such clauses in consumer contracts. The FTC holder-in-due-course rule also prohibits the use of such clauses in consumer-credit contracts.

CONTRACTS FOR THE BENEFIT OF A THIRD PARTY

In many instances, a third party will benefit from the performance of a contract. In some cases the contracting parties have actually made the agreement for the benefit of the third party. In other situations an outsider will benefit even though the parties to the agreement did not plan to benefit the third party. A common example of a contract made primarily to benefit a third party is the life-insurance policy. Its primary purpose is to provide benefits for a third party upon the insured's death. The contract, however, is between the insured and the insuring company.

Donee Beneficiary

If a contract is primarily for the benefit of a third party, and the promisee's primary interest is to confer a gift upon the third party, the third party is referred to as a *donee beneficiary*. Life insurance is a good example of a situation involving a donee beneficiary. The typical policy requires the insurance company to pay a certain amount of money in the event of the death of the insured. The insured purchased this policy with the intent to benefit the third party. If the insurance company refuses to pay, the donee beneficiary may sue the company for the amount of the insurance policy. The donee beneficiary is permitted to sue even though he or she is not in privity of contract with the company and has not given anything to the insurance company. In other cases involving a donee beneficiary, the promisee also may sue the promisor if the promisor fails to perform. However, in most cases the promisor receives only nominal damages. Suppose that John's wealthy uncle sold his yacht to Louise for $300,000. The uncle instructed Louise to pay the money to John because he wanted to give John a gift. If Louise fails to pay, John may sue her for the $300,000 because he is a donee beneficiary of the contract between Louise and his uncle. John's uncle, the promisee, also may sue Louise, the promisor, for breach of contract but he probably would receive only nominal damages.

Creditor Beneficiary

If the purpose of the promise is to discharge an obligation that the promisee owes or believes he or she owes to the beneficiary, the third party is called a *creditor beneficiary*. In the case of a donee beneficiary, the promisee intends to make a gift. In the case of a creditor beneficiary, the promisee wishes to discharge an obligation owed to the creditor beneficiary. Suppose that Tina owes Cindy $1,000. Tina sells her automobile to Sam, who promises to pay $1,000 to Cindy in order to discharge the debt between Tina and Cindy. Cindy is a creditor beneficiary of Sam's promise and has an enforceable claim against Sam for $1,000.

Incidental Beneficiary

If a promisee neither intends to confer a gift on the third party nor is trying to discharge an obligation to the third party, the third party is called an *incidental beneficiary*. He or she has no rights under the contract. Suppose that McDonald's contracted to build a store next to Louise's dress shop. Because the McDonald's would attract many people to the area, Louise anticipated she would do more business than ever. The contract between McDonald's and the builder was not intended to benefit Louise. If the builder breaches the contract, and the McDonald's is never built, does Louise have a cause of action against the builder? No. This contract was not intended to benefit Louise in any way. She would have no cause of action against the builder even though, had the store been built, her business might have increased.

Intended Beneficiary

The Second Restatement of Contracts no longer uses the terms donee or creditor beneficiary, but instead substitutes the term *intended beneficiary* to describe any beneficiary who receives rights under the contract. Even so, some courts still frequently use the terminology donee/creditor beneficiary.

A question that the courts have frequently had to face is whether a third party who will benefit from an agreement has a right to sue if the agreement is not carried out. This question is especially troublesome when the parties to the contract did not contemplate benefiting another; or if they did, this was not their primary concern. What they were interested in doing was benefiting themselves.

Although the law varies from state to state, most jurisdictions take a positive view about allowing the third party to sue. In spite of the fact that the third party was not involved in the agreement, the legal system in general recognizes that it is both just and practical to allow an outsider to recover if it is clear that this will effectuate the intentions of the parties.[7] A third party who has a right to sue is ordinarily referred to as an *intended* beneficiary. Beneficiaries who do not have a right to sue are referred to as *incidental*.

To determine if a party is an intended beneficiary, the courts first look at the intention of the parties. If it is clear that the parties intended to benefit the outsider, a right to sue is recognized. This will be the case whenever the promisor has agreed to perform directly to or for the third party.

The third party also has a right to sue in some jurisdictions as long as the main purpose of the contract is for his or her benefit. This right exists even if the promisee and promisor also benefit.

In these cases it is the promisee's intention that is significant, not the promisor's. This makes good sense because, if the promisee could sue, the third party that the promisee intended to benefit should have the same right. In either case the promisor is in the same position. A question of greater complexity occurs when the third party can show that it will benefit but is unable to convince the court that the parties intended that it should.

United States v. Ogden Technology Laboratories

U.S. District Court
406 F. Supp. 1090 (1973)

The U.S. Atomic Energy Commission, acting for the federal government, the plaintiff, entered into a contract with 3M. Ogden, the defendant, through a series of subcontracts, was hired to test six prototype units for thermoelectric supply systems. Asserting that the government may not bring suit against it because the government is not in privity of contract with Ogden, Ogden moved to dismiss the case. The District Judge denied the motion to dismiss because he found the government not to be merely an incidental beneficiary.

Bartels, District Judge

Plaintiff alleges that through its agent, the Atomic Energy Commission, it entered into a contract with Minnesota Mining and Manufacturing Company ("3M") for the development and testing of certain thermoelectric power-supply systems. In turn, 3M entered into a subcontract with the Linde Division of Union Carbide Corporation ("Linde") under which Linde was to design and fabricate and perform certain analytical work on "high temperature vacuum insulation system" ("HTVIS") units. Finally, plaintiff alleges that Linde entered into a contract with Ogden for the latter to test, in its laboratory, six prototype HTVIS units by subjecting them to prescribed shocks and programs of vibration and to report to Linde how the tests were conducted and their results.

After a number of successful tests on various units had been completed, a test of unit B–10–4 resulted in severe damage. Plaintiff alleges that the damage was caused not by any defect in the design of the HTVIS unit, but rather by Ogden improperly administering a shock greatly in excess of that specified in the contract.

Defendant, it is alleged, did not report to Linde the reason for the test failure, i.e., the excess shock. Plaintiff, not knowing of the excess shock administered and believing that the design of the units might have been faulty, caused 3M and Linde to reevaluate the design and determine the cause of failure. Because of the cost plus nature of the contracts between plaintiff, 3M and Linde, and because of clauses in these contracts placing risk of loss or damage to the units on the plaintiff, the plaintiff allegedly expended $500,000 for the reevaluation necessitated by Ogden's breach of its contractual duty to make a proper report of its shock treatment.

While we cannot be certain without further evidence, it appears from the complaint that there is a sufficient nexus between the plaintiff and Ogden to justify a claim for relief despite the fact that Ogden is not named as a party in any contract with the United States Government.

We reach this conclusion under the ancient theory of recovery for third-party beneficiaries which was first propounded in Lawrence v. Fox, in that plaintiff in this case is an intended beneficiary of the testing contract between Ogden and Linde. The parties agree that New York contract law on third-party beneficiaries controls their rights under the Linde-Ogden contract, and that under New York law ". . . it is well settled that before a third party can enforce a contract in his favor it must clearly appear that the contract was made and intended for his benefit. . . . [T]here must have been an intention on the part of the contracting parties to secure some direct benefit to him." But Ogden does not agree that plaintiff Government was a contractual beneficiary of its contract with Linde. Its relation to the Government, it claims, is too far removed to infer or permit such an intention.

We are aware that in the present case there is no pecuniary obligation running from the promisee, Linde, to the third-party Government, as is typically the case where third parties are permitted to recover on a contract. However, any third party to whom the promisee owes any duty may be a third party beneficiary of a contract to perform that duty. It is immaterial whether the duty of the promisee to the third-party beneficiary arises from a bargain between them or is created by an assumption by the promisee, acting as promisor in a previous contract, of some duty by another to the third-party beneficiary or is a non-contractual duty. Therefore, since Linde was obligated to report to the Government, albeit by way of an intervening contract with 3M, the Government is entitled to state a claim as a third-party beneficiary as long as the requisite intent to benefit the Government is shown.

It has long been recognized that the obligation to perform to the third-party plaintiff need not necessarily be expressly stated in the contract. It may be implied where the contracts and the surrounding circumstances indicate a clear intent on the part of the parties to obligate the promisor. Further, if the terms of the contract require the conferring of a benefit upon a third person, then such a benefit is to be considered as contemplated by the parties and invokes a third-party beneficiary right, even though the major motivation for the contract may be the parties' own advantage. Under these tests, plaintiff clearly is an intended beneficiary. The terms of the writings which form the agreement between Linde and Ogden evidence the fact that the Government was not just an incidental beneficiary of the Ogden obligations to Linde to test and report.

Therefore, the motion to dismiss the first cause of action in the amended complaint must be, and hereby is, denied without denying Ogden an evidentiary hearing to otherwise defeat plaintiff's claim.

Martinez v. Socoma Companies, Inc.

Supreme Court of California
521 P.2d 841 (1974)

Plaintiffs brought this class action on behalf of themselves and other disadvantaged unemployed persons, alleging that defendants Socoma Companies, Inc. and others failed to perform contracts with the U.S. government under which defendants agreed to provide job training and at least one year of employment to certain numbers of such persons. The lower court found the plaintiffs lacked standing to sue because they were not third-party beneficiaries. The California Supreme Court affirmed the judgment for the defendants.

Wright, Chief Justice

The complaint alleges that under 1967 amendments to the Economic Opportunity Act of 1964 "the United States Congress instituted Special Impact Programs with the intent to benefit the residents of certain neighborhoods having especially large concentrations of low-income persons and suffering from dependency, chronic unemployment and rising tensions." . . .

On January 17, 1969, the corporate defendants allegedly entered into contracts with the Secretary of Labor, acting on behalf of the Manpower Administration, United States Department of Labor (hereinafter referred to as the "Government"). Each such defendant entered into a separate contract and all three contracts are made a part of the complaint as exhibits. Under each contract the contracting defendant agreed to lease space in the then vacant Lincoln Heights jail building owned by the City of Los Angeles, to invest at least $5,000,000 in renovating the leasehold and establishing a facility for the manufacture of certain articles, to train and employ in such facility for at least 12 months, at minimum wage rates, a specified number of East Los Angeles residents certified as disadvantaged by the Government, and to provide such employees with opportunities for promotion into available supervisorial-managerial positions and with options to purchase stock in their employer corporation. Each contract provided for the lease of different space in the building and for the manufacture of a different kind of product. As consideration, the Government agreed to pay each defendant a stated amount in installments. Socoma was to hire 650 persons and receive $950,000; Lady Fair was to hire 550 persons and receive $999,000; and Monarch was to hire 400 persons and receive $800,000. The hiring of these persons was to be completed by January 17, 1970.

Plaintiffs were allegedly members of a class of no more than 2,017 East Los Angeles residents who were certified as disadvantaged and were qualified for employment under the contracts. Although the Government paid $712,500 of the contractual consideration to Socoma, $299,700 to Lady Fair, and $240,000 to Monarch, all of these defendants failed to perform under their respective contracts, except that Socoma provided 186 jobs of which 139 were wrongfully terminated, and Lady Fair provided 90 jobs, of which all were wrongfully terminated. . . .

Plaintiffs contend they are third party beneficiaries under Civil Code section 1559, which provides: "A contract, made expressly for the benefit of a third person, may be enforced by him at any time before the parties thereto rescind it." This section excludes enforcement of a contract by persons who are only incidentally or remotely benefited by it. American law generally classifies persons having enforceable rights under contracts to which they are not parties as either creditor beneficiaries or donee beneficiaries. California decisions follow this classification.

Unquestionably plaintiffs were among those whom the Government intended to benefit through defendants' performance of the contracts which recite that they are executed pursuant to a statute and a presidential directive calling for programs to furnish disadvantaged persons with training and employment opportunities. However, the fact that a Government program for social betterment confers benefits upon individuals who are not required to render contractual consideration in return does not necessarily imply that the benefits are intended as gifts. Congress's power to spend money in aid of the general welfare authorizes federal programs to alleviate national unemployment. The benefits of such programs are provided not simply as gifts to the recipients but as a means of accomplishing a larger public purpose. The furtherance of the public purpose is in the nature of consideration to the Government, displacing any governmental intent to furnish the benefits as gifts.

Even though a person is not the intended recipient of a gift, he may nevertheless be "a donee beneficiary if it appears from the terms of the promise in view of the accompanying circumstances that the purpose of the promisee in obtaining the promise . . . is . . . to confer upon him a right against the promisor to some performance neither due nor supposed or asserted to be due from the promisee to the beneficiary." The Government may, of course, deliberately implement a public purpose by including provisions in its contracts which expressly confer on a specified class of third persons a direct right to benefits, or damages in lieu of benefits, against the private contractor. But a governmental intent to confer such a direct right cannot be inferred simply from the fact that the third persons were intended to enjoy the benefits. The Restatement of Contracts makes this clear in dealing specifically with contractual promises to the Government to render services to members of the public:

> A promisor bound to the United States or to a State or municipality by contract to do an act or render a service to some or all of the members of the public, is subject to no duty under the contract to such members to give compensation for the injurious consequences of performing or attempting to perform it, or of failing to do so, unless . . . an intention is manifested in the contract, as interpreted in the light of the circumstances surrounding its formation, that the promisor shall compensate members of the public for such injurious consequences . . . [Restatement of Contracts Section 145]

The present contracts manifest no intent that the defendants pay damages to compensate plaintiffs or other members of the public for their nonperformance. To the contrary, the contracts' provisions for retaining the Government's control over determination of contractual disputes and for limiting defendants' financial risks indicate a governmental purpose to exclude the direct rights against defendants claimed here.

The fact that plaintiffs were in a position to benefit more directly than certain other members of the public from performance of the contract does not alter their status as incidental beneficiaries.

Affirmed.

REVIEW PROBLEMS

1. Rosier was a frequent purchaser of large quantities of oil on open account from Chanute Refining. A federal statute required inspection of oil before shipment; Chanute Refining had been doing this for Rosier, charging him an inspection fee. The statute was declared invalid and Rosier demanded a refund of the inspection fees that had been paid to Chanute Refining.

On June 19 Rosier purchased additional oil from Chanute Refining for $3,500. On June 29 Chanute assigned Rosier's account along with several others to Sinclair Co. When Rosier refused to pay, he was sued by Sinclair. At the trial Sinclair offered to present evidence to prove that it did not know of the dispute regarding the inspection fees. Is this evidence admissible? Why or why not? Sinclair Refining Co. v. Rosier, 180 Pac. 807.

2. In the preceding case, what are Sinclair's rights, if any, against Chanute Refining?

3. Bull Dog Insurance issued a policy of insurance to D'Alassano against loss by theft of an automobile. The automobile was stolen and never recovered. D'Alassano assigned his claim under the policy to Ginsberg. The policy provided that "no assignment of interest under this policy shall be or become binding upon the association unless the written consent . . . is endorsed thereon and an additional membership fee is paid." Present arguments supporting Ginsberg's right to collect under the policy. Ginsberg v. Bull Dog Auto Fire Ins. Assn., 160 N.E. 145.

4. In situations in which an assignor has assigned the same right twice, (a) some states' law gives priority to the assignment first made. Present arguments in support of this rule. (b) Other states give priority to the assignee who first notifies the obligor. Present arguments in support of this rule.

5. MGM contracted to pay Selznick royalties upon the first TV broadcast of "Gone with the Wind." Later, Selznick obtained a large loan from Haas by assigning his right to payment of the royalties to Haas as security for the loan. Selznick notified MGM of the assignment and asked that Haas be notified in advance of any royalty payments to be made to Selznick. MGM refused but neither Selznick nor Haas pursued the matter. Haas died, Selznick defaulted on the loan, and Haas's estate obtained a judgment against Selznick. When the movie was broadcast, MGM paid Selznick, but Haas did not receive notice or a payment. Haas's estate sued MGM to recover the royalty payment. Was the royalty payment effectively assigned by Selznick to Haas under the UCC? Haas Estate v. Metro-Goldwyn-Mayer, Inc., 617 F.2d 1136 (Tex. Civ. App. 1980)

6. Dooley contracted with Rose to provide enough stone to meet Rose's business requirements for ten years at favorable listed prices. In return, Rose promised not to compete with Dooley in the rock-crushing business. Later, Dooley assigned the contract to Vulcan Materials Co. Is Vulcan required to supply stone to Rose at the original contract prices? Rose v. Vulcan Materials Co., 194 S.E.2d 520 (Sup. Ct. N.C. 1973)

7. McDonald's granted a franchise in the Omaha-Council Bluffs area to Copeland, a reputable and highly successful businessman. *In a separate agreement,* Copeland was granted a right of first refusal, that is, the right to receive the first offer of additional McDonald's franchises to be developed in the area. Subsequently, Copeland assigned his franchise contracts to Shupack, with McDonald's consent. When McDonald's later offered a new area franchise to someone else, Shupack sued, claiming that the right of first refusal was included in the assignment from Copeland so that he should have been offered the new restaurant first. McDonald's had previously written Shupack stating that the right was personal to Copeland and had not passed to Shupack. Was the right assignable? How can you determine whether it was personal to Copeland? Schupack v. McDonald's System, Inc., 264 N.W.2d 827 (Nebr. Sup. Ct. 1978)

8. Cunningham played basketball for the Cougars, a professional team owned by Southern Sports Corp. His contract prohibited assignment to another club without his consent. When Southern Sports assigned the Cougars franchise and Cunningham's contract to Munchak Corp., Cunningham protested, claiming that his contract was personal and therefore not assignable. Is the assignment of Cunningham's contract effective? Munchak Corp. v. Cunningham, 457 F.2d 721 (4th Cir. 1972)

9. For a 5 percent commission fee, Hurly promised to find someone to buy Adams Sales, Inc. stock or assets. Adams Sales was experiencing financial difficulties, so the principal stockholder, Lano, agreed to indem-

nify Adams Sales for losses in its accounts payable in exchange for more Adams stock. Hurley later found a buyer, but Adams Sales could not afford to pay him the commission. Can Hurley force Lano to pay on the grounds that Hurley is a third-party beneficiary of the indemnity agreement between Lano and Adams Sales? Hurley v. Lano International, Inc., 569 S.W.2d 602 (Tex. Civ. App. 1978)

FOOTNOTES

[1]Henningsen v. Bloomfield Motors, Inc., 161 A.2d 69 (1960).
[2]UCC Section 9-318(4).
[3]New York Personal Property Law, Art. 3-A, Sec. 48-a.
[4]Allhusen v. Caresto Const. Co., 303 N.Y. 446 (1952).
[5]UCC Section 9-318.
[6]The holder in due course doctrine is discussed in greater detail in Chapter 20.
[7]Restatement (Second) of Contracts Section 133 (1973).

Performance, Discharge, and Remedies

T he discussion of contract law to this point has been concerned with the issues of whether or not a valid contract has been entered into by the parties. Now the focus shifts to what happens after the contract has been made: the consequences of performance and nonperformance of the contractual obligations. Some contracts are made and performed simultaneously—for example, when someone buys a newspaper from a street vendor. However, other contracts are entered into by the parties with a view to performance by one or both of them sometime in the future. Between the making of the contract and its time of performance, changed circumstances may make performance no longer desirable for one of the parties. For example, if a building contractor agrees to build a house for a buyer and the costs of supplies and labor increase significantly between the time the contract is made and the time the house is to be built, the builder may have second thoughts about the deal, particularly if another buyer is willing to pay the builder more than the current contract provides. Under these circumstances, the level of per-formance by the builder may be something less than was anticipated by the first buyer. Suppose the builder uses lower-grade materials and hires other than journeymen workers to construct the building. What are the buyer's rights? Can the buyer require the contractor to fire the workers, tear down the construction made of lower-grade materials, and rebuild the house using quality materials and journeymen workers? Suppose the builder, having laid the foundation, learns of the other buyer who is willing to pay more. Can the builder negotiate a contract with the second buyer and start work on that buyer's house using workers taken off the first project with a view to finishing the first house after he has built the second? The contract may or may not deal explicitly with such possibilities. Where it does not, or if the parties disagree about their interpretations of how the contract is to resolve such issues, litigation may result. The practice of the courts is to place a commonsense construction on the intention of the parties respecting performance of a contract and to fashion a reasonable and just remedy for the breach of a duty to perform. The task of a manager is to determine what performances are due under a contract, when they will be due, and what consequences will result if the performances are not rendered at the proper time or in the proper manner.

PERFORMANCE DEPENDENT UPON CONDITIONS

Conditional Promises

Sometimes the parties to a contract will condition their respective performances upon the occurrence of an event. For example, a seller may condition its duty to deliver ordered goods upon the buyer's making a specified down payment. Similarly, the buyer may condition its obligation to pay the remainder of the price owed upon its being able to obtain financing for the purchase or upon its satisfaction with the delivered merchandise, or both. In these examples, the contract does not create a duty to perform unless and until some event occurs. Such promises are termed conditional.

Similarly, a duty of performance may be conditioned upon the nonoccurrence of an event. An example is a promise to cut a lawn if it does not rain on Saturday.

An event may create or extinguish a present duty of performance. For example, the making of the down payment by the buyer in the example above gives rise to a present duty in the seller to deliver the merchandise. On the other hand, in the lawn-mowing example, rain on Saturday extinguishes the mower's present duty to cut the lawn.

An event that must occur in order to give rise to a duty of performance is called a *condition precedent*. An event that extinguishes a duty of performance is called a *condition subsequent*. The nonoccurrence of a condition precedent excuses nonperformance by the party whose duty of performance was to arise only after the condition precedent materialized. The occurrence of a condition subsequent excuses the nonperformance of a party whose duty of performance was extinguished by the condition subsequent. In both cases, the party relying upon the condition is not liable to the other party for breach of contract because the nonperformance was excused. However, if the condition precedent happens to be the other party's performance, the nonoccurrence of the condition precedent gives the party relying upon that condition a claim against the other for breach of contract. In such a case, the party relying upon the condition has its nonperformance excused, whereas the other nonperforming party remains liable for breach of contract.

Approval or Satisfaction

Contracts sometimes contain provisions requiring that a party's performance be approved by the other party or by a person who is not a party to the contract. In such cases, the approval of the other party or the third person is a condition to the performance of one of the parties to the contract. For example, a contract for the sale of real estate may require that title be approved by an attorney. The attorney's approval is a condition precedent to the buyer's duty to purchase the property. If the attorney concludes that the seller does not have title to the property, the buyer's obligation to purchase is excused by virtue of the failure of the condition (the attorney's approval) to materialize.

A common example of a contract requiring the approval of a third party is the typical construction contract. Construction contracts frequently require outside approval of the work before the owner is obligated to pay. Usually the job must be inspected by an architect or an engineer who issues a certificate for payment if the construction is satisfactory, meaning that the construction has met the specifications contained in the architect's or engineer's building plans. Until this certificate is issued, the owner has no obligation to make payment, because the architect's or engineer's certificate is a condition precedent to performance by the owner.

Just as a party's duty of performance may be conditioned upon the other party's performance being approved by a third person, so can a party's duty to perform be conditioned upon its own satisfaction with the other party's performance. That is, one of the parties may bargain that its performance will personally satisfy the other party. Although there is considerable risk to the person or firm making this kind of commitment, it is relatively common. Contracts for the sale of goods often give the purchaser the right to return the goods if not satisfied. Employment contracts for a specific period of time sometimes allow the employer to terminate employment if the employee's service is not personally satisfactory to the employer.

Because of the potential danger of forfeiture in a contract in which one party does not have to keep its end of the bargain unless it or a third party is satisfied, courts have generally interpreted these provisions narrowly. They have consistently held that the dissatisfaction or refusal to approve must be in good faith and not left to the will or idiosyncrasies of the interested party. This means that the dissatisfaction is not to be feigned but must be based upon some valid reason.

For example, suppose that an artist agrees to paint a portrait of Penelope to her satisfaction. Any dissatisfaction expressed by Penelope must be made in good faith—that is, it must be an honest dissatisfaction. Proving Penelope's bad faith may be difficult because her dissatisfaction is a subjective state involving artistic taste and personal feeling. But suppose that the artist can show that Penelope expressed dissatisfaction with the portrait only after she had suffered severe financial reversals. The artist might succeed in arguing that Penelope was really responding to her changed financial

condition rather than to the quality of the artist's work.

When performance can be measured against an objective standard—for example, if a reasonable person would be satisfied—the party to the contract must also be satisfied. Suppose that Bigdome, Inc. contracts to buy certain tools from Ace Tool that are to be satisfactory to Bigdome. If Ace can establish that the tools meet certain standards in Bigdome's industry—for example, that they have been calibrated according to industry standards—Bigdome's dissatisfaction will not excuse its nonpayment for the tools.

SUBSTANTIAL PERFORMANCE AND MATERIAL BREACH

The normal manner in which the parties' contractual expectations will be satisfied is through complete and exact performance of the contract. This, of course, is the purpose of the bargain. As a factual matter, most contracts are fully performed and the relationships end. However, there may be a failure of performance, and the injured party must determine what remedy is available.

Substantial Performance

The most satisfactory manner of performance of contractual obligations is for both parties to perform exactly as promised. However, this is not always what happens. One party may perform erroneously as a result of misinterpreting the contract. Or exact performance may be prevented by circumstances that cannot be controlled. Clearly, a party is entitled to the promised performance. Just as clearly, justice dictates that the injured party should not be unjustly enriched by the penalty imposed on the defaulting party.

When one party fails to render a part of the promised performance, the following questions may arise:

1. Is the other party privileged to refuse to render a reciprocal promised performance?
2. Is the other party discharged from its contractual duty?
3. Can the other party sue for damages, regarding the breach as "total"?
4. Can the other party sue for damages for a "partial" breach?

Under the older common law, an express contract had to be completed to the last detail before a party could enforce the performance of the other party. Under the newer concept of "substantial performance," a party who has failed to provide exact performance may nevertheless enforce the performance of the other party if (1) there was substantial performance of the contract, (2) there was an honest effort to comply fully to the contract's requirements, and (3) there was no willful or intentional departure from the terms of the contract. The rationale for what is often called the substantial-performance doctrine is that justice does not demand full, literal fulfillment of contractual obligations but only substantial fulfillment.

Where one of the contracting parties has substantially performed its contractual duties, it is entitled to enforce performance by the other party. That is, the injured party may not refuse to render a reciprocal promised performance; it is not discharged from its contractual duties. However, the party that rendered substantial performance rather than exact performance is nevertheless in breach of contract. The breach is a partial breach, not a material breach; nevertheless, it remains a breach of contract. Where there has been a breach of contract, the injured party may sue and recover damages for the breach. Thus, although the injured party is not excused from its promised reciprocal performance, it is entitled to recover damages for the other party's failure to perform exactly as promised. If the injured party's promised performance is payment, it would be entitled to deduct from the contract price the amount that will compensate for the damages sustained.

Material Breach

The antithesis of substantial performance is a level of nonperformance tantamount to a material breach of contract. That is, a party who fails to substantially perform its contractual obligation is deemed to have materially breached the contract and is thereby liable to the injured party for damages. However, a material breach carries with it a further legal consequence. The injured party is excused from rendering any reciprocal promised performance. That is, a material breach of contract by one party entitles the injured party to treat its contractual duties as discharged—any nonperformance by the innocent party is excused—and further entitles the injured party to sue and recover damages resulting from the material breach.

Whether a party's failure to exactly perform a contractual duty amounts to a material breach or substantial performance is an issue of considerable importance. The test of substantial performance is whether the performance met the essential purpose of the contract and whether the nonperformance was willful. Thus a party who relies on the substantial-performance doctrine must show that its departure from the contract was slight and unintentional.

In the following case, the court wrestles with the problem of balancing a policy against unjust enrichment with a policy of ensuring that a party gets what the contract promises. While reading the case, keep in mind that a business firm should never enter a contract with the intention of providing only a substantial performance. That is an unethical strategy that could easily destroy the firm's reputation.

Plante v. Jacobs

Supreme Court of Wisconsin
103 N.W. 2d 296 (1960)

Eugene Plante contracted with Frank and Carol Jacobs to furnish the material and construct a house upon their lot in Brookfield, in accordance with plans and specifications, for the sum of $26,765. During the course of construction Plante was paid $20,000. Disputes arose between the parties, the Jacobses refused to continue payment, and Plante did not complete the house. He sued to establish a lien on the property as a way of recovering the unpaid balance of the contract price plus extras. The owners answered with allegations of faulty workmanship and incomplete construction. The trial court entered judgment for Plante in the sum of $4,152.90. The Jacobses appealed to the Supreme Court of Wisconsin, which affirmed. Plante is the plaintiff; the Jacobses are the appellants.

Hallows, Justice

The defendants argue the plaintiff cannot recover any amount because he has failed to substantially perform the contract. The plaintiff conceded he failed to furnish the kitchen cabinets, gutters and down-spouts, sidewalk, closed clothes poles, and entrance seat amounting to $1,601.95. This amount was allowed to the defendants. The defendants claim some 20 other items of incomplete or faulty performance by the plaintiff and no substantial performance because the cost of completing the house in strict compliance with the plans and specifications would amount to 25 or 30 per cent of the contract price. The defendants especially stress the misplacing of the wall between the living room and the kitchen, which narrowed the living room in excess of one foot. The cost of tearing down this wall and rebuilding it would be approximately $4,000. The record is not clear why and when this wall was misplaced, but the wall is completely built and the house decorated and the defendants are living therein. Real estate experts testified that the smaller width of the living room would not affect the market price of the house.

The defendants rely on *Manitowoc Steam Boiler Works* v. *Manitowoc Glue Co.,* for the proposition there can be no recovery on the contract as distinguished from *quantum meruit* unless there is substantial performance. This is undoubtedly the correct rule at common law. . . . The question here is whether there has been substantial performance. The test of what amounts to substantial performance seems to be whether the performance meets the essential purpose of the contract. In the *Manitowoc* case the contract called for a boiler having a capacity of 150 per cent of the existing boiler. The court held there was no substantial performance because the boiler furnished had a capacity of only 82 per cent of the old boiler and only approximately one-half of the boiler capacity contemplated by the contract. In *Houlahan* v. *Clark,* the contract provided the plaintiff was to drive pilings in the lake and place a boat house thereon parallel and in line with a neighbor's dock. This was not done and the contractor so positioned the boat house that it was practically useless to the owner. *Manthey* v. *Stock* involved a contract to paint a house and to do a good job, including the removal of the old paint where necessary. The plaintiff did not remove the old paint, and blistering and roughness of the new paint resulted. The court held that the plaintiff failed to show substantial performance. The defendants also cite *Manning v. School District No. 6*. However, this case involved a contract to install a heating and ventilating plant in the school building which would meet certain tests which the heating apparatus failed to do. The heating plant was practically a total failure to accomplish the purpose of the contract.

Substantial performance as applied to construction of a house does not mean that every detail must be in strict compliance with the specifications and the plans. Something less than perfection is the test of specific performance unless all details are made the essence of the contract. This was not done here. There may be situations in which features or details of construction of special or of great personal importance, which if not performed, would prevent a finding of substantial performance of the contract. In this case the plan was a stock floor plan. No detailed construction of the house was shown on the plan. There were no blueprints. The specifications were standard printed forms with some modifications and additions written in by the parties. Many of the problems that arose during the construction had to be solved on the basis of practical experience. No mathematical rule relating to the percentage of the price, of cost of completion or of completeness can be laid down to determine substantial performance of a building contract. Although the defendants received a house with which they are dissatisfied in many respects, the trial court was not in error in finding the contract was substantially performed.

The next question is what is the amount of recovery when the plaintiff has substantially, but incompletely, performed. For substantial performance the plaintiff should recover the contract price less the damages caused the defendant by the incomplete performance. Both parties agree *Venzke v. Magdanz* states the correct rule for damages due to faulty construction amounting to such incomplete performance, which is the difference between the value of the house if it had been constructed in strict accordance with the plans and specifications. This is the diminished-value rule. The cost of replacement or repair is not the measure of such damage, but is an element to take into consideration in arriving at value under some circumstances. The cost of replacement or the cost to make whole the omissions may equal or be less than the difference in value in some cases and, likewise, the cost to rectify a defect may greatly exceed the added value to the structure as corrected. The defendants argue that under the *Venzke* rule their damages are $10,000. The plaintiff on review argues the defendants' damages are only $650. Both parties agree the trial court applied the wrong rule to the facts.

The trial court applied the cost-of-repair or replacement rule as to several items, relying on *Stern v. Schlafer*, wherein it was stated that when there are a number of small items of defect or omission which can be remedied without the reconstruction of a substantial part of the building or a great sacrifice of work or material already wrought in the building, the reasonable cost of correcting the defect should be allowed. However, in *Mohs v. Quarton* the court held when the separation of defects would lead to confusion, the rule of diminished value could apply to all defects.

In this case no such confusion arises in separating the defects. The trial court disallowed certain claimed defects because they were not proven. This finding was not against the great weight and clear preponderance of the evidence and will not be disturbed on appeal. Of the remaining defects claimed by the defendants, the court allowed the cost of replacement or repair except as to the misplacement of the living-room wall. Whether a defect should fall under the cost-of-replacement rule or be considered under the diminished-value rule depends upon the nature and magnitude of the defect. This court has not allowed items of such magnitude under the cost-of-repair rule as the trial court did. Viewing the construction of the house as a whole and its cost we cannot say, however, that the trial court was in error in allowing the cost of repairing the plaster cracks in the ceilings, the cost of mud jacking and repairing the patio floor, and the cost of reconstructing the non-weight-bearing and nonstructural patio wall. Such reconstruction did not involve an unreasonable economic waste.

The item of misplacing the living room wall under the facts of this case was clearly under the diminished-value rule. There is no evidence that defendants requested or demanded the replacement of the wall in the place called for by the specifications during the course of construction. To tear down the wall now and rebuild it in its proper place would involve a substantial destruction of the work, if not all of it, which was put into the wall and would cause additional damage to other parts of the house and require replastering and redecorating the walls and ceilings of at least two rooms. Such economic waste is unreasonable and unjustified. The rule of diminished value contemplates the wall is not going to be moved. Expert witnesses for both parties, testifying as to the value of the house, agreed that the misplacement of the wall had no effect on the market price. The trial court properly found that the defendants suffered no legal damage, although the defendants' particular desire for specified room size was not satisfied. For a discussion of these rules or damages for defective or unfinished construction and their application see *Restatement, 1 Contracts,* pp. 572–573, sec. 346 (1), and illustrations.

On review the plaintiff raises two questions: Whether he should have been allowed compensation for the disallowed extras, and whether the cost of reconstructing the patio wall was proper. The trial court was not in error in disallowing the claimed extras. None of them was agreed to in writing as provided by the contract, and the evidence is conflicting whether some were in fact extras or that the defendants waived the applicable requirements of the contract. The plaintiff had the burden of proof on these items. The second question raised by the plaintiff has already been disposed of in considering the cost-of-replacement rule.

It would unduly prolong this opinion to detail and discuss all the disputed items of defects of workmanship or omissions. We have reviewed the entire record and considered the points of law raised and believe the findings are supported by the great weight and clear preponderance of the evidence and the law properly applied to the facts.

Affirmed.

Sale of Goods

In contracts for the sale of goods, the doctrine of substantial performance is not applicable. Both case law and statute require the seller to make what is often referred to as "perfect tender." In one case a federal court stated that "there is no room in commercial contracts for the doctrine of substantial performance." Section 2-601 of the Uniform Commercial Code states that "if the goods or the tender of delivery fail in any respect to conform to the contract, the buyer may (a) reject the whole; or (b) accept the whole; or (c) accept any commercial unit or units and reject the rest."

Several other provisions of the UCC, however, ameliorate the harsh effect of the perfect-tender rule. The buyer who rejects goods as nonconforming must disclose the nature of the defect to the seller. The seller is then entitled to a reasonable time to "cure the defect." If the buyer accepts a tender of goods, it cannot revoke that acceptance if there has been substantial performance in good faith. A similar rule applies in installment contracts, where the buyer may reject any installment only "if the non-conformity substantially impairs the value of that installment and cannot be cured."

Time of Performance

Contracts often stipulate a time by which performance must be completed. A common example is a contract for goods that states the date upon which delivery will be made. Sometimes the time of performance is important to the parties. In other instances performance by a particular time, even though stated in the agreement, really does not make much difference.

Ordinarily, unless the nature of a contract is such as to make performance by an exact date vital, failure of a party to perform on or before the agreed-upon day does not discharge the duty of the other party. This rule may be viewed as simply an application of the substantial-performance doctrine to the time-of-performance issue. Contracts for the sale of real estate usually come within this rule. If a real estate contract sets a closing date of February 15, the inability of the buyer to close because the necessary financing has not been approved does not excuse the seller from performing. The buyer would be able to enforce the contract later, but the seller would be entitled to interest on the purchase price from the originally scheduled closing date as well as actual damages, if any, that could be proved.

Some courts say that time is always of the essence in contracts for the sale of goods. This means that if a seller misses the date upon which delivery has been promised even by a day or two the buyer has the right to refuse delivery and sue for damages. Although it is true that delay is more apt to be fatal in contracts for the sale of goods, not every delay will discharge the other party of its contractual duties. In most jurisdictions the courts will weigh all aspects of the situation before determining whether time was of the essence even in a contract for the sale of goods.

If performance on or before a particular time is important to one or both parties, they should include a provision in the contract that clearly indicates this. Ordinarily this is indicated by the words "time is of the essence." A statement of this kind is often included in contracts. To be of any value, the statement must indicate clearly which part of the performance is of the essence of the agreement.

If the parties do not agree specifically that time is of the essence, then determining whether it is in a particular situation requires consideration of the circumstances. A wholesaler who promises delivery to a retailer before April 1 and knows that the retailer plans a major advertising campaign to begin April 1 would have to perform on or before that date even though the contract did not include a "time is of the essence" clause. If the situation, the subject matter of the contract, or a clearly written provision that time is of the essence makes time a material factor, performance by that time is essential. Late performance can be rejected even though benefit has been conferred, and the injured party can refuse to meet its own commitment as well as sue for damages.

DISCHARGE OF CONTRACTUAL OBLIGATIONS

One question that managers must frequently deal with is whether a contractual obligation has terminated. Sometimes management is concerned with this question because it believes that a performance to which the firm is entitled has not been completed. In other situations the question is whether the firm has met its own contractual commitments.

When a contract is said to be discharged, one or more of the legal relations of the parties have been terminated. Most commonly this means that the legal duty of one of the parties has been terminated. A party who is under a legal duty by virtue of his or her contract may assert that the duty has been "discharged" by some event that has occurred since the making of the contract.

Seldom are all the legal relations of the contracting parties terminated at the same time. A party may be discharged from further contractual duty, by an act of the other party or some other event, and continue to retain all the rights, powers, and privileges that he or she possessed. It is indeed possible for all the contractual obligations to be terminated at once, as where contract duties are discharged by the agreement of the parties.

Contract duties may be discharged in a variety of ways. Some of these have already been discussed, although not in the context of discharge. The following discussion focuses on the primary methods of discharge.

Discharge by Complete Performance

The most obvious method of discharge of a contractual duty is by complete performance. Most contracts are discharged in this way. Complete performance means full and exact performance—not only of the character, quality, and amount required, but also within the time agreed upon.

Discharge by Occurrence of a Condition Subsequent

As mentioned earlier, a condition subsequent is an event that terminates a present duty of performance. If a condition subsequent occurs, it discharges a duty of performance. Because of their potentially harsh effect, conditions subsequent expressed in a contract are narrowly construed by the courts.

Discharge by Mutual Agreement

Rescission. A contract still executory on both sides may be discharged by an express agreement that it shall no longer bind either party. Such an agreement, called mutual rescission, is itself a contract to discharge a prior contract. Its purpose is to restore the parties to the positions they occupied before entering into the first contract.

Substitution of New Contract. A contract may be discharged by the substitution of a new contract. The difference between discharge by a substituted contract and discharge by rescission is that a rescission is a total obliteration of the contract whereas a substitution provides a new contract in place of the old one. Discharge by substitution results by expressly substituting a new contract for the old one or by making a new contract inconsistent with the old one, with new terms agreed upon by both sides.

Novation. A contract duty of a party may be discharged by the substitution of a new party for one of the original parties. Such a substitution is known as a *novation*. In a novation a new contract is created whose terms are the same as the old contract's but whose parties are different. For a novation to be valid, all three parties must agree to the substitution. A novation need not be of express agreement. It may arise from the conduct of the parties indicating acquiescence in a change of liability.

Discharge by Impossibility of Performance

After a contract has been formed, but prior to full performance, an event may occur that makes performance by one of the parties difficult, unprofitable, impracticable, or impossible or that frustrates the very purpose for which one of parties entered into the contract. Given this state of affairs, the party who views its own performance as no longer desirable may be expected to not perform its contractual obligation, and the other party may be expected to sue, claiming such nonperformance to be a breach of contract. When a party is sued for nonperformance, it may defend on the basis that supervening events made its performance impossible or that the purpose for which it made the contract had become frustrated. Before examining what constitutes discharge by impossibility or frustration of purpose, it may prove helpful to view the question as one involving the issue of how the risks of loss should be distributed. That is, when some supervening event makes a party's performance impossible, the legal and policy problem that is presented is: Who should bear the risk of loss occasioned by the occurrence of the unexpected event? Thus the role of the contract in society may be seen as an allocation of the risks of loss, and the rules regarding discharge by reason of impossibility provide an example of how the courts fashion rules allocating the risks of loss in a manner that best serves society and reflects the presumed intent of the parties where the parties have failed to state their intent precisely.

Risk of Loss. Fundamental questions of public policy are involved in many cases in which the issue of discharge of contractual obligation and its relationship to performance are considered. These policies, although often at the root of the problem as well as the solution, are generally not discussed by the opinions. A basic premise of Anglo-American contract law is that competent adults should be allowed freely to enter contracts for legitimate purposes. Connected to this premise of freedom of contract is the notion that a person should not be discharged from contractual obliga-

tions unless these commitments have been carried out exactly as promised. The emphasis given to freedom of contract and the attendant obligation to perform are reasons that contracting is used as a means of allocating many types of risks. The possibility of fluctuating price is a risk involved in many contracts. Consider a typical business agreement, tens of thousands of which are made each year. The manager of the student dining service contracts with National Dairy to have delivered to the main dining hall at the university 1,500 pints of milk each day during October at $0.08 per pint. She has accepted the risk that the market price of milk will decrease as well as numerous other risks incident to disposing of the milk. The dairy has accepted the risk of a price increase and numerous risks incident to delivery.

The bargaining underlying decisions to assume particular risks is influenced by factors such as economic power, friendship, persuasiveness, and habit. Although these and other considerations are important, the major element in arms-length negotiations is the decision makers' anticipation and evaluation of events that might affect their ability to perform. In some transactions, however, events occur that were neither anticipated by the parties nor could reasonably have been contemplated when they made the agreement. These events often create new or different risks that materially affect the ability of a party to perform.

This can be illustrated by the oil embargo imposed by the Arabs in 1973. Manufacturers dependent upon oil found costs of production substantially increased. Many were parties to contracts made when the price of oil was low. In agreeing to sell at a particular price, they had assumed a risk under conditions that were reasonably well known. The new conditions were not only different but were also unexpected.

If performance is prevented or becomes more costly because of unexpected new conditions, what should the law's position be? Must a promise be fulfilled insofar as possible even if the result is a crushing loss to one party and a windfall profit to the other? Or should the party who will suffer because of the unexpected new conditions be allowed to avoid performance at the expense of the other who has relied upon the promised performance and given something in exchange for it? This question arises in many cases and is frequently answered only with great difficulty. The court must balance the desirability of enforcing agreements freely made against the injustice of requiring a party to suffer losses of which the risks could not have been foreseen.

When a party to a contract anticipates a risk, its consequences can be limited by contractual provisions. For example, the parties might agree to excuse a late delivery if delivery should be prevented by a railroad strike or by inclement weather. Many types of insurance are also used by firms to protect themselves from some of the risks incident to contract.

Strict or Objective Impossibility.

The early common law of contract disregarded unanticipated events and required a party to carry out a promised performance in spite of the fact that it was more difficult, expensive, or demanding than either party had contemplated when the agreement was made. A promise was considered absolute. If it was impossible to perform, the defaulting party was required to pay damages.

This doctrine was so harsh that in a number of common situations the courts began to excuse a promisor on grounds that performance had literally become impossible. Although this interfered with voluntarily assumed risk allocations, justice and fair play clearly supported the courts' position.

Thus the rule developed that if, after a contract has been formed but before full performance, some unforeseeable event occurs that makes performance objectively impossible, the promisor's duty to perform is discharged.

By "objectively impossible" the courts mean that no person could legally or physically perform the contract. If the event that arises makes performance impossible only for the particular promisor, it is merely a subjective impossibility and is insufficient to discharge the promisor's duty of performance. Objective impossibility has been found in the following three circumstances: (1) the death or serious illness of a promisor whose personal performance is required, (2) a change of law making the promised performance illegal, and (3) the destruction of the subject matter of the contract.

Commercial Impracticability and Frustration of Purpose.

The trend in the law is toward an enlargement of the definition of impossibility. As a result, a fourth circumstance has been frequently allowed in recent years: where impossibility is due to the existence of a certain state of affairs, the nonoccurrence of which was a basic assumption on which the contract was made. Impossibility is probably an inappropriate word to use in such circumstances. Thus courts have used the terms commercial impracticability and frustration of purpose to describe such a circumstance. The two concepts are different but closely related.

The concept of commercial impracticability describes a situation where a party claims that some circumstance has made its own performance impracticable. Performance may be impracticable because extreme and unreasonable difficulty, expense, injury, or loss to one of the parties will occur. A severe shortage of raw materials or of supplies, due to war, embargo, local crop failure, unforeseen shutdown of major sources of supply, or the like, which either causes a marked increase in cost or prevents performance altogether may constitute impracticability.

The concept of frustration of purpose deals with a situation that arises when a change in circumstances makes one party's performance virtually worthless to the other, frustrating its purpose in making the contract. Frustration of purpose differs from commercial impracticability in that there is no impediment to performance by either party. For the concept of frustration of purpose to excuse a party's nonperformance, the purpose that is frustrated must have been a principal purpose of the party in making the contract, the frustration must be substantial, and the nonoccurrence of the frustrating event must have been a basic assumption on which the contract was made.

The *Second Restatement of Contracts* has endorsed both the concept of commercial impracticability (Section 261) and the concept of frustration of purpose (Section 265). The revisers of the *Restatement* were influenced by UCC Section 2-615, which excuses a seller from making timely delivery when the seller's performance has become commercially impracticable "by the occurrence of a contingency the nonoccurrence of which was a basic assumption on which the contract was made. . . ."

The following case concerns the application of UCC 2-615.

Mishara Construction Co. v. Transit Mixed Concrete Co.

Supreme Judicial Court of Massachusetts
310 N.E. 2d 363 (1974)

Mishara Construction Company was the general contractor for a construction project. It contracted with the Transit Mixed Concrete Company to supply all the ready-mixed concrete needed for the project. Under the contract, Mishara was to specify the dates and amounts of deliveries. In April 1967, a labor dispute stopped work on the project. Work resumed in June, but the workers maintained their picket line for two more years. Transit Mixed Concrete made few deliveries during the two-year period, and Mishara had to obtain concrete from other sources. Mishara sued for damages as a result of Transit's delays and the higher cost of purchasing concrete elsewhere. Transit defended on the basis of impossibility of performance. The trial court entered judgment for Mishara. The Supreme Judicial Court of Massachusetts affirmed. Mishara Construction Company is the plaintiff; Transit Mixed Concrete Company is the defendant.

Reardon, Justice

The plaintiff's exceptions relate to the introduction of certain evidence and the failure of the trial judge to give certain requested instructions.

There was no error in the refusal to give request 13, that on the evidence the jury "must find that [the] defendant breached its contract with [the] plaintiff by failing to deliver" Mishara's concrete requirements. The principal issue in the case was the defendant's claimed excuse of impossibility of performance. The determination of that issue depended on facts and circumstances which were for the jury to decide. While we suppose one could develop a nice technical argument that impossibility does not nullify a breach but rather provides an excuse for it, to give the instruction requested would surely have misled the jury on the ultimate question of liability. Moreover, the failure to give it was of no detriment to the plaintiff of which it can complain. See Howes v. Grush, 131 Mass. 207 (1881). Dixon v. New England R.R., *supra*.

The remainder of the plaintiff's exceptions relate to the proffered defense of the impossibility of performance. Objection was made to the introduction of all evidence regarding the existence of a picket line at the job site and the difficulty which Transit did encounter or might have encountered in attempting to make deliveries through that picket line. Furthermore, Mishara requested an instruction that Transit "was required to comply with the contract regardless of picket lines, strikes or labor difficulties" As a result Mishara would have completely withdrawn the question of impossibility resulting from the picket line from the jury. We are asked to decide as matter of law and without reference to individual facts and circumstances that "picket lines, strikes or labor difficulties" provide no excuse for nonperformance by way of impossibility. This is too sweeping a statement of the law and we decline to adopt it.

The excuse of impossibility in contracts for the sale of goods is controlled by the appropriate section of the Uniform Commercial Code, § 2-615. That section sets up two requirements before performance may be excused. First, the performance must have become "impracticable." Second, the impracticability must have been caused "by the occurrence of a contingency the non-occurrence of which was a basic assumption on which the contract was made." This section of the Uniform Commercial Code has not yet been interpreted by this court. Therefore it is appropriate to discuss briefly the significance of these two criteria.

With respect to the requirement that performance must have been impracticable, the official Code comment to the section stresses that the reference is to "commercial impracticability" as opposed to strict impossibility. This is not a radical departure from the common law of contracts as interpreted by this court. Although a strict rule was originally followed denying any excuse for accident of "inevitable necessity," e.g., Adams v. Nichols, 19 Pick. 275 (1837), it has long been assumed that circumstances drastically increasing the difficulty and expense of the contemplated performance may be within the compass of "impossibility." By adopting the term "impracticability" rather than "impossibility" the drafters of the Code appear to be in accord with Professor Williston who stated that "the essence of the modern defense of impossibility is that the promised performance was at the making of the contract, or thereafter became, impracticable owing to some extreme or unreasonable difficulty, expense, injury, or loss involved, rather than it is scientifically or actually impossible." Williston, Contracts (Rev. ed.) § 1931 (1938). See Restatement: Contracts, § 454 (1932); Corbin, Contracts, § 1339 (1962).

The second criterion of the excuse, that the intervening circumstance be one which the parties assumed would not occur, is also familiar to the law of Massachusetts. The rule is essentially aimed at the distribution of certain kinds of risks in the contractual relationship. By directing the inquiry to the time when the contract was first made, we really seek to determine whether the risk of the intervening circumstance was one which the parties may be taken to have assigned between themselves. It is, of course, the very essence of contract that it is directed at the elimination of some risks for each party in exchange for others. Each receives the certainty of price, quantity, and time, and assumes the risk of changing market prices, superior opportunity, or added costs. It is implicit in the doctrine of impossibility (and the companion rule of "frustration of purpose") that certain risks are so unusual and have such severe consequences that they must have been beyond the scope of the assignment of risks inherent in the contract, that is, beyond the agreement made by the parties. To require performance in that case would be to grant the promisee an advantage for which he could not be said to have bargained in making the contract. "The important question is whether an unanticipated circumstance has made performance of the promise vitally different from what should reasonably have been within the contemplation of both parties when they entered into the contract. If so, the risk should not fairly be thrown upon the promisor." Williston, Contracts (Rev. ed.) § 1931 (1938). The emphasis in contracts governed by the Uniform Commercial Code is on the commercial context in which the agreement was made. The question is, given the commercial circumstances in which the parties dealt: Was the contingency which developed one which the parties could reasonably be thought to have foreseen as a real possibility which could affect performance? Was it one of that variety of risks which the parties were tacitly assigning to the promisor by their failure to provide for it explicitly? If it were, performance will be required. If it could not be so considered, performance is excused. The contract cannot be reasonably thought to govern in these circumstances, and the parties are both thrown upon the resources of the open market without the benefit of their contract.

With this backdrop, we consider Mishara's contention that a labor dispute which makes performance more difficult never constitutes an excuse for nonperformance. We think it is evident that in some situations a labor dispute would not meet the requirements for impossibility discussed above. A picket line might constitute a mere inconvenience and hardly make performance "impracticable." Likewise, in certain industries with a long record of labor difficulties, the nonoccurrence of strikes and picket lines could not fairly be said to be a basic assumption of the agreement. Certainly, in general, labor disputes cannot be considered extraordinary in the course of modern commerce. Admitting this, however, we are still far from the proposition implicit in the plaintiff's requests. Much must depend on the facts known to the parties at the time of contracting with respect to the history of and prospects for labor difficulties during the period of performance of the contract, as well as the likely severity of the effect of such disputes on the ability to perform. From these facts it is possible to draw an inference as to whether or not the parties intended performance to be carried out even in the face of the labor difficulty. Where the probability of a labor dispute appears to be practically nil, and where the occurrence of such a dispute provides unusual difficulty, the excuse of impracticability might well be applicable. Thus in discussing the defense of impossibility, then Chief Judge Cardozo noted an excuse would be provided "conceivably in some circumstances by unavoidable strikes." Canadian Industrial Alcohol Co. Ltd. v. Dunbar Molasses Co., 258 N.Y. 194, 198, 179 N.E. 383, 384 (1932). The many variables which may bear on the question in individual cases were canvassed by Professor Williston in Williston, Contracts (Rev. ed.) § 1951A (1938), and he concluded that the trend of the law is toward recognizing strikes as excuses for nonperformance. We agree with the statement of the judge in Badhwar v. Colorado Fuel & Iron Corp., 138 F. Supp. 595, 607 (S.D.N.Y. 1955), affd. 245 F. 2d 903 (2d Cir. 1957), on the same question: "Rather than mechanically apply any fixed rule of law, where the parties themselves have not allocated responsibility, justice is better served by appraising all of the circumstances, the part the various parties played, and thereon determining liability." Since the instructions requested by the plaintiff and the conclusion of the evidence objected to would have precluded such a factual determination, the requests were more properly refused, and the evidence was properly admitted.

Exceptions overruled.

Discharge by Breach of Contract

A contract is breached when a party under a present duty of performance fails to perform. As already discussed, a material breach of contract by one party discharges the injured party from any further duty of performance. A partial or minor breach of contract does not operate as a discharge but does render the breaching party liable for the injuries sustained by the innocent party as a result of the breach.

Anticipatory Breach. In most instances, breach of contract occurs only after performance is due. Sometimes, however, a party to a contract repudiates a commitment to perform before the time that performance is required. This is known as an *anticipatory breach.* An anticipatory breach raises the questions whether the other party is immediately discharged from its contractual obligations and whether it can seek a remedy immediately.

Most courts allow immediate action as if the entire contract had been broken. This is justified upon the grounds that the repudiation has destroyed the good-faith relationship upon which successful performance of the contract is based and that simple justice should allow a party to take immediate action to protect its expectations.

Repudiation must be clear and unequivocal. A statement by one of the parties indicating doubt as to ability to perform or even doubt as to whether it wants to is not an anticipatory breach. Repudiation does not have to be verbal. An act is sufficient if it clearly indicates an intent not to perform in the future. A party who prevents another from performing an act that is necessary to carrying out the agreement has committed an anticipatory breach. Some courts have held that voluntary or involuntary bankruptcy is the equivalent of anticipatory breach.

When the other party to a contract has repudiated prior to performance, a firm has several options. It may treat the entire contract as broken and sue immediately for damages without complying further with its own obligations. Assume A and B have entered into an agreement in which A agrees to move a house for B. B has promised to pay A $3,000 for the job and obtain all necessary permits and road clearances. If A repudiates the agreement, it is not necessary for B to obtain the permits and clearances prior to bringing suit.

The firm may choose to ignore the repudiation and wait until performance is due before taking any action, or it may rescind the agreement and sue to recover anything it has furnished under the contract. If the contract can be specifically enforced, an immediate action requiring performance can be brought.

In goods transactions, reasonable grounds for insecurity give rise to the right to demand assurance of performance, and the failure to give such assurance is a repudiation according to Section 2-609 of the UCC. Under Section 2-610, repudiation may be treated as an immediate breach.

REMEDIES FOR BREACH OF CONTRACT

A major function of contract law is to assure that expectations based on commitments made by others will be met. Assurance that expectations will be fulfilled is especially important to business so that firms may plan future operations effectively. Individuals also, in our complicated world, must plan for the future if they are to live satisfactory lives. As both business and personal planning are often based upon commitments from others, methods of inducing people to honor their agreements are of major importance to society.

When legal remedies are available to enforce promises, society provides pressure that often induces performance. Even if the parties pay little conscious attention to what will happen if a promise is broken, the underlying threat of legal recourse has an impact. In this section we explore some of the remedies provided by the law to induce contractual performance.

Although the legal institution of contract evolved to assure that expectations based upon promises would be fulfilled, the Anglo-American courts will not usually require a party actually to perform a breached promise. There are several reasons for this. As agreements often are for long periods of time, the courts feel that the necessary continuous supervision of the compelled performance would be a difficult, if not impossible, burden. Additionally, the courts fear they would become involved in disputes as to whether the terms of the agreement were being met. They foresee that a firm ordered to perform would normally do as little as it could to complete the agreement. Objections to this minimal performance would be raised by the other party, with the court being required to settle recurring differences. Finally, in some cases, a court decree ordering a person to perform would verge on involuntary servitude.

Damages

As a result of judicial reluctance to order actual performance, contract law attempts to compensate the injured party by requiring monetary payments, called damages, from the defaulting party. The general objective of damages is to place the injured party in the position it would have been in had the agreement been carried out. If a firm has contracted to buy 1,000 units at $6.00 for delivery on January 15 and the units are not delivered, the buyer has a right to obtain the units elsewhere. If the market price is now $6.50, the buyer is placed in the position it would have been in under the contract by the award of damages of $500, the additional amount that had to be paid to obtain 1,000 units. In both instances the buyer has to pay at least $6,000, so this is not part of its damages.

In most cases damages cover reasonably anticipated losses and expenses as well as any gains and profits that might have been made. This rule, although easily stated, is often complex in application, leading to numerous legal problems.

The Reasonable-Anticipation Standard. The defaulting party is responsible for those damages that a reasonable person could foresee at the time the contract was made. In the often-cited English case of *Hadley* v. *Baxendale,* a mill was shut down because of a broken shaft. The mill's owner delivered the shaft to a cartage company that promised to return it in three days. When the shaft was not returned in three days as promised, the mill owner sued for the profits lost during the additional period that the mill was closed. The appellate court refused to allow the plaintiff to recover the lost profits, contending that it was not reasonable to anticipate that a mill would be closed completely because of a broken shaft.

Although the defendant is responsible for only reasonably foreseeable losses, anticipation of a particular loss is unnecessary. Responsibility extends to that which a reasonable person would know in the ordinary course of events as well as to knowledge of special circumstances that could result in larger-than-ordinary loss.

Certainty. Closely related and often overlapping the rule that an injured party is entitled to compensation only for losses that could reasonably have been foreseen is the additional requirement that damages be certain, not speculative. The plaintiff must establish that a particular loss was caused by the breach and that the amount lost can actually be calculated.

A problem as to the certainty of the relationship between breach and loss arises when the defendant can show that there were intervening factors that might have been responsible for plaintiff's loss. Ordinarily, this is a question of fact. If a jury finds that the breach was the "primary" or "chief" cause of the loss, the loss will be part of the damage award.

Difficult problems also arise out of the need for certainty in the actual calculation of damages. Courts generally have not equated certainty with absolute exactness. In fact, they appear to be more concerned with the need for certainty in allowing an award of damages than they are with certainty in calculating the actual amount to be awarded. Over the years, courts in commercial cases have increasingly admitted the testimony of expert witnesses who analyze business records and market summaries to satisfy the certainty requirement. One difficult question for the courts has been whether a defaulting defendant should be responsible for the loss of prospective profits stemming from a particular contract. Although most jurisdictions allow an injured party to collect prospective profits if a contract is breached with a business in operation, the rule appears to be different when the business is new or being planned. In these cases the plaintiff is not entitled to prospective profits.

Mitigation of Damages. A person injured by breach of contract has a right to recover losses that are reasonably predictable and relatively certain. The injured party, however, must limit these losses as much as possible. An injured party cannot allow damages to accumulate and then collect all that has been lost. Nor can the injured party continue to perform when the other party is in default and then recover the full contract price.

The obligation of the injured party to keep losses as low as possible is known as *mitigation of damages.* If opportunities to mitigate damages are available and plaintiff has not taken advantage of them, the court will subtract from any award the amount by which the plaintiff could have minimized his or her own losses.

The mitigation requirement forces the injured party to make numerous decisions if the contract is breached. An employee who has a contract but is fired must secure comparable employment elsewhere if possible. This raises several questions. Is any employment paying the same amount comparable? Suppose a potential job involves moving to an area that the injured party does not like; is the employment comparable?

A difficult mitigation decision for a manufacturing firm occurs when a buyer repudiates during the manufacturing of special items. The manufacturer-seller may have invested heavily in parts and materials necessary for the job. Management must decide if the buyer's losses will be less if the firm immediately halts production and sells the partially completed merchandise for salvage or if it completes the contract and sells the finished merchandise on the market. The UCC allows the manufacturer to do either as long as it uses "reasonable commercial judgment."

At some time in their careers, most business people will probably have to take action because a contract has been broken. The following case, although not a typical business problem, indicates some of the possible ramifications of mitigation decisions.

Parker v. Twentieth Century-Fox Film Corp.
Supreme Court of California
474 P. 2d 689 (1970)

Shirley MacLaine Parker, a well-known actress, was under contract with Twentieth Century-Fox Film Corporation, dated August 6, 1965, to play the female lead in Twentieth Century-Fox's production of a motion picture entitled "Bloomer Girl." The contract provided that Twentieth Century-Fox would pay Parker a minimum "guaranteed compensation" of $53,571.42 per week for 14 weeks commencing May 23, 1966, for a total of $750,000. Prior to May 1966 Twentieth Century-Fox decided not to produce the picture and by letter dated April 4, 1966, it notified Parker of that decision and informed her that it would not "comply with our obligations to you under" the written contract.

By the same letter and with the professed purpose "to avoid any damage to you," Twentieth Century-Fox instead offered to employ Parker as the leading actress in another film tentatively entitled "Big Country, Big Man" (hereinafter "Big Country"). The compensation offered was identical, as were thirty-one of the thirty-four numbered provisions or articles of the original contract. Unlike "Bloomer Girl," however, which was to have been a musical production, "Big Country" was a dramatic "western type" movie. "Bloomer Girl" was to have been filmed in California; "Big Country" was to be produced in Australia. Also, certain terms in the proffered contract varied from those of the original. Parker was given one week within which to accept; she did not and the offer lapsed. Parker then sued Twentieth Century-Fox seeking recovery of the agreed compensation.

The trial court awarded summary judgment granting to Parker the recovery of the agreed compensation. The Supreme Court of California concluded that the trial court had ruled correctly in Parker's favor and that the judgment should be affirmed. Parker is the plaintiff; Twentieth Century-Fox is the defendant.

Burke, Justice

The complaint sets forth two causes of action. The first is for money due under the contract; the second, based upon the same allegations as the first, is for damages resulting from defendant's breach of contract. Defendant in its answer admits the existence and validity of the contract, that plaintiff complied with all the conditions, covenants and promises and stood ready to complete the performance, and that defendant breached and "anticipatorily repudiated" the contract. It denies, however, that any money is due to plaintiff either under the contract or as a result of its breach, and pleads as an affirmative defense to both causes of action plaintiff's allegedly deliberate failure to mitigate damages, asserting that she unreasonably refused to accept its offer of the leading role in "Big Country."

Plaintiff moved for summary judgment under Code of Civil Procedure section 437c, the motion was granted, and summary judgment for $750,000 plus interest was entered in plaintiff's favor. This appeal by defendant followed.

As stated, defendant's sole defense to this action which resulted from its deliberate breach of contract is that in rejecting defendant's substitute offer of employment plaintiff unreasonably refused to mitigate damages.

The general rule is that the measure of recovery by a wrongfully discharged employee is the amount of salary agreed upon for the period of service, less the amount which the employer affirmatively proves the employee has earned or with reasonable effort might have earned from other employment. However, before projected earnings from other employment opportunities not sought or accepted by the discharged employee can be applied in mitigation, the employer must show that the other employment was comparable, or substantially similar, to that of which the employee has been deprived; the employee's rejection of or failure to seek other available employment of a different or inferior kind may not be resorted to in order to mitigate damages.

In the present case defendant has raised no issue of *reasonableness of efforts* by plaintiff to obtain other employment; the sole issue is whether plaintiff's refusal of defendant's substitute offer of "Big Country" may be used in mitigation. Nor, if the "Big Country" offer was of employment different or inferior when compared with the original "Bloomer Girl" employment, is there an issue as to whether or not plaintiff acted reasonably in refusing the substitute offer. Despite defendant's arguments to the contrary, no case cited or which our research has discovered holds or suggests that reasonableness is an element of a wrongfully discharged employee's option to reject, or fail to seek, different or inferior employment lest the possible earnings therefrom be charged against him in mitigation of damages.

Applying the foregoing rules to the record in the present case, with all intendments in favor of the party opposing the summary judgment motion—here, defendant—it is clear that the trial court correctly ruled that plaintiff's failure to accept defendant's tendered substitute employment could not be applied in mitigation of damages because the offer of the "Big Country" lead was of employment both different and inferior, and that no factual dispute was presented on that issue. The mere circumstances that "Bloomer Girl" was to be a musical review calling upon plaintiff's talents as a dancer as well as an actress, and was to be produced in the City of Los Angeles, whereas "Big Country" was a straight dramatic role in a "Western Type" story taking place in an opal mine in Australia, demonstrates the difference in kind between the two employments; the female lead as a dramatic actress in a western style motion picture can by no stretch of imagination be considered the equivalent of or substantially similar to the lead in a song-and-dance production.

Additionally, the substitute "Big Country" offer proposed to eliminate or impair the director and screenplay approvals accorded to plaintiff under the original "Bloomer Girl" contract, and thus constituted an offer of inferior employment. No expertise or judicial notice is required in order to hold that the deprivation or infringement of an employee's rights held under an original employment contract converts the available "other employment" relied upon by the employer to mitigate damages, into inferior employment which the employee need not seek or accept. . . .

In view of the determination that defendant failed to present any facts showing the existence of a factual issue with respect to its sole defense—plaintiff's rejection of its substitute employment offer in mitigation of damages—we need not consider plaintiff's further contention that for various reasons, plaintiff was excused from attempting to mitigate damages.

The judgment is affirmed.

Liquidated Damages. Some contracts include a provision in which the parties agree on an amount to compensate the injured party if there is a breach. This is known as a *liquidated damages clause.* Generally, when negotiating, the parties do not concern themselves with the effects of a breach. They are primarily interested in performance and its costs and benefits. There are, however, some instances when what will happen if there is a breach is an important part of the bargain. This is often the case when the contract involves large sums of money, when the time of completion is highly important, or when the amount of loss in the event of breach is unclear.

In other cases, one of the parties thinks that liquidated damages will force the other to perform. If that party has superior bargaining power, the other party might agree to pay damages that would exceed any likely loss. When liquidated damages are not reasonably related to loss, they are not damages but a penalty that violates the underlying concept of damages— that is, to place the injured party in the position it would have been in had the contract been performed. Courts have been unwilling, therefore, to accept liquidated damage provisions that penalize the defaulting party. They will not recognize a provision that is not reasonably related to losses.

Section 2-718 of the UCC provides:

Damages for breach by either party may be liquidated in the agreement but only at an amount which is reasonable in the light of the anticipated or actual harm caused by the breach, the difficulties of proof of loss, and the inconvenience or nonfeasibility of otherwise obtaining an adequate remedy. A term fixing unreasonably large liquidated damages is void as a penalty.

Punitive Damages. Punitive or exemplary damages are those that exceed the injured party's loss. In tort cases they are often a substantial portion of the plaintiff's recovery. The primary purpose of punitive damages is to deter the defendant and others from the type of act that caused the loss. Punitive damages are seldom awarded in contract cases. In those few instances in which they have been granted, plaintiffs have been able to prove something akin to fraud or that defendants acted recklessly or maliciously in breaching the agreements.

Recently some courts have allowed punitive awards in contract cases in which the plaintiff was a consumer or at least a "little guy" with limited bargaining power and the defendant, a party with appreciable economic strength, acted outrageously or oppressively.

Wright v. Public Savings Life Insurance Co.

Supreme Court of South Carolina

204 S.E. 2d 57 (1974)

Mamie Lee Wright sued to recover actual and punitive damages for the allegedly fraudulent cancellation of certain insurance policies by her insurer, Public Savings Life Insurance Company, allegedly accompanied by a fraudulent act or acts. The jury returned a verdict in her favor for $600.00 actual damages and $1,700.00 punitive damages. Public Savings Life Insurance Company appealed from the denial of its after-verdict motions. The Supreme Court of South Carolina affirmed the judgment. Mamie Lee Wright is the plaintiff-respondent; Public Savings Life Insurance Company is the defendant-appellant.

Per curiam:

In this action the plaintiff-respondent sought to recover actual and punitive damages for the allegedly fraudulent cancellation of certain insurance policies by the appellant-insurer, allegedly accompanied by a fraudulent act or acts. The jury returned a verdict in her favor for $600.00 actual damages and $1,700.00 punitive damages. The insurer appeals from the denial of its after-verdict motions.

While appellant's exceptions are 14 in number, only three questions are stated and argued and actually two of them constitute only one question to wit: was there any evidence of a fraudulent act accompanying the insurer's breach of its contract, which would support the recovery of punitive damages. The insurer apparently tacitly concedes that the judgment against it for actual damages is warranted by the evidence, but contends that it was entitled to a directed verdict as to punitive damages. In considering this contention it is elementary that the evidence and all the inferences reasonably deducible therefrom have to be viewed in the light most favorable to the respondent-plaintiff. We proceed to review the evidence and state the facts in the light of such principle.

The plaintiff Mamie Lee Wright is a resident of Lancaster, South Carolina; a person of limited education and 61 years of age at the time of the trial of this case in September, 1972. About May, 1963 she acquired from the insurer a life policy and a health and accident policy, the premium on one being 90¢ per week and the premium on the other being 60¢ per week. In 1964 she made a claim under the accident and health policy, which was paid in part, and again in 1970 she had occasion to make a claim thereunder because of illness with hypertension. In the early part of 1971, Mamie Lee was employed, apparently as a domestic or at odd jobs, working on several different jobs, and frequently getting home late at night. As a result, she and the agent collecting the debit for the insurer had some difficulty making contact, upon which Mamie Lee started making part of her premium payments at the Lancaster office of the insurer. Whenever she paid at the office she was given a temporary, conditional premium receipt, which later would be picked up by the debit agent when she was given credit by the agent for the payment on her premium receipt book. The agent on plaintiff's debit was one Shannon, who left the employment of the company on April 24, 1971, being succeeded by one Hunter.

On May 3, 1971, the Lancaster office reported to the home office of the insurer in Charleston, South Carolina that both of Mamie Lee's policies were lapsed for nonpayment of premiums. There is abundant evidence to the effect that neither of Mamie Lee's policies were subject to lapse for nonpayment as of that date. In addition to payments made to the debit agent, it is undisputed that she made the following payments to the Lancaster office: on April 15, the sum of $3.50 and on April 22 a like sum. It should be noted that the sum of $3.18 would pay the premiums on both policies for a period of two weeks. Subsequent to May 3, Mamie Lee paid at the office the sum of $10.15 on May 13, and the sum of $3.50 on May 19. On May 28, 1971, the manager of the Lancaster office informed Mamie Lee that both of her policies had been lapsed for non-payment of premiums, upon which she responded "my insurance has lapsed, as many times as I've been coming up here paying my insurance . . . My Lord, I have to work too hard to be treated like this." The response of the manager was merely "you are getting too old anyhow." She was then tendered the sum of $6.36 by way of refund and requested to sign a receipt, which she declined to sign and instead consulted counsel.

On May 13, the day that Mamie Lee made a payment in the amount of $10.15, a Multiple Revival Application was prepared without her knowledge, at least inferentially by the debit agent Hunter, which purported to apply for the revival or reinstatement of both of Mamie Lee's policies. The contents of this form purportedly show an acknowledgement by Mamie Lee Wright that the policies were properly lapsed and that no premium had been paid on either since March 29, 1971. To this application form the signature "Mamie Wright" was forged, such purported signature being witnessed by the agent Hunter. The form was forwarded to the home office in Charleston where the purported application for revival was rejected on May 20, 1971.

It is the theory and contention of the plaintiff that the insurer formed the design, because of her age and ill health, to fraudulently cancel her policies for alleged non-payment of premiums and that the acts on the part of the insurer and its agents hereinabove set forth were done in furtherance of such fraudulent scheme and design.

This Court has consistently adhered to the rule that the breach of a contract, committed with fraudulent intent, and accompanied by a fraudulent act, or acts, will entail liability for punitive as well as actual damages.

In the case of *Sullivan* v. *Calhoun,* this Court quoted with approval from 12 R.C.L. 229, the following language:

> Fraud assumes so many hues and forms, that courts are compelled to content themselves with comparatively few general rules for its discovery and defeat, and allow the facts and circumstances peculiar to each case to bear heavily upon the conscience and judgment of the court or jury in determining its presence or absence. While it has often been said that fraud cannot be precisely defined, the books contain many definitions, such as unfair dealing; the unlawful appropriation of another's property by design.

We think that the evidence hereinabove recited was quite sufficient, under settled principles of law, to warrant a finding that there was a breach of contract, with fraudulent intent, accompanied by a fraudulent act or acts on the part of the insurer and accordingly sufficient to support a verdict for punitive damages. The insurer argues, inter alia, that the breach of contract occurred on May 3, when the policies were reported for lapse to the home office and hence that any proved fraudulent acts on the part of the insurer were subsequent to and did not accompany the breach. This argument, we think, is clearly without merit. The breach had its inception, of course,

> on May 3, but, insofar as the plaintiff was concerned, was not completed until May 28 when the insurer first informed her of the cancellation and attempted to obtain from her a receipt or release upon refund of a portion of the money collected from her in recent weeks. As we view it any and all acts in furtherance of the alleged fraudulent scheme in effect accompanied the breach which did not reach its final culmination until May 28, 1971.
>
> We are not convinced that there was any prejudicial error and the judgment below is,
>
> Affirmed.

Specific Performance

Although Anglo-American law generally awards damages to a party against whom there has been a breach, under some circumstances the courts will require the defaulting party to actually perform the promised act. This remedy for breach is referred to as *specific performance.* The governing principle is that specific performance will be required when payment of damages would not adequately or completely compensate the injured plaintiff. A contract promise to pay money will ordinarily not be enforced specifically because the damage remedy is considered adequate.

Whether the damage remedy is adequate depends to a large extent on the facts of the particular case. The courts generally have held that damages are inadequate in two types of cases. First, there are those cases in which the subject matter of the contract is unique. Unusual items of personal property, such as antiques and original paintings, clearly fall into this category. Money is not considered an adequate replacement for a prized heirloom. Second, there are cases involving the sale of real estate. Because of land's economic importance, the courts historically have assumed that every piece of land is unique. As a result, contracts for the sale of real estate almost inevitably can be enforced specifically. Real estate agreements are the subject matter most commonly involved in actions for specific performance.

Other types of agreements that courts have considered unique pervade economic activity. They include contracts to sell a business, to issue a policy of insurance, to repurchase corporate stock, to act as a surety, to execute a written instrument, and even, in some instances, to lend money. In these and similar cases, if the defendant can show that plaintiff has an adequate remedy at law, specific performance will not be granted.

Section 2-716 of the UCC provides that in goods transactions "specific performance may be decreed where the goods are unique or in other proper circumstances." The Official Comment on this section states:

The present section continues in general prior policy as to specific performance. . . . However, without intending to impair in any way the exercise of the court's sound discretion in the matter, this article seeks to further a more liberal attitude than some courts have shown in connection with the specific performance of contracts of sale.

Under Section 2-716, if a buyer cannot readily find substitute goods in the market, the buyer is entitled to an award of specific performance, although the goods may not be "unique." This is because Section 2-716 allows a court to award specific performance "in other proper circumstances."

The following case illustrates the range of problems involved in the application of the specific performance remedy.

Copylease Corp. of America v. Memorex Corp.

United State District Court
408 F. Supp. 758 (1976)

The U.S. District Court determined that Memorex Corporation (Memorex) breached its contract with Copylease Corporation of America (Copylease) for the sale of toner and developer and directed the parties to submit proposed judgments relating to the availability of a specific performance remedy. In the contract, Copylease had been granted an exclusive territory by Memorex. Copylease argued that it should be awarded specific performance of the contract, that is, that it should be awarded the exclusive territory. The District Court concluded that further testimony was necessary to determine the propriety of a remedy of specific performance. Copylease is the plaintiff; Memorex is the defendant. Cal. UCC §2716(1) is the California equivalent to Section 2-716(1) of the UCC.

Lasker, District Judge

We . . . agree with Memorex that the provision in the contract granting Copylease an exclusive territory, on which Copylease places primary reliance in its request for specific performance, is not in itself an adequate basis under California law for an award of such relief. California law does not consider a remedy at law inadequate merely because difficulties may exist as to precise calculation of damages. *Long Beach Drug* and *Thayer Plymouth* . . . demonstrate the more fundamental refusal of California courts to order specific performance of contracts which are not capable of immediate enforcement, but which require a "continuing series of acts" and "cooperation between the parties for the successful performance of those acts." Absent some exception to this general rule, therefore, Copylease will be limited to recovery of damages for the contract breach.

An exception which may prove applicable to this case is found in Cal. U.C.C. § 2716(1). That statute provides that in an action for breach of contract a buyer may be entitled to specific performance "where the goods are unique or in other proper circumstances." Cal. U.C.C. § 2716(1). In connection with its claim for interim damages for lost profits from the time of the breach Copylease argues strongly that it could not reasonably have covered by obtaining an alternative source of toner because the other brands of toner are distinctly inferior to the Memorex product. If the evidence at the hearing supports this claim, it may well be that Copylease faces the same difficulty in finding a permanent alternative supplier. If so, the Official Comment to § 2716 suggests that a grant of specific performance may be in order.

Specific performance is no longer limited to goods which are already specific or ascertained at the time of contracting. The test of uniqueness under this section must be made in terms of the total situation which characterizes the contract. Output and requirements contracts involving a particular or peculiarly available source or market present today the typical commercial specific performance situation. . . . However, uniqueness is not the sole basis of the remedy under this section for the relief may also be granted "in other proper circumstances" and *inability to cover is strong evidence of "other proper circumstances."* Cal U.C.C. § 2716, Comment 2 (West 1964). [Emphasis added by the court.]

If Copylease has no adequate alternative source of toner the Memorex product might be considered "unique" for purposes of § 2716, or the situation might present an example of "other proper circumstances" in which specific performance would be appropriate.

If such a showing is made it will be necessary to reconcile California's policy against ordering specific performance of contracts which provide for continuing acts or an ongoing relationship with § 2716 of the Code. Although we recognize that the statute does not require specific performance, the quoted portion of the Official Comment seems clearly to suggest that where a contract calls for continuing sale of unique or "noncoverable" goods this provision should be considered an exception to the general proscription. Output should be considered an exception to the general proscription. Output and requirements contracts, explicitly cited as examples of situations in which specific performance may be appropriate, by their nature call for a series of continuing acts and an ongoing relationship. Thus, the drafters seem to have contemplated that at least in some circumstances specific performance will issue contrary to the historical reluctance to grant such relief in these situations. If, at the hearing, Copylease makes a showing that it meets the requirements of § 2716, the sensible approach would be to measure, with the particulars of this contract in mind, the uniqueness or degree of difficulty in covering against the difficulties of enforcement which have caused courts to refrain from granting specific performance. It would be premature to speculate on the outcome of such analysis in this case.

Injunction

An injunction is a remedy sometimes used in contract cases; however, like specific performance, its use has been limited. Injunctions have been used in employment contracts to prevent a party from performing the contract service for someone else. In a leading English case, an opera singer had contracted to sing exclusively for a particular company. When she refused to do so, the court enjoined her from singing for any other company. The court felt that it could not compel her specifically to perform her contractual obligation but that economic pressure might move her to honor her commitment.

American courts generally follow a similar rule in personal service contracts where the defendant refuses to perform. If the defendant's services expressly or by clear implication have been promised exclusively to the plaintiff, the courts will grant a decree enjoining service for anyone else. An injunction, however, will not be granted if the injured plaintiff could be compensated adequately by damages. As a result, injunctions are granted in personal service contracts only if the individual is a person with unique skills. Professional athletes who refuse to honor their contracts with one employer are often enjoined from performing for another.

The injunction is also used to enforce anciliary agreements not to compete. As discussed in Chapter 7, this type of agreement is permissible under certain circumstances. These generally involve the sale of a business and its accompanying good will, an employment contract in which the employee agrees not to work for a competitor or compete with the employer after leaving the job, or an employment contract in which the employee has access to customer lists or trade secrets that could be used by a business rival. Injunctions are also used to enforce covenants that limit land use. A deed or lease may contain a provision limiting the premises to residential use. If the tenant or owner uses the property for some other purpose, an injunction may be obtained by a party injured by the nonpermitted use.

Rescission and Restitution

Numerous situations exist in which a party has the right to rescind or cancel a contract. Rescission is available in cases involving fraud, duress, undue influence, and mistake. During the past decade a number of statutes have given consumers the right to cancel contracts under certain circumstances. One example is the home-solicitation or door-to-door-sales contract. Many states and a Federal Trade Commission rule allow a buyer three days to cancel certain types of agreements that have

been solicited and made in the buyer's residence. These laws also generally require the seller to notify the buyer in writing of this right. The three-day period does not start until notification is given. The right to cancel a home-solicitation sales contract does not depend on any wrongdoing by the seller.

When a contract is canceled, both parties must, if practicable, return any benefits received under the agreement. This is known as restitution. Restitution may involve returning specific items or compensating for benefits conferred. The principle of restitution applies even for cancellation due to fraud. The defrauded plaintiff is entitled to the return of benefits conferred because of fraud; but the law requires the defrauded plaintiff, if possible, to return the wrongdoer to the status quo. The defrauded plaintiff may, of course, elect to enforce the contract and sue for damages.

Restitution is also a remedy available in cases in which one person has been unjustly enriched at another's expense. Unjust enrichment is a fundamental concept affecting several legal areas, the theory being that justice is violated if a person is allowed to retain benefits that enrich him at another's expense. As a result, the courts may order restitution of those benefits or their value. Before the courts will order restitution, they must be convinced that retention of the benefits not only enriches the person but that the enrichment is unjust.

Restitution would be ordered by the courts when money has been paid by mistake or when a person has benefited from a contract that turns out to be unenforceable. The restitution rule applies if one party retains the benefits of a defective contractual performance when these could have been returned easily.

REVIEW PROBLEMS

1. Anderson, a carpenter, contracted with Baker to shingle the roof of Baker's house. Anderson had partially completed the work

when a hurricane destroyed a large part of the house, including the roof. Baker repaired the house, except for the roof, and demanded that Anderson honor his agreement. Is Anderson responsible?

2. Seller agreed to sell 800 bags of #1 goose down to Buyer at $10 per bag. Seller planned to obtain the down from geese housed on two large farms she owned. Buyer was not informed of this, although Buyer did know that Seller raised geese on the two farms. The main barn on one farm was struck by lightning and all the geese were destroyed. The geese on the other farm became diseased through no fault of Seller and none of the down was good enough to qualify as #1. At the time of scheduled delivery, the market price of down was $13 per bag. Discuss Seller's liability, if any.

3. Smith owned and operated a large motel in Phoenix, Arizona. To increase room occupancy, he contracted with a local tennis club to extend membership privileges and the use of its courts to guests of the motel. The agreement was to last for two years and the motel was to pay the club $500 per month. Seven months later the motel was destroyed by fire. Smith refused to continue the monthly payments; the tennis court sued. What result? Why? LaCumbre Golf & Country Club v. Santa Barbara Hotel Co., 271 P. 576 (1928).

4. Smith inherited a substantial sum of money, a portion of which she used to make the following purchases: an antique piano, the first foal sired by Secretariat, a new Mercedes, a riding horse, and a farm. In each case the seller refused to deliver the item. In which instances, if any, could Smith obtain a decree of specific performance? Explain.

5. Plaintiff's husband died. Plaintiff contracted with Defendant undertaker, who agreed to furnish a casket and a watertight vault, to conduct the funeral, and to inter the body. About three months after the funeral, plaintiff visited her husband's grave and found that very heavy rain had forced a corner of the vault to rise above the ground. Defendant, notified about the problem, met cemetery authorities and Plaintiff at the grave for the purpose of reinterring the body. When the vault was raised, it was discovered that water and mud had entered the vault because it had been improperly locked at one end. Angered at this and other complications, Defendant undertaker said in Plaintiff's presence, "To hell with the whole damned business, it's no concern of mine." Plaintiff sues for breach of contract and includes damages for mental anguish. On what grounds might Defendant defend? Who would be successful? Discuss. Lamm v. Shingleton, 55a E. 2d 810 (1949).

6. Milstead, a contractor, sued the Evergreen Amusement Company for balance due on a contract to clear and grade a site for the company's first drive-in movie theater. The court awarded Milstead the balance due less damages to the amusement company for delay in completing the work. These damages were based on the rental value of the site during the delay ($4,500). Defendant argued that the damages for delay should have been based on loss of profit during the delay ($12,500). Who is correct? Explain. Evergreen Amusement Corp. v. Milstead, 112 A. 2d 901 (1955).

7. Helen Gonzales, the chief accountant for a small New York City firm, had a twelve-month contract with the company. The contract ran from April 1 to March 31 at a salary of $1,100 per month. On December 1, 1974, Gonzales's employer wrongfully terminated the agreement. Gonzales was immediately offered a job as a bookkeeper at $800 per month. She did not accept this job. On February 1, 1975, Gonzales was offered a job as a chief accountant at $1,100 per month in Atlanta. The company also offered to pay moving expenses. Gonzales also refused this job because her family lived in New York. She finally went back to work on February 1, 1976, as a chief ac-

countant. Her salary was $1,150. Gonzales sued her original employer for breach of contract. How much will she recover? Explain.

8. The Aluminum Company of America (ALCOA) sued for relief from a burdensome toll conversion contract under which it converted alumina into molten aluminum for the Essex Group, Inc. (Essex), the supplier of the raw material. ALCOA sought a declaratory judgment that its nonperformance of the contract was excused as a result of commercial impracticability and frustration of purpose. For relief, it sought a reformation or modification of the contract.

Under the terms of the contract, entered into December 26, 1967, and labeled the Molten Metal Agreement, Essex would supply ALCOA with alumina which ALCOA would convert into molten aluminum at its Warrick, Indiana plant. Essex then would pick up the aluminum for further processing into aluminum wire products. The contract contained a complex price formula, with escalators pegged to the Wholesale Price Index—Industrial Commodities (WPI—IC), a government price index, and on the average hourly labor rates paid to ALCOA employees at the Warrick plant. The adjusted price was subject to an overall ceiling of 65% of the price of a specified type of aluminum sold on specified terms as published in a trade journal.

The price formula was designed to re-flect changes in nonlabor and labor costs. The indexing system was evolved by ALCOA with the aid of the eminent econmist Alan Greenspan. ALCOA selected the WPI—IC as a pricing element after assuring itself that the index had closely tracked ALCOA's nonlabor production costs for many years in the past and was highly likely to continue to do so in the future. However, the formula had failed to account for burgeoning energy costs. Beginning in 1973, OPEC actions to increase oil prices and unanticipated pollution control costs greatly increased ALCOA's electricity costs. Electrical power is the principal nonlabor cost factor in aluminum conversion, and the electrical power rates rose much more rapidly than did the WPI—IC. ALCOA complained that if it were compelled to perform the unexpired term of the 16 year contract, it would lose over $75 million. Essex counterclaimed for damages and specific performance of the contract, arguing that ALCOA had breached the contract. Who wins? Explain. If you decide in favor of ALCOA, should the court be allowed to reform the contract by writing a wholly new price term for the parties? If so, how would you reform the price formula? If you decide in favor of Essex, should the court award the remedy of specific performance? Aluminum Company of America v. Essex Group, Inc., 499 F. Supp. 53 (W.D. Pa. 1980).

PART III

COMMERCIAL TRANSACTIONS

Sales Law

S ales law covers all aspects of the sale of goods that may have legal consequences. Contracts for the sale of goods, commercial paper, and sellers' security interests all come within the scope of sales law. The Uniform Commercial Code is the primary source of law in this area, particularly Articles 2 (Sales), 3 (Commercial Paper), and 9 (Secured Transactions).

In many instances, the provisions of the UCC allow the parties to agree upon a rule different from that stated in the Code. Such provisions are prefaced with phrases such as "unless otherwise agreed" and "in the absence of contrary agreement." In the interest of simplicity, in discussing such sections we have omitted reference to the fact that the provisions can be altered by agreement.

GENERAL CHARACTERISTICS OF THE UCC

The drafters of the UCC sought to update the prior sales law to achieve a balance between the law and business practice. Many very specific rules were established controlling the formation and documentation of the sales transaction. Performance obligations were specifically defined, and the remedial rights of the parties were spelled out.

In addition, the UCC is based upon several important general principles, many of which represent a significant break with past law. These principles include:

1. Recognition of a general duty of good faith
2. De-emphasis of the traditional concept of title
3. Imposition of higher standards for merchants
4. Ratification of certain aspects of existing business practice

Duty of Good Faith

UCC Section 1-203 provides that "Every contract or duty within this Act imposes an obligation of good faith in its performance or enforcement."

Subsection 1-201(19) defines good faith as "honesty in fact in the conduct or transaction concerned." No direct sanction is imposed for failure to act in good faith. Instead, it is a general principle available to the courts that may be followed in dealing with other issues arising under the UCC. For example, Section 2-302 expressly provides for judicial modification or nullification of unconscionable contracts and contract terms. The good-faith provision complements the concept of unconscionability, and good faith may be used as a guideline in determining whether certain aspects of a commercial transaction may be considered unconscionable. The good-faith principle can also be used on its own—for example, to disallow an extortionate modification of a contract when the buyer has become so dependent on the seller for the supply of a commodity that the buyer cannot effectively resist the seller's demand for a higher price.

Merchant Standards

Merchants are generally held to higher standards under the UCC than are nonmerchants. The implied warranty of merchantability applies only to merchants. (Implied warranties are discussed in the chapter on warranties.) Only merchants are bound by firm offers, and only merchants may be bound, without agreement, by additional terms in an acceptance. There are many other examples of the higher standards applied to merchants.

Why discriminate between merchants and nonmerchants? Several justifications can be given. Merchants can reasonably be expected to be more sophisticated regarding the legal rules pertaining to their profession. They should know when to seek the advice of counsel and are, in fact, often guided by legal advice. Many merchants enter into sales transactions day after day. A nonmerchant seller, on the other hand, may make one major sale every two or three years. If we view the special rules for merchants from a consumer perspective, it seems appropriate that consumers should be held to a less rigorous standard.

Who is a merchant? The UCC defines a merchant in three different ways. A merchant may be a person who deals in goods of the kind in question. If a person in the hardware business sells a hammer, he or she is a merchant for purposes of the sale of the hammer because a hardware store regularly deals in goods such as hammers. A second person classified by the UCC as a merchant is one who by his occupation represents himself as having knowledge or skill peculiar to the practices or goods involved in the transaction. Suppose a mechanical contracting firm installed cooling equipment; with respect to the sale of the cooling equipment, it would be regarded as a merchant. Finally, a person may be classified as a merchant if he or she employs someone who qualifies as a merchant, under the first two definitions, to act on his or her behalf. If Mary hired a jeweler to represent her in the sale of her diamonds, the UCC treats *her* as a merchant because she employed a merchant.

The *Decatur* case discusses the problem of when a farmer is a merchant. Some courts view farmers as merchants but others reject this view, as the following case illustrates.

Decatur Cooperative Association v. Urban

Kansas Supreme Court
547 P. 2d 323 (1976)

In this case Urban (defendant) allegedly entered into an oral contract for sale of 10,000 bushels of wheat with the plaintiff, a grain elevator named Decatur Cooperative Association. The lower court ruled for Urban. The Kansas Supreme Court ruled that Urban was not a merchant for purposes of the sale of the wheat and affirmed the ruling of the trial court.

Harman, C.

Urban is a resident of Decatur County and was a member of the cooperative throughout the year 1973. He has been engaged in the wheat farming business for about twenty years. He owns about 2,000 acres of his total farmed acreage of 2,320 acreas. He is engaged solely in the farming business. Decatur contends the parties entered into an oral contract by phone whereby Urban agreed to sell to the cooperative 10,000 bushels of wheat at $2.86 per bushel, to be delivered on or before September 30, 1973. Urban denies that any contract sale was made.

During the phone conversation there was discussion of a written memorandum of sale to be prepared and sent to Urban later. A confirmation was signed by Decatur's assistant manager and was binding as against Decatur. Urban received the confirmation within a reasonable time, read it, and gave no written notice of objection to its contents within ten days after it was received.

On August 13, 1973, Urban notified Decatur that he would not deliver the wheat. The price of wheat at the cooperative on that date was $4.50 per bushel.

Under Subsection (2) of 2-201 a "merchant" is deprived of the defense of the Statute of Frauds as against an oral contract with another merchant if he fails to object to the terms of a written confirmation within ten days of its receipt. The issue presently here is whether or not appellee is, under the facts, also a "merchant." If he is not, Section 2-201 acts as a bar to the enforcement of the alleged contract. Professionalism, special knowledge and commercial experience are to be used in determining whether a person in a particular situation is to be held to the standards of a merchant.

The writers of the official UCC comment virtually equate professionals with merchants—the casual or inexperienced buyer or seller is not to be held to the standard set for the professional in business. The defined term "between merchants," used in the exception proviso to the Statute of Frauds, contemplates the knowledge and skill of professionals on each side of the transaction. The transaction in question here was the sale of wheat. Urban as a farmer undoubtedly had special knowledge or skill in raising wheat but we do not think this factor, coupled with annual sales of a wheat crop and purchases of seed wheat, qualified him as a merchant in that field. The parties' stipulation states Urban has sold only the products he raised. There is no indication any of these sales were other than cash sales to local grain elevators, where conceivably an expertise reaching professional status could be said to be involved.

We think the trial court correctly ruled under the particular facts that Urban was not a merchant for the purpose of avoiding the operation of the Statute of Frauds pursuant to K.S.A. 84-2-201(1).

Modified Concept of Title

The UCC de-emphasizes the concept of title. Under prior law, title had been used as a basic determinant of other legal rights and interests, including unallocated risk of loss, security, and insurability. Thus, before these other rights could be determined, the title to the goods had to be established. This was a very indirect way of approaching the real question of who, for example, should bear the risk of any loss of the goods. The policy implications of who most appropriately should bear the risk of loss were difficult to consider. Everything was determined by the possession of title, which not only assigned risk of loss but several other important rights as well.

The UCC now has separate sections dealing with rights related to risk of loss, insurable interests, and security interests. All matters as to the rights and obligations of the parties to a contract apply irrespective of title to the goods except where a provision of the UCC specifically refers to the question of title.

Section 2-401 determines when the buyer obtains title to goods covered by a contract. Title may not pass prior to identification of the goods. When the goods are identified to the contract, the buyer acquires certain rights in them, called a special property interest in the goods. Identification means that specific goods are somehow identified (by a mark or by being set aside or described) as the object of the particular transaction. For example, Buyer agrees to purchase a color TV. When Seller selects a particular TV in the warehouse as the one that Buyer is to get, that TV becomes identified in the contract. In a sense, prior to identification of specific goods, there is nothing on which a title can be passed.

Generally, the parties are free to arrange by explicit agreement for the transfer of title to existing goods in any manner and on any conditions. If the parties fail to specify when title is to pass, it passes at the time and place when the seller has delivered the goods. The point at which the seller has completed his obligations as to delivery is discussed in the following material.

Origin Contract. If the seller intends to send the goods to the buyer, but the contract does not require the seller to deliver the goods to a destination, title to the goods passes to the buyer at the time and place of shipment. This is called an *origin contract.* It operates as follows: Suppose a buyer in Oklahoma City wishes to purchase a lawn mower from a seller in Chicago. The seller's only obligation under the contract is to put the mower on board a truck in Chicago bound for Oklahoma City. Title to the mower remains in the seller only until he or she delivers the goods to the trucking company.

Destination Contract. If the seller is obligated under the contract to actually deliver the goods to the buyer, the title to the goods does not pass to the buyer until they are tendered to the buyer at the destination specified in the contract. This is called a *destination contract.* In the example in the last paragraph, suppose the contract required the seller to actually deliver the lawn mower to the buyer in Oklahoma City, as opposed to merely delivering it to the trucking company in Chicago. In this situation, title to the mower remains in the seller until he tenders it to the buyer. This means that if the goods arrive in Oklahoma City, and the shipper, at a reasonable time, offers to deliver the mower to the buyer's place of business, a tender has been made and title passes to the buyer—whether the buyer actually takes delivery of the goods or not.

The comments on Section 2-503 make it clear that the seller is not obligated to deliver to a named destination unless he or she has specifically agreed to such a delivery. In other words, there is a presumption that the parties intended an origin, not a destination, contract. Unless the contract calls for the seller to deliver goods at a particular destination, his or her only obligation will be to deliver them to a carrier.

Documents of Title. If delivery is to be made without moving the goods, two other rules control, as set forth in subsection 2-401(3). If the seller is to deliver a document of title (explained in the introduction to commercial paper), title passes at the time and place the seller delivers the document. Suppose the lawn mower in the earlier example has been stored in a public warehouse. When the seller left the goods, the warehousemen gave the seller a document of title called a warehouse receipt. If the receipt is negotiable, anyone in possession of the receipt has the power to receive the goods from the warehouseman. This means that if the contract that is signed by the buyer and seller specifies that a delivery will take place without moving the goods from the warehouse, whenever the seller gives the buyer the negotiable warehouse receipt, title to the mower passes to the buyer.

No Documents. If the goods are already identified to the contract (the seller has specified certain goods will be given to the buyer) and no documents are to be delivered, then title to the goods passes at the time and place of contracting. In the earlier example, suppose the seller had the mower in his or her own plant. The seller intended for the buyer to pick up the mower at the seller's plant. He or she identified a certain mower as the buyer's prior to signing the contract. In this situation, title to the mower passes to the buyer at the time of contracting.

The next case illustrates the point that, when a seller sells goods to a buyer, the seller may not retain title to the goods. Any attempt to retain title in the contract of sale will be construed by the court as a mere reservation of a security interest in the goods. (See Chapter 23 for a discussion of security interests.)

Commonwealth v. Jett

Pennsylvania Superior Court
326 A.2d 508 (1974)

The defendants, the Jetts, purchased an organ from Menchey Music Service. The store attempted to retain title to the organ after delivery of it to the Jetts. Before paying for it, the Jetts sold the organ to another person. A criminal action was brought against the Jetts based on the theory that they had committed a crime by selling the organ. The prosecution had to prove that title was in Menchey Music Service to establish the crime of fraudulent conversion. The lower court convicted the Jetts. The appeals court reversed the conviction because it found that the Jetts had had title to the organ at the time they sold it.

Cercone, Judge

This appeal arises from the appellants' (the Jetts) convictions for fraudulent conversion. The appeal raises a novel question concerning the location of title in the property allegedly converted, a Lowry organ. The appellants urge that the lower court erred when it determined that, under the terms of the installment sales contract, title to the property remained in the seller until appellant-buyers paid the balance of the installments due under the contract.

The appellants purchased the organ from the complainant, Menchey Music Service of Hanover, Pennsylvania, on December 24, 1970. After making a down payment and three monthly installments, the appellants defaulted on their payments in April 1971, and apparently have never made any further payments. The evidence indicates that after September 1971, the appellants were contacted on several occasions concerning their default and eventually were served with a writ of replevin. The property could not be replevied, however, because the appellants had sold it.

It is admitted that, with the exception of the question of title, the evidence produced at trial was sufficient to support the verdict. However, under Section 4834 of the Penal Code of 1939 (Fraudulent Conversion of Property), the Commonwealth was required to prove more than the fact that Menchey Music Service was entitled to possession of the organ because of the default in installment payments—the Commonwealth had to show that title to the organ was in Menchey Music Service. Thus, the question is, under the terms of the sale and the law in effect at the time the transaction took place, did Menchey Music Service have title to the property?

Although this is a criminal case, its resolution depends upon commercial law; to wit, the Uniform Commercial Code.

According to Professor Nordstrom, between the time of identification and shipment or delivery, the parties are free to choose, by explicit agreement, any time or incident to signal the vesting of title in the buyer. Beyond those points the parties are powerless to alter the location of title established by Section 2-401. Other commentators are in substantial agreement.

The principal reason for the Code's prohibition of retention of title by the seller under an installment sales agreement after the goods have been shipped or delivered to the buyer is that to have allowed such a retention would have created a gaping loophole in Article 9. Were the seller able to retain title to goods delivered to the buyer under an installment sales contract, it would be superfluous for him to file a financing statement to perfect a security interest or draft a security agreement which included a description of the secured property. His retention of title would establish his priority over all secured creditors or even a trustee in bankruptcy. In limiting the effect of a retention of title clause, the Code drafters sought to protect subsequent creditors of the buyer who altered their positions in reliance upon the buyer's title to the collateral. However, they also established the remedies and procedures the seller may or may not employ to realize the protection afforded by his security interest when the buyer defaults, even when there is no question of subsequent third party involvement in the transaction. Thus, the Code places attempts at reserving title uniformly into Article 9. Therefore, we hold that a reservation of title clause in an installment sales contract is inoperative as anything other than a reservation of a security interest. Since the Jetts had title to the organ when they sold it, the sale could not have constituted a fraudulent conversion.

Judgement of sentence is arrested and the appellants are dismissed.

Transfer of Title to Third Persons

Section 2-401 determines when the buyer receives title to goods from the seller. Once the buyer receives goods, he or she may choose to convey them to a third party. Section 2-403 determines the title of the third person who receives goods from the original buyer.

If the buyer receives title to the goods pursuant to Section 2-401, he or she has the power to transfer the good title to goods to a third person. But what if the buyer, for example, gives the seller a bad check—does the buyer have the power to transfer good title to a third person? Section 2-403 answers this question.

Void Title. Section 2-403 gives a purchaser all title that his or her transferor had or had power to transfer. Suppose that a person steals goods from someone, and the thief resells the goods to an innocent third party who knows nothing of the theft. The third party in this situation acquires a *void title;* that is, if the original owner demands the goods back from him or her, the third party must surrender the goods. The thief had no title to the goods, nor did he or she have any power to transfer title to the goods to anyone else.

Voidable Title. Certain persons acquire a mere *voidable title.* As between the original owner and the buyer with a mere voidable title, the owner may reclaim his or her goods. Suppose that Mary gave Alice a bad check in return for Alice's dress. As long as Mary had the dress, Alice could get it back from Mary because Mary had acquired a mere voidable title by giving a bad check.

However, if the buyer with voidable title transfers the goods to a third person, in certain instances the third person may retain possession of the goods even as against the original owner. The third person must establish several things in order to keep the goods. This person must prove that he or she was a good-faith purchaser for value. Essentially, the third

person must establish that he or she acquired the goods by paying a reasonable price and that, in doing so, the person acted in good faith. Assuming the third person establishes that he or she is a good-faith purchaser for value, he or she also must establish that the person from whom the third party acquired the goods had a voidable title.

The UCC sets out several transactions that give rise to a voidable title. If a case does not fit in one of these four transactions, the court must refer to the cases and statutes to determine whether the third person's title is voidable. The four transactions giving rise to a voidable title are:

1. When the transferor of the goods was deceived as to the identity of the purchaser
2. When the purchaser acquired the goods by giving a check which is later dishonored
3. When the transaction was one in which title was not to pass until the seller was paid
4. When the goods were procured through criminal fraud

This provision works as follows. Suppose Alfred is in the business of selling typewriters. Sam robs Alfred and takes a typewriter. Sam sells this typewriter to Alice. Alice acquires a void title. Alfred may reclaim the typewriter from Alice even if she took the typewriter in good faith, without any knowledge of the theft, and paid a reasonable price for the typewriter.

Let's change these facts somewhat so that Sam gives Alfred a check that later bounces. He sells the typewriter to Alice, who purchases it for a reasonable price and is unaware of the bad check. Alfred now demands the typewriter back from Alice. May Alice keep the typewriter? Yes, she acquired the typewriter from a person with a *voidable* title, Sam. Sam acquired a voidable title because he gave Alfred a check that subsequently bounced. As between Alfred and Sam, as long as Sam kept the typewriter, Alfred was able to get it back from Sam. Once Sam transferred the typewriter to Alice, a good-faith purchaser for value, Alfred lost his right to reacquire the typewriter. The same result would occur if Sam deceives Alfred as to his identity, or if Sam agrees to pay cash for the typewriter at some later date, or if Sam acquires the typewriter through criminal fraud. If Sam acquires a voidable title by any of these devices, or any other transfer recognized as voidable by state law, Sam has the power to transfer a title good against the original seller to a good-faith purchaser for value.

Purchasers from Someone with Good Title. The UCC protects anyone who purchases from a person who acquires a good title. In the case noted earlier, suppose Sam gives a check to Alfred that subsequently bounces, and Sam resells the goods to Alice, a good-faith purchaser for value. Alice now has the power to transfer all title she has. As she has a title good against even Alfred, she can transfer a good title to Linda—even if Linda knows that Sam acquired the goods from Alfred by passing a bad check! Linda cannot qualify as a good-faith purchaser, but she still acquires a good title since she takes it through Alice.

Entrustment. It is also possible for a merchant who deals in goods of the kind entrusted to him or her to transfer all title of the entruster to a buyer in the ordinary course of business. Entrustment is broadly defined as "any delivery and any acquiescence in retention of possession" and is covered in subsections 2-403(2) and (3).

Such a transfer might occur when a jeweler accidentally mixes a watch left with him for repair with his regular stock and sells it to a customer by mistake. Another situation in which this applies is when a manufacturer sells goods to a retailer. If the manufacturer attempts to take a security interest in the goods held by the retailer for resale, this does not prevent the retailer from cutting off the manufacturer's security interest by selling the goods to a customer. The buyer acquires a clear title if he or she qualifies as a buyer in the ordinary course of business.

To obtain a title superior to that of the previous owner of the goods, the buyer must establish several facts. The goods must have been entrusted to a merchant regularly dealing in goods of that kind. In the case of the jeweler, the jeweler regularly deals in watches so he qualifies as a merchant. (Note that the definition of merchant here is narrower than under Section 2-104.) The jeweler has the power to transfer all rights of the entruster to a buyer in the ordinary course of business. A buyer in the ordinary course of business is a person who, in good faith and without knowledge that the sale to him or her is in violation of the ownership rights or security interest of a third party, buys in ordinary course from a person in the business of selling goods of this kind. Whether a person is a buyer in the ordinary course depends on the facts and circumstances of the case. In the case of the jeweler who mixes the watch with his other stock, the jeweler has the power to transfer good title to a person who purchases the watch from him.

SCOPE OF ARTICLE 2

Article 2 of the UCC covers all transactions involving a "sale" where title passes from the seller to the buyer for a price. It also covers "contracts for sale," which include both a present sale and a contract to sell at a future time. In a present sale, the making of the contract and the completion of the sale (passing of title) occur at the same time. In a future sale the making of the contract and the completion of the sale occur at different times.

Goods

Unless the sale involves the sale of "goods," the contract is not controlled by Article 2. Section 2-105(1) of the UCC defines goods as "all things . . . which are movable at the time of identification to the contract for sale . . ." In order for an item to qualify as a good, two requirements must be met: (1) the item must be tangible (have a physical existence); and (2) it must be movable.

The UCC definition of goods also includes the unborn young of animals, growing crops, and other things attached to realty that are to be severed. A contract for the sale of growing crops, timber to be cut, or other severables is a contract for the sale of goods. If the contract covers goods that are not yet existing and identified, the goods are "future goods," and the sale of future goods operates as a contract to sell.

Contracts Not Covered

Contracts that are not covered by Article 2 are those involving the sale of real property, nongoods personal property (e.g., a contract for the sale of an investment security), or services. Where a contract involves both goods and services, the court may apply Article 2 even though the contract is not a pure "goods" contract. The sale of mixed goods and services has created a number of complex cases. Suppose you go to a dentist; if the dentist fills one of your teeth with silver, is the transaction a sale of goods? What if a plumber comes to your house and installs a new pipe; is the transaction a sale of goods? It is most likely, in both of these examples, that a court would construe the transaction as a service contract because goods are only incidentally involved in the performance of the service contract. In other words, because the service aspect of the transaction predominates, the transaction is not covered by the UCC. Conversely, an item might be sold along with a minor service. Suppose you went to a restaurant at which a waiter or waitress brought food to the table. Courts are likely to construe this situation as predominately a sale of goods and therefore covered by the UCC. Obviously, not all situations are

this clear-cut, and the mixture of goods and services gives courts some trouble in deciding whether the UCC or the common law of contracts should control a situation.

ACCEPTANCE

Method of Acceptance

Several important changes from the common law rules of offer and acceptance appear in the UCC. For example, the authors of the UCC adopted subsection 2-206(1) to make it easier for an offeree to determine in what manner he or she must accept an offer when it is felt that the offer itself does not make clear how it must be accepted. It provides that "unless otherwise unambiguously indicated by the language or circumstances, . . . an offer to make a contract shall be construed as inviting acceptance in any manner and by any medium reasonable in the circumstances." For example, one might, when faced with an offer made by telegram, accept by mail unless the circumstances warranted a more immediate reply. If the offeror has specified a particular mode of acceptance, however, even under the UCC the offeree must accept in that manner.

Shipment. Subsection (b) of section 2-206(1) permits a seller to accept an order or offer to buy goods "either by a prompt promise to ship or by the prompt or current shipment of conforming or nonconforming goods." This in effect allows for both bilateral and unilateral contracts. If the seller chooses to accept the offer by the prompt shipment of goods, an acceptance occurs whether conforming or nonconforming goods are shipped. This means the seller no longer can argue when the buyer receives nonconforming goods that there has been no acceptance of the offer, and therefore no breach of contract, because nonconforming goods were shipped in response to the buyer's order. When there has been a shipment of nonconforming goods in response to an order, there is both an acceptance of the offer and a breach of contract.

Accommodating Shipment. Of course, situations may arise where the seller is unable to supply the exact item ordered by the buyer but is in the position to ship something very similar and perhaps equally acceptable to the buyer. If the seller wishes to ship the goods to the buyer on the condition that the buyer may return them if he does not want them, the seller may ship nonconforming goods to accommodate a buyer. Section 2-206(1)(b) provides that "such a shipment of nonconforming goods does not constitute an acceptance if the seller seasonably notifies the buyer that the shipment is offered only as an accommodation to the buyer." If the buyer finds the goods unacceptable, he may return them, but the accommodating shipment will *not* be treated as a breach of contract.

Beginning Performance. It is also possible under the UCC to accept an offer by beginning performance. The offeree, rather than responding to an offer with an acceptance, might choose to perform the requested act. The UCC recognizes this as a method of acceptance where it is "a reasonable mode of acceptance," but it places an important limitation on the offeree's power to accept in this manner: "an offeror who is not notified of acceptance within a reasonable time may treat the offer as having lapsed before acceptance." The silence of the offeree will not be treated as an acceptance. Where the offeror in New York offers to purchase lawn mowers from a company in Los Angeles, the company in Los Angeles may begin to produce the mowers, but it must also notify the New York purchaser of its acceptance. If it fails to do so, the New York company may treat the offer as having been rejected. The Los Angeles company has only a reasonable time from the time it commences performance to notify the buyer of the acceptance. If the offeror doesn't hear from the offeree within a reasonable time, he may safely make other arrangements to obtain the lawn mowers without fear of being held to the contract.

Form of Acceptance

The common law requirement that the acceptance be a mirror image of the offer and the resulting "battle-of-forms" problem were discussed in Chapter 7. The explanation of the UCC modification of the common law rule in Section 2-207 that is supplied in Chapter 7 should be reviewed at this point.

CREATION OF SALES CONTRACTS

The UCC makes it much easier for a court to find that a contract for the sale of goods has been made. If the court determines that the parties intended an agreement because of something they wrote or said, or because of their conduct, it can find that a contract for sale of goods has been made even though the moment of its making is uncertain. Section 2-204(3) states the principle pertaining to "open terms" adopted in the UCC. The contract will not be set aside for indefiniteness merely because one or more terms have been left open, as long as the parties intended to make a contract and there is a reasonably certain basis for giving an appropriate remedy. The more terms the parties have left open, the more difficult it will be for a court to conclude that the parties intended to make a binding agreement. For the court to have a reasonably certain basis for giving an appropriate remedy, the parties must specify in the contract the quantity of goods sold.

Indefiniteness

Prior to the adoption of the UCC, a court would sometimes refuse to enforce a contract because parties either intentionally or unintentionally failed to cover all the terms necessary for the contract to be considered valid and enforceable. The contract might not have clearly specified the price to be paid or certain delivery or payment terms. Rather than fill in the missing terms for the parties, the courts simply refused to enforce the agreement. The UCC, in Part 3 of Article 2, provides a number of statutory terms that may be used by a court in the event the contract fails to specify particular terms.

Price. Section 2-304 states that the price can be made "in money or otherwise." A contract thus will not fail simply because it does not make the price payable in money. The price can be paid in money, goods, realty, or "otherwise."

But what if the parties leave the price term open? Section 2-305 covers this situation. It is not necessary for the contract to include the price term. If it has not been agreed upon at the time the contract is executed, then the price will be whatever a reasonable price is at the time of delivery. Any price set at a later date must be done in "good faith." If the buyer has the right to set the price at a later time, and he sets an unreasonably low price in light of the market conditions and surrounding circumstances, then the price declared will not be controlling because the buyer acted in bad faith. If one of the parties to a contract has the duty to fix a price and he or she fails to do so, the other party may cancel the contract or may set a reasonable price.

However, a contract will fail for indefiniteness if the price term is left out and if the contract clearly states that the parties do not intend to be bound by the agreement if the price is not subsequently fixed and agreed upon. Unless the contract very clearly indicates that the parties do not wish to be bound if the price cannot be agreed upon, the court may end up setting a price for them.

Delivery. The contract may also not contain directions for the time, place, or method of delivery. Even so, the contract will not fail for indefiniteness. If the time for delivery has not been specified in the contract, subsection 2-309(1) states that the time for shipment or delivery shall be a reasonable time. What is reasonable depends on the circumstances. If the contract calls for successive performances, but does not specify when the contract terminates, it is valid for a reasonable time but may be terminated at any time by either party upon reasonable notice. If the contract does not specify whether the delivery is to be in one lot or in several lots, the goods must be tendered in a single delivery and payment is due at that time.

Section 2-308 makes the seller's place of business or, if he or she has no place of business, the seller's residence the appropriate place for delivery of goods in the absence of a specified place of delivery. If the contract is for the sale of identified goods that the parties know are located at some place other than the seller's place of business or residence, the place where the goods are located is the place for delivery.

Quantity. The only term that absolutely must be stated in a contract for the sale of goods is the quantity term. Section 2-201 of the Statute of Frauds states: "a writing is not insufficient because it omits or incorrectly states a term agreed upon but the contract is not enforceable . . . beyond the quantity of goods shown in such writing." If the contract is one that must be in writing in order to be enforceable, and the writing omits the quantity term, there is no enforceable contract. If the writing incorrectly states the quantity term, there may be an enforceable contract— at least to the extent of the quantity stated in the writing.

Thus the UCC reflects the philosophy that a contract for the sale of goods should not fail, even though one or more terms have been left open, as long as the parties intended to enter into a contract and "there is a reasonably certain basis for giving an appropriate remedy" (Section 2-204[3]).

Course of Dealing, Usage of Trade, Course of Performance

In interpreting a contract, the court must take into consideration more than the literal language of the contract and the meaning that is normally associated with the words used in the contract. The UCC requires the court to examine the course of dealing, usage of trade, or course of performance between the parties.

Whenever possible, the express terms of the agreement and any course of dealing, usage of trade, and course of performance must be construed as consistent with one another. When such a construction is unreasonable, the written terms control the situation. Sections 2-208(2) and 1-205(4) make it apparent that conflicts between the express and implied terms are to be resolved in the following manner:

1. Express terms prevail over course of dealing, usage of trade, and course of performance if they cannot be reasonably construed together
2. Course of performance prevails over both course of dealing and usage of trade
3. Course of dealing prevails over usage of trade

Course of Performance. Section 2-208(1) states: "Where the contract for sale involves repeated occasions for performance by either party with knowledge of the nature of the performance and opportunity for objection to it by the other, any course of performance accepted or acquiesced in without objection shall be relevant to determine the meaning of the agreement." Course of performance involves situations where more than one performance is contemplated by the contract.

Course of Dealing. Course of performance relates to conduct *after* the execution of an agreement, whereas course of dealing relates to conduct between the parties *prior* to the execution of an agreement. "A course of dealing is a sequence of previous conduct between the parties to a particular transaction which is fairly to be regarded as establishing a common basis of understanding for interpreting those expressions and other conduct" (section 1-205[1]). Because the conduct that is material to a course of dealing occurs prior to the execution of an agreement, course of dealing cannot be used to modify or waive a written contract.

Usage of Trade. Section 1-205(2) states:

(2) A usage of trade is any practice or method of dealing having such regularity of observance in a place, vocation or trade as to justify an expectation that it will be observed with respect to the transaction in question. The existence and scope of such a usage are to be proved as facts. If it is established that such a usage is embodied in a written trade code or similar writing the interpretation of the writing is for the court.

Usage of trade is not the same as custom because the practice or method of dealing may be of recent origin or may be followed only in a particular part of the country. It simply must be observed with such regularity "as to justify an expectation that it will be observed with respect to the transaction in question." Like course of dealing, usage of trade can be used to give meaning to the particular language selected by the parties in their contract.

Filling in Terms. The UCC sets up a system to fill in the missing terms in an agreement between parties. Where a term is fully expressed in writing or by a valid oral statement, this term will control the agreement unless it conflicts with a mandatory provision of the UCC. In the absence of a particular term in a written agreement, the court will fill it in by first looking to course of performance, then to course of dealing, and finally to usage of trade to supply the missing information. If none of these enable the court to fill in a missing term, the court will examine the statutory terms in Part 3 of Article 2 of the UCC to fill in the missing information. If the UCC does not specify the term to be filled in, then the contract is enforced even though the court is unable to fill in the missing term—as long as the contract indicates that the parties intended to be bound and there is a reasonably certain basis for giving an appropriate remedy.

RISK OF LOSS

The UCC creates several methods for allocating the risk of loss between the parties:

1. By express agreement
2. By the use of mercantile terms
3. By Sections 2-509 and 2-510
4. By Section 2-326

Terms

When contracting, merchants frequently use mercantile terms or symbols as abbreviated methods of stating the delivery duties of the seller. The UCC defines these mercantile terms in Sections 2-319 to 2-325. Unless the parties to a contract specify another meaning, the UCC definitions of these terms controls.

F.O.B. The terms F.O.B. (free on board a carrier, typically a truck or train) and F.A.S. (free alongside a ship) are defined in Section 2-319. Where the contract states "F.O.B. St. Louis" and the seller is in St. Louis, then by Section 2-319(1)(a) the seller has the expense and risk of putting the goods into the possession of a carrier and shipping the goods in accordance with the provisions of Section 2-504. This is a shipment or *origin contract*. This section requires the seller, unless otherwise agreed:

1. To put the goods in the possession of the carrier
2. To make a proper contract for transportation of the goods (e.g., meat must be refrigerated)
3. To obtain and deliver or tender to the buyer any documents necessary for the buyer to obtain possession of the goods
4. To promptly notify the buyer of the shipment

If the contract states "F.O.B. New York" and the seller is in St. Louis and the buyer in New York, then the seller pays the freight and bears the risk of loss under Section 2-319(1)(b). This is a *destination contract.* The seller must at his own risk and expense transport the goods to New York and tender them to the buyer in New York. Section 2-503 requires the seller to put and hold conforming goods at the buyer's disposition and to give the buyer reasonable notification in order to enable him or her to take delivery. The tender must be at a reasonable hour and the goods must be available for a reasonable period of time.

Presumption of Origin Contract. Through an examination of the contract and the surrounding circumstances, it generally will be possible to determine whether the seller must send the goods to the buyer and whether the parties contemplated an origin or a destination contract. If the contract fails to clearly cover this point, the presumption is that the parties intended an origin contract. Suppose a contract read as follows: "Ship to ABC Corp., 1321 Redbud Lane, Mobile, Alabama." The seller's business is in Houston, Texas, and the buyer is located in Mobile. The mere fact that the label indicates where the package is to be shipped does not overcome the presumption that this is an origin contract. However, the statement "F.O.B. ABC Corp, 1321 Redbud Lane, Mobile, Alabama" creates a destination contract. The seller must at its own risk and expense transport the goods to Mobile and tender them to the buyer in Mobile.

If the contract specifies "F.O.B. vessel *St. Louis*" or "F.O.B. car or other vehicle," the seller must, in addition to bearing the expense and risk of transportation, load the goods on board.

C.I.F. The term C.I.F. stands for the words cost, insurance, and freight. When this term is used, it means that the price includes the cost of the goods, the cost of insuring the goods, and freight to a named destination. The seller must at his own expense put the goods into the possession of a carrier at the port for shipment, and obtain a negotiable bill of lading covering the entire transportation to the named destination.

C. & F. According to Section 2-320(1 and 3), when a contract includes the term C. & F., the price includes cost and freight to the named destination. The seller need not obtain insurance under a C. & F. term. The term has the same effect and imposes upon the seller the same obligations and risks as a C.I.F. term, except for the obligation to insure. The risk of loss under C.I.F. or C. & F. is on the buyer once the seller has delivered the goods to the carrier.

Ex-Ship. In a sale "ex-ship" (which means from the carrying vessel) the seller must cause the goods to be delivered to the buyer from a ship which has arrived at the port of delivery. The seller must pay freight to the named port, release the ship owner's lien, and furnish the buyer with a direction that puts the ship under a duty to deliver the goods. The risk of loss does not pass until the goods are properly unloaded from the ship.

No Arrival, No Sale. The term "no arrival, no sale" is used when the parties execute a destination contract by which the risk of loss remains on the seller during shipment. Under this term, however, the seller is not liable for breach of contract if the goods are not delivered through no fault of the seller. The parties may arrive at a different understanding, but the seller is free of liability if goods conforming to the contract fail to arrive due to the hazards of transportation. If the seller fails to ship the goods or if he ships nonconforming goods, Section 2-324 does not relieve the seller of liability.

Risk of Loss in the Absence of Terms

The Uniform Sales Act, which governed the law of sales prior to the adoption of the UCC, forced the courts to struggle with the question of who held title to the goods in order to determine which party bore the risk of loss. The UCC greatly simplifies the determination of who bears the risk of loss by treating risk of loss separately from the issue of title.

Voluntary Agreement. In general, the UCC reflects the philosophy that the parties may determine the details of a contract. The parties may arrive at an agreement on risk of loss contrary to that specified in the UCC. The agreement may shift the allocation of risk of loss, or it may divide the risk between the parties. The only restraints on the modification of the risk-of-loss provisions in the UCC are that such modifications be made in good faith and are not unconscionable.

If a seller intends to shift the risk of loss to the buyer, the contract must clearly state the manner in which risk of loss will be allocated. This is especially true when the seller tries to shift the risk of loss to the buyer before he or she takes possession of the goods. In Hayward v. Postma, 188 N.W.2d 31 (1971), the seller argued that the risk of loss for a 30-foot Revel Craft Playmate Yacht worth $10,000 that was destroyed by fire while it was still at the seller's premises should fall on the buyer. Neither the seller nor the buyer had an insurance policy covering the boat. The seller claimed that he had transferred the risk of loss to the buyer by a clause in the security agreement signed by the parties. (See Chapter 23 for an explanation of security agreements.) The court acknowledged that a risk of loss could be transferred to the buyer in this fashion, but it observed that the agreement in this case was not sufficiently clear and prominent to apprise the buyer that he bore the risk of loss on the yacht. The court noted that the usual rule in such cases was for the risk of loss to fall on the merchant-seller unless he or she had physically delivered the goods to the buyer. The rationale for this rule was that the buyer had no control over the goods and that it would be extremely unlikely that the buyer would carry insurance on goods not yet in his possession. The seller might transfer this risk to the buyer only if he or she clearly brought this matter to the buyer's attention.

Risk of loss may be specifically allocated by a clause in a contract, or the parties may allocate risk of loss through the use of a mercantile term such as F.O.B. as discussed earlier in this chapter.

No Agreement. If the contract between the buyer and the seller fails to specify how risk of loss will be allocated between the parties, Section 2-509 controls if there is a loss but no breach of contract. Section 2-510 applies if there has been a loss and a breach of contract.

The policy underlying these provisions is to place the loss on the party most likely to have insured against the loss. The person in possession of the goods normally is able to prevent a loss from occurring in the first place. For this reason, the risk of loss usually falls on the party in possession of the goods.

Section 2-509 divides risk of loss into three categories: 1. Goods shipped by carrier 2. Goods held by a bailee that are to be delivered without being moved 3. All other cases.

Identification. Risk of loss cannot pass to the buyer until the goods are identified to the contract. Section 2-501 states that, in the absence of a contrary agreement, identification occurs: when the contract is made if the goods are existing and identified; or if the goods are future goods, when the goods are shipped, marked, or otherwise designated by the seller as goods to which the contract refers.

Shipment by Carrier. When the parties enter into an origin contract and agree to delivery by carrier, risk of loss shifts to the buyer when the seller puts the goods in the possession of a carrier, makes a reasonable contract for their transportation, obtains all documents necessary for the buyer to obtain possession of the goods, and notifies the buyer of the shipment.

If a destination contract is involved, whereby the seller agrees to ship the goods to the buyer by carrier, risk passes to the buyer when the seller has put and held conforming goods at the buyer's disposition at the destination point and given the buyer any notification and documents reasonably necessary to take delivery of the goods.

Suppose a paint manufacturer sells 500 cans of paint to a retail paint store. If the parties agree for the seller to ship the goods to the buyer's store at 1011 Main, Oklahoma City, and the goods are lost in transit after the seller loads them on a common carrier (e.g., a railroad, truck, or airline), who bears the risk of loss? It must first be determined if the parties entered into an origin contract or a destination contract. Bear in mind that the UCC views an origin contract as the typical contract. The seller does not bear the risk of loss after placing the goods on the carrier unless he has specifically agreed to bear the risk of loss to the destination point. In this case, the courts probably would treat the agreement as an origin contract and place the risk of loss on the buyer. The term "ship to," attached to the goods with an address, has no significance in determining who bears the risk of loss. On the other hand, language such as "F.O.B. buyer's plant" or "Ship to buyer, risk of loss remains on seller until tender by carrier to buyer" clearly contemplates a destination contract, and the risk does not pass to the buyer until the goods are tendered to the buyer at the place of destination.

The risk of loss will not pass unless the seller makes a proper contract for transportation and ships conforming goods.

Goods Held by a Bailee. If the goods are not to be shipped by carrier but are in possession of a bailee and are to be delivered without being moved, Section 2-509(2) controls. If the bailee has issued a negotiable document of title, the risk of loss passes to the buyer when he or she receives the negotiable document of title. Risk of loss also passes to the buyer after his or her receipt of a nonnegotiable document of title, but not until the buyer has had a reasonable opportunity to present the document to the bailee. If the bailee refuses to honor the nonnegotiable document of title, risk of loss does not pass. If a nonnegotiable document of title has been issued, risk of loss passes to the buyer when the bailee acknowledges the buyer's right to the possession of the goods.

Other Cases. All other cases *not* involving a breach of contract are covered by Section 2-509(3). This section covers the situation where the seller intends to deliver the goods to the buyer in the seller's truck or the buyer intends to pick up the goods at the seller's place of business. Subsection (3) sets out two rules, one of which covers a merchant-seller and the other applies to a nonmerchant-seller. In the case of the merchant-seller, risk of loss remains on the seller until the buyer actually takes physical possession of the goods. If the seller is not a merchant, risk of loss passes to the buyer on tender of delivery. Tender means putting and holding conforming goods at the buyer's disposition and giving the buyer any notification reasonably necessary to enable him to take delivery. The tender must be at a reasonable hour and kept available long enough for the buyer to take possession.

Suppose that Acme Glass agrees to sell fifteen panels of glass to a building contractor. Nothing is said about who bears the risk of loss in the contract. If the glass is destroyed prior to the time the contractor picks up the glass, who bears the risk of loss? As Acme Glass deals in goods of this kind, it is a merchant under Section 2-104. Acme must actually deliver physical possession of the glass to the contractor. The risk of loss is on Acme.

But suppose Elmo sells fifteen panels of glass to his next-door neighbor and tenders them to his neighbor. The neighbor fails to pick up the glass, and after a week passes a fire destroys Elmo's home and the glass. Who bears the risk of loss? Because Elmo is not a merchant, and he tendered the glass to his neighbor, the risk of loss falls on his neighbor.

Note that a merchant-seller who retains physical possession of goods after selling them retains the risk of loss. This is true even after title has passed and the seller has received his or her money for the goods, as is illustrated by the following case.

Martin v. Melland's Inc.

Supreme Court of North Dakota

283 N.W.2d 76 (1979)

Plaintiff, Israel Martin, purchased a haymoving machine from Melland's, the defendant in this case. Martin traded in his old haystack mover on the new one, but he retained possession of it. The old haystack mover was destroyed while in Martin's possession. The lower court found Martin should bear the risk of loss and the North Dakota Supreme Court affirmed this decision.

Erickstad, Chief Justice

The narrow issue on this appeal is who should bear the loss of a truck and an attached haystack mover that was destroyed by fire while in the possession of the plaintiff, Israel Martin (Martin), but after the certificate of title had been delivered to the defendant, Melland's Inc. (Melland's). The destroyed haymoving unit was to be used as a trade-in for a new haymoving unit that Martin ultimately purchased from Melland's.

On June 11, 1974, Martin entered into a written agreement with Melland's, a farm implement dealer, to purchase a truck and attached haystack mover for the total purchase price of $35,389. Martin was given a trade-in allowance of $17,389 on his old unit, leaving a balance owing of $18,000 plus sales tax of $720 or a total balance of $18,720. The agreement provided that Martin "mail or bring title" to the old unit to Melland's "this week." Martin mailed the certificate of title to Melland's pursuant to the agreement, but he was allowed to retain the use and possession of the old unit "until they had the new one ready."

Fire destroyed the truck and the haymoving unit in early August, 1974, while Martin was moving hay. The parties did not have any agreement regarding insurance or risk of loss on the unit.

The district court found "that although the Plaintiff [Martin] executed the title to the . . . [haymoving unit], he did not relinquish possession of the same and therefore the Plaintiff was the owner of said truck at the time the fire occurred."

The position that the Code has taken, divorcing the question of risk of loss from a determination of title, is summed up by Professor Nordstrom in his hornbook on sales:

> "No longer is the question of title of any importance in determining whether a buyer or a seller bears the risk of loss. It is true that the person with title will also (and incidentally) often bear the risk that the goods may be destroyed or lost; but the seller may have title and the buyer the risk, or the seller may have the risk and the buyer the title. In short, title is not a relevant consideration in deciding whether the risk has shifted to the buyer." R. Nordstrom, Handbook of the Law of Sales, 393 (1970).

It is clear that a barter or trade-in is considered a sale and is therefore subject to the Uniform Commercial Code. It is also clear that the party who owns the trade-in is considered the seller. Subsection 3 of Section 2-509 is applicable in this case.

Martin admits that he is not a merchant; therefore, it is necessary to determine if Martin tendered delivery of the trade-in unit to Melland's. Tender is defined in section 2-503 UCC, as follows:

> (2-503) Manner of seller's tender of delivery.—
> 1. Tender of delivery requires that the seller put and hold conforming goods at the buyer's disposition and give the buyer any notification reasonably

necessary to enable him to take delivery. The manner, time and place for tender are determined by the agreement and this chapter, and in particular

    a. tender must be at a reasonable hour, and if it is of goods they must be kept available for the period reasonably necessary to enable the buyer to take possession; but

    b. unless otherwise agreed the buyer must furnish facilities reasonably suited to the receipt of the goods.

It is clear that the trade-in unit was not tendered to Melland's in this case. The parties agreed that Martin would keep the old unit "until they had the new one ready."

    We hold that Martin did not tender delivery of the trade-in truck and haystack mover to Melland's pursuant to section 2-509 UCC; consequently, Martin must bear the loss.

    We affirm the district court judgment.

Risk of Loss When Contract Is Breached

Section 2-510 addresses the problem of risk of loss when there has been a breach of contract by either the seller or the buyer. If for any reason the goods delivered by the seller fail to live up to the requirements of the contract, the risk of loss does not pass to the buyer.

Breach by Seller-Buyer Rejects. Section 2-510(1) covers the situation where the seller tenders or delivers goods not conforming to the contract under circumstances that give the buyer the right to reject (refuse to accept) the goods. In this case, the risk of loss remains on the seller until the buyer accepts the goods or the seller replaces the nonconforming goods with conforming goods (referred to as a "cure" by the seller).

Suppose a seller ships paper goods to the buyer. Because the goods fail to meet the standards set forth in the contract, the buyer rejects the goods. Buyer holds the goods, and while in his possession they are destroyed by fire. In this case, seller bears the risk of loss. What if the buyer accepts the paper in spite of its nonconformity? The risk of loss is then on the buyer. Likewise, if the seller takes back the nonconforming paper and substitutes conforming paper, and then the paper is destroyed, the risk of loss is on the buyer since the seller has "cured" his or her defective performance.

Breach by Seller-Buyer Revokes. Section 2-510(2) sets forth the buyer's rights when he or she revokes an acceptance. When the buyer rightfully revokes an acceptance, the risk of loss is treated as having remained on the seller from the beginning, to the extent of any deficiency in the buyer's insurance.

Suppose a seller ships groceries, which the buyer accepts. Thereafter, the buyer finds some defect in the groceries that gives him or her grounds to revoke the acceptance. When the buyer revokes his or her acceptance, the risk of loss is treated as having been on the seller from the beginning. If the goods are destroyed while in the buyer's possession, after the buyer's revocation, the loss falls on the seller entirely if the buyer has no insurance. What if the buyer has $500 worth of insurance, but the fire destroys $2,000 worth of groceries? $500 of the loss falls on the buyer's insurance company, and the other $1,500 falls on the seller. We are assuming in these examples that the goods are destroyed through no fault of the buyer or the seller—in a fire, for example.

Breach by Buyer. The final subsection of 2-510 puts the risk of loss on the buyer when he or she breaches the contract before the risk of loss passes to the buyer. In this case, the seller may, to the extent of any deficiency in his or her insurance coverage, treat the risk of loss as resting on the buyer for a commercially reasonable time. The seller must meet several conditions to put the loss on the buyer:

1. The seller must have had conforming goods
2. The goods must have been identified to the contract
3. The buyer must have breached the contract before the loss passed to the buyer
4. The loss must not have been covered, at least in part, by the seller's insurance
5. The loss must have occurred within a commercially reasonable time

Suppose on June 1 the parties enter into a contract for a delivery scheduled for June 15. On June 10, the seller segregates conforming goods and identifies them to the contract. Normally, the risk of loss remains on a merchant-seller, assuming the buyer plans to pick up the goods at the seller's place of business, until he delivers the goods to the buyer (subsection 2-509[3]). On June 12, the buyer repudiates the contract. On June 14, the goods are destroyed while in possession of the seller. If the seller has no insurance, the whole loss falls on the buyer. What if the seller keeps the goods in storage until March of the next year, at which time they are destroyed? The buyer might argue that the loss did not occur within a commercially reasonable time. Such an argument probably would be successful.

In the following case a buyer breached the contract, and the goods were destroyed by fire.

Multiplastics, Inc. v. Arch Industries, Inc.

Supreme Court of Connecticut
328 A.2d 618 (1974)

The plaintiff, Multiplastics, brought an action against Arch to recover for breach of a contract to purchase 40,000 pounds of pellets. The lower court ruled for plaintiff. The Connecticut Supreme Court affirmed the ruling for plaintiff based on Section 2-510(3).

Bogdanski, J.

The facts may be summarized as follows: The plaintiff, a manufacturer of plastic resin pellets, agreed with the defendant on June 30, 1971, to manufacture and deliver 40,000 pounds of brown polystyrene plastic pellets for nineteen cents a pound. The pellets were specially made for the defendant, who agreed to accept delivery at the rate of 1,000 pounds per day after completion of production. The defendant's confirming order contained the notation "make and hold for release. Confirmation." The plaintiff produced the order of pellets within two weeks and requested release orders from the defendant. The defendant refused to issue the release orders, citing labor difficulties and its vacation schedule. On August 18, 1971, the plaintiff sent the defendant the following letter: "Against P.O. 0946, we produced 40,000 lbs of brown high impact styrene, and you have issued no releases. You indicated to us that you would be using 1,000 lbs. of each per day. We have warehoused these products for more than forty days, as we agreed to do. However, we cannot warehouse these products indefinitely, and request that you send us shipping instructions. We have done everything we agreed to do."

On September 22, 1971, the plaintiff's plant, containing the pellets manufactured for the defendant, was destroyed by fire. The plaintiff's fire insurance did not cover the loss of the pellets. The plaintiff brought this action against the defendant to recover the contract price.

The trial court concluded that the plaintiff made a valid tender of delivery by its letter of August 18, 1971, and by its subsequent requests for delivery instructions; that the defendant repudiated and breached the contract by refusing to accept delivery on August 20, 1971; that the period from August 20, 1971, to September 22, 1971, was not a commercially unreasonable time for the plaintiff to treat the risk of loss as resting on the defendant under section 2-510(3); and that the plaintiff was entitled to recover the contract price plus interest.

The defendant contends that section 2-510 is not applicable because its failure to issue delivery instructions did not constitute either a repudiation or a breach of the agreement. The defendant also argues that even if section 2-510 were applicable, the period from August 20, 1971, to September 22, 1971, was not a commercially reasonable period of time within which to treat the risk of loss as resting on the buyer.

The trial court's conclusion that the defendant was in breach is supported by its finding that the defendant agreed to accept delivery of the pellets at the rate of 1,000 pounds per day after completion of production. The defendant argues that since the confirming order instructed the defendant to "make and hold for release," the contract did not specify an exact delivery date. This argument fails, however, because nothing in the finding suggests that the notation in the confirming order was part of the agreement between the parties. Since, as the trial court found, the plaintiff made a proper tender of delivery, beginning with its letter of August 18, 1971, the plaintiff was entitled to acceptance of the goods and to payment according to the contract.

The remaining question is whether, under section 2-510(3), the period of time from August 20, 1971, the date of the breach, to September 22, 1971, the date of the fire, was a "commercially reasonable" period within which to treat the risk of loss as resting on the buyer. The trial court concluded that it was "not, on the facts of this case, a commercially unreasonable time," which we take to mean that it was a commercially reasonable period. The time limitation in section 2-510(3) is designed to enable the seller to obtain the additional requisite insurance coverage. The trial court's conclusion is tested by the finding. Although the finding is not detailed, it supports the conclusion that August 20 to September 22 was a commercially reasonable period within which to place the risk of loss on the defendant. As already stated, the trial court found that the defendant repeatedly agreed to transmit delivery instructions and that the pellets were specially made to fill the defendant's order. Under those circumstances, it was reasonable for the plaintiff to believe that the goods would soon be taken off its hands and so to forego procuring the needed insurance.

There is no error.

Sale or Return and Sale on Approval

Section 2-326(1) states that if goods are delivered primarily for use and may be returned by the buyer to the seller even though they conform to the contract, the transaction is a *sale on approval*. If the goods are delivered to a buyer who is entitled to return conforming goods and the buyer intends to resell the goods, the transaction is a *sale or return*. In order to determine whether conforming goods that may be returned to the seller have been sold on sale-or-return or sale-on-approval terms, the court must examine whether the buyer intended to use the goods or to resell them.

When goods are purchased on sale on approval, the buyer may wish to try out the goods before accepting them. If he uses the goods in order to try them out, this does not constitute acceptance. The risk of loss and title remain with the seller until the buyer accepts the goods. Acceptance can occur automatically if the buyer fails to notify the seller of his election to return the goods within a reasonable time. Acceptance of any part of the goods is acceptance of the whole—if the goods conform to the contract. If the buyer elects to return the goods, the return is at the seller's risk and expense. If the buyer is a merchant, he must follow any instructions provided by the seller.

Under sale-or-return terms, the buyer can return all or part of the goods shipped to him as long as they are substantially in their original condition. The buyer, however, must elect to return them within a reasonable time, and he or she must return them at his or her own risk and expense.

INSURABLE INTEREST

The UCC, in Section 2-501, specifies who has an insurable interest in goods. The buyer obtains an insurable interest in existing goods as soon as they are identified to the contract. The buyer obtains an insurable interest even though the goods identified are nonconforming.

However, if the contract is for the sale of future goods, that is, goods that are not yet in existence and identified, the buyer obtains an insurable interest in the future goods when they are shipped, mailed, or otherwise designated by the seller as goods to which the contract refers.

The seller has an insurable interest in goods so long as he has title to the goods or any security interest in the goods.

BULK TRANSFERS

Article 6 of the UCC covers bulk transfers. Section 6-102 defines these as "any transfer in bulk and not in the ordinary course of the transferor's business of a major part of the materials, supplies, merchandise or other inventory . . . of an enterprise." Where a substantial part of the equipment of an enterprise is transferred, it will be a bulk transfer only if it is made in connection with a bulk transfer of inventory.

All businesses whose principal business is the sale of merchandise from stock, including businesses who manufacture what they sell, are covered by Article 6. The purpose of Article 6 is to prevent a fraud on the creditors of a going business. Creditors may extend credit to a business based on its inventory. Article 6 prevents a merchant from selling his inventory all at once without taking care of his creditors.

Requirements

Inventory may be sold in bulk without violating Article 6 if the merchant adheres strictly to the provisions of the article. A bulk transfer will not be effective against any creditor of the transferor unless:

1. The buyer obtains a list of the seller's creditors
2. The parties prepare a schedule of the property to be transferred
3. The schedule of property and list of creditors are preserved for six months following the transfer and are made available to any creditor of the transferor
4. The seller signs and swears to the list of his or her creditors.

Section 6-104(3) makes the seller responsible for the completeness and accuracy of the list of the creditors. The transfer is not rendered improper because of errors and omissions unless the buyer knew of these errors or omissions.

Notice

The buyer must notify all creditors on the list of the bulk transfer or the transfer will be ineffective against those creditors not receiving notice of it. This notice must be given at least ten days before the buyer takes possession of the goods or pays for them, whichever happens first. The purchaser does not need to provide notice of the transfer when the sale is by auction. This responsibility is transferred by Section 6-108 to the auctioneer. Some states have adopted optional Section 6-106, which specifies that the proceeds of the sale are to be applied to the debts of the seller. Other states merely require notice to the creditors.

Failure to Comply

If the buyer fails to comply with the provisions of Article 6, the transfer of goods to him is ineffective. In other words, the creditors of the seller can reach these goods even though the buyer has paid for them. If the buyer in turn sells these goods to a bona fide purchaser for value, however, this cuts off the power of the creditors to reach the goods. Section 6-111 gives the creditors of the seller six months after the date on which the transferee took possession of the goods to take action (unless the parties concealed the transfer).

REVIEW PROBLEMS

1. Weaver's contracts with Casual Slacks for the sale of teenage clothing, the order calling for delivery during "June–August." The shipment is made in August and is incomplete. Weaver's refuses to pay the full invoice price, since the shipment is received so late as to miss the major part of the preschool marketing period, making it necessary to mark the clothing from one-third to one-half off the usual retail price in order to sell it. Weaver's contends that the use of the term "June–August" has a trade meaning of delivery of a substantial portion of the goods in June, a similar delivery in July, and the balance in August. Casual Slacks, on the other hand, contends that use of the terminology "June–August" is unambiguous and means that delivery may be made at any time during the period from June 1 to August 31. Weaver's introduces parol evidence of the meaning in their trade of "June–August" at trial.

   Does the term "June–August" have a meaning given it by usage in the trade so as to explain or supplement the express terms of the written agreement, and is this testimony admissible? See Weaver's Kiddy Shoppe, Inc. v. Casual Slacks, Inc., 171 S.E. 2d 643 (Ga. App. 1969).

2. In April 1973, Val, a con artist, borrows a $25,000 Utrillo painting from Porter to hang in his town house pending a decision whether to buy it. At this time, Porter does not know that Val is a dealer. While the

Utrillo is in his possession, Val sells it to a gallery. After two subsequent sales, the painting ends up in South America. Porter now sues everyone who has possessed or purchased the painting. Does Section 2-403(2) apply? See Porter v. Werty, 23 UCC Rep 614 (N.Y. Sp. Ct. 1978)

3. Detwiller purchases a new truck from Stevens Dodge. The truck is then shipped to Bob, a dealer closer to Detwiller's home town, for pick-up. After Detwiller pays Stevens Dodge, documents of title are sent to Detwiller. Prior to the receipt thereof, the truck is destroyed by fire while sitting on Bob's lot. Detwiller and Stevens Dodge have no agreement regarding the risk of loss. Where does the risk of loss lie? Detwiller v. Stevens Dodge, 16 UCC Rep 404 (N.Y. Civ. Ct. Queens County 1975).

4. Eberhard agrees to sell and ship certain goods to Brown. The contract does not contain any F.O.B. term, nor is there any agreement on who bears the risk of loss. Certain goods are placed on board a common carrier by Eberhard but are apparently lost in transit. Eberhard now sues Brown for the price of the goods. Brown contends that the risk of loss remains with Eberhard. Is Brown's contention correct? See Eberhard Manufacturing Co. v. Brown, 232 N.W.2d 378 (Mich. 1975).

Suppose that the same facts are involved but a delivery contract has been executed requiring the goods to be delivered to a particular destination. Does this make any difference?

5. White delivers a truck to Bronx pursuant to a purchase agreement. After delivery, but before White assigns title to Bronx, the truck is stolen. Bronx contends that since it did not have a proper title to the truck, the risk of loss is on White. Is Bronx correct? See White Motor Corp. v. Bronx-Westchester White Trucks, Inc., 18 UCC Rep 382 (N.Y. Supreme Court 1975)

6. Dravo and Key enter into an oral contract for Key to sell to Dravo up to 143,000 pounds of two-inch or smaller steel punchings. No price is specified. Key provides part of the goods under the contract but Dravo refuses to pay. Dravo now contends that the contract is invalid for lack of a specified price term. Who wins? See Dravo Corp. v. Key Bellarilles, Inc., 22 UCC Rep. 333 (1976).

7. Harbach, a farmer, orally contracts in February with Continental to sell 25,000 bushels of soybeans at $3.81 per bushel, delivery and payment deferred until October, November, and December. There is some question about whether Continental sent Harbach a written confirmation of the contract. Harbach contends he did not receive such a confirmation. Harbach then refuses to make delivery, contending that no contract exists and, even if there is a contract, that the Statute of Frauds prevents enforcement. Further, Harbach claims that he, as a farmer, was not a merchant at the time of the transaction and therefore the merchant exception to 2-201 does not apply. At trial, evidence is admitted tending to show that Harbach has been engaged in agricultural pursuits for over twenty-five years and, in particular, has raised and sold grain, primarily corn, but including some small quantities of soybeans, on the type of contract here in issue for several years. It is known that Harbach is familiar with the operations of the grain market on which both corn and soybeans are traded. Is Harbach, who is a farmer, also a merchant? See Continental Grain Co. v. Harbach, 400 F. Supp. 695 (N.D. Ill. 1975)

8. Adrian Corporation is a creditor of Larry. Larry sells his business in bulk to Will, who later sells it to Climax. At the time of closing, Larry furnished an affidavit stating he had no creditors; Climax also made an inquiry of Larry's attorney to learn if there were any creditors and was assured that there were none. Adrian now sues to have

the sale declared ineffective, as it had received no notice of the sale as required by Sec. 6-105. Under UCC Sec. 6-104, is the sale effective against Adrian? See Adrian Taben Corporation v. Climax Boutique, Inc., 313 N.E.2d 66 (N.Y. 1974). Would the result be the same if Climax had discovered Adrian's existence as a creditor of Larry before the sale?

CHAPTER 16

Sales: Performance and Remedies

PERFORMANCE _____

ACCEPTANCE _____

REJECTION _____

REVOCATION _____

INSTALLMENT CONTRACTS _____

ASSURANCE OF PERFORMANCE _____

ANTICIPATORY REPUDIATION _____

IMPOSSIBILITY _____

REMEDIES _____

SELLER'S REMEDIES _____

BUYER'S REMEDIES _____

LIMITATION OR ALTERATION OF REMEDIES _____

T he formation and interpretation of sales contracts were discussed in the preceding chapter. This chapter focuses first on the performance obligations of the parties to a sales contract and then on the remedies available to the victim of a breached sales contract. The student should review Chapter 14, which deals with these matters in regard to contracts in general.

PERFORMANCE

The basic duty of the seller is to deliver or make available the goods purchased by the buyer. The buyer's basic responsibility is to pay for the goods purchased. The obligations of the seller and buyer are discussed in turn.

Delivery

Section 2-307 of the Uniform Commercial Code makes it the duty of the seller to transfer and deliver goods in accordance with the terms of the contract. But in what manner must the seller deliver the goods? Must he or she deliver all the goods at one time? The answer to this question is found in Section 2-307, which makes it clear that, unless the contract indicates a contrary agreement, all the goods must be delivered at one time. The buyer is entitled to reject a delivery that has been improperly delivered in lots—subject to the right of the seller to cure the improper tender.

Delivery in Lots. Sometimes, however, delivery in a single lot will not be possible. Suppose, for example, that the buyer does not have sufficient storage space to take delivery of the entire order at one time. Must the buyer take it anyway? Section 2-307 provides that "where the circumstances give either party the right to make or demand delivery in lots the price if it can be apportioned may be demanded for each lot." This language suggests that under certain circumstances the seller can deliver the goods in separate lots. For example, if the seller is unable to find enough trucks or railroad cars to deliver the goods in a single lot, delivery may be made in lots and the seller may demand payment for each lot.

Place for Delivery. The next question is: What is the proper place for delivery? Assuming that delivery by carrier is neither required nor authorized by the contract, Section 2-308 makes the proper place for delivery the seller's place of business or, if he or she has no place of business, the seller's residence. If the contract is for the sale of identified goods that are known by both parties to be at some other place, that place is the proper place for delivery of the goods. If the parties have agreed to delivery by carrier or have authorized delivery by carrier, the seller's duties with respect to delivery are governed by Sections 2-503 and 2-504.

Time for Delivery. If the time for shipment or delivery has not been agreed upon, the time for shipment or delivery is a reasonable time. What is reasonable depends on the nature, purpose, and circumstances of the action to be taken. Where a time has been left open for delivery, neither party may demand delivery or offer delivery at an unreasonably early

time. The performance requirements of destination and shipment contracts were described in Chapter 15.

Delivery of Nonconforming Goods. What happens if the seller delivers at the proper place and time, but the goods he or she delivers do not conform to the contract? Section 2-508(1) makes it clear that, although a tender or delivery has been rejected by the buyer because it is nonconforming, the buyer does not necessarily have a right to sue for breach of contract. If the time for performance has not yet expired, the seller may seasonably notify the buyer of his intention to cure and may then make a conforming delivery within the contract time. What is seasonable notice? Section 1-204(3) states: "an action is taken 'seasonably' when it is taken at or within the time agreed or if no time is agreed at or within a reasonable time." Thus, if the seller is to deliver goods on December 1, and he delivers nonconforming goods that the buyer rejects on November 1, the seller may notify the buyer of his intention to cure and deliver conforming goods anytime up through December 1. What if the seller delivers nonconforming goods on November 29 and notifies the buyer that he will attempt to cure? May he do so at that late date? Two days is probably not seasonable notice.

What if the seller sends a nonconforming tender that he or she reasonably believes will be acceptable to the buyer? If the seller did not anticipate at the time of sending the nonconforming goods that the buyer would reject them, and if the seller lacks the time to deliver conforming goods before the time for performance elapses, the seller has a "reasonable time" to substitute performance. Suppose a seller has agreed to deliver green, red, and blue swimsuits by December 1 and, because he or she has no blue suits in stock, sends yellow, green, and red suits. The buyer may be able to reject the goods as nonconforming. If the goods arrive on November 29 the seller will not have time to cure, so he or she may try to rely on Section 2-508(2) to obtain extra time to cure after the expiration of the time for performance. Reasonable grounds to believe that the buyer will accept the goods may be found in the prior course of dealing, course of performance, or usage of trade as well as in the circumstances surrounding the making of the contract. If the buyer has accepted a substitute color on swimsuits in the past, that is reasonable grounds for believing that the buyer will accept a substitute color now. The buyer may protect himself or herself by including a "no replacement" clause in the contract.

Payment

Cash or Check. Unless the parties have agreed to the contrary or the goods are sold on credit, payment is due at the time and place at which the buyer is to receive the goods (Section 2-310[a]). Tender of payment is sufficient when it is made by any means or in any manner current in the ordinary course of business unless the seller demands payment in legal tender (Section 2-511[2]). The buyer usually may pay by check, unless the seller demands cash. If the seller demands cash, he or she must give the buyer a reasonable time to obtain the cash. The purpose of giving the buyer additional time to collect the cash is to prevent the buyer from being unprepared at the time for payment because he or she planned to pay by check or some other instrument. This provision prevents the seller from treating the buyer's inability to pay in cash at the time for payment as a breach of contract. In the event the seller accepts the buyer's check, the payment is conditional on the check being paid by the bank when it is presented for payment (Section 2-511[3]). If the bank dishonors the check, the buyer still must pay for the goods.

Right to Inspect. The buyer generally has a right before payment or acceptance to inspect the goods at any reasonable place and time and in any reasonable manner, unless the contract provides for delivery C.O.D. or for payment against documents of title. If the seller ships C.O.D., the buyer must pay for the goods even if they do not conform to the contract unless the nonconformity appears without inspection (Section 2-512[1]). However, the buyer will have other remedies, discussed later, if the goods are nonconforming. Although the buyer must pay under these circumstances before he or she inspects the goods, the buyer still retains the right to inspect the goods after payment. The buyer is not considered to have accepted the goods until he or she has had a reasonable opportunity to inspect them. Whether the buyer has accepted or not affects the type of remedies that are available to him or her.

In the event the buyer chooses to inspect the goods, the buyer must bear the cost of inspection unless he or she discovers that the goods do not conform to the contract, in which case he or she may recover expenses from the seller if he or she rejects the goods.

Where the parties have specified a particular place or method of inspection, that place or method will be presumed to be the exclusive one. If compliance becomes impossible, the buyer can inspect the goods at any reasonable time and place and in any reasonable manner, unless the place or method fixed for inspection was clearly intended as an indispensable condition, in which case the contract fails.

Delivery by Documents of Title. If delivery is authorized and made by means of documents of title, other than as specified in Section 2-310(b), payment is due at the time and place at which the buyer is to receive the documents, regardless of where the goods are to be received. The buyer must pay for the goods when he or she is tendered the appropriate documents. He or she still retains the right to inspect the goods. No acceptance occurs until the buyer has had the opportunity to inspect them. Thus if a buyer purchased the goods C.O.D. and receives the proper documents, he or she must pay for the goods even though they are still in transit. When the goods arrive, he or she may then inspect them and exercise the right to accept or reject.

Suppose a seller in Illinois ships goods to a buyer in California. The seller receives a bearer-negotiable bill of lading from the shipper. This document permits the person in possession of it to pick up the goods from the carrier. The seller gives this bill of lading to his or her bank, which in turn transfers the document to a California bank for collection. The California bank calls in the buyer, receives payment from him or her, and releases the bill of lading to the buyer. The bank then transfers the money back to the seller's bank. The buyer may now pick up the goods from the carrier when they arrive in California. If he or she inspects the goods and finds that they do not conform to the contract, the buyer may at that point reject the goods—even though the buyer has already paid for them—and demand any money paid to the seller.

ACCEPTANCE

Acceptance may occur in one of three ways under Section 2-606 of the UCC. Acceptance is unrelated to the question of who has title to the goods, which is governed by Section 2-401.

Express Statement of Acceptance

The buyer accepts the goods if, after a reasonable opportunity to inspect them, he or she indicates that the goods are conforming or that he or she will take the goods even if they are not conforming. Suppose a buyer orders 100 blue and red swimsuits. If the seller delivers 100 blue and green swimsuits, the buyer, after inspecting them, accepts the goods by indicating that he or she will take them even though they are not blue and red. Bear in

mind that because this delivery was not conforming, the buyer could have rejected the swimsuits.

Inaction

An acceptance may also occur as a result of inaction by the buyer, that is, by the buyer's failure to effectively reject the goods after he or she has had a reasonable opportunity to inspect them. Suppose the blue and green swimsuits arrive on January 1 but, rather than opening the box immediately to inspect the goods, the buyer puts the box in the storeroom. The buyer could have inspected the goods on January 1, determined that they were not conforming, and rejected them. On April 15, the buyer opens the box. The buyer now wants to reject the suits. Because of the buyer's inaction, however, it may be too late to reject them.

Act Inconsistent with Seller's Ownership

The third method of acceptance is the buyer's commission of any act that is inconsistent with the seller's ownership. Suppose the buyer receives the blue and green swimsuits, puts them on the shelves in the store, and sells a number to the public. Selling the suits amounts to an act inconsistent with the seller's ownership.

Knowledge of Defects. In considering Section 2-606(1), which provides that a buyer has accepted when he or she has done "any act inconsistent with the seller's ownership," the courts should distinguish cases where the buyer knows of a defect from those where he or she is unaware of it. In the example in the preceding paragraph, the buyer knew the goods were nonconforming, made no attempt to reject them, and sold them to third parties. This is an act inconsistent with the seller's ownership. The same would be true if the seller attempted to reject the suits but then sold them to third persons.

Sometimes it is impossible for the buyer to avoid using the product even after rejecting it. Suppose a homeowner purchases a wall-to-wall carpet that is glued to the floor. In this situation, the homeowner may call the seller, reject the carpet, and continue to use it.

A more difficult case is the continued use of a car or mobile home after a rejection. Whether the continued use constitutes acceptance under 2-606(1)(c) is not easy for the courts to resolve. In general, it is dangerous to use the goods after a rejection because a court may construe this as an acceptance. This matter is discussed later in this chapter.

Another difficult situation arises when the buyer uses the goods prior to rejecting them although the buyer is aware of a defect. If the buyer and the seller are attempting to straighten the problem out, and this is why the buyer has delayed rejecting the goods, the use of the product at this time should not be regarded as an acceptance. The policy of the UCC is to encourage parties to work out their differences.

Similarly, the buyer's use of a product while unaware of a defect should not constitute an acceptance under 2-606(1)(c). Suppose our buyer purchases a car, drives it two days, and then the transmission fails. One could argue that the UCC gives the buyer the right to inspect goods and a reasonable time to reject them. Therefore, use of the car for two days, prior to learning of the defect, should not constitute an acceptance.

The following case illustrates what happens to a buyer who performs an act inconsistent with the seller's ownership.

Pettibone Minnesota Corp. v. Castle

Supreme Court of Minnesota
247 N.W.2d 52 (1976)

Defendant, Castle, purchased a piece of machinery from the plaintiff, Pettibone Minnesota Corporation. The defendant originally ordered an 880 Crusher, but the plaintiff substituted a Pitmaster Crusher. The trial court found the defendant accepted the Pitmaster Crusher, and was liable for the purchase price because he did an act inconsistent with the seller's ownership. The appeals court affirmed the decision of the trial court for the plaintiff.

Per Curiam

This action was brought to recover the purchase price of machine used in processing gravel, namely, an 880 Crusher and washing plant. Defendant counterclaimed for damages claiming the breach of the contract to deliver the 880 Crusher. In the course of transaction between the parties, defendant accepted delivery by plaintiff of a crusher known as a Pitmaster Crusher in the fall of 1969. There was a sharp conflict in the evidence whether the Pitmaster Crusher was accepted by the defendant on a temporary basis until the 880 Crusher was reconditioned, or whether as contended by plaintiff the Pitmaster Crusher was substituted for the 880 Crusher and purchased by defendant.

The trial court found that defendant has failed to prove the allegations of the counterclaim.

We find that the trial court was correct in determining that the parties by agreement substituted the Pitmaster Crusher for the 880 Crusher originally involved in the transaction. Defendant's counterclaim was accordingly properly dismissed, as there was no breach of a contract by plaintiff to sell the 880 Crusher to defendant.

The evidence supporting that the Pitmaster Crusher was substituted for the 880 Crusher is as follows: (1) Defendant signed a purchase order for the Pitmaster Crusher, (2) defendant never attempted to return the Pitmaster Crusher, (3) defendant insured the crusher and the washing plant and named the plaintiff as the mortgagee, and (4) defendant sold the Pitmaster Crusher and washing machine to third parties.

The admitted and unexplained retention of the machinery and subsequent sale thereof by defendant of the machine to others was an act ". . . inconsistent with the seller's ownership." The evidence justifies the finding that the defendant purchased from plaintiff the machine involved.

Affirmed.

Notice of Rejection. Assuming the buyer wants to reject a nonconforming delivery of goods, he or she must notify the seller and specify the grounds for rejection, thereby giving the seller a chance to deliver conforming goods. Should the buyer accept nonconforming goods, the buyer retains the right to sue for damages.

Suppose that Acme Lawn Equipment sends a lawn-sprinkler system on March 1 to Johnson's Lawn Supply. When the sprinkler system arrives, Johnson determines that the system fails to conform to the contract description. Johnson must reject the goods within a reasonable time after he receives them, and he must notify Acme within a reasonable time that he has done so. Suppose he receives the sprinkler system on March 5. If Johnson sends a letter to Acme on March 10 rejecting the system and specifying his reasons, he has probably complied with the requirements of Section 2-602. Since Johnson is a merchant, he must follow any instructions he receives from Acme with respect to the sprinkler system. After rejecting the goods, Johnson must be careful not to take any action inconsistent with Acme's ownership, such as selling the sprinkler to a customer. If Johnson sells the sprinkler, the courts would find he has accepted the sprinkler, even though he rejected it earlier.

Commercial Units. If the buyer chooses to accept part of a commercial unit, he or she must accept the entire unit (Section 2-606). However, the buyer does not need to accept goods that do not conform to the contract. Section 2-601 gives him or her three options if the seller tenders delivery of nonconforming goods: the buyer may (1) reject all the goods; (2) accept all the goods; or (3) accept any commercial unit or units and reject the rest. Commercial unit is defined in Section 2-105(b) as:

"Commercial unit" means such a unit of goods as by commercial usage is a single whole for purposes of sale and division of which materially impairs its character or value on the market or in use. A commercial unit may be a single article (as a machine) or a set of articles (as a suite of furniture or an assortment of sizes) or a quantity (as a bale, gross, or carload) or any other unit treated in use or in the relevant market as a single whole.

Thus, if the seller delivers 200 pairs of men's shoes, when the buyer ordered 100 pairs of men's shoes and 100 pairs of women's shoes, the buyer can accept all 200 pairs of shoes, reject the 100 pairs of women's shoes and accept the 100 pairs of men's shoes, or reject all the shoes. If the buyer elects to accept the 100 pairs of men's shoes, a commercial unit, he or she must pay at the contract rate for the shoes accepted. Section 2-717 allows the buyer to recover from the seller for the breach of contract or, as an alternative, to deduct damages from the purchase price.

REJECTION

Perfect-Tender Rule

Section 2-601 of the UCC gives the buyer of goods who has received an improper delivery the right to reject the goods "if the goods or the tender of delivery fail in any respect to conform to the contract." This is called the "perfect tender" rule. It does not apply to installment contracts, which are discussed later in this chapter, and it is limited by the seller's "right to cure."

As a practical matter, the perfect-tender rule is not very significant because of the manner in which the courts interpret Section 2-601. A buyer will be able to reject goods, as a practical matter, only where the goods or tender fail in a substantial respect to conform to the contract. Trivial defects in the tender will not give the buyer a right to reject.

To Reject

As indicated earlier, failure to make an effective rejection may constitute an acceptance. To make certain that a buyer does not unintentionally accept goods, he or she must follow the provisions of Section 2-602. The goods delivered must have been nonconforming and the seller must have failed to "cure" the nonconformity. (Cure was discussed earlier in this chapter.) The buyer must then: (1) reject the goods within a reasonable time after their delivery or tender; and (2) seasonably notify the seller of the rejection.

Timing of Notice. Actions are taken seasonably if they are taken at or within the time agreed or, if no time is agreed, within a reasonable time (Section 1-204[3]). If the buyer acts too slowly in rejecting the goods, he or she will be deemed to have accepted them. In order to determine whether the buyer acted within a reasonable time, the court will consider the surrounding circumstances.

Duties after Rejection. Once the buyer has given the requisite notice of rejection within a reasonable time, he or she must take care not to give the appearance of exercising ownership over the goods. If the goods are in the possession of a buyer who is not a merchant, his or her only duty is to hold them with reasonable care for a sufficient time for the seller to take possession.

If the buyer is a merchant, his or her duties with respect to rejected goods are set out in Section 2-603. If the seller has no agent or place of business at the market of rejection, the merchant-buyer who has the goods in his or her possession or control must follow any reasonable instructions received from the seller with respect to the goods.

In the absence of such instructions, the merchant-buyer must make reasonable efforts to resell the goods for the seller if they are perishable or threaten to decline in value speedily. If the seller chooses to resell the goods, he or she must act in good faith. The buyer is entitled to reimbursement from the seller for caring for and selling the goods, or he or she may deduct expenses from the proceeds of the sale.

A buyer in possession or control of nonperishable goods or goods that will not decline rapidly in value has several options if the seller fails to give instructions within a reasonable time after he or she learns of the buyer's rejection. The buyer may: (1) store the goods; (2) reship them to the seller; or (3) resell the goods at the seller's expense (Section 2-604).

State the Defect. It is not sufficient for the buyer merely to tell the seller that he or she rejects the goods. To be safe, the buyer must specifically state the particular defect on which he or she is basing the rejection to give the seller an opportunity to cure it. If he or she rejects the goods and fails to specify the defect, and the defect is of a nature that the seller could have cured, the buyer cannot rely on this unstated defect as a basis for rejection or to establish a breach of contract.

It is not necessary that the buyer be absolutely precise—a quick informal notice of the defects will suffice. Section 2-605(1)(b) says that a buyer must state the particular defect if both the buyer and the seller are merchants and if the seller has made a written request for a full and final written statement of all defects on which the buyer proposes to rely as justification for a rejection of the goods. If the buyer fails to list certain defects in the written statement, he or she cannot rely on these defects as grounds for rejection in a subsequent trial.

Once the buyer has accepted goods, he or she has lost the right to reject them. Whether the goods have been rejected or whether an acceptance has been revoked is important in establishing the remedies available to the buyer.

The following case discusses the question of whether a buyer who has purchased a defective mobile home may reject it after a substantial amount of time has passed and the buyer has moved it.

seller

Jones v. Abriani

Court of Appeals of Indiana
350 N.E.2d 635 (1976)

This suit arose as the result of the sale of a defective mobile home by the defendants, the Joneses, who were doing business as Jonesy's Mobile Home Sales, to the plaintiffs, the Abrianis. The lower court rendered a judgment for the plaintiffs. The defendants appealed, claiming that the judge's decision was in error. The appeals court affirmed the judgment for the plaintiffs.

Lowdermilk, Judge

An examination of the facts, viewed in the light most favorable to the trial court's judgment, reveals the following. Richard and Jayanne began shopping for a mobile home in the spring of 1971 just prior to their marriage. They viewed several models on various occasions in the Terre Haute and Indianapolis areas, and finally settled on the Spanish style Eagle mobile home that was on display at Jonesy's Mobile Home Sales because "it was fancier than most we had seen, and . . . looked to be better constructed than most we looked at for the price." Since a new mobile home could be purchased for the same price as the model home they had viewed, they decided to order a new home rather than purchasing the display unit. The new home was to be identical with the model home but for a few optional accessories and different colored sinks and carpeting.

A contract to purchase was signed by Richard. Jayanne had quickly scanned the document, but Richard himself did not read the contract, later saying "I was young, you know how everybody starts off young and I figured we could at least trust the Jones' or somebody that would watch out for us." A down payment of $1,000 was made, and the mobile home was ordered by the sellers from the manufacturer in Alabama.

When the home arrived, the Abriani's inspected the home, but were disappointed in what they found. The carpet was a different color than the one ordered, a sink was chipped, a curtain was missing, a shutter was missing, the floor plan was different from what had been ordered, the bathrooms did not have double sinks, and in general, the quality of the construction and furnishings was substantially below what they had expected. They immediately contacted Mrs. Jones to tell her that they did not want the home in that condition. She informed them that if they did not take the mobile home they would lose their down payment.

Inasmuch as the Abriani's could not afford to lose the $1,000, they decided that they had no choice but to take the mobile home on condition that the sellers would take care of their problems. Sellers installed the mobile home on a lot owned by sellers and rented to the Abriani's.

Over the next year, complaints were made to the sellers every time the rent was paid about the different problems that arose in the mobile home. Sellers eventually replaced the chipped sink, supplied the missing shutter, and connected the dryer vent free of charge. A missing curtain in the bedroom was ordered, but a correct match could not be found, so a whole new set of curtains was sent almost a year later. Although these curtains were the wrong size, the Abriani's were tired of complaining and made no further mention of the problem. Similar difficulty was experienced in gaining delivery of six missing or damaged screens, and only four were eventually received.

About four months after delivery of the home, Jayanne called Mrs. Jones to complain about a leak in the roof. Mrs. Jones informed her that the roof had to be sealed every two years, and Jayanne responded that they had only had the home for a few months, and that it should not need that kind of maintenance so soon. Mrs. Jones refused to fix the leak unless the Abriani's paid for the service. In the same call, Jayanne listed once again all of the other uncorrected problems that they had found in the home after living there for several months. They discovered that the doors were all crooked and would not shut properly. Further, the carpeting was literally falling apart and had several bald spots and a large cut. The chair was broken inside, causing the upholstery to tear. The bathtubs both leaked. All of the cabinet doors were out of alignment. The holes had been cut too large for most of the light switches. The paneling was starting to fall off, the molding was popping off, the ceiling was being damaged by the leak, there was a gas leak in the furnace, and the hot water heater element went out. There was trouble with the wiring, and a fuse was blown at least once a month. No attempt was made to remedy any of these defects.

About a year later, and after the continual assurances of repairs failed to materialize, the Abriani's wrote the Attorney General seeking help in the matter. They listed all of their complaints, including these additional problems: the bedroom windows would not raise; the window frames seemed to be out of alignment; the sliding doors on the bathtub would not fold correctly; there were no filters with the furnace; the legs on the end tables and coffee table wobbled and were about to fall off; the upholstery on the furniture was all wearing out; both mattresses were cheap and had broken springs; everytime the carpet was vacuumed the sweeper bag filled up with lint.

The only response to the letter that the Abriani's received was a printed warranty card from the manufacturer that provided that the warranty registration had to be returned within five days of purchase in order for the ninety-day warranty to be effective. Jayanne had earlier told Mrs. Jones that they had never received any information about the warranty. Since both time limits on the warranty card had long since passed, the Abriani's turned to legal counsel, and this action resulted soon thereafter.

Shortly after the Abriani's sent their letter to the Attorney General, they decided to move their home to a different lot in case any trouble arose because of the letter. At this time, the moving company pointed out a dent or bow in the A-frame hitch of the home. There was also testimony that one front panel of aluminum siding on the home "looked like it had been repaired and had buckled all up." They also discovered that the aluminum roof panel had large "wrinkles" or bulges in it, although the exact location of the leak could not be determined. . . .

We first point out that valid grounds for rejection of the mobile home existed in this case under §2–601, the Perfect Tender Rule, which provides that "if goods or the tender of delivery fail in any respect to conform to the contract, the buyer may (a) reject the whole . . . ." While tender does not necessarily have to be "perfect," the mobile home in this case clearly failed to meet the contract requirements. The seller did have a right to cure minor defects after proper notice according to the terms of §2–508, but the evidence demonstrates that no such cure was ever forthcoming within the contemplated time of performance, or at any time. . . .

Sellers also contend that the goods were in substantial compliance with the contract, except for the carpeting on which the manufacturer had retained an option to substitute different carpeting under the following clause:

> "The manufacturer has the right to make any changes in the model or the designs or any accessories and parts of any subsequent new trailer or mobile home, at any time, without creating an obligation on the part of either the dealer or the manufacturer to make corresponding changes in the trailer or mobile home described and covered by this order either before, or subsequent to, delivery of such equipment to the purchaser."

The clear import of this provision is that the manufacturer is under no duty to provide any accessory or part other than those contained within the original contract agreement. Thus, if an improvement was made in the design of a particular mobile home model, the manufacturer is under no duty to include such new design or improvement on a mobile home that had already been contracted for on the basis of the older design. There is nothing in the clause to suggest that inferior materials may be substituted at the option of the manufacturer after an agreement on the subject matter of the contract has already been reached. Further, it is clear from the facts set out above that there were other substantial defects in the home and variances from the contract terms that would amount to imperfect tender.

We hold that the evidence was sufficient to sustain a finding that a valid rejection was made by the Abriani's and that the sellers' threats to withhold the down payment were not justified under the law.

REVOCATION

As indicated in the section on rejection, once a buyer has accepted goods, he or she has lost the right to reject them. However, it still may be possible for the buyer to revoke his or her acceptance and compel the seller to take the goods back.

A buyer cannot revoke unless he or she meets one of three conditions listed in Section 2–608:

1. The buyer knew of the defect but accepted because he or she reasonably believed the nonconformity would be cured and it was not seasonably cured
2. The buyer did not discover the defect prior to his or her acceptance because the defect was difficult to discover
3. The buyer did not discover the defect prior to his or her acceptance because the seller assured the buyer there were no defects

If any of these three conditions applies, and the nonconformity substantially impairs the value of the goods to the buyer, the buyer may revoke the acceptance. The question is not whether the seller realized at the time of contracting that the nonconformity would substantially impair the value of the goods to the buyer, but whether the nonconformity in fact caused a substantial impairment of value to the buyer even though the seller did not know of the buyer's particular circumstances. Revocation is available only under these circumstances.

Reasonable Time

For the revocation of acceptance to be effective, it must occur within a reasonable time after the buyer discovers or should have discovered grounds for revocation. The buyer must act within a reasonable time to give the seller a chance to cure and to help minimize the buyer's losses. There are many cases dealing with whether the buyer's actions were taken within a reasonable time.

Substantial Change

The revocation must occur before any substantial change in the condition of the goods that is not caused by their own defects. This means that if the buyer does something to the goods to change them from their original condition, and he or she is unable to restore them to their original condition, an acceptance cannot be revoked. On the other hand, if the materials (perishable, for example) changed in condition due to their own defects, the buyer still can revoke his acceptance. In any event, a revocation of acceptance is not effective until the buyer notifies the seller of the defect.

Suppose Mrs. Smith purchased a trailer home from the Lemon Corporation. When she received the trailer on February 15, she inspected it. The carpet in the trailer was missing. When she inquired about the missing carpet, the seller told her he would see that she received a carpet at once. Mrs. Smith moved into the trailer. During the next six weeks Mrs. Smith called the seller several times about the carpet, and each time the seller assured her that he would deliver the carpet. On April 10, she sent a letter to the seller revoking her acceptance because of the failure to supply the carpet. She locked the trailer, turned the keys over to Lemon, and moved out on April 10. This revocation will probably be effective because she accepted the trailer only because the seller assured her that the nonconformity (the absence of carpet) would be cured, it was not cured within a reasonable time, and the absence of the carpet substantially impaired the value of the trailer to her. What if Mrs. Smith did not move out on April 10 but continued to occupy the trailer until December 1, at which time she attempted to revoke her acceptance? It is very likely that a court would refuse to let Mrs. Smith revoke her acceptance because she failed to revoke within a reasonable time.

Suppose that Mrs. Smith inspected the trailer on February 15, failed to detect any defects, and moved in on February 16. On February 17, she realized that a hat rack in the closet was missing. She then wanted to revoke her acceptance based on the theory that the defect was difficult to discover. Mrs. Smith must keep the trailer chiefly because any nonconformity must substantially impair the value of the trailer to her. While the absence of a hat rack might lessen the value of the trailer by a few dollars, it clearly fails to constitute a substantial impairment of value. Mrs. Smith would, however, have a right to sue the seller for the value of the hat rack.

The following case discusses an attempt by purchasers of an organ to revoke their acceptance after several attempts to repair it by the seller.

Schumaker v. Ivers

Supreme Court of South Dakota
238 N.W.2d 284 (1976)

Plaintiffs, Schumakers, purchased an electric organ from defendant, Ivers. After accepting the organ, the Shumakers experienced considerable difficulties with it. Although several months passed before the plaintiffs attempted to revoke their acceptance, the trial court found a proper revocation of acceptance and ruled for the plaintiffs. The appeals court affirmed the decision.

Wollman, Justice

On November 30, 1972, plaintiffs went to defendant's music store for the purpose of looking at electric organs. Plaintiffs looked at several models and discussed the matter with defendant, who recommended the organ in question, described in the testimony as a Story Clark Magi model. Defendant suggested that plaintiffs permit him to deliver the organ to their home on a trial basis. Plaintiffs agreed that defendant could do so, and the organ was delivered to plaintiffs' home on December 7, 1972. Mrs. Schumaker played the organ on the day it was delivered and noticed nothing unusual.

On December 11, 1972, Mrs. Schumaker went to defendant's store and paid in full the purchase price of the organ in the amount of $1,119.71. According to her testimony, she asked defendant about the warranty and service on the organ and was assured by defendant that it would all be taken care of and that he had a man who serviced organs.

Approximately two weeks after the organ was delivered, one of the bass pedals failed to play. Shortly thereafter another bass pedal also failed to play, as did two keys on the keyboard. Mrs. Schumaker called defendant on or about December 27, 1972, and told him about the problems she had been having with the organ. Defendant said that he would send out a serviceman. Nothing was done, however, until March 13, 1973, when defendant and his serviceman came to plaintiffs' home and worked on the organ. Following their visit—and here the record is rather vague with regard to dates—plaintiffs again experienced difficulty with the organ in that one key in every octave in both keyboards failed to play. Mrs. Schumaker called defendant on May 11, 1973, and told him that she was still having difficulty with the organ and that she was unhappy with it and wanted a refund of the purchase price. Defendant and his serviceman came to plaintiffs' home and after some discussion, during which defendant refused to accede to Mrs. Schumaker's request that he take back the organ and refund the purchase price, plaintiffs agreed to permit defendant to bring out a replacement organ on the condition that if it did not work, defendant would take it back and refund the purchase price of the first organ. On or about May 22, 1973, defendant brought out a replacement organ. Shortly thereafter the rhythm system on the second organ began to malfunction. In response to plaintiffs' call, defendant's serviceman attempted to repair the organ on several occasions during the period from May 24 to June 1, 1973, but was unable to remedy the problem. During his last service call the serviceman removed the rhythm system component from the organ. Following this visit the lower keyboard failed to play.

Sometime after June 1, 1973, defendant's employees attempted to return the original organ, which defendant claimed had been put into proper operating condition, to plaintiffs' home but were prevented from doing so by plaintiffs. Plaintiffs sought the advice of an attorney, who wrote to defendant on or about June 15, 1973, regarding the organ. On August 3, 1973, plaintiffs filed suit against defendant in the nature of a rescission action praying for the return of the purchase price of the organ.

Defendant contends that because the record reveals that he at all times stood ready to honor the one-year free parts and service warranty on the organ, plaintiffs should not have been permitted to summarily refuse him the opportunity to do so by revoking their acceptance of the organ. In view of the numerous unsuccessful attempts by defendant to satisfactorily repair the original organ, we conclude that the trial court did not err in holding that plaintiffs had rightfully revoked their acceptance.

As far as the adequacy of the notice is concerned, defendant acknowledged that Mrs. Schumaker had told him that plaintiffs wanted him to take the organ back and refund the purchase price. If this revocation of acceptance was in any way waived by plaintiffs' accepting delivery of the second organ, such waiver was clearly based upon the condition that the replacement organ would operate satisfactorily, a condition that failed to materialize. Plaintiffs moved promptly to send notice through their legal counsel shortly after the second organ became completely inoperable.

The judgment is affirmed.

All the Justices concur.

INSTALLMENT CONTRACTS

As noted earlier, where goods are tendered to the buyer that do not conform to the contract, the buyer has three options under Section 2-601. However, a different rule applies when the parties enter into an installment contract.

Section 2-612(1) defines an installment contract as "one which requires or authorizes the delivery of goods in separate lots to be separately accepted, even though the contract contains a clause, 'each delivery is a separate contract' or its equivalent." Assuming that the parties entered into an installment contract, what is the effect of a nonconforming delivery on one of the installments? Sections 2-612(2) and (3) set out the rules governing this situation. In general, the standard applied when one of the parties breaches an installment contract is not as rigorous as the standard applied when there has been a breach of a contract requiring delivery to take place at one time. The reason for this is that it would be unfair if a breach on an installment could always be used as grounds for canceling the entire contract.

Rejection of an Installment

Comment 5 to Section 2-612 states that "an installment delivery must be accepted if the nonconformity is curable and if the seller gives adequate assurance of cure." However, a buyer may reject a nonconforming installment if the nonconformity substantially impairs the value of that installment and cannot be cured or if the nonconformity is a defect in the required documents. Unlike rejections, which can occur if the goods fail to conform in any respect, for both revocations and installment contracts the buyer must show that the goods are substantially nonconforming.

Cancellation of Entire Contract

In certain circumstances, the nonconformity or default with respect to one or more installments may be so great that the entire contract has been impaired in value. Comment 6 to Section 2-612 makes it clear that the question is whether "the nonconformity substantially impairs the value of the whole contract." If this is the case, the entire contract may be canceled. If the aggrieved party wishes to cancel the contract, he or she must not accept a nonconforming installment without notifying the other party seasonably of the cancellation. If he or she fails to give the required notice, the contract is reinstated. Likewise, the contract is reinstated if the aggrieved party "brings an action with respect only to past installments or demands performance as to future installments."

ASSURANCE OF PERFORMANCE

What type of assurance must the seller give under Section 2-612(2) to force the buyer to accept a nonconforming installment? The standard is the same as that under Section 2-609, which deals with the right to adequate assurance of performance. Because one of the parties to a contract may become unwilling or unable to perform a contract after entering into it, this section allows the other party to demand an assurance of performance.

Comment 1 to Section 2-609 notes that the purpose of entering into a contract is to obtain actual performance of the contract rather than simply a promise to perform. Thus, when a party becomes unwilling or unable to perform, the other party to the contract is threatened with the loss of what he or she bargained for—performance. The seller who faces a buyer unable to pay, or the buyer who faces uncertain deliveries by a seller, may want to avail himself or herself of this section.

Basically, Section 2-609 allows the aggrieved party to do three things:

1. Suspend his or her own performance and all preparatory action
2. Require adequate assurance of performance
3. Treat the contract as broken if the grounds for insecurity are not cleared up within a reasonable time, not to exceed thirty days

What constitutes "adequate" assurance of due performance depends on the facts. If a seller of good repute gives a promise that a defective delivery will be straightened out, this will normally be sufficient. But if an untrustworthy seller makes the same statement, the statement alone might be insufficient.

When merchants have contracted, the question of insecurity and adequacy of any assurance offered is judged by commercial standards rather than legal standards. For example, if a reasonable merchant would believe that a buyer will not pay, this will be regarded as reasonable grounds for insecurity.

ANTICIPATORY REPUDIATION

Rather than a situation involving uncertain ability or willingness to perform, one of the parties to a contract may be faced with a direct repudiation of the contract. If one of the parties to a contract has indicated that he or she will not perform at some date in the future, must the other party wait until that date to find out if the other party actually performs or not?

Suppose two persons enter into a contract to be performed on August 1. If the seller says on June 1 that he or she will not deliver on August 1, what can the buyer do? This matter is covered by Sections 2–610 and 2–611. If either party to the contract indicates that he or she will not perform at some time in the future, and the failure to perform would substantially impair the value of the contract, the aggrieved party may (1) simply wait a commercially reasonable time for performance or (2) treat the contract as broken and seek any available remedy. This is true even if the aggrieved party has urged the other party to retract his or her repudiation. In any event, his or her own performance may be suspended.

If the aggrieved party chooses the first option, Section 2-611 permits the repudiating party to retract his or her repudiation unless the aggrieved party has canceled the contract, materially changed his or her position, or indicated that he or she considers the repudiation final. Although a retraction is possible by "any method which clearly indicates to the aggrieved party that the repudiating party intends to perform," the repudiating party must give the aggrieved party whatever assurances of performance are demanded, consistent with Section 2-609.

What if two parties enter into a contract calling for delivery of goods on May 15, and on January 1 the seller tells the buyer he will not deliver the goods pursuant to the contract? The buyer may treat the contract as having been breached on January 1, acquire the goods elsewhere, and bring a suit for damages against the seller. The buyer need not wait until May 15 to see if the seller changes his or her mind. Alternatively, the buyer may wait a commercially reasonable time for the seller to perform. The question of what is a commercially reasonable time is discussed in the following case.

Seller

Whewell v. Dobson

Supreme Court of Iowa
227 N.W.2d 115 (1975)

Defendant, Kenneth Dobson, contracted with Donald Whewell for the purchase of Christmas trees. Dobson repudiated the contract prior to the time for performance. Whewell attempted to resell the Christmas trees. The lower court found Whewell's attempted resale was within a commercially reasonable time. The appeals court affirmed the decision of the trial court for Whewell.

Mason, Justice

September 4, 1970, Donald Whewell, plaintiff-seller, and Kenneth Dobson, defendant-buyer, entered into a contract for the sale of four hundred Christmas trees. . . .

The agreed price for the trees was $3.75 apiece, or a total of $1,500 due upon delivery on or about December 1, 1970. Sometime in the latter part of September 1970, however, plaintiff received defendant's copy of the tree order with the word "cancel" written across its face. This was followed by a letter from defendant on October 2 informing plaintiff of the desire to cancel the tree order.

The trial court found that prior to receipt of the cancelled order and the October 2 letter, plaintiff had contracted with a Michigan firm to purchase four hundred Christmas trees at $3.25 apiece. Upon receiving defendant's communications, plaintiff unsuccessfully attempted to cancel the contract with the Michigan firm, which subsequently shipped plaintiff the trees.

October 30 plaintiff's attorneys wrote defendant demanding assurances of intent to perform the contract. Defendant was given until November 6 to respond after which time plaintiff would take action to minimize his damages.

November 3 defendant's attorneys responded and advised plaintiff defendant would not be able to accept delivery, whereupon plaintiff's attorneys wrote back asking that defendant advise them if he absolutely would not accept delivery. This defendant's attorneys did November 6.

Plaintiff subsequently attempted to sell the Christmas trees and was able to dispose of 124 of them at $3.00 apiece by late December. He also sent loads to Peoria and Elgin, Illinois, but was unable to sell the trees. In these attempts, plaintiff incurred $85 in trucking expenses.

At the outset, it is agreed by both parties Christmas trees are "goods" under the Uniform Commercial Code.

Thus, Article 2 of the Uniform Commercial Code on Sales should be applied in resolving this dispute, with §554.2610 being pertinent to the instant facts. . . .

As we understand the contentions of the parties, . . . one of the questions presented for review by this appeal is whether plaintiff's effort to resell the Christmas trees was attempted within a commercially reasonable time in view of the rapid rate cut Christmas trees decline in value as shown by this record. . . .

There is substantial evidence which would support a finding a repudiation of the contract did here occur, either when defendant wrote "cancel" across the face of the instrument or when the final letter was sent stating defendant would not accept delivery of the Christmas trees. It would be more logical to conclude the repudiation came to pass at the time defendant "cancelled" the tree order as it evidenced "a clear determination not to continue with performance" or a reasonable indication of a "rejection of the continuing obligation." The trial court apparently found the repudiation occurred at the earlier date.

In fact, defendant concedes in written brief and argument he repudiated the contract before the performance date—about December 1, 1970.

Under §554.2610, ". . . when such a repudiation substantially impairs the value of the contract, the aggrieved party may at any time resort to his remedies for breach, or he may suspend performance while negotiating with, or awaiting performance by, the other party. But if the aggrieved party awaits performance beyond a commercially reasonable time he cannot recover resulting damages which he should have avoided." Uniform Commercial Code Comment 1, §554.2610.

"Generally, a seller is under a duty to resell the article of sale within a reasonable time after breach or repudiation of the contract by the buyer. If the seller acts prudently and with reasonable care and judgment, the time of resale is, to a large extent, within the sellers' discretion. . . .

". . . What is such a reasonable time depends upon the nature of the goods, the condition of the market and the other circumstances of the case; its length cannot be measured by any legal yardstick or divided into degrees." (Uniform Commercial Code Comment 5, §554.2706.)

It is apparent, then, the given circumstances in a case must be taken into account in determining reasonableness. Unfortunately, there is no definite date of record indicating when plaintiff first attempted to resell. The trial transcript is singularly unhelpful. Plaintiff was asked when he began his resale attempts:

> "A. I am stating I did it immediately after I received the order of cancellation and the lawyer advised me—
> "Q. You started in October? A. After I got his cancellation."

Thus, such mitigation attempts may have commenced in October. A November 5 letter from plaintiff's attorneys indicates otherwise, however:

> "Please advise us immediately if Mr. Dobson is absolutely unwilling to accept delivery of the Christmas trees he ordered. If so, *we will attempt* to either partially cancel Mr. Whewell's order with his grower or sell the trees to another retailer so that Mr. Whewell's losses will be minimized." (Emphasis supplied).

Plaintiff was the only witness called by either side in the course of the trial.

The trial court did not specifically find that plaintiff's attempted resale was within a commercially reasonable time under the circumstances, but such finding is inherent in its conclusion that plaintiff was entitled to judgment against defendant.

In the court's ruling on defendant's motion for new trial, it is stated by the time defendant notified plaintiff of his desire to cancel the contract one-third of the time had elapsed between the signing of the agreement and the delivery date. The trial judge then opined there would have been no market for the trees after the repudiation, since the date the contract was entered into indicated other wholesalers of trees would have made arrangements at the same time.

There is substantial evidence to support the trial court's findings of fact. In this court's opinion the conclusion of law drawn therefrom by the trial court was correct.

Affirmed.

IMPOSSIBILITY

In certain instances, a party to a contract may be unable to perform because the goods have been destroyed. The UCC in Section 2-613 allows both parties to escape from the contract when goods identified to the contract have been totally destroyed without fault of either party before the risk of loss passes to the buyer. If the goods have been only partially destroyed, or have deteriorated so as to no longer conform to the contract, Section

2-613(b) gives the buyer the option to either (1) treat the contract as avoided or (2) accept the goods with due allowance for the deterioration or the deficiency in quantity but without further right against the seller.

Goods Must Be Identified

For Section 2-613 to apply, the goods must be identified when the contract is made. If just any goods are specified in the contract, as opposed to particular goods, then Section 2-613 does not apply. A seller who promises to deliver 100 lawn mowers to the buyer cannot rely on Section 2-613, but a seller who specifies 100 lawn mowers from his or her plant, which then burns to the ground along with all the mowers, may rely on the defense of impossibility (assuming that he was not responsible for the destruction). This section applies even though the goods were already destroyed at the time of contracting if neither party knew of the loss.

Impracticability

Sometimes performance will not be impossible, but will nonetheless be very difficult. Section 2-615 covers situations where performance becomes impracticable because of the occurrence of a contingency the nonoccurrence of which was a basic assumption on which the contract was made or as a result of compliance in good faith with a government regulation. This section excuses the seller from a timely delivery of goods where unforeseen supervening circumstances make performance impracticable. The mere fact that costs go up does not excuse performance; that is the type of business risk assumed in signing a contract. On the other hand, a severe shortage of raw materials or supplies due to a contingency such as war, embargo, or unforeseen shutdown of major sources of supply, which causes the goods to be significantly more expensive or impossible to obtain, is the type of situation covered.

Partial Performance

The seller is excused from the contract completely if he or she can establish that he or she is absolutely unable to perform due to the occurrence of a contingency not contemplated by the parties, but the seller must fulfill the contract to the extent possible if he or she can only partially perform. Section 2-615(b) states that when a seller can partially perform, he or she must allocate production and deliveries among the customers in a fair and reasonable manner. If the seller chooses to allocate goods, or if there will be a delay or nondelivery of goods, the seller must notify the buyer seasonably.

Section 2-616 states that a buyer, upon receipt of notification of a material or indefinite delay or of an allocation, may by written notification to the seller terminate the contract or agree to take the available allocation. The buyer must agree to this modification within a reasonable time, not to exceed thirty days, or the contract will lapse as to any deliveries affected.

Although a buyer does not have to accept the allocated goods, he or she must accept substituted performance if the agreed manner of delivery becomes commercially impossible. Likewise, if the agreed means of payment fails because of domestic or foreign government regulation, the seller under certain conditions must accept a substantially equivalent manner of payment.

REMEDIES

The first part of this chapter dealt with obligations of the parties to a contract to perform in a certain manner. The second part deals with the rights of the parties to the contract when the seller or the buyer fails to live up to his or her obligations under the contract.

Statute of Limitations

The victim of a breach in a sales transaction will often have more than one form of relief available. Some of the remedies are mutually exclusive, and others involve limiting factors such as a specific number of days within which one must act. When a breach of an important sales transaction occurs, it is imperative that the victim immediately contact a lawyer to ensure that the right to seek a remedy is not inadvertently lost.

Time Limit. This is particularly true when deciding whether to file suit or not. A person who wishes to bring an action for breach of a sales contract must bring suit within four years after the cause of action has occurred—unless the parties have agreed to a shorter period of time. The statute of limitations can be reduced to not less than one year by agreement. If a party to a contract fails to bring suit within the time stipulated in the agreement (or, if no time is stipulated, within four years), he or she is barred from ever bringing suit by the statute of limitations even though he or she may have an otherwise perfectly valid claim.

Time Statute Starts to Run. The four-year period starts to run from the date the breach of contract occurs, whether the aggrieved party knows of the breach or not, except in the case of a breach of warranty. The time limit for a breach of warranty begins to run when tender of delivery is made, except when the warranty extends to the future performance of goods. In that case, the time limit runs from the time the breach is or should have been discovered.

If, for instance, Sam purchases an air conditioner that is warranted for three years, the four years begins to run from the date on which Sam discovers or should have discovered the breach. If he tries the air conditioner on May 1 and learns of the breach on that date, the statute of limitations begins to run. On the other hand, if he fails to turn it on all summer, the statute will begin to run sometime at the beginning of the summer— the date on which he should have discovered the breach of warranty. If Sam never turns on the air conditioner and thus never learns of the breach, the time period starts to run anyway on the date he should have discovered the breach. This encourages a purchaser to be diligent in discovering defects in items purchased.

Diligence in reporting defects is important because it permits the seller to attempt to remedy the defect and helps to minimize the buyer's damages.

SELLER'S REMEDIES

If the buyer wrongfully rejects goods, improperly revokes his or her acceptance, fails to make a payment due, or repudiates part or all of the contract, the aggrieved seller has a number of remedies.

Election of Remedies

The UCC rejects the idea that a seller must elect one remedy or another. Instead, whether one remedy bars another will depend on the circumstances of a particular case. The reader should bear in mind with respect to the UCC sections on remedies that Section 1-106(1) states: "The remedies provided by this Act shall be liberally administered to the end that the aggrieved party may be put in as good a position as if the other party had fully performed. . . ." The purpose of the remedies provided for in the UCC is not to punish the wrongdoer but simply to put the aggrieved party in the position he or she would have occupied had the contract been performed.

Remedies Available

Section 2-703 gives the aggrieved seller a number of remedies:

1. Withhold delivery of goods
2. Stop delivery of goods held by a bailee
3. Resell the goods and recover damages
4. Recover damages for nonacceptance as provided in Section 2-708
5. Recover the price
6. Cancel the contract

The aggrieved seller also has certain rights with respect to unfinished goods. When the buyer breaches the contract, the seller can identify to the contract any completed conforming goods, and he or she may either stop work on unfinished goods and sell them for their scrap or salvage value or may in the exercise of reasonable commercial judgment complete the unfinished goods and identify them to the contract (Section 2-704). The reason the seller is allowed this option is to minimize the damages sustained by the buyer. If the seller chooses to complete the work on unfinished goods, the burden is on the buyer to show that it was unreasonable for the seller to complete the goods. The seller may then proceed to resell under Section 2-706 or, where resale is not practicable, bring an action for the price under Section 2-709.

Resale

The UCC contemplates the seller's principal remedy as resale. When the buyer has wrongfully rejected goods, revoked his acceptance improperly, failed to make a payment, or repudiated all or part of a contract, the seller may resell the goods in question. The seller is not obligated to resell the goods, but this is the usual manner of establishing damages since the seller is in the business of selling goods. If the seller resells the goods in good faith and in a commercially reasonable manner, he or she may recover the difference between the resale price and the contract price together with any incidental damages, but minus any expenses saved as a result of the buyer's breach (Section 2-706[1]).

Incidental Damages. Section 2-710 states that incidental damages to the seller include "any commercially reasonable charges, expenses or commissions incurred in stopping delivery, in the transportation, care and custody of the goods after the buyer's breach, in connection with return or resale of the goods or otherwise resulting from the breach." These are the typical expenses a seller might incur; however, Section 2-710 allows for all commercially reasonable expenditures made by the seller. Suppose the seller had entered into a contract for $4,650.00, and the buyer breached. If the seller incurred $29.50 in expenses in reselling the goods, and they were sold in good faith and in a commercially reasonable manner for $3,000.00, the seller would be entitled to $1,679.50 from the buyer if he or she proceeded under Section 2-706.

Manner of Resale. To assure that the resale takes place in a fair manner, Section 2-706 sets out provisions for conducting the resale. Of course, the parties may agree between themselves as to the details of the resale, but the method of resale still must be fair. In the absence of such an agreement, the resale may be at a public or private sale, as long as every aspect of the sale is commercially reasonable. In choosing whether to have a public or private sale, the character of the goods must be considered and relevant trade practices and usages must be observed. If the seller elects a private sale, he must give the buyer reasonable notification of his intent to resell. It is not necessary to give the buyer notification of the time and place of the private sale.

At a public sale, only identified goods can be sold unless the seller is able to sell them as future goods at a recognized market for public sale of future goods. These identified goods must be sold at a usual place or market for public sale if one is available. Before selling the goods, the seller must give the buyer reasonable notice of the time and place of the resale unless the goods are perishable or threaten to decline rapidly in value. This means the sale must be at a place or market where potential buyers may reasonably be expected to attend and the buyer has an opportunity to bid or notify others of the sale. In order to assure the best possible price, prospective bidders must be given an opportunity to inspect the goods. The seller is permitted to buy the goods. These measures are included to benefit the original buyer by tending to increase the resale price.

If the goods are resold improperly to a purchaser who buys in good faith at the resale, the purchaser takes free of any rights of the original buyer.

Suppose that our seller in the earlier example resold the goods for $5,000. Must he account to the buyer for the $350 above the original contract price of $4,650? Section 2-706(6) answers that the "seller is not accountable to the buyer for any profit made on any resale." The seller in this situation may keep the profit.

Failure to Comply. What happens if the seller fails to comply with the restrictions placed on the resale of goods? Does this bar him from any remedy? If he or she fails to comply with the provisions for resale in Section 2-706, the resale price cannot be used in calculating damages. However, the seller can still collect something. Comment 2 to Section 2-706 states that, if the seller acts improperly, he or she must establish damages under Section 2-708.

Damages

Market Price. Section 2-708(1) makes the seller's damages for nonacceptance or repudiation by the buyer the "difference between the market price at the time and place for tender and the unpaid contract price. . . ." In addition to this sum, the seller may recover for any incidental damages incurred, but he or she must deduct from the damages any expenses saved as a result of the buyer's breach. A seller might utilize this section to keep the goods that the buyer has refused to accept. It is not mandatory that the seller resell the goods in order to establish his or her damages although, as noted earlier, most sellers will attempt to resell the goods.

The market price is measured at the time and place for tender. To take an obvious case, if the buyer agreed by contract to pick up the goods at the seller's place of business on June 15 and the buyer breaches, the seller may be able to collect the difference between the contract price and the market price at which the goods are selling in the town where the seller's business is located. If the buyer agreed to pay $1,000 for the goods, and they are now selling for $800 in the seller's town, the seller collects $1,000 minus $800, or $200, plus incidental damages and minus any expenses saved. In this case, the seller would receive the same amount of damages whether the seller resold the goods and sued under 2-706 or collected under 2-708(1). In certain more complex situations, the seller might receive a larger amount under 2-708(1) than under 2-706. However, some scholars argue that a seller should not be able to recover any more under 2-708(1) than under 2-706.[1]

Profit. In the event that the measure of damages provided by section 2-708(1) is inadequate to put the seller in as good a position as performance would have done, the seller may collect the profit (including overhead) that he or she would have recovered had the contract been performed plus any incidental damages.

The UCC could be written more clearly on the question of when profits may be recovered. One case where 2-708(1) will not put the seller in the same position as performance would have done is that of the lost-volume seller. Suppose a retailer agrees to sell a couch for $500 to Mrs. Jones. If Mrs. Jones breaches the contract, the retailer would be entitled to the difference between the contract price ($500) and the market price ($500). This would leave the retailer with no damages as long as he or she is able to sell all the couches in stock. But what if the supply of couches exceeds the demand? In that case, because Mrs. Jones breached the contract, the seller will sell one less couch. In this situation, the seller should be able to receive the profit (including overhead) that he or she would have made on the Jones's contract.

Price. The seller can recover the price of goods sold only under certain circumstances. Price actions may be maintained when resale of the goods is impracticable, when the buyer has accepted the goods, or when the goods were destroyed or lost within a reasonable time after the risk of loss had passed to the buyer (Section 2-709). If the seller wishes to obtain the contract price, the goods that have been identified to the contract and are still in his or her possession must be held for the buyer. If the seller is able to resell them prior to collecting a judgment, he or she may do so and the proceeds will be credited to the buyer.

Once the buyer has accepted goods, the UCC permits the seller to recover the price of the goods as opposed to a recovery under Section 2-706 or Section 2-708. Whether a buyer has accepted does not depend on the passage of title nor on the date set for payment. Acceptance takes place if one of the events listed in Section 2-606 occurs. Suppose the seller delivers goods to the buyer, and the buyer states that he will take the goods. The buyer's statement constitutes an acceptance and renders him liable for the price under Section 2-709.

Likewise, if goods are lost or damaged within a commercially reasonable time after the risk of loss has passed to the buyer, the buyer is liable for the price. A seller who ships goods "F. O. B. seller's plant" need only deliver the goods to the carrier. Once the goods are in the possession of the carrier, the risk of loss passes to the buyer. In the event the goods are destroyed while in the possession of the carrier, the buyer is liable for the price of the goods.

If the goods have not been accepted by the buyer or destroyed after the risk of loss has passed, an action for the price can be maintained for goods identified to the contract only after a "reasonable effort to resell" them at a reasonable price. The seller need not try to resell, however, if circumstances indicate that it would not be possible to resell them at a reasonable price. Suppose a manufacturer custom designed a rolling steel door for a buyer. If the steel door does not fit any other building because it was custom designed, the buyer is liable for the price of the door.

Withhold Delivery

In the event the buyer becomes insolvent, the seller's ability to collect damages from the buyer under the sections previously discussed will be impaired. If the buyer has no money, a judgment against him will be of little practical value to the seller. For this reason, the UCC provides special remedies where the buyer becomes insolvent.

When the seller discovers that a buyer has become insolvent, he or she may refuse to deliver the goods to the buyer except for cash. If the buyer owes the seller for goods delivered before the seller learned of the buyer's insolvency, the seller may also demand payment for all goods previously delivered before making any further deliveries. The mere fact that the seller withholds delivery of goods pursuant to Section 2-702 does not mean that he or she is barred from exercising any remedy available for damages.

Goods in Possession of Buyer. Section 2-702(2) applies when the buyer has actually received the goods but has not yet paid for them. If the buyer received the goods on credit while he was insolvent, the seller has ten days to demand their return. Receiving goods on credit amounts to a misrepresentation of solvency by the buyer and is therefore fraudulent against the seller. If the seller learns of the buyer's insolvency and actually demands return of the goods within ten days, the seller is entitled to the goods. If the buyer misrepresented his or her solvency to the seller in writing within three months of the time the buyer received the goods, the ten-day rule does not apply. In that event, the seller may claim actual fraud by the buyer and, if he or she can establish fraud, the seller may reclaim the goods.

Goods Held by Carrier or Bailee. If the goods have already been delivered to a carrier or other bailee, the seller may wish to stop delivery upon discovering that the buyer is insolvent. It is not necessary for the buyer to be insolvent in all cases for the seller to stop delivery; however, if the seller wishes to stop shipments of less than a carload, the buyer must be insolvent. For the seller to stop delivery when the buyer breaches the contract, the amount must be a delivery as large as a carload if the buyer is solvent. This provision was adopted because it is a burden on the carriers to stop delivery. If a seller of a smaller-than-carload lot has doubts about the buyer's capacity to pay, he can ship C.O.D. There is, of course, risk in stopping any shipment because improper stoppage is a breach by the seller.

The seller can stop delivery until the buyer has received the goods, until the documents of title have been negotiated to the buyer, or until the carrier or other bailee gives notice that the goods are being held for the buyer. The seller must give notice to the bailee with sufficient time to enable the bailee by reasonable diligence to stop delivery of the goods. Assuming notice arrives in time for the bailee to act diligently, the bailee must hold and deliver the goods according to the seller's directions. If a negotiable document of title was issued, however, this must be surrendered before the bailee must obey the stop order.

BUYER'S REMEDIES

When the seller fails to make delivery or repudiates or the buyer rightfully rejects or revokes acceptance of goods, the buyer has several remedies:

1. Cancel the contract and recover any amounts paid to seller
2. Cover
3. Recover damages pursuant to Section 2-713
4. Gain possession of goods identified to the contract pursuant to Section 2-502
5. Obtain specific performance or replevy the goods pursuant to Section 2-716
6. Resell goods in his or her possession pursuant in certain circumstances

The remedy most often used is cover.

Cover

When the seller fails to make a delivery or indicates that he or she will not deliver pursuant to a contract, the buyer is faced with the situation of not having material needed to conduct business. To take care of this situation, the UCC allows the buyer to purchase goods in substitution for those covered in the contract (Section 2-712). If the buyer acts in good faith and without unreasonable delay, he or she may establish damages as the difference between the cost of cover and the contract price.

The court will not second-guess the buyer in determining the reasonableness of his or her actions but will merely examine whether the buyer's actions were reasonable at the time and place he acted. If it later turns out that a cheaper or more effective means of cover was available, this does not automatically mean that the buyer acted unreasonably. In addition to the difference between the cover price and the contract price, the buyer is entitled to any incidental or consequential damages incurred, but he or she must deduct from the claim any expenses saved as a result of the seller's breach.

Incidental Damages. Incidental damages include, but are not limited to, "expenses reasonably incurred in inspection, receipt, transportation and care and custody of goods rightfully rejected, any commercially reasonable charges, expenses or commissions in connection with effecting cover and any other reasonable expense incident to the delay or other breach" (Section 2-715[1]).

Consequential Damages. Consequential damages include all losses resulting from the general or particular requirements and needs of the buyer that the seller had reason to know of at the time of contracting and that could not reasonably have been prevented by cover or otherwise. It is not necessary that the buyer establish damages with mathematical precision, but the buyer does bear the burden of proving the loss. If the seller does not wish to assume liability for consequential damages, he or she should use Section 2-719(3), which states:

Consequential damages may be limited or excluded unless the limitation or exclusion is unconscionable. Limitation of consequential damages for injury to the person in the case of consumer goods is prima facie unconscionable but limitation of damages where the loss is commercial is not.

Consequential damages also include an injury to a person or property if it proximately results from a breach of warranty.

Suppose the seller agrees to deliver 10,000 bushels of wheat to the buyer on October 15. The price per bushel is $4.50. On October 15, the seller refuses to deliver the wheat. In this situation, the buyer may receive the difference between the contract price and the cover price if he or she acts in good faith and without unreasonable delay. If the buyer purchases 10,000 bushels of wheat on the open market on October 15 for $5.00 per bushel, the buyer should receive $50,000 minus $45,000, or $5,000 plus any incidental or consequential damages caused by the seller's breach but minus any expenses saved as a result of the breach.

Damages

If the seller has failed to deliver goods in accordance with a contract or has repudiated the contract, the buyer may establish damages by covering although it is not mandatory to cover. The buyer may, instead, elect to establish damages under Section 2-713, even if other goods have been purchased. The buyer is under no duty to use the price of the goods purchased in order to establish damages. In fact, the buyer may not wish to use the damages provided for Section 2-712 if he or she made a better deal when purchasing the goods than was made under the original contract.

Market Price. Subsection 1 makes the measure of damages the difference between the market price at the time the buyer learned of the breach and the contract price. The buyer also can collect any incidental and consequential damages incurred, but he or she must credit the seller with any expenses saved as a result of the seller's breach. The market price will be determined by examining the current market price (when the buyer learned of the breach) at the place for tender or, if the buyer rejected the goods after they arrived or revoked acceptance, by examining the current market price (when the buyer learned of the breach) at the place of arrival. Thus Section 2-713 uses as a guideline the market in which the buyer would have obtained cover had he or she attempted to cover.

If the seller was to have tendered goods to the buyer in Los Angeles, the market price to be used would be the prevailing price in the Los Angeles market at the time the buyer learned of the breach. If the buyer had attempted to cover, presumably this would have been the price he or she would have paid.

Value as Warranted. When the buyer has accepted goods and the time for revocation has passed, he or she is still entitled to damages if the seller fails to perform properly pursuant to 2-714(2). The buyer's damages are the difference between the value of the goods accepted and the value they would have had if they had been as warranted. The buyer may also collect incidental and consequential damages. For example, if the purchaser of an automobile determines that the car has a defective horn, a court might award him as damages the cost of repairing or replacing the defective horn.

Specific Performance/Replevin

Specific Performance. The buyer may wish to obtain the goods because of inability to find substitute goods elsewhere or because the seller is in poor financial condition. Section 2-716 gives the buyer the right to specific performance and replevin in certain circumstances. The buyer may obtain specific performance of the contract when "the goods are unique or in other proper circumstances." What is unique depends on the circumstances. In any event, if a buyer is unable to cover, this is good evidence of other proper circumstances that merit specific performance of the contract.

Replevin. The buyer has a right of replevin for goods identified to the contract if after a reasonable effort he or she is unable to find

substitute goods or if the circumstances indicate that he or she will be unable to find them.

Right to Resell. If the buyer rightfully rejects goods or properly revokes acceptance of them, Section 2-711(3) gives the buyer a security interest in the goods in his or her possession or control. The buyer may hold and resell these goods if he or she has paid a part of the price or has incurred expenses for the inspection, receipt, transportation, care, and custody of the goods. If the buyer resells, he or she must comply with Section 2-706 and must forward the balance of the amount received (beyond what was paid on the goods and expenses) to the seller.

Liquidated Damages

Rather than leave the determination of damages to the court, the parties may agree in advance what the measure of damages will be in the event that one of the parties to the contract breaches. When damages have been specified in the contract they are referred to as *liquidated damages*. A court will enforce the amount set by the parties only if it is a reasonable amount in light of all the circumstances. If it is unreasonably large, it is void as a penalty. This leaves the court free to award damages as seem appropriate under the circumstances (Section 2-718). If the buyer would normally sustain $500 a day in damages in the event the seller fails to deliver on time, a provision awarding the buyer $10,000 a day for every day the seller is late in delivering the goods would be void as a penalty.

LIMITATION OR ALTERATION OF REMEDIES

The UCC does not require parties to a contract to follow these rules on remedies. Section 2-719 makes is clear that the parties to a contract are free to shape their own remedies.

They may add remedies not covered in the UCC, or they may choose to substitute different remedies for those provided in Article 2. Damages recoverable under Article 2 may be limited or altered. If the parties to a contract wish to specify one particular remedy to be employed exclusively, the contract must clearly indicate that that remedy is the sole remedy available to the aggrieved party.

All attempts to modify or eliminate the remedies provided under Article 2 are subject to the charge of unconscionability. Some minimum remedy must be available to the aggrieved party. If the remedy provisions in a contract are found to be unconscionable or to deprive either party of a substantial value of the bargain, the court may strike them and apply the remedies found in Article 2.

As noted in the chapter on warranties, Section 2-719(3) permits consequential damages to be limited or excluded unless such an exclusion would be unconscionable. Where consumer goods are involved, however, a limitation of consequential damages for injury to a person is *prima facie* unconscionable (see the chapter on warranties).

REVIEW PROBLEMS

1. Davis purchased a mobile home from Colonial Mobile Homes. Davis paid cash. Upon delivery, Davis noticed that one tire was flat and was told by Colonial's employee that the driver had pulled it to the site on the flat tire "all the way" from the plant where it was manufactured. Davis had to wait three weeks to inspect the interior since no keys were delivered with the mobile home. Upon inspection, severe problems were discovered—for example, the cabinets were out of line, the doors and windows would not shut, it leaked when it rained, the floors were buckled, and there were other defects. None of these defects was visible on inspection when Davis purchased the mobile home. After living in the home for three months, Davis moved out. Prior to his vacating, his attorney sent a letter to Colonial demanding replacement or refund. Davis attempted to make repairs prior to the lawsuit's being filed. Did Davis's payment in cash for the mobile home impair his right of inspection upon delivery under Section 2-513? Davis v. Colonial Mobile Home, 220 S.E.2d 802.

2. Pace ordered a large quantity of lumber items from Sagebrush. On delivery, it was discovered that there were two truckloads of materials that had not been ordered. Pace allowed them to be unloaded without objection, but wrote "not ordered" on his copy of the invoice. Pace then attempted to correct the situation but was unable to contact Sagebrush. The nonordered lumber items were then placed in Pace's inventory, offered for sale to the public, and a portion was sold. Pace also made a partial payment on the order and made no attempt to return the nonordered lumber. Did Pace accept the nonordered lumber items? See Pace v. Sagebrush Sales Co., 560 P.2d 789 (Ariz. 1977).

3. Fablok purchased ten knitting machines of a certain type from Cocker, the sole domestic manufacturer of these machines. Shortly after delivery of the first two machines, Fablok notified Cocker of defects in the machines. Cocker assured Fablok that the defects were correctable, and Cocker attempted to correct the defects in the machines for a period of time running over about two years. Cocker failed to correct the defects. Fablok then notified Cocker of its revocation of acceptance. Was Fablock's revocation of acceptance made within a reasonable time? See Fablok Mills, Inc. v. Cocker Machine and Foundry Co., 310 A.2d 49 (N.J. Super. 1973).

4. White contracted with Continental for twenty carloads of plywood to be delivered

in separate lots. Upon receipt of the first carload, White determined that it did not meet the contract specifications. White decided to cancel the contract. White then notified Continental. In the meantime, however, Continental had shipped another carload under the contract. Upon arrival of the second car, both parties agreed to an inspection according to a U.S. government standard, per the original contract, which provides that a 5 percent variance from the specifications is too great. The second carload, however, was within the allowed variance. White paid for the first carload, but refused to pay for any others. Continental then sued for breach of contract. May White cancel the entire contract? See Continental Forest Products v. White Lumber Sales, Inc., 8 UCC Rep. 178 (Ore. 1970).

5. Mishara contracted with Transit for delivery of ready-mixed concrete to a construction site. Transit delivered concrete for seven months until a labor dispute shut down the job for two months. After work resumed, a picket line remained around the site until its completion some two years later. During this two-year period, Transit made no deliveries of concrete to the site, despite Mishara's repeated requests. Transit asserted the defense of "commercial impracticability" when Mishara sued for breach of contract. What are the elements of commercial impracticability and does the labor dispute at the jobsite excuse Transit's performance? See Mishara Construction Co., Inc. v. Transit-Mixed Concrete Corp., 310 N.E.2d 363 (Mass. 1974).

6. Waites constructs certain cabinets to Thrift's order for use in a motel under construction. The cabinets are shipped to Thrift, who, upon receipt, notifies Waites that they cannot be used because of an error in the construction plans. Thrift wishes to return them. Waites refuses to take them back, but offers to find an outlet for them. After not hearing from Waites for many months, Thrift ships the cabinets back to Waites, without Waites's authority. Thrift has made no payments to Waites. Can Waites recover the price of the goods from Thrift? R. R. Waites Co., Inc. v. E. H. Thrift Air Conditioning, Inc., 510 S.W.2d 759 (Mo. App. 1974).

7. Jimlar contracted to purchase certain boots and shoes from Armstrong to be resold by Jimlar. Armstrong does not deliver the boots and shoes. The purchase was particularly attractive to Jimlar, since the boots and shoes were offered at a price considerably below market. The market price allegedly was above the price at which Jimlar has contracted to resell the boots and shoes. What damages may Jimlar recover? Jimlar Corp. v. A. J. Armstrong, Inc., 17 UCC Rep. 108 (N. Y. Sup. Ct. 1975).

8. Hirst purchased a metal casket manufactured by Elgin, which was warranted in writing as being leakproof. Approximately three months after the burial of Hirst's father, the body was disinterred for a second autopsy. Upon opening, the casket was found to contain water. There is no evidence that the casket had been mistreated. Hirst sued for damages caused by mental suffering. May Hirst recover these damages from Elgin? Hirst v. Elgin Metal Casket Co., 438 F. Supp 906 (D. Mont. 1977).

FOOTNOTE

[1]White and Summers, Uniform Commercial Code 273 (2nd ed. 1980).

Warranties

When the seller of goods makes a representation as to the character, quality, or title of the goods as part of the contract of sale, and promises that certain facts are as represented, a warranty has been made. A seller who assures or guarantees the buyer that the goods will conform to certain standards may be liable for damages if the goods fail to meet those standards.

TYPES OF WARRANTIES

Express Warranties

Sometimes a seller, through words or actions, creates an *express warranty.* In a written document, or sometimes orally, the seller specifies precisely the terms of his or her guarantees to the buyer. Suppose Acme Machines states in literature provided with a lifting device that the machine will lift loads of up to 1,000 pounds. This is a representation of fact—either the machine will lift up to 1,000 pounds or it will not. A seller who makes such a statement creates an express warranty that the machine will lift up to 1,000 pounds. If a buyer purchases the machine and later learns that its lifting capacity does not exceed 400 pounds, the buyer can bring an action for breach of an express warranty.

Implied Warranties of Quality

Not every warranty arises out of the words or actions of the seller. Sometimes a warranty as to the quality of the goods arises by operation of law. Two warranties arise out of a sale automatically by operation of law—the implied warranty of merchantability and the implied warranty of fitness for a particular purpose.

In the example mentioned earlier, suppose the manufacturer designed and sold the lifting device for use in loading railroad boxcars. If the machine fails to function properly when used in loading boxcars, the manufacturer has breached the implied warranty of merchantability. This warranty arose, not out of any words or actions of the seller, but merely as a result of making the sale. The machine was not merchantable because it was not fit for the purposes for which such goods are sold.

Assume instead that the purchaser of this machine told the seller what his requirements were. The buyer stated that he needed a machine capable of lifting very dense packages weighing around 2,000 pounds. The buyer relied on the seller's skill and judgment to select a suitable machine for him. These facts create an implied warranty of fitness for a particular purpose.

Implied Warranty of Title

A third warranty also automatically arises from a sale—the warranty of title. What if the buyer in this example learned after purchasing the lifting device that it had been stolen? In this case, by selling stolen merchandise, the seller has breached the implied warranty of title.

These warranties are discussed in greater detail in the following material.

WARRANTY LAW

Development of the Law

Warranty cases are one of the most common types of cases arising out of the sale of a product. Sometimes a person or company who purchases a product experiences problems with it. Then the question arises: Whose responsibility is it to repair the product? The buyer naturally hopes the seller will repair the product. The actual rights of the buyer are in part governed by the wording of the warranty, if any, and in part by statutes.

For many years the law favored the seller—the law followed the doctrine of *caveat emptor* (let the buyer beware). Starting with the twentieth century, the law slowly moved in the direction of recognizing more rights for the buyer. More recently, really starting in the late 1960s, the consumer movement has pressed the courts and legislatures to strengthen the rights of purchasers. Certainly one cannot state that the doctrine of *caveat emptor* governs the law of sales today.

Source of Warranty Law

The law governing all aspects of sales law, including warranties, developed on a case-by-case basis. For many centuries the law of sales was found in the decisions of judges dealing with real cases.

Toward the end of the nineteenth century, scholars and practitioners became increasingly dissatisfied with the case-law approach. Many people advocated more uniformity in the law. This movement gave rise to the drafting of the Uniform Sales Act (1906), which some states eventually adopted. After a number of years, the Uniform Sales Act was superseded by the Uniform Commercial Code (1952), which has been adopted by every state except Louisiana. Louisiana has enacted some parts of the UCC, but not Article 2. Article 2 of the UCC covers the law of sales, including the rules relating to warranties.

While the UCC rules generally govern in the area of warranties, bear in mind that other statutes have been passed that have an impact on these rules. The discussion in the text is largely confined to the UCC rules.

Sale of Goods

In order to determine whether Article 2 of the UCC applies to a given case, an attorney must determine if the facts involve a sale of goods.

A *sale* is defined in Section 2-106 of the UCC as "the passing of title from the seller to the buyer for a price." *Goods* are tangible (having a physical existence) property that is movable at the time of identification to the contract (Section 2-105).

Suppose that Margaret agrees to sell her watch to Penelope. A watch is a tangible, movable article. If the parties intend to pass title to the watch for a price, this transaction constitutes a sale under Section 2-106.

What if Margaret *gives* the watch to Penelope? No sale is involved in such a transaction and the principles of Article 2 do not control. A gift is not a sale of property for a price.

Things Other than Goods

The mood of the courts in the 1970s, as earlier indicated, shifted in the direction of consumer rights. Many courts were confronted with cases in which the plaintiff wished to claim some warranty protection under the UCC but had not purchased goods. Such cases often arise with leases. Technically, Article 2 does not apply to leases because the parties to the transaction do not intend a transfer of title. Nonetheless, some courts have extended the warranty provisions of the UCC to nonsale transactions such as leases. These courts have reasoned that a lease is very much like a sale, so as a matter of public policy the warranty provisions of Article 2 should be extended to the lease transaction. In other cases, courts have found warranties in the sale of homes or in personal service contracts.

The point to bear in mind is that a plaintiff should not give up on pursuing a case based on Article 2 warranties simply because the transaction does not appear to be a sale under Article 2. If a court feels there is good reason to extend the protection of the UCC beyond a pure sale of goods, it may elect to do so.

WARRANTY OF TITLE

Provisions

When a purchaser buys goods, receipt of good title to the goods is expected. This belief is reflected in the provisions of Section 2-312(1), which states that the seller of goods warrants: (1) the title conveyed is good and its transfer rightful; and (2) the goods are free of any security interest or other encumbrance of which the buyer at the time of contracting has no knowledge. This warranty arises automatically by operation of law.

Exposing Buyer to a Suit

The first provision—that the title conveyed is good and its transfer rightful—assures the buyer of a good title. Certainly, if a seller conveys stolen property to a buyer, the seller has breached the warranty of title. Suppose however that a seller, believing he owns an automobile, sells this automobile to a buyer. After the sale, a third party informs the buyer that he, the third party, is the one who lawfully holds title to the automobile. A title is not good if it unreasonably exposes the buyer to a lawsuit. In this case, the buyer may be forced to litigate the issue of title in court with the third party. Whatever the resolution of the case—that is, whether or not the third party establishes that he is the lawful owner of the automobile—if the third party's claim is not frivolous the buyer may sue the seller for breach of the implied warranty of title. The seller's questionable title wrongfully exposed the buyer to a suit. The *Ricklefs* case, which follows, deals with this issue.

Ricklefs v. Clemens

Supreme Court of Kansas
531 P.2d 94 (1975)

Ricklefs purchased an automobile from Clemens. It turned out the automobile may have been stolen. Ricklefs sued Clemens for breach of the warranty of title. The trial court found a breach of warranty of title by Clemens. The Kansas Supreme Court affirmed the trial court.

Kaul, Justice

On March 26, 1971, defendant-appellee (Ronald D. Clemens) sold the automobile in question, a Chevrolet Corvette Stingray 2-door coupe titled as a 1969 model, to plaintiff-appellant (Warren Ricklefs) for $1,500.00 cash and a trade-in allowance of $2,400.00 for plaintiff's 1969 Pontiac. Clemens executed a certificate of title warranting the title to be free from all liens and encumbrances except as stated in the assignment. Ricklefs operated the automobile until December 1, 1971, when he was notified by an agent of the Federal Bureau of Investigation that the automobile was stolen. The agent also informed plaintiff that the automobile was a 1968, rather than a 1969 model. Plaintiff did not use the automobile after December 1, 1971, for the reason, plaintiff testified, that the agent had told him he might be arrested. Plaintiff claims that he made demand on Clemens for restitution but was refused.

Section 2-312, the code provision for warranty of title, does not mention, specifically, warranty of quiet possession; however, in this connection, we find the following in the official UCC comment:

> The warranty of quiet possession is abolished. Disturbance of quiet possession, although not mentioned specifically, is one way, among many, in which the breach of the warranty of title may be established.

In Amer. Container Corp. v. Hanley Trucking Corp., 111 N.J. Super. 322, 268 A. 2d 313, an action involving the sale of a stolen semitrailer wherein the court considered the language of section 2-312 of the UCC, the court had this to say:

> The purchaser of goods which are warranted as to title has a right to rely on the fact that he will not be required, at some later time, to enter into a contest over the validity of his ownership. The mere casting of a substantial shadow over his title, regardless of the ultimate outcome, is sufficient to violate a warranty of good title . . .

In this case the notice of the F.B.I. agent and the warning given to plaintiff that he might be arrested is sufficient to cast a shadow over plaintiff's title and establishes a breach of warranty of title.

Although Clemens, under the circumstances, may be said to be innocent, he is, nevertheless, liable to Ricklefs for breach of warranty of title, both express by virtue of the certificate guaranty and implied by virtue of the UCC section 2-312.

Free of Encumbrance

The seller also warrants to the buyer that the goods are free of any security interest or other encumbrance of which the buyer at the time of contracting has no knowledge. If the seller conveys mortgaged property to the buyer without informing the buyer of this fact, this violates the warranty of title.

Goods Do Not Infringe

A merchant-seller also warrants that the goods sold do not infringe upon the patent, trademark, or copyright of a third party. This is true unless the seller has manufactured the goods according to the buyer's specifications.

Circumstances Indicating No Warranty of Title

There is no warranty of title in a contract for sale when the circumstances give the buyer reason to know that the person selling does not claim title in himself or that he is purporting to sell only such right or title as he or a third person may have. This means that when the buyer purchases goods at a sheriff's sale, or from an executor or foreclosing creditor, the seller is not warranting the title.

Exclusion of Warranty

The warranty of title may be excluded or modified by specific language that makes the buyer aware that the seller is not claiming title in himself or herself or that the seller is selling only whatever right or title he or she or a third person may have. This is the only manner in which a warranty of title can be excluded or modified. Specific language must be included in the contract for sale beyond that specified in Section 2-316, which deals with exclusion of express and implied warranties, to make clear to the buyer that the seller does not warrant the title to the goods. The reason for this requirement is that the buyer normally may expect a seller to warrant the title even though the seller is excluding all other warranties.

EXPRESS WARRANTIES

Provisions

The UCC (Section 2-313) states that express warranties are created as follows:

(a) Any affirmation of fact or promise made by the seller to the buyer which relates to the goods and becomes part of the basis of the bargain creates an express warranty that the goods shall conform to the affirmation or promise.
(b) Any description of the goods which is made part of the basis of the bargain creates an express warranty that the goods shall conform to the description.
(c) Any sample or model which is made part of the basis of the bargain creates an express warranty that the whole of the goods shall conform to the sample or model.

Affirmation of Fact

Although a specific factual statement will create a warranty, a statement as to the value of goods or a statement of the seller's opinion or commendation of the goods does not create a warranty (Section 2-313[a]). It is reasonable to expect that a person selling goods will make favorable statements about the product being sold. For this reason, statements as to value or mere opinions do not create an express warranty under the UCC.

Suppose the salesman at Al's Used Car Lot states to a person looking at a 1984 Ford, "That car is the best deal in town." Such a statement is the typical positive statement a buyer expects of a seller. No one expects a seller to run his or her products down. Because the average purchaser expects these favorable comments from a seller, a buyer may not rely upon a statement like the one here dealing with the 1984 Ford. It may not be relied upon in a breach-of-warranty case.

Basis of the Bargain. However, Comment 8 to Section 2-313 indicates that the critical question remains: What statements of the seller have in the circumstances and in objective judgment become part of the basis of the bargain? All the statements of the seller are part of the basis of the bargain unless good reason is shown to the contrary.

Exactly what is meant by the phrase "basis of the bargain?" The drafters of the UCC intended for the courts to examine what the agreement between the parties actually was. What terms did the parties agree upon in striking a deal? "Basis of the bargain" is a somewhat murky concept, but it is very much like reliance. Suppose the seller of the 1984 Ford in the earlier example states: "The tires on the Ford are brand new radials and cost over $500." The buyer appears to be impressed by this statement, and says: "Well, in that case, the car is a good buy. I'll take the car." If the tires turn out to be bias-belted retreads with 7,500 miles on them, has the seller breached an express warranty? Was any warranty created by this seller's statement? The answer to both questions is yes. The seller's statement is one of fact and becomes part of the deal between the buyer and seller

because the buyer is apparently induced by these facts to enter into this agreement. The seller's statement will be treated by the courts as a part of the basis of the bargain.

Puffing. If the seller of a dining-room set says, "This is the best dining-room set in town," a buyer would not reasonably use this statement as part of the basis of the bargain between the parties. This type of language is commonly referred to as "puffing." To create an express warranty under the UCC more than mere puffing by the seller is required. If the seller instead says, "This table is solid oak," an express warranty that the table is solid oak is created. Either the table is oak or it is not; whether it is oak is a question of fact, not of opinion. If it turns out that the table is pine stained an oak color, and the buyer wanted an oak table, the buyer may bring an action for breach of an express warranty created by the seller's statement.

Many of the cases dealing with puffing do not cite a clear rule. The more specific the statement, the more likely that a court will call it one of fact and not opinion. Whether the statement is oral or written is also important. The most commonly cited rule could be called the fact-opinion rule as stated by the court in Royal Business Machines v. Lorraine Corp., 633 F.2d 34 (1980):

> The decisive test for whether a given representation is a warranty or merely an expression of the seller's opinion is whether the seller asserts a fact of which the buyer is ignorant or merely states an opinion or judgment on a matter of which the seller has no special knowledge and on which the buyer may be expected also to have an opinion and to exercise his judgment. . . . General statements to the effect that goods are "the best". . . . or are "of good quality," or will "last a lifetime" and be "in perfect condition" . . . are generally regarded as expressions of the seller's opinion or "the puffing of his wares" and do not create an express warranty.

Some cases following this test have failed to find an express warranty. For example, in Carpenter v. Alberto Culver Co., 184 N.W.2d 547 (Mich. App. 1970), the plaintiff brought suit because she suffered an adverse skin reaction after using a hair dye manufactured by Alberto Culver. The plaintiff argued that an express warranty was created by the City Drug Store through a clerk who stated to her that several of the clerk's friends used the dye and that her own "hair came out very nice" and the plaintiff "would get very fine results." The court found these rather vague statements were not express warranties. Other courts, however, have found such statements to be express warranties. In General Supply & Equipment Co. v. Phillips, 490 S.W.2d 913 (Tex. Civ. App. 1972), the plaintiff brought suit over some plastic paneling sold by the defendant to the plaintiff to cover the plaintiff's greenhouses as roofing material. The paneling had been advertised as follows: "Tests show no deterioration in 5 years normal use" and "It won't turn black or discolor . . . even after years of exposure." The paneling darkened and turned black about two years after it was installed. The court noted that the plaintiff had knowledge of the facts asserted in the advertising and would not have bought the paneling had he not seen the advertisement. It found that these statements appearing in the advertising constituted an express warranty. (See also *Interco* v. *Randustrial* later in this chapter.) Other cases in the warranty area seem to follow different tests for determining if a statement is puffing or not.

It is sometimes difficult to distinguish between a statement of fact and a statement of opinion. In making this determination, the court examines whether the seller has used words that imply or convey an express warranty to the buyer. Predicting the outcome of a puffing defense is quite difficult.

Puffing is a major defense in express-warranty cases. Ask yourself why it should be a defense at all. If a merchant makes untrue statements about his or her products, why should he or she escape from the bargain with a defense like puffing? Generally, the types of statements that are regarded as puffing are vague statements of praise not clearly relied upon by the buyer. Even so, no one can be certain about the outcome of a case.

Suppose you purchase a steak at a restaurant because an advertisement you read states: "I am sure you will find this steak to be one of the most tender and juicy steaks you have ever eaten." If you find it tough and dry, will you be able to bring a case for breach of warranty? The court would probably find such a statement by an advertiser to be mere puffing upon which you may not reasonably rely. Should this be the outcome of the case?

Description

An express warranty can also be created by describing goods if the description is part of the basis of the bargain between the parties. The seller need not use the word warranty, nor is it necessary that the buyer rely on the seller's affirmation of fact or promise in order to find that the seller made an express warranty. Comment 3 to Section 2-313 states: "In actual practice affirmations of fact made by the seller about the goods during a bargain are regarded as part of the description of those goods; hence no particular reliance on such statements need be shown in order to weave them into the fabric of the agreement." The description need not be by words. Technical specifications, blueprints, or the like, if made part of the basis of the bargain between the parties, can create an express warranty.

Sample or Model

An express warranty also can be made by a sample or model that is made part of the basis of the bargain between the parties. When the seller actually draws an item from the bulk of goods that is the subject matter of the sale, the item is referred to as a sample; when a demonstration item is offered for inspection, it is called a model.

Creation after Contracting

It is possible for an express warranty to be created after the contract has been executed by the parties. If the buyer asks the seller, for example, whether the plastic just bought will withstand freezing temperatures and the seller replies "yes," this might constitute an express warranty. Section 2-209(2) of the UCC permits modification of a contract without consideration. However, the Statute of Frauds must be complied with.

If the parties orally agree upon an express warranty, but the final executed contract fails to reflect this agreement, the party wishing to assert the warranty may encounter difficulties in establishing its existence. The parol evidence rule found in Section 2-202 prohibits any evidence that contradicts a writing intended by the parties as a final expression of their agreement.

The following facts illustrate a typical express-warranty case: A purchaser of a mobile home, John Benfer, was told that the mobile home he was interested in purchasing had quarter-inch plywood sheathing that made it better than cheaper units. A mobile home similar to the one purchased by Benfer was on the seller's lot. The seller pointed out the grade of plywood sheathing to Benfer. Among the written warranties given Benfer was one specifically warranting that his mobile home would come with quarter-inch plywood. The home delivered to Benfer did not come with this sheathing. He brought suit based on breach of an express warranty created by affirmation of fact and by model. The court agreed that these warranties were created and, because the home delivered failed to conform to the model, found a breach of express warranty by the seller (Town and Country Mobile Home v. Benfer, 527 S.W.2d 523 [Tex. Civ. App. 1975]).

The following case discusses the issues of puffing and reliance in express-warranty cases.

Interco, Inc. v. Randustrial Corp.

Court of Appeals of Missouri
533 S.W.2d 257 (1976)

Suit was brought against Randustrial Corp., the defendant, by Interco, the plaintiff, for breach of warranty. Randustrial asserted as defenses that its statements were mere puffing and that there was no evidence of reliance on the statements by Interco. The court rejected these defenses. The jury at the trial-court level decided for Randustrial and found no breach of contract. The appeals court affirmed the jury verdict of no breach of contract—although it found that the statement in question was not puffing and was relied upon by Interco.

Gunn, Judge

Interco maintains facilities consisting of 21 buildings for its International Shoe Company division in St. Louis. In 1971, Building No. 3 required floor repairs on the first story. The floor was extremely rough, rendering it difficult to move merchandise between the storage area and loading dock. Interco's Manager of Facilities Engineering read Randustrial's building maintenance supply catalogue and from it ordered a product designated as Resilihard which was designed as a floor covering to smooth rough areas. However, after a discussion with Randustrial's sales representative and upon the latter's recommendation, another of Randustrial's products, called Sylox, was selected because of its flexibility. Sylox was applied to the first floor of Building No. 3, and its use was satisfactory for Interco's purposes.

The following year—1972—a floor problem similar to that in Building No. 3 developed in Building No. 1. The second floor of Building No. 1 became rough, creating difficulty in the movement of hand-truck traffic. Because of the favorable experience with Sylox and also by reason of Randustrial's catalogue description for its use, Interco ordered and installed Sylox to the second floor of Building No. 1. The catalogue described the purpose of Sylox as "to patch or resurface old wood floors for hand-trucking or foot traffic." The order was placed and the Sylox applied without the advice of or consultation with Randustrial's representatives. The consequences were wholly undesirable, for shortly after its application, the Sylox began to deteriorate and became unserviceable; it was an impediment rather than an expedient in the movement of hand-trucking.

Interco maintains that it was entitled to judgment as a matter of law based on a breach of express warranty by Randustrial. Interco argues that the purchase of Sylox was based on the following Randustrial catalogue description of the material and asserts an express warranty thereby:

> Sylox is a hard yet malleable material which bonds firm to wood floors for smooth and easy hand-trucking. Sylox will absorb considerable flex without cracking and is not softened by spillage of oil, grease or solvents.

We have noted that Interco claims the existence of a warranty as to Sylox, and Randustrial argues the absence of a warranty. We disagree with Randustrial's contentions in this regard. Although Randustrial contends its reference to Sylox in its sales catalogue did not constitute an express warranty, if the words used in the catalogue constitute a description or an affirmation of fact or promise about Sylox and became a part of the basis of the bargain, an express warranty was created. Randustrial also asserts that there could be no breach of warranty because Interco had failed to test the material before applying it to Building No. 1 and had failed to seek advice from Randustrial on its application. The uncontradicted evidence was that the cause of the breakup of the Sylox was the movement of the floor. There was nothing vague in Interco's evidence as to the intended use of Sylox. The evidence was palpable that Interco wanted something to withstand flex without breaking. The catalogue stated that "Sylox will absorb considerable flex." Thus, there was a description or affirmation of fact or "warranty" regarding Sylox giving rise to the purpose for which it was purchased by Interco. This was not mere puffing of a product. Interco was entitled to take the catalogue description of Sylox at its face value and plain meaning. There was no need to consult Randustrial or seek its advice regarding the use of Sylox. Any suggestion that Interco was at fault for not having tested the product or sought consultation is fatuous, for the catalogue description made no such requirement. All the buyers are required to establish is that the express warranties were made and that they were false, thereby establishing a breach of the contract. Interco had no obligation to establish a defect in Sylox as Randustrial suggests. We have previously noted that there has been no contention that the Sylox was misapplied.

Randustrial's argument that Interco failed to prove reliance on any warranty is also not felicitous. There is no mention of reliance in 2-313. And the comments to that section of the UCC reveal that the concept of reliance as required in pre-UCC warranty cases was purposefully abandoned.

The fact that the language read by Interco was contained in a catalogue and was basically an advertisement does not preclude a finding that it is a warranty. A brochure, catalogue, or advertisement may constitute an express warranty. . . . However, the catalogue advertisement or brochure must have at least been read, as the UCC requires the proposed express warranty be part of the basis of the bargain. Randustrial does not dispute the fact that Interco had read the catalogue.

Randustrial relies on the pre-UCC case of *Turner* v. *Central Hardware Co.* (1964), arguing that the statement that Sylox "will absorb considerable flex" merely reflects the seller's opinion of the goods and creates no warranty. In the Central Hardware Co. case, a ladder advertised as "mighty strong and durable" collapsed under use causing injury to the plaintiff. In discussing the use of factual information vis-a-vis mere "sales talk" in advertising, the court said:

> The seller's privilege to puff his wares, enhance their quality and recommend their value, even to the point of exaggeration, is unquestionable, so long as his salesmanship remains in the field of "dealer's talk," commendation or mere expressions of opinion. . . .

We believe that the foregoing pre-UCC law continues under 2-313, which specifically excludes a seller's mere opinion or commendation from being interpreted as an express warranty. The Central Hardware Co. case does make clear, though, that the language chosen by the seller in his advertising must be interpreted in favor of the buyer in order to restrict "untruthful puffing of wares." We believe that this is the same type of approach desired by the draftsmen of the UCC. . . . An important factor is whether the seller assumes to assert a fact of which the buyer may be expected to have an opinion and be able to express his own judgment.

Although Randustrial is pertinacious in its contention that the catalogue content regarding absorbability of considerable flex is merely a reflection of opinion, we must disagree. It is manifest that the words so used were meant to induce purchases through the assurance that considerable flex would be absorbed and were not mere opinion. The words were an affirmation of fact within the meaning of 2-313.

But having determined that an express warranty as to Sylox did exist, we reach the crux of this case—whether there was a breach of that warranty by Randustrial as a matter of fact. Ordinarily—and this case is no exception—the question of whether there has been a breach of warranty is a factual matter to be determined by the trier of fact.

The keystone of this case and the basis for Randustrial's triumph before the jury and affirmation by this court continues to be the phrase "absorb considerable flex." That phrase is too imprecise to be defined as a matter of law. It was for the jury to determine as a matter of fact whether Sylox conformed to the promise to absorb considerable flex. The jury could have reasonably found on the basis of the evidence presented to it that the flex or movement in the second floor of Building No. 1 was more than considerable and more than Sylox was designed to accommodate. The fact issue as to what amounted to considerable flex in this case was proper for the jury to determine.

The jury verdict for Randustrial is affirmed.

Note that the plaintiff must have relied on the advertisement for it to be an express warranty. The advertisement thus must be part of the basis of the bargain between the parties for any express warranty to arise based on such advertising literature. The court in *Interco* required some evidence that Interco knew of the statement in the catalogue: "sylox will absorb considerable flex," and that Interco relied upon the statement in making the purchase.

The absence of reliance might prevent a plaintiff from recovering. In Hagenbuch v. Snap-On Tools Corp., 339 F. Supp. 676 (D.C. N.H. 1972), the plaintiff purchased a cross-pen hammer from a salesman of Snap-On Tools. The plaintiff argued that the Snap-On Tools 1969 catalogue created an express warranty. The catalogue stated that the hammer is "excellent for the repair work since it has plenty of beef to handle heavy tires. Also can be used for many other jobs such as straightening frames, bumper brackets, bumpers, puller work, etc. . . ." The plaintiff was struck in the eye by a chip from the hammer. He tried to collect on breach of express warranty, but the court found there was no evidence that Hagenbuch had relied on the catalogue description when he purchased the hammer. The judge therefore ruled Hagenbuch was not entitled to recover for breach of express warranty.

This case illustrates the importance for the plaintiff of establishing that the advertising became part of the basis of the bargain between the parties. Without evidence that the plaintiff was influenced by the advertising statement in ques-

tion, it is unlikely a plaintiff will be able to establish an express warranty.

IMPLIED WARRANTY OF MERCHANTABILITY

Provisions

Section 2-314 of the UCC states:

(1) Unless excluded or modified (Section 2-316), a warranty that the goods shall be merchantable is implied in a contract for their sale if the seller is a merchant with respect to goods of that kind. Under this section the serving for value of food or drink to be consumed either on the premises or elsewhere is a sale.

(2) Goods to be merchantable must be at least such as
   (a) pass without objection in the trade under the contract description; and
   (b) in the case of fungible goods, are of fair average quality within the description; and
   (c) are fit for the ordinary purposes for which such goods are used; and
   (d) run, within the variations permitted by the agreement, of even kind, quality and quantity within each unit and among all units involved; and
   (e) are adequately contained, packaged, and labeled as the agreement may require; and

(f) conform to the promises or affirmations of fact made on the container or label if any.

(3) Unless excluded or modified (Section 2-316) other implied warranties may arise from course of dealing or usage of trade.

Thus the implied warranty of merchantability arises by operation of law—not as a result of any warranty expressly stated in the contract. The requirements stated in Section 2-314(2) are *cumulative*, but subsections (e) and (f) deal with packaging, and subsection (b) deals with fungible, or interchangeable, goods. This is not an exhaustive list of what is "merchantable" but merely states that the goods must at least comply with these requirements.

Generally, the court will try to determine if the goods are fit for the ordinary purposes for which such goods are used. In making this determination, the court will consider the manner in which such goods are used. A seller who delivers shoes that come apart when the buyer walks around in them has breached the warranty of merchantability because shoes certainly should be fit for ordinary walking.

Merchants

It should be noted that Section 2-314 applies only when the seller is a merchant. If the seller is not a merchant, no such warranty arises. For example, in Siemen v. Alden, 341 N.E.2d 713 (Ill. App. 1975), the plaintiff brought suit for breach of the implied warranty of merchantability. He had purchased an old multirip saw from a man in the sawmill business. While operating the machine, the plaintiff was injured. The court refused to permit the plaintiff to recover based on the implied warranty of merchantability. It found that the defendant was not in the business of selling saws and therefore was not a merchant pursuant to Section 2-104.

If a seller is a nonmerchant, there is no implied warranty of merchantability. Nonetheless, these provisions may serve as guidelines when the nonmerchant-seller states that the goods are guaranteed.

Fungible Goods

If the sale involves fungible goods, the court will examine whether the goods are of "fair average quality." This means that the goods must be roughly of the same type as specified in the contract. Some of the lowest quality goods could be included in the delivery, but the mix must average out to be close to the standard in the contract.

Food

In determining whether food is merchantable or not, some courts follow the "foreign-natural distinction"—that is, a given food is merchantable if it contains elements that are natural to the product. A consumer who breaks his tooth on a cherry pit while eating a piece of cherry pie would be unable to recover in a jurisdiction following this test. Other jurisdictions follow the "reasonable expectation" test—that is, only those things that we reasonably expect to be in the food should be in it. In a jurisdiction following the "reasonable expectation" test, the consumer who breaks a tooth on a cherry pit in a piece of pie might be able to recover.

In a famous case involving breach of the implied warranty of merchantability, Webster v. Blue Ship Tea Room, Inc., 198 N.E.2d 309 (Mass. 1964), the plaintiff brought suit because, while she was eating fish chowder at the Blue Ship Tea Room, a fish bone became lodged in her throat. This led to two esophagoscopies and the eventual extraction of a fish bone. The question in this case was whether there had been a breach of the implied warranty of merchantability. The court delved into the culinary traditions of New England and determined that fish chowder normally contains large chunks of fish in which a consumer ought to expect bones. The court ruled that the occasional presence of fish bones should be anticipated by a customer, and therefore it decided for the Tea Room.

IMPLIED WARRANTY OF FITNESS FOR A PARTICULAR PURPOSE

Particular Purpose

If the seller knows at the time of contracting the particular purpose for which the buyer wants the goods and the buyer relies on the seller's skill or judgment to select or furnish suitable goods, there is an implied warranty that the goods will be fit for the purpose the buyer specifies at the time of contracting (Section 2-315).

A particular purpose differs from the ordinary purpose for which goods are used. If a buyer wishes to purchase climbing shoes and asks the seller to select a pair for him or her, the seller breaches this warranty if he or she sells the buyer shoes used only for ordinary walking. The shoes might be suitable for walking and therefore merchantable, but they would not be suitable for the particular purpose the buyer specified. It is not necessary that the buyer state how he or she intends to use the product as long as the circumstances should make the seller aware of the needs of the buyer.

Simply because the goods are merchantable does not mean they are fit for the buyer's particular purpose. If the buyer wishes to purchase a furnace for use at home and tells the seller that he or she wants to heat a house of 2,000 sq. ft., the seller has breached the implied warranty of fitness for a particular purpose if the heater is inadequate to heat the buyer's house, even though it operates properly and would heat a much smaller house quite nicely.

Unlike the implied warranty of merchantability, this warranty applies to both merchants and nonmerchants.

Reliance

Reliance is critical under Section 2-315. If the buyer supplies specifications to the seller, there is no reliance and hence no breach of the warranty, even if the seller knows the purpose for which the goods are to be used.

Gates v. Abernathy
Court of Appeals of Oklahoma
11 U.C.C. 491 (1972)

Plaintiff, Gates, brought suit against Abernathy, the owner of the shop, Penelope's. Gates purchased a dress at Penelope's for his wife. He was assured that the dress was suitable for his wife. It was not, and Gates sued to receive his money back. The trial and appeals court decided for Gates.

Neptune, Justice

One of the plaintiffs, Dr. Paul Gates, wished to purchase some clothes to give his wife (the other plaintiff) as a Christmas present. Dr. Gates had never before bought any clothing for his wife and was ignorant of what size she wore. He was aware, however, that his wife had frequently shopped at "Penelope's," a shop owned by defendant, and that she had been waited on there by the store manager, Penny. Therefore, he went to "Penelope's," spoke to Penny and explained to her that he wished to buy some clothes to give to his wife as a Christmas present. Penny showed Dr. Gates certain items in sizes that she said she was certain would be proper for Mrs. Gates. Dr. Gates picked out three pant suits in the size that Penny had recommended and purchased them. It was understood that if the suits did not fit or if there "was any problem" they could be returned.

When she received the gifts, Mrs. Gates tried them on and discovered that they were much too big. Shortly after Christmas, Dr. Gates returned the pant suits to "Penelope's" and received a credit slip. When Mrs. Gates came to the shop with the credit slip she was unable to find anything in her size. She was directed to another store owned by defendant but found nothing acceptable in her size. She demanded the money back but this was refused. Dr. and Mrs. Gates brought this action to recover the purchase price of the suits plus attorney fees.

Plaintiffs sued under section 2-315 claiming breach of an implied warranty of fitness for a particular purpose. Defendant entered a general denial. The trial court sitting without a jury entered judgment for plaintiff in the sum of $192.62 plus an attorney's fee of $50 plus $4 for costs. Defendant appeals.

Appellant asserts that this is not a situation where appellees could recover on an implied warranty of fitness. There is no merit in this contention. The statute upon which the action is based, section 2-315 states:

> Where the seller at the time of contracting has reason to know any particular purpose for which the goods are required and that the buyer is relying on the seller's skill or judgment to select or furnish suitable goods, there is unless excluded or modified under the next section an implied warranty that the goods shall be fit for such purpose.

It is hard to imagine a case which fits into the outline of the statute as well as this one. It is uncontested that the buyer here was relying on the judgment of the seller to furnish the kind of goods he wanted, nor is there any question that the seller was aware that the seller's expertise was being relied on by the buyer. Appellees did not sue on the basis that the clothes were not merchantable or useable as clothes. Rather, appellees claimed that they were not useable for the particular purpose for which they were bought, that is, for Mrs. Gates to wear.

The statute gives relief to a buyer who relies on a seller's expertise to buy a product to be used in a particular manner. Even before the statute was enacted the Oklahoma Supreme Court gave relief in analogous circumstances. In *Ransom* v. *Robinson Packer Co.* (1926), the court said:

> Where an article of personal property is sold for a definite purpose made known to the seller, and the seller represents that the article will perform that particular purpose, there is a warranty of fitness which protects the purchaser and for which the seller is liable, in the event the article fails to do what it was sold to do.

In that case, pumps sold to the buyer operated in the manner expected, but they did not perform the job that the seller had promised. In the case at bar, the clothes were good clothes but they did not fit Mrs. Gates as the seller had represented. We conclude that the instant case is controlled by section 2-315.

The judgment of $192.62 against appellant and in favor of appellees is affirmed and the case is remanded to the trial court for hearing to fix the amount of the attorney's fee.

Affirmed and remanded.

CONFLICT OF WARRANTIES

When a purchaser buys a product, it may have only one warranty or it may have several warranties. Warranties on a product should be construed by the court in such a fashion as to give effect to every warranty. On the other hand, if it is impossible to give effect to all warranties, the intention of the parties will determine which warranty is controlling. Section 2-317 sets forth three rules to determine the intention of the parties:

(a) Exact or technical specifications displace an inconsistent sample or model or general language of description.
(b) A sample from an existing bulk displaces inconsistent general language of description.
(c) Express warranties displace inconsistent implied warranties other than an implied warranty of fitness for a particular purpose.

These rules control unless one of the parties introduces evidence indicating that the rules would lead to an unreasonable result. It should be noted that if the seller misleads the buyer by implying that all the warranties can be performed, and they cannot all be performed, the seller will be estopped from setting up the inconsistency of the warranties as a defense.

EXCLUSION OR MODIFICATION OF WARRANTIES

Express Warranties

Express warranties, as noted earlier, can be created by an affirmation of fact or promise made by the seller, or by a description, or by a sample or model that is made part of the basis of the bargain between the parties. Once an express warranty has been created, it is very difficult to disclaim. Section 2-316(1) states:

Words or conduct relevant to the creation of an express warranty and words or conduct tending to negate or limit warranty shall be construed wherever reasonable as consistent with each other; but subject to the provisions of the Article on parol or extrinsic evidence (Section 2-202) negation or limitation is inoperative to the extent that such construction is unreasonable.

Conflict Between Warranty and Disclaimer.
Once an express warranty comes into existence, any language in the contract suggesting that express warranties have been disclaimed will create a conflict between the warranty and the disclaimer. If it is possible to read the warranty and disclaimer as consistent, the court must do so, but if such a reading is unreasonable, then the express warranty prevails over the disclaimer. The drafters of the UCC were trying to protect the buyer from hidden

disclaimers by making any language inconsistent with the express warranty ineffective. In this way, the buyer is not misled.

Thus any contract that uses language excluding "all warranties, express or implied," but that also contains an express warranty in direct conflict with this attempted disclaimer, will not succeed in eliminating the express warranty. If the seller provides the buyer with a sample but tries to exclude all express warranties in the contract, it is unlikely that the express warranty created by the sample can be disclaimed through use of such language.

Suppose a person signs a contract for the purchase of steel pipe. The contract explicitly states that the pipe will withstand temperatures down to 30 degrees below zero. This statement is an affirmation of fact and constitutes an express warranty. The contract also attempts to exclude "all warranties, express and implied." Is such a clause effective to eliminate the warranty that the pipe will withstand temperatures at least as low as 30 degrees below zero? The court must read the warranty and disclaimer as consistent if possible. Here such a reading would not be possible. If the buyer purchases the pipe, and it fails to withstand a temperature of 30 degrees below zero, he or she has a cause of action against the seller for breach of warranty. The express warranty and the exclusion directly conflict. The express warranty has not been effectively excluded.

Problems of Proof. Subsection (1) of Section 2-316 is subject to the provisions on parol or extrinsic evidence (Section 2-202). These relate to the problem of proving an express warranty. Although the parties may have in fact agreed upon a particular express warranty, they may not have incorporated it into the final written contract. The question then becomes: Can the person asserting the existence of an express warranty introduce evidence of an oral agreement arrived at before the contract was signed (but not expressed in the contract) when the contract disclaims the existence of any express warranties? The parol evidence rule, found in Section 2-202, may prevent this evidence from being introduced at trial because it contradicts the written terms of the contract.

Suppose in our pipe example the salesman tells the purchaser orally that the pipe will withstand temperatures at least as low as 30 degrees below zero. However, the contract the buyer signs explicitly states that the seller will not guarantee the performance of the pipe in temperatures below zero. The contract states that it is intended as the final agreement of the parties and is a complete and exclusive statement of the terms of the agreement. Clearly, this contract is not silent or ambiguous on the question of the pipe's ability to withstand temperatures. The court will not permit introduction of the salesman's statement to alter or vary the explicit terms of this written contract.

Implied Warranties

Implied Warranty of Merchantability. The implied warranty of merchantability may be disclaimed if the disclaimer mentions the word "merchantability" and, in case of a writing, is conspicuous. Explicitly stating in a written contract "There is no implied warranty of merchantability," in larger type than the rest of the contract, will call the buyer's attention to the exclusion of this warranty. This may also be excluded by other language, as is discussed in the following material.

Implied Warranty of Fitness for a Particular Purpose. To exclude the implied warranty of fitness for a particular purpose, the exclusion must be in writing and conspicuous. It can be disclaimed by the language: "There are no warranties which extend beyond the description on the face hereof." Note that subsection (2) of 2-316 does not specifically require that language excluding the implied warranty of fitness must use the phrase "implied warranty of fitness." A seller might state in a written contract "There is no implied warranty of fitness." If this appears in larger type than the rest of the contract, it will call the buyer's attention to the exclusion of this warranty. This warranty may also be excluded by other language, as discussed in the next paragraph.

Language that Excludes All Implied Warranties. Excluding or modifying either of the implied warranties of quality can easily be accomplished by using the language specified in Section 2-316(2), as discussed in the two preceding paragraphs.

Phrases such as "as is" or "with all faults," can exclude all implied warranties (Section 2-316[3]). The seller need not use these exact phrases as long as the language used "in common understanding calls the buyer's attention to the exclusion of warranties and makes plain

that there is no implied warranty." By using the phrases provided, a seller can be certain of protection. It should be noted that subsection (3)(a) says nothing about the phrase being conspicuous. Because there are differing court decisions on this point, a prudent seller will make such a disclaimer conspicuous.

Conspicuous Language. To make certain that disclaimer language is conspicuous, the seller probably should use bold type (type larger and darker than that of the rest of the contract) and the disclaimer should appear on the first page of the contract. An extremely careful seller might use a different color type for the disclaimer and have the buyer initial the paragraph containing the disclaimer. If this course is followed, there will be little doubt that the buyer was aware of the disclaimer of all warranties. The following case discusses the need for the term "as is" to be conspicuous.

Fairchild Industries v. Maritime Air Services, Ltd.

Court of Appeals of Maryland
333 A.2d 313 (1975)

Maritime purchased a helicopter from Fairchild. The contract indicated that the helicopter was sold "as is." Maritime claimed a breach of the implied warranties. Fairchild claimed the implied warranties had been disclaimed. The court rejected Fairchild's argument that it had effectively excluded the implied warranties by use of the phrase "as is" in the contract. The court found that the legislature intended for the exclusion of warranties to be brought to the buyer's attention. In ruling for Maritime, it found Fairchild had failed to exclude the implied warranties because the phrase "as is" must be conspicuous in order for it to be effective. It was held not to be conspicuous in this case.

Levine, Judge

On May 9, 1969, the parties entered into a lease agreement in which Fairchild leased a helicopter to Maritime for an initial term of one year, with options to extend the lease for an additional two years, subject to an option to purchase the aircraft during the term of the lease. Maritime exercised the option to purchase on March 19, 1970. The parties entered into a purchase agreement which consisted of a printed form, furnished by Fairchild, on which relevant provisions were inserted by typewriter. Among those typewritten provisions was the following:

> It is specifically understood and agreed by the parties that the Aircraft is sold in an "as is" condition. Seller makes no representation or warranties express or implied whatsoever except Warranty of Title. Buyer acknowledges that before entering into this Agreement he has examined the Aircraft as fully as he desires.

The interposition of this "disclaimer" to Maritime's allegations that Fairchild had breached implied warranties of merchantability and fitness in the sale of the aircraft led to the certification of these questions:

> 1. Does the requirement found in section 2-316(2) . . . that "to exclude or modify the implied warranty of merchantability or any part of it the language must mention merchantability and in case of a writing must be conspicuous, and to exclude or modify any implied warranty of fitness the exclusion must be by a writing and conspicuous" apply to the provisions for exclusion of warranties set forth in section 2-316(3)(a) . . . ?

The purpose of section 2-316 is set forth in Official Comment 1 to that section:

> This section is designed principally to deal with those frequent clauses in sales contracts which seek to exclude "all warranties, express or implied." It seeks to protect a buyer from unexpected and unbargained language of disclaimer by denying effect to such language when inconsistent with language of express warranty and permitting the exclusion of implied warranties only by conspicuous language or other circumstances which protect the buyer from surprise.

In light of the legislative purpose of section 2-316 to insure that exclusions of warranties are brought to the attention of the buyer, we are persuaded by the argument that, while expressions like "as is" put the buyer on notice of the disclaimer, they do so only when brought to the buyer's attention. This means that in the case of a written disclaimer, the writing must be conspicuous. Acceptance of the argument advanced by Fairchild (that the phrase "as is" need not be conspicuous) would mean that a written exclusion of the implied warranty of merchantability, expressly mentioning that word, would be ineffective unless conspicuous; and that the written language, "There are no warranties which extend beyond the description on the face hereof," would be equally ineffective to exclude a warranty of fitness unless conspicuous. Yet, the words *as is,* even if buried in the fine print of a lengthy document, would exclude all implied warranties. We fail to see how this anomalous result would further the avowed purpose of section 2-316 "to protect a buyer from unexpected and unbargained language of disclaimer."

Nor is there any merit in Fairchild's argument that had the drafters intended the expression *as is* to be conspicuous, they would have employed the uppercase "AS IS" or "WITH ALL FAULTS" rather than the lowercase. The same lowercase is also used in the exclusions mentioned in Subsection (2); yet, even Fairchild would concede that they must be conspicuous.

Examination of Goods. Section 2-316(3)(b) permits a seller to exclude the implied warranties by giving the buyer an opportunity to examine the goods or a sample or model. If a seller wishes to rely upon subsection (3)(b), he or she must demand that the buyer examine the goods and give the buyer the opportunity to inspect the goods before entering into the contract; and the buyer must have examined the goods as fully as he or she desires. The seller, by demanding that the buyer examine the goods, puts the buyer on notice that he or she is assuming the risk of defects that an examination would reveal. Merely telling the buyer the goods are available for inspection is not sufficient; the seller must demand that the buyer examine them.

When the buyer examines the goods, a sample, or a model, the buyer's skill and method of examining will determine what defects are excluded by the examination. Defects that the buyer is unable to discover because they are latent or beyond his or her power of discovery through reasonable examination will not be excluded.

The following case illustrates the consequences of a failure to examine the goods after a demand has been made on the buyer.

Tarulli v. Birds in Paradise
New York Civil Court, Queens County
26 U.C.C. 872 (1979)

Plaintiff Tarulli brought suit for the death of an exotic bird he had bought from a bird dealer called Birds in Paradise. He asserted a breach of the implied warranty of merchantability and argued that the defendant had failed to exclude this warranty. The court disagreed, saying that the defendant had asked Tarulli to have the bird examined by a veterinarian, but he had failed to do so. Because Tarulli failed to have the bird examined the court ruled he was bound by the agreement even though the exotic bird was ill at the time Birds in Paradise delivered it to Tarulli. The court ruled for Birds in Paradise.

Posner, Justice

This is a small claims action which involves a defendant doing business as Birds in Paradise and a plaintiff whose purchase of an exotic bird turned into a veritable Miltonian "Paradise Lost."

On Dec. 18, 1978, the plaintiff, Bart Tarulli signed an agreement with the defendant, a dealer in birds, for the sale of one Moluccan Cockatoo. The agreed upon consideration was $400 cash and one Mexican Yellow Head Parrot. The agreement of sale, specifically signed and agreed to by plaintiff, Tarulli, stated as follows:

"This bird is guaranteed to be in good health, to the best of our knowledge, at the time of sale. The customer has a health guarantee extending to close of business 12-20-78, in which to have the bird checked by a licensed veterinarian and is urged to do so. If the veterinarian finds anything seriously wrong with the bird, it will be exchanged for another bird of equal value of the customer's choice, at once or when available, provided a letter from the examining veterinarian is offered as evidence of the bird's illness, and the bird is returned within the guarantee period. No exchange will be made after this period."

Plaintiff testified during trial that he never took the cockatoo to a veterinarian during the period permitted in the agreement. On or about Jan. 12, 1979 the cockatoo showed symptoms of illness and plaintiff brought said bird to Dr. B. J. Schiller, a veterinarian. Despite the extensive care and treatment administered by Dr. Schiller, the cockatoo died that same evening.

Dr. Schiller, as an expert witness for the plaintiff, testified that a post-mortem examination revealed the cause of death as anemia which she would guess existed for more than three weeks, but wasn't sure how long.

It is the plaintiff's contention that the defendant breached the implied warranty of merchantability under the Uniform Commercial Code section 2-314, and [that plaintiff] should be entitled to the sum of $800 ($400 plus the value of the Mexican Yellow Head Parrot), and $50 for veterinary fees.

The plaintiff bolsters this contention by arguing that birds fall within the definition of "goods" as contained in UCC section 2-105(1). Furthermore, the defendant satisfied the definition of a "merchant" under the UCC section 2-104. Thus, the plaintiff maintains that he bought "goods" from a "merchant" and said goods were defective at the time of sale, thereby breaching the implied warranty of merchantability, which was not excluded or modified as per UCC section 2-316. The plaintiff emphasizes UCC section 2-316(2) that to exclude or modify the implied warranty of merchantability, there must be specific mention of the word "merchantability" and the writing must be conspicuous. The plaintiff argues that the defendant failed expressly to exclude the implied warranty of merchantability by failing to specifically mention merchantability in the conditions of sale.

However, subsection 2 of UCC section 2-316 is not the exclusive mechanism to exclude or modify the implied warranty of merchantability. Subsection (3) provides as follows:

"Notwithstanding subsection (2)
"(b) when the buyer before entering into the contract has examined the goods or the sample or model as fully as he desired or has refused to examine the goods there is no implied warranty with regard to defects which an examination ought in the circumstances to have revealed to him."

The Official Comment 8 of section 2-316 of the Code states that this subsection goes to the nature of the responsibility assumed by the seller at the time of the making of the contract.

"Of course if the buyer discovers the defect and uses the goods anyway, or if he unreasonably fails to examine the goods before he uses them, resulting injuries may be found to result from his own action, rather than proximately from a breach of warranty.

"In order to bring the transaction within the scope of 'refused to examine' in paragraph (b), it is not sufficient that the goods are available for inspection. There must in addition be a demand by the seller that the buyer examine the goods fully. The seller by the demand puts the buyer on notice that he is assuming the risk of defects which the examination ought to reveal."

This court finds that the defendant did in fact make such a demand upon the plaintiff to have the cockatoo checked by a licensed veterinarian before Dec. 20, 1978, and it was specifically for the purpose of having the veterinarian determine whether there is "anything seriously wrong with the bird," which only then would entitle the plaintiff to certain relief.

Here, the defendant by the demand for an examination of the cockatoo by a veterinarian put the plaintiff on notice that he is assuming the risk of defects which the examination ought to reveal. Not only was there testimony by the plaintiff that he never took the cockatoo to a veterinarian within the designated period; in effect, bringing the transaction within the scope of a refusal to examine, as per section 2-316(3)(b). But, there is also plaintiff's expert testimony of Dr. Schiller, who on cross-examination was asked: "If the bird had been brought in during the guarantee period, could the anemia have been detected?" And in answer to that question, Dr. Schiller stated unequivocally "yes." In other words, the burden of examination was on the plaintiff, who by not exercising his obligation which would have uncovered the anemia, forfeited any claim for damages based on discoverable defects. The plaintiff's own expert witness testified that had the cockatoo in fact been examined within the designated period the latent anemia would have been detected; and this neglect on the part of the plaintiff, in the opinion of the court, precludes any implied warranty of merchantability.

Judgment for defendant.

Implied Warranty of Title

Special language must be used to exclude the implied warranty of title. A buyer expects this warranty when buying goods, and a seller must comply with the provisions of Section 2-312(2), as discussed earlier, to exclude the warranty of title.

Limitation of Remedies

The reader should distinguish the attempt to exclude or modify a warranty from an attempt by the seller to limit the remedies of the buyer under Section 2-719 or 2-718. Section 2-316(4) states that remedies for breach of warranty can be limited in accordance with these two sections.

Liquidated-Damages Clauses. A liquidated-damages clause provides for the payment of a particular sum by a party if he or she breaches the contract. Section 2-718 deals with an attempt by the parties to provide for liquidated damages. Such agreements will be enforceable only if the contract provides for an amount that is reasonable in the light of the anticipated or actual harm caused by the breach, the difficulties of proving loss, and the inconvenience or nonfeasibility of otherwise obtaining an adequate remedy. A term fixing unreasonably large liquidated damages is void as a penalty. Section 2-718 allows the parties to agree in advance that the seller will pay the buyer a particular sum if there is a breach of warranty, as long as the sum is reasonable.

Limitation or Modification of Remedies. Section 2-719 allows the parties (subject to certain limitations) to modify or limit the remedies provided in Article 2. Subsection (3) is worthy of further consideration here. It recognizes the validity of clauses limiting or excluding consequential damages, unless the limitation or exclusion is unconscionable. (See the chapter on illegality of contracts for a discussion of unconscionability.)

Consequential damages include any loss resulting from general or particular requirements and needs of the buyer that the seller had reason to know about at the time of contracting and which could not reasonably have been prevented by the buyer's obtaining the goods elsewhere or otherwise, and injury to person or property proximately resulting from any breach of warranty (Section 2-715[a]).

If the seller attempts to limit consequential damages for injury to a person by consumer goods, the clause is prima facie unconscionable. Any limitation on damages when the loss is commercial is not prima facie unconscionable. Even though an attempt to limit consequential damages for injury to a person is prima facie unconscionable, the seller can still attempt to disclaim all warranties, as provided in Section 2-316. In this respect, note the limitations placed on a seller's power to disclaim as discussed in the section of this chapter on the Magnuson-Moss Act.

Consider Posttape Associates v. Eastman Kodak Co., 537 F.2d 751 (3d Cir. 1976). Posttape Associates produced a documentary film

using Kodak film. ~~the~~ the legend:

READ THIS NOTICE placed if defective in ma~~box bore~~ or packaging, or if damaged any subsidiary company even ligence or other fault. Except placement, the sale, processing, or dling of this film for any purpose is warranty or liability. . . .

Posttape used the film but, because it turned out to be defective, the movie had to be reshot. Posttape wished to recover consequential damages to compensate it for the cost of the second filming of the documentary.

The court noted that an agreement that limits damages in this fashion must clearly indicate that no other damages are available to the buyer other than those listed on the cannister. It remanded the case for retrial on the issue of whether the cannister provided for an exclusive remedy. In making the determination whether the remedy provided by Kodak eliminated consequential damages of this nature, the circuit court instructed the lower court to take into consideration the trade practices in the film industry and the nature of the agreements.

FEDERAL TRADE COMMISSION WARRANTY RULES

In the Magnuson-Moss Warranty-Federal Trade Commission Act, which became effective in July 1975, Congress expanded the power of the Federal Trade Commission, specified minimum disclosure standards for written consumer-product warranties, and set certain minimum standards for those warranties. The act can be enforced by the FTC, by the U.S. Attorney General, or by a private party. The act gives consumers an opportunity to learn in advance of a purchase the nature of the warranty and to provide for effective en-

...arranty in case of breach. ...t does not *require* warranties
424 ...products.

...ts Covered

...act applies to any consumer product accompanied by a written warranty. A consumer product is any tangible personal property normally used for personal, family, or household purposes, including personal property intended to be attached to real estate. Service contracts are also covered by the act. Goods that are purchased for commercial or industrial purposes or for resale in the ordinary course of business are not covered by the FTC warranty rules.

The FTC warranty rules require compliance only if the consumer product costs $15 or more and is accompanied by a written warranty. If a company does not wish to be bound by the act or the FTC rules, it should not offer a written warranty on its consumer products. Oral warranties are not covered by the act.

Information That Must Be Disclosed

A written warranty must be in terms easily understood by the average consumer. It must disclose to consumers before the sale of the product such information as:

1. The name and address of the warrantor
2. The products or parts covered
3. A statement of what the warrantor will do, at whose expense, and for what period of time
4. The step-by-step procedure that the consumer should follow to enforce the warranty

Full or Limited Warranty

The act requires that a product be labeled as having either a "limited" or a "full" warranty. This labeling system allows a consumer to compare products before making a final purchase. Prior to the act, the consumer frequently did not even know what type of warranty the product carried until arriving home, opening the box, and finding the warranty.

A written full warranty must provide the following:

1. Any defects, malfunctions, or inability to conform to the terms of a written warranty must be corrected by the warrantor without charge and within a reasonable length of time
2. The warrantor cannot limit the period within which the implied warranties will be effective with respect to the consumer product
3. The warrantor cannot limit or exclude consequential damages on a consumer product unless noted conspicuously on the face of the warranty
4. The warrantor must allow the consumer to choose between a refund of the purchase price or replacement of the defective product or part after a reasonable number of attempts to remedy the defect or malfunction.

A limited warranty does not give the consumer these guarantees. A product must be clearly and conspicuously labeled as having a limited warranty if a written warranty is provided and the full warranty conditions are not met.

Disclaimer of Implied Warranty

The provision that a warrantor cannot disclaim any implied warranty is important. The act prohibits the disclaimer or modification of an implied warranty if a written warranty is given or if a service contract is entered into with the purchaser within ninety days after the sale. A "full" warranty cannot disclaim, modify, or even limit the basic implied warranties. The purchaser of a consumer product with a "limited" warranty also is assured that the implied warranties cannot be disclaimed or modified. But the implied warranties can be limited in duration to that of the written warranty—as long as the limitation is reasonable, conscionable, and conspicuous.

Consequential Damages

A full warranty may limit consequential damages. The Magnuson-Moss Act permits such a limitation, although UCC Section 2-719 states that the consequential damages may be limited or excluded only as long as the limitation is conscionable. The limitation of consequential damages for injury caused by consumer goods is prima facie unconscionable under Section 2-719(3).

WARRANTIES AND PERSONAL-INJURY CLAIMS

Warranties may be used by a person injured by a product to establish a personal-injury claim. If an injured party is able to establish that the defendant made a warranty, failed to live up to the warranty, and as a result of the breach of warranty the plaintiff was injured by the product, he or she may be able to collect damages based on breach of warranty. One of the major problems associated with warranties was the absence of privity of contract, as discussed in the next section.

Privity of Contract and Section 2-318

Today, the trend is away from requiring the plaintiff to establish privity of contract with the defendant. Privity is a direct contractual relationship between the parties. Section 2-318 states the UCC's limited rule on privity. The drafters of the UCC presented three alternative sections for the states to consider adopting.

Alternative A. Many states have adopted Alternative A, which states:

A seller's warranty whether express or implied extends to any natural person who is in the family or household of his buyer or who is a guest in his home if it is reasonable to expect that such person may use, consume or be affected by the goods and who is injured in person by breach of the warranty. A seller may not exclude or limit the operation of this section.

Any natural person in the buyer's family or household, or one who is a guest in his or her home, may sue the seller directly for injuries sustained. This provision does not help all persons injured by a defective product, for example, a bystander. If a man is mowing his lawn, and the mower blade flies off and strikes his neighbor, the neighbor may not avail himself of Section 2-318 in states that have adopted only Alternative A.

Alternative B. Alternative B extends to "all natural persons who may reasonably be expected to use, consume or be affected by the goods and who are injured in person by breach of the warranty." A number of states have adopted this alternative. Both A and B limit the damages recoverable as a result of a breach of warranty to personal damages.

Alternative C. Alternative C extends the warranty protection to "any person, natural or otherwise." This would include damage to a corporation. Thus Alternative C covers injury of any type, not just personal injuries.

Suits Against Someone Other than the Buyer's Seller. The UCC does not take a direct position on suits against someone more remote in the distributive chain than the buyer's immediate seller. If a man is injured by his defective mower, he can clearly bring suit against the retail merchant from whom he purchased the mower. The UCC does not take a position whether the man can sue the wholesaler or manufacturer of the mower. However, most courts today allow suit to be brought under Section 2-318 against the manufacturer and wholesaler, and thus privity does not pose a serious problem to an injured party who wishes to bring suit for breach of warranty. Injured parties typically try to sue the manufacturer because the manufacturer is often in a better position to pay than a local retailer.

Notice

There can be a problem under the UCC, however, if notice is not given of the breach of warranty. Section 2-607(3) clearly states that the buyer must, in a reasonable time after he or she discovers or should have discovered any breach of warranty, notify the seller of the breach or be barred from any remedy. Therefore, notice must be given to the seller and everyone in the distributive chain for the injured party to sue under the UCC.

Assuming that the plaintiff establishes a warranty and a breach of that warranty, and that as a result of the breach he or she was injured, a successful case may be pursued against the seller. Today, many personal-injury suits arising out of the use of a defective product are based on warranty theory. This area of law is called products liability. The other theories on which suit may be brought are discussed in the next chapter. The following case discusses warranty theory as a basis for a personal-injury suit.

Cantrell v. Amarillo Hardware Company

Supreme Court of Kansas

602 P. 2d 1326 (1979)

Cantrell was injured while using a ladder manufactured by Werner. He sued Werner, the manufacturer, Amarillo Hardware, the wholesaler, and Moore, the retailer. The trial court entered a judgment for Cantrell against Werner for breach of warranty. The Kansas Supreme Court affirmed the judgment of the trial court.

Holmes, Justice

This is an appeal in a products liability case, by defendant R. D. Werner Company, Inc., from a jury verdict granting plaintiff judgment for $13,500.00 actual damages and $18,500.00 punitive damages. The jury found no liability on the part of the codefendants, Raymond H. Moore, d/b/a Gambles, and Amarillo Hardware Company. Underwriters Laboratories, Inc., also a defendant, was granted summary judgment on the second day of trial. We find no error in the trial court's rulings and affirm the judgments.

Werner asserts that the court erred in failing to sustain its motion for a directed verdict on the grounds of insufficient evidence. The evidence revealed that the Mark V ladder was an aluminum sixfoot stepladder warranted to be satisfactory under loads of up to 200 pounds. Plaintiff weighed 165 pounds. The ladder, at the time in question, was in the same condition as when it left defendant's factory. The cardboard box covering the top of the ladder bore the following message:

> "GOOD QUALITY; LIGHT-STRONG-SAFE; RATED LOAD 200 LBS; FOR SAFETY'S SAKE BUY ME. I'M LIGHT AND STRONG! FIVE YEAR GUARAN-TEE, SEE BACK PANEL. The manufacturer guarantees the ladder, under normal use and service to be free from defects in material and workmanship, for five years from date of purchase."

The ladder had not been misused or abused. At the time it collapsed it was being used upon a clean cement floor with all braces extended and locked. The ladder had two knee braces below the first step located at the front of the side rails and while this type ladder was in use, it had a tendency to twist resulting in both front legs buckling inward. The front legs of the ladder in question buckled inward throwing plaintiff to the cement floor. While the Mark V had previously been approved by Underwriters and met their requirements and those of the American National Standards Institute, defendant had been advised by Underwriters early in 1973 that certification would be withdrawn unless modifications were made and additional braces installed below the first step. Such notice had been received by Werner several months prior to the manufacture of the ladder. As early as 1973, Werner did install on other models two additional knee braces at the rear of the front rails below the first step, but continued to manufacture the model in question with only two braces. Records were admitted showing at least five prior claims against Werner where the front rails on similar ladders had collapsed inward below the first step. No attempt has been made to summarize all the evidence favorable to plaintiff.

It has long been the rule that when a verdict is attacked for insufficiency of the evidence, the duty of the appellate court extends only to a search of the record for the purpose of determining whether there is any competent substantial evidence to support the findings. The appellate court will not weigh the evidence or pass upon the credibility of the witnesses. Under these circumstances, the reviewing court must review the evidence in the light most favorable to the party prevailing below.

Werner argues there is no evidence in the record indicating that any component, design feature or material used in the ladder was defective. Relying on Wilcheck v. Doonan Truck & Equipment, Inc. 220 Kan. 230, 552 P.2d 938 (1976), Werner contends that the proof of a defect is the basic element necessary for recovery in an action founded upon breach of contract. We have no quarrel with the broad general statement in *Wilcheck* that "[r]egardless of the theory upon which recovery is sought for injury in a products liability case, proof that a defect in the product caused the injury is a prerequisite to recovery."

The cause of action at bar is based on a breach of express warranty.

When plaintiff purchased the ladder in question there was a cardboard cover on the top of the ladder which expressly warranted the ladder to be of good quality, light, strong and safe. It also stated that the manufacturer (Werner) "guarantees the ladder, under normal use and service to be free from defects in material and workmanship, for five years from date of purchase.

Werner argues that since plaintiff showed no specific defect in the ladder that an essential element necessary for the recovery of damages is lacking.

In Huebert v. Federal Pacific Electric Co., Inc., 208 Kan. 720, 494 P.2d 1210, this court discussed the scope of express warranties by manufacturers as follows:

"A manufacturer may by express warranty assume responsibility in connection with its products which extends beyond liability for defects. All express warranties must be reasonably construed taking into consideration the nature of the product, the situation of the parties, and surrounding circumstances. However, defects in the product may be immaterial if the manufacturer warrants that a product will perform in a certain manner and the product fails to perform in that manner. Defects may be material in proving breach of an express warranty, but the approach to liability is the failure of the product to operate or perform in the manner warranted by the manufacturer."

Considering our scope of review, we have no hesitancy in finding there was sufficient competent evidence to support the jury's award of actual damages and that there was a violation of the express warranty of the appellant which was the cause of plaintiff's injuries.

[The Court's discussion of punitive damages was omitted.]

The judgment is affirmed.

REVIEW PROBLEMS

1. Autzen contracted to purchase a used 50-foot boat from Taylor for $100,000. After agreeing on the price, but during the process of negotiating, Autzen was assured that the boat was in good condition, and Taylor's agent had the boat inspected for dry rot prior to Autzen's purchase, although Autzen felt it was unnecessary to do so. Upon completion of the inspection, the inspector concluded that the hull was very sound "and that the boat should be well suited for its intended purpose." Autzen then gave Taylor's agent $20,000 and took possession. Approximately two months later, Autzen discovered that parts of the boat's flying bridge had been weakened by dry rot. A further inspection of the boat revealed that there was an enormous amount of dry rot and insect infestation. Was there an express warranty made as to the condition of the boat? Autzen v. John C. Taylor Lumber Sales, Inc., 572 P.2d 1322 (Ore. 1977).

2. Wex Corporation contracts with Axion Corporation for the production and purchase of three valve-testing machines. Two were paid for, the third was not, as it proved to be unsatisfactory because it failed to meet the specifications when delivered and tested. The machines were complicated, and one of the first of their kind produced. Wex Corporation now contends that Axion Corporation breached the implied warranty of merchantability under Section 2-314. Upon which Subsection(s) of Section 2-314 does it appear that Wex was relying? From the given facts, does it appear Wex will recover for breach of warranty? Axion Corp. v. G.D.C. Leasing Corp., 269 N.E.2d 664 (Mass. 1971).

3. Lewis orders a quantity of enamel-lined steel pipe from Key for an Alaskan construction project. The pipe as ordered was delivered in March, a time of extremely low temperatures. In April, Lewis began laying the pipe. By early May, some 5,000 feet of the pipe had been installed. An inspection of the pipe at this time revealed that portions of the interior enamel lining had cracked away from the steel outer casing

and were hanging down in sheets. Lewis brought suit for breach of the implied warranty of fitness for a particular purpose under Section 2-315. Was there an implied warranty of fitness for a particular purpose? Lewis and Sims, Inc. v. Key Industries, Inc., 577 P.2d 1318 (Wash. App. 1976).

4. Testo purchased a used 1969 Camaro Z-28 from Ross for $2,697. Testo was unaware that the automobile had been highly modified for racing purposes. In the dealings for the car, Testo took a test drive but did not experience any problems. He was not told that the car had been modified. On the purchase order, there was a printed disclaimer of all warranties express or implied, including the implied warranty of merchantability. There was no discussion of this provision during the negotiations to purchase the car. After the deal was closed, Testo received a card that provided for a 15 percent discount on any necessary parts and labor for two years, but otherwise the vehicle was sold "as is." About three hours after the purchase, Testo experienced troubles starting the engine. It overheated and would not start until it cooled down. Testo replaced the battery and the starter himself in a futile attempt to correct the problem. He then determined the name of the former owner, and after talking to him, learned of the racing modifications. After much more trouble and attempted repairs, Testo asked for rescission of the contract and return of the purchase price. Ross refused. Was the disclaimer of warranties effective? Testo v. Ross Dunmire Oldsmobile, Inc. 554 P.2d 349 (Wash. App. 1976). Does the fact that the Z-28 was test-driven by Testo prior to purchase have any bearing on the issue of the disclaimer?

5. Christopher purchased a motor home from Larson for $16,000. Christopher was assured by Larson's salesman that the motor home would meet the requirements Christopher expressed to the salesman. This all led up to Christopher's purchasing the motor home. On the backside of the contract was a disclaimer of warranties, including the implied warranty of merchantability among other fine-print provisions. This disclaimer was never called to Christopher's attention. Christopher and his family took a trip in the motor home, which proved to be defective in a number of ways. Some repairs were needed to make it back home. Was the disclaimer of warranties effective? Christopher v. Larson Ford Sales v. Condor Coach Corp. 557 P.2d 1009 (Utah 1976). What should Larson have done in order for the disclaimer to be effective?

6. George is the owner of a 1971 Mustang, purchased from Pettigrew, a retail Ford dealer. Browder, George's mother-in-law, is injured when the right front wheel of the Mustang collapses. Ford Motor Company, the manufacturer of the Mustang, validly disclaimed all implied warranties as to George. Browder sues Pettigrew and Ford for, among other things, breach of the implied warranties, alleging her status as a third-party beneficiary. Was Browder a third-party beneficiary of any implied warranties? Browder v. Pettigrew, 17 UCC Rep. 741 (Tenn. App. 1975). If Browder is a third-party beneficiary of the implied warranties, is Ford's disclaimer also valid against her?

7. M&A leased several business machines from Quality, the lease payments being $222.07 per month for sixty months. Part of the lease agreement provides, in capital letters, that Quality made no express or implied warranties of merchantability with respect to the leased equipment and that Quality disclaimed all such warranties. The lease provision also provides that, at the end of the sixty-month period, title to the equipment would pass to M&A, if all conditions of the lease had been complied with, upon payment of a lump sum. Approximately six months after the beginning of the lease,

M&A quit making payments, alleging that Quality had breached the implied warranty of merchantability and the implied warranty of fitness for a particular purpose. Do the UCC implied warranties arise in this situation? Quality Acceptance Corporation v. Million and Alkers, Inc., 367 F. Supp. 771 (D. Wyo. 1973). Was the disclaimer of warranties in the lease agreement effective, assuming the warranties do arise?

Products Liability

P roducts liability encompasses several theories of recovery, of which the most important are negligence, strict liability, and warranty. Each theory may be used by a plaintiff injured as a result of a mishap involving a product. If possible, all three theories may be asserted to further the chances of recovery.

Over the past few decades there has been a trend toward increased consumer protection. Often innocent persons have been injured by products through no fault of their own. Society is faced with the question of whether a person who is injured by a dangerous product should bear the loss caused by the product or whether this loss should be sustained by the manufacturer, distributor, or seller of the product—parties arguably better able to guard against or absorb the costs of such losses. The scales appear to be tipping in favor of the consumer as responsibility for losses is increasingly imposed on manufacturers, distributors, and sellers.

In the absence of some legal liability, is there any economic incentive for a company to make a product as safe as possible? Were it not for civil damage actions, many companies might be economically pressured into marketing products that appeared to be safe to the consumer but were actually quite dangerous. Because of the possibility of large judgments, a company can no longer safely decide that a cheap, unsafe product will bring the greatest profits.

HISTORICAL BACKGROUND

In the past, absence of privity limited the power of an injured party to recover. That is, a direct contractual relationship between the injured party and the defendant was required for the injured party to recover from the defendant. A manufacturer producing a defective product was liable only to the wholesaler, the party to whom the product was sold. An injured consumer could not recover from the manufacturer. Suit generally was possible only against the retailer with whom the consumer had dealt. The requirement of privity was generally upheld throughout the nineteenth century, although some inroads were made in cases involving food, drugs, and other ultrahazardous products.

In 1916, a major departure from the requirement of privity occurred in MacPherson v. Buick Motor Co., 111 N.E. 1050 (1916). In that case, the New York Court of Appeals held

431

a manufacturer liable for injuries resulting from the use of a product, irrespective of whether the product was "inherently dangerous," because there was evidence of negligence in the manufacture or assembly of the product. This was true even though the plaintiff was unable to establish privity of contract with the manufacturer. The *MacPherson* decision influenced the decisions of other state courts. In 1960, a further step was taken in the landmark case of *Henningsen* v. *Bloomfield Motors, Inc.*

Henningsen v. Bloomfield Motors, Inc.

Supreme Court of New Jersey
161 A.2d 69 (1960)

The plaintiff, Claus Henningsen, purchased a Plymouth automobile from defendant Bloomfield Motors, Inc. His wife, Helen, was injured while driving the car. Claus and Helen brought suit against Bloomfield and Chrysler Corporation. The case was tried on the issue of implied warranty of merchantability. Chrysler had attempted to limit the warranty protection to replacement of defective parts for ninety days or 4,000 miles. Chrysler claimed this barred a claim for personal injury based on breach of a warranty. The trial court decided for the plaintiffs against both defendants. Chrysler claimed that because it was not in privity of contract with the Henningsens, no warranty of merchantability existed between Chrysler and the Henningsens. The New Jersey Supreme Court found that the absence of privity of contract would not bar the suit. It affirmed the judgment against Chrysler and Bloomfield Motors based on implied warranty of merchantability.

Francis, Justice

Plaintiff Claus H. Henningsen purchased a Plymouth automobile, manufactured by defendant Chrysler Corporation, from defendant Bloomfield Motors, Inc. His wife, plaintiff Helen Henningsen, was injured while driving it and instituted suit against both defendants to recover damages on account of her injuries. Her husband joined in the action seeking compensation for his consequential losses. The cause was submitted to the jury for determination solely on the issues of implied warranty of merchantability. Verdicts were returned against both defendants and in favor of the plaintiffs. Defendants appealed and plaintiffs cross-appealed from the dismissal of their negligence claim.

The testimony of Claus Henningsen justifies the conclusion that he did not read the two fine print paragraphs referring to the back of the purchase contract. And it is uncontradicted that no one made any reference to them, or called them to his attention. With respect to the matter appearing on the back, it is likewise uncontradicted that he did not read it and that no one called it to his attention.

The reverse side of the contract contains 8½ inches of fine print.

In the seventh paragraph, about two-thirds of the way down the page, the warranty, which is the focal point of the case, is set forth.

> 7. It is expressly agreed that there are no warranties, express or implied, *made* by either the dealer or the manufacturer on the motor vehicle, chassis, or parts furnished hereunder except as follows . . .

We come to a study of the express warranty on the reverse side of the purchase order signed by Claus Henningsen. At the outset we take notice that it was made only by the manufacturer and that by its terms it runs directly to Claus Henningsen.

The terms of the warranty are a sad commentary upon the automobile manufacturers' marketing practices. Warranties developed in the law in the interest of and to protect the ordinary consumer who cannot be expected to have the knowledge or capacity or even the opportunity to make adequate inspection of mechanical instrumentalities, like automobiles, and to decide for himself whether they are reasonably fit for the designed purpose. But the ingenuity of the Automobile Manufacturers Association, by means of its standardized form, has metamorphosed the warranty into a device to limit the maker's liability.

The manufacturer agrees to replace defective parts for 90 days after the sale or until the car has been driven 4,000 miles, whichever is first to occur, *if the part is sent to the factory, transportation charges prepaid, and if examination discloses to its satisfaction that the part is defective.* It is difficult to imagine a greater burden on the consumer, or less satisfactory remedy.

What relief is provided when the breach of the warranty results in personal injury to the buyer? In this instance, after reciting that defective parts will be replaced at the factory, the alleged agreement relied upon by Chrysler provides that the manufacturer's "obligation under this warranty" is limited to that undertaking: further, that such remedy is "in lieu of all other warranties, express or implied, and all other obligations or liabilities on its part." The contention has been raised that such language bars any claim for personal injuries which may emanate from a breach of the warranty.

A question of first importance to be decided is whether an implied warranty of merchantability by Chrysler Corporation accompanied the sale of the automobile to Claus Henningsen.

Chrysler points out that an implied warranty of merchantability is an incident of a contract of sale. It concedes, of course, the making of the original sale to Bloomfield Motors, Inc., but maintains that this transaction marked the terminal point of its contractual connection with the car. Then Chrysler urges that since it was not a party to the sale by the dealer to Henningsen, there is no privity of contract between it and the plaintiffs, and the absence of this privity eliminates any such implied warranty.

Under modern conditions the ordinary layman, on responding to the importuning of colorful advertising, has neither the opportunity nor the capacity to inspect or to determine the fitness of an automobile for use; he must rely on the manufacturer who has control of its construction, and to some degree on the dealer who, to the limited extent called for by the manufacturer's instructions, inspects and services it before delivery. In such a marketing milieu his remedies and those of persons who properly claim through him should not depend upon the intricacies of the law of sales. The obligation of the manufacturer should not be based alone on privity of contract. It should rest, as was once said, upon 'the demands of social justice.'

Accordingly, we hold that under modern marketing conditions, when a manufacturer puts a new automobile in the stream of trade and promotes its purchase by the public, an implied warranty that it is reasonably suitable for use as such accompanies it into the hands of the ultimate purchaser. Absence of agency between the manufacturer and the dealer who makes the ultimate sale is immaterial.

What effect should be given to the express warranty in question which seeks to limit the manufacturer's liability to replacement of defective parts, and which disclaims all other warranties, express or implied? In assessing its significance we must keep in mind the general principle that, in the absence of fraud, one who does not choose to read a contract before signing it, cannot later relieve himself of its burdens.

But in the framework of modern commercial life and business practices, such rules cannot be applied on a strict, doctrinal basis. The conflicting interests of the buyer and seller must be evaluated realistically and justly.

In these times, an automobile is almost as much a servant of convenience for the ordinary person as a household utensil. For a multitude of other persons it is a necessity. What influence should these circumstances have on the restrictive effect of Chrysler's express warranty in the framework of the purchase contract? It seems obvious in this instance that the motive was to avoid the warranty obligations which are normally incidental to such sales. The language gave little and withdrew much. In return for the delusive remedy of replacement of defective parts at the factory, the buyer is said to have accepted the exclusion of the maker's liability for personal injuries arising from the breach of the warranty, and to have agreed to the elimination of any other express or implied warranty. An instinctively felt sense of justice cries out against such a sharp bargain. But does the doctrine that a person is bound by his signed agreement, in the absence of fraud, stand in the way of any relief?

The traditional contract is the result of free bargaining of parties who are brought together by the play of the market, and who meet each other on a footing of approximate economic equality. But in present-day commercial life the standardized mass contract has appeared. It is used primarily by enterprises with strong bargaining power and position.

The gross inequality of bargaining position occupied by the consumer in the automobile industry is thus apparent. There is no competition among the car makers in the area of the express warranty.

In the context of this warranty, only the abandonment of all sense of justice would permit us to hold that, as a matter of law, the phrase "its obligation under this warranty being limited to making good at its factory any part or parts thereof" signifies to any ordinary reasonable person that he is relinquishing any personal injury claim that might flow from the use of a defective automobile.

The reasonable inference to be drawn from the whole context is that a preliminary finding against the binding effect of the disclaimer would have to be made, i.e., that the disclaimer was not "fairly procured," before an implied warranty could be deemed to exist. Even assuming that the duty to make such a finding was not as explicit as it should have been, in view of our holding that the disclaimer is void as a matter of law, the charge was more favorable to the defendant than the law required it to be. The verdict in favor of the plaintiffs and against Chrysler Corporation establishes that the jury found that the disclaimer was not fairly obtained. Thus, this defendant cannot claim to have been prejudiced by a jury finding on an aspect of the case which the court should have disposed of as a matter of law.

Both defendants contend that since there was no privity of contract between them and Mrs. Henningsen, she cannot recover for breach of any warranty made by either of them. We are convinced that the cause of justice in this area of the law can be served only by recognizing that she is such a person who, in the reasonable contemplation of the parties to the warranty, might be expected to become a user of the automobile.

Affirmed.

NEGLIGENCE

Manufacturer's Negligence

An injured party might choose to bring suit for negligence—that is, the breach or nonperformance of a legal duty, through neglect or carelessness, resulting in damage or injury to another. In essence, the plaintiff must establish that the defendant failed to exercise due care in the manufacturing or handling of the product. Today, it is not necessary to establish privity of contract in order to make a case for negligence against the defendant. In other words, the plaintiff need not have purchased the product from the defendant. The plaintiff, however, must establish that his or her injury is a result of a breach of duty on the part of the defendant. The defendant's duty is to exercise that degree of care that would be exercised by a reasonably prudent person under the same circumstances.

The main problem with using negligence as a theory of recovery is the substantial burden of proof that falls on the plaintiff. The seller (the defendant) may be able to establish that he or she exercised all due care that was possible under the circumstances.

Negligence of Manufacturer in Assembly

Section 395 of the *Restatement of Torts Second* sets forth a standard by which the courts may judge the actions of a manufacturer. It states:

A manufacturer who fails to exercise reasonable care in the manufacture of a chattel which, unless carefully made, he should recognize as involving an unreasonable risk of causing physical harm to those who use it for a purpose for which the manufacturer should expect it to be used and those whom he should expect to be endangered by its probable use, is subject to liability for physical harm caused to them by its lawful use in a manner and for a purpose for which it is supplied.

The *Restatement* in this section covers the problem of a product that for one reason or another leaves the manufacturer's premises in an unsafe condition because reasonable care was not taken in assembling it. For example, a manufacturer of automobiles fails to carefully inspect a vehicle and so does not notice that one of two bolts necessary to the safe operation of the car is missing. As a result, while the automobile's purchaser is driving it down the highway the car veers out of control and crashes into a lamp pole.

In this case, the manufacturer's failure to exercise reasonable care in manufacturing the automobile created an *unreasonable* risk of physical harm to persons using the automobile. The purchaser in this example used the car in a lawful manner and for a purpose for which automobiles are supplied—that is, driving. The manufacturer is liable to the purchaser for his or her injuries due to its negligence in the manufacture of the automobile.

Bear in mind that if the manufacturer is able to convince a court that it exercised reasonable care in manufacturing its product, no liability arises under Section 395 of the *Restatement.*

Contrast this example with one involving an automobile that should have had a second bolt but did not because the company failed to provide for it in the design. In this situation, if the vehicle ends up in an accident, the manufacturer is not liable for negligence in assembling the automobile. Instead, it may be liable for negligence in designing the automobile, as discussed in the next section.

A great number of cases today involve the issue of defective design.

Manufacturer's Negligent Design

An important aspect of the current law of product liability relates to the manufacturer's liability for a defectively designed product. Unlike negligence in production, which may affect one or a few products, defective design may affect an entire class of products and may involve potential liability to thousands of individuals. Several federal agencies charged with regulating certain types of products are increasingly using mandatory recall as a corrective device.

A manufacturer can be held liable for injuries to a person caused by a product defective because of poor design or improper construction or assembly. The *Restatement of Torts Second* in Section 398 announces a standard for the design of products:

A manufacturer of a chattel made under a plan or design which makes it dangerous for the uses for which it is manufactured is subject to liability to others whom he should expect to use the chattel or to be endangered by its probable use for physical harm caused by his failure to exercise reasonable care in the adoption of a safe plan or design.

This means that a manufacturer must exercise due care in the design of all products. Putting a product on the market that later is determined to be unsafe for normal use may result in liability for physical injuries caused by the product.

Suppose a manufacturer adopts a design for its product that is obviously unsafe—for example, an electric fan that does not have a screen to protect users from the rotating metal blade. A young child, unable to comprehend the danger involved, sticks his hand into the path of the blade and the blade clips off a few fingers. The manufacturer may be liable for the child's injuries because it failed to exercise reasonable care in the adoption of a safe design for the fan.

There is also the problem of misuse of a product. A manufacturer today must design its products to be safe when they are used improperly as well as properly—if the improper use is foreseeable.

The problem of improper use came up in Larsen v. General Motors Corp., 391 F.2d 495 (8th cir. 1968). General Motors' defense involved the intended use of a vehicle that was involved in an accident. The court in that case wrote:

Where the manufacturer's negligence in design causes an unreasonable risk to be imposed upon the user of its products, the manufacturer should be liable for the injury caused by its failure to exercise reasonable care in the design. These injuries are readily foreseeable as an incident to the normal and expected use of an automobile. While automobiles are not made for the purpose of colliding with each other, a frequent and inevitable contingency of normal automobile use will result in collisions and injury-producing impacts. No rational basis exists for limiting recovery to situations where the defect in design or manufacture was the causative factor of the accident, as the accident and its resulting injury, usually caused by the so-called "second collision" of the passenger with the interior part of the automobile, all are foreseeable. Where the injuries or enhanced injuries are due to the manufacturer's failure to use reasonable care to avoid subjecting the user of its products to an unreasonable risk, that failure should be eliminated and reasonable steps in design taken to minimize the injury-producing effects of impacts.

The following case illustrates the issue of negligent design in the context of an automobile suit.

Mickle v. Blackmon

Supreme Court of South Carolina
166 S.E.2d 173 (1969)

The plaintiff in this suit, Janet Mickle, was seriously injured by the gearshift lever on the 1949 Ford automobile in which she was riding when it was involved in a collision with another vehicle driven by Larry Blackmon, a defendant in this case. Mickle also sued the Ford Motor Company for alleged negligence in the design and composition of the gearshift lever. The trial court decided for the plaintiff against Ford. The appeals court affirmed the judgment of the trial court.

Brailsford, Justice

On May 29, 1962, in the City of Rock Hill, seventeen-year-old Janet Mickle was a passenger in a 1949 Ford automobile, driven by Kenneth Hill. At the intersection of Jones Avenue and Black Street, this vehicle was involved in a collision with an automobile driven by Larry Blackmon.

Janet was impaled on the gearshift lever, which entered her body behind the left armpit, penetrated to her spine, damaged the spinal cord at about breast level and caused complete and permanent paralysis of her body below the point of injury. She sued Ford Motor Company, alleging negligence in the design and composition of the gearshift lever and of the knob or ball affixed thereto.

Plaintiff's case against Ford rests upon the claim that Ford was negligent in the design and placement of the gearshift lever, which, without an adequate protective ball or knob, created an unreasonable risk of injury to a passenger upon the happening of a collision; and that this risk was realized when the protective knob shattered on the impact of plaintiff's body and she was impaled on the spear-like lever. Ford, while defending the suitability of its gearshift lever assembly at the time of the production and initial sale of the car, disclaims any duty to manufacture an automobile in which it is safe to have a collision, or to exercise care to minimize the collision-connected hazards presented to occupants by the design of the passenger compartment. Ford urges that its only duty in this respect is to manufacture a product which is free of latent defects and reasonably fit for its intended use, and that such use does not include colliding with other vehicles or objects.

It is a matter of common knowledge that a high incidence of injury-producing motor vehicle collisions is a dread concomitant of travel upon our streets and highways, and that a significant proportion of all automobiles produced are involved in such smash-ups at some time during their use. Thus, an automobile manufacturer knows with certainty that many users of his product will be involved in collisions, and that the incidence and extent of injury to them will frequently be determined by the place-ment, design and construction of such interior components as shafts, levers, knobs, handles and others. By ordinary negligence standards, a known risk of harm raises a duty of commensurate care. We perceive no reason in logic or law why an automobile manufacturer should be exempt from this duty.

Having resolved the legal question of Ford's duty to exercise care in plaintiff's favor, we now examine the sufficiency of the evidence to support the jury's factual finding that there was a breach of that duty.

The 1949 Ford was equipped with a manual transmission. The gearshift lever was mounted on the right of the steering shaft below the wheel. It was a slender, cylindri-cal, steel rod about 12 inches in length, with a slight taper to a diameter of $5/16$ of an inch at the end of which a plastic knob or ball was mounted. This rod protruded some two inches beyond the rim of the wheel and was pointed generally in the direction of a passenger on the right side of the front seat. Without an adequate protective knob, the lever was quite capable of piercing the body of any person who might be thrown upon it, and the jury could reasonably have concluded that the rod presented an unreasonable risk of injury unless effectively guarded.

The end of the gearshift lever was covered by a knob or ball of a plastic material manufactured by Tennessee Eastman Company of Kingsport, Tennessee, labeled ten-nite butyrate, also referred to in the record as acetate butyrate. The ball was moulded by Ford in two hollow sections, the bottom section with a hole slightly smaller in diameter than the end of the lever. The two sections were glued together and the slightly heated ball was force-fitted over a series of annular grooves around the end of the rod. This resulted in a firm, permanent attachment. The knob could not be removed without rupturing it.

The plastic material was available in a wide range of colors, including black. Ford chose to use white tennite butyrate for the knobs in its 1949 model. Exposure to the ultraviolet rays of sunlight caused this material to deteriorate. Carbon, which is the coloring agent used to produce black tennite butyrate, is highly resistant to ultraviolet rays. Ford switched to black butyrate for the knobs in its 1950 model. After exposure to sunlight for an undetermined length of time, the greater the exposure the more rapid the deterioration. Hairline cracks which developed on the surface in this process destroyed the force distributing quality of the plastic knob and caused it to shatter easily on impact. After developing these cracks, a 1949 white ball was of no value as a protective guard but remained serviceable as a knob. The presence of the hairline cracks was apparent on visual inspection. However, their deteriorating effect would not necessarily be comprehended by a person of ordinary reason. The black 1950 balls never developed these cracks. Rigidly attached to the gearshift lever, they were not subject to wear, as are moving parts of machinery, and there is no evidence that the black knobs deteriorated with age or normal use.

When questioned about the expected life of the material furnished to Ford for the

1949 knobs, an Eastman expert testified: "That is a hard question to answer because it is dependent on the type of exposure, but, generally speaking, I think it would be expected to last six or eight years without any question. More if it had less exposure to ultraviolet." However, accompanying detailed specifications furnished to the users of this material by its producer was a statement of its general characteristics, including the following: "Articles moulded from this formula are generally commercially unaffected by 12 or more months of continuous outdoor exposure."

Ford knew that the white plastic from which the 1949 gearshift ball was moulded would deteriorate on exposure to the sun's rays, and counsel disclaims that the ball was attached to the lever as a safety device. Without regard to the reason for affixing the ball, however, counsel argues that the burden was on plaintiff to prove that the assembly was "unreasonably dangerous at the time this automobile was first sold." Counsel urges that the absence of evidence "that this knob would have shattered if this impact had occurred in 1949, 1950 or subsequent thereto during the normal life expectancy of this plastic material," results in a failure of proof.

It is implicit in the verdict that the gearshift lever presented an unreasonable risk of injury if not adequately guarded. At the time of plaintiff's injury the knob on the Hill car continued to serve its functional purpose as a handhold, but it had become useless as a protective guard. It is inferable that the condition of the knob did not arise from ordinary wear and tear, but from an inherent weakness in the material of which Ford was aware when the selection was made. In the light of the insidious effect on this material of exposure to sunlight in the normal use of an automobile, it could reasonably be concluded that Ford should have foreseen that many thousands of the one million vehicles produced by it in 1949 would, in the course of time, be operated millions of miles with gearshift lever balls which, while yet serving adequately as handholds, would furnish no protection to an occupant who might be thrown against the gearshift lever. The jury could reasonably conclude that Ford's conduct, in manufacturing a needed safety device of a material which could not tolerate a frequently encountered aspect of the environment in which it would be employed, exposed many users of its product to unreasonably great risk of harm. Therefore, the issue of Ford's negligence was submissible under elementary common law principles, unless other considerations relied upon by Ford require a different conclusion.

In a products liability case against the manufacturer, plaintiff does, of course, have the burden of establishing that the defect complained of existed at the time the product was sold by the defendant. There is no duty on a manufacturer to furnish a machine that will not wear out. We subscribe to the following statement of the law which is applicable to the facts of this case:

> If the chattel is in good condition when it is sold, the seller is not responsible when it undergoes subsequent changes, or wears out. The mere lapse of time since the sale by the defendant, during which there has been continued safe use of the product, is always relevant, as indicating that the seller was not responsible for the defect. There have been occasional cases in which, upon the particular facts, it has been held to be conclusive. It is, however, quite certain that *neither long continued lapse of time nor changes in ownership will be sufficient in themselves to defeat recovery when there is clear*

evidence of an original defect in the thing sold.'' (Emphasis added.) Prosser on Torts, 667 (3d ed. 1964).

Here, there was evidence of an original weakness in the gearshift assembly which caused the collapse of the protective knob. The deterioration of the product and its consequent failure was the very risk created by the negligent choice of material, or the jury could so find. The rule relied upon, that a manufacturer is not liable for the failure of a product due to deterioration from ordinary wear and tear or misuse, simply does not fit these facts.

We readily concede that the passage of thirteen years between the marketing of a product and its injury-producing failure is a formidable obstacle to fastening liability upon the manufacturer. However, it may reasonably be inferred in this case that the advanced age of the ball was coincidental with its failure rather than the cause of it, and that the knob would have shattered upon a comparable impact had it occurred much earlier in the life of the car. The important inquiry is not how long the knob lasted but what caused its failure. Mere passage of time should not excuse Ford if its negligence was the cause. Since this conclusion finds support in the evidence, the issue was for the jury.

Manufacturer's Duty to Inspect, Test, and Warn

Testing and Inspecting. The manufacturer generally must exercise due care to make certain a product placed on the market is safe. This includes reasonable tests and inspections to discover present or latent defects in a product before putting it on the market. For example, the manufacturer of a chair was held liable when it failed to discover a defect that it could have ascertained by inspecting the chair (Sheward v. Virtue, 126 P.2d 345 [1942]).

Suppose a manufacturer of lamps exercises reasonable care with respect to the design and assembly of its lamps. Will this be sufficient to relieve it of any legal liability to someone injured by a lamp? What if the cord on the lamp was frayed when manufactured and as a result the purchaser was electrocuted when he plugged the lamp cord into a socket? One could argue that the manufacturer had failed to exercise due care in inspecting the lamp cord.

Warning. It is not sufficient for a manufacturer merely to test and inspect a product. Sometimes the manufacturer also has a duty to warn the public of the dangerous potential of a product. The *Restatement of Torts Second* in Section 388 suggests the following standard with respect to a duty to warn:

One who supplies directly or through a third person a chattel for another to use is subject to liability to those whom the supplier should expect to use the chattel with the consent of the other or to be endangered by its probable use, for physical harm caused by the use of the chattel in the manner for which and by a person for whose use it is supplied, if the supplier

(a) knows or has reason to know that the chattel is or is likely to be dangerous for the use for which it is supplied, and

(b) has no reason to believe that those for whose use the chattel is supplied will realize its dangerous condition, and

(c) fails to exercise reasonable care to inform them of its dangerous condition or of the facts which make it likely to be dangerous.

Suppose the manufacturer of a chemical knows that the chemical is highly caustic and that users may not be aware of that fact. In this situation, the manufacturer should exercise reasonable care to inform users of the chemical of its causticity. This might be accomplished by putting a prominent warning on the containers in which the chemical is supplied. If the manufacturer fails to supply any warning, it will be liable to any person injured by the chemical who the manufacturer could expect to use or be endangered by the probable use of the product—for example, someone transferring the chemical to another container. The manufacturer must exercise reasonable care to inform such a person of the caustic nature of the chemical. If it fails to give such a warning, and the person is injured, the manufacturer will be liable for the injuries that person sustains.

The defect in the product must be the *proximate cause* of the injury—that is, there must be a connection between the defect in the product and the injury sustained. If a chemical in a drum explodes when exposed to heat, but the specific injury was caused by the drum's falling on a workman's foot, it would not be possible to say that failure to warn of the chemical's flammability was the proximate cause of the worker's injury.

Subsection (a) of the *Restatement* indicates that the manufacturer must be able to foresee that the product may be dangerous if used improperly. Foreseeability is very important in duty-to-warn cases. The phrase "for which it is supplied" can be a problem where the injured party misuses the product. Must the manufacturer warn consumers not only of dangers inherent in the proper use of the product but also of dangers inherent in its misuse? Many courts have required this of a manufacturer.

A warning must be clear and intelligible.

Even if a warning makes clear the dangers inherent in using or misusing the product, there still is the problem of to whom the warning should be given. Suppose, for example, that a warning appears in literature supplied by the manufacturer to purchasers of its products but not directly on the dangerous article itself. In Griggs v. Firestone Tire and Rubber Co., 513 F2d 851 (8th cir. 1975), the court held that even under these circumstances the jury could have found that Firestone did not properly discharge its duty to warn because, although it provided a warning with literature that accompanied a dangerous tire rim, it could have put the warning directly on the rim. Some cases do, however, hold that adequate warning to the purchaser of the product is sufficient. The *Griggs* case illustrates the point that it is probably safer to put a warning in a place where it will be seen by all persons who might be endangered by the product. For example, if the seller of a lawn mower wants to warn purchasers not to put their hands in the mower's exhaust chute while the mower is in operation, it could put such a warning in the instructions for operating the mower. A warning decal on the exhaust chute, however, would be more likely to be seen by users of the mower.

Subsection (b) of Section 388 deals with the problem of whether the defect in the product is *obvious*. If the chattel is in an obviously dangerous condition, it may be unnecessary to warn of the danger. On the other hand, if the danger is not likely to be discovered by persons using the product (in other words, if the danger is *latent*) a duty to warn exists. The manufacturer should then exercise reasonable care to inform users of the latent danger.

In addition to Section 388 of the *Restatement of Torts Second*, a number of statutes and regulations (for example, the Food, Drug, and Cosmetic Act and the Federal Hazardous Substances Act) require warnings on certain products.

Martin v. Bengue

Supreme Court of New Jersey
136 A. 2d 626 (1957)

The plaintiff, Martin, was injured as a result of burns caused by a cigarette igniting an ointment, Ben-Gay, that he had applied to his chest. The plaintiff contends that the defendant, Bengue, is liable to him because it failed to warn him of the flammability of its product, Ben-Gay. The trial court and the appeals court decided for Martin on the basis of negligent failure to warn.

Jacobs, Justice

The plaintiff had a heavy cold and had been home for several days. About twice each day his wife had rubbed a medium amount of Ben-Gay on his chest, shoulders, and neck substantially in accordance with the directions for its use. On the morning of February 4, after a customary application, the plaintiff seated himself in a living room chair. He was then dressed in the same cotton pajamas which he had been wearing for several days and his pajama top had become rather greasy from its contact with the Ben-Gay. While listening to the radio and talking to his wife, who was in the kitchen, he attempted to light a cigarette. After striking the match he suddenly realized that its head had fallen off and that the lower part of his pajama top was burning. Still seated, he unsuccessfully tried to pat the fire out. He then jumped up still continuing his patting motion. The fire spread rapidly across the portions of his body which had been covered with Ben-Gay. In the plaintiff's language "it like exploded, you might say." He immediately called to his wife, who found him "completely enveloped in flames." She tore off the pajama top, applied a home remedy for his burns, called the doctor, and took him to the hospital where he remained for over a month. He suffered very severe burns, particularly about his "chest, shoulder, face and ears."

The plaintiff started to use Ben-Gay many years ago and testified that he had probably then read its accompanying literature. Similarly his wife testified that she was "an old user of Ben-Gay," had read the legend on the package, was familiar with the directions which accompanied it, and found "nothing that said it was dangerous to use." The tube which contained the Ben-Gay and the directions which accompanied it contained nothing whatever as to flammability. The directions did contemplate that the pajama top would be worn after the ointment had been applied and the plaintiff's position is that the vapors emitted by the Ben-Gay, when confined between the pajama top and the body, were flammable. In support he introduced testimony by Messrs. Bechtoldt and Kanengieser, both graduate chemists.

The testimony indicated that the methylsalicylate in Ben-Gay has a flash point (produces a puff of flame, not a fire) at about 225°F and that its vapors burn continuously at about 235°F. It also indicated that the temperature of a burning match and burning cotton is between 1200° and 2000°F. From this, coupled with the remaining evidence in the record, the Appellate Division found that it could reasonably be inferred that Ben-Gay vapors would burn at about 235°F "only when the oxygen in the air is limited in quantity, as where it is confined by some article, such as a pajama coat, so as to form with the vapors a combustible mixture . . .''

Products may not be defective but the manufacturers and suppliers may negligently fail to warn of concealed dangers with resulting foreseeable injury.

In Tomao v. A. P. DeSanno & Son, 209 F.2d 544, 546 (3rd Cir., 1954), the court properly noted that ''if the manufacturer owes a duty to use due care in making his products, he owes also the companion duty to warn of the latent limitations of even a perfectly made article, the use of which, however, is dangerous if the user is ignorant of those limitations and the manufacturer has no reason to believe he will recognize the danger.''

While the manufacturer of a product is not an insurer of its safety, he is under a duty of care to avoid all unreasonable risks of harm from its use. When such risks are foreseeable, he must take reasonable precautions to avoid them. Within broad outer limits fixed by the court, the issue of foreseeability is properly left to the jury. Professors Harper and James have put it this way:

> The courts, of course, set the outer boundary to what a man may reasonably be held to foresee. But a judgment upon this question, in the nature of things, may be exercised within wide limits, and this is one of the focal points where the concept of negligence is being expanded. Not only have the scientific advances noted above enlarged the scope of what a jury may find to be foreseeable, but a quickening social conscience and the general trend towards wider liability have led the courts to perceive risks in ordinary activities of men where not so long ago they ruled them out of the permissible range of what might be found. 2 Harper & James, at p. 916.

The fact that the product may have been used by many people over a considerable period of time without prior injury would not preclude the finding of foreseeability and negligence.

And the fact that the injury may have followed upon the application of an intervening force such as fire would not preclude the finding that the intervening force was itself a foreseeable risk which the defendant should have guarded against.

The totality of the evidence, viewed most favorably towards the plaintiff at this preliminary stage, was legally sufficient to enable a jury to find that when Ben-Gay is applied it emits vapors, which, when confined between the body and a pajama top, will burn with very high intensity and rapidity when ignited; that the defendant Bengue, Inc., as the manufacturer, and the defendant Thos. Leeming Co., Inc., as its sole United States distributor, had employed chemists to analyze the product and knew or should have known of the described flammability of its vapors; that the defendants knew or should have known that users of the product might indulge in smoking or otherwise incur the danger of igniting the confined Ben-Gay vapors; that in the exercise of reasonable prudence they would have warned the users of the danger; and that their failure thus to warn the users constituted actionable negligence. The defendants strenuously urge that ''the risk of injury from the ignition of Ben-Gay is so far beyond the realm of probability and of normal experience as to excuse the defendants from foresight thereof.'' While a jury might so find, it might also reasonably find otherwise. The number of smokers has been estimated to be between 55 and 60 millions.

It seems to us that the danger of igniting the confined vapors, by a match, cigarette or otherwise, cannot fairly be said to have been so patently remote as to justify the court's withdrawal from the jury of its normal function of passing on the issue of foreseeability.

Negligence of Assemblers and Submanufacturers

Many products are composed of parts manufactured by several companies. To what extent is a company that uses the products of another company in making its own product liable if a component part malfunctions? Take the case of an airplane company. If a malfunctioning altimeter causes the plane to crash, can the manufacturer escape liability by pointing to the altimeter manufacturer?

Assemblers. An assembler generally must make reasonable tests and inspections to discover latent defects. In MacPherson v. Buick Motor Co., 111 N.E. 1050 (1916), Buick, the manufacturer, was held liable for a defective wheel used on the automobile even though Buick bought the wheel from another company. The court held Buick liable because the defect could have been discovered had Buick made a reasonable inspection of the wheel. Thus an assembler must make reasonable inspections and tests of parts to be incorporated into the finished product to protect itself from liability.

Makers of Component Parts. The manufacturer of a component part is also liable for negligence. The *Restatement of Torts Second* follows this position, indicating that the manufacturer of parts to be incorporated in a product is liable if the parts "are so negligently made as to render the product in which they are incorporated unreasonably dangerous for use" (Comment m to Section 395). Similarly, the manufacturer of materials to be used in products that would be dangerous unless the materials are carefully made is also liable if it fails to exercise reasonable care. In Schwalbach v. Antigo Electric & Gas, Inc., 135 N.W.2d 263 (1965) the manufacturer of a safety device incorporated in a furnace was held liable when the device failed to function properly and injuries resulted.

Retailer's Negligence

Design and Construction. If a plaintiff wishes to recover from the retailer for injuries sustained in using a defective product, negligence will not be an effective theory of recovery in most instances. (See, however, the discussion of strict liability.) When a retailer receives a product from a manufacturer, he or she knows very little about it beyond what the buyer may know. Quite frequently, the product is packaged when the retailer receives and sells it. As the retailer actually has very little control over the product's design or fabrication, it makes sense not to hold him or her liable for negligence. The retailer's duty with regard to design or construction of products is minimal.

Inspections, Tests, Warnings. Normally a retailer need not inspect or test the items sold if he or she neither knows nor has reason to know that the product is dangerous. The courts tend not to impose a duty to inspect or test under these circumstances. On the other hand, if the retailer should have known that the product was dangerous and could have inspected the item or tested it, he or she may be liable. Two classes of retailers who must pay special attention to the products they sell are food retailers and druggists.

Suppose a grocery store received a shipment of frozen TV dinners. When the trucker delivered the load, he informed the manager that the truck's refrigeration unit failed to function properly during part of the trip. The truck driver believed that the dinners may have thawed although they were frozen at the time of delivery. Without inspecting them, the manager ordered the stock boys to load the dinners in the store's freezers. In such a case, although a grocery store would generally not be expected to inspect the TV dinners, here it clearly should. If a purchaser became ill after eating one of the TV dinners, the store might be liable for its failure to inspect.

The same is true of the duty to warn. If the retailer should know that a product is dangerous, and that the danger is of a type the purchaser is not likely to discover, the retailer should warn the purchaser.

In the earlier example, the grocery store probably should warn purchasers that the TV dinners had defrosted in transit if it sells them.

Representing Products as Own. If the retailer advertises, labels, or packages a product in such a fashion that it appears that the re-tailer is the manufacturer, the retailer will be held to the same standards as the manufacturer.

Many companies market under their own names products manufactured by someone else. Sears, Roebuck, for example, sells floor scrubbers manufactured by another company but labeled "Kenmore"—the Sears trade name.

The *Restatement of Torts Second*, Section 400, states: "one who puts out as his own product a chattel manufactured by another is subject to the same liability as though he were its manufacturer." Comment d indicates that when one puts his or her name or affixes his or her trade name or trademark, one puts out the product as his or her own. If the seller marks the goods as "made for" the seller, this rule still applies unless the real manufacturer is clearly indicated. In Schwartz v. Macrose Lumber & Trim Co., 50 Misc. 2d 547, 272 N.Y.S. 2d 227 (1966), the court held the distributor of masonry nails liable to a person injured when a nail shattered. The package containing the nails indicated that they were made for the distributor but did not indicate who the manufacturer was. Conversely, where the distributor clearly indicated that a can of pineapple was manufactured by another company, the consumer was not permitted to recover from the distributor (Elmore v. Grenada Grocery Co., 197 So. 761 [1940]).

The following warranty case illustrates the potential liability of such sellers.

Smith v. Regina Manufacturing Corporation
U.S. Court of Appeals, Fourth Circuit
396 F.2d 826 (1968)

The plaintiff, Smith, was injured while using an electric floor polisher-scrubber manufactured by Regina but sold by Sears. Plaintiff sued Regina and Sears. The district court found Sears liable because it sold the polisher-scrubber under its trade name "Kenmore." The Fourth Circuit affirmed Sears's liability.

Sobeloff, Circuit Judge

Briefly stated, the facts are that plaintiff Cole L. Smith, a citizen of South Carolina, purchased from Sears' catalog store in Camden, S.C., an electric floor polisher-scrubber manufactured by Regina but sold under the Sears' trade name "Kenmore." After taking the polisher home and assembling it in his kitchen, Smith filled a special dispenser attached to the unit with a scrubbing solution, poured water on the floor and plugged the appliance into the nearest socket. Upon flipping the switch, Smith received a violent electric shock which threw him across the room and against a stove, causing a severe back injury.

Appellants insist that even if the manufacturer's stringent safety standards failed to disclose any defects before the machine left the plant, the proximate cause of the accident was Smith's contributory negligence in turning the polisher on while it was standing on a wet floor. The jury found that the polisher was defective at the time Smith threw the switch, and that the accident would not have occurred but for this defect. The trial transcript clearly supports this finding. Moreover, the manufacturer's instructions gave no warning against using the polisher on a wet floor.

Since it is not the manufacturer of the defective polisher, Sears further contends that under South Carolina law, which clearly governs this action, it may not be held liable for plaintiff's injuries. We disagree.

In Carney v. Sears Roebuck & Co., 309 F.2d 300 (4th Cir. 1962), this court, relying heavily on Judge Soper's opinion in Swift & Co. v. Blackwell 84 F.2d 130 (4th Cir. 1936), recognized the doctrine that a retailer (in that case also Sears) who sold as its own a product manufactured by a third party could be held responsible for injuries resulting from defects arising in the course of manufacture, and we concluded that Virginia had adopted this rule. While it is true that the state of South Carolina had not at the time of this trial adopted the rule per se, the pronouncements on products liability emanating from the highest court of that state clearly demonstrate a desire to protect consumers and correspondingly to impose stringent duties on sellers. Revealingly, the state has never recognized the rule of caveat emptor and has held nonwarranty clauses inapplicable unless clearly brought to the buyer's attention.

For over 130 years, South Carolina has held to the principle that a retailer, "whether he was ignorant of the defect or conscious of it, is bound to take back the thing or to abate the price, *and to make good the damages which the buyers shall have suffered*" Stevenson v. B.B. Kirkland Seed Co., 180 S.E. at 201. Moreover, in 1966 the South Carolina legislature adopted its version of the Uniform Commercial Code which provides:

> (1) Unless excluded or modified, a warranty that the goods shall be merchantable is implied in a contract for their sale if the seller is a merchant with respect to goods of that kind. [S.C. Code section 10.2-314 (Supp. 1966).]

Although the statute did not become effective until after the transaction in the instant case, its presence in the South Carolina Code at the time of this trial, with no authority to the contrary, further evidences the state's receptivity to the doctrine enunciated in *Carney, supra.* Applying South Carolina law, as we think the Supreme Court of that state would declare it, we hold that by selling the product under its trade name, Sears warranted its merchantability and assumed the responsibilities of a manufacturer.

For the reasons stated, the judgment of the District Court is

Affirmed.

Statutory Violations as Proof of Negligence

Some federal and state statutes, such as the Federal Food, Drug, and Cosmetic Act, specify a certain standard of conduct. If a party injured by a product is able to point to a statute or regulation that has not been complied with, this may create a statutory right of action independent of the common-law action. A manufacturer who ignores safety standards promulgated by a government agency may leave the company open to liability. For this reason, a company must keep well informed of governmental statutes and regulations pertaining to the qualities of products it manufactures.

Defenses Available in Negligence

Contributory Negligence. A number of defenses are available to a company in a product-liability suit. One defense frequently urged in such suits is contributory negligence. Contributory negligence is any conduct on the part of the plaintiff that falls below the standard of care a reasonably prudent person would exercise in the interest of his or her own safety and that contributes to the plaintiff's injury.

In Tulkka v. Mackworth Rees, Division of Avis Industries, Inc., 257 N.W.2d 128 (Mich. App. 1977), the plaintiff, injured while operating a press, had failed to use all the available safety equipment. Because of his contributory negligence, he failed to recover. The court felt that a reasonably prudent person would have used the safety equipment provided by the employer. Contributory negligence is a complete bar to recovery in a negligence suit.

Some states have replaced the doctrine of contributory negligence with that of comparative negligence, which also applies in product-liability cases. While contributory negligence bars recovery by the plaintiff, comparative negligence does not.

When a court applies the comparative-negligence doctrine, the court or jury weighs the relative negligence of the parties and reduces the amount of recovery in proportion to the plaintiff's negligence. It bars recovery only if the plaintiff's negligence was proportionally greater than the defendant's.

For example, suppose a jury decided that the employer was 80 percent responsible for a given injury but that the employee was 20 percent responsible. If the court followed the doctrine of contributory negligence, the plaintiff would recover nothing. If, however, the court applied the doctrine of comparative negligence, the jury would determine how much the plaintiff's injuries were worth (for example, $100,000) and then reduce this amount by 20 percent—the extent of the plaintiff's responsibility for the accident. The plaintiff would therefore receive $80,000.

Assumption of Risk. In assumption of risk, the defendant asserts that the plaintiff acted voluntarily with full knowledge and appreciation of the risk involved. In Goblirsch v. Western Land Roller Co., 246 N.W.2d 687 (Minn. 1976), for example, a farmworker was injured by a corn-grinding machine that had to be fed by hand when the corn was wet. The court here applied the doctrine of assumption of risk and the plaintiff failed to recover.

In general, contributory negligence and assumption of risk are available to defendants in product-liability suits based on negligence. This makes negligence a less appealing doctrine for the plaintiff than other theories discussed later in this chapter.

Obvious Danger/Abnormal Use. Some courts have also denied relief to the plaintiff on the theory that the danger presented to the plaintiff was obvious, and other courts have denied recovery on the theory that the plaintiff made an abnormal use of the product.

MISREPRESENTATION *for fraud or negligence*

Innocent Misrepresentation

Sometimes by oral statements or through advertising, brochures, catalogues, and the like, a seller may incorrectly state something about its product. When a seller misrepresents its product, and a buyer relies upon the misrepresentation, the buyer who is injured by the product may have a cause of action based on the misrepresentation. Innocent misrepresentation is defined by the *Restatement of Torts Second*, section 402B:

> One engaged in the business of selling chattels who, by advertising, labels or otherwise, makes to the public a misrepresentation of a material fact concerning the character or quality of a chattel sold by him is subject to liability for physical harm to a consumer of the chattel caused by justifiable reliance upon the misrepresentation, even though
> (a) it is not made fraudulently or negligently, and

> (b) the consumer has not bought the chattel from or entered into any contractual relation with the seller.

A material fact, for the misrepresentation of which the *Restatement* holds a seller accountable, is one that was taken into consideration by the buyer in deciding to purchase the product.

Many statements have been found to be misrepresentations of material facts concerning the character or quality of a product. In Hauter v. Zogarts, 534 P.2d 377 (Calif. Sp. Ct., 1975), Hauter brought suit for injuries he sustained while using a training device for golfers called the "Golfing Gizmo." On the first day of use, while practicing his golf swing, he was seriously injured by the product. He brought suit on the grounds of innocent misrepresentation—among other theories of recovery. Hauter had relied upon the manufacturer's statement "Completely Safe Ball Will Not Hit Player," which the California Supreme Court found to be a factual representation. Because the statement was false, Hauter recovered even though the manufacturer in this case believed the statement to be true.

Defenses

Two defenses frequently asserted by defendants in innocent-misrepresentation cases are puffing and absence of reliance.

Puffing. Puffing is a statement of mere opinion or loose general praise. If a statement is mere puffery, the plaintiff will not recover. For example, in Berkebile v. Brantly Helicopter Corp., 337 A.2d 893 (Sup. Ct. Penn., 1975), Berkebile's heirs brought suit for his death when the helicopter he was piloting crashed. Brantley had described the helicopter in an advertisement as "safe, dependable," not "tricky to operate," and one that "beginners and professional pilots alike agree . . . is easy to fly." The Pennsylvania Supreme Court characterized these statements as mere puffery and refused to allow the plaintiffs to collect damages based on innocent misrepresentation.

Determining which statements are puffing and which are not is often difficult. Courts differ in their willingness to characterize statements as puffing.

Reliance. To recover on grounds of innocent misrepresentation, not only must the manufacturer's misrepresentation of a material fact not be puffing but the buyer must prove that the misrepresentation was *justifiably relied upon* by him. If the buyer was unaware of the misrepresentation or indifferent to it, or if the statement did not influence his purchase or subsequent conduct, the buyer may not recover. The misrepresentation must have been a *substantial* factor in inducing the purchase or use of the product.

The plaintiff need not point to a specific statement of misrepresentation but may rely upon a picture. A police officer named Winkler acquired a discarded police helmet used in riot control from the department for his personal use. On the carton, the manufacturer depicted a motorcyclist wearing the helmet. Winkler was familiar with the carton and believed that the helmet was intended for motorcycle use. While riding his motorcycle, he collided with a pickup truck. He sustained head injuries because the helmet was not in fact suitable for motorcycle riding. In Winkler v. American Safety Equipment Corp., 604 P.2d 693 (Colo. Ct. of Appeals, 1979), the Colorado Court of Appeals found evidence to support a jury verdict of misrepresentation in light of Winkler's justifiable reliance on the picture on the carton.

The following case provides another example of innocent misrepresentation.

Klages v. General Ordnance Equipment Corporation

Superior Court of Pennsylvania
367 A.2d 304 (1976)

Plaintiff, John R. Klages, was employed as a night auditor at Conley's Motel. After once being held up by armed robbers, Klages purchased the defendant's mace pen for protection. The promotional literature for the weapon stated in part: "Rapidly vaporizes on face of assailant effecting 'instantaneous incapacitation' . . . an attacker is 'subdued—instantly' . . . An advertisement in Time Magazine stated the Chemical Mace is '. . . a weapon that disables as effectively as a gun and yet does no permanent injury' . . ." When Klages was again held up soon thereafter, he removed the mace pen from the cash register where it was stored. Using the cash register as a shield, he squirted the mace, hitting the intruder right beside the nose. He immediately ducked below the register, but the intruder shot him in the head. As a result of the injury, Klages suffered complete loss of sight in his right eye. He later instituted suit against the retailer and manufacturer of the mace pen. The lower court submitted the case to a jury based on innocent misrepresentation and the jury decided for the plaintiff. The Superior Court affirmed the trial court's decision.

Hoffman, Judge

Having adopted section 402B of the Restatement (Second) of Torts as the law of this Commonwealth, we must determine whether the appellant misrepresented "a material fact concerning the character or quality of a chattel sold by him . . ."

The comments to section 402B are helpful in this regard. First, Comment f states that "[t]he fact misrepresented must be a material one, upon which the consumer may be expected to rely in making his purchase . . ." Comment g states that section 402B "does not apply to statements of opinion, and in particular it does not apply to the kind of *loose general praise* of wares sold which, on the part of the seller, is considered to be 'sales talk', and is commonly called 'puffing'—as, for example, a statement that an automobile is the best on the market for the price . . . In addition, the fact misrepresented must be a material one, of importance to the normal purchaser by which the ultimate buyer may justifiably be expected to be influenced in buying the chattel." (Emphasis supplied).

The facts and circumstances surrounding the purchase of a product are helpful in determining whether the representation is of a material fact. In this case, the appellant sold a product designed as a tool to deter violence. Its sole anticipated use was to protect the purchaser from harm under extremely dangerous circumstances and the appellee specifically purchased the product with these explicit purposes in mind. Specific representations about the effectiveness of the weapon under such dangerous circumstances are clearly material. The mace weapons were described as effecting an instantaneous, immediate, complete incapacitation of an assailant. This is not "loose, general praise"; rather it is specific data on the capability of a product. This situation is thus distinguishable from Berkebile v. Brantly Helicopter Corporation, where the representation that the purchaser was assured of a safe, dependable helicopter was held to be mere "puffing." The lower court, therefore, properly submitted the issue of liability under section 402B to the jury.

Affirmed.

STRICT LIABILITY

Strict Liability in Tort Generally

The law of torts has for years recognized the doctrine of strict or absolute liability if a person or company engages in certain types of activities. For example, if a company engages in blasting as part of its business, and this blasting causes an injury to someone, the company may be held liable to the injured party under the concept of strict or absolute liability.

Strict liability in the product-liability area is different from the concept of strict liability discussed in the material on torts earlier in this book. Strict liability in the products-liability area originated only in the 1960s. Today most states have accepted the doctrine of strict liability in product liability. The doctrine does not make the seller of a defective product absolutely liable. The injured party must demonstrate that the product was defective and that it was the proximate cause of injury. The rule is set out in the *Restatement of Torts Second,* section 402A:

(1) One who sells any product in a defective condition unreasonably dangerous to the user or consumer or to his property is subject to liability for physical harm thereby caused to the ultimate user or consumer, or to his property, if
  (a) the seller is engaged in the business of selling such a product, and
  (b) it is expected to and does reach the user or consumer without substantial

change in the condition in which it is sold.

(2) The rule stated in Subsection (1) applies although

   (a) the seller has exercised all possible care in the preparation and sale of his product, and

   (b) the user or consumer has not bought the product from or entered into any contractual relation with the seller.

Caveat:

The Institute expresses no opinion as to whether the rules stated in this Section may not apply

(1) to harm to persons other than users or consumers;

(2) to the seller of a product expected to be processed or otherwise substantially changed before it reaches the user or consumer; or

(3) to the seller of a component part of a product to be assembled.

Distributors/Retailers/Lessors

Across the United States the law varies with respect to the liability of distributors under strict liability in tort. In general, most jurisdictions have not held a distributor liable where he or she merely sends the product on to someone else. Strict liability in tort may, however, be applied to retailers. Some courts have applied the doctrine of strict liability in tort to lessors even though no sale is involved. In Cintrone v. Hertz Truck Leasing & Rental Service, 212 A.2d 769 (1965), for example, the court held a lessor subject to strict liability in tort.

Manufacturers

Today, many product-liability suits are brought against manufacturers on the basis of strict liability in tort.

Unlike the plaintiff in a negligence case, the plaintiff in a case of strict liability in tort need not concern himself or herself with whether the defendant's actions were reasonable or not. Manufacturers are liable even though they exercised all possible care in the preparation and sale of their products. Furthermore, strict liability in tort has fewer problems of proof than negligence. Contributory negligence is a good defense in a negligence case but not in a case of strict liability in tort.

As a cause of action strict liability is superior to warranty theory because warranty law is still burdened with the technical procedural requirements of the law of sales. For example, the Uniform Commercial Code requires that notice be given to persons under certain circumstances. There is no such requirement under the *Restatement.*

It may also be superior to innocent misrepresentation because the defendant may not have misrepresented its product.

The elements that a plaintiff must establish are:

1. The defendant is in the business of selling the product
2. The product was expected to and in fact reached the injured party without substantial change in the condition in which it was sold
3. The product was in a defective condition
4. This defective condition rendered the product unreasonably dangerous to the user or consumer or his property
5. There was a causal relationship between the defect and the damage done to the plaintiff
6. This resulted in physical harm to his person or property.

If the plaintiff succeeds in establishing all these elements, the plaintiff will prevail at trial.

The plaintiff must establish the existence of a defect in the product and prove that the defect caused his or her injuries. If there is no defect in the product, the plaintiff may not recover. Furthermore, if there is a defect but the injury sustained by the plaintiff was not related to the defect, the plaintiff will not win at trial.

The following case illustrates the application of strict liability in an automobile accident case.

Buehler v. Whalen
Illinois Court of Appeals
355 N.E.2d 99 (1976)

In the following case, Buehler, the plaintiff, brought an action against the driver of a vehicle, Whalen, for injuries sustained in an automobile accident. Buehler also sued Ford Motor Company, another defendant in this case, based on the contention that the design of the vehicle rendered it unreasonably dangerous to a user. The trial court decided for Buehler against Ford, and the appeals court affirmed the judgment.

Eberspacher, Justice.

On January 3, 1971, at approximately 4:20 P.M., the Rudolph Buehler family was returning to their home in their automobile, a 1966 Ford Fairlane sedan. They stopped at a gas station in Carlyle, Illinois, and had the fuel tank filled to within two or three inches from the top of the gas tank's filler spout. After the gas cap was secured to the filler neck, they then proceeded homeward, by traveling south on Illinois Route 127 until they came to their driveway, which intersects the highway. Route 127 is a two-lane highway which runs in a north-south direction; at that time the posted speed limit was 65 miles per hour and the road surface was wet from a recent shower. The Buehler residence was east of the highway and the collision occurred as they were making a left turn from the highway onto their driveway.

As Rudolph Buehler, the driver, approached his driveway he put his left turn signal on about 300–400 yards in front of it. He reduced his speed to 10–15 miles per hour and ultimately to three to five miles per hour. A line of five cars formed behind the Buehler auto. The last car in the line was that of Whalen. She entered the north-bound lane and proceeded to pass all the cars in the line.

Buehler had made a 30° to 40° angle left turn and his auto was one-half to two-thirds onto the driveway upon being struck by the Whalen vehicle. Whalen testified that she was two car lengths behind Buehler when she became aware of his intention to turn. She estimated her speed as 65 miles per hour. She hit her brakes and started to pump them. She tried to miss the Buehler auto by swerving right, back into the southbound lane. The left front of Whalen's auto struck the left rear of the Buehler car. Plaintiff Gerrell Forth, who was driving one of the cars in line behind the Buehlers, estimated that the impact speed of Whalen's car was 30 miles per hour. Upon impact, fire was immediately seen by occurrence witnesses inside the passenger compartment of the Buehler auto and coming out the center of the back bumper. The trunk lid was closed and the windows were rolled up at this time. Mrs. Marie Buehler, one of the plaintiffs, who was riding in the front seat, smelled gasoline upon impact and saw flames engulf the back seat area where her niece and sons were riding.

After impact the Buehler auto spun into a ditch bordering the highway and it came to a rest approximately 35 feet south of the driveway; it was lying on its right side and pointing southward. The windows had not broken. Plaintiff Gerrell Forth was the first person to approach the Buehler auto. With the aid of others who arrived, he righted the auto back onto its wheels. He then helped the passengers out of the car. From the time of the impact to the time the last living person left the burning auto, only 45–60 seconds elapsed. Gerrell Forth was burned while helping Michael Buehler out of the rear door and into the water in the ditch. Due to the intense fire he was unable to rescue the Buehlers' niece in time. He testified that he only saw fire in the interior of the auto. Several of the firemen who arrived at the scene thought that the fire was of a gasoline origin. It was stipulated by the parties that all of the plaintiffs' injuries were burns and there was testimony to the effect that these burns were of a gasoline origin.

The vehicle driven by the Buehlers was a 1966 Ford Fairlane. This vehicle was one of several Ford cars that, since 1960, had been equipped with a flange mounted fuel tank. The flange mounted tank is different from strap mounted fuel tanks used on other cars in that the top of the flange mounted tank serves as the floor of the trunk whereas the strap mounted tank is placed beneath the floor of the trunk and is therefore separated from the trunk compartment. The flange mounted tank is also screwed into place and it is held rigidly to the car structure, whereas the strap mounted tank is held by metal bands which allow it to be displaced to some extent under stress.

The tank's nonflexible gas filler spout runs through the luggage compartment to a license plate bracket above the bumper. The flange of the tank is about two and one-half inches from the bumper while the rear of the tank itself is four inches from the bumper.

The flange mounted tank was not used in American cars prior to 1960. In that year Ford began using that type of tank in some of its cars. General Motors and Chrysler stayed with the strap mounted tank. Since 1970 Ford changed back to strap mounted tanks for all its automobiles.

In the 1966 Ford Fairlane, the only shield separating the trunk compartment, where the fuel tank and filler spout are located, from the passenger compartment, is a fibreboard panel and the rear seat padding. It was undisputed that neither of these materials significantly limits the passage of fire.

After the collision, the gas cap to the Buehler auto was found near the scene of the impact. The ears to the cap, which secure it to the filler spout, were missing. Similar ears were found inside the Buehlers' fuel tank. The filler spout was found to be no longer extending through the opening in the license bracket area, but was instead below the bumper or about flush with it.

For the reasons enunciated in *Suvada* v. *White Motor Co.*, strict liability is imposed against a manufacturer in cases involving products where a defective condition makes them unreasonably dangerous to a user. Defectively designed products are unreasonably dangerous because they fail to perform in a manner reasonably to be expected in light of their nature and intended functions.

A manufacturer's duty to design a product which is reasonably fit for its intended use encompasses foreseeable ancillary consequences of normal use, which in the case of automobiles includes collisions. The environment in which an automobile is used must be taken into consideration by a manufacturer when designing its product. In an automobile dependent society, involving extensive usage, crowded highways, heavy loads, and high speeds, the statistically inevitable consequences of normal use of an auto entail the proven hazard of injury producing collisions of different kinds. Since injury producing impacts are foreseeable, the manufacturer is under a duty to design its vehicle to avoid subjecting the user to an unreasonable risk of injury in the event of a collision.

Viewing the evidence in its aspect most favorable to the plaintiffs, it appears clear that an impact to the trunk of the Buehlers' 1966 Ford Fairlane was an occurrence that was objectively reasonable to expect. In the event of such an impact it is also reasonable to expect that fire could develop in the trunk where the fuel system was located and could spread to the passenger compartment. In such a situation there would exist a high probability of serious burns or death resulting from an intense gasoline fed fire originating in the trunk. Testimony showed that Ford could have used a strap mounted tank that would have greatly reduced the risk of fire upon a rear-end impact. This type of tank was in fact used by Ford in prior as well as subsequent comparable models. Chrysler and General Motors had always used the strap mounted fuel tank. Moreover, there was testimony that the cost of placing a shield, in the 1966 Ford Fairlane, between the passenger compartment and the fuel containing system would only be one dollar plus one-half hour of labor time. Such a shield would have substantially reduced the risk of injury to the plaintiffs by providing additional time to effectuate an escape. We note that in the instant case it took less than one minute for the occupants to be removed from the burning vehicle. We are therefore of the opinion that the risks of harm to the plaintiffs were not so improbable or extraordinary as to be unforeseeable to Ford and that Ford owed the plaintiffs a duty to design its vehicles so as to reduce the probability of the injuries suffered.

We are now led to determine if the plaintiffs made a *prima facie* case that one or any design defect proximately caused the plaintiffs' injuries. Ford contends that the plaintiffs failed to sustain their burden of proof. Causation is primarily a question of fact for a jury to determine. If there was sufficient evidence from which a jury could find that an unreasonably dangerous condition existed in the Ford Fairlane by reason of its design and that the fire or the instantaneous spread of fire into the passenger compartment resulted from that condition, then the jury's verdict must be left undisturbed.

The evidence viewed in the light most favorable to the plaintiffs shows that upon impact the Buehler auto immediately burst into flame from a gasoline source in the interior of the car. Expert testimony showed that the location of the fuel tank, filler spout, and gas cap in the trunk made them extremely vulnerable in the event of a rear-end impact; that the flange mounted tank was susceptible to stress; and that the filler spout tended to be displaced into the trunk and the gas cap could break off in the event of a rear-end impact. In addition, the lack of any shielding device between the passenger compartment and the trunk permitted any fire that would develop in the trunk to spread without resistance into the passenger compartment. In the experts' opinion these conditions were unreasonably dangerous and were causally related to plaintiffs' burns. They believed that upon impact the spout was displaced into the trunk and that the configuration change of the fuel tank broke the gas cap off and forced gasoline to spray into the trunk. The fire that resulted from a spark from the impact instantly spread into the passenger compartment because no barrier protected that compartment and therefore the plaintiffs suffered serious burns, even though they were extracted in one minute or less.

We are satisfied that there was sufficient evidence to support the jury's verdict.

Affirmed.

Privity

The privity requirement developed because the courts reasoned that a person should not be able to recover for a breach of contract unless he or she was a party to the contract. Because the warranty theory of recovery was an extension of the contractual theory of recovery, the courts for many years required the plaintiff to demonstrate that he or she was in privity of contract with the defendant. Under the tort theory, however, there is no need to establish a contractual relationship because this theory of recovery is not based in contract.

Today, a plaintiff generally does not have to establish privity of contract to recover for personal injuries caused by a defective product. There are still a few jurisdictions, however, that require it in certain cases.

Privity of contract is not an issue in strict liability in tort. Section 402A(2)(b) of the *Restatement* states that strict liability applies whether or not the user or consumer has entered into a contract with the seller. An injured party may proceed under Section 402A against retail sellers, distributors, manufacturers, of component parts, and general manufacturers. The only seller an injured buyer will be unable to collect from is the seller who is not engaged in the business of selling such a product (Section 402A [1][a]). If you were to sell your lawn mower to your next-door neighbor, he or she could not sue you under this theory of liability because you would not be regarded as a person in the business of selling lawn mowers.

General Manufacturers. Clearly, if a manufacturer sells a product in a defective condition unreasonably dangerous to the user or consumer or to his or her property, the manufacturer may be liable under strict liability in tort if the product was expected to and in fact did reach the user or consumer without substantial change in the condition in which it was sold.

Manufacturers of Component Parts. Not only may an injured party sue the manufacturer of a product under strict liability in tort, but in many jurisdictions he or she may also sue the manufacturer of any defective part incorporated into the finished product.

Bystanders. Suppose that the injured person did not purchase the product or qualify as a member of the buyer's household or a guest. Such a person is nevertheless able to collect under the theory of strict liability in tort. Section 402A of the *Restatement* makes the seller liable "to the ultimate user or consumer, or to his property." The Institute did not express an opinion on whether the rule should be extended to persons other than users or consumers, but a number of court decisions have extended strict liability to bystanders. In a Michigan case, a hunter was allowed to proceed under this theory when his companion's gun exploded and injured him (Piercefield v. Remington Arms Co., Inc., 133 N.W.2d 129 [1965]). In a Delaware case, the court held that a lease of a motor vehicle, entered into in the regular course of a truck-rental business, was subject to application of the doctrine of strict liability in tort in favor of an injured bystander (Martin v. Ryder Truck Rental, 353 A.2d 581 [Del. Sup. Ct. 1976]).

Duty to Warn

What if a manufacturer produces a product that, although carefully manufactured, could cause injury to a person because of some latent danger? For example, suppose a drain cleaner could not safely be used with liquid bleach—

two articles a person might commonly use in housecleaning—but the manufacturer failed to warn users of this fact. Under the *Restatement,* such a manufacturer could be held liable because the product was in a "defective condition unreasonably dangerous to the user or consumer."

One cannot escape liability under Section 402A by giving an incomplete or inadequate warning of the dangers inherent in using a product. The following case illustrates the problems of an inadequate warning.

Jackson v. Coast Paint & Lacquer Co.

U.S. Court of Appeals, Ninth Circuit
499 F.2d 809 (1974)

The plaintiff, Jackson, was injured while using paint sold by Coast Paint & Lacquer Co., the defendant. Jackson contended that the manufacturer, Reliance, also a defendant, failed to adequately warn him of the dangers associated with use of the paint. The plaintiff challenged the instructions given by the trial court. The Court of Appeals agreed that the instructions of the trial court were erroneous and ordered a new trial for the plaintiff.

Merrill, Circuit Judge

In 1964 plaintiff, a citizen of Utah, was a journeyman painter employed by a Utah painting contractor. His employer entered into a contract with a Montana manufacturing company to paint some railroad tank cars that were to be used for the shipment of bulk quantities of honey. Plaintiff was sent by his employer to Billings, Montana, to do the work.

The paint used to coat the inside of the tank cars, "Copon EA9," was manufactured and sold by defendant Reliance Universal, Inc., a Texas manufacturer of industrial paints and coatings. It is an epoxy paint which is highly flammable. While plaintiff was spray painting the inside of one of the tanks a fire occurred and he was very severely burned. The fuel of the fire consisted of the paint fumes which had accumulated in the tank. The cause of ignition is uncertain and was a disputed issue at trial.

An officer of Reliance testified that Reliance was aware of the fact that Copon EA9 is hazardous if not properly used under proper conditions. Two hazards are recognized to be associated with use of the paint: breathing the toxic vapors and fire.

The label on the paint used by plaintiff was introduced into evidence. It contains a warning which first refers to the toxicity of the paint if ingested, and then states:

> Keep away from heat, sparks, and open flame. USE WITH ADEQUATE VENTILATION. Avoid prolonged contact with skin and breathing of spray mist. Close container after each use. KEEP OUT OF REACH OF CHILDREN.

Plaintiff testified that he and other painters of his acquaintance understood the warning regarding adequate ventilation to refer only to the danger of breathing toxic vapors. While painting the tanks he had contrived and used a tube and mask which enabled him to breathe fresh air from outside the tank. Otherwise plaintiff took no precautions in the nature of "ventilation." He testified that he had been unaware of the possibility that flammable vapors permitted to accumulate in a closed, inadequately ventilated area could be touched off by a spark resulting in a fire or explosion. There was, however, other evidence that some persons in plaintiff's company were aware that such a danger existed.

It is not essential to strict liability that the product be defective in the sense that it was not properly manufactured. If the product is unreasonably dangerous that is enough. A product may be perfectly manufactured and meet every requirement for its designed utility and still be rendered unreasonably dangerous through failure to warn of its dangerous characteristics.

Comment j to section 402A of the Restatement states in part:

> *Directions of warning.* In order to prevent the product from being unreasonably dangerous, the seller may be required to give directions or warning, on the container, as to its use . . .
> But a seller is not required to warn . . . when the danger, or potentiality of danger, is generally known and recognized.

The district court's instructions to the jury included the following:

> [D]efendant had a duty to supply plaintiff or his employer with proper and adequate directions for the use of the paint and proper and adequate warnings concerning the dangers inherent in the paint.
> If the defendant had reason to believe that plaintiff or his employer knew or would discover the hazards inherent in the paint, then defendant had no duty to warn plaintiff or his employer of these dangers.

In our judgment this instruction was erroneous in three respects.

First. It suggests that liability is based on negligence rather than strict liability. (It is in fact patterned upon section 388(b) of the *Restatement,* which sets forth the elements of liability on the part of a supplier of a chattel for *negligent* failure to warn of dangers known to the supplier.) In strict liability it is of no moment what defendant "had reason to believe." Liability arises from "sell[ing] any product in a defective condition unreasonably dangerous to the user or consumer." It is the unreasonableness of the condition of the product, not of the conduct of the defendant, that creates liability.

Second. Plaintiff has contended that a more specific warning of the fire hazard ought to have been given, namely, that accumulated fumes or vapors in an inadequately ventilated area may be ignited by a spark resulting in a violent fire or explosion. His position is that the absence of such a specific warning rendered the paint as marketed by the defendant "unreasonably dangerous to the user or consumer"; in other words, that there was a "duty to warn" of the particular hazard. Defendant contends, in this regard, that it had no duty to warn of this particular hazard because, in the words of Comment j to section 402A, "the danger, or potentiality of danger, is generally known and recognized."

On the evidence presented, this was an issue for the jury. The challenged instruction, however, presents the wrong issue. It is not the knowledge actually possessed by the plaintiff, individually, that determines whether the absence of warning renders a product unreasonably dangerous. On the issue of duty to warn, however, the question to be put to the jury is whether "the danger, or potentiality of danger, is *generally* known and recognized"; whether the product as sold was "dangerous to an extent beyond that which would be contemplated by the ordinary consumer who purchases it, with *the ordinary knowledge common to the community* as to its characteristics" [*Restatement* section 402A, Comments *j, i* (emphasis added)].

Third. The most serious error in the challenged instruction is the statement that knowledge of the hazard on the part of plaintiff's *employer* would obviate any duty to warn plaintiff. Besides improperly focusing on the knowledge of an individual rather than general or common knowledge, this erroneously conceives the "community" whose common knowledge the jury is to ascertain. The seller's duty under section 402A is to "the ultimate user or consumer." At least in the case of paint sold in labeled containers, the adequacy of warnings must be measured according to whatever knowledge and understanding may be common to painters who will actually open the containers and use the paints; the possibly superior knowledge and understanding of painting contractors is irrelevant.

Accordingly we hold that the duty to warn runs, on these facts, directly to the painter, and is not discharged when the employer alone is informed of the danger.

Reversed and remanded for new trial.

Defective Condition

The requirement of establishing a defect is an element in every product-liability cause of action except innocent misrepresentation. In a negligence case, the plaintiff must establish that the defect was the result of the defendant's failure to exercise reasonable care. In an express warranty case, the defect is established by showing that the goods did not conform to the warranties made by the seller. Evidence that the seller breached the implied warranty of merchantability or the implied warranty of fitness for a particular purpose is sufficient to establish a defect under those causes of action.

In strict liability cases, a plaintiff must establish that the product was defective, that the defect caused the injury in question, and that the defendant is the party responsible for the defect. The *Restatement of Torts Second* in comment j to section 402A states:

The rule [of strict liability] stated in this Section applies only where the product is, at the time it leaves the seller's hands, in a condition not contemplated by the ultimate consumer, which will be unreasonably dangerous to him. The seller is not liable when he delivers the product in a safe condition, and subsequent mishandling or other causes make it harmful by the time it is consumed. The burden of proof that the product was in a defective condition at the time that it left the hands of the particular seller is upon the injured plaintiff. And unless evidence can be produced which will support the conclusion that it was then defective, the burden is not sustained.

The problem of establishing what the term "defect" means has been a difficult one for the courts. One of several tests used by the courts is to examine what the expectations of the consumer were with respect to a product, and then to determine whether the injured party was surprised by the danger associated with the product. This area is likely to continue to create problems for the courts, and other tests for what a defect is will undoubtedly be adopted by the courts in the future.

Unreasonable Danger

Not only does the *Restatement* require evidence of a defect in the product that caused injuries to a consumer, it also requires the plaintiff to establish that the danger posed by the product was unreasonable—that is, more dangerous than would be contemplated by an ordinary consumer.

The drafters of the *Restatement* included this requirement because some products are obviously defective but still not unreasonably dangerous. A stove that gets foods too hot may be defective but not necessarily unreasonably dangerous. A new car delivered with grease on its upholstery is defective but not dangerous.

Some courts do not require the plaintiff to establish unreasonable danger in order to recover. The California Supreme Court, for example, adopted this position in Cronin v. J. B. E. Olson Corp., 501 P.2d 1153 (1972), because the court thought the requirement was too similar to the concept of negligence.

Defenses

One defense available to a defendant being sued under a negligence theory is not available when suit is brought under strict liability in tort. In general, contributory negligence is not available as a defense.

Most courts recognize assumption of the risk as a valid defense in a strict-liability case.

REVIEW PROBLEMS

1. Simpson was a passenger in an automobile equipped with a bench seat and was sitting in the middle of the seat when the automobile was involved in a head-on collision with another vehicle. The automobile was equipped with a floor shift, manufactured by Hurst, that had been installed by a previous owner. As a result of the collision, Simpson, who was not wearing any seatbelt or other restraint, was impaled on the shift, suffering personal injuries. Simpson sues Hurst, claiming Hurst was negligent in failing to warn of the danger of installing the shift in an automobile with a bench seat. Will Simpson prevail in her action against Hurst? On what grounds might the court find for Hurst on the issue? Simpson v. Hurst Performance, Inc., 437 F. Supp. 445 (D.C. N.C. 1977).

2. Spruill, a 14-month-old infant, died of chemical pneumonia as a result of ingesting a small quantity of furniture polish manufactured by Boyle. The incident occurred when Spruill, left alone for a few minutes by

his mother in a room in which she was polishing furniture, managed to reach the bottle containing the furniture polish and then opened it and drank from it. On the back of the label, red letters ⅛-inch high warned of the combustible nature of the product; several lines below this, brown letters 1/32-inch high warned that the product was harmful if swallowed, especially by children. In fact, ingestion of one teaspoonful by an infant is fatal. Did the accident in question arise from the normal use of the product? Was the accident foreseeable to the manufacturer? Was the manufacturer's warning of the harmful effects of the polish, if swallowed, sufficient? Spruill v. Boyle-Midway, Inc., 308 F.2d 79 (4th Cir. 1962).

3. Chappuis was injured when hit in the eye by a fragment of steel from the edge of a previously chipped hammer. Neither Chappuis nor anyone else on the job was aware of the damage to the hammer. At the time of the accident, Chappuis's use of the hammer was its "normal use." Sears, the seller, and Vex, the manufacturer of the hammer, knew that once the hammer became chipped it should be discarded, as it could likely chip again. At the time the hammer was sold, it carried a label stating that safety goggles should be worn while using the hammer, that it should be used only to drive and pull common nails, and that the hammer would chip if used for other purposes. Are Sears and Vex strictly liable for Chappuis's injuries? Why or why not? Chappuis v. Sears Roebuck & Co., 358 So.2d 926 (Supreme Court of La. 1978).

4. Comstock, a mechanic, was injured at work when struck by an auto manufactured by General Motors. The auto was in the shop for repair of defective brakes. Prior to the incident, General Motors had discovered that the defect existed in all similar autos and had warned its dealers thereof but had not warned any purchaser. The defect was caused by the failure of a component part manufactured by Rex, which was part of another unit designed by General Motors, and supplied to General Motors by King. General Motors also tested the product. May General Motors be held liable for Comstock's injury? If so, upon what theory? Comstock v. General Motors Corporation, 99 N.W.2d 627 (Supreme Court of Michigan, 1959).

5. Moody was injured as the result of the failure of the side rail of an aluminum ladder sold by Sears under its trade name. The ladder in fact was manufactured by Wex, but there was nothing connected with the sale to show that anyone but Sears was involved. The defect in the ladder was a latent one. May Moody recover from Sears for his injury? What legal theory, if any, would impose liability on Sears? Moody v. Sears, Roebuck & Co., 324 F. Supp. 844 (S.D. Ga. 1971).

6. Greenman was injured when using a power tool, manufactured by Yuba as a lathe, when the piece of wood he was turning suddenly flew out of the machine and struck him in the forehead. The machine was a gift to Greenman from his wife. Examination of the machine revealed that inadequate set screws were used in construction, which allowed the tailstock to move away from the wood, permitting the wood to fly out of the lathe. Yuba's brochure contained statements as to its ruggedness and high quality of construction. On what theories may Greenman seek recovery of damages from Yuba? May Greenman actually so recover? If so, under which of the above theories is recovery easier and why? Greenman v. Yuba Power Products, Inc., 377 P.2d 897 (California Supreme Court 1963).

7. Suvada purchased a used, reconditioned truck from White. The airbrake unit was manufactured by Bendix and installed by White. The brake unit proved defective when it subsequently failed and the truck collided with a bus, causing a number of

injuries to bus passengers and much property damage. May Suvada recover damages from Bendix in a lawsuit arising from the above collision? What legal theory may Suvada utilize in order for him to so recover and why? Suvada v. White Motor Co., 210 N.E.2d 182 (Supreme Court of Illinois 1965).

8. West died from injuries suffered when he was struck and run over by a road grader manufactured by Caterpillar. At the time of the accident, West was waiting for a bus on the corner of a street being graded. As the bus approached, West walked across the street, not looking in the direction from which the grader was backing. The grader was not equipped with mirrors or any device warning of its operation while in reverse; it was designed with a "blind spot" behind the operator; and rearward visibility was obstructed by various parts of the grader. What was West's status in relation to the grader at the time of the accident? Will Caterpillar be liable for any damages resulting from George's death and, if so, under what legal theory? West v. Caterpillar Tractor Co., Inc., 336 So.2d 80 (Supreme Court of Fla. 1976).

9. Stroud was injured at a construction site when a metal structure manufactured by Dorr collapsed while Stroud was working on it. The collapse was caused by the placing of a compression ring upside down at the top of the structure. Stroud welded the compression ring to the top of the structure's center pole. After doing this, he noticed that it was upside down, reported it to his supervisor, and continued working on the structure. May Stroud recover damages against Dorr for his injuries? What defense does Dorr have in Stroud's action against it? Stroud v. Dorr-Oliver, Inc., 542 P.2d 1102 (Supreme Court of Arizona 1975).

10. Ralston, an employee of Illinois Power, was injured when using trencher equipment manufactured by Don to bore holes under a street. The injury occurred while Ralston was standing on a rotating rod that had buckled as a result of striking hard material. The operator of the machine had reversed the rod, causing Ralston's pant-leg and foot to be caught in the rotating rod, injuring Ralston's leg. Ralston knew about the danger involved in this procedure, and had done it several times before. He further had realized the possibility of an accident occurring as a result of the procedure involved here. If Ralston sues Don in strict liability in tort, does Don have any defense? If so, what is it? Ralston v. Illinois Power Co., 299 N.E. 2d 497 (Appellate Court of Illinois 1973).

CHAPTER 19

Commercial Paper: Introduction and Negotiability

During the latter half of the nineteenth century, the law relating to commercial transactions became very confused because the states were following different rules. This resulted in an outcry for general commercial rules that would apply everywhere in the United States.

The National Conference of Commissioners on Uniform State Laws set about drafting some suggested rules for all states to follow. One product of this effort was the Uniform Negotiable Instruments Law, which was finished in 1896. Other uniform acts soon followed. The Uniform Negotiable Instruments Law was an attempt to encourage the states to codify (put in statutory form) in a uniform manner their laws in this area. The hope was

that this would simplify the conduct of business.

Unfortunately, this hope was not realized. The law was construed over a period of years in different ways in different states. Furthermore, years of experience under this and other uniform acts suggested a need for some changes in the law.

In the 1940s work was begun on a new set of rules for the commercial law area. The American Law Institute, working with the National Conference of Commissioners on Uniform State Laws, succeeded in producing a final draft of a new model act in 1952. This act is called the Uniform Commercial Code (UCC), which has been adopted in all states except Louisiana—which has adopted part of it. Article 3 of the UCC deals with commercial paper and Article 4 covers bank deposits and collections. For the most part, the material covered in this and the following chapters on commercial paper deals with provisions of Article 3, although Article 4 is mentioned in places. Article 3 covers checks, drafts, notes, and certificates of deposit, which are called commercial paper. Commercial paper is a written promise or obligation to pay certain sums of money.

This chapter deals primarily with the basics of commercial paper and the law dealing with the transfer of such paper. Before examining the law as it relates to checks, drafts, notes, and certificates of deposit, we first cover another important type of document used in commercial transactions—documents of title.

DOCUMENTS OF TITLE

A *document of title* is any document that

in the regular course of business or financing is treated as adequately evidencing that the person in possession of it is entitled to receive, hold and dispose of the document and the goods it covers. To be a document of title, a document must purport to be issued by or addressed to a bailee and purport to cover goods in the bailee's possession, which are either identified or are fungible portions of an identified mass (UCC Section 1-201 [15]).

These documents are usually issued by professional bailees who are in the business of either delivering or storing goods. A bailee is one who takes temporary possession of the property of another for a particular purpose.

Warehouse Receipts

Definition. If a seller wishes to store goods temporarily, he or she may deliver the goods to a "warehouseman." A "warehouseman" is one type of bailee. The seller receives a *warehouse receipt*. This receipt enables the seller, or anyone to whom the seller transfers the document, to pick up the goods from the warehouseman. A seller might decide to ship goods instead of storing them. When the seller delivers the goods to a carrier (another type of bailee) for purposes of delivery, the carrier will give the seller a *bill of lading*. This document enables its possessor to receive the goods from the carrier. Warehouse receipts and bills of lading are the most familiar documents of title.

Form. A warehouse receipt need not be in any particular form, but it must contain certain information. Among other things, the warehouse receipt must contain information about the location of the warehouse, the date of issue of the receipt, to whom the goods are to be delivered, the storage or handling charges, a description of the goods or their containers, and a statement that advances have been made or liabilities incurred for which the warehouseman claims a lien or security interest.

In the event the warehouseman improperly prepares the warehouse receipt, he or she may be liable—to anyone who purchases the document for value and in good faith—for any damages caused by the nonreceipt or misdescription of the goods.

Duties of Warehouseman. A warehouseman must exercise such care with respect to goods in his or her possession as a reasonably careful person would exercise under like circumstances.

Absent a contrary agreement, a warehouseman must keep separate the goods covered by each receipt so as to permit at all times identification and delivery of those goods, except that different lots of fungible goods may be commingled. Fungible goods are goods of which any unit is treated as the equivalent of any other like unit, such as wheat or corn.

Rights of Warehouseman. On notifying the person on whose account the goods are held and any other person known to claim an interest in the goods, a warehouseman may require payment of any charges and the removal of the goods from the warehouse at the termination of the period of storage fixed by the document. If no period is fixed in the warehouse receipt for the removal of the goods, the notice may specify their removal at a certain time after the lapse of thirty days. If the goods are not removed by such date, the warehouseman may sell the goods in accordance with UCC Section 7-210.

The warehouseman has a lien on any goods stored in his or her possession for charges for storage, transportation, insurance, labor, or other expenses relating to the goods, and for expenses necessary for preservation of the goods or reasonably incurred in their sale.

A warehouseman's lien may be enforced by public or private sale of the goods in blocks or in parcels, at any time or place and on any terms that are commercially reasonable, after notifying all persons known to claim an interest in the goods (Section 7-210).

The following case considers the constitutionality of such liens.

Flagg Brothers, Inc. v. Brooks

U.S. Supreme Court
436 U.S. 149 (1978)

Flagg Brothers, respondent and defendant, stored furniture belonging to Brooks, petitioner and plaintiff. Flagg Brothers sold her furniture pursuant to a lien created by Section 7-210. Brooks claimed the actions of Flagg Brothers violated the U.S. Constitution. The trial court found no constitutional violation. The Court of Appeals found a violation of the Fourteenth Amendment. The Supreme Court agreed with the trial court and found for Flagg Brothers.

Justice Rehnquist

The question presented by this case is whether a warehouseman's proposed sale of goods entrusted to him for storage, as permitted by New York Uniform Commercial Code section 7-210, is an action properly attributable to the State of New York.

According to her complaint, the allegations of which we must accept as true, respondent Shirley Brooks and her family were evicted from their apartment in Mount Vernon, N. Y., on June 13, 1973. The City Marshal arranged for Brooks' possessions to be stored by petitioner Flagg Brothers, Inc. in its warehouse. Respondent was informed of the cost of moving and storage, and she instructed the workmen to proceed, although she found the price too high. On August 25, 1973, after a series of disputes over the validity of the charges being claimed by Flagg Bros., Brooks received a letter demanding that her account be brought up to date within 10 days "or your furniture will be sold." A series of subsequent letters from Brooks and her attorneys produced no satisfaction.

Brooks thereupon initiated this class action in the District Court under 42 U.S.C. section 1983, seeking damages, an injunction against the threatened sale of her belongings, and the declaration that such a sale pursuant to section 7-210 would violate the Due Process and Equal Protection Clauses of the Fourteenth Amendment.

A claim upon which relief may be granted to respondents against Flagg Brothers under section 1983 must embody at least two elements. Brooks must first show that she has been deprived of a right "secured by the Constitution and the laws" of the United States. Secondly, that Flagg Brothers deprived her of this right acting "under color of any statute" of the State of New York. She must establish not only that Flagg Brothers acted under color of the challenged statute, but also that its actions are properly attributable to the State of New York. It is apparent that she has not alleged facts which constitute a deprivation of any right "secured by the Constitution and the laws" of the United States.

It must be noted that Brooks has named no public officials as defendants in this action. The City Marshal, who supervised her evictions, was dismissed from the case by consent. This total absence of overt official involvement plainly distinguishes this case from earlier decisions imposing procedural restrictions on creditors' remedies. In those cases, the Court was careful to point out that the dictates of the Due Process Clause "attach only to the deprivation of an interest encompassed within the Fourteenth Amendment's protection." Thus, the only issue presented by this case is whether Flagg Brothers' action may fairly be attributed to the State of New York. We conclude that it may not.

Brooks' primary contention is that New York has delegated to Flagg Brothers a power "traditionally exclusively reserved to the State." She argues that the resolution of private disputes is a traditional function of civil government, and that the State in section 7-210 has delegated this function to Flagg Brothers. She has read too much into the language of our previous cases. While many functions have been traditionally performed by governments, very few have been "exclusively reserved to the State."

The proposed sale by Flagg Brothers under section 7-210 is not the only means of resolving this purely private dispute. Brooks has never alleged that state law barred her from seeking a waiver of Flagg Brothers' right to sell her goods at the time she authorized their storage. The challenged statute itself provides a damage remedy against the warehouseman for violations of its provisions. This system of rights and remedies, recognizing the traditional place of private arrangements in ordering relationships in the commercial world, can hardly be said to have delegated to Flagg Brothers an exclusive prerogative of the sovereign.

Whatever the particular remedies available under New York law, we do not consider a more detailed description of them necessary to our conclusion that the settlement of disputes between debtors and creditors is not traditionally an exclusive public function.

We conclude that our sovereign function cases do not support a finding of state action here.

Brooks further urges that Flagg Brothers' proposed action is properly attributable to the State because the State has authorized and encouraged it in enacting section 7-210. Our cases state "that a State is responsible for the . . . act of a private party when the State, by its law, has compelled the act." This Court, however, has never held that a State's mere acquiescence in a private action converts that action into that of the State.

It is quite immaterial that the State has embodied its decision not to act in statutory form. If New York had no commercial statutes at all, its courts would still be faced with the decision to prohibit or to permit the sort of sale threatened here the first time an aggrieved bailor came before them for relief. A judicial decision to deny relief would be no less an "authorization" or "encouragement" of that sale than the legislature's decision embodied in this statute. It was recognized in the earliest interpretations of the Fourteenth Amendment "that a State may act through different agencies,—either by its legislative, its executive, or its judicial authority; and the prohibitions of the Amendment extend to all action of the State" infringing rights protected thereby. If the mere denial of judicial relief is considered sufficient encouragement to make the State responsible for those private acts, all private deprivations of property would be converted into public acts whenever the State, for whatever reason, denies relief sought by the putative property owner.

The State of New York is in no way responsible for Flagg Brothers' decision, a decision which the State in section 7-210 permits but does not compel, to threaten to sell these belongings.

Here, the State of New York has not compelled the sale of a bailor's goods, but has merely announced the circumstances under which its courts will not interfere with a private sale. Indeed, the crux of Brooks' complaint is not that the State has acted, but that it has refused to act. This statutory refusal to act is no different in principle from an ordinary statute of limitations whereby the State declines to provide a remedy for private deprivations of property after the passage of a given period of time.

We conclude that the allegations of the complaint do not establish a violation of her Fourteenth Amendment rights by either Flagg Brothers or by the State of New York. The District Court properly concluded that the complaint failed to state a claim for relief under 42 U.S.C. section 1983. The judgment of the Court of Appeals holding otherwise is Reversed.

Bills of Lading

Definition. When a shipper puts goods in the hands of a carrier, he or she receives a receipt called a bill of lading. The bill of lading is a document between the carrier and the shipper covering the terms and conditions of the arrangement between them. It is a document issued by the carrier to transport the goods. Thus the parties contemplate some movement of the goods from one place to another, whereas parties using a warehouse receipt plan to store the goods. UCC Section 1-201(6) defines bill of lading as follows:

"Bill of lading" means a document evidencing the receipt of goods for shipment issued by a person engaged in the business of transporting or forwarding goods and includes an airbill. "Airbill" means a document serving for air transportation as a bill of lading does for marine or rail transportation, and includes an air consignment note or air waybill.

Duties of Carrier. A carrier who issues a bill of lading must exercise the degree of care in relation to the goods that a reasonably careful person would exercise under the circumstances.

The warehouseman and carrier generally have a duty to deliver the goods to the person entitled to them under the document. Before the goods are delivered, the bailee's lien must generally be satisfied and the document of title must be surrendered for cancellation or notation of partial deliveries. A bailee has no liability if he or she delivers goods in good faith and if there has been compliance with the provisions of Article 7 of the UCC and the terms of the document. The UCC in Section 1-201(19) defines good faith as "honesty in fact in the conduct or transaction concerned."

Transferability. Section 3-103 specifically provides that Article 3 of the UCC, which deals with negotiable instruments, does not apply to documents of title. This is true even though bills of lading, warehouse receipts, and other documents of title may be negotiable. These documents are negotiable if by their terms the goods are to be delivered to the bearer or to the order of a named person. This allows documents of title to be exchanged freely between persons. Unlike a negotiable instrument, a document of title does not contain an unconditional promise or order to pay a sum of money.

A bill of lading is both a contract and a receipt and is usually transferable to another party. The person who ships goods may transfer the document to a third person. The third person may present the document to the carrier at the destination and obtain the goods.

A seller who wishes to deliver goods to a buyer in a distant location may arrange for the goods to be shipped by carrier. The carrier will deliver a bill of lading to the seller. It would be possible merely to mail the bill of lading to the purchaser. Assuming that the bill of lading is negotiable and made out to bearer, the buyer could receive delivery of the goods merely by presenting the bill of lading to the carrier. This is fine when the buyer has already paid for the goods. What if the buyer has not yet paid the seller, and the seller wants to be paid in full before he or she delivers the goods? The seller may deliver the bill of lading to his or her bank, along with a commercial instrument called a draft. The draft and the bill of lading are forwarded by the seller's bank to a bank in the buyer's town. The bank in the buyer's town requires the buyer to pay the draft (in essence, to pay for the goods) and it then turns over the bill of lading to the buyer. The bank then sends the buyer's money to the seller's bank. In this manner, a seller receives payment prior to the time the buyer receives the goods. The buyer, having paid for the goods and received the bill of lading, may now claim the goods from the carrier.

LETTER OF CREDIT

Another document used by business men and women is a letter of credit. The UCC defines a letter of credit as an engagement by a bank or other person made at the request of a customer that the issuer will honor drafts or other demands for payment upon compliance with the conditions specified in the credit.

A buyer in one country may wish to purchase goods from a seller in another country. The seller may not be willing to extend credit to the buyer. In order to receive the goods, the buyer may arrange for a letter of credit from a bank. The bank agrees to pay the seller when the bank is presented the appropriate documents. This agreement makes the bank, rather than the buyer, the party obligated to pay. By using a letter of credit, the buyer may obtain goods from the seller because the seller is assured of payment from the buyer's bank.

In certain instances, the bank will be forced to pay even though the buyer is unhappy with the goods delivered under the contract. The bank's obligation to pay under the letter of credit is independent of its customer's obligations under the contract of sale.

COMMERCIAL PAPER

The law dealing with assignments, as discussed in Chapter 13, affects commercial paper. Many aspects of commercial paper are governed by the law of assignments. In particular, the law of assignments governs any instrument that fails to qualify as a negotiable instrument.

Contracts and Commercial Paper

A person may enter into a contract with another person for the payment of money. Suppose Smith agrees to pay Jones $100, and they enter into a contract that reflects Smith's obligation to pay $100 to Jones. In general, Jones's right to receive $100 may be assigned by Jones to a third person. Jones in this case is referred to as the *assignor or transferor,* and the person to whom he has transferred this right to receive money is referred to as the *assignee or transferee.* There is nothing improper about assigning a contractual right to receive money to a third party.

Rather than sign a contract to pay $100, Jones might instead ask Smith to sign a negotiable instrument in which Smith agrees to pay the $100 to Jones. Jones may then transfer the instrument to a third person. When a negotiable instrument is given by Smith to Jones, the UCC refers to the transfer as an *issuance* of the instrument. If Jones properly transfers the instrument to a third party, the UCC calls this a *negotiation.*

A right to receive money may be created by contract and *assigned* to a third party, or it may be created by a negotiable instrument and *negotiated* to a third party. In either case, the third party may collect. Why would a person enter into a negotiable instrument rather than a contract to pay money?

Advantages of Negotiable Instruments

There are a number of advantages associated with a negotiable instrument as opposed to a simple contract to receive money. A person in possession of a negotiable instrument may actually be in a better legal position than the person from whom he or she took the instrument. On the other hand, an assignee of a simple contractual right to receive money is never in any better position than his or her assignor. The courts often state that the assignee "steps into the shoes" of the assignor. By this, the courts mean that the assignee is in the same position with respect to enforcing the contract as was the assignor.

Let us take a look at how this might occur. Suppose Smith agrees to pay Jones $100. Jones then assigns his right to receive $100 to Robinson. Robinson has the same rights as her transferor or assignor, Jones. If Jones agreed to deliver a 1970 Chevrolet in return for the $100, but he never delivered it, Robinson would be subject to the defense that the car was never delivered. Because Smith could assert the failure to deliver the car against Jones, he may assert it against Robinson. But what if Smith signed a negotiable instrument and issued it to Jones instead of a contract and Jones then negotiated it to Robinson? If Robinson qualified as a holder in due course (discussed in the next chapter), she would take the instrument free of the defense that Jones never delivered the automobile to Smith.

Another situation in which the holder in due course of a negotiable instrument stands in a better position than an assignee of a contractual right to receive money is when a thief

FIGURE 19–1

Contractual Right to Receive Money	Negotiable Instrument
1. A agrees to pay B (assignor)	1. A agrees to pay B (transferor)
2. B assigns to C (assignee)	2. B negotiates to C (transferee)
3. C steps into the shoes of the assignor, B	3. If C is a holder in due course, C takes free of certain defenses A has against B

transfers the instrument. Suppose in the prior example that a thief steals the negotiable instrument from Robinson. If the instrument qualifies as *bearer paper* (discussed in the next chapter), the thief has the power to transfer good title to the instrument, under certain circumstances, to an innocent third party who gives value for the instrument and is unaware that he or she is dealing with a thief. If the thief in this example transfers the instrument to Moore, Moore may receive good title to the instrument. In this case, she may enforce the instrument against the original person obligated to pay, that is, Smith. Smith may not assert against Moore the defense that the instrument was stolen if Moore qualifies as a holder in due course of a bearer-negotiable instrument. Had Moore taken a contractual right to receive money from the thief, rather than a negotiable instrument, she would be subject to Smith's claim that the contract was stolen. The assignee of a contractual right to receive money steps into the shoes of the assignor. Whatever defenses could be asserted against the assignor may be asserted against the assignee. Because the thief (the assignor) had no interest in the contract, he or she could not transfer any interest in the contract to Moore (the assignee). The same rules apply if a finder, rather than a thief, transfers a bearer-negotiable instrument or a contractual right to receive money.

There are a number of other advantages to holding a negotiable instrument rather than a contractual right to receive money. For this reason, people prefer to acquire negotiable in-

FIGURE 19–2

Contractual Right to Receive Money	Negotiable Instrument
1. A agrees to pay B (assignor)	1. A agrees to pay B (transferor) (by bearer instrument)
2. B assigns to C (assignee)	2. B negotiates to C (transferee) (bearer instrument)
3. Stolen by D who sells it to E	3. Stolen by D who sells it to E
4. E is subject to the defense the contract was stolen	4. E is a holder in due course (if E holds bearer paper, he or she takes free of defense instrument was stolen)

struments rather than take a contractual right to pay money.

Why does the law permit certain persons in possession of negotiable instruments to enforce them when their transferors could not enforce the instruments? The UCC reflects the policy that negotiable instruments should be freely transferable. By giving a holder in due course these additional rights, the UCC encourages the transfer and acceptability of negotiable instruments.

TYPES OF COMMERCIAL PAPER

Commercial paper is a document or instrument evidencing an obligation on the part of a certain party to make a designated payment in the future. There are four basic types of commercial paper: promissory notes, drafts, checks, and certificates of deposit.

Promissory Notes

A promissory note is a written *promise* to pay money. It must contain an unconditional promise to pay a sum certain in money. It must be payable on demand or at a definite time. It must be payable to order or to bearer. It must be signed by the person making the promise (Section 3-104).

There are two parties to the instrument: (1) the *maker*, who agrees to pay a certain sum of money; and (2) the *payee*, the person the maker promises to pay.

A demand note is one that is payable on demand. A time note is one that is payable at some definite time. If a note states that it is payable on demand, the person in possession of the instrument knows that he or she may collect on the instrument immediately by demanding payment from the maker. If the note states that it is payable ninety days after date, the person in possession of the instrument knows that the maker must pay ninety days from the date on the note.

In the note in Figure 19–3, Douglas Whitman, the *maker*, promises to pay a certain sum of money to Thomas Dunfee, the *payee*. The payee knows he will be able to demand payment on this instrument two years from January 1, 1984. Because this instrument is not payable on demand, it is a time note.

Suppose that Thomas Dunfee wishes to transfer this instrument to Bartley Brennan. Dunfee may transfer his rights under this note to Brennan by indorsing it, usually on the back of the instrument, and delivering it to Brennan. In this case, Dunfee is called the *indorser* (or transferor) and Brennan is referred to as the *indorsee* (or transferee).

Drafts

A draft is a written *order* to pay money. It is a written, unconditional order by one person addressed to another person, signed by the

FIGURE 19–3

PROMISSORY NOTE

$100.00	Kansas City, Kansas January 1, 1984

Two (2) years after date I promise to pay to the order of Thomas Dunfee

One Hundred and no/100 -- Dollars

Payable at the First National Bank of Kansas City

Douglas Whitman
SAMPLE

FIGURE 19–4

DRAFT

$100.00   January 1, 1984
                                                                 SAMPLE

Thirty days after date----------------------------
Pay to the order of Frank Gibson
One Hundred and no/100--------------------------------Dollars
To: *William McCarty*   Charge the same to the
       Kalamazoo, Michigan   account of *John Blackburn*

person giving the order, requiring the person to whom it is addressed to pay a sum certain in money, on demand or at some specific time, to the order of bearer or some specific person. The person giving the order is called the *drawer*. The person to whom the order is addressed is the *drawee*. The person who is to receive the money is the *payee*. The drawer may name himself or herself as the payee.

In the draft shown in Figure 19–4, John Blackburn, the *drawer*, orders William McCarty, the *drawee*, to pay a sum of money to Frank Gibson, the *payee*. It is an unconditional order, in writing, signed by John Blackburn (the party who gives the order), to William McCarty. It orders William McCarty to pay a sum certain in money ($100) to the order of a specific person, Frank Gibson. The draft in this case is not payable immediately, as it would be in the case of a demand instrument. This draft is a time instrument, as opposed to a demand instrument, since it is not payable until thirty days after January 1, 1984.

While John Blackburn has ordered William McCarty to pay $100, McCarty is not obligated to pay anything until McCarty agrees to pay this draft. If he agrees to pay the draft, he becomes an *acceptor*. A drawee becomes an acceptor of a draft by signing his or her name across the face of the draft. The acceptor may also write on the instrument the date on which he or she accepted the instrument as well as the place where it will be paid. Once the drawee has accepted the draft, he or she is obligated to pay it when it becomes due.

As was the case for the note, if Frank Gibson, the payee, wants to transfer this instrument to Tom Dunfee, he may do so. Gibson may transfer his rights under this draft to Dunfee by indorsing the draft and delivering it to Dunfee. In this case, Gibson is called the indorser (or transferor) and Dunfee is called the indorsee (or transferee).

Checks

A check is a special form of draft that is written by a depositor (drawer) directing a bank (drawee) to pay a designated sum of money on demand to a third party (payee).

The check in Figure 19–5 is payable on demand. Whenever the person named on the check presents it for payment, he or she is entitled to payment of the $100. (See Chapter 22, "Checks," for an extensive discussion of the law relating to checks.) The drawer of the check is Bartley Brennan, who signed it. The drawee is the First National Bank of Chicago. The payee is Douglas Whitman. Clearly, this check contains an unconditional order directed to the bank to pay a sum certain in money at a definite time to the order of a specific person.

A special form of check called a cashier's check is a check drawn by a bank on itself.

FIGURE 19–5

CHECK

SAMPLE	No. *101*
	January 1, 1984
Pay to the order of *Douglas Whitman*	*$100.00*
One Hundred and no/100------------------------Dollars	
The First National Bank of Chicago	*Bartley Brennan*

Certificates of Deposit

A certificate of deposit represents an acknowledgement by a financial institution of the receipt of a designated sum of money plus a promise to repay this sum at an agreed rate of interest.

PARTIES TO COMMERCIAL PAPER

Accommodation Party

An accommodation party is one who signs an instrument in any capacity for the purpose of lending his or her name and credit to another party to the instrument. An accommodation party may sign as a maker, acceptor, drawer, or indorser.

Why would a person need to have an accommodation party sign an instrument? The person taking the instrument wants an assurance that he or she will be paid and refuses to accept the instrument without the signature of an accommodation party. Suppose a student wants to purchase a motorcycle but because he has not yet developed a satisfactory credit history the bank refuses to lend him the money. The bank might agree to lend him the money if his parents agree to sign a note as co-makers. In this case, the bank is assured that it will receive its money back either from him or his parents. Obviously there is some risk in signing as an accommodation party.

The accommodation party may end up paying off someone else's debts, although he has a right of reimbursement as a surety from the party he accommodates, who in this example is the maker.

Guarantor

A guarantor is a person who signs an instrument and agrees to pay the instrument under certain circumstances. Normally, the guarantor does this by signing, in addition to his or her name, "payment guaranteed," "collection guaranteed," or similar words.

USING COMMERCIAL PAPER

Commercial paper generally is used in several ways: to borrow money, as a substitute for money, as a credit device, or to create some evidence of a debt.

To Borrow Money

If Brown goes to the bank to borrow money, the bank will probably ask Brown to sign a note in which Brown promises to repay the money over a certain period of time at a stated rate of interest. Suppose Brown wants to purchase an automobile with the proceeds of the loan. The bank will ask him to sign a note and a security agreement. (See Chapter 23, "Secured Transactions," for a discussion of security agreements.) The note obligates Brown to repay the money to the bank over a period of time or on a fixed maturity date. The security agreement gives the bank an interest in the automobile Brown intends to purchase. In the event Brown fails to comply with his obligations under the note, the bank will exercise its rights under the security agreement. The bank may repossess the automobile, resell it, and pay off the note with the proceeds of the sale.

To Create Evidence of a Debt

In the example discussed in the previous paragraph, the note signed by Brown serves as written evidence of Brown's obligation to the bank. The fact that Brown signed a note simplifies the bank's burden of establishing that a debt exists between Brown and it. The note constitutes proof that Brown in fact owes the bank a certain amount of money, which must be repaid at a certain time.

As a Substitute for Money

Commercial paper also serves as a substitute for money. When a person goes into a store to purchase an item, she might pay for it by presenting a check to the store. If she is purchasing a very expensive item, she will probably prefer to use a check because it eliminates the need to carry a large sum of money. It also provides a record of payment.

As a Credit Device

Commercial paper may also be used as a credit device. Suppose a seller wanted to sell goods to a buyer in another part of the country. The seller could insist that the buyer send a certified check before it ships the goods. In this way, the seller would be certain of payment. Alternatively, the seller might sell the goods to the buyer on credit. The seller would bill the buyer for the goods at a later date. Of course, if the buyer does not pay at that time, the seller may have to sue. In the suit, the seller would have to prove that the buyer owed it

money. If the buyer had signed a commercial instrument, it would greatly simplify the case since the seller would have evidence of the obligation.

Another possibility open to the seller is to utilize a draft. The draft may be utilized to finance a sale. A draft is an order by the drawer to the drawee to pay a certain sum of money. Suppose an Ohio seller wishes to ship goods to a buyer in Kansas. The seller will load the goods on a carrier, such as a truck, and the trucking company will provide him or her with a bill of lading—a document giving the person holding it the power to claim the goods. The seller then ships the goods to the buyer in Kansas. At the same time, the seller prepares a draft. If the seller wants to be paid at once, he or she will prepare a demand draft. The seller (the drawer of the draft) draws a draft ordering the buyer (the drawee) to pay a certain sum of money to the seller's bank (the payee). As noted earlier, at this point the buyer has no obligation on the draft. Only when he or she *accepts* the draft does the drawee incur any obligation to pay the draft. The seller will then give the draft and the bill of lading to its bank for collection. The seller's bank transfers the draft through banking channels to the buyer's bank in Kansas. The Kansas bank presents the draft to the buyer, and the buyer accepts and pays it. The buyer then receives from the bank the bill of lading, which enables the buyer to receive the goods from the carrier. The Kansas bank forwards the money back to the Ohio bank through banking channels.

When a seller uses a draft with an attached bill of lading, it is called a *documentary draft*. If a draft alone is utilized, the draft is called a *clean draft.*

The seller may also use a time draft, called a *trade acceptance.* It serves as a credit device to enable the buyer to receive the goods immediately without paying for them at once. In this instance, the seller follows the same procedure outlined above. The seller names himself or herself on the draft as the payee, and sets a time at which the draft is payable. The bank in Kansas asks the buyer to accept the draft, which he or she does by signing his or her name across the face of the instrument or in a space provided for the acceptor's signature. At this point the drawee buyer becomes an acceptor of the draft. This obligates the buyer to pay the draft at whatever date it becomes due. The bank releases the bill of lading to the buyer. It then returns the draft to the seller. The seller may retain the draft until its due date, then present the draft to the buyer for payment at that time. If the seller uses a time draft payable June 1, which the buyer signs on January 1, he or she then waits until June 1. On June 1, the seller presents the draft to the buyer for payment. Alternatively, the seller may want cash at once. In this case, the seller takes the draft to a third party, such as a bank, and negotiates it to the bank. The bank pays the seller its money at once. The bank then waits until June 1 to collect the draft. On June 1, the bank presents the draft to the buyer for payment.

Drafts, notes, and checks may be used in other ways. But in general they are used as credit-extension devices, to borrow money and to create some evidence of a debt.

Negotiability

The UCC seeks to encourage the free transferability of negotiable instruments. The holder-in-due-course device is the basic method by which such transferability is encouraged. A holder in due course of a negotiable instrument is given preferred status.

For example, Merchant purchases goods from Manufacturer and signs a negotiable promissory note. Manufacturer negotiates the note to Financial Institution. Merchant never receives the goods and raises that fact as a defense against Financial Institution. Because Financial Institution is a holder in due course, Merchant cannot successfully raise the defense of failure of consideration and refuse to pay Financial Institution. Instead, Merchant's only recourse is to sue Manufacturer for breach of contract.

Some modifications of the rule relating to the holder-in-due-course doctrine have been made in the area of consumer transactions. Some states have adopted the Uniform Consumer Credit Code, which prohibits the use of promissory notes when consumer goods are purchased. A major modification of the holder-in-due-course device in consumer transactions was created by a Trade Regulation Rule adopted by the Federal Trade Commission. This rule is discussed in Chapter 20.

To qualify as a holder in due course, one must be:

(1) a proper holder
(2) in possession of a negotiable instrument
(3) that was properly negotiated

REQUIREMENTS OF NEGOTIABLE INSTRUMENTS

The requirements of a negotiable instrument are formal, and considerable emphasis is placed upon the use of special words. The courts will look to the document itself to determine whether it is negotiable. The UCC requires that the document be:

1. a signed
2. writing
3. containing a promise or order to pay
4. that is unconditional
5. relating to a sum certain
6. in money

Further, it must:

7. contain no other promise or order
8. be payable on demand or at a certain time
9. be payable to order or to bearer (or words of similar meaning)

The instrument must then be duly negotiated in order for the transferee to obtain the status of a holder in due course. Negotiation requires that:

1. the instrument be transferred
2. to a proper holder
3. with any required proper indorsement.

Transfer may be achieved either through physical delivery or, more rarely, a constructive delivery of the instrument. Constructive delivery occurs when the transferee, with intent to effect a transfer, performs a symbolic act representing the transfer. For example, delivery of the keys to a safe containing the instrument may constitute a constructive transfer.

Reexamine the promissory note in Figure 19–3 (p. 470). Does it meet all the requirements of negotiability?

1. The instrument is signed by the maker (Doug Whitman).
2. The instrument is in writing.
3. The instrument contains a promise to pay.
4. The promise is unconditional.
5. The maker promises to pay a sum certain.
6. The amount of this note is in money.
7. The instrument contains no other promise or order.
8. The instrument is payable at a certain time.
9. This instrument is payable to order.

Because all the elements of negotiability are present, this note qualifies as a negotiable instrument.

If some of these elements are missing, the instrument could still be transferred but it would *not* be governed by the rules in Article 3 of the UCC. (However, if the only defect in the instrument is that it is not payable to either order or bearer, Article 3 still governs, but no one can be a holder in due course of the instrument [Section 3-805].) This instrument would be governed by the law of contracts as discussed earlier in this book, and in particular by the law relating to assignments. If the instrument were transferred to a third party, the maker of this instrument would be able to assert any defenses against the person holding the instrument. If this instrument qualified as a negotiable instrument, and if it were validly negotiated to a holder in due course, the maker of the note would not be able to assert a personal defense against the holder in due course, though real defenses could be successfully raised to defeat him. (Defenses are discussed in Chapter 21.)

Even if an instrument is negotiable, so long as the instrument is in the hands of the payee the obligor (person obligated to pay the instrument) may set up any defenses he or she has against the payee, unless the payee qualifies as a holder in due course. Whether the instrument is negotiable or nonnegotiable, the obligor may assert any defenses he or she has against the original parties to the instrument. Only when a negotiable instrument is validly negotiated to a third party who qualifies as a holder in due course are personal defenses of the obligor cut off.

Signed

To be negotiable, an instrument must be signed by the maker or drawer. It is not necessary to actually sign an instrument by handwriting; a signature may be made by printing, stamping, writing, or initialing. The question is whether the symbol on the instrument was executed or adopted by the party signing the instrument with the present intention of authenticating the writing.

Agent. It is not necessary to sign an instrument personally. The principal may designate an agent or representative to sign for him or her (subsection 3-403[1]). When an agent has authority to sign documents, he or she has the power to bind the principal.

In the following case, the owner of a business permitted his agent to write checks on the business account. The name of the business was printed on the check, but the agent merely signed his name. This was an action by a holder of the instrument against the business.

drawer gives order
drawee writes chk

payee

Jenkins v. Evans
New York Supreme Court
295 N.Y.S.2d 226 (1968)

Albert Stickler wrote checks on the Glass Lake House account, on which he was authorized to write checks. He gave his check to Payne, who transferred it to Jenkins, the plaintiff in this case. Jenkins sued Evans, the owner of the Glass Lake House and the defendant, to recover on the check. Evans claimed he was not liable because neither his signature nor the words Glass Lake House appeared on the signature line on the checks. The lower court ruled in favor of Jenkins because he was a holder in due course of the check. The appellate court affirmed this decision.

Staley, Justice

The respondent, Jenkins, sues to recover the sum of $295, the face amount of two checks drawn upon the account of the Glass Lake House which were delivered to one William Payne as payee, by Albert L. Stickler, the managing agent of the Glass Lake House at Averill Park, New York. Thereafter, the said William Payne endorsed and delivered the checks to the respondent in payment of an obligation. The checks were subsequently dishonored by the National Exchange Bank of Castleton-on-Hudson, New York.

Jenkins moved for summary judgment upon the ground that he is a holder in due course, since he took the checks for value and in good faith, and without notice of any defense of it. Evans cross moved for summary judgment upon the grounds that the checks were signed by Albert L. Stickler, individually, and nowhere on the face of the instrument does it indicate that Stickler signed on behalf of the Glass Lake House; that Albert L. Stickler was the maker of the checks, and is personally liable on the checks; that the checks were drawn without the authority of Evans and that upon information and belief, the said checks were used for personal obligations of Albert L. Stickler.

The appellant, Evans, admits that Albert L. Stickler was authorized to sign checks drawn upon the account of the Glass Lake House, and does not deny that the checks were drawn upon the check forms used by the Glass Lake House. Appellant does not deny that Jenkins is a holder in due course.

Evans' contention that he is not liable on the checks, since his signature does not appear thereon and the words "Glass Lake House" do not appear above the signature line on the checks, is without merit. Any writing to be a negotiable instrument must be signed by the maker or drawer. No person is liable on an instrument unless his signature appears thereon, and a signature may be made by the use of any name.

Appellant authorized the use of the name and signature, and nothing upon the face of the check would indicate that it was necessary for Albert L. Stickler to indicate that he was signing in a representative capacity, or that his capacity to sign the checks was limited. It thus appears that the appellant's printed name and address at the top of the check establishes he is named in the instrument and that he clothes his agent, Albert L. Stickler, with authority to possess, issue, and sign checks drawn upon his account, and respondent took the checks in question without notice of any defense against them.

Jenkins then is a holder-in-due-course and took the checks free from any and all defenses on the part of the Evans.

> "The indication of agency or representation may appear in the body of the instrument as well as in the signature so as to preserve the person signing from individual liability. Thus, an instrument may be regarded as that of a principal although the name of the principal appears, not in the signature or promise, but on the blank or form on which the instrument is written."

The appellant is, therefore, bound to the obligation represented by the checks, and summary judgment was properly granted in favor of the respondent.

Order affirmed, with costs.

Capacity of Signer A person may sign an instrument in a number of capacities—as a drawer of a draft, as an acceptor of a draft, as a maker of a note, or as an indorser of an instrument. No one has any liability on an instrument unless his or her name appears on it (subsection 3-401[2]). A note to be enforceable must be signed by the maker. A draft to be enforceable must be signed by the drawer.

It is necessary to determine in what capacity a person signed an instrument. In order to clarify this issue, the UCC adopted some rules. A person who signs a *note* in the lower-right-hand corner is presumed to be a maker, while a person who signs a *draft* in the lower-right-hand corner is presumed to be a drawer. When the drawee of an instrument signs his or her signature across the face of the draft, the signature is regarded as an acceptance. Section 3-402 adopts a presumption that, if a person's signature is ambiguous, it is deemed an indorsement. Normally, an indorsement appears on the reverse side of an instrument.

Signature of a Representative. While it is true that a person's signature must appear on an instrument before he or she has any liability on the instrument, the signature may be made by someone on behalf of someone else. If an agent authorized to sign on another's behalf signs a negotiable instrument, this binds the principal. A person who is incapacitated might appoint a person to sign documents on his or her behalf. Likewise, an agent of a corporation (such as the treasurer or president) may sign commercial paper on behalf of the corporation if that agent is authorized to do so.

The power to sign for another may be an express authority granted to the agent, or it may be implied in law or in fact, or it may rest merely upon apparent authority. It is not necessary for there to be any particular form of appointment in order to establish such appointment.

An agent must sign an instrument properly, otherwise he or she may be liable under certain circumstances for the face amount of the instrument. The correct way for a person to sign an instrument in a representative capacity on behalf of another is as follows:

Peter Pringle
by Arthur Adams, Agent

A signature in this manner clearly indicates to any person taking it that the agent signed on behalf of the principal and did not intend to incur any personal liability on the instrument. If an officer of the corporation is signing on behalf of the corporation, he or she should sign the instrument as follows:

Book Corporation
by Doug Whitman, President

This signature clearly indicates that Whitman signed on behalf of the corporation and intended to bind *only* the corporation and not himself. This becomes significant when a corporation is unable to pay its debts. Normally, shareholders and officers are not liable for the debts of the corporation. However, when a corporation is unable to pay its debts, the holders of instruments may attempt to enforce the instruments against anyone whose signature is on them. A small corporation owned by the person who signed a note might go bankrupt. In that case, the holder of the note may sue the officer who signed the note. If that person failed to sign the note in the manner suggested above, he or she might end up paying a debt of the corporation.

A very dangerous manner of signing an instrument would be for an agent to sign but fail to name the person represented or the fact that the agent signed in a representative capacity. If Arthur Adams signs an instrument on behalf of Peter Pringle, but the only signature appearing on the instrument is "Arthur Adams," Peter Pringle is not liable on this instrument. Arthur Adams, however, is liable.

What if, rather than signing his name, Adams signs only the principal's name on the instrument: "Peter Pringle." In this case, only

the principal is liable. However, a signature in this manner by an agent may create problems for persons taking the instrument, who must establish that an authorized agent signed on behalf of its principal. To avoid legal problems, the agent should sign the principal's name together with his or her own name, along with some indication that the agent is signing the instrument in a representative capacity.

An agent might neglect to sign the principal's name, but he or she might sign his or her name along with some indication of the capacity in which he or she is acting, for example: "Arthur Adams, agent." So long as this instrument remains in the hands of the payee, the agent may introduce evidence that the parties were aware that the agent signed in a representative capacity. In this case, the agent is not liable. However, if the instrument is negotiated to a holder in due course, the agent will be personally liable on the instrument. The agent will not be permitted to introduce evidence that he signed the instrument only in a representative capacity. In any event, the principal will not be liable because his or her name does not appear on the instrument.

What if the agent signs the instrument as follows: "Peter Pringle, Arthur Adams"? In this case, as long as the instrument is in the possession of someone with whom the agent has dealt, the agent may introduce evidence that he or she signed in a representative capacity. But as in the preceding example, this evidence may not be introduced against a holder in due course. The agent must pay a holder in due course.

Once again, the proper manner to sign an instrument, when acting in a representative capacity, is to sign the name of the principal, then sign the name of the agent with some indication that the agent is signing in a representative capacity. In signing for an organization, the name of an organization should be preceded or followed by the name and office of the individual authorized to sign on behalf of ·the organization—for example:

"XYZ Corporation, by Douglas Whitman, President."

In the following case, the president of a cor-poration signed some notes on behalf of the corporation without indicating that he was signing in a representative capacity.

Rotuba Extruders, Inc. v. Ceppos

Court of Appeals of New York

385 N.E.2d 1068 (1978)

Suit was brought against Kenneth Ceppos on seven notes he signed. Ceppos was president of Kenbert Lighting Industries, Inc. Ceppos signed these notes to enable Kenbert to receive goods. The trial court granted a summary judgment in favor of the plaintiff, Rotuba, on the notes. The Appellate Division reversed the decision of the trial court. The New York Court of Appeals reversed the decision of the Appellate Division and reinstated the summary judgment on the notes for Rotuba.

Fuchsberg, Judge

This appeal, in an action between the immediate parties to a series of negotiable instruments, calls upon us to determine what measure of proof is required to free from personal liability an authorized representative who signs his own name to a series of negotiable instruments showing the name of the principal represented but that do not show that the representative signed in a representative capacity. The issue falls squarely within section 3-403.

Suit was brought against Kenneth Ceppos on seven promissory notes in the aggregate face amount of $33,898.80. These notes had been delivered to plaintiff between February and May, 1976, in payment for goods sold and delivered to Kenbert Lighting Industries, Inc., a close corporation of which Kenneth Ceppos was the chief executive officer and of which Robert Ceppos and Daniel Ceppos were the other principals. Rotuba apparently then considered Kenbert so precarious a credit risk that it was insistent that one of the three Ceppos' guarantee payment for goods sold to Kenbert. When the first notes went unpaid upon presentation for payment, Rotuba first brought an action against Kenbert. Shortly thereafter, as the due date of the remaining notes approached, Kenbert filed a voluntary petition under chapter 11 of the Federal Bankruptcy Laws. Rotuba thereupon initiated the present action against the individual defendants.

On the single printed line provided for a signature in the lower right-hand corner of each note appeared the signature of Kenneth Ceppos and, in a space immediately above this, in what is apparently a different handwriting, were the words "Kenbert Lighting Ind. Inc." No word or symbol, not even as much as "by" or "for" appeared to signify that Kenneth Ceppos was acting in a representative capacity in affixing his signature. Nor was there any designation of any office or position that Kenneth Ceppos held with Kenbert.

It is Rotuba's position that the notes indicate on their very faces that Kenneth Ceppos is personally liable on them. In opposition, Ceppos contends that a triable issue of fact exists because, as he asserts, the notes are ambiguous on their faces and his intention was only to sign them in a representative capacity.

Section 3-403 aims to foster certainty and definiteness in the law of commercial paper, requirements deriving from the "necessity for takers of negotiable instruments to tell at a glance whose obligation they hold". To make commercial paper "freely negotiable without undue risk" the basic law is that resort to extrinsic proof is impermissible when the face of the instrument itself does not serve to put its holder on notice of the limited liability of a signer.

As the statute states, the only exception has to be one that is "otherwise established between the immediate parties".

But the type of showing needed to bring the note within the "except" clause of section 3-403 must necessarily amount to more than the mere self-serving allegation of the signer's subjective intent to sign as representative. To escape personal liability, the signer has the burden to "establish" an agreement, understanding or course of dealing to the contrary. Thus, without an affirmative demonstration that the taker of the note knew or understood that the signer intended to execute the instrument in a representative status only, there can be no defense that, notwithstanding the form of the note, representative liability was "otherwise established between the parties."

Clearly, the notes in this case fall within the situation contemplated by the statute and, in factual circumstances that meet its requirements, would have permitted Ceppos to rebut the presumption of individual liability. Yet, Ceppos neither alleged nor made any evidentiary showing of the intent necessary to constitute such an agreement or understanding and, consequently, his affidavit does not serve to deny Rotuba summary judgment.

The undisclosed intention of Ceppos, without more, does not establish the understanding between the parties required by section 3-403. Ceppos' affidavit does not even disclose such elementary facts as who acted for Rotuba in accepting the notes, what disclosure was made of Ceppos' unilateral intention, or what manifestation or knowledge of such intention, if any, was made anywhere or to anyone on behalf of Rotuba.

In short, Ceppos pointed to nothing that would tend to show that the parties regarded the obligation as a corporate one alone. The nature of the transaction here gives no indication that regardless of the faces of the notes, corporate liability and none other was intended by the parties. Certainly, there was nothing unusual about it. It is common business practice to treat such an obligation as a corporate one, and creditors of small corporations often demand that officers personally obligate themselves on corporate notes.

Therefore, the order of the Appellate Division should be reversed and the order granting summary judgment on the first cause of action must be reinstated.

Unconditional Promise or Order

An instrument, in order to be negotiable, must contain an unconditional promise or order to pay. Notes and certificates of deposit must contain an unconditional *promise* to pay.

Drafts and checks must include an unconditional *order* to pay. If the language in an instrument states that the obligor *promises* to pay someone, the instrument cannot be a draft or check.

Suppose John Doe wrote out the following statement on a piece of paper: "I.O.U. $100 (signed) John Doe." This piece of paper obviously has some characteristics of a negotiable instrument. But it lacks one important element: a promise or an order to pay. While John Doe acknowledges his obligation to pay a debt of $100, he does not promise to pay it or order someone else to pay it. This missing element renders the I.O.U. nonnegotiable. In the typical note, a statement appears such as "I promise to pay." In the case of a draft, some language must appear that orders someone or some institution to pay. In the draft in Fig. 19–4, this requirement is fulfilled by placing the drawee's name after the word "To," or as it appears in that instrument: "To: William McCarty." On a check, the name of the drawee bank will appear on the face of the check. The check illustrated in Fig. 19–5 has the words "The First National Bank" in the lower-left-hand corner of the check.

The negotiability of an instrument must be determinable by an examination of the face of the instrument itself. It must not be necessary for anyone who wishes to take the instrument to refer to any other document in order to determine if an instrument is negotiable.

So long as the instrument is in the possession of the original obligee (the party the obligor must pay) or any transferee who fails to qualify as a holder in due course, an instrument may be modified or affected by any other written agreement executed as part of the same transaction. A holder in due course is not affected by any limitation of his or her rights arising out of a separate written agreement if he or she had no notice of the limitation at the time of receiving the instrument.

It is common for persons to execute several documents at the same time. Suppose a person wishes to borrow $5,000 from a bank in order to purchase a new automobile. The bank will probably ask the borrower to sign a promissory note and a security agreement. (Security agreements are covered in Chapter 23, "Secured Transactions.") The security agreement will contain information that does not appear in the note. The UCC requires that all writings executed as parts of the same transaction are to be read together as a single agreement—in this instance, both the note and the security agreement. If the note is negotiated to a holder in due course who is unaware of any defense or claim arising under the terms to the security agreement, he or she will not be affected by any defense or claim arising out of the security agreement.

The negotiability of an instrument is always to be determined by what appears on the face of the instrument alone. If it is negotiable in itself, a purchaser without notice of a separate writing is not affected by the other writing (Section 3-119[2]). If the instrument states it is subject to or governed by any other agreement, it is not negotiable. If the instrument merely refers to a separate agreement or states that it arises out of such an agreement, it is negotiable.

Section 3-105 lists certain matters that may appear in an instrument without making the promise or order to pay conditional. Section 3-112 also identifies some terms and omissions that do not affect the negotiability of an instrument. The following material discusses several important points covered in Section 3-105.

To determine whether the negotiable instrument includes an unconditional promise or order to pay, one need only examine the instrument itself. Oral statements do not affect the negotiable character of an instrument. Suppose that McGrew tells Allison at the time she executes a promissory note that she will pay the note only if Allison delivers a 1959 Ford to her. This statement has no effect on the negotiable character of the instrument. A party examining the face of the instrument would be unaware of the oral condition put on the instrument by McGrew at the time she executed the note.

In the case mentioned earlier between the bank and the borrower, we noted that the bank might ask its customer to sign several documents at the same time. Insofar as third persons who were not parties to the original transaction are concerned, whether the instrument is negotiable depends on what appears in the instrument. Negotiability is not influenced by what appears in a separate written document.

Take the case of Allison and McGrew. If the note McGrew signs indicates that McGrew is giving this note to Allison in consideration for the 1959 Ford, or if it indicates that the note is being transferred because Allison sold her 1959 Ford to McGrew, McGrew's promise to pay Allison is *not* rendered conditional. Such recitals only explain why the note is issued—but the note stands regardless of the recitals. On the other hand, if McGrew writes into the note that the terms of the note are subject to or governed by the contract signed between McGrew and Allison for the sale of the 1959 Ford, the promise to pay is rendered conditional. The instrument would be nonnegotiable. This type of statement requires any person who wishes to acquire this note to examine some other document than the note between McGrew and Allison. The negotiability of an instrument must be determinable by an examination of the face of the instrument in question.

Some instruments indicate that they are payable *only* from a particular account. Such a statement makes an instrument nonnegotiable. If language in the instrument states "Pay only out of the Acme account," the language renders the instrument nonnegotiable. However, if the instrument merely indicates a particular account to be debited, the instrument is negotiable. If a person writes on the bottom of a note "Pay out of Acme account," this would be treated as a mere reference, not a statement that conditions or limits payment of the instrument from the Acme account.

Sum Certain in Money

To be negotiable, an instrument must also contain a sum certain in money. If it is possible for a holder to determine at the time of payment the amount payable merely by examining the instrument itself, the amount payable is certain. If it is necessary to make computations in order to determine the amount payable, the sum is certain if the computation can be made from the instrument itself without reference to any outside source. The fact that the sum is payable with stated interest, or with different rates of interest before and after default, will not make the note nonnegotiable (Section 3-106[1]). All of this information can be determined from the face of the instrument. On the other hand, if the note is payable "at the current rate," the instrument is not negotiable because the holder would not know the current rate by examining the instrument itself.

An instrument is payable in money if "the medium of exchange" in which it is payable is money at the time the instrument is made. An instrument payable in "currency" or "current funds" is payable in money (Section 3-107[1]). The promise to pay may be stated in foreign currency rather than in dollars.

Payable on Demand or at Certain Time

To be negotiable, an instrument must be payable on demand or at a definite time. An instrument is payable on demand if it is payable at sight or on presentation or if it contains no time for payment (Section 3-108). It must be paid whenever the holder presents it for payment.

An instrument payable at a definite time must state the date on which it is payable. The note in Fig. 19–3 is payable two years after its date—that is, two years after January 1, 1984. If the maker of this note failed to insert a date, the note would not be negotiable because it would not be payable at a definite time. However, Section 3-115 permits a holder of an instrument to fill in the date before negotiating the instrument. Not all instruments are this simple, but they may still be payable at a definite time.

According to Section 3-109, an instrument is payable at a definite time if by its terms it is payable:

COMMERCIAL PAPER: INTRODUCTION AND NEGOTIABILITY

1. On or before a stated date or at a fixed period after a stated date
2. At a fixed period after sight
3. At a definite time subject to acceleration
4. At a definite time subject to extension at the option of the holder
5. At a definite time subject to extension to a further definite time at the option of the maker or acceptor or automatically upon or after a specified act or event

The instrument in Fig. 19–3 is payable at a fixed period after a stated date. A draft payable "30 days after sight" is also payable at a definite time. When the holder presents it to the drawee and the drawee accepts it (thereby becoming the acceptor of the draft), the thirty-day period begins to run.

The time for payment must be determinable from the face of the instrument. An instrument may contain an *acceleration clause,* which, in an instrument payable at a definite time, permits the entire draft to become due immediately upon the option of one of the parties or the occurrence of some specified event. The option to accelerate may be exercised only if the party in good faith believes the prospect of payment or performance is impaired (Section 1-208). A clause in an instrument that reads "payable June 1, 1985, but the entire sum is due and payable immediately in the event the maker dies" is a valid acceleration clause. The payee of this instrument knows he or she will be paid on June 1, 1985, at the latest, or earlier if the maker dies before

that time. An instrument can also be written in such a fashion that the holder can accelerate the time for payment. However, as noted before, the holder must reasonably believe that the prospect of payment or performance has been impaired.

The instrument also may be made payable at a definite time subject to extension at the option of the holder, at the option of the maker or acceptor, or automatically upon the occurrence of an act or event.

If the instrument is payable only upon an act or event whose occurrence is uncertain, the instrument is not payable at a definite time even though the act or event has occurred (Section 3-109[2]). For instance, if the note is payable "upon the marriage of my daughter," and the daughter has now married, the note is still not payable at a definite time. It must be possible to determine, at the time a person takes the instrument, whether the instrument is payable at a definite time or on demand. The specified event (the daughter's marriage) may never occur. She may never marry, or she may die before the note comes due. In such cases, the instrument would never be payable. No one would want to take an instrument unless he or she was certain that it would be paid either immediately or at some definite time in the future.

The following case concerns a note that the court determines is not negotiable because it was not payable on demand or at a definite time.

Barton v. Hudgens Realty and Mortgage, Inc.

Court of Appeals of Georgia
222 S.E.2d 126 (1975)

Plaintiff, Hudgens Realty, brought suit upon what it purported to be a "promissory note" signed by the defendants, the Bartons, and containing the following pertinent language: "By execution of this document the undersigned hereby acknowledges and promises to pay to the order of Scott Hudgens Realty & Mortgage, Inc., a Delaware corporation, at Atlanta, Georgia, or at such other place or to such other party or parties as the holder hereof may from time to time designate, the principal sum of three thousand dollars ($3,000). This amount is due and payable upon evidence of an acceptable permanent loan of $290,000 for Barton-Ludwig Cains Hill Place Office Building, Atlanta, Georgia, from one of SHRAM's investors and upon acceptance of the commitment by the undersigned." In the answer, the Bartons admitted execution of the "promissory note," and further admitted execution of the loan commitment, but denied that an "acceptable permanent loan" was obtained and therefore denied that the "promissory note" was due and payable on the date alleged. Hudgens Realty moved for judgment on the pleadings, based upon the Bartons' admission of execution of the "note" and the loan commitment, and the motion was granted. The Appeals Court affirmed the decision of the trial court for Hudgens Realty.

Deen, Presiding Judge

Hudgens Realty relies upon *Freezamatic Corporation* v. *Brigadier Industries Corporation,* wherein it was held that under our Uniform Commercial Code when execution of a promissory note is admitted but an affirmative defense is not raised, judgment on the pleadings in favor of the holder is proper. While it is true that Code provides for such a circumstance, what the plaintiff (and also the defendants) overlooked is that the provisions of Code Ann. Ch. 109A-3 apply only to negotiable instruments and the "promissory note" here in issue does not so qualify. This "promissory note" by its terms was made payable "upon evidence of an acceptable permanent loan . . . and upon acceptance of the [loan] commitment"; however under Code Ann. Section 109A-3-104(1)(c) a negotiable instrument must "be payable on demand or at a definite time." The "note" here was not payable on demand under the language of section 109-A-108 and under section 109A-3-109(2) "[a]n instrument which by its terms is otherwise payable only upon an act or event uncertain as to time of occurrence is not payable on demand or at a definite time even though the act or event has occurred." The language of the "promissory note" therefore reveals that it was not payable on demand or at a definite time, was therefore not negotiable and thus the Freezamatic Corporation case is not controlling authority.

The "promissory note" is rather *a contract to pay money* when certain contingencies are satisfied—"upon evidence of an acceptable permanent loan . . . and upon acceptance of the [loan] commitment." There is no dispute that the loan commitment was accepted by the Bartons. Hudgens contends that this commitment itself, without more, wherein one of its investors agreed to make the loan in the desired amount, satisfied the requirement of evidence of an acceptable permanent loan. Barton, apparently relying on the fact that the loan was never finally consummated, denies that "an acceptable permanent loan was obtained." Thus the controversy between the parties turns upon the construction of the contract language making the amount due and payable "upon evidence of an acceptable permanent loan."

Under Code Ann. section 20-704(4) the whole contract should be looked to in arriving at the construction of any part. The contract provides specifically that it is for a loan origination fee; there is nothing which requires as a prerequisite to recovery evidence that the loan in fact be accepted. All that is required is that there be "evidence of an acceptable permanent loan." The record reveals that by their signatures, the Bartons signified their "acceptance of the terms and conditions" of the loan commitment. We agree with the Hudgens' construction of the document, that the loan commitment is evidence of a permanent loan in the desired amount and that the admission by the Bartons of its execution acknowledges its acceptability and further supplies the necessary requirement for recovery under the contract. In short, the Bartons contracted for the procurement of a loan and the signed loan commitment is "evidence of an acceptable permanent loan." The broker having successfully originated a loan, its fee was earned and the Bartons were bound by their contract.

To Order or Bearer

To Order. To be negotiable, an instrument must also be payable to order or to bearer. "Order" and "bearer" are *words of negotiability*. "An instrument is payable to order when by its terms it is payable to the order or assigns of any person therein specified with reasonable certainty, or him or his order . . ." (Section 3-110). Thus a check payable "to the order of John Jones" is negotiable. The courts interpret this requirement strictly: a check "payable to John Jones" is not negotiable because it does not say "to the order of John Jones." The printed checks issued by banks have "to the order of" printed on them. An instrument alternatively might state "to John Jones or order" or "to John Jones or assigns."

An instrument must specify a particular person or organization so that it will be clear who is entitled to payment. It can be made payable to more than one person. For example, an instrument can be "payable to the order of John Doe and Acme Car Repair." In this case, the instrument may be properly negotiated to a third party only if *both* parties to the instrument indorse it. An instrument made payable to two parties in this fashion may not be properly negotiated if only John Doe or Acme Car Repair indorses it. People often use this device when they want to make certain that all parties to whom they are obligated have been paid. On the other hand, if an instrument is made payable to the order of "John Doe *or* Acme Car Repair," the signature of *either* party as an indorser, along with a delivery of the instrument, will result in a proper negotiation.

An instrument payable to the order of "John Doe and/or Acme Car Repair" may be negotiated by the indorsement of either party along with delivery of the instrument to a third party. Suppose the instrument reads "John Doe/Acme Car Repair." In this case, the check will be treated as a check payable to both of these parties, and it will require the signature of both John Doe and Acme Car Repair.

To Bearer. Even though an instrument fails to qualify as an order instrument, it is negotiable if it is payable to bearer. An instrument is payable to bearer when by its terms it is payable to bearer or to the order of bearer, or to a specified person or bearer, or to cash or to the order of cash, so long as it does not purport to designate a specific payee. If an instrument is payable "to order of bearer" or "cash," it is bearer paper. Anyone who gets possession of this instrument has the power to negotiate it.

An instrument payable "to order of bearer," although it sounds as if it is payable to order, is treated as an instrument payable to bearer (Section 3-111[a]). An instrument that reads "pay bearer" also is treated as payable to bearer.

Under Section 3-110(3), an instrument that is made payable "to order and to bearer" is payable *to order* unless the bearer words are handwritten or typewritten. A drawer might write "Pay to the order of John Doe" and fail to note that the form has the phrase "or bearer" printed on it. In this situation, the instrument is treated as payable *to order*. However, if a form contains the words "Pay to order of ————————————," and the drawer writes in the blank space "John Doe or bearer," the intent of the maker or drawer to create a bearer instrument is assumed (Section 3-110, Comment 6).

Instruments containing phrases like "Pay cash," "Pay to the order of cash," "Pay bills payable," or others that do not designate a specific payee are treated as instruments payable to bearer.

Incomplete Instrument. An instrument that merely states "to the order of" followed by a blank space is an *incomplete* order instrument. The following case illustrates what happens if the instrument fails to specify a payee.

Gray v. American Express Co.

Court of Appeals of North Carolina
239 S.E.2d 621 (1977)

Joseph Faillance gave several American Express Traveler's Checks to Ernie's Truck Stop, which in turn transferred the checks to Charles Gray, the plaintiff in this case. American Express refused to honor the checks on the grounds that they were incomplete because they were not payable to anyone. The trial court ruled for American Express and the appeals court affirmed the decision of the trial court.

Clark, Judge

Plaintiff, owner of Charles L. Gray Company, a wholesale grocery company located in Rocky Mount, received an order on 9 August 1967 from Ernie's Truck Stop for about $4,900 worth of cigarettes. He delivered the cigarettes to the manager of Ernie's. The manager gave the cigarettes over to Joseph Faillance of New York. Faillance paid the manager with $4,800 in American Express Traveler's Checks. Plaintiff saw Faillance sign and countersign the checks. Faillance did not date the checks or make them payable to anyone. The signature and countersignature were similar. The manager gave the checks to plaintiff in payment for the cigarettes. The checks remained blank as to date and payee. The manager did not indorse the checks over to plaintiff. On 10 August 1967 plaintiff turned the checks over to a local bank, still blank as to date and payee, and was refused payment on the ground that the checks were stolen. Payment was similarly refused after plaintiff forwarded the checks to Chase Manhattan Bank. Plaintiff never filled in the blanks.

A traveler's check is a negotiable instrument within the purview of Article III of the Uniform Commercial Code. 3-114 explicitly permits an instrument to be undated. Dating therefore is not a necessary element, the absence of which makes the instrument incomplete and unenforceable under 3-115. However, the name of the payee is an essential element. The payee's name is not one of the "[t]erms and omissions not affecting negotiability" under 3-112. 3-104 demands "[a]ny writing to be a negotiable instrument within this article must . . . be payable to order or to bearer" 3-104(1)(d). Under old law of commercial paper and now incorporated into the Uniform Commercial Code, a note payable neither to order nor to bearer is not negotiable. Specificity on the face of the instrument is required whether payment be to order or to bearer 3-111(b). Therefore, it is clear that the checks were legally incomplete because they lacked the name of the payee.

3-115 permits completion of an incomplete instrument if done "in accordance with authority given. . . ." *Jones* v. *Jones* (1966), construing the old law now incorporated into the Uniform Commercial Code, considered that the instrument's primary makers had the authority to complete the instrument by inserting the name of the payee. The holder had final authority. *Lawrence* v. *Mabry* (1830), held that a bill of exchange drawn and issued in blank for the name of the payee may be filled in by a bona fide holder in his own name, and will bind the drawer. It is clear that plaintiff had the authority to complete the instruments, had nine years so to do, and did not. The instruments remained incomplete and unenforceable as a matter of law.

An incomplete instrument is payable neither to order nor to bearer and is not negotiable. No one can become a holder in due course of such an instrument.

No Other Promise, Order, Obligation, or Power

Even if an instrument is a signed writing containing an unconditional promise or order to pay a sum certain in money, payable on demand or at a definite time, and payable to order or bearer, it still may not be negotiable if the maker or drawer gives any other promise, order, obligation, or power except as authorized by Article 3.

Certain additional information may be given in an instrument without impairing its negotiability. A statement that collateral has been given to secure the obligation will not impair the negotiability of an instrument. For example, a person obtaining a loan to purchase an automobile will sign a note for the bank indicating that the maker is using the automobile as collateral—that is, if he or she fails to make the payments specified under the note, the bank may repossess the automobile. (See Chapter 23, "Secured Transactions," for a complete discussion of the use of collateral.) Merely mentioning this information does not impair the negotiability of the instrument. Similarly, the note may indicate that the maker must protect the collateral. Other information that may appear in a note without impairing its negotiability appears in UCC Section 3-112.

Section 3-112 also states that the negotiability of an instrument is not affected by the omission of the place where the instrument is drawn and payable.

Date

In most cases, the negotiability of an instrument is not affected by the fact that it is undated. However, if an instrument states that it is "payable 15 days after date," the instrument will not be negotiable if it is undated. It is an incomplete instrument. Under Section 3-115, the instrument may be completed as authorized. The instrument is not negotiable until the date is filled in.

An instrument also is not rendered nonnegotiable because it is dated sometime in the past (an antedated instrument) or at some time in the future (a postdated instrument).

RULES OF CONSTRUCTION

The UCC, in Section 3-118, lists several rules of construction that apply if the writing is ambiguous or leaves out certain information. When one is in doubt as to how to interpret an instrument, these rules should be consulted.

Among other provisions, Section 3-118 provides that if there is doubt whether an instrument is a note or a draft the holder may treat the instrument as either. It also specifies that handwritten terms control typewritten and printed terms, and typewritten control printed. Words generally control figures, except that if the words are ambiguous the figures control.

REVIEW PROBLEMS

1. Defendant executed and delivered two promissory notes to Consumer Foods, Inc., who subsequently assigned the notes to Aetnor Acceptance Corporation. The notes simply stated, in part, "Buyer agrees to pay to Seller. . . ." In light of this wording, are these promissory notes negotiable? Locke v. Aetnor Acceptance Corporation, 309 So.2d 43 (Court of Appeals Florida 1975)

2. Max Williams signed and delivered a note to Glenn W. Cooper that, among other things, contained the following statement: "At the earliest possible time after date, without grace, for value received, I promise to pay to the order of Glenn W. Cooper, payable at Seymour, Texas, Five Thousand Dollars." Is this a negotiable instrument in light of this language? Williams v. Cooper, 504 S.W.2d 564 (Court of Civil Appeals Texas 1973)

3. William Feldman drew a check payable to "Interstate Steel Corp. General Pipe & Supply." These are two different companies. There was no "or" or "and" between the names, but one name was on one line and the other name was on another line. Interstate Steel deposited the check to its account, withdrew the funds credited to its account, and then became insolvent. Was the check, signed only by Interstate, properly negotiated? Feldman Construction Company v. Union Bank, 104 Cal. Rptr. 912 (California Court of Appeals 1972)

4. Davis Aircraft Engineering, Inc., entered into a loan agreement with Bank A. On the face on each note was printed: "This note evidences a borrowing made under, and is subject to, the terms of the loan agreement." There is nothing in the loan agreement that would impose any contingency upon the obligation to pay. Davis contends that the notes are nonnegotiable because there is not an unconditional promise to pay. Will Davis win? United States v. Farrington, 172 F. Supp. 797 (D.C. Mass. 1959)

5. Hotel Evans contracted with A. Alport & Son to construct a hotel and in return gave Alport certain promissory notes. The notes contained the notation "with interest at bank rates." At the time of payment, the bank wrote "8 ½%" above the words "bank rates." Are the notes negotiable? A. Alport & Son Inc. v. Hotel Evans, Inc., 317 N.Y.S.2d 937 (New York Supreme Court 1970)

6. Knoxville Casket Co. entered into a loan agreement with Acme Metals. On the face of the note appears the following provision: "90 days after date, for value received, Knoxville Casket Co. promises to pay to the order of Acme Metals the face amount of the note." The signature of the president of Knoxville Casket Co. appears on the face of each note without designating that he is president or agent for Knoxville Casket Co. Acme asserts that the president is person-

ally liable for debt. At the trial, there is testimony that the president intended to sign only in his representative capacity and that Acme knew of his intentions. Will the president be held liable? Acme Metals Inc. v. Weddington, 575 S.W.2d 15 (Court of Appeals of Tennessee 1978)

7. Griffin, the president of Greenway Co., signs checks to pay for a project for the company. The company's name and address appear on the check. There is nothing on the check to indicate Griffin's office or capacity to sign for the corporation. Should he be held personally liable? Griffin v. Ellinger, 538 S.W.2d 97 (Supreme Court of Texas 1976)

Transfer, Negotiation, and Holder in Due Course

 s noted in the preceding chapter, several conditions must be met in order for a person to qualify as a holder in due course:

1. He or she must be in possession of a *negotiable* instrument (as explained in Chapter 19).
2. The instrument must be issued or *negotiated* to the holder.
3. The person in possession of the negotiable instrument validly issued or negotiated to him or her must also *comply with Section 3-302* of the Uniform Commercial Code.

When these three conditions are met, the person in possession of a negotiable instrument attains the preferred status of a holder in due course. This chapter examines the concepts of negotiation and holder in due course.

TRANSFER AND NEGOTIATION

Issue

When a negotiable instrument has been drawn up and signed by the parties, one more step must take place for the instrument to become enforceable: It must be *issued* by the maker or drawer to the holder. In the typical transaction, issuance occurs when the maker or drawer of the instrument hands the instrument to the payee. This delivery of the instrument by the drawer or maker to the payee is called an *issuance* of the instrument.

The maker or drawer of an instrument is *not* liable on an instrument until he or she delivers or issues the instrument. Delivery of an instrument simply means the voluntary transfer of the instrument. Transfer may be achieved either by physical delivery or, in rare instances,

490

by constructive delivery of the instrument. Constructive delivery occurs when the maker or drawer, with the intent to effect a transfer, performs a symbolic act representing the transfer. For example, delivery of the keys to a safe containing the instrument may constitute a constructive transfer.

In determining whether a delivery took place, the courts must examine the *intent* of the parties. However, if someone other than the assignee of the instrument has physical possession of it, there is a rebuttable presumption that delivery has occurred. If the maker or drawer still has physical possession of the instrument, there is a rebuttable presumption that delivery was not intended.

Suppose Smith signed a note payable to Jones, and he placed it on his desk. If Jones burglarized Smith's office and took the instrument, may she enforce it against Smith? No. Clearly, although he signed the instrument, Smith did not issue (voluntarily deliver) it to Jones. If a thief stole the note, however, and transferred it to a holder in due course, the holder in due course could enforce the note against Smith—even though Smith never voluntarily transferred it to Jones. This is because the absence of delivery is a *personal* defense. Personal defenses may not be asserted against a holder in due course. On the other hand, if the person in possession of the instrument did not qualify as a holder in due course, Smith could assert the personal defense of no delivery against that person. In that case, Smith would not have to pay the note.

This example illustrates why it is so critical for a person to qualify as a holder in due course. Persons who attain this preferred status can then take instruments free of all *personal* defenses. (Personal defenses are discussed in the next chapter.) Anyone who is not a holder in due course takes the instrument subject to all defenses or claims by any party.

Transfer

Once the original maker or drawer of an instrument has signed and issued the instrument, the instrument may be transferred to a third party. If the transfer constitutes a *negotiation,* the person to whom the instrument is transferred becomes a *holder* of the instrument. If the transfer fails to qualify as a negotiation, the person to whom the instrument is transferred (the assignee) will never attain the status of a holder in due course. Such a person takes the instrument by *assignment* (as opposed to taking it by negotiation) and therefore may not become a holder of the instrument. A person must be a holder of an instrument in order to qualify as a holder in due course. This is true even if the instrument assigned qualifies as a negotiable instrument under Section 3-104(1).

If a person in possession of an instrument takes it by *assignment,* the transaction is governed by the law of contracts rather than Article 3 of the UCC. The person to whom the instrument is assigned is a mere *assignee* of a contractual right to receive money. The transfer gives the assignee all the rights of the assignor (the person who transferred the instrument to the assignee). However, the assignee also takes the instrument subject to any defenses or claims that might have been asserted against his or her assignor or any prior party to the instrument.

A person who takes a nonnegotiable instrument also is governed by the law of contracts rather than Article 3 of the UCC. Article 3 applies only to negotiable instruments that have been validly negotiated to a third party.

To take an example, suppose Smith signs a note payable to Jones and issues it to her. Jones wishes to transfer the note to her daughter, Mary. If Jones fails to properly transfer the note (as discussed later in this chapter), her daughter becomes a mere assignee of a contractual right to receive money from Smith.

This means that Mary acquires all the rights her mother had (the right to receive money from Smith) but takes the instrument subject to any claims or defenses Smith might have against Jones. Suppose Jones acquired the note from Smith in return for her promise to give Smith a 1959 Ford. After acquiring the note, Jones refuses to transfer the title to the Ford to Smith. So long as the note was in Jones's hands, Smith had a defense on the instrument— breach of contract. If sued by Jones on the instrument, he could refuse to pay the note because Jones failed to live up to her part of the bargain. Because Mary "steps into the shoes of her assignor," she takes the note subject to the defense of breach of contract. If Mary sues Smith on the note, Smith may assert against Mary the failure of her mother to deliver the Ford as a reason for his refusal to pay the note.

Negotiation

Section 3–202 defines a *negotiation* as "the transfer of an instrument in such form that the transferee becomes a holder." Section 1–201(20) defines a holder as a "person who is in possession of a[n] . . . instrument . . . drawn, issued, or indorsed to him or to his order or to bearer or in blank."

How does one become a holder? The person in possession of the instrument must in some cases have (1) the indorsement of the prior holder of the instrument and (2) delivery of the instrument. In other cases, the delivery of the instrument alone will be sufficient to negotiate the instrument. If the instrument qualifies an an *order instrument* the former is required, but a *bearer instrument* may be negotiated by delivery alone. As explained in the prior chapter, an order instrument generally is one made payable to the order of someone. A bearer instrument is one made payable to bearer or cash.

Suppose Smith writes a note, but makes it payable to bearer as shown in Figure 20–1.

FIGURE 20–1

$100.00	Chicago, Illinois January 1, 1984

On demand I promise to pay to the order of *bearer*
One hundred and no/100 - - - - - - - - - dollars
Payable at First National Bank, Chicago, Illinois

John Smith
SAMPLE

Smith now physically delivers the note to Jones. The act of transferring the note to Jones is an *issuance* of the instrument. What if Jones now wants to transfer this note to her daughter, Mary? What must she do to validly negotiate the note so that Mary becomes a holder of the instrument? All Jones must do is deliver the note to Mary because this is a bearer instrument, which may be negotiated by delivery alone.

Suppose instead that this note was made payable to the order of Mrs. Jones as in Figure 20–2. If Jones merely delivers this instrument to Mary, there has not been a negotiation of the instrument. This note must be indorsed on the back by Jones and delivered to Mary to negotiate it because it is an *order instrument*.

Let us re-examine the definition of a holder in Section 1–201(20). In the two notes appearing earlier, once Jones takes delivery of either note she is a holder. The first note is "drawn to bearer." All she need do to become a holder is take delivery of the note. To become a holder of the second note she again need only take delivery because the second note was drawn payable to her order. Mary becomes a holder of the first note when it is delivered to her because it was "drawn to bearer." To become a holder of the second note, Mary not only must take delivery but also must obtain her mother's indorsement, because the instrument originally was "drawn . . . to the order" of Jones. As it was not originally drawn to Mary's order, she must first obtain her mother's signature to effectively negotiate the instrument.

FIGURE 20–2

$100.00   Chicago, Illinois January 1, 1984
On demand I promise to pay to the order of Grace Jones
One hundred and no/100------------------------dollars
Payable at First National Bank, Chicago, Illinois

John Smith
SAMPLE

Because they may be negotiated by delivery alone, there is some risk in creating instruments that are payable to bearer. What if Smith signed the first note, which was payable to bearer, and a thief stole it from him? There is no delivery of the instrument to the thief because Section 1–201(14) defines a delivery as a *"voluntary* transfer of possession" of the instrument. No negotiation takes place, and the thief does not acquire an interest in the note. However, the thief may transfer this instrument to a subsequent innocent purchaser. The UCC permits such a person taking bearer paper to become a holder of the instrument. In other words, while the thief may not acquire title to stolen bearer paper, the thief has the power to transfer good title to a third party. A party who is unaware of the theft may become a holder of the instrument who may enforce the instrument against the original maker.

The same rules also apply if a person *finds* a bearer instrument and transfers it to an innocent third party. Bearer instruments must be handled very carefully because of the power given by the UCC to an illegitimate possessor to transfer good title to an innocent third party.

While bearer instruments expose the maker or drawer to some risks, the same is not true of order instruments. Take the note illustrated in Fig. 20–2. It is payable to the order of Jones and therefore qualifies as an order instrument. Suppose a thief or finder comes into possession of this instrument. If the thief signs Jones's name, and transfers the instrument to an innocent third party, Quinn, does Quinn become a holder of the instrument? No. This instrument was drawn payable to the order of Jones. To negotiate it, there must be a delivery of the instrument, and the instrument must be indorsed by Jones. The forged *indorsement by the thief* is ineffective. No title to the instrument passes to Quinn; she does not become a holder. The note has not been negotiated to Quinn because she lacks Jones's indorsement. Because Quinn holds the instrument through a forged indorsement, when she presents it to Smith for payment, Smith may refuse to pay the instrument if he detects that Jones did not sign it. Not only does Quinn not qualify as a holder of the instrument, but anyone Quinn transfers the instrument to also will not become a holder. No one may qualify as a holder under a forged indorsement of an order instrument.

To review negotiation: (1) If the instrument is a bearer instrument, delivery alone is sufficient to negotiate the instrument; (2) If the instrument is an order instrument, to negotiate it the appropriate party must indorse and deliver it to someone.

An indorsement must be written by or on behalf of the holder. In most cases, the indorsement is written on the back of the instrument. If for some reason there is no space on the reverse side of the instrument, the indorsement may appear on a paper firmly affixed to the instrument. Such a paper is called an *allonge.* It will not be sufficient to pin or clip the allonge to the instrument. The allonge must be firmly attached in such a manner that it will not become separated from the instrument—as by gluing the allonge to the instrument.

When a person transfers an order instrument for value, he or she has an obligation (absent a contrary agreement) to indorse the instrument. However, a negotiation of the instrument does not take place until the instrument has been indorsed. When a person receives an order instrument that lacks the indorsement of the transferor, the transferee may require the transferor to indorse the instrument. The transferee of an order instrument without the requisite indorsement is not a holder.

INDORSEMENTS

Negotiable instruments are indorsed for two reasons: (1) the indorsement may be necessary to negotiate the instrument; and (2) the indorsement may be required to obligate the indorsee to pay the instrument under certain circumstances discussed in the next chapter.

Blank Indorsement

A blank indorsement specifies no particular indorsee and may consist of a mere signature. This is the most common type of indorsement. How would Jones indorse in blank the note in Figure 20–2 that was payable to her order? On the reverse side of the note she would sign it as shown in Figure 20–3.

FIGURE 20–3

Grace Jones

When Jones signs the instrument in this fashion, and delivers it to another person, there has been a negotiation of the note. The person to whom she transfers the note becomes a holder of the note. Jones has transferred title to the instrument to the third person. By indorsing the instrument in this fashion, she also promises to pay the instrument, under certain circumstances, if Smith fails to pay.

When an instrument is payable to order and it is indorsed in blank, it becomes payable to bearer and may be negotiated by delivery alone. Just as in the case of an instrument originally payable to bearer, an instrument that is indorsed in blank may be negotiated by delivery alone. This means that the same risks associated with an instrument that is originally payable to bearer also apply to an instrument that is indorsed in blank. A thief or finder has the power to negotiate the instrument indorsed in blank to an innocent third party so that the third person becomes a holder of the instrument.

Special Indorsements

A special indorsement specifies the person to whom or to whose order the instrument is payable. Jones could indorse the note discussed earlier as shown in Figure 20–4.

FIGURE 20–4

Pay Mary Jones

Grace Jones

The note in question was originally payable to the order of Jones and therefore was an order instrument. When Jones indorsed the note in this manner it became payable to the order of the special indorsee (Mary Jones) and may be further negotiated only by Mary Jones's indorsement and delivery of the note to a third person. A note remains an order instrument when it is indorsed with a special indorsement.

Jones could also have indorsed the note with the words "Pay to the order of Mary Jones, (signed) Grace Jones" or "Pay to Mary Jones or order, (signed) Grace Jones." In other words, it is not necessary to include the words of negotiability in the special indorsement. While it is true that an instrument originally must be payable to order or to bearer for it to be negotiable, the special indorsement need not include the words of negotiability.

It is possible to convert an instrument indorsed in blank into a special indorsement by writing over the signature of the indorser in blank words such as "Pay to Mary Jones." If Mary's mother simply indorsed the note over to Mary by signing "Grace Jones" on the reverse side, Mary could convert the indorsement into a special indorsement by writing the words "Pay to Mary Jones" above her mother's signature. The instrument would then need to be indorsed by Mary Jones and delivered to someone in order for there to be a valid negotiation of the instrument.

By specially indorsing bearer paper, and thereby converting it to order paper, the person taking possession of the instrument avoids the risks associated with bearer paper. If a thief then steals the instrument, the thief must forge the signature of the special indorsee to whose order the instrument is payable. Because a forged indorsement will be ineffective, the special indorsee has protected himself or herself.

The following case illustrates the use of special indorsements.

Klomann v. Sol K. Graff & Sons

Appellate Court of Illinois
317 N.E.2d 608 (1974)

Robert Graff executed three notes for the defendant partnership, Sol K. Graff & Sons. The notes were made payable to Fred Klomann. Klomann transferred the notes to his daughter and then back to his wife, Georgia. When Georgia Klomann, plaintiff, attempted to enforce these instruments, the lower court ruled in her favor. On appeal, the appellate court ruled for the defendant because the instruments had not been properly indorsed to Georgia Klomann.

Dieringer, Justice

Sol K. Graff & Sons, a partnership conducting business as real estate brokers, negotiated the trade and sale of certain parcels of real estate on behalf of Fred Klomann. The transactions culminated in the purchase by Fred Klomann of the Countryside Shopping Plaza, and the partnership, Sol K. Graff & Sons, owing Fred Klomann $13,000. On August 31, 1967, the defendant, Robert J. Graff, one of the partners of Sol K. Graff & Sons, executed three promissory notes naming Fred Klomann as payee on each note.

Fred Klomann held the three notes in question for a period of time and then by special indorsement gave the notes to his daughter, Candace Klomann. Fred Klomann signed the notes and handed them to Candace. She examined the notes and then handed them back to Fred for collection. In April, 1970, Fred Klomann scratched out Candace's name in the special indorsement, inserted the name of his wife, Georgia Klomann, and delivered the three notes to Georgia.

On May 18, 1971, the plaintiff, Georgia Klomann, brought suit against Sol K. Graff & Sons and Robert J. Graff in two counts for the value of the three notes.

The defendant contends the plaintiff has no right, title or interest in the promissory notes, thereby raising an issue of fact which precluded the entry of summary judgment in favor of the plaintiff.

The plaintiff maintains the defense of whether Georgia Klomann has an interest in the notes is not available to the defendant. In support of her contention, the plaintiff relies on Section 3-306(d) of the Uniform Commercial Code which provides:

> "Unless he has the rights of a holder in due course any person takes the instrument subject to (d) the defense that he or a person through whom he holds the instrument acquired it by theft or that payment or satisfaction to such holder would be inconsistent with the terms of a restrictive indorsement. *The claim of any third person to the instrument is not otherwise available as a defense to any party liable thereon unless the third person himself defends the action for such party."* (Emphasis Added).

We believe that the plaintiff has no right, title or interest in the promissory notes. Section 3–204 of the Uniform Commercial Code provides:

> "(1) A special indorsement specifies the person to whom or to whose order it makes the instrument payable. Any instrument specially indorsed becomes payable to the order of the special indorsee and may be further negotiated only by his indorsement."

A review of the record in the instant case reveals Fred Klomann specially indorsed the promissory notes to his daughter, Candace, in August, 1967. The notes, therefore, could only be further negotiated by Candace. Examination of the record further reveals Candace, the special indorsee, has never negotiated the notes. Fred Klomann, in April, 1970, improperly scratched out Candace's name in the special indorsement and inserted the name of his wife Georgia. Section 3–201 of the Uniform Commercial Code provides in pertinent part:

"(1) Transfer of an instrument vests in the transferee such rights as the transferor has therein . . ."

When Fred Klomann signed the notes in question to his daughter he no longer had any interest in them. His attempted assignment to Georgia approximately three years later conveyed only that interest which he had in the notes, which was nothing. Plaintiff, therefore, has no interest in the notes sued on in the instant case. We do not believe, as the plaintiff contends, that the Uniform Commercial Code intends a situation where there is an indorsement to a second party (Candace Klomann) and delivery; second party gives the note back to the payee for collection, payee subsequently strikes the name of the indorsee and puts in the name of a third party (Georgia Klomann), to not allow the maker of the note to look into the situation and see where title really lies.

For the reasons stated herein, the judgment of the Circuit Court of Cook County is reversed and remanded.

Reversed and remanded.

Qualified Indorsements

The two indorsements discussed above, in blank and special, are also *unqualified* indorsements. This means that the in-blank or special indorser is promising to pay the holder of the instrument under certain circumstances. For example, suppose Jones received the $100 note from Smith. Jones then indorsed the note in blank and delivered it to Mary Jones. If Mary attempts to collect from Smith when the note comes due, but Smith refuses to pay, Mary could sue Jones for the $100 because Jones indorsed with an unqualified indorsement. The unqualified indorser in effect guarantees payment of the instrument if the holder is unable to collect from the maker, drawer, or acceptor when the instrument comes due.

A person who wishes to sign as a qualified indorser does so by adding "without recourse" or similar words to the indorsement as in Figures 20–5 and 20–6. The indorsement in Figure 20–5 is a qualified, in-blank indorsement. The indorsement in Figure 20–6 is a qualified, special indorsement. When Jones signs in either of these ways, she eliminates her secondary or conditional liability as an indorser. The secondary or conditional liability is the agreement of an unqualified indorser to pay the instrument if the party primarily obligated to pay fails to pay the instrument when it comes due. The concept of secondary liability is discussed in greater depth in the next chapter.

FIGURE 20–5

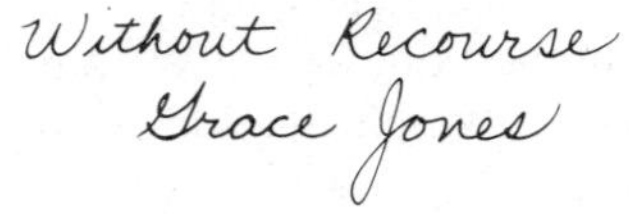

Without Recourse
Grace Jones

FIGURE 20–6

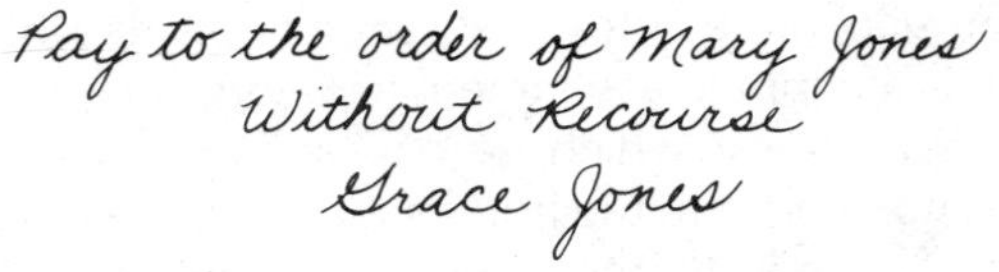

Pay to the order of Mary Jones
Without Recourse
Grace Jones

Both a qualified and an unqualified indorser, however, give certain warranties to the persons to whom they transfer their instruments. This warranty liability is not excluded by signing an instrument with a qualified indorsement.

Restrictive Indorsements

In addition to in-blank, special, and qualified indorsements, the UCC also creates a category of indorsements called restrictive indorsements. The UCC creates several types of restrictive indorsements.

Conditional Restrictive. If the indorsement imposes a condition on the right of the indorsee to collect, it is a conditional restrictive indorsement. Suppose that Jones, when she received the note from Smith payable to her order, indorsed the note over to her daughter Mary in the following fashion: "Pay to Mary Jones when she delivers her 1959 Ford to me, (signed) Grace Jones." This is actually a conditional restrictive indorsement. Jones then hands the note to Mary.

Why would Jones indorse the note in this manner? She wants to make certain that she receives the 1959 Ford before Mary is paid. In effect, she is putting a restriction on the ability of Mary to collect on this note. Once Mary delivers the Ford to her mother, she may collect on the note—but not before.

As with all types of restrictive indorsements, the conditional restrictive indorsement does not prevent the further transfer or negotiation of the instrument. This means that if Mary wishes to transfer the note from her mother to Laura, she may do so. This is true whether or not Mary has delivered the 1959 Ford to her mother.

However, the purpose of the conditional restrictive indorsement is to impose an obligation on the indorsee—in this case, Mary's (the indorsee's) obligation is to deliver the 1959 Ford to her mother. What if Mary presents the note to Smith, and Smith pays Mary the $100 even though Mary has not yet delivered the Ford to her mother? In this situation, neither Mary nor Smith has complied with Section 3–206(3), which requires any transferee to "pay or apply any value given by him for . . . the instrument consistently with the indorsement. . . ." Because the Ford has not yet been delivered, Mary (the restrictive indorsee) and Smith (the maker) remain liable to Jones for the amount of the instrument.

Intermediary banks are not bound by conditional restrictive indorsements. An intermediary bank is any bank to which the instrument is transferred in the course of collection except the depository bank or payor bank. For example, when a check is deposited to an account for collection, the bank at which it is deposited is called the *depository* bank. The depository bank may then transfer the instrument to an *intermediary* bank, which in turn may transfer it to the *drawee* bank. If the drawee bank pays the check, it becomes the *payor* bank.

A conditional indorsement is not the same as a conditional promise or order to pay. If the maker or drawer of an instrument writes the instrument in such a fashion that his or her promise or order is conditional, this renders the instrument nonnegotiable under Section 3-104. This is not true of a conditional indorsement. If an instrument had an unconditional promise or order to pay someone originally, it is negotiable. The conditional indorsement will not have any impact on the negotiability of the instrument.

Conditional restrictive indorsements are very uncommon.

Prohibit Further Transfer. Indorsements that attempt to prohibit further transfer of an instrument also are highly uncommon. Such an indorsement might read: "Pay to Mary only." The indorser is attempting to prohibit further transfer of the instrument through such an indorsement. But such an indorsement does not prevent the further transfer or negotiation of the instrument. It is treated as if it were an unrestrictive indorsement.

For Deposit or Collection. The most common restrictive indorsement is the indorsement that includes words such as "for collection," "for deposit," "pay any bank," or like terms signifying a purpose of deposit or collection. For example, if Smith gave Jones a check for $100, she might indorse the check "For deposit, (signed) Grace Jones." This is an in-blank, restrictive, unqualified indorsement.

The indorsement "pay any bank" specifies that only banks are to receive the proceeds of the instrument. When a person deposits a check to his or her bank account, the bank may restrictively indorse the check in this manner. Only a bank could then become a holder of an instrument so indorsed, unless a bank specially indorsed the check to someone who is not a bank. A bank might use such an indorsement when putting a check through the collection process.

Suppose Jones takes the $100 check from Smith, indorses it "For deposit, (signed) Grace Jones," and deposits it to her account. The bank will indorse the check "for collection" or "pay any bank" and forward it to an intermediary bank for collection. The intermediary bank will present the check to the drawee bank, which, if it pays the check, becomes the payor bank. Both of these indorsements are restrictive indorsements.

To the extent that a transferee pays or applies any value given by the transferee consistently with the indorsement, he or she becomes a holder for value. If the transferee otherwise complies with Section 3-302, he or she qualifies as a holder in due course. If Jones's bank credits her account for the $100, it has applied the value consistent with the "For deposit" indorsement and is therefore a holder. When the payor bank pays the intermediary bank, it has paid the check consistent with the "For collection" or "Pay any bank" indorsement, and the payor bank qualifies as a holder.

Trust Indorsements. A restrictive indorsement that states that it is for the benefit or use of the indorser or another person is a trust indorsement. It is the fourth type of restrictive indorsement recognized under Section 3–205. Such an indorsement might read "Pay Lance only in trust for Mary." In this case Lance, the restrictive indorsee, is acting as a representative of Mary and holds any money paid on the instrument in trust for Mary. To the extent that Lance applies the proceeds consistent with the terms of the indorsement, he qualifies as a holder.

Trust indorsements affect only the immediate transferee—in this case, Lance. A later holder for value of this instrument is neither given notice nor otherwise affected by such a restrictive indorsement unless he or she has *knowledge* that a fiduciary or other person has negotiated the instrument in any transaction for his or her own benefit or is otherwise in breach of duty (Section 3–206[4]).

As with the three other types of restrictive indorsements, a trust indorsement does not prevent the further transfer or negotiation of the instrument.

Restrictive Indorsements Generally. Most restrictive indorsements require the indorsee to take some action with respect to the proceeds of an instrument—such as holding it in trust for someone or depositing it to someone's account.

Unlike most transferees, intermediary banks and payor banks that are not depository banks are neither given notice nor affected by a restrictive indorsement of any person except the bank's immediate transferor or the person presenting the instrument for payment (Section 3–206[2]).

HOLDER IN DUE COURSE

In order to become a holder in due course of a negotiable instrument, a holder must take the instrument: (1) for value; (2) in good faith; and (3) without notice that the instrument is overdue or has been dishonored, or of any defense against or claim to it on the part of any person (Section 3–302).

Even assuming a person in possession of an instrument fulfills the three requirements set out in Section 3–302, he or she still may not qualify as a holder in due course. A person wishing to claim the status of a holder in due course must also establish that he or she holds a *negotiable* instrument (as defined in Section 3–104) and that he or she is a *holder* of the instrument.

As discussed in the preceding chapter, several elements must be complied with for an instrument to qualify as negotiable. It must be: (1) a writing, (2) signed by the drawer or maker, (3) containing a promise or order to pay, (4) that is unconditional, (5) a sum certain, (6) in money, (7) without any other promise, (8) payable on demand or at a definite time, and (9) payable to order or bearer. An instrument that fails in any respect to fulfill these nine requirements is *not* negotiable. A person in possession of such an instrument may not qualify as a holder in due course. A person who wishes to qualify as a holder in due course will therefore examine the instrument carefully before taking it to determine if it is negotiable.

The mere fact that a person holds a nonnegotiable instrument does not mean that he or she will not recover. As we noted earlier, the right to receive money is generally assignable to third persons. The only problem for the assignee is that he or she steps into the shoes of the assignor—that is, the assignee acquires only the rights the assignor had. If a defense existed between the original parties to a contract to pay money, that defense may be asserted against the assignee of the contractual right to receive money.

In the event the party originally obligated to pay has no defenses that could have been asserted against the assignor, he or she must pay the assignee. The mere fact that the assignee is in possession of a nonnegotiable instrument is not a defense. If Smith gives Jones a $100 bearer note, but it in some respect fails to comply with Section 3–104, it is nonnegotiable. Suppose that Jones transferred the note to Mary. Under these facts, it appears that Smith must pay Mary when the note comes due even though the instrument is not negotiable. What if Jones defrauded Smith? Because Smith could assert the defense of fraud against Jones (the assignor), he may assert fraud to avoid paying the note against Mary (the assignee).

Instead of a non-negotiable instrument, suppose the parties were dealing with a negotiable instrument. Smith could refuse to pay Mary, even if the instrument was negotiable, if he could establish that Mary was not a holder of the instrument. Once again, a holder is anyone in possession of an instrument drawn, issued, or indorsed to him or to his order or to bearer or in blank. If the instrument was not properly negotiated to Mary, she would not qualify as a holder of the instrument. Suppose the original note was negotiable and was payable to the order of Jones (rather than payable to bearer) and Jones delivered the note to Mary but failed to indorse it. Mary is not a holder of the note. In order to negotiate an order instrument, the holder must indorse it and deliver it to someone. Jones failed to indorse the note. (Mary may be able to require Jones to indorse the note but, until Jones indorses it, Mary may not qualify as a holder of the note.)

Assuming that the note is negotiable, and the person attempting to enforce it is a holder, that person may qualify as a holder in due course if he or she otherwise complies with Section 3–302. The following material discusses these requirements.

For Value

A holder takes an instrument for value when he or she gives a negotiable instrument for it or makes an irrevocable commitment to a third person, or to the extent that the agreed consideration has been performed, or when he or she acquires a security interest in or a lien on the instrument otherwise than by legal process, or when he or she takes the instru-

ment in payment of or as security for an antecedent claim (Section 3–303).

Let us examine the various ways in which a person may give value.

Executory Promise. The UCC, in Section 3–303, completely separates the concepts of *value* and *consideration*. Consideration is defined as something of value given in return for a performance or a promise of performance. While a mere promise to perform is sufficient consideration to support a contract, such a promise does not amount to a giving of value under Section 3–303. An executory promise to give value is not value. Thus, if an attorney is given a note for $200,000 for $10,000 in legal services already rendered, with the rest of the services to be rendered in the future, the attorney would be a holder in due course of the note only to the extent of $10,000. The promise of the attorney to perform services could serve as consideration to support a contract, but a promise to perform services does not qualify as giving value. Had the attorney in this case already performed services worth $200,000, he or she would have given value.

Suppose that Smith executes the $100 note payable to Jones. What if Jones gives the note to Mary, who promises to pay her mother $100 in return for the note? May Mary qualify as a holder in due course? No. Mary has not given value in exchange for the note. This is a mere executory promise to give value. Until Mary pays the $100, she has not given value. If she sues Smith before she pays the $100 to her mother, Smith may assert any defense he has on the instrument against Mary because Mary is not a holder in due course.

Why does the UCC adopt this position with respect to executory promises? Comment 3 to Section 3–303 states that a person giving an executory promise does not need the protection afforded by the status of a holder in due course. When such a person learns of a defense on the instrument or of a defect in the title, the purchaser may rescind the transaction for breach of the transferor's warranty.

There are, however, instances in which an executory promise may be regarded as value. Section 3–303(c) states that a holder takes an instrument for value when he or she "gives a negotiable instrument for it or makes an irrevocable commitment to a third person." Consequently, while it may not constitute value to promise to do something, giving an instrument for an instrument constitutes value.

Suppose that Jones transfers Smith's $100 note in return for Mary's check for $100. When Mary gives the check to her mother, she has given value for the note. Section 3–303 recognizes a negotiable instrument as value because it carries the possibility of negotiation to a holder in due course, after which the party who gave it cannot refuse to pay.

The same rationale applies to any irrevocable commitment by the holder to a third party. Suppose that company X gives its bank a $1000 note. In return, the bank issues a letter of credit in which it promises to pay a seller from whom X wishes to purchase goods. Because a letter of credit constitutes an irrevocable commitment by the bank to the seller, the bank has given value for the $1000 note.

In the following case the court found an executory promise to constitute value.

Saka v. Mann Theatres

Supreme Court of Nevada
575 P.2d 1335 (1978)

Suit was brought by Mann Theatres, the plaintiff and respondent, against Saka, the defendant and appellant, for the amount of a dishonored check tendered by Saka to Mann. The trial court found Saka liable on the check. The supreme court of Nevada affirmed the judgment for Mann.

Manoukian, Justice

An agreement was reached by respondent and Affinity Pictures whereby respondent was to rent one of its theaters to Affinity to exhibit a film for two weeks. Appellant was one of the producers of the film. The rental fee was $10,884 or $5,442 for each seven day period. Appellant Saka tendered to Boulevard Theatre, the theater within the Mann Theatre chain which was rented, two checks each for $5,442. One check was honored, but the second check did not clear. Respondent sued for the amount of the dishonored check and prevailed in the district court. The material facts involving the tendered check were sharply disputed and the trial judge chose to believe respondent's version of the case.

Testimony was proffered that in June of 1974, Saka had contacted a Mark Rosen of Mann Theatres regarding the rental of Boulevard Theatre. One month later in July, Rosen met with several parties in Los Angeles and was given two checks drawn by Saka. Appellant contends that he wrote the two checks at the request of an officer of Affinity Pictures who stated that the money was needed to cover the rental fees for the theater.

Rosen testified that he contacted Saka during the first week of the film exhibition concerning the returned check and that Saka stated that a temporary hold had been placed on the account which would be lifted in a matter of days. Rosen, following assurances by Saka that the check would be later honored, permitted the film to be shown the second week. Rosen testified that Saka offered to even make periodic payments on the check. The check was never made good and respondent initiated suit.

The central question is whether the trial court properly found appellant liable on the check.

Saka contends that he is not liable for two reasons. First, he argues respondent was not a holder in due course, and, second, appellant did not receive any consideration from respondent upon which to base individual liability. He claims that Mann Theatres was not a holder in due course because it did not take the instrument "for value" as required by 3–302. His argument is that because the check was tendered and accepted for the second week's showing of the film, Mann Theatres merely gave an executory promise to give value. Korzenik v. Supreme Radio, Inc., 347 Mass. 309, 197 N.E.2d 702 (1964). The underlying policy reason is that when a transferee becomes aware of a defense, he need not enforce the instrument but may elect to rescind the transaction based upon the breach. Korzenik, supra. Nevertheless, one is considered a holder in due course to the extent he has performed such "executory promise." Coventry Care, Inc. v. United States, 366 F.Supp. 497 (W.D.Pa.1973). Here, testimony indicated that respondent had already begun performance when notified that the check did not clear. For this reason alone, respondent qualified as a holder in due course. This determination is dispositive of the appeal, and we find it unnecessary to discuss the issue of want of consideration.

The judgment of the lower court is affirmed.

What happens if a person who gives an executory promise learns of a defense or claim to the instrument before he or she performs the promise? The person may become a holder in due course only to the extent that he or she has fulfilled the promise. In the case mentioned earlier in which Mary promises to pay her mother $100 for Smith's note, suppose Mary pays her mother $50 on June 1. On June 2, Mary learns from Smith that her mother defrauded him. May Mary enforce the note? Mary is a holder in due course only as to the amount she has already paid her mother— $50. As to the other $50, she will not be able to collect it if Smith establishes his defense of fraud by Mary's mother. What if Mary on June 3 pays her mother the other $50; could she then claim to be a holder in due course for the entire sum of $100? No. Paying off the executory promise at this point is too late because she already has learned of a defense against the instrument. Mary takes the instrument for value only to the extent the agreed consideration has been performed before she learns of any claims or defenses. As noted earlier, Mary may rescind the transaction when she learns of Smith's defense. This should be adequate protection for her.

Banks and Value. When a person receives a check from someone and deposits it to his or her account, the bank will credit the depositor's account. Probably the check was written on an account at another bank, so the depositor's bank will act as an agent for purposes of collection. Does the mere fact that a customer deposits a check to his or her account, and the bank credits the account, mean that the bank has given value for the check? No. The mere crediting of an account by a bank does not constitute the giving of value. A bank has given value to the extent that it has a security interest in an instrument (Section 4–209). A bank has a security interest in an instrument to the extent that credit given by the bank for the instrument has been withdrawn (Section 4–208[1][a]). The UCC means by this that, to the extent the depositor draws against an instrument, the bank has given value. If the bank otherwise complies with Section 3–302, it qualifies as a holder in due course of this check.

In most cases, a depositor will have some money in his or her account when a check is deposited. If the bank permits the depositor to write a check on the account, how do we know whether the bank is permitting the customer to draw against the check? To simplify this matter, the UCC adopts a rule in Section 4–208 that "credits first given are first withdrawn." In other words, the UCC adopts a "first in, first out" rule.

Suppose that Alice gives Frank a check for $100. Frank takes the check to his bank and deposits it on June 1. At that time Frank already has $200 in his account. On June 2 Frank receives another $100 check from Alice, which he deposits to his account that day. On June 3 Frank withdraws $200 from his account. At this point, has the bank given value for either of Alice's checks? No. Because the UCC applies a first-in-first-out rule, the $200 is treated as a withdrawal of the $200 initially in Frank's account. On June 4, Frank withdraws another $100. In this case, the bank has now given full value for Alice's first check, which was deposited to Frank's account on June 1. If the bank otherwise complies with Section 3–302, it will be treated as a holder in due course of Alice's first check deposited June 1. On June 5, Alice notifies the bank of a defense on the second check. On June 6, the bank permits Frank to withdraw the final $100 from his account. Has the bank given value for Alice's second check? No. Applying the first-in-first-out rule, Frank's final $100 withdrawal is treated as a withdrawal against Alice's second check. Because the bank gave value *after* it learned of Alice's defense, it has not given value for the second check and cannot qualify as a holder in due course of the second check.

Negotiable Instrument as Security. If a person acquires a security interest in an instrument (other than by legal process), he or she takes the instrument for value. Suppose that Jane receives a note for $100 from Linda. In order to obtain a $100 loan at the bank, Jane gives the bank Linda's note. The bank has given value for Linda's note to the extent it holds Linda's note as security to make certain Jane repays her loan.

However, if the bank had acquired Linda's note by legal process, it would not be a holder for value. For example, if the bank obtained a judgment against Jane, and then attached Linda's note, it would not be regarded as having given value for Linda's note. Consequently, the bank could not qualify as a holder in due course of Linda's note.

Instrument in Payment or as Security for Antecedent Claim. The final category in which a person is treated as having given value is when the person "takes the instrument in payment of or as security for an antecedent claim against any person whether or not the claim is due" (Section 3–303[b]).

Suppose that Alice purchases some goods from Jane in March for $100. Several months elapse. In May, Alice gives Jane a $100 note. Jane is treated as having given value for the note. But what if Jane merely asked for some security in May, and Alice gave Jane a $100 note executed by Tom? The UCC treats Jane as having given value for Tom's note, even though she does not extend the time in which

Alice must pay her or make any other concession to Alice. If Alice fails to pay Jane, Jane might attempt to collect on the note from Tom. Jane will be treated as having given value for Tom's note even though she took it as security for an antecedent claim against Alice, and even though she made no additional concessions to Alice at the time she took Tom's note. If Jane otherwise has complied with Section 3–302, she will be treated as a holder in due course of Tom's note and will take the note free of certain defenses Tom might have been able to assert against Alice.

Good Faith

To be a holder in due course, the holder of the instrument must also have taken the instrument in good faith. Section 1–201(19) defines good faith to mean honesty in fact in the conduct or transaction concerned. The drafters of the UCC, in defining good faith as honesty in fact, left judges fairly wide discretion in determining what is an acceptable level of behavior. However, they clearly selected a *subjective* test as opposed to an objective test. The UCC thus does not adopt the standard of the behavior of a reasonably prudent person acting under the same circumstances. Instead, it adopts a standard that examines the actual behavior of the person taking the instrument. In order to determine if a person took an instrument in good faith, the court must determine if he or she acted honestly, even though his or her actions were not those of a reasonable person.

The UCC rejected the objective test as it developed in England under *Gill* v. *Cubitt*. This means that a person who, for example, takes an instrument under suspicious circumstances has not necessarily acted in bad faith. If this person acts honestly, although perhaps not reasonably, he or she qualifies under the UCC definition of good faith. As noted earlier, the manner in which the UCC has defined good faith gives the courts some discretion in this area.

Whether an individual took an instrument in good faith is determined at the time of taking the instrument. If a person acted in good faith at that time, and then *later* learns of facts that make him or her suspicious, he or she still is regarded as having taken the instrument in good faith.

The question of good faith is dealt with in the following case.

Manufacturers & Traders Trust Co. v. Murphy
U.S. District Court, Western District, Pennsylvania
369 F. Supp. 11 (1974)

In this federal trial court case, the defendant Murphy was sued by the plaintiff, Manufacturers & Traders Trust Co. Murphy gave a check to Brownsworth, who in turn cashed the check at Manufacturers. Murphy claims Manufacturers did not take the check in good faith and therefore could not be a holder in due course. The court ruled for Manufacturers.

Knox, District Judge

This diversity action arose out of a contract between the defendant C. E. Murphy (hereinafter Murphy), a Pennsylvania resident, and the third party defendant, David

Brownsworth (hereinafter Brownsworth). On September 27, 1972, a personal check for $15,000 was given by Murphy at Meadville, Pennsylvania, to Brownsworth in consideration of monies (including a $5,000 profit on Murphy's investment) expected to be derived within a short time from the purchase and resale of carpet fabric by Brownsworth. On September 28, 1972, in the afternoon, Murphy became suspicious of the transaction and placed a stop payment order on the check.

Meanwhile, Brownsworth, on the morning of September 28, 1972, went to the Silvercreek, New York, branch of the plaintiff bank, Manufacturers and Traders Trust Company, a New York corporation (hereinafter M & T) and received a cashier's check for $15,000 to replace Murphy's personal check in that amount. Although the Silvercreek manager vaguely knew Brownsworth, he nevertheless called Murphy's bank, The First National Bank of Pennsylvania in Meadville, Pennsylvania, to verify the check and determine if monies were available in the Murphy account. The Meadville bank told the Silvercreek manager that there were sufficient funds to cover the $15,000 check. Thereafter, the Silvercreek manager issued a cashier's check for the full amount to Brownsworth. It is important to note that the transaction occurred prior to Murphy placing a stop payment on his check.

Later, on September 28, Brownsworth took this $15,000 cashier's check to the Fredonia, New York, branch of the plaintiff bank and received $3,000 in cash and four cashier's checks for $3,000 each. Finally, on September 28, Brownsworth cashed two of these $3,000 cashier's checks at the plaintiff's branch bank at the Buffalo New York International Airport and received $6,000 in cash. The remaining two cashier's checks were cashed later in Las Vegas, Nevada. Plaintiff Bank then sued Murphy in this district court upon the original check given to Brownsworth.

The plaintiff, in this motion, requests summary judgment on the grounds that it is a holder in due course of defendant's personal check for $15,000 and thus entitled to recovery. The defendant disputes plaintiff, citing a lack of good faith by plaintiff which would destroy its status as a holder in due course.

M & T claims that it is a holder in due course in compliance with the requirements of section 3–302 of the Uniform Commercial Code. Under that section, plaintiff claims it gave value (its cashier's check for $15,000) in good faith (having contacted Murphy's Meadville Bank to verify account and the sufficiency of funds) and had no notice of defenses or claims against the instrument when taken (the stop payment order by Murphy was not made until later). M & T has presented the check and its evidence of being a holder in due course which it has the burden of establishing. At that point, the defendant, Murphy, must come forward with evidence which would establish, if believed, that plaintiff is not a holder in due course.

The defendant contends that M & T is not a holder in due course since it lacked the good faith required to be such a holder. In support of this proposition, Murphy advances two theories:

First, that because Brownsworth was not a regular customer at M & T bank that the cashing or giving of a cashier's check was not in good faith generally. This argument overlooks the fact that the Silvercreek manager of plaintiff's branch bank called Murphy's bank in Meadville to verify the account and the sufficiency of funds on this check which appeared authentic on its face. Therefore, we reject this argument. It must be kept in mind that the law favors the negotiability of a negotiable instrument.

Second, that a lack of good faith is shown on plaintiff's part by the conflicting stories given by Brownsworth to two of the branch bank managers. This, defendant alleges, gave some type of notice to the bank generally which would make them suspicious and destroy any good faith in dealing with Brownsworth. This notice to the branch offices fails on its face to convince us but it furthermore lacks merit for the reason that the plaintiff bank was irrevocably committed on the $15,000 personal check for Murphy prior to a different story being given by Brownsworth at the Fredonia branch office. M & T became liable to pay on its $15,000 cashier's check immediately upon issuing it. It became a holder in due course at that moment and later events would mean no difference in that status. Therefore, we reject this theory of defendant as well.

Without Notice

We now know that a person, to qualify as a holder in due course, must be the holder of a negotiable instrument who took the instrument for value and in good faith. In order to qualify as a holder in due course, this person must establish one last element as set forth in Section 3–302(a)(c): that he or she took the instrument without notice that it was overdue or had been dishonored or of any defense against or claim to it on the part of any person. It therefore appears that the holder of an instrument must take it without notice of four things:

1. that the instrument is overdue
2. that the instrument has been dishonored
3. a defense by any person
4. any claim to it by any person

Assuming the holder does not have notice of any of these four points, he or she may qualify as a holder in due course. But what did the drafters of the UCC mean when they wrote that the holder must take without notice?

Notice. The UCC defines notice in Section 1–201. Section 1–201(25) states that a person has notice of a fact when he or she has actual notice of it; or if he or she has received notice or notification of it; or if from all the facts and

circumstances known to the person at the time in question, he or she has reason to know a fact exists.

A person knows or has knowledge of a fact when he or she has actual knowledge of the fact. If Smith takes a note knowing that the maker of the note has a valid defense against the payee, he clearly has notice and does not take the instrument as a holder in due course. However, merely because he does not qualify as a holder in due course does not mean he will not collect on the note. All we are saying is that Smith takes subject to any defenses on the instrument. The maker still must *prove* the defense.

A person receives notice when: (1) it comes to his or her attention; or (2) the notice was duly delivered at the place of business through which the contract was made or at any other place held out by the person as the place for receipt of such communications. If the maker of the note discussed above calls Smith and tells him of a defense on the instrument, Smith clearly has received notice of the defense under Section 1–201(25)(b).

By also providing that a person has notice if by the facts and circumstances known to the person he or she has reason to know a fact exists, the drafters gave the courts substantial discretion as to whether a person has notice.

When notice is received by an organization is discussed in Section 1–201(24). In general, notice must be brought to the attention of the individual in that organization conducting the transaction in question.

In any event, notice must be received at such time and in such manner as to give the person or organization a reasonable opportunity to act on the notice.

Any notice received after the person has acquired the instrument does not prevent the person from qualifying as a holder in due course. The critical issue is what the person knew at the time he or she took the instrument. Information learned at a later time is not relevant as to whether the person took with notice.

Notice Instrument Overdue. By examining the face of an instrument a person may learn important information. One of the most critical things revealed by the face of the instrument is whether the instrument is overdue.

Basically, there are two types of instruments: demand instruments and time instruments. The latter is payable at a specific time —for example, a note "payable June 1, 1984." A demand instrument is one that is payable "on demand," "at sight," "on presentation."

A taker of a negotiable instrument is denied status as a holder in due course if he or she takes an instrument that is overdue. The very fact that the instrument is still in circulation after it is payable should make anyone taking it suspicious. When instruments are due, one assumes that the party entitled to collect will attempt to collect.

An instrument that is payable at a definite time, such as one payable June 1, 1984, is overdue at the beginning of the day after it is due. In this case, the instrument is overdue on June 2, 1984.

Section 3–304(3) lists several situations in which a person is deemed to have notice that an instrument is overdue. One of these is when he or she is taking a demand instrument after demand has been made or *more than a reasonable length of time after its issue.* The

UCC sets forth a relatively clear rule as to checks: a reasonable time for presentation of a check for collection is presumed to be thirty days. Suppose Linda issues a check to Alice on September 1. This means Alice has thirty days from the date of issue (September 1) to present the check. Anyone taking the check later than thirty days after issue may not qualify as a holder in due course.

Demand instruments other than checks create more of a problem as to when they are overdue. The UCC merely states that a person has notice that such an instrument is overdue if he or she takes it more than a reasonable length of time after its issue. It is not possible to state a clear-cut rule when such an instrument is overdue.

Notice Instrument Dishonored. In general, a dishonor of an instrument occurs when a demand for payment or acceptance has been made and the party expected to pay or accept refuses to do so. Suppose a note payable September 1, 1984, is presented by the payee to the maker on that date. If the maker refuses to pay at that time, there has been a dishonor of the instrument. (See the next chapter for an in-depth discussion of the issue of dishonor.)

A person who takes an instrument knowing of such a dishonor cannot qualify as a holder in due course. In many cases, a simple examination of the instrument will reveal that it has been dishonored. For example, a check that has been dishonored by a bank might be stamped "insufficient funds." Clearly, a person taking such a check would have notice of the dishonor.

However, in some cases the instrument may not indicate on its face that it has been dishonored, and the transferor may not tell the transferee of the dishonor. In such a case, the court must determine whether there is any other evidence that the transferee had notice of the dishonor. If it finds that the transferee had such notice, he or she will not qualify as a holder in due course.

Notice of Claim or Defense. A purchaser has notice of a claim or defense if the instrument is incomplete; appears to have been forged or altered or is so irregular as to call into question its validity, terms, or ownership; creates an ambiguity as to the party to pay; the purchaser has notice that the obligation of any party is voidable or that all parties have been discharged.

A defense to an instrument is typically something that is asserted as a reason not to pay it. A claim, on the other hand, is an argument asserted by a person claiming the instrument.

Some defenses or claims are obvious from the face of the instrument, such as a crude alteration or a forgery. If such an alteration or forgery calls into question the validity, terms, or ownership of the instrument, a person holding the instrument could not qualify as a holder in due course.

It does not follow that merely because the holder knew an incomplete instrument was completed that he or she had knowledge of any defense or claim unless the holder had notice of an *improper* completion. An instrument might be blank as to some unnecessary fact, might contain minor erasures, or might even have an obvious change such as the date. For example, "January 2, 1983" could be changed to "January 2, 1984" without exciting suspicion. If a check had no date, the holder would not have notice of a defense or claim merely because the transferor filled in the date.

So long as an instrument is blank it is an incomplete instrument, and the taker may not qualify as a holder in due course. Any person taking such an incomplete instrument takes it subject to any defenses or claims. An instrument may be completed in accordance with the authority given, however, and once it is completed as authorized, it is effective as completed.

Is there anything about the check in the following case that would cause the taker to have notice that it was overdue or had been dishonored or that any defense against or claim to it had been made by anyone?

Jaeger & Branch, Inc. v. Pappas

Supreme Court of Utah
433 P.2d 605 (1967)

Pappas, the defendant in this case, bought some materials from Allo. In order to get Allo to release these materials, Pappas gave Allo a check, which Allo gave to Jaeger. Jaeger had spoken to Pappas before receiving the check. When sued by Jaeger, the plaintiff claimed Jaeger took the check with notice of a defense. The trial court ruled for Jaeger, and the appeals court affirmed.

Crockett, Chief Justice

In connection with his construction and furnishing of the C'est Bon Hotel in Park City, Utah, the defendant, Jim Pappas, had been purchasing materials from the Allo Distributing Company of North Hollywood, California. On January 11, 1966, a shipment of carpet from that company, consigned to the defendant was being held up in Ogden, Utah. On that date Pappas had two telephone conversations with Allo in California about this shipment and why it was not being delivered. Allo requested Pappas to call the plaintiff, Jaeger, to whom Allo owed money for materials. In compliance with that request, on that same day, January 11, Pappas called Jaeger and inquired about the holding up of the shipment of carpet and whether Allo was meeting its obligations to Jaeger. Jaeger answered that it knew nothing about the tie-up of the shipment and stated that for reasons of business ethics it would not divulge whether or not Allo owed them money. Incidentally, but of no legal significance here, in the conversation it was nevertheless made plain that Allo was indebted to Jaeger.

Sparing the detail of and contradictions in the testimony as to the content of the telephone conversations just referred to, and two more between Pappas and Allo the next day, January 12, these facts emerge: Pappas apparently gave sufficient assurance of forthcoming payment to get the shipment of carpet released. On January 12, he made out a check for $6,500 drawn on Walker Bank in Salt Lake City, payable to Allo, and forwarded it to them. Two days later, on January 14, Allo endorsed the check and delivered it to make payment to Jaeger, who in turn deposited it in its bank account in Los Angeles. It is significant that in neither of the conversations of January 11 referred to did Pappas say anything about placing any conditions upon a check he would send. It was not until the next day or the day after (testimony is somewhat uncertain) that it is claimed that he informed Allo by telephone that if the latter did not send him "everything you say you're going to" that he would stop payment on the check he sent. But it is not shown that this statement was communicated to the plaintiff, Jaeger. The important facts are that the only conversation with Jaeger had occurred a day or two before the alleged threat about stopping the check; and that this record is devoid of any indication that anything was said to Jaeger about any condition or limitation upon any such check, which, the fact is, did not come into existence until the 12th.

In the meantime, the carpet had been released and was received by the defendant on January 14. It was not until four days later, on January 18, that the defendant filed with his bank a stop-payment order indicating as the reason: "Overpayment." Inasmuch as the check had not been cleared for payment with defendant's bank, payment was refused and the check was returned to the plaintiff, hence this lawsuit.

We have no disagreement with certain postulates inherent in plaintiff's position: that when one who takes a negotiable instrument is aware of any fact which should alert him that there is a defense, he cannot close his eyes and ignore it. He must act in good faith and exercise such caution as a reasonable person would under those circumstances and is chargeable with knowledge of such facts as reasonable inquiry would disclose. However, the converse of that proposition is equally true, that in the absence of anything to warn him to the contrary, he may assume that persons with whom he deals are themselves acting honestly and in good faith. A very high proportion of the commerce of the world is carried on through credit, which is necessarily based on confidence in the honesty and integrity of those who engage in it. To impose upon one who is offered commercial paper the duty of inquiring in each instance whether obligations have been satisfactorily performed by prior holders would so burden such transactions as to create insuperable impedimenta to the free exchange of negotiable paper, an indispensable part of modern business.

From our survey of the facts in this case in the light of the principles we have discussed herein, we have discovered nothing which would compel the finding contended for by the defendant; that the plaintiff was aware of facts which precluded him from being a holder in due course. To the contrary, the evidence provides ample support for the trial court's rejection of that contention in favor of what impresses us as a reasonable view of the situation: that what the defendant Pappas attempted to do was to get the shipment of carpet released by the use of this check, and that when he accomplished that purpose, he sought to renege on his commitment by stopping payment on the check.

Affirmed.

Holder Through a Holder in Due Course

While a person who holds an instrument may not qualify as a holder in due course, he or she may have all the rights of a holder in due course. The so-called shelter provision of the UCC, found in Section 3–201(1), states that the "transfer of an instrument rests in the transferee such rights as the transferor had therein." The drafters of the UCC adopted this provision to encourage the free transferability of negotiable instruments. A person who for one reason or another knows that he or she cannot qualify as a holder in due course may take an instrument if the transferor is a holder in due course. If the transferor is a holder in due course, the transferee has the *rights* of a holder in due course.

For example, suppose on June 5 Briscoe offers to sell a note "payable on June 1" to Knott. Knott cannot qualify as a holder in due course because she knows that the instrument is overdue—it is payable June 1. She may safely take the note, however, if Briscoe is a holder in due course. In that case, Knott will have all the rights of her transferor.

STATUS OF HOLDER IN DUE COURSE

A holder in due course occupies a very special position. When he or she takes an instrument, he or she takes it free of any claim of legal title or liens. Furthermore, the holder in due course generally takes the instrument free from all defenses of any party to the instrument *with whom the holder has not dealt*. This point is illustrated by the following case.

Wilmington Trust Co. v. Delaware Auto Sales
Supreme Court of Delaware
271 A.2d 41 (1970)

Delaware, the plaintiff in this case, received a treasurer's check from Wilmington, the defendant. When Delaware presented the check for payment, Wilmington refused to pay. It asserted the defense of failure of consideration against Delaware. Delaware claimed the status of a holder in due course. The lower court found for Delaware. The appeals court reversed the judgment for Delaware because Wilmington had previously dealt with Delaware.

Carey, Justice

The facts are essentially undisputed: Robert Hoopes, of Seaford, purchased a used car from Delaware Auto Sales and paid for it with a personal check drawn on Wilmington Trust Company in the amount of $1,550. Early the next morning, due to dissatisfaction with the car, which he later returned, Hoopes called the Seaford branch of the bank and stopped payment on his check. This order was noted in the Wilmington office at 8:35 A.M. That same morning, Al Kutner, owner of Delaware Auto Sales, went to the Greenville branch of the bank between 9:00 and 9:30 A.M., and exchanged the personal check of Hoopes for a treasurer's check in the same amount. The Assistant Treasurer investigated the adequacy of Hoopes' funds, failed to discover or had not yet received notice of the stop-payment order. At 9:24 A.M., the Hoopes account was charged with a "hold" for the amount of the treasurer's check. Later, when the treasurer's check was presented for payment, the stop-payment order was noticed and the check was cancelled. Defendant below alleged want or failure of consideration and mistake. Plaintiff below contended that it was a holder in due course and therefore not subject to those defenses.

It is clear that Delaware Auto Sales cannot assert the rights of a holder in due course as against Wilmington Trust Company. The rights of a holder in due course are defined in section 3–305:

> "To the extent that a holder is a holder in due course he takes the instrument free from. . . .
> "(2) all defenses of any party to the instrument *with whom the holder has not dealt. . . ."* (emphasis added).

In other words, personal defenses are available between immediate parties. Delaware Auto Sales dealt directly with Wilmington Trust Company; even if the auto dealer was a holder in due course, it is not immune to the defense of want or failure of consideration, as set forth in section 3–306(c).

We find that there was a failure of consideration here. Since the bank received the stop-payment order before it issued the treasurer's check, it had no right to charge the account of Hoopes, its depositor. A complete failure of consideration for the treasurer's check resulted and the bank had the right to refuse to honor it when presented by the payee.

We need not consider the defense of mistake also asserted by the bank.

Judgment reversed.

Abuses of Holder-in-Due-Course Doctrine

Although designed to facilitate the transfer of commercial documents, the holder-in-due-course doctrine has hurt consumers. Fly-by-night businesses have induced consumers to sign contracts obligating them to pay installments over several years in return for the business's promise to deliver goods over time. The business then negotiates the consumer's promissory note to a financial institution, the business is abandoned, and the consumer is left with no legal defense against the financial institution and no recourse against the defunct merchant. The following case is a classic in-volving a situation of this type and demonstrates how a few courts have sought to protect the consumer in such situations.

Unico v. Owen

Supreme Court of New Jersey
232 A.2d 405 (1967)

The defendant, Owen, purchased some goods from Universal. Universal sold its note to Unico, the plaintiff. When Owen refused to pay, Unico brought suit on the note. The lower courts and the New Jersey supreme court found Unico was not a holder in due course and therefore took the note subject to Owen's defense.

Francis, Justice

The issue to be decided here is whether plaintiff Unico, a New Jersey partnership, is a holder in due course of defendant's note. If so, it is entitled to a judgment for the unpaid balance due thereon, for which this suit was brought. The District Court found plaintiff was not such a holder and that it was therefore subject to the defense interposed by defendant, maker of the note, of failure of consideration on the part of the payee, which endorsed it to the plaintiff. Since it was undisputed that the payee failed to furnish the consideration for which the note was given, judgment was entered for defendant. The Appellate Division affirmed, and we granted plaintiff's petition for certification in order to consider the problem.

The facts are important. Defendant's wife, Jean Owen, answered an advertisement in a Newark, N.J. newspaper in which Universal Stereo Corporation of Hillside, N.J., offered for sale 140 albums of stereophonic records for $698. This amount could be financed and paid on an installment basis. In addition the buyer would receive "without separate charge" (as plaintiff puts it) a Motorola stereo record player. The plain implication was that on agreement to purchase 140 albums, the record player would be given free. A representative of Universal called at the Owens' home and discussed the matter with Mr. and Mrs. Owen. As a result, on November 6, 1962 they signed a "retail installment contract" for the purchase of 140 albums on the time payment plan proposed by Universal.

Under the printed form of contract Universal sold and Owen bought "subject to the terms and conditions stipulated in Exhibit 'A' hereto annexed and printed on the other side hereof and made part hereof, the following goods . . .: 12 stereo albums to be delivered at inception of program and every 6 months thereafter until completion of program," a "new Motorola consolo [sic]" and "140 stereo albums of choice . . ." a downpayment of $30 was noted; the balance of $668, plus an "official fee" of $1.40 and a time price differential of $150.32, left a time balance of $819.72 to be paid in installments. Owen agreed to pay this balance in 36 equal monthly installments of $22.77 each beginning on December 12, 1962, "at the office of Universal Stereo Corp., 8 Hollywood Avenue, Hillside, N.J., or any other address determined by assignee." The contract provided:

> If the Buyer executed a promissory note of even date herewith in the amount of the time balance indicated, said note is not in payment thereof, but is a negotiable instrument separate and apart from this contract even though at the time of execution it may be temporarily attached hereto by perforation or otherwise.

It was part of Universal's practice to take notes for these contracts, and obviously there was no doubt that it would be done in the Owen case. Owen did sign a printed form of note which was presented with the contract. The name of Universal Stereo Corporation was printed thereon, and the note provided for the monthly installment payments specified. On the reverse side was an elaborate printed form of endorsement which began "Pay to the order of Unico, 251 Broad St., Elizabeth, New Jersey, with full recourse," and which contained various waivers by the endorser and an authorization to the transferee to vary the terms of the note in its discretion in dealing with the maker . . .

At this point the hyper-executory character of the performance agreed to by Universal in return for the installment payment stipulation by Owen must be noted. Owen's time balance of $819.72 was required to be paid by 36 monthly installments of $22.77 each. Universal's undertaking was to deliver 24 record albums a year until 140 albums had been delivered. Completion by the seller therefore would require 5⅓ years. Thus, although Owen would have fully paid for 140 albums at the end of three years, Universal's delivery obligation did not have to be completed until 2⅓ years thereafter. This means that 40% of the albums, although fully paid for, would still be in the hands of the seller. It means also that for 2⅓ years Universal would have the use of 40% of Owen's money on which he had been charged the high time-price differential rate. In contrast, since Universal discounted the note immediately with Unico on the strength of Owen's credit and purchase contract, the transaction, so far as the seller is concerned, can fairly be considered as one for cash. In this posture, Universal had its sale price almost contemporaneously with Owen's execution of the contract, in return for an executory performance to extend over 5⅓ years. And Unico acquired Owen's note which, on its face and considered apart from the remainder of the transaction, appeared to be an unqualifiedly negotiable instrument. On the other hand, on the face of things, by virtue of the ostensibly negotiable note and the waiver or estoppel clause quoted above which was intended to bar any defense against an assignee for the seller's default, Owen had no recourse and no protection if Universal defaulted on its obligation and was financially worthless.

Owen received from Universal the stereo record player and the original 12 albums called for by the contract. Although he continued to pay the monthly installments on the note for the 12 succeeding months, he never received another album. During that period, Mrs. Owen endeavored unsuccessfully to communicate with Universal and finally ceased making payments when the albums were not delivered. Nothing further was heard about the matter until July 1964, when the attorney for Unico, who was also one of its partners, advised Mrs. Owen that Unico held the note and that payments should be made to it. She told him the payments would be resumed if the albums were delivered. No further deliveries were made because Universal had become insolvent. Up to this time Owen had paid the deposit of $30 and 12 installments of $22.77 each, for a total of $303.24. Unico brought this suit for the balance due on the note plus penalties and a 20% attorney's fee.

Owen defended on the ground that Unico was not a holder in due course of the note, that the payment of $303.24 adequately satisfied any obligation for Universal's partial performance, and that Universal's default and the consequent failure of consideration barred recovery by Unico. As we have said, the trial court found plaintiff was not a holder in due course of the note and that Universal's breach of the sales contract barred recovery.

This brings us to the primary inquiry in the case. Is the plaintiff Unico a holder in due course of defendant's note?

In the field of negotiable instruments, good faith is a broad concept. The basic philosophy of the holder in due course status is to encourage free negotiability of commercial paper by removing certain anxieties of one who takes the paper as an innocent purchaser knowing no reason why the paper is not as sound as its face would indicate. It would seem to follow, therefore, that the more the holder knows about the underlying transaction, and particularly the more he controls or participates or becomes involved in it, the less he fits the role of a good faith purchaser for value; the closer his relationship to the underlying agreement which is the source of the note, the less need there is for giving him the tensionfree rights considered necessary in a fast-moving, credit-extending commercial world.

The Universal-Unico financing agreement serves as evidence that Unico not only had a thorough knowledge of the nature and method of operation of Universal's business, but also exercised extensive control over it. Moreover, obviously it had a large, if not decisive, hand in the fashioning and supplying of the form of contract and note used by Universal, and particularly in setting the terms of the record album sales agreement, which were designed to put the buyer-consumer in an unfair and burdensome legal straight jacket and to bar any escape no matter what the default of the seller, while permitting the note-holder, contract-assignee to force payment from him by enveloping itself in the formal status of holder in due course. To say the relationship between Unico and the business operations of Universal was close, and that Unico was involved therein, is to put it mildly. There is no case in New Jersey dealing with the contention that the holder of a consumer goods buyer's note in purchasing it did not meet the test of good faith negotiation because the connection between the seller and the financer was as intimate as in this case.

There is a conflict of authority in other jurisdictions but we are impelled for reasons of equity and justice to join those courts which deny holder in due course status in consumer goods sales cases to those financers whose involvement with the seller's business is as close, and whose knowledge of the extrinsic factors—i.e., the terms of the underlying sale agreement—is as pervasive, as it is in the present case.

For purposes of consumer goods transactions, we hold that where the seller's performance is executory in character and when it appears from the totality of the arrangements between dealer and financer that the financer has had a substantial voice in setting standards for the underlying transaction, or has approved the standards established by the dealer, and has agreed to take all or a predetermined or substantial quantity of the negotiable paper which is backed by such standards, the financer should be considered a participant in the original transaction and therefore not entitled to holder in due course status.

Few state courts have been as progressive as New Jersey's in dealing with this problem. Many jurisdictions have harshly applied the doctrine against consumers, and literally thousands of consumers have been affected. The Office of Economic Opportunity (OEO) Office of Legal Services handled 13,781 holder-in-due-course cases during a one-year period beginning May 1, 1970.

Financers have argued that the cost of credit would go up if the doctrine of the holder in due course were to be abolished in consumer transactions. Consumer groups have replied that the real issue is how to control the misdealing merchants who, by their wrongful actions, cause the legal dispute to arise between the consumer and the financing agency. Consumer advocates reason that the financers are better able to control the merchants. After all, the financing agency sees the merchant on a recurring basis and may be vital to the merchant's continued existence. The financer is in a good position to judge the merchant's integrity and honesty. The single consumer, on the other hand, usually deals with a merchant in a few isolated transactions and thus has little opportunity for judging the merchant's behavior.

Many persons confronted by a holder in due course have been forced to pay for goods they never received (complete failure of consideration), goods that the seller refused to repair (breach of warranty), goods that did not meet the seller's representations (fraud in the inducement), and so forth. The purchaser could assert a claim against the seller, but since the note had been negotiated to a holder in due course, he or she had to pay the note. When the seller went bankrupt or skipped town, the buyer lost out completely.

Some state courts attempted to help a purchaser by finding that the holder of the instrument failed to qualify as a holder in due course. Other states adopted the Uniform Consumer Credit Code, which gives consumers more protection. On the whole, the state approach led to a gross lack of uniformity. The states tried to deal with the problem, but innumerable cases cluttered court dockets across the country. What was needed was a sweeping, uniform rule that applied everywhere in the United States. Thanks to the Federal Trade Commission, we now have such a rule for consumer-credit contracts.

FTC Modification of the Doctrine

The FTC adopted a Trade Regulation Rule effective May 14, 1976, which, as far as consumers are concerned, virtually eliminated the problem of being forced to pay on an obligation when the seller failed to live up to his or her part of the bargain. The FTC rule provides that:

In connection with any sale or lease of goods or services to consumers, in or affecting the Federal Trade Commission Act, it is an unfair or deceptive act or practice within the meaning of Section 5 of that Act for a seller, directly or indirectly, to:

(a) take or receive a consumer credit contract which fails to contain the following provision in at least ten point, bold face, type:

NOTICE
ANY HOLDER OF THIS CONSUMER CREDIT CONTRACT IS SUBJECT TO ALL CLAIMS AND DEFENSES WHICH THE DEBTOR COULD ASSERT

AGAINST THE SELLER OF GOODS OR SERVICES OBTAINED PURSUANT HERETO OR WITH THE PROCEEDS HEREOF. RECOVERY HEREUNDER BY THE DEBTOR SHALL NOT EXCEED AMOUNTS PAID BY THE DEBTOR HEREUNDER.

or, (b) accept, as full or partial payment for such sale or lease, the proceeds of any purchase money loan (as purchase money loan is defined herein), unless any consumer credit contract made in connection with such purchase money loan contains the following provision in at least ten point, bold face, type:

NOTICE
ANY HOLDER OF THIS CONSUMER CREDIT CONTRACT IS SUBJECT TO ALL CLAIMS AND DEFENSES WHICH THE DEBTOR COULD ASSERT AGAINST THE SELLER OF GOODS OR SERVICES OBTAINED WITH THE PROCEEDS HEREOF. RECOVERY HEREUNDER BY THE DEBTOR SHALL NOT EXCEED AMOUNTS PAID BY THE DEBTOR HEREUNDER.

This amendment was designed to protect the rights of consumers who purchase on credit and incur obligations to financial institutions by preserving the consumers' claims and defenses.

Note that the Act precludes *sellers* from taking a consumer-credit contract or proceeds of a purchase-money loan, unless the consumer-credit contract contains the above-cited provision. This takes care of the situation where a seller arranges for financing a sale, or the situation where the seller refers a buyer to a finance company to obtain a loan for the goods. A purchase-money loan basically refers to a situation where a consumer receives a cash advance for which he or she will pay a finance charge to purchase goods and services from a seller who (1) refers the consumer to the creditor or (2) is affiliated with the creditor by common control, contract, or business arrangement. A consumer-credit contract is an instrument that evidences or embodies a debt arising from a "purchase money loan" transaction or a sale in which credit is extended to a consumer.

This rule does not apply to a person who acquires goods for use in his or her business but rather to people who purchase goods for personal, family, or household use. Such consumers now may purchase goods on credit, and if a defense, either real or personal, arises that can be asserted against the seller, this defense can be asserted against the holder of the consumer-credit contract even though the holder qualifies as a holder in due course.

What would happen if a consumer entered into a consumer-credit contract, and signed the contract, but the FTC notice was not included in the language of the contract? At least one court has decided that, while such a contract violates the FTC rule, in the absence of such a notice a holder in due course takes free of all personal defenses. This is true even though the contract should have included the FTC notice. Of course, this is an unfair trade practice.

The FTC rule does not apply to a credit-card transaction. However, the Fair Credit Billing Act protects buyers utilizing a credit card. There are two requirements: the merchandise must cost more than $50, and the consumer must live within 100 miles of the place where the original transaction took place. If both conditions are met, the consumer need only make an effort to return the item and ask for a refund or replacement. The consumer can then hold off on payment of the credit-card company's bill until the problem is ironed out with the retailer.

REVIEW PROBLEMS

1. The defendant signed a paper with Economy Exterminating Company entitled "Retail Installment Contract/Including Promissory Note and Security Agreement." It called for a cash price of $250 to be paid in monthly installments. On the same day, the defendant also signed a paper that stated that the agreed services had been satisfactorily performed. Although her house was to be sprayed every other month, it was in fact sprayed only once. The instrument in question, among other things, granted the holder the power to waive particular defaults or remedies without waiving others and to require its written consent for any transfer of the buyer's obligations (while keeping its own freely transferrable). It also contained an application for insurance. This instrument was transferred to a finance company. Can it claim status as a holder in due course? Geiger Finance Company v. Graham, 182 S.E.2d 521 (Court of Appeals of Georgia 1971).

2. Barrett issued a check in the amount of $1,500 drawn on his joint banking acount with his wife to the order of Acquatic Industries. His bank paid the check even though Acquatic failed to indorse the check. The bank debited his account for $1,500. No stop payment order had been issued by Barrett prior to payment. He is now suing the bank for unauthorized payment of the check. Should he prevail in light of the fact that Acquatic did not indorse the check? First National Bank of Guinnett v. Barrett, 233 S.E.2d 24 (Ct. of Appeals of Georgia 1977).

3. Flett drew a check for $9,000, dated March 26, 1964, payable to J. J. Ryan Construction Co., Inc. Ryan indorsed and deposited the check into his checking account at the Waltham Citizens National Bank. The bank allowed Ryan to draw against the check immediately. Ryan subsequently went bankrupt. Flett in the meantime stopped payment on the check. Can the bank recover the $9,000 from Flett? Has the bank given value? Waltham Citizens National Bank v. Flett, 234 N.E.2d 739 (Supreme Judicial Court of Mass. 1968).

4. Anthony and Dolores Angelini entered into a contract with Lustro Aluminum Products, Inc. for repair work on their home. They signed an installment-payment contract. Payments were to begin "60 days after completion" of the work on their home. Anthony was told the payments on the note would not begin until the work was satisfactorily completed. When they executed the note, it contained no date for payments to begin. Lustro indorsed the note to General Investment Corporation ten days after it was executed. Lustro warranted as part of the indorsement that it "has furnished and installed all articles and materials and has fully completed all work which constitutes the consideration for which this note was executed and delivered by the maker." General dealt regularly with Lustro. Lustro never finished the job and eventually became insolvent. When General took the note, it also received the contract. It did not inquire of the Angelinis if the work had been completed although a contractor could obtain from the owner and submit to a finance company a certificate of completion if the work had been completed. Did General Investment Corporation qualify as a holder in due course? (Note, that this case was litigated before the adoption of the FTC rules.) General Investment Corp. v. Angelini, 278 A.2d 193 (Supreme Court of N.J. 1971).

5. Eldon's Stores, Inc. is a closely held corporation engaged in the retail grocery business. Merrill Lynch is a national stock brokerage

firm. Drexler was the attorney for Eldon's Stores, Inc. From January, 1968 through January 1970, Drexler maintained a trading account in his name with Merrill Lynch by which he purchased and sold stock at various times. Eldon's Stores, Inc. had no account with Merrill Lynch. In 1969, Eldon's Stores, Inc. gave Drexler a check written to Merrill Lynch to purchase stock for the corporation. The check was drawn by the corporation and contained corporate identification by way of the business. Drexler took the check and purchased stocks for his own accounts. Merrill Lynch took the check as payment for Drexler's stock. After discovering the misapplication of the funds, Eldon's claimed that Merrill Lynch had no better title than Drexler, its transferor. Merrill Lynch claimed it took the check as a holder for full value and that it had no notice of any defense or claims to the check on the part of any person. Is Merrill Lynch's claim that it was a holder in due course a good defense to the claims of Eldon's Stores, Inc.? Eldon's Super Fresh Stores v. Merrill Lynch, Pierce, Fenner & Smith, Inc. v. Drexler, 207 N.W.2d 282 (Supreme Court of Minnesota 1973).

6. Korzenik was an attorney for Southern New England Distributing Corporation. Southern obtained by fraud some notes from Supreme Radio. Southern then indorsed the notes over to Korzenik as a retainer for future legal services. Supreme Radio discovered the fraud and demanded the notes back from Korzenik. Korzenik claimed he was a holder in due course. Supreme Radio claimed he was not because he had given no value in exchange for the note. Who will win as to the notes? Korzenik v. Supreme Radio, Inc., 197 N.E.2d

702 (Supreme Judicial Court of Massachusetts 1964).

7. Pazol drew a check on Fulton National bank for payment to Eidson. Eidson deposited the check into his account at Sandy Springs Bank. On the same day, Eidson withdrew the amount of the check from his account. On the next day, Sandy Springs discovered the dishonorment of this check. Sandy Springs claims it is a holder in due course and demands payment from Pazol. Pazol claims Sandy Springs does not qualify as a holder in due course because it gave no value for the check. Is Sandy Springs a holder in due course? Pazol v. Citizen National Bank of Sandy Springs, 138 S.E.2d 442 (Ct. App. Ga. 1964).

8. Villa had a corporate account under the name of Villa Auto Sales. The manager of the bank was personally acquainted with Villa. Corporate authority stating Villa was authorized to sign or indorse any check held by the corporation was on file on the bank. Villa cashed two checks given to him by Leo Used Cars. These checks were written on another bank. The checks were cashed by the teller at Industrial and sent though the bank collection procedure. The teller did not follow the bank's set procedure of obtaining a manager's approval before cashing a corporate check. Meanwhile, Leo Used Cars stopped payment on the checks because Villa had sold them defective used cars. The bank now claims that it is a holder in due course and not subject to the claims against Villa Auto Sales. Is the bank's claim a valid one? Industrial National Bank of Rhode Island v. Leo's Used Car Exchange, Inc., 291 N.E.2d 603 (Supreme Judicial Court of Mass. 1963).

Liability of Parties and Defenses

C hapters 19 and 20 discussed the different types of commercial paper as well as the significant legal doctrines that support commercial paper as a vital component of the economy of the United States. This chapter investigates further the liability of parties who use commercial paper in business transactions and the defenses available against honoring these instruments.

TYPES OF LIABILITY

Unconditional or Primary Liability

Liability of the maker, drawer, drawee, and endorser of commercial paper differs appreciably. The liability of the maker of a promissory note is the most easily understood. A note, as indicated in Chapter 19, is a two-party instrument. The maker of a note assumes an unconditional responsibility based upon the instrument's promise to pay. This responsibility

is often referred to as primary, although the Uniform Commercial Code does not use that term. Potentially, the drawee of a draft also assumes a similar liability, but the manner in which this arises is more complicated. Remember that a draft is a three-party instrument in which a drawer orders a drawee to pay a payee. When the drawee accepts this order, the drawee becomes the acceptor, assuming a liability comparable to that of the maker of a note.

Both the maker of a note and the acceptor of a draft contract to pay the instrument according to its terms at the time they become parties. Neither is excused from paying even if the holder presents the instrument long after it becomes due. As a primary party, the maker or acceptor is bound to pay, and the holder need resort to no one else first. This obligation continues until the statute of limitations prevents the holder from recovering.

Until the drawee's acceptance—that is, his or her signed engagement to honor the draft as presented (Section 3–410[1])—the drawee has no liability on the instrument; upon acceptance, unconditional liability is established. A common example of acceptance is the certification of a check by a bank. By accepting, the drawee agrees to honor the instrument according to its terms as presented. The mechanics of acceptance were discussed in Chapter 19.

Although it is not an advisable practice, a drawee sometimes accepts an incomplete instrument. When doing so, the drawee accepts liability on the completed instrument to the extent that he or she authorized completion. If, however, the instrument is completed in an unauthorized manner and is transferred to a holder in due course, the acceptor's liability may increase if the holder in due course enforces the instrument as completed (Section 3–407[3]). In addition to becoming primarily liable by accepting, the drawee by this action admits the existence of the payee and the payee's capacity to endorse. The maker of a note also admits these same facts (Section 3–413[3]).

Secondary Liability

The liability of the drawer of a draft and of endorsers of commercial paper is not absolute. Responsibility of these parties for payment is conditioned upon certain events taking place. Accordingly, the UCC refers to endorsers and drawers as secondary parties (Section 3–102[1][d]). A secondary party is not expected to pay the instrument, whereas a primary party is.

Drawer's Commitment. Recall that a drawer initiating a draft is ordering the drawee to pay. The drawer expects the drawee to do so. This expectation is generally based upon a contractual relationship between the two. By accepting, the drawee agrees to be bound as ordered.

Endorser's Commitment. When commercial paper is transferred by endorsement, the endorser expects that the primary party, the drawee/acceptor or maker, will pay. The endorser's commitment, like that of the drawer of a draft, is to pay only if the primary party fails to do so.

Dishonor. The trigger for establishing secondary liability is dishonor. An instrument is dishonored if it is properly presented for acceptance or payment and the party upon whom presentment is made refuses to comply (Section 3–507[1][a]). A draft is dishonored by the drawee's either refusing to accept or refusing to pay, but a note is dishonored only if the maker refuses to pay.

ESTABLISHING SECONDARY LIABILITY

Generally, the following events must occur to establish the secondary liability of endorsers as well as that of the drawer of a draft: (1) presentment, (2) dishonor, and (3) notice of dishonor. A fourth step called protest is required in some situations.

Presentment

Presentment is the term describing the procedure in which the holder of commercial paper or the holder's agent submits the instrument to the drawee or maker for acceptance or payment. For many drafts, presentment is made twice—once for acceptance and once for payment. A note is not presented for acceptance as the party who is liable for payment has already promised to do so.

Presentment for Acceptance. Presentment for acceptance is often a critical step in a transaction involving a draft. Initially, presentment for acceptance is necessary to establish the drawee's primary liability. Additionally, the secondary liability of the drawer and endorsers frequently depends upon a proper presentment for acceptance.

According to the UCC, presentment for acceptance is required in three instances. It must be made where the draft so provides, where it is payable at some place other than the drawee's residence or place of business, or where the time of payment depends upon the acceptance date (Section 3–501[1][a]). The holder may, however, present any draft payable at a stated date for acceptance. A common example would be the trade acceptance, which is discussed in Chapter 19.

Presentment for Payment. Practically, a holder of commercial paper must present the instrument to the proper party in order to collect. Presentment for payment is also a necessary step in establishing the liability of secondary parties if the instrument is dishonored. Unless presentment is accomplished correctly, all endorsers are discharged completely, and drawers to a limited extent if the drawee becomes insolvent during any delay in presentment (Section 3–502[1][b]). In the following case, the drawer of a number of checks argues that he is discharged because the checks were not presented for payment for several months.

Kaiser v. Northwest Shopping Center, Inc.

Court of Civil Appeal of Texas
544 S.W.2d 785 (1976)

Robert G. Kaiser (defendant-appellant) and Northwest Shopping Center, Inc. (plaintiff-appellee) were parties to a lease agreement under which Kaiser was obligated to pay $500 per month rent plus a pro rata share of property taxes, a maintenance fee, and a percentage of gross sales over $200,000.

The lease gave Kaiser the exclusive right to operate a drug store in the shopping center. The original lease term was to expire on December 31, 1973; however, a letter dated June 1, 1971, gave Kaiser an option to extend the lease on the same terms, except that his rent would be increased to $750 per month. By another letter dated January 22, 1974, Northwest Shopping Center, Inc. informed Kaiser that, since Kaiser had not elected to extend his lease, he would be considered a month-to-month tenant at a rate of $600 per month. Kaiser then took the position that he had extended the lease by tendering checks in the amount of $750 per month. Commencing in January 1974, Northwest held Kaiser's rent checks without presenting them while another tenant, a large grocery chain, was attempting to renegotiate its lease to permit it to install a pharmaceutical department, which, if permitted by Northwest, would have been contrary to a covenant in Kaiser's lease. When these negotiations collapsed, Northwest decided to acquiesce in Kaiser's lease extension. Acting on this decision, Northwest presented the accumulated checks to Kaiser's bank on October 29, 1974. The bank honored some of the checks but refused to honor others because they were stale or because the account contained insufficient funds. On October 31 Northwest again presented the dishonored checks, but payment had been stopped on them. Northwest then sued to recover the unpaid rent.

The trial court held that neither the checks nor the underlying rent obligation was discharged by the landlord's failure to make timely presentment of the checks for payment and entered judgment against Kaiser. Kaiser appeals. Held: Affirmed.

Akin, Justice

Kaiser contends that because the checks were not presented within a reasonable period of time, the checks and the underlying debt are discharged [Sections 3–601 and 3–802]. These sections of the Code do not support such a contention. Section 3.802 provides:

> (a) Unless otherwise agreed, where an instrument is taken for an underlying obligation . . .
>   (2) . . . If the instrument is dishonored action may be maintained on either the instrument or the obligation; discharge of the underlying obligor on the instrument also discharges him on the obligation.

This section allows a creditor, after a check is dishonored, to choose whether he wants to sue on the check or the underlying debt. However, it goes on to provide that if the debtor's liability on the check has been discharged under another provision of the Code, then the underlying debt is also discharged. The methods by which the obligation on a check can be discharged are specified in 3.601. Kaiser apparently relies upon 3.601(b), to wit:

> Any party is also discharged from his liability on an instrument to another party by any other act or agreement with such party which would discharge his simple contract for the payment of money.

Kaiser argues that retention of the checks longer than a reasonable time is an "other act" constituting a discharge under the section. Apparently he relies on the cases holding that ". . . a creditor's retention for an unreasonable length of time of a check tendered in full payment of an unliquidated or disputed claim, without cashing or otherwise using it and without indicating a refusal to accept the check in accord and satisfaction, constitutes an acceptance of the check in settlement for payment of the claim, so as to bar any action for an alleged balance due."

The flaw in this argument is that "acceptance," as used in these cases, means that the creditor treats the check as cash, subject to payment by the bank on which it was drawn, and is bound by any conditions upon which the check was delivered. By merely holding the check, the creditor does not lose his right to be paid. If the check is not honored by the bank on which it is drawn, the debtor loses the benefit of his tender by check. Retention of the check, even beyond a reasonable time, does not discharge either the check or the underlying debt under 3.601(b) or under 3.802.

Kaiser also relies on 3.503(b)(1), which provides that instruments shall be presented for payment within a "reasonable" time, defined as thirty days from the date of issue or the date of the check, whichever is later. This section does not relieve the drawer, however, of his liability on the stale check. The only penalty the Code provides for such a delay as between the drawer and the holder is under 3.502, which provides that a drawer's liability on a stale check may be discharged if the bank on which it is drawn has become insolvent. Since no question of the bank's solvency is presented here, 3.502 and 3.503 do not assist Kaiser.

Accordingly, the judgment of the trial court is affirmed. . . .

If an instrument indicates the date on which it is due, presentment for payment is due on that day. An accepted draft payable a specified number of days after sight is due at that time. If a note is payable on demand in order to fix the liability of secondary parties, presentment for payment is due within a reasonable time after the party becomes liable (Section 3–503[1][e]). A reasonable time is determined by the nature of the instrument, customs of the trade, and the facts of the particular case (Section 3–503[2]).

Presentment for either payment or acceptance must be made at a reasonable hour. If presentment is required at a bank, the presentment must be made during the banking day (Section 3–503[4]). If presentment is due on a day that is not a full business day for either party, presentment is due on the next following day that is a full business day for both parties (Section 3–503[3]). Presentment may be made by mail, through a clearing house, or at the place of acceptance or payment specified in the instrument. When nothing is specified, presentment may be at the place of business or residence of the party who is to accept or pay (Section 3–504[2][1]).

The party to whom presentment is made may require the presenter to

(1) exhibit the instrument

(2) identify himself or herself
(3) sign a receipt on the instrument for any partial payment
(4) surrender the instrument upon full payment (Section 3–505[1])

If these requirements are not met, the person upon whom presentment is made may refuse to accept or pay without dishonoring.

Dishonor

Dishonor, as previously mentioned, is the refusal of a party upon whom a proper demand for payment or acceptance is made to comply within the required time. Payment of an instrument may be deferred without dishonor to provide the person upon whom demand is made an opportunity to examine it to determine if it is properly payable (Section 3–506[2]); however, payment must be made before the close of business on the day of presentment (Section 3–506[2]). Subject to any required notice of dishonor and protest, a holder has upon dishonor an immediate right of recourse against the drawers and endorsers. (Section 3–507[2]). In the following case the holder of an improperly dishonored check loses a suit against the drawee bank.

J. E. B. Stewart v. The Citizens and Southern National Bank

Court of Appeals of Georgia

225 S.E.2d 761 (1976)

J. E. B. Stewart (plaintiff-appellant) received a check in the amount of $185.48 in payment of a fee from a client. The check was that of a corporation drawn on an account with The Citizens and Southern National Bank (defendant-respondent) and made out to an employee who was Stewart's client. The client endorsed the check and delivered it to Stewart. Stewart presented the check to The Citizens and Southern National Bank and to Barbara Eschwig, manager of its North Avenue branch. The bank and Eschwig refused to cash the check, although stating that the check was good— that is, that there were sufficient funds in the corporation's account.

Stewart then sued the bank and Eschwig for actual damages in the amount of $185.48 arising out of their refusal to cash a valid check drawn against a solvent account and for $50,000 punitive damages for alleged aggravating circumstances growing out of the transaction. He also sought reasonable attorney fees.

Defendants moved to dismiss the complaint and contended there were no contractual or other duties existing between them and plaintiff under which defendants were obligated to cash the check presented by the plaintiff. They asserted that the payorbank and a drawee was not liable to an endorser on the check; that defendant Eschwig owed no duty to plaintiff to negotiate the check that Stewart presented; and that defendants were not personally liable to the plaintiff. Motion to dismiss was granted, and plaintiff appeals. Held: Affirmed.

Evans, Judge

1. Defendants base their reasoning of owing no duty to the plaintiff upon Code Ann. Sec. 109A-3-409 which provides that a check or other draft does not of itself operate as an assignment of any funds in the hands of the drawee available for payment, and that the drawee is not liable on the instrument until it accepts it.

2. While a check is merely an order upon a bank to pay from the drawer's account, it may be revoked at any time by the drawer before it has been certified, accepted, or paid by the bank, and may be revoked by operation of law upon the death of the drawer.

3. But upon presentment of the check as to which payment was refused, the check was dishonored, and plaintiff's remedy, as a holder, was "against the drawers and indorsers," not the defendant bank and its agent, neither of whom owed him a duty. In such circumstances, the refusal to cash the check and creating liability against the "drawers and indorsers" would not create a liability by the bank to the person who presented the check for payment, and such person would have no course of action against the defendant bank. The lower court did not err in dismissing the claim.

4. Plaintiff cites as authority for his position, and relies heavily upon the case of *Mason* v. *Blayton*. . . . But the *Blayton* case is authority *against* plaintiff's position and not

in support of same. Blayton gave Mason a check and when it was not paid Blayton sued Mason on the check; and then Blayton moved for summary judgment which was denied by the trial court. On appeal the entire discussion is taken up with the proposition that the holder of the check (the drawee) had the right to sue the person who gave the check, and the trial court was reversed because of its failure to so hold. But never a word is found therein to the effect that the holder of the check *had a right of action against and could lawfully sue the bank.* It is difficult to understand how plaintiff here can place his reliance upon the above authority.

Judgment affirmed.

Notice of Dishonor

In most cases the final step in establishing the liability of secondary parties is to provide notice that the instrument has been dishonored. A holder has until midnight of the third business day after dishonor to notify his or her immediate transferor of the dishonor. Prior holders are required to give notice before midnight of the third business day after themselves receiving notice of dishonor (Section 3–508[2]). A bank is required to give notice before midnight of the banking day following the banking day on which it received the item or notice of dishonor (Sections 3–508[2], 4–104[1][h]).

Although the time within which notice must be provided is relatively short, other requirements for notice are more liberal. Notice of dishonor may be given orally in a face-to-face conversation or over the telephone; however, both of these practices should be avoided because the party providing notice may have to prove later that it was given. If oral notice is given, it should be followed by a written notice within the statutory period.

The most common type of notice of dishonor is the check that has been returned through a clearinghouse because the drawer has insufficient funds or has stopped payment for some reason; but notice of dishonor is frequently given by mail or telegram. The UCC allows notice of dishonor in any reasonable manner as long as the instrument is identified and the fact of dishonor clearly indicated.

Notice of dishonor does not have to be given in any particular order. Usually the holder notifies the person who transferred the instrument to him or her. This triggers that person's liability. That person in turn would notify the individual from whom the instrument was received and so on down the line. The holder might, however, notify other transferors in order to initiate their responsibility in the event collection from the immediate transferor is not accomplished. Once a party has been notified of dishonor, no further notice need be given, for the notice operates for the benefit of all parties who have rights on the instrument (Section 3–508[8]).

Protest

Protest is an official certificate of dishonor given by a consular officer of the United States, a notary public, or other person authorized to certify dishonor by the law of the place where dishonor occurs (Section 3–509[1]). Protest is required on dishonored drafts drawn or payable outside of the United States. A draft of this type is generally referred to as a *foreign bill.*

The purpose of a certificate of protest is to provide acceptable evidence of dishonor. Since a certificate of protest provides a rebuttable presumption that notice of dishonor has been given, dishonored commercial paper is often protested although no requirement exists to do so (Section 3–510[a]).

EXTENT OF SECONDARY LIABILITY

As previously indicated, an endorser's liability is secondary. This liability is conditioned upon the instrument's being dishonored when properly presented and notice of dishonor provided the endorser. Unless excused, a holder's failure to meet these conditions as directed by statute discharges the endorser both completely and immediately (Section 3–502[1][a]).

The liability of the drawer of a draft is also secondary, as it depends upon certain conditions being fulfilled; but a critical difference exists between the position of the drawer of a draft and that of an endorser. The drawer usually receives a consideration from the payee. This is the reason that the drawer has ordered the drawee to honor the instrument. To allow a drawer to escape liability because the holder fails to make due presentment or provide notice of dishonor would result in the drawer receiving an unjustifiable gain. As a result, in general if the drawee refuses to accept or pay, policy dictates that the drawer be liable. However, if the drawer were to suffer a loss because the holder fails to make proper presentment or provide notice of dishonor, that loss should be the holder's.

The drawer will suffer a loss if it leaves funds on deposit with the drawee to cover a draft and the drawee becomes insolvent. If the drawee's insolvency occurs after the draft is due, the drawer's loss is a result of the holder's failure to make the necessary presentment or give notice of dishonor in a timely manner. With this in mind, the UCC limits the drawer's liability on the draft to the extent that the drawee's insolvency deprives the drawer of funds. This result is accomplished by providing the drawer with a right to obtain a discharge of liability by assigning his or her right against the drawee to the holder (Section 3–502[1][b]).

UNIVERSAL DEFENSES

Commercial paper is a substitute for money. Although not as acceptable generally as currency, checks, drafts, and promissory notes transfer readily in the economy. In some situations the use of commercial paper is preferable to the use of money. Individuals and business firms pay many obligations with checks because to do so is safer and more convenient than to use currency.

The doctrine of holder in due course, described in the previous chapter, is the major reason that commercial paper is readily acceptable in most transactions. Recall that the holder in due course enjoys a special position, since with limited exceptions a holder in due course takes the instrument free of defenses of any party to it with whom he or she has not dealt.

Defenses that may be asserted against a holder in due course are called *universal* or *real* defenses. Some defenses are recognized even against a holder in due course because the holder in due course never agreed to the obligation indicated by the instrument. Negotiable instruments are a form of contract. If no contractual liability has been assumed, the instrument is a nullity.

A note upon which the maker's signature is forged is an example. Even if the instrument is proper in form and duly negotiated to a holder in due course, the victim of the forgery should not be liable. A similar result follows when an instrument is materially altered after being executed. The party liable is not responsible for the instrument in its altered state, since this was not the contract that person agreed to.

Other universal defenses exist because the

public policy underlying each is considered more important to society than the public need for the ready transferability of commercial paper. Universal defenses of this kind include infancy; certain other types of incapacity; duress and illegality when these render the underlying transaction void; discharge in bankruptcy; and fraud in the execution.

Forgery

A person whose signature is used on a negotiable instrument without authority is not liable on it. If, however, the person's negligence substantially contributed to the use of the unauthorized signature, he or she is precluded from asserting the lack of authority against a holder in due course (Section 3–406).

K & K Manufacturing, Inc. v. Union Bank

Court of Appeals of Arizona
628 P.2d 44 (1981)

K & K Manufacturing, Inc. and Bill J. Knight, the firm's president and majority stockholder (plaintiffs-appellants) brought this action against Union Bank (defendant-appellee) seeking repayment of funds paid on checks with Knight's unauthorized signature. The forgeries were the work of Eleanor Garza, the firm's bookkeeper, who also handled Knight's personal finances.

The total amount of forgeries on the K & K account was $49,859.31; on Knight's personal account, $11,350. After a trial, judgment was entered in Knight's favor for $5,500. This amount was the total paid out of his personal account on forged checks prior to his receiving the bank statement containing the first forged items plus the fourteen days stated in UCC Section 4–406(2)(b) as a reasonable time to notify the bank. At that time no forged checks on K & K Manufacturing had been paid. As a result, judgment was entered for Union Bank against K & K. Both plaintiffs appealed. Held: Affirmed.

Hathaway, Chief Judge

In this case we must apply articles three and four of the Uniform Commercial Code to determine who should bear the risk of loss when a dishonest employee forges her employer's name as drawer on a number of checks on his business and personal checking accounts, then appropriates the proceeds for her personal use.

The bookkeeper's duties at K & K Manufacturing were very broad, including picking up the company mail and Knight's personal mail from a common post office box, preparing checks for Knight's signature to pay both company and personal bills, and making entries in a cash disbursement journal reflecting the expenses for which the checks were written. Most importantly, it was her responsibility to reconcile the monthly statements prepared and sent by appellee Union Bank, where Knight kept both his business and personal checking and savings accounts. No one shared these duties with Miss Garza.

Between March 1977 and January 1978, Miss Garza forged Knight's signature on some 66 separate checks drawn on his personal or business accounts at Union Bank.

The majority of these checks were made payable to her. The bank paid each such check and Miss Garza received or was credited with the proceeds.

Eventually an in-house audit showed the discrepancies in the 1977 disbursements. Appellants brought this action against appellee for breach of contract, seeking repayment of the funds the bank paid out on checks with unauthorized signatures. . . . [T]he trial court made findings of fact and conclusions of law.

Appellants contend that findings 13, 14 and 15 are not supported by the evidence. They argue the record shows their actions were not negligent and that the bank's practices and procedures were negligent as a matter of law. The disputed findings are as follows:

13. Defendant bank (appellee) paid all the checks in good faith and in accordance with reasonable commercial standards.
14. Defendant bank did not fail to exercise ordinary care in paying the checks.
15. The plaintiffs (appellants) did not exercise reasonable care and promptness to examine the bank statements and cancelled checks in order to discover the forgeries.

Our duty begins and ends with the inquiry of whether the trial court had before it evidence which reasonably supports its actions, viewed in a light most favorable to sustaining its findings. The determination of which actions are commercially reasonable and what constitutes ordinary care on the part of the bank, as well as reasonable care and promptness on the part of the depositor, are questions of fact for the trier of fact.

The concept of which party bears the loss in a forgery situation such as the one presented here is addressed in articles three and four of the Uniform Commercial Code, covering commercial paper and bank deposits and collections. A.R.S. Sec. 44-2543 (U.C.C. Sec. 3-406) provides:

Negligence contributing to alteration or unauthorized signature
Any person who by his negligence substantially contributes to a material alteration of the instrument or to the making of an unauthorized signature is precluded from asserting the alteration or lack of authority against a holder in due course or against a drawee or other payor who pays the instrument in good faith and in accordance with the reasonable commercial standards of the drawee's or payor's business.

A.R.S. Sec. 44-2632 (U.C.C. Sec. 4-406) provides in part:

Customer's duty to discover and report unauthorized signature or alteration
A. When a bank sends to its customer a statement of account accompanied by items paid in good faith in support of the debit entries or holds the statement and items pursuant to a request or instructions of its customer or otherwise in a reasonable manner makes the statement and items available to the customer, the customer must exercise reasonable care and

promptness to examine the statement and items to discover his unauthorized signature or any alteration on an item and must notify the bank promptly after discovery thereof.

B. If the bank establishes that the customer failed with respect to an item to comply with the duties imposed on the customer by subsection A the customer is precluded from asserting against the bank:

1. His unauthorized signature or any alteration on the item if the bank also establishes that it suffered a loss by reason of such failure; and

2. An unauthorized signature or alteration by the same wrongdoer on any other item paid in good faith by the bank after the first item and statement was available to the customer for a reasonable period not exceeding fourteen calendar days and before the bank receives notification from the customer of any such unauthorized signature or alteration.

C. The preclusion under subsection B does not apply if the customer establishes lack of ordinary care on the part of the bank in paying the item(s).

These provisions impose a duty on the depositor to check his monthly statement for unauthorized signatures or alterations on checks. If the depositor fails to do so, after the first forged check and statement relating thereto is sent to him, plus a reasonable period not exceeding 14 days, he is precluded from asserting the unauthorized signature or alteration against the bank. The burden of proof of depositor's negligence is on the bank. Even if the bank succeeds in establishing the depositor's negligence, if the customer establishes that the bank failed to exercise ordinary care in paying the bad checks, the preclusion rule does not apply.

We first address the issue of whether appellee met its burden of proof of showing that appellants "substantially contributed" to the forgeries or failed to exercise "reasonable care and promptness" in examining the monthly statements. The record shows that appellants trusted Miss Garza completely with both writing checks and reconciling the monthly statements. No spot checks were made by Knight or the controller at Knight Foundry, both of whom had access to the banking records. Knight was informed by a bank officer that his personal account was overdrawn on 12 occasions in 1977, yet did nothing to discover the reasons therefor. Knight testified he was aware Miss Garza's work was often inaccurate as well as tardy in 1977 and 1978.

Appellants argue they were not negligent in relying on a previously honest employee. . . . Misplaced confidence in an employee will not excuse a depositor from the duty of notifying the bank of alterations on items paid from the depositor's account. We adopt the majority view that the depositor is chargeable with the knowledge of all facts a reasonable and prudent examination of his bank statement would have disclosed if made by an honest employee. The trial court's finding number 15 is amply supported by the evidence.

Secondly, we turn to the question of whether appellants met their burden of proof of demonstrating appellee did not exercise ordinary care in paying the bad checks, and did not act in good faith and in accordance with reasonable commercial standards. There appears to be no dispute regarding the good faith of appellee in paying the forgeries. The issue is whether its methods of ascertaining unauthorized signatures on its depositor's checks met the standard of care under the circumstances.

Implied in the debtor/creditor relationship between a bank and its checking account depositor is the contractual undertaking on the part of the bank that it will only discharge its obligations to the depositor upon his authorized signature. The mere fact that the bank has paid a forged check does not mean the bank has breached its duty of ordinary care, however.

At trial, an operations officer for appellee testified as to the methods employed during the period the forgeries occurred to discover unauthorized signatures on depositor's checks. She testified that checks were organized so that a bundle from the same account could be compared with the authorized signature on the bank's signature card. A staff of five filing clerks handled an average of approximately 1,000 checks each per hour in this manner. She testified it was common for a file clerk to become familiar with the drawer's signature in large accounts such as appellants'. An official of a large Arizona bank testified that tellers and file clerks are not trained to be handwriting experts. He testified that in his opinion, because most large banks have completely abandoned physical comparison of checks with the signature card, the system employed by appellee was better than the norm of the banking community in Southern Arizona.

In view of this and other evidence, we conclude that there was sufficient evidence to support findings 13 and 14 and the judgment entered below. Similar methods of comparing drawer's signatures have been upheld as constituting ordinary care and being within reasonable commercial standards across the country.

Affirmed.

Material Alteration

A material alteration is one that changes the contract of any of the parties. Changes that do not affect the agreement of the parties are not considered material. An example would be the addition of a co-maker or surety (Section 3–407, Comment 1).

A holder in due course who takes after a material alteration may enforce the instrument but only according to its original tenor (Section 3–407). If a person who is obligated on the instrument is negligent and that negligence contributes substantially to the instrument's being materially altered, the holder in due course may enforce the instrument in its altered form (Section 3–406).

In protecting the rights of a holder in due course, the UCC treats an incomplete instrument as it does one that has been materially altered. A holder in due course may enforce the instrument as it has been completed, even though it was completed in a manner that was not authorized (Section 3–407[3]). This means that a check signed by the drawer in blank and stolen or lost is enforceable by a holder in due course against the drawer as it is completed by the thief or finder.

Fraud in the Execution

The basis of this defense is similar to that underlying forgery and material alteration. A holder in due course attempting to recover on a forged instrument is not allowed to recover because the defendant never agreed to be bound. Where a material alteration has occurred, the defendant's liability is limited because he or she did not agree to the instrument's terms as they now appear. In fraud in the execution, also called fraud in the factum, the party defending escapes liability because he or she was misled as to what was being signed.

This might happen in a number of ways. Extreme cases exist in which a promissory note was cleverly hidden under another document that a person supposedly signed. Upon removal of the cover document, the signature is on the note, which the payee then negotiates. The more usual situation is one in which a buyer signs a promissory note or some other type of commercial paper, being assured by the seller that the instrument is merely an authorization to conduct a credit investigation or a receipt. In these situations, because the signer never intended to make a promise, no liability exists. For this defense to be successful, the defendant must be able to show that no reasonable opportunity existed to discover what was actually being signed. If the defendant acted carelessly either in not reading the instrument being signed or in some other manner, the defense will fail.

Fraud in the execution differs from the false statement made to induce a person to enter into a contract. This is called fraud in the procurement or fraud in the inducement. Fraud in the inducement is not a defense against a holder in due course. Although it is a defense in a contract case, contractual defenses of this kind may be asserted only against ordinary holders. These defenses are examined in some detail later in this chapter.

Infancy

As indicated in Chapter 10, a minor has the right to rescind most contractual obligations. The extent to which this right exists depends upon state law. Under the UCC, a minor may raise the defense of infancy against a holder in due course to the same extent that infancy is a contractual defense according to state law governing the transaction (Section 3–305[2][a]). For example, in most states a minor purchasing a stereo is allowed to disaffirm the contract since the item is not a necessity. If the minor signs a note as payment for the stereo, the note is not enforceable even if transferred to a holder in due course who has no knowledge of the maker's minority.

Other Incapacity

Mental incapacity and incapacity as a result of intoxication can be used as defenses against a holder in due course in limited instances. Incapacity other than infancy is available against a holder in due course if applicable state laws "render the underlying obligation a nullity" (Section 3–305[1][b]). In effect this means that the underlying contract must be void, not just voidable, if incapacity is to be used successfully against a holder in due course. In most states contracts by mental incompetents are void only if the incompetent has been adjudicated insane. A similar rule applies to intoxication. If the promisor's intoxication was so extreme that he or she could not have intended to contract, the agreement is void. In a similar situation a person obligated on commercial paper has a good defense against the holder in due course.

Duress and Illegality

Duress and illegality are treated by the UCC in a manner similar to incapacity other than infancy (Section 3–305[1][b]). In both instances, if applicable state law renders the contract void, duress or illegality can be asserted against a holder in due course. In most states a contract secured by duress is voidable, not void; thus duress is generally unavailable as a defense against a holder in due course. If, however, the duress is so extreme that the agreement is void from the beginning, duress is a good defense. Illegality is treated in a comparable manner, as the following case indicates.

New Jersey Mortgage & Investment Corp. v. Berenyi

Superior Court of New Jersey, Appellate Division

356 A.2d 421 (1976)

New Jersey Mortgage and Investment Corp. (plaintiff-respondent) was the holder in due course of a negotiable promissory note. Andrew and Anna Berenyi (defendants-appellants), the makers, refused to pay and the holder in due course sued on the note. Berenyi argued that no liability existed because the transaction was illegal. The trial court entered judgment for plaintiff and defendant appealed. Held: Affirmed.

Before Judges Kolovsky, Bischoff and Botter

Per Curiam

Defendant Anna Berenyi appeals from a judgment for plaintiff based on the following stipulated facts:

1. On May 25, 1964, in a proceeding brought by Arthur J. Sills, Attorney General of the State of New Jersey, against Kroyden Industries, Inc., a corporation of the State of New Jersey, in the Superior Court of New Jersey, Chancery Division, Essex County, a Consent Order was made by Honorable Ward J. Herbert, J.S.C., which Order enjoined the said Kroyden Industries, Inc. from committing certain acts or making certain representations with its customers in connection with the sale of carpeting.
2. In August, 1964, the defendants, Andrew Berenyi (now deceased) and Anna Berenyi, were referred from a participant in a sales scheme of Kroyden Industries, Inc., for the purchase of carpeting.
3. An employee of Kroyden Industries, Inc. offered, in violation of the injunction aforesaid, to give to the defendants carpeting which, if the contract price of $1,100.00 was paid, was worth $44.00 per square yard without making any payments as long as they referred prospective buyers to Kroyden Industries, Inc.
4. The defendants agreed to this plan since the carpeting would not cost them anything as long as they made the required referrals.
5. The defendants, relying upon the above offer and representations signed a negotiable promissory note for $1,521.00. Said instrument was negotiated to the plaintiff herein.
6. The plaintiff is a holder in due course for value of the negotiable promissory note sued upon and had no knowledge or notice of the proceedings brought against Kroyden Industries, Inc.; and had no knowledge or notice of the entry of the Order in the Chancery Division by Judge Herbert; and had no knowledge or notice that Kroyden Industries, Inc., violated the aforementioned injunctive Order.

The trial judge ruled that the fact that the note was obtained as part of a transaction entered into by Kroyden Industries, Inc. (Kroyden) in violation of the injunctive order was not a defense in an action brought by plaintiff, whose status as a holder in due course, with no knowledge or notice of the injunctive order, was admitted.

The controlling issue presented is whether the defense here asserted is a "real" defense or a "personal" defense. Real defenses are available against even a holder in due course of a negotiable instrument; personal defenses are not available against such a holder. We affirm since we are satisfied that the defense presented is not a "real" defense.

Defendant argues that since the transaction which resulted in the execution and delivery of defendant's note was engaged in by Kroyden in violation of the injunctive order, the transaction was "illegal and thus a nullity under N.J.S.A. 12A:3-305," which provides in pertinent part as follows:

> To the extent that a holder is a holder in due course he takes the instrument free from . . .
> (2) all defenses of any party to the instrument with whom the holder has not dealt except . . .
> (b) such other incapacity, or duress, or illegality of the transaction, as renders the obligation of the party a nullity; and . . .

However, the fact that it was illegal for Kroyden to enter into the transaction did not by reason of that fact render defendant's obligation under the note she executed a nullity.

On the contrary, as noted in the New Jersey Study Comment on N.J.S.A. 12A:3-305(2)(b):

> In New Jersey, a holder in due course takes free and clear of the defense of illegality, unless the statute which declares the act illegal also indicates that payment thereunder is void. . . . (See *e.g.,* N.J.S.A. 2A:40-3 which specifically provides that notes given in payment of a gambling debt "shall be utterly void and of no effect.") . . . where no such statute is involved, it has been held that a negotiable instrument which is rooted in an illegal transaction or stems from a transaction prohibited by statute or public policy is no reason for refusing to enforce the instrument in the hands of a holder in due course.

There being no statute ordaining that a note obtained in violation of an injunction is void and unenforceable, the illegality involved is not a "real" defense; the note is enforceable in the hands of a holder in due course who had no knowledge or notice of the injunction.

The judgment is affirmed. No costs.

CASE NOTE:

This case is an example of the manner in which negotiable instruments used in consumer transactions can injure unsophisticated buyers. A substantial number of states have adopted statutes requiring that notes executed in connection with a retail installment contract be labeled "Consumer Note" and additionally providing that such a note should not be negotiable. The Federal Trade Commission also has adopted a rule limiting the use of negotiable instruments in consumer transactions.

Discharge in Bankruptcy

Providing individuals and firms that are insolvent with an opportunity to make a fresh start has long been an important public policy. Where a holder in due course is a creditor of the bankrupt and for one reason or another the claim of the holder in due course is not asserted until the bankrupt is discharged, the discharge provides a good defense.

LIMITED DEFENSES

An ordinary holder of commercial paper is entitled to payment unless a signature necessary to liability is missing or the obligor establishes some defense. The ordinary holder is subject to all the universal defenses as well as a wide variety of additional claims and defenses. These additional defenses are usually referred to as limited or personal defenses.

Limited defenses differ from universal defenses in that they are based upon legally acceptable reasons for not performing a contract while the universal are based generally upon the idea that no contract ever existed. For example, fraud in the execution is a universal defense good even against a holder in due course because the defendant never intended to execute a negotiable instrument. On the other hand, fraud in the procurement is merely a personal defense. It is not good against a holder in due course but is good against an ordinary holder because the defendant intended to contract, although wrongfully induced to do so.

Under the UCC, an ordinary holder of commercial paper is subject to all valid claims against it as well as the following defenses:

1. Breach of contract
2. Lack or failure of consideration
3. Nonperformance of a condition precedent
4. Nondelivery
5. Acquisition of the instrument through theft by any person

Although these are the chief personal defenses, other defenses may also be asserted against the ordinary holder.

The fact that numerous defenses can be raised against a holder does not limit the viability of commercial paper appreciably. In most instances the obligor has no defense and the holder collects. Additionally, as the status of holder in due course is relatively easy for the good faith transferee of commercial paper to attain, people in the business community are generally not reluctant to use these instruments in their transactions.

REVIEW PROBLEMS

1. Henry Jaroszewski and his wife agreed to purchase frozen food from Merit Food Corporation to be delivered in three deliveries. At the time they entered into this agreement, they signed a "purchase and sales agreement." They also signed a form entitled "Request for a personal loan"; the second page was a promissory note; the third

page was a credit application; and the fourth provided for an authorization by the purchasers for the bank to pay the proceeds of the loan ($1,850) to Merit. The purchasers became dissatisfied with the food after receiving $200 worth, and they refused to accept further deliveries. The bank in the meantime had paid Merit the $1,850. The purchasers now claim Merit's representatives fraudulently represented the nature of the forms they were signing. They also claim the bank knew of Merit's misconduct because it had dealt with Merit on similar transactions in the past. Must Jaroszewski pay the bank? Waterbury Savings Bank v. Jaroszewski, 238 A.2d446 (4th Cir. 1967).

2. Linda Mesnik opened a checking account with the Hempstead Bank in the name of Linda Mesnik Agency. During the next eighteen months approximately $60,000 was deposited and paid out by checks. The account was then closed. Mesnik claims that the signatures on many of the checks were not hers but unauthorized forgeries and the checks were cashed as part of a conspiracy between her husband and a bank employee. The bank contends that Mesnik's claim is barred by the statute of limitations since she did not report the unauthorized signatures within one year. Mesnik's response is that the statements were intercepted by her husband. Would Mesnik be successful? Discuss. (Mesnik v. Hempstead Bank, 443 N.Y. S2d 579 (1980).

3. Citizens and Southern National Bank sued R. C. Bell and Ruby Bell as co-makers of several collateral installment notes. R. C. Bell filed a petition in bankruptcy and proceedings against him were stayed. Ruby Bell admitted that she executed the notes along with R. C. Bell, but she claimed she did so as a "mere accommodation indorser." Ruby Bell's pretrial deposition indicated that she did not directly receive the proceeds from the notes and that the bank failed to proceed against the collateral. She

argued that as a result she was discharged. Would Citizens and Southern be successful in its action against her? Discuss. Bell v. Citizens and Southern Nat'l Bank, 258 S.E. 2d 774 (1979).

4. Bergfield contracted to sell Kirby a parcel of real estate for $352,560. The contract called for a $20,000 payment at the closing. The closing was completed in the office of Bergfield's attorney and all necessary documents were executed by both parties. All of the documents except the check were retained by Bergfield's attorney until Bergfield could ascertain whether or not the check was good. The following day Bergfield went to his bank and requested the cashier to phone Kirby's bank to determine if there were sufficient funds in Kirby's account to cover the check. The person who answered the phone indicated that Kirby's account did not contain sufficient funds. Unknown to this person, the bank's president had arranged with Kirby to cover the check when it was presented. As the contract contained a "time is of the essence" clause Bergfield treated the contract as breached and refused to allow his attorney to deliver the deed. He also retained Kirby's deposit. Kirby now sues for specific performance. Would he be successful? Kirby v. Bergfield, 182 N.E.2d 205 (1970).

5. About 9:30 A.M. on July 17, 1952, Evern Jones got his mail at the post office in the City of Jackson. In one of the letters was a payroll check of American Book Company in the sum of $432.53, payable to the order of Jones. He wrote his name on the back of the check in the post office and started across the street to a nearby bank. He had several other pieces of mail in his hands. The wind, blowing at almost gale proportions, blew the mail out of his hands. Passers-by came to his assistance, but he was not successful in retrieving his check. He immediately reported his loss to

the bank, and asked the Book Company to stop payment. This was done.

Between two and three o'clock that afternoon, Mrs. Tommie Davis, an employee of the White System of Jackson, Inc., took a telephone call ostensibly from Leon Orman, at Five Point Service Station, who advised that one of their customers, with a check larger than they could handle, wished to buy some tires, and inquired if the System would cash it. She asked Mr. White, the president, what to do, and he advised that, if it was a company check, to cash it. About twenty or thirty minutes later, a man came into the office and presented the check.

Mrs. Martha Lewis, another employee, took the check, and Mrs. Davis explained the previous telephone conversation. In addition to the name Jones, there purported to be an endorsement of Five Point Service Station and Leon Orman. Mrs. Lewis thought the man was Leon Orman. Because of the size of the check, she asked Mr. Taylor, the office manager, about it, but he bade her get Mr. White's approval. The White System frequently accommodated people by cashing checks for them, and generally the checks were brought into the office by errand boys or employees.

White System seeks to recover the amount of the check on which American Book Company had stopped payment. Would White System be successful? Explain. American Book Company v. White System of Jackson, 78 So.2d 582 (1955).

Checks and Electronic Fund Transfers

T his chapter discusses two important subjects dealing with the transfer of funds: checks and the electronic transfer of funds.

A check is a specialized type of draft, which is an instrument ordering one person to pay another. In the case of a check, the drawer of the check orders a bank to pay someone on the drawer's behalf. Thus a check is a draft drawn on a bank and payable on demand.

In the last few years, electronic fund transfers have become another method of transferring funds to take the place of checks. An electronic fund transfer involves the transfer of funds from one account to another account, not through the use of a piece of paper, but through an electronic transfer generated by plugging the appropriate data into a machine. This new form of transferring money poses special problems, some of which are discussed in this chapter.

CHECKS

The Bank and Its Customers

The relationship between a bank and its customer depends upon the status of the customer. Section 4–104(1)(e) of the Uniform Commercial Code defines a customer as "any

538

person having an account with a bank or for whom a bank has agreed to collect items and includes a bank carrying an account with another bank." Thus a customer can be someone other than a depositor. Generally, though, a customer is thought of as a depositor.

The Bank as Debtor. Ordinarily, when a person makes a deposit to his or her checking or savings account, the bank becomes a debtor of the depositor, who is then a creditor of the bank. If the depositor makes a special deposit, however, the bank will become the agent or trustee for the depositor. A deposit is general unless there is a specific agreement or understanding between the parties that the deposit is to be a special deposit. Whether a deposit is special or general depends on the bona fide contract between the depositor and the bank. For a special deposit to exist, there must be an express or clearly implied agreement that the deposit is made for some particular purpose—for example, safekeeping. Otherwise, the deposit is general.

As a debtor of the general depositor, the bank is bound by an implied contract to repay the deposit, which may be money or other items, on the depositor's demand or order. The relationship between the bank and its depositor is determined by the terms of the deposit agreement, which is an express contract between the parties and is binding on them. An example of such a contract is the signature card signed by a depositor when opening his or her account at the bank. The debtor-creditor relationship attaches immediately upon the depositor's making the deposit. (Note that the provisions of Article 4 may be varied by agreement, but no agreement can disclaim a bank's responsibility for its own lack of good faith or failure to exercise ordinary care.)

The Bank as Agent. Even though the bank is a debtor, in discharging its obligations to the depositor the bank is also his or her agent and is bound by the rules of principal and agent. In

this situation, the bank is the agent and the customer the principal. This relationship arises, for example, when the bank pays checks drawn upon it. Thus the bank's relationship to a depositor is twofold: debtor-creditor and principal-agent.

Another situation where a principal-agent relationship arises between a bank and its depositor is when the bank seeks to obtain collection of an item for its depositor, who is the owner of the check. It should be noted that the status as agent is only a presumption and may be rebutted by evidence of a clear contrary intent.

Death or Incompetence of a Customer

In light of the principal-agent relationship between a bank and its customer, one might conclude from agency law that the bank's authority to act terminates upon the death or declaration of incompetency of the principal. Because of the large number of items handled by a bank, and the possible liability of the bank for a wrongful dishonor, the UCC instead relieves a bank of liability for payment of any instrument before it has notice of the death or incompetency of the drawer. The bank may pay (and another bank consequently may accept) an item until it knows of the death or of the adjudicated incompetence and has a reasonable opportunity to act on it.

Even if the bank knows of the death of a customer, the UCC permits the bank to pay or certify a check drawn on it for ten days after it receives notice. The bank may pay or certify a check unless a person claiming an interest in the account orders the bank to stop payment during this ten-day period. Suppose Smith writes a check on March 10, and someone presents it for payment on March 15. Even if Smith dies on March 11, and the bank knows it, the bank may honor the check. On the other hand, if an heir notifies the bank to stop payment of the check, the bank must comply.

CHECKS GENERALLY

Failure to Indorse

If a customer deposits a check written by someone else, the bank will credit the customer's account for the amount of the check. The bank (called a depository bank) will then attempt to collect the check from the drawee bank (the bank on which the check was written). The customer could, of course, go directly to the drawee bank and cash the check, but this would be very time-consuming. By depositing the check, the customer authorizes the bank to collect the check for him or her.

What if the customer fails to indorse the check? Must the bank obtain the customer's signature? An order instrument must be indorsed in order for a proper negotiation to occur. Since we all make mistakes, the UCC has a special provision to speed up the collection process in this situation. Generally, the depository bank may simply supply the customer's indorsement (Section 4–205[1]). This eliminates the necessity of calling the customer back to the bank to indorse the check.

Not an Assignment of Funds

Merely because one receives a check from someone else does not mean that one is entitled to the funds in the other's account. A check does not operate as an assignment of funds in the hands of the drawee (Section 3–409[1]). A bank is not liable on a check until it accepts it. As for the holder of the check, he or she has no recourse against the bank when it fails to accept a check. The holder of a check that has been dishonored must attempt to collect from the drawer of the check or from one of the indorsers.

Overdrafts

If the bank decides to honor a check, it may do so even though the charge creates an overdraft. A customer who writes a check for $550, but who has deposited only $500 in his or her account, has in effect authorized the bank to pay $550 to the payee. By implication, the customer has agreed to reimburse the bank for the other $50. The bank has no obligation to honor such a check because it creates an overdraft. At most banks, the customer will soon discover that his or her check has bounced.

Postdating

Sometimes, a customer will postdate a check —that is, he or she will issue the check before the date on the check has arrived. For example, the customer may give a check to the payee on March 1 but date it March 15. This is done when the person giving the check does not intend the check to be presented before March 15 (and very likely does not have sufficient funds in his or her account to cover the check on March 1). The UCC indicates that the negotiability of an instrument that is undated, antedated, or postdated is unaffected (Section 3–114[1]). The time such a postdated check is payable is determined by the stated date on the instrument. Thus, if a customer writes a check on March 1 dated March 15, it is not payable until March 15. This is true even though a check is generally a demand instrument—that is, one payable on the demand of the payee or other holder of the instrument. The drawer hopes in this situation to pay his or her obligations on March 15. As the payee has physical possession of the instrument, the payee may run the check through on March 15. Unfortunately, this arrangement is filled with danger.

First, there is at least the argument that if the check goes through on March 15 and there are no funds to cover it, the drawer has issued an insufficient-funds check. A second possibility is that the payee will wrongfully cash the check before the date on the check. This also may result in the check's not being honored if the drawer does not have sufficient funds in his or her account. The drawer could be prosecuted in this situation. The more prudent practice is to not write checks until one has sufficient funds in the account to cover them. The Fair Debt Collection Practices Act makes it illegal for a debt collector to take a post-dated check.

Failure of the Bank to Honor a Check

What if the bank fails to pay a check written by the drawer when it ought to have done so? The bank will be liable to the drawer for any damages proximately caused by a wrongful dishonor of the check. If the bank merely made a mistake, its liability is limited to actual damages proved. The UCC explicitly recognizes damages for arrest and prosecution and other consequential damages proximately caused by the wrongful dishonor. If a drawer wrote a check that the bank wrongfully failed to honor, he or she could be prosecuted. (In most states the drawer probably would not be arrested. Most states require that notice of the dishonor be given to the drawer and an opportunity to make the check good. During this period, the drawer probably would be able to straighten the matter out with the bank.)

A wrongful dishonor is different from a failure to exercise ordinary care in the handling of an item. See UCC 4–103(5) for the damages stipulated when a bank fails to exercise ordinary care.

Stale Checks

A bank also has no obligation to its checking-account customers to honor uncertified checks presented more than six months after date. Such a check is referred to as a stale check (Section 4–404). On the other hand, the bank may honor such a check if it acts in good faith. If one receives a dividend check from GM on August 1 but neglects to cash it until March 1 of the following year, the check is stale. Nonetheless, it would seem reasonable to cash such a check, as GM presumably would want the check paid.

STOP PAYMENT

Right to Stop

Section 4–403 of the UCC gives a bank customer the right to stop payment of a check. Subsection 1 requires the customer to notify the bank in such time and manner as to give the bank a reasonable opportunity to act on the stop-payment order. The order must be received by the bank before it has paid a check in cash, accepted the check, or certified it.

Under Section 4–403(2), an oral order is effective for fourteen days; a written order is effective for six months. A written stop-payment order can be renewed for additional periods of six months. In the event a check is paid over a binding stop-payment order, the burden is on the bank's customer to establish any loss incurred as a result of paying the check.

The right to stop payment is that of the drawer alone. An indorsee or payee has no right to order payment stopped on a check.

Section 4–405(2) does provide, when a bank's customer has died, that any person claiming an interest in the account of the deceased may stop payment on checks drawn on his or her account.

Defenses

Even though the drawer of the check has the right to stop payment, he or she remains liable to any holder of the instrument unless the drawer has a defense good against the holder. The drawer of a check cannot issue a check to a payee and expect to escape liability simply by stopping payment on the check. The drawer must establish a defense that can be successfully asserted against the holder of the instrument—for example, failure of consideration. If one writes a $450 check to an appliance store for a refrigerator, but the store never delivers the refrigerator, one would be able to stop payment on the check. If the store sued, one could successfully assert failure of consideration as a defense against the store. The store may not proceed against the bank for refusing to honor the check because a check is not an assignment of funds in the account of the drawer.

If the drawer of a check is so unfortunate as to write a check like the drawer in the example above, and it is transferred to a holder in due course, or someone having the rights of a holder in due course, he or she may be liable on the check even if he or she stopped payment on it. The defense of failure of consideration is a personal defense and therefore may not be asserted successfully against a holder in due course. On the other hand, a real defense, like adjudicated insanity, may be asserted against a holder in due course.

When a bank pays a check over a stop-payment order, Section 4–407 gives the payor bank a right of subrogation. Subrogation means the bank acquires whatever rights in the check the drawer had in that instrument. This right is given to prevent unjust enrichment to the extent necessary to prevent a loss to the bank by reason of its improper payment of a check.

Payment Over Stop-Payment Order

What if the bank pays a holder in due course over a stop-payment order? Section 4–407(a) gives the bank the rights of the person it pays. As the drawer has no defense against that person unless he or she has a real defense, the bank will be able to collect the amount paid from its customer, even though the check was paid over a stop-payment order. (Note that the burden of establishing a loss is on the customer under Section 4–403[3].)

Conversely, if the bank reimburses its customer when it pays a check over a stop-payment order, it receives any rights of the drawer against the payee or any other holder of the check with respect to the transaction out of which the check arose.

What if a drawer issues a check as indicated earlier for a refrigerator but the store never delivers the refrigerator? If the bank honors the check over a stop-payment order, the bank may proceed against the store for the amount it received under the check. This section does not permit, of course, a double recovery by the bank.

Comment 8 to Section 4–403 recognizes inferentially that a bank and its customer may agree under Section 4–103(1) to waive or *limit* the bank's liability for improper payment over a stop-payment order, as long as the payment is not due to a lack of ordinary care or a lack of good faith. There is a split of authority regarding the validity of these agreements. A few cases hold that such a provision is not binding because it was not supported by consideration. The general rule seems to be that these agreements are, in fact, valid.

The following case discusses the issue of stop payment orders.

THOMAS v. MARINE MIDLAND TINKERS NATIONAL BANK

Civil Court of the City of New York
381 N.Y.S.2d 797 (1976)

Plaintiff Thomas commenced this action to recover the sum of $2500 from the defendant bank, claiming that defendant wrongfully paid a check drawn against his account after receiving a proper and timely stop-payment order. The court ruled for Thomas.

Shanley N. Egeth, Judge

On Dec. 8, 1973, plaintiff entered into agreement to purchase two rugs from one Ralph Gallo for a price of $10,500. A $2500 deposit was given by delivery of a post-dated check, #221, dated Dec. 10, 1973, and drawn upon plaintiff's account at the defendant bank's 140 Broadway, New York City branch. Plaintiff agreed to pay the balance of the purchase price, to wit: $8000, by Dec. 30, 1973, and took the smaller rug home that day. At opening, on Dec. 10, 1973, plaintiff went to the branch of defendant bank where his account was maintained, spoke to an officer, Kenneth Hurley, with whom he had prior business relations, and directed that payment be stopped upon the subject check. All required information was correctly given (except the check was described as #22 rather than #221, the correct number), and a stop payment memo was issued by the bank. On the afternoon of the next day, Dec. 11, 1973, the check was presented for payment at the very same branch, and it was cashed. Thereafter, plaintiff's account was debited the $2500 paid on the check. The same day, without knowledge that the check had been cashed, plaintiff telephoned Gallo, told him the contract was rescinded, and asked him to pick up his rug. Two or three days later, the rug was picked up at plaintiff's apartment. Plaintiff had no knowledge that the check had been cashed until he received his January bank statement. He called Gallo, demanding return of the $2500. The request was refused with an indication that Gallo might seek to enforce the purchase agreement. The defendant bank rejected plaintiff's request to restore the $2500 to his account. At present plaintiff has no rug in his possession nor does he have his $2500.

UCC Sec. 4–403(1) explicitly provides:

> A customer may by order to his bank stop payment of any item payable for his account but the order must be received at such time and in such manner as to afford the bank a reasonable opportunity to act on it prior to any action by the bank with respect to the item described in Section 4–303.

It is undisputed that a detailed direction was given to the defendant to stop payment on the check in question (except for a single digit mistake on the check number), the order was confirmed in writing early in the morning, and the subject check was paid at the very same branch in the afternoon of the following day. Under these circumstances, I find that adequate notice and a reasonable opportunity was given to the bank, and that it must be held accountable for its act in making payment of the check in contravention of the stop payment order.

A day and one half is more than reasonable notice to enforce a stop order on a check presented at the very same branch, and payment of the item by the bank thereafter constitutes a breach of its obligations to honor the stop order. The normal problem of reasonable computer lag when dealing with a great number of other branches of a large bank has no relevancy to the facts at bar, where all transactions occurred in a single branch. The single digital mistake in describing the check in the stop order is deemed trivial, and insignificant. Enough information was supplied to the bank to reasonably provide it with sufficient information to comply with the stop payment order. The bank is therefore held responsible for its act of improperly making payment upon the check.

Defendant bank has virtually rested on plaintiff's case, in that no affirmative defense has been asserted or proved and no real evidence has been adduced by said defendant. The defendant contends that plaintiff has failed to prove a prima facie case in that no evidence was introduced in the plaintiff's case to negate the ultimate right of the payee of the stopped check to retain the proceeds thereof.

In this case, the defendant bank chose to try its case against the plaintiff alone without asserting any affirmative defense as to non loss, or adducing any evidence to negate the claimed loss at trial. The defendant bank chose rather to maintain a position that plaintiff was required to come forward with evidence as to the underlying transaction to negate any inference of non loss or lesser loss in order to prove plaintiff's prima facie case.

As previously stated the bank's position in this regard is in error under the law existing before and after the enactment of the Code. Therefore plaintiff has proven his prima facie case and defendant's motion to dismiss on that ground must be denied.

Plaintiff's good faith act of surrendering possession of the rug to the payee after giving defendant a stop payment order, and his assumption of compliance therewith by the defendant, is understandable and reasonable. Unless done without good faith, such surrender certainly may not defeat defendant's statutory accountability under UCC, section 4–403(1) for failure to comply with a proper stop order. The existence of defendant's subrogation right to stand in the shoes of the payee (UCC section 4–407[b]) does not negate the obligation of the subrogee bank to come forward with some evidence in support of any such claimed right. In this case defendant chose not to do so. Defendant therefore failed to produce any evidence to negate plaintiff's prima facie case. Under the circumstances, there are no issues of fact to be determined regarding plaintiff's failure to meet his burden of establishing the fact and amount of loss under UCC section 4–403(3) because of the defendant's failure to come forward with anything which controverts plaintiff's prima facie showing of loss.

Accordingly, defendant's motions are denied and plaintiff is granted judgment against the defendant in the sum of $2500 together with interest, costs, and disbursements as demanded in the complaint.

CERTIFICATION

As clearly stated in Section 3–411, certification is an acceptance. A bank has no obligation to certify a check in the absence of a specific agreement to do so. But once a bank has certified a check, it is obligated to honor it. When it certifies a check, the bank becomes primarily liable on the instrument. That being the case, there is no right as far as the drawer is concerned to stop payment of a certified check.

Certification of a check by a bank at the drawer's request does no more than affirm the genuineness of the drawer's signature and to indicate that there will be funds on deposit to meet the item when the check is presented for payment. If the drawer obtains certification of his or her check, the drawer remains secondarily liable, although the bank is primarily liable.

The holder of a check may also have the check certified. The drawer and all prior indorsers will be released from liability if the holder takes this action. Of course, a holder could present the check for payment in this situation; thus it seems reasonable to release the drawer and indorsers from liability.

It is possible for a certified check to be indorsed after the bank has certified it. In this instance, the certification remains effective, and the indorser will have all the duties imposed by Section 3–414.

UNAUTHORIZED SIGNATURES AND ALTERATIONS

Customer's Duty to Discover and Report

The customer of a bank has a duty to discover and report to the bank forgeries and alterations on his or her checks. This duty arises once the bank has sent its customer both a statement of his or her account and the items honored by the bank (Section 4–406[1]). The customer must exercise "reasonable care and promptness" in examining the statement and items to discover unauthorized signatures or any alterations. If he or she discovers an improper signature or an alteration, the next step is to notify the bank "promptly." This means the customer must contact the appropriate person at the bank to enable the bank to take action on the check. Thus, after a customer receives a statement accompanied by the checks honored by the bank, he or she must review them to make certain they are proper.

If the customer fails to comply, he or she may not assert an unauthorized signature or any alteration as a defense against the bank if the bank establishes that it suffered a loss as a result of the customer's failure to comply with Section 4–406(1). The burden of proof is on the bank to establish that it suffered a loss.

Acts by the Same Wrongdoer

Once a customer has received a statement and an item on which there has been an unauthorized signature or alteration, a second rule comes into play that covers additional acts by the same wrongdoer. This rule covers indorsements as well as unauthorized signatures of the customer and alterations. A customer has a reasonable period of time not exceeding fourteen calendar days to notify the bank of any unauthorized signature or alteration. If the customer fails to notify the bank, any loss caused by an unauthorized signature or alteration by the same wrongdoer after this fourteen-day period will be borne by the customer.

This puts the burden on the customer to police his or her account in order to prevent a wrongdoer from continuing his or her improper actions. Once a customer notifies the bank of any such unauthorized signature or alteration, the risk of loss shifts back to the bank to guard against future unauthorized signatures or alterations by the same wrongdoer.

Bank's Burden of Proof

Before a bank may charge its customer's account pursuant to either Section 4–406(2)(a) or (b), the bank must establish that the customer failed to exercise reasonable care and promptness in examining his or her statement and the items included with the statement and that the customer failed to promptly notify the bank. Even if the bank succeeds in establishing this, however, the risk of loss shifts back if the customer proves a lack of ordinary care on the part of the bank in paying an item (Section 4–406[3]).

If the bank loses the suit against its customer on an unauthorized drawer's signature, it may proceed against anyone who broke the presenter's warranty that he or she had no knowledge that the drawer's signature was unauthorized (Section 4–207).

FORGED SIGNATURE OF THE DRAWER

Signature of Drawer Required

For an instrument to be negotiable, it must be signed by the maker or drawer. Section 3–401(1) clearly indicates that no one is liable, even to a holder in due course, on an instrument unless his or her signature appears on it. Thus, where someone forges the signature of the drawer on his or her checks, the drawer is not liable. Only if a customer's authorized signature appears on a check may the bank charge his or her account.

The UCC assumes that the bank will recognize the signatures of its customers and will not honor forgeries. If a bank honors a check that the customer alleges to be a forgery, the bank must establish that the signature is genuine. Even so, Section 3–307(1)(b) states that "the signature is presumed to be genuine or authorized" except if the signer died or has become incompetent. This means that, until evidence is introduced supporting a finding that the signature is a forgery or unauthorized, the plaintiff is not required to prove that it is authentic.

Other Persons Liable

Assuming that the bank paid a check, and the customer establishes that his or her signature was unauthorized, the bank may not charge his or her account. It may be, however, that the bank can collect from someone other than its customer.

One possibility is for the bank to bring suit based on the theory of breach of warranty. Section 4–207 indicates that each customer or collecting bank who obtains payment of a check and each prior customer and collecting bank warrants to the payor bank that he or she has no knowledge that the signature of the drawer is unauthorized (Section 4–207[1][b]).

Another possibility is to sue the forger. Section 3–404(1) states that, even though an unauthorized signature does not bind a customer of the bank, it operates as the signature of the unauthorized signer in favor of any person who in good faith pays the instrument or takes it for value.

Of course, if a customer ratifies an unauthorized signature, the bank may charge the customer's account.

Negligence by Customer

The bank may also charge the customer's account if the customer was negligent. Section 3–406 states that if a drawer's negligence substantially contributes to a material alteration of an instrument or to the making of an unauthorized signature, he or she may not assert the lack of authority against a bank who pays the instrument in good faith and in accordance with reasonable commercial standards. Comment 7 to Section 3–406 indicates that the most obvious case of negligence is a drawer who uses an automatic signing device and is negligent in looking after it.

Section 4–406 imposes a duty on a bank's customers to examine their checks and notify the bank promptly of any forgeries. Failure to comply with this rule may result in a customer's being unable to raise the defense of forgery against the bank.

The following case illustrates a customer's duty to examine his or her checks.

ZENITH SYNDICATE, INC. v. MARINE MIDLAND BANK

Civil Court, New York County
23 UCC Rep. 1267 (1978)

The defendant, Marine Midland Bank, charged certain checks to the account of Zenith Syndicate, the plaintiff. The plaintiff failed to examine its monthly statement and report the forgery of its signature on these checks. The court ruled, therefore, that the bank was entitled to charge Zenith Syndicate's account for the amount of the checks.

Sorkin, J.

This is an action to recover the amounts of forged checks drawn on a bank and charged to its customer's account. Plaintiff corporation maintained an account with defendant bank in which either its president or vice president was authorized to sign checks. Between February and November of 1972, plaintiff's bookkeeper drew approximately twenty checks on which she forged the signature of the then president. These checks were paid by the bank and charged to plaintiff's account.

During the period in which the account was maintained, monthly bank statements with cancelled checks were sent to plaintiff's office. The task of examining the cancelled checks and reconciling the account was delegated to the bookkeeper, the same person who forged the checks. Not until the account was transferred to another bank in November of 1972 did plaintiff's principals learn of the forgeries. Defendant was unable to recover the sum of $4,278.68 paid on those checks and refused to credit plaintiff's account in this amount.

The duties and liabilities of the parties in a case such as this are governed by UCC Section 4–406. That statute, in its relevant part, provides that

> when a bank sends to its customer a statement of account accompanied by items paid in good faith in support of the debit entries . . . or otherwise . . . makes the statement and items available to the customer, the customer must exercise reasonable care and promptness to examine the statement and items to discover his unauthorized signature . . . and must notify the bank promptly after discovery thereof. (Subdivision 1)

If the bank customer fails to comply with the duties imposed on it by subdivision (1) of the section, it is precluded under subdivision (2) from asserting against the bank:

> (a) his unauthorized signature . . . if the bank also establishes that it suffered a loss by reason of such failure; and (b) an unauthorized signature . . . by the same wrongdoer on any other item paid in good faith by the bank after the first item and statement was available to the customer for a reasonable period not exceeding fourteen calendar days and before the bank receives notification from the customer of any such unauthorized signature. . . .

Subdivision (3) of the section renders the preclusion imposed by Subdivision (2) inapplicable "if the customer establishes lack of ordinary care on the part of the bank in paying the item." In other words, even if the customer was negligent or for any other reason failed to discover the forged signatures after the bank had sent a statement, if the customer proves the bank was negligent also, the preclusion rule does not apply.

In the present case, after defendant sent plaintiff its monthly statements, it was plaintiff's duty to discover the forgeries and plaintiff was not relieved thereof merely because a dishonest employee concealed the wrongdoing. "A depositor cannot be charged with the knowledge which the dishonest employee had gained while he was stealing from him but 'a depositor must be held chargeable with knowledge of all the facts that a reasonable and prudent examination of the returned bank statements, vouchers and certificates would have disclosed had it been made by a person on the depositor's behalf who had not participated in the forgeries.' " In other words, the fact that an employee of a bank customer conceals a forgery does not obviate the customer's responsibility to examine his or her own bank statement.

Plaintiff, therefore, is precluded from recovering against defendant for the losses occasioned by the forgeries unless it establishes that defendant was negligent in paying the forged items.

In this regard, plaintiff relies on a claim that during the period in question, defendant employed two persons whose job it was to check that the items presented to the bank for payment were signed by persons authorized to do so; that these two individuals possessed no specialized knowledge of the art of handwriting comparison, had no specialized training that field, and were not checked for accuracy of performance. This alone does not warrant a finding of negligence in the paying of these particular checks. While a bank has a duty to use due care in detecting forgeries, its employees cannot be held to the degree of expertness of a handwriting expert.

Plaintiff thus having failed to establish that the bank was negligent in paying the checks, defendant is entitled to judgment dismissing the complaint.

ALTERED AND IMPROPERLY COMPLETED CHECKS

Material Alteration

Any alteration of an instrument is material if it changes the contract of any party to an instrument (Section 3–407[1]). If someone were to come into possession of a check and improperly raise the amount of the check, he or she would have materially altered the instrument.

The consequences of this action vary depending on whether the check falls into the hands of a holder in due course. If someone other than a holder in due course possesses the check, a fraudulent and material alteration by the holder generally discharges anyone whose contract is changed by this action. All other alterations have no effect on the parties to the instrument; the instrument may be enforced according to its original tenor or, in the case of incomplete instruments, according to the authority given.

On the other hand, a subsequent holder in due course may always enforce the instrument according to its original tenor. When an incomplete instrument has been completed, he or she may enforce it as completed.

The following case concerns an instrument that was allegedly altered by its holder.

BLUFFESTONE v. ABRAHAMS

Court of Appeals of Arizona
607 P.2d 25 (1979)

In this case the plaintiff and appellee, Pearl Bluffestone, held a $5,000 note signed by Gary Abrahams. Following Pearl's husband's death, her son-in-law, Alan Gilenko, helped Pearl settle the estate. Gilenko took this demand note and added monthly payments and a provision for attorney's fees. The note was signed by Bert and Lee Abrahams, Gary Abrahams's brother and father, with knowledge of the changes. A second note for $10,000 was also signed by Bert and Lee. Gary, Bert, and Lee all contended that they were not liable because both notes had been materially altered. The trial court found for the plaintiff. The court of appeals also ruled for plaintiff, but disallowed the award for attorney's fees in Gary Abrahams's note.

Howard, Judge

This is a suit on two promissory notes. David and Pearl Bluffestone were husband and wife. Prior to his death in January of 1976, David lent money to the Abrahams in connection with a carwash business. A corporation was eventually formed by the parties known as ABCO Car Washing Company, Inc., (ABCO) and the business was commenced.

After David Bluffestone died, his son-in-law, Alan Gilenko, came to Tucson to help Pearl straighten out her financial affairs. A promissory note of $5,000 was found among David's personal possessions. According to the testimony of Gilenko, this note did not, at the time it was found, have any provision for monthly payments or for attorney's fees. It was signed by Gary Abrahams. Gilenko added monthly payments to the note and a provision for attorney's fees. Bert and Lee Abrahams then signed the note with knowledge of the alterations to the instrument.

A second note, in the amount of $10,000, was then prepared by Gilenko and signed by Bert and Lee Abrahams. Both notes bore interest at 6% per annum.

It was the position of Lee and Bert Abrahams at trial that they signed the $10,000 note as a corporate obligation of ABCO and therefore were not personally liable.

Gary Abrahams contended that he was not liable on the $5,000 note because it was materially altered without his consent or knowledge. All the Abrahams contended that neither note had a provision for interest or attorney's fees when they signed the notes and that they were thus materially altered.

They also contend the trial court erroneously failed to offset certain sums which they claimed were owed to them by Bluffestone. The trial court awarded Pearl judgment against Lee and Bert Abrahams on both notes and against Gary Abrahams on the $5,000 note.

The $10,000 note does not show that Bert and Lee Abrahams signed in a representative capacity. They are therefore personally obligated. There was a conflict in the evidence as to whether Bluffestone owed any money to appellants and we therefore defer to the conclusion reached by the trial court.

The testimony of Alan Gilenko and the documentary evidence support a conclusion that the provisions for interest and attorney's fees were not added after Lee and Bert Abrahams had signed the $10,000 note and that the $5,000 note already had a provision for the interest when originally signed by Gary. We therefore affirm the judgment of the trial court against Lee and Bert Abrahams on both notes.

The liability of Gary Abrahams on the $5,000 note presents a more serious problem. The effect of the alteration of the $5,000 promissory note is governed by U.C.C. Sec. 3–407.

Appellee contends that the evidence shows that the alterations were accomplished with Gary's knowledge and consent. She further contends that Gary's $100 payments on the note after alteration constituted a ratification of the alterations. We do not agree with either contention. Mr. Gilenko's answers to written interrogatories, admitted into evidence show that after David's death, Gilenko had discussions with all of the Abrahams concerning the monies that were due and owing to David. As a result of these discussions Gilenko altered the $5,000 promissory note and prepared the $10,-000 note. Gilenko's answers to the interrogatories do not disclose what, if anything, was said to Gary Abrahams about the $5,000 note and its alterations. However, the record shows that Gilenko did completely discuss the alterations with Bert and Lee Abrahams and the note was changed with the consent and approval of both.

A change made with the consent of the parties to the instrument does not avoid it, but will be binding on the consenting parties in its altered form. Consent to the alteration of an instrument may be implied by the acts of the parties. In order to be binding, however, an implication of consent arising from the circumstances must be plain and unambiguous. We are unable to find anything in the evidence which indicates that Gary Abrahams expressly or impliedly consented to the alterations.

It is also the rule that by making payment of the principal or interest, with knowledge of an alteration, a party is held to ratify the instrument as altered. For this rule to be operable mere payment is not enough, there must be a showing of payment with knowledge of the alteration. Direct evidence is not required and the trier of fact may indulge all reasonable inferences from the facts shown by the evidence, or which unbiased and rational minds can properly deduce from the facts proved. The record does not show that the note either before or after alteration was ever in the possession of Gary. He did make a $100 payment on the note after the death of David, but $100 payments had been made on the note before it had been altered. We do not believe the evidence shows Gary made the payment with knowledge of the alteration.

A.R.S. Sec. 44–2544(B)(1) requires that the alteration be both fraudulent and material. Fraud requires a dishonest and deceitful purpose to acquire more than one was entitled to under the note as signed by the maker rather than only a misguided purpose. We believe that the trial court, as the trier of fact, could legitimately have concluded that no fraud was shown, and that Gilenko was merely misguided in not obtaining Gary's consent when the $5,000 note was altered under a mistaken belief that Gary's consent was not necessary as long as the consent of the parties who were adding their names to the note, to-wit, Gary's brother and father, had been obtained.

Because the note was a demand note, prior to its alteration, the trial court was correct in awarding appellee the balance of the principal and interest on the note. However, since the note, prior to its alteration, contained no provision for attorney's fees, none should have been awarded as against Gary Abrahams.

The judgment is modified by striking the award of attorney's fees against Gary Abrahams and Barbara Abrahams, husband and wife. The judgment is affirmed as modified.

Right of Bank to Charge Customer's Account

Payment in Good Faith of Altered Check. Section 4–401(2) adopts a position similar to that found in Section 3–407(3). A bank that makes a payment in good faith to a holder can charge its customer's account according to the original tenor of an altered item.

Let us suppose that the bank pays in good faith a check written by the drawer on August 1. The drawer wrote the check for $250, but when the bank cashed it, the amount read $2500. Can the bank charge the drawer's account for $2500, $250, or nothing at all? The answer is the bank may charge its customer's account for the original tenor of the altered check, or $250. This section parallels Section 3–407(3), which gives the bank similar protection to that given a holder in due course who takes an altered instrument.

Payment in Good Faith of Improperly Completed Check. If an item was improperly completed, rather than altered, the bank may enforce it according to the tenor as completed. This is true even though the bank knows that the item was completed, unless the bank has notice that the completion was improper.

Suppose a drawer of a check casually dates and signs a check, making it payable to cash, but fails to fill in the amount. This check eventually falls into the hands of a holder in due course. In the meantime, someone has filled in the amount of the check as $500. The holder in due course presents the check to the drawer's bank and the bank cashes the check. May the bank charge the drawer's account for $500? Yes, the bank may charge the account of its customer according to the tenor of the completed check. This, of course, assumes that the bank did not have knowledge that the completion was improper. This section of the UCC gives the bank rights analogous to those given to a holder in due course who takes an item that has been completed without authorization.

Customer's Duty to Exercise Care

A customer must exercise reasonable care with respect to his or her checks. If by his or her negligence, the drawer substantially contributes to a material alteration of the check, he or she may not assert this alteration against a holder in due course or a drawee or payor who pays the instrument in good faith and in accordance with the reasonable commercial standards of the drawee's business (Section 3–406). Thus, if a customer's negligence results in an alteration, the bank may enforce the instrument as altered. Although the UCC does not define negligence, it indicates that negligence has been found where spaces are left in the body of the instrument so that it is possible to insert words or figures.

When a drawer receives his or her checks, even though he or she was not negligent, the drawer has an obligation to inspect the checks for alterations and to promptly notify the bank of any alterations (Section 4–406). Failure to notify the bank may preclude the drawer from asserting any alteration against the bank.

Bank's Rights Against Others

Simply because a bank is unable to collect from the drawer of the instrument does not mean it must bear the loss for a check. A bank may at this point try to collect from anyone who broke the presenter's warranty.

PAYMENT ON A FORGED INDORSEMENT

In order for a drawee bank to properly charge a drawer's account when it honors one of his or her checks, the bank must pay only a holder of the check. With respect to bearer paper, this does not create a problem. But what if the drawer wrote a check to a specific payee, whose indorsement was forged or unauthorized? No one who comes into possession of the check can be a holder because of the forged indorsement. (As no one could become a holder of the check, no one could become a holder in due course with respect to the check.) That being the case, it would be improper for the bank to charge its customer's account.

In the event a bank charges its customer's account in this situation, it must recredit the customer's account for the amount of the check. In this case, the bank has breached its contract with the drawer or has breached the customer–depository-bank relationship. This assumes that after the bank honors the check, the drawer discovers the forgery and notifies the bank within a reasonable time. The bank, in turn, could sue its transferors for breach of warranty of title or genuineness of signatures.

In addition to a suit by the drawer against the drawee (payor) bank, there is also the possibility of a suit by the owner of the instrument when a bank has paid on a forged indorsement. Section 3–419(1)(a) stipulates that an instrument is converted when it is paid on a forged indorsement. This means that any person who pays a check bearing a forged indorsement will be liable to the true owner of the instrument. In effect, there will be a series of conversions. Section 3–419(2) indicates that,

if suit is brought against the drawee, the drawee's liability is the face amount of the instrument. On the other hand, a collecting bank is not liable in conversion or otherwise to the true owner beyond the amount of any proceeds remaining in its hands.

In certain instances, even though the name of the payee is forged, there can be a valid negotiation of the check (Section 3–405). In this case, the above rules concerning forgery do not control. Also, if a customer fails to indorse a check, his or her bank may indorse the check for him or her (Section 4–205).

ELECTRONIC FUND TRANSFERS

At the present time, the UCC's Permanent Editorial Board is considering revisions of the UCC to cover problems created by electronic fund transfers. In the future, the American Law Institute will propose revisions to the UCC for adoption by the states. Congress has already passed legislation of interest to anyone dealing with this area of law.

Electronic fund transfers will be of increasing importance in the future as more and more financial institutions begin to utilize this method of transferring funds. Checks and cash may someday virtually disappear. This will be both good and bad for consumers. On the one hand, it will be much easier and quicker to transact business and to transfer funds at all hours of the day. On the other hand, such systems will generate a great deal of information, much of which could conceivably be used against persons maintaining such accounts.

Types of Electronic Fund Transfers

There are several types of electronic fund transfers (EFTs) currently in use. Typically, in order to initiate a transaction on any of the machines involved, the consumer has a card that gives him or her access to the machine. Often, the consumer also has a secret number to prevent others from using the card should it fall into the wrong hands.

Point-of-Sale Terminals. In some places around the country, point-of-sale (POS) terminals are utilized. Typically, these terminals are located in a business. This permits the business to transfer funds from an individual's account to the account maintained by the business. Thus a point-of-sale terminal might be found in a grocery store. When a customer purchases groceries, the terminal at the grocery store permits the customer to transfer money from his or her account to the store account.

Automated Tellers and Cash Dispensers. A second type of EFT device is the automated-teller machine (ATM) or the cash dispenser (CD). The automated-teller machine permits the user to withdraw cash, make deposits, and transfer money from one account to another without dealing with bank personnel. Automated-teller machines provide a number of benefits for consumers, the foremost of which is twenty-four-hour banking. A card-holder may make deposits or withdrawals, for example, at any time of day or night.

The cash dispenser merely dispenses cash. These machines may be either on-line or off-line. If they are on-line, the machine is connected to a central processing computer that has access to the consumer's account. Thus the entire transaction may be completed immediately. In off-line machines, the machine stores the data for collection at a later time. This means that the on-line system is much more complex, but it completes all transactions at the time a consumer initiates them.

Pay-by-Phone Systems. A third EFT device is the pay-by-phone system. Here, the consumer calls his or her bank and orders the bank to pay the persons or businesses he or she specifies, thereby eliminating the need for writing a check. This system is frequently used to pay utility bills.

Preauthorized Direct Deposits and Automatic Payments. Finally, there are preauthorized direct deposits and automatic payments. An employer might enter into an agreement with its employee to deposit his or her wages periodically in the employee's account at a bank. This is a preauthorized direct deposit. Such a deposit saves a trip to the bank for the employee.

Conversely, the buyer of a product might agree with a seller to have monthly payments automatically withdrawn from the buyer's account and transferred to the seller's. Such an arrangement is frequently made between the buyer of a house and the mortgage company. The buyer need not worry about forgetting to make a payment because each payment is withdrawn from the buyer's account automatically.

The Electronic Fund Transfer Act

Congress in 1978 passed the Financial Institutions Regulatory and Interest Rate Control Act. One part of this legislation is the Electronic Fund Transfer Act (EFTA), which regulates financial institutions that offer electronic fund transfers involving an account held by a consumer. The act, which became effective in 1980, establishes some rules by which the parties to these transactions will be governed.

Definitions. The primary objective of the Electronic Fund Transfer Act (EFTA) is to protect certain rights of consumers dealing with such electronic systems. A consumer under the act is any *natural* person. The term *electronic fund transfer* under the act means "any transfer of funds, other than a transaction originated by check, draft, or similar paper instrument, which is initiated through an electronic terminal, telephonic instrument, or computer or magnetic tape so as to order, instruct, or authorize a financial institution to debit or credit an account." Specifically included under the act are point-of-sale transfers, automated-teller-machine transactions, direct deposits or withdrawals of funds, and transfers initiated by telephone.

An electronic terminal is defined by the EFTA as "an electronic device, other than a telephone operated by a consumer, through which a consumer may initiate an electronic fund transfer. Such term includes, but is not limited to, point-of-sale terminals, automated-teller machines, and cash-dispensing machines." The term *financial institutions* refers to banks, savings and loan associations, credit unions, "or any other person who, directly or indirectly, holds an account belonging to the consumer." Generally, an account is a demand or savings account or other asset account, established primarily for personal, family, or household purposes. In his or her relationship with a financial institution the consumer is referred to as a customer.

Regulations and Standards.

The EFTA authorized the board of governors of the Federal Reserve System to formulate regulations to carry out the purposes of the act. The board issued Regulation E, which must be consulted for a complete understanding of the act.

The board also drafted model clauses for use by financial institutions that utilize electronic systems. In certain cases under the act, use of these clauses is a defense to a suit brought by a customer.

The act sets certain standards governing transactions involving electronic fund transfers by customers. Among other things, the standards require documentation of all transfers, permit preauthorized transfers, provide means for resolving disputes, and limit customer liability.

Disclosure of Terms and Conditions.

The EFTA requires that the terms and conditions of electronic fund transfers be disclosed at the time a customer contracts for such services. The financial institution must disclose:

1. The liability incurred in the event of an unauthorized transfer and, at the option of the financial institution, notice of the advisability of prompt reporting of any loss, theft, or unauthorized use of a card, code, or other means of access
2. The telephone number and address of the person or office to be notified in the event of an unauthorized transfer
3. The type and nature of electronic fund transfers that the customer may initiate, including any limitations on this right
4. Any charges involved
5. The customer's right to stop payment and the procedure that must be followed
6. The customer's right to receive documentation of transactions
7. A summary of the error-resolution provisions of the act and the customer's rights thereunder (this must be provided at least once per calendar year)
8. The financial institution's liability to the customer
9. Under what circumstances the financial institution will in the ordinary course of business disclose information concerning the customer's account to third persons

A financial institution must notify a customer in writing at least twenty-one days prior to the effective date of any change in any term or condition required to be disclosed as noted above if such change would result in greater cost or liability for such customer or decreased access to the customer's account. (In certain instances, a change may be implemented without notifying the customer.)

Documentation.

Each time a customer initiates an electronic fund transfer, the financial institution must make available to the customer written documentation of the transfer.

The documentation must indicate the amount involved and the date of the transfer, the type of transfer, the identity of the customer's account from which or to which funds are transferred, the identity of any third party to whom or from whom funds are transferred, and the location or identification of the electronic terminal involved.

The financial institution must provide each customer with a periodic statement for each account that may be accessed by electronic means. Generally, such a statement must be provided every three months. The statement must include all the information stipulated above plus the amount of any fee or charge assessed, the balances in the account at the beginning and end of the period, and the address and telephone number to which a customer may direct inquiries or give notice of account error. The act has special provisions covering preauthorized transfers that credit only a customer's passbook account.

Preauthorized Transfers. A preauthorized electronic fund transfer is an electronic fund transfer authorized in advance to recur at substantially regular intervals. When a customer's account is scheduled to be credited by such a transfer from the same payor at least once in each successive sixty-day period, the financial institution must either elect to provide notice to the customer when the credit is made as scheduled or to provide negative notice to the customer when the credit is not made as scheduled. This notice need not be given by the financial institution if the payor provides notice of the transfer. The manner in which notice of such a preauthorized electronic fund transfer will be handled must be disclosed to a customer at the time the customer contracts for electronic fund transfer service.

A preauthorized electronic fund transfer that debits a customer's account may be utilized only if the customer agrees in writing and is furnished a copy of the authorization. The customer can stop payment on such preauthorized transfers if he or she notifies the financial institution orally or in writing at any time up to three business days preceding the scheduled date of such transfer. If the financial institution requests it when the oral notice is given, the customer must provide written confirmation of the oral notice within fourteen days of an oral notification.

In the event the preauthorized transfers vary in amount, the financial institution or the payee must give the customer reasonable advance notice of the amount to be transferred and the scheduled date of the transfer.

Error Resolution. Within sixty days after receiving a financial statement, a customer may notify his or her financial institution of any errors in the report. Such notice obligates the financial institution to investigate the alleged error and report the results of the investigation to the customer within ten business days. (If notice of error is given to the financial institution orally, the institution may require the customer to provide written confirmation within ten business days.)

In the event the results of the investigation reveal that an error occurred, the financial institution must promptly correct the error. This must be done within one business day after such an error is discovered.

Alternatively, the financial institution may provisionally recredit the customer's account pending an investigation of the account. This must be done within ten business days after receiving notice of error. The financial institution then has forty-five days after receipt of the notice to conclude the investigation. If during this period it determines that an error did not occur, the financial institution has three business days after arriving at this conclusion to deliver or mail an explanation to the customer.

If the financial institution fails to follow this procedure, or if contrary to the evidence it knowingly and willfully concludes that the customer's account was not in error, the customer is entitled to treble damages.

Customer Liability for Unauthorized Transfers. The EFTA defines "unauthorized electronic fund transfer" as

an electronic fund transfer from a consumer's account initiated by a person other than the consumer without actual authority to initiate such transfer and from which the consumer receives no benefit, but the term does not include any electronic fund transfer (A) initiated by a person other than the consumer who was furnished with the card, code, or other means of access to such consumer's account by such consumer, unless the consumer has notified the financial institution involved that transfers by such other persons are no longer authorized, (B) initiated with fraudulent intent by the consumer or any person acting in concert with the consumer, or (C) which constitutes an error committed by a financial institution.

Obviously, if a customer has authorized a transfer, he or she must bear the cost of the transfer. On the other hand, if the transfer was not authorized by the customer, the act nevertheless imposes some liability on him or her.

Before a customer can be liable at all, it must be established that the transfer was the result of the use of an accepted means of access and that the customer had been provided with a means of identifying himself or herself to that means of access. For example, a bank's customer will not incur any liability under the act until the bank has provided the customer with a card and a secret number for access to the bank's electronic terminal.

Once the customer is in possession of such means of access as a card and a secret number, his or her liability, in the event of an unauthorized transfer, will not exceed the lesser of $50 or the amount obtained prior to the time the financial institution becomes aware that an unauthorized electronic fund transfer has been or may be effected.

If a bank learns on June 1 that an unauthorized transfer from a customer's account has occurred, the maximum that the customer can lose is $50. If the transfer was for $25, the customer loses $25. But if the transfer was for $75, the customer loses only $50.

The customer, however, has a duty to examine the periodic statements provided to him or her. If the financial institution establishes that the losses would not have occurred but for the failure of the customer to report within sixty days of the transmittal of the statement (or, in extenuating circumstances, within a reasonable time) any unauthorized electronic fund transfer or account error on the statement, the loss is borne by the customer. This section of the EFTA is similar to UCC 4–406, which puts the burden on customers to examine their bank statements.

The financial institution need not reimburse its customer when the loss would not have occurred but for the customer's failure to report any loss or theft of a card or other means of access within two business days after learning of the loss or theft. (In certain circumstances, a reasonable period, rather than two days, is allowed.) The customer's liability in this situation is limited to the lesser of $500 or the amount of unauthorized transfers that occur after two business days (or such longer period) following the customer's discovery of the loss or theft but prior to his or her notifying the financial institution.

Suppose the customer loses his card on June 1 but fails to report the loss until June 10. If a thief manages to make a withdrawal from the customer's account on June 2 for $100 and another withdrawal on June 8 for $300, the customer would owe the bank $300, if the bank can establish that the customer learned of the loss on June 1.

In order to recover, the financial institution must meet its burden of proof and establish that the customer and the financial institution had an agreement under which the customer agreed to this liability. The EFTA does not impose liability on a customer in excess of his or her liability under any agreement with the customer's financial institution.

Liability of the Financial Institution. Under the EFTA a financial institution is liable to a customer for all damages proximately caused by its failure to make an electronic fund transfer, in accordance with the terms and conditions of an account, in the correct amount or in a timely manner when properly instructed to do so by the consumer.

There are certain exceptions to this rule—for example, if the electronic terminal does not have sufficient cash to complete the transaction or the customer does not have sufficient funds in his or her account. If the failure was not intentional and resulted from a bona fide error, the financial institution is liable for the actual damages proved.

The financial institution is also liable for damages proximately caused by its failure to credit a deposit of funds and to fail to stop payment of a preauthorized transfer from a customer's account.

Other than the failure to stop payment, a financial institution is not liable if it shows that its failure to act resulted from an act of God or other circumstances beyond its control or from a technical malfunction that was known to the customer at the time he or she attempted to initiate an electronic fund transfer or, in the case of a preauthorized transfer, at the time such transfer should have occurred.

Issuance of Cards or Other Means of Access. In general, cards or other means of access may be issued only in response to a request or as a renewal. Unsolicited cards, codes, or other means of access may be distributed only if the cards, codes, or other means of access are not validated and the financial institution makes a complete disclosure of the customers' rights and liabilities. There must also be a clear explanation that the cards, codes, or other means of access are not validated and how the customer may dispose of the material if he or she chooses not to validate it.

Miscellaneous. If a person agrees to accept payment by means of an electronic fund transfer, and a system malfunction prevents such a transfer, the customer's obligation to the other person is suspended until the malfunction is corrected and the electronic fund transfer may be completed. This is the case unless the other person subsequently makes a written request for payment by a means other than an electronic fund transfers.

No one may condition the extension of credit to a consumer on such consumer's repayment by means of preauthorized electronic fund transfers. Nor may a consumer be required to establish an account for receipt of electronic fund transfers with a particular institution as a condition of employment or receipt of a government benefit.

No writing or other agreement between a consumer and any other person may contain any provision that waives any right conferred or cause of action created by the EFTA. However, the act does not prohibit a writing or agreement that gives the consumer more extensive rights or remedies or greater protection than is afforded by the act or a waiver that is given in settlement of a dispute or action.

As noted earlier, the EFTA provides extensive penalties, both civil and criminal, for noncompliance.

REVIEW PROBLEMS

1. Kidwell had a checking account with Exchange Bank, upon which the president of Kidwell was authorized to draw. Smith, the corporate secretary of Kidwell, forged the president's signature on sixty-five checks made payable to her. This occurred over a three-year period. These forgeries were not reported by Kidwell to Exchange Bank until after the end of the three-year period. The facts disclose that the quality of the forgeries ranged from crude to fair; that Exchange Bank handled a large volume of checks compared to other banks; and that Exchange Bank may not have compared all the signatures on the checks against the signature card bearing the signature of Kidwell's president. Will Kidwell's failure to report the forgeries to Exchange Bank excuse any liability of the bank for improper payment? Will Exchange Bank be liable at all for the improper payments? See Exchange Bank and Trust Co. v. Kidwell Construction Co., Inc., 463 S.W.2d 465 (Tex. Civ. App. 1971).

2. Nu-Way had a checking account with Mercantile Bank. Nu-Way hired Jones, a former convict, as night manager. Among Jones's duties was that of ordering automotive parts from parts companies. Smith, the president of Nu-Way, would on occasion date and sign checks and fill in the name of the payee (which was always a parts company) for payment of parts used by Jones. The president would leave the amount blank for Jones to fill in as needed for parts. Jones, on seven of these checks, altered the checks to substitute his own name as payee and cashed the checks for his own benefit. The facts disclose that the alterations were obvious and should have been discovered. Mercantile Bank cashed the checks, charging Nu-Way's account for them. Upon discovery of the alterations,

Nu-Way sued Mercantile Bank for the wrongful payment of the altered checks. What will be the result in this case? Assume that it took Nu-Way several months to notify Mercantile Bank of the alterations; does this have any effect on your answer? See Nu-Way Services, Inc. v. Mercantile Trust Company National Association, 530 S.W. 2d 743 (Mo. App. 1975).

3. A welfare check drawn on Franklin Bank was issued to Smith in the amount of $13.50. After it was issued, and before it was cashed, the amount of the check was raised to $313.50, in which amount it was cashed at Westbury Bank, and then paid to Westbury Bank by Franklin Bank. In what amount may Franklin Bank charge the drawer's account? Who, if anyone, will be liable for the amount by which the check was altered, i.e., $300? See Franklin National Bank v. Bank of Westbury Trust Co., 318 N.Y.S. 2d 656 (District Court of New York 1971).

4. Newman paid Erron $1200 in 1955, using two checks drawn on Trustee Bank. The checks were left undated, i.e., _____, 195____. The 195____ was printed. Later that year, Trustee Bank merged with Manufacturers Bank. In 1964, Erron presented the two checks drawn by Newman on Trustee Bank to Manufacturers Bank for payment. The dates on the checks were completed in pen and ink to read April 16, 1964. The printed 5 had been crossed out and a handwritten 6 had been substituted. Manufacturers Bank paid the checks, charging Newman's account for $1200. It appears that Manufacturers Bank customarily honored Trustee Bank checks. Newman sues for wrongful payment. Was the bank correct in honoring the checks? What should Newman have done to prevent this? See Newman v.

Manufacturers National Bank of Detroit, 152 N.W.2d 564 (Mich. App. 1967).

5. McKay issued a postdated check to Smith in connection with a building contract. Bank accepted the check for deposit three days before the date on the check. The check was returned to Bank by McKay's bank, with a stop-payment notation on it. McKay had issued a stop-payment order on the check because of some difficulties he and Smith had as a result of the contract. Bank demanded payment of the check from McKay, who refused. Between whom is a stop-payment order effective? Does the stop-payment order have any effect on Bank's rights against McKay? See First National Bank of Trinity v. McKay, 521 S.W.2d 661 (Tex. Civ. App. 1975).

6. Manis leased certain premises from Kersh. Upon Manis's default under the lease, Kersh demanded and received from Manis a certified check in the amount of $700. On the back of the check appeared a statement to the effect that acceptance and indorsement of the check would constitute a full and final settlement between Manis and Kersh with regard to any obligations under the lease. Kersh did not indorse the check, but had it certified by the issuing bank and received payment on it. Kersh subsequently sued Manis on further obligations under the lease. Manis defends on the ground that he has been released from any further liability. What is the effect of obtaining certification of a check? Is Manis correct in his defense? See Kersh v. Manis Wholesale Co. 219 S.E.2d 604 (Ga. App. 1975).

7. Smith, Whalley's bookkeeper, forged and cashed a series of checks, drawn on Whalley's business account with Bank. This occurred between January and May. Smith was in complete charge of Whalley's books and records. Whalley's president routinely examined the bank statements to determine the account balance but did not examine any of the canceled checks. After examining the statements, the president returned the statements and checks to Smith. No one reported the forgeries to Bank until Smith was discharged in June, when irregularities were found. Bank acted in good faith in paying the forged checks. May Whalley recover the amount of the forged checks from Bank? Was Whalley's procedure with respect to the canceled checks and bank statement an exercise of reasonable care? See George Whalley Co. v. National City Bank of Cleveland, 380 N.E.2d 742 (Ohio App. 1977).

8. P made out a check to Mr. and Mrs. B, intending that the money go to the Bs as an investment in a joint venture. P gave the check to Mrs. B, who indorsed it, signing her and Mr. B's names. She then deposited the check to her account. Mr. B, upon learning from P that the money did not go into the joint venture as intended, sued the bank for conversion. Mrs. B, in the meantime, died. May Mr. B recover from the Bank for the Bank's payment of a forged indorsement? Could P have sued under UCC 3–419?

9. What are the four types of electronic fund transfer services?

10. On June 1 Jones received her Zip Card in the mail from her bank. The Zip Card is utilized by her bank's automated teller machine. Before she received the means of identifying herself (her secret number) from the bank, a bank employee stole her card on June 4. The employee somehow gained access to her account and withdrew $1,000. On these facts, does Jones have any liability? What would be the result if Jones failed to report the loss of her card until August 1? If Jones had received both the card and the means of identification, what would be her maximum liability?

Secured Transactions

Much of the nation's economy is based on transactions involving credit. Credit is often provided to buyers by manufacturers, wholesalers, and retailers who are willing to accept payment in the future in order to market their products. In addition, institutions such as commercial banks, factors, and finance companies make loans to finance business inventories, business operations, and consumer sales.

Sometimes providing credit for individuals or business firms subjects the lender to considerable risk because of the possibility that the debt will not be paid. This risk is reduced if the lender can obtain an interest in property as assurance that the debtor will meet his or her obligation. When a creditor establishes a valid security interest and the debtor fails or refuses to pay, the creditor can take the property or have it sold and the proceeds applied against the debt. A creditor who acquires a security interest in personal property is known as a *secured creditor*. The property providing the security is called *collateral*.

This chapter discusses the nature and scope of security interests in personal property and fixtures. Chapter 35 deals with transactions in which real property is the collateral. Much of the law dealing with secured transactions in which personal property is the collateral is based on Article 9 of the Uniform Commercial Code.

ARTICLE 9

Background of Article 9

Article 9 of the UCC provides a comprehensive scheme for administering the many different types of financing using personal property as security. Prior to the adoption of Article 9, secured financing in the United States was carried out in a variety of different ways. This caused a great deal of confusion and increased the expense of secured transactions. In addition, the rights of the parties were often adversely influenced by legal technicalities arising from the differences in the methods used to establish the creditor's rights to the security. The confused state of the law is indicated by the following selection from the Official Comment that accompanied the original version of Article 9 in 1958:

> Existing law recognizes a wide variety of security devices, which came into use at various times to make possible different types of secured financing. Differences between one device and another persist, in formal requisites, in the secured party's rights against the debtor and third parties, in the debtor's rights against the secured party, and in filing requirements, despite the fact that today many of those differences no longer serve any useful function.

One of the major objectives of the drafters of Article 9 was to provide a uniform and simple system for creditors to establish a security interest. To accomplish this, Article 9 eliminates the traditional distinctions that existed among security devices. Article 9 supersedes prior legislation dealing with such security devices as chattel mortgages, conditional sales, trust receipts, factor's liens, and assignments of accounts receivable. For these devices the drafters substituted the single term "security interest."

Terminology of Article 9

In addition to *security interest,* a number of other terms have specific meanings as they are used in Article 9. The following are important for understanding how a creditor protects an interest in particular personal property or fixtures. Most of these will be discussed in greater detail as they relate to particular provisions of Article 9.

Purchase Money Security Interest. A security interest taken by a seller in items sold to a buyer to secure all or part of the price is a purchase money security interest (PMSI). This term also encompasses a security interest taken by a person who gives value to a debtor to acquire rights in or the use of collateral if the collateral is so used (Section 9–107). If a retail merchant sells goods to a purchaser and retains a security interest in these goods, it is a PMSI. Similarly, if a bank makes a loan to a man to purchase a boat and he buys a boat with the money, a PMSI in the boat may have been created. Under the UCC, purchase money obligations often have priority over other obligations.

Secured Party. A lender, seller, or other person in whose favor there is a security interest, including a person to whom accounts or chattel paper have been sold (Section 9–105[m]).

Security Agreement. This is an agreement that creates or provides a security interest (Section 9–105[2]).

Financing Statement. This document gives notice to all persons searching the records that the secured party claims an interest in certain collateral owned by the debtor (Section 9–402). Subject to certain requirements to be discussed later, the security agreement may be filed instead of a separate financing statement.

Although the UCC no longer retains distinctions based on form, for purposes of filing the financing statement in the appropriate place it is extremely important to understand what type of collateral is involved. If the secured party improperly classifies the collateral, he or she may file the financing statement in the wrong place and lose whatever protection the secured party might have had against other creditors of the debtor.

Goods. "Goods" are defined in Section 9–105(h) as all things that are movable at the time the security interest attaches or those things that are *fixtures.* Goods become fixtures when they become so related to particular real estate that an interest in them arises under real estate law (Section 9–313[1][a]).

Goods are classified in one of four categories: *consumer goods, equipment, farm products,* or *inventory.* The classification of goods depends on their use, but goods cannot be classified in more than one category in any single transaction.

Goods are *consumer goods* if they are used or bought for use primarily for personal, family, or household purposes (Section 9–109[1]). A TV bought from a retail merchant for use in the home is a consumer good.

Goods are *equipment* when they are used primarily in business if they are not inventory, farm products, or consumer goods (Section 9–102[2]). An example is machinery used in operating a plant.

Goods are *inventory* if they are held by a person for sale or lease or to be furnished under service contracts or if they are raw materials, work in process, or materials used or consumed in business (Section 9–109[4]). If materials used or consumed in a business have a long life span, they are equipment; but if they are consumed in the manufacture of a product, they are inventory. For example, bolts used in manufacturing a car are inventory, but a drill used in manufacturing a car is equipment.

Goods are *farm products* if they are crops, livestock, or supplies used or produced in farming operations, or if they are products, crops, or livestock in their unmanufactured states (e.g., maple syrup), and if they are in possession of a debtor engaged in raising, fattening, grazing, or other farming operations. When crops or livestock or their products come into the hands of someone not engaged in farming operations, they cease to be farm products. Eggs in the hands of a farmer are farm products, but when the farmer sells those eggs to a dairy company they become inventory in the hands of the dairy company. If a rancher has a meat-packing plant on his or her ranch, once the cattle have been slaughtered the beef is classified as inventory held for sale.

Instrument. According to Section 9–105(i), instrument means a negotiable instrument (as defined in Section 3–104, e.g., a note) or a security (as defined in Section 8–102, e.g., stocks) or any other writing that evidences a right to the payment of money and is not itself a security agreement or lease and is of a type that is, in the ordinary course of business, transferred by delivery with any necessary endorsement or assignment.

Document of Title. A document of title is a written instrument issued by or addressed to a person who holds goods for another. It identifies those goods unless they are fungible, that is, part of an identifiable mass (Section 1–201[15]). For example, an order from a farmer who has stored corn addressed to the storage facility to deliver 10,000 bushels of the corn to a railroad is a document of title. Other documents of title are bills of lading, dock warrants, dock receipts, and warehouse receipts.

Chattel Paper. A writing or writings that evidence both a monetary obligation and a security interest in or a lease of specific goods is chattel paper. If the transaction consists of a security agreement or a lease and an instrument or a series of instruments, the *group* of writings taken together constitutes chattel paper.

When a merchant sells goods to a consumer, the merchant may retain a security interest in the goods sold. Suppose a retail merchant sells a television set to a consumer and retains a security interest in it. The contract by which he retains a security interest in the TV is a security agreement: the merchant is the secured party; the buyer is the debtor; and the TV is the collateral. If the merchant wishes to finance his operations, he may sell a number of such contracts to a bank. With respect to the bank, these contracts are collectively referred to as *chattel paper.* The retail dealer is a debtor with respect to the bank, and the bank is the secured party. The customers are referred to as *account debtors*.

Account. An *account* is any right to payment for goods sold or leased or for services rendered that is not evidenced by an instrument or chattel paper, whether or not it has been earned by performance (Section 9–106). Accounts are not evidenced by writing. This term covers the ordinary account receivable. If a clothing store sells clothes to customers on an open account and gives them thirty days to pay, the accounts of the customers can be sold to a financer. The financer would be a secured party, the clothing store the debtor, and the customers the account debtors.

General Intangibles. These are any personal property other than goods, accounts, chattel paper, documents, and money (Section 9–106). The term covers the various contractual rights and personal property that are used as commercial security—for example, goodwill, trademarks, and patents.

Scope of Article 9

Article 9 applies primarily to security interests in personal property and fixtures arising out of agreements. The article does not apply to statutory liens such as the mechanic's or artisan's lien. These liens are created by legislation to protect contractors and others who provide improvements to real property. Article 9 does, however, cover priority problems between statutory liens and secured transactions (Section 9–310). Additionally, the article applies to transactions involving the sale of accounts and chattel paper.

Although Article 9 applies to consumer transactions, its provisions do not replace other state legislation such as small loan acts, retail installment sales statutes, and other regulatory measures applicable to consumer financing.

The major exclusion from Article 9 coverage is security interest in real estate. Fixtures, however, are covered, and in some circumstances real estate and Article 9 transactions are connected. For example, if Jones owns a promissory note and a real estate mortgage securing funds he has advanced to Smith, Jones may use them as collateral when borrowing from Brown. Section 9 also applies to transactions in which the collateral is minerals, standing timber, or growing crops.

Purpose of Article 9

In order to limit risk in secured financing, the creditor has two major objectives. First, he or she needs assurance that security rights in the collateral are protected if the debtor defaults. This is accomplished if the creditor obtains an enforceable security interest. Second, the creditor needs protection against third parties establishing superior rights in the collateral. To prevent this, the creditor must take steps in addition to those required to establish rights against the debtor. In both cases, however, the initial step is to establish a security interest.

ESTABLISHING AN ENFORCEABLE SECURITY INTEREST

Three events must take place before a creditor obtains a security interest in the collateral. These events do not have to occur simultaneously or in any particular order. Once they have occurred, the secured party's right in the collateral is said to *attach*. Attachment establishes the secured party's right to the collateral against the defaulting debtor.

The secured party's right attaches:

1. When the parties agree that the secured party has a security interest

2. The debtor receives value
3. The debtor has rights in the collateral.

The Security Agreement

A *security agreement* creates or provides a security interest (Section 9–105[1]). Unless the collateral is in the possession of the secured party, the security agreement must be in writing. The agreement must contain a description of the collateral and be signed by the debtor. A description that reasonably identifies the collateral is sufficient; however, care should be taken to describe the collateral since insufficient identification can lead to litigation.

In the Matter of Charles O. Cooley, Bankrupt
United States Court of Appeals
624 F.2d 55 (1980)

Charles O. Cooley, Jr., borrowed funds from the First National Bank of Louisville (appellee) to finance Cooley's business. To complete this transaction, Cooley and his wife executed documents giving the bank a security interest in certain collateral. When Cooley became bankrupt, Michael Clare (trustee-appellant) brought an action in the bankruptcy court asserting that the security agreement was invalid. The bankruptcy judge decided that the security agreement was enforceable; the U.S. District Court affirmed; and the trustee in bankruptcy, Clare, appeals. The Court of Appeals affirmed.

Lively, Circuit Judge

The record contains the following written instruments: A Loan and Security Agreement dated April 9, 1974, given "to secure the payment and performance of all liabilities of the Borrower (Charles O. Cooley, Jr., dba Cooley's Lawn Service) to the Bank . . . ," A Financing Statement bearing the same date, and a promissory note from Charles O. Cooley, Jr., and Patricia E. Cooley, his wife, to the bank for $10,000 base amount plus a finance charge of $4,301.60, dated November 7, 1974. The bankruptcy judge conducted a hearing and made a finding of fact that the bankrupts executed and delivered to the bank on April 9, 1974, a promissory note for $3,000 and that the security agreement of that date granted the bank a security interest in collateral which included the personal property of Cooley's Lawn Service that is in dispute.

The trustee . . . argues that the security agreement of April 9th was insufficient because it did not disclose the amount of the loan or the maturity date. The Uniform Commercial Code (UCC), as adopted by Kentucky, sets forth the requirements of a valid security agreement. There is no requirement that the amount secured or the date of maturity be shown. These are essential contents of the underlying debt instrument (the promissory note) but not of the security instrument. The security agreement here specifically provided for future advances. The flexibility intended by the UCC would be severely limited by a requirement that a security agreement state a fixed amount and maturity date. We know of no authority for the appellant's position.

Finally, the trustee asserts that the security agreement is invalid because the description of the collateral is insufficient under Kentucky law. He relies principally upon the decision in *Mammoth Cave P.C.A.* v. *York,* where it was held that a security agreement which listed "farm equipment" as collateral and stated that it included "replacements of and additions to equipment" was not adequate to perfect a security interest in a subsequently acquired tractor.

The collateral was described in the security agreement before us as follows:

    (a) All inventory of the Borrower, now owned or hereafter acquired;

    (b) All contract rights of the Borrower, now existing or hereafter arising;

    (c) All accounts receivable of the Borrower, now existing or hereafter arising;

    (d) All goods, instruments, documents of title, policies and certificates of insurance, securities, chattel paper, deposits, cash or other property owned by the Borrower or in which it has an interest which are now or may hereafter be in the possession of the Bank or as to which the Bank may now or hereafter control possession by documents of title or otherwise;

    (e) Proceeds and products of all of the foregoing; (and)

    (f) All machinery and equipment, including machinery and equipment which are or will become fixtures, office supplies, furniture, office and store fixtures, raw materials, work in process, and the proceeds and products of all of the foregoing.

K.R.S. Section 355.9–110 provides that any description of property is sufficient "whether or not it is specific if it reasonably identifies what is described." Construing this requirement in a case where the adequacy of the description of collateral was challenged, Chief Judge Charles M. Allen wrote . . .

> We believe that since the financial statement does accurately describe the type of collateral which the creditor was holding, and since it is obvious from the description set out in the statement that the debtor was an on-going business whose various types of assets were being used as security, this was sufficient to suggest inquiries or means of identification which, if pursued, would disclose the property which was secured. [Citation omitted.]

In his opinion Judge Allen distinguished *Mammoth Cave P.C.A.* v. *York, supra,* and a case decided by the district court in which the description of collateral was found to be inadequate.

We believe *Mammoth Cave P.C.A.* v. *York* is distinguishable from the present case. Here the borrower was a going business, shown in the security agreement and the recorded financing statement as "Charles O. Cooley, Jr., DBA Cooley's Lawn Service." The listing of collateral, described by categories, included all the usual assets of a going business. It would be contrary to the purpose of the UCC to hold that lawn tending equipment of this borrower was not sufficiently described by the language used in the security agreement.

The judgment of the district court is affirmed.

Although the formal requirements of a security agreement are minimal, most also contain references to the following items:

After-Acquired Property. This is collateral that becomes the subject of a security interest after the parties have reached an initial agreement. One example would be a retailer's inventory purchased to replace goods subject to the original security agreement. When an after-acquired property clause is included in a security agreement, the secured party acquires a "continuing general lien" in property acquired to replace the original inventory.

Future Advances. Security agreements may include a clause covering advances of credit made by the secured party after the agreement is signed. This is necessary if the advance is to be secured by the original agreement. The clause might read: "This security agreement shall include future advances or other indebtedness that debtor may owe to secured party during the time that the security agreement is in force, whenever incurred." Rights of the debtor established by an after-acquired property clause and a future advance clause are often referred to as a *floating lien* (Section 9–204, Comment z). Combining the after-acquired property and future advances clauses facilitates the financing of inventory and accounts receivable where the collateral is goods being retailed or raw materials being manufactured.

A number of other subjects are covered in most security agreements. They include, but are not limited to, the following:

1. Amount of the debt
2. Terms of payment
3. Responsibility for care and maintenance of the collateral
4. Acceleration of payment rights
5. Right to additional collateral

Additional Requirements

In addition to a valid security agreement, two other conditions must be met before the creditor can obtain a security interest in the collateral. First, the debtor must receive value. If the secured party extends credit, makes a loan to the debtor, or provides the debtor any consideration sufficient to support a simple contract, this requirement has been fulfilled. Second, the debtor must have rights in the collateral. The debtor does not have to have title to the collateral. A purchaser acquiring property under an agreement in which the seller retains title has rights in the collateral sufficient to support a creditor's security interest.

PERFECTION OF A SECURITY INTEREST

A security interest that has attached may be enforced by the secured party against the debtor. The secured party also needs protection against claims to the collateral that others might assert arising out of their transactions with the debtor. To secure this protection, the secured party must *perfect* his or her security interest in the collateral. By perfecting the security interest, the secured party puts the world on notice that he or she claims a special interest in the collateral. Other people dealing later with the debtor may realize that the secured party has a superior interest in the property that may well be used to satisfy the debt.

Methods of Perfecting a Security Interest

The secured party may perfect a security interest by any of the following methods:

1. Filing a financing statement in the appropriate public office
2. Taking possession of the collateral

In some transactions, security interests are automatically perfected when they attach to the collateral. Whether the secured party may perfect by filing, by taking possession, or by relying upon automatically obtaining a perfected security interest depends to a large extent upon the classification of the collateral involved.

In certain instances, the secured party automatically obtains a perfected security interest without taking possession of the collateral or filing. Article 9 provides that a merchant who sells consumer goods to a buyer on credit does not need to file a financing statement or take possession of the goods to perfect interest in the items sold. With the exception of motor vehicles and fixtures, a perfected security interest arises automatically when the merchant's security interest in the collateral attaches (Section 9–302[d]). The merchant's security interest is a purchase money security interest.

Additionally, Article 9 establishes temporary automatic security interests in two situations. The most important is a ten-day security interest in any proceeds a debtor receives from the sale of the collateral. A twenty-one-day security interest measured from the time of attachment is automatically perfected in certain negotiable interest and stocks in the debtor's possession (Sections 9–304, 9–306[3]).

Perfection by Filing

The most common method of perfecting a security interest is by filing a financing statement. This document, when properly filed, gives the public notice of the secured party's interest in the collateral. Public notice needs to be provided so other creditors or transferees of the debtor may learn of the creditor's claims to the collateral.

The Financing Statement. A financing statement must give the names of the debtor and the secured party and their respective addresses, be signed by the debtor, and contain a statement indicating the types—or describing the items—of collateral. A financing statement is effective even if it contains minor errors. When the financing statement covers crops, timber to be cut, minerals, or goods that are to become fixtures, the financing statement must describe the real estate involved. Normally a standard form is used for the financing statement; however, under the UCC a copy of the security agreement may be used if it contains all of the information listed above and is signed by the debtor. Parties usually do not file the security agreement. If the parties wish to amend the financing statement, the UCC requires filing of a writing signed by both debtor and secured party.

FIGURE 1
Financing Statement (Approved Form U.C.C. Sec. 9–402)

This financing statement is presented to a filing officer for filing pursuant to the Uniform Commercial Code.

Name of Debtor (or Assignor) ....
Address ....
Name of Secured Party (or Assignee) ....
Address ....

1. This financing statement covers the following types (or items) of property:
   (Describe)..
2. (If collateral is crops) The above described crops are growing or are to be grown on:
   (Describe Real Estate and specify Name of Record Owner) ....
3. (If collateral is goods which are or are to become fixtures) The above described goods are affixed or to be affixed to:
   (Describe Real Estate and specify Name of Record Owner) ....
4. (If proceeds or products of collateral are claimed) Proceeds—Products of the collateral are also covered.
   Signature of Debtor (or Assignor) ....
   Signature of Secured Party (or Assignee) ......

Many financing statements are filed incorrectly because the wrong name is used for the debtor. Section 9–402(7) provides that the name on a financing statement is sufficient if it gives the individual, partnership, or corporate name of the debtor, whether or not it adds other trade names or names of partners. Suppose that Alfred Zimmer operates a business under the name Southern Pit Barbeque. Should the statement be filed under Z or S? Here, it should be filed under the name of the debtor—Zimmer. If Zimmer changed his name, or if he were operating a corporation that changed its name, must the secured party refile its financing statement? Yes; if the filed financing statement becomes seriously misleading, it will not be effective to perfect a security interest in collateral acquired by the debtor more than four months after the name change.

Place of Filing. The place of filing depends upon the type of collateral covered by the security agreement. If the secured party improperly classifies the collateral and files in the wrong office, secured status as to the described collateral does not exist.

For collateral related to land such as fixtures, goods that are to become fixtures, timber to be cut, or minerals, filing generally is required in the county where the land is located. For other types of collateral, the states have different rules concerning the proper place to file. A number of states direct that filing take place in the county of the debtor's residence or, if the debtor is not a resident of the state, in the county where the goods are kept. Other states take the position that filing is most effective when centralized on a state-wide basis. This reduces costs and facilitates the acquisition of credit information. These states generally require that filing, except for land-related collateral, be done in the office of the Secretary of State, located in the state capital.

Time and Duration of Filing. A financing statement can be filed at any time—even before a security agreement is made or before a security interest attaches to the collateral (Section 9–402[1]). A secured party might want to file before attachment because this may aid in getting a higher priority than other parties claiming an interest in the same collateral by filing.

A filed financing statement is effective for five years from the date of filing. To assure its continuing validity after five years, the secured party must file a *continuation statement;* otherwise, the security interest becomes unperfected. A continuation statement may be filed by the secured party within six months prior to the expiration of the five-year period. The continuation statement makes the original statement valid for an additional five years. Succeeding continuation statements may be filed. The continuation statement need be signed by only the secured party.

What if the secured party allows the financing statement to lapse at the end of five years, although the debtor is still obligated to him, and an intervening creditor files an effective financing statement? Section 9–403(2) states that the security interest "is deemed to have been unperfected as against a person who became a purchaser or lien creditor before lapse." Suppose a bank lends money to A and properly perfects a security interest in A's collateral; then four years later a finance company also lends money to A and perfects its security interest in the same equipment. If the bank allows the filing to lapse, the finance company is entitled to priority over the bank's security interest, which became unperfected by the lapse.

Once all the obligations of the parties have been completed under the security agreement, the secured party must file a termination statement with each filing officer with whom the financing statement was filed. If consumer goods are involved, this statement must be filed within one month or, following written demand by the debtor, within ten days. If other than consumer goods are involved, and the debtor demands in writing a termination statement, the secured party must furnish a termination statement for each filing officer with whom the financing statement was filed. If the secured party fails to file as specified or to send a termination statement within ten days after a proper demand, he or she will be liable to the debtor for one hundred dollars and for any loss caused the debtor by such failure (Section 9–404).

Perfection by Possession

For most types of collateral, an alternative to perfection by filing is for the secured party to take possession of the property. Article 9 permits a secured party to perfect a security interest in goods, negotiable documents, or chattel paper by taking possession of them. The secured party may choose, however, to perfect an interest in these items by filing a financial statement.

A security interest in money or in negotiable instruments, such as shares of stock, can be perfected only by the secured party's taking possession. For instance, if A borrows money from B bank with the security being 100 shares of General Motors stock, the bank must hold the stock in order to have a perfected security interest. A security interest in accounts or general intangibles must be perfected by filing.

A secured party in possession of collateral is under a duty to use reasonable care in its custody and preservation. The secured party must keep the collateral identifiable unless it is fungible, in which case it may be commingled. The secured party responsible for a loss to the collateral through failure to use reasonable care bears that loss, but the security interest is retained. Reasonable expenses incurred to preserve the collateral and insurance costs are borne by the debtor.

PRIORITY

In some situations, other people besides the secured creditor claim an interest in the collateral. A secured creditor may have to compete with someone who has purchased the collateral from the debtor, holders of statutory liens, general creditors, a trustee in bankruptcy, other secured creditors, and even the government. Because of the different interests involved, numerous state and federal statutes influence the solution to these conflicts.

Article 9 of the UCC does, however, provide the rules for resolving many of them.

The Unperfected Security Interest

As a general rule, Article 9 establishes a priority for the holder of a perfected security interest against other creditors and transferees from the debtor. Although the key to the secured creditor's protection is perfection of the security interest, limited protection is afforded an unperfected security interest. The unperfected security interest does enjoy priority over general creditors of the debtor who have established no lien on the collateral.

General creditors, however, have little difficulty in overcoming this priority. The general creditor may obtain a judgment against the debtor and have the sheriff levy on the property the creditor wishes to claim, even though the creditor knew of the secured party's interest in the collateral. Because of the relative ease with which a general creditor can establish a priority over an unperfected security interest, the prudent secured creditor will always perfect to obtain maximum safety.

Conflicting Security Interests

When two or more persons claim security interests in the same collateral, the general rule of priority is stated in Section 9–312(5)(a) as follows:

a) conflicting security interests rank according to priority in time of filing or perfection—*Priority dates from the time a filing is first made covering the collateral or the time the security interest is first perfected*, whichever is earlier, *provided* that there is no period thereafter when there is neither filing nor perfection [emphasis added].

Under Article 9, a party may file with respect to particular collateral before it comes into existence. A security interest cannot be perfected, however, until the security interest attaches to the collateral; this means that the secured party must have taken possession of the collateral or that the debtor must have signed a security agreement and received value from the secured party and have rights in the collateral. There can be no perfection of the security interest until these events occur.

Section 9–312(5)(a) specifies that priority occurs when a filing is first made covering the collateral *or* when the security interest is first perfected, whichever is earlier. This rule makes it advantageous for a secured party to file its financing statement as soon as possible. The date of the filing will control if the security interest is subsequently perfected. It is also possible to perfect by taking possession of certain types of collateral. In this case, the perfection is effective from the time the secured party takes possession of the collateral.

Taking into consideration the times at which perfection is effective and the rules stated in Section 9–312(5), consider the following examples: A perfects his security agreement against collateral held by X on January 1. B perfects a security interest in the same collateral on February 1. Because A perfected his interest on January 1, A has priority (Section 9–312[5][4]). Suppose that A's security interest in X's collateral attaches on January 1 and B's security interest in X's collateral attaches on February 1, but neither secured party perfects his interest. Whichever secured party first perfects his interest (by taking possession of the collateral or by filing) takes priority, and it makes no difference whether or not he knows of the other interest at the time he perfects his own. Thus if B perfects by filing before A, his interest has priority over A's. Section 9–312(5)(b) states the rule where neither party perfects. This rule is somewhat theoretical, but if neither perfects, the first interest to attach wins—this would be A, whose interest attached on January 1.

Suppose instead that a secured party files a financing statement on June 1 but fails to perfect his or her security interest at that time because the security interest has not yet attached to the collateral. On July 1 a second secured party perfects an interest in the same collateral. On August 1 the first secured party's interest attaches to the collateral, and the security interest is thus perfected on August 1. In this situation, the first secured party has priority because the filing was on June 1 and this was before the second secured party's interest became effective on July 1. Once again, there is an advantage under the UCC to filing as soon as possible.

Purchase Money Security Interest

The UCC places the holder of a purchase money security interest (PMSI) in a beneficial position. Article 9 provides a claimant with a PMSI priority over a conflicting security interest in the same collateral if the PMSI is perfected within ten days of the time the debtor takes possession of the collateral (Section 9–312[4]). Priority for a PMSI may be justified on grounds that the party enabling property to be purchased deserves to be protected.

A PMSI provides protection for the seller in the following situation, although a perfected security interest already exists in the collateral: First State Bank advances funds to Jones Manufacturing and perfects a security interest in all the firm's equipment. The security agreement contains a provision extending the bank's interest to any after-acquired equipment. At a later date Jones purchases a new machine on credit from Smith Machine Company. As long as Smith Machine files a financing statement within ten days of the machine's delivery, its security interest has priority over that of First State Bank.

Consumer Goods. The holder of a PMSI in most types of consumer goods has extensive protection. Perfection is automatic for the retailer who obtains a security agreement from a customer. No filing is necessary to establish the seller's priority. One exception to this rule is automobile financing. To perfect a security interest in an automobile, the secured party must file a security agreement or comply with a state's certificate of title law.

Inventory. A PMSI in inventory has priority even though another creditor has previously perfected a security interest in the debtor's inventory if the following events occur (Section 9–312[3]):

1. The PMSI is perfected at the time the debtor receives possession of the inventory
2. The purchase money secured party gives notification in writing to the holder of the conflicting security interest if the holder had filed a financing statement covering the same types of inventory (i) before the date of the filing made by the purchase money secured party or (ii) before the beginning of the twenty-one-day period where the PMSI is temporarily perfected without filing or possession
3. The holder of the conflicting interest receives notice within five years *before* the debtor receives possession of the inventory
4. The notification states that the person giving notice has or expects to acquire a PMSI

in inventory of the debtor, describing such inventory by item or type

It is not necessary to notify secured creditors who have not filed financing statements, even if the person claiming a PMSI has knowledge of their interests.

Problems arising under Section 9–312(3) usually involve a conflict between a secured party claiming interest in certain collateral under an after-acquired property clause and a person claiming a PMSI in the same collateral. The rationale for this section is that a secured party typically will make advances on new inventory or releases of old inventory as new inventory is received. If the inventory financer learns of the PMSI in particular inventory, he or she may not make an advance against it (Section 9–312[3][b]).

The priority of the PMSI in inventory extends only to *identifiable cash proceeds* received on or before the inventory is delivered to the buyer. If the goods are sold to a buyer on account, the PMSI priority does not extend to these proceeds. Suppose a secured party makes a loan to a retailer to finance his or her operations and the perfected security agreement retains a security interest in after-acquired accounts receivable. After this, a manufacturer sells goods to the retailer and perfects a PMSI in this inventory and the proceeds from their sale. Between the two parties, whose security interest has priority if the only assets of the retailer are accounts receivable generated by the sale of merchandise sold by the manufacturer? The secured party claiming a security interest in after-acquired accounts receivable has priority because accounts are not cash proceeds.

Chattel Paper and Instruments

When chattel paper is sold by the seller to a secured party, the secured party may choose to have the retail merchant collect the accounts, or the secured party may collect the accounts. The secured party may leave the chattel paper with the dealer, or the secured party may take possession of the paper. As noted previously, an interest in chattel paper may be perfected either by filing or by taking possession of it. Leaving it in the hands of the retail merchant is dangerous: if the secured party leaves the paper in the hands of the merchant and perfects an interest by filing, a subsequent secured party who takes possession of this chattel paper may gain priority over the secured party who merely files to perfect. Certain purchasers of chattel paper left in the debtor's possession take free of the security interest that has been perfected by filing. This is one of the limitations on the otherwise protected status of a party with a perfected security interest.

In general, the rules applicable to chattel paper also apply to the purchase of instruments. Recall, however, that a security interest in instruments generally can be perfected only by possession. The only types of perfected nonpossessory security interest that can arise in an instrument are the temporary twenty-one-day perfection provided for in Section 9–304(4) and (5) or the ten-day perfection in proceeds of Section 9–306. If a security interest is temporarily perfected under either of these sections, a person taking possession of them during this period without knowledge that they are subject to a security interest has priority over the conflicting security interest (Section 9–308[a]).

Protection of Buyers of Goods

The UCC gives some buyers of goods protection against perfected security interests. When a person in "good faith and without knowledge that the sale to him is in violation of the ownership rights or security interest of a third party in the goods buys in ordinary course from a person in the business of selling goods of that kind" (excluding pawnbrokers), he qualifies as a "buyer in ordinary course of business." Under Section 9–307(1) a buyer in the ordinary course of business takes free of a security interest created by his or her seller even if it is perfected and the buyer knows this.

This section permits the ordinary consumer to buy goods from a retail merchant without being liable to a secured party of the merchant who claims a security interest in the goods purchased by the buyer. Normally, of course, a security agreement permits a merchant to sell from inventory. This section therefore applies to the situation in which the security agreement between the seller and the secured party does not permit such sales.

A special rule exists for purchase of consumer goods—that is, goods used primarily for personal, family, or household purposes (Section 9–109[1]). Remember that a PMSI in consumer goods can be perfected without filing (other security interests in consumer goods must be filed). As long as the buyer buys without knowledge of the security interest for his or her own personal, family, or household purposes before a financing statement is filed, he or she takes free of even a perfected security interest (Section 9–307[2]).

If a person buys goods from someone not in the business of selling goods of that kind, he or she is *not* a buyer in ordinary course of business. This means that the buyer-in-the-ordinary-course-of-business rule stated in Section 9–307(1) does not apply. Suppose a finance company lends money to a retail merchant and obtains a perfected security interest in the merchant's equipment. Since the merchant is not in the business of selling equipment, but rather is in the business of selling inventory, someone who purchases this equipment from the merchant is *not* a buyer in the ordinary course of business.

Cunningham v. Camelot Motors, Inc.
Superior Court of New Jersey
351 A.2d 402 (1975)

James Cunningham (plaintiff) and Eugene Koblentz (plaintiff) each purchased a Triumph from Camelot Motors, Inc. (defendant). Both purchasers paid in full and took possession of their automobiles, receiving temporary registration certificates. In each case Camelot promised to procure the required certificates of ownership for permanent registrations. Camelot failed to deliver these documents to either purchaser.

Three years prior to either of the above transactions, Camelot had entered into a floor plan financing agreement with Hudson United Bank (defendant). Under the terms of the agreement Hudson advanced moneys to Camelot and received a security interest in all motor vehicles then owned or thereafter acquired by Camelot. A UCC financing statement was filed reflecting Hudson's security interest in Camelot's inventory, and Hudson obtained possession of all of the certificates of origin issued by the manufacturer of new automobiles in Camelot's inventory. The agreement further authorized Camelot to sell any vehicles from its inventory in the regular course of its business, and Camelot was obligated to remit to Hudson the loan balances owing to Hudson on the vehicles that Camelot sold.

Camelot failed to make the required remittance to Hudson on the automobiles that are the subject of these actions, and Hudson has refused to surrender the certificates of origin to Camelot or to either of the plaintiffs. The result is that neither plaintiff has been able to obtain a certificate of ownership or to register his vehicle.

Plaintiffs move for summary judgment and seek an order directing Camelot and Hudson to surrender and endorse the certificates of origin to them. While assuming that Hudson has a perfected security interest in the vehicles, plaintiffs urge that under UCC Section 9–307(1) Hudson's security interest is invalid as to them. They argue that as buyers in the ordinary course of business they take free of a security interest created by the seller even though the security interest is perfected and even though the buyer knows of its existence.

Gelman, J.S.C.

UCC Section 1–201(9) defines a "buyer in ordinary course of business" as

> . . . a person who in good faith and without knowledge that the sale to him is in violation of the ownership rights or security interest of a third party in the goods buys in ordinary course from a person in the business of selling goods of that kind but does not include a pawnbroker. "Buying" may be for cash or by exchange of other property or on secured or unsecured credit and includes receiving goods or documents of title under a pre-existing contract for sale but does not include a transfer in bulk or as security for or in total or partial satisfaction of a money debt.

The purpose of Section 9–307(1) is obvious: to protect bona fide purchasers for value who acquire goods in the ordinary course of business from a merchant's inventory. To meet the conditions imposed by Section 9–307(1), plaintiffs must show only that they purchased the automobiles (1) in good faith; (2) without knowledge that the sale was in violation of Hudson's security interest; (3) from a person in the business of selling goods of that kind; and (4) for present value, i.e., cash or by a present exchange of other property. The facts set forth in the moving papers establish that these conditions have been met by these plaintiffs and that under Section 9–307(1) they take free of Hudson's security interest in the automobiles.

An order will be entered directing Hudson to surrender the certificates of origin to Camelot and directing Camelot to execute and deliver the certificates to plaintiffs.

Statutory Liens

If a person furnishes services or materials in the ordinary course of his business, any lien upon goods in his or her possession given by state law for such materials or services takes priority over a perfected security interest (Section 9–310). This means that when a mechanic repairs a vehicle, if state law gives him or her a mechanic's lien on the car for services rendered, this interest is superior to that of a bank that has a security interest in the car.

Security Interests in Fixtures

Goods are "fixtures" when they become so attached to a particular piece of real estate that an interest in them arises under real estate law (Section 9–313[1]). Article 9 recognizes three categories of goods:

1. Those that retain their *chattel* character entirely and are not part of the real estate, which should be perfected by filing in accordance with the rules on personal property

2. *Ordinary building materials* that have become an integral part of the real estate, which should be perfected by recording a real estate mortgage

3. *Fixtures* that are perfected by making a "fixture filing," a financing statement filed in the office where a mortgage on the real estate would be filed or recorded, covering goods that are or are to become fixtures (Section 9–313[1][b])

The financing statement covering a fixture filing must contain a description of the real estate sufficient to identify it. Applying this test, a description is adequate if a person searching the real estate records would discover the filing. In some states the description is adequate if it sufficiently describes real estate for purposes of a mortgage.

A fixture filing gives to the fixture security interest priority as against other real estate interests based upon the principle that the first to file or record prevails. This is the usual rule with respect to conflicting real estate interests. An additional requirement is that the debtor must have an interest of record in the real estate or be in possession (such as a tenant). This later requirement restricts a valid fixture filing where the creditor is a contractor.

An exception to the first-to-file rule exists for a PMSI in a fixture. This interest has priority over previously recorded real estate interests as long as the security interest is perfected by a fixture filing before the goods become fixtures or within ten days thereafter (Section 9–314[4][a]).

Another exception to the first-to-file rule covers readily removable factory or office machines or readily removable replacements of domestic appliances that are consumer goods. If an interest in these goods is perfected by any method in Article 9 before they become fixtures, the fixtures filing prevails over a conflicting interest of most claims that are acquired in the real estate or the conflicting interest of the owners.

The final exception to the first-to-file rule for filing gives a perfected security interest in fixtures priority over a conflicting interest that is a lien on the real estate obtained by legal or equitable proceedings after the security interest was perfected (Section 9–313[4][c]).

Accessions and Commingled or Processed Goods

A secured party who claims an interest in goods installed or affixed to other goods ("accessions") is entitled to priority with certain exceptions over anyone else claiming an interest in the whole goods, if the security interest attaches before the goods are installed or affixed to other goods (Section 9–314[1]).

If a security interest in goods is perfected and the goods subsequently become part of a product or mass and their identity is lost in the product or goods, the security interest continues in the product or mass (Section 9–315).

ASSIGNMENT

A common business practice is for a seller of goods holding an installment contract with an accompanying security interest to transfer these to a finance company. In return, the finance company advances funds that the seller uses in the operation of its business.

Rights of an Assignee

When an installment contract and security interest are sold to a finance company, the finance company becomes the secured party.

As this transaction is usually an assignment, the finance company is often referred to as the *assignee.* The original seller, who is the assignor, is now a *debtor* since it has received an advance from the finance company. The original purchaser is referred to as an *account debtor.* In general, the UCC does not permit the original purchaser to restrict the assignment of an installment contract (Section 9–318[4]). Even if the parties include a provision restricting assignment in the installment contract, the contract may be assigned.

In the absence of a contrary provision, the rights of an assignee are subject to all terms of the contract between the account debtor and assignor and any defense or claim arising therefrom. The assignee takes the contract subject to any claims the account debtor has against the assignor that arise independently of the contract and accrue *before* the account debtor receives notification of the assignment (Section 9–318[1][a] and [b]).

Waiver of Defenses

Quite often a seller, anticipating the documents will be used in financing, asks the buyer to sign an installment contract and security agreement containing words similar to the following:

> Buyer hereby agrees to waive as against any assignee of this contract all claims or defenses buyer may have against secured party to the full extent permitted by law.

This clause facilitates the seller's assignment of the installment contract to a financer, for the buyer has waived its rights to sue and set up defenses against the financer (assignee). If a buyer accepts this terminology, it must settle any dispute arising over the goods with the seller, although the seller has transferred all its rights to a finance company. The UCC permits waiver-of-defense clauses as long as the assignee takes the assignment for value, in good faith, and without notice of a claim or defense.

A waiver-of-defense clause is effective against the account debtor unless his or her defense is one that could be asserted against a holder in due course of a negotiable instrument (see Chapter 21) or a statute or decision establishes a different rule for consumer goods. A Federal Trade Commission rule, discussed in Chapter 21, abolishes the use of such clauses in consumer contracts everywhere in the United States, but the clause is still effective in business transactions that do not involve sales to a consumer.

DEFAULT

When the debtor defaults under a security agreement, a secured party has the rights and remedies provided in Article 9 and whatever rights and remedies the security agreement itself gives the secured party—subject to certain limitations specified in Section 9–501(3). In general, the secured party may reduce the claim to a judgment, foreclose, or otherwise enforce the security interest by any available judicial procedure. The secured party may elect to reduce the claim to a judgment and then levy on the collateral. In this case, the judgment lien relates back to the date of perfection of the security interest (Section 9–501[5]). When there is a judicial sale following judgment, execution, and levy, the judicial sale is a foreclosure of the security interest, but the sale is not governed by Article 9.

Secured Party's Right to Possession after Default

In the absence of a contrary agreement, if the debtor defaults, the secured party has a right to possession of the collateral. Section 9–503 permits a secured party to take possession of the collateral if it may be done without breach of the peace. This means the secured party may go to the place where the collateral is and take possession of it. Although the UCC permits self-help repossession, the process is not without legal risk. One problem involves the meaning of the term "breach of peace," which is used in the statute but not defined. If the secured party commits a breach of the peace in repossessing the collateral, he or she is subject to tort liability. Generally, courts have construed this term broadly in a manner that protects the debtor, as the following case indicates.

General Electric Credit Corp., et al. v. Timbrook

Supreme Court of Appeals of West Virginia
291 S.E.2d 383 (1982)

"Donna June Timbrook (plaintiff-appellant) purchased a mobile home from Winchester Mobile Home Sales, Inc., a Virginia corporation (defendant-appellee), on September 10, 1974. . . . In 1979, Timbrook became delinquent in her payments. She contacted West Virginia Legal Services Plan, Inc., which wrote several letters to Winchester trying to arrange an agreeable payment schedule; but in April, 1980, Winchester sued in Mineral County Circuit Court for judgment for her indebtedness. Timbrook answered, counterclaimed, and raised a bona fide defense."

In mid-May Timbrook found a handwritten note on her door requesting that she call Winchester's collection department. The next day she purchased a new lock for her front door, but on May 29, 1980, while she was at work, representatives of the creditor broke her lock (to release a household pet) and removed her home and all her possessions from its cinder-block foundation (destroyed in the process) and carried it back to old Virginia.

Timbrook obtained a preliminary injunction to prevent further disposition of her property, but after full hearing, the trial court dissolved it and ruled that the repossession was proper because there had been no breach of peace. Timbrook appealed from the trial court's order. Reversed and remanded.

Harshbarger, Justice

A creditor's common law right to self-help repossession has been codified in the Uniform Commercial Code, Article 9, Section 503:

> Unless otherwise agreed a secured party has on default the right to take possession of the collateral. In taking possession a secured party may proceed without judicial process if this can be done *without breach of the peace* or may proceed by action. If the security agreement so provides the secured party may require the debtor to assemble the collateral and make it available to the secured party at a place to be designated by the secured party which is reasonably convenient to both parties. Without removal a secured party may render equipment unusable, and may dispose of collateral on the debtor's premises under section 9-504.

We have never defined what a breach of peace is, that would vitiate a self-help repossession. Several authorities make criminal "breach of peace" analyses, but we believe the term has a broader Uniform Commercial Code meaning.

Tortious activity incites or tends to incite breaches of the peace. The use or threat of violence impairs the tranquility to which our citizens are entitled in their homes and possessions.

White and Summers, leading scholars on the Uniform Commercial Code, have resolved:

> To determine if a breach of peace has occurred, courts inquire mainly into: (1) whether there was entry by the creditor upon the debtor's premises; and (2) whether the debtor or one acting on his behalf consented to the entry and repossession.
>
> In general, the creditor may not enter the debtor's home or garage without permission. . . .

We agree with those courts that have recognized breakings and unauthorized entries of debtors' dwellings to be breaches of the peace that deprive creditor or repossessors of self-help default remedies.

A creditor has a legitimate interest in getting collateral from a defaulting debtor. That strong interest, however, must be balanced against a person's right to be free from invasions of his home.

Creditors have other options that do not threaten rights that our laws have always jealously protected. If there can be no repossession without peace breaching, they can sue.

And, of course, if repossessions result in breaches of the peace, creditors are responsible for any torts they commit.

This record revealed that Timbrook's mobile home door was locked, evincing lack of owner consent to enter. An unauthorized entry into a debtor's dwelling is a breach of peace. . . .

The trial court erred in finding that the peace had not been breached. We remand for further proceedings consistent with this opinion.

Reversed and remanded.

Disposition of Collateral

After default the secured party may sell, lease, or otherwise dispose of the collateral. The disposition may be by public or private proceedings—but every aspect of the disposition, including the method, manner, time, place, and terms, must be commercially reasonable. Prior to public sale, the secured party usually must notify the debtor of the time and place of the sale or, if it is a private sale, the debtor must be notified of the time. If nonconsumer goods are involved, the secured party must also notify any other secured party from whom he or she has received written notice of a claim of an interest in the collateral.

The purchaser of the collateral generally takes free of any security interest or lien subordinate to that of the secured party. If the purchaser bought at a public sale, he or she must not have had knowledge of any defects in the sale and must not have bought in collusion with the secured party, other bidders, or anyone else conducting the sale. In any other case, the purchaser must simply act in good faith.

As a general rule, the secured party may retain the collateral in satisfaction of the obligation. If a secured party wishes to do this, the debtor and other appropriate parties, such as those with security interests in the collateral, must be notified. In the absence of objections within twenty-one days from the date of notifi-cation, the secured party may keep the collateral. If objections are received, he or she must dispose of the collateral as directed by the UCC.

If the collateral is sold, the proceeds are distributed in the following order: The reasonable expenses incurred in repossessing and disposing of the collateral are deducted. Next, the secured party collects the unpaid debt and other lawful charges agreed to in the security agreement. Finally, if the secured party receives written demand from any subordinate security interests, these are paid. Any remaining funds go to the debtor. For example, if the debtor owed the secured party $50,000 and put up his or her equipment as collateral for a loan, the distribution would be as follows if the secured party got $90,000 for the equipment: The secured party's reasonable administrative expenses would first be deducted (suppose they were $2,000), leaving $88,000. Then the $50,000 would be deducted, leaving $38,000. If he or she had received a written demand from a subordinate party who also claimed that the debtor owed him or her $50,000, the subordinate party would get the balance of the $38,000.

Right of Redemption

Although rarely done in actual practice, the collateral may be redeemed by the debtor or any other secured party any time before the secured party has disposed of it, or entered into a contract to dispose of it, or completed the process for retaining the collateral under Section 9–505(2). The party redeeming, however, must pay all money owed and perform all obligations owing at the time he or she attempts to redeem the property.

Liability of Secured Party for Noncompliance

Clearly, if the secured party is not performing as required by the UCC, he or she may be restrained from disposing of the collateral. If the disposition has already occurred, the secured party is liable for any loss caused by a failure to comply with Part 5 of Article 9.

Of particular significance is the penalty when consumer goods are used as collateral. If the secured party fails to meet the requirements of the UCC in this instance, he or she will be liable for an amount not less than the finance charge together with 10 percent of the principal.

Citizens State Bank v. Hewitt

Court of Appeals of Georgia

279 S.E.2d 531 (1981)

Citizens State Bank (plaintiff-appellant) sought a judgment against Walter C. Hewitt (defendant-appellee) for $4,225. Plaintiff alleged that defendant had failed to make payments for a boat and automobile as agreed upon by contract and that it had exercised its right to foreclose. Defendant answered in general, denying plaintiff's claim and, as affirmative defenses, claimed that reasonable notice of foreclosure sale was not provided as required by law. The court directed a verdict in favor of plaintiff on the automobile and in favor of defendant with respect to the boat. Plaintiff appealed. The appellate court affirmed.

McMurray, Presiding Judge

On July 24, 1975, Walter C. Hewitt executed and delivered a combination note and security agreement creating a security interest in favor of Citizens State Bank, Kingsland, Georgia, in a 1975 Dodge pickup truck. On October 7, 1976, Hewitt executed and delivered a second combination note and security agreement creating a security interest in favor of the bank in a 135 horsepower Evinrude motor, a 2000 Gator trailer, and a McKee Craft boat. Hewitt thereafter became in default in his payments on the two notes. On July 11, 1978, the bank . . . repossessed Hewitt's truck, boat, motor, and trailer, returning same to its parking lot where a "For Sale" sign was displayed on each item.

On July 12, 1978, a standard form letter correspondence was forwarded to Hewitt, titled "Notice of Intention to Pursue Deficiency Claim" with reference to the personal items secured. However, in the body of the correspondence it advised Hewitt with reference to *the automobile* [all emphases by the court] repossessed after default it would be sold "in order for Citizens State Bank to recover the amounts owed under your contract plus any expenses allowed by law." Further, if the proceeds from the sale are not sufficient to pay the entire amount owed plus any expenses, the bank intended to pursue a deficiency claim against Hewitt. The letter further advised that he had a *right to redeem the automobile* and terminate the contract by paying the bank a certain amount at any time prior to the first day on which *the automobile* would be offered for sale, "if not redeemed, or at any time thereafter until it is sold." The letter also advised him he had a *right to demand a public sale of the automobile* by so advising the bank of his demand "in writing by registered or certified mail . . . within ten . . . days of the posting of this notice." There was no mention in the body of the letter that the boat, motor and trailer had been repossessed, would thereafter be sold and a deficiency judgment sought in the event the proceeds from the sale were not sufficient to pay off the indebtedness; the right to redeem same and terminate the contract or that Hewitt had a right to demand a public sale of these items. The items were then sold at separate private sales, that is, the "Dodge pickup" to one business concern and the boat, motor and trailer to another some 6 months later.

Citizens State Bank, as plaintiff, then sought judgment against the defendant for $4,225 with interest as provided by law and reasonable attorney fees. . . .

The defendant answered in general denying the claim, admitting only jurisdiction and the execution of the two separate notes executed by him in favor of the plaintiff. Defendant added other affirmative defenses that all notices were not reasonable as required by law and the private sale of the collateral was not commercially reasonable as required by Code Ann. Section 109A-9-504.

After discovery and the issuance of the pretrial order in which the issues were narrowed to whether or not an actionable deficiency exists in the amount owed plaintiff by defendant under the promissory notes and whether the sale of the property was accomplished in a commercially reasonable manner, the case proceeded to trial. At the completion of the evidence defendant moved for a directed verdict contending the plaintiff had failed to carry the burden of proof that it had "reasonably notified the debtor" that it would seek a deficiency judgment; that it intended to sell the goods at a private sale and when that sale was to take place, and that the defendant had never waived his right to notification; further, that the sale must be commercially reasonable and that plaintiff failed to prove that every aspect of the sale, including the method, manner, time, place and terms were commercially reasonable and that the resale was a fair and reasonable value of the collateral at the time of the repossession, thereby precluding plaintiff from a deficiency judgment. The plaintiff in its argument and response to the motion contends that the letter was satisfactory to all purposes as to every item of personal property even though it is quite clear from the letter that *only the automobile* was mentioned. The trial court then denied the motion with respect to the Dodge motor vehicle but granted the motion with respect to the boat, motor, and trailer inasmuch as the language in the letter "your indebtedness" was insufficient under the law to supply notice as to the intentions of the secured party with reference to the boat, motor, and trailer and the notice did not notify the debtor that the plaintiff was going to dispose of them in a commercially reasonable manner in a public or private sale. The court stated to counsel that the Uniform Commercial Code, being in derogation of the common law it must be strictly construed and that the plaintiff failed to give proper notice with respect to the boat, motor, and trailer that plaintiff intended to seek a deficiency judgment after sale, either public or private.

Thereafter, plaintiff moved for a directed verdict with reference to the deficiency on the promissory note involving the motor vehicle, and the court directed a verdict in the amount of $1,666.60 (including statutory attorney fees), with reference thereto instructing the jury to eliminate plaintiff's claim for $2,731 plus statutory attorney fees, plus costs, with respect to the boat, motor and trailer, based upon the evidence in the case. A judgment was then entered reciting that the jury had been directed to render a verdict to the plaintiff with reference to the promissory note executed July 24, 1975, and in favor of the defendant with regard to the note executed October 7, 1976, and granted plaintiff judgment against the defendant for the sum of $1,666.60. Both plaintiff and defendant filed notices of appeal, but the defendant later dismissed his appeal. *Held:*

Code Ann. Section 109A-9-504, sets forth in detail the secured party's right to dispose of collateral after default. As to the effect of the disposition and its right to seek a deficiency, paragraph (3) states clearly that the disposition of the collateral may be by public or private proceedings and may be made by way of one or more contracts. Sale or other disposition may be as a unit or in parcels and at any time and place and on any terms *"but every aspect of the disposition including the method, manner, time, place and terms must be commercially reasonable . . . (and) . . . reasonable notification of the time and place of any public sale or reasonable notification of the time after which any private sale or other intended disposition is to be made shall be sent by the secured party to the debtor,"* if he has not after default signed a statement waiving, renouncing, or modifying his right to notification of the sale. Compliance with this Code section is a condition precedent to recovery of any deficiency between the sale price of the collateral and the amount of the unpaid balance. The secured party, in failing to strictly comply with the statutory law (Code Ann. Section 109A-9-504, supra, with reference to the reasonable notification of the time after which any private sale or other intended disposition is to be made) cannot recover the deficiency.

The trial court did not err in directing the verdict against the plaintiff where it is clear from the notice that there was noncompliance with Code Ann. Section 109A-9-504(3).

Judgment affirmed.

REVIEW PROBLEMS

1. Norton bought a used tractor from Hodges for $12,500, giving Hodges a security interest in the tractor to secure the unpaid portion of the purchase price. Three months later, after paying $370, Norton defaulted and returned the tractor. Hodges then sold the tractor at a public auction for $2,500 and sued Norton for the balance.

At the trial there was evidence that Hodges's attorney had posted a notice of the auction on the courthouse door as required by state law. This notice was posted two weeks prior to the sale. No notice of the sale was sent to Norton, nor was there any evidence of additional publicity. When returned, the tractor had been subject to ordinary wear and tear. The UCC requires that a creditor's disposition of the collateral be done in a commercially reasonable manner. Is Hodges entitled to a deficiency judgment? Discuss. Hodges v. Norton, 223 S.E.2d 848 (1976)

2. Bristol, Inc. entered into an agreement leasing a store premises to the Commonwealth of Pennsylvania. Two years later Bristol, Inc. borrowed from Girard Trust and as security assigned its interest in the lease to Girard. Girard did not record its security interest under Article 9 or make any other public record of the assignment.

   The following year Bristol, Inc. filed a petition in bankruptcy. A receiver was appointed. The receiver retained all rentals from the store and applied them to Bristol's business operations. Girard Trust thereupon filed a petition with the bankruptcy court to recover the rentals paid to the receiver under the lease that has been assigned. Should the petition be granted? Discuss. In Re Bristol Associates, Inc. 505 F.2d 1056 (1974)

3. Peco leased an electronic cutting machine to Hartbauer for 36 months for a rental of $26,399.96. The rental included an $8,000 "lease deposit" to be paid by work performed by Hartbauer for Peco, with the balance in regular monthly installments of $511.11, each. The lease gave Hartbauer an option to purchase the equipment any time after the 36 months, if not then in default, for a purchase price of $1,000. Peco never filed a financing statement.

   Within the 36-month period, Hartbauer, being insolvent, executed an assignment for the benefit of creditors to Dodge. Dodge intends to sell the machine leased by Peco to Hartbauer at an auction. Peco brings a suit to enjoin the sale. There is proof that at the end of the lease the value of the machine would be $10,000. Would the injunction be granted? Explain, indicating the issue involved. Peco, Inc. v. Hartbauer Tool & Die Co., 500 P.2d 708 (1972)

4. F purchased a mobile home from L, executing an installment contract and a security agreement. The security agreement gave L a purchase money security interest in the mobile home. L eventually sold this to M. On the date that F purchased the mobile home he acquired title; however, pursuant to an understanding with L, F left the mobile home on L's lot. The trailer was to be picked up later, at which time F would make the down payment.

   In the meantime, R, who financed L's purchase of inventory and held a security interest therein, seized all of L's inventory, including F's trailer as L had defaulted. R eventually sold the mobile home to another. F, upon returning to L's lot, found the mobile home gone and refused to pay M. M asserts its right to the mobile home as a secured creditor of F.

   A. In order for M to prevail, the security interest under F's security agreement must have attached. Had the security interest in fact attached? Discuss.

   B. What effect, if any, did the fact that the mobile home was left on L's lot have on any attainment of the security interest? Rex Financial Corp. v. Mobile American Corp., 23 U.C.C. Rep. 788 (Ariz. 1978)

5. A purchased a motor home from L by installment contract. The contract signed by A contained an agreement not to assert any claims or defenses A might have with respect to the contract against any assignee of the contract should L assign it. Shortly after the contract was entered into, L assigned it to Bank. Approximately one year later, A ceases to make payments under the contract, asserting that the motor home was in fact used and not new as represented by L and that L had failed to rectify defects on the motor home.

   Is A bound by his agreement waiving all claims and defenses against Bank? ARE v. Barrett Bank, 300 So.2d 250 (1976)

6. R obtained a judgment against M. Upon attempting to levy execution against a herd of cattle, R discovered M's interest therein was subject to a security interest in favor of a third party. The financing statement on file in the county court house lacked the signature of the secured party and the addresses of both M and the secured party. R then challenged the validity of the security interest, as it otherwise had priority over the judgment lien. All parties involved are residents of the same small town—R knew M and the secured party and where they each lived.

A. Was the failure of the secured party to sign the financing statement fatal to his or her security interest?

B. Was the omission of the secured party's and M's address fatal to the security interest? Riley v. Miller, 549 S.W.2d 314 (1977)

Bankruptcy

T he use of credit for the purchase of property, goods, and services has become common for both consumers and businesses. In difficult economic times, when interest rates soar and unemployment and loss of income are experienced by consumers and businesses alike, many borrowers are forced into bankruptcy. Approximately 200,000 bankruptcies are filed each year in the United States, 85 percent of them personal bankruptcies.

Bankruptcy laws provide relief and protection to the debtor while fairly distributing the debtor's assets among creditors. Bankruptcy laws are provided for in Article I, Section 8 of the U.S. Constitution: "The Congress shall have the power . . . to establish . . . uniform laws on the subject of bankruptcies throughout the United States." Thus bankruptcy laws are entirely federal; states do not have the power to enact bankruptcy laws. State laws do, however, play a role in bankruptcy proceedings in defining the nature of liens, secured transactions, and other property interests.

THE BANKRUPTCY ACT OF 1978

Bankruptcy Courts

The Bankruptcy Reform Act of 1978, which became effective on October 1, 1979, is the source of the present law on bankruptcies. This act made a number of reforms in the previous law, including the creation of a separate system of federal bankruptcy courts presided over by bankruptcy judges. Previously, bankruptcy cases had been the responsibility of the federal district courts. Unlike other federal judges, who are appointed for life by the President with the advice and consent of the Senate, bankruptcy judges are appointed by the President, with the advice and consent of the Senate, for fourteen-year terms.[1]

While a bankruptcy judge has broad powers, he or she does not in fact administer the debtor's estate. That power is given to a trustee in bankruptcy. A temporary trustee is initially appointed by the bankruptcy judge; later the creditors are allowed to select a permanent trustee of their own choosing at their initial meeting. The trustee represents the debtor's estate and administers it by collecting the property, investigating the financial status of the debtor, and making reports to the court concerning the distribution of the estate.

Types of Bankruptcy Proceedings

Liquidation. The bankruptcy laws provide for three kinds of proceedings. Liquidation or straight bankruptcy is the most common type and will be the primary focus for our discussion.

Reorganization. A reorganization is a type of bankruptcy proceeding frequently used by corporate debtors. Essentially, this type of proceeding allows the debtor to stay in business rather than liquidate. In the reorganization, the debtor and creditors agree on a plan that provides for the debtor to pay some portion of its debts while being discharged from paying the remaining portion. The main features of this form of bankruptcy will be noted and compared to the liquidation proceedings near the end of the chapter.

Regular Income. A third type of bankruptcy proceeding, provided for in Chapter 13 of the bankruptcy laws, permits the adjustment of debts of an individual with a regular income. This proceeding is often referred to as either a Chapter 13 or regular-income plan, since it provides relief for an individual who has a regular income but does not result in the debtor becoming bankrupt. The regular-income plan will be briefly discussed at the end of this chapter.

THE BANKRUPTCY PROCEEDING

The liquidation or straight bankruptcy proceeding is either voluntary (started by the debtor) or involuntary (started by the creditors). The debtor can be an individual, a corporation, or a partnership that has a residence, domicile, place of business, or property in the United States. Corporations that are subject to extensive regulation by administrative agencies are not subject to the bankruptcy law. The financial failures of insurance companies, banks, savings and loan associations, and similar institutions are subject to special regulatory proceedings rather than the bankruptcy laws. Railroads and municipal corporations are not subject to the liquidation or straight bankruptcy proceedings. Railroads are subject to the reorganizations referred to at the end of this chapter, while municipal corporations can seek adjustment of their debts under another section of the bankruptcy laws if state laws authorize such action.

Commencement of the Proceeding

Voluntary Proceeding. The filing of a voluntary proceeding automatically subjects the debtor and its property to the jurisdiction and supervision of the bankruptcy court. Once the petition is filed, creditors cannot start a suit or seek the enforcement of an existing judgment against the debtor. The filing of the petition for a voluntary bankruptcy by the debtor acts as a *stay* upon other proceedings. However, some actions such as criminal proceedings and the collection of alimony or child support are excluded from the effect of the stay.

Involuntary Proceeding. Creditors can file an involuntary proceeding against any debtor who could have filed a voluntary proceeding, with two exceptions: an involuntary proceeding cannot be filed against farmers or nonprofit corporations. If the debtor has twelve or more creditors, at least three of the creditors must join in filing the petition. If there are fewer than twelve creditors, any one of them can file the petition. Regardless of how many creditors file, their unsecured claims against the debtor must total at least $5,000. Thus two irate creditors, with claims against a debtor totaling $3,000, cannot force the debtor into involuntary bankruptcy; neither can 200 such creditors having a total of less than $5,000 in claims.

If the debtor does not challenge the creditors' petition, the debtor's property is subjected to the jurisdiction and supervision of the bankruptcy court. However, if the debtor does challenge the petition, the creditors must prove that the debtor has not been paying his debts as they become due or that the debtor's property has been placed in receivership or assignment for the benefit of the creditors within 120 days before the petition was filed. Once the creditors prove either requirement, the debtor's property is subjected to the court's supervision. But if neither requirement is proven, the creditors' petition is dismissed.

The *Jenkins* case that follows concerns the filing of an involuntary proceeding against a debtor who claimed he was a farmer. While the case was decided under the old law, its analysis of this question would probably be followed by a court interpreting a similar provision of the new law.

Jenkins v. Petitioning Creditor—Ray E. Friedman
8th Circuit Court of Appeal
664 F.2d 184 (1981)

Friedman, the petitioning creditor, filed a petition seeking to have Jenkins adjudicated an involuntary bankrupt. The petition was filed after Jenkins transferred some of his property to other creditors, a transfer that Friedman said was fraudulent and constituted a preference. Jenkins contended that he was a farmer and thus exempt from being adjudged bankrupt as a result of an involuntary proceeding.

The bankruptcy court determined that Jenkins was not a farmer, but its decision was reversed by the District Court. The Court of Appeals found that Jenkins was a farmer and affirmed the decision of the District Court.

McMillian, Circuit Judge

Friedman, a Chicago-based brokerage firm, commenced this involuntary bankruptcy proceeding on June 28, 1978, alleging that Jenkins had fraudulently and preferentially transferred certain assets and property to local creditors during the months of February and March, 1978. In part, these transfers were accomplished through the foreclosure and sale of property encumbered in favor of the local creditors. At this time, Jenkins was allegedly indebted to Friedman in the amount of $224,280. The debt resulted from losses incurred by Jenkins in commodities futures trading, mainly pork bellies, with Friedman acting as his broker. Jenkins' trading activities consistently resulted in losses; through his trading with Friedman in the first three months of 1978, Jenkins suffered a net loss exceeding $560,000. Funds were advanced by Friedman to cover margin call deficits incurred by Jenkins, who in turn borrowed a total of $330,000 from a local bank to repay the brokerage firm.

Following the transfer of property by Jenkins, Friedman initiated this action, seeking to have Jenkins adjudicated an involuntary bankrupt. Jenkins filed a motion to dismiss, contending he was a "farmer" and was therefore exempt from an adjudication of involuntary bankruptcy under § 4(b) of the Bankruptcy Act, 11 U.S.C. § 22(b). The Act, §1(17) defines a "farmer" as

> an individual *personally engaged in farming or tillage of the soil,* and shall include an individual personally engaged in dairy farming or in the production of poultry, livestock, or poultry or livestock products in their unmanufactured state, *if the principal part of his income is derived from any one or more of such operations.* (emphasis supplied).

We believe the definitional standard of § 1(17) is satisfied in this case. The bankruptcy court specifically found that Jenkins was "personally engaged in farming" from 1963 through the 1978 season; Friedman apparently does not challenge this finding. Further, examination of Jenkins' income at the time in question supports the district court's conclusion that the principal part of Jenkins' income was derived from farming. The record indicates that Jenkins earned gross income of approximately $60,000 from his farming operations during the first three quarters of 1978. During this period, Jenkins also received $2,820 from the sale of hail insurance, a business he maintained in addition to farming. Jenkins did not realize any income from his commodities trading. Like the district court, we do not believe that the term "income" as used in § 1(17) was intended to include borrowed funds. Consequently, it is clear that the principal part of Jenkins' income during 1978 was derived from farming. The requirements of § 1(17) are therefore satisfied in this case.

Friedman contends, however, that § 1(17) must not be applied literally, arguing instead that factors in addition to income, particularly the source of the alleged bankrupt's indebtedness, must be considered in determining whether a debtor falls within the "farmer" exemption. In this case, the company asserts, consideration of the source of Jenkins' indebtedness, his commodities trading losses, would evidence an occupational pursuit other than farming. Friedman cites several decisions in which source of indebtedness was considered important in determining applicability of the "farmer" exemption. . . . Although Jenkins' commodities trading occurred on a regular basis and resulted in substantial losses, Friedman has not established that his trading activities were more than a collateral venture, albeit an unsuccessful one.

In sum, we conclude that the requirements of § 1(17) are satisfied in this case. Accordingly, the order of the district court is affirmed.

The Role of Creditors

Within a reasonable time after a petition in bankruptcy has been filed, the debtor must file with the court a schedule of assets and liabilities, a statement of financial affairs, and a list of creditors. The creditors listed by the debtor are then notified of the bankruptcy petition. Those who have claims against the debtor file proofs of claims with the court. The court generally allows the claims unless they are objected to by the debtor or other creditors. The creditors who are claimants in the bankruptcy proceeding are generally unsecured creditors.

If a creditor has a claim secured by a security interest or other lien on specific property of the debtor, that creditor, and only that creditor, can use the property to pay off the debt. If the value of that property is equal to the value of the debt, he need not be concerned with the debtor's remaining assets and liabilities. An unsecured creditor is a person whose claim must be paid from the general property of the debtor; this creditor has no right or legal interest to any specific property of the debtor. It is this creditor who usually is most affected by the debtor's bankruptcy.

After the claims of the creditors have been filed and allowed, the court calls a meeting of the unsecured creditors. The judge cannot appear at the creditors' meeting, but a temporary trustee appointed by the judge does attend. At their first meeting, the creditors normally do several things. First, they usually elect a permanent trustee. The permanent trustee may be the person appointed by the court to serve on a temporary basis or it may be someone else. At least 20 percent of the total amount of unsecured claims that have been filed and allowed must be represented at the meeting. The vote of creditors holding more than half of the total value of the unsecured claims represented at the meeting elects the trustee.

The second function performed by the creditors at their first meeting is the examination of the debtor. The debtor is placed under oath and is asked questions by the creditors and the trustee. The questions usually concern the nature of the debtor's assets and matters relevant to the potential discharge of the debts listed by the debtor.

THE DEBTOR'S ESTATE

Property in the Estate

The trustee is responsible for administering the debtor's estate. He or she collects all the property in the estate, reduces the property to money, and closes the estate after distributing the money according to the priorities established by the bankruptcy law. The debtor's estate consists of all property owned by or on behalf of the debtor as of the date of the filing of the bankruptcy petition. The *Turpin* case that follows involves the determination of whether certain employee benefits held for the debtor constitute property that should be included in the debtor's estate.

Matter of Turpin

5th Circuit Court of Appeals
644 F.2d 472 (1981)

Turpin filed for bankruptcy and did not include in his estate his interest in a pension plan and a profit-sharing plan established by his employer. The trustee in bankruptcy sought to have Turpin's interest in the plan transferred to the trustee, since the bankruptcy laws provide that the trustee takes title to all "property" of the debtor who files for bankruptcy. The bankruptcy court concluded that the title to the pension and profit-sharing funds belonged to the trustee. That decision was affirmed by the District Court. However, the Court of Appeals found that pension and profit-sharing funds such as those held for Turpin were similar to future wages, since he was not entitled to them on the date of the filing of the petition. As future wages and benefits, they pass to the bankrupt free of claims of creditors so that the bankrupt can leave the bankruptcy proceeding with a clean slate and some assets with which to support himself and his family. The decision of the bankruptcy court and of the District Court was reversed and remanded for proceedings consistent with the opinion of the Court of Appeals.

Per Curiam

Appellant William R. Turpin filed a voluntary petition in bankruptcy on December 16, 1976. On April 6, 1977, Appellee, the trustee in bankruptcy, filed a complaint against Turpin and City National Bank of Austin in the bankruptcy court. The complaint asserted that the bankruptcy trustee was entitled to certain funds held for the credit of Turpin by the bank as trustee of the Austin Neurosurgical Association Profit Sharing Plan Trust and the Austin Neurosurgical Association Money Purchase Pension Plan Trust.

These two trusts had been created by Turpin's employer, the Austin Neurosurgical Association (a professional corporation), in order to provide retirement benefits to its employees. Both funds are qualified pension plans under the Employee Retirement Income and Security Act of 1974, and the Internal Revenue Code. At the time the bankruptcy petition was filed, Turpin had been employed by the Association for seven years and pursuant to the trust agreements, the Association had contributed $66,-931.82 to the Profit Trust and $42,780.56 to the Pension Trust on Turpin's behalf.

In his answer appellant admitted that these funds were held in trust for his benefit but denied that the bankruptcy trustee had acquired any rights to these sums upon his declaration of bankruptcy.

The bankruptcy court concluded that title to the trust funds credited to Turpin as of the date the petition was filed had passed to the bankruptcy trustee pursuant to § 70(a)(5) of the Bankruptcy Act. The judgment of the bankruptcy court was affirmed by the district court.

On appeal, Turpin argues that his interest in the trusts was not property which passed to the trustee under § 70(a)(5) and that the trustee has no present claim or future right to any of the funds. We agree.

Section 70(a)(5) of the Bankruptcy Act formerly provided that

> (a) The trustee of the estate of a Bankrupt . . . shall . . . be vested by operation of law with the title of the bankrupt as of the date of the filing of the petition [to] . . . (5) property, including rights of action, which prior to the filing of the petition he could by any means have transferred or which might have been levied upon and sold under judicial process against him, or otherwise seized, impounded or sequestered. . . .

This circuit has previously examined the question whether retirement benefits which a bankrupt is entitled to receive in the future fall within the category of property which passes to the trustee under § 70(a)(5). *In re Nunnally*, 506 F.2d 1024 (5th Cir. 1975). In *Nunnally*, we concluded that the trustee had no claim upon such benefits, and we adhere to that conclusion today.

Our decision in *Nunnally* was guided by three Supreme Court opinions which articulated principles for determining whether a particular asset is property transferred to the trustee under § 70(a)(5). In these cases the court emphasized that the scope of the term "property" as used in § 70(a)(5) must be determined with reference to the distinctive purposes of the Bankruptcy Act. Although the primary purpose of the Bankruptcy Act may be "to secure for creditors everything of value that the bankrupt may possess in alienable or leviable form," . . . the Act is also designed to provide the bankrupt with a clean slate—"to leave the bankrupt free after the date of his petition to accumulate new wealth in the future" and thus to enable the bankrupt to "make an unencumbered fresh start." . . .

In light of this policy of providing the bankrupt with a clean slate, the Supreme Court has reasoned that the bankrupt's future wages and assets "designed to function as a wage substitute at some future period and during that future period to 'support the basic requirements of life for [the debtors] and their families. . . .' '', do not fall within the category of property which passes to the trustee pursuant to § 70(a)(5).

In *Nunnally* we concluded that retirement benefits were assets designed to provide the bankrupt with a substitute for wages at some point in the future and thus the bankruptcy trustee had no claim to them under § 70(a)(5). We reach the same conclusion with regard to the benefits at issue here. . . .

In *Nunnally* we concluded awarding the bankrupt's retirement benefits to the trustee would deprive the bankrupt of a genuine fresh start not because of the bankrupt's immediate need for the funds but because to recognize the trustee's claim against the funds would leave a cloud of pre-bankruptcy debt hanging over the bankrupt's future. Providing the bankrupt with a "fresh start" means assuring him that assets to which he may become entitled *in the future* will be acquired free of any pre-bankruptcy obligations. Future wages may not be garnished to pay those obligations and pension benefits received in the future, even though they may be the product of pre-bankruptcy contributions to a pension fund, are a substitute for future wages and thus pass to the bankrupt free of the claims of pre-bankruptcy creditors.

Our conclusion in *Nunnally* that the bankruptcy trustee may not claim title to a bankrupt's future retirement benefits under § 70(a)(5) still strikes us as a sound one and, in any event, it controls the outcome of this case. We reaffirm it today, we order that the judgment entered by the bankruptcy court and affirmed by the district court be reversed and we remand for proceedings consistent with this opinion.

Reversed and remanded.

Property Added to the Estate

After-Acquired Property. Certain property acquired by the debtor after the petition has been filed will be added to the debtor's estate. Specifically, property acquired within 180 days after the date of the filing of the petition is added to the estate if the debtor acquired the property by inheritance, as a result of a property settlement or divorce decree with the debtor's spouse, or as a beneficiary on a life-insurance policy.

Preference Property. The trustee has the right under some circumstances to avoid or recall certain transfers of property made by the debtor. If the debtor transferred property to one creditor in prejudice to other creditors at a time when the debtor was insolvent, the property transferred may, under certain circumstances, be recovered and added to the debtor's estate. The transfer must have been made by the debtor within ninety days prior to the filing of the bankruptcy petition. It must have been made at a time when the debtor was insolvent, that is, when his debts were greater than his assets. The transfer must have given the creditor more than the creditor would have received through the bankruptcy proceeding in order to constitute a preference. Thus not all transfers of property to creditors prior to the filing of the petition constitute preferences; however, if the transfer does constitute a preference, it can be added to the debtor's estate.

Lien Creditor's Property. A third type of property that may be added to the debtor's estate is the property obtained by the trustee acting as a lien creditor. Thus, if the debtor had given to a creditor a lien on certain property and if that lien had not been perfected or had not become effective as of the date of the filing of the petition, the trustee could add that property to the debtor's estate. The trustee, as of the date of the filing of the petition, has the status of a lien creditor, and if that status gives the trustee a better claim on certain property than the claims of other creditors, the property that those creditors thought they had an interest in can be added to the debtor's estate. Those creditors would then not have any preference on the specific property added to the debtor's estate. Instead, they would become unsecured creditors who would file a claim and receive whatever portion of their debt that is eventually distributed to them by the trustee. Review the *Schalk* case, below, in which the trustee's status as a lien creditor is discussed. Note the importance of state law in determining the rights to the property that the trustee seeks to add to the debtor's estate.

Voidable Transfers. The trustee also has the power to restore to the debtor's estate certain property transferred by or on behalf of the debtor to third parties. First, any transfer made *after* the filing of the bankruptcy petition, whether by or on behalf of the debtor, can be voided by the trustee within two years after the transfer or before the bankruptcy case is concluded, whichever occurs first. Second, the trustee may void any transfer made by the debtor within one year prior to the filing of the petition if the transfer was a fraudulent transfer or was made with the intent of hindering, delaying, or defrauding a creditor. Finally, since the trustee administers the property of the debtor, any property that can be returned to the debtor due to someone else's fraud, mistake, duress, or undue influence can be reached by the trustee and added to the estate.

Matter of Schalk

8th Circuit Court of Appeals

592 F.2d 993 (1979)

The trustee for the estate of Robert Schalk sought to compel the Belle-Bland Bank to turn over a 1972 mobile home trailer to the trustee. The trustee claimed that its rights as a hypothetical lien creditor, whose lien was perfected as of the date of the filing of the petition in bankruptcy, gave it a better ownership claim to the property than that of the bank. The bankrupt Schalk had acquired an interest in the trailer by paying $1,000 and agreeing to pay the bank the balance owed by Limberg, the original purchaser of the trailer. However, since Limberg never transferred a certificate of title to Schalk, as required under state law, Schalk did not have title to the trailer on the date the petition was filed. Thus the trustee did not have title to the property, and the decision of the bankruptcy court, affirmed by the District Court, was also affirmed by the Court of Appeals.

Ross, Circuit Judge

In July 1971 a dealer, V. L. Long Mobile Homes, Inc., received the manufacturer's statement of origin for the trailer and on November 22, 1972, sold the vehicle to Lenora Limberg for $10,474.80. Limberg's purchase was financed by the Belle-Bland Bank which took a purchase money security interest in the vehicle.

V. L. Long did not assign the manufacturer's statement of origin to Limberg until October 26, 1973. On October 31, 1973, Limberg sent an application for Missouri title to the Missouri Department of Revenue with the bank's lien noted on the application. The department issued a certificate of title on November 8, 1973, showing Limberg as owner, with the bank's lien noted as of October 26, 1973.

In the meantime, after the sale to Limberg but before her application for a new certificate of ownership, Limberg executed a document on October 18, 1973, purporting to sell all of her interest in the trailer to Robert Stephen Schalk. However, she never assigned a certificate of title to Schalk. Schalk paid $1,000, took possession of the trailer and agreed to pay the remaining installments on Limberg's debt to the bank. He made twenty-four payments of $87.29 each to the bank until March 1976. Later the bank repossessed the trailer, and in October 1976 Schalk instituted bankruptcy proceedings.

The trustee, who succeeded under section 70(a) of the Bankruptcy Act to such title to personal property as the bankrupt had on the date of bankruptcy, claims title to the vehicle based on the October 18, 1973 sale to Schalk and his subsequent payments. However, we agree with the district court that Schalk did not obtain title to the trailer in October 1973 or at any time thereafter because of Limberg's failure to deliver an assigned certificate of title to Schalk.

Under Mo.Ann.Stat. § 301.210 (Vernon), a buyer's failure to obtain an assigned certificate of ownership in connection with his purchase of a registered motor vehicle or trailer in the state precludes title from passing to him and renders the sale void. The Missouri courts have construed section 301.210 strictly.

Mo.Ann.Stat. § 301.210(4) (Vernon) states:

> It shall be unlawful for any person to buy or sell in this state any motor vehicle or trailer registered under the laws of this state, unless at the time of the delivery thereof, there shall pass between the parties such certificate of ownership with an assignment thereof, as herein provided, and the sale of any motor vehicle or trailer registered under the laws of this state, without the assignment of such certificate of ownership, shall be fraudulent and void.

The Missouri courts have consistently held that absolute technical compliance with Sec. 301.210 is required, otherwise the sale is fraudulent and void. * * * Failure to strictly comply with the statute means no title passes and the purported buyer has no ownership. * * * This is true, painful as it may be, even where the buyer was guilty of no intentional wrongdoing, i. e., has acted in good faith. . . . The fact that the title to plaintiff's truck was of Maryland origin does not alter the necessity of compliance with § 301.210. * * * The statute is applicable to all sales made in Missouri, irrespective of the origin of the certificate of title. The purpose of the statute is aimed to hamper traffic in stolen motor vehicles and to prevent fraud and deceit in the sale of used cars and trucks.

Limberg did not hold legal title in trust for Schalk. At most, Schalk acquired a right to compel Limberg to assign the certificate of title to him. However, he never exercised this right. As Schalk did not have title to the trailer on the date of bankruptcy in October 1976, the trustee's claim based on section 70(a) must fail.

In the alternative, the trustee claims that the bank's lien on the trailer is subordinate to his rights arising under section 70(c) of the Bankruptcy Act, 11 U.S.C. § 110(c). Under section 70(c) and Mo.Ann.Stat. § 400.9-301(1)(b), (3) (Vernon), the trustee is vested with the rights of a hypothetical lien creditor whose lien was perfected as of the date of bankruptcy and who is deemed without notice of prior unperfected liens on the bankrupt's property.

We hold, however, that the bank had perfected its security interest in the trailer by November 1973. Thus the bank's lien, perfected before the date of bankruptcy, has priority over the trustee's section 70(c) lien which arose when bankruptcy proceedings were instituted in October 1976.

Mo.Ann.Stat. § 301.600 (Vernon) governs perfection of security interests in motor vehicles and trailers. That section states in part:

> 2. A lien or encumbrance on a motor vehicle or trailer is perfected by the delivery to the director of revenue of the existing certificate of ownership, if any, an application for a certificate of ownership containing the name and address of the lienholder and the date of his security agreement, and the required certificate of ownership fee. *It is perfected as of the time of its creation if the delivery of the aforesaid to the director of revenue is completed within thirty days thereafter, otherwise as of the time of the delivery.*

Therefore, the bank's security interest was perfected on October 31, 1973, when Limberg's application for a certificate of ownership noting the bank's lien was sent with the required fee to the Missouri Department of Revenue, or at the latest on November 8, 1973, when the certificate of title was issued showing Limberg as owner and the bank as lienholder as of October 26, 1973.

Accordingly, the judgment of the district court is affirmed.

Exemptions from the Estate

An individual debtor can claim certain exemptions that are not available to corporations or partnerships. The exempt property will not be included in the debtor's estate and thus will not be subject to distribution to the creditors. Instead, the debtor is allowed to keep the exempt property and still be discharged from the debts and liabilities he has listed.

The Bankruptcy Reform Act of 1978 made available to all debtors a list of properties exempt under federal bankruptcy laws. However, the debtor need not rely on that list if he or she desires instead to select the exemptions available under the law of the state where the debtor lives. Furthermore, the bankruptcy laws permit the state to require that the debtor use the exemptions listed under the state law. Thus the debtor has the choice of following either the state or the federal exemption list unless the law of the state where the debtor lives requires the debtor to follow the state list.

Federal Exemptions. The list of properties exempted by federal law from the debtor's estate in bankruptcy includes:

1. The debtor's residence, up to a value of $7,500
2. The debtor's interest in a motor vehicle, up to $1,200 in value
3. The debtor's interest in household furnishings, wearing apparel, appliances, books, musical instruments, animals, or crops held for personal, family, or household use up to $200 in value for each item
4. Up to $500 in jewelry
5. The debtor's interest in implements, tools of the trade, or professional books
6. Any unmatured life insurance policy owned by the debtor, except for credit life policies
7. Prescribed health aids
8. The debtor's right to certain public benefits, including unemployment compensation, social security, veteran's benefits, and disability benefits
9. The debtor's right to certain private benefits, including alimony, child support, pension and profit-sharing plans to the extent reasonably necessary for the support of the debtor or the debtor's dependents
10. The debtor's interest in any other kind of property up to a value of $400 plus any amount not used under the first exemption listed (thus, if a debtor does not own a residence, he can exempt $7,900 of property under this exemption)

State Exemptions. The properties exempt for a debtor under state law vary, depending on the state of the debtor's residence. Some state laws are more liberal than the federal law, particularly states where there is no dollar limit placed on the residence or homestead exemption. Compare this part of the federal exemptions to the homestead exemption law in Kansas as found in *Belcher* v. *Turner*.

Belcher v. Turner

10th Circuit Court of Appeals

579 F.2d 73 (1978)

Carl and Esther Belcher filed a voluntary petition for bankruptcy. They claimed that the duplex in which they lived was exempt property under the Kansas homestead exemption law. The bankruptcy judge found that only half of the duplex was exempt. The District Court agreed and the Court of Appeals affirmed the judgment of the District Court. While this case arose under prior law, where no federal exemptions were available, under present law, if the debtor sought to use the state exemptions, the law of the state where the debtor resided for the greater part of the preceding six months would be considered.

Lewis, Circuit Judge

This appeal arises out of bankruptcy proceedings in the district court for the District of Kansas. Appellants Carl and Esther Belcher filed a voluntary petition for bankruptcy in which they claimed as exempt property a side-by-side duplex which they own. The claim was made under the homestead exemption set out in the Kansas Constitution, art. 15, § 9 and Kan.Stat.Ann. § 60-2301.*

In a memorandum decision the bankruptcy judge found that each unit in the duplex has a separate entrance, driveway, garage, and address. There is no common entrance except through an unfinished attic. The Belchers had resided in one unit since purchasing the property and had always leased the other unit. After finding the above facts the bankruptcy judge discussed the applicable law and determined that only the half occupied by the Belchers was exempt. The district court affirmed.

Under 11 U.S.C. § 24, the Bankruptcy Act makes available to bankrupts those exemptions prescribed by state law. The scope and application of such exemptions are defined by the state courts and we are bound by their interpretations.

The Kansas cases which are most analogous on their facts are those considering an application of the exemption to property used by an owner partly as a residence and partly for business purposes. The most recent statement of the general rule [is] that

> [t]he test for determining whether a structure is a homestead is determined by its use or occupancy as a residence, and an incidental departure for business purposes does not deprive it of its homestead character. . . .

Of course, if [the building] should practically become a business house rather than a home, it would then cease to be exempt.

*Kan.Stat.Ann. § 60-2301 provides in pertinent part:
A homestead to the extent of one hundred and sixty (160) acres of farming land, or of one acre within the limits of an incorporated town or city, occupied as a residence by the family of the owner, together with all the improvements on the same, shall be exempted from forced sale under any process of law. . . .
The above exemption is made applicable to bankruptcy proceedings by 11 U.S.C. § 24.

Appellants argue the overriding purpose of this duplex was to provide them with a home. They suggest the rental of half the building was consistent with this purpose because the rent was used to pay the mortgage on the entire property. We believe these arguments ignore the underlying fact that half of the duplex has always been rented out and was never intended or expected to serve as appellants' residence. The unit was intended to produce income. Reduced to its essential, appellants' claim of exemption is based only on the fact that the two units are part of the same physical structure. This one factor is not and should not be dispositive. The Kansas cases cited by appellants which inferentially support exempting the entire duplex did not involve bankruptcy. The purpose and intent of the Bankruptcy Act and its allowance of the homestead exemption counsel a different result. The aim is to protect and preserve the residence of the debtor; exempting the half of the duplex in which appellants reside will fully achieve that purpose. The district court judgment is

Affirmed.

DISTRIBUTION OF DEBTOR'S ESTATE

Priority Claims

After the trustee has collected all the debtor's property and reduced it to money, the money is distributed to the creditors. (Secured creditors can proceed against the property with which their debt is secured. If any portion of their debt is unsecured, that portion must be considered along with other unsecured claims.) Some claims are given a higher priority than others. Claims are paid in order of their priority. Thus each class of claims is paid in full before any payment is made of claims of lower priority. If there is not enough money to pay fully all claims in any class, the money available is prorated among the creditors in that class.

The highest priority is assigned to the costs and expenses involved in administering the bankruptcy proceeding. These include legal fees, accountants' fees, trustee fees, and court costs. The next class of claims pertains only to involuntary proceedings: expenses occurring in the ordinary course of the debtor's business or financial affairs after filing of the case but prior to the appointment of the trustee make up the second class of claims. The third class consists of claims for wages, salaries, or commissions earned by employees within ninety days before the filing of the petition or the cessation of the debtor's business, whichever occurs first. Claims in this class are given priority up to $2,000 per individual.

Three other categories of claims have some priority over general claims. The fourth class consists of claims for contributions to an employee benefit plan arising from services rendered within 180 days before the filing of the petition or the cessation of the debtor's business. The limit per claimant in this category is also $2,000, and no individual can receive more than $2,000 from a combination of claims falling in the third and fourth priority classes. The fifth class is for claims for deposits made on consumer goods or services that were not received; the limit for claims in this class is $900. The sixth and last class consists of tax claims submitted by governmental units.

General Claims

If a claim exceeds the amount allowed as a priority, the excess becomes a general claim.

After all classes of priority claims have been paid, any remaining property is distributed on a pro-rata basis to all unsecured creditors with general claims against the debtor's estate. Often, there will be little, if any, distribution to creditors who have only a general claim against the debtor. Thus it is important to creditors who can do so to have their claims classified as priority claims.

Review the *Pan American Paper Mills* case relating to claims of what is now the sixth priority level. While the case was decided under prior law, which assigned tax claims to the fourth priority class, determination of whether the claim is a priority or a general claim would also have to be made by a court interpreting the new law. Note that this case actually involves a reorganization type of bankruptcy proceeding rather than a liquidation proceeding. Since the classification of claims is treated similarly in both types of proceedings, the case is inserted at this place for its discussion of claims classification.

In re Pan American Paper Mills, Inc.,
1st Circuit Court of Appeals
618 F.2d 159 (1980)

Pan American Paper Mills, Inc. (Pan Am) filed a Chapter 11 reorganization petition. Two claims were filed against Pan Am by the Puerto Rico Workmen's Compensation Act Insurance Fund. The Fund claimed that the first of the two claims was entitled to priority as taxes; the bankruptcy judge agreed. Pan Am then appealed, saying that its obligation to pay a premium to the Fund, because it had missed payments for several years, was a penalty assessed on it and that a penalty cannot be a tax. The District Court affirmed the decision of the bankruptcy judge and the Court of Appeals also affirmed.

Wyzanski, Senior District Judge

This appeal involves a tax priority claim made in bankruptcy proceedings. The question presented is whether unpaid "premiums" assessed under the Puerto Rico Workmen's Accident Compensation Act, for a period when an employer was covered but not insured constitute "taxes" entitled to priority under § 64(a)(4) of the Bankruptcy Act, 11 U.S.C. § 104(a)(4).

§ 64(a)(4) of the Bankruptcy Act, 11 U.S.C. § 104(a)(4) provides:

> (a) The debts to have priority, in advance of the payment of dividends to creditors, and to be paid in full out of bankrupt estates, and the order of payment, shall be . . . (4) taxes legally due and owing by the bankrupt to the United States or any State or any subdivision thereof. . . .

The Puerto Rico Workmen's Accident Compensation Act, (hereinafter the "WAC Act") establishes a comprehensive, compulsory insurance system which the parties agree covered Pan American Paper Mills, Inc., (Pan American) and its employees during the years relevant to this case. § 8 provides that the act shall be administered by a Manager who shall create a State Insurance Fund (hereinafter called "the Fund"). § 19 obliges every covered employer to insure his employees "in" the Fund. § 28 makes it the duty of every covered employer to file no later than July 20 of each year a "statement" or report showing the wages paid during the fiscal year that ended on the previous June 30. § 26 authorizes the Manager to assess premiums for the year following the report period, and provides that "said premiums shall be collected semi-annually in advance." However, the premium for the first semester (July 1 to December 31) is not due until a date specified in the notice of assessment, and the premium for the second semester (January 1 to June 30) is not due until January 2.

If the employer does not pay the premium before the end of the relevant semester the employer is not insured against any accident that occurs during that semester. Under the original form of the WAC Act, as enacted in the Puerto Rico Act of April 18, 1935, if the employer did not pay the premium before the end of the semester, then, because he was not insured for that semester, he was totally excused from any obligation to pay the premium at any time. [A] covered employee of a covered employer had the benefits of the WAC Act even though his employer was uninsured because he had failed promptly to pay a premium he owed. That is, the employee was free to proceed to recover from the Fund accident compensation for any covered injury and, in turn, the Fund was entitled to be compensated by the uninsured, but covered employer for all costs thus incurred by the Fund.

Pan American failed to pay its WAC Act premiums amounting to $68,250.61 for the years 1972 through 1976. On account of covered injuries which Pan American employees sustained during those years, the Fund paid them $50,897.05.

June 26, 1975 Pan American filed a petition for relief under Chapter XI of the Bankruptcy Act, 11 U.S.C. § 701, et seq. The Bankruptcy Judge allowed the petition and continued Pan American as a debtor in possession. The Fund filed two claims which were consolidated; the first or priority claim sought $68,250.61 on account of unpaid premiums which the Fund alleged were "taxes" entitled to priority under § 64(a)(4) of the Bankruptcy Act, 11 U.S.C. § 104(a)(4); and the second or unsecured claim sought $50,897.05 on account of compensation for what the Fund had paid to Pan American employees.

The Bankruptcy Judge entered an order allowing both claims and according a § 64(a)(4) tax priority to the first claim. The District Judge affirmed the order, and Pan American appealed.

Pan American's appeal is based on its argument that an obligation imposed upon an uninsured employer to pay a "premium" to the Fund established under the Workmen's Accident Compensation Act would be a penalty, and that therefore such an obligation cannot be a tax under § 64(a) of the Bankruptcy Act. We reject Pan American's argument and affirm the District Court.

The question whether an obligation is a tax entitled to priority under § 64(a)(4) of the Bankruptcy Act is a federal question.

The Supreme Court, taking a broad view of what constitutes "taxes" within the meaning of § 64(a)(4), has ruled that "the priority commanded by § 64 extends to those pecuniary obligations laid upon individuals or their property, regardless of their consent, for the purpose of defraying the expenses of government or of undertakings authorized by it."

That broad approach led lower courts to hold that where, pursuant to an unemployment compensation law, a state exacts from an employer so-called "contributions" a state's claim for such contributions is entitled to priority as a claim for taxes under Bankruptcy Act § 64(a)(4).

We see no reason not to apply the same approach to situations where pursuant to a workmen's compensation law a state or subdivision of the United States exacts from an employer so-called "premiums." The reason that such premiums should be treated as taxes within § 64(a)(4) of the Bankruptcy Act is that they are pecuniary obligations imposed by the government for the purpose of defraying the expenses of an undertaking which it authorized.

Appellant's argument in the case at bar that the Fund's priority claim of $68,250.61 for premiums is not a tax because in return for the premiums involved in the claim Pan American received no insurance protection rests upon a misconception. Bankruptcy Act § 64 gives priority to a premium claim if it has certain tax characteristics not because it has insurance characteristics. The pertinent questions about a so-called premium are whether the government compelled the employer to pay the exaction and whether the payment was for a public purpose.

In determining whether the premiums were "taxes" under Bankruptcy Act § 64(a)(4) it is of no consequence that had Pan American been prompt in paying the premiums it would have had as a *quid pro quo* insurance protection; nor is it of any consequence that since the corporation failed to make prompt payment it had no insurance protection. Pan American is not, except in a colloquial and inexact sense, punished in any way because of its delay. . . .

The decision of the district court is affirmed.

DISCHARGE OF DEBTS

After the debtor's estate has been liquidated and distributed among the creditors, the bankruptcy court conducts a hearing to determine if the debtor should be discharged from the remaining debts. A discharge can be granted to an individual petitioner, but a partnership or a corporation cannot be discharged from its debts under the bankruptcy laws. Those business entities may seek to reorganize under Chapter 11 of the federal bankruptcy laws or they may seek liquidation under state laws.

Exceptions to Discharge

Under certain circumstances, the court will deny a discharge to a debtor. If this occurs, the debtor remains liable for the unpaid portion of the creditors' claims. A debtor will be denied a discharge if a prior discharge was granted within six years of the filing of the petition. A discharge will not be granted if the debtor, within one year before the filing of the petition, or at any time thereafter, intentionally concealed or transferred assets with the intent to hinder, delay, or defraud creditors.

Other reasons for refusing a discharge to a debtor include the debtor's concealment, destruction, falsification, or failure to keep records related to the debtor's financial condition or business transactions. A debtor who fails to adequately explain the loss of assets or who refuses to obey a lawful order of the bankruptcy court or who makes any fraudulent statement or claim in connection with the bankruptcy case can be denied the discharge of unpaid debts, as the *Horton* case indicates. Since the new bankruptcy law has virtually the same provisions as those of the old law referred to in the *Horton* case, the determination made in *Horton* would probably be followed by courts reviewing the new law.

Matter of Horton
9th Circuit Court of Appeals
621 F.2d 968 (1980)

The debtor Horton appealed the decision of the bankruptcy judge, which was affirmed by the District Court, to refuse to grant a discharge of his debts. The bankruptcy judge refused a discharge because the debtor had failed to keep adequate records or accounts from which his financial condition and business transactions could be ascertained. In all his business transactions, the debtor dealt almost exclusively in cash. The fact that the debtor did not like banks did not absolve him from the duty under the bankruptcy laws to keep sufficient records of his financial conditions. The Court of Appeals affirmed the judgment of the bankruptcy judge and the District Court's denial of a discharge to the debtor.

Grant, District Judge

The defendant, Robert Jackson Horton, sought a discharge of his debts in bankruptcy. This was refused by the bankruptcy judge in December 1974. The reason for refusing discharge was "Horton's unjustified failure to keep adequate books of accounts or records from which his financial condition and business transactions could be discerned." Maintaining such records is required. This decision was affirmed by the district court which entered judgment against Horton after a consideration of the merits of his claim. Horton now appeals to this court, contending that the lower courts erred in not granting him relief.

Horton is no stranger to the Bankruptcy Court. He has made his appearance there like clockwork every seven years. He was first granted a discharge in 1960 and again in 1967. This latest petition in bankruptcy was filed in 1973. At that time the case was routinely assigned to Judge Downey. The judge immediately disqualified himself, however, since he had presided over the previous discharges and felt he did not have the requisite impartiality in Horton's latest cause. The case was accordingly assigned to Judge Hughes.

The Bankruptcy Act provides that a discharge cannot be granted if the bankrupt has failed to keep sufficient records of his financial transactions. Although this failure may be deemed justifiable under the particular circumstances of the bankrupt, in this case the failure was found unjustified. Horton alleges that the findings of fact and law were insufficient under the requirements of Bankruptcy Rule 752(a).

The record reveals that the bankruptcy judge filed a five-page memorandum in which he reduced a convoluted and often contradictory factual record into findings of law and fact. This memorandum assessed (1) the records Horton kept, (2) the sufficiency of those records, and (3) once the records were found to be insufficient, whether the keeping of insufficient records was excusable in this particular case. The memorandum is more than sufficient to satisfy the requirements of Rule 752(a).

Horton's essential disagreement is not with the sufficiency of the findings, but with their correctness and the appropriateness of the legal standard applied. Therefore, we turn our attention to determining whether these findings are supported by the record. Unless they are clearly erroneous, they will not be disturbed on appeal.

Using these standards, we have assessed the record in this case. It shows that Horton dealt almost exclusively in cash during all his business transactions, keeping little or no verifiable records. He was unable to show where his salary was spent. As the bankruptcy judge and the district court concluded, his dislike of banks did not absolve him from keeping records. These fact findings are not clearly erroneous.

Against this general backdrop of scanty record keeping, we have examined Horton's contention that certain of his daughter's records provide the information Horton cannot supply. Horton built a house for his daughter, acting as a general contractor and paying suppliers and builders over Twenty Thousand Dollars in cash payments, without keeping any financial records of these dealings. Horton alleges that his daughter's records should be substituted for his own, to satisfy the provisions of Section 14(c)(2).

Legally, however, Horton had a duty to maintain his own records of such a transaction, even if his daughter's records were complete.

Even if we accepted the dubious contention that Horton could rely upon his daughter's records, they are not sufficient for that purpose. The transcript reveals that these records do not differentiate between payments made to Horton to reimburse him and those which were made directly to suppliers for the materials. Therefore, even if they are considered, they do not clarify Horton's financial position. Furthermore, the testimony of Horton and his daughter and her roommate were found to be "incredible" and replete with inconsistencies and contradictions.

Once the Trustee has shown that the bankrupt's records are inadequate, the burden shifts to the bankrupt to justify the nonexistence of these records. The record explicitly and implicitly indicates that the bankruptcy judge correctly applied these presumptions and burden of proof. Horton's argument to the contrary is without merit.

For the foregoing reasons, the decision below is Affirmed.

Nondischargeable Claims

If none of the exceptions apply, the discharge relieves the debtor from any obligation for the payment of the debts that arose prior to the filing of the petition. A judgment entered by a court on a debt that is discharged becomes void; no action can be taken to collect that debt. Nevertheless, there are some claims for which the debtor continues to be liable; these are known as nondischargeable claims. Claims that are not dischargeable include:

1. Claims for back taxes accrued within three years prior to the bankruptcy
2. Claims arising out of the debtor's embezzlement, fraud, or larceny
3. Claims based on the debtor's willful or malicious torts
4. Claims for alimony or child support

5. Unscheduled claims
6. Certain fines and penalties payable to governmental units
7. Educational loans that became due and payable less than five years prior to the filing of the bankruptcy petition

Reaffirmations

While the discharge of debts owed by the debtor to creditors relieves the debtor of any legal obligation to pay those debts, the debtor may agree to reaffirm or reassume the debts after the bankruptcy proceeding. However, since the debtor may be under a great deal of pressure from former creditors to reaffirm the discharged debts, the bankruptcy laws make the reaffirmation of debts somewhat difficult. A simple promise by the debtor, even in writing, is not sufficient for a valid reaffirmation. First, the court must conduct a hearing at which the debtor is informed of the consequences of such action. Second, the debt must usually be approved by the court as not imposing an undue hardship on the debtor and being in the debtor's best interest. If these conditions are not met, the reaffirmation of the debt is not valid and its discharge is effective.

BUSINESS REORGANIZATION

Instead of filing a petition for liquidation, a business may elect to file for reorganization under Chapter 11 of the Bankruptcy Act. As in a liquidation proceeding, a petition for reorganization may also be filed by the creditors. Most of the rules that apply to the to the liquidation proceeding also apply to the reorganization. Railroads, however, are not subject to liquidation because of the public's dependence on their services. Reorganization allows a financially troubled firm or railroad to continue to operate while its financial resources and obligations are put in order.

Under Chapter 11 reorganizations, the court must appoint a creditors committee. This committee usually consists of the seven largest unsecured creditors and is appointed as soon as practicable after the order for relief has been entered by the court. The task of the creditors committee is to examine the affairs of the business and decide whether the business should continue in operation. The committee also usually determines whether to request of the court that a trustee should take over the the management of the business. If necessary, the committee may employ attorneys, accountants, and other agents to assist it in performing these tasks. Generally, the debtor or any other interested party may file a plan for reorganization. While only the debtor may file a plan during the first 120 days after the petition has been filed (unless a trustee has been appointed), the debtor's plan is usually developed in consultation with the creditors. A debtor who files a plan within the 120 days has an additional sixty days to have the plan approved by the creditors. The court can extend or reduce these time periods for good cause. If the debtor does not meet the deadline or is unable to obtain the consent of the creditors, any party in interest (a creditor or the trustee) may propose a plan.

The plan that is proposed must classify claims and ownership interests. It must specify the treatment of each class of claims and must provide for the same treatment for all persons in the same class unless the holder of a particular claim agrees to less favorable treatment. The plan must also provide adequate means for carrying out the plan's payment terms. If the debtor is a corporation, the plan must also protect stockholder voting rights, ensure that nonvoting stock will not be issued, and provide that in the selection of officers and directors the interests of creditors and stockholders will be protected.

The plan may modify the rights of some of the creditors. It may specify that some property be transferred to other creditors, that some creditors will be partially paid over an extended time, and even that some creditors will not be paid. The only requirement is that all the debtor's claimants must receive as much as they would have received in a liquidation proceeding.

Those who hold claims or interests in the debtor's property are allowed to vote on the proposed plan. If creditors representing more than one-half of the number of claimants and at least two-thirds of the value of the claims in a class vote in favor of the plan, that class of creditors has accepted the plan.

Normally, a plan will not be approved unless all those whose claims or interests have been impaired—those whose rights have been altered or who are to receive less than the full value of their claims or interests—have agreed to it. It is, however, possible for the court to confirm a plan even when those with impaired claims don't consent if the court determines that all persons in a particular class are treated fairly and equitably. Confirmation of the plan binds debtor and creditors. The property of the debtor is released from the claims of the creditors, and the debtor is given a Chapter 11 discharge.

The following article concerns the reorganization of Braniff International Corporation. It appeared in *The Wall Street Journal* on January 13, 1983. What does the article suggest regarding the court's role in approving the plan? How are the secured creditors treated under the plan? How does that compare to the treatment of unsecured creditors?

Braniff Is Opposed by Creditors, Others On Eve of Hearing on Reorganization

By DEAN ROTHART, *Staff Reporter of* THE WALL STREET JOURNAL

On the eve of a federal bankruptcy court hearing that could lead to a final reorganization plan for Braniff International Corp., new problems have arisen that are likely to complicate further the grounded airline's difficulties and delay a settlement with creditors.

Tomorrow, in Fort Worth, Texas, federal bankruptcy Judge John Flowers is slated to hear arguments on Braniff's plan to lease or sell some of its assets to PSA Inc., and to settle the majority of Braniff's claims with its secured creditors. The proposals, if approved by the court, would serve as the foundation of Braniff's reorganization plan under Chapter 11 of federal bankruptcy laws.

Under Chapter 11, a company has court protection from its creditors while it works out a plan to pay its debts.

But opposition to both the PSA plan and the settlement snowballed yesterday, the deadline for filing objections to the plan with the court. Among those objecting to the proposals were Braniff's unsecured creditors' committee, some competing airlines, three Braniff labor unions and some individual creditors.

Late yesterday, the airline's secured creditors still were haggling among themselves about details of the proposals. Braniff's unsecured creditors reported that they rejected the settlement proposal at a meeting held in Dallas Tuesday. At least one unsecured creditor went so far as to say that he would "declare war" on his secured counterparts, who he believes are selling out the unsecured creditors.

Recently Braniff appeared to be reaching the end of its long reorganization ordeal that began in May when the airline filed for Chapter 11. As reported, Braniff last week proposed a settlement with its secured creditors to give them title to its 62 aircraft, as well as some engines and spare parts. In return, Braniff asked the creditors to drop their secured claims of more than $400 million, and settle for a claim of $250 million, which would be treated as an unsecured claim.

The proposal incorporated an agreement reached earlier with PSA, under which PSA can lease or buy Braniff equipment facilities in 16 cities where Braniff had operated. As part of the earlier agreement, Braniff would make available to PSA $30 million in "cash and cash equivalents" to be repaid in five years. If the secured creditors accept the proposal, they also would be required to lease 30 aircraft to PSA in fulfillment of Braniff's agreement with that airline.

A 'Quintessential Rip-off'

In the final hour, however, Braniff is meeting stiff resistance. The Braniff proposals are a "quintessential rip-off," said a member of the official unsecured creditors committee. "Everybody gets something in the process, but the unsecured creditors would get nothing," he said. Some unsecured creditors estimate that they would receive about one penny for each dollar of unsecured claims that they have against Braniff under its proposals.

Judge Flowers could approve the Braniff proposals over the objections of the unsecured creditors and others, but some think that such a move would be difficult to justify.

CHAPTER 13 REGULAR INCOME PLANS

Chapter 13 proceedings are used by individuals with regular incomes who owe debts and want to pay them without harassment by creditors. While the prior law made this bankruptcy proceeding available only to wage earners, under the present law any individual (except a stockbroker or commodity broker) who has a regular income (whether from wages, investments, social security, or pensions) and unsecured debts of less than $100,000 and secured debts of less than $350,000 may use Chapter 13. Unlike liquidation or reorganization, Chapter 13 proceedings can be begun only by a voluntary petition filed by the debtor.

Upon the filing by the debtor of a Chapter 13 proceeding, an automatic stay stops creditors from taking action against the debtor. The debtor then proposes a plan providing for the use of future income for the payment of creditors. That income will be subject to control by a trustee, and the plan must ensure that all claims entitled to priority are paid in full. Unsecured claims may be divided into classes, but all claims within any class must be treated the same. Claimants may be paid in full or paid an amount not less than what they would receive in a liquidation proceeding. Usually, the plan provides for the payment of creditors over three years or less; however, the court may extend the period of payment to five years.

In order for the plan to be confirmed by the court, priority claimants must be paid in full, to the extent that money is available, unless they agree to accept less than the full amounts of their claims. Secured creditors vote on whether to accept the plan. If these creditors do not accept the plan, but either retain their liens or receive the properties securing their claims, the court will still confirm the plan. Unsecured creditors do not vote on the plan, but they must receive at least the amounts they would have received in a liquidation proceeding. The statutory concept underlying the treatment of secured claims by a Chapter 13 proceeding is discussed in the *Whitman* case. Note the court's comparison of Chapter 13 under the new code with the prior law for Chapter 13 proceedings and with the straight bankruptcies.

Memphis Bank & Trust Co. v. Whitman

6th Circuit Court of Appeals

692 F2d 427 (1982)

The debtor, Ms. Whitman, filed a Chapter 13 complaint in bankruptcy court two months after she purchased a car and took out an automobile loan with Memphis

Bank. Her loan of $9,799 was for a principal amount of $5,659 plus $2,922 of interest (at 21%) and $1,217 in insurance and other charges. The bankruptcy court ordered her to pay the bank the value of the car ($4,800) plus interest at 10% plus an unsecured claim of $2,171.74. The court reduced the interest note on the contract from 21% to 10%. The District Court affirmed the bankruptcy judge's determination and the Bank appealed to the Court of Appeals.

In its opinion, the Court of Appeals reviews the purpose of Chapter 13 of the new Code and contrasts it with the straight bankruptcy or liquidation proceedings detailed in Chapter 7 of the Code and discussed in the beginning of this Chapter. The Court also reviews the requirement that the debtor's plan be proposed in good faith. Since the Court of Appeals found the 10% interest note used by the bankruptcy judge to be arbitrary and was unsure that the bankruptcy judge's decision about the good faith of the debtor's plan was correct, the decisions of the bankruptcy judge and the District Court were reversed and remanded.

Merritt, Circuit Judge

This secured claim case arises under the newly revised Chapter 13 of the Bankruptcy Code which sets out principles for courts to follow in composing the debts of distressed wage earners. It is a case of first impression under the new Code. The "confused state of the law concerning the treatment of secured claims" caused major problems under the old Chapter 13, and led to a radical revision of the treatment of wage earner plans in the new Code. We first explain the legal framework in which the case arises and then deal with the facts and applicable law.

I. THE STATUTORY CONCEPT UNDERLYING TREATMENT OF SECURED CLAIMS

Chapter 13 of the new Code is considerably more helpful to debtors than either the old Chapter 13 or the old or new straight bankruptcy provision under Chapter 7. Creditors no longer have to agree to the Chapter 13 plan; it is court imposed. Business debtors are eligible to file now. Creditors may not file an involuntary proceeding as in Chapter 7 cases. Creditors are not necessarily entitled to full but delayed payment as under the old Chapter 13 but only to an amount equal to what they would have received in a straight bankruptcy. The stay and retention of property provisions are more protective than Chapter 7; and Chapter 13 also provides more favorable treatment of liens, defaults and taxes than Chapter 7.

On the question of discharge, under Section 1328(a) of the new Chapter 13, the only debts excepted from discharge are alimony and child support, claims not included in the plan and certain long-term obligations voluntarily excepted from the plan. Thus except for alimony and child support the nine exceptions to discharge, including fraud, applicable to Chapter 7 are not applicable to Chapter 13. A debtor who obtains credit by fraud or other dishonesty receives a discharge under Chapter 13 but not under Chapter 7.

The concept behind the treatment of secured claims under the new Chapter 13 is fairly simple. The total claim of the secured creditor which is to be allowed is divided into two parts, the secured portion and the unsecured portion. These two are called in section 1325 the "allowed secured claim" and the "allowed unsecured claim." The secured portion of the total claim represents the present value of the collateral and the unsecured portion is the remainder, i.e., the amount the allowed claim exceeds the value of the collateral. The House Report on the new Code explains the reason for this division:

> Most often in a consumer case, a secured creditor has a security interest in property that is virtually worthless to anyone but the debtor. The creditor obtains a security interest in all of the debtor's furniture, clothes, cooking utensils, and other personal effects. These items have little or no resale value. They do, however, have a high replacement cost. The mere threat of repossession operates as pressure on the debtor to repay the secured creditor more than he would receive were he actually to repossess and sell the goods.

Current Chapter 13 does little to recognize the differences between the true value of the goods and their value as leverage. Proposed Chapter 13 instead views the secured creditor-debtor relationship as a financial relationship, and not one where extraneous, non-financial pressures would enter. The bill requires the court to value the secured creditor's interest. To the extent of the value of the security interest, he is treated as having a secured claim, entitled to be paid in full under the plan, unless, of course, he accepts less than full payment. To the extent that his claim against the debtor exceeds the value of his collateral, he is treated as having an unsecured claim, and he will receive payment along with all other general unsecured creditors.

Section 1325(a)(5)(B) seems to require the Bankruptcy Court to assess interest on the secured claim for the present value of the collateral (if it is not to be paid immediately) in order not to dilute the value of that claim through delay in payment. In effect, the law requires the creditor to make a new loan in the amount of the value of the collateral rather than repossess it, and the creditor is entitled to interest on his loan.

II. THE FACTS OF THE INSTANT CASE

The instant case involves an automobile loan in the principal amount of $5,659, which was to have been paid over 42 months at $233 per month, making a total debt of $9,799, consisting of interest at 21% in the amount of $2,922 and insurance and other charges of $1,217. Having made no payments under the contract, the debtor, a divorced woman with three children, filed a Chapter 13 complaint two months after incurring the debt. The judge found that although the debtor "puffed" her income somewhat on her loan application, the basic reason for her default was a reduction in wages. He declined to find that she acted dishonestly in securing the loan. She filed a payment plan asking to reduce the monthly payment on the automobile from $233 to $157 and to extend the time to 60 months. The judge at the confirmation hearing found that her conduct in securing the loan and immediately filing under Chapter 13 for a reduction in payments made the proposed plan lack good faith. He indicated he would approve a plan that continued monthly payments at $233 until the contract debt was paid in full, and the debtor amended her plan to embody this proposal.

The Bankruptcy Court then wrote an opinion in which it apparently changed its mind. The reasons for the change are not clear. Yet at the end of its opinion the Court orders payment of a secured claim of $4,800 (the value of the collateral), plus interest on this amount at a 10% rate, plus an unsecured claim of $2,171.74, a figure that omits any contract interest. The Court states that it is subtracting the contract interest because under Chapter 13 contract interest stops upon the filing of the petition. The District Court affirmed.

III. THE APPROPRIATE PROCEDURE TO FOLLOW IN A SECURED CLAIM CASE

Although there are as yet few court of appeals and district court cases touching on the new Chapter 13, there are already many bankruptcy court cases. A reading of those cases suggests a composite set of procedures followed implicitly by most bankruptcy courts in secured claim cases:

1. Determine the present value of the collateral under the secured claim provisions of 1325.
2. Determine the amount allowable under applicable law to the creditor by virtue of the debtor's default including unpaid principal, finance charges, interest earned prior to filing but unpaid, etc.
3. Subtract the amount of the secured claim determined in step 1 from the amount calculated in step 2. This represents the unsecured claim.
4. Determine the appropriate interest rate to be applied to the secured claim, as more fully discussed below. Add the secured claim and the interest to be paid.
5. Determine, based on the debtor's ability to pay and his conduct, how much of the "allowed unsecured claim" should be paid, provided this amount is not less than the value the creditor would receive in straight bankruptcy.
6. Determine whether the debtor's proposed plan, based on his ability to pay and conduct, is reasonable and in good faith.
7. Confirm, deny confirmation or suggest modifications in the plan depending on the outcome of step 6.

This procedure seems to fit well with the statutory framework and statutory purpose in Chapter 13 cases. It eliminates the confusion under the old law and had the Bankruptcy Court followed it, we would not have the present confusion about what it intended to do in this case. We reverse and remand the case to the Bankruptcy Court with instructions to follow this procedure.

IV. INTEREST RATE TO BE ALLOWED ON SECURED CLAIM

Rather than tying the interest rate to an arbitrary ten per cent rate, the Bankruptcy Court's solution, or some other arbitrary rate, we hold that in the absence of special circumstances, bankruptcy courts should use the current market rate of interest used for similar loans in the region. Bankruptcy courts are generally familiar with the current conventional rates on various types of consumer loans. And where parties dispute the question, proof can easily be adduced.

The reason we do not use an arbitrary rate is that such a rate may vary widely from the current market rate. The theory of the statute is that the creditor is making a new loan to the debtor in the amount of the current value of the collateral. Under this theory, the most appropriate interest rate is the current market rate for similar loans at the time the new loan is made, not some other unrelated arbitrary rate.

V. THE "GOOD FAITH" REQUIREMENT

We cannot tell exactly what the Bankruptcy Court did on the issue of whether "the plan has been proposed in good faith" under section 1325(a)(3) of Chapter 13. Despite the fact that this subsection says only that the wage earner plan must be "proposed" in good faith, not that the debt in question be incurred in good faith, it is clear from the record that the Bankruptcy Court assessed the automobile payment plan in light of the debtor's pre-plan conduct in creating the debt. In light of its comments at the confirmation hearing and in other parts of its written opinion, it is unclear why the Bankruptcy Court changed its mind. We, therefore, remand the case to the Bankruptcy Court for clarification on this subject as well.

On the "good faith" issue, the creditor and the debtor appear to have diametrically opposed positions. The creditor says that the debt in question was fraudulently obtained and that a plan composing such a debt is necessarily in bad faith. The debtor claims that under the "good faith" provision the Court can only look to see whether the proposed plan or arrangement is made in good faith, i.e., whether it is in line with the debtor's inability to pay, and not whether the debt was incurred in good faith.

The "good faith" requirement is neither defined in the Bankruptcy Code nor discussed in the legislative history. The phrase should, therefore, be interpreted in light of the structure and general purpose of Chapter 13. Obviously the liberal provisions of the new Chapter 13 are subject to abuse, and courts must look closely at the debtor's conduct before confirming a plan. We should not allow a debtor to obtain money, services or products from a seller by larceny, fraud or other forms of dishonesty and then keep his gain by filing a Chapter 13 petition within a few days of the wrong. To allow the debtor to profit from his own wrong in this way through the Chapter 13 process runs the risk of turning otherwise honest consumers and shopkeepers into knaves. The view that the Bankruptcy Court should not consider the debtor's pre-plan conduct in incurring the debt appears to give too narrow an interpretation to the good faith requirements.

One way to refuse to sanction the use of the bankruptcy court to carry out a basically dishonest scheme under Chapter 13 is to deny confirmation to the proposed plan. When the debtor's conduct is dishonest, the plan simply should not be confirmed. Unless courts enforce this requirement, the debtor will be able to thwart the statutory policy denying discharge in Chapter 7 cases for dishonesty.

Another way to deal with the problem when the conduct is questionable but is not shown to be dishonest, as the Bankruptcy Court found it to be in the instant case, is to require full payment in accordance with the contract. This is the position the Bankruptcy Court apparently intended to take until it wrote the last paragraph of its opinion. On remand the Bankruptcy Court should make clear whether it is, in fact, taking this position and state on the record its reasons for its decision on the good faith issue.

Accordingly, the judgment of the District Court is reversed and the case remanded for further proceedings consistent with the opinion.

REVIEW PROBLEMS

1. The two defendants, Kapela and Brovenick, were the sole shareholders of a corporation that borrowed money from a bank. Each personally guaranteed to the bank the loan made to the corporation. Later, the corporation lent money to Brovenick, one of the shareholders; he gave the corporation a promissory note for that loan. The corporation assigned that note to the bank.

   One week prior to the corporation's filing for bankruptcy, Brovenick paid money to the bank; he claimed that payment reduced his debt to the corporation and also reduced his guarantor obligation to the bank. Five months after the bankruptcy petition was filed by the corporation, Newman, the corporation's trustee in bankruptcy, brought suit against both shareholders and sought to recover for the corporation the money paid by Brovenick to the bank. The trustee claimed the payment constituted a voidable preference, benefiting the shareholder/guarantors at the expense of other creditors of the same class. Do you agree? Kapela v. Newman, 649 F.2d 887 (1st Cir., 1981)

2. Crown Sportswear owed $51,000 to Bassett Walker. Bassett Walker, as a creditor, filed a petition for an involuntary bankruptcy for the debtor, Crown Sportswear. Bassett Walker's petition alleged that Crown had less than twelve creditors. The bankrupt sought to dismiss the petition, alleging that it had twelve or more creditors and thus an involuntary petition could not be filed by a single creditor. The evidence submitted indicated that the attorney for the creditor, after talking with his client and with a person in the credit bureau, was unsure as to the number of creditors. The bankrupt says the creditors must be able to prove the number of his creditors. The creditor, Bassett Walker, said he filed in good faith and the bankruptcy laws put on the bankrupt the burden of proving the number and identity of his creditors. Who do you think is right? Should the petition of Bassett Walker be dismissed if he was mistaken but did not act in bad faith? In re Crown Sportswear, Inc., 575 F2d 991 (1st Cir., 1978)

3. The bankrupt, Keidel, borrowed $3,500 from the bank to finance the purchase of a mobile home she was buying from its seller, Mitchell. She signed a security agreement with the bank and gave it her promissory note. The bank gave her a check, issued to her and to Olin Employees' Credit Union, the prior lienholder. The bankrupt was advised to get a new certificate of title showing that she, instead of the seller Mitchell, had the title to the mobile home.

   Keidel began to apply for a certificate of title, but didn't complete her application. Five months later, she filed a petition in bankruptcy. One month after that date, the bank applied for and obtained a new certificate of title, showing Keidel's ownership of the mobile home and the bank's lien interest. Under the state law, the bank had a security interest in the mobile home as of the date of its loan to Keidel, but that security interest was not perfected until the date the bank applied for the new certificate of title. Does the trustee in bankruptcy, standing in the position of a lien creditor, prevail over the bank that had a security interest created prior to the date of the petition in bankruptcy, but perfected after that date? Matter of Keidel 613 F.2d 172 (7th Cir., 1980)

4. Emily Westhem's original engagement ring had belonged to Andrew Westhem's grandmother. A number of years ago it was stolen and the insurance proceeds were used to purchase the ring here in question. The present ring is a diamong ring having a fair market value of more than $3,000 and described as one emerald-cut diamond of approximately four carats with two side diamonds.

The present California Code of Civil Procedure exempts "[n]ecessary household furnishings and appliances and wearing apparel, ordinarily and reasonably necessary to, and personally used by, the debtor and his resident family." The bankrupt claims the ring is exempt as wearing apparel, reasonably necessary to and personally used by his wife. The trustee claims it is not exempt. Who is correct? In re Westhem 642 F.2d 1139 (9th Cir., 1981)

5. The defendant filed a voluntary proceeding in bankruptcy. Six weeks later, his mother died and he became entitled to money from a trust fund that had been created by defendant's father. After his mother's death, the debtor filed a disclaimer, which under state law disclaimed his interest in that money and passed it instead to his children. The trustee in bankruptcy claims that the property that the debtor was entitled to was part of his estate and that the state law allowing him to disclaim it is inconsistent with and subject to the federal bankruptcy law. Is the trustee correct? Mickelson v. Detlefsen, 466 F.Supp 161 (D. Minn., 1979)

6. The debtor, Dennis Mazzola, a builder and contractor who owned his own construction company, filed a voluntary petition in bankruptcy. The plaintiffs claimed that, since some of the statements made by Mazzola on the debtor's schedule and statement of affairs were false, the debtor's discharge should be denied. Mazzola conceded that false statements existed, but said that they were mere mistakes and not fraudulent, as is necessary to bar his discharge.

The debtor was asked if he had transferred any property during the year preceding the filing of the petition. The debtor answered no, saying that he had interpreted the question to ask if he currently owned property. In fact, he had transferred property to his corporation. The debtor also failed to disclose his ownership of the stock of the construction company because he didn't believe the stock to be of any value. Should the discharge be denied to Mazzola? In re Mazzola, 4 B.R. 179 (D. Mass, 1980)

7. Sotello was the principal officer and major stockholder of a corporation that was liable to withhold money from employees of the corporation for payment of taxes. The Internal Revenue Code states that any person who is required to but fails to pay over taxes to be withheld shall be liable to a penalty equal to the amount of taxes due. Sotello, his wife, and the corporation were all adjudged bankrupt. Sotello claims that the amount owed to the IRS is a corporate debt for which he is not liable. He further claims that even if he is liable, the amount owed is a penalty, not a tax, and therefore is a debt from which his bankruptcy discharges him. The IRS says that since he has always been the corporation's president, director, and majority stockholder, he is a person who the Internal Revenue Code states "has a duty to collect, account for and pay over the taxes" due from employees. Furthermore, it says that the amount owed by him to the IRS is a tax that is not dischargeable pursuant to the bankruptcy laws. Is the IRS correct? United States v. Sotello, 436 U.S. 268 (1978)

8. Petitioners are claims adjustors and attorneys who provided professional services to an insurance company that has been liquidated under state law. The statutory scheme for distributing assets of an insolvent insurance company gives priority status, after expenses of administration are paid, to claims owed to employees. The language of the state law is very similar to that in the federal bankruptcy statutory provision. The other general creditors claim that the attorneys and claims adjustors are not employees but are independent contractors. Thus amounts owed to them are not due as "wages" and are not entitled to priority status. Assume that this provision in the state law is interpreted in the same way as is the provision in the federal bankruptcy laws. Should the claims adjusters' and attorneys' claims, or a part of them, be granted priority status? White v. State ex Rel Block, 597 P.2d 172 (1979)

FOOTNOTE

[1]In a 1982 decision the U.S. Supreme Court determined that some of the provisions of the Bankruptcy Act of 1978 were unconstitutional. Since bankruptcy judges were neither given life tenure nor granted salaries that could not be diminished by Congress, the Court held the grant of judicial authority to them conflicted with Article III of the Constitution. Congress was given until the end of 1982 to revise the law and the organization of the bankruptcy courts. While legislation clarifying the status of the bankruptcy court system had not been enacted by August of 1983, it is likely to be in place early in 1984. Northern Pipeline Construction Co. v. Marathon Pipe Line Co. 102 S.Ct. 2858 (1982)

PART IV

BUSINESS ORGANIZATIONS

The Agency Relationship

T he agency relationship has increased in importance during the last 100 years. Several factors account for this development. Probably the most significant is that a large percentage of business in the United States is done by corporations. Since a corporation is unable to act for itself, it must conduct its operations through agents. A partnership, too, unable to act for itself, must function through agents. Finally, an independent entrepreneur wishing to expand the scope of his or her operation to any significant degree must turn to someone for assistance and representation. That someone is an agent.

This chapter considers several aspects of the agency relationship. It begins by describing how the relationship is created and the authority that agents enjoy. Next it briefly examines the status of employees as independent contractors or agents. The chapter then discusses at length the rights and liabilities of the parties. Finally, the chapter reviews the ways in which the relationship is terminated.

AGENTS AND PRINCIPALS

Agency Defined

Agency is a legal relationship in which one person, called the principal, authorizes another, called the agent, to act in the principal's behalf. The relationship is created either by express or implied contract or by law. In the relationship, the principal has the right to control the agent's conduct concerning the delegated activity. The term "agency" applies to personal or business transactions conducted between the principal and third parties through the agent. In agency relations, the principal delegates to the agent the management of some activity that the principal may lawfully do in person. The agent then has the power to bind legally

615

the principal to third persons as though the principal had personally transacted the business.

Types of Agents

Agents are classified as either *general agents* or *special agents*. The general agent is more or less continuously employed by the principal to conduct a series of transactions. He or she can be the manager of the principal's business or a sales clerk working on a part-time basis. A special agent is hired for a particular transaction, a particular purpose, or a particular occasion. There is no continuity in the special agent's employment. Realtors and investment brokers are examples of special agents. The distinction between general and special agents is primarily a matter of degree, depending on the agent's continuity of employment.

Types of Principals

Principals are classified as either *disclosed* or *undisclosed*. In the usual agency transaction, the third person knows that the agent is acting for a principal and knows the principal's identity. The principal's identity may be important, since the third person may be relying on the principal's credit and reputation. The agent's identity is unimportant since the transaction is between the principal and the third person, and the agent is not a party to the deal. When the third person knows the principal's identity, the principal is referred to as a disclosed principal.

Sometimes a principal may not wish to be identified or to reveal the existence of the agency to the third person. When the third person has no knowledge that the agent is working for a principal, the principal is called an undisclosed principal. In these situations the agent's identity becomes more important than the principal's identity. Since the agent purports to be acting on his or her own, the agent is a party to the contract along with the principal. Undisclosed principals are not necessarily sinister persons. People frequently have honest reasons for not wishing their connection with a transaction known. In some dealings the principal's identity is simply unimportant. For example, in sales and purchases of stock, buyer and seller normally are unaware of the identity of the other, each knowing only his or her broker.

The disclosed-undisclosed terminology is significant in a later discussion of the rights and obligations involved in agency transactions. Generally, agents for disclosed principals are not liable on the contracts they negotiate; agents for undisclosed principals are liable.

CREATION AND AUTHORITY

A business person needs to know if an agency relationship exists; for if it does, the principal is bound through negotiations by the agent. The contracts made by an authorized agent for the principal are as binding on the principal as they would have been had the principal entered into them in person.

An agent's authority is conferred by various methods. The principal may expressly authorize the agent's action by explicitly stating to the agent what he or she is authorized to do. The principal may indicate to the agent by conduct that the agent has authority to undertake certain transactions. Authority is established also if other persons can reasonably infer from the principal's conduct that the principal authorizes the agent's activity. Even when the principal does not authorize someone to act as an agent, a third party may establish authority if the principal ratifies transactions done for him.

Actual Authority

Actual authority is the power of an agent to affect the principal's legal relations by acts done according to the principal's manifestations of consent to the agent. The principal may manifest consent by any means that causes the agent to understand what the principal wants the agent to do. If the agent's actual authority is stated in words, it is referred to as express authority. If the agent's actual authority is communicated by the principal's conduct toward the agent, it is called implied authority. The legal effect is the same whether actual authority is expressly or impliedly manifested: the agent is empowered to change the principal's legal relations with third persons by performing according to the principal's manifestations. For example, if a business person tells his or her secretary to accept customer payments, the secretary has express authority to collect payments as instructed. If additionally the secretary purchases office supplies and the principal pays without objection, the secretary or the seller may reasonably infer that the principal authorizes continued purchases of office supplies. In both situations the principal is obligated to others by the secretary's actions.

Express Authority. The clearest example of express authority is the *power of attorney*. A power of attorney is a formal written instrument conferring authority upon an agent. Powers of attorney are often used because a third person entering into a specific, major transaction with an agent may require evidence of the agent's authority. In these situations, the authority may be set forth in a form that is familiar and convenient to persons in the business. The acts authorized usually require the execution of specifically described documents. For example, banks and other professional lenders that deal regularly with borrowers' agents have standard forms for the purpose of assuring themselves of the authority of agents to borrow on their principals' credit. Because of absence, sickness, age, or disinterest, individuals widely use powers of attorney to delegate the management of their affairs to others. Interpretation of the activi-

ties included in these powers is frequently a problem.

Informal written expressions of authority are often included in standard form contracts that the agent negotiates with third persons. Known as merger, integration, or exculpatory clauses, these statements serve to explicitly limit an agent's authority to make only those agreements contained in the standard form contract. A typical merger clause is: "It is hereby further agreed that there are no prior writings, verbal negotiations, understandings, representations or agreements between the parties not herein expressed, and no agent of Seller is authorized to make or enter into on Seller's behalf any writings, verbal negotiations, understandings, representations or agreements not here expressed." Unauthorized transactions made by the agent with a third person who has notice of this limitation on the agent's authority are not binding on the principal. Obligations undertaken in violation of this express limitation of authority are the agent's.

Verbal commands expressing the principal's authorization of an agent to transact certain business are quite common. If the transactions do not require written authorization, such statements confer upon the agent the power to bind the principal. For example, the principal may say to someone, "Manage my business," and by this oral statement delegate the management of the business to an agent.

Implied Authority. In most agency relations it will not be possible to express every detail of the agent's authority. For example, if a store-owner hires someone to manage his or her business, it may not be practical to describe every management function involved in the enterprise. To provide flexibility in these situations, the agent is allowed additional implied authority to perform activities that he or she or a third party might reasonably infer are incidental or necessary to carry out the principal's instructions.

Several factors determine whether implied

authority exists. The circumstances generally considered by courts are customary trade usages, the principal's practices regarding other agents in similar situations, and previous experiences involving the principal and the particular agent. For example, a question of whether a particular salesperson has the implied authority to extend warranties on merchandise sold to third persons may be answered by examining what similar salespeople in the trade normally do, what generally is practiced by other salespeople employed by the principal, and what the principal historically has permitted that particular salesperson to do.

While the principal impliedly authorizes the agent to do whatever is normally required to accomplish the job, sometimes as the job progresses the agent confronts an emergency. In such an emergency, the agent can reasonably infer that the principal consents to the agent's undertaking whatever is required to protect the principal's interests. Authorization of the agent's activity is implied in these situations. This implied authority exists only when the threat to the principal's business is sudden and unexpected and when contact with the principal or superior officer is impracticable. It extends only to activities necessitated by the emergency.

Apparent Authority

Authority also exists if the principal's conduct causes third persons reasonably to believe that the agent is authorized. This permits third parties to rely upon the principal's manifestation in dealing with an agent. This type of authority is called apparent authority. Its effect on the principal's liability to third persons is the same as actual authority, since both types empower the agent to affect the principal's legal relations with others. The adjectives "actual" and "apparent" denote only the viewpoints used in interpreting the principal's conduct. Actual authority is determined from the agent's viewpoint; apparent authority is determined from the third person's viewpoint.

The agent's apparent authority may arise in various ways. It may result from the principal's statement to a third person or from the principal's acquiescence to the agent's activities. It may be established from the principal's permission to the agent to do something under circumstances creating a reputation of authority in the area in which the agent acts. Prior dealings between the agent and third persons might lead a third person reasonably to infer that the agent is authorized. For example, a customer might reasonably believe that a salesperson in a department store is authorized to transact business in an adjacent department. Apparent authority, however, cannot be established by the agent's statements alone. This would allow anyone to confer upon himself or herself authority to obligate others simply by acting and talking like an agent.

Ratification of Unauthorized Activity

Authorization of the agent need not occur before the agent transacts the principal's business. If the principal earlier has not authorized someone to act as an agent, the principal may supply the authority later by ratifying the transaction. Ratification is the subsequent approval by the principal of an earlier unauthorized act by someone claiming to act as an agent. Ratification may occur when the agent exceeds his or her original authority and enters into unauthorized transactions or when a stranger supposely acts as another's agent. The difference between the principal's liability created by ratification rather than prior authorization is the timing of the principal's consent to be bound. Where actual or apparent authority exists, the principal manifests his or her consent before the agent conducts any business. When ratification occurs, the principal's consent comes after the business is conducted.

Because ratification treats the transaction as if it were originally authorized, only those acts that could originally be authorized can be ratified. For this reason the ratifier must have been in existence and competent to be a principal at the time the transaction took place. Only those acts purportedly undertaken for the principal may be ratified. No ratification can occur for acts done by someone acting on his or her own.

Any conduct of a principal manifesting the principal's complete, knowledgeable affirmance of the supposed agent's acts can constitute a ratification. However, the principal's affirmance must be complete. He or she cannot affirm part of a transaction while disaffirming the rest. Any acts, words, or conduct reasonably indicating an intent to ratify may constitute a ratification. For example, a principal receiving benefits of an agent's unauthorized bargain or suing to enforce a contract made by a bogus agent may constitute a ratification.

Effect of Agent's Knowledge

An important consequence of the agency relation is that the principal is charged with knowing everything regarding the agency that is known by the agent. This is because one incident of the agent's employment is the communication to the principal of information regarding agency matters. Presumably the agent tells the principal everything relating to the agent's performance. Whether this actually is done is unimportant, because the reason for imputing the agent's knowledge to the principal is to protect innocent third persons. When determining the principal's liability to innocent third persons, the principal and not the third person bears the risk of the agent's failure to inform.

Notification is the act of informing the agent, which has the same legal effect as if the principal had received it. For example, filing a claim with an insurance company's claims agent is a form of notification to the company. To be effective, notification must be made to an agent authorized to receive it. Frequently

the terms of a contract specify the person authorized to receive notice, but the agent also may be impliedly or apparently authorized to receive notification. Notice given to an agent who is unauthorized to receive it is not effective notification to the principal unless the principal later ratifies its receipt.

An agent's knowledge is not imputed to the principal when the agent and a third party conspire to cheat or defraud the principal or when the agent is otherwise acting against the principal's interests. In these situations the agent's knowledge is not imputed because it cannot be presumed that the agent will normally communicate the information to the principal. For example, an insurance company is not prevented from rescinding an insurance contract when there is collusion between the insured and the company's agent to defraud the company.

AGENCY DISTINGUISHED

Power of Control

Many situations exist in which one person acts for another. Not all of these create an agency relationship. This is legally significant, for if a relationship is an agency, certain legal consequences attach; if the relationship is something else, the legal result may be quite different.

In deciding whether a relationship is an agency, the name the parties give it is not controlling. The substance of the relationship, not the parties' characterization, is determinative.

What distinguishes agency from similar relationships is the power of control retained by the principal over the agent's activities. Relations normally distinguished from agency may become agency relations if this power of control is present. Frequently called the "power of control" test, the concept is a useful tool, although not the only one, for determining the existence of agency.

Independent Contractors

People who work for others but are not controlled as to the essential elements of completing the task are referred to as independent contractors. Independent contractors agree only to furnish certain results and are responsible only for their final product. Since independent contractors are not normally agents, their employers are not generally liable to the contractors' creditors or to persons harmed by the contractors' negligence. In addition, employers are not responsible for making social security and unemployment compensation contributions on contractors' behalf or for withholding taxes from sums paid to contractors.

An individual contractor, however, may become an agent or servant if the employer retains control over the details of performance. Whether an independent contractor becomes an agent or servant depends on the degree and character of the control retained by the employer over the work done, and no absolute dividing line can be drawn between the two. Additionally, an employer who hires an independent contractor to perform inherently dangerous work, or to assume duties that by law cannot be delegated to others, remains liable for injuries caused by the contractor.

Columbia Broadcasting System Inc. v. Stokely–Van Camp, Inc.

U. S. Court of Appeals, Second Circuit
552 F.2d 369 (1975)

Columbia Broadcasting System, Inc. (CBS or the medium, plaintiff-appellant) instituted this action against Stokely–Van Camp, Inc. (Stokely, defendant-appellee) for payment of $428,497.33 for advertising. The advertising was placed by an advertising agency, Lennen & Newell, Inc. (Lennen or the agency), which went bankrupt. Since Stokely had paid the agency but the agency had not paid CBS, the question is on which party the loss must fall.

The U.S. District Court dismissed CBS's complaint upon Stokely's cross-motion for summary judgment. The District Court held that the agency had no actual or apparent authority to bind Stokely. CBS appealed. Held: Reversed and Remanded.

Oakes, Circuit Judge

Stokely . . . is an Indiana corporation engaged in the production, sale and distribution of food products throughout the United States. . . .

Lennen was a so-called "full service" advertising agency, which had handled Stokely's account for over 17 years on the basis of an unwritten arrangement. On behalf of Stokely, Lennen would produce television commercials, with Stokely's approval, pursuant to an advertising budget approved by Stokely. Lennen gave Stokely advertising advice and made the arrangements for the advertising. Stokely did not know what contracts, if any, were made by Lennen with the media but did know that Lennen was being paid by means of a 15 per cent commission based on the gross amount of the invoices. Stokely never asked for or received copies of the agency-media contracts and simply paid Lennen on its invoices.

CBS sold time for Stokely commercials both on its network under so-called network agreements . . . and on the five specific CBS stations under a series of 13 specific contracts. . . . Lennen would prepare and send to Stokely schedules containing the station, date, program and time for each Stokely commercial to be shown during the forthcoming three months on network television and would also advise Stokely of the station, date and time for each Stokely commercial to be shown locally on the CBS television stations. At all times in question under both the network and the station contracts CBS would bill Lennen for the cost of the advertising time less 15 per cent, which was the standard commission in the trade for an advertising agency. . . . The Lennen invoices to Stokely did not refer to the CBS invoices and were on a Lennen invoice form showing a gross, sales tax, cash discount and net. The invoices did not reflect the credit terms in the CBS contracts.

The network and the station billings were separately made by CBS to Lennen, separately accounted for in the CBS books and separately paid by Lennen. . . .

It should also be pointed out preliminarily that in respect to the network contracts here relied upon by CBS, the first was initiated by Lennen by verbal order confirmed by letter of Lennen to CBS dated May 4, 1971, stating that Lennen was purchasing "in behalf of" Stokely.

CBS then sent to Lennen a "Network Television Agreement" with a covering letter dated May 25, 1971. The covering letter stated that if the agreement were in order, Lennen should return it to CBS for countersignature, after which "a fully signed copy" would be returned to Lennen. The covering letter, Exhibit C, said, however, "Until any modifications have been mutually agreed upon, the enclosed Agreement shall constitute the understanding between us with respect to this purchase." . . . The agreement specifically refers to Lennen as "acting as agent for Stokely-Van Camp, Inc." The agreement incorporates certain obligations running to and from the advertiser, Stokely. Among other things it provides that "Agency and Advertiser will indemnify and hold harmless CBS and any stations" from and against various claims arising out of the broadcast of the "Agency Package," and conversely provides that CBS will indemnify and hold harmless "Agency and Advertiser" from and against claims arising out of the particular programs which it supplies. The agreement also provides that "if this Agreement is with a recognized advertising agency each payment hereunder shall be subject to the deduction therefrom of an advertising agency commission in an amount equal to 15% thereof." The agreement further provides in Paragraph 5: "(it being understood that Agency acting as agent for disclosed principal)."

The second network contract is the same as the first and was handled in the same way with a covering letter containing the same language and no signatures to the agreement. It seems clear enough in regard to the network contracts that they were in full force and effect despite the fact that they were never signed, the forwarding of the commercials constituting acceptance of the terms by Lennen.

The station contracts were all in writing and signed by CBS and Lennen. . . . These station contracts are on a standard form styled "CBS Television Stations National Sales Schedule Agreement." Each refers to Lennen as ("Agency") acting as agent for: Stokely-Van Camp, Inc. ("Advertiser"), and each was signed by Lennen "As Agent for Stokely-Van Camp, Inc." In the basic terms and conditions incorporated in the agreements by reference, each contract is said to have been "entered into by Agency as agent for Advertiser for the broadcast of Announcements over Station. . . ." Unlike the network contracts in respect to payment of the invoices there is a specific provision reading as follows:

> CBS shall bill Advertiser via Agency monthly or weekly whenever CBS shall so elect, for the charges due hereunder for such period. Advertiser shall pay CBS, in accordance with such billing, within ten calendar days after receipt thereof. Any failure whatsoever by Advertiser to make timely payment charges under this Agreement or any other breach whatsoever by Advertiser or Agency of this Agreement shall give CBS the right in addition to its other rights, to cease performance of this Agreement.

In the event that the station omits to broadcast the commercials in question under Paragraph 3D of the station contract the advertiser—not the agency—has the right to terminate the contract. Assorted warranties, indemnity agreements and cross obligations run from the advertiser and agency to CBS and vice versa. . . .

AGENCY

We come to the legal issues. The first question is whether the advertising agency, Lennen, was, in its negotiations with CBS under the contracts here involved, acting as an agent for the advertiser or as an independent contractor. If the latter, the matter ends and CBS is entitled to no recovery. . . .

The first question depends on whether the action of the agency on behalf of the advertiser was either authorized or apparently authorized or was by virtue of "a power arising from the agency relation and not dependent upon authority or apparent authority." . . .

We are thus required to look at the general rules of agency law to determine whether there was here any express or apparent authority or "power arising from the agency relation" on the part of Lennen to bind Stokely as it purported to do on the contracts executed with CBS. We start with the assumption that a person who employs an agent normally intends that he himself shall be a party to the transaction or contract in question, and a third person dealing with the agent normally intends to contract with the principal if the latter is disclosed. . . . We also are fully aware that an independent contractor, one who is not subject to the right of another to control his physical conduct in the performance of the undertaking, may or may not be an agent. . . . Here by virtue of 17 years of dealings there was a mutual manifestation of consent that Lennen would act on Stokely's account in connection with the latter's advertising. To determine the extent of an authorization, a court must look to the accompanying circumstances, including the situation of the parties, their relations to one another, and the business in which they are engaged; the general usages of the business in question and the purported principal's business methods; the nature of the subject matter and the circumstances under which the business is done. . . . Professional agents can properly assume that they have the authority usually exercised by others in the same field. . . . So, too, a principal, say in Indiana, who does business through an advertising agency on Madison Avenue, can ordinarily expect his agency to do business in accordance with the usages in New York. . . . As to authorization to contract, it may be inferred from authority to conduct a transaction if the making of the contract is incidental thereto, usually accompanies such a transaction or is reasonably necessary to accomplish it. . . .

So saying, it is evident that we have to reverse Judge Wyatt to the extent that he held there was no disputed question of fact and that Lennen had no actual authority to contract with CBS to bind Stokely. Rather, we find there are disputed facts which, if found in CBS's favor, tend to show an agency relation between Stokely and Lennen and the latter's authority to bind the former to pay for advertising procured on the former's account and for its benefit. Here, for example, when media salesmen called on Stokely soliciting purchase of their particular services, Stokely would indicate that Lennen was its agency and that Lennen should be contacted. How much money was being spent on each particular network, moreover, was left entirely to the discretion of the agency and was unknown by Stokely. From the medium's point of view, it seems to appear that it generally does not sell to an agency without selling to a client; that is to say, sales of time are made only for specific advertisers and not to the agency as a broker for the medium's time. The dealings between CBS and the agency were for purposes of preparing a "package" best suited to the advertising needs of the client in terms of either prime time or daytime, depending on the client and its products to be advertised.

At the same time, particularly because this is a case for all practical purposes of first impression, we believe that we should remand for full factual findings as to the customs and usage of the trade, particularly the usages of the Madison Avenue advertising business as they existed at the time of the execution of the contracts in question, and whether the making of a contract such as the one here purporting to bind the principal is incidental to or usually accompanies or is reasonably necessary to accomplish the business of supplying commercial television time for purposes of sponsors' advertising. What we might assume and what may be found on trial are two different matters.

Accordingly, we remand to the district court for the purpose of determining whether there was an agency relationship. . . .

CASE NOTE

Upon remand, the U.S. District Court determined that no evidence existed that advertising agencies generally executed contracts binding their clients. The evidence established that CBS did not believe and could not reasonably have believed that Lennen was authorized to bind Stokely. The court also was unable to find any actual or apparent authority from Stokely to Lennen to bind Stokely to pay CBS and that there was no agency relationship. As a result the court entered judgment for Stokely (456 F.Supp. 539 [1977]).

CONTRACTUAL DEALINGS BETWEEN AGENTS AND THIRD PARTIES

Contractual liability depends on whether a person is a party to the contract. Generally, an agent who negotiates an authorized contract for the principal is not a party to the agreement and, therefore, is neither liable on the contract nor able to enforce it against the third person. The agent may agree to become a party, but in most situations the agent acts only for the principal. However, even if not a party to the agreement, an agent is responsible for unauthorized dealings, based upon an implied warranty of authorization to act for the principal.

Undisclosed Agency

Where the agent acts for an undisclosed principal, the third person has no notice of the agency relation or the principal's identity. From the third person's viewpoint, the person negotiating the contract is the party to the contract. For this reason, an agent purporting to act alone, but in fact acting for an undisclosed principal, becomes a party to the contract, along with the principal. However, while outwardly appearing to be a party, in reality the agent is still acting for another. This transforms the agent into a peculiar form of contracting party with special rights and duties. For example, if the agent enforces the contract against the third person, the principal is entitled to any proceeds or performance, since that is what the principal and agent originally agreed. Once the undisclosed principal's identity is revealed, the agent may force the third person to elect which party is responsible for performance. If the agent is forced to perform, he or she is entitled to reimbursement from the principal.

Disclosed Agency

The agent who contracts in the name of a disclosed principal does not become a party to the contract unless he or she personally agrees to do so. The principal and third person are directly liable to each other, and the agent is not involved. An agent seeking to avoid personal liability under a contract must fully disclose the principal's identity.

The agent for a disclosed principal must exercise care when a negotiated agreement is put in writing. When the names of both the principal and the agent appear on the written contract, to avoid liability the agent should make certain his or her signature indicates the agency relation and identifies the principal. For example, "Peter Principal by Arthur Adams, his agent" is sufficient. Parol evidence may be used to explain an ambiguous signature. Currently the courts do not uniformly interpret a signature in the form of "Arthur Adams, agent." The trend is to treat the signature as sufficiently ambiguous to permit parol evidence to explain whether the agent was intended to be a party. However, some states still prohibit any explanation and hold the signer personally liable.

Agent's Warranty Liability

The agent for a disclosed principal may be liable to a third person even without becoming a party to the contract. If the agent purports to act with authority but actually exceeds this authorization, the principal is not bound on the transaction unless it is ratified. However, the agent is not a party to the contract because he or she purported to contract for someone else. While not liable as a contracting party, the agent is responsible for damages to the third person for breach of an implied warranty of authority. This is because the agent is better able to know the limits of his or her authorization, and a third person is permitted reasonably to rely on the agent's representation of authority. The agent may avoid liability by informing the third person that he or she makes no warranty or is unsure of his or her authority.

AGENT'S TORTIOUS ACTIVITY

Besides performing contract negotiations, the agent's activity may involve a tort against others. This tort may be intentional or negligent. Either way, the innocent victim may recover damages for the resulting injury. Damages may be recovered from the agent, since every person is responsible for his or her own torts unless acting under a cloak of governmental immunity. Additionally, the principal is sometimes also financially responsible for the agent's torts. The result is that the victim gets a windfall in the form of an additional responsible party.

Doctrine of Respondeat Superior

The principal is liable for any torts the agent commits during the agent's employment. This concept, called the doctrine of respondeat superior ("let the superior respond"), is an application of strict liability theory, meaning that liability is imposed regardless of the principal's fault or blame. Strict liability is used in other areas of tort law where significant policy reasons require discarding traditional fault ideas in favor of no-fault liability. However, unlike other applications of strict liability, the principal's liability is based on some original fault of the agent. Thus the principal's responsibility is often referred to as vicarious.

Scope of Vicarious Liability

While respondeat superior is recognized because it is believed desirable and expedient to make the principal responsible for injuries inflicted by the agent, the principal is not made responsible for every tort the agent commits. Only where the agent commits a tort in the scope of employment is the principal liable under respondeat superior. The phrase "scope of employment" indicates the limits of the principal's liability for another's wrongdoing. The principal is liable only for accidents that are incidental to agency purposes. To make the principal responsible for acts that are in no way connected with agency goals would be unfair; the principal can be expected to bear only those costs that are closely associated with the business.

This limit on the principal's liability is easier to state than to apply. Determining if the agent is acting within the scope of employment often is difficult because the agent may temporarily be performing a personal errand or doing the principal's work while also serving a personal purpose, or the agent may be performing the principal's work in a forbidden manner. No precise formula exists to determine whether at a particular moment a particular agent is engaged in the principal's business. Whether the agent is inside or outside the scope of employment is often a matter of degree. Since the scope-of-employment test determines whether respondeat superior applies, as a guide in close cases, courts often refer to the policy purposes that respondeat superior is supposed to serve.

Agent's Liability to Third Parties

In conducting the principal's business, the agent may, of course, harm third persons. The fact that the agent acts in a representative capacity does not make the agent immune from tort liability to third persons. Although the doctrine of respondeat superior extends the principal's liability by making the principal liable to third persons for the agent's torts, the doctrine does not affect the agent's liability. An agent's tort liability to another is the same as if the agent were not employed. The doctrine of respondeat superior does not repeal the law of torts, which makes individuals liable for the torts they commit; respondeat superior makes both the principal and the agent liable to the victim. Thus the agent's tort liability differs from the agent's usual liability in contract. Since the agent for a disclosed principal normally is not a party to the agreement, the agent is not liable on the contract.

PRINCIPAL'S CRIMINAL RESPONSIBILITY

Early common law courts generally did not impose criminal liability upon a faultless principal for the agent's unauthorized criminal conduct. The principal could be guilty only as an accomplice or accessory to the agent's crime when the principal directed, participated in, or ratified the agent's conduct. No guilt was attributed to a principal not otherwise involved in the agent's activity.

Today statutes sometimes impose criminal liability on the principal for the agent's criminal conduct. These statutes create regulatory or public-welfare offenses classified as misdemeanors and punishable by fines. An example of such a regulatory statute is one stating that "whoever, by himself or by his agent, sells or permits to be sold, intoxicating liquors to a minor is punishable by a fine of $100."

Regulatory Crimes

Early courts also held that corporations could not be criminally liable for the acts of their agents. As a fictitious legal entity, a corporation lacked both a mind to form the required criminal intent and a body to be imprisoned. Today it is almost universally recognized that a corporation may be criminally liable for its agent's regulatory offenses. However, courts often qualify the doctrine by permitting the corporation to defend successfully by showing that the high managerial officer having supervisory responsibility over the subject matter of the offense employed due diligence to prevent its commission.

Nonregulatory Crimes

When a nonregulatory crime requiring some criminal intent is involved, corporate criminal liability is often limited to situations where the criminal conduct is participated in or performed by the board of directors or a high management official. Courts reason that these directors and officers actually operate as the corporation's mind by establishing corporate policy. This limitation is called the superior-officer rule and applies only to nonregulatory offenses.

The corporate agent who commits a crime is personally liable even though he or she acted for the corporation. However, generally a corporate officer is not personally liable for the corporation's crimes merely because he or she is an officer. Normally such a supervisory agent is guilty only when the criminal acts are done under the executive's direction or with the executive's permission. Currently a trend toward expanding the criminal liability of corporate executives is emerging. Some jurisdictions hold corporate executives criminally responsible for their companies' regulatory offenses even when the executives do not personally participate in the unlawful activity. In a limited number of states, the corporate officer having primary responsibility for discharging a duty imposed by law on the corporation is accountable for the reckless failure to perform the required act.

In the following case, the U.S. Supreme Court ruled that the president and chief executive officer of a large national food chain, by virtue of the power and responsibility of his position, was criminally liable for unsanitary storage conditions in one of the company's warehouses. The case illustrates the evolving criminal liability of corporate executives. The decision came at a time when serious questions, both philosophic and legal, were being raised concerning the nature and scope of personal accountability (and liability) for actions taken, or not taken, while exercising authority.

United States v. Park

U.S. Supreme Court
421 U.S. 658 (1975)

The United States (plaintiff-appellant) brought this criminal action against Acme Markets, Inc. (Acme) and John Park (defendants-appellees) for violation of the Food, Drug, and Cosmetics Act. The defendants were charged with the unsanitary storage of food in Acme's Baltimore warehouse. Acme pleaded guilty, but Park contested the charge.

Evidence at the trial indicated that Park, Acme's chief executive officer and president, had been advised by letter at least twice of heavy rodent infestation at the warehouse. Park testified that he identified those responsible for sanitation and was assured that the Baltimore division vice president "would be taking corrective action." The criminal suit was instituted when inspection indicated continued unsanitary conditions. A jury found Park guilty. He appealed to the Court of Appeals, which reversed and remanded. That court viewed the government as arguing "that the conviction may be predicated solely upon a showing that . . . [Park] was the president of the offending company." The court then stated that as "a general proposition, some act of commission or omission is an essential element of every crime." The United States filed a motion for certiorari which the Supreme Court granted. Held: Reversed.

Chief Justice Burger

We granted certiorari because of an apparent conflict among the courts of appeals with respect to the standard of liability of corporate officers under the Federal Food, Drug, and Cosmetic Act . . . and because of the importance of the question to Government's enforcement program.

The rule that corporate employees who have "a responsible share in the furtherance of the transaction which the statute outlaws" are subject to the criminal provisions of the Act was not formulated in a vacuum. Cases under the Federal Food and Drugs Act of 1906 reflected the view both that knowledge or intent were not required to be proved in prosecutions under its criminal provisions, and that responsible corporate agents could be subjected to the liability thereby imposed. Moreover, the principle had been recognized that a corporate agent, through whose act, default, or omission the corporation committed a crime, was himself guilty individually of that crime. The principle had been applied whether or not the crime required "consciousness of wrongdoing," and it had been applied not only to those corporate agents who themselves committed the criminal act, but also to those who by virtue of their managerial positions or other similar relation to the actor could be deemed responsible for its commission.

In the latter class of cases, the liability of managerial officers did not depend on their knowledge of, or personal participation in, the act made criminal by the statute. Rather, where the statute under which they were prosecuted dispensed with "consciousness of wrongdoing," an omission or failure to act was deemed a sufficient basis for a responsible corporate agent's liability. It was enough in such cases that, by virtue of the relationship he bore to the corporation, the agent had the power to have prevented the act complained of.

The rationale of the interpretation given the Act . . . , as holding criminally account- able the persons whose failure to exercise the authority and supervisory responsibility reposed in them by the business organization resulted in the violation complained of, has been confirmed in our . . . cases. Thus, the Court has reaffirmed the proposition that "the public interest in the purity of its food is so great as to warrant the imposition of the highest standard of care on distributors." In order to make "distributors of food the strictest censors of their merchandise," the Act punishes "neglect where the law requires care, or inaction where it imposes a duty." "The accused, if he does not will the violation, usually is in a position to prevent it with no more care than society might reasonably expect and no more exertion than it might reasonably exact from one who assumed his responsibilities." Similarly, . . . the courts of appeals have recognized that those corporate agents vested with the responsibility, and power commensurate with that responsibility, to devise whatever measures are necessary to ensure compliance with the Act bear a "responsible relationship" to, or have a "responsible share" in, violations.

Thus . . . the cases . . . reveal that in providing sanctions which reach and touch the individuals who execute the corporate mission—and this is by no means necessar- ily confined to a single corporate agent or employee—the Act imposes not only a positive duty to seek out and remedy violations when they occur but also, and primarily, a duty to implement measures that will insure that violations will not occur. The requirements of foresight and vigilance imposed on responsible corporate agents are beyond question demanding, and perhaps onerous, but they are no more stringent than the public has a right to expect of those who voluntarily assume positions of authority in business enterprises whose services and products affect the health and well-being of the public that supports them.

The Act does not . . . make criminal liability turn on "awareness of some wrongdo- ing" or "conscious fraud." The duty imposed by Congress on responsible corporate agents is, we emphasize, one that requires the highest standard of foresight and vigilance, but the Act, in its criminal aspect, does not require that which is objectively impossible. The theory upon which responsible corporate agents are held criminally accountable for "causing" violations of the Act permits a claim that a defendant was "powerless" to prevent or correct the violation to "be raised defensively at a trial on the merits." If such a claim is made, the defendant has the burden of coming forward with evidence, but this does not alter the Government's ultimate burden of proving beyond a reasonable doubt the defendant's guilt, including his power, in light of the duty imposed by the Act, to prevent or correct the prohibited condition. Congress has seen fit to enforce the accountability of responsible corporate agents dealing with products which may affect the health of consumers by penal sanctions cast in rigorous terms, and the obligation of the courts is to give them effect so long as they do not violate the Constitution.

We cannot agree with the Court of Appeals that . . . the Government had the burden of establishing "wrongful action". . . . The concept of a "responsible relationship" to, or a "responsible share" in, a violation of the Act indeed imports some measure of blameworthiness; but it is equally clear that the Government establishes a prima facie case when it introduces evidence sufficient to warrant a finding . . . that the defendant had, by reason of his position in the corporation, responsibility and authority either to prevent in the first instance, or promptly to correct, the violation complained of, and that he failed to do so. The failure thus to fulfill the duty imposed by the interaction of the corporate agent's authority and the statute furnishes a sufficient causal link. The considerations which prompted the imposition of this duty, and the scope of the duty, provide the measure of culpability.

We are satisfied that the Act imposes the highest standard of care and permits conviction of responsible corporate officials who, in light of this standard of care, have the power to prevent or correct violations of its provisions.

Reversed.

RIGHTS AND DUTIES BETWEEN PRINCIPAL AND AGENT

Agent's Right to Compensation

Unless the agent's services are intended to be gratuitous, the agent is entitled to compensation for the general value of his or her services. The agent's right to compensation usually is provided by contract, with matters of interpretation determined according to the ordinary rules of contract law. An important issue ordinarily is whether the agent performed the specified services according to the contract. Since the contract's terms and conditions governing the agent's compensation often are a source of misunderstanding and disputes between the parties, these provisions should be established clearly in writing. The matters to be considered will vary with each agency, but parties to most agencies should normally consider the amount and the basis of compensation. For example, whether the compensation is to be by salary, wages, commission, a share of profits, bonuses, or in a form other than money should be expressly provided in writing. Additionally, the agent should consider including some provision to compensate for extra services and to reimburse expenses. The principal should consider including conditions governing the right of compensation. For example, he or she may wish to provide that the agent is to achieve certain results or render specified services before becoming entitled to compensation. Both parties should consider providing for compensation in the form of liquidated damages in the event of a breach of contract or other misconduct.

Agencies involving practices peculiar to a trade will require special attention to avoid misunderstanding. For example, sales agents may wish to stipulate that commissions are deemed earned even if the principal fails to fill orders or if the customer rejects delivery or does not pay for ordered merchandise. Principals of sales agents may wish to provide that commissions are earned when orders are either obtained, accepted, delivered, or paid for.

In the absence of an agreement, there is an implied obligation on a principal to pay for services rendered by the agent where the services are customarily paid for. If the agency contract does not provide for compensation, a promise to pay is inferred from the fact that the agent's services are rendered at the principal's request or have been accepted by the principal.

When customary and practical, the principal is obligated to keep and render accounts of the compensation owed to the agent. This allows the agent to know what he or she is entitled to and serves to implement the agent's right to compensation. Like the right to compensation, this right to an accounting depends upon custom and usage. For example, principals employing traveling sales agents whose compensation is based on completed sales are in a better position to maintain sales records; therefore, they customarily keep the accounts. However, agents such as real estate brokers and lawyers, who own their own businesses and have complete knowledge of all transactions, will ordinarily keep their own accounts. Principals employing them are relieved of accounting responsibilities. A principal, however, may be required to maintain certain records for tax purposes. Additionally, the parties may stipulate in their agency contract who is to maintain and render accounts.

In addition to compensating the agent for services rendered, the principal is obligated to indemnify or reimburse the agent for any authorized expenses or losses suffered by the agent while acting for the principal. An *indemnity* obligates one person to make good any loss or damage incurred by another while acting for that person's benefit. The principle upon which the theory of indemnity rests is that the true benefactor should bear the ultimate burden of payment. In agency relations, the agent customarily makes expenditures for the principal in executing the agency. Also, the agent may be exposed to liability when carrying out his or her authorized tasks. Since the principal put the agent initially in this position, the principal should bear the financial burden.

The agency agreement sometimes establishes the agent's right to indemnity; however, the parties may agree that the agent will bear the risk of loss and the expenses of performance of his or her duties. If no provision is made for indemnity, courts infer the right when the agent incurs an expense, suffers a loss, or assumes a liability while acting in an authorized manner. For example, the agent is entitled to reimbursement from the principal for any authorized payment that is necessary to the agent's performance. This right to reimbursement does not arise until payment is made.

The agent's right to indemnity extends to losses and expenses incurred in legal proceedings initiated by a third party against the agent regarding an authorized transaction. For the agent to receive indemnification for losses and expenses resulting from legal proceedings, the agent must notify the principal of the proceeding within a reasonable time. This allows the principal to respond by defending his or her interest in the legal proceeding. If the principal is notified but fails to defend, the agent may recover any expenses reasonably incurred in a good-faith defense or reasonable settlement of the legal proceedings.

When the principal is liable to the agent for compensation, reimbursement, or indemnity, the agent is permitted a lien or security interest in the principal's goods or money lawfully possessed by the agent. This lien extends only to the amount of the agent's compensation or indemnity and entitles the agent to retain possession of the property or the proceeds from its sale until the agent is paid what is owed.

Agent's Fiduciary Duties

Since the agent acts solely for the principal's benefit in all matters connected with the agency, the principal-agent relationship is called a fiduciary relationship, and the agent is referred to as the principal's fiduciary. In the fiduciary relationship the fiduciary acts not for himself or herself but for another person. Since someone else reposes trust and confidence in the fiduciary, the fiduciary is held to very high standards of conduct. Fiduciary duties are imposed for the protection of the other person's property and interests, and the courts do not tolerate any abridgement of these duties without the consent of the other person. The judicial posture is best summarized by Justice Cardoza's classic statement:

> Many forms of conduct permissible in a workaday world for those acting at arm's length, are forbidden to those bound by fiduciary ties. A trustee is held to something stricter than the morals of the marketplace. Not honesty alone, but the punctilio of an honor the most sensitive, is then the standard of behavior. As to this there has developed a tradition that is unbending and inveterate. Uncompromising rigidity has been the attitude of the courts of equity when petitioned to undermine the rule of undivided loyalty by the "disintegrating erosion" of particular exceptions. . . . Only thus has the level of conduct for fiduciaries been kept at a higher level than that trodden by the crowd (FN *Meinhard* v. *Salman*, 164 N.E. 545, 546 [N.Y. 1926]).

A fiduciary is under a general duty to act for the other person's benefit on matters within the relationship. The agent, therefore, must act solely for the principal's benefit in all matters affecting the agency relation. Other fiduciary duties imposed on the agent are: the duty of loyalty to the principal, the duty to obey the principal's instruction, the duty to use reasonable skill and care in the performance of his or her job, and the duty to inform the principal of matters affecting the agency. Violation of these duties terminates the agency relation and results in a forfeit of the agent's compensation.

Agent's Duty of Loyalty

A demanding duty of the agent is to be loyal to the principal. Fidelity is fundamental to the agency relationship, because without it no assurance exists that the principal's interests would be promoted. The agent must not allow personal interests to conflict with the principal's. He or she may not compete directly with the principal, or indirectly by working for the principal's competitor, without the principal's consent.

Since the agent is under a duty to act solely for the principal, the agent must pay all agency profits to the principal. All benefits, even bribes, resulting from the agency relation belong to the principal. An agent may not take advantage of an opportunity rightfully belonging to the principal. For example, a purchasing agent, authorized to buy property for the principal, cannot buy for himself or herself any property that the principal would be interested in buying. Any such property bought belongs to the principal even though held by the agent.

It follows that the agent cannot deal with the principal as an adverse party, unless the principal consents to such a transaction. For example, a sales agent authorized to sell the principal's property to third persons cannot buy the property for himself or herself without the principal's consent. Even if the agent pays a fair price, the principal may rescind the sale and recover the property or obtain any profits made by the agent in any resale of the property to an innocent purchaser. Since the agent cannot deal with the principal as an adverse party, the agent also cannot represent an adverse party in a transaction with the principal unless both parties are fully informed and agree to the arrangement. Any transaction negotiated by a double agent is voidable at the option of the party having no knowledge of the agency.

The agent's duty of loyalty also extends to the use of confidential information, such as the principal's trade secrets and customer lists. The agent may not use or communicate information confidentially given to him or her by the principal.

Agent's Duty to Obey

The agent must obey any reasonable instruction from the principal regarding the agent's performance. The reasonableness of an instruction depends on ethical and legal considerations. For example, a sales agent need not obey an order to misrepresent the quality of merchandise, since such an order is illegal.

If the principal issues an ambiguous instruction, the agent should seek clarification while giving it a reasonable interpretation consistent with trade practice and prior dealings. Reasonable instructions that are clear, precise, and imperative must be strictly followed, or the agent will be liable in either contract or tort for any losses resulting from the disobedience. Any violation of such a clear directive is not excused by custom or usage in the business. Furthermore, the agent's motives are immaterial to his or her liability. The fact that the agent disobeys in good faith, intending to benefit the principal, will not relieve the agent of liability for any resulting loss. However, the agent may disobey instructions in order to respond to an emergency that the agent did not create if communication with the principal is impractical.

Agent's Duty to Use Skill and Care

The agent must use skill and care in performing the principal's business. If the agent fails to exercise reasonable skill and care, the principal may recover for any loss or damage resulting from the agent's negligence. This permits the principal to rely on the agent to perform properly the assigned responsibilities. The duty of skill and care arises from what is commonly accepted as the customs and experiences of everyday living. If someone hires another to perform a job, the employer usually expects that the job will be done skillfully and carefully. Thus the agent should possess and exercise the necessary skill and care to perform the principal's business. For example, an insurance broker should know something of the trade, the form of policy, the nature of the risk, the solvency of the underwriter, and all general matters affecting the contract. A broker without these skills will be liable if he or she negligently fails to provide adequate insurance protection for the insured.

The agent is required to exercise reasonable and ordinary skill and care in the performance of the agency objectives. The standard of skill and care is that ordinarily possessed by persons engaged in the same business or occupation. However, if the agent claims special skills, he or she is held to a higher standard of care that is commensurate with the claimed specialization.

The agent is not the insurer of his or her acts. For example, an agent who sells the principal's merchandise to a buyer on credit does not impliedly guarantee the buyer's solvency. All that is required is that the agent use skill and care in determining the purchaser's ability to pay for the merchandise. Thus, if the agent sells merchandise on credit to someone the agent knows or should know is a poor credit risk, the agent will be liable to the principal for any losses resulting from the purchaser's nonpayment.

If the agent carelessly performs the principal's business, resulting in loss or damage to the principal, the agent's liability is for the tort of negligence. The principal will have to establish in court all the elements of negligence and will be subject to the defense of contributory negligence where, notwithstanding the agent's negligence, the principal could have avoided any loss by exercising ordinary care for his or her own protection. If the parties have entered into an agency contract, they may either enlarge or limit the agent's duties in their agreement. If the agent violates these duties, the agent additionally will be liable for breach of contract.

The following case shows the duty of diligence in a contemporary setting. The court applies age-old policy to help resolve a current problem.

Bucholtz v. Sirotkin Travel Ltd.

District Court, Nassau Co.

343 N.Y.S.2d 438 (New York, 1973)

Bucholtz (plaintiff) engaged Sirotkin Travel Ltd. (defendant) to arrange a trip to Las Vegas. The agency made hotel reservations and arranged flights; however, these were not confirmed. The flight was changed and the reservation unavailable. Plaintiff was forced to stay in a motel a half mile out of town. This resulted in both additional expense and inconvenience, and plaintiff brought a small claims proceeding against the travel agency. The plaintiff asked for damages of $106 for inconvenience and discomfort. The court awarded damages.

Donovan, Judge

The law presently lacks clarity with respect to the relationship between the travel agency and its clients. Obviously the travel agency is an agent, but the question comes, whose agent? Is it the agent of a hotel or other innkeeper with whom, or for whom, the agency transacts business? Or the steamship line or airline with whom it does business? Generally the travel agency is neither an agent nor an employee of the common carriers and innkeepers with whom it may do business. . . . Nor do we see any justification for holding the travel agent to be the agent of any intermediate wholesaler who may put together a "package" of accommodations.

The travel agent deals directly with the traveler. He must be charged with the duty of exercising reasonable care in securing passage on the appropriate carrier and lodging with an innkeeper. The money was paid over by the traveler to the defendant agency for that specific purpose.

News reports are constantly appearing with stories of travelers—many of them quite young—being stranded far from home or having vacation plans ruined because passage or lodging for which they have paid has not been provided. Who is to bear the responsibility? Is it some remote "wholesaler" who is unknown to the traveler, or the traveler himself, or the travel agency in whom the traveler has reposed his confidence?

Sometimes we must go deep into the past to find ancient principles and mold them to take care of new problems. The policy of the common law from ancient times has been to safeguard the traveler.

In this case nothing was done by the travel agency to verify or confirm either the plane reservations or the hotel reservations. If this duty is the responsibility of the travel agency, then the travel agency is liable in negligence for its failure to exercise reasonable care in making the reservations.

It may be urged that the default in this respect is that of the remote "wholesaler."

Where, as here, the agent is selected because he is supposed to have some special fitness for the performance of the duties to be undertaken, the traveler is entitled to rely on the judgment and discretion of that agent as well as his honesty and financial responsibility. The agent may not evade responsibility by delegating to a subagent the carrying out of the task which has been committed to him. . . . Travel agencies may find it convenient, in the course of transacting their business, to deal with wholesalers.

> The news reports are so voluminous that we may take judicial notice of the vice inherent in conducting business in so loose a fashion. The wholesaler may fail to pay for accommodations or may even fail to book the accommodations and the traveler is left in a helpless situation. He either has no recourse because of financial insufficiency or he may be required to travel to a distant jurisdiction in order to maintain a suit.
>
> Unless the principal, here the traveler, has expressly or impliedly authorized the travel agency to delegate responsibility to a second agency or "wholesaler," the responsibility must remain on the defendant travel agency. In an area so fraught with danger to the traveler, public policy demands that the travel agency be held responsible to: (a) verify or confirm the reservations and (b) use reasonable diligence in ascertaining the responsibility of any intervening "wholesaler" or tour organizer.
>
> This duty parallels, or is analogous to, the duty of an insurance broker in obtaining insurance coverage for his client. . . .
>
> The defendant is liable to the claimant for the breach of its fiduciary responsibility in failing to use reasonable care to confirm the reservations. . . .

Agent's Duty to Inform and Account

Parties in agency relations must keep each other informed; therefore, a duty is imposed on the agent to communicate to the principal regarding anything affecting the principal's interests. The agent must make a reasonable attempt to inform the principal of matters relating to any agency transaction that the agent should realize the principal would want to know about. For example, a real estate agent who is authorized to sell the principal's property at a specified price and on specified terms must inform the principal if he or she knows of someone who will pay a higher price or agree to better terms. Furthermore, the agent should disclose any information that disqualifies the agent from effectively promoting the principal's interests. If the agent is unable to undertake the principal's interests, the principal must be informed. Even if the agent is merely ill for a day, the duty to inform requires the agent to notify the principal so that the principal may make other arrangements.

The agent's duty to inform the principal of information relevant to agency affairs extends to information acquired outside the agent's scope of employment or before entering the agency relation. Although some courts have held that the agent's duty to inform includes matters learned of after the agency relation is terminated, the current trend is to not require the disclosure of such information. Furthermore, the agent need not reveal any information received in confidence, since that would require the agent to violate a duty to another. For example, an agent who leaves the employ of one principal to go to work for another need not inform the new employer about trade secrets used by the former employer.

The agent must keep and render an account of money or other property that the agent receives. This includes anything received from the principal as well as anything obtained from third persons for the principal. The agent is liable to the principal for all funds belonging to the principal coming into the agent's possession during the agency relation. Although it is ordinarily the principal's duty to keep his or her own accounts, the duty shifts to the agent if the agent is entrusted with funds or property or is required to make collections and expenditures. The manner of accounting need not be formal or meet technical accounting requirements. The method of bookkeeping depends on what is normally done in the business or is accepted by the principal.

The agent must not mix the principal's money or property with his or her own. This makes any accounting more accurate. Thus the agent may not put the principal's money in his or her own bank account or in a joint account unless the principal agrees to such an arrangement. To allow otherwise would make it difficult to determine whether it was the principal's or the agent's money that was deposited.

The following case illustrates the agent's duty to inform as well as other duties the agent owes to the principal.

McKeehan v. Wittels

Missouri Court of Appeals
508 S.W. 2d 277 (1974)

Dorothy M. McKeehan (plaintiff-appellee) brought an action seeking punitive damages from Jacob M. Wittels, Malcolm Wittels, Ilene Wittels, and Wittels Investment Company (defendants-appellants). Plaintiff's case was based upon breach of fiduciary duty. The trial court awarded plaintiff $29,942.65 actual damages and $25,000 in punitive damages. Defendants appealed, challenging the sufficiency of the evidence to support a breach of fiduciary duty. The appellate court affirmed the judgment of the lower court for all defendants except Ilene Wittels.

McMillian, Judge

As the first element of her cause of action, plaintiff Dorothy McKeehan pleads the creation and existence of a confidential relationship between herself and defendants, Malcolm, Jacob, and Ilene Wittels and Wittels Investment Co., Inc. The fiduciary duty or "fiduciary relationship" discussed in this case is usually referred to as applicable to suits in equity, but the principles underlying the doctrine in equity are also applicable to cases at law where the relation is sometimes referred to as a "confidential relation." A fiduciary relationship is created and established where there has been "a special confidence reposed in one who in equity and conscience is bound to act in good faith, and with due regard to the interests of the one reposing the confidence. . . ."

We believe that the record supports a finding that a fiduciary relationship existed between plaintiff Dorothy McKeehan and defendants Malcolm and Jacob Wittels and Wittels Investment Co., Inc. The transcript reflects that from the outset of the series of transactions in question, plaintiff dealt directly with Malcolm and Jacob Wittels who constantly assured her that they would take care of her investments. Plaintiff also testified that Malcolm Wittels urged her to intrust her funds with the Company and claimed that the Company had extensive experience and knowledge in handling such investments. Defendant Malcolm Wittels denies in his deposition that he or anyone made such promises to Dorothy McKeehan. However, this fact issue turns completely on the credibility of the witnesses. Consequently, we defer to the trial court's finding that Dorothy McKeehan's testimony was the more credible.

As the second element of her cause of action, plaintiff pleads that defendants breached their fiduciary duty by deliberately failing to follow her instructions, failing to disclose essential information affecting the security of her investments, and misrepresenting certain facts for the purpose of furthering their own financial position. It is established law in this state that ". . . [w]hen a loss results to a principal from his agent's failure to pursue the instructions given to him, a cause of action arises in favor of the former. . . .".

> ". . . [S]ometimes instructions are violated in such a way as to authorize a principal to proceed directly against the agent as a debtor or for conversion. Loyalty to their trust is firmly exacted of all agents by law, and when one uses his position for his own ends, regardless of the welfare of his principal, he becomes responsible for a resultant loss, as if he unscrupulously handles money or property confided to him to benefit himself. . . . [A]n agent cannot ignore the directions given to him as to how the business put into his hands shall be transacted, and cannot use his agency for his own advantage, to the detriment of the principal."

Likewise, a fiduciary relationship between principal and agent obligates the agent to fully disclose all material facts to the principal, to strictly avoid misrepresentation and in all respects to act with utmost good faith. If plaintiff presented sufficient evidence to prove either that defendants deliberately ignored her instructions in order to further their own financial position, or failed to disclose material facts to plaintiff or actively misrepresented material facts to plaintiff, she will have produced sufficient evidence to support the trial court's finding of proof of the second material element of her cause of action, breach of fiduciary duty arising out of a confidential or fiduciary relationship.

Plaintiff has demonstrated with direct evidence in the form of exhibits and testimony that she entrusted to defendants Malcolm and Jacob Wittels and Wittels Investment Co., the sum of $28,813.00. Plaintiff testified that she repeatedly demanded of both Malcolm and Jacob Wittels that her funds be returned to her after the various deeds of trust had matured. Plaintiff's attorney, Fred Reichman, testified that he related to defendant Malcolm Wittels that plaintiff was interested in disposing of her investments. Reichman testified that he received personal assurances from Malcolm Wittels that Dorothy McKeehan's investments would be returned to her. Consequently, the evidence indicates that both Malcolm and Jacob Wittels had personal knowledge of plaintiff's instructions and knowingly disregarded them. Secondly, both plaintiff and her attorney testified that Malcolm and Jacob Wittels renewed the deeds of trust on several parcels of property without her consent and against her expressed wishes. Such evidence is sufficient to sustain a finding that defendants Malcolm and Jacob Wittels and Wittels Investment Co., knowingly failed to follow plaintiff's explicit instructions regarding the handling of her investments.

We also find ample evidence to sustain a finding that Malcolm and Jacob Wittels and Wittels Investment Co., breached their fiduciary duty to plaintiff by failing to disclose material facts regarding her investments. It is the established law in this jurisdiction that the existence of a confidential or fiduciary relationship between principal and agent obligates the agent to make a complete and full disclosure of all material facts concerning the transaction which might affect the principal's decision regarding his or her investments. Similarly, it is a breach of fiduciary duty for an agent to occupy a position antagonistic to his principal.

Plaintiff's evidence strongly supports the trial court's finding that the defendants Malcolm and Jacob Wittels and Wittels Investment Company did occupy a position antagonistic to plaintiff and consequently failed to disclose all necessary facts to plaintiff regarding her investments. The record is clear that as to certain parcels of property, defendants sold the first deeds of trust to plaintiff and held on to the more profitable second deeds themselves. This arrangement is highly suspect since it is usually the first deeds of trust which pay interest and principal, not the second. Taking into consideration the evidence of plaintiff's lack of sophistication in the area of real estate transactions, and of defendants' knowledge of her dependence (both physical and intellectual) on their judgment, it is not unreasonable to conclude that she was totally unaware of the Wittels' ownership of the second deeds of trust which operated to her disadvantage. Plaintiff also introduced exhibits and testimony that tax liens existed on all of the parcels of property held under the deeds of trust purchased from defendants. Malcolm Wittels testified that he knew that a tax lien was considered to be a first lien on the property. There is strong evidence that Malcolm and Jacob Wittels were aware of the existence and accrual of tax liens on the properties at the time plaintiff purchased and held the deeds of trust. When the deeds of trust were given to Dorothy McKeehan under the circumstances shown in the evidence, she was justified in believing she was purchasing a first deed of trust constituting a first lien on the property and not subject to any prior tax liens. The record clearly reflects the extreme unlikelihood that defendants Malcolm and Jacob Wittels were unaware of these tax liens. Their failure to disclose the tax liens to plaintiff at the time of sale and the failure to disclose the accrual of these tax liens was more than sufficient evidence to sustain the trial court's finding and judgment with respect to these defendants.

We have carefully read the record and have concluded that there is substantial evidence to support the trial court's finding that defendants Malcolm and Jacob Wittels and Wittels Investment Company breached their fiduciary duty to plaintiff. However, we find no evidence in the record, either direct or circumstantial, of Ilene Wittel's participation in either the creation of the fiduciary relationship or the subsequent breach of duty.

Judgment affirmed as to Malcolm Wittels, Jacob Wittels and Wittels Investment Company. Judgment reversed as to Ilene Wittels.

Smith, P.J., and Clemens, J., concur.

TERMINATION OF AGENCY

Probably a majority of agencies terminate by the accomplishment of the objective for which the agency was created or by the expiration of time allotted for completing performance. The agency can, however, be terminated in numerous other ways. Termination of the relationship occurs by events or conditions that destroy the agent's power to act for the principal. An example would be the bankruptcy of the principal or of the agent, if the agent's financial status is important to the relationship. Another example would be the destruction of the subject matter. In addition, as the agency relationship is consensual, either party may terminate the agency at any time by withdrawing his or her consent. The death or incompetency of the principal will also terminate the agency; however, some states permit the relationship to continue after the principal's incompetence if a power of attorney expressly so provides or if the power of attorney is approved by the court.

Power vs. Right to Terminate

When the principal withdraws consent, the principal is said to revoke the agent's authority. When the agent withdraws consent, the agent is said to renounce authority. Since the principal originally had the power to manage his or her own business before delegating that job to the agent, the principal has the power to resume control of the business by firing the agent. The agent also may renounce at any time, since forcing someone to work against his or her will is unconstitutional slavery. However, because someone has a legal power to do something does not mean that he or she has a legal right to do it. For example, a person has the power to breach a contract, but exercising the power is wrong and renders the breaching party liable to the other party for damages. So while either party to an agency relation has the power to terminate the agency at will, the termination may subject the terminating party to contractual liability if it amounts to a breach of its agency contract.

Agency of Indefinite Duration

Some agency contracts do not specify precisely how long the parties intend their relation to last. This raises the question of whether either party may terminate the agency at will without liability for wrongful termination.

This usually occurs in distributorship and employment agreements.

It is common for a local dealer to build a business as the distributor of a manufacturer's products. These distributorship agreements, sometimes in the form of franchise contracts, are entered into by both parties in contemplation of a continuing relationship, often without any express term. Usually the distributor incurs start-up costs at the outset of the relationship. For sales of goods involving application of the Uniform Commercial Code, the manufacturer may terminate a distributorship only for due cause, and then only after giving the dealer reasonable notice of the termination (Sections 1–203 and 2–309). Thus the manufacturer must show a justifiable reason for terminating the distributorship, such as the dealer's noncompliance with the distributorship agreement, and must give the dealer sufficient notice of termination to permit the distributor to make an orderly phase-out by liquidating inventories, collecting accounts receivable, and finding new product lines to handle.

Employment contracts are often contracts of indefinite duration. Assurances of "steady," "regular," or even "permanent" employment are usually held to create an employment at will, which either party may terminate at any time without liability. A few courts consider this unduly harsh to the employee who may have suffered serious detriment in taking the employment by quitting a former job and relocating at the new place of employment. In these jurisdictions the employer can fire an employee only in good faith. Since not many courts have adopted this approach, what is a suitable good-faith termination is not yet defined.

Notifying Agent of Termination

Before an attempted termination is effective, the other party to the relation normally must be notified of the termination. Thus, if the principal wishes to fire the agent, notice to the agent of the termination is required to revoke the agent's authority. Notification may be made in any way that tells the agent that his or her services are no longer desired. For example, if a realtor who has been hired by a homeowner to sell the owner's house hears that the owner has sold the house on his or her own, the realtor should realize the agency relation has been terminated. In this way, revocation of an agent's authority is like revocation of an offeror's contract offer. Actual notice is needed, but no particular form of notice is required. All that is needed is for the agent to realize that the agency is over.

Notifying Third Parties of Termination

Although revocation of the agent's real authority may be accomplished by notifying the agent, third parties must also be notified. If they do not know of the termination, they may think the agency still exists and continue to transact business with the agent and hold the principal responsible since to them the agent apparently is still authorized to transact the principal's business. To revoke the agent's apparent authority, the principal must give suitable notice of the agent's termination to third parties.

What constitutes suitable notice depends on what is reasonable under the circumstances. In some cases, no notice need be given at all. Generally, no notice need be given to third parties when the principal terminates the employment of a special agent, such as a realtor, because this type of agency gives notice to third parties of its limited authority. People dealing with special agents should seek assurance of the agent's continued authority. Normally this may be done by seeking written authorization. Principals giving their agents written authority should invalidate the writing upon terminating the agency.

When the principal terminates a general agent, normally the principal must actually notify all persons whom the principal has dealt with through the agent. This may require consulting appropriate records for determining the agent's customers, although sometimes it is impossible to notify every person who has dealt with the agent. Additionally, others who might rely upon the agency relationship deserve to know that the agency has been terminated. In these situations, reasonable notice requires some compromise between the principal's duty to notify third parties and the difficulty of doing so. Suitable notice is any means reasonably designed to reach all third parties. Publication in a newspaper is the typical method. After publication, all persons except those who dealt with the agent on a regular basis are considered to have constructive notice of the termination.

A number of changes in circumstances automatically terminate the agent's authority. These include events such as the loss or destruction of the subject matter, the bankruptcy of the principal or under some circumstances the bankruptcy of the agent, and the death or incompetency of the principal. When the agency is terminated because of changes of this nature, generally neither the agent nor the third party need be notified of the termination. This is because the courts entertain the fiction that these events are notorious facts known to all. Since everybody in the world knows about the event all at once, its occurrence automatically revokes the agent's authority. This results in excusing the principal from liability to anyone and in making the agent liable to the third party for breach of the agent's warranty of authority.

A sizeable minority of states allows the agent's authority to continue after the principal dies or is declared incompetent until the agent or the third party learns of the death or incompetency. In these jurisdictions, the agent is able to bind the estate of a deceased or incompetent principal and will be able to avoid any warranty liability. In the case of banks, the UCC provides that neither the death nor the incompetence of the customer revokes a bank's authority to accept, pay, or collect an item until the bank knows of the death or the adjudication of incompetency and has a reasonable opportunity to act on it.

Irrevocable Agency

In some agency relations, the principal cannot revoke the agent's authority because the agent has an interest in continuing the relation. Courts sometimes say the agent possesses a property right in the relation or has an "agency coupled with an interest." Actually, these are not true agencies. Normally, an agency exists to permit the principal to accomplish something through the agent. However, an irrevocable agency is designed to allow the agent to do something for himself or herself.

An irrevocable agency is like a contract that must be specifically performed. Someone breaching a contract must perform the agreed undertaking if money is no substitute for performance. Similarly, if the agent must continue performing as an agent to protect an interest because money will not pay for the principal's breach of a promise not to revoke, the agency is irrevocable. An example of an irrevocable agency is when a debtor borrows money, giving property as collateral by granting the creditor authority to sell the property in event of default. The creditor is the debtor's agent. Money cannot substitute for continuing the agency relation since the agency initially is created to protect the creditor against the debtor's financial default.

REVIEW PROBLEMS

1. Arthur Murray, Inc., engages in the licensing of persons to operate dance studios using its registered trade name and the Arthur Murray method of dancing. Burkin, Inc., obtained a license to use the Arthur Murray name and method in connection with a dancing school in San Diego. The franchise agreement between Arthur Murray and Burkin provided that Arthur Murray would: (1) fix minimum tuition rates; (2) designate the school's location and layout; (3) make pupil refunds and charge the amounts to Burkin; and (4) collect 5 percent of the school's weekly gross receipts to be used to pay any suits against Arthur Murray's. Additionally, the agreement provided that Burkin would: (1) obey Arthur Murray's rules regarding the qualifications and conduct of instructors and discharge any employee found unacceptable to Arthur Murray; (2) submit advertising for Arthur Murray's approval; (3) maintain and manage the school according to Arthur Murray's general policies; and (4) submit weekly financial records to Arthur Murray. Gertrude Nichols entered into several contracts with the San Diego school and made prepayments for lessons that were never furnished because Burkin, Inc., discontinued its operations. Nichols brought suit against Arthur Murray, Inc., claiming that the San Diego school was its agent. Do you think Nichols is right? Nichols v. Arthur Murray, Inc., 56 Cal.Rptr. 728 (1967)

2. Porter had been employed by the Brinn & Jensen Company for many years as a traveling salesman and had been assigned to cover a definite territory. Porter used his own automobile as a means of transportation and covered his territory once every five weeks. He worked on a commission basis but had a drawing account with the company, which was treated as an ad-

vance on commissions earned. He also made collections for the company and performed other services when so directed by the home office. The company could discharge Porter at any time it became dissatisfied with the manner in which he was doing his work. The company required Porter to furnish an automobile to be used in covering his territory, and he would not have been retained if he could not have provided one. It was generally left to Porter to determine the route to be used in covering his territory, but the company retained the right to direct him where to go within the territory if it desired to do so. Porter was required to make personal calls on customers and send in his orders daily. The company instructed him concerning the merchandise to be pushed. He was required to devote all of his time to company business. While driving on company business, Porter was killed when his automobile crashed into another automobile driven by Peterson, who was seriously injured. At the time of the accident, Porter had with him a sample case, forms, catalogues, and a number of orders signed by customers. Peterson sued the company, claiming that Porter was its agent. The company claimed it had no liability since it did not control the physical movements of the automobile being driven by Porter. Who is right? Peterson v. Brinn & Jensen Co., 280 N.W. 171 (1938)

3. Mary Dyer, a minor, executed a power of attorney appointing her father as her agent to act for her in all matters pertaining to her ownership of 100 shares of stock in the Union Electric Company. To obtain information regarding the management of the company, Mary, through her father, requested to inspect and copy certain company records. She wanted this information in order to advise other stockholders and obtain their proxies to bring about a change in company management by electing a new board of directors. The company refused to honor her father's power of attorney and also denied him permission to attend meetings of the board of directors. Mary, through her father as guardian, brought suit to compel the company to recognize her father as her agent and comply with his requests. The company argued that the power of attorney was void because Mary, as a minor, lacked the legal capacity to appoint an agent. Is Mary or the company correct? Dyer v. Union Electric Company, 309 S.W.2d 649 (1958)

4. Owner listed his house with Penelope, a real estate broker, granting Penelope an exclusive right to sell Owner's house. Penelope entered negotiations with Buyer, who manifested an interest in purchasing the property. Buyer found the price agreeable; however, he insisted upon including a clause in the sales contract giving him the right to cancel the contract if he could not obtain a loan to finance his purchase. At the closing of the land sale contract, Buyer exercised his right to cancel, giving as his reason the inability to procure a loan. Penelope turned to Owner and claimed that she was entitled to her commission even though the sale did not go through. Must Owner pay Penelope a commission? A.A. Realty Co. v. Albright, 186 N.E.2d 137 (1961)

5. Robert Desfosses owned and operated a corporation engaged in selling mobile homes and developing mobile-home parks. He employed Steve Notis, a licensed real estate broker, to negotiate the purchase of a tract of land suitable for the company to develop as a mobile-home park. When Notis related that the land was available, Desfosses directed Notis to purchase the land as a straw man and then to convey the land to Desfosses. While Notis was negotiating the purchase of the land, he repeatedly told Defosses that the land

would cost $32,400, although he knew the land could be purchased for $15,474.62. Notis made these false statements for the purpose of inducing Desfosses to deliver to him the sum of $32,400. Relying on Notis's statements as to the land's cost, Desfosses delivered $32,400 to Notis, intending to deliver only the amount necessary to make the purchase. Using Desfosses's money, Notis paid the owner of the land $15,474.62 to close the sale, took title in his own name, and promptly conveyed the land to Desfosses. After paying out the sum necessary to complete the purchase of the land, Notis retained the balance of the $32,400 that Desfosses had given him. Desfosses later learned of Notis's actions and brought suit to recover his money. He also refused to pay Notis any commission for his efforts. Notis claimed that Desfosses was entitled only to a rescission of the resale contract, thereby entitling Notis to the return of the land in exchange for money. Who is right? Desfosses v. Notis, 333 A.2d 83 (1975)

6. Julius and Olga Sylvester owned an unimproved piece of land near King of Prussia, Pennsylvania. They were approached by George Beck, a real estate broker, who asked if they were willing to sell their land, stating that an oil company was interested in buying, renting, or leasing the property. The Sylvesters said that they were interested only in selling, and they authorized Beck to sell the property for $15,000. Several weeks later, Beck phoned the Sylvesters and offered to buy the property for himself for $14,000. Olga asked, "What happened to the oil company?" and Beck responded, "They are not interested; you want too much money for it." The Sylvesters sold the property to Beck. A month later Beck sold the property to David Epstein for $25,000. When the Sylvesters learned that Beck had realized a huge profit in a quick resale of the property,

they sued Beck, claiming that he owed them the $11,000 profit. Does Beck owe the Sylvesters the money? Sylvester v. Beck, 178 A.2d 755 (1962).

7. The directors of the Tulsa Industrial Loan and Investment Company instructed its secretary-treasurer to secure an indemnity bond indemnifying the company for losses that might be caused by embezzlement by any of its employees. The secretary-treasurer did so, signing the application for the company. The application included a statement that, to the best of the company's knowledge and belief, all employees who would be bonded had always performed their duties faithfully, and that no act had come to the company's knowledge indicating that the employees who would be bonded were unreliable, deceitful, dishonest, or unworthy of confidence. Before the application was signed, the secretary-treasurer, in collusion with other agents, had embezzled substantial amounts from the company. Upon discovering this, the company filed a claim to collect under its indemnification policy. The insurer refused payment, stating that the company misrepresented facts in its application. The insurer argued that since the secretary-treasurer was the company's agent and he knew of the embezzlement, his knowledge was imputed to the company, making its statement in the application a knowing misrepresentation. Is the company entitled to payment? Maryland Casualty Co. v. Tulsa Industrial Loan & Investment Co., 83 F.2d 14 (10th Cir. 1936)

8. From May 17, 1973, to June 1973, Bob Harvey was employed by the Magnolia Health Center as a laboratory technician. While at Magnolia, Harvey ordered laboratory testing services from Bio-Chem Medical Laboratories, Inc. Harvey left Magnolia on June 13, 1973, to assume an administrative position with another

clinic. Later that month, he received a bill from Bio-Chem for the testing services he had ordered while at Magnolia. Harvey claimed that he contracted for these services in a representative capacity for his employer and therefore was not obligated to pay the bill. Must Harvey pay? Explain. Bio-Chem Medical Laboratories, Inc. v. Harvey, 310 S.2d 173 (1973)

9. All-Pro Reps, Inc., is engaged in the business of representing professional athletes in contractual dealings and in providing financial-management services to athletes. John Jones contacted Nate Archibald to make a one-day appearance at Jones's boys' camp and was told by Archibald to contact All-Pro. All-Pro informed Jones that Archibald would appear at the camp on August 15, 1973. A timely payment of the agreed compensation was made by Jones. On August 10, five days before the scheduled appearance, All-Pro, which had been notified by Archibald on the night of August 9 that circumstances prevented him from making the appearance, sent this information by mail to Jones and refunded the consideration paid by Jones. This letter was received by Jones on August 14. Jones filed suit against All-Pro. His complaint alleged that All-Pro was Archibald's authorized agent in the transaction, that Archibald willfully breached the contract, that All-Pro knew or should have known that Archibald would not appear, that All-Pro knew or should have known that its method of communication would not allow sufficient time to secure a replacement, that All-Pro breached its duty to supply to Jones a replacement of a person of equal stature and reputation as Archibald and to give timely notice of Archibald's nonappearance, and that the consequence of all this was that Jones incurred damages in the amount of $200,000 for loss of reputation. Who wins and why? Jones v. Archibald, 360 N.Y.S.2d 119 (1974).

10. Harold, the owner of Harold's Department Store, directed Julius, his stockhandler, to arrange a display containing lightbulbs. Julius arranged the display in a negligent manner. Penelope, a purchaser, was injured when the display fell over, causing the lightbulbs to explode. Penelope brought suit against both Harold and Julius for damages. Harold went bankrupt before the case went to court. Julius claimed that he should not be liable because he had acted under Harold's direction. Is Julius right? Explain. Restatement of Agency 2D, Sections 343, 350 (1957).

11. Bob Barber and Peter Pratt were employees of the Household Finance Company. Woody Woodcock was an executive vice president and a director of the Liberty Finance Company. Fred Farrell and George Glen were neither directors, officers, nor employees of the Beneficial Finance Company. Over a seven-year period Barber, Pratt, Woodcock, Farrell, and Glen conspired to bribe two public officials of the Commonwealth of Massachusetts. The purpose of the conspiracy and the payment of the bribe money was to ensure the maintenance of a maximum interest rate that loan companies licensed to do business in Massachusetts were permitted to charge. Each individual and corporation was named in an indictment alleging the commission of an unlawful conspiracy to bribe a public official. The three corporations argued that they should not be held criminally responsible for the conduct of Barber, Pratt, Woodcock, Farrell, and Glen. Discuss the criminal responsibility of each of the indicted corporations. Commonwealth v. Beneficial Finance Co., 275 N.E.2d 33 (1971)

Nature and Formation of Partnerships

For the army of hopefuls annually entering the ranks of the self-employed, three questions dominate most of the early planning: How do I get started in business? How do I form a company? Should I form a partnership, corporation, or some other type of business organization? Confused by the comparative benefits of each, many business owners automatically choose the corporate form. Call it myth, error, or popular misconception, the general consensus holds that the corporate form is always superior. The facts, however, do not bear this out. Forming a corporation may not always be the wisest course.

Selecting the wrong business form may cut deeply into the owner-manager's financial rewards. It is therefore critical for an entrepreneur to examine all the alternatives with a lawyer and a financial adviser before making the final choice. This and the following chapters examine the partnership and corporate forms of business organization.

This chapter considers the nature of partnerships and how they are created. Partnerships involve the pooling of talent, money, and experience of two or more people. This type of business is easy to start, requires only simple registration, and is untaxed—partnership income being taxed only as the personal incomes of the partners.

Historically partnerships have often been informal associations because most partners did not give their organizational structure much attention. Partnership agreements have sometimes been unwritten. As a result, partnership law has developed to include the most diverse and unexpressed organizational structures. Some associations may not be recognized as partnerships by their participants; nevertheless they are treated as partnerships for legal purposes. Although a partnership contract is not always necessary, one is recommended. The contract should clearly distinguish each partner's rights and responsibilities in the operation of the firm. This precaution decreases the likelihood of legal disputes.

NATURE OF PARTNERSHIPS

Known to the ancients, the partnership is the oldest form of business association. The partnership concept is traceable from Babylonian sharecropping through classical Greece and Rome to the enterprise of the Renaissance. In the Middle Ages, it was a method of bringing financier and merchant together to avoid usury laws. Today the partnership still is an important form of business organization, especially in areas outside of manufacturing. Table 26–1 presents data on U.S. partnerships in 1977 reported by the *Statistical Abstract of the United States 1982.*

TABLE 26–1. PARTNERSHIP DISTRIBUTION AND PRODUCTIVITY, 1982

Industry	Number (in thousands)	Receipts (in billions of dollars)
Manufacturing	30	13.1
Wholesale & Retail	205	58.2
Finance, Insurance, & Real Estate	577	76.3
Services	239	83.3

Partnerships are usually thought of as small enterprises like real estate and security brokerages, accounting firms, mom-and-pop retail establishments, and family farms. This stereotype of the partnership is not always accurate. While most general partnerships are small, so are most corporations.

Although partnerships can be described by firm size and participant profile, of greater importance is their legal nature. How partnerships are legally defined and distinguished from other forms of business association is important for liability purposes. The tax laws often determine whether the partnership or another form of business organization is preferable for financial reasons.

Sources of Partnership Law

Modern partnership law originated in the mercantile courts of Elizabethan England. Confusion during the nineteenth century regarding its requirements led to passage by Parliament of the Partnership Act in 1890. The Uniform Partnership Act (UPA), drafted in 1914, and the Uniform Limited Partnership Act (ULPA), completed two years later, are its American cousins. They represent American efforts to make the law of partnerships uniform throughout the states. These acts were products of the Commission on Uniform State Laws, the source as well of the Uniform Commercial Code. The two acts are positive law in virtually every state and are referred to throughout the text.

Section 4 of the UPA contains rules for construing the act's provisions. Its declaration that "The law of agency shall apply to this act" ties in the material presented in Chapter 25 regarding agency law. In many ways, partnership law is the law of agency applied to partnerships.

Partnership Defined

The UPA defines a partnership as "an association of two or more persons to carry on as co-owners a business for profit" (Section 6[1]). This statutory definition governs whether a partnership exists. Anyone entering a relation satisfying this definition incurs the liability of a partner to the firm's creditors.

Types of Partnerships. Partnerships are either general or limited. A general partnership is the ordinary partnership governed by the UPA. To constitute a general partnership, nothing more is needed than to satisfy the definition of a partnership provided by Section 6(1). All the participants in a general partnership incur unlimited personal liability to partnership creditors.

A limited partnership carries many characteristics of a general partnership except that the liability of some members is limited. Governed by the ULPA, it offers some of the benefits of both partnerships and corporations, and may be used to attract investors willing to put up money but unwilling to risk personal liability. A limited partnership protects a special partner by exempting him or her from personal liability. It consists of one or more general partners who conduct the business and are personally liable to creditors as in an ordinary partnership. Additionally, it includes one or more limited partners who contribute capital and share in profits but who do not participate in the firm's management or operation and who assume no liability beyond a fixed amount, usually their capital contribution. The reason for requiring at least one general partner in a limited partnership is to provide someone answerable to the public for all partnership obligations. Limited partnerships were originally devised to enable persons to engage in business without being known or named. Today they are employed to provide the privilege of investing without the assumption of managerial responsibility or personal liability. Because of the many similarities to the corporate form, use of the limited partnership is diminishing. However, for real-estate investing, federal law on tax sheltering still makes the limited partnership an attractive alternative.

Other Unincorporated Associations. Partnerships traditionally have been distinguished from two other unincorporated business associations: the agency and the joint venture. It is often said that these relations are different from the partnership. However, it is more accurate to describe the partnership as a particular form of agency and the joint venture as a special type of partnership.

The partnership is a species of agency. Section 9 of the UPA provides that "Every partner is an agent of the partnership for the purpose of its business. . . ." This makes the partnership a mutual agency. Each partner acts as the agent of his or her copartners. However, unlike the true agency, each partner also is a principal, because UPA Section 6 provides that a partnership consists of co-owners. Thus each partner is simultaneously both principal and agent of the partnership. True agents usu-

ally are not co-owners of their principal's business and are entitled only to compensation for services rendered.

The joint venture is a partnership limited in duration and scope. While a partnership under UPA Section 6(1) must be an association of two or more persons to "carry on a business," the joint venture is an association of two or more persons for a single undertaking. For example, several promoters combining to bring a rock group to town for a single concert constitute a joint venture. Although it is often said that the partnership and the joint venture are different, in many respects they are analogous. The main difference is their respective scope and duration. It is difficult to distinguish between the two since some joint-venture undertakings are quite long, such as the promoting of a real-estate development, and some partnerships are short, such as where one of two partners dies shortly after starting the business. Theoretically, there should be no difference between the two associations under the UPA. Section 2 of the UPA defines "business" to include "every trade, occupation or profession." Thus there may be a doing of business within the UPA during a joint venture. While it is often said that the two relations are different, in reality it is a distinction without a difference. The same legal rules applicable to partnerships govern joint ventures.

Aggregate and Entity Nature of Partnerships

There are two conceptions of partnership: one that it is an aggregate of persons associated together to share its profits and losses, owning its property and liable for its debts; the other that it is an artificial being, a distinct entity, separate in rights and responsibility from the partners who compose it. The first conception is referred to as the aggregate theory of partnership, and the second is called the entity theory.

Aggregate Theory. The aggregate theory considers the partners to be co-owners of the enterprise and the property used in it, each owning an individual interest in the partnership. The consequence of this is to hold each partner personally liable for partnership debts. Creditors can reach each partner's personal assets if partnership assets are insufficient to discharge a debt.

Entity Theory. The entity theory treats the partnership as a separate legal entity, distinct from the individual partners. This theory holds that the partnership has juristic personality, meaning that it is a "person" for legal purposes. Since the partnership is a separate legal person, individual partners may enter into transactions with the firm, such as lending money or equipment to the enterprise. Accountants and businesspeople generally regard and treat a partnership as a business, separate and distinct from its individual partners.

UPA Approach. Historically, European countries held to the entity theory, while the English common law adhered to the aggregate theory. Draftsmen of the UPA faced the dilemma of which theory best described a partnership's legal nature. Succinctly describing this dilemma, one of the draftsmen, William Draper Lewis, stated:

The issue is whether the group of activities carried on by the partners should be regarded as being carried on by them—which is the actual fact—or as being carried on by a legal personality distinct from the legal personalities of the partners. Thus under the aggregate theory the partners own in common the partnership property, and they are joint principals in partnership transactions. Under the legal person theory the partnership legal person owns the partnership property, and the partners are merely its agents.[1]

The draftsmen resolved their dilemma by creating a hybrid legal personality, embracing both aggregate and entity characteristics. For example, Section 6(1)'s definition of a partnership as an "association of two or more persons" describes it as an aggregate association. However, Section 2's inclusion of partnerships in its definition of "person" suggests that a partnership possesses juristic personality. Thus the legal nature of a partnership as either an aggregate or an entity is not clearly delineated.

The UPA strikes a balance between both theories. Generally speaking, under the UPA a partnership is an aggregate, but in certain limited circumstances it is treated as an entity. For example, UPA Section 8 recognizes the partnership as an entity for owning its own property by authorizing conveyances of real estate to or by the partnership in the partnership name (8[3]) and by creating the presumption that all property acquired with partnership funds is partnership property (8[1]). Thus the UPA adopts both the aggregate and entity theories of partnership, depending upon the particular problem involved.

Other rules and statutes similarly treat partnerships as entities for specific purposes. For example, under the Federal Rules of Civil Procedure a partnership is an entity for litigation purposes; it may sue or be sued in its own name. Under the Federal Bankruptcy Act a partnership is also a distinct entity and may be adjudged a bankrupt. In situations where it is doubtful whether the partnership should be treated as an aggregate or an entity, courts adopt whichever theory best suits the purposes of public convenience and commercial utility or best conforms to the expectations of the business community.

In the following case, the court adopts the entity theory for a particular situation while maintaining the aggregate theory as a general rule.

McKinney v. Truck Insurance Company

Missouri Court of Appeals
324 S.W. 2d 773 (1959)

A suit was brought by an individual partner, McKinney, against his worker's compensation insurer for expenses incurred in defending a worker's compensation suit filed against him by one of his employees, Davis. The trial court rendered a judgment against the partner and he appealed. The appellate court affirmed. McKinney is the plaintiff-appellant; the Truck Insurance Company is the defendant-appellee.

Stone, Presiding Judge

Cut to the quick by the indignity inflicted upon him, a bull calf being castrated by one Davis, "sort of an expert" at such matters, rebelled and grievously injured his tormentor, by reason of which Davis filed a claim for benefits under the Missouri Workmen's Compensation Law against Paul McKinney, as employer, and Truck Insurance Exchange (hereinafter referred to as the Exchange), his alleged insurer. The Exchange theretofore had issued a "standard workmen's compensation and employers' liability policy" to "Ralph McKinney & Paul McKinney dba Acme Glass Co., 1647 St. Louis, Springfield, Missouri," as "employer," described in the policy declarations as a "co-partnership"; but, claimant Davis having been employed by Paul in connection with operation of a 167-acre farm in another county owned by Paul and his wife and Davis' castration of the calf having been wholly unrelated to the business conducted by Acme Glass Company (even though the castrated calf had wreaked as much havoc as the proverbial bull in a china closet), the Exchange insisted that its policy issued to Acme afforded no coverage to Paul with respect to his farm operation and refused to defend him in the compensation proceeding instituted by Davis, although Davis' joinder of the Exchange as a party to the proceeding necessitated a defense on its own behalf. After counsel employed by Paul personally and counsel for the Exchange, presenting a united front against their common antagonist, had concluded upon appeal to this court a successful defense of Davis' claim . . . and thus had put out of the way (if not out of mind) the castrated calf and the contentious claimant, Paul turned on the Exchange and brought the instant suit to recoup the expenses (primarily attorneys' fees) incurred by him personally in such defense. Cast in the trial court on the Exchange's motion to dismiss his petition, Paul appeals from the adverse judgment.

Paul's earnest contention that the Exchange owed him a defense in the compensation proceeding rests on his theory that, by issuing a workmen's compensation policy to "Ralph McKinney & Paul McKinney dba Acme Glass Co." described as a "co-partnership," the Exchange became obligated to "step in and afford a full defense to these two named individuals on any workmen's compensation claim which may be filed against either of them and the Exchange's obligations to the two named individuals are the same as though two separate policies were issued, one to each of the individuals," because (as Paul's counsel put it) "a partnership cannot be considered as a separate entity and the effect of this policy was to fully insure all workmen's compensation obligations of the two named individuals." Although other jurisdictions reflect a sharp conflict of authority as to whether or not a partnership is a legal or juristic entity separate and distinct from the individuals who compose it . . . , the courts of this state usually have regarded a partnership as a mere ideal entity with no legal existence apart from its members, and have followed the so-called aggregate or common-law theory of partnership rather than the entity theory. There may be a judicial tendency toward the entity theory . . . ; and, as counsel for the Exchange assert, the Uniform Partnership Act adopted in Missouri in 1949 . . . may have "wrought decided changes in the common-law conception" of a partnership. However, the persuasive opinion of informed scholars is that the Uniform Partnership Act does not transform a partnership into a separate legal or juristic entity . . . but "adopts the common-law approach with 'modifications' relating to partnership property" so that the Act "is consistent with the entity approach for the purposes of facilitating transfers of property, marshalling assets, and protecting the business operation against the immediate impact of personal involvements of the partners." Mazzuchelli v. Silberberg, 1959, 29 N.J. 15, 149 A. 2d 8, 11. Accordingly, we cannot agree with counsel for the Exchange that the Uniform Partnership Act "makes a partnership a legal entity."

But, grave danger lurks in unquestioning acceptance and unguarded application of potentially deceptive generalities; and, although our Missouri courts usually follow the aggregate or common-law theory as to partnerships, we think that it should not and cannot be announced, as an arbitrary, absolute, unqualified and unyielding rule, that under no circumstances and for no purposes may a partnership be considered and treated as an entity. We read that the partnership entity sometimes is recognized with reference to its contracts with third persons . . . ; and we like and adopt the logical, forthright, common-sense reasoning of the Supreme Court of Tennessee in United States Fidelity & Guaranty Co. v. Booth, 164 Tenn. 41, 45 S.W. 2d 1075, 1076–77(2), a case involving a workmen's compensation policy, where it was said that, in construing and giving effect to contracts made by and with partnerships, it may appear from the subject-matter or otherwise that the parties dealt with and treated the partnership as if it were an entity, separate and distinct from the individuals composing it; and, to the extent that this is so, the intention of the parties can only be given effect, in the enforcement of the contract, by judicial recognition of the partnership entity as contemplated by the parties."

Thus, in jurisdictions where, as in Missouri, the aggregate or common-law theory as to partnerships usually is followed, the courts have given effect to the intention of contracting parties by treating a partnership as an entity in determining and delimiting the coverage afforded by insurance policies issued to the partnership. . . .

The employer, to whom the Exchange issued the policy contract under consideration, was "Ralph McKinney & Paul McKinney dba Acme Glass Co., 1647 St. Louis, Springfield, Missouri," identified and described as a "co-partnership"; the employer's "operations" were classified and described as "glass merchants—including bending, grinding, beveling or silvering of plate glass" and "glaziers—away from shop—including drivers, chauffeurs and their helpers"; and, the policy "declarations" contained the statement that "this employer is conducting no other business operations at this or any other location not herein disclosed." Since the unambiguous provisions of the policy contract establish beyond room for reasonable doubt that the parties thereto intended and undertook to provide workmen's compensation coverage for Acme Glass Company, and since nothing in the policy suggests that thereby such coverage would be provided for any employee of either individual partner engaged in work wholly unrelated to the partnership operation, we believe that we should recognize the partnership entity of Acme Glass Company as the employer with whom the Exchange contracted, thereby giving effect to the plain intent of the contracting parties and following the general rule that an insurer may afford workmen's compensation coverage for a partnership and its business activities without exposing itself to liability for all of the unrelated business operations of each individual partner.

Affirmed.

Partnership Taxation

A partnership is both an entity and an aggregate for federal income-tax purposes. For accounting and reporting purposes, a partnership is treated as an entity. For tax liability purposes, it is an aggregate.

Partnership Return. Partnerships are tax-reporting, not tax-paying, entities. A partnership is not a taxable entity for federal income-tax purposes. It is not subject to federal income tax. Partnerships are treated as conduits through which the income and losses of the individual partner flow and are reported. The partnership must file an informational tax return with the Internal Revenue Service. This return is used for informational purposes and as the vehicle for making certain elections, like that of accounting method. The return states the partnership's income and expenditures and specifies each partner's individual share of profits or losses.

Individual Partner's Return. Although the partnership is not subject to federal income tax, the individual partners pay the tax. Each partner is taxed directly on his or her share of the partnership income, which is reported on his or her individual tax return. Each partner's share of partnership income is added to any other income he or she may have. Thus partnership income is taxed once, as the individual income of the partner. This differs from corporate income, which is taxed twice—once as corporate income and again as dividends to the individual shareholder.

The conduit nature of a partnership for tax treatment applies to losses as well as income. Each partner may deduct from other income whatever loss he or she has suffered through the partnership. Corporate shareholders cannot do this because any corporate loss belongs to the corporation, which is the taxable entity. The partnership thus may be the preferred organizational form whenever it appears that the business will lose money initially.

Subchapter S Corporations. Subchapter S of the Internal Revenue Code provides that certain qualifying corporations may elect to be taxed as partnerships. This privilege is limited to organizations having ten or fewer shareholders, and certain limitations on kinds of income along with other restrictions apply. Since Subchapter S treatment is not available for businesses having more than ten participants, the partnership form may be an attractive alternative to incorporation.

PARTNERSHIP FORMATION

No particular steps are required to form a general partnership. Although customarily each partner's rights and responsibilities are established in an instrument called the "partnership agreement" or the "articles of partnership," usually this is not mandatory. A partnership may result from any arrangement of facts fulfilling UPA Section 6(1)'s definition of a partnership. The requisites and essential elements of a partnership are implied in the definition. It is possible for an association that is not recognized as a partnership by its participants to be treated as a partnership by the courts and third parties for liability purposes. This risk of inadvertent partnership liability may be minimized by considering the extent to which any associated business activity satisfies Section 6(1)'s definition of a partnership and by carefully avoiding establishing those elements. Helpful here are the rules for determining the existence of a partnership provided in Section 7. Additionally, partnership liability can result from people representing themselves to be partners or consenting to others representing them as partners. Section 16 governs when partnership liability results from such representations. To avoid unintended liability where a partnership is contemplated, partners should reduce their agreed-upon relation to a written partnership agreement. Those wishing to further restrict their liability to outsiders by forming a limited partnership must file a certificate of limited partnership with the appropriate public official.

Factors Establishing Partnership Existence

UPA Section 6(1)'s definition of a partnership as "an association of two or more persons to carry on as co-owners a business for profit" establishes the essential elements of a general partnership. To understand how Section 6(1) determines partnership existence, the meaning of each phrase of the definition must be examined. The following paragraphs dissect the definition of a partnership and explain the reasons for the words employed in it.

"An Association." Association denotes the voluntary nature of the partnership arrangement. Because a partnership is a voluntary association, the participants must intend to enter into a partnership. Whether or not a partnership is created depends on the intent of the participants to create one. Their intent is the primary test of partnership existence. This intent may be expressed by either a written or an oral agreement, or it may be inferred from conduct. As with contractual intent, partnership intent is measured objectively. Subjective intent is immaterial.

While the parties' designation of their relationship as a "partnership" or some other business form is entitled to some weight, it is not conclusive. Using partnership language in partnership papers is highly persuasive, even though the agreement may contain tools unusual to a partnership. If the manifested intent is present, a partnership is created. However, the mere existence of an agreement, labeled "partnership agreement," that characterizes the signatories as "partners" does not conclusively establish partnership existence. The parties' conduct must conform with their expressed intent. Similarly, calling by another name what for all intents and purposes is a partnership will not destroy the existence of a partnership. To paraphrase the Bard, a partnership by any other name is still a partnership. Because laypeople frequently misuse legal terminology when describing their legal relations, courts ignore clever draftsmanship when it is inconsistent with the parties' conduct. The judicial function of ascertaining partnership intent was best described by Judge Andrews in the landmark partnership case of *Martin* v. *Peyton* (1927):

Assuming some written contract between the parties, the question may arise whether it creates a partnership. If it be complete, if it express in good faith the full understanding and obligation of the parties, then it is for the court to say whether a partnership exists. It may however be a mere sham intended to hide the real relationship. Then other results follow. In passing upon it, effect is to be given to each provision. Mere words will not blind us to realities. Statements that no partnership is intended are not conclusive. If as a whole a contract contemplates an association of two or more persons to carry on as co-owners a business for profit, a partnership there is . . . . On the other hand, if it be less than this, no partnership exists.[2]

"Of Two or More Persons." One person alone cannot form a partnership. A sole proprietor cannot convert his or her sole proprietorship into a partnership by drafting articles of partnership, filing a partnership tax return, or otherwise conducting the business as a partnership. It takes two to tango, and it takes at least two to partner. Although a minimum number of persons is required, the UPA imposes no maximum limit on the number of persons who may form a partnership. A thousand persons may create a partnership.

The intention of one person alone cannot create a partnership. Where someone wishes to join an already existing partnership, all the partners must consent to the new member's admission. Under UPA Section 18(g), "no person can become a member of a partnership without the consent of all the partners." The intent to form a partnership must by shared by all. Section 18(g) is called the *delectus personae* ("choice of the person") provision of the UPA, meaning that each person may freely select his or her own partners. A partner may not be forced upon someone. This follows from the highly personal nature of the partnership relation.

Section 2 states that a person "includes individuals, partnerships, corporations, and other associations." Thus the definition of a partnership provides that any of these entities may form a partnership. Any individual having contractual capacity may become a partner. By including partnerships as persons in Section 2, the UPA permits a partnership to be a member of another partnership. Similarly, two corporations should be able to form a partnership. However, there is some disagreement on this point. The courts are divided regarding whether a corporation can become a partner. The official comment to UPA Section 6 provides that "the capacity of corporations to contract is a question of corporaton law." The prevailing view holds that, absent some statutory authorization by a state corporation code, a corporation cannot become a partner. The trend recently has been to permit this. Many contemporary corporation codes, including the Model Business Corporation Act (Section 4[p]) and the Delaware Corporate Code (Section 122[11]) empower corporations to become partners. Some states permit a corporation to become a partner only if it is empowered to do so by the corporation's charter or articles of incorporation.

"To Carry On." It is often said that the carrying on of a business, not an agreement to carry on business at a future date, is the test of partnership existence. The official comment to UPA Section 6 indicates that this is not the intended meaning of the phrase "to carry on." Section 6(1) does not provide that persons are not partners until they participate in the carrying on of the business. The words "to carry on," not "carrying on," are used.

The requirement that a partnership be an association to carry on a business should exempt joint ventures from becoming partnerships. For example, if several grocery-store owners take advantage of lower prices for volume purchases by combining to buy a truckload of coffee, dividing it among themselves, their arrangement would not form a partnership. "To carry on" contemplates a series of transactions, not a single endeavor. As mentioned earlier, the trend is to treat joint ventures as partnerships by applying similar principles of law as provided by the UPA.

"As Co-Owners." To form a partnership, the associates must co-own the business. Co-ownership distinguishes partnership from nonpartnership relations such as employment. For example, if a general manager is not a co-owner of the enterprise, he or she is an employee, not a partner.

While including elements of property rights, co-ownership under UPA Section 6(1) entails management rights in the firm. Co-ownership describes the community of interest each partner shares in the firm's operations. It includes the power of ultimate control each partner possesses in the firm's management. For an association to consist of co-owners, the associates must have equal rights in the decision-making process. Section 18(e) states that "all partners have equal rights in the management and conduct of the partnership business." Factors reflecting co-ownership include giving instructions, hiring and firing employees, and determining how money is spent. However, Section 18 permits partners to agree to delegate their managerial rights to a managing partner. This complicates the determination of co-ownership existence, but courts consider this when ascertaining why a partner failed to assert his or her management rights.

Since co-ownership involves control of business operations, not just co-ownership of business property, a capital contribution is not required to enter a partnership. A person can be a co-owner of a partnership without making a capital contribution if he or she shares the power of ultimate control in the firm's operations.

"A Business." Co-ownership of property by itself does not establish a partnership (UPA Section 7[2]). The co-ownership required by Section 6(1) is co-ownership of a business. A partnership must be formed as a business. Section 2 states that a business includes "every trade, occupation, or profession." The official comment to Section 6 describes a business as "a series of acts directed toward an end." Thus if two persons together inherit real estate that remains unimproved and idle, they are co-owners, but not of a business. However, if they improve the property by erecting an apartment complex, their actions constitute a business.

"For Profit." A partnership must be formed as a business for profit. The term "business" connotes a profit-maximizing objective. Nonprofit organizations cannot be formed as partnerships under the UPA. The official comment to Section 6 explains:

> Lastly, the definition asserts that the business is for profit. Partnership is a branch of our commercial law; it has developed in connection with a particular business association, and it is, therefore, essential that the operation of the act should be confined to associations organized for profit.

Courts require only an expectation, not the actual making, of profit for the existence of a partnership. Profit motive, not profit making, is the test. To allow otherwise would permit parties engaged in losing enterprises to avoid the provisions of the UPA by claiming not to be engaged in partnership activity. Thus if two individuals decide to go into business as a partnership, but instead of making profits actually lose money, their association still is a partnership.

The importance of profit sharing to the determination of partnership existence is reflected in UPA Section 7(4)'s declaration that "the receipt by a person of a share of the profits of a business is prima facie evidence that he is a partner in the business. . . ." By stating that profit sharing is prima facie evidence of partnership existence, Section 7(4) requires a court to direct a verdict that a partnership is created, unless there is additional evidence rebutting the presumption of partnership. Where this additional evidence is shown, a court must decide the issue of partnership existence by examining the additional tests of partnership, such as the parties' intent and co-ownership or control of business operations. Thus the profit sharing test of Section 7(4) is presumptive, not conclusive, on the issue of partnership existence.

While profit sharing is prima facie evidence of partnership existence, the sharing of gross returns is not. Section 7(3) states that "the sharing of gross returns does not of itself establish a partnership. . . ." A sales commission is an example of the sharing of gross returns.

When launching an enterprise, daring entrepreneurs frequently fail to reflect upon the possibility of the firm's failing to generate profit. Even farsighted associates who consider how each will share in the profits sometimes prefer not to dwell upon the possibility of losing money. While someone sharing in the firm's profits is presumed to have an interest in the partnership necessitating the status of partner, one who is committed to sharing the losses may be participating in the venture to an even greater degree. The phrase "a business for profit" is interpreted to mean that partners share in the losses as well as the profits of the business. Sharing losses may be sufficient to establish partnership status. Section 18(a) states that each partner "must contribute towards the losses, whether of capital or otherwise, sustained by the partnership according to his share of the profits." Although Section 18 permits partners to provide a different rule by agreement, a specific agreement not to share losses may negate the existence of a partnership.

Protected Relations

Certain business relations frequently involve the sharing of profits by parties not intending to create a partnership. For example, creditors, employees, and landlords sometimes are paid in profits without any intent that they become partners in the firm. These arrangements provide much-needed flexibility in business dealings. Thus the fears of an uneasy creditor or landlord may be allayed by providing that loan or rent payments be taken from the firm's profits. The UPA recognizes the utility of these profit-sharing arrangements and provides for their protection against the risk of partnership liability. While providing that profit sharing is presumptive of partnership existence, Section 7(4) enumerates certain situations in which profit sharing does not create a partnership. These include situations in which

1. Profits are received to discharge a debt
2. Profits are received as wages or rent
3. Profits are paid to a widow or an estate as an annuity
4. Profits are paid for the purchase of a partnership asset

This protection against the risk of unwanted partnership formation can be lost if the protected party becomes too involved in the firm's operation. Frequently an uneasy creditor or landlord, unsatisfied with simply a share of the profits, seeks to protect his or her interests by controlling the firm's operations. If the control reserved over business operations is merely that necessary to protect the creditor's or landlord's interests, the relation should remain protected from becoming a partnership. However, if the control is affirmative or goes beyond what is necessary to protect the creditor's or landlord's interests, the risk of unwanted partnership formation increases. No clear-cut rule exists for determining when the protected status is lost and partnership status is gained. A sliding scale, not a rigid rule, is the measure. The greater the participation in the business and the greater the degree of unnecessary control, the greater the risk of partnership formation. For example, a landlord, receiving 50 percent of a firm's profits as rent for the use of a business building, may choose to retain certain controls over the firm's operations to protect his or her interests. If the landlord merely retains inspection rights over financial records, requires the daily reporting of business activity, requires that the firm's banking be done at a particular bank, and requires that the firm be run on a cash operation basis, he or she should not lose the protection granted by Section 7(4)(b). However, if the landlord appoints a representative to keep the firm's books and act as cashier, requires that money be received in the landlord's name, and additionally provides that all payments be made by the landlord, the risk of partnership formation is great. In the first situation, the landlord possesses only negative checks against mismanagement that protect his or her interest in receiving the rent. In the second situation, the landlord's action is affirmative and amounts to the kind of control usually possessed by partners acting as co-owners of a business. Participation to a significant degree may be sufficient to show the necessary co-ownership and control of a partner and thus evidence a partnership relation. People desiring not to enter into a partnership should draft documents demonstrating the relation as one of those specified in Section 7(4) to come within the section's protection. For example, if a rental relationship is intended, the profit payments should be denoted as "rent." Similarly, if a debtor-creditor relation is contemplated, the documents should declare the profit payments to be "interest" and "principal" repayments. Care should be taken that the documents reflect the parties' real relation. As Judge Andrews remarked, mere words will not blind a court to the existence of a partnership. Where possible, sound legal counsel should be sought.

The following case shows the operation of UPA Sections 6 and 7.

P & M Cattle Company v. Holler

Supreme Court of Wyoming
559 P. 2d 1019 (1977)

A partnership, the P & M Cattle Company, brought an action against a property owner, Rusty Holler, seeking recovery for losses incurred in 1974 under an alleged "oral joint venture agreement" to purchase, lease, and sell livestock. The property owner filed a counterclaim. Judgment for $2,219.40 was entered on the counterclaim and the partnership appealed. The Wyoming Supreme Court affirmed. The P & M Cattle Company is the plaintiff-appellant; Rusty Holler is the defendant-appellee.

Raper, Justice

[I]t appears that the only real issue is whether the parties to this appeal were parties to a joint venture or partnership agreement to share losses as well as profits from a cattle purchase, feed and sell operation.

In 1971, the defendant was looking for someone to pasture cattle on the defendant's land at $3.00 per head per month. One of two partners in the plaintiff partnership expressed an interest and invited defendant to talk. As a result, the following written agreement was entered into:

> "2–23–1971
> "Contract—Rusty Holler (60 Bar Ranch)—L.W. Maxfield and Bill Poage
> "Rusty to furnish grass for est 1000 yr st and 21 heifers—
> "Maxfield & Poage to furnish money for cattle plus trucking & salt—and max of $300.00 per month for labor
> "Rusty to take cattle around May 1st and cattle to be sold at a time this fall agreed upon by all parties involved
> "Cost of cattle plus freight—salt and labor to be first cost
> "Net money from sale of cattle less first cost to be split 50–50 between Rusty (½) and Maxfield and Poage (½) (death loss to be part of first cost)
> "/s/ L.W. Maxfield
> "/s/ Bill Poage
> "LM
> "/s/ Rusty Holler"

The 1971 agreement was orally renewed for the years 1972, 1973, and 1974. Plaintiff and defendant each realized substantial returns in the first three years but in 1974 there was not enough realized from the sale of cattle to pay first costs and a loss resulted. Plaintiff insists that the defendant is bound to pay it $44,500.00 representing one-half of the total cash loss in the sum of $89,000.00. The defendant personally expended first costs for expenses (salt) over and above the amount received from sale of cattle in the sum of $3,967.76, The contract clearly states that plaintiff was to "furnish money for . . . salt."

The parties never discussed nor is there any mention in the contract of what would happen if the cattle sold at a loss. Nor was any mention made of reimbursement or credit to the defendant for the value of his services and pasture or grass he contributed, in the event cattle sold at a loss.

A broad overview of the entire record suggests that this case involves only a contract in which plaintiff agreed to put up the money and defendant agreed to put up grazing land and grass, along with services, with a view to profit to both, each to bear their own losses. Before confirming that position, we must examine the law of joint venture.

In Wyoming, a joint adventure partakes of the nature of a partnership and is governed substantially by the same rules of law, the principal distinction being that a joint adventure usually relates to a single transaction, though it may be continued over a period of years. Even though a joint adventure and a partnership are not identical, the relationship of co-adventurers is controlled largely by the law of partnership. A concise distinction between joint venture and partnership is drawn in 1 Cavitch, Business Organizations, §13.05 (2), pp. 677–678:

> "It is apparent that the comparatively modern legal concept of joint adventure is intended to identify business ventures which, but for their limited scope and duration, would be partnerships. To date, however, there is no discernible legal difference between the two types of associations. As a result, the courts have held that the joint adventure is subject to the same rules of law

which are applied to partnerships, especially when determining the rights of the parties *inter se.*"

Since joint adventures, also frequently referred to as joint ventures, are a species of and governed by the law of partnerships, we must go to the Uniform Partnership Act . . . , adopted by the Wyoming State Legislature in 1917. Section 6 defines a partnership as follows: "A partnership is an association of two or more persons to carry on as *co-owners* a business for profit." (Emphasis added.) Section 7 lays out the criteria for resolving the question as to whether a partnership obtains:

> "In determining whether a partnership exists, these rules shall apply:
> "(1) Except as provided by section 16 persons who are not partners as to each other are not partners as to third persons;
> "(2) Joint tenancy, tenancy in common, tenancy by entireties, joint property, common property, or part ownership does not of itself establish a partnership, whether such co-owners do or do not share any profits made by the use of the property;
> "(3) The sharing of gross returns does not of itself establish a partnership, whether or not the person sharing them have a joint or common right or interest in any property from which the returns are derived;
> "(4) The receipt by a person of a share of the profits of a business is prima facie evidence that he is a partner in the business but no such inference shall be drawn if such profits were received in payment:
> "(a) As a *debt* by installments or *otherwise,*
> "(b) As *wages* of an employee or *rent* to a landlord,
> "(c) As an annuity to a widow or representative of a deceased partner,
> "(d) As an interest on a loan, though the amount of payment vary with the profits of the business,
> "(e) As the *consideration* for the sale of the good-will of a business or other *property* by installments *or otherwise.*"
> (Emphasis added.)

As can be seen from § 7, an agreement to share profits is far from decisive that a partnership is intended.

As in any contractual relationship, the intent of the parties is controlling. The parties must intend to create the relationship of joint adventure or partnership. . . . Superimposed upon the rule of intent, it is frequently held that where there is no express agreement to form a partnership, the question of whether such a relation exists must be gathered from the conduct, surrounding circumstances and the transactions between the parties. . . . There is no automatic solution to the question of the existence of a partnership but it turns upon the facts and circumstances of association between the parties. . . . No single fact may be stated as the complete and final test of a partnership. . . . Even a written agreement, designating the parties as partners and providing for a sharing of the profits, is only evidential and not conclusive of the existence of a partnership.

In the case before us there was no express agreement to form a partnership. True, there was an agreement but nowhere in that document is there anywhere mentioned the term partnership. Nor is there anywhere mentioned any sharing of losses, which is normally concomitant with a sharing of profits in a partnership. While § 7 creates an inference, that inference is not conclusive. . . .

In the first place, the agreement is not labeled a "partnership agreement" nor is the term "partnership" anywhere mentioned within its terms. The plaintiff was itself a partnership made up of two ranchers well acquainted with that arrangement, one of whom drew the contract. From its inception, then, none of the parties ever identified it as such. The pact was conceived in an atmosphere created by defendant's desire to sell grass. The division of losses was never discussed between the parties until the plaintiff delivered the bad news to the defendant following fall cattle sales in 1974. No partnership federal income tax return in any of the years 1971–74 was prepared and submitted to the Internal Revenue Service of the United States. On the income tax returns made by the plaintiff during the period in question, the part of profits paid to the defendant was carried as a business expense listed as "contract feeding." The defendant included such payments on his individual income tax return as a sale of "crops," nor were the cattle grazed on his place by the defendant carried on defendant's income tax return livestock inventory. On the check given by plaintiff to defendant in 1973, for defendant's share of profits at the end of the season, it was shown as being for "pasture."

Within the framework of the Uniform Partnership Act, we find rules available to the trial judge to determine that there was no partnership. The division of profits was only a measure—a standard of payment by plaintiff to defendant in discharge of a debt for services and grass under § 7(4)(a) or in payment to defendant for wages of an employee in caring for the cattle while on his ranch and rent to him as landlord for his pasture under § 7(4)(b) or sale of grass as personal property under § 7(4)(e) or through a combination of those lettered subsections for wages and rent or sale of property. We need not determine precisely what it was as long as outside the pale of partnership. We are satisfied that no partnership was intended. The agreement was only an apparatus to pay defendant for his grass and services. . . .

Affirmed.

Partnership Established by Representation

The existence of a true partnership depends on the intent of the parties to associate as partners. However, in certain situations persons who actually are not partners will be liable to third parties as though they are. People who represent themselves to be partners or consent to others' representing them as partners are liable as partners to third parties who rely upon those representations in their dealings with the purported partnership. This is called *partnership by estoppel*. Represented partners are called partners by estoppel or ostensible partners. The statutory basis for this doctrine is provided by UPA Section 4(2), which states that "the law of estoppel shall apply . . . ," and Section 16's more detailed declaration that:

When a person . . . represents himself, or consents to another representing him to any one, as a partner . . . he is liable to any such person to whom such representation has been made, who has, on the faith of such representation, given credit to the apparent partnership. . . .

Liability is imposed on the represented partner in these situations because he or she is in a better position to avoid injury to others by correcting the misconception. Liability rests on the person most capable of preventing any loss from occurring. Two elements are the essence of estoppel: representation and reliance.

Representation. Partnership by estoppel results either from someone representing himself or herself as a partner or from consenting to such a representation by another. A signature on a letter or check can constitute a representation. Liability resulting from someone's own representation simply is another application of the principle, well established in contract law, that a person is responsible for the apparent or objective manifestations of intent. Someone behaving like a partner is liable as a partner. It is immaterial that a person may secretly deny all connection with the partnership or even be unaware of the significance of the behavior.

Liability also results from someone consenting to being represented as a partner by another. However, it is not enough that a person knows he or she is being portrayed as a partner. UPA Section 16 imposes liability only where there is some consent to the other person's representation. Consent may be manifested by an affirmative act, as when someone expressly permits his or her name to be listed among the partners on a company's stationery. Consent also may be manifested by silence, as when someone says nothing while being introduced as another's partner. However, knowledge of a representation alone does not establish estoppel. For example, suppose that, after reading in the morning paper an advertisement naming Penelope a partner

in a business, a supplier agrees to sell merchandise on credit to the firm. If upon reading the advertisement that morning, Penelope waits until the afternoon to protest the publication, she will not be liable to the seller if the price is not paid. While learning of the advertisement that morning, Penelope's knowledge alone does not make her a partner by estoppel. Section 16 calls for consent, which is not present since Penelope protested the advertisement that very day. However, consent can be inferred from someone's continued acquiescence in another's representation. Thus, if after reading the advertisement, Penelope acquiesces in its continued publication, her consent can be inferred.

Reliance. Someone seeking to hold another liable as a partner by estoppel must have extended credit in reliance upon the representation of that person as a partner. UPA Section 16 requires that the duped person must have "on the faith of such representation, given credit to the actual or apparent partnership. . . ." The party asserting liability must have been induced by the misleading appearance to change his or her position. Thus not every creditor of the purported partnership relation may hold the bogus partner responsible as a partner by estoppel. Only creditors who have economically relied to their detriment upon the represented partnership have reason to require payment from the ostensible partner. An ostensible partner's liability extends only to those creditors who rely upon his or her represented position in the firm. A creditor who does not rely upon the representation has no reason for holding the represented partner responsible, because the creditor did not extend credit on the basis of that person's financial position in the firm to begin with. Having initially not relied upon the represented partner's financial status when dealing with the firm, the creditor cannot later claim repayment from that person.

This reliance requirement further limits an

ostensible partner's liability where a creditor has previously dealt with the firm. Prior dealings make it difficult to determine whether the creditor did anything he or she otherwise would not have done had the creditor known the truth about the bogus partnership relation. Prior extensions of credit negate any presumption that the creditor later forwarded credit upon the financial status of the purported partner. Thus, where prior dealings occur, a creditor can collect from the purported partner only if he or she can show that the dealings would not have continued without the advent of the ostensible partner.

A creditor's reliance must be reasonable under the circumstances. This requirement of reasonable reliance may impose upon a creditor a duty to investigate the relationship before assuming the existence of a partnership. In certain circumstances a creditor may have no obligation to inquire further, such as where the representations of partnership are made directly to the creditor by one of the purported partners.

The following case illustrates the nature of the consent and reliance requirements.

Cox Enterprises, Inc. v. Filip
Court of Civil Appeals of Texas
538 S.W. 2d 836 (1976)

A newspaper, Cox Enterprises, Inc., doing business as the Austin-American-Statesman, filed suit against two individuals, Richard Filip and Jack Elliott, doing business as Trans Texas Properties. Cox Enterprises' suit was to recover an account for newspaper advertising services furnished to Trans Texas Properties allegedly at the request of Filip and Elliott. The trial court rendered judgment against Filip for $622.78 but in favor of Elliott, and the newspaper appealed the judgment in favor of Elliott. The Texas Civil Court of Appeals affirmed. Cox Enterprises, Inc., is the plaintiff-appellant; Elliott is the defendant-appellee.

Shannon, Justice

Appellee's basic defense to appellant's suit was that he had no financial interest in Trans Texas Properties and was not liable for debts of that business. With regard to appellee's defense, the court found that Filip was owner of Trans Texas Properties and that appellee Elliott had no character of ownership interest therein. In order to obtain credit for Trans Texas Properties, its employee, Tracey Peoples, represented to appellant that appellee Elliott was an owner of the business. Peoples had no authority to make that representation. Although appellant relied upon Peoples' representation in extending credit and rendering the advertising services to Trans Texas Properties, appellant made no effort to verify the accuracy of the representation. Moreover, appellee did not hold himself out to appellant as having an ownership interest in Trans Texas Properties.

The court concluded that Filip, as owner of Trans Texas Properties, was liable to appellant for the advertising services. The court concluded further that Elliott was not liable because he was not an owner of Trans Texas Properties, because he did not hold himself out as an owner of that business, and because he did not authorize anyone to represent him as an owner of Trans Texas Properties.

. . . [T]he court found that in the exercise of ordinary care, Elliott should have known that Peoples told appellant that he was an owner of Trans Texas Properties.

Appellant's point of error is that the court erred in not entering judgment for appellant predicated upon the court's finding of Elliott's failure to exercise ordinary care to discover that he had been held out to appellant as an owner of Trans Texas Properties.

Appellant's argument is bottomed upon the Texas Uniform Partnership Act, Tex. Rev. Cit. Stat. Ann. art. 6132b, §16 (1) (1970). Section 16(1) provides as follows:

> "§16. Partner by Estoppel
> "Sec. 16. (1) When a person, by words spoken or written or by conduct, represents himself, or consents to another representing him to any one, as a partner in an existing partnership or with one or more persons not actual partners, he is liable to any such person to whom such representation has been made, who has, on the faith of such representation, given credit to the actual or apparent partnership, and if he has made such representation or consented to its being made in a public manner he is liable to such person, whether the representation has or has not been made or communicated to such person so giving credit by or with the knowledge of the apparent partner making the representation or consenting to its being made. . . ."

Prior to the enactment of the Texas Uniform Partnership Act, the rule in Texas was that for liability to be based upon partnership by estoppel, it must be established that the person held out as a partner knew of, and consented in fact to the holding out. . . .

Section 16(1) codifies and enlarges upon the common law of partnership by estoppel. That section imposes a duty on a person to deny that he is a partner once he knows that third persons are relying on representations that he is a partner. We do not read section 16(1) as creating an affirmative duty upon one to seek out all those who may represent to others that he is a partner.

Appellant argues that §16(1) means that one who negligently holds himself out or permits himself to be held out as a member of a partnership relationship is estopped to deny such partnership relationship as against third persons who in good faith relied on the existence of such apparent partnership and extended credit thereon. Branscome v. Schoneweis, 361 F. 2d 717 (7th Cir. 1966). In *Branscome,* the Seventh Circuit construed Ill.Rev.Stat. ch. 106 ½ §16(1) (1952), which is identical to the Uniform Partnership Act and Tex.Rev.Civ.Stat.Ann. art. 6132b, §16(1)(1970). The court held Schoneweis personally liable for debts of the company because *he* negligently held *himself* out to be a partner.

In the case at bar, and in the terms of §16(1), appellant's factual theory was that appellee consented to Peoples' representation to appellant that appellee was a partner in Trans Texas Properties. Appellant, however, failed in its burden to convince the trier of fact that appellee consented for Peoples to represent that appellee was a partner in Trans Texas Properties.

Affirmed.

Formalities

Although under the UPA no formalities are required to create a general partnership, some may be required by other statutes. Certificates, licenses, and permits may have to be obtained. A name should be selected and in some cases must be registered. While not usually required, the execution of a partnership agreement is often advisable. Additionally, technical formalities do accompany the formation of limited partnerships.

License, Permit, and Certificate Requirements. Partnerships engaging in certain types of activity usually do need to obtain state or local licenses to do business. Occupational licensing is a well known fact of professional life among doctors and lawyers. However, license requirements frequently fall on those pursuing other callings. Certified public accountants, real estate brokers, and construction contractors are only a few of the many business people required to obtain licenses. Failure to obtain the necessary licenses and permits may deprive a partnership of the ability to enforce its contracts. This is just another application of the rule of contract law regarding the nonenforcement of illegal agreements.

Name Selection and Registration. It is customary, but not necessary, to use a firm name for the partnership. The partnership should have a business name because of the good will that may develop from its use. As a practical matter, a name may be required upon the opening of the partnership's bank account.

Unless prohibited by statute, the partners may use any name they desire so long as fraud, trade-name infringement, and unfair competition are not involved. Thus the partnership cannot employ a name that is deceptively similar to the name of another business.

Most businesses operate under fictitious names. A fictitious name is one that does not disclose the surnames of all the firm's owners.

For example, if Julius Jones and Penelope Smith operate a cafe under the name of "The Bottoms Up Bar," their business name is fictitious. By statute in most states, fictitious names must be registered so creditors of the partnership can enforce their rights against all the firm's members. A nonfictitious name is one containing the surnames of all the partners and does not have to be registered. Any form of expression may be employed for the fictitious name; however, some states prohibit use of the word "Company" or any other word that might confuse the partnership with a corporation.

Registration provides public notice of the names and addresses of all partners. It usually involves the filing of a certificate with the county recorder where the partnership is located and, in some states, in each county in which partnership real estate is situated. A few states, such as California, require the information supplied on the certificate to be published in a local newspaper for a designated period of time. A new certificate or amendments to the old certificate must be filed for every change in the firm's composition.

Noncompliance normally results in the partnership's being unable to sue on its contracts until the registration requirement is satisfied. This is easily done and does not usually result in hardship to the partnership. Fines and penalties are also authorized but seldom levied since prosecutors and police usually have more important matters to look after than pursuing nonregistered partnerships.

Partnership Articles. Although not normally required, it is customary to define the rights and duties of the members of a partnership in an instrument called "the partnership agreement" or "articles of partnership." There are advantages to a writing. A written partnership agreement avoids the problem of later proving that the agreement to enter into partnership was actually made. Drafting articles of partnership with the guidance of good legal counsel can focus the parties' attention on potential problem areas in their relationship. The written agreement also helps avoid future disagreements by clarifying the parties' relationship for future reference. Additionally, there are tax advantages to reducing the partnership relation to a writing, since the Internal Revenue Code permits partners to allocate their tax burden among themselves.

The partnership agreement usually takes the form of a series of numbered paragraphs addressing important aspects of the parties' relationship. Partnership agreements range from fairly simple instruments to rather complex documents, depending on the nature of the business and the number and character of the associates. The following items may be considered when drafting the partnership agreement. The list is not exhaustive, but it provides a good start.

1. Name of the partnership
2. Names of the partners
3. Date of the agreement
4. Purpose of the partnership
5. Location of the business
6. Duration of the enterprise
7. Investment of each partner, whether capital, realty, services, etc.
8. Any loans to the partnership of assets or cash
9. Sharing of profits and losses
10. Whether there will be any remuneration to the partners for services rendered to the partnership
11. Management and voting powers of each partner
12. Whether there will be arbitration for the disposition of disagreements
13. Whether there will be voluntary or involuntary retirement
14. The method of disposing of any dead partner's share in the partnership, and the method of evaluation
15. Cross-insurance of the partners
16. Respective duties of each partner
17. How books of account are to be established and maintained, and what the period of accounting will be
18. What the banking arrangements will be
19. Who has authority to borrow money
20. Method of hiring and firing—who does it, and who determines pay

Written partnership articles are necessary if the partnership agreement qualifies as a contract coming under the statute of frauds, which requires a written memorandum signed by the party against whom enforcement is sought for certain contracts. If a partnership is to continue for longer than one year, or involves the transfer of an interest in real estate to or by the partnership, written articles must be executed.

Limited Partnerships. While under the UPA no formalities are required to form general partnerships, technical formalities do accompany the formation of limited partnerships. Formation of limited partnerships is governed by the ULPA. Drafted in 1916, the ULPA is positive law in thirty-three states. In 1976, the Commission on Uniform State Laws substantially revised the ULPA to reflect modern usage. As of the date of this book's publication, seventeen states have adopted the Revised ULPA.[3]

Under ULPA Section 2, persons forming limited partnerships must file a certificate of limited partnership with a designated governmental official, usually the county clerk or recorder. The certificate provides public information about the general and limited partners and the nature of their firm, including the partnership name and the character of the business, the names and addresses of all general and limited partners, and information regarding each limited partner's capital contribution (ULPA Section 2). The certificate must be amended to reflect any changes in the character or composition of the limited partnership (Section 24). Although technical defects in the certificate will not defeat the formation of a limited partnership, a limited partner may lose the protection of limited liability if he or she knows of any false statements contained in the certificate. Under Section 6, any person detrimentally relying upon false statements in the certificate may hold liable any party to the certificate who knew that the statement was false. To avoid liability as a general partner in this situation, the limited partner must promptly renounce his or her interest in the profits of the business upon ascertaining the mistake (Section 11).

Filing the certificate restricts the limited partner's liability to his or her capital contribution (ULPA Section 7), which may be cash or other property but not services (Section 4). If the limited partner contributes capital in the form of services, or takes part in the control of the business, he or she becomes liable as a general partner (Sections 5 and 7). Under the 1976 revision, present contributions of service and promises to make future cash payments, property contributions, or performances of service are permissible forms of capital contribution (Rev. ULPA Section 101[2]). Accordingly, the services or promise must be accorded a value in the certificate of limited partnership, and that value determines the limited partner's liability.

Under Section 5 of the ULPA, the surname of a limited partner cannot appear in a limited partnership's name unless that name is also the name of a general partner or unless the partnership operated under that name before that person became a limited partner. Section 5 additionally provides that "a limited partner whose name appears in a partnership name . . . is liable as a general partner to partnership creditors who extend credit to the partnership without actual knowledge that he is not a general partner." Many firms avoid this liability by including, wherever the firm's name is printed, the notation "limited partner" or "ltd." after the limited partner's name. By so designating the limited partner, the firm gives creditors "actual knowledge that he is not a general partner."

Under the 1976 revision of the ULPA, the name of each limited partnership has to contain without abbreviation the words "limited partnership," and additionally "may not contain any word or phrase indicating or implying that it is organized other than for a purpose stated in its certificate of limited partnership" (Rev. ULPA Section 102). To facilitate the selection of a name, the revised ULPA provides for the reservation of the intended partnership name. Anyone intending to form a limited partnership may apply to the secretary of state for the desired name. If the name is available, it may be reserved for exclusive use by the partners for 120 days while the partnership is being formed.

The following case shows the loss of limited liability when a limited partner asserts control over the business. The case also discusses the power of corporations to enter partnerships.

Delaney v. Fidelity Lease Limited

Supreme Court of Texas
526 S.W. 2d 543 (1975)

In February 1969 Neil G. Delaney and others leased land to Fidelity Lease Ltd., a limited partnership consisting of a corporate general partner and twenty-two limited partners. Three of Fidelity's limited partners were officers, directors, and shareholders of the corporate general partner. The lessors sued for breach of the lease, claiming that the three limited partners who served as corporate officers were personally liable as general partners because of their involvement in the management and control of the partnership business. The trial court held, on motion for summary judgment, that three limited partners were not personally liable. The court of civil appeals affirmed and the lessors appealed. The Texas Supreme Court reversed and remanded. Delaney and others are the plaintiffs-appellants; Fidelity Texas Limited and the limited partners are the defendants-appellees.

Daniel, Justice

The question here is whether limited partners in a limited partnership become liable as general partners if they "take part in the control of the business" while acting as officers of a corporation which is the sole general partner of the limited partnership.

Fidelity Lease Limited is a limited partnership organized under the Texas Uniform Limited Partnership Act, Article 6132a, to lease restaurant locations. It is composed of 22 individual partners, and a corporate general partner, Interlease Corporation. Interlease's officers, directors and shareholders were W. S. Crombie, Jr., Alan Kahn, and William D. Sanders, who were also limited partners of Fidelity. In February of 1969, plaintiffs Delaney, et al. entered into an agreement with the limited partnership, Fidelity, acting by and through its corporate general partner, Interlease, to lease a fast-food restaurant to the partnership. In accordance therewith, plaintiffs built the restaurant, but Fidelity failed to take possession or pay rent.

Plaintiffs brought suit for damages for breach of the lease agreement, naming as defendants the limited partnership of Fidelity Lease Limited, its corporate general partner Interlease Corporation, and all of its limited partners. On plaintiffs' motion the cause against the limited partners individually, insofar as it relates to their personal capacities and liabilities, was severed from the cause against Fidelity and Interlease. In this severed cause, the trial court granted a take nothing summary judgment for the limited partners. Plaintiffs appealed only as to limited partners Crombie, Kahn and Sanders. Plaintiffs sought to hold these three individuals personally liable under Section 8 of Article 6132a, alleging that they had become general partners by participating in the management and control of the limited partnership.

Pertinent portions of the Texas Uniform Limited Partnership Act, Article 6132a, provide:

> "Sec. 8. A limited partner shall not become liable as a general partner unless, in addition to the exercise of his rights and powers as a limited partner, he *takes part in the control of the business.*
>
> "Sec. 13. (a) A person may be a general partner and a limited partner in the same partnership at the same time.
>
> "(b) A person who is a general, and also at the same time a limited partner, shall have all the rights and powers and be subject to all the restrictions of a general partner; except that, in respect to his contribution, he shall have the rights against the other members which he would have had if he were not also a general partner." (Emphasis added.)

It was alleged by plaintiffs, and there is summary judgment evidence, that the three limited partners controlled the business of the limited partnership, albeit through the corporate entity. The defendant limited partners argue that they acted only through the corporation and that the corporation actually controlled the business of the limited partnership. In response to this contention, we adopt the following statements in the dissenting opinion of Chief Justice Preslar in the court of civil appeals:

> "I find it difficult to separate their acts for they were at all times in the dual capacity of limited partners and officers of the corporation. Apparently the corporation had no function except to operate the limited partnership and Appellees were obligated to their other partners to so operate the corporation as to benefit the partnership. Each act was done then, not for the corporation, but for the partnership. Indirectly, if not directly, they were exercising control over the partnership. Truly 'the corporation fiction' was in this instance a fiction." 517 S.W.2d at 426–27.

Thus, we hold that the personal liability, which attaches to a limited partner when "he takes part in the control and management of the business," cannot be evaded merely by acting through a corporation. . . .

The defendant limited partners also contend that the "control" test enumerated in Section 8 of Article 6132a for the purpose of inflicting personal liability should be coupled with a determination of whether the plaintiffs relied upon the limited partners as holding themselves out as general partners. Thus, they argue that, before personal liability attaches to limited partners, two elements must coincide: (1) the limited partner must take part in the control of the business; and (2) the limited partner must have held himself out as being a general partner having personal liability to an extent that the third party, or plaintiff, relied upon the limited partners' personal liability. . . . They observe that there is no question in this case but that the plaintiffs were in no way misled into believing that these three limited partners were personally liable on the lease, because the lease provided that the plaintiffs were entering into the lease with "Fidelity Lease, Ltd., a limited partnership acting by and through Interlease Corporation, General Partner."

We disagree with this contention. Section 8 of Article 6132a simply provides that a limited partner who takes part in the control of the business subjects himself to personal liability as a general partner. The statute makes no mention of any requirement of reliance on the part of the party attempting to hold the limited partner personally liable.

Crombie, Kahn, and Sanders argue that, since their only control of Fidelity's business was as officers of the alleged corporate general partner, they are insulated from personal liability arising from their activities or those of the corporation. This is a general rule of corporate law, but one of several exceptions in which the courts will disregard the corporate fiction is where it is used to circumvent a statute. . . . That is precisely the result here, for it is undisputed that the corporation was organized to manage and control the limited partnership. Strict compliance with the statute is required if a limited partner is to avoid liability as a general partner. . . . It is quite clear that there can be more than one general partner. Assuming that Interlease Corporation was a legal general partner, a question which is not before us and which we do not decide, this would not prevent Crombie, Kahn, and Sanders from taking part in the control of the business in their individual capacities as well as their corporate capacities. In no event should they be permitted to escape the statutory liability which would have devolved upon them if there had been no attempted interposition of the corporate shield against personal liability. Otherwise, the statutory requirement of at least one general partner with general liability in a limited partnership can be circumvented or vitiated by limited partners operating the partnership through a corporation with minimum capitalization and therefore minimum liability. We hold that the trial court erred in granting summary judgment for the defendants, Crombie, Kahn, and Sanders. If, upon trial on the merits it is found from a preponderance of the evidence that either of these three limited partners took part in the control of the business, whether or not in his capacity as an officer of Interlease Corporation, he should be adjudged personally liable as a general partner.

In affirming the trial court, the majority opinion of the court of civil appeals stated:

> "It is permissible in this State to form a limited partnership where a corporation is the only general partner, provided that the purpose to be carried out by the limited partnership is lawful." 517 S.W.2d at 423.

The court had no point of error before it requiring such statement to be made. Its accuracy depends upon the scope of the corporate charter. . . . We reserve any decision on these questions until they are properly presented for our determination.

REVIEW PROBLEMS

1. The A & P Trucking Company, a partnership, was prosecuted for violation of the federal Motor Carrier Act and Interstate Commerce Commission regulations. The partners did not participate in or have knowledge of the alleged criminal acts. The prosecution charged that the partnership, as a person, knowingly violated federal law. The partnership defended that it was not a "person" and therefore the charges should be dismissed. What result and why? United States v. A & P Trucking Co., 358 U.S. 121 (1958)

2. A partner is served with a subpoena requiring the production of partnership financial records. May the partner invoke his personal privilege against self-incrimination provided in the Fifth Amendment of the United State Constitution to justify his refusal to comply with the subpoena? Bellis v. United States 417 U.S. 85 (1974)

3. Friends of a brokerage firm lent the firm $200,000 in liquid securities. In return the creditors were to receive 40 percent of the firm's profits, but not less than $100,000 nor more than $500,000. The creditors established the right to be informed of all transactions affecting the loaned securities. The creditors also established: the right to be informed of all partnership transactions, to inspect the books, and to veto any speculative business transactions. They also established a prohibition on further loans by the firm and a limitation of the distributions to

firm members. There was a provision that profits be realized. The creditors also retained a power of resignation over the firm's partners. By the retention of such extensive control, have the creditors become partners in the firm? Martin v. Peyton, 158 N.E. 77 (N.Y. 1927)

4. United Foods, a food broker, was an authorized buyer of produce from Minute Maid. It realized profits by purchasing Minute Maid inventories at bargain prices. United entered into an agreement with Cold Storage, as follows: Cold Storage would lend money to United to purchase produce; the produce would be collateral for the loans; a special account would be established and managed by Cold Storage; the books were to be credited with advances by Cold Storage and debited by advances made by Minute Maid; and at the year's end the books were to be closed and the profits divided. Over the year, United became overextended and indebted to Minute Maid, which sued Cold Storage rather than United because it was a more attractive defendant, alleging that Cold Storage was United's partner. What result? Minute Maid Corp. v. United Foods, Inc., 291 F. 2d 577 (5th Cir. 1961)

5. Ralph Presutti approached his father, Claude, in April, 1969, saying, "Dad, if you put up the money, we'll go partnership in a gas station." However, since the oil company whose station they were to operate frowned on partnership stations, Ralph explained that Claude could not sign any dealer agreements or leases or any other partnership documents such as tax returns. Claude agreed to the arrangement. He withdrew $8,000 from his bank account, which he and Ralph used to open a joint account under the service station's trade name. From time to time, Claude drew checks upon the account for payment of merchandise at the station. In July, Ralph returned $2,000 to Claude. In September, Claude began working at the station and

continued for one year. For these services, Claude drew salary of $125 each week. Occasionally he received additional sums that were from partnership profits, as well as free gas, tires and automobile accessories. During his one-year tenure, Claude managed the station whenever Ralph was away and participated in such policy decisions as whether they should purchase a truck and whether they should distribute trading stamps. After a year, Ralph still refused to sign a written partnership agreement, so Claude stopped working at the station. Despite this, he continued to receive payments of money and car repairs from the station until January 1972. As of January 1972, Claude had received approximately $17,000 as salary, partial return of his capital contribution, and distribution of profits. When Ralph finally refused to affirm the partnership's existence, Claude filed suit for an accounting of his share of the partnership profits. What result? Presutti v. Presutti, 310 A. 2d 791 (Md. App. Ct. 1973)

6. A barber-shop owner executed two separate but similar partnership agreements with two barbers in his shop. Under the agreements, the owner provided the barber chair, supplies, and licenses while the others provided the tools of their trade. Upon dissolution, ownership of these items was to revert to the party providing them. Income was divided 30–70 percent between the owner and one barber and 20–80 percent between the owner and the other barber. The agreements further required the owner to hold and distribute all receipts and stated the work hours and holidays of the two barbers. Additionally, the agreements provided that all policy was to be decided by the shop owner, and it also forbade any assignment of the agreement without the owner's permission. By state law, employers are to file an assessment report with the state employment commission and make unemployment compensa-

tion contributions. Partnerships, however, are not subject to unemployment compensation assessment when no nonpartner employees are involved. Must the barber-shop owner file the forms and make the assessed contributions? Chaiken v. Employment Security Comm. 274 A. 2d 707 (Del. Sup. Ct. 1971)

7. Francis and Thelma Gosman were an ambitious and industrious young couple, married in 1945 when he was twenty-one and she was eighteen. He drove a milk truck and she was a clerk-typist. After several years of marriage, when their first child was expected and Thelma could no longer keep her job, she began to raise chickens at home and planted a garden to supplement the family income—selling chickens, eggs, and garden produce from the house. The sale proceeds were deposited in the Gosmans' joint bank account, which was subject to the order of either of them. Ultimately, Francis gave up his milk route, and his participation in the family business increased while Thelma's decreased. This was followed by the removal of the business from their residence to a business complex, where the business ultimately became a grocery store, a liquor store, a restaurant, and a night club, which grossed almost $500,000 in 1969, close to $600,000 in 1970, and over $600,000 in 1971. Francis managed the enterprise and, although Thelma's duties were less onerous, she continued stocking grocery shelves, waiting tables in the restaurant and night club, bartending, counting money and making bank deposits, managing the club when Francis was sick or out of town, decorating the building interior, and running errands. In 1972 Francis filed for divorce against Thelma, and she counterclaimed seeking a divorce and alleging that, since she was a "partner" with Francis in the family business, her property rights should be determined pursuant to the Partnership Act, awarding her 50 percent of the partnership's fair market value and 50 percent of the balance of the checking account. What result? Gosman v. Gosman, 318 A. 2d 821 (Md. 1974)

8. Can someone wishing to prove a partnership relation with another under UPA Sections 6 and 7 use public representation of their relation to prove the partnership relation à la Section 16? In other words, can Section 16 be used to elevate an ostensible partner into an actual partner? Garner v. Garner, 358 A. 2d 583 (App. Ct. Md. 1976)

FOOTNOTES

[1]Lewis, "The Uniform Partnership Act—A Reply to Mr. Crane's Criticism," 29 *HARV.L.REV.* 158, 162 (1915).
[2]158 N.E. 77, 78 (N.Y. 1927).
[3]The states that have adopted the Revised ULPA are: Arkansas, California, Colorado, Connecticut, Delaware, Idaho, Iowa, Maryland, Massachusetts, Michigan, Minnesota, Montana, Nebraska, Washington, West Virginia, and Wyoming.

Operation and Dissolution of Partnerships

T his chapter explores the rights and duties resulting from the operation and dissolution of partnerships. It first focuses on the property rights created by the partnership relation. Partnerships generally involve the use of property, either furnished by the partners or acquired by the firm. The partnership, its partners and creditors both of the partnership and of the individual partners may acquire rights in this property.

This chapter further examines the rules governing the relations among partners, and their relations with persons dealing with the partnership. Once the partnership starts operating, it sometimes is necessary to settle managerial disputes between partners. These issues may be covered by a partnership agreement; however, the Uniform Partnership Act and the Uniform Limited Partnership Act address them when they are not. In addition to regulating the relations among partners, the UPA and ULPA further regulate the rights and liabilities resulting from dealings with third persons.

Finally, the day may come when the part-nership must be dissolved. Changing circumstances may necessitate a change in the firm's structure; the retirement of one of the partners is an example. Or conditions may call for a complete transformation to some other form of doing business, such as a corporation. Or it simply may be time for the partnership's termination. This chapter concludes with an explanation of how partnerships are dissolved and wound up.

PROPERTY RIGHTS IN PARTNERSHIPS

According to Section 24 of the Uniform Partnership Act, "the property rights of a partner are (1) his rights in a specific partnership property, (2) his interest in the partnership, and (3) his right to participate in the management." The following paragraphs discuss the first two types of property rights. The partner's right to participate in the firm's management is discussed separately with the rules regarding a partner's managerial rights and responsibilities.

Property rights in partnerships pose two problems: (1) distinguishing partnership property from an individual partner's personal assets and (2) distinguishing partnership property from the related type of property known as the partner's interest in the partnership. Partnership property is property that the partners agree belongs to the partnership and must be used for partnership purposes. It differs from a partner's personal assets because it belongs to all the partners as tenants in partnership. Partnership property differs from a partner's interest in the partnership, which is the partner's share of the profits and surplus. In lay language, a partner's interest is commonly called a partner's share.

Partnership Property

Most partnerships require property for their operation. This may be either real property (land) or personalty (movable items). Usually the partnership acquires its original property from individual partners as their capital contributions. The partners may contribute specific assets to the firm, such as land, equipment, or patents; or they may contribute money that is used to purchase assets. These assets, including money, usually become partnership property.

However, persons engaged in business as partners may have property that is not partnership property. This property may remain the sole property of an individual partner even though it is used by the firm. For example, an individual partner's real estate may be used by the firm for its business premises without becoming the partnership's property if the partner providing it intends only to lend it to the firm. Similarly, nothing prevents a partner from lending equipment to the firm while retaining ownership of it.

What Constitutes Partnership Property. Although a partner's personal assets may be vulnerable to partnership obligations, distinguishing partnership property from a partner's personal assets is essential for several reasons. If property belongs to the partnership, its use by individual partners is restricted; if it is sold, any capital gain or loss is distributed to each partner in the same proportion as profits, unless otherwise agreed; and if the property must be applied to satisfy creditor claims, partnership creditors have priority over an individual partner's personal creditors. However, if the property is an individual partner's personal asset, his or her use of it is unrestricted; the entire capital gain or loss from its sale belongs to the partner and is includable on his or her individual income-tax return; and if the partner dies, the property belongs to his or her estate and is distributed to the heirs or beneficiaries.

While no hard and fast rules exist for distinguishing partnership property from an individual partner's assets, certain guidelines may be extracted from the UPA. Section 8(1) provides that "all property originally brought into the partnership stock or subsequently acquired by purchase or otherwise, *on account of the partnership*, is partnership property" (emphasis added). The provision that partnership property be acquired "on account of the partnership" means that the controlling criterion for deciding if certain property is the partnership's is the partners' intent that it belong to the firm and be devoted to its purposes. The partners' intent is the primary consideration. They may decide among themselves what will be owned by all as partnership property and what will be retained by each as his or her own.

One measure of the partners' intent is the way the property is acquired. UPA Section 8(2) states that "unless a contrary intention appears, property acquired with partnership funds is partnership property." Thus property bought with the firm's money is considered the partnership's; if it is bought with individual funds, it is considered that individual's property. Additional factors may strengthen this presumption. Repairing and improving the property at partnership expense, paying insurance premiums from partnership accounts, or listing the property on partnership financial statements may reinforce Section 8(2)'s presumption. However, Section 8(2)'s statement, "unless a contrary intention appears," qualifies the presumption. The presumption can be explained away if an intention of individual ownership appears.

One way for the partners to explain away the presumption is to establish their intent at the outset in their partnership agreement. The partnership agreement can state what is partnership and what is individual property. Generally this governs, since it is the clearest indication of intent. Usually this is done by describing the partnership property and its agreed-upon value in a separate schedule incorporated by reference into the agreement. Property used by the firm but owned by an individual partner can also be identified in this way. Thus where an individual partner's property is loaned to the partnership, a copy of the lease may be attached to the agreement and incorporated by reference. The partnership agreement can provide that acquired property be recorded as partnership property in the partnership accounts. A well-kept set of books will identify the partnership's assets, and the property listed there will be considered partnership property.

Tenancy in Partnership. Assuming that certain property belongs to the partnership, the UPA describes the nature of a partner's ownership rights in it. "A partner is a co-owner with his partner of specific partnership property as a tenant in partnership" (UPA Section 25[1]). This tenancy in partnership is a unique property concept created by the UPA especially for partnerships. It recognizes that a partner's co-ownership rights in specific partnership property differ from other types of co-ownership. For example, many of the incidents of land ownership do not fit the needs of

partnerships. The UPA's tenancy in partnership recognizes that the rights of a partner as a co-owner of specific partnership property should depend on the needs of the partnership relation, which are not necessarily the same as other forms of co-ownership.

The special needs of the partnership relation require that an individual partner's ownership rights in specific partnership property be restricted. Although the partners are co-owners of partnership property, they have limited ownership rights. Generally, a partner cannot sell or encumber specific partnership property or dispose of it by will. The theory is that the partnership property is to remain intact. It reflects recognition of the business primacy of the partnership relation.

Under UPA Section 25, "a partner . . . has an equal right with his partners to possess specific partnership property for partnership purposes, but he has no right to possess such property for any other purpose without the consent of his partners." A partner's use of partnership property is limited to partnership purposes. He or she may not use partnership property for personal or other nonpartnership purposes unless all the other partners agree. Their agreement may be implied by a continued acquiescence to the individual partner's personal use of partnership property, or the partners may expressly provide their consent in their partnership agreement.

Since a partner cannot possess partnership property for personal purposes, he or she cannot claim that specific partnership property as part of his or her homestead and thus free from seizures by creditors in a bankruptcy proceeding. Homestead laws permit a bankrupt to keep property free from creditor claims if the property is part of the debtor's homestead. Under UPA Section 25, a partner "cannot claim any right under the homestead or exemption laws" for specific partnership property.

The UPA further restricts a partner's power to assign his or her rights in specific partnership property. A partner cannot assign his or her rights in partnership property unless it is an assignment of the rights of all the partners in the same property (Section 25). For example, a partner cannot mortgage specific partnership property for a personal obligation. This aspect of the tenancy in partnership is necessary since partnerships are voluntary, personal relations. If the law recognized the possibility of individual assignments, the assignee would become a partner in the firm with the rights to possess the property for partnership purposes. But partnerships are voluntary relations, and people cannot have partners thrust upon them (UPA Section 18).

Since a partner's right in specific partnership property is not voluntarily assignable for a separate purpose of the partner, it follows that his or her separate creditors should not be able to force an involuntary assignment through a judicial seizure of the property. UPA Section 25 prohibits any seizure of specific partnership property by a partner's personal creditor to satisfy a nonpartnership obligation. Thus a partner's rights to partnership property are not subject to creditor claims except upon a claim against the partnership.

When a partner dies, his or her ownership of specific partnership property passes to the surviving partners. It is not included in the deceased partner's estate (UPA Section 25). This is called the right of survivorship. It fits nicely the needs of the partnership, because it permits the partnership to be dissolved without interference from the dead partner's estate. Since a deceased partner's ownership rights in specific partnership property is not distributed to the heirs or beneficiaries, a partner cannot effectively include it in a will.

Partner's Interest in the Partnership

Section 26 of the UPA states that "a partner's interest in the partnership is his share of the profits and surplus, and the same is personal property." This interest is an intangible economic right. Its value appears on the partnership's balance sheet as each partner's capital account. Unlike specific partnership property, which belongs to the firm and is collectively held by the partners, each partner's interest belongs to him or her individually. Since it is each partner's individual property, a partner's interest has most of the ownership qualities that are denied to a partner in specific partnership property: it is assignable; it may be seized by creditors; and, when a partner dies, it becomes a part of the estate.

Assignment of Partner's Interest. Since a partner's interest is assignable, a partner may convey it to another. An attempted assignment by a partner of his or her ownership in specific partnership property, void under UPA Section 25, is regarded as a valid assignment of the partner's interest in the partnership. The person the partner transfers the interest to does not become a partner in the firm but only receives a right to share in the firm's profits. The assignee does not enjoy the usual rights and privileges possessed by partners. He or she may not interfere with the firm's management, require information regarding firm transactions, or inspect the partnership books (Section 27[1]). However, if the partnership is dissolved, the assignee may require an accounting of the interest from the date it was acquired (Section 27[2]). These restrictions place the assignee of a partner's interest in an insecure position and, as a practical matter, make it difficult to find a buyer.

Creditor's Rights. Unlike specific partnership property, which is shielded from attack by a partner's personal creditors, a partner's interest in the partnership may be seized by his or her individual creditors to satisfy a debt resulting from a transaction outside of the firm business. Since a partner may voluntarily assign his or her interest to creditors, it follows that the partner's personal creditors should be able to force an involuntary assignment by a judicial seizure of the interest. The creditors may accomplish this by seeking a *charging order* provided by UPA Section 28, which is similar to the garnishment of someone's wages. Under the charging order, a personal creditor may reach the partner's interest without interfering with firm business.

The charging order attaching the partner's interest is the exclusive remedy for a partner's personal creditors. It is available only to a partner's personal judgment creditors, those who earlier obtain a judgment against the partner. UPA Section 28 provides that a court "may charge the interest of the debtor partner with payment of the unsatisfied amount of such judgment debt. . . ."

UPA Section 28 additionally permits a creditor to ask a court to appoint a receiver, an independent person who receives the partner's share of profits for the creditor. The receiver enters into the partnership and acts as a partner. Section 28 permits the receiver to make "orders, directions, accounts and inquiries which the debtor partner might have made, or which the circumstances of the case may require." From the other partners' perspective, the appointment of a receiver is not desirable. Under Section 28, they may redeem the charged interest and get rid of the receiver by paying off the judgment creditor. Section 28 further provides that they can use partnership property to do this, provided there is approval among all the partners whose interests are not subject to the charging order.

Inheritance. When a partner dies, his or her interest in the partnership passes to the heirs or beneficiaries of his or her estate. Since a partner individually owned the partnership interest while living, it follows that it should become a part of the estate upon death. A partner may convey the interest by will. This may be done by a specific bequest of the interest to a particular beneficiary. However, since UPA Section 28 categorizes a partner's interest as personal property, a bequest of all a partner's personal property includes a transfer of the partnership interest.

In addition to transfers by will, a partner may provide in the partnership agreement that his or her interest in the partnership will pass to one or more surviving partners. Normally this is done by a "buy-sell" provision in the partnership agreement. Under a buy-sell agreement, the partners agree that the survivors will purchase the deceased partner's interest by paying the representative of the deceased partner the value of the deceased's interest in the firm. This payment may be either in a lump sum or in installments, and it may be aided by insurance. Usually this is done by stipulating in the partnership agreement that partnership proceeds be used to purchase life insurance for each partner covering the value of each partner's interest. The insurance proceeds are then used to pay the value of the deceased partner's interest to the deceased's representative.

Limited Partnerships

A limited partner's property rights are similar to a general partner's, except there is no right to participate in the management of the limited partnership. Distinguishing partnership property from a limited partner's individual property is seldom a problem. The nature of a limited partner's interest in a limited partnership is similar to the general partner's; however, the assignee of a limited partner's interest may become a substitute limited partner, enjoying more protection than the assignee of a general partner's interest.

Partnership Property. Confusion regarding the distinction between partnership property and a limited partner's personal assets is less likely, since the certificate of limited partnership must describe and state the agreed value of the property that each limited partner contributes to the firm (ULPA Section

2[a][vi]). ULPA Section 13 provides that "a limited partner may also lend money to and transact other business with the partnership. . . ." If additional property belonging to the limited partner is used by the firm, the presumption is that it has been loaned to the firm.

Limited Partner's Interest. A limited partner's interest in a limited partnership is the same as a general partner's. It is the partner's share of the profits of the limited partnership and the right to receive distributions of partnership assets (Rev. ULPA Section 101[10]). Like the interest in a general partnership, it is personal property (Section 18); assignable and subject to a charging order (Sections 19 and 22); and when the limited partner dies, it is included in the estate (Section 21).

Under ULPA Section 19, the assignee of a limited partner's interest acquires whatever rights the limited partner had to the firm's profits and the return of the partner's capital contribution. This differs from the assignment of a partner's interest in a partnership under the UPA, where the assignee acquires only the partner's share of the profits.

The assignee of a limited partner's interest in the partnership potentially has more protection than the assignee of a general partner's interest. Although the assignee of a general partner's interest is denied the inspection and accounting privileges enjoyed by partners, the assignee of a limited partner's interest may become a *substitute limited partner*. A substitute limited partner acquires all the rights and privileges enjoyed by the assignor. This may be done only if it is authorized by the certificate of limited partnership and if all the partners consent to the substitution. Once the substitution occurs, the certificate must be amended to reflect the change. If an assignee does not become a substitute limited partner, his or her inspection and accounting rights remain restricted (ULPA Section 19).

RELATIONS AMONG PARTNERS

Sections 18 through 23 of the UPA contain rules governing the relations of the partners to each other. These rules reflect the partners' presumed intent regarding their relationship. In providing general rules for determining the rights and obligations of the partners, Section 18 states that "the rights and duties of the partners in relation to the partnership shall be determined, *subject to any agreement between them,* by the following rules . . ." (emphasis added). The phrase "subject to any agreement between them" permits the partners to alter or waive the rules governing their relationship where that is their actual intent. This is usually done in the partnership agreement, since its function is to express the intention of the partners with regard to substantive law and tax considerations. Where no partnership agreement exists, or where an existing agreement is silent, the UPA provisions are implied. Thus the UPA serves as a backdrop and as a point of departure for the drafting of the partnership agreement.

As discussed in the previous chapter, astute business people appreciate the advantages of a written partnership agreement. Because a partnership is an extremely intimate relationship, perhaps the greatest potential problem is the risk of future disagreement among those who start out with the highest mutual regard. This risk may be diminished by reducing the partners' relation to a written instrument. By focusing attention on potential trouble spots, a carefully drafted partnership agreement may avoid future disagreements and litigation. Since the UPA provides the basic rules governing the partners' relation to each other, and also provides that these rules may be varied by the partners, the following paragraphs discuss these rules and the extent that they may be altered by agreement. In short, Sections 18 through 23 define: the fiduciary duties of partners, their rights to compensation, their management rights, and their right to information. Special rules exist for limited partners, reflecting the differences between the limited and general partnership relations.

Partners' Fiduciary Duties

Section 21 of the UPA provides that partners owe a fiduciary duty to each other. The fiduciary duties of agents were discussed in Chapter 25. Since UPA Section 9 provides that "every partner is an agent of the partnership for purposes of its business," and Section 4(3) states that "the law of agency shall apply under this act," it follows that partners share fiduciary duties similar to those of agents. A partnership is just a special type of agency, and partnership law is simply the application of agency principles to partnerships.

The intimate nature of the partnership association also makes the application of the fiduciary rule to partnerships appropriate from a business-policy perspective. Someone should not have to deal with his or her copartners as though they were opposite parties in an arm's-length transaction. A partner should be able to trust his or her copartners, to expect that they are pursuing a common goal and not working at cross-purposes. As one judge wrote of the business rationale underlying the application of the fiduciary rule to partnerships:

> If fiduciary relation means anything I cannot conceive a stronger case of fiduciary relation than that which exists between partners. Their mutual confidence is the life blood of the concern. It is because they trust one another that they are partners in the first instance; it is because they continue to trust one another that business goes on.[1]

The partner's fiduciary status basically embodies a duty of loyalty to his or her copartners that arises from the fundamental nature of partnership. In a partnership, each partner is the confidential agent of his or her copartners. Therefore, no one may act at his or her copart-

ners' expense. The fiduciary relation prohibits all forms of trickery, secret dealings, and self-preference in matters relating to the partnership. For example, a secret profit may not be made to the exclusion of copartners.

The duty of loyalty resulting from a partner's fiduciary position is such that the severity of a partner's breach will not be questioned. Rather, the question will be whether there has been any breach at all. The requisite degree of loyalty must be maintained at all times. From the first exploratory discussions through formal association in partnership to final severance of the relationship, partners are required to exercise scrupulous loyalty and good faith. A partner's duty of loyalty most frequently operates in two areas: (1) instances where a partner engages in transactions with his or her copartners and the firm and (2) instances where partnership opportunities are presented to a partner.

Nothing prohibits partners from dealing with each other at arm's length, as ordinary business people, when negotiating a nonpartnership transaction. However, when the transaction concerns any aspect of the partnership relation, the requisite degree of loyalty must be maintained. Transactions of this type include instances when one partner purchases the partnership share of another and when a partner sells his or her own property to the partnership.

Whenever a person buys the partnership share of a copartner, the purchasing partner must inform the selling partner fully of any information he or she possesses that would affect the value of the partnership share. The purchaser may not conceal or fraudulently represent material facts to his or her copartner. Similarly, when a partner sells his or her own property to the partnership there must be no misrepresentation to the firm nor concealment of the seller's identity.

Just as a person is held to a high standard of loyalty when engaging in transactions with copartners or the firm, he or she is held to an equally strict standard when presented with a partnership opportunity. Occasionally, a third party will refuse to deal with the partnership and will offer a partnership opportunity to a partner in his or her individual capacity. A partner cannot accept such an offer while still a member of the firm, unless his or her copartners grant permission.

When a partner learns of or is offered any opportunity in his or her capacity as a member of the partnership, he or she cannot appropriate this opportunity for personal benefit without first offering it to the firm. A partner may not, for example, purchase the rights to manufacture a product that would fit into the firm's product line. When the firm is presented with a business opportunity, a partner may take the opportunity for himself or herself if the partnership does not have sufficient funds to take advantage of the opportunity or if the firm simply fails to take action on it. Otherwise, a partner may take advantage of a partnership opportunity only when it has been completely abandoned by the firm.

Because a partner is a fiduciary, he or she is held accountable for profits made in competition with the business. However, a partner may engage in additional enterprises in his or her own behalf as long as the venture is not within the scope of the partnership and is done in good faith. When litigation develops, it is not always easy to determine what the partners intended as the scope of the business. For example, partners in real estate may intend to retain some freedom to deal on their own accounts. Failure to delineate the scope of the partnership business in a partnership agreement invites later quarrels. This is usually avoided by including a purpose clause in the partnership agreement. A closely allied problem is the amount of time each partner must spend on firm business. If outside interests of one or more partners are to be permitted, a partnership agreement can provide for this.

The classic case of *Meinhard* v. *Salmon* demonstrates the very high degree of loyalty required from a partner.

Meinhard v. Salmon

Court of Appeals of New York
164 N.E. 545 (1928)

Salmon secured a twenty-year lease to the Hotel Bristol, at 42nd Street and Fifth Avenue in New York City, which provided that the hotel should be altered by him to be suitable for shops and offices. Needing capital for the work, he enlisted the financial assistance of Meinhard. Under a joint-venture agreement, Meinhard was to furnish one-half of the cost of alteration, upkeep, and repair in return for 50 percent of the profits. Losses were to be shared equally. Salmon retained sole management responsibility and authority. The project was highly successful. Four months before the end of the twenty-year term, the lessor made a new lease, having renewal provisions up to eighty years, with the Midpoint Realty Company, under which it was to develop the one-time hotel property and adjoining lots on both streets and construct a $3-million building. Salmon owned the Midpoint Company and personally guaranteed the performance of its covenants under the new lease. About a month later, Meinhard learned of the project and demanded that the lease be held in trust for the joint venture, which had not yet expired. When Salmon refused, Meinhard sued. The referee found for Meinhard, limiting his interest in the new lease to 25 percent, the proportion that his interest under the joint venture bore to the new project. On cross-appeals, the Appellate Division enlarged his interest to 50 percent. On Salmon's further appeal, the Court of Appeals of New York affirmed and modified the judgment to give Salmon 51 percent interest.

Cardozo, C. J.

Joint adventurers like copartners, owe to one another, while the enterprise continues, the duty of the finest loyalty. Many forms of conduct permissible in a workaday world for those acting at arm's length, are forbidden to those bound by fiduciary ties. A trustee is held to something stricter than the morals of the market place. Not honesty alone, but the punctilio of an honor the most sensitive, is then the standard of behavior. As to this there has developed a tradition that is unbending and inveterate. Uncompromising rigidity has been the attitude of courts of equity when petitioned to undermine the rule of undivided loyalty by the "disintegrating erosion" of particular exceptions. . . . Only thus has the level of conduct for fiduciaries been kept at a level higher than that trodden by the crowd. It will not consciously be lowered by any judgment of this court.

The owner of the reversion, Mr. Gerry, had vainly striven to find a tenant who would favor his ambitious scheme of demolition and construction. Baffled in the search, he turned to the defendant Salmon in possession of the Bristol, the keystone of the project. He figured to himself beyond a doubt that the man in possession would prove a likely customer. To the eye of an observer, Salmon held the lease as owner in his own right, for himself and no one else. In fact he held it as a fiduciary, for himself and another, shares in a common venture. If this fact had been proclaimed, if the lease by its terms had run in favor of a partnership, Mr. Gerry, we may fairly assume, would have laid before the partners, and not merely before one of them, his plan of reconstruction. The pre-emptive privilege, or, better, the pre-emptive opportunity, that was thus an incident of the enterprise, Salmon appropriated to himself in secrecy and silence. He might have warned Meinhard that the plan had been submitted, and that either would be free to compete for the award. If he had done this, we do not need to say whether he would have been under a duty, if successful in the competition, to hold the lease so acquired for the benefit of a venture then about to end, and thus prolong by indirection its responsibilities and duties. The trouble about his conduct is that he excluded his coadventurer from any chance to compete, from any chance to enjoy the opportunity for benefit that had come him alone by virtue of his agency. This chance, if nothing more, he was under a duty to concede. The price of its denial is an extension of the trust at the option and for the benefit of the one whom he excluded.

No answer is it to say that the chance would have been of little value even if seasonably offered. Such a calculus of probabilities is beyond the science of the chancery.

We have no thought to hold that Salmon was guilty of a conscious purpose to defraud. Very likely he assumed in all good faith that with the approaching end of the venture he might ignore his coadventurer and take the extension for himself. He had given to the enterprise time and labor as well as money. He had made it a success. Meinhard, who had given money, but neither time nor labor, had already been richly paid. There might seem to be something grasping in his insistence upon more. Such recriminations are not unusual when coadventurers fall out. They are not without their force if conduct is to be judged by the common standards of competitors. That is not to say that they have pertinency here. Salmon had put himself in a position in which thought of self was to be renounced, however hard the abnegation. He was much more than a coadventurer. He was a managing coadventurer. Clegg v. Edmondson, S D. M. & G. 787, 807. For him and for those like him the rule of undivided loyalty is relentless and supreme. . . . A different question would be here if there were lacking any nexus of relation between the business conducted by the manager and the opportunity brought to him as an incident of management. . . . For this problem, as for most, there are distinctions of degree. If Salmon had received from Gerry a proposition to lease a building at a location far removed, he might have held for himself the privilege thus acquired, or so we shall assume. Here the subject-matter of the new lease was an extension and enlargment of the subject-matter of the old one. A managing coadventurer appropriating the benefit of such a lease without warning to his partner might fairly expect to be reproached with conduct that was underhand, or lacking, to say the least, in reasonable candor, if the partner were to surprise him in the act of signing the new instrument. Conduct subject to that reproach does not receive from equity a healing benediction.

A question remains as to the form and extent of the equitable interest to be allotted to the plaintiff. The trust as declared has been held to attach to the lease which was in the name of the defendant corporation. We think it ought to attach at the option of the defendant Salmon to the shares of stock which were owned by him or were under his control. The difference may be important if the lessee shall wish to execute an assignment of the lease, as it ought to be free with the consent of the lessor. On the other hand, an equal division of the shares might lead to other hardships. It might take away from Salmon the power of control and management which under the plan of the joint venture he has to have from first to last. The number of shares to be allotted to the plaintiff should, therefore, be reduced to such an extent as may be necessary to preserve to the defendant Salmon the expected measure of dominion. To that end an extra share should be added to his half.

Affirmed.

Profits and Compensation

Unless there is an agreement to the contrary, under the UPA partners "share equally in the profits" (Section 18[a]). This equal sharing in profits results regardless of unequal contributions of capital, skills, or services by the partners.

Under UPA Section 18(f), "no partner is entitled to remuneration for acting in the partnership business, except that a surviving partner is entitled to reasonable compensation for his services in winding up the partnership affairs." Thus, absent agreement, a partner is not entitled to compensation for services rendered for the firm's business. The reason for this is that what a partner does for the firm's business is presumed to be in his or her own interest. Absent any agreement, it is ordinarily expected that each partner will devote himself or herself to the promotion of the firm's business without compensation. This is so even when a comparison of services rendered by the partners shows one partner performing more than the others. This rule rests on the presumed intent of the partners, so if there is a provision for compensation included in the partnership agreement, it will be enforced.

From an economic perspective, the rules governing profits and compensation may be considered sound where the partners contribute equally to the venture. To the extent that contributions are unequal, different rules may be needed. For example, the senior partner in an accounting firm may demand more of the earnings than the other partners on the basis of his or her experience and reputation. Or contributions to a manufacturing enterprise may vary widely in terms of equipment, good will, and time. By fixing the percentages of each partner's share of the profits in the partnership agreement, some of these differences may be taken into account. Thus, if the chief variation in contribution is the amount of capital contributed to the firm, the proportion of capital contributed may determine the proportion of the profits received. However, in many situations it may be felt wise to reflect economic contributions by providing in the partnership agreement for salaries, as for example where one partner contributes managerial talent. The important point is that, unless the partners want the UPA's rules governing equal sharing of profits and no compensation to apply, the partnership agreement should specify the partners' intent.

Management

Under UPA Section 18(e), "all partners have equal rights in the management and conduct of the partnership business." From this concept of equality, it follows that a majority of the partners may decide ordinary partnership matters, provided no agreement between them makes a different rule (Section 18[n]). A majority of the partners can determine firm action in ordinary affairs regardless of each partner's comparative investment in the firm. Thus a majority will govern over a minority in such matters as borrowing money, hiring and discharging employees, collecting debts, and determining when and how profits are to be divided.

Individual partners and those who comprise a minority are protected from majority oppression by two exceptions to the general principle of majority rule in management matters: (1) no partner may be excluded from participating in the firm's management and (2) the majority must act in good faith for the firm's interest and not out of self-interest. Since each partner has an equal right to take part in the management of the firm's business, it makes sense that one partner may not exclude another partner from his or her full share in the management of the partnership. The requirement that the majority act in good faith and not for private advantage springs from the fiduciary duty of loyalty each partner owes to the other. Practically speaking, fairness requires consulting with the minority before taking action.

Individual partners and minorities are also protected by the requirement of unanimous approval on extraordinary matters, admission of incoming partners, and changes in the partnership agreement. Because UPA Section 18(h) permits majority rule regarding *"ordinary matters* connected with the partnership business" (emphasis added), majority control does not extend to unusual or extraordinary transactions. These require unanimous approval. For example a majority cannot engage the firm in a different business or change the firm's location if any partner objects.

UPA Section 18(g) provides that "no person can become a member of a partnership without the consent of all the partners." This reflects the intimate nature of partnership relations. No person need have a partner thrust upon him or her. Each partner may choose his or her associates.

Under UPA 18(h), "no act in contravention of any agreement between the partners may be done rightfully without the consent of all the partners." Nothing contravening the partnership agreement may be undertaken without unanimous approval. This is just another application of contract law, since an act contravening the partnership agreement will constitute a breach of contract, and any modification of a contract requires agreement among all parties.

Both majority and unanimous actions may be taken with complete informality, such as an exchange of letters or a telephone call.

Since either majority rule or unanimous approval will normally govern the firm's operations regardless of each partner's contribution, the partners may prefer to specify a different rule in the partnership agreement. For example, majority rule may be replaced by a provision in the partnership agreement leaving ordinary business decisions to a "majority in interest" of either the earnings or the capital contributions of the partners, meaning to the partners who together are entitled to more than half the profits or who together contributed more than half the capital. A major contributor may insist on complete control. This, too, may be provided in the partnership agreement. Where the partners contemplate that one of them will assume most of the managerial duties, the partnership agreement may designate a "managing partner," specify-

ing the responsibilities entrusted to his or her discretion. Where a firm has many partners, such as a large, national accounting firm, provisions for centralizing management in an executive committee may be considered. If there is an even number of partners, the agreement may provide for arbitration to resolve deadlocks.

Information

Section 20 of the UPA provides that "partners shall render on demand true and full information of all things affecting the partnership to any partner or to the legal representative of any deceased partner or any partner under legal disability." Thus each partner has the right to all information concerning partnership affairs. Although Section 20 conditions the duty to render information on a "demand," the courts hold that the duty is an affirmative one, meaning that partners must perform a duty of disclosure regardless of demand. This is because the duty to inform springs from the partner's fiduciary duty of loyalty. As part of the duty of loyalty, partners must not conceal information from each other.

A partner's right to information continues even if a partner lets others manage the firm. To protect his or her investment and to guard against exposure to potential liability, a partner needs access to all partnership information whether or not the partner actively participates in the firm's management.

To implement this right to information, UPA Section 19 requires that "the partnership books shall be kept, subject to any agreement between the partners, at the principal place of business of the partnership, and every partner shall *at all times* have access to and may inspect and copy *any* of them" (emphasis added). Although the UPA does not specify what type of books and records are to be kept, federal income-tax regulations will require a detailed balance sheet, statements of partnership income and each partner's share of income and deductions, and a reconciliation of the partners' capital accounts (Income Tax Regs. 1.446–1[a][4][1961] and 1.6001–1[1959] and Form 1065). A partner need not be a bookkeeper or an accountant to maintain the records, nor need he or she follow standard accounting practice. However, it may be wise to hire a competent accountant or bookkeeper when the partners lack this expertise. If keeping partnership records at the principal place of business and making them available at all times seems inconvenient, the partnership agreement may provide a different location and specify times when the records may be inspected.

To further protect a partner's right to partnership information, UPA Section 22 gives each partner the right to a formal accounting of partnership affairs. A formal accounting is a comprehensive, court-ordered investigation of partnership transactions by a court-appointed investigator. The UPA gives the right to an accounting when specific circumstances justify it even though there is no dissolution of the partnership. Under Section 22, a partner can seek an accounting without dissolving the partnership when

1. He or she is wrongfully excluded from partnership business
2. A partner withholds profits from a secret transaction
3. It is provided for in the partnership agreement
4. Other circumstances render it just and reasonable

Except in these situations, one partner does not have a right to an accounting from his or her copartners unless the partnership is dissolved. The reason for this is that the partner already has access to the firm's books and property.

A partner's only recourse against his or her copartners for breaching a duty owed under either the UPA or the partnership agreement is to bring an action for an accounting. A partner cannot otherwise sue his or her copartners or the partnership for claims arising out of the partnership's affairs because the partner would be both the plaintiff and defendant in the case. Outside of an action for an accounting, a partner can sue his or her copartners only when the problems at issue have nothing to do with partnership affairs or where an accounting has already taken place and the partner's share has been determined.

Limited Partners

Limited partners are not subject to the same rules as general partners. Limited partners owe no fiduciary duties, have different rights regarding compensation, are prohibited from participating in the management of the partnership, but generally have the same rights to information as general partners. The law regarding the relations between general and limited partners is in a transitional state. The Revised ULPA has been recommended by the Conference on Uniform State Laws; however, it has been adopted by only seventeen states.[2] The following paragraphs discuss both the ULPA and the Revised ULPA.

Unlike a general partner, a limited partner owes no duty of loyalty and may, for example, operate a business in competition with the partnership.

Under the ULPA, a limited partner may receive any profits or compensation stipulated in the certificate of limited partnership (Section 15); however, the ULPA fails to provide any basis for profit sharing in the absence of agreement. The Revised ULPA provides that, in the absence of agreement, profits shall be allocated according to the value of each partner's contribution to the partnership (Section 503).

The limited partner's management rights

are less than those of a general partner. The trade-off for obtaining limited liability is the surrender of any right to participate in the management of the partnership. This prevents a creditor from mistaking a limited partner for one of the general partners with full potential liability. Under the ULPA, a limited partner loses the protection of limited liability if he or she "takes part in the control of the business" (Section 7). Difficulty in determining when the "control" line is crossed has created substantial uncertainty as to when the rights of review, consultation, and veto become participation in the firm's management. Under the Revised ULPA, if a "limited partner's participation in the control of the business is not substantially the same as the exercise of the powers of a general partner," he or she loses the limited liability "only as to persons with actual knowledge of his participation in control" (Section 303). Under this rule, a limited partner may participate in the firm's management so long as he or she refrains from exercising all the powers of a general partner and avoids direct dealings with third parties. To further provide a "safe harbor" for limited partners, the Revised ULPA lists certain activities—such as consulting, being a contractor, or being an agent of the firm—that a limited partner may perform without being deemed to be taking part in the control of the business. The Revised ULPA expands and clarifies the permissible participation of limited partners in the management of the firm.

Although limited partners may not participate in the firm's management as much as general partners, their passive position requires that they have access to information in order to protect their investment. Under ULPA Section 10, a limited partner may demand "true and full information *of all things affecting the partnership* and a formal account of partnership affairs whenever circumstances render it just and reasonable . . ." (emphasis added). Furthermore, the limited partner has the right to "have the partnership books kept at the principal place of business of the partnership, and *at all times* inspect and copy *any of them* . . ." (emphasis added). The Revised ULPA conditions the right to information "from time to time upon reasonable demand" and limits the available information to records "regarding the state of the business and the financial condition of the limited partnership," tax returns, and "other information regarding the partnership as is just and reasonable" (Section 305).

The Revised ULPA also states what records are to be kept by the partnership. Although it does not require a standard form of financial report, it does require that certain basic documents, including the certificate of limited partnership and any partnership agreement, be kept along with tax returns and other financial statements (Section 105).

RELATIONS WITH THIRD PARTIES

Because partnerships exist to conduct business, partners need to interact with third parties who deal with the partnership. This interaction may be by making contracts or, as an inevitable incident of doing business, committing torts. The problem is to what extent a partner's conduct binds the firm and fellow partners.

As mentioned earlier, partnership law is a particular application of agency law. A partner's power to bind the firm in dealings with third parties is determined by the general rules of agency law as provided in the UPA. Because each partner is an agent of the partnership for the purpose of its business (Section 9), his or her acts may result in the firm's being: liable for contracts made and torts committed by a partner; bound by a partner's admissions; and charged with the knowledge of or notice to a partner. Agency rules provided in the UPA also apply for determining the liability of incoming and withdrawing partners for obligations incurred by the partnership. A limited partner is not an agent of the partnership and therefore has no authority to act for the firm and bind it to third parties.

Contracts

The power of a partner to bind the partnership to contracts with third parties may be either actual or apparent. The partner may have actual authority as expressly provided in the partnership agreement. If no actual or express authority is provided there, the partner may have apparent authority. Where a partner's acts are unauthorized, they may be ratified by a majority of the copartners and made binding on the firm. Thus the power of a partner to bind the firm by contract to third parties may be found either in the partnership agreement or, by implication, in his or her conduct or the conduct of the copartners.

Section 9 of the UPA provides that any act of a partner is binding on the partnership if it is "for apparently carrying on in the usual way the business of the partnership." This is just a restatement of the agency rule regarding apparent authority. Partners have apparent authority consistent with the nature of the partnership business. The usual authority possessed by partners in similar businesses is the measure of a particular partner's apparent authority. Section 9(2) further provides that any "act of a partner which is not apparently for the carrying on of the business of the partnership in the usual way does not bind the partnership unless authorized by the other partners." For acts unrelated to the partnership's business, a partner needs actual authority. This may be provided informally or in the partnership agreement.

Sometimes a partnership agreement restricts a partner's authority to bind the partnership. For example, a partnership agreement may provide that "no partner shall incur any indebtedness of the firm in excess of five hundred dollars." What effect should this have on third parties? Under UPA Section 9, third parties are not limited or bound by secret restrictions of a partner's authority, or by restrictions in a partnership agreement, unless they know of them. Thus any contracts made by a partner for the firm and related to its business are binding on the partnership notwithstanding any secret restrictions on the partner's authority if they are unknown to the third party.

Torts

Under UPA Section 13, the partnership is liable for the torts "of any partner acting in the ordinary course of the business of the partnership or with the authority of his co-partners." Thus all members of a partnership are liable for a partner's torts committed within the scope and course of the partnership business. This liability also ensnares absent partners who did not participate in, ratify, or know about the tort. The determining factor for invoking partnership liability is whether the tort was committed within the reasonable scope of and in behalf of the partnership business. If the wrongful conduct was clearly outside the scope of the partnership business, the nonparticipating partners may still be liable if they authorize, ratify, or consent to the tort. Thus the requisites of consent and of scope and course of business provide the principal channels through which vicarious liability attaches to a partnership for a partner's torts. This usually occurs where a partner's negligence injures a third party. In comparison to negligent conduct, a willful and malicious tort is generally held not to be within the scope of an ordinary partnership, and the partnership is not liable unless the nonparticipating partners authorize, ratify, or consent to their copartner's willful tort. For example, if a copartner in a tavern commits an unprovoked assault upon a customer, liability would not extend to the absent copartner who had neither consented to nor authorized the attack.

The following case demonstrates the tort liability of partners.

Kelsey-Seybold Clinic v. Maclay

Supreme Court of Texas
466 S.W. 2d 716 (1971)

For several years, John Dale Maclay and his wife and children had been under the medical care of the Kelsey-Seybold Clinic, including treatment by a pediatrician, Dr. Brewer, who was a partner in the clinic. Claiming that the pediatrician was engaging in conduct designed to alienate the affections of his wife, Maclay notified Dr. Kelsey, a senior partner at the clinic, of the allegedly tortious relationship. Maclay claimed that, in spite of such notice, the physician's relationship with Maclay's wife continued unabated. Maclay brought suit against the physician and the clinic for the tort of alienation of affections. The trial court rendered summary judgment in favor of the clinic. The Texas Court of Civil Appeals reversed. The clinic appealed further to the Supreme Court of Texas, which affirmed.

Walker, J.

We are unwilling to believe that plaintiff seriously expects to prove in a conventional trial that the acts alleged to have been committed by Dr. Brewer were in the course and scope of the partnership business or were either authorized or ratified by the Clinic. . . . [W]e assume for the purpose of this opinion that Dr. Brewer was not acting in the ordinary course of the Clinic's business and that his conduct was neither authorized nor ratified by the partnership. This will enable us to reach questions that may well arise at the trial of the case.

The Court of Civil Appeals reasoned that the summary judgment was improper because the Clinic had not conclusively negated consent on its part to the alleged wrongful conduct of Dr. Brewer. In reaching this conclusion, it relied on our opinion in K & G Oil Tool & Service Co. v. G & G Fishing Tool Service, 158 Tex., 314 S.W. 2d 782, where it was stated that:

"A non-participating partner is ordinarily not personally liable for the wrongful, tortious or criminal acts of the acting partner unless such acts are within the scope of the partnership's business or were consented to, authorized, ratified or adopted by the non-participating partner."

There was no question of consent in K & G, and it was held that the non-participating partner was not liable. . . .

Where a partner proposed to do, in the name or for the benefit of the partnership, some act that is not in the ordinary course of the business, consent by the other partners may constitute his authority to do the act for the partnership. . . . We also recognize that even a wilful or malicious act outside the ordinary scope of the partnership business may be so related to the business that tacit consent of the other partners could fairly be regarded as a grant of authority. In this instance, however, Dr. Brewer was acting solely for his own personal gratification. His conduct could not benefit the Clinic in any way, and no one would have supposed that he was acting for the partnership. It is our opinion that in these circumstances the "consent" that might be inferred from the silence or inaction of the Clinic after learning of his conduct does not render the Clinic vicariously liable for the damages claimed by plaintiff.

On the basis of the present record and the facts we are assuming in this case, the liability of the Clinic must rest, if at all, upon some theory akin to that recognized by the court in Williams. [Williams v. F. & W. Grand Five, Ten and Twenty-five Cent Stores, 273 Pa. 131, 116 A. 652]. The Clinic was under a duty, of course, to exercise ordinary care to protect its patients from harm resulting from tortious conduct of persons upon the premises. A negligent breach of that duty could subject the Clinic to liability without regard to whether the tortious conduct immediately causing the harm was that of an agent or servant or was in the ordinary scope of the partnership business. For example, it might become liable, as a result of its own negligence, for damage done by a vicious employee while acting beyond the scope of his authority. . . .

We are also of the opinion that the Clinic owed a duty to the families of its patients to exercise ordinary care to prevent a tortious interference with family relations. It was not required to maintain constant surveillance over personnel on duty or to inquire into and regulate the personal conduct of partners and employees while engaged in their private affairs. But if and when the partnership received information from which it knew or should have known that there might be a need to take action, it was under a duty to use reasonable means at its disposal to prevent any partner or employee from improperly using his position with the Clinic to work a tortious invasion of legally protected family interests. This duty relates only to conduct of a partner or employee on the premises of the Clinic or while purportedly acting as a representative of the Clinic elsewhere. Failure to exercise ordinary care in discharging that duty would subject the Clinic to liability for damages proximately caused by its negligence.

The rather meager information in the present record does not necessarily indicate that the Clinic was under a duty to act or that it could have done anything to prevent the damage when Dr. Kelsey first learned of the situation. On the other hand, it does not affirmatively and clearly appear that the Clinic could or should have done nothing. Mrs. Maclay's affections may have been alienated from her husband before anyone talked with Dr. Kelsey, but the facts in that respect are not fully developed. There is not proof as to when, where or under what circumstances the misconduct, if any, on Dr. Brewer's part occurred. Dr. Kelsey testified that he did not believe anything improper occurred at the Clinic, but the proofs do not establish as a matter of law that he was justified in not making further inquiry after his conversations with plaintiff and Mr. Maclay's uncle. The record does not show whether there is a partnership agreement that might have a bearing on the case, and we have no way of knowing the extent to which the Clinic might have determined which patients were to be seen by Dr. Brewer or controlled his actions while on duty. Dr. Kelsey's testimony suggests that the partners might have been in a position to prevent improper conduct by one of their number on the premises of the Clinic. In our opinion the Clinic has failed to discharge the heavy, and in a case of this character virtually impossible, burden of establishing as a matter of law at the summary judgment stage that it is not liable under any theory fairly presented by the allegations.

The judgment of the Court of Civil Appeals is affirmed.

Dissenting opinion by Greenhill, J.

I am unable to agree that the partners of Dr. Brewer or the Kelsey Clinic are even potentially liable.

This suit was brought by a husband for the alienation of his wife's affections. The acts alleged to have occurred were not any sort of assault or battery as in the Williams case from Pennsylvania relied upon by the majority opinion. The alleged acts involved here between Dr. Brewer and the plaintiff's wife were between consenting adults; and obviously, they were committed in secret. The majority opinion correctly finds that Dr. Brewer was acting solely for his own personal gratification; that his conduct could not benefit the clinic in any way; and it assumes that his conduct was neither authorized nor ratified by the partnership. The Uniform Partnership Act provides for liability of the partnership for wrongful acts of a partner "acting in the ordinary course of the business of the partnership." Article 6132b, §13, Vernon's Annotated Civil Statutes. I find no such action here. [The rest of Justice Greenhill's opinion regarding the tort of alienation of affections is omitted.]

Admissions, Knowledge, and Notice

Agency rules make the partnership responsible for the admissions or representations of any partner concerning partnership affairs within the scope of his or her authority (UPA Section 11). Also as in agency law, knowledge or notice to any partner of matters relating to partnership affairs is imputed to the partnership (Section 12). Thus notice to a partner concerning a matter of firm business, such as notice to a partner of a prior mortgage on property acquired by the firm, is notice to the partnership and all its members. However, knowledge or notice is not imputed when the partner acquires it while acting fraudulently or adversely to the firm or when the knowledge was acquired by the partner before joining the firm.

Withdrawing and Incoming Partners

As frequently occurs, one partner will withdraw or retire from the firm and be replaced by an incoming partner. When this happens, care must be taken to consider how the change in membership will affect the liabilities of each. A retiring partner remains liable to third parties unless he or she notifies third parties who know of the partnership and have extended credit to it. This may be done informally by letter or phone, or by a novation, substituting the incoming partner for the retiring partner as responsible to the partnership's creditors. (A novation is a contract that discharges a previous contractual obligation and creates a new contractual duty by substituting another person for the original obligor. It is the substitution by mutual agreement of one debtor for another.) Constructive notice, such as publication in a newspaper, is essential to adequately notify third parties who know about the partnership but never extended credit to it.

An incoming partner is liable for all partnership obligations arising before his or her admission as though the incoming partner had been a partner when such obligations were incurred. However, this liability may be satisfied only out of the partnership property (UPA Section 17). A judgment for such an obligation cannot be satisfied out of the incoming partner's individual property. An incoming partner may promise the partners that old creditors will be paid. When this happens, the promise can be enforced by the creditors as third-party beneficiaries to the contract and subject the incoming partner's individual property to satisfy the debt. Another way to accomplish the same result is for the creditors to enter into a novation, substituting the incoming partner for any withdrawing partner.

PARTNERSHIP DISSOLUTION

The day may finally come when the partnership is dissolved. The partners may wish to withdraw from the firm or simply to change to the corporate form. Or the partnership may be bankrupt, although business failure is only one of many possible reasons for partnership dissolution. Unlike corporations, partnerships lack continued existence. Like humankind, they also are mortal. However, with a little wizardry the partnership business may be born again to continue its commercial course in a new guise. The following paragraphs visit the deathbed of the partnership, view its "dissolution," and witness its "winding up." To conclude on a happier note, the chapter considers how the business may be continued.

Dissolution, Winding Up, and Termination

The UPA distinguishes among a partnership's dissolution, winding up, and termination, which are the three phases of ending a partnership. Phase 1, the partnership's dissolution, represents the point in time when the partners cease being associated with one another as partners. It has nothing to do with the discontinuation of the partnership *business* but refers only to a change of *relation* among the partners. The partnership does not automatically cease doing business upon dissolution. A partnership continues after dissolution until the business is liquidated and the partnership terminated, unless continued by agreement or pursuant to the UPA. Phase 2 is the winding up of partnership affairs. Winding up is the process of bringing the partnership business to an end. Phase 3 is the partnership's termination. Upon termination the partnership is legally and functionally dead.

Dissolution. UPA Section 29 defines dissolution as the "change in the relation of the partners caused by any partner's ceasing to be associated in the carrying on as distinguished from the winding up of the business." According to the section's official comment, dissolution is a legal event, a point in time when the partners cease doing business together. The partnership, consisting of a particular group of individuals, has technically dissolved.

Winding Up and Termination. UPA Section 30 cautions that "on dissolution the partnership is not terminated, but continues until the winding up is completed." The winding up, otherwise called by business people "liquidation," is the process of ending partnership affairs. It is the process through which termination is reached. It is the administration of assets to discharging the firm's obligations to its creditors and members. When that process is completed, the partnership is terminated.

Causes of Dissolution

Partnership dissolution is caused (1) by the acts of the partners or (2) by operation of law.

Acts of the Partners. Any partner can cause a dissolution of the partnership at any time. Each partner has the power to dissolve the partnership. However, the distinction between the power to dissolve and the right to dissolve should be carefully noted. A power is the ability to affect the legal status of another —for example, a partner's ability to alter his or her associates' status as members of a partnership by dissolving the firm. However, a person may incur a liability for exercising a power wrongfully. When the right to do something exists, there is no liability for its exercise. A partner may possess the power to dissolve but not the right. Thus, while a partner can cause a dissolution of the partnership at any time, if the dissolution is wrongful, the errant partner may be liable to his or her copartners for the misconduct.

Whether the partner has the right to dissolve is determined by the agreement among the partners. Consent to future dissolution may be manifested in their partnership agreement. The agreement may confer the right to dissolve the firm upon a partner, or it may withhold the right under certain circumstances. Any act by a partner that causes the firm's dissolution is rightful if it complies with the agreement. An act of a partner that causes the firm's dissolution is wrongful if it contravenes the agreement. Under UPA Section 31, dissolution is caused without violating the agreement between the partners:

1. When the partnership term expires, which may be upon the completion of a specified time period or a particular project
2. If no definite time or particular undertaking is specified, at the express will of any partners
3. By mutual agreement of all the partners, or by less than all where one or more of the partners has assigned his or her interest or it has been subjected to a charging order
4. By expelling a partner according to the terms of the partnership agreement.

A dissolution is in contravention of the agreement among the partners when the circumstances do not permit one under Section 31 by the express will of any partner at any time.

When a dissolution is caused in contravention of the partnership agreement, the remaining partners may recover damages from the partner who wrongfully dissolves the firm (UPA Section 38[2]). This is just another application of the contract-law principles regarding the rights of contracting parties in the event of a breach of contract. The UPA also protects the remaining partners from summary dissolution by permitting them to continue the partnership without the errant partner. To do this, the remaining partners must pay to the dissolving partner the value of his or her interest in the partnership, less damages, and must

indemnify him or her against all partnership liabilities.

Operation of Law. Dissolution of a partnership also may be caused by operation of law. Under UPA Section 31, dissolution is caused by operation of law in the following ways:

1. By any event that makes it unlawful to carry on the partnership business
2. By the death of any partner
3. By the bankruptcy of any partner or the partnership
4. By court decree under Section 32

Section 32 empowers dissolution by judicial determination. On application by or for a partner, a court will order a dissolution on one of the following grounds:

1. Incapacity, that is, where the partner is incapable of performing as a partner
2. Improper conduct detrimental to the business, such as continually breaching the partnership agreement
3. The business can only be carried on at a loss, that is, the partnership has been wiped out
4. Where the circumstances and equities indicate a dissolution is necessary

Limited Partnerships. The causes of dissolution of limited partnerships are substantially the same as ordinary partnerships. For example, a limited partnership is dissolved by the completion of its term or undertaking. However, there are some differences due to the limited partners' narrow roles. Thus while in an ordinary partnership the ceasing of a partner to carry on the business may bring about dissolution, this is not true with limited partners. The death, incapacity, bankruptcy, or withdrawal of one of the limited partners does not dissolve a limited partnership.

Winding Up the Partnership Business

The winding up is the process by which the partnership business is brought to an end. After the partnership relation has dissolved, the partnership's affairs must be wound up if business is to be terminated. This winding up of firm affairs, sometimes called liquidation, is the process of reducing assets to pay creditors and members of the partnership. During winding up, all uncompleted transactions are finished, debts are settled or paid, claims and accounts receivable are collected or settled, and the remaining assets are either sold or distributed along with any surplus to the partners. During this process the partnership continues for the limited purpose of liquidation, and the partners retain only those powers that are incidental to winding up the business.

Right to Wind Up. The surviving partners who are not bankrupt and who have not wrongfully dissolved the partnership have the right to wind up the affairs of the partnership. When the partners agree to a dissolution, or when the partnership's term expires, all the partners have the right to wind up the firm's affairs. Frequently, upon dissolution the partners will designate a fellow partner to be in charge of winding up the business. This person is usually called the "liquidating partner" or "liquidator." The partners may appoint the liquidating partner by agreement in the articles of partnership.

If the partnership is dissolved because of the bankruptcy or death of a partner, the remaining or surviving partners are entitled to wind up the partnership. Under the UPA, a surviving partner is entitled to reasonable compensation for his or her winding-up services. If the last surviving partner dies before the business is wound up, the executor or administrator will have the right to wind up. Otherwise, the legal representative of a deceased partner does not have the right to participate in the winding-up process. If dissolution is by court order, a court-appointed receiver will wind up the firm.

Partners' Powers During Winding Up. Two needs arise upon dissolution of the partnership: (1) the need to wind up firm affairs and (2) the need to protect third parties who do business with the firm without knowing of its dissolution. Both needs are satisfied by two agency-law concepts: actual and apparent authority.

To prevent partners from engaging in any new business that might delay the winding-up process, a partner's actual authority upon dissolution is limited to doing only what needs to be done to bring about a termination of the business. Thus a partner may do only what is necessary and incidental to winding up the firm's affairs.

Whether a transaction is necessary and incidental to winding up the partnership depends on the circumstances. Generally, the partners who are winding up the partnership may sell partnership property to liquidate firm assets, may receive payment for obligations owed to the partnership, and may enter into compromises with creditors in order to release the partnership from its obligations. Actions that at first may seem inappropriate nevertheless are appropriate if they are necessary and incidental to the partnership's winding up.

The concept of apparent authority protects third parties who deal with a partner without knowing about the partnership's dissolution and winding up. A partner's apparent authority may serve to bind the firm to a transaction that would have been binding before dissolution where a third party deals with a partner without knowledge or notice of the dissolution. UPA Section 35 incorporates the concept of apparent authority by providing that after dissolution a partner may still bind the partnership to transactions with persons who formerly extended credit to the firm if the former creditor has no notice of the dissolution. Persons who never extended credit to the firm are considered to have notice of the dissolution if the fact of dissolution has been advertised in a newspaper of general circulation.

Distribution of Assets

Order of Claims. After partnership assets are liquidated, the proceeds are distributed to pay any claims against the firm. Claims against the partnership are paid in the following order:

1. Claims of partnership creditors
2. Claims of partners for loans or advances
3. Partners' capital contributions
4. Remaining assets distributed as profits and surplus to the partners

If the partnership is solvent, no problems are presented since everyone gets paid. However, if the partnership assets are insufficient to pay the partnership creditors, the partners must make up the loss in the same proportion as they shared profits. If some of the partners are insolvent but others are able to pay, the firm's creditors will be paid by the solvent partners (UPA Section 40).

In the distribution of the assets of a limited partnership, the limited partners under the ULPA follow creditors but precede general partners, and they receive their share of the profits before the return of their capital contributions. Thus after dissolution the obligations of a limited partnership are paid in the following order:

1. Creditors
2. Limited partners' share of profits and other compensation
3. Limited partners' return of capital contributions
4. Loans or advances from general partners
5. Profits due to general partners
6. Return of general partners' capital contribution (ULPA Section 23).

Under the Revised ULPA, loans or advances from partners rank on the same level with claims by other creditors, and general and limited partners are treated together rather than ranked separately (Section 804).

Marshalling of Assets. A partnership creditor has a claim against partnership assets; and where partnership assets are insufficient to pay the claim, the creditor has a claim against the individual partners' property. A problem is presented when there are both individual and partnership creditors. What are their relative rights with respect to a partner's partnership and individual property? Individual creditors have priority to the partner's individual property and partnership creditors have priority to partnership property (UPA Section 40). Under the doctrine called "marshalling of assets," a partnership creditor must pursue his or her claim against partnership property before pursuing a partner's individual property. By compelling partnership creditors to exhaust partnership property before pursuing a partner's individual property, the doctrine enables both individual and partnership creditors to satisfy their claims if there are substantial assets.

Continuing the Partnership Business

Depending on the particular business involved, dissolution and subsequent liquidation without the right to continue the partnership business can be economically disastrous to the remaining partners. Consequently, one of the major reasons for having a partnership agreement is to provide for the firm's continuation by the remaining partners despite dissolution. In large accounting and brokerage firms, for example, partners are continually joining and withdrawing from the firm. Technically, this dissolves the partnership. However, through carefully considered provisions in their partnership agreements, they avoid any termination of activities. Thus while dissolution may require terminating the partnership through the process of liquidation, this can be circumvented by a continuation provision in the partnership agreement that allows the remaining partners to carry on the partnership by buying out the withdrawing partner. While this technically is a dissolution of the partnership, the partnership *business* continues despite dissolution.

The Right to Continue. Pursuant to the UPA, partners may have the right to continue the partnership business although their agreement contains no continuation provision. As mentioned earlier, when dissolution is caused by an act in contravention of the agreement, the partners not wrongfully causing the dissolution may continue the business by (1) paying the dissolving partner the value of his or her interest minus an amount attributable to any damages resulting from the breach and (2) indemnifying the wrongful partner against all partnership liabilities. The value of the partner's interest is generally determined by reference to its market value at dissolution rather than its book value.

While the UPA grants the right to continue to the innocent partners when there is a wrongful dissolution, the partners should still provide for the situation in their partnership agreement. Minimum provisions in their agreement concerning continuation should include:

1. A valuation method for the errant partner's interest
2. An agreed method of indemnification
3. An agreed method of payment if other than in cash

Continuation by Agreement. The dissolved partnership may be continued by an agreement between the withdrawing and remaining partners at the time of dissolution or may be provided for in advance by a provision in the partnership agreement. For example, a clause in the partnership agreement may provide: "In the event of dissolution caused by the retirement of a partner, the remaining partners shall have the right to continue the partnership business under the same name by themselves or with any other persons they may choose; however, they shall pay to the retiring partner the value of his interest as of the date of dissolution." When the dissolution-causing event occurs, the liquidation process will consist of bookkeeping entries and the purchase of the withdrawing partner's interest by the remaining partners.

Providing for the firm's continuation in the partnership agreement requires foresight and care by the partners. They will want to:

1. Determine which dissolution-causing event, such as death, retirement, bankruptcy, etc., will give rise to the right to continue
2. Determine which partners will have the right to continue
3. Determine the manner of disposing of the withdrawing partner's interest—for example, purchase by the remaining partners or another party, such as an incoming partner
4. Determine the method of paying for the withdrawing partner's interest, such as the use of cash, insurance proceeds, or deferred payments made from future earnings
5. Determine the manner of allocating the price of the withdrawing partner's interest

On the last point, a valuation method should be determined. For example, an appraisal may be good for a real estate partnership but not for a service or professional partnership. Whatever valuation method is used, it must be fair. This fairness requirement is a result of each partner's fiduciary duty of loyalty, which requires fair dealings among partners. An agreed dollar value, even with periodic adjustments, is not considered fair. Similarly, using book value is unfair, unless provisions require periodic reappraisal of assets, such as real estate and inventories. Even a provision using a valuation method that is fair may result in a value that is unfair when implemented. For example, in one case the partnership agreement provided that the surviving partners could use their discretion in valuing the partnership's good will. However, the partners abused their discretion and stated that the business had no good will. The court held that this resulted in an unfair value given to the deceased partner's interest.[3]

The partnership provision calling for the purchase of a withdrawing partner's interest is usually referred to as a "buy-sell" agreement. When the death of a partner is contemplated, the buy-sell agreement usually provides for the purchase of a deceased partner's interest at death and is frequently funded by insurance. In a growing business where the partners have reinvested their profits, the surviving partners may be without immediate funds to pay the deceased partner's interest. Furthermore, the only source of funds for paying the deceased partner's interest in installments may be the future profits of the business, which will then not be available for reinvestment. In such a situation, the buy-sell provision in the partnership agreement may provide for the funding of the purchase price with insurance. The insurance premiums may be paid by the partners or the partnership. On the death of a partner, the insurance-policy proceeds are used to pay the deceased partner's interest.

Continuation's Effect on Existing Liabilities. Where the partnership is continued, creditors of the former partnership remain as creditors of the continuing partnership. The creditors may enforce their claims against a withdrawing partner, since a retiring partner remains liable for any obligations incurred by the partnership before he or she withdrew from the firm. The remaining partners may relieve the withdrawing partner of existing liabilities, but third parties are not bound by the arrangement unless they agree to the change through a novation.

Continuation's Effect on Later Liabilities. Just as it is important to notify third parties of the partnership's dissolution when it is terminated, it is equally important to provide notice when the business continues. Failure to notify third parties of the dissolution when the business continues may increase the liability of the continuing partners. Thus if the continuing partners fail to notify third parties of the partnership's dissolution when a partner withdraws from the firm, the continuing partners may be bound by later acts of their former partner. If the business is continued as a corporation, failure to notify former creditors may result in the former partners being held personally liable for new obligations as if they were still partners.

The following case illustrates how a dissolution may not lead to the termination of the partnership business.

Ramseyer v. Ramseyer
Supreme Court of Idaho
558 P. 2d 76 (1976)

From approximately 1959 to 1969, Homer Ramseyer and his sons, Duane and Donald, conducted a cattle-ranching business as equal partners pursuant to an oral agreement. The partnership, Ramseyer Cattle Co., owned and operated two ranches,

Antelope Springs Ranch and Grassy Hills Ranch. Homer's second wife, Ebony, filed for divorce in May 1969. On June 12, 1969, Homer executed a deed conveying to his sons his interest in the Antelope Springs Ranch and sold to his sons his interest in the cattle owned by the partnership. On the same date, Duane and Donald executed a deed conveying Grassy Hills to Homer and agreed orally to pay $20,000 to Homer's daughter. Duane and Donald also assumed certain partnership debts. After June 12, 1969, Duane and Donald continued to operate a cattle-ranching business as a partnership under the name of Ramseyer Cattle Co. In October 1973, Homer sued his sons, seeking a judicial dissolution of the old partnership and an accounting for transactions since 1969 involving the assets of the old partnership. Duane and Donald answered by alleging that the old partnership had been dissolved by mutual, oral agreement in 1969. The trial court found in favor of Duane and Donald and dismissed the complaint. Homer appealed. The Supreme Court of Idaho affirmed. Homer Ramseyer is the appellant; Donald and Duane Ramseyer are the respondents.

Hagan, District Judge

Does the evidence support the finding of a dissolution of the partnership? . . . .

There is no dispute the Ramseyer partnership is governed by applicable provisions of the Uniform Partnership Law (UPL). . . . However, it should be noted some specific provisions of the UPL are applicable only in the absence of an agreement to the contrary by the parties. I.C. §53–329, defines "dissolution" as follows:

> "The dissolution of a partnership is the change in the relation of the partners caused by any partner ceasing to be associated in the carrying on as distinguished from the winding up of the business."

So defined "dissolution" is a legal term of art. It does not refer to the other steps in the process of completing and finishing a partnership relationship.

> "On dissolution the partnership is not terminated, but continues until the winding up of partnership affairs is completed." I.C. 53–330.

A partnership relationship is legally ended and its affairs completed when the three steps of (1) dissolution, (2) winding-up or liquidation, and (3) termination are finished. Initially we are concerned solely with the question of the dissolution of the Ramseyer partnership.

Appellant's complaint sought a judicial dissolution pursuant to I.C. § 53–332. Judicial dissolution is provided for in several situations. Here, however, the trial court found that the Ramseyers had effected a dissolution of their partnership by their voluntary acts of June 12, 1969. I.C. § 53–331 specifies several non-judicial causes of dissolution, both voluntary and involuntary. In pertinent part those causes include:

> "53–331. Causes of Dissolution.—Dissolution is caused:
> 1. Without violation of the agreement between the partners.
>   a. . . . .

        b. By express will of any partner when no definite term or particular undertaking is specified.

        c. By the express will of all the partners who have not assigned their interests or suffered them to be charged for their separate debts, either before or after the termination of any specified term or particular undertaking.

      . . . . . .

     2. In contravention of the agreement between the partners, where the circumstances do not permit a dissolution under any other provision of this section, by the express will of any partner at any time. . . .''

The trial court here did not conclude which specific section governed the dissolution it found, though its conclusion that the dissolution was by the mutual agreement of the partners would bring the dissolution within I.C. § 53–331(1)(c).

The assets exchanged by the Ramseyers on June 12, 1969, constituted the assets of the partnership. After that date, appellant no longer participated in the management of the Antelope Springs Ranch, no longer wrote checks on the partnership checking account, and no longer shared in the profits or losses of the operation as the respondents organized and continued it. This "ceasing to be associated in the carrying on . . . of the business" is uncontradicted evidence of a dissolution of the partnership.

Appellant contends the exchange of property was not made pursuant to any "agreement" to dissolve the partnership. Rather he asserts the purpose of the exchange was to minimize his community estate in view of a pending divorce action. We know of no principle of community property law by which either spouse could achieve such a result, considering the fact the husband, as manager of the community under the law at the time the divorce was granted, owed a fiduciary duty to the wife to account for the community property. . . . The evidence is clear appellant and respondents understood that the exchange of property was final. The details of the exchange and the documentation were arrived at by appellant and an attorney of his choosing. Respondents testified the exchange was not their idea and they just went along with their father and his attorney.

Appellant also contends the old partnership was not dissolved because respondents continued to conduct a similar operation under the same name and with the same assets after June 12, 1969. However, the assets of the new partnership were not the same as those of the old partnership. Appellant himself was in possession of a sizeable portion of the real property formerly used as partnership real property. Moreover, appellant was no longer liable on the old partnership's debts. Respondents also assumed a new obligation to their sister on appellant's behalf. In these circumstances, we find no error in the court's determination the old partnership had been dissolved.

. . . [W]e must [now] consider the contention the old partnership had not been wound-up.

Where partners to a dissolved partnership have agreed upon a settlement and disposition of their partnership accounts, liabilities inter se, and obligations to partnership creditors, they have accomplished a winding-up of partnership affairs. An agreement of this nature—whether denominated a private settlement and account, or extrajudicial agreement, and whether oral or in writing—is presumed to include all disputed matters among the partners, and will be final and conclusive upon them in the absence of fraud, mistake or duress. . . . There is no allegation of fraud, mistake or duress in appellant's complaint, nor is there evidence of any in the record. All the partnership assets were divided, so far as the record shows, the partners' respective interests were settled, and agreement was reached on the assumption by respondents of outstanding partnership liabilities.

We find no error in the trial court's conclusion the transactions of June 12, 1969, constituted both a dissolution of the partnership and a winding-up of partnership affairs.

Affirmed.

REVIEW PROBLEMS

1. Two partners purchased insurance policies on each other's lives. This was done to provide enough money to pay the partnership's debts and continue the business in case one died. Premiums were paid from each partner's personal funds. One partner died. Is the policy's proceeds the personal asset of the surviving partner or a partnership asset? Silva v. Cohn, 200 Cal.App.2d 651, 19 Cal.Rptr. 469 (1962)

2. Ranton and his brother Vinnie owned parcels of real estate as partners. Ranton moved the frame of his house onto one of the lots and started to build and make improvements on it. Because of hard feelings between the brothers, Vinnie drove a bulldozer into the house. Ranton filed a claim with his insurer. The insurer refused to pay the claim on the ground that the property was no longer Ranton's but belonged to the partnership. Had Ranton's house become the property of the partnership, thus precluding him from collecting on his insurance policy? Brouillette v. Phoenix Assurance Co., 340 S.2d 667 (La.Ct. App. 1977)

3. What is the difference between partnership property and a partner's interest in a partnership?

4. Eight partners operated a coal mine. One of the partners loaned his truck to the partnership. Due to the negligence of one of the partnership's employees, the truck was destroyed while being used in the operation of the coal mine. The owner of the truck sued all the partners, including himself, as members of the partnership. What result? Smith v. Hensley, 354 S.W.2d 744 (Ky.Ct. App. 1961)

5. How is a partner's power to bind the partnership similar to an agent's authority to bind a principal?

6. Hugo and Charles did business as partners. After several years, Hugo died and Charles, his brother, was appointed administrator of his estate. Tax returns disclosed that the partnership business was being continued just as it had been before Hugo's death, whose estate was receiving the profits and being charged with the losses of the business. Did Charles have the authority to continue the partnership business after the dissolution of the partnership brought on by Hugo's death, and are the assets of Hugo's estate chargeable with the liabilities of the partnership incurred after Hugo's death? Blumer Brewing Co. v. Mayer, 223 Wis. 540, 269 N.W. 693 (1936)

7. Betty and Martha were partners in a real

estate business. Both contributed personal services, which were the primary source of profits. Martha withdrew from the partnership, and Betty continued to run the business. To what extent is Martha entitled to share in the profits earned after her withdrawal? Hilgendor v. Denson, 341 S.2d 549 (Fla. Ct. App. 1977)

8. Dissolution of a partnership does not necessarily and usually does not mean that the business of the partnership is discontinued. Why?

FOOTNOTES

[1]Helmore v. Smith, 35 Ch.D. 436, 444 (1887).
[2]See note 3, Chapter 26, *supra*.
[3]Curtis v. Campbell, 336 S.W.2d 355 (Ky. App.Ct. 1960).

Nature and Formation of Corporations

O ne of the most important tools of modern business is the corporate form of organization. For some businesses, the corporate structure is ideal. That is because corporations offer two major benefits: (1) the corporation has an identity of its own, separate and distinct from its human operatives, who are not held personally liable; and (2) it may continue to function regardless of the death or departure of its management. If limited liability and business continuity are not important objectives for a firm, however, the corporate form may be inefficient. Corporations are more administratively complex than other types of business organization, they are often expensive to set up, and they are frequently taxed at higher rates than individuals.

This chapter and the four that follow complete our discussion of the law of business associations begun in Chapter 25 with agency law. A functional approach to corporate law is developed here. The present chapter examines the formation of a corporation; the following chapters discuss corporate financing (Chapter 29) and corporate operations (Chapter 30). Examination of the law of corporations is completed with chapters on how the Securities and Exchange Commission regulates some corporations (Chapter 31) and on theories of corporate social responsibility (Chapter 32).

HISTORICAL PERSPECTIVE

The corporation as a form of business organization was well known to the Romans. It was Elizabethan England, however, that gave birth to the modern business corporation. Two forerunners of contemporary corporations were the overseas trading company and the joint stock company. (Recall from high-school history the role that joint stock companies like the British East India Company played in colonizing America.) Even in their infancy corporations had their critics. In 1720 a panic-stricken British Parliament passed the "Bubble Act," establishing as criminal the "acting or presuming to act as a corporate body or bodies" without being incorporated, which at that time was an expensive and cumbersome process. The act did not stem the corporate tide, however, as imaginative lawyers created new forms of business organization to circumvent the law. It was not until 1825 that Parliament officially recognized the reality of corporate existence and repealed its anticorporate law.

The United States has evolved from a midnineteenth-century nation of farmers, shopkeepers, and small manufacturers into a highly industrialized society dominated by corporations. During the twentieth century, several changes have occurred in the nature of corporations and corporate law. As corporate size has increased, so has the need for capitalization, usually obtained through the sale of securities to investors. The focus of the law in recent decades has been to provide investors with protection in the securities market. At the same time, legislatures have sought to attract corporations to their states by adopting corporate codes that give management more and shareholders less control over corporate activities. Currently the focus of attention is on the problems of small, privately owned corporations (called close corporations), which have different needs from those addressed by state laws directed toward large corporations. For example, one recent change has been the modification of state corporate law to permit the creation of single-shareholder corporations.

NATURE OF CORPORATIONS

As the discussion of partnership law made clear, partnerships have two distinct disadvantages: (1) the partners share unlimited personal liability for partnership obligations; and (2) a technical dissolution of the partnership results from any change in the partnership relation, such as the retirement or death of one of the partners. These features of personal liability and lack of business continuity add risks to partnership ventures that potential investors may be unwilling to assume. This is particularly true when the potential investors do not wish to participate in the management of the business.

Even a limited partnership may be unattractive to such investors, since limited partnership statutes require the filing of information revealing the involvement of each limited partner; thus a publicity-shy investor may have information regarding his or her financial support become part of the public record. Further, a limited partner runs some risk of losing his or her limited liability if there is not strict compliance with the statutory prohibitions regarding participating in the control of the firm.

The corporation was conceived as a means of avoiding the risks and discontinuities of partnership and of achieving business objectives beyond the reach of individuals. When capital needs are great, risks are high, and the enterprise's duration is long, the corporation is the preferred form of business organization. The corporation is the legal institution that can hold over a period of time the aggregated capital of many, unaffected by the death or withdrawal of individuals.

Corporate Characteristics

The chief attributes of a corporation are: (1) its entity status, sometimes called juristic or corporate personality; (2) the limited liability of its owners; (3) its continued existence, meaning that a corporation may be established in perpetuity; (4) the transferability of its ownership; and (5) the centralization of its management in its officers and directors rather than in its shareholders/owners. These corporate characteristics are descriptive only. They are not, generally, "tests" of corporate existence, and they are not necessarily found in all corporations. However, most corporations share these characteristics. Furthermore, for federal income tax purposes, the presence or absence of these characteristics determines whether an enterprise is taxed as a corporation.

Juristic Personality. The principal characteristic of a corporation that distinguishes it from all other business organizations is its status as a legal entity. Because of that status, the law treats the corporation as a person. This convenient fiction permits the corporation to enter into and execute contracts, own and convey property, and sue and be sued as a separate entity distinct from its owners and managers.

To the uninitiated, the concept of the corporation as a legal person separate from its members may seem mysterious. But in fact it is a very practical solution to an important societal problem. Because human beings must be the subjects of the law's commands, it is necessary for the law to personify the corporation—treat it like a person—in order to regulate it for beneficial social and economic purposes. One such purpose is to permit the efficient conduct of business. To imagine life without the concept of the corporation as a legal entity, imagine a transaction between the Ford Motor Company and B.F. Goodrich. Treating the transaction as involving two partnerships would involve millions of people as "partners" with hundreds changing every day. Keeping track of the potentially liable people would be a burdensome task even in a computer society.

Limited Liability. A major consequence of the corporation's entity status is the limited liability it accords to its shareholders. Corporate rights and liabilities are not to be confused with those of its owners. Generally, shareholders are not liable for corporate debts beyond the amount of their investment, and the corporation is not liable for the debts of its shareholders. The limited liability includes tort and criminal as well as contractual liability. This is a major business incentive for investors because they can avoid personal liability for corporate activities. Similarly, personal creditors of shareholders cannot reach the corporate property, although they may reach the shares of the debtor shareholder.

Continued Existence. Another key advantage of the corporation that stems from its separateness from the shareholders is its capacity for continuous life, sometimes called perpetual succession. In his *Commentaries,* Blackstone described corporations as "artificial persons who enjoy a kind of legal immortality," and compared them to the River Thames that flows with constantly changing water but continues as the same stream. Similarly, shareholders may come and go with no effect upon the corporate entity. A corporation such as the Ford Motor Company can continue long after its founder and major stockholder has died. As Peter Drucker wrote, "The corporation is permanent, the shareholder is transitory."

Although in most states corporations enjoy continuous existence, a few jurisdictions, such as Mississippi and Oklahoma, limit the life of a corporation to a certain number of years. Furthermore, the corporation's articles of incorporation and bylaws, which are its governing instruments, may limit its duration if that is deemed desirable by its incorporators. Thus the Revised Model Business Corporation Act (RMBCA) provides: "Unless its articles of incorporation provided otherwise every corporation . . . has without limitation power to have perpetual duration and succession in its corporate name" (Section 3.02).

Transferability of Ownership. Ownership interest in a corporation, which generally takes the form of shares of corporate stock, can be traded readily. This permits investors to place a value on their investment and to liquidate it if their investment objectives change. Because ownership interest in a corporation may be transferred by a shareholder while living, upon his or her death it is possible to distribute the interest to the shareholder's beneficiaries or heirs. Thus a shareholder may convey by will his corporate stock to another just as he or she could have given that stock away while alive. When the stockholder dies without leaving a will, the shares pass to the heirs as a part of the estate.

Restrictions on the transferability of shares provided in the corporate governing instruments are permitted if they are reasonable. This usually occurs in corporations having only a few shareholders who wish to limit the corporation's ownership to themselves. Generally this takes the form of a right of first refusal being conferred upon the corporation or the other shareholders in the event of any sale of the corporate stock. A right of first refusal generally means that before any stock may be sold it must first be offered to the corporation or other stockholders who have the right to purchase the stock for fair value, thereby preventing outsiders from obtaining an ownership interest in the corporation.

Centralized Management and Control. The final characteristic of a corporation is the separation of its management from its ownership. Shareholders have no direct control over the daily business of the corporation. While this may not be as true of those corporations that have only a few shareholders, individual shareholders are generally powerless to affect corporate affairs in the case of large organizations where the ownership of stock is dispersed. This is because shareholder control is generally limited to electing the corporation's directors and approving major changes in the corporation's structure and operation.

The corporation's management rests with its officers and directors. By statute in most states, the management function is centralized in the board of directors. The board of directors often delegates its duties to several officers, such as a president and vice presidents, whom the board appoints to manage the daily corporate business and to report to the directors for guidance. The only control usually possessed by the shareholders is the power to elect and remove the directors. Shareholders, of course, can achieve power if they join together, but in many large corporations this is often difficult and involves large-scale organization.

There are obvious efficiencies in centralized management since direct participation of shareholders in management decision making is likely to create more problems than it solves. Thus the centralized management promotes large-scale organization, not individual rights. The result has been the emergence in recent years of an increasingly professionalized and frequently self-perpetuating class of corporate managers who merely go through the formalities of accounting to shareholders. It would not be unfair to characterize the government of a large corporation as "oligarchical" in the sense that the small group running it accounts only to itself or to a few large shareholders. Considering, however, that management selection is often meritocratic and that there is a community of interest and outlook in most instances between management and shareholders, the virtual disenfranchisement of the shareholder is not as oppressive as it appears. In partial recognition of these realities, corporate law in recent times has sought to protect the shareholder—viewed primarily as investor rather than owner—against fraud and has substantially strengthened the obligations of management to act honestly and to disclose all material facts.

Corporations and the Constitution

The legal personification of the corporation raises questions as to whether and how the rights and protections that the U.S. Constitution extends to "persons," "people," and "citizens" apply to corporations. For example, the Fifth and Fourteenth Amendments provide that no "person" shall be "deprived of life, liberty or property, without due process of law," and the Fourteenth Amendment prohibits any state to "deny to any person within its jurisdiction the equal protection of the laws." The Fifth Amendment also provides that no person "shall be compelled in any criminal case to be a witness against himself . . ." and the Fourth Amendment guarantees "the right of the people to be secure in their persons, houses, papers, and effects against unreasonable searches and seizures. . . ." Furthermore, Article IV and the Fourteenth Amendment secure the privileges and immunities of the "citizens" of each state and the United States.

Are corporations "persons" and "citizens" under these constitutional provisions? Is a corporation one of "the people" entitled to the Fourth Amendment's protection against unreasonable searches and seizures? The answer to these questions depends not on semantics but on the purposes underlying these various constitutional provisions.

The U.S. Supreme Court has specifically held that a corporation is a "person," entitled to the equal protection of the law, whose property cannot be taken without legal due process. However, a corporation is not a "person" entitled to the Fifth Amendment's privilege against self-incrimination, although it is considered one of the "people" entitled to the Fourth Amendment's protection against unreasonable searches.

This apparent inconsistency rests on the different purposes underlying these constitutional guarantees. The constitutional provision against self-incrimination is considered essentially a personal one, applying only to natural persons. It is not applicable to corporations because its original purpose was to protect individuals against the use of legal process to obtain self-incriminating testimony. Thus a corporation cannot oppose the subpoenaing of its books and records by asserting the privilege. Further, an officer or employee of a corporation cannot withhold testimony or documents on the ground that the coroporation would be incriminated, although it would be permissible for such an officer or employee to refuse such evidence on the ground that he or she might be incriminated by its production.

Unlike the privilege against self-incrimination, the Fourth Amendment's protection against unreasonable searches and seizures applies to corporations as well as individuals. However, the protection is not absolute; only *unreasonable* governmental searches are prohibited. Hence, the protection yields in the face of a valid search warrant or subpoena.

Thus, under the Fourth and Fifth Amendments, the books and records of a corporation cannot be insulated from governmental inspection unless the scope of the governmental intrusion is unreasonable under the Fourth. The determination of which governmental intrusions are reasonable and which are not is a judicial function. In appraising the reasonableness of an intrusion, the courts attempt to balance the expectation of privacy with the government's need for information before issuing warrants or subpoenas.

Although the word "person" impliedly includes "citizen," a corporation is not considered to be a citizen entitled to the protection of the privileges and immunities clauses of the federal Constitution since these also apply only to natural persons. The consequence of a corporation not being a citizen under these clauses is that it may be compelled to comply with the corporation laws of a state in which it intends to do business but in which it is not incorporated. It may even be kept out of the state entirely if the state so wishes, unless the corporation is an interstate business. A state's "doing business" requirements cannot burden interstate commerce because of overriding provisions in the federal Constitution. Thus a state may usually require out-of-state corporations to register and pay fees for the privilege of doing business within the state or to designate an agent within the state for the acceptance of service of legal process.

Recently the U.S. Supreme Court, treating the corporation as a "person," resolved the question of whether it possesses freedom of expression under the First Amendment.

First National Bank of Boston v. Bellotti

U.S. Supreme Court
435 U.S. 765 (1978)

First National Bank and other corporations (appellants) brought suit against Bellotti, attorney-general of the Commonwealth of Massachusetts (appellee), to have Section 8 of the state's criminal statute declared unconstitutional. Section 8 forbade expenditures by banks and business corporations for purposes of influencing or affecting the vote on any question submitted to the voters other than one materially affecting any of the property, business, or assets of the corporation. Further, the statute specifically stated that "questions submitted to the voters solely concerning taxation of income, property or transaction of individuals shall not be considered to materially affect the property, business or assets of corporation." Violations of the statute were punishable by a maximum fine of $50,000 to be levied against each corporation, and a fine of $10,000 and/or one year in prison for corporate officers, directors, or agents of the corporation.

When First National Bank and other corporations sought to spend money to publicize their opposition to a referendum proposed to amend Massachussett's constitution to authorize the legislature to enact a graduated personal income tax, the appellee, Attorney-General Bellotti, informed appellants that he intended to enforce the statute. The appellants then brought this suit. The Massachusetts courts held Section 8 to be constitutional. First National and other corporations appealed to the U.S. Supreme Court. Held: Reversed.

Powell, Justice.

The court below framed the principal question in this case as whether and to what extent corporations have First Amendment rights. We believe that the court posed the wrong question. The Constitution often protects interests broader than those of the party seeking their vindication. The First Amendment, in particular, serves significant societal interests. The proper question therefore is not whether corporations "have" First Amendment rights and, if so, whether they are coextensive with those of natural persons. Instead, the question must be whether § 8 abridges expression that the First Amendment was meant to protect. We hold that it does.

The speech proposed by appellants is at the heart of the First Amendment protection. In appellants' view, the enactment of a graduated personal income tax, as proposed to be authorized by constitutional amendment, would have a seriously adverse effect on the economy of the State. The importance of the referendum issue to the people and government of Massachusetts is not disputed. Its merits, however, are the subject of sharp disagreement.

As the Court said in *Mills* v. *Alabama,* "there is practically universal agreement that a major purpose of [the First] Amendment was to protect the free discussion of governmental affairs." If the speakers here were not corporations, no one would suggest that the State could silence their proposed speech. It is the type of speech indispensable to decisionmaking in a democracy, and this is no less true because the speech comes from a corporation rather than an individual. The inherent worth of the speech in terms of its capacity for informing the public does not depend upon the identity of its source, whether corporation, association, union, or individual.

The court below nevertheless held that corporate speech is protected by the First Amendment only when it pertains directly to the corporation's business interests. In deciding whether this novel and restrictive gloss on the First Amendment comports with the Constitution and the precedents of this Court, we need not survey the outer boundaries of the Amendment's protection of corporate speech, or address the abstract question whether corporations have the full measure of rights that individuals enjoy under the First Amendment. The question in this case, simply put, is whether the corporate identity of the speaker deprives this proposed speech of what otherwise would be its clear entitlement to protection. We turn now to that question.

We (thus) find no support in the First or Fourteenth Amendments, or in the decisions of this Court, for the proposition that speech that otherwise would be within the protection of the First Amendment loses that protection simply because its source is a corporation that cannot prove, to the satisfaction of a court, a material effect on its business or property. The "materially affecting" requirement is not an identification of the boundaries of corporate speech etched by the Constitution itself. Rather, it amounts to an impermissible legislative prohibition of speech based on the identity of the interests that spokesmen may represent in public debate over controversial issues and a requirement that the speaker have a sufficiently great interest in the subject to justify communication.

Section 8 permits a corporation to communicate to the public its views on certain referendum subjects—those materially affecting its business—but not others. It also singles out one kind of ballot question—individual taxation—as a subject about which corporations may never make their ideas public. The legislature has drawn the line between permissible and impermissible speech according to whether there is a sufficient nexus, as defined by the legislature, between the issue presented to the voters and the business interests of the speaker.

In the realm of protected speech, the legislature is constitutionally disqualified from dictating the subjects about which persons may speak and the speakers who may address a public issue. If a legislature may direct business corporations to "stick to business," it also may limit other corporations—religious, charitable, or civic—to their respective "business" when addressing the public. Such power in government to channel the expression of views is unacceptable under the First Amendment. Especially where, as here, the legislature's suppression of speech suggests an attempt to give one side of a debatable public question an advantage in expressing its views to the people, the First Amendment is plainly offended. Yet the State contends that its action is necessitated by governmental interests of the highest order. We next consider these asserted interests.

Appellees (nevertheless) advance two principal justifications for the prohibition of corporation speech. The first is the State's interest in sustaining the active role of the individual citizen in the electoral process and thereby preventing diminution of the citizen's confidence in government. The second is the interest in protecting the rights of shareholders whose views differ from those expressed by management on behalf of the corporation. However weighty these interests may be in the context of partisan candidate elections, they either are not implicated in this case or are not served at all, or in other than a random manner, by the prohibition in § 8.

Appellee advances a number of arguments in support of his view that these interests are endangered by corporate participation in discussion of a referendum issue. They hinge upon the assumption that such participation would exert an undue influence on the outcome of a referendum vote, and—in the end—destroy the confidence of the people in the democratic process and the integrity of government. According to appellee, corporations are wealthy and powerful and their views may drown out other points of view. If appellee's arguments were supported by record or legislative findings that corporate advocacy threatened imminently to undermine democratic processes, thereby denigrating rather than serving First Amendment interests, these arguments would merit our consideration. But there has been no showing that the relative voice of corporations has been overwhelming or even significant in influencing referenda in Massachusetts, or that there has been any threat to the confidence of the citizenry in government.

Finally, the State argues that Section 8 protects corporate shareholders, an interest that is both legitimate and traditionally within the province of state law. The statute is said to serve this interest by preventing the use of corporate resources in furtherance of views with which some shareholders may disagree. This purpose is belied, however, by the provisions of the statute, which are both under- and over-inclusive.

The under-inclusiveness of the statute is self-evident. Corporate expenditures with respect to a referendum are prohibited, while corporate activity with respect to the passage or defeat of legislation is permitted, even though corporations may engage in lobbying more often than they take positions on ballot questions submitted to the voters. Nor does § 8 prohibit a corporation from expressing its views, by the expenditure of corporate funds, on any public issue until it becomes the subject of a referendum, though the displeasure of disapproving shareholders is unlikely to be any less.

The fact that a particular kind of ballot question has been singled out for special treatment undermines the likelihood of a genuine state interest in protecting shareholders. It suggests instead that the legislature may have been concerned with silencing corporations on a particular subject. Indeed, appellee has conceded that "the legislative and judicial history of the statute indicates . . . that the second crime was 'tailor-made' to prohibit corporate campaign contributions to oppose a graduated income tax amendment.''

Nor is the fact that § 8 is limited to banks and business corporations without relevance. Excluded from its provisions and criminal sanctions are entities or organized groups in which numbers of persons may hold an interest or membership, and which often have resources comparable to those of large corporations. Minorities in such groups or entities may have interests with respect to institutional speech quite comparable to those of minority shareholders in a corporation. Thus the exclusion of Massachusetts business trusts, real estate investment trusts, labor unions, and other associations undermines the plausibility of the State's purported concern for the persons who happen to be shareholders in the banks and corporations covered by § 8.

The over-inclusiveness of the statute is demonstrated by the fact that § 8 would prohibit a corporation from supporting or opposing a referendum proposal even if its shareholders unanimously authorized the contribution or expenditure. Ultimately shareholders may decide, through the procedures of corporate democracy, whether their corporation should engage in debate on public issues. Acting through their power to elect the board of directors or to insist upon protective provisions in the corporation's charter, shareholders normally are presumed competent to protect their own interests. In addition to intra-corporate remedies, minority shareholders generally have access to the judicial remedy of a derivative suit to challenge corporate disbursements alleged to have been made for improper corporate purposes or merely to further the personal interests of management.

Assuming, *arguendo,* that protection of shareholders is a ''compelling'' interest under the circumstances of this case, we find ''no substantially relevant correlation between the governmental interest asserted and the State's effort'' to prohibit appellants from speaking.

Because § 8 prohibits protected speech in a manner unjustified by a compelling state interest, it must be invalidated.

Held. Reversed.

Classes of Corporations

The corporate form of organization has many dimensions. A corporation may be either public or private, profit or nonprofit, publicly issued or closely held, professional or nonprofessional, and foreign or domestic. Thus there are many different kinds of corporations, each bearing a generally accepted label. Because a court may refer to a corporation by its label, familiarity with the common types of corporations and the terminology used to describe them is useful. Moreover, comparison of various kinds of corporations that at first appear to be dissimilar often reveals certain commonly shared characteristics.

Public and Private Corporations. A corporation may be broadly classified as either public or private. The distinction refers to its purposes and powers. A public corporation is created and funded by the government to act as its instrumentality for the carrying out of some public purpose. Examples of public corporations include municipal, school, and water districts and various public-benefit corporations such as the U.S. Legal Services Corporation. Many state colleges and universities are organized as public corporations.

Private corporations are all corporations other than those that are public. They are created for private rather than public purposes. The General Motors Corporation is an example of a private corporation.

Profit and Nonprofit Corporations. A corporation for profit is primarily a business corporation, one engaged in commercial enterprises. Thus a corporation for profit is organized to conduct a business with a view to realizing gains to be distributed as dividends among its shareholders. A nonprofit corporation is not organized to make a profit for its members and does not conduct a business. Because they are not organized with a view to distributing gains, nonprofit corporations are usually expressly forbidden by statute to issue certificates of shares. They may issue membership certificates, if they so desire. Thus they are sometimes characterized as membership rather than shareholder corporations. Social, philanthropic, religious, and cultural corporations are examples of nonprofit corporations.

Public-Issue and Closely Held Corporations. A public-issue corporation is one whose stock ownership is diffused and whose management is divorced from its owners. "Going public" is a phrase frequently used to describe the process by which a privately owned firm issues stock to the public. This process is usually accompanied by increased governmental regulation, most notably from the Securities and Exchange Commission (SEC), which administers federal legislation regulating the issuance and trading of corporate securities.

In contrast to a public-issue corporation, in which stock is often widely held and management is normally unrelated to stock ownership, a "close" or "closely held" corporation is one whose stock is not publicly traded and whose stock ownership and management usually intertwine. A close corporation usually has only a few shareholders, most or all of whom participate in its management. Thus there is a striking resemblance to a partnership.

Many corporate concepts and principles created with public-issue corporations primarily in mind are ill-adapted to close corporations. Although the nature and methods of operation of the two kinds of corporations are different, in the past, and especially before 1960, state corporate codes generally established the same rules for governing both corporations. Great Britain and some countries of continental Europe have long had special statutes governing the "private company." Since World War II, strong pleas have been made to enact in this country similar comprehensive statutes to govern close corporations. Since 1960, a legislative breakthrough has occurred, with many states adding to their corporation statutes provisions designed to meet the problems of close corporations. Even now, however, only a handful of states, most notably Florida, Delaware, and Maryland, have adopted separate statutes for close corporations.

Professional Corporations. Until recently, every state prohibited professionals, such as accountants, architects, doctors, and lawyers, from incorporating their professional practices. A recent trend in some states has been to authorize professionals to practice their professions in the corporate form of organization. An individual or group of persons licensed in some kind of professional service may now organize as a corporation in these states. However, restrictions are imposed to protect the public. Thus stock may usually be issued only to duly licensed professionals engaged in the service for which the corporation has been organized.

Foreign and Domestic Corporations. A corporation is domestic to the state where it is created. It is considered foreign in all other states and countries where it does business. Thus a corporation incorporated in Delaware is considered a "foreign" corporation in Ohio. This is true even if the corporation's principal place of business is in Ohio.

REGULATION OF CORPORATIONS

Since the beginning of the Republic, the activities of corporations have been enmeshed in government regulation. Before the middle of the nineteenth century, corporations were generally created pursuant to the granting of a corporate charter or franchise by the state in the form of special legislation. However, as the corporate form of organization became popular, the states enacted general corporate codes that governed the creation and operation of corporations.

Although the commerce clause and the necessary and proper clause of the federal Constitution empower the U.S. government to grant corporate charters, the federal government has no corporate code. On occasion, however, the federal government has chartered certain corporations, such as the Postal Service Corporation, by the enactment of special legislation. Virtually all corporations are the creations of the states. Various federal laws, such as the securities and exchange laws, the tax code, the labor statutes, and the antitrust laws, are noteworthy for their impact upon corporations. These may be viewed as constituting a "federal law of corporations" even though there is no single comprehensive federal corporate code.

State Corporation Codes

Corporate law is basically statutory. Each state has its own corporation statutes, usually consisting of a general corporation statute for commercial corporations and several supplemental or special statutes governing certain specific corporations such as banks, insurance companies, nonprofit corporations, and other categories of corporations. Although there is no uniformity among the various state general corporation laws, the Model Business Corporation Act (MBCA) has served as the basic guideline for the majority of states, and the corporate law principles employed in the remaining state statutes are sufficiently similar to permit a degree of generalized discussion.

Because it has affected the majority of state statutes, the MBCA will provide the primary statutory basis for discussion. Drafted by the American Bar Association in 1946 and substantially revised in 1969, the MBCA has widely influenced recent statutory revisions. Because it is a "model" statute, states are not discouraged from adopting it with modifications, as opposed to a "uniform" statute such as the UCC, which, in the interests of uniformity, is encouraged by its drafters to be adopted by the states in its completed form with only a few suggested alternative provisions. A major revision of the MBCA was set forth in 1983 by the Bar Association. It is entitled the "Revised Model Business Corporation Act" (RMBCA). It will be the primary statutory basis for discussion in this chapter and the two that follow.[1]

Federal Regulation of Corporations

State corporate codes are having diminishing effects on corporate management as various federal regulatory laws increasingly impact upon the corporation. Although there is no federal corporate code, there has been a tremendous upsurge of federal law affecting corporate activities in such areas as antitrust, labor-management relations, taxation, the securities markets, civil rights, and consumer protection. The Sherman Antitrust Act has been in existence since the late nineteenth century, but most federal regulation of corporations has occurred since 1933, when the

Securities Act was enacted as one response to the Great Depression. Taken together, these various federal regulatory laws constitute a federal corporation law.

Proposals for federal chartering of corporations date from the creation of the Republic. Federal chartering was advocated early in this century by Louis Brandeis in his book *Other Peoples' Money.* The main contemporary support for the proposal derives from those who most vocally criticize the social performance of corporations, the foremost of whom is Ralph Nader. In his book *Taming the Giant Corporation,* Nader argues that sweeping federal legislation is needed rather than piecemeal reforms of the existing regulatory framework in response to particular problems. Federal chartering proposals vary from proposals for the federal licensing of large corporations to a full-scale federal corporate code complete with an "employee bill of rights." The serious proponents of federal chartering so far have limited their proposals for the most part to large interstate corporations.

Taxation of Corporations

Unlike the partnership, which is merely a tax-reporting entity under the federal income tax law, the corporation is a taxpayer. It is required to file returns and pay income taxes in a manner similar to that required of individual taxpayers. This produces what is known as a "double tax effect"; income is taxed to the corporation as earned and taxed again to the shareholders when distributed.

An exception to this double-tax treatment is the Subchapter S corporation, which is not taxed. Subchapter S of the Internal Revenue Code allows certain corporations to elect special tax treatment and thereby avoid any income tax at the corporate level. As long as it remains qualified, the Subchapter S corporation may elect to pay virtually no federal income tax and have its income included in the personal incomes of its shareholders and taxed

directly to them. However, a Subchapter S corporation is heavily restricted as to the number and kind of shareholders. To qualify as a Subchapter S corporation, the corporation must (1) have only thirty-five or fewer individual shareholders, (2) limit its stock to a single class, and (3) obtain from every shareholder a written consent, which is filed with the Internal Revenue Service. Although there is a limit on the number of shareholders of a Subchapter S corporation, there is no limit on the size of corporate assets; even large corporations may qualify for Subchapter S treatment although the provisions of the tax law were designed to allow certain small businesses to be treated as tax conduits in which income flows through the corporation to the shareholders in much the same way as income to a partnership passes through it to the partners and is not taxed to the firm. Because shareholders of Subchapter S corporations must be individuals, partnerships and corporations are excluded from holding stock in such a corporation.

CORPORATE FORMATION

Modern incorporation procedures are not nearly as cumbersome and time-consuming as they were when incorporators had to shepherd special corporate charters through state legislatures. Today, thousands of corporations are formed each year without much intellectual effort on the part of the incorporators and without raising any significant legal issues.

Preincorporation Activity

Corporation formation starts with certain preincorporation activity on the part of those who are promoting the yet-to-be-formed corporation. Before the corporation is formally launched, contracts must sometimes be made, legal relations created, and business activities undertaken with a view to creation of the corporation. Preincorporation problems are not as common as they once were, because modern corporation laws making incorporation relatively easy have all but eliminated the need for much work to be done in advance of actual incorporation. The preincorporation problems that do arise result from the activities of promoters.

The Promoter.

A promoter is someone who undertakes to form a corporation. Corporations do not spring into existence spontaneously. They result from planning and preliminary work by promoters. It is the promoter who transforms an idea into a business. The promoter plans the development of a corporate business venture, brings together people who are interested in the projected enterprise, effectuates its organization and incorporation, and establishes the newly formed corporation as a fully functioning business. Although promoters are sometimes called "preincorporators," their activities often reach beyond the point of formal incorporation.

The promoter's efforts are largely devoted to making contracts on behalf of the proposed corporation. Sometimes these contracts are self-serving—for instance, when the promoter conveys property to the corporation in exchange for shares of the corporation's stock. Frequently, the contracts are with third persons for materials and services that are necessary to launch the enterprise. Problems arising from these promoter contracts involve: (1) the duties of promoters toward the unborn corporation; and (2) the contractual liabilities of both the promoter and the newborn corporation to third parties.

Promoter's Duties to the Corporation.

Since at the time of the promoter's activities no corporation is yet in being, the promoter is not the corporation's agent. No agency can be said to exist because there is no principal. Furthermore, someone cannot serve another as a self-appointed agent. Nevertheless, a promoter is under certain obligations.

Because they are joint venturers in forming the corporation, all promoters occupy a fiduciary relationship with any other co-promoters. Promoters also occupy a fiduciary relationship to the corporation they form. This fiduciary relationship casts upon the promoter an affirmative duty of full disclosure to the corporation regarding any dealings with the corporation in which the promoter has a personal interest and, further, a duty to enter any transactions with the corporation in good faith. Thus the promoter may not obtain any secret profits out of transactions with or on behalf of the corporation to be formed.

A typical case of promoter liability for failing to fully disclose material information to the corporation occurs when, after organizing the new corporation, the promoter sells to it his own property. If the promoter conveys property to the corporation, he or she must fully disclose any personal interest, the extent of any profit on the transaction, and any other material factors that might affect the corporation's decision whether to purchase. This disclosure must be made to either an independent board of directors, meaning a board that is not controlled by the promoter, or to all existing shareholders.

The usual case of promoter liability for failing to deal in good faith with the corporation is when "watered stock" has been issued to the promoter. The term "watered stock" refers to stock issued by a corporation in excess of any fair and adequate consideration received in exchange for it. This results in a diminution of the value of the stock held by other shareholders and further damages creditors of the corporation who may have relied on the belief that the corporation had received assets equivalent in value to the value of the issued shares. Stock watering occurs when promoters cause the overvaluation of their contribution to the corporation, resulting in the issuance of stock by the corporation for less than fair consideration. When there is stock watering, innocent shareholders whose stock has been devalued by the issuance of the watered stock may bring suit on behalf of the corporation to recover the lost value. Further, any injured creditors may force the promoter to pay to the corporation the unpaid value of the shares.

Preincorporation Contracts. A contract made by the promoter with a third party on behalf of the proposed corporation raises the question of whether the promoter, the corporation, or both are contractually liable. Generally, the promoter remains liable as a party to the contract unless relieved of the liability by the corporation. On the other hand, the corporation generally is not bound by the contract of the promoter until the corporation affirmatively assents to the contractual obligation.

The usual case of promoter liability on preincorporation contracts occurs when the proposed corporation never comes into existence or the corporation completely disavows the contract. In such a situation the other party to the contract will usually attempt to hold the promoter liable. Because the promoter acts for the corporation before its organization, under the general rules of agency law he or she is the principal on the contract. Under agency law, an agent for an undisclosed or, more aptly, a nonexistent principal becomes a party to any contracts made with third parties. Similarly, the promoter is held bound by his or her contracts. If this were not so, any agreement made by the promoter on behalf of the future corporation would be inoperative until after the corporation were formally organized, thereby depriving the third party of any remedy until that time. Personal liability for the promoters on preincorporation contracts is not unfair, since the promoter is in the best position to bring about incorporation and the adoption of the contract by the corporation. Thus it is only fair that the risk that the corporation may not be formed should be the promoter's and not the third party's, even if the third party is advised of the exact state of affairs.

Nevertheless, it is possible that those dealing with the promoter may be said to be looking to the corporation and not the promoter for performance of the contractual obligation. If the promoter clearly negates liability, the agreement is considered to be a continuing offer to the corporation rather than a contract. Thus, if the promoter specifically states that he or she is contracting in the name of the proposed corporation and not individually, the other party must rely entirely on the credit of the proposed corporation and has no claim against the promoter. This is simply a matter of recognizing the intention of the parties.

Generally, a corporation is not liable on a contract made by the promoter for its benefit unless it takes some affirmative action to adopt the contract when it formally comes into existence. Mere incorporation does not of itself render the promoter's contracts binding on the company; there must be some action by the corporation indicating its assent. This adoption may be by express words or writing or may be inferred from the corporation's knowingly accepting the contract's benefits. Thus adoption of the contract need not be express but may be implied. The rationale for this rule of corporation nonliability on preincorporation contracts, unless the circumstances indicate an intent to be bound, is to avoid any injustice to the corporation's shareholders and subsequent creditors that would result if the corporation were forced to come into existence burdened with the obligation to perform its promoters' promises. The case below illustrates this general rule of corporate nonliability with regard to promoters' contracts.

Solomon v. Cedar Acres East, Inc.

Supreme Court of Pennsylvania

317 A.2d 283(1974)

The plaintiff-appellant, Jerome Solomon, is an architect who sought specific perform-ance of a contract for architectural services against the corporate defendant-appellee, Cedar Acres East, Inc. The corporation joined Frank Millmond, promoter of the corporation, as an additional defendant. On August 3, 1966, the promoter signed an option to buy a fifty-two-acre tract of land for a corporation primarily controlled and owned by the promoter (this corporation is not the corporate defendant involved in this case). Soon thereafter, the promoter engaged the appellant, who did certain preliminary architectural work for the site during August, September, and October of 1966. The defendant corporation was not contemplated and was not in existence at that time.

On November 13, 1966, the promoter entered into an agreement with four other men for the creation of the defendant corporation. The agreement provided for the issuance of 100 percent of the stock of the proposed corporation. Two days later, on November 15, 1966, the appellant and the promoter entered into a contract whereby the appellant was to perform architectural services as required for the development of the tract of land. The appellant was to be a 5-percent owner of any corporation formed for the development of the tract, was to receive 5 percent of the profits of any corporation formed, and was to receive $50 for each one-family living unit erected on the tract. The agreement did not make any reference to the defendant corporation. The appellant performed additional services after the signing of his agree-ment, but performed no services after December 8, 1966.

On December 21, 1966, the promoter assigned to the defendant corporation the option to buy the fifty-two-acre tract.

On June 30, 1967, the appellant sent an itemized bill for architectural services to the defendant corporation stating "Amount due as of this invoice . . . $1,500." A second notice of the $1,500 billing was sent to the defendant corporation on August 10, 1967. A letter followed on December 7, 1967, in which the appellant requested payment of the $1,500 in "complete settlement." This letter referred to the terms of the agreement that the appellant had entered into with the promoter on November 15, 1966. This letter was the first notice that the defendant corporation had received concerning the appellant's agreement with the promoter. The defendant corporation refused to honor the agreement or to pay for the architectural services that had been rendered by the appellant at the promoter's request. The appellant then filed this equity action for specific performance requesting 5 percent of the stock in defendant corporation and damages. The trial court denied specific performance of the contract against both the corporate defendant and the promoter, but ordered the defendants to pay $2,000 in quantum meruit for architectural services. The architect, Solomon, appealed. Held. Reversed.

Manderino, Justice

We shall first discuss the issue raised concerning the corporate defendant. The trial court concluded that the corporate defendant was not bound by the contract entered into on November 15, 1966, between the appellant and the promoter. . . . The trial court did find, however, that the corporate defendant had received some benefit from the architectural services rendered by the appellant and, therefore, held that the corporate defendant was liable in quantum meruit.

The sole claim in this appeal, concerning the corporate defendant, is that the record does not support the trial court's conclusion that the corporate defendant did not ratify the November 15, 1966 agreement. The appellant admits that no express ratification ever occurred. He argues, however, that ratification can be inferred because the corporate defendant benefited from the use of architectural plans knowing that such plans were prepared by the appellant. The corporate defendant had no knowledge of the agreement or that it provided for the issuance of stock to the appellant and for profit sharing by the appellant. These material facts were unknown to anyone except the promoter and the appellant. Ratification of a contract by one not a party to the contract requires that the ratifying party be in possession of all the material facts and act with such knowledge . . . The only shareholder of the corporate defendant who had knowledge of all of the material facts concerning the November 15, 1966 agreement was the promoter. His knowledge, however, cannot be imputed to the corporate defendant. Knowledge possessed by a single promoter having only a minority interest cannot bind the corporate defendant.

In this case, the promoter was not a majority stockholder. His stock interest was only twenty-five per cent. In *Beltz v. Garrison,* cited by the appellant, a ratification was inferred because the corporation received benefits from a contract signed by four persons who, after the signing of the contract, became members of the corporation's board of directors and constituted eighty per cent of the directors and owned all of the stock of the corporation. *Beltz* is of no help to the appellant.

The other issue raised by the appellant concerns the promoter defendant. Although the trial court found that the promoter had entered into the November 15, 1966 agreement with the appellant, the trial court did not award damages based on that agreement. Instead, the trial court awarded damages only in quantum meruit. The trial court further granted to the appellant, "without prejudice, the right to pursue any claim he may have with regard to these shares or compensation therefrom against [the promoter] in a separate proceeding."

Appellant contends that the trial court erred in its refusal to allow full recovery against the promoter. We agree. The trial court concluded that the appellant and the promoter entered into an agreement on November 15, 1966. That conclusion was fully supported by the record. In fact, the promoter admitted that he entered into that agreement with the appellant and said that it was a personal contract. Under these circumstances, the trial court should have determined the amount of damages to which the appellant was entitled under the agreement. . . . Complete relief should have thus been given to the appellant against the promoter in the same manner as though the promoter had been the original defendant.

Since the promoter was no longer a shareholder in the corporate defendant, the trial court could not direct specific performance. Full recovery, however, could have been awarded in the form of money damages. Although such recovery is a legal remedy rather than an equitable remedy, such relief would have been proper. Once equity has assumed jurisdiction of an action, money damages may be awarded to insure a just result. . . . There is no reason why this dispute should not be settled in the present action.

Held. Reversed.

Incorporation Procedure

The modern mechanics of incorporation are much more streamlined than they once were. However, because corporate existence continues to be a privilege conferred by the state, the proper papers must be filed and certain formalities attended to in order to bring about incorporation. Business people will continue to require the assistance of an attorney during this process.

The first step taken in incorporating a business is the selection of the state of incorporation. Once that has been decided, the incorporators must prepare and file the articles of incorporation, along with any fees and taxes, with the secretary of state. If all is in order, the secretary issues a certificate of incorporation, sometimes called the corporate charter. After the issuance of the certificate, an organizational meeting must be held to adopt the corporate bylaws, elect officers, and transact any initial corporate business.

Selecting the State of Incorporation. After determining to incorporate, the first decision to be made is where to incorporate. Most small corporations usually incorporate in the state where they are to be located. If the business is of an interstate nature, consideration is sometimes given to other states if the local state corporation and tax laws have restrictions. Delaware is often the first state considered because the climate of opinion prevalent in its legislature and courts is generally favorable to

corporate management and unfavorable to dissident minority shareholders. Delaware's corporation statute is considered "liberal" because of its flexibility, which enables management to conduct corporate business with few restrictions.

Delaware is not the only state that may be attractive to incorporators. Although early state corporation codes were hostile to the corporation, states later encouraged corporations by enacting unrestrictive legislation. New Jersey and New York competed with Delaware by offering "liberal" corporation codes. Today, many corporations are incorporated in these states even though their principal places of business are elsewhere. Thus the official state residences of many Delaware corporations are mailboxes. This practice has led to the characterization of some state corporation laws as "for export only." On the other hand, California has a corporate code that attempts to limit the discretion of corporate management.

One disadvantage of out-of-state incorporation is that the corporation will incur double taxation in the form of a franchise tax for doing business in the state where its business is done. Out-of-state incorporation also subjects the corporation to liability for suits in a jurisdiction removed from its principal place of business. Furthermore, in the event of litigation, there may be an issue of which state's law applies. The general rule is that the law of the incorporating state will be applied to issues relating to the internal affairs of the corporation. However, there is a trend toward making this determination on the basis of whether the state of incorporation has an interest in having its law applied.

Articles of Incorporation. After the state of incorporation is selected, the incorporators must prepare and file the articles of incorporation, which are to be submitted, along with any fees, to the secretary of state (RMBCA Section 2.03). Among the items to be included in the articles is the corporation's name (RMBCA Section 2.02). This name must include the word "corporation," "company," "incorporated," or "limited" or an abbreviation of one of those words. The RMBCA prohibits using any word or phrase that indicates that the corporation is organized for any purpose other than the one stated in its articles. It requires a corporate name to be distinguishable upon the records of the secretary of state from that of other corporations authorized to transact business (RMBCA Section 4.01). If a name is available, the RMBCA permits incorporators to apply to the secretary of state in advance to reserve the name for 120 days while the corporation is being organized (Section 4.02).

Additional information regarding the corporation's capital structure must also be provided, such as the number and classes of authorized shares (RMBCA Section 2.02). Although many states require a minimum stated capital for starting the business (usually $1,000), the RMBCA does not.

The articles must also state the name and address of the corporation's initial registered agent and initial office and the names and addresses of all incorporators (RMBCA Section 2.02). Although many states still require that there be three incorporators and three directors, the RMBCA permits the corporation to have only one incorporator and one director, thus enabling sole proprietors to incorporate their businesses without needlessly involving others (Sections 2.01 and 8.03).

Organizational Meeting. After issuance of the certificate of incorporation by the secretary of state, an organizational meeting of the board of directors must be held for the purpose of adopting the bylaws, electing officers, and transacting initial corporate business, such as the adoption of any preincorporation contracts (RMBCA Section 2.05). The corporate bylaws provide private legislation for the regulation and management of corporate affairs and must not be inconsistent with the articles or state law (RMBCA Section 2.06). Unless the articles provide otherwise, adoption of the initial bylaws as well as any later amendments rests with the board of directors. Many states permit shareholder adoption and amendment of the bylaws.

Incomplete Incorporation

Problems may arise when there has been some defect in the incorporation process, such as a failure by one of the incorporators to sign the articles or a failure to provide sufficient information in the articles as required by statute. Streamlined incorporation procedures make this less of a problem. However, when it does occur, it raises the possibility of personal liability for the shareholders. Because the consequences of failing to comply with the technical requirement of incorporation are potentially so dire, three mitigating doctrines have been developed by the courts to shield shareholders from being treated as partners. These doctrines are: (1) de jure incorporation; (2) de facto incorporation; and (3) corporation by estoppel.

De Jure Incorporation. In construing the requirements of incorporation statutes, courts have generally held that no useful purpose will be served by a strict technical interpretation that converts every detailed requirement into a prerequisite of corporate existence. Thus, if there has been substantial compliance with the provisions of a statute authorizing the formation of a corporation—that is, if the noncompliance is slight—a "de jure" corporation results. A de jure corporation is recognized as a corporation for all purposes and as to all parties, including the state of incorporation. No one, not even the state, may challenge the organization's corporate status, notwithstanding a technical noncompliance with the incorporation procedures.

To obtain de jure status, there must be literal compliance with all mandatory requirements of incorporation and substantial compliance with all directive requirements. What constitutes a mandatory as opposed to a directive requirement is a matter of statutory construction and depends upon the nature of the incorporation defect. Requirements that are merely formalities, such as the requirement that a seal be affixed on the articles, are considered directive only. Their absence is not sufficient to defeat corporate existence. However, the more important a requirement is, the more likely it will be considered a mandatory requirement. Thus the requirement that the articles be filed would be mandatory; failure to file the articles could not result in de jure corporate status.

De Facto Incorporation. Where there are significant defects in the incorporation to prevent a de jure existence, courts may nevertheless recognize the organization as a de facto corporation. In the case of a de facto corporation, third persons cannot take advantage of the defects to charge the shareholders with unlimited liability or to avoid contracts with them. The state, however, can maintain proceedings to attack the corporate existence directly to have its charter revoked. This is because the defect is significant enough that the law cannot ignore it, and the state is permitted to take any necessary steps to remedy the situation. Thus, whereas a de jure corporation cannot be challenged by anyone, a de facto corporation can be challenged by the state.

Generally, a de facto corporation results if

there is a law in the state under which a corporation might be formed, there has been a colorable or apparent attempt in good faith to incorporate under such law, and the organization has conducted business as a corporation. An example of de facto corporate existence might be when articles are drafted in due form and turned over to an attorney who neglects to file them through no fault of the incorporators. Although there is not sufficient compliance for de jure existence, the de facto corporate status thus achieved will nevertheless shield the shareholders from personal liability to third parties.

The statutory trend is to eliminate the de facto doctrine because it is believed that modern incorporation statutes are sufficiently streamlined to justify stricter compliance than the doctrine requires. Further, it is believed that the continued viability of the de facto doctrine at a time when it is not needed only encourages noncompliance with incorporation procedures. Thus the RMBCA has eliminated the doctrine (Section 2.03).

Incorporation by Estoppel. Where a third person deals with a defectively organized corporation as if it were in fact incorporated, he or she may be estopped to challenge the corporate status of the organization upon later learning of the defective incorporation. It is generally considered to be unfair to allow the third party to hold the shareholders personally liable when he or she originally dealt with the organization as though it were a corporation, knowing that a corporation is an entity of limited liability. However, unlike the de facto doctrine, which recognizes a corporate status as to all third parties, the estoppel theory recognizes the corpoation only for the particular third-party transaction. The case below illustrates a court's use of de facto and estoppel theories of incorporation, as well as the RMBCA's most recent statements as to when de jure incorporation takes place.

Timberline Equipment Co., Inc. v. Davenport

Supreme Court of Oregon

514 P.2d 1109(1973)

Plaintiff-appellee brought this complaint to recover rentals on equipment leased to defendant-appellant, Bennett and others. In addition to making general denial, Bennett alleged as a defense that the rentals were to a de facto corporation, Aero-Fabb Corp., of which Bennett was an incorporator, director, and shareholder. He also alleged that plaintiff was estopped from denying the corporate character of the organization to whom plaintiff rented the equipment.

On January 22, 1970, Bennett signed articles of incorporation for Aero-Fabb Co. The original articles were not in accord with the statutes and, therefore, no certificate of incorporation was issued for the corporation until June 12, 1970, after new articles were filed. The leases were entered into and rentals earned during the period between January 22 and June 12. The lower court ruled in favor of the plaintiff. Bennett appealed. Held. Affirmed.

Denecke, Justice.

Prior to 1953 Oregon had adopted the common-law doctrine that prohibited a collateral attack on the legality of a defectively organized corporation which had achieved the status of a de facto corporation.

In 1953 the legislature adopted the Oregon Business Corporation act. Oregon Laws 1953, ch. 549. The Model Business Corporation Act was used as a working model for the Oregon Act.

ORS 57.321 of the Oregon Business Corporation Act provides:

> Upon the issuance of the certificate of incorporation, the corporate existence shall begin, and such certificate of incorporation shall be conclusive evidence that all conditions precedent required to be performed by the incorporators have been complied with and that the corporation has been incorporated under the Oregon Business Corporation Act, except as against that state in a proceeding to cancel or revoke the certificate of incorporation or for involuntary dissolution of the corporation.

This selection is virtually identical to § 56 of the Model Act. The Comment to the Model, prepared as a research project by the American Bar Foundation and edited by the American Bar Association Committee on Corporate Laws, states:

> "Under the Model Act, de jure incorporation is complete upon the issuance of the certificate of incorporation, except as against the state in certain proceedings challenging the corporate existence. In this respect, the Model Act provisions are the same as those in many states, although in a number of them some further action is required before the corporation has legal existence, such as local filing or recording or publication."
>
> "Under the unequivocal provisions of the Model Act, any steps short of

securing a certificate of incorporation would not constitute apparent compliance. Therefore a de facto corporation cannot exist under the Model Act."

"Like provisions are made throughout the Model Act in respect of the conclusiveness of the issuance by the secretary of state of the appropriate certificate in connection with filings made in his office. . . .

"In some states, however, issuance of the certificate of incorporation and compliance with any additional requirements for filing, recording or publication is not conclusive evidence of incorporation.

"In those states, such action is stated to be only prima facie evidence of incorporation, and in others the effect is merely one of estoppel preventing any question of due incorporation being raised in legal actions by or against the corporation." Model Business Corporation Act annotated § 56, p. 305 (2nd ed. 1971).

ORS 57.793 provides:

"All persons who assume to act as a corporation without the authority of a certificate of incorporation issued by the Corporation Commissioner, shall be jointly and severally liable for all debts and liabilities incurred or arising as a result therof."

This is merely an elaboration of § 146 of the Model Act. The Comment states:

"This section is designed to prohibit the application of any theory of de facto incorporation. The only authority to act as a corporation under the Model Act arises from completion of the procedures prescribed in sections 53 to 55 inclusive. The consequences of those procedures are specified in section 56 as being the creation of a corporation. No other means being authorized, the effect of section 146 is to negate the possibility of a de facto corporation.

"Abolition of the concept of de facto incorporation, which at best was fuzzy, is a sound result. No reason exists for its continuance under general corporate laws, where the process of acquiring de jure incorporation is both simple and clear. The vestigial appendate should be removed." 2 Model Business Corporation Act Annoted § 146, pp. 908–909 (2nd ed. 1971)

We hold the principle of defacto corporation no longer exists in Oregon.

The defendant also contends that the plaintiff is estopped to deny that it contracted with a corporation. . . . Corporation by estoppel is a difficult concept to grasp and courts and writers have "gone all over the lot" in attempting to define and apply the doctrine. One of the better explanations of the problem and the varied solutions is contained in Ballentine, Manual of Corporation Law and Practice §§§§28–30 (193):

"The so-called estoppel that arises to deny corporate capacity does not depend on the presence of the technical elements of equitable estoppel, viz. misrepresentations and change of position in reliance thereon, but on the nature of the relations contemplated, that one who has recognized the organization as a corporation in business dealings should not be allowed to quibble or raise immaterial issues on matters which do not concern him in the slightest degree or affect his substantial rights." Ballentine, supra, at 92.

We need not decide whether the doctrine of corporation by estoppel would apply in such a case as this. The trial court found that if this doctrine was still available under the Business Corporation Act defendants did not prove all the elements necessary for its application, and, moreover, it would be inequitable to apply the doctrine.

Under the explanation stated above for the application of the doctrine of estoppel in this kind of case, it is necessary that the plaintiff believe that it was contracting with a corporate entity. The evidence on this point is contradictory and the trial court apparently found against defendants.

A final question remains: Can the plaintiff recover against Dr. Bennett individually?

In the first third of this century the liability of persons associated with defectively organized corporations was a controversial and well-documented legal issue. The orthodox view was that if an organization had not achieved de facto status and the plaintiff was not estopped to attack the validity of the corporate status of the corporation, all shareholders were liable as partners. This court, however, rejected the orthodox rule. In *Rutherford* v. *Hill* we held that a person could not be held liable as a partner merely because he signed the articles of incorporation though the corporation was so defectively formed as to fall short of de facto status. The court stated that under this rule a mere passive stockholder would not be held liable as a partner. We went on to observe, however, that if the party actively participated in the business he might be held liable as a partner.

This controversy subsided 30 or 40 years ago probably because the procedure to achieve de jure corporate status was made simpler; so the problem did not arise.

The Model Act and the Oregon Business Corporation Act, ORS 57.793, solve the problem as follows:

> "All persons who assume to act as a corporation without the authority of a certificate of incorporation issued by the Corporation Commissioner, shall be jointly and severally liable for all debts and liabilities incurred or arising as a result thereof."

We have found no decisions, comments to the Model Act, or literature attempting to explain the intent of this section.

We find the language ambiguous. Liability is imposed on "[a]ll persons who assume to act as a corporation." Such persons shall be liable "for all debts and liabilities incurred or arising as a result thereof."

We are of the opinion that the phrase, "persons who assume to act as a corporation" should be interpreted to include those persons who have an investment in the organization and who actively participate in the policy and operational decisions of the organization. Liability should not necessarily be restricted to the person who personally incurred the obligation.

The trial court found that Dr. Bennett "acted in the business venture which was subsequently incorporated on June 12, 1970."

The proposed business of the corporation which was to be formed was to sell airplanes, recondition airplanes and give flying lessons. Land was leased for this purpose. Equipment was rented from plaintiff to level and clear for access and for other construction.

There is evidence from which the trial court could have found that while Drs. Bennett and Gorman, another defendant, entrusted the details of management to Davenport, they endeavored to and did retain some control over his management. All checks required one of their signatures. Dr. Bennett frequently visited the site and observed the activity and the presence of the equipment rented by plaintiff. He met with the organization's employees to discuss the operation of the business. Shortly after the equipment was rented and before most of the rent had accrued, Dr. Bennett was informed of the rentals and given an opinion that they were unnecessary and ill-advised. Drs. Bennett and Gorman thought they had Davenport and his management "under control."

This evidence all supports the finding that Dr. Bennett was a person who assumed to act for the organization and the conclusion of the trial court that Dr. Bennett is personally liable.

Held. Affirmed.

DISREGARDING CORPORATE PERSONALITY

Once incorporation is complete, shareholders reasonably expect to be insulated from liability for the corporation's debts. One of the main purposes of incorporating is to enable the stockholders to engage in a business without incurring any personal liability beyond the loss of their investments. However, if the recognition of the corporate entity will result in some injustice, such as defrauding creditors, evading statutory obligations, or defeating the interest of the public, the corporate entity will be disregarded. In such a case, personal liability will be imposed on the stockholders.

The rapid growth of closely held corporations and diversified corporate organization consisting of a single parent and several subsidiaries has compelled the courts recently to re-examine the entity status of some corporations. Like most statutes, the RMBCA confers liability on the corporation for corporate debts (Section 3.02). As a legal entity, the corporation normally bears sole liability for debts

created in its name. However, limited liability protection is a privilege granted to shareholders for the convenience of conducting business in the corporate form. It is a privilege that must be used to promote decent and fair objectives. The corporate entity will be disregarded, resulting in a loss of limited liability, when the privilege is abused. Shareholders will be held personally liable for corporate debts when such a solution is necessary to avoid an injustice.

Courts have used colorful language in holding shareholders liable. The most common phrase is "piercing the corporate veil," meaning that the corporate entity, which is normally an effective veil shielding shareholders from liability on corporate debts, will be "pierced" to reach the shareholders and hold them liable. Another phrase frequently found is that the corporate entity is merely the "alter ego" or "instrumentality" of the shareholder, meaning that there is in reality no distinction between the corporation's and the shareholder's legal personalities. Stripped of this verbiage, and irrespective of any enunciated formulas, the end result is that shareholder liability will be imposed to reach an equitable result.

The question of the status of a corporation often arises when a liability has been incurred in the name of the corporation but the corporation has become insolvent. The creditor, seeking to find a solvent defendant, may sue all or some of the shareholders, arguing that for some reason they should be called upon to pay the corporation's debts. The issue presented is whether the loss should be imposed on third persons or shareholders. A blind application of the entity approach would mean that the creditor inevitably suffers the loss. In most cases this is a reasonable result since the creditor extended credit to a corporation, which he or she should realize is a creature of limited liability. However, this result often does not occur when it would be unjust to the creditor. This is more likely to be true in cases of involuntary creditors, such as tort victims. Creditors who made contracts with the corporation have greater difficulty in obtaining shareholder liability because they presumably dealt with the corporation voluntarily and should have known whether the corporation lacked substance.

Significant considerations in deciding whether to disregard the corporate entity are whether there has been a lack of observance of corporate formalities resulting in a commingling of shareholder and corporate assets and whether there has been inadequate capitalization of the corporation. When control by the stockholders or a parent corporation is carried out in a normal manner, with due regard for all necessary formalities and for the rights of creditors, separate entity status will normally be sustained. However, when the corporation is totally without any voice in its own affairs, when there is a manipulation of the assets of the corporation and the shareholders, and when corporate and personal activities are so intertwined that no separation is discernible, then the courts will look behind the façade and consider the identities as one. In doing this, the courts sometimes say that the corporate entity is merely a "sham" or a mere shadow of the shareholder's personality. Closely held and parent-subsidiary corporations are particularly vulnerable to this attack because frequently close corporations fail to follow the formalities of corporate existence and parent-subsidiaries often share the same directors. Undercapitalized corporations are also targets for "piercing" litigation, because a grossly undercapitalized corporation may be considered a fraud upon creditors. The case below illustrates this point.

DeWitt Truck Brokers, Inc. v. W. Ray Flemming Fruit Company

U.S. Court of Appeals, Fourth Circuit

540 F. 2d 681 (1976)

DeWitt Trucking Company (plaintiff) seeks to recover transportation charges from Flemming (defendant), who is the president of a fruit company for which plaintiff hauled produce. The plaintiff seeks to pierce the corporate veil and hold defendant personally liable. Flemming owned approximately 90 percent of the corporation's stock. It began in 1962 with a capitalization of 5,000 shares issued for a consideration of $1 each. Approximately 2,000 shares were retired. The corporation has one director other than Flemming. The corporation engaged in the business of a commission agent selling fruit for growers in the South Carolina area. It would additionally arrange for and pay the transportation from the grower's warehouse to the purchaser. The failure to pay such charges owed to the plaintiff led to this suit. The District Court ruled in favor of the plaintiff. The defendant appealed. Held. Affirmed.

Russell, Donald

At the outset, it is recognized that a corporation is an entity, separate and distinct from its officers and stockholders, and that its debts are not the individual indebtedness of its stockholders. This is expressed in the presumption that the corporation and its stockholders are separate and distinct. . . . And this oft-stated principle is equally applicable, whether the corporation has many or only one stockholder. But this concept of separate entity is merely a legal theory, "introduced for purposes of convenience and to subserve the ends of justice," and the courts "decline to recognize [it] whenever recognition of the corporate form would extend the principle of incorporation 'beyond its legitimate purposes and [could] produce injustices or inequitable consequences.' " *Krivo Industrial Supp. Co.* v. *National Distill. & Chem. Corp.* Accordingly, "in an appropriate case and in furtherance of the ends of justice," the corporate veil will be pierced and the corporation and its stockholders "will be treated as identifiable."

The circumstances which have been considered significant by the courts in actions to disregard the corporate fiction have been "rarely articulated with any clarity." Perhaps this is true because the circumstances "necessarily vary according to the circumstances of each case," and every case where the issue is raised is to be regarded as *"sui generis* [to] . . . be decided in accordance with its own underlying facts."

Contrary to the basic contention of the defendant, however, proof of plain fraud is not a necessary element in a finding to disregard the corporate entity. This was made clear in *Anderson* v. *Abbott* where the Court, after stating that "fraud" has often been found to be a ground for disregarding the principle of limited liability based on the corporate fiction, declared:

". . . The cases of fraud make up part of that exception [which allow the corporate veil to be pierced, citing cases]. *But they do not exhaust it.* An obvious inadequacy of capital, measured by the nature and magnitude of the corporate undertaking, has frequently been an important factor in cases denying stockholders their defenses of limited liability."

On the other hand, equally as well settled as is the principle that plain fraud is not a necessary prerequisite for piercing the corporate veil is the rule that the mere fact that all or almost all of the corporate stock is owned by one individual, or a few individuals, will not afford sufficient grounds for disregarding corporateness. But when substantial ownership of all the stock of a corporation in a single individual is combined with other factors clearly supporting disregard of the corporate fiction on grounds of fundamental equity and fairness, courts have experienced "little difficulty" and have shown no hesitancy in applying what is described as the "alter ego" or "instrumentality" theory in order to cast aside the corporate shield and to fasten liability on the individual stockholder.

But, in applying the "instrumentality" or "alter ego" doctrine, the courts are concerned with reality and not form, with how the corporation operated and the individual defendant's relationship to that operation. . . . And the authorities have indicated certain facts which are to be given substantial weight in this connection. One fact which all the authorities consider significant in the inquiry, and particularly so in the case of the one-man or close-held corporation is whether the corporation was grossly undercapitalized for the purposes of the corporate undertaking. . . . Other factors that are emphasized in the application of the doctrine are failure to observe corporate formalities, nonpayment of dividends, the insolvency of the debtor corporation at the time, siphoning of funds of the corporation by the dominant stockholder, nonfunctioning of other officers or directors, absence of corporate records, and the fact that the corporation is merley a façade for the operations of the dominant stockholder or stockholders. The conclusion to disregard the corporate entity may not, however, rest on a single factor, whether undercapitalization, disregard of corporation's formalities, or what-not, but must involve a number of such factors; in addition, it must present an element of injustice or fundamental unfairness. But undercapitalization, coupled with disregard of corporate formalities, lack of participation on the part of the other stockholders, and the falure to pay dividends while paying substantial sums, whether by way of salary or otherwise, to the dominant stockholder, all fitting into a picture of basic unfairness, has been regarded fairly uniformly to constitute a basis for an imposition of individual liability under the doctrine.

If these factors, which were deemed significant in other cases concerned with this same issue, are given consideration here, the finding of the District Court that the corporate entity should be disregarded was not clearly erroneous. Certainly the corporation was, in practice at least, a close, one-man corporation from the very beginning. Its incorporators were the defendant Flemming, his wife and his attorney. It began in 1962 with a capitalization of 5,000 shares, issued for a consideration of one dollar each. In some manner which Flemming never made entirely clear, approximately 2,000 shares were retired. At the times involved here, Flemming owned approximately 90% of the corporation's outstanding stock, according to his own testimony, though this was not verified by any stock records. Flemming was obscure on who the other stockholders were and how much stock these other stockholders owned, giving at different times conflicting statements as to who owned stock and how much. His testimony on who were the officers and directors was hardly more direct. He testified that the corporation did have one other director, Ed Bernstein, a resident of New York. It is significant, however, that whether Bernstein was nominally a director or not, there were no corporate records of a real directors' meeting in all the years of the corporation's existence and Flemming conceded this to be true. Flemming countered this by testifying that Bernstein traveled a great deal and that his contacts with Bernstein were generally by telephone. The evidence indicates rather clearly that Bernstein was, like the directors in *G. M. Leasing,* "nothing more than [a] figurehead[s]," who had "attended no directors meeting," and even more crucial, never received any fee or reimbursement of expenses or salary of any kind from the corporation.

The District Court found, also, that the corporation never had a stockholders' meeting. . . . It is thus clear that corporate formalities, even rudimentary formalities, were not observed by the defendant.

Beyond the absence of any observance of corporate formalities is the purely personal manner in which the corporation was operated. No stockholder or officer of the corporation other than Flemming ever received any salary, dividend, or fee from the corporation, or, for that matter, apparently exercised any voice in its operation or decisions. In all the years of the corporation's existence, Flemming was the sole beneficiary of its operations, and its continued existence was for his exclusive benefit. During these years he was receiving from $15,000 to $25,000 each year from a corporation, which, during most of the time, was showing no profit and apparently had no working capital. Moreover, the payments to Flemming were authorized under no resolution of the board of directors of the corporation, as recorded in any minutes of a board meeting. Actually, it would seem that Flemming's withdrawals varied with what could be taken out of the corporation at the moment: If this amount were $15,000, that was Flemming's withdrawal; if it were $25,000, that was his withdrawal.

Under the arrangement with the drawers, it was to remit to the grower the full sale price, less any transportation costs incurred in transporting the products from the growers' farm or warehouse to the purchaser and its sales commission. An integral part of these collections was represented by the plaintiff's transportation charges. Accordingly, during the period involved here, the corporation had as operating funds seemingly only its commissions and the amount of the plaintiff's transportation charges, for which the corporation had claimed credit in its settlement with its growers. At the time, however, Flemming was withdrawing funds from the corproation at the rate of at least $15,000 per year; and doing this, even though he must have known that the corporation could only do this by withholding payment of the transportation charges due the plaintiff, which in the accounting with the growers Flemming represented had been paid the plaintiff. And, it is of some interest that the amount due the plaintiff for transportation costs was approximately the same as the $15,000 minimum annual salary the defendant testified he was paid by the corporation. Were the opinion of the District Court herein to be reversed, Flemming would be permitted to retain substantial sums from the operations of the corporation without having any real capital in the undertaking, risking nothing of his own and using as operating capital what he had collected as due to the plaintiff.

Finally, . . . Flemming stated to the plaintiff, according to the latter's testimony as credit by the District Court, that "he (i.e., Flemming) would take care of [the charges] personally, if the corporation failed to do so. . . ." When one, who is the sole beneficiary of a corporation's operations and who dominates it, as did Flemming in this case, induces a creditor to extend credit to the corporation such an assurance as given here, that fact has been considered by many authorities sufficient basis for piercing the corporate veil.

Held. Affirmed.

REVIEW PROBLEMS

1. Triplett, his partner, and their secretary acted as incorporators and signed articles of incorporation for Air Capital International, Inc. None served as officers or directors of

the corporation. Air Capital violated two then-existing sections of the Kansas Corporation statute. The statute provided that articles of incorporation had to be filed with the secretary of state and the registrar of deeds in the county where the corporation's office was located. Air Capital's articles of incorporation were filed with the secretary of state but not with the county registrar of deeds, thus it never became a legally existing corporation. A second section of the Kansas statute provided that a corporation cannot do business until it legally existed. Air Capital did not meet this requirement before it began doing business in 1967. Air Capital, Inc., declared bankruptcy in 1971. The State of Kansas brought action against Triplett, his partner, and their secretary to recover employment taxes due. What result? State ex rel. Carlton v. Triplett, 517 P. 2d 135 (Kan. 1973)

2. The Illinois incorporation statute provided that persons desiring to form a corporation in that state must "sign, send and acknowledge" the articles of incorproation before a notary public. Edward Ford and Andrew Fisher signed and filed articles of incorporation with the secretary of state, but failed to affix any seal to the document. Later, the Illinois attorney general brought legal proceedings against the two men, claiming that they were doing business under an illegal corporate certificate and attempting to revoke the corporate status. What result? People v. Ford, 294 Ill. 391(1920)

3. Carlton owned the stock of ten taxi corporations, each owning two cabs and carrying the minimum insurance required by state law. Walkovsky was injured in an accident as a result of the negligence of one of the drivers of the cabs. Can Walkovszky successfully sue Carlton and hold him personally liable for his injuries, or must he satisfy any claim he has against the assets of the particular two-cab corporation involved in the accident? Walkovszky v. Carlton, 18 NY 2d.414(1966)

4. Seller entered into a contract for the sale of plants to the "Denver Memorial Nursery, Inc." The contract was signed by John Parr as Denver's president. Seller knew that the corporation was not yet formed and the contract recited this fact, but Seller insisted that the contract be executed this way rather than wait until the corporation was organized. The corporation was never formed. Seller sued John Parr to hold him personally liable on the contract. What result? Quaker Hill v. Parr, 148 Colo. 45(1961)

5. A, B, and C signed articles of incorporation in New Jersey whereby the corporation was to engage in the trucking business. Before filing the articles with the secretary of state, one of the association's trucks injured Frawley. At the time of the accident was the company a corporation and liable on that basis, or is there individual liability? Frawley v. Tenafly Transport Co., 95 N.J. Law 405(1921)

6. A suffered an on-the-job injury. She sued the Heritage Building Company to recover workmen's compensation benefits at a time when the company's liabilities exceeded its debts. Shortly after she sued all the company's assets were transferred to B, the president and sole stockholder, in consideration of the company's indebtedness to him. He, in turn, on the same day transferred these assets to another of his corporations, Heritage Corporation. A won a judgment against Heritage Building Company but the company had no assets from which to satisfy a judgment. A then filed a suit against B and the Heritage Corporation. What result? Will B be held personally liable? Tigrett v. Pointer, 580 W 2d 375(1979)

FOOTNOTE

[1]The 1969 Model Business Corporation Act has undergone a major revision and has been tentatively adopted by the Committee on Corporate Law of the Section of Corporation, Banking and Business Law of the American Bar Association as of this writing. It has been set forth for comments as the Revised Model Business Corporation Act of 1983. The final version will be published as part of the Model Business Corporation Act Annotated (Third Edition). See Goldstein and Hamilton, *The Revised Model Business Corporation Act,* 38 *Business Lawyer* 1019 (1983) for an explanation of the work of the Committee and the changes brought about by this major work. Excerpts are reprinted in the Appendix of this text. The authors acknowledge here the assistance of the American Bar Foundation and the Committee on Corporate Law.

CHAPTER 29

Financing the Corporation

KINDS OF SECURITIES ⎯⎯⎯⎯⎯⎯⎯⎯⎯⎯⎯⎯⎯⎯⎯

STOCK SUBSCRIPTIONS ⎯⎯⎯⎯⎯⎯⎯⎯⎯⎯⎯⎯⎯

I n most states, before a corporation can begin conducting business it must have money to finance its operations. Financing, or capitalizing, a corporation is the process of assembling funds in exchange for issued shares of stock. These funds are collectively called the corporation's capital. Although capitalization is an accounting term, it is used by courts to refer to the financing of the corporate enterprise. In addition to funds raised from issued shares, courts often consider loans to a corporation from its shareholders, or even accumulated earnings not withdrawn from the corporation, as capital. The reader should be aware of the imprecise use of this term.

Financing may occur initially during the launching of the corporation, or it may occur later when the corporation needs more capital for expansion, for resuscitation, or for operation. The process has two components: (1) short-term financing and (2) long-term financing. Short-term funds are assembled largely by use of promissory notes and mortgages. The common source is the commercial bank, which will extend lines of credit. Long-term funds are raised by the selling of securities (stocks and bonds). If the financing is public, the securities are sold in the formal capital market.

This chapter focuses primarily on the legal problems involved in the assembling of long-term funds. The material falls roughly into three parts: (1) the kinds of securities and their provisions, (2) the method of acquiring initial capital through subscription contracts, and (3) the method of acquiring capital following incorporation.

KINDS OF SECURITIES

The sale of securities is the usual method of corporate financing. Most financing comes from investors who receive securities in return for their investments. The security is usually represented by a certificate, such as a share of stock or a bond, that evidences the security holder's rights in the corporate business. However, a security need not necessarily involve this type of formal paper. The two main types of securities are: (1) debt securities and (2) equity securities.

Debt Securities

The Revised Model Business Corporation Act authorizes corporations to borrow money, incur liabilities, and issue bonds (Section 3.-02[8]); none of these expedients needs shareholder approval (Section 12.01). The funds generated by this borrowing must be used only for corporate purposes. Debt securities evidence a debt of the corporation and become corporate liabilities.

Types of Debt Securities. Debt securities include *notes, debentures,* and *bonds.* Notes usually represent short-term borrowing of the corporation. They are payable upon order to a bank or person. Interest payments are due periodically. Debentures are unsecured corporate obligations backed by the general credit of the corporation and its assets. If the corporation defaults, creditors will attempt to seize the assets. A bond (used interchangeably with debentures) is usually a long-term debt security secured by a lien or mortgage on corporate property. Bonds are bearer instruments. Interest payments are made periodically upon submission of coupons by the bondholders.

Debt securities have two important characteristics. They are subject to *redemption* and *conversion.* Redemption means the corporation reserves the right to call in and pay off its obligations at any time before they are due, usually at a premium over face value. Debt securities may also be convertible—that is, they may be converted into equity securities (e.g., common stock) at a certain ratio.

Tax Advantages of Debt Securities. Debt securities offer significant tax advantages for the corporation that issues them. Interest payments on bonds or notes are tax deductible for the corporation, while dividend payments on equity securities (such as common stock) are not. Payments of a debt by a corporation may be considered a nontaxable return on capital for the investor, while a redemption of equity securities from a shareholder by the corporation may be taxed as ordinary income. The Internal Revenue Service (IRS) has often investigated corporations' debt structures to determine if they are excessive. If the IRS finds that a debt structure is excessive, it attempts to treat the excessive debt as a form of corporate equity for tax purposes. Thus the substantial advantages associated with corporate debt financing has led to considerable litigation. Because the courts have treated each situation as unique, no overriding legal principle has evolved to determine when a corporation's debt is excessive. Courts have considered the ratio of debt to equity as relevant but have rejected a purely quantitative approach.

Equity Securities

Every business corporation must issue equity securities, usually called shares or stock. Stockholders (shareholders) own the corporation. Authorization for the issuance of equity is contained in the corporation's articles of incorporation. Unless authorized, the sale of shares is void.

The money raised by the corporation from the sale of stock is the fund out of which the corporation may meet its obligations to creditors; it represents the corporation's stated capital. The corporation is not bound to return to the shareholders their investment before liquidation of the enterprise. The shares usually have no maturity date. Return on the shareholders' investment takes two forms: dividends, which are dependent upon the availability of profits and the discretion of the board of directors; and capital gains, which result from the shareholders' ability to sell their stock for a higher price than was originally paid. Shareholders' claims are subordinate to the claims of debt-security holders because debt holders stand as creditors of the corporation, not as its owners. Upon corporate liquidation following dissolution, shareholders receive only those funds available after all corporate creditors have been paid.

Common and Preferred Stock. Most states authorize the issuance of more than one class of corporate stock and permit the corporation to vary the rights, preferences, and restrictions among the different classes. The two classes most frequently issued are: (1) common stock and (2) preferred stock.

If the corporation issues only one class of stock, that stock will be common stock. Because common stockholders assume the most risk and have the most to gain from the corporate venture, they receive none of the preferences that the holders of other classes of stock may receive. Common stockholders stand behind bondholders and holders of other classes of stock when corporate distributions are made. However, common stockholders are able to participate in the corporate management. (See Chapter 30 for a discussion of the shareholders' role in management.)

Preferred stock is given special rights and preferences when corporate distributions are made. Because of these preferences, preferred shareholders assume less risk than common shareholders. They do not usually participate in corporate management.

Under the RMBCA, the preferences of any class of stock must be stated in the articles of incorporation (Section 6.01). Thus the extent that preferred stock differs from common stock depends on the provisions of the articles of incorporation. However, Section 6.03 permits the articles to authorize the board of directors to issue preferred stock in series and to determine the relative rights and preferences of the shares of each series regarding:

1. The dividend rate
2. The amount payable to shareholders upon liquidation
3. Any redemption rights along with any provisions for sinking funds for redeeming preferred shares
4. The conditions for convertible shares
5. Any voting rights

As a practical matter, the special rights and preferences accorded preferred shareholders by either the articles or the board will be printed on the preferred stock certificates.

Preferred stock usually has a stated dividend rate. Although it is not mandatory that a corporation pay a dividend in any given year, if it does declare a dividend the preferred shareholders will receive the rate stipulated by the articles and will be paid before the common shareholders. Preferred shareholders also have superior standing in the distributions of corporate assets upon the corporation's liquidation (RMBCA Section 6.02).

Preferred stock may be made redeemable. The RMBCA permits the articles to provide that preferred stock may be redeemed by the corporation at the price fixed by the articles. This is usually done by establishing a sinking fund for the redemption of preferred stock.

Preferred stock may also be convertible into shares of another class or into another type of security, such as a bond. However, the RMBCA provides that the shares of one class of stock may not be converted into those of another class that has superior or prior rights and preferences regarding corporate distributions (Section 6.02.) Thus preferred stock may be converted into common stock, but not vice versa.

As noted above, preferred shareholders generally participate less in corporate management than common shareholders. This balances the lower risk assumed by preferred shareholders. Thus preferred stock is generally nonvoting. The RMBCA permits the elimination of voting rights for particular classes of stock (Section 6.03).

Stock Options and Warrants. In addition to common and preferred stock, the RMBCA authorizes the issuance of stock options and rights (Section 6.24). These securities entitle their holders to purchase from the corporation shares of the corporation's stock. If the option is a negotiable instrument giving the owner the right to purchase stock of the corporation at a specified price, it is called a warrant. Warrants are usually issued to make the issue of some other security more attractive. The owner of the warrant is not only guaranteed the right to buy a number of shares but also is permitted to trade it freely. Often warrants are issued to present shareholders to prevent a dilution of ownership. Shareholders are able to buy a new issue in the form of warrants and thus get an opportunity to buy the stock at a price lower than its market price.

Stock options are often issued by a corpora-tion to an officer or employee to compensate him or her for work done or to provide an incentive for further effort. Under the RMBCA, if options or warrants are to be is-sued to the directors, officers, or employees of the corporation, shareholder approval is not required (Section 6.24 and Official Com-ment). Below is a well-reasoned decision illus-trating the law as applied to stock options granted to executives as part of a compensa-tion package.

Lieberman v. Koppers Co., Inc.

Court of Chancery of Delaware.

149 A.2d 756, affd. sub. nom. Lieberman v. Becker, 155 A.2d 596 (1959)

Lieberman (plaintiff), a stockholder of Koppers Co., Inc. (defendant) brought a deriva-tive action against the company to have declared invalid a deferred-compensation unit plan approved by the stockholders. The purpose of the plan was to attract and retain persons of outstanding competence and to give key employees a stockholder's point of view of the company. The plan provided for the issuance of units in lieu of options to purchase stocks. The value of each unit on the date of issue was that of one share of common stock on the same date. Each unit was subject to being increased in value by the crediting to it of dividends paid on a share of stock as well as any increase in the market value of a single share before a participant's right to a unit occurred. As a condition to the award of units, each participant agreed to remain in the company's employ for five years from the date of his award or until retirement and to be available for consultation for a ten-year period after retirement, during which time a participant might not compete with Koppers. The plan was administered by three or more board members declared ineligible to participate. Both parties moved for summary judgment. Held. For defendant.

Marvel, Vice Chancellor

The complaint alleges that as of December 31, 1957, 89,800 units had been awarded under the plan to various employees and that to the extent that the plan provides for awards to participants based on the increased market value of common stock of the defendant corporation it is invalid for the reason that such awards bear no reasonable relation to the value of services rendered by a participant, and that such awards thus constitute a waste and gift of corporate assets. No complaint, however, is made concerning the provisions of the plan dealing with dividend credits. It is further alleged that since the adoption of the plan the stock of Koppers has fluctuated widely, that such fluctuations bear little or no relation to the services to the corporation and its stockholders and so are invalid.

In addition to the enjoining of the operation of the plan the complaint seeks an accounting for all payments made by Koppers under the plan and for general equitable relief, but admittedly those persons who have become eligible for and received payments under the plan by reason of severance of employment are not before the Court, and no accounting is presently sought.

The answer admits the pleaded facts as to the adoption of the plan, sets forth the vote on stockholder approval and concludes that the plan was adopted and given effect by directors of Koppers in the exercise of their best business judgment as directors and was approved by substantially all of the stockholders who voted thereon in the belief the plan is a fair, reasonable, appropriate and valid plan in furtherance of the welfare and success of Koppers and for the advantage of all its shareholders.

There being no doubt but that the plan here under attack is reasonably calculated to insure the receipt of services by the corporation, it is not subject to the Kerbs ruling (Kerbs v. California Eastern Airways).

Furthermore, while it is alleged that certain directors are beneficiaries of the plan, no real attack is made nor could such be made on the basis of director self-dealing in view of the existence of an impartial committee and stockholder approval.

In short, it is my considered opinion that the plan is reasonably and fairly designed to achieve a legitimate business purpose, namely to retain or obtain qualified executive personnel through the medium of deferring compensation until retirement. While a substantial block of stock has been reserved for financing the plan, corporate reserves, if any, may be allocated to the payment of deferred compensation, thereby probably reducing what would have been the stock demands of a comparable stock option plan. Furthermore, while moneys are not paid out by participants for units, there is no reason advanced why a reasonable and impartial committee may not be expected to take this factor into consideration in the award of units, and when need be, in the reduction of units already awarded. Plaintiff also declines to give proper recognition to the dividend credit provision, the most tangible and perhaps the most attractive feature of the plan in the eyes of participants. Finally, the so-called speculative or capital gains features of the plan are by no means absent from conventional option plans and certain types of incentive plans based on earnings, and it would be unrealistic not to recognize that the plan, if fairly operated, will add to job satisfaction and induce added effort on the part of participants with resulting benefits to the corporation.

Admittedly, the market value of stock of any substantial corporation cannot be isolated from broad economic trends, wars, rumours and many other factors both direct and indirect which affect stock prices. However, earnings are the mark of corporate success and the main factor in stock appreciation, and I do not believe it can be dogmatically said that the services of employees given in response to an incentive plan based in substantial part on the appreciation in the market value of their employer's common stock bear no reasonable relation to such appreciation, and I decline to strike down the plan as per se unreasonable and invalid.

While it may be established in the future that the award of specific units under the plan may in an individual case ultimately pose the threat of payment of illegally excessive compensation, such a case is not now before me.

Held: For Defendant.

STOCK SUBSCRIPTIONS

A method of corporate financing more common with small corporations than with large is the stock subscription. A stock subscription is an agreement between a corporation and a prospective shareholder whereby the corporation agrees to issue shares and the subscriber agrees to pay for them. In a majority of states, an offer by the prospective shareholder and an acceptance by the corporation must exist in order to bring the stock subscription contract into existence. Stock subscriptions may be executed either before or after incorporation. The issue raised by both preincorporation and postincorporation subscriptions is whether the subscriber attains shareholder status in the corporation. If the subscriber does, he or she will be liable for whatever consideration was promised under the subscription agreement in payment for the shares.

Preincorporation Subscriptions

Persons interested in the formation of a business corporation frequently desire to begin the process of financing the proposed enterprise before the formal steps resulting in the formation of the corporation are complete. One of the devices employed in this process of assembling funds is the preincorporation subscription, by which one or more investors make known to the promoter their intention to purchase shares of a designated class and number in the proposed corporation at an agreed upon sum.

A preincorporation subscription may take many forms. Although a few states, such as Delaware and Kansas, require that stock subscriptions be in writing and signed by the subscriber, most states do not require that a subscription be written. A preincorporation subscription may be an individual transaction or it may be a class of transactions by a number of persons, as when a "subscription list" is signed. The word "subscriber" need not appear, and other language such as "I hereby purchase, etc." may be employed. The agreement may include definite provisions as to the time and manner of payment of the agreed amount, the time when the subscriber is to become entitled to a stock certificate, and the legal relations between the subscriber and other shareholders; but usually it gives little or no indication of the intent of the parties with respect to these matters.

Authorities disagree whether a subscriber may withdraw his or her subscription before the corporation comes into existence. The older rule, which still prevails in many jurisdictions, is that a preincorporation subscription may be withdrawn at any time prior to acceptance by the corporation, which cannot occur until the corporation comes into existence. Because there is no corporation in existence at the time the subscription is executed, the subscription is merely an expression of intent to purchase shares and has no legal effect. Furthermore, under general contract law, the subscriber's death, insanity, or bankruptcy will terminate the subscription offer in accordance with the usual rules relating to an unaccepted offer. Newer statutes, including the RMBCA (Section 6.20), make preincorporation subscriptions irrevocable for a stated period of time, typically six months, unless the subscription agreement provides otherwise or all the subscribers consent to the revocation. Although by statute in some states acceptance of the subscription offer is deemed to occur upon incorporation, most statutes, including the RMBCA, require that the corporation act affirmatively to accept the preincorporation subscription offers. Thus, to make a binding subscription contract under these statutes, not only must the corporation be completely organized but there must be an acceptance by the corporation after coming into existence, either expressly by issuing shares to the subscribers or impliedly by recognizing the subscriber as a stockholder.

The realities of corporate finance require an

exception to the general principles of contract law. The function of preincorporation subscriptions is to raise capital with which to finance the future corporation. The status of preincorporation subscriptions is of great concern to the incipient corporation. A practical disadvantage of preincorporation subscriptions presented by the revocable-offer rule is that such subscription agreements may be illusory before incorporation. The practical consequences of subscribers' right to revoke is not only uncertainty as to the amount of funds a proposed corporation will have available upon incorporation but even the possibility that there will not be sufficient funds to permit its formal organization. If a subscriber who happens to be one of the major contributors to the proposed corporation revokes his or her subscription, the whole venture may collapse even before it gets started.

The RMBCA recognizes that some corporations must be financed before actual incorporation and that preincorporation subscribers should therefore be bound for a limited time so that the articles may be filed, unless the agreement provides otherwise. The effect of the RMBCA's approach is that the ultimate receipt of capital by the corporation is better assured, since each potential investor is obligated to put up a specific amount of money for a specific number of shares as soon as the corporation is formed and the subscriptions are accepted.

Postincorporation Subscriptions

When the subscription agreement is made between the subscriber and a corporation already in existence, there exists a binding obligation for the subscriber to purchase, and the corporation to sell, shares of the corporate stock. Ordinary contract principles of offer and acceptance are determinative. Thus a stock subscription made with a corporation already in existence is a contract between the subscriber and the corporation. The contract may result either from an offer made by the corporation and accepted by the subscriber or from an offer made by the subscriber and accepted by the corporation.

A postincorporation subscription agreement must be distinguished from an executory contract to purchase stock. A subscription agreement confers shareholder status instantly on the subscriber even though no stock certificate has yet been issued. Under an executory contract for the purchase of shares, shareholder status is suspended until the contract is fully executed—that is, until a stock certificate has been issued to the purchaser.

Shareholder status under a stock subscription contract does not depend on the issuance of a stock certificate. Under a subscription contract, the subscriber is liable for the subscription payment even though the corporation has not delivered the stock certificate. When the subscription is made, the subscriber is instantly vested with all the rights and obligations of a shareholder, even though some shareholder rights, such as voting and receiving dividends, may be suspended until full payment of the subscription price is made.

However, when the agreement is an executory contract for the purchase of stock, the purchaser does not become a stockholder until the purchase price is fully paid and the stock certificate has been issued. Thus an executory purchaser of shares is relieved of the duty to pay in the event of the corporation's bankruptcy because the corporation cannot perform its duty to deliver shares in a going concern. This is simply an application of the contract law principle that a material breach of an executory contract will discharge the nonbreaching party of any obligation of performance under the contract.

The problem presented by postincorporation subscriptions and by executory contracts to purchase stock is to distinguish between the two transactions. Because both are contracts, the intent of the parties is controlling. Although not conclusive, calling the contract a "subscription agreement" or a "purchase contract" will be highly persuasive. Beyond this, courts look to the nature of the transaction and the rights conferred by the corporation.

Consideration to Be Paid by Subscriber

The issuance of shares by a corporation implies that it has received consideration equal in value to the stated value of the shares. Once the corporation has set a formal valuation on its shares, it cannot sell them below that price. Stockholders who have been issued shares for consideration below the fixed value are liable for any unpaid consideration.

The value of shares to be received as consideration by the corporation is determined by the Board of Directors. Under the RMBCA the board may set a minimum price or establish a formula or any other method to determine price (Section 6.21). Although the RMBCA eliminates the distinction between *par* and *no par* stock and the use of the term *stated capital* (Section 6.21 and Official Comment), most state statutes continue to use such terms. Traditionally, Boards of Directors have designated the value of shares as the par value or stated value of the stock. The total of the par and stated values of the corporation's issued shares constitutes the stated capital of the corporation.

Par value is the price established by either the articles or the directors below which a share may not be originally issued by the corporation. The dollar value is usually quite low —$1 is typical—but the par value has little practical effect on the issuance of shares. Shareholders who do not contribute an amount at least equal to the par value of the stock issued are liable to creditors for the balance. The extent of liability is the difference between the par value and the amount actually contributed. Creditors, including bond-holders, can seek to have this amount paid to the corporate treasury or, sometimes in the event of dissolution and a deficiency, paid to them to satisfy their claims.

The RMBCA provides that payment for shares may be made with money or other property of any description actually transferred to the corporation or with labor or other services actually rendered to the corporation. Also, the RMBCA allows promissory notes and agreements to provide future services to constitute payment for shares (Section 6.21). Most state statutes presently will not allow these latter items to serve as consideration. Because shares may be issued for a consideration other than cash, a question sometimes arises over whether the corporation received full value for its stock.

Authorities disagree regarding the valuation of property or services transferred to the corporation in consideration for its shares. A few states follow the "true value" rule. Under this rule, whether a shareholder is liable for any unpaid value depends upon whether the assets given in consideration for the shares were actually worth the price of the stock. The shareholder is held liable for any substantial variance between the fair market value of the property or service transferred to the corporation and the price of the stock.

Most states (including those that adopt the RMBCA), follow the "good faith" rule, which is based on the assumption that people may honestly differ about the value of property and service rendered to a corporation in consideration for its stock. Under this rule, the valuation made by the corporation will be upheld as long as it was honestly made, no fraud or bad faith exists on the part of the directors (Section 6.21), and they have exercised the degree of care that an ordinary, prudent person in their position would exercise (Section 8.30). The case below is the landmark opinion of the U.S. Supreme Court that originally set forth the "good faith" rule.

Coit v. Amalgamating Company

U.S. Supreme Court

119 U.S. 343 (1886)

Coit (plaintiff), holder of a judgment for $5,489 against Gold (defendant), brought this suit to compel the stockholders to pay what he claimed to be due and unpaid on the shares of the capital stock held by them. Coit was unable to obtain execution of his judgment against the corporation itself because it was insolvent. The defendant, the North Carolina Gold Amalgamating Company, was incorporated under the laws of North Carolina, on January 30, 1874, for the purpose, among other things, of working, milling, smelting, reducing, and assaying ores and metals, with the power to purchase such property, real and personal, as might be necessary in its business and to mortgage or sell the same. By its charter, the minimum capital stock was fixed at $100,000, divided into 1,000 shares of $100 each; the corporation was empowered to increase it from time to time, by a majority vote of the stockholders, to $2.5 million. The charter provided that the subscription to the capital stock might be paid "in such installments, in such manner and in such property, real and personal," as a majority of the corporators might determine, and that the stockholders should not be liable for any loss or damages or be responsible beyond the assets of the company. Previously to the charter, the corporators had been engaged in mining operations, conducting their business under the name and title which they took as a corporation. When the charter was obtained, the capital stock was paid by the property of the former association, which was estimated to be of the value of $100,000, the shares being divided among the stockholders in proportion to their respective interests in the property. Each stockholder placed his estimate upon the property; and the average estimate amounted to $137,500. This sum they reduced to $100,000, inasmuch as the capital stock was to be of that amount. The lower courts ruled in favor of the defendant, and it is from these decisions that plaintiff appealed. Held. Affirmed.

Field, Justice

The plaintiff contends, and it is the principal basis of his suit, that the valuation thus put upon the property was illegally and fraudulently made at an amount far above its actual value, averring that the property consisted only of a machine for crushing ores, the right to use a patent called the Crosby process, and the charter of the proposed organization; that the articles had no market or actual value, and, therefore, that the capital stock issued thereon was not fully paid, or paid to any substantial extent, and that the holders thereof were still liable to the corporation and its creditors for the unpaid subscription. If it were proved that actual fraud was committed in the payment of the stock, and that the complainant had given credit to the company from a belief that its stock was fully paid, there would undoubtedly be substantial ground for the relief asked. But where the charter authorizes capital stock to be paid in property, and the shareholders honestly and in good faith put in property instead of money in payment of their subscriptions, third parties have no ground of complaint. The case is very different from that in which subscriptions to stock are payable in cash, and where only a part of the instalments has been paid. In that case there is still a debt due to the corporation, which, if it become insolvent, may be sequestered in equity by the creditors, as a trust fund liable to the payment of their debts. But where full paid stock is issued for property received, there must be actual fraud in the transaction to enable creditors of the corporation to call the stockholders to account. A gross and obvious overvaluation of property would be strong evidence of fraud.

But the allegation of intentional and fraudulent undervaluation of the property is not sustained by the evidence. The patent and the machinery had been used by the corporators in their business, which was continued under the charter. They were immediately serviceable, and therefore had to the company a present value. The corporators may have placed too high an estimate upon the property, but the court below finds that its valuation was honestly and fairly made; and there is only one item, the value of the chartered privileges, which is at all liable to any legal objection. But if that were deducted, the remaining amount would be so near to the aggregate capital, that no implication could be raised against the entire good faith of the parties in the transaction. In May, 1874, the company increased its stock, as it was authorized to do by its charter, to $1,000,000 or 10,000 shares of $100 each. This increase was made pursuant to an agreement with one Howes, by which the company was to give him 2000 shares of the increased stock for certain lands purchased from him. Of the balance of the increased shares, 4000 were divided among the holders of the original stock upon the return and delivery to the company of the original certificates—they thus receiving four shares of the increased capital stock for one of the original shares returned. The other 4000 shares were retained by the company. The land purchased was subject to three mortgages, of which the plaintiff held the third; and the agreement was that, under the first mortgage, a sale should be made of the property, and that mortgages for a like amount should be given to the parties according to their several and respective amounts, and in their respective positions and priorities. The plaintiff was to be placed by the company, after the release of his mortgage, in the same position. Accordingly he made a deed to it of all his interest and title under the mortgage held by him, the trustee joining with him, in which deed the agreement was recited. The company, thereupon, gave him its mortgage upon the same and other property, which was payable in installments. The plaintiff also received at the same time an accepted draft of Howe's on the company for $1000. When the first instalment on the mortgage became due, the company being unable to pay it, he took its draft for the amount, $3000, payable in December following. It is upon these drafts that the judgment was recovered in the Court of Common Pleas of Philadelphia, which is the foundation of the present suit. It is in evidence that the plaintiff was fully aware, at the time, of the increase in the stock of the company, and of its object. Six months afterwards, the increase was cancelled, the outstanding shares were called in, and the capital stock reduced to its original limit of $100,000. Nothing was done after the increase to enlarge the liabilities of the company. The draft of the Howes was passed to the plaintiff and received by him at the time the agreement was carried out upon which the increase of the stock was made; and the draft for $3000 was for an instalment upon the mortgage then executed. The plaintiff had placed no reliance upon the supposed paid-up capital of the company on the increased shares, and, therefore, has no cause of complaint by reason of their subsequent recall. Had a new indebtedness been created by the company after the issue of the stock and before its recall, a different question would have arisen. The creditor in that case, relying on the faith of the stock being fully paid, might have insisted upon its full payment. But no such new indebtedness was created, and we think, therefore, that the stockholders cannot be called upon, at the suit of the plaintiff, to pay in the amount of the stock, which, though issued, was soon afterwards recalled and cancelled.

Held: Affirmed.

REVIEW PROBLEMS

1. Henry Molina attended a meeting with Rudy Largosa to discuss the formation of a corporation to engage in selling stereo equipment. At the meeting, Molina signed a subscription form for the purchase of forty shares at $50 per share for a total investment of $2,000 in the proposed corporation. The subscription form did not set forth the capital of the proposed corporation or the extent of Molina's proportionate interest in it. Molina later paid Largosa $2,000, which was deposited in a bank account under the name of the proposed corporation. Shortly after the corporation was officially organized, it failed. Molina sued Largosa to recover his $2,000, contending that, because the subscription form did not set forth the total capital of the proposed corporation and his proportionate interest in it, there was no valid subscription contract. What result would you expect? Molina v. Largosa, 456 P.2d 293 (1970)

2. D Corporation was organized by S, who transferred property for preferred stock and then caused $1.5 million in par value common stock to be issued. D and S agreed that there would be no consideration paid for the common stock. D subsequently incurred liabilities, became insolvent, and entered receivership. P, a corporation organized to purchase the assets of D and carry on the business, bought the claims of creditors and sued to collect from S the par value of the common stock. What will be the result? Hospes v. Northwestern Mfg. & Car Co., 48 Minn. 174 (1892)

3. The Columbia Straw Paper Company purchased thirty-nine paper mills from Emanuel Stein for $5 million, for which it issued to Stein $1 million of the corporation's bonds, $1 million worth of its preferred stock, and $3 million worth of common stock. The value of the mills was arrived at by analyzing the expected profits to be derived from the property. Columbia later became insolvent, and creditors of the company sued Stein, claiming that the mills he sold to the corporation were not worth $5 million; that the directors acted in bad faith by basing the value of the mills on an extravagant estimation of prospective profits rather than the appraised value of the mills' property. May a corporation make an exchange for its stock on the basis of an estimation of prospective profits to be derived from that property? See v. Heppenheimer, 61 A.843 (1905)

4. Citizens of Schuyler, Nebraska, sought to form a corporation for the processing of chicory. Lednicky signed a subscription agreement to purchase five shares of stock, par value $50, in the proposed company. Articles of incorporation were obtained. Lednicky agreed to pay for his five shares at the rate of $10 a month. After paying $80 he refused to continue payment, and the cor-

poration sued for the balance. The defense was that the subscription agreement was not an enforceable contract. What will be the result? Nebraska Chicory Co. of Schuyler, Nebraska v. Lednicky, 113 N.W. 245 (1941)

5. The Clifton Coal Co. was organized with 1,200 shares, par value $100, with power to increase the shares to 2,000 by a majority vote of the stockholders. This increase was later voted, but the corporation was unable to sell the additional 800 shares. The corporation then issued $50,000 worth of bonds and was able to dispose of them by offering the buyers $50,000 worth of stock as a bonus; the remaining $30,000 worth of stock was given to the original stockholders of the corporation. The stock certificates bore the statement that the shares were "fully paid and non-assessable." Stutz and other creditors of the corporation brought an action to compel an assessment upon the 800 shares. What should the result be? Handley v. Stutz, 139 U.S. 417 (1891)

6. Sherman, to whom certain creditors of the Oleum Development Co. had assigned their judgments, sued the stockholders of Oleum to recover amounts alleged due on unpaid subscriptions to the capital stock of the corporation. The stock had a par value of $1 a share and was issued as fully paid-up stock, but in no instance was it actually fully paid for, and in some cases the corporation had received no more than 10¢ a share. These facts were fully known to the creditors when they extended credit to the corporation. What will be the result? Sherman v. Harley et al., 174 P. 901 (1921)

CHAPTER 30

Operating the Corporation

CORPORATE PURPOSES AND POWERS _____

CORPORATE MANAGEMENT_____

MANAGEMENT'S FIDUCIARY OBLIGATIONS _____

O nce the corporation has been formed and financed, it is ready to commence the operation of its business. Just what that business may be depends upon the purpose of the corporation as reflected by its charter and articles of incorporation. Thus, in discussing corporate operation, this chapter focuses first on the subject of permissible corporate activity as circumscribed by the corporation's purposes and powers. Then it turns to the three groups who participate in operating the corporation: the shareholders, the board of directors, and the corporate officers or executives. These three groups are examined separately, but their roles are closely interrelated. Generally speaking, those who comprise the corporation's management (the board of directors and the corporate executives) are permitted much flexibility in operating the corporation, and are protected from shareholder involvement in management affairs. This protection against shareholder interference is offset by certain fiduciary obligations imposed upon corporate management for the protection of shareholder interests. This chapter thus concludes by examining management's fiduciary duties.

CORPORATE PURPOSES AND POWERS

Both business and legal theory hold that a corporation must have a purpose. Business theorists speak of corporate purpose in terms of "strategy," which is defined as the determination of fundamental long-term goals for the company and the adoption of courses of action and the allocation of resources necessary to achieve them. Strategy includes selecting target markets, defining products or services to address these markets, and determining the distribution system in a manner that is within the corporation's resources and capabilities.

Legal theorists view corporate purpose differently. A corporation's purpose is defined in the articles of incorporation and state statutory law under which the corporation is formed.

Closely related to the subject of proper purposes is the subject of proper powers. State law often sets forth the acts that a corporation may legally perform. These acts should be consistent with proper corporate purposes. If the corporation engages in an improper purpose or exercises an improper power, the purpose or act is declared to be "ultra vires" (beyond the corporation's power) and unenforceable. This is known as the *ultra vires* doctrine. Recent legislative developments have attached a declining role to this doctrine.

Corporate Purposes

The corporation's purpose is the reason for which the corporation is organized. This establishes the nature of its business and circumscribes the range of permissible corporate activities. Corporations need not be formed for a single purpose only; they may be organized to undertake as many purposes as the incorporators deem desirable. Section 3.01 of the Revised Model Business Corporation Act (RMBCA) provides that "Every corporation incorporated under this Act has the purpose of engaging in *any* lawful business unless a narrower purpose is set forth in the articles of incorporation." Implicit in this statement also is the requirement that a corporation formed under the general corporate law must have a profit-making purpose, since nonprofit corporations are usually organized under a separate statute.

Earlier in the evolution of corporation law, detailed descriptions of corporate purposes were required to be included in the articles of incorporation. This reflected the general mistrust of unchecked corporate activity. Under modern corporate codes, including the RMBCA, a generally worded purpose clause may be provided in the articles (Section 2.02).

Sometimes incorporators desire to limit the activities of the corporation to the furtherance of a particular purpose. When this is the case, a narrower purpose clause may be included in the articles, or a specific prohibition against certain activities may be stated. Because most modern corporate codes permit a "full purpose" clause to be included in the articles, the subject of what is a proper corporate purpose is of diminishing importance.

Corporate Powers

Closely related to the subject of corporate purposes is that of corporate powers. Corporate powers are those powers granted to the corporation by articles and statute to implement its overall objectives. Because corporate purposes and powers are to be compatible, the corporation's powers must be consistent with the corporation's stated purpose.

A corporation's powers may be express or implied. A corporation has express power to perform those acts authorized by the general corporation law of the state of incorporation and those acts authorized by its articles. Most states have express statutory provisions allowing corporations to sue and be sued, own property, borrow money, etc. Corporations also have implied powers to do whatever is reasonably necessary to promote their express powers, unless such acts are expressly prohibited by law. The trend is to construe broadly what is meant by reasonably necessary. Two current issues involving proper corporate powers are whether a corporation may join a partnership and whether a corporation may guarantee the debt of another—for example, one of its key employees.

Section 3.02 of the RMBCA codifies most of the permissible powers of a corporation. Two additional powers—the ability to indemnify directors, officers, and other employees, and the ability to purchase and dispose of its own shares—are provided in Sections 8.51 and 6.-31. Many of the powers included in these sections were provided to remove doubt that existed with regard to certain activities. For example, Section 3.02(10) permits the corporation to become a partner and Section 3.02(9) empowers it to lend money and invest its funds. By statute, the RMBCA also expands the scope of a corporation's implied powers. As mentioned, a corporation's implied powers usually include whatever is reasonably necessary to effectuate the corporation's express powers. Under RMBCA Section 3.02(16) the corporation is allowed "to . . . do any other act not inconsistent with law, that furthers the business and affairs of the corporation."

The Ultra Vires Doctrine. Corporate transactions outside the corporations' purposes and powers are ultra vires (beyond the power). Under the doctrine of ultra vires, the corporation is not responsible for transactions that were not authorized by its charter, the articles of incorporation, or the law of the state of incorporation. The older view was that ultra vires acts were void for lack of legal capacity, the reason being that the state had not given the corporation the power to do the particular act. Under this view, the shareholders could not subsequently ratify the unauthorized corporate act because the transaction was void. The present view is that ultra vires transactions are voidable. If completely unperformed on both sides, neither party can bring an action on the contract. However, if the ultra vires transaction has been fully performed or executed on both sides, either party can bring an action on the contract. The doctrine does not apply to tortious or criminal conduct, because the lack of authorization is not considered an excuse for such conduct.

Two legal consequences *attach* to an ultra vires transaction: (1) the doctrine may serve as a *basis of liability* asserted by the state or shareholders to enjoin or set aside a corporate act, and (2) the doctrine may serve as a *defense to liability* by the corporation arising from an unauthorized transaction, much in the same manner as a minor can defend against a contract claim by raising the defense of lack of contractual capacity. This second consequence has been criticized because it permits a corporation to reap the benefits from an ultra vires transaction while avoiding any of its burdens by raising the doctrine as a defense.

Because the use of the doctrine as a defense threatens the security of commercial transactions, the doctrine is in decline. Most statutes, including the RMBCA (Section 3.04), severely limit the ultra vires doctrine by stating that "corporate action may not be challenged on the ground that the corporation lacks power or lacked power to act" (Section 3.04[a]). The RMBCA limits challenges to the corporation's power to act to suits brought by the state Attorney General; suits by the corporation against officers or directors for previously authorizing an ultra vires act; and shareholder suits to enjoin ultra vires acts (Section 3.04[b]).

Additional Areas of Ultra Vires Vitality. As seen above, two legislative developments have resulted in the decline of the doctrine of ultra vires: (1) the elimination of the doctrine as a defense to creditor claims and (2) the expansion of permissible corporate powers. The doctrine retains vitality where the general corporation statute is silent on the subject. For example, the corporation's right to make charitable contributions is still uncertain in some states. According to the older view, corporations existed solely for the economic benefit of the shareholders; thus corporate charitable contributions were considered ultra vires unless a benefit to the corporation could be shown. Under this "corporate benefit rule," a corporate contribution to a business college, for example, would have to be supported by showing that the act was intended to create good will between the corporation and the college, which might provide the corporation with a pool of potential employees. Some state corporation codes are still silent on the subject of corporate charitable contributions, thus necessitating this type of analysis. However, present provisions in the federal income tax law allowing deductions for charitable contributions, along with the current concern for corporate social responsibility, have resulted in the amendment of three-quarters of states' corporation statutes to allow gifts for "the public welfare or for charitable, scientific or educational purposes" (RMBCA Section 3.02[14]).

Another area where the doctrine of ultra vires is presently applicable is that of corporate political activity. Although federal legislation currently regulates this kind of corporate activity, the courts have held that shareholders are not permitted to bring private suits under the federal law, thus relegating shareholders to state law and the doctrine of ultra vires. Presently, the power to make political contributions is not specifically included in the RMBCA or most corporate statutes. The following case illustrates the application of the doctrine of ultra vires in the area of corporate political activity.

Marsili v. Pacific Gas and Electric Company
California Court of Appeals
124 Cal. Rptr. 313 (1975)

Marsili and two other stockholders initiated a derivative suit challenging the propriety of a $10,000 contribution made by Pacific Gas and Electric Company (PG&E) to Citizens for San Francisco, an unincorporated association that advocated the defeat of Proposition T appearing on the ballot in the November 2, 1971 election for the city and county of San Francisco. (Proposition T was a nonpartisan initiative proposal that, if adopted, would have prohibited construction in San Francisco of any building more than 72 feet high without prior approval of the voters.) Plaintiffs argued that the contribution was ultra vires because neither PG&E's articles of incorporation nor the law of California permitted PG&E to make political contributions. They argued that the individual members of the board of directors of PG&E should be compelled to restore the $10,000 contribution to the Corporation. The lower court granted a motion for summary judgment made by the defendants and dismissed the complaint. Held, affirmed.

Kane, Associate Justice

By definition adopted by plaintiffs themselves, "ultra vires" refers to an act which is beyond the powers conferred upon a corporation by its charter or by the laws of the state of incorporation.

The parties are in agreement that the powers conferred upon a corporation include both express powers, granted by charter or statute, and implied powers to do acts reasonably necessary to carry out the express powers. In California, the express powers which a corporation enjoys include the power to "do any acts incidental to the transaction of its business . . . or expedient for the attainment of its corporate purposes."

The articles of PG&E are manifestly consistent with this statutory imprimatur. Thus, for example, they authorize all activities and endeavors incidental or useful to the manufacturing, buying, selling, and distributing of gas and electric power, including the construction of buildings and other facilities convenient to the achievement of its corporate purposes, and the performance of "all things whatsoever that shall be necessary or proper for the full and complete execution of the purposes for which . . . [the] corporation is formed, and for the exercise and enjoyment of all its powers and franchises."

In addition to the exercise of such express powers, the generally recognized rule is that the management of a corporation, "in the absence of express restrictions, has discretionary authority to enter into contracts and transactions which may be deemed reasonably incidental to its business purposes." In short, "a corporation has authority to do what will legitimately tend to effectuate . . . [its] express purposes and objects." California is in accord with this general rule also: " 'Whatever transactions are fairly incidental or auxiliary to the main business of the corporation and necessary or expedient in the protection, care and management of its property may be undertaken by the corporation and be within the scope of its corporated [sic] powers.' "

No restriction appears in the articles of PG&E which would limit the authority of its board of directors to act upon initiative or referendum proposals affecting the affairs of the company or to engage in activities related to any other legislative or political matter in which the corporation has a legitimate concern. Furthermore, there are no statutory prohibitions in California which preclude a corporation from participating in any type of political activity. In these circumstances, the contribution by PG&E to Citizens for San Francisco was proper if it can fairly be said to fall within the express or implied powers of the corporation.

The crux of the controversy at bench, therefore, is whether a contribution toward the defeat of a local ballot proposition can ever be said to be convenient or expedient to the achievement of legitimate corporate purposes. Appellants take the flat position that in the absence of express statutory authority, corporate political contributions are illegal. This contention cannot be sustained. We believe that where, as here, the board of directors reasonably concludes that the adoption of a ballot proposition would have a direct, adverse effect upon the business of the corporation, the board of directors has abundant statutory and charter authority to oppose it.

The law is clear that those to whom the management of the corporation has been entrusted are primarily responsible for judging whether a particular act or transaction is one which is helpful to the conduct of corporate affairs or expedient for the attainment of corporate purposes. . . . Indeed, a court cannot determine that a particular transaction is beyond the powers of a corporation unless it clearly appears to be so as a matter of law. With respect to the means which the corporation may adopt to further its objects and promote its business, its managers are not limited in law to the use of such means as are usual or necessary to the objects contemplated by their organization, but where not restricted by law, may choose such means as are convenient and adapted to the end, though they be neither the usual means, nor absolutely necessary for the purpose intended. . . .

Neither the court nor minority shareholders can substitute their judgment for that of the corporation "where its board has acted in good faith and used its best business judgment in behalf of the corporation."

Plaintiffs, as mentioned earlier, do not contend that the individual defendants acted in bad faith, or that they acted unreasonably or for an improper purpose. Accordingly, the judgment of the board of directors cannot be disturbed by the court unless it is held, as a matter of law, that the contribution could not be construed as incidental or expedient for the attainment of corporate purposes. For several reason which we shall set forth, such a holding would simply not be reasonable in the light of the uncontradicted record below.

First, the Executive Committee of PG&E based its decision to authorize the contribution upon its judgment that the adoption of Proposition T would have an adverse impact upon the corporation and, in particular, would increase the tax rate applicable to the company's facilities and interfere with present and future building plans of the company, including the construction of the Embarcadero Substation.

Second, the Executive Committee considered the adoption of Proposition T to be detrimental to the City and County of San Francisco: specifically, by increasing taxes, it would have depressed business growth and, by imposing an immutable proscription on building heights, it would have rendered the Urban Design Plan ineffective.

Third, by requiring voter approval for the construction of any building more than 72 feet in height, the decision to construct necessary corporate facilities would depend upon the mood of the electorate rather than upon relevant business considerations. The corporation would thereby become embroiled in a contested political campaign every time it determined that it was in the corporation's interest to construct a building more than 72 feet in height.

Not only would the business judgment of the board of directors be subservient to the vagaries of an election campaign, but the cost of submitting such a proposal to the voters would undoubtedly be considerable. This is demonstrated by the very case at bench where in excess of $68,000 was spent by the supporters of Proposition T, and an even greater sum was spent by its opponents. These figures attest to the high cost of submitting a proposal to the voters and demonstrate the severe economic burden that the proposition would have imposed upon those seeking to comply with its terms.

The members of the Executive Committee of PG&E reasonably sought to avoid these consequences. Their judgment was not arbitrary or capricious but was based upon pertinent business considerations that were of direct and immediate concern to the corporation.

Held: Affirmed.

CORPORATE MANAGEMENT

Three groups participate in operating the corporation: the shareholders, the board of directors, and the corporate officers and executives. The following pages examine the management role of each of these groups. The material begins with a discussion of the role of shareholders, whose involvement in corporate management is indirect and therefore minimal. It proceeds to a discussion of the role of the board of directors, which is charged with the responsibility of setting corporation policy, and concludes with a look at the function of corporate officers and executives, to whom the day-to-day management of the corporation is delegated.

The Role of Shareholders

Shareholders have no direct control over corporate operations. They cannot command the board of directors or the corporate executives to undertake an activity or decide a matter in a particular way. Though ultimate control resides with the shareholders, they usually do not participate actively in corporate affairs. They can take action only by voting during a shareholders meeting. Shareholder suffrage at these meetings is usually confined to selecting the membership of the board of directors and approving certain extraordinary transactions. Little more than this minimal involvement is permitted of investors. If they are dissatisfied with their investment, they may sell their stock. However, if the corporate management has violated the corporate documents or otherwise incurred a liability toward the investors, the shareholders may bring suit against the responsible parties to recover any loss on behalf of the corporation or to recoup any loss to their invesmtent.

Areas of Shareholder Involvement. There are usually two areas of shareholder involvement in corporate affairs: (1) the election of members of the board of directors and (2) the approval of certain extraordinary corporate transactions. Thus, under the RMBCA, shareholder participation is restricted to the annual election or removal of corporate directors (Sections 8.03 and 8.08), loans to employees and directors (Section 8.32), sale of the corporation's assets outside the usual course of corporate business (Section 12.02), any plan of merger or share exchange (Section 11.03), and a voluntary dissolution of the corporation (Section 14.03). Although some statutes require shareholder approval of bylaw amendments, the RMBCA does not (Section 2.06). Of course, it is always permissible to increase the areas of shareholder involvement by appropriate provisions in the corporate articles and bylaws.

Shareholders Meetings. Because they are not agents of the corporation, shareholders cannot act individually; they can act only collectively at shareholders meetings. The RMBCA requires that an annual shareholders meeting be held at the times specified in the corporate bylaws (Section 7.01). Sometimes it is necessary to have a special meeting of the shareholders for a particular purpose. The RMBCA further permits special meetings to be called by the board of directors, by the holders of more than 5 percent of the shares entitled to vote at the meeting, or by any person authorized to do so in the articles or bylaws (Section 7.02).

Most statutes, including the RMBCA, require that notice of any shareholders meeting be provided to each shareholder of record entitled to vote at such a meeting. The RMBCA stipulates that the notice be in writing, stating the place, day, and hour of the meeting. In the case of a special meeting, the notice must also include the purpose or purposes for which the meeting is called. The notice must be delivered not less than ten days or more than fifty days before the date of the meeting (Section 7.05).

Unless the required notice is waived, failure to provide it voids any action taken at the meeting. A waiver may be made by a signed writing or evidenced by conduct, such as attending the meeting without objecting to the lack of notice. The RMBCA permits action to be taken without a shareholders meeting if written consent specifying the action to be taken is signed by all the shareholders entitled to vote on the matter (Section 7.04).

A quorum of the shares entitled to vote, represented in person or by proxy, must be present before any action can take place at the shareholders meeting. Section 7.25 of the RMBCA provides that a majority of the voting shares shall constitute a quorum, unless the articles provide otherwise. However, the articles cannot provide for a quorum consisting of less than one-third of the voting shares.

The shareholders meeting is usually conducted according to the provisions of the corporate articles or bylaws, which generally provide that the board chairman or corporate president preside. Minutes of the meeting are customarily recorded by the corporate secretary. Shareholders are entitled to submit and speak upon proposals and resolutions during the meeting. Recently, shareholders who are concerned about social issues and politically active have used the shareholders meeting to submit proposals to limit the involvement of their corporations in certain activities, such as investing in countries that violate human rights or practice apartheid.

Because most voting at shareholders meetings is done by proxy and therefore the result is normally a foregone conclusion, the typical shareholders meeting is a well-orchestrated occasion designed to fulfill the formalities of corporate law. For this reason, some scholars seriously question the continued practice of requiring an annual shareholders meeting. In what may very well be a harbinger of future development, Delaware no longer requires an annual meeting.

Voting. Shareholders function by voting on matters at the shareholders meeting. Each share of stock entitles its holder to one vote on each matter submitted to a vote, unless the corporate articles provide for more or less than one vote per share (RMBCA Section 7.21). Thus the holder of fifty shares is generally entitled to cast fifty votes. The RMBCA also authorizes the issuance of nonvoting shares (Sections 6.01 and 7.21). For example, preferred stock generally has no voting rights. However, even nonvoting stock is entitled to vote on certain extraordinary transactions, such as amendments to the corporate articles (Section 10.04), mergers and consolidations (Section 11.03), and dissolution of the corporation (Sections 14.02 and 14.03). To determine who is entitled to vote, the directors may set a date of record, and the person having legal title to the stock on the record date is entitled to vote the shares (Section 7.07). A person acquiring legal title to the shares after the record date must obtain the proxy of the record title holder in order to vote them at the shareholders meeting.

Because a shareholder is entitled to one vote for each share held, the holder of 51 percent of the voting shares will have complete control over corporate operations. To assure minority shareholders some voice in corporate affairs, most statutes permit a shareholder to cumulate his or her votes for directors, meaning that the shareholder can cast as many votes for one candidate for director as there are directors to be elected, multiplied by the shareholder's number of shares. This form of proportional representation usually applies only to the election of directors. In some states, cumulative voting is required by statute and cannot be refused in any election or eliminated in the corporate articles or bylaws. In other states it is permissive, meaning that cumulative voting can be eliminated in the corporate documents. Under the RMBCA, cumulative voting is permissive (Sections 7.21 and 7.24).

Cumulative voting for directors is controversial. Proponents claim that it is necessary to assure minority voice in corporate affairs. Opponents claim that minority representation means dissent in the boardroom.

A device for diluting the effect of cumulative voting is the staggered election of directors, because the fewer directors there are to be elected, the greater the number of shares that will be necessary to assure representation. This is allowed by the RMBCA, which permits boards consisting of nine or more directors to be divided into two or three classes, with each class being elected to a staggered three-year term (Section 8.06). Since the RMBCA is permissive on the subject of cumulative voting, requiring the staggered election of directors in classes poses no problems. However, in states where cumulative voting is mandatory, the staggered election of directors is often prohibited.

A shareholder may vote either in person or by proxy. A proxy is a delegation of authority given by a shareholder to another person to vote his or her stock. A proxy is basically a special type of principal-agent relationship and is therefore subject to the rules of agency law as modified by special state statutes or by federal regulations under Section 14 of the Securities Exchange Act of 1934.

The RMBCA requires that a proxy be in writing (Section 7.22). A telegram or cablegram should be sufficient. Some states, like California, require that the proxy be filed with the corporation before or at the shareholders meeting. A few states allow oral proxies.

Because the proxy is an agency, every appointment of a proxy is revocable. One way a shareholder may revoke a proxy is to attend and vote at the shareholders meeting. A proxy is not revocable if it is coupled with an interest, meaning that some consideration has been received by the shareholder for his or her delegation of voting rights—for example, an option or pledge to purchase the stock.

Even when proxies are irrevocable, statutes generally limit their duration. The RMBCA provides that the appointment of a proxy is valid for only eleven months after it is made unless otherwise provided in the proxy (Section 7.22). Thus a proxy can extend beyond eleven months only if the writing specifies the date on which it is to expire or the length of time it is to continue in force.

Proxy solicitation by corporate management, insurgent shareholder groups, competing shareholder factions, or even outsiders has become a common and effective method of establishing or maintaining control over a corporation without actually purchasing enough stock to exert control. Section 14 of the Securities Exchange Act of 1934 and Rule 14a of the Securities and Exchange Commission (SEC) regulate proxy solicitation. Their purpose is to protect shareholders from misleading or concealed information in the solicitation of proxies. These proxy rules apply to corporations having more than 500 shareholders and assets of more than $1 million. They are discussed in detail in Chapter 31.

Because proxies are revocable, other devices for combining votes for control of the corporation are frequently used. Two such devices are the pooling agreement and the voting trust. A pooling agreement, sometimes called a voting agreement, is a contract entered into by several shareholders who mutually promise to vote their shares in a certain manner. In most states such agreements are specifically enforceable. Section 7.31 of the RMBCA provides that "a voting agreement under this section is specifically enforceable."

A voting trust is an agreement among shareholders to transfer their voting rights to a trustee, who is permitted to vote the shares in a block at the shareholders meeting according to the terms of the trust instrument. Courts are divided as to the legality of voting trusts at common law, but most statutes, including the RMBCA (Section 7.30), provide for and limit them. Under the RMBCA a voting trust must be in writing. This writing, termed the "voting trust agreement," must specify the terms and conditions of the voting trust, and a copy of it must be deposited with the corporation. The shareholders must transfer their shares to the trustee and receive in return trust certificates, sometimes called certificates of beneficial ownership. The RMBCA also limits the life of a voting trust to ten years (Section 7.30).

Inspection Rights. For a shareholder to intelligently exercise his or her voting rights, it may be necessary to have access to certain corporate information. Most statutes, including the RMBCA (Section 7.20), recognize that the opposition to corporate management must be able to obtain a list of existing shareholders if it is ever to be successful in ousting management; therefore they grant shareholders an absolute right to examine and copy shareholder lists. Under the RMBCA, the shareholder list must be available at the shareholders meeting.

The shareholder may also be able to obtain

information contained in the corporate records. The RMBCA provides that a shareholder has a qualified right to certain corporate information. Section 16.01 requires that the corporate records of account, the minutes of shareholders and directors meetings, and a shareholders list are to be kept, usually at the corporation's principal place of business. Upon written demand five business days before the date on which a shareholder wishes to inspect, he or she may examine any of the relevant corporate records during reasonable working hours. The RMBCA permits an attorney or an agent, who could be an accountant, to accompany the shareholder or to make the inspection for the shareholder if the shareholder so wishes. The written demand must be in good faith and for a proper purpose. The right of inspection is limited to three classes of corporate records: minutes of meetings of the board and committees of the board, accounting records, and a record of shareholders (Section 16.02).

What is a "proper purpose" or a request made in good faith is an issue left for the courts to decide. The following case illustrates the judicial approach to defining these terms.

National Consumers Union v. National Tea Company

Appellate Court of Illinois
302 N.E. 2d 118 (1973)

Plaintiffs Jan Schakowsky and the National Consumers Union (NCU), shareholders of defendant, National Tea Company (National), filed a petition for a writ of mandamus to compel National to permit them to examine the books and records of the corporation. Schakowsky was the owner of one share of the corporation for more than six months. NCU also owned one share but for less than six months. Plaintiffs argued that demands for records, minutes, books, and records of account were made in a reasonable manner, in good faith, and for a proper purpose. Defendant argued that NCU was seeking to "sensitize" National to NCU's brand of "consumer" demands by their own admission in a discovery deposition. The defendants argued that their motion for summary judgment should be granted as NCU expressed no proper purpose for inspecting the documents they wished to examine. The trial court granted defendants' motion for summary judgment. Held, affirmed.

Lorenz, Justice

Plaintiffs first contend that the trial court erred in holding that N.C.U. had no rights of its own to examine defendants' books and records. Section 45 of the Business Corporation Act . . . gives shareholders the right to examine a corporation's books and records of account, its minutes, and its record of shareholders, if they hold their shares of record for at least six months preceding their demand or if they hold at least five percent of the corporation's outstanding shares. Furthermore, the books and records must be examined at a reasonable time and for a proper purpose. Shareholders may examine the books and records in person or through an agent or attorney. Section 45 also gives courts of competent jurisdiction discretion, upon a showing of proper purpose, to compel a corporation to allow shareholders, who do not otherwise meet the requirements of the section, to examine the books and records. Since the complaint does not allege that N.C.U. held its single share of stock for more than six months, it is clear that it had no right of its own to examine defendant's books and records.

The claim then made by both plaintiffs is that they showed a proper purpose for examining National's books and records, namely—to solicit proxies and that the court abused its discretion in denying them this right. We recognize that soliciting proxies is a proper purpose for examining shareholders lists and for examining a corporation's books and records.

We also agree with plaintiffs and the trial court that a single proper purpose is sufficient to satisfy the requirements of the statute. However, we also recognize that shareholders no longer have an absolute right to examine shareholders lists or corporate books and records. Now, the rights of minority stockholders must be balanced with the needs of the corporation upon the facts of each case.

In the instant case, the trial court determined that the evidence before it showed that plaintiffs had a speculative purpose at best. Although plaintiffs assert that they wanted to examine the books and records because they desired to solicit proxies, the evidence clearly showed that N.C.U. and Schakowsky had actually engaged in a course of conduct inimical to National's interest. Schakowsky admitted that they had urged shoppers not to frequent National's stores. On the basis of single shares of stock, the plaintiffs desire to go on a fishing expedition through National's books and records apparently searching for further ammunition to "sensitize" National to N.C.U.'s brand of "consumer" demands. Numerous cases . . . relied on by the trial court, indicate that such speculative purposes do not satisfy the requirements of having a proper purpose. On these facts we cannot say that the trial court erred in holding that plaintiffs had no proper purpose for examining National's books. Furthermore, although plaintiffs contend that they satisfied the statutory requirements for examining National's books, it is clear that they cannot satisfy those requirements without having a proper purpose.

Held: Affirmed.

Dividends. A dividend is a distribution paid to shareholders because of their stock ownership. It may be in cash, property (including the stock of other corporations), or the stock of the corporation itself. This latter type of dividend is referred to as a "stock dividend."

The RMBCA prohibits the declaration or payment of a dividend when the corporation is insolvent or when such a payment would render the corporation insolvent, meaning that the corporation is unable to pay its debts

as they become due (Section 6.40). Dividends can be lawfully declared and paid only out of the corporation's earned surplus under the traditional approach now used in most states. Earned surplus represents the profits realized on operations and investments. However, the RMBCA would permit dividends to be paid out by the board of directors based on financial statements prepared on the basis of accounting principles and practice that are "reasonable" under the circumstances, or on a fair evaluation, or other method that is reasonable under the circumstances (Section 6.40[d]). The RMBCA retains an equity insolvency test but allows directors wider discretion in making judgments as to the future ability of the corporation to generate funds and remain solvent.

The directors have wide discretion concerning whether or not to declare a dividend. The shareholders ordinarily have no right to a dividend. The directors alone determine the amount of dividends and when they are to be distributed. A shareholder's "right" to a dividend normally materializes only after a dividend has been declared by the board.

Although courts usually do not disturb the discretion of directors with regard to a dividend declaration, there is an exception to this general rule. When there is a bad-faith refusal by the board of directors to declare a dividend, a court may use its equitable powers to compel a distribution. However, courts do not possess any equitable power to require a board of directors to declare dividends out of abundant earnings in the absence of fraud or abuse of discretion.

Preemptive Rights. If the articles of incorporation so provide, a shareholder has an option called a preemptive right that entitles the shareholder to subscribe to a newly authorized issue of shares in the same proportion that his or her present shares bear to all outstanding shares before new shares are offered to the public. Preemptive rights are aimed at preventing the dilution of the shareholder's equity in the corporation against his or her wishes (RMBCA Section 6.30). Under most state statutes presently on the books, preemptive rights usually do not apply to treasury shares (meaning shares previously issued and reacquired by the corporation), previously authorized but unsold and unissued shares, or shares that are issued or agreed to be issued upon the conversion of convertible shares. Preemptive rights do not apply to these shares because such shares are not new issues but are part of previous offerings.

Since preemptive rights often interfere with the disposition of large issues of shares, many corporations restrict or eliminate this right. How preemptive rights may be restricted or eliminated depends on the particular statutory provision governing their application. Some statutes provide that preemptive rights exist unless otherwise provided in the articles. Under these statutes, preemptive rights can be eliminated or limited only by an appropriate provision in the corporate articles. Other statutes provide that preemptive rights do not exist unless otherwise provided in the corporate articles. Under this approach, for shareholders to have preemptive rights such rights must be expressly included in the articles of incorporation. The RMBCA adopts this latter approach.

Transfer of Shares. Generally, a shareholder who is dissatisfied with corporate operations may freely transfer his or her shares to someone else. Such transfers traditionally have been governed by Article 8 of the Uniform Commercial Code as adopted by most states today.

Under Article 8 of the UCC, a stock certificate can be validly transferred only by the delivery of the certificate and its indorsement by the registered owner. The indorsement may be either on the certificate itself or on a separate instrument called a "stock power." The signature of the registered owner on the back of the certificate constitutes a valid indorsement (Section 8–308). An indorsement of the certificate on a stock power alone does not transfer any rights unless the certificate is also delivered to the transferee (Section 8–309). When a certificate has been delivered to a purchaser without the necessary indorsement, a transfer has been completed and the purchaser has a specifically enforceable right to compel any necessary indorsement (Section 8–307). The effect of a valid transfer is to make the transferee the complete legal and equitable owner of the shares, and the corporation must register the transfer and recognize the transferee as the rightful owner (Section 8–401).

Because it is considered to be sound public policy to promote the free transfer of property, a shareholder may freely transfer his or her shares. This is known as the doctrine of free alienability of property, or the doctrine of free alienation. Under this doctrine, free alienability is considered an inherent attribute of corporate securities, and unreasonable restraints on alienation are invalid. However, the doctrine invalidates only unreasonable restraints on transfer; reasonable restrictions are permitted. To be valid, any such reasonable restriction must be noted conspicuously on the certificate (Section 8–204).

Most jurisdictions recognize the right of corporations to impose restrictions giving the corporation or other shareholders the option to purchase the shares at an agreed upon price before they are offered to third parties. This type of restriction is known as a "right of first refusal" and is most commonly imposed by close corporations in an attempt to restrict control if not total membership to a homogeneous shareholder group. However, restrictions giving the directors an option to purchase the shares at a price to be fixed at the directors' sole discretion are generally considered to be unreasonable restraints and therefore invalid.

Transfer restrictions are increasingly being resorted to today to police enforcement of the registration requirements of the Securities Act of 1933 against persons purchasing their securities in a transaction exempt from that act's registration requirements as one "not involving a public offering." Under the Securities Act, shares issued pursuant to this private offering exemption must be held by the issuee as an investment and not for resale or public distribution. A subsequent sale may render the seller liable as an underwriter under the act and destroy the private offering exemption and render the issuer liable as well. To protect themselves, corporate issuers often require the issuee to sign a letter indicating his or her investment intent. Stock sold in this fashion is known as "lettered stock," but the letter alone is not an effective transfer restriction, because the restriction is not conspicuously included on the certificate pursuant to UCC Section 8–204. As additional protection, corporate issuers must print a legend on the face of the certificate stating that the shares are not transferred until registered, thus notifying potential purchasers that the corporation may refuse to recognize any transfer that will impair the exemption.

The RMBCA has added a provision seeking to codify court decisions that have ruled both for and against transfer restrictions. Section 6.27 authorizes transfer restrictions when imposed by the articles of incorporation, bylaws, and agreements among shareholders. Transfer restrictions are authorized to maintain the corporation's identity, to preserve exemptions under federal or state securities laws, and "for any other reasonable purpose" (Section 6.27[c]).

Appraisal and Buy-Out Rights of Dissenting Shareholders. Certain kinds of extraordinary transactions, even though lawfully authorized and validly effected, entitle dissenting shareholders to have their shares purchased by the corporation at a fair cash value. This is referred to as the shareholder's appraisal and buy-out right. Its purpose is to effect a compromise between the overwhelming majority who desire a fundamental change in the corporate venture and the insistence of a dissenter not to be forced into a position different from that bargained for when he or she bought the stock.

The RMBCA (Section 13.02) recognizes five extraordinary transactions that give rise to an appraisal and buy-out right:

1. A merger or consolidation
2. A sale or exchange of all or substantially all of the corporate property and assets not in the regular course of business
3. The acquisition of the corporation by another through the exchange of the corporate stock
4. An amendment to the articles of incorporation that materially and adversely affects rights of a dissenter's shares
5. Any other corporate action that by virtue of the articles of incorporation, bylaws, or board resolution entitles shareholders to dissent, and be paid for their shares

However, the right does not apply to the shareholders of a surviving corporation in a merger if a vote of that corporation's shareholders is not necessary to authorize the merger. The right also does not apply when the corporation's shares are registered on a national securities exchange. Some states, such as Ohio, additionally grant appraisal rights when certain amendments to the corporate articles change the purpose of the corporation or adversely affect the class of shares owned by the dissenter.

Under the RMBCA, the shareholder must take certain procedural steps to effectuate an appraisal and buy-out remedy. If one of the transactions noted here is to be voted on, and dissenter rights are created, the dissenting shareholder must notify the corporation prior to the shareholders meeting that he or she intends to demand payment if the proposed action of management is approved. Then the shareholder must vote against the proposed action at the meeting. After majority approval has been obtained, the dissenting shareholder must be notified how to demand payment and then make a written demand on the corporation for payment of the fair value of the shares. The corporation must respond with an offer to the shareholder of what it considers to be the fair value of the shares plus interest. If no agreement is reached, either party may petition the court in the county where the registered office of the corporation is located for an appraisal of the fair value of the shares. All dissenting shareholders will be made parties to the proceeding and will be bound by any judgment. In such a case, the court may appoint one or more appraisers to recommend a fair value of the shares. The costs of the proceeding, including the expenses of the appraisers, will be assessed against the corporation unless the court determines that the shareholders' failure to accept the corporation's offer was arbitrary, vexatious, or not in good faith, in which case the cost and expenses will be apportioned among the dissenting shareholders (Sections 13.21 through 13.31).

Shareholder Suits. Sometimes in order to enforce a right or to protect his or her investment, a shareholder must resort to legal action in the form of a lawsuit. Although the procedural aspects of shareholder litigation are of more concern to lawyers than to business people, some awareness of the fundamentals of shareholder litigation is appropriate.

Shareholder litigation falls into two broad categories: (1) direct suits by shareholders on their own behalf and (2) derivative suits on behalf of the corporation. Direct actions by shareholders on their own behalf may be further subdivided into two additional categories: (a) individual actions and (b) class actions.

Direct suits by shareholders on their own behalf are limited to the enforcement of claims belonging to the shareholder based on his or her share ownership. When the injury is primarily to the shareholder, the shareholder may bring an action on his or her own behalf. If the injury is peculiar to the shareholder, the action will be an individual one. If the injury affects several shareholders or a class of shares, a class action may be pursued, with the shareholder initiating the action representing the entire class. In a shareholder class action, the representative of the class brings suit on behalf of himself or herself individually and on behalf of all other shareholders who are similarly situated. Some examples of shareholder suits that may be brought individually or by way of class action are suits:

1. To enforce the right to vote
2. To sue for breach of a shareholder agreement
3. To enforce the right to inspect corporate books and records
4. To compel the payment of lawfully declared dividends
5. To protect preemptive rights
6. To compel corporate dissolution

When the injury to the shareholder's investment results from a wrong to the corporation rather than a wrong directed against the shareholder, a shareholder cannot bring a direct suit on his or her own behalf but must bring a derivative action on behalf of the corporation to enforce a right belonging to the corporation. Any judgment will go directly to the corporation, not to the shareholder who brings the action. The reason for this restriction is to avoid a multiplicity of litigation that might otherwise occur if all shareholders were permitted to bring direct actions on their own behalf for wrongs committed against the corporate entity. The restriction also is consistent with the separateness of corporate and shareholder interests recognized by the courts when the corporation is sued as a defendant. Although any remedy belongs to the corporation, theoretically the shareholder will also benefit from the judgment because any corporate remedy should also enhance the shareholder's investment.

The shareholder's derivative suit involves the assertion by a shareholder of a corporate cause of action against persons either in or out of the corporation who have allegedly wronged it. Such suits are brought where the corporation has failed to enforce such claims itself. Some examples of derivative suits would be actions:

1. To recover damages resulting from a consummated ultra vires act
2. To enjoin corporate officials from breaching their fiduciary duty to the corporation
3. To recover improperly paid dividends
4. To enjoin outsiders from wronging the corporation or to recover from such a wrong

Certain procedural prerequisites must be met in a shareholder's derivative suit. The plaintiff must have been a shareholder at the time the wrong was committed against the corporation or have acquired the shares by operation of law (such as through the distribution of a decedent's estate) from someone who was a holder of record at that time. The shareholder must also show that he or she has exhausted internal corporate remedies describing with particularity the efforts, if any, made to obtain the desired action from the directors and, if necessary, from the shareholders, and providing the reasons for any failure to obtain the action or for not making the effort. A derivative proceeding, once begun, cannot be discontinued or settled without court approval (RMBCA Section 7.40).

The Role of the Board of Directors

Although the shareholders are the owners of the corporation, the board of directors is the supreme power in the management of the corporation. The following pages examine the nature of the board's authority, the appointment of directors to the board, and the formalities of board functions.

Nature of Board Authority. Although the board of directors is charged by statute with the duty of managing the corporation, it is generally recognized that the purpose of the board is only to establish policy and to provide direction to the corporation. Recent legislative developments reflect a trend toward recognizing this reality.

Most state statutes say that the business affairs of the corporation "shall be managed by a board of directors." Recently, many commentators have voiced concern that such language may be interpreted to mean that the directors must become involved in the detailed administration of the corporation's affairs. Although requiring such involvement is reasonable in closely held corporations, recent developments make such an expectation unreasonable in today's complex corporations. Noteworthy among these developments is the advent of outside directors, who are individuals from outside the corporate management and not otherwise involved with the corporation. The RMBCA seeks to clarify board responsibility and bring it into accord with the realities of today's corporations, particularly the large diversified enterprise. Section 8.01 now provides that the business and affairs of the corporation shall be managed *"under the direction"* of a board of directors. The RMBCA eliminates any ambiguity regarding the role of the board of directors in formulating major management policy as opposed to direct day-to-day management. Only a few state statutes, such as Delaware's and California's, have similar provisions, although a trend exists toward adopting such language.

Generally, the board's responsibility may be broadly described as establishing basic corporate objectives, selecting competent senior executives, monitoring personnel policies and procedures with a view to assuring that the corporation is provided with other competent managers in the future, reviewing the performance of senior executives, and monitoring the corporation's performance. Typical matters over which the board has control include dividends, financing, and corporate policy as to the prices of its products, expansion, and labor relations. More specifically, the board of directors is also required or authorized to: call special shareholders meetings, elect corporate officers, declare dividends, recommend dissolution, approve any merger or consolidation, change the registered office or registered agent, allocate to capital surplus consideration received for shares having no par value, cancel reacquired shares, and approve amendments to the corporate bylaws.

Appointment of Directors. Under the RMBCA, the initial directors may be named in the articles of incorporation. These directors may be "dummy directors" who serve only until the first shareholders meeting and then resign (Section 2.02[b]). The RMBCA does not require that the number and names of the directors constituting the initial board be stated in the articles. Except for the first board, the number of directors may be established either by the corporate articles or the bylaws (Section 8.03). The effect of this is to permit the directors to retain for themselves the power to change the number of directors without seeking shareholder approval. This is because under Section 2.06 of the RMBCA, the power to amend the bylaws is vested solely in the board unless reserved to the shareholders by the articles, while amendments to the articles require shareholder approval. Thus, by providing for the number of directors only in the bylaws, the directors may reserve for themselves the power to determine their number.

Until recently, most state statutes required a minimum of three directors. However, the trend, as illustrated by Section 8.03 of the RMBCA, is to allow for only one director. This eliminates the need for single shareholder corporations to enlist superfluous directors.

Although traditionally shareholders elect the directors from among their ranks, most statutes, including the RMBCA (Section 8.-02), specifically provide that directors need not be shareholders of the corporation. Furthermore, few statutes impose age and residency requirements upon directors. For example, the RMBCA specifically states that "directors need not be residents of this State . . ." (Section 8.02). However, these and other requirements may be prescribed in the corporate articles. Thus, if it is felt that a real financial stake in the success of the enterprise will likely increase both vigilance and diligence, the articles may provide a requirement of substantial stock ownership by directors. Such stock is generally called a director's qualifying stock.

Federal legislation affecting board composition may disqualify some individuals from becoming directors. Interlocking directorates of competing corporations are restricted by Section 8 of the Clayton Act. This statute forbids someone from serving as a director of two or more competing corporations if one corporation has capital, surplus, and undivided profits aggregating more than $1 million and if the elimination of competition between them would constitute a violation of federal antitrust laws.

Aside from the members of the initial board, directors are elected at the annual shareholders meeting and usually hold office until the next annual meeting. Section 8.03 of the RMBCA provides, "Directors are elected at the first annual meeting of shareholders and at each annual meeting thereafter. . . ." However, under the RMBCA, directors may serve staggered terms in corporations having nine or more directors if the articles authorize the classification of directors. When there is a classification of directors, the terms of the classes into which the directors are divided will expire serially and will be longer than one year. For example, a board of nine directors may be divided into three classes with three directors in each class. After the first two years, each director will serve for three years, and three directors will be elected each year.

Vacancies may occur on the board as the result of the resignation, death, or removal of an incumbent director or as the result of an increase in the number of directors. Many statutes provide that any vacancy on the board must be filled by a vote of the shareholders. The RMBCA (Section 8.10) allows the shareholders or the remaining directors to fill the vacancy. Under the RMBCA, a director elected to fill a vacancy created by an incumbent is elected until the next shareholders meeting at which directors are elected. Any director elected to fill a vacancy created by an increase in the number of directors serves only until the next election of directors by shareholders (Section 8.05).

Although directors may be removed from the board by failure to obtain reelection at the annual shareholders meeting, a stickier question is presented when the removal is to occur during the director's term of office. In the absence of a statute or a provision in the articles, the courts do not permit shareholders to remove a director without cause. Thus, at common law, directors can be removed during their terms only for cause. Exactly what constitutes cause is often unclear. Today, most statutes, including the RMBCA (Section 8.08), permit a majority of the voting shareholders to remove a director or the entire board "with or without cause" before the end of his or her term at a special shareholders meeting called expressly for that purpose.

Formalities of Board Functions. The general common law rule is that a director can act as a part of the board of directors only at a proper meeting of the board. Under this approach the board cannot act unless it is formally convened. Informal action is insufficient; the directors have to be physically present at the meeting and cannot vote by proxy. The reason for this is to encourage consultation among board members as a body. Today, most statutes, including the RMBCA (Section 8.21), establish a contrary rule and allow board members to act informally without a meeting upon the written consent of all board members. The RMBCA also allows board members to participate in board meetings via a telephone conference call (Section 8.20).

Under the RMBCA, board meetings may be held either in or outside the state of incorporation. The time for board meetings is included in the corporate bylaws; therefore, a director is considered to have constructive notice of all regular board meetings. Many statutes provide that if there is no provision to the contrary in the bylaws, the directors must be given notice of the time and topic of all specially called meetings. The RMBCA provides only that such notice as required by the bylaws must be given, and it also states that neither the business to be transacted nor the purpose of any special meeting must be specified in the notice unless required by the bylaws (Section 8.22). When notice is required by the bylaws, the RMBCA states that a director's attendance at the meeting constitutes a waiver of the required notice, unless the director attends to object to the meeting.

Under the RMBCA, unless the articles or bylaws provide a greater number, a majority of the board members constitutes a quorum for a meeting of the directors (Section 8.24). A majority vote of the quorum constitutes a binding act of the board.

The RMBCA permits the articles or bylaws to authorize the board to designate an executive committee or other committees composed of board members to exercise all the authority of the board except in extraordinary matters, such as article amendments, mergers, etc. (Section 8.25). Executive committees function between board meetings and are especially useful when the board of directors is large and when consideration of specific matters by the smaller group will facilitate decision making. Finance and audit committees, with duties relating to corporate finance and the selection of auditors, are less common.

The Role of Officers and Executives

It is generally recognized that the board of directors is not expected to operate the corporate business. The board delegates the day-to-day management to the corporate officers and executives, who are elected by the board and serve at the board's discretion. The RMBCA provides that "A corporation has the officers described in its bylaws or appointed by the board of directors . . ." (Section 8.40). Unlike most state statutes today, the RMBCA does not require that there be a President, Vice-President, and Treasurer, but leaves the number and titles of officers to the bylaws or the board. This is especially important for small corporations. The officers are regarded as agents of the corporation, having such authority as is conferred by the bylaws or by a board resolution.

MANAGEMENT'S FIDUCIARY OBLIGATIONS

As already observed, those who control and manage modern corporations are protected against interference from shareholders in the handling of corporate affairs. Thus individual shareholders are generally powerless to affect corporate affairs in the case of large-scale organizations. However, this virtual disenfranchisement of the shareholder is not as oppressive as it appears. In partial recognition of these realities, corporate and securities law in recent times have substantially strengthened the fiduciary obligations of management and of other controlling persons to both the corporation and to the shareholder.

Fiduciary Duty to the Corporation

Directors and officers owe fiduciary duties to the corporation similar to the fiduciary duties that agents owe their principals. These fiduciary duties fall broadly into two categories: (1) the duty of loyalty and (2) the duty of care.

Duty of Loyalty. Corporate directors and officers occupy a fiduciary relationship with the corporation, which requires the exercise of good faith and loyalty in any dealings with and for the corporation. The basic principle is that corporate directors and officers should not use their positions to make personal profits or to gain other personal advantages. In principle, this duty of loyalty is similar to the duty of loyalty exercised by agents and partners; however, this duty is owed to the corporate entity, not to the shareholders. The duty arises most frequently in transactions between the corporation and the corporate official involving possible conflict of interest or when a corporate opportunity comes to the attention of the corporate official.

Conflicts of interest between officers and directors and their corporations can occur whenever a transaction takes place between the corporation and them. The RMBCA does not prohibit a transaction between a director and the corporation in which the director has a financial interest as long as the transaction was fair when authorized, or was ratified by the board of directors. When a transaction is contested the burden of proof to establish fairness falls on the person charged with having a conflict. The person charged has the burden to show there was full disclosure of the conflict and approval by disinterested directors or shareholders (Section 8.31 and Official Comments).

The general rule is that a corporation has a prior claim to opportunities of business and profits that may be regarded as incidental to its business. Such an opportunity is called a "corporate opportunity," and directors and officers cannot acquire this business opportunity to the detriment of the corporation. Usurpation of a corporate opportunity is normally dealt with by imposing a constructive trust on the wrongful director or officer, meaning that he or she is deemed to hold the benefits of the bargain for the corporation. When an opportunity that is relevant to the corporation's present or prospective business activities comes to the attention of a corporate director or officer, he or she must first offer it to the corporation. Only after a disinterested board determines that the corporation should not pursue the opportunity may the corporate officer or director pursue the matter for his or her own account. However, if the corporation is financially unable to take advantage of the opportunity, the officer or director need not present it to the corporation. The following case clearly illustrates the corporate opportunity doctrine.

Guth v. Loft, Inc.

Supreme Court of Deleware

5 A. 2d 503 (1939)

Loft filed a complaint in the Court of Chancery against Charles Guth, Grace Company, and Pepsi-Cola Company seeking to impress a trust in favor of Loft upon all shares of capital stock of Pepsi-Cola registered in the name of Guth and Grace (approximately 91 percent of the capital stock).

Guth became the president and general manager of Loft in 1931. Loft manufactured and sold candies, syrups, and beverages in 115 retail stores along Middle Atlantic seaboard and had wholesale activities amounting to $800,000 in sales. Its total assets exceeded $9,000,000 in 1931. When Coca-Cola refused to give Guth a jobber's discount based on volume of purchases made by Loft, Guth found out that Pepsi-Cola could be purchased for considerably less. When Pepsi-Cola was adjudicated bankrupt in 1931, one Megargel, an officer and major stockholder of that company, and Guth entered into an agreement whereby 50 percent of the stock of Pepsi-Cola went to Grace, a corporation owned by Guth's family that made syrups for soft drinks and that sold some syrup to Loft. Through several other transactions with Megargel, Guth came to own another 41 percent of Pepsi-Cola stock. During this period 1931–35, Guth borrowed heavily from Loft, and Grace became insolvent. Additionally, without the knowledge of the board of directors, Guth used Loft's facilities, materials, credit, executives, and employees at will. Some reimbursement was made for wages to workers. Loft suffered a loss of profits in its retail stores estimated at $300,000. Guth had discarded Coca-Cola and spent $20,000 advertising Pepsi-Cola.

Guth claimed that in 1931 he had offered Loft's board of directors the opportunity to take over Pepsi-Cola but they had declined for the following reasons: Pepsi-Cola was a failure, they did not wish to compete with Coca-Cola, the proposition was not in line with Loft's business, and it was not equipped to carry on such a business on the extensive scale needed. Guth also claimed that the board in August, 1933 consented to Loft's extending to Guth its facilities and resources without limit upon Guth's guarantee of all advances and upon Guth's contract to furnish Loft a supply of syrup at a favorable price. No record of these actions was found in contract form or in the minutes of meetings of Loft's board of directors. The lower court found in favor of Loft. Held: affirmed.

Layton, Chief Justice

Corporate officers and directors are not permitted to use their position of trust and confidence to further their private interests. While technically not trustees, they stand in a fiduciary relation to the corporation and its stockholders. A public policy, existing through the years, and derived from a profound knowledge of human characteristics and motives, has established a rule that demands of a corporate officer or director, peremptorily and inexorably, the most scrupulous observance of his duty, not only affirmatively to protect the interests of the corporation committed to his charge, but also to refrain from doing anything that would work injury to the corporation, or to deprive it of profit or advantage which his skill and ability might properly bring to it, or to enable it to make in the reasonable and lawful exercise of its powers. The rule that requires an undivided and unselfish loyalty to the corporation demands that there shall be no conflict between duty and self-interest. The occasions for the determination of honesty, good faith and loyal conduct are many and varied, and no hard and fast rule can be formulated. The standard of loyalty is measured by no fixed scale.

If an officer or director of a corporation, in violation of his duty as such, acquires gain or advantage for himself, the law charges the interest so acquired with a trust for the benefit of the corporation, at its election, while it denies to the betrayer all benefit and profit. The rule, inveterate and uncompromising in its rigidity, does not rest upon the narrow ground of injury or damage to the corporation resulting from a betrayal of confidence, but upon a broader foundation of a wise public policy that, for the purpose of removing all temptation, extinguishes all possibility of profit flowing from a breach of the confidence imposed by the fiduciary relation. Given the relation between the parties, a certain result follows; and a constructive trust is the remedial device through which precedence of self is compelled to give way to the stern demands of loyalty.

The rule, referred to briefly as the rule of corporate opportunity, is merely one of the manifestations of the general rule that demands of an officer or director the utmost good faith in his relation to the corporation which he represents.

The real issue is whether the opportunity to secure a very substantial stock interest in a corporation to be formed for the purpose of exploiting a cola beverage on a wholesale scale was so closely associated with the existing business activities of Loft, and so essential thereto, as to bring the transaction within that class of cases where the acquisition of the property would throw the corporate officer purchasing it into competition with his company. This is a factual question to be decided by reasonable inferences from objective facts.

The facts and circumstances demonstrate that Guth's appropriation of the Pepsi-Cola opportunity to himself placed him in a competitive position with Loft with respect to a commodity essential to it, thereby rendering his personal interest incompatible with the superior interests of his corporation; and this situation was accomplished, not openly and with his own resources, but secretly and with the money and facilities of the corporation which was committed to his protection.

Although the facts and circumstances disclosed by the voluminous record clearly show gross violations of legal and moral duties by Guth in his dealings with Loft, the appellants make bold to say that no duty was cast upon Guth, hence he was guilty of no disloyalty. The fiduciary relation demands something more than the morals of the market place. Guth's abstractions of Loft's money and materials are complacently referred to as borrowings. Whether his acts are to be deemed properly cognizable in a civil court at all, we need not inquire, but certain it is that borrowing is not descriptive of them. A borrower presumes a lender acting freely. Guth took without limit or stint from a helpless corporation, in violation of a statute enacted for the protection of corporations against such abuses, and without the knowledge or authority of the corporation's Board of Directors. Cunning and craft supplanted sincerity. Frankness gave way to concealment. He did not offer the Pepsi-Cola opportunity to Loft, but captured it for himself. He invested little or no money of his own in the venture, but commandeered for his own benefit and advantage the money, resources and facilities of his corporation and the services of its officials. He thrust upon Loft the hazard, while he reaped the benefit. His time was paid for by Loft. The use of the Grace plant was not essential to the enterprise. In such manner he acquired for himself and Grace ninety one percent of the capital stock of Pepsi, now worth many millions. A genius in his line he may be, but the law makes no distinction between the wrong doing genius and the one less endowed.

Upon a consideration of all the facts and circumstances as disclosed we are convinced that the opportunity to acquire the Pepsi-Cola trademark and formula, goodwill and business belonged to the complainant, and that Guth, as its President, had no right to appropriate the opportunity to himself.

Held: Affirmed.

Duty of Care. Corporate officers and directors are charged with affirmative duties concerning the management and control of the business of their corporations, and they are liable for any corporate losses resulting from their negligence. As recently amended, the RMBCA sets forth the duty of care for corporate directors as follows:

[a] A director shall discharge his duties as a director, including his duties as a member of a committee:

1. in good faith;
2. with the care an ordinary prudent person in a like position would exercise; and
3. when exercising his business judgment with the belief, premised on a rational basis, that his decision is in the "best interests of the corporation" Section 8.30

The drafters' comment explains the applications of this standard as follows:

By combining the requirement of good faith with the statement that a director must act (1) "with such care as an ordinary prudent person in a like position would use under similar circumstances" and (2) "when exercising his business judgment . . . ," Section 8.30(a) incorporates the familiar concept that a director should not be held liable for an honest mistake of business judgment if these criteria are satisfied (Official Comment).

This is known as the "business judgment rule."

Section 8.30 further permits a director to rely on information, opinions, and statements prepared by corporate officials and consultants whom the director reasonably believes are reliable and competent, and any board committees on which he or she does not serve regarding matters within their designated authority.

The following case illustrates the business judgment rule.

Miller v. American Telephone & Telegraph Company
Third Circuit Court of Appeals
507 F. 2d 759 (1974)

Plaintiffs, stockholders in American Telephone and Telegraph Company (AT&T), brought a stockholders' derivative action in the Eastern District of Pennsylvania against AT&T and all but one of its directors. The suit centered upon the failure of AT&T to collect an outstanding debt of some $1.5 million owed to the company by the Democratic National Committee (DNC) for communications services provided by AT&T during the 1968 Democratic national convention. Federal diversity jurisdiction was invoked under 28 U.S.C. §1332.

Plaintiffs' complaint alleged that "neither the officers or directors of AT&T have taken any action to recover the amount owed" from on or about August 20, 1968, when the debt was incurred, until May 31, 1972, the date plaintiffs' amended complaint was filed. The failure to collect was alleged to have involved a breach of the defendant directors' duty to exercise diligence in handling the affairs of the corporation, to have resulted in affording preference to the DNC in collection procedures in violation of §202 (a) of the Communications Act of 1934 and to have amounted to AT&T's making a "contribution" to the DNC in violation of a federal prohibition on corporate campaign spending, 18 U.S.C. §610 (1970).

Plaintiffs sought permanent relief in the form of an injunction requiring AT&T to collect the debt, an injunction against providing further services to the DNC until the debt was paid in full, and a surcharge for the benefit of the corporation against the defendant directors in the amount of the debt plus interest from the due date. A request for a preliminary injunction against the provision of services to the 1972 Democratic convention was denied by the district court after an evidentiary hearing.

On motion of the defendants, the district court dismissed the complaint for failure to state a claim upon which relief could be granted. The court stated that collection procedures were properly within the discretion of the directors whose determination would not be overturned by the court in the absence of an allegation that the conduct of the directors was "plainly illegal, unreasonable, or in breach of a fiduciary duty. . . ." Plaintiffs appeal from dismissal of their complaint.

Seitz, Chief Judge

The sound business judgment rule, the basis of the district court's dismissal of plaintiffs' complaint, expresses the unanimous decision of American courts to eschew intervention in corporate decision-making if the judgment of directors and officers is uninfluenced by personal considerations and is exercised in good faith. Underlying the rule is the assumption that reasonable diligence has been used in reaching the decision which the rule is invoked to justify.

Had plaintiffs' complaint alleged only failure to pursue a corporate claim, application of the sound business judgment rule would support the district court's ruling that a shareholder could not attack the directors' decision. Where, however, the decision not to collect a debt owed the corporation is itself alleged to have been an illegal act, different rules apply. When New York law regarding such acts by directors is considered in conjunction with the underlying purposes of the particular statute involved here, we are convinced that the business judgment rule cannot insulate the defendant directors from liability if they did in fact breach 18 U.S.C. §610 as plaintiffs have charged.

The alleged violation of the federal prohibition against corporate political contributions not only involves the corporation in criminal activity but similarly contravenes a policy of Congress clearly enunciated in 18 U.S.C. §610. That statute and its predecessor reflect congressional efforts: (1) to destroy the influence of corporations over elections through financial contributions and (2) to check the practice of using corporate funds to benefit political parties without the consent of the stockholders.

The fact that shareholders are within the class for whose protection the statute was enacted gives force to the argument that the alleged breach of that statute should give rise to a cause of action in those shareholders to force the return to the corporation of illegally contributed funds. Since political contributions by corporations can be checked and shareholder control over the political use of general corporate funds effectuated only if directors are restrained from causing the corporation to violate the statute, such a violence seems a particularly appropriate basis for finding breach of the defendant directors' fiduciary duty to the corporation. Under such circumstances, the directors cannot be insulated from liability on the ground that the contribution was made in the exercise of sound business judgment.

> Since plaintiffs have alleged actual damage to the corporation from the transaction in the form of the loss of a $1.5 million increment to AT&T's treasury, we conclude that the complaint does state a claim upon which relief can be granted sufficient to withstand a motion to dismiss. Reversed for plaintiffs.

Fiduciary Duty to Shareholders

In early court decisions the directors and officers of a corporation were said to have no fiduciary duty to existing or potential stockholders but solely to the corporation. More recently there has been a trend in decisions finding a duty on the part of officers, directors, employees of the corporation, as well as employees of investment banking firms retained by the corporation to disclose information obtained as a result of being insiders. At the federal level, the Securities Exchange Act addressed itself to disclosure requirements for officers and directors and to what constitutes insider trading. Chapter 30 on the Securities and Exchange Commission will discuss these and other topics in detail.

While the "business judgment" rule has given officers and directors wide latitude in managing a corporation, minority shareholders have recently been filing suits alleging that they have been "frozen out" of the corporation. Minority shareholders often seek injunctions or damages in cases where corporate boards have ratified high salaries for majority or controlling shareholders who are also officers of the corporation. A minority shareholder suit may also result when the board fails to declare dividends and it can be shown that there was not a "good faith" reason. For example, if the controlling shareholders seek to force the minority to sell their stock by not declaring a dividend, or to depress the price of the stock to serve the interest of officers or directors, the courts will see a wrongful purpose and a violation of the "business judgment" rule.

Other circumstances in which minority shareholders have charged "oppression" involve mergers and amendments to the corporate charter altering voting rights of a class of stock.

REVIEW PROBLEMS

1. Biltmore Tissue Corporation was organized in 1932 with an authorized capitalization of 1,000 shares of stock. The adopted bylaws of the corporation contained provisions limiting the number of shares available to each stockholder and restricting stock transfers during both the life of the stockholder and in case of death. According to the bylaws, if a stockholder wanted to sell or transfer shares, he or she had to give the corporation or other stockholders the chance to purchase the stock from the stockholder at the price paid when the stock was originally purchased. If the option was not exercised within 90 days, the stockholder was then free to sell the stock. Henry Kaplan had purchased shares with restrictions of sale and transfer, as detailed above, printed on the stock certificates. When Kaplan died, Biltmore's board of directors voted to exercise its option to repurchase the shares from Kaplan's estate and agreed to pay a sum greater than what Kaplan paid for the stock. Kaplan's executors declined to sell

and wanted the stock transferred to the estate. They brought a lawsuit to compel the corporation to transfer the stock according to the estate's wishes, claiming that the limitation on sale and transfer was an unreasonable restraint. They further argued that the ownership in Kaplan could not be coupled with the right of alienation in another person. The corporation argued that due to the restriction of sale and transfer of the stock, it was not prohibiting the transfer of stock but merely putting a reasonable restriction on the transfer. Does the provision in the corporate bylaws giving the corporation a right or first option to purchase the stock at the price that it originally received for it amount to an unreasonable restraint on the transfer of the stock? Allen v. Biltmore Tissue Corp. 2 NY.2d 534, 141 N.E.2d 812 (1957)

2. Gilbert, the owner of record of seventeen shares of Transamerica Corporation, wrote the management of the company and submitted four proposals that he wanted to be presented for action by shareholders at the next annual stockholders meeting. The Securities and Exchange Commission demanded that Transamerica comply with Gilbert's request, but the company refused. The SEC brought an action to forbid Transamerica from making use of any proxy solicited by it for use at the annual meeting, from making use of the mails or any instrumentality of interstate commerce to solicit proxies, or from making use of any soliciting material without complying with the SEC's demands. Transamerica claimed that the shareholder may interest himself only in a subject in respect to which he is entitled to vote at a stockholder's meeting when every requirement of state law and of the provisions of the charter and bylaws has been fulfilled. State law states that a certificate of incorporation may set forth provisions that limit, regulate, and define the powers and functions of the directors and stockholders.

A bylaw of Transamerica vested in the board of directors the power to decide whether any proposal should be voted on at an annual meeting of stockholders. Three of Gilbert's proposals were: (1) to have independent public auditors of the books of Transamerica elected by the stockholders; (2) to eliminate from a bylaw the requirement that notice of any proposed alteration or amendment of the bylaws be contained in the notice of meetings; (3) to require an account or a report of the proceedings at the annual meetings to be sent to all stockholders. Is Gilbert entitled to make such demands? What are the reasons for and against the proposals made by Gilbert? Will the power of shareholders go to an extreme if small shareholders like Gilbert can exert so much pressure? Securities and Exchange Commission v. Transamerica Corp., 163 F.2d 511 (3d Cir. 1947), *cert. denied,* 332 U.S. 847 (1948)

3. The directors of Acoustic Products Company concluded that it was essential for the success of the company to purchase the rights to manufacture under certain patents held by the DeForest Radio Company. Acoustic was already involved in the manufacture of phonographs and radios. A contract was entered into between an agent of Acoustic and the major shareholder of DeForest providing that Acoustic could purchase one-third of the DeForest stock. This would increase the possibility for Acoustic to obtain the needed patent rights. The directors of Acoustic were not able to acquire enough funds for Acoustic to perform the contract. Thus they personally purchased the DeForest stock. When Acoustic later went bankrupt, the trustee in bankruptcy brought this action against the directors, claiming that by purchasing the DeForest shares they had violated the fiduciary duty owed to the corporation. The parties agreed that the acquisition of the rights under the DeForest patents were essential

for Acoustic's success. Conceding that there existed a close relation between Acoustic and DeForest, the directors argued that, since the company did not have the money to purchase the shares, the directors had violated no duty by purchasing the shares themselves. Who should win? Should the directors suffer financially even though they made their effort to help Acoustic? Or is this possibility for suffering by the directors part of the game in order to prompt directors to use their best efforts in uncovering financial resources to be used by their companies in acquiring an attractive opportunity? Irving Trust Co. v. Deutsch, 73 F.2d 121 (2d Cir. 1934), *cert. denied*, 274 U.S. 708 (1935)

4. Emerson Electric Company acquired 13.2 percent of the outstanding common stock of Dodge Manufacturing Company through a tender offer made in an unsuccessful attempt to take over Dodge. Shortly thereafter, the shareholders of Dodge approved a merger with Reliance Electric Company. Emerson decided to dispose of enough of its shares to bring its holdings below 10 percent in order to immunize the disposal of the remainder of its shares from liability under section 16(b) of the Securities Exchange Act of 1934. Section 16(b) provides that a corporation may recover for itself the profits realized by an owner of more than 10 percent of its shares from a purchase and sale of its stock within any six-month period, provided the owner held more than 10 percent at the time of both purchase and sale. Emerson sold some shares of Dodge, reducing its holdings in Dodge to 9.96 percent of the outstanding shares. Several weeks later Emerson sold the remainder of the Dodge shares to Dodge. Reliance demanded the profits realized on both sales, since the purchase and two sales all occurred within a three-month period. Emerson does not dispute the fact that the profits from the first sale should now be turned over. It contends that after the first sale it no longer held more than 10 percent and should not be treated as an "insider" but like any other investor and consequently, should be able to keep its profit. Who should prevail? If Emerson should lose, is there any time it can keep its profit, or will it always be penalized since it once held more than 10 percent of Dodge's stock? Reliance Electric Co. v. Emerson Electric Co., 404 U.S. 418 (1972)

5. Pillsbury had long opposed the Vietnam war. He learned that Honeywell, Inc. had a substantial part of its business in the production of munitions used in the war and also that Honeywell had a large government contract to produce antipersonnel fragmentation bombs. Pillsbury was determined to stop this production. He bought one share of Honeywell in his name in order to get himself a voice in Honeywell's affairs so he could persuade the company to cease producing munitions. Pillsbury submitted demands to Honeywell requesting that it produce its original shareholder ledger, current shareholder ledger, and all corporate records dealing with weapons and munitions manufacture. Honeywell refused. Pillsbury brought suit to compel Honeywell to let him inspect the requested records. Pillsbury claimed that he wished to inspect the records in order to correspond with other shareholders, with the hope of electing to the board one or more directors who represented his particular viewpoint. Should the court let Pillsbury inspect the records? Does Pillsbury have a proper purpose germane to his interest as a shareholder? Should a shareholder be allowed to persuade a company to adopt his social and political views? State ex rel. Pillsbury v. Honeywell, Inc., 291 Minn. 322, 191 N.W.2d 406 (1971)

6. Cole Real Estate Corporation was a closely held corporation that owned, managed, and rented residential apartment properties.

Mrs. Helen Cole was the majority stockholder, owning all but 86 of the 4,120 outstanding shares of common stock. Peoples Bank & Trust Company of Indianapolis held the remaining 86 shares in a trustee capacity. Mrs. Cole had been a director, the president, and treasurer of the corporation since its organization in 1935. Cole Corporation was a "one-woman corporation," and little evidence of corporate identity was maintained. The most recent board of directors meeting was held in 1954, when the corporation was reorganized. At that meeting the last stock dividend was declared on previously outstanding preferred shares. Mrs. Cole testified that a shareholder meeting had not been held due to lack of interest, even though she knew Indiana law required annual shareholder meetings. As the corporation's sole employee, Mrs. Cole lived in a home owned and operated by the corporation. The home also was the corporate office, and she paid no rent or utilities. Two automobiles—owned, operated, and maintained by the corporation—provided Mrs. Cole with her only means of transportation. She set her own salary during the years 1964–70 without consulting the board of directors. Peoples Bank & Trust, as minority shareholder, brought a lawsuit for an accounting, recovery of corporate assets, and a declaration of dividends. Mrs. Cole argues that a close corporation should be justifiably distinguished from a public corporation when questions of corporate formality and internal operations are at issue. Peoples Bank contends that corporate law prevents an officer and a director of a corporation from using the assets of a corporate entity for their personal gain. Who should win? Was there excessive compensation and/or converted corporate assets? Should a dividend be declared? Cole Real Estate Corp. v. Peoples Bank & Trust Co., 310 N.E. 2d 275 (Court of Appeals of Indiana, 1974)

7. Wiberg, a director of Gulf Coast Land and Development Company, and another director contracted with the corporation to devote their full time to selling a new line of its stock, for which they were to receive a commission on sales. The corporate resolution creating this contract was passed by the votes of these two directors and by a third director. The resolution was later ratified by holders of a majority of the shares at a special meeting in which the three directors, who were the majority shareholders, voted to ratify their action as directors. After two years, the corporation terminated the contract and refused to pay Wiberg his commission. Wiberg sued to recover his commission. Defendant contends that the contract was void as against public policy because two of the three directors who had voted for it had personal interest in the transaction and because it had not been ratified by 100 percent of the shareholders. Wiberg argues that the contract is enforceable, even when the corporation makes a contract with a director; that the director's vote is necessary to authorize the contract if the contract appears to be fair, just, and beneficial to the corporation; and that the director personally made a full disclosure and the contract was then ratified by a majority of the stockholders. Assuming that the contract is what Wiberg contends it is—that is, fair, just, and beneficial to the corporation—should Wiberg prevail? Even though Wiberg has a personal interest in the contract, do you think he will act fairly and honestly in the corporation's interests? Wiberg v. Gulf Coast Land and Development Company, 360 S.W.2d 563 (Tex. Civ. App. 1962)

Securities Regulation

I n Chapter 29, two types of securities (stocks and bonds) were described and their roles in raising capital for corporate financing were analyzed. The importance of securities to our society cannot be overemphasized. Not only are they a means of raising capital for corporate expansion but they also serve as instruments by which individual citizens accumulate wealth through interest received on bonds and dividends paid on stocks. This wealth is often passed on to heirs or contributed to nonprofit organizations such as universities to be used for student scholarship funds and faculty research. Additionally, securities are an integral part of the private sector of our economy with its emphasis on individual decision making in the marketplace. Individual investors, by themselves or through their pension and mutual funds, determine which segments of the economy and which industries within segments will grow. For example, if investors believe that solar power rather than nuclear power will be the energy source of the future, they will move their capital in that direction, stimulating the growth of the solar industry. Further, security holders are the owners of corporations. Through their election of boards of directors they determine which officers will govern and what direction the corporations will take. For example, stockholders through derivative suits may force officers and directors to personally return to the corporation funds illegally spent or wasted. When over 400 corporations in the mid 1970s confessed to the Securities and Exchange Commission that they had made questionable payments overseas and illegal political contributions in this country, many stockholder derivative suits were filed.

This chapter discusses the role of government in regulating securities. Initially, the Securities Act of 1933 (1933 Act) is examined. It sets forth rules governing the *issuance* of securities and their registration. While the 1933 Act prescribes requirements for registration, it does not seek to evaluate the worth of a particular stock or bond offering made to the investing public. Its primary purpose is to force publicly held corporations to disclose all material information to potential investors so the latter can make prudent judgments on whether to invest or not. Second, the chapter examines the 1934 Securities Exchange Act (Exchange Act). This act sets forth rules governing the *trading* in securities once issued. With the Exchange Act, Congress established the Securities and Exchange Commission (SEC) to protect the securities market from fraudulent conduct and to ensure full disclosure for investors trading in securities. The 1933 Act and the Exchange Act are often referred to as the "Securities Acts." While they are the most significant federal legislation regulating securities, Congress has passed additional specialized security statutes.[1] This chapter concludes with an analysis of the role of state legislation in regulating securities issued and traded in intrastate commerce.

THE SECURITIES ACT OF 1933

Definition of a Security

Section 2(1) of the 1933 Act defines a security as

> any note, stock, treasury stock, bond, debenture, evidence of indebtedness, certificate of interest or participation in any profit-sharing agreement, collateral-trust certificate, preorganization certificate or subscription, transferable share, investment contract, voting-trust certificate, certificate of deposit for a security, fractional undivided interest in oil, gas, or other mineral rights, or, in general, any interest or instrument commonly known as a "security," or any certificate of interest or participation in, temporary or interim certificate for, receipt for, guarantee of, or warrant or right to subscribe to or purchase, any of the foregoing.

The interpretation of this definition has been left to the SEC, through its rule-making power and advisory releases, as well as to the courts in individual decisions. In a landmark case, *SEC v. W. J. Howey Co.*,[2] the U.S. Supreme Court outlined a test that is presently used in determining whether a particular instrument or transaction can be termed a "security" and thus falls within the federal security statutes. The Court stated that

1. A contract or scheme must exist where a person invests money in a common enterprise.
2. The investors must have some expectation of profits.
3. The profits must be derived *solely* from the efforts of a promoter or third party but not the investors themselves.

The third element in this test has been the focus of further court concern. It has been interpreted to mean that notes formalizing a debt incurred in a business[3] or shares of stock entitling a purchaser to lease an apartment in a state-subsidized nonprofit housing cooperative[4] are *not* securities. More recently, the courts have modified their interpretation of the words "solely from the efforts of those other than investors." This is particularly true when the efforts made by noninvestors are the significant ones. The case below involving a fraudulent pyramid sales scheme illustrates this trend.

SEC v. Glenn W. Turner Enterprises

U.S. Court of Appeals, Ninth Circuit
474 F.2d. 476 (1973)

This is an action by the Securities and Exchange Commission to enjoin Glenn W. Turner from violating the securities law by selling securities that were not registered. Dare To Be Great (Dare) was a subsidiary of Glenn W. Turner Enterprises, Inc. It offered courses in self-motivation that were entitled Adventures I, II, III. The initial course (Adventure I) included a portable tape recorder, twelve tape-recorded lessons, and some printed material. The purchaser also was entitled to attend a twelve-to-sixteen-hour series of group meetings. The initial cost was $300. For Adventure II, which included more tapes and an additional eighty hours of meetings, the purchaser paid $700. If he or she paid $2,000 more, Adventure III was made available with more tape recordings, more group sessions, and a notebook called "The Fun of Selling." The purchaser of Adventure III could also become an "independent sales trainee" for the purpose of selling Adventures I, II, and III. For an additional $5,000, he or she also received Adventure IV and the right to sell Adventure IV. The purchaser also had the option of selling a $1,000-plan that was similar to Adventure II. The SEC claimed that all these plans were "securities" within the meaning of the 1933 and 1934 Securities Acts. The federal district court decided in favor of the SEC. Defendant, Turner Enterprises, Inc. appealed.

Held. Affirmed for SEC.

Duniway, Justice

The trial court's findings, which are fully supported by the record, demonstrate that Turner Enterprises' scheme is a gigantic and successful fraud. The question presented is whether the "Adventures" or "Plans" enjoined are "securities" within the meaning of the federal securities laws.

It is apparent from the record that what is sold is not of the usual "business motivation" type of courses. Rather, the purchaser is really buying the possibility of deriving money from the sale of the plans by Dare to individuals whom the purchaser has brought to Dare. The promotional aspects of the Plans, such as seminars, films, and records, are aimed at interesting others in the Plans. Their value for any other purpose is, to put it mildly, minimal.

Once an individual has purchased a Plan, he turns his efforts toward bringing others into the organization, for which he will receive a part of what they pay. His task is to bring prospective purchasers to "Adventure Meetings."

These meetings are like an old-time revival meeting, but directed toward the joys of making easy money rather than salvation. Their purpose is to convince prospective purchasers, or "prospects," that Dare is a sure route to great riches. Films are shown, usually involving the "rags-to-riches" story of Dare founder, Glenn W. Turner. The goal of all this is to persuade the prospect to purchase a plan, especially Adventure IV, so that he may become a "salesman," and thus grow wealthy as part of the Dare organization. It is intimated that as Glenn W. Turner Enterprises, Inc., expands, high positions in the organization, as well as lucrative opportunities to purchase stock, will be available. After the meeting, pressure is applied to the prospect by Dare people, in an effort to induce him to purchase one of the Adventures or the Plan. In *SEC v. W. J. Howey Co.,* the Supreme Court set out its by now familiar definition of an investment contract: "The test is whether the scheme involves an investment of money in a common enterprise with profits to come solely from the efforts of others."

In *Howey* the Court held that a land sales contract for units of a citrus grove, together with a service contract for cultivating and marketing the crops, was an investment contract and hence a security. The Court held that what was in essence being offered was "an opportunity to contribute money and to share in the profits of a large citrus-fruit enterprise managed and partly owned by respondents." The purchasers had no intention themselves of either occupying the land or developing it; they were attracted only "by the prospects of a return on their investment." It was clear that the profits were to come "solely" from the efforts of others.

For purposes of the present case, the sticking point in the *Howey* definition is the word "solely," a qualification which of course exactly fitted the circumstances in *Howey.* All the other elements of the *Howey* test have been met here. There is an investment of money, a common enterprise, and the expectation of profits to come from the efforts of others. Here, however, the investor, or purchaser, must himself exert some efforts if he is to realize a return on his initial cash outlay. He must find prospects and persuade them to attend Dare Adventure Meetings, and at least some of them must then purchase a plan if he is to realize that return. Thus it can be said that the returns or profits are not coming "solely" from the efforts of others.

We hold, however, that in light of the remedial nature of the legislation, the statutory policy of affording broad protection to the public, and the Supreme Court's admonitions that the definition of securities should be a flexible one, the word "solely" should not be read as a strict or literal limitation on the definition of an investment contract, but rather must be construed realistically, so as to include within the definition those schemes which involve in substance, if not form, securities. Within this context, we hold that Adventures III and IV and the $1,000 Plan are investment contracts within the meaning of the 1933 and 1934 Acts.

Securities Markets

Securities markets are not easily defined because, unlike goods (e.g., clothes) that are manufactured, distributed, and consumed by the public, securities as defined above are not consumed directly by the purchaser/investor. Securities become a form of currency in which an initial investor may trade for other securities in what are known as "securities markets." These may have a physical location, such as the New York Stock Exchange (NYSE) with its trading floor, or none, such as the over-the-counter (OTC) market. There is a marked contrast to their operations. The NYSE acts in a very formal manner, determining who will be allowed to trade on the exchange (who has a "seat") and the function of each member. Until 1975, it prescribed the commissions to

be charged. In a NYSE transaction, a buyer or seller goes to an investment firm, which acts as a broker. The broker transmits the customer's order to the exchange floor, where only a registered specialist may buy or sell as a dealer in the security. The broker's firm charges the customer a commission.

In contrast, the OTC market has no physical facilities and no specialists. Most work is done by a computer network or phone, and anyone can act as a dealer. If a customer orders a particular stock on the OTC market and the firm is not a dealer in the stock, it will purchase it as a broker from another dealer, making a market in the stock.

With satellite communication and data-transmission networks, some have argued that there is no longer a need for physical facilities like the NYSE. In effect they argue that computerized national and international marketing systems for securities will soon be in place and that stock exchanges will be outmoded.

Registration of Securities

The 1933 Act forbids the public offer or sale through the mail or other means of interstate commerce of any instrument or transaction defined as a security unless it has been registered with the SEC or meets one of the exemptions set out in Section 3 or 4 of the Act. When a corporation wishes to issue securities (issuer or issuing corporation), it files a registration statement with the SEC that contains a prospectus and additional exhibits and information. A copy of the prospectus must be provided to every purchaser. The additional exhibits and information are kept on file. The SEC staff examines the prospectus and exhibits to see if they include such information as the nature of the registrant's business, properties held, the management, control, and operation of the business, the securities to be offered for sale, and certified financial statements. The SEC has authority to request additional information or to issue a "refusal order" not permitting a registration to become effective if it contains serious deficiencies. Usually a letter of comment ("deficiency letter") by the SEC staff is sufficient to correct deficiencies. If no action is taken by the staff, registration automatically becomes effective twenty days after a registration statement has been filed. As noted previously in this chapter, the purpose of the 1933 Act is to provide public disclosure of material information to potential investors so they will have an adequate basis for determining whether to invest in an issuer's securities offering. The registration statement is a vehicle for implementing this goal. The SEC does not evaluate the merit or worth of the securities registered and to be issued.

After the securities are registered and the effective date for issuance has arrived, the issuer, usually through underwriters and dealers, sells its securities to individual and institutional investors. It should be noted that after filing but before the effective date ("waiting period") oral offers by underwriters to dealers and the public are permitted, but no written offers or sales are allowed until the effective date. During this waiting period the SEC allows notices to appear in newspapers of potential offerings by the issuer as long as such notices clearly specify that they are not offers to sell. It should be emphasized that the SEC can shorten the time between registration and effectiveness to forty-eight hours. This has become common, especially with volatile markets.

Traditionally, corporations that issue securities have worked through investment-banking firms (underwriters), which buy or offer to buy securities and in turn employ dealers as agents to sell securities to the public. In an attempt to cut red tape and help issuers raise capital at opportune moments, the SEC adopted Rule 415 on an experimental basis. Effective March 1982, the rule allows over 2,000 large publicly traded corporations to file single "shelf registration" statements with the SEC, designating the amount of bonds and stocks they want to put on the "shelf" for a two-year period. This statement covers all potential sales of securities, so the individual company does not have to publish a new, detailed prospectus each time it wants to raise capital. It can simply refer investors to data published in its annual or quarterly reports and enter the market with its "shelf securities" at an opportune time. Corporations such as American Telephone and Telegraph have applauded the new rule for the flexibility it provides, especially in a period of fluctuating market conditions. Large investment banking firms and regional underwriters have opposed Rule 415, claiming that the investor will have little opportunity to learn of new offerings before issued. Regional securities firms fear that they will be squeezed out of the underwriting business. Historically, the regional underwriters have relied upon big investment firms such as Morgan Stanley to include them in large syndicates selling securities for an issuer. In May 1982, under Rule 415, AT&T sold its entire offering of $110.8 million in stock to an investment-banking firm, Morgan Stanley, which in turn sold the securities to institutional investors. If this experimental rule becomes permanent, it could add impetus to the merging of regional firms with financial giants like American Express and Prudential Insurance. This trend, combined with large corporations like Phillip Morris doing their own in-house underwriting, may lead to a different marketing style and greater concentration in the investment-banking industry.

Exempted Securities

Section 3 of the 1933 Act, and regulations implementing it, exempt from the registration provision certain types of securities. It should be noted that the Section 3 securities discussed here are *not* exempted from the antifraud provisions of either the 1933 or 1934 Securities Acts.

Section 3(a) exempts from registration commercial paper such as drafts, notes, and bankers' acceptance provided they arise out of current transactions, have maturity dates of not more than nine months, and are not advertised for sale to the public.

Section 3(b) authorizes the SEC to exempt relatively small offerings of securities that do not exceed $5 million. Using this authority, the SEC promulgated Regulation A and Rules 240 and 242.

Rule 240 allows a small issuance of a closely held corporation to be exempt from registration under the following conditions:

1. The total sales within twelve months do not exceed $100,000
2. No general advertising to the public takes place in offer or sale

3. All the stock of the issuing corporation is owned by 100 people or fewer
4. The securities offered have certain restrictions with regard to their resale
5. The issuing corporation notifies the SEC within 10 days after each issue

Rule 242 provides further relief from the costly registration process for small businesses. Promulgated in February 1980, it allows sales by small issuers up to $2 million per issue in a six-month period without registration. However, the following conditions must be met:

1. The $2 million figure would include sales made under Rule 240 and Regulation A (discussed below)
2. Sales would be made to certain "accredited persons" and thirty-five "other purchasers" (accredited persons generally include banks, insurance companies, investment companies, and certain officers or directors of the issuing corporation)
3. If no accredited purchasers are involved, others must be provided with all material information
4. The issuer may not engage in any general advertising
5. The issuer must take precautions and notify the SEC of any resale of the exempt securities similar to Rule 240's precautions

Regulation A, also promulgated pursuant to Section 3(b), exempts small public offerings of securities that do not exceed $1.5 million over a twelve-month period. The issuing company must file a notification and offering circular with a regional SEC office ten days before each proposed offering of securities. The SEC may follow with some informal comments similar to the regular registration process.

Section 3(b) also provides an exemption for a public offering of "any security which is part of an issue sold only *within the border of a single state* and to residents of that state." The issuer must be a resident or a corporation incorporated or doing business in that state. The courts and the SEC under Rule 147 have emphasized that *all* purchasers must be residents of the state. If one is not, the securities offering will not be exempted. Additionally, Rule 147 requires that 80 percent of the gross revenues of the issuer must come from operations within the state.

Certain other securities are also exempt from registration by virtue of Section 3 of the 1933 Act and SEC interpretations of that section—for example, securities issued by the U.S. Government, nonprofit organizations, and domestic banks, as well as securities regulated by agencies other than the SEC. Securities are exempted if issued pursuant to mergers or reorganizations where no cash is involved and the issuer offers securities solely in exchange for other securities.

Exempted Transactions

Section 4(1) of the 1933 Act exempts transactions by persons other than an issuer, underwriter, or dealer. Sections 4(3) and 4(4) allow qualified exemptions for dealers and brokers. In reality, underwriters are the only ones not exempted. Rule 144 promulgated by the SEC sets forth the conditions that determine when a person is not an underwriter and not involved in selling restricted securities and is therefore exempt.

Section 4(2) involves transactions that are exempt because they do *not* involve any public offering of securities. Approximately 25 percent of all corporate securities fall under this exemption. As noted in the case below, there are several factors that the courts and the SEC consider in determining whether one qualifies for a private-placement exemption.

Hill York Corp. et al. v. Gurn H. Freeman et al. and American International Franchises, Inc. et al.

U.S. Court of Appeals, Fifth Circuit
448 F. 2d 680 (1971)

Freeman and Browne, defendants, had developed a franchise promotion scheme designed to funnel funds from the sale of stock in certain franchise sales centers to themselves as stockholders of American International Franchises, Inc. (American). The Freemans formed American in Springfield, Mo., in July 1967; Browne joined one month later as executive vice president. These three individuals comprised all the officers and stockholders of American.

The franchising concept conceived by the Freemans involved the marketing of two restaurant franchises called Hickory Corral and Italian Den. The chairman of the board of directors of Hickory Corral was Gurn Freeman, and the chairman of the board of Italian Den was Jack Freeman. The only restaurant of either type to be operated was one Hickory Corral, which opened in Springfield, Mo., and closed shortly thereafter. Under the plan commonly used, American would seek out local investors to incorporate a state-wide or regional franchise sales center. The payment of a franchise fee to American conferred upon the purchaser the exclusive right to sell Hickory Corral and Italian Den franchises within the state or region. The local investors who formed the franchise sales center corporation would sell stock in the corporation to a small number of persons who would be most likely to furnish supplies and services to the restaurants—for instance, a real estate firm, an air conditioning company, a builder.

American was also in the franchise consulting business and was to assist the local investors in organizing and developing the business of the sales center. During the first year of operation, the defendants formed six state franchising systems, one of which involved a plaintiff in this case, Florida Franchise Systems, Inc. As in other transactions, Browne, the defendant, sought out the plaintiff, solicited capital from it, and provided sales brochures designed by the defendants to secure additional capital. American International advised the franchisees on every step, purchasing $10,000 worth of stock out of the $70,000 available. Additionally, two of the five directors were required by the agreement with Florida Franchise to be representatives of American. On October 4, 1968, American and Florida Franchise entered into a franchise agreement, utilizing a form agreement drafted by American. The price to Florida Franchise for this exclusive right to sell was $25,000. Subsequent to the payment of the $25,000, on October 22, American insisted that Florida Franchise enter into a new agreement that provided for an additional franchise fee of $1,000 per month.

Plaintiffs, alleging that these activities amounted to a pyramiding scheme to funnel money to American, brought this suit for rescission of the stock sales and the return of their investments. A jury in the lower court awarded rescission of the agreement and a return of the monies paid. Punitive damages of $85,000 were assessed against the defendants individually. They appealed.

Held: Affirmed for plaintiffs as to rescission of stock sales and return of purchase price. Reversed as to punitive damages.

Clark, Judge

It is conceded that no registration statement had been filed with the SEC in connection with this offering of securities. The defendants contend, however, that the transactions come within the exemptions to registration found in 15 U.S.C.A. § 77d(2) (commonly known as Section 4(2)). Specifically, they contend that the offering of securities was not a public offering.

At the threshold of this contention we deem it appropriate to consider the instructions under which the public offering phase of the exemption was decided.

The SEC has stated that the question of public offering is one of fact and must depend upon the circumstances of each case. We agree with this approach. It is of course apparent that presenting an issue of fact to SEC analysts is totally different from presenting a question of fact to a jury unsophisticated and untrained in the niceties of securities law. Although courts accord a marked deference to the expertise of such an agency which is charged with broad regulation of a specific field when reviewing their regulatory action, we do not intimate that their procedures are binding precedent. However, to be consistent—which is the constant aim if not the invariable result of the law—and, most vitally, because we find SEC criteria both legally accurate and meaningfully sufficient for testing the issue, we hold that a jury should consider the factors enumerated below which the SEC considers, together with the policies embodied in the Act.

The following specific factors are relevant:

1. The number of offerees and their relationship to each other and to the issuer.

In the past the SEC has utilized the arbitrary figure of twenty-five offerees as a litmus test of whether an offering was public. A leading commentator in the field has noted, however, that in recent years the SEC has increasingly disavowed any safe numerical test. Initially, the figure of twenty-five was probably no more than a rule of administrative convenience. In any case, such an arbitrary figure is inappropriate as an absolute in a private civil lawsuit. The Supreme Court has put it thus: "No particular numbers are prescribed. Anything from two to infinity may serve: perhaps even one." SEC v. Ralston Purina Co., 346 U.S. 119, 73 S. Ct. 981, 97 L.Ed.2d 1494 (1953). Obviously, however, the more offerees, the more likelihood that the offering is public. The relationship between the offerees and the issuer is most significant. If the offerees know the issuer and have special knowledge as to its business affairs, such as high executive officers of the issuer would possess, then the offering is apt to be private. The Supreme Court laid special stress on this consideration in *Ralston Purina* by stating that "[t]he focus of the inquiry should be on the need of the offerees for the protections afforded by registration. The employees here were not shown to have access to the kind of information which registration would disclose." Also to be considered is the relationship between the offerees and their knowledge of each other. For example, if the offering is being made to a diverse and unrelated group, i.e. lawyers, grocers, plumbers, etc., then the offering would have the appearance of being public; but an offering to a select group of high executive officers of the issuer who know each other and of course have similar interests and knowledge of the offering would more likely be characterized as a private offering.

2. The number of units offered.

Here again there is no fixed magic number. Of course, the smaller the number of units offered, the greater the likelihood the offering will be considered private.

3. The size of the offering.

The smaller the size of the offering, the more probability it is private.

4. The manner of offering.

A private offering is more likely to arise when the offer is made directly to the offerees rather than through the facilities of public distribution such as investment bankers or the securities exchanges. In addition, public advertising is incompatible with the claim of private offering.

Even an objective testing of these factors without determining whether a more comprehensive and generalized prerequisite has been met, is insufficient. "The natural way to interpret the private offering exemption is in light of the statutory purpose. The design of the statute is to protect investors by promoting full disclosure of information thought necessary to informed investment decisions." Thus the ultimate test is whether " 'the particular class of persons affected need the protection of the Act'." *SEC* v. *Ralston Purina Co.* The Act is remedial legislation entitled to a broad construction. Conversely, its exemptions must be narrowly viewed. Thus, only where the practical need for the enforcement of the safeguards afforded by the Act or the public benefit derived from such enforcement can confidently be said to be remote with respect to the transactions is the private offering exemption met.

It is well-settled law that the defendants have the burden of proving their affirmative defense of private offering. *SEC* v. *Ralston Purina Co.* The defendants, however, adduced no evidence on this issue, relying instead on the evidence introduced by the plaintiffs to prove these sales were exempt from registration. The evidence indicates that this offering was limited to sophisticated businessmen and attorneys who planned to do business with the new firm. The thirteen actual purchasers paid 5,000 dollars each for their stock. In order to be exempt from the Florida Blue Sky Law, the total number of purchasers in the first year of stock sales was deliberately kept below fifteen and the number of original subscribers below five, pursuant to advice these plaintiff-purchasers obtained from independent legal counsel who they retained to render advice on the Blue Sky and SEC laws. Finally, the defendants assert that the plaintiffs had access to all the information they desired. We take this to mean that the plaintiffs had access to all information concerning Florida Franchise. We also interpret it to mean that the plaintiffs could have obtained any information they desired concerning American and the background of the individual defendants if they had just asked.

The defendants rely most strongly on the fact that the offering was made only to sophisticated businessmen and lawyers and not the average man in the street. Although this evidence is certainly favorable to the defendants, the level of sophistication will not carry the point. In this context, the relationship between the promoters and the purchasers and the "access to the kind of information which registration would disclose" become highly relevant factors. Relying specifically upon the words just quoted from *Ralston Purina,* the SEC has rejected the position which the defendants posit here, stating: " 'The Supreme Court's language does not support the view that the availability of an exemption depends on the sophistication of the offerees or buyers, rather than their possession of, or access to, information regarding the issuer.' " Obviously if the plaintiffs did not possess the information requisite for a registration statement, they could not bring their sophisticated knowledge of business affairs to bear in deciding whether or not to invest in this franchise sales center. There is abundant evidence to support the conclusion that the plaintiffs did not in fact possess the requisite information. The plaintiffs were given:

1. a brochure representing that the defendants had just left the very successful firm of Nationwide, but without disclosing the fact that Nationwide was then under investigation by the SEC;
2. a brochure representing Browne as an expert in capitalization consulting, when in fact he had no expertise in such consulting;
3. a brochure stating that the franchise fee would be 25,000 dollars, when in fact the franchise fee turned out to be 25,000 dollars plus a 1,000 dollar per month royalty;

4. a brochure representing that the existing sales centers were successfully operating, without disclosure of the fact that most of them were under investigation by various state securities commissions.

No reasonable mind could conclude that the plaintiffs had access to accurate information on the foregoing points since the only persons who reasonably could have relieved their ignorance were the ones that told them the untruths in the first instance. This proof, as an *a priori* matter, inexorably leads to the conclusion that even the most sanguine of the purchasers would have entertained serious, if not fatal, doubts about investing in this scheme if completely accurate information had been furnished.

Following this case, and a decision against granting a private placement exemption in the *Continental Tobacco Company* case,[5] the SEC published Rule 146, which sought to clarify the standard for obtaining a private-placement exemption. The following criteria assure an exemption from registration:

1. The number of purchasers cannot exceed 35. If one purchaser buys more than $150,000 worth of securities, he is not counted within this number.
2. Each offeree has access to the same kind of information that would be furnished if the registration process took place.
3. The issuer can sell only to purchasers it has reason to believe are capable of evaluating the investment risks and benefits, or able to bear the risk and have services of a representative with knowledge and experience to evaluate the risk.
4. No general advertising or solicitation may be done.
5. The issuer must take precautions against nonexempt, unregistered resale of their securities, unless certain regulations are met.

Liability Under the 1933 Act

The 1933 Act seeks to assure full disclosure for potential investors. The registration process, as noted above, is the major tool for carrying out this statutory policy. Congress provided civil liability for the failure of issuing corporations to meet the provisions of the 1933 Act in Sections 11, 12, 17. It should be noted that both private and public remedies are provided.

Section 11 provides for a statutory cause of action allowing purchasers who have relied on material misstatements or incorrect data in the registration statement to sue and obtain civil damages. Since Section 11 was promulgated, case law has pointed to certain individuals as most likely to be held liable. For example, losses have been recouped from

1. The issuer
2. All who signed the registration statement
3. Lawyers, engineers, and accountants who participated in the preparation of the registration statement
4. Every director
5. Every underwriter

The issuing corporation and all those involved in the preparation of a registration statement should therefore exercise great care. It should be noted that all but the issuer are allowed a due-diligence defense. This defense requires the individual defendant to show that he or she had reasonable grounds to believe that there were no misstatements or material omissions. In the landmark case *Escott* v. *Bar Chris Corp.,*[6] the court treated each of the defendants' pleas of due diligence individually, considering their relationships to the issuing corporation and their areas of expertise. Based on *Bar Chris,* an "inside" director of a corporation who is also a lawyer will have greater difficulty establishing a "due diligence" defense than will an outside director, especially if he or she is a nonlawyer.

Section 12(1) imposes liability for the sale of an unregistered security that fails to meet any of the Section 3 or 4 exemptions. The sale of securities prior to the filing of a registration statement or before the effective date subjects the issuer to liability from the person who purchased the securities. The standard for recovery set out by the courts is the purchase price paid for the security, plus interest, less income received. The purchaser must return the security to the seller.

Section 17 imposes liability on all those who aid and abet any fraud in connection with the offer or sale of securities. It is a general fraud section, bolstered by Section 24, which imposes criminal sanctions where it can be shown that there were any *willful* violations of any provision of the 1933 Act or rules and regulations made by the SEC pursuant to that statute. An individual convicted can be imprisoned for up to five years and/or fined up to $10,000. The reach of Section 17 is illustrated in the case below.

United States v. Naftalin
Supreme Court of the United States
441 U.S. 768 (1979)

Naftalin was president of a registered broker-dealer firm. In July and August 1969, he selected stocks that had peaked in price and were entering declines. He placed five broker orders to sell shares of these stocks, although he did not own the shares he pretended to sell. Gambling that the price of securities would decline before he was requested to deliver them to the broker, he planned to make offsetting purchases through other brokers at lower prices. His profit would be the difference between the price at which he sold and the price at which he covered. Naftalin was aware, however, that had the brokers who executed his sell orders known that he did not own the securities, they would either not have accepted the orders or would have required a margin deposit. He therefore falsely represented that he owned the shares he directed them to sell.

Unfortunately for Naftalin, the market prices of the securities he "sold" did not fall prior to the delivery date but instead rose sharply. Naftalin was unable to make covering purchases and never delivered the promised securities. Consequently, the five brokers were unable to deliver the stock they had "sold" to investors and were forced to borrow stock to keep their delivery promises. Then, in order to return the borrowed stock, the brokers had to purchase replacement shares in the open market at the now-higher prices. The five brokers suffered substantial losses, although the persons to whom the stocks were sold suffered no losses.

The brokers reported the scheme to the SEC, which in turn reported it to the Department of Justice. The Justice Department instituted criminal proceedings against Naftalin for violating Section 17 of the Securities Act of 1933. Naftalin was found

778 BUSINESS ORGANIZATIONS

guilty, but the Court of Appeals reversed, citing that the act was designed to protect investors rather than brokers. The government appealed to the Supreme Court.
Held: Reversed for United States.

Brennan, Justice

Section 17 of the Securities Act of 1933 states: "It shall be unlawful for any person in the offer or sale of any security by the use of any means or instruments of transportation or communication in interstate commerce or by the use of the mails, directly or indirectly:

(1) to employ any device, scheme, or artifice to defraud, or

(2) to obtain money or property by means of any untrue statement of a material fact or any omission to state a material fact necessary in order to make the statements made in the light of the circumstances under which they were made not misleading, or

(3) to engage in any transaction, practice, or course of business which operates or would operate as a fraud or deceit upon the purchaser."

Naftalin claims he did commit fraud but the fraud was against the brokers, not the investors who purchased the securities. He claims brokers are not investors under the Act. Nothing in the Act supports this view. Subsection (1) makes it unlawful for any person in the offer or sale of any securities directly or indirectly to employ any device to defraud. This language does not require that the victim of the fraud be an investor —only that the fraud occur in an offer or sale.

An offer and sale occurred here. Naftalin placed orders to sell with the brokers, the brokers acted as his agent and executed the orders and the results were contracts of sale. The fraud can occur at any stage of the selling transaction. Section 17 of the Act applies not only to the issuance of new securities but to the subsequent resale of those securities. This section was intended to cover any fraudulent scheme in an offer or sale of securities, whether in the course of an initial distribution or in the course of ordinary market trading.

THE SECURITIES ACT OF 1934

Purpose and Scope

As stated in the introduction to this chapter, the Securities Exchange Act of 1934 established the SEC to ensure fair trading practices for investors and others in the securities market. It sets forth rules governing the trading of securities, not initial offerings, which are governed by the 1933 Act. Following enactment of the Exchange Act, congressional and SEC investigations continued to reveal abuses in the marketplace. The Exchange Act was amended in major ways in 1964, 1968, 1975, and 1977. Aspects of the act discussed here include:

1. Requirements for detailed registration and reporting

2. Rules governing the use of proxies
3. Provisions governing tender offers
4. Provisions relating to short swing profits
5. Provisions relating to securities fraud in the marketplace
6. Provisions governing corrupt practices of American-based corporations abroad (included in the Foreign Corrupt Practices Act of 1977)

Registration and Reporting Requirements

Section 12 of the Exchange Act requires all publicly held companies regulated by the SEC to register two classes of securities: debt and equity. This requirement pertains to all companies with assets of $1 million or more and a class of equity securities having at least 500 shareholders of record. Such securities must be registered or they will not be allowed to be traded on a national securities exchange. Registration of a class of securities under the Exchange Act should not be confused with the registration of an initial offering of nonexempt securities within a class under the 1933 Act. A company registering a class of securities under the Exchange Act will always have to meet the requirements of the 1933 Act when making an initial public offering that does not meet any of the exemptions noted previously in this chapter. The 1933 Act regulates the initial sale of securities, while the Exchange Act governs its trading on national exchanges.

Over the years since 1934 the SEC has promulgated rules and prescribed forms for registering classes of securities. Much of the information requested is similar to that required by the 1933 Act.

The SEC through its rule-making power has also devised periodic refiling requirements for corporate registrants to ensure that the potential investor has continuing access to information about securities that are being traded on the exchanges. Annual reports (Form 10–K)

and quarterly reports (Form 10–Q) have been updated to provide increasing amounts of information for potential investors. Additionally, current reports (Form 8–K) can be requested and must be filed by the registering company within fifteen days if the SEC perceives that a material event has taken place that a reasonably prudent investor should know about in order to make an investment decision. A significant change in a company's assets or a potential merger have been considered material events.

The American Law Institute recently proposed to Congress a codification of the federal securities law that attempts to streamline the present registration requirements under the 1933 Act and the Exchange Act, where much duplication exists. The proposed code would provide for an annual company registration requirement with continuous disclosure when securities are registered and traded.

Section 18 of the Exchange Act makes a registering company liable for civil damages to anyone who buys or sells securities and relies on misleading statements contained in the registration statement or any of the reports noted above.

Proxy Solicitations

A proxy is best defined as a writing whereby a holder of registered securities gives permission to another person to vote the stockholder's shares at a stockholders meeting. In many cases, inside management seeks proxies from its shareholders to defeat a particular issue that has been placed before the board by dissident shareholders. Proxies are also given by shareholders who will not be present for the purpose of electing new directors or preventing a takeover of a company. Since the proxy solicitation process often involves the future direction of the corporation, full disclosure is required by the Exchange Act and the SEC. Ten days prior to mailing a proxy statement to shareholders, the issuing company must file it with the SEC. The Commission often issues informal letters of comment requiring some changes before proxies are mailed. SEC rules require the solicitor of proxies to furnish shareholders with all material information concerning the matter being submitted to them for their vote. A form by which shareholders may indicate their agreement or disagreement must be provided as well. In the case of proxies solicited for the purpose of voting for directors, shareholders must be furnished an annual report.

Often shareholders will request that a certain proposal be placed on the agenda at an annual meeting. Under the Exchange Act and SEC rules, if timely notice is given by the shareholder(s), management must include such proposals in its proxy statement and allow shareholders to vote for or against it. If management opposes the proposal, it must include a statement in support of the shareholder's proposal, not to exceed 200 words, along with its statement of opposition. This shareholder prerogative has been used to oppose the making of napalm, to force companies to deal with forms of discrimination, and to deal with company-caused environmental problems. SEC rules allow management to exclude shareholder proposals for the following reasons:

1. The matter is moot
2. The matter is not significantly related to the issuing company's business
3. The matter relates to ordinary business operations
4. The matter would violate state or federal law if included in a proxy proposal passed by the board of directors[7]

Any issuing company who supplies a proxy statement that is misleading to its shareholders may be held civilly liable under Section 18 of the Exchange Act to any person who relies on such statements in the buying or selling of registered securities. The SEC is authorized to force compliance with proxy rules by invoking injunctive relief. Additionally, the U.S. Supreme Court had held that a private right of action exists for damages and other relief under Section 14 in light of Section 27, which grants federal district courts jurisdiction over actions "to enforce any liability or duty rendered by the Exchange Act."[8]

Tender Offers

A tender offer is an offer by an individual or a corporation to the shareholder of another corporation to purchase a number of shares at a specified price. Tender offers are sometimes referred to as "takeover bids" and are usually communicated through newspaper advertising.

In the 1960s, following a large number of conglomerate mergers, many of which involved bitter struggles between acquiring and targeted corporations, Congress became concerned with charges of fraud, insider trading, and manipulation of markets. As a result, it passed the Williams Act, which amended the Exchange Act by adding provisions giving the SEC authority over tender offers, particularly those involving cash. The three most important provisions governing tender offers are set out in Sections 13(d), 14(d), and 14(e).

Under Section 13(d), any person or group that acquires more than 5 percent of a class of securities registered under the Exchange Act is required to file a statement with the SEC and the issuing company within ten days. It must include:

1. The person or group background and the number of share owners
2. Its purpose in acquiring the stock
3. The source of funds used to acquire the securities
4. Its plans for the targeted company
5. Any contracts or understanding with individuals or groups relevant to the targeted company

It should be noted that if there is a hostile tender offer or takeover bid, the targeted company must also file a statement in its attempt to defeat the takeover.

Section 14(d) sets forth procedural and substantive requirements that must be met in making a tender offer. For example, no tender offer that would result in the ownership of 5 percent or more of a class of securities, may be made unless the offeror furnishes each offeree a statement concerning the information required by Section 13(d). Certain substantive requirements dealing with the term of the tender offer are also provided for, as well as such matters as the right of withdrawal of a tender offer, terms of its acceptance, and payment of consideration.

Section 14(e) makes it unlawful for any person to misstate or omit a material fact or to engage in fraudulent or deceptive practice in connection with a tender offer. The federal courts have implied a private right of action for a targeted corporation that alleges a violation of 14(e),[9] but the Supreme Court limited this right when it refused to allow a defeated tender offer or to sue for damages resulting from misleading statements by a competitor who was successful in acquiring the targeted company.[10]

Additionally, tender offer requirements must meet state regulations in the states where the companies are incorporated. This aspect of securities regulation is discussed at the end of the chapter.

Short-Swing Profits

Section 16(b) of the Exchange Act seeks to further the goal of full disclosure for potential investors by preventing certain insiders from realizing profits solely by virtue of their access to material information. It prevents directors, officers, and owners of 10 percent of the securities of an issuing corporation that has securities registered with the SEC or a national exchange from realizing profits on stocks by buying and selling within a six-month period. Any such profits must be returned to the corporation. If the corporation fails to sue for recovery of profits, shareholders may file on behalf of the corporation. The SEC seeks to monitor insider short-swing profits by requiring officers, directors, and 10-percent owners to file forms with the SEC within ten days of a sale or purchase. It should be noted that major newspapers also report such buying or selling by insiders.

Securities Fraud

Section 10(b) and Rule 10b–5. As stated in the introduction to this chapter, the Securities Act seeks to ensure full disclosure of material information for potential investors. Therefore, it is important that any form of fraudulent conduct that would distort the free flow of information to investors in the securities market be made unlawful.

Section 10(b) of the Exchange Act is referred to as a "catchall" provision to deal with securities fraud. It makes illegal the use of the mails or other facilities of interstate commerce to do the following:

To use or employ, in connection with the purchase or sale of any security, any manipulative or deceptive device or contrivance in contravention of such rules and regulations as the Commission may prescribe as necessary or appropriate in the public interest or for the protection of investors.

This statutory provision's broad language encompasses all possible forms of fraud that the Commission may proscribe using its rule-making powers. In 1942, the Commission set forth Rule 10b–5, which has been the foundation for most SEC and private enforcement action dealing with fraudulent conduct. It states:

It shall be unlawful for any person, directly or indirectly, by the use of any means or instrumentality of interstate commerce, or of the mails, or of any facility of any national securities exchange,

(1) to employ any device, scheme, or artifice to defraud,
(2) to make any untrue statement of a material fact necessary in order to make the statements made, in the light of circumstances under which they were made, not misleading, or
(3) to engage in any act, practice, or course of business which operates or would operate as a fraud or deceit upon any person, in connection with the purchase or sale of any security.

The reader should be aware that the rule applies to *any* purchase or sale by *any* person of *any* securities. Whether a company is registered under the Exchange Act or not is unimportant. Thus all the exempted securities and transactions previously set forth in this chapter are *not* exempted from Rule 10b–5. Privately held corporations, as well as those publicly held, can be held liable under the rule.

It should be noted that the conduct of purchaser as well as seller is covered by Rule 10b–5.

The rule is basically an antifraud provision designed to prohibit manipulative or deceptive practices. Both the SEC and private parties alleged to have been injured may bring actions because no specific standards for determining fraud under Rule 10b–5 were set out by the Commission. It was left to the federal courts to develop criteria. In the 1960s and early 1970s, federal district and appellate courts developed a broad interpretation of fraud under 10b–5, imposing liability for negligent conduct as well as for intended or deliberate acts. With a change in the makeup of the Supreme Court in the mid-1970s, private and SEC actions alleging fraud were held to a narrower *intent* (scienter) standard, with some federal courts imposing liability for knowing or reckless behavior.[11] An illustration of the present standard of liability for fraud under Rule 10b–5 is provided by the case below. This case has special importance for the accounting profession.

Ernst & Ernst v. Hochfelder
Supreme Court of the United States
425 U.S. 185 (1976)

Ernst & Ernst (defendant-appellant) is a "big eight" accounting firm retained by First Securities Company (First Securities), a small brokerage firm, to audit its books and records, to prepare annual reports for SEC filing, and to respond to questionnaires from the Midwest Stock Exchange.

Plaintiff-respondents were customers of First Securities who invested in a fraudulent securities scheme perpetrated by Leston B. Nay, president of the firm and owner of 92 percent of its stock. Nay induced the respondents to invest funds in "escrow" accounts that he represented would yield a high rate of return. Respondents did so from 1942 through 1966, with the majority of the transactions occurring in the 1950s. In fact, there were no escrow accounts since Nay converted respondents' funds to his own use immediately upon receipt. These transactions were not in the customary form of dealings between First Securities and its customers. The respondents drew their personal checks payable to Nay or a designated bank for his account. No such escrow accounts were reflected on the books and records of First Securities, and none was shown on its periodic accounting to respondents in connection with their other investments. Nor were they included in First Securities' filings with the SEC or the Exchange.

The fraud came to light in 1968 when Nay committed suicide, leaving a note that described First Securities as bankrupt and the escrow accounts as "spurious." Respondents subsequently filed this action for damages against Ernst & Ernst in the U.S. District Court for the Northern District of Illinois under §10(b) of the 1934 Act. The complaint charged that Nay's escrow scheme violated §10(b) and Commission Rule 10b–5, and that Ernst & Ernst had "aided and abetted" Nay's violations by its "failure" to conduct proper audits of First Securities. As revealed through discovery, respondents' cause of action rested on a theory of negligent nonfeasance. The premise was that Ernst & Ernst had failed to utilize "appropriate auditing procedures" in its audits of First Securities, thereby failing to discover internal practices of the firm said to prevent an effective audit. The practice principally referred to was Nay's rule that only he could open mail addressed to him at First Securities or addressed to First Securities to his attention, even if it arrived in his absence. Respondents contended that if Ernst & Ernst had conducted a proper audit, it would have discovered this "mail rule." The existence of the rule then would have been disclosed in reports to the Exchange and to the SEC by Ernst & Ernst as an irregular procedure that prevented an effective audit. This would have led to an investigation of Nay that would have revealed the fraudulent scheme. Respondents specifically disclaimed the existence of fraud or intentional misconduct on the part of Ernst & Ernst.

The District Court granted Ernst & Ernst's motion for summary judgment and dismissed the action. The Court of Appeals for the Seventh Circuit reversed and remanded, holding that one who breaches a duty of inquiry and disclosure owed another is liable in damages for aiding and abetting a third party's violation of Rule 10b–5 if the fraud would have been discovered or prevented but for the breach. The court stated in its reasoning that Ernst & Ernst had both a common law and statutory duty of inquiry into the adequacy of First Securities' internal control system by virtue of its contractual duties to audit and prepare filings with the SEC.

Held: Reversed for appellants.

Powell, Justice

We granted certiorari to resolve the question whether a private cause of action for damages will lie under §10(b) and Rule 10b–5 in the absence of any allegation of "scienter"—intent to deceive, manipulate, or defraud. We conclude that it will not and therefore we reverse.

Section 10(b) makes unlawful the use or employment of "any manipulative or deceptive device or contrivance" in contravention of Commission rules. The words "manipulative or deceptive" used in conjunction with "device or contrivance" strongly suggest that §10(b) was intended to proscribe knowing or intentional misconduct.

In its "amicus curiae" brief, however, the Commission contends that nothing in the language "manipulative or deceptive device or contrivance" limits its operation to knowing or intentional practices. In support of its view, the Commission cites the overall congressional purpose in the 1933 and 1934 Acts to protect investors against false and deceptive practices that might injure them.

The Commission then reasons that since the effect upon investors of given conduct is the same regardless of whether the conduct is negligent or intentional, Congress must have intended to bar all such practices, not just those done knowingly or intentionally.

In addition to relying upon the Commission's argument with respect to the operative language of the statute, respondents contend that since we are dealing with "remedial legislation," it must be construed " 'not technically and restrictively, but flexibly to effectuate its remedial purposes.' " They argue that the "remedial purposes" of the Acts demand a construction of §10(b) that embraces negligence as a standard of liability.

Although the extensive legislative history of the 1934 Act is bereft of any explicit explanation of Congress' intent, we think the relevant portions of that history support our conclusion that §10(b) was addressed to practices that involve some element of scienter and cannot be read to impose liability for negligent conduct alone.

The section was described rightly as a "catch all" clause to enable the Commission "to deal with new manipulative (or cunning) devices." It is difficult to believe that any lawyer, legislative draftsman, or legislator would use these words if the intent was to create liability for merely negligent acts or omissions. Neither the legislative history nor the briefs supporting respondents identify any usage or authority for construing "manipulative (or cunning) devices" to include negligence.

We have addressed to this point, primarily the language and history of §10(b). The Commission contends, however, that subsections (b) and (c) of Rule 10b–5 are cast in language which—if standing alone—could encompass *both intentional* and *negligent* behavior. These subsections respectively provide that it is unlawful "[t]o make any untrue statement of a material fact or to omit to state a material fact necessary in order to make the statements made, in the light of the circumstances under which they were made, not misleading . . ." and "[t]o engage in any act, practice, or course of business which operates or would operate as a fraud or deceit upon any person . . ." Viewed in isolation the language of subsection (b), and arguably that of subsection (c), could be read as proscribing, respectively, any type of material misstatement or omission, and any course of conduct, that has the effect of defrauding investors, whether the wrongdoing was intentional or not.

We note first that such a reading cannot be harmonized with the administrative history of the Rule, a history making clear that when the Commission adopted the Rule, it was intended to apply only to activities that involved scienter. More importantly, Rule 10b–5 was adopted pursuant to authority granted the Commission under §10(b). The rule-making power granted to an administrative agency charged with the administration of a federal statute is not the power to make law. Rather, it is " 'the power to adopt regulations to carry into effect the will of Congress as expressed by the statute.' " Thus, despite the broad view of the Rule advanced by the Commission in this case, its scope cannot exceed the power granted the Commission by Congress under §10(b). For the reasons stated above, we think the Commission's original interpretation of Rule 10b–5 was compelled by the language and history of §10(b) and related sections of the Acts. When a statute speaks so specifically in terms of manipulation and deception, and of implementing devices and contrivances—the commonly understood terminology of intentional wrongdoing—and when its history reflects no more expansive intent, we are quite unwilling to extend the scope of the statute to negligent conduct.

Insider Trading. Over the past forty years, Rule 10b–5 has been most frequently applied to three forms of conduct: (1) insider trading; (2) corporate misstatements; (3) corporate mismanagement.

Insider trading may be defined as the buying or selling of securities by individuals who have access to nonpublic information that, if known by a potential investor, would affect the latter's trading decision. The SEC and courts originally defined "insiders" as corporate officers, directors, and major stockholders. Over the years Rule 10b–5 has been interpreted to include anyone who receives nonpublic material information from a corporate source. Courts have found insider trading by partners in a brokerage firm,[12] broker-dealers acting as underwriters,[13] and even an employee of a financial printing firm who worked on documents that involved a contemplated tender offer.[14]

In the financial printing firm case, which is set out below, the U.S. Supreme Court appeared to limit the scope of the rule by defining "insiders" as those who "have a relationship of trust and confidence with shareholders."

Vincent F. Chiarella v. United States

Supreme Court of the United States

445 U.S. 222 (1980)

In 1975 and 1976, Chiarella, a printer, worked as a "markup man" in the composing room of Pandick Press, a New York financial printer. Among documents that the defendant handled were five announcements of corporate takeover bids. When these documents were delivered to the printer, the identities of the acquiring and target corporations were concealed by blank spaces or false names. The true names were sent to the printer on the night of the final printing.

The defendant, however, was able to deduce the names of the target companies before the final printing from other information contained in the documents. Without disclosing his knowledge, defendant purchased stock in the target companies and sold the shares immediately after the takeover attempts were made public. By this method, the defendant realized a gain of slightly more than $30,000 in the course of fourteen months. Subsequently, the SEC began an investigation of his trading activities. In May 1977, the defendant entered into a consent decree with the Commission in which he agreed to return his profits to the sellers of the shares. On the same day, he was discharged by Pandick Press.

In January 1978, the defendant was indicted on seventeen counts of violating

§10(b) of the Securities Exchange Act of 1934 (1934 Act) and SEC Rule 10b–5. After the defendant unsuccessfully moved to dismiss the indictment, he was brought to trial and convicted on all counts.

The Court of Appeals affirmed his conviction.

Held: Reversed for defendant.

Powell, Justice

The question in this case is whether a person who learns from the confidential documents of one corporation that it is planning an attempt to secure control of a second corporation violates §10(b) of the Securities Exchange Act of 1934 if he fails to disclose the impending takeover before trading in the target company's securities.

In this case, the defendant was convicted of violating §10(b) although he was not a corporate insider and he received no confidential information from the target company. Moreover, the "market information" upon which he relied did not concern the earning power or operations of the target company, but only the plans of the acquiring company. Defendant's use of that information was not a fraud under §10(b) unless he was subject to an affirmative duty to disclose it before trading. In this case, the jury instructions failed to specify any such duty. In effect, the trial court instructed the jury that defendant owed a duty to everyone; to all sellers, indeed, to the market as a whole. The jury simply was told to decide whether defendant used material nonpublic information at a time when "he knew other people trading in the securities market did not have access to the same information."

The Court of Appeals affirmed the conviction by holding that "anyone—corporate insider or not—who regularly received material nonpublic information may not use that information to trade in securities without incurring an affirmative duty to disclose." Although the court said that its test would include only persons who regularly receive material, nonpublic information, its rationale for that limitation is unrelated to the existence of a duty to disclose. The Court of Appeals, like the trial court, failed to identify a relationship between defendant and the sellers that could give rise to a duty. Its decision thus rested solely upon its belief that the federal securities laws have "created a system providing equal access to information necessary for reasoned and intelligent investment decisions." The use by anyone of material information not generally available is fraudulent, this theory suggests, because such information gives certain buyers or sellers an unfair advantage over less informed buyers and sellers.

This reasoning suffers from two defects. First, not every instance of financial unfairness constitutes fraudulent activity under §10(b). Second, the element required to make silence fraudulent—a duty to disclose—is absent in this case. No duty could arise from petitioner's relationship with the seller of the target company's securities, for petitioner had no prior dealings with them. He was not their agent, he was not a fiduciary, he was not a person in whom the sellers had placed their trust and confidence. He was in fact, a complete stranger who dealt with the sellers only through impersonal market transactions.

In this case, as we have emphasized before, the 1934 Act cannot be read " 'more broadly than its language and the statutory scheme reasonably permits.' " Section 10(b) is aptly described as a catch-all provision, but what it catches must be fraud.

When an allegation of fraud is based upon nondisclosure, there can be no fraud absent a duty to speak. We hold that a duty to disclose under §10(b) does not arise from the mere possession of nonpublic market information. The contrary result is without support in the legislative history of §10(b) and would be inconsistent with the careful plan that Congress has enacted for regulation of the securities markets.

Following this decision, the SEC adopted Rule 14e–3, which makes it illegal for "any person to purchase or sell a security while in possession of material nonpublic information about a prospective tender offer, if he/she knows or has reason to know that such information emanates from either the offering person or the issuer or person acting on their behalf."

In September 1982, the SEC extended its enforcement scope with regard to insider trading in American stocks to individuals who use Swiss bank accounts to trade in stocks illegally. In a memorandum of understanding negotiated with Swiss officials, a system was established in Switzerland to process SEC requests for information about bank clients suspected of insider trading. A special three-member Swiss commission was set up to review these inquiries. Upon receipt of a SEC request for information, the Swiss bank involved freezes assets in a client's account equal to his/her alleged trading profits, studies the SEC allegations, and reports to the Swiss special commission. That panel then makes a decision as to whether the bank should honor the SEC request. If the SEC loses, it may appeal to the Swiss Federal Banking Commission. Prior to this agreement, bank secrecy legislation in Switzerland provided insiders with a shield against disclosure of trading in American stocks based on nonpublic information. The SEC sees this agreement as a model for future understandings with countries like the Bahamas, Panama, Bermuda, and the Cayman Islands that also have bank secrecy laws.

Corporate Misstatements. In addition to disclosure required by the Securities Act of 1933 (Sections 13 and 14) when dealing with proxies and other documents filed with the SEC, Rule 10b–5 prohibits misstatements in the form of overoptimistic profit reports or press releases as to earnings if they would affect the prudent judgment of potential investors. In the landmark case of *SEC* v. *Texas Gulf Sulfur*,[15] executives were held liable for releasing pessimistic, not overoptimistic, statements concerning the possible success of Texas Gulf's (TGS) exploration for ore. After denying the company's success in its Timmens, Ontario, operation, executives purchased stock, or calls on the stock, knowing of a potential ore discovery. The same information was undisclosed to the investing public, to sellers, the stock option committee of TGS, or the TGS board of directors. TGS argued that the press release denying ore discoveries was not issued "in connection with the purchase or sale of securities." Since the company was not engaged in buying or selling securities at the time of the release, there was no violation of Rule 10b–5. The Second Circuit Court of Appeals rejected this argument, stating that prices of TGS stock had been artificially held down by the pessimistic press release, enabling the executives and their tippees, acting on information not available to potential investors, to purchase stock and options at low prices. The court, basing its decision on the legislative history of 10(b), found that the SEC was correct in stating that there was a connection between the press release and the investing public's transactions if it "would cause reasonable investors

BUSINESS ORGANIZATIONS

to rely thereon, and in connection therewith, so relying, cause them to purchase or sell a corporation's security." In that case, the court deemed that a misleading statement needed a "wrongful purpose" for it to be a violation of Section 10(b) and Rule 10b–5.

Corporate Mismanagement The *Hochfelder* case previously set out in this chapter is an obvious illustration of corporate mismanagement and fraud upon shareholders. Shareholder derivative suits or minority stockholders' actions have become common in attacking transactions dealing with mergers and reorganizations, and sales and purchases of corporations of their own securities. State incorporation laws provide for a fiduciary duty between shareholders and a corporation's officers and directors. Suits have been based on breaches of this duty. When attempts have been made by shareholders to avoid state corporation law and sue on the basis of fraud under Section 10(b), the Supreme Court has been reluctant to "federalize" state corporate law.[16] The courts have refused to allow actions for mismanagement under Rule 10b–5 unless the plaintiffs (shareholders) have bought or sold securities in the transactions under question and there exists some connection between the alleged fraud and the transactions.[17]

THE FOREIGN CORRUPT PRACTICES ACT OF 1977

Background

In 1973, during the Watergate hearings, Americans learned for the first time about illegal domestic political contributions made by corporations to President Nixon's 1972 reelection campaign. The SEC undertook a study in 1974 of these secret payments, viewing the companies' failures to disclose as violations of the Exchange Act of 1934. The SEC found upon further investigation that corporations had made questionable payments overseas as well. The Commission's staff concluded that there were clear patterns of illegal or questionable payments both domestically and overseas. The SEC considered these payments *material* information under the Securities Acts because they affected the integrity of both management and the record-keeping procedures of the companies involved. This undisclosed information, in the eyes of the Commission, would in all likelihood have altered the judgment of a reasonably prudent investor. The corporations argued that disclosure was not required because the amounts involved were small compared to sales or earnings and thus not material. The SEC interpretation of materiality was accepted by the Supreme Court in 1976. The Court defined "material information" as that which a "reasonable investor would consider important in deciding how to vote, or whether to buy, sell or hold securities."[18] The SEC brought thirty-nine enforcement actions prior to passage of the Foreign Corrupt Practices Act, alleging violations of the Exchange Act. The Commission also set up in 1975 a volunteer disclosure program whereby companies were encouraged to conduct investigations of their operations and, upon finding questionable payments, to discuss appropriate disclosure methods with the SEC staff. More than 450 companies admitted making questionable or illegal payments totaling more than $300 million; 117 of the *Fortune* 500 were involved.[19] Payments had been made to high-level officials for the purpose of obtaining contracts. In the enforcement actions, as well as in the voluntary disclosure program, corporate officials testified that these "bribes" or "commissions" were a means of doing business. They were "facilitating" or "grease" payments that were often necessary to meet the competition of other American firms as well as of foreign multinationals. In many cases, it was learned that the payments were treated by corporate accountants as expense items and illegally deducted as business expenses on income-tax returns filed with the Internal Revenue Service.

Although the Justice Department was able to prosecute some payments under currency-transaction regulations and mail-wire fraud statutes, statutory authority to reach questionable payments overseas for foreign political bribery was only indirect. The SEC had forced disclosure under Exchange Act provisions, but by 1977 Congress felt a need to take further action.

Provisions

The Foreign Corrupt Practices Act was enacted because Congress considered corporate bribes to foreign officials to be (1) unethical, (2) harmful to our relations with foreign governments (Korean and Japanese officials were forced to resign after disclosure of payments from American-based multinational corporations), and (3) unnecessary to American companies doing business overseas.

Passed in 1977, the act applies to all "domestic concerns" whether doing business overseas or not and whether registered with the SEC or not. Examined here are its antibribery and accounting provisions.

The act's antibribery provisions[20] prohibit all domestic concerns, whether registered with SEC or not, from offering or authorizing corrupt payments to:

1. A foreign official (or someone acting in an official capacity for a foreign government)
2. A foreign political party official or a foreign political party
3. A candidate for political office in a foreign country

A payment is "corrupt" if its purpose is to get the recipient to act or refrain from acting so the American firm can retain or get business.

The standard that corporate officials are held to is "knowing" or "has reason to know." If he or she knows or should know that a payment violates the provisions of the act, the official and the company will be held liable.

Officers, directors, stockholders, employees, and U.S. agents who act on behalf of the company and willfully violate the act's antibribery provisions can be fined up to $10,000 per violation and imprisoned for not more than five years. Companies cannot directly or indirectly pay fines for convicted officers or employees.

The Foreign Corrupt Practices Act prohibits the "offer" or "promise" of a bribe even if it is not consummated. It prohibits the payment of "anything of value." The *Congressional Record* indicates that small gifts and tokens of hospitality that are customarily given in a foreign country do not fall within the prohibitions of the FCPA, even if made to officials. Only "political" payments are prohibited. This raises the question of whether a bribe paid to a company owned by a foreign official is illegal. "Foreign officials" are not clerical or ministerial employees. Thus payments to a clerk in order to get goods through customs *may* not be prohibited by the act. There is no maximum set on these "grease payments" as long as the recipient is merely "clerical or ministerial." The "reason to know" standard of liability for directors and officers of corporations indicates that all domestic companies must be aggressive in setting and enforcing strict ethical standards for doing business.

The accounting provisions of the act apply only to companies subject to the Securities Acts—that is, only public nonexempt companies. The SEC, in its report to Congress on illegal and questionable payments,[21] requested some reforms. Congress enacted record-keeping and internal-control provisions. The accounting provisions were enacted as amendments to the Exchange Act, sections 13(b)2(A) and 13(b)2(B).

Section 13(B)2(A) requires that all publicly held, registered companies "make and keep books, records and accounts in reasonable detail" that "accurately and fairly" reflect transactions and disposition of assets. Concern has been expressed whether inaccuracies involving small amounts would violate the FCPA.

Section 13(b)(2)B requires publicly held companies to maintain systems of internal controls sufficient to provide "reasonable assurances" that transactions are executed in accordance with management's authorization, that transactions are recorded to permit preparation of financial statements in accordance with generally accepted accounting principles, and that at regular intervals management compares records with the actual assets available. There exists no particular definition of "reasonable assurances," although the *Congressional Record* indicates that Congress intended that the cost of maintaining the system should not exceed its benefits.[22]

The penalties for willful violation of the accounting provisions are those imposed by the Exchange Act. They include fines of up to $10,000 and imprisonment up to five years. In all cases brought by the SEC for violations of the accounting provisions, only civil remedies have been sought.

Enforcement

The SEC and the Justice Department share responsibility for enforcing the Foreign Corrupt Practices Act. SEC is charged with investigating suspected violations of the bribery and accounting provisions. The SEC can bring only civil actions, but it may recommend criminal enforcement to the Justice Department's Multinational Fraud Branch. The Justice Department has authority to proceed civilly and criminally against domestic concerns alleged to have violated the antibribery provisions.

Proposed Amendments

Many complaints have been directed at the bribery and accounting provisions of the For-

eign Corrupt Practices Act. A Senate committee held hearings in 1981 on proposed amendments to the act introduced by Senator John Chaffee (Senate Bill 708).[23] The amendments were approved by the full Senate but were not acted upon by the House in the Ninety-third Congress.

The Chaffee amendments provided for the following changes in the FCPA:

1. The title of the act would have been changed to the Business Practices and Records Act.
2. Enforcement responsibilities for the antibribery provisions would have been assigned entirely to the Justice Department. Authority to obtain injunctive relief would also have been placed in the Justice Department rather than divided, as at present, between the SEC and the Justice Department.
3. The "reason to know" language in the bribery provisions would have been replaced by a standard holding officers, directors, and employees liable only if they "corruptly direct or authorize, expressly or by a course of conduct, an offer of a bribe."

Additionally, the proposed amendments sought to clarify whether payments were corruptly made by listing five situations where the act would *not* apply:

1. When a payment was made to facilitate
2. When it was lawful under the laws and regulations of the foreign country
3. Any payment that was a courtesy or token of hospitality
4. Any expenditures associated with selling, purchasing, or demonstrating a good
5. Any ordinary expenditure associated with performance of a contract with a foreign government or agency

Proponents of amendments to the act's anti-bribery provisions argue that the act has resulted in lost business opportunities, exports, and employment for this country because companies are afraid to risk committing violations. Opponents of the amendments argue that the Act has not been in place long enough to know its long-term impact. They argue that the proposed amendments would legalize bribery and revive the pre-1977 abuses that led to the enactment of the Act.

The Chaffee amendments would have changed the Act's accounting provisions by imposing cost-benefit and prudent-individual standards in defining "reasonable assurance" and "reasonable detail." Corporations would not have to adopt internal-control systems that were not cost effective. A cost-benefit defense would also be available when a company was charged with a violation. Additionally, the amendments would have eliminated separate provisions of the act requiring accurate books and records and incorporated the principle of record-keeping into the statutory objective of the internal-control requirements. Finally, criminal liability for failure to meet the internal-control provisions would have been eliminated. Proponents of the amendments argue that standards for control, including cost-benefit analyses, are more reasonable and cost effective. Opponents argue that cost-benefit analysis is not a term of art and means different things to different people.

STATE SECURITIES LAWS

State regulation of securities began in 1911 when Kansas enacted a securities statute. The U.S. Supreme Court in 1917 called such regulations of securities "blue-sky" laws, describing their purpose as "the prevention of speculative schemes which have no more basis than so many feet of blue sky."[24] In enacting the 1933 Securities Act, Congress specifically preserved the power of the states to regulate securities transactions of an *intrastate* nature. All fifty states, the District of Columbia, and Puerto Rico have enacted securities statutes. A corporation issuing securities in interstate commerce must meet the registration requirements of each of the states in which its securities are sold as well as the federal requirements. The cost and time involved in meeting various state requirements has led to the adoption of the Uniform Securities Act (USA), in whole or in part, by some thirty states.

Common Provisions

Almost all state statutes contain provisions covering: registration of securities, broker-dealer registration, and fraud in issuance and trading of securities.

Registration of Securities. The 1933 Securities Act has served as a model for state statutes with regard to types of information required for registration. There are generally three methods of registration: notification, qualification, and coordination. Unlike the federal securities acts, state laws provide that securities may be registered by notification when the issuing corporation meets certain tests of reliability and earnings. In most states notification is effective if the state administrator of the securities law does not take action within a number of days after filing. When an issuing company registers in a "coordination" state, the same procedure is followed except that, generally, a prospectus is all that is required. In "qualification" states, following the filing of information, registration of the securities is not effective until the state administrator has approved. It should be noted that this power is in sharp contrast to that of the SEC under the 1933 Act. The SEC has no power to determine the worth of a particular filing. The sole purpose of the federal securities acts is to provide full disclosure of material information for potential investors. State administrators, however, may evaluate the securities being issued as well as the issuing corporation. Most states exempt from registration those securities exempted by the 1933 Securities Act—for example, governmental securities and securities issued by institutions subject to different federal regulatory statutes. Additionally, state securities legislation exempts securities listed on major stock exchanges.

Broker-Dealer Registration and Fraud.

Almost every state statute requires registration by brokers and agents. Some establish licensing requirements and reserve the right to deny or revoke licenses. Issuers or broker-dealers must post surety bonds in many states.

Most states have adopted antifraud provisions similar to those set forth in Section 10–b of the Exchange Act and Rule 10b–5. States generally use some form of injunctive relief as a remedy for fraud, but many also have criminal provisions in their statute. The USA would permit individual investors to recover money damages.

Conflict Between Federal and State Security Statutes

As noted above, fifty-two separate jurisdictions in addition to the Federal government have statutes governing securities registration and trading. Often securities statutes apply to any offer or sale of securities in a state, but many transactions involve a seller or securities-issuing company incorporated or doing business in one state and a buyer located in another state. Besides the question of which state law governs the particular sale of a security, serious federal-state constitutional questions have arisen. For example, at what point do state statutes interfere with federal securities laws and become a burden on interstate commerce? In a landmark case set out below, the U.S. Supreme Court for the first time fully discussed this question. The reader should examine the importance the Court attaches to the commerce clause first discussed in Chapter 2 of this text.

James Edgar v. Mite Corporation and MITE Holdings, Inc.

Supreme Court of the United States

457 U.S. 624 (1982)

Appellee, Mite Corporation, and its wholly owned subsidiary, MITE Holdings, Inc., are corporations organized under the laws of Delaware with executive offices located in Connecticut. Appellant, James Edgar, is the secretary of state of Illinois and is charged with the administration and enforcement of the Illinois Securities Act. Under the Illinois Act, any takeover offer for the shares of a target company must be registered with the secretary of state. A target company is defined as a corporation or other issuer of securities of which shareholders located in Illinois own 10 percent of the class of equity securities subject to the offer or for which any two of the following three conditions are met: the corporation has its principal executive office in Illinois, is organized under the laws of Illinois, or has at least 10 percent of its stated capital and paid-in surplus represented within the state. An offer becomes registered twenty days after a registration statement is filed with the secretary unless the secretary calls a hearing. The secretary may call a hearing at any time during the twenty-day waiting period to adjudicate the substantive fairness of the offer if he believes it is necessary to protect the shareholders of the target company, and a hearing must be held if requested by a majority of a target company's outside directors or by Illinois shareholders who own 10 percent of the class of securities subject to the offer. If the secretary does hold a hearing, he is directed by the statute to deny registration to a tender offer if he finds that it "fails to provide full and fair disclosure to the offerees of all material information concerning the take-over offer, or that the take-over offer is inequitable or would work or tend to work a fraud or deceit upon the offerees."

On January 19, 1979, Mite initiated a cash tender offer for all outstanding shares of Chicago Rivet and Machine Co., a publicly held Illinois corporation, by filing a Schedule 14D–1 with the Securities and Exchange Commission in order to comply with the Williams Act. The Schedule 14D–1 indicated that Mite was willing to pay $28 per share for any and all outstanding shares of Chicago Rivet, a premium of approximately $4 over the then-prevailing market price. Mite did not comply with the Illinois Act, however, and commenced this litigation on the same day by filing an action in the U.S. District Court for the Northern District of Illinois. The complaint asked for a declaratory judgment that the Illinois Act was preempted by the Williams Act and violated the commerce clause. In addition, Mite sought a temporary restraining order and preliminary and permanent injuctions prohibiting the Illinois secretary of state from enforcing the Illinois act.

After Chicago Rivet's efforts to obtain relief in Pennsylvania courts proved unsuccessful, both Chicago Rivet and the Illinois Secretary of State took steps to invoke the Illinois act. On February 1, 1979, the Secretary of State notified Mite that he intended to issue an order requiring it to cease and desist further efforts to make a tender offer for Chicago Rivet. Mite renewed its request for injunctive relief in the District Court, and on February 2 the District Court issued a preliminary injunction prohibiting the secretary of state from enforcing the Illinois act against Mite's tender offer for Chicago Rivet.

Mite then published its tender offer in the February 5 edition of the *Wall Street Journal*. The offer was made to all shareholders of Chicago Rivet residing throughout the United States. The outstanding stock was worth over $23 million at the offering price. On the same day Chicago Rivet made an offer for approximately 40 percent of its own shares at $30 per share. The District Court entered final judgment on February 9, declaring that the Illinois act was preempted by the Williams Act and that it violated the commerce clause. Accordingly, the District Court permanently enjoined enforcement of the Illinois statute against Mite. The U.S. Court of Appeals for the Seventh Circuit affirmed the District Court's decision.

Held: Affirmed for Mite.

White, Justice

The Commerce Clause provides that "Congress shall have Power . . . [t]o regulate Commerce . . . among the several states." U.S. Const., Art. 1, § 8, cl. 3. Not every exercise of state power with some impact on interstate commerce is invalid. A state statute must be upheld if it regulates even-handedly to effectuate a legitimate local public interest, and its effects on interstate commerce are only incidental unless the burden imposed on such commerce is clearly excessive in relation to the putative local benefits. The Commerce Clause, however, permits only incidental regulation of interstate commerce by the states; direct regulation is prohibited. The Illinois Act violates these principles for two reasons. First, it directly regulates and prevents, unless its terms are satisfied, interstate tender offers which in turn would generate interstate transactions. Second, the burden the Act imposes on interstate commerce is excessive in light of the local interests the Act purports to further.

States have traditionally regulated intrastate securities transactions, and this Court has upheld the authority of states to enact "blue-sky" laws against Commerce Clause challenges on several occasions. The Court's rationale for upholding blue-sky laws was that they only regulated transactions occurring within the regulating states.

The Illinois Act is also unconstitutional under the test of *Pike* v. *Bruce Church, Inc.,* for even when a state statute regulates interstate commerce indirectly, the burden imposed on that commerce must not be excessive in relation to the local interests served by the statute. The most obvious burden the Illinois Act imposes on interstate commerce arises from the statute's previously-described nationwide reach which purports to give Illinois the power to determine whether a tender offer may proceed anywhere.

The effects of allowing the Illinois Secretary of State to block a nationwide tender offer are substantial. Shareholders are deprived of the opportunity to sell their shares at a premium. The reallocation of economic resources to their highest-valued use, a process which can improve efficiency and competition, is hindered. The incentive the tender offer mechanism provides incumbent management to perform well so that stock prices remain high is reduced.

Appellant claims the Illinois Act furthers two legitimate local interests. He argues that Illinois seeks to protect resident security holders and that the Act merely regulates the internal affairs of companies incorporated under Illinois law. We agree with the Court of Appeals that these asserted interests are insufficient to outweigh the burdens Illinois imposes on interstate commerce.

While protecting local investors is plainly a legitimate state objective, the state has no legitimate interest in protecting nonresident shareholders. Insofar as the Illinois law burdens out-of-state transactions, there is nothing to be weighed in the balance to sustain the law. We note, furthermore, that the Act completely exempts from coverage a corporation's acquisition of its own shares. Thus Chicago Rivet was able to make a competing tender offer for its own stock without complying with the Illinois Act, leaving Chicago Rivet's shareholders to depend only on the protections afforded them by federal securities law, protections which Illinois views as inadequate to protect investors in other contexts. This distinction is at variance with Illinois' asserted legislative purpose, and tends to undermine appellant's justification for the burdens the statute imposes on interstate commerce.

We are also unconvinced that the Illinois Act substantially enhances the shareholders' position. The Illinois Act seeks to protect shareholders of a company subject to a tender offer by requiring disclosures regarding the offer, assuring that shareholders have adequate time to decide whether to tender their shares, and according shareholders withdrawal, proration and equal consideration rights. However, the Williams Act provides these same substantive protections. As the Court of Appeals noted, the disclosures required by the Illinois Act which go beyond those mandated by the Williams Act and the regulations pursuant to it may not substantially enhance the shareholders' ability to make informed decisions. It also was of the view that the possible benefits of the potential delays required by the Act may be outweighed by the increased risk that the tender offer will fail due to defensive tactics employed by incumbent management. We are unprepared to disagree with the Court of Appeals in these respects, and conclude that the protections the Illinois Act affords resident security holders are, for the most part, speculative.

We conclude with the Court of Appeals that the Illinois Act imposes a substantial burden on interstate commerce which outweighs its putative local benefits. It is accordingly invalid under the Commerce Clause.

REVIEW PROBLEMS

1. Maresh, a geologist, owned some oil and gas leases on land in Nebraska. He entered into an oral agreement with Garfield whereby the latter would provide some investment funds for Maresh to drill for oil. Garfield, a businessman, knew a great deal about oil stocks and the securities market. He promised to wire the money to Maresh, who began drilling immediately. Maresh found out that the land was dry before he received Garfield's money. Garfield refused to invest as he had promised, claiming that the offered lease investment was a "security" within the meaning of the Securities Act of 1933 and that it had not been registered. What result? Garfield v. Strain, 320 F. 2d 116 (10th Circuit, 1963)

2. Continental Tobacco Company, a manufacturer of cigarettes, sold some unregistered five-year debentures, paying 6 percent common stock, to thirty-eight persons between June 1969 and October 1970. All investors prior to purchase signed an agreement with Continental that acknowledged receipt of unaudited financial statements, other information about the corporation, access to officers of the company, knowledge of the risk involved, and that they were experienced investors. Purchasers went to meetings in a room where telephones were manned and orders for securities continually came in. One investor called the meetings a "boiler plate operation" where high-pressure tactics were used to sell the securities. The SEC brought suit against Continental claiming that it was selling unregistered securities. The company claimed that its sale of securities was a private offering and thus was exempt from registration under the 1933 Act. SEC v. Continental Tobacco Co., 463 F. 2d 137 (5th Cir., 1972)

3. Truckee Showboat, a California corporation, offered to sell its common stock to residents of California through the use of the U.S. mail. Its offer to sell was advertised in the *Los Angeles Times* on June 18, 1957, and the offer was made exclusively to residents of the State of California. The proceeds of the sale of the stock, minus commission, were to be used to acquire the El Cortez Hotel in Las Vegas, Nevada. Truckee Showboat, Inc. was incorporated and kept all its records in California. All its directors and officers were Californians. The SEC charged the company with issuing unregistered nonexempt securities under the 1933 Act. Truckee Showboat claimed an intrastate exemption. What result? SEC v. Truckee Showboat, Inc., 157 F. Supp. 824 (S.D. Calif., 1957)

4. Livingston was a twenty-year employee of

Merrill Lynch, a large securities investment firm. Livingston was a securities salesman who was given the title "account executive." In January 1972, the company gave Livingston and forty-seven other account executives the title "vice president" as a reward for outstanding sales records. All of their duties and responsibilities were the same as before this recognition. Livingston never acquired any executive duties and never attended board of directors meetings. In November and December 1972 Livingston sold 1,000 shares of Merrill Lynch stock. In March 1973 he repurchased the same number of shares, making a profit of $14,836.37. The company sued for the profits, claiming that Livingston by virtue of his inside information made short-swing profits in violation of Section 16(b) of the Securities Exchange Act of 1934. The defendant denied this charge. What result? Merrill Lynch, Pierce, Fenner, Smith v. Livingston, 566 F. 2d 1119 (9th Circuit, 1978)

5. Mills was a minority shareholder of Electric Auto-Lite Company. Prior to the merger of Auto-Lite and Mergenthaler into the Mergenthaler Linotype Co., Mergenthaler owned 50 percent of Auto-Lite and dominated its board of directors. American Manufacturing Company in turn had control of Mergenthaler and through it controlled Auto-Lite. Auto-Lite's management at the time of the merger sent out a proxy statement to shareholders of Auto-Lite telling them that their board of directors recommended that they vote for approval of the merger. They failed to include in the proxy statement information as to the fact that Morgenthaler dominated the board and that American Manufacturing through Morgenthaler controlled Auto-Lite. Mills and other minority shareholders filed a class-action and derivative suit claiming that management had sent out a misleading proxy in violation of Section 14 of the Exchange Act of 1934 and that the merger should be set aside. Management and the board of directors of the merged company claimed that there was no material omission in the proxy statement. What result? Mills v. Auto-Lite, 396 U.S. 375 (1970)

6. Lakeside Plastics and Engraving Company (LPE) was a closed corporation incorporated in the State of Minnesota in 1946. It suffered losses until 1952, when it showed a yearly profit but still a large overall deficit. Fields and King in 1946 had each purchased thirty shares, which they held. Myzel, a relative of the Levine family, founders of the company, advised Fields and King in 1954 that the company stock was not worth anything and the company was going out of business. Both sold their shares to Myzel, who sold them to the Levine family at a substantial profit. Myzel failed to disclose before purchasing the shares that there were increased sales in 1953, a new Blatz contract, and profits of $30,000, along with the potential of 1954 sales. Fields, King and others in separate actions sought damage for violation of 10(b) of the Exchange Act of 1934. What result? Myzel v. Fields, 386 F. 2d 718 (8th Circuit, 1967)

FOOTNOTES

[1]Statutes affecting securities that are not discussed in this chapter include: The Public Utility Holding Company Act of 1935, The Trust Indenture Act of 1939, The Investment Company Act of 1940, Bankruptcy Reform Act of 1978 (Chapter 11), The Securities Investor Protection Act of 1970.

[2]328 U.S. 293 (1946).

[3]Exchange National Bank v. Touche Ross & Co., 544 F. 2d 1126 (2d Circuit 1976).

[4]United Housing Foundation v. Foreman, Inc., 421 U.S. 837 (1975).

[5]SEC v. Continental Tobacco, 463 F. 2d 137 (5th Circuit, 1972).

[6]283 F. Supp. 643 (S.D. N.Y., 1968).

[7]In August 1983 the SEC amended Regulation 14a to define for the first time "matters not significantly related to business" as those accounting for than 5 percent of the assets, earnings, and sales of a company. Shareholder proposals can now be excluded if a stockholder does not own more than $1,000 worth of stock, or 17 percent of the shares outstanding, for a period of one year or more. Also, a proposal can be excluded when it has been previously submitted, and has received less than 5 percent of the vote. Shareholders are limited to one proposal per company per annual meeting.

[8]See J.I. Case Co. v. Berak, 377 U.S. 426 (1964).

[9]See Electronic Speciality Co. v. International Controls Corp., 409 F. 2d 937 (2d Circuit, 1969).

[10]See Piper v. Chris-Craft Industries, 97 S. Ct. 926 (1977).

[11]See Santa Fe Industries v. Green, 430 U.S. 462 (1977); Aaron v. SEC 446 U.S. 680 (1980).

[12]Cady Roberts and Co., 40 S.E.C. 907 (1961).

[13]Investors Management Co., 44 S.E.C. 633 (1971).

[14]Chiarella v. U.S., 45 U.S. 222 (1980).

[15]401 F. 2d 833 (2d Circuit, 1968).

[16]See Santa Fe Industries v. Green, 430 U.S. 462, 467 (1977).

[17]See Superintendent of Insurance v. Bunkers Life and Casualty Co., 404 U.S. 6 (1971), Blue Chip Stumps v. Manor Drugstore, 421 U.S. 723 (1976).

[18]TSC Industries, Inc. v. Northway, 426 U.S. 438, 449 (1976).

[19]See U.S. Congress, House Committee on Interstate and Foreign Commerce, *Unlawful Corporate Payments Act of 1977,* H.R. Rep 640, 95th Congress, 1st Session, 1977, p. 4.

[20]15 U.S.C., 78 dd-1, 78 dd-2, 78 ff.

[21]Securities and Exchange Commission, *Report on Questionable and Illegal Corporate Payments and Practices,* May 12, 1976. SEC Release 34-15570.

[22]Senate Report on S. 3664, 94th Congress, 2d Session, 1977, p. 12.

[23]See Joint Hearings before Subcommittee on Securities and Subcommittee on International Finance and Monetary Policy, Ninety-Seventh Congress, S. 708. To Amend and Clarity the Foreign Corrupt Practices Act of 1977, May 20, 21 and July 23, 24, 1981.

[24]Hall v. Geiger Jones Co., 24 U.S. 539 (1917).

CHAPTER 32

Corporate Social Responsibility and Business Ethics

I n the last quarter of the twentieth century, the role of the corporation in society has undergone renewed examination. Despite extensive writings on corporate social responsibility, no one definition of what it means has been generally accepted. Not only is there debate about what the term means, but many people continue to view the corporation as having no responsibility other than to its owners. While the term seems to mean different things to different people, each of the words in the term contributes something to its overall definition. This chapter will discuss the legal issues raised by the differing definitions of social responsibility, with emphasis on their implications for corporate managers. It concludes with a discussion of business ethics.

DEFINING CORPORATE SOCIAL RESPONSIBILITY

The term "corporate," when used to modify social responsibility, suggests that the business firm, separate and distinct from its officers and employees, can (and perhaps should) in some way assume responsibility for some actions. Are ethical standards always personal and never institutional? Can corporations, like individuals, be held accountable for their actions? Shouldn't society's rules for institutional behavior originate from sources outside the business enterprises?

The term "social" suggests that the corporation's responsibility is owed to society. To whom in society should the corporation be responsible? Is the corporation responsible to those in society who are in no way connected to the corporation—persons who are not employees or owners or customers or suppliers? Does the corporation's responsibility concern only its products or services or does it also have responsibility to help solve general social problems?

The term "responsibility" usually has several meanings.[1] In the *causal* sense, responsibility usually means accountability. If someone causes an action or event, that person should be held responsible for whatever damage or injury results.

Responsibility is also used in a *normative* sense. A parent has socially sanctioned responsibilities to children, a citizen to the law, a doctor to patients. Society expects people to behave according to norms associated with their social roles. Acting according to these norms is the responsibility of the parties involved.

Finally, the term responsibility is used in a *decision-making* sense. Persons who are reliable and trustworthy are considered responsible. Such people make decisions and judgments based on factors deemed appropriate by others. A responsible decision or action may evoke an attitude of trust from those interacting with the decision-maker even though there is disagreement with the decision itself.

The term "corporate social responsibility" is used in many different ways. Perhaps by examining two different definitions, we can extract a single serviceable definition for use in this chapter.

The first definition, found in the text *Corporate Social Responsibility*, by Farmer and Hogue, focuses on actions that ". . . when judged by society in the future, are seen to have been of maximum help in providing nec-

essary amounts of desired goods and services at minimum financial and social costs, distributed as equitably as possible."[2] The second definition, expressed by William Frederick, focuses on "a willingness (by the corporation) to see that human and economic resources are utilized for broad social ends and not simply the narrowly-circumscribed interest of private persons and firms."[3] Different points of emphasis are found in these definitions. The first makes society the judge of what actions are socially responsible, whereas the second focuses on the willingness of the corporation to take beneficial actions.

The first definition incorporates the classical view that the role of the corporation is to provide "goods and services." However, it also suggests that these should be provided at "minimum financial and social costs" rather than at maximum profit. The second definition doesn't focus on the firm's output of goods and services, but emphasizes the purposes for which its resources are utilized. Both definitions seem to require the corporation to consider how it uses a variety of resources, "human and economic," to provide "maximum help . . . at minimum financial and social costs" for the benefit of society.

SOCIAL RESPONSIBILITY AS A CORPORATE CONCERN

Social responsibility has emerged as a growing concern for today's corporation. An annual survey of *Fortune* 500 companies that seeks to determine how many of the nation's largest companies include social-responsibility statements in their annual reports has been conducted since 1971 by Ernst and Ernst, one of the nation's largest accounting firms. That survey covers seven categories of social problems: the environment, energy, fair business practices, human resources, community involvement, products, and other. The surveys reveal that during the late 1970s approximately 90 percent of the top 500 industrial companies, the top 50 banks, and the top 50 life-insurance companies made social-responsibility disclosures in their annual reports.[4]

While social responsibility has become a business concern, it is unclear how the business enterprise is to respond. To determine what social role a corporation should undertake, we first need to identify the basic theories of social responsibility. Each of the theories will be briefly examined to see how a business corporation could organize its resources to ensure that its actions are socially responsible.

We also know from an examination of our own actions that ethical standards may influence behavior as much as legal standards do. A corporation's "business ethics" can be examined by reviewing individual actions taken by corporate managers and employees. Advertising may be misleading. Gifts to politicians, buyers, or other persons of influence may edge close to becoming bribes. Careless or false reporting by employees of their business expenses may be overlooked. The pursuit of profits may overshadow all other standards or values unless the people in the corporation have a clear sense of ethical standards that affect their business activities. Thus this chapter concludes with a focus on the development and application of ethical standards for the business corporation.

A large segment of American society seems to distrust the business community, particularly the mammoth multinational corporations.[5] This public distrust often leads to increasing legal restrictions on corporations, although sometimes corporations may move in response to societal pressures rather than wait for legal controls to be enacted. While the terms "social responsibility" and "business ethics" are difficult to define and mean different things to different people, the definitions of both terms usually include not only voluntary actions (taken without reference to legal requirements) but also certain of the responsibilities that are placed on the business enter-

prise by the legal system. It is for this reason that we include this chapter in a text dealing with the legal environment of business.

THEORIES OF CORPORATE SOCIAL RESPONSIBILITY

While there are numerous theories advanced to support recognition of corporate social responsibility, they seem to have several common components. We have grouped various subcategories together and will discuss five basic theories for socially responsible business behavior.

Coping-Strategy Theory

Simply stated, the coping-strategy theory is that business should take just enough steps toward social responsibility to ensure that government regulatory officials and business critics do not succeed in infringing on major business prerogatives. This position is purely defensive. It is based on the assumption that if business does nothing on its own toward accepting social responsibility, public pressure will bring about increased regulation by government. Thus business is urged to do enough (or to appear to do enough) to prevent or restrict further legal regulation of business. Under this approach, business would take actions selected to be highly visible and to counter specific instances of public discontent with business.

Humanist Theory

The humanist theory has its roots in general concepts of social justice. Business is viewed as a natural component of the social life of mankind. In that context, business is considered to have certain basic obligations. It is expected to act in a manner that would enhance the general welfare. According to this theory, each business unit should take a broad view to determine how it might contribute to the betterment of society. Some businesses may undertake programs designed to aid the handicapped, to hire former prisoners, or to assist in medical research efforts involving particular diseases. Such activities may be based on general humanist concerns and are representative of this theory of corporate social responsibility.

Profit-Making Theory

According to the profit-making theory, social responsibility is a public-relations tool. Steps toward social responsibility are taken only when a direct correlation with profitability or increased corporate goodwill can be shown. Under this view, corporate social responsibility is considered to be good business. For example, a corporation that makes a large charitable donation to a major school of business might hope that the school's administration and faculty would develop a positive attitude toward the company. This attitude would, in turn, be transferred to the students, who might be more likely to consider the company favorably when weighing competing job offers.

Certainly a corporation's goodwill can be influenced by intangible assets. Although the dollar value of goodwill is very hard to assess, it may shift significantly upward or downward as a result of specific corporation actions (or inactions). Increase in goodwill may come from the recognition of a firm's efforts in social responsibility by trade, professional, or educational groups. Socially responsible actions based on the profit-making theory may, in fact, be aimed at such groups.

Institutional Theory

A basic tenet of the institutional theory is that business enterprises, along with labor unions, government, the media, and organized religions, must be viewed as major institutions of our society. Each of these institutions is considered to have a particular social role that generates expectations regarding its rights and responsibilities within the society.

The Shingle Theory. One way of defining the societal role of a major business enterprise is to view it the way a small community might view a retail merchant or local professional. This can be described as "the shingle theory." The small-town merchant or professional hangs out a "shingle" and thereby represents to the community that certain quality standards will be observed and that the business will stand behind its product or service. The shingle theory is thus similar to the legal principle of implied warranty. By virtue of engaging in certain transactions, business is considered by law to have made certain representations. Liability may be imposed by the legal system if the products or activities involved do not meet the standards established by the implied representation.

The Power Theory. A second approach to defining business's role is to equate the responsibility of the institution with the power it possesses. The greater the power, the greater the responsibility to see that the social good is served. It is probably for this reason that the public's view and the law's regulation of business often distinguish between large and small business firms.

The Economic Theory. A final way of defining the institutional responsibility of business firms is to look solely at the economic dimension of the firm's activities. Business is expected to be economically efficient, to produce and distribute effectively quality goods in accord with consumer desires. Thus, if a business does good deeds in the society, but also makes products that are defective or inferior to those of its competitors, it will not be performing its corporate social responsibility according to the institutional theory.

Professional-Obligation Theory

The traditional professions such as medicine and law are characterized by: (1) limited entry; (2) a required process of licensing; and (3) a formal and legally enforceable ethical code. Business management is not a traditional profession when tested against these standards. The violation of the legal profession's Code of Ethics by most of the lawyers who were criminally involved in the Watergate scandal led to their disbarment (removal of their licenses to practice law). Yet many of the executives involved in the Koreagate or similar scandals who pleaded guilty to having violated the law by making improper political payments nevertheless retained their managerial positions. The business executives did not lose their managerial posts because no formal ethical standards existed by which their conduct could be measured.

Nevertheless, access to positions of senior management responsibility with major business enterprises is generally restricted by rigorous performance requirements. In addition, there is a growing demand for development of more formalized codes of ethics for business managers. A number of firms—IBM, Xerox, and Whirlpool, for example—have developed internal ethical codes for their managers. Thus business management may be seen as evolving toward professional status.

The argument supporting the professional-obligation theory notes that commensurate with professional status is a high standard of public responsibility. For example, lawyers are expected to perform works of public service and/or to engage in providing free some of their professional services. This obligation is usually expressed in the lawyers' Code of Conduct. The rules of the American Bar Association are known as the "Model Rules of Professional Conduct," while those of state bar associations are often referred to as a "Code of Professional Conduct."[6] As the movement toward professional status evolves, business managers may also be considered to have responsibilities to society to do public-service work. Some corporations, such as IBM, do give paid sabbatical leaves for public-service activities to some of their employees.

EVALUATION OF CORPORATE SOCIAL RESPONSIBILITY THEORIES

Basic Challenge to Corporate Social Responsibility

The basic challenge to the idea of social responsibility has been closely identified with Milton Friedman, the well-known conservative economist and Nobel laureate. Some of his statements on social responsibility follow:

There is no such thing as *corporate* social responsibility because only individuals have responsibilities.

In an economic system based on private property, the corporate executive is employed by the owners (shareholders) to make as much money as possible while conforming to the basic rules in society, both those embodied in law and those embodied in ethical custom.

The corporate executive acting as an agent for the stockholders should not make decisions about social responsibilities and social investment because those represent tax decisions and the imposition of taxes and the expenditure of tax proceeds are governmental functions.

The doctrine of social responsibility involves the acceptance of the socialist view that political mechanisms, not market mechanisms, are the appropriate way to determine the allocation of scarce resources to alternate uses.[7]

While few would argue with Professor Friedman that the aim of business is to maximize profits, it does not seem realistic to limit the purpose of a corporation to that one objective. We cannot so easily compartmentalize the economic, social, and political dimensions of our society. Furthermore, Friedman ignores the separation of ownership and control existing in large corporations. In fact, management is usually granted wide authority by shareholder owners, who seldom intervene in running the business. Thus it is management, not shareholders, who shape the company's stance on social responsibility. Finally, the distinction between corporate and individual social responsibility apparently is based on the separation of corporate ethics from individual ethics. Yet the choices and decisions made by the individuals who act as corporate managers are impossible to separate from corporate actions. The transfer of values and ethical standards by individual managers to corporate decisions is going to happen, consciously or unconsciously, and Friedman's idea of separating personal ethics from actions taken by corporate executives may be unrealistic.

Evaluation of Coping-Strategy Theory

The coping-strategy theory assumes that the business will know what action to take to avoid government intervention. It also assumes that business will act as a monolithic unit, with each industry and firm agreeing on the strategy that needs to be taken. Should all chemical manufacturers increase their expenditures for and requirements regarding waste disposal? What kind of voluntary action should they take? Will that change the level of government regulation? What if foreign firms do not increase their expenditures and company requirements? How do we ensure common action among different businesses in the same industry without allowing the companies to reach agreements that might violate antitrust laws? Will all financial institutions disclose the same information, in a similar manner, to the applicant for a loan? The coping strategy theory appears to be defective in assuming that all businesses will have the same information and concern regarding possible government

regulation and that all will react in a similar manner. History suggests otherwise.

Evaluation of Humanist Theory

The humanist theory expects business to act in a manner that would enhance the general welfare of society. Yet one manager motivated by humanist concerns might want to use corporate assets to sponsor the development of a certain type of art, while other managers might feel that such an expenditure would not benefit society. Some might prefer to donate money to specific charitable organizations. Should the money be used to encourage cancer research, aid the blind, or assist teenagers with drug habits? Are all or any of these activities proper concerns for corporations? How should corporations judge among competing societal needs? The humanist theory appears to be too general to be applied to specific situations.

Evaluation of Profit-Making Theory

The profit-making theory of social responsibility views socially responsible activities as necessary to aid the corporation in its search for profits and increased goodwill. This view seeks to balance the quest for short-term profits with socially responsible activities that will generate long-term profitability for the firm. The corporate manager is thus charged with planning how to trade off short-run cash profits for long-term general profitability that will provide greater overall benefit to the firm.

But what if economic conditions limit the company's flexibility? While a corporation may benefit in the long term through increased employee loyalty and productivity if it does not reduce employees' wages during bad economic times, the company may be so strapped for cash that it has no alternative. The profit-making theory of social responsibility might not work in an industry where all firms are not similarly motivated or during times when economic conditions require attention only to short-term profits.

Evaluation of Institutional Theory

The institutional theory sees business as one of the major institutions in society. As such, it is responsible for taking actions that will be consistent with the basic goals and needs of society. One of the most obvious problems with this theory has been noted in the discussion of the coping-strategy theory, namely, that business is not monolithic but is composed of thousands of organizations with differing needs and views. Many of these organizations are involved in severe economic struggles with their counterparts.

Small business enterprises sometimes sense that they are unfairly burdened by government regulation caused by public distrust of large business enterprises. The manufacturer feels that, since it may be subject to significant liability if its products cause injury, it should be able to control the terms, conditions, and prices at which its products are sold. The retailer feels it provides all the services and receives most of the consumer complaints so that it, not the manufacturer, should establish all terms related to the sale of the product. The confrontations between and among business organizations make it difficult for all businesses to subscribe to the same institutional role. Similarly, this diversity makes it difficult to agree on the role of business in society. The institutional theory cannot stand alone as a basis for encouraging socially responsible business behavior because neither the businesses nor the society to which it may seek to be responsible is monolithic or unified.

Evaluation of Professional-Obligation Theory

The professional-obligation theory assumes that a code of conduct for socially responsible action can be standardized for all businesses. How will the code be developed? If it is done by individual companies, as is the case now for some of our large business enterprises, the code may not be agreed to by others in the same industry. If a professional obligation is imposed by an association, such as is the case with the bar association and its member lawyers, will the code also be imposed on nonmembers? Will all corporations agree to abide by the code and allow an association to enforce it against their executives?

Managers do have some professionally based codes of responsibility to identify and serve general societal needs. One business association asks its members to test their actions by these four questions: "Is it the truth? Is it fair to all concerned? Will it build goodwill and better friendship? Will it be beneficial to all concerned?"[8] While many managers and executives follow such an ethical code and professionally based standard, some do not.

IMPLEMENTATION OF CORPORATE SOCIAL RESPONSIBILITY STANDARDS

The five theories of corporate social responsibility are not mutually exclusive. Although they overlap or conflict in certain contexts, they may be synthesized into a flexible set of evaluative criteria to guide very different types of corporations through the maze of issues surrounding social responsibility. Even if we assume that a synthesized, operational standard of appropriate social responsibility can be formulated, there are problems that must be considered in implementing the standards.

There appear to be three basic choices. One is for the individual corporation to adopt its own version of the standards as corporate policy and then for that corporation to develop its own internal means to induce its managers to implement it. A second is to attempt to incorporate the standards into some type of enforceable rules or laws. We would then leave it to designated institutions or to the legal system to force business to act in a socially responsible manner. A third choice is for the standards to become adopted by the public as desirable policy. This method of implementing standards assumes that the public will then mobilize behind actions that are consistent with the policy and will react negatively when the standards are not adhered to by business firms. There are problems with each of these alternatives, as the following discussion indicates.

Individual Corporations and Social Responsibility

The problem of implementing social-responsibility standards raises problems for individual corporations. What priorities should the firm establish? What specific problems should the corporation seek to address? What resources does the corporation have that could be allocated to aid in the solving of social problems? Aside from the legal standards imposed on the corporation, there are usually no societal standards to refer to for aid in answering the questions.

Thus the individual corporation is left to determine its own standards. Of course, the determination of what constitutes socially responsible behavior by corporate managers raises the problem of accountability. As Milton Friedman asked: "What right do managers of private corporations have to determine public policy for their organizations?"[9] Without some kind of accountability, an individual corporation's decisions about what actions are socially responsible may be arbitrary.

On the other hand, if corporations are able to choose from among alternatives the actions that they themselves determine are best able to be undertaken by their particular organizations, those actions may more effectively deal with social problems. Actions that respond to internally established standards could accomplish more for society than would actions that instead react to industry-wide standards.

The diversity of actions taken by individual firms might prove to be beneficial rather than detrimental. Some corporations might lend some of their managers to aid neighborhood groups seeking to establish associations to address problems in particular geographic areas. Other firms might want to provide special services to disadvantaged youth or senior citizens with special economic programs. Financial assistance to the community at large might be available from one corporation while another would seek to provide funds for specific programs. Of course, if participating in socially responsible activities adversely affects a corporation's profits, that corporation could be placed at a competitive disadvantage with other corporations that do not participate. However, there is no indication that taking socially responsible actions adversely affects a firm's profitability.[10] Thus the sum total of the actions taken by individual corporations in order to fulfill their social responsibility may be more far-reaching than if standardized actions were mandated through laws and regulations.

The Boards of Directors. The board of directors has the primary responsibility for establishing a corporation's social-responsibility standards. Structural changes have been made in the composition of the boards of directors of many large corporations. (Such changes are discussed in greater detail in the corporate governance section of this chapter.) A study conducted by the Center for Research in Business and Social Responsibility at the University of Texas at Dallas found that, in 1979, ninety companies had social-responsibility committees in their boards of directors.[11]

Top Management. A second level of corporate commitment to social responsibility is found in the involvement of top management with issues and groups normally considered external to the company's primary activities. One survey indicates that chief executive officers spend from 20 to 75 percent of their time on such involvement, with the average being 40 percent.[12] These figures show the importance of social responsibility to the top management of corporations.

The involvement of chief corporate executives in socially responsible actions takes many forms. Of course, such involvement may arise from different motivations. According to one study, the persons external to the corporation with whom chief executives deal are generally government representatives, investor analysis groups, consumer representatives, media reporters, and community leaders.[13]

All Levels of Management. A third level of commitment by individual corporations to social responsibility probably represents the key to the implementation by the firm of the corporate-established standards. All levels of management must be aware of how the functions they perform may be viewed by the society to which their corporation is responsible. A variety of efforts have been made by many companies. Among these efforts are the following:

1. Encouraging managers to attend continuing education programs that focus on understanding how governmental organizations, bureaus, and agencies function
2. Preparing company publications devoted to discussion of societal problems of concern to the corporations
3. Involving employees and managers in creating social programs and developing social responsibility standards for the corporation
4. Promoting participation in seminars and conferences which provide information on how to deal with environmental or public policy problems.[14]

The management of a corporation's socially responsible actions can involve a series of activities that constitute a management system.

The author of one of the leading textbooks focusing on the implications for management of the emergence of social-responsibility concerns lists seven states of such a system:[15]

1. Identification of public issues and trends in public expectations
2. Evaluation of their impact and setting priorities
3. Research and analysis of issues
4. Development of corporate options regarding issues
5. Development of strategy
6. Implementation of strategy
7. Evaluation and assessment of corporate activites

Public Mobilization of Corporate Social Responsibility Standards

Public opinion is usually slow to form and often can have only an indirect effect on corporate actions. Thus no element of "control" exists for specific situations. Further (and fortunately), there is no means by which public opinion on ideological issues may be quickly shaped toward a particular end. Instead, opinion on ideological matters seems to form gradually over a period of time. Factors influencing its development include teaching in educational institutions, particularly schools of business and economics; statements and positions of politicians, government officials, and business leaders; related economic and political events; and popular writings on ideological issues.

All of these forces now appear to be oriented toward raising the public's consciousness of social-responsibility issues. But it will take a great deal more time for public opinion to become dominant. The likelihood that public opinion will influence corporations to follow some established social-responsibility standard for particular corporate activities is not very great.

Legal Controls and Corporate Social Responsibility Standards

How can our legal system control and/or direct corporate behavior? Is the legal system effective in prohibiting antisocial action by business firms? How can the existing legal structure be changed to increase its effectiveness as a force shaping business behavior? These questions all have become critically important in the last few years.

The legal system is basically a negative force when it acts to punish wrongdoers. Ideally, there is voluntary compliance with most legal rules, and when this occurs the legal system operates in a positive manner. Compliance with rules of law may be motivated by a desire to do the "right thing" or by a fear of sanctions for violating the law.

Does the legal system produce the type of behavior on the part of large business enterprises that our society desires? Some recent writers have argued that the answer is no.

These critics contend that the legal system is ineffective in controlling corporate behavior because of the corporation's special legal characteristics. As a legal entity, the corporation is an "actor" whose intent is difficult to discern and whose "conscience" is hard to reach. Ultimately, to be effective, a legal sanction must be imposed on responsible and human corporate managers.

The following two decisions are dramatic example of courts holding corporations responsible for the social consequences of their actions. Both opinions describe the "facts" of the same event. Compare the two opinions carefully. What legal sanctions could effectively be imposed on a corporation whose actions are not socially responsible? Would criminal sanctions be effective? What about assessing punitive damages or fines against the corporation? Do you think the alternatives presented by the two cases would equally affect both the individual manager and the corporate entity?

Roginsky v. Richardson-Merrell, Inc.

Second Circuit Court of Appeals

378 F.2d 832 (1967)

In this action, Roginsky sought to recover compensatory and punitive damages for personal injuries, primarily cataracts, resulting from taking a drug, MER/29, developed by Richardson-Merrell Company for lowering blood cholesterol levels. The jury gave affirmative answers to all the questions relating to liability and fixed compensatory damages at $17,500 and punitive damages at $100,000, which the judge later declined to eliminate or reduce. On appeal, defendant complained that the award of punitive damages violated due process. The court of appeals affirmed the judgment of compensatory damages but reversed the trial court's award of punitive damages.

Friendly, Circuit Judge

. . . MER/29 was developed in the late 1950's by the Wm. S. Merrell Company, a division of defendant, for the purpose of lowering blood cholesterol levels. . . .

Before the drug was placed on the market there had been 246 experiments involving 3907 animals and it had been administered to over 2000 human patients under close clinical observation. Eighty percent of these patients who had used the drug for 90 days or longer experienced a reduction of cholesterol levels averaging 20 percent. The only reported side effects were dermatitis of several different types, two reports of hair loss, some nausea and vomiting, one report of a drop in white blood cell count, two cases of vaginal bleeding or spotting, three cases of tearing or watering of the eyes, and one of blurred vision. . . .

Marketing began June 1. During the balance of 1960 over 100,000 persons used the drug, with no reports of cataracts.

In January 1961, Merck & Co., which had borrowed a sample of MER/29 and then synthesized its own supply, reported that test animals had developed cataracts. Defendant, after sending a team to Merck's laboratory, decided to make a further experiment on animals selected by it but did not reveal the Merck report to the FDA or the medical profession. . . .

On defendant's rerun of the Merck experiment, its dogs developed cataracts in October, 1961. At the same time the Mayo Clinic reported cataracts in two, later three, patients who were using MER/29. The combined effect of these two incidents was to cause the defendant, on October 18, 1961, to request the FDA's permission to issue a warning letter to all physicians. . . . About April 1, the Mayo Clinic reported cataracts in a six year old boy who had been given high dosages to counteract a severe case of excessive cholesterol unusual in a child. Early in April defendant decided to withdraw MER/29 from the market; this was done on April 17, 1962.

Plaintiff, then aged 60, began using MER/29 in February 1961. In June he noticed scaling, rashes and falling hair which he reported to his physician. These conditions became aggravated despite treatment; around the year-end he noted disturbing eye symptoms and stopped taking the drug. In about six months the skin and hair conditions disappeared but the eye ailment, later diagnosed as cataracts, became somewhat worse; however, it has not become sufficiently serious for him to have them removed. . . .

We thus came to the issue of punitive damages, an issue of extreme significance not only in monetary terms to this defendant in view of the hundreds of pending MER/29 actions and to the plaintiff as well, but from a longer range, to the entire pharmaceutical industry and to all present and potential users of drugs. Plaintiff, of course, does not claim that defendant intended to harm him; his contention is that defendant's negligence rose to such a level of irresponsibility or worse as to invite this extraordinary sanction. . . .

The legal difficulties engendered by claims for punitive damages on the part of hundreds of plaintiffs are staggering. If all recovered punitive damages in the amount here awarded these would run into tens of millions, as contrasted with the maximum criminal penalty of "imprisonment for not more than three years, or a fine of not more than $10,000, or both. . . ." We have the gravest difficulty in perceiving how claims for punitive damages in such a multiplicity of actions throughout the nation can be so administered as to avoid overkill. . . . We know of no principle whereby the first punitive award exhausts all claims for punitive damages and would thus preclude future judgments; . . . While jurisprudes might comprehend why Toole in California should walk off with $250,000 more than a compensatory recovery and Roginsky in the Southern District of New York and Mrs. Ostopowitz in Westchester County with

$100,000, most laymen and some judges would have some difficulty in understanding why presumably equally worthy plaintiffs in the other 75 cases before Judge Croake or elsewhere in the country should get less or none.

Although multiple punitive awards running into the hundreds may not add up to a denial of due process, . . . we would wish to consider very seriously whether awarding punitive damages with respect to the negligent—even highly negligent—manufacture and sale of a drug governed by federal food and drug requirements, . . . would not do more harm than good. A manufacturer distributing a drug to many thousands of users under government regulation scarcely requires this additional measurement for manifesting social disapproval and assuring deterrence. Criminal penalties and heavy compensatory damages, recoverable under some circumstances even without proof of negligence, should sufficiently meet these objectives. . . .

The parties are in substantial agreement on one point—that New York does not impose punitive damages on a corporation unless, as charged by Judge Croake, "the officers or directors, that is, the management" of the company or the relevant division "either authorized, participated in, consented to or, after discovery, ratified the conduct" giving rise to such damages. . . .

Obviously this definition would be met if a manufacturer placed a drug on the market without any test program, a practice now rendered unlawful by federal legislation, or when its management knew the program had disclosed dangers of serious mischance or was incomplete in some material respect. Sufficient proof would also be furnished if, after the drug had been placed on the market, the manufacturer was shown to have become aware of danger and to have done nothing, deliberately closing its eyes. On the other hand, error in failing to make what hindsight demonstrates to have been the proper response—even "gross" error—is not enough to warrant submission of punitive damages to the jury.

An attempt to analyze every item of evidence relied on by plaintiff would prolong this opinion to a length even more inordinate than it has assumed; we limit ourselves to the evidence deemed most significant and helpful to the plaintiff.

One of the earliest and most inflammatory items was this: As part of the New Drug Application submitted to the FDA, defendant reported on a 16 month study of three pairs of monkeys, one of each pair being given the drug and the other being a control. The plan was to start the dosage at two and a half times the anticipated human dose, and then to raise it first to five and then to ten times. The experiment had been conducted by a toxicologist, Smith, who had left the company's employ before reporting on it; the writeup by his successor, Dr. King, contained numerous errors—none, however, shown to have been known to management—and one thing that was much worse. A laboratory technician testified to an occasion when she had submitted a final graph of the weights of the monkeys to a Dr. Van Maanen who directed her to increase the weight shown for one monkey whose weight had dropped 25 percent and to show weights for others for two weeks after they had in fact been autopsied; after complaining to Dr. King, her immediate supervisor, she made the changes. But Dr. Van Maanen, Merrell's Director of Biological Science, was also a subordinate who reported to the vice president and research director, Dr. Werner, and there was not the slightest evidence that the latter or any higher authority knew of his dictating this change in the observed data. Equally irrelevant to the issue of punitive damages was another error by Dr. King in reporting an experiment on female rats, all of which were shown to have died under exceptionally heavy dosage. Here also there was no proof of management complicity, nor was there any showing that Dr. King's error was deliberate. Moreover, it has not been clearly shown that either of these mis-reports was truly material.

. . . This brings us to the receipt of the report from Merck & Co. in January 1961 as to cataracts in dogs which we mentioned at the outset. Since this, to our minds, was the first information reaching management which might indicate that MER/29 could have such serious side effects as to make it unsafe despite its beneficial qualities, the officers' action must be severely scrutinized.

Defendant's immediate response was to send Dr. Werner, its research vice-president, Dr. Van Maanen and Dr. King to the Merck laboratory. The decision made on their return was to rerun the experiment. On its face this was not heedless or reckless conduct; on the contrary, to have accepted the Merck report as conclusive would have been irresponsible. Apart from the possibility of chemical differences in the Merck synthesized drug, a point on which defendant heavily relies but to which plaintiff effectively responds that Merrell did not ask for a sample, significance of the Merck results was called in question by the dogs' being beagles, which are known to be cataract prone, and defendant's suspicion of inbreeding which would have further invalidated the results.

Indeed, the serious criticism is not over what defendant did but what it failed to do —notify the FDA, the medical profession, or both. Plaintiff does not contend that FDA regulations required defendant to report the Merck results, the requirements then being limited to reporting results of experiments done in the manufacturer's own laboratory or by an investigator who had been furnished the drug. The claim is rather that, even though there is no direct proof that such notification was considered and rejected, its logic was so apparent as to permit an inference that defendant didn't want the FDA to know of the Merck results for fear it might order the warning accompanying the drug to be stiffened or the drug withdrawn, and didn't want physicians to know for fear they would be unduly frightened. Assuming a jury could find that this was so and that defendant was motivated by commercial considerations as well as by a desire to benefit potential victims of atherosclerosis and granting that management knew its own experiments have disclosed corneal opacities in rats, we fail to see how this meets the definition of reckless indifference to human life or health. . . .

The judgment as to compensatory damages is affirmed; the judgment as to punitive damages is reversed.

Toole v. Richardson-Merrell, Inc.

California Court of Appeals
60 Cal.Rptr. 398 (1967)

Toole, 43 years of age, developed cataracts in both eyes as a result of taking the drug triparanol, manufactured and sold by appellant under the trade name "MER/29."

Acting under his doctor's direction, he began using MER/29 in July 1960. He developed a condition known as ichthyosis, characterized by dry, flaky, red and inflamed skin. He also suffered hair loss over his entire body. He stopped using the drug in December 1961. His skin returned to normal, most of his hair regrew, but cataracts developed, his eyes became opaque, and it was necessary to operate and remove the lenses of both eyes. As a result, his sight was distorted, peripheral vision was reduced, his eyes lost their ability to adjust for distances and became painfully sensitive to light, and he was required to wear corrective glasses. There was also evidence that he was more apt to suffer detached retinas, which could lead to blindness. He had an emotional overlay of fear that the drug might have some long-term ill effect that would manifest itself later in life.

Toole filed suit against Richardson-Merrell, Inc., seeking compensatory and punitive damages for injuries he suffered as a result of using its drug. The jury awarded Toole $175,000 in compensatory damages and $500,000 as punitive damages. The trial judge, with the plaintiff's approval, reduced the punitive damages to $250,000. The defendant appealed both aspects of the trial court's final judgment.

The California court of appeals in this opinion affirmed the trial court's award of both compensatory and punitive damages.

Salsman, Associate Justice

MER/29 was developed by the Wm. S. Merrell Co., Inc., a division of appellant Richardson-Merrell Inc. Frank N. Getman was president of the division; Robert Woodward was executive vice president (succeeded later by E.R. Beckwith, Jr.); Dr. Harold Werner was vice president and director of research; Phillip Ritter was vice president in charge of marketing, and Dr. Joseph Murray was liaison officer to the Food and Drug Administration, working under Vice President Werner. Below this level of management were two divisions. One, the Medical Science Division, was headed by Dr. Pogge, assisted by Drs. Bunde and McMaster, the latter in charge of medical research on MER/29. The other division was the Biological Science Division, in charge of Dr. Van Maanen. This division had five departments, one of which was the Toxicology Department headed first by Knox Smith and later by William King. Mrs. Beulah Jordan also worked in the Toxicology Department, and under the direction of Mr. King and Dr. Van Maanen compiled some of the records hereafter mentioned.

THE EVIDENCE

Appellant's Toxicology Department began animal testing of MER/29 in 1957. In the first six-week test, all female rats on a high dosage died. All were found to have suffered abnormal blood changes. There was evidence that unusual blood changes in animals tested with drugs are regarded as a major danger signal.

A second rat study was begun, using a reduced dosage of MER/29. This test also produced abnormal blood changes in the rats. Vice President Werner was informed of these results.

In 1958 William King was hired by appellant and put in charge of the Toxicology

Department, replacing Knox Smith. He was assigned to review the blood findings reported in the rat tests conducted by Smith.

In March 1959 a test of MER/29 in monkeys was completed. Again, abnormal blood changes were found. But Dr. Van Maanen ordered Mrs. Beulah Jordan, the laboratory technician, to falsify a chart of this test by recording false body weights for the monkeys, by extending their records beyond dates after which the monkeys had been killed, and by adding data for an imaginary monkey that had never been in the test group at all. Mrs. Jordan protested to King but was told: "He (Van Maanen) is higher up. You do as he tells you and be quiet."

Knox Smith had prepared a brochure reflecting Merrell's test results of MER/29 on rats. This literature was intended for use of medical doctors clinically testing the drug on human beings. King revised this brochure, and eliminated all reference in it to the abnormal blood findings previously recited. Dr. McMaster, of the Medical Science Division, who was in charge of medical research on MER/29, had knowledge of the deletions, and consented to them.

On July 21, 1959 appellant filed a new drug application with the FDA seeking permission to place MER/29 on the market. The application contained many false statements, among them these:

(1) It was reported that only four out of eight rats had died during a certain study, whereas in truth all had died.
(2) Wholly fictitious body and organ weights and also blood tests were reported for dead rats as if they had continued to live and to take MER/29.
(3) None of the abnormal blood changes encountered in experiments was disclosed.
(4) False data was related for a monkey being tested with the drug, and also data was stated for a monkey that was never part of the test group.
(5) The falsified chart, prepared by Mrs. Jordan under protest was included in the application.

At the time appellant filed its new drug application it knew that MER/29 would require long-term use, because when use was discontinued cholesterol levels rose, but appellant had no data on the long-term effects of MER/29 in humans. At the time of its new drug application only 116 persons had taken MER/29 on an experimental basis, and none had used the drug for more than six months. There was evidence that before a drug such as MER/29 is marketed initial studies should be made to establish its toxicity, followed by a three-year test in humans, to be followed by a final period of testing in humans before placing the drug on the market.

The FDA informed appellant that its new drug application was incomplete; that a low margin of safety was indicated and that a two-year study in rats and a three-month study in dogs should be undertaken. This information was conveyed to President Getman and the vice-presidents and division heads under him. Dr. Murray, appellant's liaison officer, replied to the FDA and specifically informed it that there had been no blood changes in appellant's tests of MER/29 on rats or monkeys, and that a 16-month study in monkeys had adequately demonstrated the safety of MER/29. These statements concerning absence of blood changes in animals were of course untrue.

In January 1960 appellant completed another study on the effect of MER/29 in rats.

Nine out of ten rats in this study developed eye opacities. Appellant's report to the FDA of the results of this study was false or misleading because it reported that eight out of twenty rats had developed mild inflammation of the eye, but did not disclose the eye opacities seen in the test animals. . . .

In April 1969 the FDA granted appellant's application to market MER/29. There was testimony at trial, however, that placing the drug on the market at that time was not in line with the general practice of reputable drug firms, in view of appellant's knowledge of the results of its animal studies and clinical investigations.

MER/29 was introduced to the market by the greatest promotional and advertising effort ever made by appellant in support of a product. There was testimony that doctors had never before seen so much promotion of a single drug. Doctors were bombarded with sales promotion, and subjected to brainwashing sessions with detailmen (salesmen). One advertising brochure stated that MER/29 was ". . . virtually nontoxic and remarkably free from side effects even on prolonged clinical use."

Two months after MER/29 was placed on the market, appellant received a letter from Dr. Loretta Fox, of Florida, who said she had used MER/29 experimentally on rats, and had thereafter observed lenticular and corneal eye opacities in her subjects. Dr. Fox gave the same information to the FDA, who in turn asked appellant to review her experiment and to comment on it. Dr. Murray replied to the FDA inquiry. He enclosed a memorandum from King, head of appellant's Toxicology Department, which stated that MER/29 had been used on thousands of rats, and "In only one group of animals, in one experiment, and at only one time, did we observe eye changes." King's memorandum also stated "We have no evidence from our experience or from the literature that MER/29 would in itself, produce such changes." These statements were essentially false.

On October 10, 1960, Dr. Murray again wrote to the FDA enclosing a copy of his letter of September 29th to Dr. Fox. He asserted that Dr. Fox's observations were ". . . most surprising to us" and that ". . . our pathologist states that he has never seen such involvement of the lens. . . ." At the time this letter was written, King, appellant's pathologist, had proceeded with the chronic study of MER/29 in rats, and had found an even greater percentage of rats on the lower dosage blind than when Dr. Murray's earlier letter had been sent to the FDA. All of the rats on the higher dosage of MER/29 were blind by October 1960. There was expert testimony at trial to the effect that, with all this information in hand, appellant should have withdrawn the drug from the market.

In April 1962 FDA officials made an unannounced visit to appellant's laboratories and took all of appellant's records relating to its animal experiments. After the records were seized, President Getman drafted a letter to the FDA requesting withdrawal of MER/29 from the market, and on May 22, 1962 the agency issued its order suspending permission for the marketing of the drug on the ground that it was unsafe for its intended use.

MER/29 was administered to approximately 400,000 persons during its relatively short market life. In its first year at large it contributed $7,000,000 to appellant's gross sales. 490 cases of cataracts caused by use of the drug were reported. The majority of those on the drug maintained its use for less than three months. There was evidence that a very high percentage of those taking the drug would have developed cataracts if the drug had remained on the market and they had continued its use.

Appellant does not directly challenge the sufficiency of the evidence to support the compensatory damage award. It is clear from those portions of the record we have heretofore recited that the jury could infer that appellant did not exercise ordinary care adequately to test MER/29 before placing it on the market, and did not give adequate warning to the medical profession, and through it to respondent, of known dangerous side effects of the drug. Thus the award of compensatory damages may readily be sustained on the ground of negligence.

Appellant next argues that a verdict should have been directed in its behalf on respondent's causes of action for fraud and breach of express warranty. Appellant says first that the statements it made about MER/29 were mere expressions of scientific opinion made to physicians, and second that there is no evidence that respondent relied upon any of the statements made by appellant. The jury's verdict, however, necessarily contains implied findings that appellant's statements were misrepresentations of material facts and that respondent relied upon them to his injury and damage. These findings are supported by the record.

Appellant represented that: (a) MER/29 is virtually non-toxic; (b) it is remarkably free from side effects; (c) it is a proven drug; (d) it has been administered under controlled conditions to more than 2,000 patients for periods up to three years; (e) there is no longer any valid question as to its safety or lack of significant side effects; (f) MER/29 has a unique, specific and completely safe action.

Appellant next says there is no evidence to show that respondent relied upon any of its representations. But there was evidence from which the jury could readily infer reliance on the presentations. Respondent's doctor, his agent, relied upon them.

Appellant contends that as a matter of law a verdict should have been directed for it on the issue of punitive damages. It argues that if wrongful acts were done by its agents it must be shown that such acts were authorized or ratified by responsible management in order to hold the corporation liable.

A corporation may be held liable for punitive damages for the acts of its agents and employees when the act is done in ill will, or is motivated by actual malice, or done under circumstances amounting to fraud or oppression, providing that the act is done with the knowledge or under the direction of corporate officials having power to bind the corporation. . . .

. . . There was ample evidence from which the jury could infer that high level management had knowledge of wrongdoing on the part of department heads and other employees and agents.

. . . Appellant says there is no showing of any deliberate intent to do harm to respondent, and that in the absence of a showing of deliberate intention on the part of appellant to injure respondent the award of punitive damages must fall. But malice in fact, . . . as that term is used in Civil Code section 3294, may be established by showing that the defendant's wrongful conduct was wilful, intentional, and done in reckless disregard of its possible results. Where, as here, there is evidence that the conduct in question is taken recklessly and without regard to its injurious consequences, the jury may find malice in fact. . . .

The judgment is affirmed.

CORPORATE GOVERNANCE AND CORPORATE SOCIAL RESPONSIBILITY

Society's changing expectations for business corporations have to a significant degree been incorporated into new laws and regulations. Laws related to health and safety in the workplace, equal employment opportunity, product safety, and pollution control exemplify this focus on social regulation. Government agencies that did not exist several decades ago—the Occupational Safety and Health Administration, Environmental Protection Agency, Consumer Product Safety Commission, Equal Employment Opportunity Commission—are now of major concern to many business corporations.

Furthermore, some recent proposals seek to make corporations more socially responsible by changing the legal requirements affecting the corporation's organizational structure. These proposals are based on the assumption that changes in the structure of corporate governance would make it more likely that corporations would act in a socially responsible manner than is now true.

The Board of Directors

Significant attention has been focused on the composition of the corporate board of directors. Since it is the board of directors that is legally responsible for the actions taken by the corporation, many proposals have sought to require that persons on the board of directors of major publicly held business corporations be persons who are not affiliated with the corporation's daily management. Some members of the board of directors, perhaps a majority, would have to be "outside" directors, not corporate officers. The outside directors are thus seen as performing an oversight function; they ensure that the insiders are performing in the manner that the board of directors determines to be socially responsible.

Audit Committees

Other proposals seek to assign to some outside directors an audit function. Committees of selected outside directors are entrusted with monitoring specific corporate activities. Often, such a committee is established to monitor the company's accounting procedures and ensure the accuracy of the firm's annual report.

Some outside directors may be given personnel responsibilities. They are charged with determining executive compensation policies or are asked to nominate other outside directors. Thus management officers may be unable to nominate their own friends and associates for membership on their corporation's board of directors. Some of these proposals have been adopted by the Securities and Exchange Commission as requirements that must be adhered to by corporations with a certain number of public shareholders.

Disclosure Requirements

Finally, some proposals that indirectly affect corporate governance relate to the disclosure of information by the corporation to its owners. The primary purpose behind the increased disclosure regulations that the Securities and Exchange Commission has adopted in recent years is to make the corporation more responsible to its stockholders. Secondarily, these disclosures provide information to society as a whole.

Examples of required disclosures include disclosure of the effects of inflation on corporate profits, of payments to foreign officials (some of which have been made illegal by the Foreign Corrupt Practices Act), and of executive "deferred compensation" agreements. Of course, there is no assurance that the disclosure of such information actually is useful to shareholders or to the public at large. The additional corporate expense in providing the information may outweigh its benefit for the shareholder or potential investor.

Other Concepts

Several more controversial concepts also have been advanced. For example, Harold Williams, once the chairman of the SEC, has suggested that corporations might experiment with having a chairman of the board who is not the chief executive officer.[16] This idea has not received much support. A chairman unfamiliar with day-to-day executive functions probably would have difficulty handling the board meeting. He or she certainly would have difficulty with some of the questions that require daily contact with the corporation's managers. Such a proposal is unlikely to gain voluntary support, and its imposition by regulation is improbable.

Others have suggested appointing constituent directors or special-interest directors. In Europe, this practice is widespread; representatives of organized labor frequently are included on corporate boards. The main criticism of this approach is that it changes the nature of the board and of the roles performed by the corporation's constituent groups. First, a board of directors must function with cohesion and ease of communication. Those characteristics develop through time as common problems and difficulties are faced and handled. Procedures, both formal and informal, are carefully established and it is felt that only insiders will feel entirely comfortable in a meeting. Similarly, single-issue directors might have difficulty in working effectively on behalf of management rather than in a more narrow and perhaps more adversarial role.

A variety of other proposals for reforming the present method of corporate governance have been advanced. One recent approach seeks to alter the role of corporate legal counsel. There have been instances in which a cor-

poration's management systematically has concealed illegal activity from its legal counsel. Even where the legal counsel has the necessary information, there are conflicts in the dual role of an attorney who is also an employee. Proposals to change the attorney's professional obligation, as found in the Model Rules of Professional Conduct, have been made at recent meetings of the American Bar Association.

It is beyond the scope of this chapter to attempt to detail all the proposals to reform the corporate organizational structure to make the corporation more responsible to society. Several questions are as yet unanswered. Will changes in corporate governance structures change the degree to which a corporation acts in a socially responsible manner? Is there a need for more laws and more regulation or will desirable goals best be accomplished by deregulation? Can we even determine how we want corporations to behave and act toward society? Only one thing can be certain about these questions; there are no simple and easy answers.

BUSINESS ETHICS

Defining Ethics

Ethics are usually defined as standards of behavior. Some people rely on personal values and emphasize the subjective standard of "What I think is right." Other people refer to some external standard, perhaps found in laws, religious teachings, or customary practices. The personal standards and the external guides are frequently combined in order to reach a more comprehensive definition of ethics.

Dr. Albert Schweitzer defined ethics as "the name we give to good behavior." He noted that ethics spring from an obligation to consider not only our personal well-being but also that of others and of human society as a whole.[17] Schweitzer's emphasis on our obligation to others is also the theme embodied in the Golden Rule: "Do unto others as you would have them do unto you."

Other definitions of ethics also express concern with the relationship between our actions and their effects on other people. Ivan Hill, former Director of the Ethics Resource Center in Washington, D.C., has stated that "ethical behavior recognizes and rests with a shared interest. On a practical level, this shared interest effects an ordering of society's economic means by which the individual can pursue his own ends. It is the recognition and personal acceptance of this behavior that we call ethical behavior."[18] The compiler of *A Bibliography of Business Ethics* notes that "ethics deals with the 'what should be done?' questions with reference to actions that might harm or benefit human beings . . . and aims at maximizing human benefit."[19]

Sources of Ethics

Certainly, the cumulative individual values of business people form the basis for what could be defined as "business ethics." But individuals differ significantly in the values they hold. The formation of ethical standards by individuals is influenced by a variety of sources. Among the sources most commonly referred to are:

Parents. Parents can suggest guidelines for the actions of their children. "You aren't to have other children over to our house when there are no adults present." "While you are in high school, you are not to stay out past eleven o'clock during the week." "You can't bring your friends in here and serve them alcoholic beverages if they are not legally of age."

Parents can also establish standards by example. Do parents who tell children not to call other children bad names violate that stan-

dard in family discussions about their "friends and neighbors"? If children are not to take property belonging to someone else, do the parents take hotel towels or fail to return items lent to them? Are all laws to be followed except the income tax laws, the speeding laws, and others with which a parent may disagree?

Peers. Is it all right to follow prevailing practices? If others cheat on exams, does that make it right? A recent *Wall Street Journal* article notes that while cheating on the college campus is hardly new, educators say today's students may be different in several ways. "Nobody is afraid about saying they do it." "They seem to feel it's part of the game, they feel less guilty about it."[20]

Many of the Watergate defendants stated that they had followed the orders and practices of others who suggested covering up illegal and unethical practices because of the examples of and pressure from their peers.

Education. While the ethical standards of most people reading this text no doubt have been well-developed for years, the teachings in classrooms and schools are important sources for our values. Education may of course also come from books we read, movies we watch, or television programs we tune in to. The "permissive society" of the seventies may have been influenced by the writings of baby doctor Benjamin Spock or by the "atmosphere" on the college campuses. In any event, whether proper or not, many in society attribute to our educational institutions a great deal of influence in forming society's values.

Religion. Religious doctrines on abortion, contraception, and a woman's role in society are influential standards for millions of people. Is it enough to say we follow prevailing religious teachings? Puritanical New Englanders burned witches for violating their doctrines. Mass suicide was suggested and apparently practiced because of the orders of religious leaders in the New Guinea People's Temple in 1979. In Iran, opponents of the ruling Ayatollah are executed. While religious teachings and practices often do establish needed standards of conduct necessary for life in a civilized society, the variety of teachings and practices can be confusing and bewildering.

Law. Much growth in law in recent years has involved the application of legal sanctions to what formerly were purely questions of ethics and morality. A contract that provided one party an unfair advantage was once rather routinely enforced in the law courts. The only question that could be raised regarding its fairness was an ethical one. However, the law courts have recently adopted the view that since the parties didn't really bargain with one another unconscionable contracts will not be enforced.

Similarly, the business merchant must meet the "good faith" standard in performing contracts governed by the Uniform Commercial Code. This standard brings to the law courts a concern that was once left to the ethical standards of the contracting parties. Legal duties have been imposed in a variety of places where ethical obligations once were controlling.

Abraham Maslow has suggested that there is a hierarchy of needs that motivate people and influence their value development. The hierarchy Maslow suggests is illustrated in Figure 32–1. According to Maslow, as the individual rises in the hierarchy, the needs become cumulative. Thus an individual who is concerned with the fourth level of self-esteem must also satisfy the lower levels of socialization, safety, and physiological concerns.

FIGURE 32–1

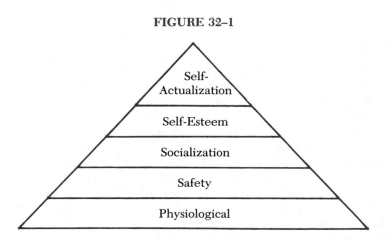

Ethical values presumably become more important as the individual progresses beyond concern with basic needs. Ethical standards reflect changes in society. As society has developed, the ethical standards affecting business have changed. In the early twentieth century, legal and ethical standards placed on the buyer the responsibility of

checking to see that the products being purchased were well made and fairly priced. As we near the end of this century, society increasingly places on the seller the obligation to ensure that its product is safe and fairly priced. Laws relating to product liability, recall of defective products, implied warranties, and unconscionable pricing are but a few examples of the shift in society's expectations regarding the concern that business should have with the effect of its actions on other people.

Business Ethics and Corporate Social Responsibility

While business ethics and corporate social responsibility are often discussed together, the two are not the same. Ethics, according to one author,[21] is a practical science, based on the rightness and wrongness of human action. Thus business ethics is concerned with corporate actions and policies that seek to minimize harm and maximize benefit in conformity with the corporation's determination of rightness and wrongness. Corporate social responsibility is concerned with the corporation's role in society. The corporation's responsibility to society is determined by examining the demands made by society, not by focusing on what the corporation believes is the right action to take. Thus action by a corporation taken to pursue social-responsibility standards might not be identical with actions that the corporation's managers believe to be ethical.

There is, of course, a close relationship between business ethics and social responsibility. To be acceptable to society, a business ethic must be compatible with prevailing social-responsibility standards. Corporate social responsibility has been described as the "fit" between society's expectations of the business community and the ethics of business.[22] The fit has two components. The first is concerned with what the corporation does in relation to what society expects it to do; are its actions in line with society's expectations? The second component focuses on the attitudes of the officers and managers of the corporation. What are their ethical standards and attitudes as to what are or are not socially responsible actions for their corporation?

Ethics and Business Corporations

If ethics are standards for behavior, how can these standards be developed and institutionalized by business corporations? There seem to be several approaches to integrating ethical standards into corporate policies and practices. The most common method of institutionalizing ethical standards has been the development of corporate ethical codes.

Sixty-seven percent of the firms surveyed in one study had developed ethical codes.[23] A code of ethics can offer some guidance, particularly if it is written in specific terms, includes effective sanctions, and is accompanied by formal enforcement mechanisms. The advantage of a code is that it standardizes definitions of acceptable conduct. If this is true, a code may make it easier for a manager to act ethically and more difficult to behave in a clearly unethical manner.

Other methods by which ethical standards can be institutionalized by business corporations have been noted in various writings. A formally designated ethics committee may be established on the board of directors or at the highest levels of corporate management. Management-development programs that incorporate ethics into seminars and training sessions are also used in some corporations.

Codes of Ethics

A corporate code of ethics must be sensitive to special concerns affecting the nature of the corporation's activities. Multinational corporations must consider issues related to compliance with differing national laws, customs, and accepted practices. Companies producing consumer products need to address advertising policies, consumer relations, and product-safety standards.

The writing and development of a code

should involve many corporate levels, from the board of directors through middle management and sales personnel. The writers must be aware that no set of standards can possibly cover every single ethical development.

Two ethical areas are included in almost all existing corporate codes. According to a survey conducted for the Ethics Resource Center in Washington, D.C., 94 percent of the codes prohibit outside activities that are considered to involve conflict of interest with corporate activities, while 97 percent of the codes prohibit the giving or taking of favors to influence business decisions.[24] The Ethics Code for the Securities and Exchange Commission, for example, prohibits a staff member from accepting "food and refreshment" from a company being investigated by the SEC.[25]

The second ethical issue, which has received a great deal of media coverage in the past few years, concerns the matter of making payments to obtain services, permits, licenses, or contracts in foreign markets. In its dealings with Japanese firms, Lockheed made large payments to Japanese officials for the purpose of obtaining contracts. Some Lockheed officials were fined and disciplined, and the Japanese officials who were involved were removed from their positions. While the Foreign Corrupt Practices Act now establishes some legal standards for some of these practices, there are still ethical problems related to the payment or receipt of gifts or services.

Ethical Problems for Business

While our discussion of business ethics has considered a variety of means by which ethical standards may be adopted and used in business, we have not attempted to define how the ethical standards should be used in specific situations. No doubt we would find it impossible to agree on one ethical value system. Rather than seek such agreement, it may be helpful to present several court cases and a variety of problem situations that raise ethical questions; they can serve as a basis both for classroom discussion and for individual thought. First review the two cases that follow. What ethical questions do they raise? Do they represent situations you encounter in business dealings? Would you like the company you work for to be involved in similar cases? Finally, seek to answer the questions posed by the problem situations[26] presented at the end of this chapter. How would you deal with similar problems?

Vokes v. Arthur Murray, Inc.
Florida District Court of Appeals, Second District
212 So. 2d 906 (1968)

The plaintiff, a 51-year-old widow, brought this action against the defendant dance-instruction corporation to recover damages caused by the defendant's fraud. The defendant argued that there was no fraud or misrepresentation on its part, that its statements were mere "trade puffing." The trial court found for the defendant and dismissed plaintiff's amended complaint; from that decision, the plaintiff appealed. The court of appeals found the statements made by plaintiff in her complaint could be the basis for finding that the defendant committed fraud. Accordingly, it reversed the trial court's dismissal of the plaintiff's complaint.

Pierce, J.

This is an appeal by Audrey E. Vokes, plaintiff below, from a final order dismissing with prejudice, for failure to state a cause of action, her fourth amended complaint, hereinafter referred to as plaintiff's complaint.

Defendant Arthur Murray, Inc., a corporation, authorizes the operation throughout the nation of dancing schools under the name of "Arthur Murray School of Dancing" through local franchised operators, one of whom was defendant J. P. Davenport whose dancing establishment was in Clearwater.

Plaintiff Mrs. Audrey E. Vokes, a widow of 51 years and without family, had a yen to be "an accomplished dancer" with the hopes of finding "new interest in life." So, on February 10, 1961, a dubious fate, with the assist of a motivated acquaintance, procured her to attend a "dance party" at Davenport's "School of Dancing" where she whiled away the pleasant hours, sometimes in a private room, absorbing his accomplished sales technique, during which her grace and poise were elaborated upon and her rosy future as "an excellent dancer" was painted for her in vivid and glowing colors. As an incident to this interlude, he sold her eight ½-hour dance lessons to be utilized within one calendar month therefrom, for the sum of $14.50 cash in hand paid, obviously a baited "come-on."

Thus she embarked upon an almost endless pursuit of the terpsichorean art during which, over a period of less than sixteen months, she was sold fourteen "dance courses" totalling in the aggregate 2302 hours of dancing lessons for a total cash outlay of $31,090.45, all at Davenport's dance emporium. All of these fourteen courses were evidenced by execution of a written "Enrollment Agreement—Arthur Murray's School of Dancing" with the addendum in heavy black print, "No one will be informed that you are taking dancing lessons. Your relations with us are held in strict confidence," setting forth the number of "dancing lessons" and the "lessons in rhythm sessions" currently sold to her from time to time, and always of course accompanied by payment of cash of the realm.

These dance lesson contracts and the monetary consideration therefor of over $31,000 were procured from her by means and methods of Davenport and his associates which went beyond the unsavory, yet legally permissible, perimeter of "sales puffing" and intruded well into the forbidden area of undue influence, the suggestion of falsehood, the suppression of truth, and the free exercise of rational judgment, if what plaintiff alleged in her complaint was true. From the time of her first contact with the dancing school in February, 1961, she was influenced unwittingly by a constant and continuous barrage of flattery, false praise, excessive compliments, and panegyric encomiums, to such extent that it would be not only inequitable, but unconscionable, for a Court exercising inherent chancery power to allow such contracts to stand.

She was incessantly subjected to overreaching blandishment and cajolery. She was assured she had "grace and poise"; that she was "rapidly improving and developing in her dancing skill"; that the additional lessons would "make her a beautiful dancer, capable of dancing with the most accomplished dancers"; that she was "rapidly progressing in the development of her dancing skill and gracefulness," etc., etc. She was given "dance aptitude tests" for the ostensible purpose of "determining" the number of remaining hours instructions needed by her from time to time.

At one point she was sold 545 additional hours of dancing lessons to be entitled to award of the "Bronze Medal" signifying that she had reached "the Bronze Standard", a supposed designation of dance achievement by students of Arthur Murray, Inc.

Later she was sold an additional 926 hours in order to gain the "Silver Medal," indicating she had reached "the Silver Standard," at a cost of $12,501.35.

At one point, while she still had to her credit about 900 unused hours of instructions, she was induced to purchase an additional 24 hours of lessons to participate in a trip to Miami at her own expense, where she would be "given the opportunity to dance with members of the Miami Studio."

She was induced at another point to purchase an additional 126 hours of lessons in order to be not only eligible for the Miami trip but also to become "a life member of the Arthur Murray Studio," carrying with it certain dubious emoluments, at a further cost of $1,752.30.

At another point, while she still had over 1,000 unused hours of instruction she was induced to buy 151 additional hours at a cost of $2,049.00 to be eligible for a "Student Trip to Trinidad," at her own expense as she later learned.

Also, when she still had 1100 unused hours to her credit, she was prevailed upon to purchase an additional 347 hours at a cost of $4,235.74, to qualify her to receive a "Gold Medal" for achievement, indicating she had advanced to "the Gold Standard."

On another occasion, while she still had over 1200 unused hours, she was induced to buy an additional 175 hours of instructions at a cost of $2,472.75 to be eligible "to take a trip to Mexico."

Finally, sandwiched in between other lesser sales promotions, she was influenced to buy an additional 481 hours of instruction at a cost of $6,523.81 in order to "be classified as a Gold Bar Member, the ultimate achievement of the dancing studio."

All the foregoing sales promotions, illustrative of the entire fourteen separate contracts, were procured by defendant Davenport and Arthur Murray, Inc., by false representations to her that she was improving in her dancing ability, that she had excellent potential, that she was responding to instructions in dancing grace, and that they were developing her into a beautiful dancer, whereas in truth and in fact she did not develop in her dancing ability, she had no "dance aptitude," and in fact had difficulty in "hearing the musical beat." The complaint alleged that such representations to her "were in fact false and known by the defendant to be false and contrary to the plaintiff's true ability, the truth of plaintiff's ability being fully known to the defendants, but withheld from the plaintiff for the sole and specific intent to deceive and defraud the plaintiff and to induce her in the purchasing of additional hours of dance lessons." It was averred that the lessons were sold to her "in total disregard to the true physical, rhythm, and mental ability of the plaintiff." In other words, while she first exulted that she was entering the "spring of her life," she finally was awakened to the fact there was "spring" neither in her life nor in her feet.

It is true that "generally a misrepresentation, to be actionable, must be one of fact rather than of opinion." . . . But this rule has significant qualifications, applicable here. It does not apply where there is a fiduciary relationship between the parties, or where there has been some artifice or trick employed by the representor, or where the parties do not in general deal at "arm's length" as we understand the phrase, or where the representee does not have equal opportunity to become apprised of the truth or falsity of the fact represented.

". . . A statement of a party having . . . superior knowledge may be regarded as a statement of fact although it would be considered as opinion if the parties were dealing on equal terms."

It could be reasonably supposed here that defendants had "superior knowledge" as to whether plaintiff had "dance potential" and as to whether she was noticeably improving in the art of terpsichore. And it would be a reasonable inference from the undenied averments of the complaint that the flowery eulogiums heaped upon her by defendants as a prelude to her contracting for 1944 additional hours of instruction in order to attain the rank of the Bronze Standard, thence to the bracket of the Silver Standard, thence to the class of the Gold Bar Standard, and finally to the crowning plateau of a Life Member of the Studio, proceeded as much or more from the urge to "ring the cash register" as from any honest or realistic appraisal of her dancing prowess or a factual representation of her progress.

Even in contractual situations where a party to a transaction owes no duty to disclose facts within his knowledge or to answer inquiries respecting such facts, the law is if he undertakes to do so he must disclose the *whole truth*. . . . From the face of the complaint, it should have been reasonably apparent to defendants that her vast outlay of cash for the many hundreds of additional hours of instruction was not justified by her slow and awkward progress, which she would have been made well aware of if they had spoken the "whole truth."

We repeat that where parties are dealing on a contractual basis at arm's length with no inequities or inherently unfair practices employed, the Courts will in general "leave the parties where they find themselves." But (in) . . . our view, from the showing made in her complaint, plaintiff is entitled to her day in Court.

It accordingly follows that the order dismissing plaintiff's last amended complaint with prejudice should be and is reversed.

Reversed.

Kenworth v. Huntley

Colorado Court of Appeals

537 P. 2d 1087 (1975)

Plaintiff Kenworth sued Huntley for the balance of the purchase price of a 1960 Peterbilt truck-tractor that Huntley agreed to purchase from Kenworth. It was undisputed that the total price was $6,000 and that Huntley made a $3,000 cash down payment, the balance being the trade-in value of a truck owned by Huntley. Kenworth, alleging that Huntley refused to deliver title to his truck, sought judgment for the balance due on the purchase price. Huntley counterclaimed and alleged that Kenworth had falsely represented that the Peterbilt truck-tractor had recently had a major overhaul. Prior to trial, the parties stipulated that Huntley's truck had been sold by Kenworth and that the proceeds would be held by Kenworth's attorney for payment to the party who prevailed in the lawsuit.

The trial court found that the alleged representation had been made and that it was false. It entered judgment for Huntley in the amount of $3,000. Kenworth appealed, contending that the essential elements of fraud were not established by the evidence. The appellate court disagreed and affirmed the judgment of the trial court.

Kelly, Judge

Kenworth argues that the evidence was insufficient to establish every element of fraud. The record here does not support this argument. There was ample testimony to support the finding that the plaintiff falsely represented a material fact to defendant, with knowledge that it was false, and that defendant relied on the representation and was damaged thereby.

Before coming to Denver, Huntley telephoned Kenworth from South Dakota to inquire about a truck in the $6,000 range, and Kenworth's representative told him that they had a truck suitable to his needs. After arriving in Denver, Huntley and his wife spent an entire day on the Kenworth used truck lot, inspected the truck, and asked numerous times about its condition. Both Huntley and his wife testified that Kenworth's salesman told Huntley several times that the truck had recently had a major overhaul. The evidence is uncontroverted that the truck engine had not been overhauled and that the salesman was fully aware of the truck's repair record.

It is clear that the defendant was without knowledge of the truth of the matter. The evidence shows that the engine had a clean appearance and the only way Huntley could have tested the veracity of the salesman's statements would have been to remove and inspect the engine. Huntley asked the salesman to allow him to test drive the truck, but the salesman refused, telling him that the truck needed some minor repairs before it could be taken out on the road. In addition, there were repair records on the truck, but Huntley neither knew nor was informed about them.

There can be no question that the defendant relied on plaintiff's false representation. Both Huntley and his wife testified that they would not have considered buying the truck if they had not been told that it had been recently overhauled. Moreover,

Huntley had recently talked to other dealers and was satisfied that this truck, with a major overhaul, was worth the asking price.

The record also shows that defendant suffered damages. Soon after he bought the truck, it developed major engine problems. Huntley was told by a mechanic who inspected the engine that it was worn out. He was advised either to have it overhauled or to install a rebuilt engine, and he chose the latter course of action.

A proper measure of damages in an action for fraud is the difference between the actual value of the property and the value it would have had if it had been as represented at the time and place of the sale. Evidence to establish this measure of damages may take different forms. In this case, there was testimony by an expert that the fair market values of similar trucks ranged from $3,500 for a truck without a major overhaul to $7,500 for one with an overhaul, at the time and place of the sale. This was sufficient evidence to support the trial court's award of $3,000 damages to Huntley for his loss of bargain.

Affirmed.

Business Ethics Problems

Bribery and Facilitating Payments. 1. You are a purchasing manager for Alpha Corporation. You are responsible for buying two $1 million generators. Your company has a written policy prohibiting any company buyer from receiving a gratuity in excess of $50 and requiring that all gratuities be reported. The company has no policy regarding *whistle-blowing*. A salesperson for a generator manufacturer offers to arrange it so that you can buy a $12,000 car for $4,000. The car would be bought from a third party. You decline the offer.

Do you now report it to your superior? To the salesperson's superior?

2. You are the general manager of a construction company. Your company has a very important contract that requires you to obtain certain permits from the city by June 1 or the job will be relet. The city inspector demands a $20,000 cash payment for issuing the permits. The financial security of the firm will be endangered if you lose the job.

What do you do?

Duty of Loyalty. 1. You are the responsible executive for River City Engineering (RCE) and in its behalf are preparing a bid for a U.S. Government contract. If you fail to secure it, you will have to close your operation and 90 employees will be out of work. The welfare rolls of Near Lost, Michigan, will more than double and many small enterprises will be forced to close. RCE is the town's leading employer and taxpayer.

Your principal competitor is Multilarge Engineering International (MEI), a company that is reported to have good political connections and that is best situated to take the contract. If you can underbid its price, you can probably get the contract.

Your chief assistant proposes to discover in advance the terms of MEI's secret bid. His assistant, Bill, proposed to marry Sue, the assistant to MEI's chief executive officer's executive secretary, whom she hates. Sue would be delighted to help Bill get a promotion. She will be typing the proposal, or part of it, and is secretly planning to leave MEI anyway. She is trustworthy (Bill says) and no one would ever know. All that is needed is your okay *today.* The bids will be submitted in two days.

A. What is your reply?

B. What about the *method* used in intelligence gathering? Obviously, use of burglars, à la Watergate, involves criminals (the burglars, those who employ them, and those who knowingly accept what was stolen). Is your position better here since breaking and entering is not necessary because a confidential agent of MEI is willing to be disloyal?

2. An elderly lady who now lives in a nursing home hires you to sell her old house for her. She suggests she would take $40,000 for it. She owned the house for forty years but has not seen it for several years. She is unaware that it is now located by a new shopping center near a new expressway where similar properties have been selling for $75,000.

A. Assume you are a friend of the owner but are not a realtor. You know she trusts you a great deal. You also know of several possible buyers, one of whom is a close friend of yours. What would you do?

B. Suppose you wanted to buy the house as an investment for your church/fraternity/social club. Would you? How much would you pay? Do you sell it to your brother-in-law? Are these questions of law or of ethics?

C. Suppose you face this situation described above not as a friend but as a realtor employed by the lady. Would your answers be different? What if you weren't assisting her but were a buyer recently transferred to the city looking for residential property. Would you take advantage of the lady's ignorance? Is this a question of law or ethics?

Whistle-Blowing. 1. You are a lab technician for the Standard Ethical Drug Company. You run tests on animals and prepare a summary that is then doctored by your superior to make a drug appear safe when in fact it is not. Your superior determines your salary and has a significant influence on whether you retain the job. You are the sole source of support of your two children. You have no close relatives to help you, and you are just making it financially. Jobs equivalent to the one that you now hold are very difficult to come by. You are convinced that if the company markets the drug, the risk of cancer to the drug users will increase significantly. The drug provides significant relief for hemorrhoids.

What do you do?

2. Smith hires you to prepare his federal and state tax returns. When you have nearly completed the job, he tells you he sold a share of a business interest to a partner, incurring a capital gain of $50,000. He asks you how he can avoid or minimize the tax. After you review the law and facts you report it is not possible. He owes the tax. He tells you, "Okay, just don't report it then; they have no way of ever finding out about it."

A. Do you follow his instructions and sign the form as the tax preparer? If you refuse, you know you probably won't get paid and won't get any of Smith's business in the future.

B. Suppose you are the partner who bought the interest. Smith asks you to keep the transaction a secret until next year so he won't have to pay the tax until then, when his rates will be lower. Do you agree?

C. Are your answers different if you are an attorney? A CPA? A full-time H&R Block employee? A part-time H&R Block employee?

Advertising. 1. Your company sells only in the state of New Wyoming. State law allows you to market your cola in "giant quarts." A quart is a standard measure, so a giant quart is the same size as an ordinary quart. A survey conducted by your firm indicates that 40 percent of cola buyers think that a giant quart is larger than a regular quart. Do you call your bottle a giant quart?

2. You are an advertiser of a soft-drink product

that has 10 percent of the total soft-drink market. Your product is the only one of the five leading products that does not contain arzine, an additive that enhances its taste. Some medical research indicates that the presence of arzine may cause some people who take it in very heavy doses (the equivalent of 15 drinks of your product each day for at least two or three years) to develop high blood pressure. The majority of studies conducted during the last ten years, however, show no adverse effects to people who drink products containing arzine.

Your assistant suggests the following advertising campaigns:

A. A campaign citing the medical research showing that the arzine in your competitors' products could be harmful; no mention would be made of the contradictory research.

B. A campaign mentioning that your product does not contain arzine and shows several healthy and youthful people endorsing it for that reason. Several movie stars and athletes would endorse your product; no mention of medical research would be made.

REVIEW PROBLEMS

1. Which of the five theories of corporate social responsibility do you think are most influential for U.S. corporations? Why?

2. Do you think corporations in other countries have greater or less concern for social responsibility than do U.S. corporations? What do you know about the social responsibility of Japanese, German, Korean, or Saudi Arabian corporations?

3. Review the three methods noted for implementing corporate-social-responsibility standards. What specific actions would you suggest business leaders take in order to broaden the adoption and implementation of such standards?

4. What do you think is the general public view of the social responsibility and ethical standards of business managers and their corporations? How do your views compare with those of other business students or those of nonbusiness students?

5. Compare and contrast the facts in the *Toole* case with those in the *Roginsky* case. How do you account for the difference? Is the same law regarding punitive damages applied in each case?

6. Do *you* think Arthur Murray, Inc., has violated a legal standard in selling dance lessons to Mrs. Vokes? Has it violated an ethical standard? Would it bother your ethical standards to work for Arthur Murray? Is there any corporation or organization you would not want to work for because of ethical standards?

7. If you owned the Kenworth car and truck dealership, what would you tell your salespeople regarding representations or statements they make to prospective purchasers? Realizing that your objective is to sell cars and trucks at a profit, what ethical standards would you seek to have your salespeople follow? How would you try to ensure that *they* follow the ethical standards *you* think they should follow? What would you do if some other car and truck dealers with whom you compete do not follow similar standards?

8. Read the *Wall Street Journal* for at least one week. Note the articles that you think relate to the social responsibility and business ethics concerns raised by this chapter. Write a short summary of how the corpo-

rate-social-responsibility theories or business ethical standards noted in the chapter could affect the behavior of one of the firms referred to in a *Journal* article.

FOOTNOTES

[1]Goodpaster and Matthews, "Can a Corporation Have a Conscience?" 60 *Harvard Business Review,* 132, 133 (January-February 1981).

[2]Farmer and Hogue, *Corporate Social Responsibility.* (Chicago, Ill., Science Research Associates, 1973), p. 6.

[3]W. Frederick, "The Growing Concern Over Business Responsibility," *California Management Review,* 1, No. 4 (1960), 54.

[4]"Social Responsibility Disclosure," *Public Relations Journal,* 35 (April 1979), 35.

[5]A Gallup Poll taken in 1979 revealed that 45 percent of teenagers and 47 percent of adults felt that American business corporations were interested only in profits and cared little about the quality of life and well-being of society. Joseph A. Pickler and Richard DeGeorge, "Ethics: Principles and Disclosures," *Peat, Marwick and Mitchell World,* Spring 1979, pgs. 28–32.

[6]See "Model Rules of Professional Conduct—Final Draft," *American Bar Association Journal* (November, 1982), 1411; and "Code of Professional Responsibility of the Michigan Bar Association," 62 *Michigan Bar Journal* 30R (April, 1983).

[7]Milton Friedman, "The Social Responsibility of Business Is To Increase Its Profits," *New York Times,* September 13, 1970, p. 142.

[8]This is the "Four Way Test" of Rotary International.

[9]Milton Friedman, "The Social Responsibility of Business Is To Increase Its Profits," *New York Times,* September 13, 1970, pgs. 122–123.

[10]Abbott and Monsen, "On the Measure of Social Responsibility: Self-Reporting Disclosures as a Method of Measuring Corporate Social Responsibility," *Academy of Management Journal,* Vol. 22, 501–515, at 514 (1979).

[11]P. Sethi, Cunningham and Miller, "Corporate Governance: Public Policy–Social Responsibility Committee of Corporate Board: Growth and Accomplishment." (Dallas: University of Texas Center for Research in Business and Social Policy, 1979), p. 49.

[12]Rogene A. Buchholz, *Business Environment and Public Policy: Implications for Management* (Englewood Cliffs, N.J., Prentice-Hall, Inc., 1982).

[13]Phyllis S. McGrath, *Managing Corporate External Relations: Changing Perspectives and Responses* (New York, the Conference Board, 1976), p. 51.

[14]Buchholz, *Business Environment and Public Policy,* supra.

[15]Ibid., at 469.

[16]Harold Williams, "Corporate Accountability—One Year Later," paper delivered at the Sixth Annual Securities Regulation Institute, San Diego, CA, January 18, 1979.

[17]See M. Stearns, "What are Business Ethics?" *Data Management,* 19 (May 1981), p. 26.

[18]Ibid.

[19]Donald G. Jones, *A Bibliography of Business Ethics, 1971–75* (Charlottesville, University of Virginia Press, 1977), p. 16.

[20]"Why are They Cheating?" *The Wall Street Journal,* June 10, 1982, p. 24, col. 4.

[21]James Weber, "Institutionalizing Ethics into the Corporation," *MSU Business Topics* (Spring 1981), p. 47.

[22]Zenisek, "Corporate Social Responsibility: A Conceptualization Based on Organizational Literature," *Academy of Management Review* (1979), 362.

[23]Weber, "Institutionalizing Ethics Into the Corporation," *supra,* 48.

[24]M. Stearns, "What are Business Ethics?" *supra,* p. 27.

[25]"Lunch Can't Be Free When the S.E.C. Staff is Inspecting a Firm," *The Wall Street Journal,* June 5, 1982, p. 8, col. 2.

[26]Several of these problems were developed by my colleague at Western Michigan University, Professor James Bliss. I am indebted to him for allowing me to use them in this textbook.

PART V

PROPERTY

Personal Property

W hen a person speaks of property, he or she usually refers to something he or she owns—a piano, an automobile, a house. From a legal standpoint, however, the things themselves are not significant. What is important are the rights the individual has in them. Traditional legal usage defines property as the bundle or aggregate of rights that people have in things they own. These include the right to use, sell, or even destroy the thing if the person wishes to do so.

PROPERTY AND GOVERNMENT

The very existence of property depends upon government. State and federal laws create and maintain the "bundle of rights" that the legal system refers to as property. A trademark, for example, has value because the government establishes certain guarantees and protections for its owner. The mutual promises of a contract have economic significance because courts will award damages if a promise is not kept. A trademark and a contract are property because society, through law, supports the owner's capacity to control the actions of others through them.

Conversely, although a person's right to travel is important, it is not property. The state establishes no aggregate of rights relating to one's passport. All that the individual can do is travel or refrain from traveling. This can also be said of other civil rights, such as the right to vote.

Whether or not something is property has important constitutional ramifications, since federal and state constitutions prohibit government from taking property without due process of law. More will be said about this in the following chapter on real property.

REAL AND PERSONAL PROPERTY

One of the points stressed throughout this book is that legal institutions often reflect dominant economic, political, and social values. Property law is convincing illustration of this point.

833

Until about a hundred and fifty years ago, land was the most important source of wealth and a major determinant of social position both in England and in the United States. Ownership of land also had important political significance, since often only landowners were permitted to vote.

Real Property

One result of the historic importance of land is a distinction in Anglo-American law between it and other forms of wealth. Because of land's economic significance, the early common law provided extensive protection to landowners. A landowner ousted from possession could immediately bring an action to recover the land. This was known as a real action, and it is the reason that land is called real property or real estate. On the other hand, a person who lost control of something of economic value other than land, usually a movable item, initially could sue only for money. This was known as a personal action and the item involved as personal property. In modern law the distinction between real and personal property continues to be recognized.

Personal Property

Personal property generally is characterized as movable. Historically, personal property consisted of items that had substance. These items were often referred to as goods or chattels. In the agrarian economy that existed in the United States until this century, livestock, farm equipment, and the tools of a person's trade were common examples. Along with land, these items were major forms of wealth. As the nature of the American economy changed, new forms of wealth were created. Today an appreciable amount of wealth is intangible. It consists of rights that a person has that represent value. An intangible right, often referred to as a chose (French, "thing") in action, is also personal property.

Intangible Personal Property

A stock certificate is an example of intangible personal property. The certificate is evidence of value, although it has no intrinsic worth itself. The owner of the stock can sell it, use it as security, or give it away. He or she also has numerous rights in relation to the firm, other owners, and creditors. Intangible property figures in many business transactions. Patents, copyrights, trademarks, and contracts, as well as stock, are examples of intangible property important in business.

As new forms of wealth have been created, personal property has become more equivalent to real property in economic significance. This has led to a narrowing of the legal distinction between the two, but differences continue to exist and to influence decisions that business people must make.

The distinction between real and personal property raises numerous insurance, tax, financing, and inheritance questions. In the case that follows, the distinction between the two types of property determined the outcome of the litigation.

Barron v. Edwards

Court of Appeals of Michigan
206 N.W.2d 508 (1973)

Barron (plaintiff-appellee) entered into an oral agreement to sell sod to Edwards (defendant-appellant). The land on which the sod was growing was condemned by the State Highway Department, and Barron sued to restrain Edwards from removing the sod. Edwards counterclaimed for specific performance or, in the alternative, damages. Barron moved to dismiss the counterclaim on grounds that the contract covered an interest in land and was not enforceable because not reduced to a writing. The trial court granted the plaintiff's motion. Edwards appealed. Held: Reversed and remanded.

Bashara, Judge

Plaintiff owned and operated a sod farm in Wayne County. Defendant was in the business of selling sod and had purchased sod from plaintiff on several prior occasions. Defendant alleges that on November 10, 1969, he entered into an oral contract with plaintiff whereby he agreed to purchase the plaintiff's entire crop of sod, consisting of approximately 30 acres, for $350.00 per acre. Defendant paid $700.00 in 1969 and removed approximately 1½ acres of sod. His answer alleged that the understanding between the parties was that he would remove the remaining 28 acres in the spring of 1970.

On April 9, 1970, plaintiff notified defendant that the State Highway Department had condemned and taken title to the entire farm. He offered to return the $700.00 and reimburse the defendant for any funds expended on maintaining the sod. This payment was refused by defendant.

The statutory provisions applicable to the solution of this problem are M.C.L.A. Section 440.2105(1); M.S.A. Section 19.2105(1), and M.C.L.A. Section 440.2107(2); M.S.A. Section 19.2107(2), which provide:

"Sec. 2105. (1) 'Goods' means all things (including specially manufactured goods) which are moveable at the time of identification to the contract for sale other than the money in which the price is to be paid, investment securities and things in action. 'Goods' also includes the unborn young of animals and *growing crops and other identified things attached to realty as described in the section on goods to be severed from realty.* [Emphasis supplied by the court.]

"Sec. 2107. (2) A contract for the sale apart from the land of growing crops or other things attached to realty and capable of severance without material harm thereto but not described in subsection (1) is a contract for the sale of goods within this article whether the subject matter is to be severed by the buyer or by the seller even though it forms part of the realty at the time of contracting, and the parties can by identification effect a present sale before severance."

Although these provisions do not specifically state what is to be included within the meaning of growing crops, the Official Comment to 2–105 of the Uniform Commercial Code contains the following statement:

"Growing crops are included within the definition of goods since they are frequently intended for sale. The concept of 'industrial' growing crops has been abandoned, for under modern practices fruit, perennial hay, nursery stock and the like must be brought within the scope of this Article."

Thus, if sod can be considered a crop rather than a part of the realty, it is within the above-cited statutory provisions. The factors used in determining this issue are stated in 21 Am. Jur.2d, Crops, Sec. 3, pp. 581–582:

"The primary and most easily recognizable distinction is that between fructus naturales and fructus industriales. Apart from statutes or peculiar circumstances requiring a contrary conclusion, it is stated in many cases that those products of the earth which are annual, raised by yearly manurance and labor, and which owe their annual existence to cultivation by man, may be treated as personal chattels, for some purposes at least, even while still annexed to the soil and irrespective of their maturity. Conversely, and also in the absence of statutory provisions or peculiar circumstances requiring a contrary conclusion, fructus naturales—grasses growing from perennial roots and, according to some courts, the fruit or other products of trees, bushes, and plants growing from perennial roots—are regarded as realty while they are unsevered from the soil."

Here the sod owed its existence to yearly fertilizing and cultivation by man. It is also significant that plaintiff raised this sod on several prior occasions and apparently treated it as a commercial product. Thus, this sod cannot be considered "growing grass" as the plaintiff contends. We therefore hold that the sod in the instant case was personalty.

This result is supported by recent decisions which have interpreted the above-cited statutory provisions. In *Groth* v. *Stillson,* this Court held that Christmas trees were growing crops. Our Court relied on the fact that the trees required annual care, and that such trees were a fruit of industry. Likewise, in the instant case, the sod owed its existence to annual maintenance and fertilization.

Also applicable is *Azavedo* v. *Minister.* . . . In *Azevedo* that Court used the following reasoning in holding that hay is within the meaning of "growing crops".

"The sale of hay is included within the definition of the sale of 'goods' as defined by NRS 104.2105(1) and NRS 104.2107(2), which when read together provide that the sale of 'growing crops,' when they are to be 'severed by the buyer or by the seller,' constitutes the sale of goods within the definition of that expression in the Uniform Commercial Code."

Plaintiff further argues that even if this Court finds that the sod in question is personalty, the contract is nevertheless unenforceable due to M.C.L.A. Sec. 440.-2201; M.S.A. Sec. 19.2201, which provides in relevant part:

"Sec. 2201. (1) Except as otherwise provided in this section a contract for the sale of goods for the price of $500.00 or more is not enforceable by way of action or defense unless there is some writing sufficient to indicate that a contract for sale has been made between the parties and signed by the party against whom enforcement is sought or by his authorized agent or broker. A writing is not insufficient because it omits or incorrectly states a term agreed upon but the contract is not enforceable under this paragraph beyond the quantity of goods shown in such writing.

"(2) Between merchants if within a reasonable time a writing in confirmation of the contract and sufficient against the sender is received and the party receiving it has reason to know its contents, it satisfies the requirements of subsection (1) against such party unless written notice of objection to its contents is given within 10 days after it is received."

Defendant does not dispute the fact that the contract was for the sale of goods valued at more than $500.00 but contends that subsection (2) controls the instant case. We agree.

The record indicates that both parties were merchants. Defendant was in the business of selling and installing sod and the plaintiff had sold sod on numerous occasions. The record further indicates that a confirmatory memorandum was sent by the defendant to the plaintiff and that the plaintiff did not send a written notice of objection until the 10-day period had elapsed.

The appellee counters that this provision is not controlling of the instant case since the confirmatory memorandum was not delivered within a reasonable time as required by statute.

As to what constitutes a reasonable time, M.C.L.A. Sec. 440.1204(2); M.S.A. Sec. 19.1204(2), states:

"What is a reasonable time for taking any action depends on the nature, purpose and circumstances of such action."

We agree that, under the circumstances present in the instant case, there is a factual question as to whether the defendant sent the memorandum within a reasonable time. Since an accelerated judgment was granted, there was no testimony with regard to this question. We remand so as to allow the trier of fact to determine this issue. Reversed and remanded. Costs to defendant.

FIXTURES

As the previous case indicates, the classification of property as real or personal has important legal consequences. In many situations, conflicting arguments exist for classifying property one way or the other. Naturally, individuals and firms wish to have the property classified in the manner most beneficial to them. This classification problem is further complicated by the fact that the property's designation can change, depending upon how it is used.

A common example is material used in home construction. Cement blocks are personal property when part of a building supplier's inventory. When used as part of a dwelling, however, the blocks become real property. On the other hand, trees growing in a forest are real property, but if a tree is cut to be milled into lumber or stacked as firewood it becomes personal property. Personal property that has become real property through attachment to land or buildings is called a *fixture*.

Determination of Fixtures

The chief test in determining whether personal property has become a fixture is the intention of the party who attached the item to real property. This intention, however, is not the secret intention of that person but the intention determined by the manner in which the person acted. Other factors that courts consider are the manner in which the item is attached and its application and use as a permanent part of the realty. Often attachment and use are considered only as evidence of what was intended. The Wisconsin case that follows indicates the importance of intention. The case of *In Re Park Corrugated Box Corp.*, on page 840, discusses alternative approaches to determining fixtures. In both cases, intention plays a dominant role.

George v. Commercial Credit Corp.

U.S. Court of Appeals, Seventh Circuit

440 F.2d 551 (1971)

George (petitioner-appellant), trustee in bankruptcy, claimed an interest in a mobile home owned by Foskett, the bankrupt, and mortgaged to the Commercial Credit Corp. (respondent-appellee). George argued before a referee in bankruptcy that a mobile home is not a fixture. The referee rejected this argument and dismissed George's claim. The district court affirmed and George appealed. Held: Affirmed.

Duffy, Senior Circuit Judge

Dale Wallace Foskett owned five acres of land in Jefferson County, Wisconsin. On December 6, 1968, he purchased a Marshfield Mobile Home, No. 9090, from Highway Mobile Home Sales, Inc. He signed an installment contract and paid $880 on the purchase price of $8,800. Added was a sales tax and interest covering a ten-year period.

Sometime in December 1968, Foskett executed a real estate mortgage to Highway Mobile Home Sales, Inc. The mortgage recites the sum of $14,227.70 and described the real estate in metes and bounds. The mortgage was assigned to Commercial Credit Corporation, the respondent-appellee herein.

The mobile home here in question could not move under its own power. It was delivered to Foskett's real estate property by Mobile Sales. This mobile home was never again operated on or over the highways as a motor vehicle.

The mobile home here in question was 68 feet in length, 14 feet in width, and 12 feet in height. It contained six rooms and weighed 15,000 pounds.

The bankrupt owned no other home and he and his wife occupied the mobile home continuously from December 6, 1968 until forced to vacate same by order of the Trustee in Bankruptcy.

The home was set on cement cinder blocks three courses high. It was connected with a well. It was hooked up to a septic tank. It also was connected with electric power lines.

The bankrupt never applied for a certificate of title from the Wisconsin Motor Vehicle Department. However, he did apply for a homeowner's insurance policy and he asked the seller to remove the wheels from his home. He also applied for a building permit and was told he had to construct a permanent foundation for the home. The permit was granted upon condition that the foundation be constructed within one year. However, within that period, the petition for bankruptcy was filed.

The issue before us can be thus stated: Commercial Credit Corporation argues that the mobile home was a fixture under applicable law and is not personalty. The trustee insists that the mobile home was and still is a "motor vehicle" and is personalty.

The mobile homes industry has grown rapidly in the last few years. There has been a great demand for relatively inexpensive housing by middle income families. In Wisconsin, a distinction is now recognized between mobile homes (those used as homes) and motor homes (those often used as vehicles).

In the recent case of *Beaulieu* v. *Minnehoma Insurance Company,* the Wisconsin Supreme Court pointed out the unique character of mobile homes: "As indicated by the plaintiff, a mobile home has a dual nature. It is designed as a house; yet, unlike a house, it is also capable of being easily transported. In the instant case, it was employed solely as an economical means of housing. It was never moved, nor was moving contemplated at the time the insurance coverage was procured."

We look to state law to determine the applicable standards for determining when personalty becomes affixed to real property.

(1) The Wisconsin law on the question is found in *Auto Acceptance and Loan Corp.* v. *Kelm,* where the Wisconsin Supreme Court reaffirmed its decision in *Standard Oil Co.* v. *LaCrosse Super Auto Service, Inc.* That case held that the three tests for determining whether facilities remain personalty or are to be considered part of the realty are (1) actual physical annexation to the realty; (2) application or adaptation to the use or purpose to which the realty is devoted, and (3) intention of the person making annexation to make a permanent accession to the freehold.

In the *Standard Oil Company* case, the Court pointed out that "physical annexation" is relatively unimportant and "intention" of the parties is the principal consideration.

In *Premonstratensian Fathers* v. *Badger Mutual Insurance Co.,* the Court reaffirmed its adherence to the three-fold test saying, "It is the application of these tests to the facts of a particular case which will lead to a determination of whether or not an article, otherwise considered personal property, constitutes a common-law fixture, and hence takes on the nature of real property."

Viewed in light of these Wisconsin tests, the finding of the referee and the District Court that this mobile home had become a fixture must clearly stand. The bankrupt's actual intention pointed definitely toward affixing the mobile home to the land as a permanent residence, as seen in his application for a building permit (which, by law, required him to erect a concrete slab as a permanent foundation within one year), his purchase of a homeowner's insurance policy, and his requests made to the seller to have the wheels of the home removed. Moreover, the home was clearly adapted to use as the permanent residence of the bankrupt and was never moved off of his five-acre plot.

The fact that it may have been physically possible for this mobile home to have been more securely attached to the ground should not alter our position. Physical attachment did occur by means of cinder blocks and a "C" clamp, while connections for electricity, sewage and natural gas were provided as well. Finally, we note that the very size and difficulty in transporting this mobile home further highlight the fact that this was a vehicle which was intended primarily to be placed in one position for a long period of time and to be used as an intended permanent home.

Affirmed.

Trade Fixtures

The rule that personal property annexed to real estate becomes a part of it has serious ramifications to tenants. Unless the tenant and owner agree, a tenant making permanent additions to real property may not remove a fixture at the end of the term. This greatly hampers a business from leasing a building if the firm needs to add items—such as display cases or machinery—to operate effectively. Because of this, the legal system differentiates between fixtures and personalty attached to real estate to carry on a trade or business.

Items of this latter nature are called trade fixtures and generally may be taken by the tenant at the end of the term. Agricultural fixtures are treated in a similar manner. In order to remove a trade or agricultural fixture, the tenant must restore the premises to its original condition and must remove the item while in possession.

Allowing tenants to remove trade fixtures has social benefits. It encourages both the use of land and efficiency in business. Tenants will be more apt to invest in new and improved equipment if they can remove these items after they have been attached to the realty. In a number of states, statutes establish tenant's rights to remove trade fixtures.

Because the doctrine of trade fixtures is important to tenants, parties to a commercial lease should include provisions clearly expressing their intentions. They might agree that the tenant shall not remove items that ordinarily would be trade fixtures. On the other hand, a lease provision stating the tenant's right to remove items added to carry out its business or trade would clearly show the intention of the parties and would lessen possibilities of disagreement.

The case that follows illustrates the trade fixture doctrine and discusses an additional approach to determining when an item is a fixture.

In Re Park Corrugated Box Corp.

U.S. District Court (D. N. J.)

249 F. Supp. 56 (1966)

Manufacturers Leasing Corporation (Manufacturers) petitioned a referee in bankruptcy for an order allowing Manufacturers to reclaim a machine from Park Corrugated Box Corp. (Park), the bankrupt. The referee denied this order and Manufacturers appeals. Held: Affirmed.

Augelli, District Judge

On February 8, 1965 Park filed a petition for an arrangement under Chapter XI of the Bankruptcy Act. Manufacturers was listed in Park's schedules as a security-holding creditor in the amount of $34,952.60. On March 8, Manufacturers filed its petition to reclaim from Park the machine above mentioned, which was used in the manufacture of corrugated boxes, and known as a "Hooper Combined Printer Slotter, Model WSG2P-200-E, size 50 × 103½ inches".

On September 4, 1963, Manufacturers and Park entered into a "Conditional Sale and Security Agreement," whereby Park purchased the subject machine from Manufacturers for the sum of $47,405.00. The agreement stated that Manufacturers was to have a purchase money security interest in the collateral to secure the balance due, that Manufacturers was to have all the rights of a secured party under applicable state law, and that Manufacturers was to retain title to the collateral until the balance was paid in full.

The agreement between Manufacturers and Park was filed twice with the Register of Deeds of Passaic County, on September 10, 1963 and again on October 10, 1963. It had not been filed with the Secretary of State in Trenton, New Jersey.

Under the Uniform Commercial Code as adopted in New Jersey, N.J.S.A. 12A:9–401(1) provides that:

> "The proper place to file in order to perfect a security interest is as follows:
> (a) . . . (not applicable);
> (b) when the collateral is goods which at the time the security interest attaches are or are to become fixtures, then in the office where a mortgage on the real estate concerned would be filed or recorded;
> (c) In all other cases, in the office of the Secretary of State."

Manufacturers contends that the machine was a fixture, that under N.J.S.A. 12A:9–401(1)(b), the agreement was properly filed in the County Register's Office, and that therefore Manufacturers has a perfected security interest in the machine prior to the rights of the Trustee. The Trustee argues, as the Referee has found, that the machine was not a fixture, that under N.J.S.A. 12A–401(1)(c), the agreement should have been filed in the office of the Secretary of State, and that therefore Manufacturers' security interest was not perfected. The issue in this case is thus simply whether the machine in question is or is not a fixture within the meaning of N.J.S.A. 12A–401(1)(b).

N.J.S.A. 12A:9–313(1) provides that the law of New Jersey determines whether and when goods become fixtures. The law in New Jersey concerning fixtures has most recently been reviewed in the case of *Fahmie* v. *Nyman*. In that case, the court discussed the two tests used in New Jersey to determine whether and when a chattel becomes a fixture. They are known as the "traditional test" and the "institutional doctrine."

Under the "traditional test," intention is the dominant factor. A chattel becomes a fixture when the party making the annexation intends a permanent accession to the freehold. This intention may be "inferred from the nature of the article affixed, the relation and situation of the party making the annexation, the structure and mode of annexation, and the purpose or use for which the annexation was made."

The testimony before the Referee at the reclamation proceeding shows that there was no intention to annex the machine permanently to the freehold. A witness for Manufacturers testified that although the machine was annexed to the building, it could easily be removed in one hour without material physical damage to the building. He described the machine as being about 125 inches wide by 8 feet long, weighing 45,000 pounds, anchored by two or three leg screws on each side, and connected to a 220 volt electric line. This same witness testified that a rigger could remove the machine quite easily by merely unbolting the screws, disconnecting the 220 volt line, jacking it up, putting it on rollers and taking it out. Park's president testified that the machine had been moved two or three times to other sections of the plant by employees of Park during the time it was located in the plant.

Under the "institutional doctrine," the test is whether the chattel is permanently essential to the completeness of the structure or its use. A chattel is a fixture if its severance from the structure would cause material damage to the structure or "prevent the structure from being used for the purposes for which it was erected or for which it has been adapted." Thus, in *Temple Co. v. Penn. Mutual Life Ins. Co.,* the Court stated, in holding lighting equipment and seats to be fixtures under the "institutional doctrine," that "[t]he building was erected and used as a theatre, and whatever was incorporated with the building to fit it for use as a theatre became part of the realty."

Again, the testimony before the Referee shows that the machine in question was not essential to the structure or its use, and that the severance of the machine would not prevent the structure from being used for the purposes for which it was erected or could be adapted. There was testimony that after the machine was removed from the building, the structure could be used for industrial uses generally; also testimony that different prior uses had been made of the structure. Thus, both before the machine was installed and after it was removed, the structure was and could be used for any number of different purposes. Finally, there was attached to the agreement between the parties a statement by Manufacturers that the machine is "to be affixed to real property . . . by removable screw joints or otherwise, so as to be severable from the realty without material injury to the freehold."

While the machine in question does not appear to be a fixture under either the "traditional test" or the "institutional doctrine," Manufacturers makes the further contention that the machine is a "trade fixture" under New Jersey law, and therefore a "fixture" pursuant to N.J.S.A. 12A:9–401(1)(b). However, the term "trade fixture" is generally applied only in landlord and tenant cases to describe a chattel which the tenant has installed on the landlord's premises for trade purposes, and which the tenant is allowed to remove if it can be severed without material injury to the freehold. Otherwise, the chattel would be a fixture and belong to the landlord. Thus, a "fixture" is just the opposite of a "trade fixture" under landlord and tenant law; the latter can be removed by the tenant without material injury to the freehold. A "trade fixture" is not a fixture within the meaning of N.J.S.A. 12A:9–401(1)(b).

Since the machine here involved was not a fixture under N.J.S.A. 12A:9–401(1)(b), and the agreement between Manufacturers and Park was not filed in the office of the Secretary of State pursuant to N.J.S.A. 12A:9–401(1)(c), Manufacturers' security interest was not perfected prior to the filing of the Chapter XI petition. Therefore the Trustee's rights to the machine take priority over the rights of Manufacturers.

Under the circumstances, and for the reasons so well stated in the Referee's opinion, the order denying reclamation in this case will be affirmed. Counsel for the Trustee, on notice to counsel for Manufacturers, will please submit an appropriate order.

BAILMENTS

The designation of personal property as a fixture causes problems in some business transactions. Other legal problems involving personal property may arise when one person holds property owned by another. This is common in many business relationships. Usually if the property has been placed in the holder's control to accomplish something about which both have agreed, a legal relationship called bailment exists. The owner who has surrendered the property is called the *bailor;* the person who controls it is called the *bailee.*

Examples of bailment in commercial transactions include leasing an automobile or equipment, storing goods in a warehouse, or delivering goods to a trucker for shipment. A bailment exists when a person takes an automobile to a garage for repairs or checks a coat in a restaurant. Common personal transactions such as borrowing a friend's golf clubs also create bailments.

Bailments have extensive legal ramifications for both parties, and they also often give rise to difficult legal problems. Since bailments are important in business, the business manager must know the rights and duties of the parties to a bailment and be able to distinguish bailments from other transactions.

Essential Elements

As with most legal relationships, generalizations about bailments are dangerous. Although the following statements about bailments indicate the essential elements of the relationship, each will require clarification:

1. A bailment's subject matter is personal property.
2. The bailee must have possession of the property.
3. An intention to possess the property must exist or be implied by law.
4. The property must be returned or accounted for when the bailment is completed.

Personal Property. The subject matter of a bailment must be personal property. The property can be either tangible or intangible, but it must be in existence at the time the bailment is created. The promise of a company to deliver stock to an employee is not a bailment when the only notation of the transaction is an indication on the company's books that the agreement exists. If, however, the stock has been issued, but the company retains the certificates until the employee obtains funds to pay applicable taxes, the relationship is a bailment.

Possession. Possession of the goods or chattels by the bailee is a major element in any bailment. Possession is generally determined by the control that the bailee exercises over the property. In most bailments the property is actually in the bailee's possession, but constructive possession is sufficient. For example, most states regard a bank that supplies safe-deposit facilities as a bailee in spite of the fact that the bailee does not have control of the bailor's property. The reasoning underlying this rule apparently is that the bank controls admission to the vault where the property is stored.

Agreement. Although many cases indicate that a bailment requires agreement, an express agreement is unnecessary. A bailment can be created by actions indicating that the parties intended to agree, and some courts have found agreements in situations in which they believed that the parties should have agreed.

Return of Property. Ordinarily the item bailed or a substitute for the item, usually money, is to be returned or accounted for by the bailee. A transaction in which the recipient of personal property is under no obligation to return or account for it is a sale or a gift. In both a sale and a gift, title passes to the recipient. The distinction between sale and bailment is important since the legal rights and obligations of a bailee and vendee differ markedly.

Delivery of an item to another with payment over a period of time at the end of which title vests in the buyer is a *conditional sale*, not a bailment. This transaction remains a conditional sale even if the seller can retrieve the specific item if payment is not made. On the other hand, a transaction in which the party to whom property is delivered has an option to purchase or holds the property for sale to another is a bailment. A bailment of this nature is generally referred to as a *consignment*.

Legal Principles

Before discussing some common legal problems involving bailors and bailees, two fundamental legal maxims must be reviewed. First, like other legal relationships, bailment results from the manner in which the parties act. The relationship is not created merely because the parties label their transaction a bailment. If the essential elements exist, a bailment is created no matter how the parties designate what they are doing. Second, subject to statute, the rights and obligations of the bailor and bailee are determined by their agreement. Courts look first to the agreement to determine how responsibility is allocated, although an agreement that violates public policy will not be enforced.

Classification

In many bailments the parties either fail to indicate how duties and obligations will be performed or they do so inadequately. In these cases courts have had to work out solutions to the problem of where the equities lie between the parties. One method that has been used is to relate rights and duties to the benefits received by the parties. To facilitate this, a threefold classification of bailments has developed. The most common type of bailment in business is one in which both parties benefit. This is referred to as a *mutual-benefit bailment*. A bailment in which the bailee furnishes no consideration for the property is referred to as a bailment for the *sole benefit of the bailee* or a *gratuitous bailment*. In this situation, someone lends an item to another, expecting no payment in return. If only the owner benefits, the bailment is said to be for the *sole benefit of the bailor*. This type of bailment exists if someone who is not paid holds another's property for safekeeping.

Not all legal problems involving bailments can be solved using these classifications. Recently a number of courts have rejected this system of classification, especially when attempting to decide the bailee's responsibility for care and use of the property, but the classification helps to solve some problems.

Bailor's Responsibility for Defective Goods

In bailments for the sole benefit of the bailee (gratuitous bailments), courts traditionally have required only that the bailor warn the bailee of known dangers exposing the borrower to an unreasonable risk of harm. In a mutual-benefit bailment or a bailment for the sole benefit of the bailor, the bailor's responsibility for defective goods is much more extensive.

Most courts in the United States apply a negligence standard. Thus the bailor is responsible for damages caused by its careless conduct. For example, if the bailment involves a leased item, the damaged plaintiff-lessee can recover by showing that the lessor knew of the defect that caused the damage or that the lessor failed to make a proper inspection that would have disclosed the flaw.

Some states recognize an implied warranty of fitness or suitability if the bailee relies upon the bailor's expertise and the bailor has reason to know the use for which the property is required. In these states the bailor's exposure to liability is potentially greater than in states that apply only a negligence standard since the bailor is responsible in some instances even if not careless—for example, if the bailor makes a reasonable inspection but does not discover a defect that renders the item unfit for the bailee's use. As the implied warranty of suitability of purpose in a bailment is similar to the Uniform Commercial Code warranty of fitness for a particular purpose, most states allow the bailor to disclaim this warranty in the same manner as a seller.

In *Bona* v. *Graefe*, the case that follows, the court wrestles with the problem of applying new theories of liability in the sale of goods to cases that involve not a sale but a lease. The Maryland court probably reflects the majority opinion in the United States, which imposes a negligence—not a strict liability or implied warranty—standard (see Chapter 4), but many courts would take a different view from Maryland's on the implied-warranty-of-fitness argument.

Bona v. Graefe

Court of Appeals of Maryland
285 A.2d 607 (1972)

Bona (plaintiff-appellant) sustained serious injuries when thrown from a runaway golf cart driven by Carrigan (defendant-appellee). Bona sued Royce Distributors (Royce) (defendant-appellee), the owner of the cart; Graefe (defendant-appellee), manager of the golf course, to whom the cart had been leased by Royce, and by whom it was subleased to Bona; and Carrigan, who was operating the cart. The trial court entered a directed verdict in favor of Royce and Graefe and a jury found in favor of Carrigan. Bona appealed. Held: Affirmed.

Singley, Judge

The appeal comes to us on a narrow question: was the trial court in error when it entered directed verdicts in favor of Royce and Graefe on the second (breach of warranty) and the third (strict liability) counts of the declaration?

On a Sunday in August of 1969, Bona, who had been a member of the South Sherwood Forest Golf Club for several years, where he played two or three times a week, was a member of a foursome which planned to play the course that day. Two golf carts were rented: one by Bona, which Carrigan operated; another by Fred A. Dammeyer and Theodore B. Foster, which Dammeyer operated. An employee of Graefe's removed Bona's cart from the storage area, and drove it around the putting green. It was there that the employee said he tested the brake and found it working properly. Carrigan said he saw the employee test the cart; Bona said that he was not aware of this. The cart was delivered to Carrigan near the first tee. He drove it to the first tee; he and Bona teed off, and both of them got in the cart and headed for the first green, following the cart occupied by Dammeyer and Foster. There was testimony that players customarily took a macadam-covered path about 60 feet long, which descended a steep grade and then made a left turn at the foot of the descent where the path ended, in order to reach the fairway.

Carrigan had testified on deposition that he applied the brake when he reached the crest of the hill and "there wasn't any." He shouted to the occupants of the other golf cart, which Carrigan thought was about 10 feet ahead of him. They pulled to the right, he passed them and ultimately struck an earth embankment, where Bona was thrown out just before the cart tipped over.

It will be remembered that Bona's appeal does not question the correctness of the jury verdict entered in Carrigan's favor, or of the directed verdicts entered in favor of Royce and Graefe on the negligence count, but rather rests on the argument that the case against them should have gone to jury on breach of warranty and strict liability. Unhappily for Bona, the route which he must take to achieve his goal is steeper than the path where the accident occurred.

Perhaps no uniform act was the subject of more extensive study and debate prior to its adoption than the Uniform Commercial Code (the UCC), Maryland Code (1957, 1964 Repl.Vol.) Art. 95B. The express warranty provisions of Sec. 2–313 and the warranty of fitness implied by Sec. 2–315 are parts of Article 2 of the UCC, which is clearly limited to sales of goods. Bona would have us read the sections as being also applicable to bailments for hire. Perhaps one answer to this contention, like A. P. Herbert's Lord Mildew's, is that if the draftsmen had intended the sections to apply to leases of goods as well as to sales, they should have said so.

A hint of what the draftsmen may have had in mind can be found in Official Comment 2 to UCC Sec. 2–313, which says, in part:

> Although this section (dealing with express warranties) is limited in its scope and direct purpose to warranties made by the seller to the buyer as part of a contract for sale, the warranty sections of this Subtitle are not designed in any way to disturb those lines of case law growth which have recognized that warranties need not be confined either to sales contracts or to the direct parties to such a contract. They may arise in other appropriate circumstances such as in the case of bailments for hire, whether such bailment is itself the main contract or is merely a supplying of containers under a contract for the sale of their contents. . . . [T]he matter is left to the case law with the intention that the policies of this Act may offer useful guidance in dealing with further cases as they arise.

It seems anomalous to us that many authors of the texts and commentaries seem to take the stance that there should be no differentiation between sales and bailments under Article 2 of the UCC, reasoning either by analogy or by interpretation.

For us to accept Bona's contention would take us beyond the limits of judicial legislation, a journey which we refused to make in *Howard* v. *South Baltimore General Hospital*. In similar vein, we declined to extend by analogy the warranty implied by the UCC to the sale of goods to the sale of real estate, saying that if there were to be a change, it should be by the legislature and not by the courts.

Concededly, a few courts have read UCC Sec. 2–315 as being applicable to cases where a chattel is the subject of a lease rather than a sale. Most frequently these are instances where the arrangement, although called a lease, is analogous to a sale in that the rental installments are equivalent to the purchase price plus interest, or a purchase is contemplated at the end of the lease period, and the lessee assumes obligations more consistent with ownership than with bailment.

Another class of bailor-bailee cases is bottomed on strict liability in tort; although on occasion, passing reference may be made to the implied warranties of the UCC, *Cintrone* v. *Hertz Truck Leasing & Rental Service* invoked the doctrine of strict liability in a case involving what the defendant claimed to be a gratuitous bailment.

There is a third type of case in which one who leases goods has been held to have impliedly warranted either under common law concepts or by analogy to the UCC the suitability of the chattel leased.

Other cases may give lip service to breach of warranty but usually require proof co-extensive with that required in a negligence action.

Another case to which we have been referred which applied UCC thinking to the lease of a chattel is *Baker* v. *City of Seattle,* which also involved an injury suffered by the lessee of a golf cart when there was a brake failure. There the court struck down a disclaimer contained in a lease, analogizing the lease to a sale, by applying UCC Sec. 2–316 and Sec. 2–719.

Maryland seems never to have adopted what has been the general rule elsewhere: that the bailor of a chattel to be used by the bailee for a particular purpose known to the bailor impliedly warrants the reasonable suitability of the chattel for the bailee's intended use of it. Perhaps the reluctance of our predecessors to embrace this rule reflects a preoccupation with analogous principles which are well established in our landlord and tenant cases: that generally the lessor of real property does not impliedly warrant that it is fit for habitation, that a landlord does not impliedly covenant to make repairs, and that ordinarily, a landlord will be answerable in damages in tort only if his tenant is injured on the demised premises as a result of the landlord's negligent breach of a contractual duty to make repairs.

Consequently, the liability of the lessor of a chattel, as distinguished from that of a vendor, if it is to be imposed at all in Maryland, must be imposed in a tort action for negligence. It is not enough for a plaintiff to prove that a lessor failed to make proper inspections; he must prove either that the lessor knew of the defect or that a reasonable inspection, if made, would have disclosed the defect.

Bona has not appealed from the entry of a directed verdict in favor of Royce and Graefe on the negligence count, with the consequence that the question whether Royce and Graefe used reasonable care is not directly before us. There was testimony, however, that the carts were inspected and serviced by employees of Royce on a weekly basis, and that Graefe's employee, as was his custom, drove Bona's cart from the storage shed to a point near the first tee, during the course of which he tested the brake and found it working properly. This evidence, taken with the lack of proof that the service and inspection procedures if properly done would have detected the defect, or that there was a defect of which Royce or Graefe had knowledge, would seem to have amply justified the trial court's conclusion that there was no evidence that Royce and Graefe had failed to use ordinary care.

As regards Bona's contention that the court below was in error in not permitting the case to go to the jury on the question of strict liability in tort, we have, on two occasions in the past declined to espouse the doctrine formulated by 2 Restatement, Torts 2d Sec. 402 A. Despite the fact that the principle enunciated by Sec. 402 A is gaining acceptance, there is even less reason why it should be adopted in this case.

Here again the difficulty is that Sec. 402 A is directed at one who *sells* a product which, because of its defective condition, is unreasonably dangerous to the user, and reaches the user without substantial change in the condition in which it is sold. *Speyer, Inc.* v. *Humble Oil & Refining Co.,* quite properly we think, held that Sec. 402 A is not applicable to a lessor.

By positing his appeal on breach of implied warranty and strict liability in tort, Bona would seem to concede that he had not and could not adduce the proof required by Sec. 408. We conclude that the trial court correctly applied the law when it entered directed verdicts in favor of Graefe and Royce on the implied warranty and strict liability courts.

Affirmed.

Bailee's Responsibility for Care and Use

Although the bailee is in possession of the bailor's property, the bailee does not guarantee the safety of the property against loss or injury. Almost all courts have stated that a bailee is not an insurer. A bailee is, however, responsible for any loss caused by its negligence, but traditionally the courts have measured the degree of care that must be exercised by the type of bailment.

In a mutual-benefit bailment, the general rule requires the bailee to take ordinary and reasonable care of the subject of the bailment. Liability occurs if the bailee does not exercise the same degree of care that an ordinarily prudent person would use in caring for his or her own property.

Some jurisdictions allow the bailee to escape or limit its liability by agreement with the bailor; however, in a number of states an agreement of this nature is against public policy and not enforceable. These kinds of agreements are especially apt to be unenforceable if the bargaining power of the bailee is substantially greater than that of the bailor. As it is possible for the bailee to limit its liability by agreement, the bailor, too, can increase the bailee's responsibility by contract. A common example would be a requirement that the bailee insure the property for the bailor's benefit.

Negligence or the absence of due care is also the standard in a bailment for the sole benefit of the bailor or one that solely benefits the bailee. In each case, however, the degree of care that the bailee must exercise in order to escape liability differs. In a situation where only the bailor benefits, the bailee need exercise only slight diligence. Thus the bailee is liable only if its neglect of duty amounts to willfulness and evidences a reckless disregard for the rights of others. Conversely, if the bailment is for the sole benefit of the bailee, slight negligence is enough to establish the bailee's responsibility for injury or loss. Courts feel that it is reasonable to expect that a person who borrows another's property will take extraordinary care to protect it. This degree of care has been defined as that which the prudent person would exercise in his or her own affairs of great importance.

Although classification of bailments based upon benefit has traditionally aided courts in determining liability, the current trend is to consider the type of bailment as only one factor in measuring whether conduct is reasonable under the circumstances. Whether a bailee has exercised the proper degree of care is determined by this and factors such as the type of property, the reason for the bailment, custom of the trade, and prior dealings between the parties.

Bailee's Use of Property

A bailee who treats the property in a manner not authorized by the agreement becomes absolutely liable for any loss or damage. This responsibility exists in spite of the bailee's exercise of due care or of a result that actually benefits the bailor. A bailee who uses the property in an unauthorized manner, stores it someplace other than that agreed upon, or fails to return it according to the contract is liable to the bailor even though injury or loss is caused by an accident or act of God.

In many transactions, the bailee's authority to deal with the property is not expressed clearly by the parties. In these cases, the court must consider a number of factors to determine the bailee's liability. These include:

1. The purpose of the transaction
2. The type of property
3. The relationship between the parties
4. The custom of the business

In some cases a bailee who acquires property for repairs cannot allocate this responsibility to another; in others, by considering factors such as the above, clearly this can be done.

TRANSFER OF TITLE TO PROPERTY

Sale

Sale is the most important method of transferring title to property. Although the methods of selling both real and personal property have developed along somewhat different lines, both are governed extensively by statute and case law. The sale of goods is the subject of Article 2 of the Uniform Commercial Code, which is discussed in detail in Chapters 15 and 16. Some of the legal problems inherent in the transfer of title to real property by sale are discussed in Chapter 35.

In general the process involved in selling real property is much more formal than that involved in the sale of goods. Additionally, statutes in all states require public recording of the transfer of title to real property if the owner's title is to be valid against claims of third parties who might acquire an interest in the real estate.

Gift

Title to property frequently is transferred by gift. In dollar value the vast majority of gifts are made through the testamentary disposition of a deceased person. Gifts by living persons, however, are very important. A gift by a living person is usually an *inter vivos* gift. If a living person makes a gift in expectation of impending death, the gift is said to be *causa mortis*. In an inter vivos gift, the recipient or donee receives an irrevocable title; while if a gift is causa mortis, the gift may be revoked if the donor does not die.

For a gift by a living person to be valid, the donor must intend to make a gift, and delivery of the item must take place. In addition, the donee must be willing to accept the gift. Ordinarily this last requirement causes few problems, although the other essential elements of a gift sometimes result in litigation, as the following case illustrates.

In re the Estate of Alfred V. Sipe, Deceased

Supreme Court of Pennsylvania

422 A.2d 826 (1980)

Eleanor A. Sipe (petitioner-appellee), executrix of the estate of Alfred V. Sipe, petitioned for an order directing Mary Drabik (respondent-appellee) to turn over to the estate money she had withdrawn after decedent's death from a joint savings account.

The lower court entered a decree in favor of the executrix and Drabik appealed. Held: Reversed.

Flaherty, Justice

The trial court concluded that a gift had not been made because the decedent, when he opened the account, filled out the entire signature card himself by signing both his name and the appellant's name and their Social Security numbers on the card. Appellant's failure to sign the joint signature card was "fatal to her case" according to the trial court. We do not agree.

Although this Court has held on numerous occasions that the "[e]xecution of a signature card creating a joint savings account with a right of survivorship is *sufficient* to establish an inter vivos gift to the joint tenant by the depositor of the funds" and "introduction into evidence of a duly executed joint account signature card shifts the burden of proof to those who seek to bar enforcement of the survivorship terms of the writing" [emphasis added by the court], it is not the law and we have never held that such proof is the only proof which can establish a gift. All of the circumstances must be considered in determining whether a gift was made or whether the joint account was established for some other purpose.

Sometime prior to September 17, 1975, decedent had opened a savings account in his own name at a branch of the Union National Bank. On the above date, decedent went to the bank and told an employee of the bank that he wanted to close the account in his own name and open a new account in his name and the name of the appellant into which was deposited approximately $8,000.00, which included the $3,000.00 balance in his old account. Decedent signed a temporary signature card for the account and was given a permanent signature card to be signed by himself and the appellant and returned to the bank. The court found that decedent, not appellant, signed appellant's name on the signature card.

About eighteen months later, on February 20, 1977, decedent, who was about to enter the hospital for surgery, gave the passbook for the joint account to appellant. After his discharge from the hospital about a month later, decedent, who needed care, went to the residence of his nephew Vernon Sipe, which was next door. Decedent died about six weeks later on April 30, 1977. After his discharge from the hospital, decedent was not confined to bed. Although he could not drive himself, he visited the hospital for treatments, went shopping on various occasions and was in the bank where the joint account existed sometime in early April, although he did not transact any business, but was there in the company of his nephew Vernon Sipe, who had business at the bank.

The requirements for a gift are intent, delivery and acceptance in all cases. This is so whether we are concerned with monies, a bank account, a stock certificate, or a horse. Accepting the trial judge's conclusion that the appellant did not sign the signature card herself, the issue remains whether or not a valid gift was established.

As to the first requirement for a valid gift—intent—there is no question that the evidence satisfies that requirement. Decedent was not opening a savings account for the first time. He specifically asked that that account be closed and a new joint account be opened in his name and the name of appellant. He was given an explanation of the account and a signature card which he signed and returned to the bank. That signature card clearly states that a joint account is being established with the right of either party to withdraw and with the right of survivorship. The only conclusion possible is that the decedent intended to make a gift.

Appellee seems to attach great significance to the lower court's finding that appellant did not sign the signature card. It cannot be overemphasized that appellant's signing or not signing of the signature card does not control the disposition of this case. Signing the card would have shifted the burden of proof to the challenger that joint ownership was not created. Not signing the card merely means that we must consider all the circumstances in determining whether a joint account was intended to exist, whether the requirements of the law pertaining to the creation of gifts have been met, not whether the parties to this intended gift have complied with the rules and regulations designed for the legitimate protection of Union National Bank, not a party to this dispute.

In addition to donative intent, the law of gifts also requires acceptance of the gift, but acceptance is presumed. The acceptance requirement was met when appellant received the passbook from decedent. It has never been required that a donee sign a document acknowledging acceptance, which is what appellee's position would dictate.

Finally, the law of gifts also requires a delivery. Without reaching the question of whether a delivery was effected when decedent gave the signature card to the bank, it is clear that delivery was made when decedent gave the passbook to appellant.

Appellee has suggested that this was a convenience account. There is almost no evidence so to indicate. Evidence to establish that such a joint account was a convenience account is not sufficient unless the evidence is clear, precise and convincing. The evidence must not be general but must be detailed and specific as to when and under what circumstances the decedent manifested that the account was a convenience account. Such evidence is lacking in this case.

The only conclusion warranted on the basis of the undisputed facts, coupled with the facts as found by the trial court, is that the decedent made a valid gift to the appellant.

The decree of the trial court is reversed and a decree entered in favor of appellant. Each party to pay own costs.

In addition to sale or gift, title to property is transferred in several other ways. Some of these, such as adverse possession and eminent domain, are more commonly associated with real property. Adverse possession and eminent domain will be discussed in Chapter 35.

Judicial Sale

Most courts have the power to order the sale of a defendant's real or personal property in order to satisfy a judgment. Sometimes the court's order is based upon an agreement in which one of the parties has used specific property as a security. Usually the property secures a loan or is used to finance the purchase of the property. A real estate mortgage or a security agreement executed by the purchaser of goods are examples. In addition, many states allow designated officials to seize various assets of a defendant and to sell them to satisfy a money judgment. Usually state statutes establish a category of property that is exempt from seizure. This is generally property necessary to earn a livelihood or sustain life.

Abandoned and Lost Property

Abandoned property is that which the owner has intentionally relinquished, intending to terminate any interest he or she possessed. Lost property is that which the owner had no intention of giving up but has parted with inadvertently through carelessness. The title acquired to each differs. The first person to acquire abandoned property obtains absolute title. A finder, however, acquires an interest that is good against all the world but the true owner.

At common law, the finder of lost property was required to search for the rightful owner. Some states require the finder to make a diligent search, while others merely require that the finder follow procedures prescribed by statute. Finders who take possession of lost property are gratuitous bailees as far as responsibility to the owner for any damage to the property.

Descent and Distribution

When a person dies without leaving a will, that person's real and personal property is divided among his or her heirs as directed by statute. In all American jurisdictions, the legislative policy has been to provide a statutory scheme for distribution of the intestate decedent's property that reflects what he or she presumably would have done had a will been written.

As a result, the largest shares are provided the surviving spouse and children. In most of these statutes, if there is a surviving wife or children, more distant relatives do not participate.

CHANGING CONCEPTS OF PROPERTY

Property is a dynamic concept continually being reshaped by society to meet new economic and social needs. In the United States today, two movements modifying traditional rights associated with property are discernible. One of these involves the restructuring of property rights in their relationship to civil rights. This is illustrated by legislation and cases that attempt to ensure the fundamental interests of minorities. In most instances, where traditional property rights conflict with basic civil rights, property rights have been limited.

The 1948 U.S. Supreme Court opinion in *Shelly* v. *Kramer*, 334 U.S. 1 (1948) exemplifies this trend. This case involved an agreement by certain owners of real estate not to sell or lease their homes to "any person not of the Caucasian race." When Shelly, a black, purchased a parcel covered by this restriction, Kramer and others sued to restrain him from taking possession. The Supreme Court held that state courts could not enforce a private agreement depriving a person of a constitutional right. In effect, the Supreme Court limited the right of Kramer and the others to restrict the use of their real estate in this manner.

A second direction that the law is taking is to extend property rights to a person's employment or the facilities necessary to practice a chosen profession. Although the movement in this direction is slow, the trend is clear. Recently, status and reputation have been treated as property, as in the following case.

Memphis Development Foundation v. Factors Etc., Inc.

U.S. Court of Appeals, Sixth Circuit
616 F.2d 956 (1980)

Memphis Development Foundation (Foundation) (plaintiff-appellant) sued in U.S. District Court to enjoin Factors Etc. Inc. (defendant-appellee) from interfering with Foundation's attempt to erect a large bronze statue of Elvis Presley in downtown Memphis. Foundation solicited public contributions to pay for the sculpture. Donors of $25 or more received an eight-inch pewter replica of the proposed statue.

During his lifetime, Presley had conveyed the exclusive right to exploit the commercial value of his name to Boxcar Enterprises in exchange for royalties. These rights had been assigned to Factors Etc., Inc. (Factors) two days after Presley's death. Factors by counterclaim sought damages and an injunction against distribution of the replicas by Foundation.

The district court granted Foundation's injunction prohibiting interference with its efforts to erect the statue but prohibited it from distributing any statue bearing the image or likeness of Elvis Presley. Foundation appealed.

Held: Reversed and remanded.

Merritt, Circuit Judge

This appeal raises the interesting question: Who is the heir of fame? The famous have an exclusive legal right during life to control and profit from the commercial use of their name and personality. We are called upon in this diversity case to determine whether, under Tennessee law, the exclusive right to publicity survives a celebrity's death. We hold that the right is not inheritable. After death the opportunity for gain shifts to the public domain, where it is equally open to all.

At common law, there is a right of action for the appropriation or unauthorized commercial use of the name or likeness of another. An individual is entitled to control the commercial use of these personal attributes during life. But the common law has not heretofore widely recognized this right to control commercial publicity as a property right which may be inherited.

Tennessee courts have not addressed this issue directly or indirectly, and we have no way to assess their predisposition. Since the case is one of first impression, we are left to review the question in the light of practical and policy considerations, the treatment of other similar rights in our legal system, the relative weight of the conflicting interests of the parties, and certain moral presuppositions concerning death, privacy, inheritability and economic opportunity. These considerations lead us to conclude that the right of publicity should not be given the status of a devisable right, even where as here a person exploits the right by contract during life.

Recognition of a post-mortem right of publicity would vindicate two possible interests: the encouragement of effort and creativity, and the hopes and expectations of the decedent and those with whom he contracts that they are creating a valuable capital asset. Although fame and stardom may be ends in themselves, they are normally by-products of one's activities and personal attributes, as well as luck and promotion. The basic motivations are the desire to achieve success or excellence in a chosen field, the desire to contribute to the happiness or improvement of one's fellows and the desire to receive the psychic and financial rewards of achievement. As John Rawls has written, such needs come from the deep psychological fact that the individuals want the respect and good will of other persons and "enjoy the exercise of their realized capacities (their innate or trained abilities), and this enjoyment increases the more the capacity is realized, or the greater its complexity." According to Rawls:

> [Such] activities are more enjoyable because they satisfy the desire for variety and novelty of experience, and leave room for feats of ingenuity and invention. They also evoke the pleasures of anticipation and surprise, and often the overall form of the activity, its structural development, is fascinating and beautiful. *A Theory of Justice* 426–27 (1971).

Fame is an incident of the strong motivations that Rawls describes. The desire to exploit fame for the commercial advantage of one's heirs is by contrast a weak principle of motivation. It seems apparent that making the right of publicity inheritable would not significantly inspire the creative endeavors of individuals in our society.

On the other hand, there are strong reasons for declining to recognize the inheritability of the right. A whole set of practical problems of judicial line-drawing would arise should the courts recognize such an inheritable right. How long would the "property" interest last? In perpetuity? For a term of years? Is the right of publicity taxable? At what point does the right collide with the right of free expression guaranteed by the first amendment? Does the right apply to elected officials and military heroes whose fame was gained on the public payroll, as well as to movie stars, singers and athletes? Does the right cover posters or engraved likenesses of, for example, Farah Fawcett Majors or Mahatma Gandhi, kitchen utensils ("Revere Ware"), insurance ("John Hancock"), electric utilities ("Edison"), a football stadium ("RFK"), a pastry ("Napoleon"), or the innumerable urban subdivisions and apartment complexes named after famous people? Our legal system normally does not pass on to heirs other similar personal attributes even though the attributes may be shared during life by others or have some commercial value. Titles, offices and reputation are not inheritable. Neither are trust or distrust and friendship or enmity descendible. An employment contract during life does not create the right for heirs to take over the job. Fame falls in the same category as reputation; it is an attribute from which others may benefit but may not own.

The law of defamation, designed to protect against the destruction of reputation including the loss of earning capacity associated with it, provides an analogy. There is no right of action for defamation after death. The two interests that support the inheritability of the right of publicity, namely, the "effort and creativity" and the "hopes and expectations" of the decedent, would also support an action for libel or slander for destruction of name and reputation after death. Neither of these reasons, however, is sufficient to overcome the common law policy terminating the action for defamation upon death.

Fame often is fortuitous and fleeting. It always depends on the participation of the public in the creation of an image. It usually depends on the communication of information about the famous person by the media. The intangible and shifting nature of fame and celebrity status, the presence of widespread public and press participation in its creation, the unusual psychic rewards and income that often flow from it during life and the fact that it may be created by bad as well as good conduct combine to create serious reservations about making fame the permanent right of a few individuals to the exclusion of the general public. Heretofore, the law has always thought that leaving a good name to one's children is sufficient reward in itself for the individual, whether famous or not. Commercialization of this virtue after death in the hands of heirs is contrary to our legal tradition and somehow seems contrary to the moral presuppositions of our culture.

There is no indication that changing the traditional common law rule against allowing heirs the exclusive control of the commercial use of their ancestor's name will increase the efficiency or productivity of our economic system. It does not seem reasonable to expect that such a change would enlarge the stock or quality of the goods, services, artistic creativity, information, invention or entertainment available. Nor will it enhance the fairness of our political and economic system. It seems fairer and more efficient for the commercial, aesthetic, and political use of the name, memory and image of the famous to be open to all rather than to be monopolized by a few. An equal distribution of the opportunity to use the name of the dead seems preferable. The memory, name and pictures of famous individuals should be regarded as a common asset to be shared, an economic opportunity available in the free market system.

These same considerations also apply to the Presley assigns' more narrow argument based on the fact that Presley entered into contracts during his life for the commercial use of his image. It is true that the assignment of the right of publicity during life shows that Presley was aware of the value of the asset and intended to use it. The assignment also suggests that he intended to convert a mere opportunity or potential for profit into a tangible possession and consciously worked to create the asset with, perhaps, the hope of devising it.

The question is whether the specific identification and use of the opportunity during life is sufficient to convert it into an inheritable right after death. We do not think that whatever minimal benefit to society may result from the added motivation and extra creativity supposedly encouraged by allowing a person to pass on his fame for the commercial use of his heirs or assigns outweighs the considerations discussed above.

Accordingly, the judgment of the District Court is reversed and the case is remanded for further proceedings consistent with the principles announced above.

REVIEW PROBLEMS

1. Cogliano owned a nursery business on land taken by the state to build a highway. The nursery stock consisted principally of young trees of varying ages and heights, some

shrubbery, rose bushes, and perennials. The value of the land apart from the stock was $10,000. The value of the nursery stock was $40,000. The state Department of Public Works awarded Cogliano $10,000 for the land. This award did not include the nursery stock, which Cogliano was given 30 days to remove. (a) Indicate the legal basis that the Department of Public Works might use in support of the limited award. (b) On what grounds might Cogliano argue that he was entitled to $50,000? (c) Who has the best argument? Why? Cogliano v. Commonwealth of Massachusetts, 135 N.E. 2d 648 (1956)

2. Tillotson purchased a drying bin from the B. C. Manufacturing Co. The bin was erected on property owned by the Newman Grove Grain Co. The bin was anchored to a concrete base and became an integral part of the grain corporation's elevator, to which it was attached with loading and unloading ducts, electrical wiring, etc. The Newman Grove Grain Co. mortgaged the real estate to the Battle Creek State Bank. Is the bin a fixture? What difference does this make? Explain. Tillotson v. Stephens, 237 N.W. 2d 108 (1975)

3. Amerson wished to borrow an electric drill from Howell. Howell was aware that the drill had previously shocked three people, none of whom was injured. This information was conveyed to Amerson. In addition, before giving the drill to Amerson, Howell changed the plug and tested the drill, receiving no shock. When Amerson used the drill, he suffered a fatal shock. Would Amerson's estate be able to recover from Howell? Discuss. Howell v. Amerson, 156 S.E. 2d 371 (1967)

4. California Artists is a publisher and distributor of Christmas greeting cards. Its policy is to destroy cards that are not sold after two seasons. For a number of years destruction had been accomplished by delivering boxed cards to Salvage, Inc., a private concern that conducted a dump and salvage operation.

Material delivered to Salvage was treated in two ways. If a person specified that the material was to be covered, Salvage would immediately cover it and certify that this had been done. Other material was dumped but subject to salvage. The material not salvaged was covered later. The fee for this was much less than the fee for immediate covering.

In January 1955, California Artists sent 877,000 cards packaged in cartons to the dump. Its employee was ordered to "Take the cards to the dump and dispose of them." The employee did not indicate that California Artists wanted the cartons covered immediately. The cartons were marked California Artists.

Salvage, Inc. sold some of the cartons to McFadden, who planned to sell them. When California Artists learned of this, they brought suit to recover the cards, arguing that Salvage had no right to sell them since it was a bailee for destruction. What might McFadden argue to counter the California Artists' position? Who would win? H. S. Crocker Co. v. McFadden, 307 P. 2d 429 (1957)

5. Dundas owned four horses that were stabled temporarily in an old barn at the fairgrounds. Usually the horses were stabled in a newer barn but had been moved with Dundas's knowledge for a short time because of the county fair. The old barn had no telephone, automatic sprinkler system, or smoke or heat detector. A dry-chemical fire extinguisher was placed at each end of the barn. Owners with horses in the barn were responsible for care and feeding of the horses as well as for cleaning the stalls. The barn was open for horse owners and the public each day. Owners could remove horses at any time the barn was open and substitute others at their discretion.

A fire occurred in the barn because a 13-

year-old boy, whose parents had horses stabled there, was setting off caps and a burning cap set fire to bedding in one of the stalls. Although the boy tried to extinguish the fire, he was unable to do so. By the time he reached a telephone and fire-fighting equipment arrived, none of the horses could be saved. Dundas sued the county. What is the basis of her action? What defense would the county have? Who would win? Support your answer. Dundas v. Lincoln County, 618 P. 2d 978 (1980)

6. Snowden was employed by Osborne, a general contractor on a project to construct a building. Oliver was the subcontractor for plastering work on the building. To aid in the performance of his work, Oliver erected a scaffold on the outside of the building. Oliver was under no duty to furnish scaffolding for employees of other contractors; however, customarily employees of other contractors used scaffolding in place to complete their own work. The scaffolding constructed by Oliver had walkways that were 1 inch thick; generally boards 1⅝ inches thick were used.

Snowden was injured when he rested a 300-pound mold on the scaffold erected by Oliver. This exceeded weights that Oliver's employees ordinarily used. The injury to Snowden was the direct result of a fall caused by a plank breaking at a knot. Was Oliver liable to Snowden for injuries resulting from the fall? Discuss. Oliver v. Snowden, 426 S.W. 2d 545 (1968)

Interests in Real Property

R eal property law deals with ownership of land and those things that are permanently attached to it. Because land is an unusual commodity and for centuries has been of great economic importance in the Western world, the legal relationships involving real property are extensive and complicated. This chapter discusses some of the many interests that exist in real estate.

SCOPE OF REAL PROPERTY

As traditionally defined by courts and commentators, land ownership encompasses the surface of the earth, everything above that surface, and all that is below. The space over which the surface owner has dominion is compared to an inverted pyramid extending upward indefinitely into space and downward to the center of the earth. As air travel became an important means of transportation, the traditional rule has gradually been modified. Today the general rule is that the surface owner's air rights are limited to the space that can be reasonably used and enjoyed.

Air space and natural resources such as oil and gas, water, and minerals can be separated from the land and treated as independent commodities. In cities, landowners, while retaining ownership of the surface, sell the air space above it for the construction of commercial buildings. Ownership of high-rise condominiums is based on divided ownership of air space. In mining regions, the right to extract natural resources is frequently separated from ownership of the surface and leased or sold. In the arid areas of the West, water rights are very often separated from surface ownership of land.

858

ESTATES IN LAND

Interests in land may be divided in many different ways. One way, as the previous section indicates, is to divide use and enjoyment of the land itself horizontally in relation to space. Another way is to separate the land from possible rights in it and allow numerous interests to exist simultaneously. This is the basis of the doctrine of estates. This doctrine was important in the historic development of English and American land law and continues to influence real property law today.

The word estate as used in real property law indicates the nature, quantity, and quality of an ownership interest. As an estate refers to an ownership interest, it is or must have the potential for becoming possessory. The extent of an estate is determined by the duration of the interest and the time when the right to possess and enjoy the land begins.

For example, a wife might provide by will that her real property go to her husband for the duration of his life and then to her daughter. Upon the wife's death, both husband and daughter would have existing estates. The husband's estate would be measured by the duration of his life; the daughter's estate could last forever, but it does not begin until her father dies.

Fee Simple Estates

A fee simple estate, also called a fee simple absolute or simply a fee, is the most extensive interest that a person can have in land. This is the type of estate held by most owners of real property. The estate is potentially infinite in duration. It may be transferred to others during the lifetime of the owner. Upon the owner's death, his or her interest does not end but passes by will or the laws of intestate succession, if the owner dies without leaving a will. This is the type of estate held by the wife in the previous example. The only restrictions upon this estate are those imposed by government. If a question exists as to the type of estate that is transferred, the courts presume that a fee simple is intended.

Fee Simple Defeasible

A defeasible fee is less extensive than a fee simple, since the defeasible fee terminates if certain events occur. Until these events occur, however, the owner of a defeasible fee possesses the same interests as those possessed by the owner of a fee simple. For example, a defeasible fee might be used if a person wished to give land to a municipality for recreational purposes. The grantor might execute a deed with the following language: "to the City of Columbus, Georgia, and its successors and assigns so long as the property is used for recreational purposes." If the land is not used for the stated purpose, the city's interest terminates automatically and reverts to the grantor or the grantor's heirs. Not all defeasible fees terminate automatically. Some require the grantor or the grantor's successors to take steps to terminate them. Although the defeasible fee is not used extensively today, it has played a significant role historically in property law.

Life Estates

A life estate is one whose duration is measured by the life of a person, typically the owner but possibly some other person. This latter type of estate is called an estate *pur autre vie*. Life estates may be created by deed or will. They are also created by statute and case law. A life estate may be sold or mortgaged, but the acquiring party's interest is terminated by the life tenant's death. The following case illustrates the type of legal problem that sometimes arises when a life estate is created.

Sauls v. Crosby

District Court of Appeals of Florida
258 So.2d 326 (1972)

Annie L. Sauls (plaintiff-appellant), a life tenant, appealed from a lower-court judgment denying her the right to cut merchantable timber and enjoy the proceeds. Dan S. and Bertha Mae Crosby (defendants-appellees) successfully argued that Sauls did not have the right to cut merchantable timber unless the proceeds were held in trust for the benefit of those entitled to the estate after Sauls's life estate terminated.

Rawls, Judge

On the 9th day of October 1968, appellant conveyed to appellees certain lands situated in Hamilton County, Florida, with the following reservation set forth in said conveyance: "The Grantor herein, reserves a life Estate in said property." By this appeal appellant now contends that the trial court erred in denying her, as a life tenant, the right to cut merchantable timber and enjoy the proceeds.

The English common law, which was transplanted on this continent, holds that it is waste for an ordinary life tenant to cut timber upon his estate when the sole purpose is to clear the woodlands. American courts today as a general rule recognize that an ordinary life tenant may cut timber and not be liable for waste if he uses the timber for fuel; for repairing fences and buildings on the estate; for fitting the land for cultivation; or for use as pasture if the inheritance is not damaged and the acts are conformable to good husbandry; and for thinning or other purposes which are necessary for the enjoyment of the estate and are in conformity with good husbandry.

In this jurisdiction a tenant for life or a person vested with an ordinary life estate is entitled to the use and enjoyment of his estate during its existence. The only restriction on the life tenant's use and enjoyment is that he not permanently diminish or change the value of the future estate of the remainderman. This limitation places on the "ordinary life tenant" the responsibility for all waste of whatever character.

An instrument creating a life tenancy may absolve the tenant of responsibility for waste, unless it is wanton or malicious, by stating that the life tenant has the power to consume or that the life tenant is without impeachment for waste. Thus, there is a sharp distinction in the rights of an ordinary life tenant or life tenant without impeachment for waste or life tenant who has the power to consume. An ordinary life tenant has no right to cut the timber from an estate for purely commercial reasons and so to do is tortious conduct for which the remainderman may sue immediately.

In the case of *In re Paine's Estate*, the Florida Supreme Court incidentally concerned with the timber rights of a life tenant, by dictum, noted that a life tenant without impeachment for waste could cut and sell the timber on the estate. The rule pronounced in *Paine* conforms with the general authorities on the subject and is limited to a life tenant with power to consume or a life tenant without impeachment for waste. It does not apply to an ordinary life tenant. In the cause sub judice, the trial court was concerned with the rights of an ordinary life tenant and correctly concluded that appellant "does not have the right to cut merchantable timber from the land involved in this suit unless the proceeds of such cutting and sale are held in trust for the use and benefit of the remaindermen. . . ."

The judgment appealed is affirmed.

Legal Life Estates

Despite their many potential legal problems, life estates have been used to provide financial security for one spouse upon the death of another. At common law, dower and curtesy were estates that widows and widowers enjoyed in their spouse's real property by virtue of the marriage.

Dower. At common law, upon the death of her husband a wife acquired a one-third life interest in lands that he had owned during marriage. Although most states have abolished dower, it continues to exist in a few. In several of these states, dower has been expanded to include the husband, and in others the one-third share has been increased to one-half. Where dower has been abolished, if the surviving spouse is not provided for by will, state statutes generally allow that person to elect a share in both the real and personal property of the deceased.

Curtesy. At common law, a surviving husband acquired a life interest in all his wife's real property if a child had been born of the marriage. Curtesy has been abolished in most states, but a few still allow the surviving husband a life interest in his deceased wife's realty.

LEASEHOLD ESTATES

Leasehold estates are among the most significant interests that exist today in real property. In business, the lease provides a method for obtaining land with far less capital than fee simple ownership requires. In housing, the lease entails lower immediate costs than fee simple ownership and allows the holder both mobility and freedom to try different life styles.

A leasehold interest is created when the owner of real property, usually referred to as the landlord or lessor, conveys possession and control of the property to another, called the tenant or lessee, in exchange for a payment called rent. The possessory right granted by the owner is temporary. Upon termination of the lease, possession and control revert to the owner.

Both real property and contract law apply to leases. Generally at common law, courts applied real property principles to the lease, treating it as a conveyance or transfer of land ownership. This was significant to the relationship between the parties for, as long as the tenant was in possession of the land, he or she was required to pay the rent. This rule applied even if the lessor breached promises in the lease or failed to maintain the premises.

Treating the lease as a transfer of land ownership probably was justified in the agrarian society existing in the United States until the 1840s; however, the gradual transition to an urban industrial society required reconsideration of the fundamental nature of the lease. In an urban environment, the building or unit of the building rented is more important to the lessee than the land upon which the building rests. Rules ignoring this economic fact of life could not long survive. Thus during this century the trend has been for courts and legislatures to emphasize the contractual aspect of the lease in order to provide increased protection, especially for residential tenants. The following case illustrates this trend.

Javins v. First National Realty Corp.

U.S. Court of Appeals, D.C. Circuit

428 F.2d 1071 (1970)

First National Realty Corp. (plaintiff-appellee) brought suit against Javins and others (defendants-appellants) seeking possession of rented apartments on grounds that each of the defendants had defaulted in payment of rent due for April. The defendants admitted they had not paid rent for the month in question, but defended on grounds that approximately 1,500 violations of the District of Columbia housing regulations affected their apartments either directly or indirectly. The Landlord and Tenant Branch of District of Columbia Court and the District of Columbia Court of Appeals ruled proof of such violations inadmissible. Defendants appealed to the U.S. Court of Appeals. Held: Reversed.

J. Skelly Wright, Circuit Judge

Because of the importance of the question presented, we granted appellants' petitions for leave to appeal. We now reverse and hold that a warranty of habitability, measured by the standards set out in the Housing Regulations for the District of Columbia, is implied by operation of law into leases of urban dwelling units covered by those Regulations and that breach of this warranty gives rise to the usual remedies for breach of contract.

Since, in traditional analysis, a lease was the conveyance of an interest in land, courts have usually utilized the special rules governing real property transactions to resolve controversies involving leases. However, as the Supreme Court has noted in another context, "the body of private property law * * *, more than almost any other branch of law, has been shaped by distinctions whose validity is largely historical." Courts have a duty to reappraise old doctrines in the light of the facts and values of contemporary life—particularly old common law doctrines which the courts themselves created and developed.

The assumption of landlord-tenant law, derived from feudal property law, that a lease primarily conveyed to the tenant an interest in land may have been reasonable in a rural, agrarian society; it may continue to be reasonable in some leasing involving farming or commercial land. In these cases, the value of the lease to the tenant is the land itself. But in the case of the modern apartment dweller, the value of the lease is that it gives him a place to live. The city dweller who seeks to lease an apartment on the third floor of a tenement has little interest in the land 30 or 40 feet below, or even in the bare right to possession within the four walls of his apartment. When American city dwellers, both rich and poor, seek "shelter" today, they seek a well known package of goods and services—a package which includes not merely walls and ceilings, but also adequate heat, light and ventilation, serviceable plumbing facilities, secure windows and doors, proper sanitation, and proper maintenance.

Some courts have realized that certain of the old rules of property law governing leases are inappropriate for today's transactions. In order to reach results more in accord with the legitimate expectations of the parties and the standards of the community, courts have been gradually introducing more modern precepts of contract law in interpreting leases.

In our judgment the trend toward treating leases as contracts is wise and well considered. Our holding in this case reflects a belief that leases of urban dwelling units should be interpreted and construed like any other contract.

Modern contract law has recognized that the buyer of goods and services in an industrialized society must rely upon the skill and honesty of the supplier to assure that goods and services purchased are of adequate quality. In interpreting most contracts, courts have sought to protect the legitimate expectations of the buyer and have steadily widened the seller's responsibility for the quality of goods and services through implied warranties of fitness and merchantability. Thus without any special agreement a merchant will be held to warrant that his goods are fit for the ordinary purposes for which such goods are used and that they are at least of reasonably average quality. Moreover, if the supplier has been notified that goods are required for a specific purpose, he will be held to warrant that any goods sold are fit for that purpose. These implied warranties have become widely accepted and well established features of the common law, supported by the overwhelming body of case law. Today most states as well as the District of Columbia have codified and enacted these warranties into statute, as to the sale of goods, in the Uniform Commercial Code.

Implied warranties of quality have not been limited to cases involving sales. The consumer renting a chattel, paying for services, or buying a combination of goods and services must rely upon the skill and honesty of the supplier to at least the same extent as a purchaser of goods. Courts have not hesitated to find implied warranties of fitness and merchantability in such situations. In most areas product liability law has moved far beyond ''mere'' implied warranties running between two parties in privity with each other.

The rigid doctrines of real property law have tended to inhibit the application of implied warranties to transactions involving real estate. Now, however, courts have begun to hold sellers and developers of real property responsible for the quality of their product. For example, builders of new homes have recently been held liable to purchasers for improper construction on the ground that the builders had breached an implied warranty of fitness. In other cases courts have held builders of new homes liable for breach of an implied warranty that all local building regulations had been complied with.

In our judgment the common law itself must recognize the landlord's obligation to keep his premises in a habitable condition. This conclusion is compelled by three separate considerations. First, we believe that the old rule was based on certain factual assumptions which are no longer true; on its own terms, it can no longer be justified. Second, we believe that the consumer protection cases discussed above require that the old rule be abandoned in order to bring residential landlord-tenant law into harmony with the principles on which those cases rest. Third, we think that the nature of today's urban housing market also dictates the abandonment of the old rule.

Since a lease contract specifies a particular period of time during which the tenant has a right to use his apartment for shelter, he may legitimately expect that the apartment will be fit for habitation for the time period for which it is rented. We point out that in the present cases there is no allegation that appellants' apartments were in poor condition or in violation of the housing code at the commencement of the leases. Since the lessees continue to pay the same rent, they were entitled to expect that the landlord would continue to keep the premises in their beginning condition during the lease term. It is precisely such expectations that the law now recognizes as deserving of formal, legal protection.

Even beyond the rationale of traditional products liability law, the relationship of landlord and tenant suggests further compelling reasons for the law's protection of the tenants' legitimate expectations of quality. The inequality in bargaining power between landlord and tenant has been well documented. Tenants have very little leverage to enforce demands for better housing. Various impediments to competition in the rental housing market, such as racial and class discrimination and standardized form leases, mean that landlords place tenants in a take it or leave it situation. The increasingly severe shortage of adequate housing further increases the landlord's bargaining power and escalates the need for maintaining and improving the existing stock. Finally, the findings by various studies of the social impact of bad housing has led to the realization that poor housing is detrimental to the whole society, not merely to the unlucky ones who must suffer the daily indignity of living in a slum.

Thus we are led by our inspection of the relevant legal principles and precedents to the conclusion that the old common law rule imposing an obligation upon the lessee to repair during the lease term was really never intended to apply to residential urban leaseholds. Contract principles established in other areas of the law provide a more rational framework for the apportionment of landlord-tenant responsibilities; they strongly suggest that a warranty of habitability be implied into all contracts for urban dwellings.

We believe, in any event, that the District's housing code requires that a warranty of habitability be implied in the leases of all housing that it covers. The housing code —formally designated the Housing Regulations of the District of Columbia—was established and authorized by the Commissioners of the District of Columbia on August 11, 1955. Since that time, the code has been updated by numerous orders of the Commissioners. The 75 pages of the Regulations provide a comprehensive regulatory scheme setting forth in some detail: (a) the standards which housing in the District of Columbia must meet; (b) which party, the lessor or the lessee, must meet each standard; and (c) a system of inspections, notifications and criminal penalties.

We therefore hold that the Housing Regulations imply a warranty of habitability, measured by the standards which they set out, into leases of all housing that they cover.

The judgment of the District of Columbia Court of Appeals is reversed and the cases are remanded for further proceedings consistent with this opinion.

Classification by Duration of Term

Leasehold estates are classified in several different ways. A traditional classification is by the duration of the term. Major legal differences exist between leases that are for fixed terms and those of indefinite duration. A second method of classifying leases is by the manner in which the rent is determined. Probably the most common classification is by the use made of the property, commercial or income-producing leases being differentiated from residential leases. This classification has become particularly significant in recent years, since many states have adopted legislation that applies specifically to residential leases.

Term Tenancy. A term tenancy, sometimes called an estate for years, exists for a fixed period of time. The agreement creating the term establishes particular beginning and ending dates. A lease written to commence on February 1, 1984, and to terminate on January 31, 1987, would be a term tenancy. The term may be as short as a week or a month, but most term tenancies are for a year or more. A few leases have been written with terms of 999 years.

A principal characteristic of a term tenancy is that it ends automatically at the time designated in the agreement. The owner is not required to notify the tenant of the termination of the lease. Generally in the United States a term tenancy for more than a year must be in writing to be enforceable.

Periodic Tenancy. A periodic tenancy, also referred to as a tenancy from month-to-month or year-to-year, is a rental agreement that continues for successive periods until terminated by proper notice from either party.

A periodic tenancy is created in several ways. If a tenant is in possession under a term tenancy unenforceable because it is not in writing, courts generally hold that a periodic tenancy exists. More commonly, the periodic tenancy is created by the express agreement of the parties to enter into an agreement of this type. Periodic tenancies are also created when a tenant holds over after a term tenancy. The holdover tenancy is discussed later in the chapter. The major factor distinguishing the periodic tenancy from the term tenancy is that the periodic tenancy continues until one of the parties gives proper notice of termination.

The determination of the time period for proper notice varies considerably from state to state. At common law, the general rule was to measure notice by the period of the tenancy —that is, a week-to-week tenancy required a week's notice, a month-to-month tenancy required a month's notice. Proper notice for a year-to-year tenancy, however, was six months. In the United States today, over a quarter of the states have adopted the Uniform Residential Landlord and Tenant Act. This act requires a written notice of ten days for a week-to-week tenancy and sixty days for a month-to-month tenancy. Year-to-year tenancies are not mentioned in the act since they are used almost exclusively for the rental of agricultural lands. Probably the prevailing American rule for year-to-year tenancies is the common law requirement of six months' notice.

Tenancy at Will. A tenancy at will is created when the owner of property gives someone permission to occupy it for an unspecified period of time. This type of tenancy may be created by express agreement or by implication. The key factors are that the tenant is lawfully in possession of the property but that the duration of possession is uncertain. An example of a tenancy at will would be a situation in which the landlord allows a tenant to remain in possession of space in a building scheduled to be torn down until actual demolition commences.

A tenancy at will terminates by any action of either party indicating that he or she no longer wishes to continue the tenancy. A number of states have passed legislation requiring the person wishing to terminate the tenancy to give proper notification to the other. Generally the time required for notification is thirty days. The death of either party or the sale or lease of the property also terminates a tenancy at will.

Tenancy at Sufferance. A tenancy at sufferance exists when a person, initially a lawful occupant, unlawfully occupies another's property. The landlord owes this tenant no duties other than not to injure him or her wantonly or willfully. A tenancy at sufferance may be created if a person who has sold the real estate remains in possession after the time he or she agreed to vacate. The most common example of the tenancy at sufferance is when a person holds over after the expiration of his or her term. This person becomes a holdover tenant if the landlord elects to treat him as such; however, until this decision is made and acted upon, the tenancy is at sufferance.

Holding Over. When a term tenant remains on the premises at the expiration of the term without the owner's consent, the owner has the option of either evicting the tenant or treating the tenant as a holdover. If the owner decides to treat the tenant as a holdover, in most states a periodic tenancy is created. If the original tenancy was for a year or more, almost all states treat the new term as a periodic tenancy for a year. If the original term was for less than a year, the term of holdover tenancy is for a similar period. For example, a month-to-month tenancy is created if the original term tenancy was for a month. An interesting legal problem arises when a tenant holds over after being notified of a rent increase. Most states hold the tenant responsible for the increased rent.

Classification by Method of Determining Rent

A wide range of methods exists for determining the amount of the rent the tenant must pay. In residential leases the rent is usually a fixed amount, but in commercial leases different arrangements are often used to establish the tenant's obligation. These arrangements are primarily the result of the lessor's desire to shift as many economic risks as possible to the tenant. A lessor leasing property for a long term naturally wishes to limit the effect of inflation on rental income. If the rent is a fixed amount and property expenses increase, the owner's income from the property is drastically reduced. Rental payments can be negotiated that protect the owner from this possibility. In other situations an owner might wish to share in the increased productive use of a parcel of real estate without assuming the risk of investing in a building or a business to utilize the property. Like protection against inflation, this objective can be attained through various types of rental payments. A few of the more common methods for determining rent in commercial leases to accomplish the objectives are the percentage lease, the net lease, and the revaluation or appraisal lease. Many variations and combinations of these basic patterns have been used.

Percentage Leases. A percentage lease provides the lessor with a rent determined by a fixed percentage of the gross sales or net profits from a business operated on the leased premises. Some percentage leases are written with a fixed minimum rental. Percentage leases protect the lessor against inflation and also provide him or her with a share in the productive use of the property.

Net Leases. A net lease is a lease in which the tenant pays a fixed rent and in addition agrees to pay the taxes, insurance, and maintenance expenses. A variation of the net lease is the net-net lease. In the net-net lease the tenant agrees to pay all costs attributed to the property. The net lease protects the lessor against inflation.

Revaluation or Appraisal Leases. Some long-term leases provide for adjustment of rental payments based on periodic revaluation of the property. Several different methods of revaluation are used. Revaluation allows the lessor to share in any increase in the value of the land.

Rights and Duties of the Parties

Most problems that arise in a tenancy can be solved by the parties if they have a well-drafted lease. In the lease, landlord and tenant may allocate rights and duties in any manner that they choose as long as what they do is not illegal or against public policy (see Chapter 11). Sometimes parties who enter into a lease do not anticipate a problem that occurs during the term. If a dispute arises that is not settled by the lease, the solution must be found in state statutory or case law.

Understanding how the law allocates the rights and duties of the parties absent agreement in the lease is complicated by the dual nature of the lease and by developments in landlord-tenant law during the past fifty years. The case of *Javins* v. *First National Realty Corp.*, above, illustrates a trend in American law to provide residential tenants with rights not generally available to commercial tenants. This increased protection for residential tenants is also reflected in the statutory law, since many states have expanded the duties of landlords of residential property.

Duty to Repair and Maintain. The allocation of the duty to repair and maintain the premises illustrates the different treatment states sometimes afford commercial and residential leases. At common law, in the absence of agreement, the landlord had a limited duty to repair and maintain the property. If he or she knew of a latent defect, this had to be corrected prior to the commencement of the term. No duty existed to maintain the premises except for the common areas of multiunit buildings. A number of states retain the common law rule for commercial leases, but in most states the rule has been modified for residential property. In these states, if residential property is not maintained in habitable condition, tenants have various remedies against landlords. These remedies include lease rescission, rent abatement, and rent withholding. In a few states, tenants are permitted to make necessary repairs and deduct the cost from the rent.

Use of the Premises. Because a lease is a conveyance as well as a contract, during the term the lessee has the right to possession and control of the property. This means that with few exceptions the lessor may not enter the premises unless the parties have agreed to the contrary. Thus at common law the landlord's right of access to inspect, to make alterations or repairs, or to show the premises is limited. Three principal exceptions exist to the rule

limiting the landlord's right of access. First, he or she may enter to collect the rent if the lease fails to state where rent shall be paid. Next, the Uniform Residential Landlord-Tenant Act and similar state statutes extend the landlord's right of access to inspect the condition of the property and to make necessary repairs in emergencies. Inspection requires notice to the tenant and must be done at reasonable times and intervals. Finally, even absent a statute, the landlord has a right of access to prevent material damage or loss to the property resulting from the the tenant's negligence or misconduct.

As the tenant has the right of possession and control of the premises, he or she can use the property for any reasonable purpose in view of the surrounding circumstances. However, the tenant cannot use the property for an illegal purpose, for a purpose that violates public policy, or in a manner that would result in substantial or permanent damage to the property. In most commercial leases, covenants limit the use that the tenant can make of the property.

Transfer of Leased Premises. A tenant transfers his or her interest in a leasehold by assignment or sublease. As the legal consequences of the two types of transfer differ, the parties should be certain that documents effecting the transfer clearly indicate what type they intend.

A transfer is an assignment if the tenant conveys all of his or her remaining interest. If this is the case, both the new tenant and the landlord are liable to each other according to the terms of the original lease. The original tenant becomes a guarantor that the provisions of the lease will be carried out.

A transfer is a sublease if the tenant transfers less than his or her remaining interest. An example would be a tenant with a lease running from January 1 to December 31 renting the premises during June and July. Since this transfer is a sublease, neither subtenant nor landlord can sue the other directly for breach of the original lease. If the landlord breaches a lease provision, the subtenant must seek relief by bringing an action against the original tenant on the sublease. If the rent is not paid, the landlord must look to the original tenant.

Termination of Lease

Most leases terminate by expiration of the term or by agreement of the parties. Many leases contain provisions providing for their termination under certain conditions. A common example is a provision terminating the lease if the premises are destroyed. Absent a provision of this nature, the tenant remains responsible for the rent. Another example would be a provision terminating the lease if the tenant files for bankruptcy. Without this provision, the trustee of the debtor's estate acquires the lease.

A lease is also terminated by condemnation, but the tenant is entitled to compensation for the value of the leasehold interest. In some instances statutes provide for the termination of a lease. Generally death does not terminate the obligations of either party, but a few states allow the estate of a decedent to cancel a lease covering the deceased's residence.

NONPOSSESSORY INTERESTS IN REAL PROPERTY

Easements

Sometimes people have interests in land that are limited to use and do not extend to posses-sion. These are referred to as nonpossessory interests. Easements are nonpossessory interests that are used extensively in the development of land. They are also essential to operation of utilities and to effective production in industries such as mining and gas extraction.

Easement Appurtenant. An easement appurtenant involves two parcels of land, usually but not necessarily adjoining. The easement allows the possessor of one parcel to benefit by using the other parcel of land. The parcel that benefits is referred to as the dominant tenement. The property that is subject to the easement is known as the servient tenement. If an easement is appurtenant, any transfer of the dominant tenement includes the easement. The easement cannot be separated and transferred independently of the dominant estate. Use by the dominant tenement is limited to the terms of the easement.

Unless the document creating the easement indicates that the easement is exclusive, the owner of the servient estate may also use the land upon which the easement has been dedicated. The servient owner's use must not conflict with the purpose and character of the easement. The cost of maintenance is a problem that sometimes arises when an easement has been created without the parties' agreement as to how this burden should be allocated. The following case deals with this problem.

Island Improvement Association of Upper Greenwood Lake v. Ford
Superior Court of New Jersey, Appellate Division
383 A.2d 133 (1978)

Island Improvement Association of Upper Greenwood Lake (plaintiff-appellant) was organized to raise funds to maintain roads in a privately developed residential area. The association brought a class action against Ford and others (defendants-appellees) to compel them to contribute road maintenance costs. The trial court granted defendant's motion to dismiss and plaintiff appealed. Held: Affirmed in part; reversed in part.

Fritz, P.J.A.D.

There seems to be no factual question but that (1) title to the roads is in a private association, the grantor of the deeds to the individual purchasers, (2) an express easement to use the roads was conveyed to each property owner and (3) none of the deeds to the individual owners imposes any contractual obligation on the owners to maintain the roads.

At the end of the plaintiff's case the trial judge granted defendants' motions to dismiss. He came to this conclusion with respect to the individual owners on the ground that there was no contractual obligation imposed on or assumed by those owners and he lacked the authority to "clothe the (plaintiff) association with quasi municipal authority."

No contractual obligation having been undertaken by the individual owners, we look to see if any obligation is imposed on the dominant tenement by law. While *Ingling* v. *Public Service Elec. & Gas Co.* concerns itself with a different type easement and with problems of a somewhat different nature, we are satisfied that it correctly imposes upon the owner (or owners) of a dominant tenement—in the case before us an easement over lands of another—the duty of maintenance and repair. The *right* [sic] of the dominant tenant to maintain and repair has been recognized as an incident to the beneficial use of the easement. Convinced that with the benefit ought to come the burden, absent agreement to the contrary, we hold that the *obligation* to maintain devolves upon the dominant tenant. This is certainly the rule where the easement is solely for the benefit of the dominant estate. In our judgment there are compelling equitable reasons to apply the rule to the situation before us even though there may well be incidental use of these roads by others than the individual landowners.

We make it abundantly clear that by the enunciation of this rule we are not establishing plaintiff-appellant as a *"quasi*-municipal" agency. As a matter of fact we do not even suggest what the relationship or obligations, administrative or otherwise, of the appellant association should be in the scheme of things. Further we are not mandating [a joining] of the association by those of the individual owners who are not members. We are merely declaring the obligation of all the individual owners to contribute to the repair and maintenance of the easement in question.

Affirmed. The matter is remanded to the Chancery Division for further proceedings consistent with the foregoing, including the fashioning of a remedy.

Easement in Gross. An easement in gross exists independently of a dominant estate. The privileges given by the easement belong to an individual independently of ownership or possession of any specific land. Because of the personal nature of the easement, many American jurisdictions will not allow a non-commercial easement in gross to be transferred. Commercial easements in gross, because of their importance to the public, are transferable.

Creation of Easements. Because an easement is an interest in land, it can be created only by a written instrument or by prescription. Most easements are created by an express grant or reservation in a deed or similar instrument, but an easement may be implied in connection with a conveyance. In order to establish an easement by prescription, the claimant must prove that the use of the property was adverse, open, notorious, and continuous throughout the statutory period. Prescription is discussed in the following chapter.

Profit à Prendre and License

Other important nonpossessory interests are the profit à prendre, the license, and the lien.

A profit à prendre or profit is an interest in real property similar in many ways to an easement in gross. The distinguishing difference is that the owner of a profit has the right to take something of supposed value from the land. The right to cut and remove timber or to quarry and take gravel are examples of a profit. The profit carries with it the right to enter upon the land. Since a profit is an interest in land, it is irrevocable.

A license differs from a profit in that the license is merely a personal privilege to enter upon the land of another for a particular purpose. A license is not an interest in real property. Holding a ticket to an athletic event or occupying a motel room are examples of license. Most licenses are revocable at the will of the owner of the property on which the license is exercised; however, if a license is coupled with an interest in the land, license may not be revoked.

Liens

A lien is a very important nonpossessory interest in land. It is a right existing in the property of another to secure payment of a debt or performance of some obligation. Some liens are created by statute, others by agreement of the parties. Liens can exist in both real and personal property. A real property lien with which most people are familiar is the mortgage. Mortgages are discussed in the following chapter.

CO-OWNERSHIP

A third division of rights in land exists when several people own undivided interests in a parcel of land at the same time. Generally in this type of ownership each person is entitled to a specific fraction of the parcel but also shares with the others a single right to possession and profits from the land. This is generally referred to as concurrent ownership or co-ownership. Co-ownership is often used for holding investment real estate.

Co-ownership was important to the common law, and the various concurrent estates that developed at common law remain important today. A number of legal problems are associated with these common law concurrent estates. These problems are reduced or eliminated if multiple owners use a partnership, corporation, or trust to hold title to the property. As a result, such devices are becoming increasingly important in real estate, replacing the common law forms of multiple ownership.

Joint Tenancy

The principal feature of a joint tenancy is the right of survivorship. This means that upon the death of one of the co-owners, that person's interest passed automatically to surviving joint owners. Historically, the joint tenancy was important in real property law because of the right of survivorship. As the political and economic systems in England developed, ownership of an estate by a single individual enhanced the ability of the aristocracy to retain power. Eventual ownership by only one of the co-owners was encouraged by recognizing an automatic transfer of the interest of other co-owners upon death. Although joint tenancy has had a role in American law, it was never as important in this country as it was in England because of the different social and economic conditions in the two countries.

Today, in some states, statutes prohibit the creation of a joint tenancy with the right of survivorship. In most states it is still possible to have a joint tenancy, but the person establishing it must clearly indicate that this is the intention.

Rights of Joint Tenants. Each co-owner who holds a joint tenancy has an equal right to possession of the entire property. This is referred to as an undivided interest. Although a joint tenant may not exclude other joint tenants from possession, the law considers occupancy by one as occupancy by all. If each tenant is to benefit, all must agree to share the property. Where agreement cannot be reached, the tenancy must be terminated.

Termination of Joint Tenancy. A joint tenancy is terminated if one of the owners sells his or her interest. In some states a joint tenancy is terminated if an owner's interest is mortgaged. The joint tenancy is also terminated if the interest of a joint tenant is sold to satisfy a debt. In any case, a person who acquires the interest of a joint tenant becomes a tenant in common with the remaining co-owners.

Tenancy in Common

A tenancy in common is a form of co-ownership in which each owner possesses an individual interest in a parcel of land, but other than that each owner's rights are the same as those possessed by a sole owner. Although the joint tenancy was for centuries the favored form of co-ownership, today English and American law favor the tenancy in common. In almost all states, a tenancy in common is implied unless a joint tenancy is clearly indicated by the instrument creating the concurrent estate.

Rights of Tenants in Common. Like joint tenants, each tenant in common has an undivided right to possession of the entire parcel. Normally, a tenant in common will not be responsible to his co-owners for any benefits obtained through exclusive occupancy. At the same time, no tenant in common is entitled to the exclusive use of any part of the land. The result is that problems arise when one co-tenant wrongfully excludes the others or when the property can be practically occupied only by a single tenant. Under the circumstances, in a number of states, the co-tenants not in occupancy will be entitled to a fair compensation for the use of the property. Similar problems arise where a co-tenant not in possession receives benefits from the property exceeding those of his or her co-owners. These types of problems can best be solved by agreement among the parties, as can problems involving liability of co-tenants for upkeep and improvements. When agreement cannot be reached, partition of property may be the only solution.

Partition. An action by which a co-owner obtains a division of property terminating any interest of other co-owners in the divided portion, partition is the historic method by which unwilling concurrent owners of real property may terminate the interests of fellow co-owners. Although courts traditionally ordered partition even when no statute authorized them to do so, today partition exists in some form by statute in every state. In a few states, statutory language is broad enough to include partition when owners are divorced. Many states also make the remedy available to some holders of future interests. Under the law of almost all states, co-owners of personal property enjoy the right to partition to the same degree as co-owners of realty.

Tenancy by the Entirety

Nearly half the states recognize tenancy by the entirety, a type of co-ownership existing only between husband and wife. This type of co-ownership is based upon an ancient legal fiction by which the common law regarded husband and wife as a single legal person. One result was that if the two acquired equal interests in real estate by the same instrument, the property was considered owned as an indivisible legal unit. Upon the death of either, the survivor remained as the parcel's sole owner. This result has also been accepted by modern law. Today a right of survivorship exists for the tenancy by entirety similar to that existing for the joint tenancy. In a small estate this right benefits the surviving spouse as it avoids the necessity and cost of probate proceedings.

A tenancy by the entirety is a more stable type of co-ownership than the joint tenancy. Because the marital partners are considered as a single unit, neither husband nor wife can sever the tenancy without the other's consent. Unlike the joint tenancy, a sale by either husband or wife does not terminate the tenancy nor end the right of survivorship.

In many jurisdictions a tenancy by the entirety cannot be terminated by the forced sale of the husband's or wife's interest. This means that if either spouse refuses to pay an individually incurred debt, the creditor cannot attach —that is, judicially seize—his or her interest in the property. This rule has been criticized for permitting the debtor to escape responsibility while owning an interest in a valuable asset. In a few states, creditors of the husband, but not of the wife, may reach the income, profits, and title of the property. Whatever interest these creditors acquire is lost if the wife survives. Other states permit the separate creditors of either spouse to levy upon and sell the share of the debtor, whether husband or wife. If the opposite spouse survives, the creditor is deprived of his or her interest. If the creditor holds a joint judgment against both spouses, the creditor can attach the estate held by the entirety.

Tenancies by the entireties are terminated primarily by divorce because the marital relationship is essential to this form of co-ownership. Upon divorce the parties become tenants in common.

Tenancy in Partnership

Most states have adopted the Uniform Partnership Act, which creates the tenancy in partnership. This act permits a partnership to buy, hold, and sell real estate in the partnership name. Individual partners share ownership in particular property only as members of the firm. Spouses, heirs, and creditors of individual partners have no rights in partnership property. Although an individual partner can transfer partnership real property, any transfer is made only as an agent for the firm. Upon the death of any partner, that person's share passes to surviving partners.

Community Property

Community property is a form of co-ownership between husband and wife in which each has a half interest in property acquired by the labor of either during marriage. A number of jurisdictions in the United States apply the doctrine of community property to property owned by a husband or wife. The states in which community property is an integral part of the legal system are Arizona, California, Idaho, Louisiana, Nevada, New Mexico, Texas, and Washington. Since community property ownership is statutory, each state varies the characteristics of the system to fit its own needs.

Community property is based on the marital relationship. In community property jurisdictions, the husband and wife are regarded as partners. Each becomes a co-owner with the other in all property acquired by the labor or skill of either while the two are married. This rule applies even though title to the property is individually held by the husband or wife.

Property owned by the husband or wife prior to marriage and property acquired during marriage by gift, inheritance, or will does not become community property. In addition, any real property purchased with the separate property of one spouse who takes title in his or her name remains separate property.

Condominiums and Cooperatives

Condominiums and cooperatives are nontraditional forms of co-ownership that have become significant factors in the real estate market since World War II. In both cooperatives and condominiums, owners enjoy individual control over designated units in a facility, usually an apartment or office building, while sharing portions of the facility with other owners. This type of ownership is generally found in urban areas where land values have increased because of the concentration of population. Condominium and cooperative ownership is based on statutes, which vary considerably from state to state.

Condominiums. In condominium ownership, a person individually owns part of a building. At the same time, he or she has ownership rights as a tenant in common with other condominium owners in elements of the real estate necessary for effective utilization of the entire structure. This includes land, walls, halls, lobbies, and service facilities such as elevators and heating and plumbing systems. Because each unit is owned separately and the owner possesses an undivided interest in the common elements, a person may sell, mortgage, or lease his or her unit individually.

The condominium is created by a declaration, a document describing the parcel, units in the structure, and the rights and duties of condominium owners. A set of bylaws regulates the operation and maintenance of the building. Owners of the units share in the costs of maintaining the common elements of the real estate. The case that follows illustrates one type of problem that arises in condominium ownership.

Ritchey v. Villa Nueva Condominium Association

Court of Appeals, California

146 Cal.Rptr. 695 (1978)

Joe B. Ritchey (plaintiff-appellant) purchased a two-bedroom unit in the Villa Nueva condominium project. He rented the unit to Dorothy Westphal, a woman with two young children. This violated a bylaw of the condominium restricting occupancy to persons 18 years of age and older. The Villa Nueva Condominium Association (defendant-respondent) brought suit to remove Westphal, who moved out before an answer could be filed. Ritchey then commenced this action seeking an injunction and declaratory relief, as well as damages for malicious prosecution, abuse of process, and interference with a contractual relationship. Both parties filed for summary judgment. The court denied Ritchey's motion and granted Villa Nueva's. Ritchey appealed. Held: Affirmed.

Caldecott, J.

Appellant challenges the validity of an amendment to the bylaws of the Villa Nueva Condominium project which restricts occupancy in the high-rise portion of the project to persons 18 years of age and older. Appellant contends that such an age restriction is per se unreasonable. In addition, he argues that under the circumstances of the present case, the occupancy restriction cannot reasonably be enforced against him.

Appellant urges that an age restriction is patently unreasonable in that it discriminates against families with children. Age restrictions in condominium documents have not been specifically tested in our courts. Nevertheless, we conclude on the basis of statutory and case authority that such restrictions are not per se unreasonable.

In *Flowers* v. *John Burnham & Co.,* an apartment house restriction limiting tenancy to adults, female children of all ages, and male children under the age of five was held not to violate the Unruh Act guaranteeing equal access to "accommodations, advantages, facilities, privileges, or services in all business establishments of every kind whatsoever." The court noted that arbitrary discrimination by a landlord is prohibited by the act, but held: "Because the independence, mischievousness, boisterousness and rowdyism of children vary by age and sex . . . [the defendant], as landlord, seeks to limit the children in its apartments to girls of all ages and boys under five. Regulating tenants' ages and sex to that extent is not unreasonable or arbitrary."

Similarly, in *Riley* v. *Stoves,* the Arizona Court of Appeals upheld a covenant in a deed restricting occupancy of a subdivision to persons 21 years of age or older: "The restriction flatly prevents children from living in the mobile home subdivision. The obvious purpose is to create a quiet, peaceful neighborhood by eliminating noise associated with children at play or otherwise. . . .

"We do not think the restriction is in any way arbitrary. It effectively insures that only working or retired adults will reside on the lots. It does much to eliminate the noise and distractions caused by children. We find it reasonably related to a legitimate purpose and therefore decline to hold that its enforcement violated defendants' rights to equal protection."

It should also be noted that the United States Congress has adopted several programs to provide housing for the elderly, setting an age minimum of 62 years for occupancy. As the Riley court observed, "These sections represent an implicit legislative finding that not only do older adults need inexpensive housing, but also that their housing interests and needs differ from families with children."

Under Civil Code section 1355, reasonable amendments to restrictions relating to a condominium project are binding upon every owner and every condominium in that project "whether the burdens thereon are increased or decreased thereby, and whether the owner of each and every condominium consents thereto or not." Whether an amendment is reasonable depends upon the circumstances of the particular case.

The amendment of the bylaws here in issue operates both as a restraint upon the owner's right of alienation, and as a limitation upon his right of occupancy. However, for the reasons hereinafter discussed, we conclude that under the facts of this case the amendment is reasonable. For the sake of simplicity, we will address each of these aspects of the amendment independently.

THE RESTRAINT UPON ALIENATION

Article IX of the bylaws expressly provides that, to the extent that the bylaws conflict with applicable federal and state statutes and regulations, the provisions of such statutes or regulations will apply. This provision is in accordance with the general rule that all applicable laws in existence when an agreement is made necessarily enter into the contract and form part of it.

Title 10 of the Administrative Code provides that restrictions in the bylaws may limit the right of an owner to sell or lease his condominium unit so long as the standards are uniform and objective, and are not based upon the race, creed, color, national origin or sex of the purchaser or lessee. It thus appears that a restriction upon alienation can be based upon the age of the vendee or lessee, or his family.

THE LIMITATION UPON OCCUPANCY

Appellant purchased his condominium unit approximately 16 months prior to the enactment of Article XI, section 3, of the bylaws. At that time, the enabling declaration establishing a plan for condominium ownership, the model form of subscription and purchase agreement, and the report issued to the public by HUD, consistently referred to units in the condominium project as "family home units" or "family units" located in "multi-family structures," and emphasized their suitability for families with children. Appellant states that he relied upon these representations when he purchased his unit.

Appellant, however, does not claim that any of these representations were false or were made to mislead him. As far as the record shows, appellant, at the time of his purchase and for several months thereafter, could lease the premises to a person with children under 18 years of age. Furthermore, appellant does not contend that it was represented to him that the conditions of occupancy would not be changed. In fact, at the time of his purchase, the enabling declaration specifically provided that the bylaws could be amended, and that he would be subject to any reasonable amendment that was properly adopted. Thus, the amendment is reasonable.

Appellant contends that the association exceeded the scope of its authority in enacting an age restriction on occupancy. He argues that the association was established for the sole purpose of operating and maintaining the common areas and facilities of the condominium project, and that any attempt to limit or prescribe the use of the individually owned units was ultra vires. This argument is without merit.

The authority of a condominium association necessarily includes the power to issue reasonable regulations governing an owner's use of his unit in order to prevent activities which might prove annoying to the general residents. Thus, an owners' association can prohibit any activity or conduct that could constitute a nuisance, regulate the disposition of refuse, provide for the maintenance and repair of interiors of apartments as well as exteriors, and prohibit or regulate the keeping of pets.

Therefore, a reasonable restriction upon occupancy of the individually owned units of a condominium project is not beyond the scope of authority of the owner's association

The judgment is affirmed.

Cooperatives. In cooperative (often called a co-op) ownership, an individual controls a unit in a building, but the land and building itself are owned by some type of association, often a corporation. The corporation's shareholders are the building's tenants. An individual's right to a particular unit is based upon a lease from the association, available only because he or she is a shareholder. The bylaws of the corporation detail the rights and duties of the tenants. Although the building is maintained by the association, maintenance expenses are shared by the shareholder-tenants. Because the individual does not own the unit to which he or she is entitled, individual financing is not available. Most bylaws restrict the individual's right to transfer his or her lease.

Real Estate Investment Trusts

The trust is a device that has been used in the United States and England for centuries. The premise upon which the trust is based is the division of property interests among owners. In a trust, one person or an institution is given specific property that is managed for the benefit of others. The property may be real or personal. The trust has been an important instrument for law reform and the legal basis for some significant economic innovations. One of these is the Real Estate Investment Trust (REIT).

A REIT is an organization in which trustees own real estate or loans secured by real estate that they manage for beneficiaries who hold transferable shares representing their respective interests.

Business trusts such as REITs developed during the first three decades of the twentieth century because they enjoyed some tax advantages over the corporate form of business organization. Income earned by the trust was not taxable as long as it was distributed to the trust beneficiaries. Of course, the distributed income was taxable to each of them. Income earned by a corporation is taxable both to the corporation and to shareholders when distributed. This tax advantage of REITs was eliminated by court decision in 1935 but restored by statute after World War II, when Congress approved legislation allowing investment trusts dealing in real estate to serve as a conduit through which income passes without being taxed twice.

LAND AND THE LAW

The variety of interests that can exist in real property illustrate the interrelationships between legal, economic, and social systems, a point developed throughout this text. Land has always been a critical factor in economic and social life in the Western world. Until the nineteenth century, for most people, survival depended upon access to land, and land was the principal source of wealth in both Europe and the Americas. In addition, both political power and social status were often dependent upon land ownership.

Land's importance in the past and today is reflected in real estate law. Innovative use of air rights which is basic to condominium and cooperative ownership exemplifies the dynamic vitality of the legal system as it responds to a world of changed social, economic, and political conditions. At the same time the historic interests in real property that continue to be useful to society—such as the concept of estates—are links that join the past and present.

REVIEW PROBLEMS

1. May conveyed to Tenneco, Inc., an easement crossing a portion of his land. Using this easement, Tenneco constructed and put into service an underground natural gas pipeline. Several years later May constructed a road over a portion of Tenneco's easement. Federal regulations require installation of a protective encasement around pipe where it passes under a street. Tenneco installed the encasement at a cost of $4,903.39 and billed May for this amount. May refuses to pay and Tenneco sues. Would Tenneco be successful? Discuss. Tenneco, Inc. v. May, 512 F.2d 1381 (1975)

2. Cushman is developing Blackacre as a residential subdivision. Prior to Cushman's acquisition of the property, Blackacre had been an apricot orchard. A roadway based upon an easement ran from the orchard to a public street. This property subject to the roadway easement was owned by Davis. The road had existed for many years. Its primary use was to move spraying and picking equipment into the orchard. This was done about ten times each year. Davis also used the road for access to his home and to a water tank. From time to time others used the road to reach the orchard. Cushman seeks to quiet title to the easement for access to the subdivision and Davis strenuously objects. Will Cushman be successful in his quiet title action? Discuss. Cushman v. Davis, 145 Col.Rptr. 791 (1978)

3. The will of Alma H. Rand contained the following provision: "3rd. That the share of the Estate of Henry Rand of the town of Southport, Lincoln County, State of Maine, shall be left to John Freeman Rand in fee simple *with the proviso that he shall never deny access or occupation to the several heirs hereinafter named during their lifetime.*" What kind of estate did John Rand have as a result of this provision? Explain. Babb v. Rand, 345 A.2d 496 (1974)

4. The Chelsea Yacht Club owned a clubhouse that had been erected on piles driven into the bed of the Mystic River. The land was owned by the state, but the club had secured a license to construct the building. The only access to the clubhouse was over the Chelsea North Bridge. Both clubhouse and bridge were over sixty years old. Because of the age of the bridge, the state constructed a new bridge several miles away. The old bridge was removed. This left the clubhouse surrounded by water. The club sued the bridge authority for damages occasioned by the loss of access over the bridge. On what theory might the club sue the bridge authority? Would the club be successful? Discuss. Chelsea Yacht Club v. Mystic River Bridge Authority, 116 N.E.2d 153 (1953)

5. Luithle and his wife owned real estate as joint tenants. Luithle purchased cattle from Schlichenmayer, paying for the cattle with a worthless check. Luithle immediately sold the cattle. Part of the proceeds were used to make a $1,100 mortgage payment on the real property that the couple owned. A short time later Luithle died and Schlichenmayer sued the wife to recover the $1,100 on grounds that she was unjustly enriched. Would Luithle be successful? Discuss. Schlichenmayer v. Luithle, 221 N.W.2d 77 (1974)

CHAPTER 35

Acquisition, Financing, and Control of Real Property

T he previous chapter explained the concept of title or ownership and outlined some of the interests that can exist in real property. This chapter discusses the various ways of acquiring title, some methods of financing its acquisition, and common means for controlling how real property is used.

Title or ownership of real property may be acquired in a number of ways. Although purchase is the most common, individuals and sometimes business firms become owners of real property by gift from living donors or by inheritance. Acquisition of real property as a result of the death of the owner is treated in Chapter 36. Gifts are discussed in Chapter 33.

Governments or those authorized by government can acquire title to real property by exercising the power of eminent domain, and in limited instances a person or firm can obtain title to property by adverse possession or unauthorized occupancy.

ADVERSE POSSESSION

Obtaining title by adverse possession is a legal anomaly, for the doctrine allows a person occupying land as a trespasser to defeat the rights of the true owner. The justification for this unusual policy is that society benefits when idle land is put to use. The legal system encourages the use of land by providing a person occupying land wrongfully with a means to establish clear title.

Balanced against the policy of encouraging land use is the traditional concern of Anglo-American law with the protection of private property rights. The law does not favor the derogation of these rights by unlawful actions adverse to the owner's interests. Because of the importance of protecting private property, an adverse occupant acquires title only if prescribed conditions are met and certain acts occur. These acts and conditions exist to ensure that the owner has an opportunity to discover challenges to his or her title and a reasonable chance to protect it.

Statutes of Limitations

Basic to all adverse possession claims are state statutes of limitations. These statutes establish a period of time during which the rightful owner of land must bring an action to oust the trespasser.

At common law the owner had to bring suit within twenty years, and several states have adopted this as the limitation period. Although only a handful of states allow the owner more than twenty years to act, a substantial number apply shorter periods. These range from five to eighteen years. Many of the states with short limitation periods are in the sparsely populated western United States. This reflects the public policy underlying adverse possession, which is to encourage land use. In some states the limitation period is reduced if the adverse possessor has paid taxes or occupies the land on the basis of a document such as an invalid deed or will.

A number of states allow occupancy of two or more successive adverse possessors to be added together to establish possession for the necessary period. This is called tacking, since the periods are "tacked" together. Although tacking is probably permitted in a majority of

states, some jurisdictions limit it to cases involving heirs, spouses, or blood relatives.

Elements of Adverse Possession

Generally five elements must exist for title to be acquired by adverse possession. In addition to proving continuous possession for the statutory period, the claimant must establish that possession is open and notorious, hostile, actual, and exclusive.

Open and Notorious. Open and notorious acts are those that will alert the true owner to claims that are adverse to his or her rights. Although the true owner does not have to acquire actual knowledge of what is taking place, the acts must be such that a diligent owner would become aware of them.

Hostile. As the elements of adverse possession are not mutually exclusive, acts that are open and notorious are often hostile. The requirement that possession be hostile does not connote ill will or evil intent but merely that the person in possession of the property claims to occupy as the owner. Most state courts accept that possession is hostile for purposes of adverse possession if the occupant claims ownership whether by mistake or willfully. A person who enters into property with the owner's permission cannot claim successfully by adverse possession unless he or she repudiates the owner's title.

Actual Possession. Actual possession consists of exercising dominion over land, making ordinary use of it, and taking the ordinary profit the land is capable of yielding. Courts determine actual possession by looking at the character of the land that is involved. Residence upon the property is not necessary unless this is the use that would be expected. In a few states the adverse possessor must enclose the land to establish a claim; however, in most states enclosure, while a good indication of possession, is not required.

Exclusive Use. Exclusive use means that the claimant possesses the land for his or her own use. Total exclusion of others is not required, but the adverse possessor must exclude others as would be expected of an owner under the circumstances. Occasional use by others, even the rightful owner, does not negate exclusiveness if the use permitted by the adverse possessor is consistent with his or her claims of ownership. The following case involves the element of exclusive use and several other aspects of adverse possession.

Porter v. Posey

Missouri Court of Appeals
592 S.W. 2d 844 (1979)

This was an action brought by Eugene and Grace Porter (plaintiffs-appellees) to quiet title to .18 acres of land. The land in dispute was within property described in a deed to Donald E. and Edna Posey (defendants-appellants). The Poseys had purchased their property in October 1975. In July 1976, the Porters purchased the adjoining land from the Englemeyers.

The Englemeyers had purchased this land in three parcels between June 1955 and January 1956. Soon after the Englemeyers acquired the three parcels, they cleared the disputed tract with a bulldozer and built a graveled turnaround roadway on it. The Englemeyers maintained and used the turnaround until 1976, when they transferred their property to plaintiffs. In addition to the turnaround, the Englemeyers used the disputed tract as a means of access to their property and as a site for volleyball games and overflow parking. The Englemeyers believed they owned the turnaround and the land upon which it was built.

Sometime prior to purchasing their land in October 1975, the Poseys had the property surveyed and discovered that the turnaround was within the property lines described in their deed. Sometime later, apparently in the summer of 1976, the father of defendant Donald Posey threatened Mr. Englemeyer with a shotgun and told him to get off the land in dispute.

Shortly after the Porters took title to the property purchased from the Englemeyers, defendant Donald Posey installed a cable blocking access to the turnaround. The Porters then sued to quiet title to the disputed tract. The lower court quieted title in them and the Poseys appealed. Held: Affirmed.

Satz, Judge

Limited by the record to plaintiffs' theory, the crucial questions in this case are: (1) was title to the tract in dispute vested in the Englemeyers; (2) if so, was their title subsequently extinguished or divested; and (3) if not divested or extinguished, was their title properly transferred to plaintiffs.

In order for the trial court to have vested title in plaintiffs on the present record, it must have found that title first vested in the Englemeyers by adverse possession.

Thus, implicit in the court's ultimate decision is a finding that the Englemeyers occupied the tract in dispute intending to possess it as their own, or, more specifically, that the Engelmeyers occupied or used the tract and their occupation or use of the tract was (1) actual (2) open and notorious (3) hostile (4) exclusive and (5) continuous for ten years. Defendants limit their attack on these implicit findings to an attack on the open and notorious, hostile and exclusive elements of the Engelmeyers' adverse possession.

Open and notorious occupancy or possession is an essential element of adverse possession because the openness and notoriety of the occupancy or possession gives the owner cause to know that an adverse claim of ownership is being made by another. The determination of openness and notoriety centers on whether the particular acts in question are acts of ownership and are sufficient to give the existing owner notice of the claim being made. Thus, the element of open and notorious is satisfied by a showing that the occupancy or possession manifested a claim of ownership and was conspicuous, widely recognized and commonly known.

In the instant case, the Engelmeyers entered the disputed tract with a bulldozer, cleared the land, built the turnaround, then maintained it and the land surrounding it. The family also played volleyball and parked on this land. In addition, a neighbor testified that he believed the Engelmeyers to be the owners of this tract of land because they were the only ones who maintained it and used it with any regularity for a period of 18 years. Changing the physical structure of the land by clearing it, building a turnaround and then using and maintaining the turnaround was sufficient evidence to support the court's finding that the Engelmeyers' acts were acts of ownership, sufficient to give the then existing owner notice of this claim and were commonly known so as to constitute open and notorious occupancy or possession.

Defendants argue that the playing of volleyball and the parking of cars on the land in question were so "friendly in character" that these acts failed to give the then existing owner—defendants' predecessors in title—notice of a claim of ownership. Defendants, however, conveniently omit the fact that the parking of cars and playing of volleyball were not isolated acts or incidents but were combined with the noted clearing of the land, the building of the turnaround and the continuous use and maintenance of this turnaround and its surrounding land.

Defendants next argue that the Engelmeyers' use and possession was not hostile. Hostility of possession does not imply ill will or acrimony. Moreover, to prove hostility, an expressed declaration of hostility need not be made. Hostile possession is simply an assertion of ownership adverse to that of the true owner and all others; i.e., "the claimant must occupy the land with the intent to possess it as his own and not in subservience to a recognized, superior claim of another." Thus, as with other elements of adverse possession, the element of hostility is founded upon the intent with which the claimant held possession and, since the elements of adverse possession are not mutually exclusive, acts which are open and notorious, supporting a claim of ownership, may and often do logically satisfy the element that the claim be hostile.

In the present case, as we have previously noted, there was sufficient evidence for the trial court to find that the Engelmeyers occupied and used the disputed tract with the intent to possess it as their own and, thus, clearly their use and occupancy was hostile.

Defendants' next attack on adverse possession is that the Engelmeyers' possession was not exclusive because others occasionally used the turnaround and, thus, defendants contend, plaintiffs' evidence, at best, merely established a common easement by prescription. This argument ignores the fact that the element of exclusivity is also required to establish an easement by prescription; and, therefore, if there were exclusive use to satisfy that element for a prescriptive easement, arguably that use would satisfy the element of exclusive use required by adverse possession.

Be that as it may, possession or use is exclusive when the claimant occupies or uses the land for his own use and not for that of another. The present record reveals that the Engelmeyers built the turnaround believing it to be on their property. The fact that travelers occasionally also used this roadway to turn around does not imply nor indicate that the Engelmeyers occupied the land for the benefit of these travelers. Indeed, even occasional use of disputed property by the record owner will not of itself negate the exclusive use by an adverse claimant, if the record owner's knowledge or notice of the adverse claim is not otherwise altered. For these reasons, defendants' argument against exclusivity is not persuasive.

The remaining question, then, is whether the Engelmeyers properly transferred title to plaintiffs. As noted, the principle urged by plaintiffs to support the Engelmeyers' transfer of title to plaintiffs, in effect, permits title to property acquired by adverse possession to be transferred without a written conveyance, and simply requires the title owner to intend to transfer the property so acquired and the transferee to receive or take possession of that property. In addition, this principle implicitly permits a person acquiring title by adverse possession to convey it to another without having title quieted in him prior to the conveyance; and it also permits an oral conveyance of title which seemingly violates the requirement that land may only be conveyed by a written instrument. Moreover, facially, the principle parallels and is similar to the doctrine of ''tacking'' which permits an adverse possessor, in possession of land for less than the prescriptive period, to add his period of possession to that of a prior adverse possessor in order to establish a continuous possession for the requisite prescriptive period.

Defendants do not directly attack the validity or propriety of this principle. Rather, as we understand defendants' argument, they argue the principle is inapplicable here because the Engelmeyers' intent to transfer ownership or title to the disputed tract could only support a valid conveyance of that ownership or title if, but only if, the Engelmeyers and plaintiffs did not recognize that another party, the defendants, owned a deed describing the tract; i.e., the Engelmeyers' and plaintiffs' recognition of record title in defendants precluded plaintiffs, in defendants' language, from ''tacking'' their possession to the Engelmeyers' possession. We do not agree.

In the present case, Mrs. Engelmeyer's unrefuted testimony was that she and her husband intended to convey the disputed tract to plaintiffs. Moreover, this was plaintiffs' understanding, and the fact that plaintiff Eugene Porter sought legal advice to carry out that intention merely enforces the weight to be given to Mrs. Engelmeyer's testimony. Further, there was sufficient explicit testimony and inferential evidence for the trial court to find that, after the transfer, plaintiffs took possession of the disputed tract. Thus, the Engelmeyers transferred their title to the disputed tract to plaintiffs.

The judgment of the trial court is affirmed.

Prescription

The previous chapter described the easement, a nonpossessory right to use the land of another for a particular purpose. Most easements are created by written instruments; however, an easement may be created by prescription, a legal doctrine similar in several ways to adverse possession. Both are based upon wrongful invasion of the property rights of the true owner, but prescription is based on adverse use, not occupancy. As a result, a person acquiring a prescriptive easement merely acquires a right to use another's land, while the successful adverse possessor actually acquires title. Another common difference between the two is that the time necessary to acquire an easement by prescription is frequently less than the time required to acquire title by adverse possession.

EMINENT DOMAIN

Eminent domain is the power of the sovereign to acquire private property without the owner's consent. Although this power is inherent in the sovereign, both state constitutions and the Constitution of the United States place limitations upon it. Three principal limitations exist: the property must be used for a public purpose; the owner must be adequately compensated; and the property cannot be taken without due process of law. The latter limitation in effect guarantees the owner an opportunity to be heard before a fair, competent tribunal on questions such as the amount of compensation or whether the property is being acquired for "public use." Both the United States and the individual states may delegate the power of eminent domain. Authority to exercise this power is frequently conferred upon political subdivisions such as cities and counties as well as public service corporations. Individuals and private corporations may also be authorized to exercise the power of eminent domain.

PURCHASE AND SALE OF REAL PROPERTY

The purchase and sale of real property should be of special interest to business students because they will probably participate in several such transactions. The large amounts of money, long-term financial commitments, and technical legal procedures that are incidental to most real estate sales make knowledge of these transactions particularly important.

Buying and selling real estate involves several legal areas. Agency and contract law are especially important. Agency is significant, since a brokerage system plays a major role throughout the United States in the real estate business. Many real estate sales are negotiated by brokers, and brokers are involved in leasing, property management, and appraisal of real estate. The importance of the contract in the real estate business can hardly be overemphasized. It is the critical document in a real estate sale, and it governs the relationship between brokers and clients and between landlords and tenants.

Anatomy of a Real Estate Sale

The typical real estate sale in the United States is usually the result of a period of negotiation between buyer and seller, often with the help of a real estate broker. In some areas, especially for residential real estate, a person desiring to buy will submit an offer to the seller. This is often referred to as a "purchase offer" or "offer to purchase." Buyers should realize that this document's terms become the contract if the seller accepts. The seller, however, can reject or make a counteroffer if not satisfied with the purchase offer terms. In this case the negotiations often continue, and a contract on different terms may or may not eventuate.

Another procedure, probably more frequently used in commercial transactions, is for the parties, at a point when agreement appears to have been reached, to meet, settle any remaining terms, and execute a document expressing the terms of their agreement. Whatever procedure is used, statutory provisions in all states require that a contract for the sale of real property be in writing to be enforceable.

Equitable Title. When a contract for the sale of real estate is completed, the buyer acquires equitable title. This gives the buyer the right to sue for damages or specific performance if the seller refuses to perform. Simultaneously, the seller acquires a right to enforce the contract.

Whatever process of contract formation is used in a real estate sale, almost inevitably an interval of time takes place between the making of the contract and its performance. Customarily during this period, the buyer completes the necessary arrangements for financing and examines the seller's title. If the title is defective, the seller has an opportunity to cure defects prior to the date set for title closing. When title closes, the buyer obtains legal title by a deed and the seller gets the purchase price.

Risk of Loss. As the buyer has equitable title during the period between contract signing and title closing, in some states the buyer must bear the risk of loss or damage to the property. If the property is damaged by fire, the buyer in these states is required to complete the transaction as agreed. A number of jurisdictions reject this rule as unfair, especially when the buyer is not in possession. These states allow the buyer an adjustment in the price to compensate for the loss. The allocation of the risk of loss should not be left to state law. The problem can and should be settled by the parties in their contract.

Title Closing. Two types of title closing are common in the United States. In most areas the parties involved in the transaction meet as a group and exchange the funds and documents required to complete the transfer. Ordinarily, buyer, seller, brokers, a representative of the institution financing the sale, and attorneys for each party are present.

In some localities, real estate sales close through a third party called an escrow agent. In an escrow closing, buyer and seller submit the necessary documents and funds to the escrow agent, who is responsible for seeing that the transaction closes on the terms agreed upon in the contract. When the seller delivers a properly executed deed to the escrow agent and the agent is assured that the seller is passing a good title, the funds and mortgage documents are turned over to the proper parties and the transaction is completed.

Deeds

Ownership of real property is transferred by an instrument called a deed. A deed is a two-party instrument. The person conveying the property is called the *grantor;* the person to whom the property is conveyed, the *grantee.* Several types of deeds are in common use in the United States. Ordinarily, the type of deed a seller will use is agreed upon in the contract of sale.

Warranty Deed. A warranty deed conveys title and warrants that the title is good and free of liens and encumbrances. The warranties are also referred to as covenants. They provide the purchaser with some protection against claims that might interfere with ownership.

Although the use and wording of particular covenants vary from one jurisdiction to another, four covenants are common in the

United States. One of these is called the *covenant of seisin* or *covenant of right to convey.* By this covenant the seller guarantees that he or she has good title and the right to transfer it. A second covenant used in many jurisdictions is the *covenant against encumbrances.* In making this covenant, the seller affirms that no encumbrances exist against the property. The *covenant of quiet enjoyment* and the *covenant of general warranty* are guarantees that the buyer will not be evicted from the property by someone with a title superior to the seller's. As a result of these two covenants, the seller agrees to defend the buyer's title against all lawful claims.

Warranty deed covenants do not assure the buyer that the seller has title, but they do provide a right to sue if a covenant is broken. This is a valuable right if the seller is solvent and still within the jurisdiction; however, a buyer should never rely upon a warranty deed.

Bargain and Sale Deed. A bargain and sale deed conveys title but contains no warranties. Although no formal guarantees of title are made, the bargain and sale deed is by nature contractual, and the seller implies that he or she has a title to convey. This deed has a number of variations. It will sometimes contain covenants against the seller's acts. If this is the case, the seller guarantees that he or she has done nothing that might adversely affect the title.

Quitclaim Deed. A quitclaim deed merely releases whatever interest the grantor has. Unlike the warranty deed and bargain and sale deed, the transferor by a quitclaim does not purport to convey title. If, however, the grantor has title, this interest is conveyed as effectively as it would be by a warranty or bargain and sale deed. Quitclaim deeds are commonly used to correct defective titles.

A deed is a complicated legal instrument that should be drafted by an attorney. To be valid, a deed must contain words of conveyance. These are words that indicate an intention to convey title. In addition, the instrument must identify a competent grantor and grantee, contain a legal description, and be properly signed and executed. A final requirement is a valid delivery and acceptance. Most legal problems involving deeds arise because someone claims the deed has not been properly delivered. The case that follows is an example.

Bennett v. Mings

Court of Civil Appeals of Texas
535 S.W.2d 408 (1976)

Nellie Mings (plaintiff-appellee) brought suit against Cyril C. Bennett (defendant-appellant) seeking the cancellation of a deed. Upon a jury verdict favorable to Mrs. Mings, the trial court ordered the deed canceled. Bennett's motion for a new trial was dismissed and he appealed. The court of civil appeals affirmed.

Ray, Justice

Appellant Bennett contends that the appellee failed to introduce any evidence to support the jury finding that Mrs. Mings did not intend for the deed to become operative as a conveyance, or in the alternative, that the evidence was insufficient to support the jury's verdict.

The evidence shows that on September 7, 1972, Nellie Mings, a lady ninety-one years of age at that time, signed a warranty deed conveying a tract of land with her home and furnishings located thereon, to her nephew, Cyril C. Bennett. Manual delivery of the deed was made to appellant and he put it in his safety deposit box. In December of 1973, appellee requested the return of the deed and appellant Bennett returned it to Mrs. Mings. A few days later, Bennett regained possession of the deed and recorded it. Upon learning of this, Mrs. Mings again demanded return of her deed, and upon Bennett's refusal, she brought this suit. The evidence is undisputed that originally both parties agreed that the deed would not be recorded until Mrs. Mings's death and that "delivery" was not then complete. Appellant stated that the deed still belonged to Mrs. Mings though he had it in his safety deposit box. Bennett testified that he got the deed the second time with the permission of Mrs. Mings because she wanted things cleared up before her death. Mrs. Mings testified that she surrendered the deed to Bennett only with the permission that he could use the deed for security, but that under no circumstances was the deed to be recorded. She further testified that she gave up the deed under Bennett's insistent demand and that she was put in fear.

Appellant contends that once there has been a complete and effective delivery of a deed, the delivery is absolute and unconditional and is operative immediately.

The jury found that Mrs. Mings signed the deed, but that Mrs. Mings did not intend the deed to become operative as a conveyance of her land, home and furnishings when it was delivered to Bennett and further, the jury found that no consideration was paid to Mrs. Mings.

Whether a deed has been delivered is a question for the jury's determination, . . . and the question is primarily one of the grantor's intent. . . .

In order to constitute delivery, a deed of conveyance must be placed in the hands of the grantee, or within his control, with the intention that it is to become presently operative as a conveyance. Without such intention manual delivery to the grantee is insufficient to pass title. . . .

The issue in the present case is whether or not at either time Bennett obtained possession of the deed that Mrs. Mings intended that the deed become immediately operative as a conveyance. The evidence is clear that when Bennett obtained possession of the deed the first time neither he nor Mrs. Mings felt that the deed constituted such delivery as to become immediately operative as a conveyance and Bennett so testified. However, when Bennett obtained the deed the second time he testified that she gave him the deed with permission to record it. Her testimony is in direct conflict with his and the jury could have properly inferred that Mrs. Mings gave Bennett the deed out of fear or that she let Bennett use the deed as security, but with no present intent that it become immediately operative as a conveyance. We conclude that it was the duty of the jury to weigh the conflicting evidence as it did, and to determine whether the requisite intent was present for the conveyance to be effective when Bennett obtained possession of the deed the second time. We have reviewed the evidence and hold that the jury was justified in finding that Mrs. Mings did not intend the deed to become operative as a conveyance of her land, home and furnishings.

The judgment of the trial court is affirmed.

Recording Statutes

All states have statutes requiring that important instruments affecting the title to real property be entered as part of the public record. In addition to deeds and mortgages, the statutes generally require that long-term leases, easements, assignments, and similar instruments be recorded. The purpose of these statutes is to notify third parties of interests that exist in a particular piece of land. This protects the third party from loss that might occur if he or she were to acquire an interest in land subject to unknown claims of another. It is important to note, however, that the recording statutes do not affect the validity of the instrument. An unrecorded deed or mortgage is enforceable between the original parties.

Recording statutes are based on the premise that if a real property interest is not recorded, a person acquiring a conflicting interest will have superior rights in the land. For example, if X conveys real property to Y, Y is required to record the deed. If Y does not and X fraudulently conveys to Z, Z may acquire an ownership interest superior to Y's. In order for this to occur, Z must be a good-faith purchaser. This means that Z must not have knowledge of the sale to Y and must give value for the property.

Constructive Notice. Constructive notice is knowledge that the law implies a person has. Constructive notice exists if a person without actual knowledge is in a position to have acquired it by reasonably investigating available sources. If a person acquiring an interest in realty knows something that would induce a reasonable person to make further inquiry, and none is made, the law presumes actual knowledge exists. In addition, any information that might be discovered by a careful check of the record is presumed known. A person with actual or constructive knowledge of a prior conflicting interest does not acquire his or her interest in good faith. The result is that a person who does not examine the record is penalized and the recording statutes operate effectively.

Fong v. Batton

District Court of Appeals of Florida
214 So.2d 649 (1968)

Catherine Batton (plaintiff-appellee) brought this action against Joe and Amy Fong (defendant-appellant) for breach of the covenant of seisin in a warranty deed dated July 31, 1966. Plaintiff alleged that the Fongs breached this covenant because the public record did not contain a deed showing title in Audrey Donaldson, their predecessor in title. The trial court granted plaintiff's motion for summary judgment and awarded her damages of $4,695. Defendant appealed. Reversed.

Hendry, Judge

This appeal was taken by the appellants who were the defendants in the Circuit Court of Dade County, from a final summary judgment in favor of the plaintiff. The action arose on the following facts: In 1948, according to the public records of Dade County, Florida, certain property at issue in this case was owned by Daisy A. Vitale; the public records show the recordation of a mortgage executed in 1949 by Audrey Donaldson and delivered to Daisy Vitale . . . . The next transaction shown in the public records was a conveyance of the property by Audrey Donaldson to the defendants in December, 1952. Public records do not show a deed from Vitale to Donaldson.

This appeal treats the two basic issues of law raised in this cause: first, whether the defendants complied with the covenant of seisin by conveying to the plaintiff title in the transaction of July 31, 1966; and secondly, whether the court below applied the proper measure of damages.

The plaintiff's cause of action was predicated upon defendant's having breached the covenant of seisin. The covenant of seisin is an assurance that a grantor has the very estate in quantity and quality which he purports to convey. Thus, seisin is breached if the grantor has no title at all or if part of the land is in the adverse possession of another. . . .

When the defendants delivered title to the plaintiff, the chain of title was imperfect for the reason that the conveyance from the grantor Vitale, to the grantee Donaldson, was not a matter of public record. We hold that this imperfection in the chain of title is insufficient to sustain a cause of action for breach of the covenant of seisin.

The record shows that the only pleading entered in this cause relating to the Vitale-Donaldson conveyance was an affidavit by the grantee Donaldson, in which she stated that she had been the grantee of all title and interest in the property, but had lost the actual deed and subsequently failed to record it in the public records. Both the affidavit and the public record presented the trial court with the factual and legal effect of a chain of title containing an unrecorded conveyance. Applying the rules of law to this set of facts, the court erred in holding that a breach of the covenant of seisin had occurred. Rather, the law is settled that, in the absence of a contractual provision calling for "marketable *record* title," or "marketable *abstract* title," an unrecorded link in the chain of title does not, in and of itself, create unmarketable title. In De Huy v. Osborne, . . . this distinction was discussed:

> "Every valid undertaking to convey land implies the conveyance of a good title, unless of course such an obligation is excluded by other provisions of the contract. . . . That obligation, however, where the contract does not in effect require the conveyance of a good marketable title 'of record,' may be discharged by the conveyance of a title resting partly in parol, but free from doubt upon questions of both law and fact. . . . But the distinction between 'a good marketable title,' and 'a good marketable title of record' or 'as shown by an abstract,' is obvious. . . . A vendor's obligation to deliver a good marketable title *of record* is not fulfilled when the validity of the title tendered depends upon material facts not susceptible of reasonably definite ascertainment or proof by record evidence, at any and all times, by those who may need to prove them for the protection of the title, or, in other words, when the title tendered is not deductible of record with reasonable certainty."

. . . The recordation statute, Sec. 695.01 Fla.Stat., F.S.A., has always been primarily intended to protect the rights of bona fide purchasers of property, and creditors of property owners, rather than the immediate parties to the conveyance to the property.

In Moyer v. Clark, . . . the Supreme Court stated that, "The statute obviously was not intended to have the result of requiring a grantee to record his own deed within a specified time, or lose an otherwise valid title."

In Luria v. Bank of Coral Gables, . . . the recording statute was the subject of this discussion:

"Our recording statute . . . requires deeds to be recorded to be effectual in law or equity against creditors or subsequent purchasers for a valuable consideration and without notice, and was never intended to affect the rights of anyone else. The record of deed is notice only to those who are bound to search for it (sic) to creditors and those who have subsequently acquired some interest or right in the property under the grantor or mortgagor."

Accordingly the summary final judgment appealed is reversed.

REAL PROPERTY AS SECURITY

Real property is often used to secure payment of a debt. Most purchases of a home or commercial real estate involve the use of real property as security. Because these transactions require large amounts of money, many buyers must borrow in order to complete them. When borrowing is necessary, the loan ordinarily is secured by an interest in the property. The security interest provides the lender with the right to have the property sold and the proceeds applied against the debt if the borrower fails to pay or defaults in some other manner. Security interests in real estate are established by mortgages and deeds of trust.

The Mortgage Transaction

Financing based upon a mortgage involves two instruments—the mortgage and a note or bond. The mortgage provides the lender with a security interest in the real estate; the note or bond contains the terms of the loan and establishes the borrower's personal obligation to pay.

The existence of the mortgage and note provides the lender alternative remedies in the event of default. Suit may be brought on the note and a personal judgment obtained against the debtor, or the real property may be sold and the proceeds applied against the debt. The latter remedy is called foreclosure.

If the lender wins a judgment on the note, the judgment may be collected by attaching other property or by garnisheeing the debtor's wages. If the security when sold does not bring enough to pay the debt, the lender may sue for the difference, using the note. A few states require the lender to choose either to foreclose against the collateral to pay the debt or to sue on the note.

Lien and Title Theories of Mortgages

Modern mortgage law can be traced to the early use of the mortgage in England. At common law a borrower who mortgaged real property as security actually transferred title to the lender. The lender obtained a deed just as if he had purchased the property. As the mortgage was given as security, the title that the lender acquired was not absolute. A provision in the mortgage called the defeasance clause provided that, if the debt was paid when due, transfer of title to the lender was voided. Title reverted to the borrower.

The historical theory that the mortgage conveys title to the mortgagee continues to be used in some states, referred to as *title theory* states. Even in these states, however, although the lender acquires title, the lender does not acquire the right of possession unless the mortgagor defaults.

Most states recognize that in reality a mortgage is a lien. It is a device used by debtors and creditors to secure a debt. The creditor is primarily interested in having the security sold and the proceeds applied to the debt if the debtor fails to pay or violates some other mortgage provision. States taking this position are called *lien theory* states.

Deed of Trust

In a number of states the typical real estate security instrument involves three parties and is based on the law of trusts. Instead of executing a mortgage in favor of a lender, the borrower transfers title to a trustee by a deed of trust. The important difference between a mortgage and a deed of trust is that in the latter legal title to the real estate passes to the trustee.

The trustee holds the property for the benefit of both the borrower and the lender. When the debt secured by the deed of trust is repaid, the trustee must reconvey title to the borrower.

The trustee has the power to sell the property if the borrower fails to maintain payment on the debt or breaches some other condition of the loan agreement. The power-of-sale provision makes foreclosure unnecessary, although the trustee usually can elect that procedure. Because foreclosure can be avoided, applying the security to a defaulted debt is more rapid and economical than through the judicial procedure. Lawyers in states where the deed of trust is common argue that the ability to sell the security efficiently is the deed of trust's major advantage over the mortgage.

Installment Land Contracts

An alternative to financing the purchase of real estate by mortgage or deed of trust is the installment land contract. In this type of agreement, the buyer contracts to pay for the property over a period of time. The seller retains title to the property until the purchase price is paid; however, the buyer is entitled to possession and to rents and profits. Installment land contracts in some states are regulated by statutes designed to protect buyers. These statutes often treat the installment contract as if it were a mortgage. For example, a common statutory provision requires the seller to have the property sold if the buyer defaults even though the seller has retained title to the property conditioned upon payment of the debt.

FORECLOSURE

Foreclosure is the legal procedure by which a lender who has advanced funds with real property as security recovers in the event of default. The ultimate result of a foreclosure action is the sale of the property with the proceeds applied to pay the debt. Any balance after paying the expenses of the sale and the debt is turned over to the borrower. If the sale does not bring enough to pay the debt, in most states the lender can sue for the deficiency.

Judicial Foreclosure

In the United States foreclosure generally is accomplished by a judicial decree ordering the mortgaged real estate sold to pay the debt. This process is known as judicial foreclosure and is what most people have in mind when they use the term "foreclosure." Judicial foreclosure entails a complicated and costly legal action. Because the procedure results in a court order, due process and the procedural requirements of litigation designed to protect the parties are necessary. In obtaining the court order and selling the premises, the lender must adhere strictly to statutory requirements.

Power-of-Sale Foreclosure

Legal complications, expenses, and delays associated with judicial foreclosure have encouraged alternative methods of foreclosure. Many mortgages contain provisions granting a mortgagee or third party power to sell the real estate without resorting to judicial foreclosure if the mortgagor defaults. The deed of trust, also, normally is enforced by a nonjudicial sale since the deed empowers the trustee to sell the security if the borrower defaults.

Statutes in most states provide some protection for the mortgagor whose property is subject to a power-of-sale foreclosure. These statutes require a public sale, notice of the action to be taken, usually by advertisement, and a sale that is fairly conducted in order to produce the best price. Trustees are subject to the same statutory regulations in carrying out a power-of-sale provision. In addition, the trustee must conform to an extensive body of law that regulates fiduciaries generally.

Due-on-Sale Clause and Foreclosure

Many mortgages contain provisions allowing the lender to treat the unauthorized sale of the security as a default. A clause of this nature permits the lender to demand payment of the entire debt if the property is sold. Originally these "due-on-sale" clauses were included in mortgages to provide the lender with an opportunity to evaluate the potential purchaser. As interest rates rose in the mid-1960s, financial institutions began to use the clause to escape from low-interest loans. The clause provided the lender an opportunity to negotiate a higher rate of interest or to declare the entire balance due and payable. The following case is one of a number brought in state courts by borrowers arguing that the due-on-sale clause is unenforceable.

Occidental Savings and Loan Association v. Venco Partnership

Supreme Court of Nebraska
293 N.W.2d 843 (1980)

Occidental Savings and Loan (plaintiff-appellee) brought an action to foreclose mortgage on property owned by Venco Partnership (defendant-appellant). The trial court directed foreclosure and defendant appealed.

Krivosha, Chief Justice

The instant appeal presents the court with its first opportunity to consider the validity and enforceability of what is commonly referred to as a "due on sale" clause frequently found in a real estate mortgage. The trial court concluded that the "due on sale" clause was both valid and enforceable and, accordingly, ordered foreclosure of the mortgage containing the questioned clause. We have reviewed the files and records and the law applicable to such matters and conclude that the trial court was correct in its conclusions. . . .

While "due on sale" clauses take a number of forms, essentially they are, in form, similar to the clause involved in the instant case, which provided "(I)n the event of a sale of said premises without the written approval of said (lender), then the whole indebtedness hereby secured shall, at the option of said (lender), immediately become due and collectible without further notice, and this mortgage may then be foreclosed to recover the amount due on said note or obligation. . . ."

While this is our first opportunity to examine the validity of "due on sale" clauses, many other courts have already made such an examination and reached varying results. . . .

Most of the cases which have considered this issue have started their analysis by concluding without much discussion that the "due on sale" clause is a restraint on alienation. They have then either upheld the clause or struck it down depending on whether they thought that, under the particular facts, the restraint was reasonable. Likewise, appellants herein urge this court to find that the "due on sale" clause is an unreasonable restraint on alienation, absent the mortgagee pleading and proving that the security is impaired; while the appellees urge us to find that the clause is a reasonable restraint on alienation. We believe that the error committed by most jurisdictions in deciding this matter is their willingness to assume that a "due on sale" clause is a restraint on alienation and that the only issue is reasonableness. In our view, the "due on sale" clause is not a restraint on alienation as that concept is legally defined.

An example of the law pertaining to restraints on alienation makes it clear that a "due on sale" clause is not a restraint on alienation and cannot be so considered for any purpose, theoretical or practical.

The questioned clause in no manner precludes the owner-mortgagor from conveying his property. The owner is free to convey without legal restraint and the conveyance does not cause a forfeiture of the title, but only an acceleration of the debt.

It is true that the possibility of acceleration may impede the ability of an owner to sell his property as he wishes; nonetheless, not every impediment to a sale is a restraint on alienation, let alone contrary to public policy. It is a fact that zoning restrictions, building restrictions, or public improvements may impede the sale and substantially affect the ability of an owner to realize a maximum price. Yet no one suggests that such restrictions or covenants, as a class, are invalid simply because they affect the ease with which one may dispose of one's property.

Appellants next argue that, if a "due on sale" clause is not a direct restraint on alienation and, therefore, void, it is, at least, an unreasonable *indirect* restraint on alienation which should be declared invalid and unenforceable as a matter of public policy unless a mortgagee pleads and proves that his security is in jeopardy.

The difficulty in attempting to determine the validity of a contract based upon some notion of an indirect restraint on alienation and a concept of "practical inalienability" is that there is no framework within which a court may operate. Parties to a contract can never know, absent litigation, whether the contract is valid or not. Such a result is undesirable and should be avoided if possible.

The facts of the instant case further establish that the clause did not restrain the alienation. The transfer of title was made without any obvious difficulty resulting from the terms of the mortgage. The seller-mortgagor did not even answer the petition to foreclose the mortgage and was declared in default by the court. Moreover, the seller-mortgagor has not appeared in this court and apparently is completely unconcerned with the outcome of this case. How does one argue in light of those facts that the "due on sale" clause was a practical restraint on the alienation of title in this case? . . . The landmark case involving modern day restraints on alienation is said to be the 1964 case of *Coast Bank* v. *Minderhout.* . . . In the *Coast Bank* case, the California Supreme Court concluded that, while a "due on sale" clause was a practical restraint on alienation, it was a reasonable restraint and, therefore, was valid per se. This was then followed by a series of other California decisions, each of which narrowed the conditions under which a "due on sale" clause would be considered valid. . . . California's latest encounter with this problem was the 1978 decision by the California Supreme Court in the case of *Wellenkamp* v. *Bank of America.* . . . By the time the California court decided the *Wellenkamp* case, it had come full circle from its initial position in the *Coast Bank* case and determined that a "due on sale" clause was invalid and unenforceable unless the lender could demonstrate that enforcement was reasonably necessary to protect the lender against the impairment of its security or the risk of default.

A more interesting aspect of the *Wellenkamp* decision is the basis upon which the court reached its conclusion. Relatively few legal principles are relied upon as authority. The decision is based primarily on considerations of social need and the assumed effect of a "due on sale" clause in the marketplace. The rights and needs of the seller, as seen by the court, are detailed and balanced against the rights and needs of the lender, as seen by the court. The court concludes that the rights and needs of the seller outweigh those of the lender, notwithstanding the fact that the parties have freely entered into a contract to the contrary.

. . . It is difficult to understand why an institutional lender using private funds of individual depositors should be treated differently than an individual lender using his own funds.

While the immediate result obtained by the California court may seem to be in the best interest of everyone except the lender, one need only give some careful thought to the results which must flow from such a decision to recognize that whatever relief may be provided for the seller is momentary and fleeting. Decisions such as *Wellenkamp* place an unreasonable burden upon lenders and call upon courts to act as periodic arbitrators in the sale of real estate.

. . . Appellants further argue that the only purpose of the "due on sale" clause is to protect the lender's interest in the security and it should not be used as a device to permit the lender to rearrange its loan portfolio. While there is no evidence in this record to support the former conclusion, there is support for the appellee's position that "due on sale" clauses are the main vehicle for increasing interest rates when money is scarce.

The restraint, if any, in this case does not attach itself to the title and the conveyance thereof but rather to the mortgage and the assumption thereof. The lender never promised the seller that another could assume the mortgage; as a matter of fact, it told the seller the contrary. Should we, therefore, ignore the plain terms of the contract and look for some hidden intention, unsupported by evidence?

A further inequity of declaring all "due on sale" clauses invalid occurs when, as in the instant case, the note and mortgage contain no prepayment penalty. In the event that the market should decline below the established mortgage rate, the seller and his subsequent buyer are at liberty to pay off the lender without penalty and adjust their loan by seeking another, lower interest, mortgage. A "due on sale" clause allows a lender to adjust its portfolio in a rising market. The effect of a rising interest market and an invalid "due on sale" clause would be to permit a seller to obtain a premium for the sale of its property at the expense of the lender. We know of no principle in law or equity which would sustain such a position. We must find, as a matter of law, that "due on sale" clauses are neither direct nor indirect restraints on alienation and, therefore, are not void as such.

The only remaining basis for declaring the questioned clauses invalid would be a finding that they are repugnant to public policy. This should not be done lightly or without sufficient compelling reason.

Not only are we convinced that a "due on sale" clause is not repugnant to public policy but, to the contrary, we recognize that, under certain economic circumstances, they may favor the public interest and, therefore, be supportive of public policy. On the one hand, the assets of savings and loan associations are principally invested in long-term mortgages, while, on the other hand, the funds necessary to make such loans are obtained from short-term and demand savings accounts and certificates. As the cost of obtaining deposits rises, the spread widens between what the association must pay for funds by way of interest and what the association receives from borrowers. Once the spread gets too great, the association will be unable to meet the standards set by government regulations and will fail. The potential failure of savings and loan associations and the loss of their depositors' funds should be of no less a concern to the courts than the inability of a property owner to transfer its mortgage at a premium when selling its property. Balancing portfolio return with cost of money is an important factor in the survival of lending associations. The "due on sale" clause is an important device in maintaining that balance.

Affirmed.

CASE NOTE

The controversy surrounding the enforcement of the due-on-sale clause provides an interesting illustration of the manner in which economic developments affect the law. During the 1970s rapidly escalating interest rates were a significant economic phenomenon in the United States. Savings and loan associations were caught in a financial crunch, since they had many outstanding loans at low rates and were experiencing difficulty paying higher rates to depositors. In order to do this they argued that they needed the due-on-sale clause to help bring their loan portfolios up to current market rates. At the same time, owners and those in the real estate industry involved in selling contended that the enforcement of the due-on-sale clause depressed real estate sales since the clause limited the buyer's ability to finance at low rates.

This controversy was further complicated because savings and loan associations are chartered by either state or federal governments. Federally chartered savings and loans are regulated by the Federal Home Loan Bank Board, state savings and loans by state law.

During the 1970s, as mentioned in the previous case, a number of states took the position that the due-on-sale clause could not be enforced because it limited the owner's ability to sell his or her real estate. The clause, they contended, was against public policy since it established a restraint on alienation. Federally chartered savings and loans countered by arguing that they were exempted from these state laws because they were regulated by a federal agency. In 1976, the Federal Home Loan Bank Board promulgated a regulation providing that a federal savings and loan association had the power to include a due-on-sale clause in its loan instrument.

The controversy between the Board's authority and state law was settled by a U.S. Supreme Court decision in 1982. In *Fidelity Federal Savings & Loan Association* v. *De La Cuesta* (__U.S.__; 102 S.Ct. 3014 [1982]), the Court stated that the federal regulation preempted state law. The result of this decision is that in states like California, which had declared the due-on-sale clause a violation of public policy, state savings and loans cannot enforce the clause but federal savings and loans can. In Nebraska, the jurisdiction involved in the principal case, both state and federal savings and loans may enforce a due-on-sale clause.

CONTROL OF LAND USE

An owner's rights in real property are not absolute. Often these rights are subject to restrictions imposed by government and/or by private agreements. The most common type of public control of land use is zoning. Private agreements limiting land use are called restrictive covenants.

Restrictive Covenants

Restrictive covenants are usually placed in a deed by the seller when conveying land to a buyer. The buyer, of course, must have agreed to accept these limitations on use of the land. Restrictive covenants can be made part of a plan for the development of real property. When this is done, the covenants are included in the plot plan, which must be filed with the proper authorities.

In developing real property, restrictive covenants are used to ensure that property owners will not suffer a loss in property value because of the unorthodox activity of a neighbor. Restrictive covenants in a residential development might limit the use of land to single-family dwellings or require houses to exceed a minimum square footage. Restrictive covenants are also used when an individual sells a portion of his or her property to ensure that the buyer will not use the land in a manner objectionable to the seller who remains as a neighbor.

Restrictive covenants run with the land. This means that the limitations on the use of the land are not dependent on the continued ownership of the buyer who agreed to the restriction. In general, enforcement of restrictive covenants has not been favored by courts because they interfere with the free transferability of property. In order for a restrictive covenant to run with the land it must have been the intention of the original grantor and grantee, and the covenant must to a substantial degree affect the essential nature of the land. The idea that property, both real and personal, should be freely transferable is an important concept in Anglo-American law.

Restrictive covenants can be terminated in several ways. One way is to have all concerned parties agree in writing to the termination. This, however, is difficult if the number involved is large. Covenants can also be terminated by condemnation or by not being enforced when they are violated. The longer violations of covenants are ignored, the less likely a court is to enforce them.

Zoning

Zoning is the division of an area, usually a municipality, into districts in order to control land use. Zoning ordinances regulate such things as the structure and design of buildings, lot size, setback requirements, and uses to which land may be put. Limitations on the use of land through zoning are of recent vintage. Comprehensive control of land use is a product of the twentieth century. The notion of comprehensive zoning was first approved by the U.S. Supreme Court in 1926.

Although nuisance was the original basis for zoning regulations, today zoning is based on the states' police power. On the basis of this power, land use can be regulated to protect the health, safety, and welfare of the public. Like all regulation based upon the police power, zoning ordinances to be valid must not be unreasonable or arbitrary.

Traditional zoning ordinances divide the municipality into districts for residential, commercial, and industrial uses. Over the years these basic zoning classifications have expanded considerably. As a result, many localities now have fifteen to twenty or more zones. Because use within these zones is restricted, multiplication of zones promotes inflexibility in land use and gives rise to criticism of the traditional zoning process. In response to this criticism, other techniques for controlling land use have developed since World War II.

Planned Unit Developments (PUDs) are an example of innovative use of the zoning power. In a PUD, zoning regulations are applied to an area larger than the traditional subdivision. The objective of a PUD is to permit mixed use of an area within a development while providing a maximum amount of land for open space. Various types of housing such as townhouses, apartments, and single-family dwellings are permitted within the same tract. In some instances the zoning plan permits commercial as well as residential use. In addition, the plan provides for extensive open areas. A major advantage of the PUD is the flexibility it provides in planning for community growth.

The extension of public control of real property through zoning is illustrative of major changes that have occurred in real property law since the 1960s. Other examples include the development of such new forms of ownership as condominiums and cooperatives, major modifications in financing and investing techniques, and limitations upon the rights of owners to deal with their property in a manner interfering with the civil rights of other citizens. In spite of these and other changes, traditional legal concepts and terminology remain important in the field.

REVIEW PROBLEMS

1. Eva Corley and other heirs of George Johns sued the estate of J. W. Johns and legatees under J. W.'s will. They sought to have title to forty acres willed by J. W. to these legatees declared in them. George Johns had deeded the forty acres to J. W. in 1924. Corley alleged that the deed was invalid because there was no proof of delivery; the deed, never recorded, had been found in a trunk belonging to J. W. after his death in 1972. Would an argument that J. W. did not have title because the deed was never recorded be effective? Explain. Corley v. Parson, 223 S.E.2d 708 (1976)

2. Linmont purchased a corner lot from Amoco in order to construct and operate a

filling station. At the time of the purchase, Linmont and Amoco entered into an agreement by which Linmont agreed to take all its requirements of gas and oil from Amoco. The agreement also obligated subsequent owners and tenants of the station to purchase all requirements of petroleum products from Amoco. This agreement and the deed were properly recorded in the office of the County Clerk. Linmont sold the property to Chock Full of Power, which refused to comply with the agreement. Amoco sues. Would Amoco be successful? Discuss. Bill Wolf Petroleum Corp. v. Chock Full of Power, 333 N.Y.S.2d 472 (1972)

3. On December 1, 1960, Robert L. Glass executed and delivered a promissory note to Sumner G. Whittier as Administrator of Veterans Affairs. The note, in the amount of $13,400 with interest, was secured by a mortgage on property purchased by Glass. In 1962 Glass sold the property to Andrew Crane, who assumed the indebtedness of Robert L. Glass. In 1964 Crane defaulted on the note and the property was foreclosed. The property when sold did not bring enough to pay the balance of the note, and the Veterans Administration sued Glass for the deficiency, amounting to $1,711.34 plus interest. Glass defended on grounds that the debt had been assumed by Crane. Would the VA be successful? Discuss. United States v. Glass, 298 F. Supp. 396 (1969)

4. Stephens and his wife had two sons. They quarreled with the older son and as a result wished to deny him any interest in a farm they owned. In order to accomplish this, they conveyed the farm to their younger son, retaining a life estate for themselves. The younger son gave no consideration for the farm. A few months later Stephens and his wife wished to vacate the deed to the younger son because they believed he had conspired against them with his brother. They brought an action to cancel the deed on grounds that no consideration had been paid. Would they be successful? Discuss. Stephens v. Stephens, 193 So.2d 755 (1967)

5. The Village of Northbrook approved a zoning ordinance permitting the construction of a large shopping center in an area along its boundary with Highland Park. Residents of Highland Park and the municipality of Highland Park sued to block construction of the shopping center on grounds that it would cause massive congestion in the area, destroying the quiet residential character of their community. They argued that this violated the equal protection clause of the Constitution since the shopping center actually protected much of the residential character of Northbrook. The reason for this was that the chief highway leading to the site ran through Highland Park. Would the suit be successful? Support your answer. City of Highland Park v. Train, 519 F.2d 681 (1975)

CHAPTER 36

Wills, Trusts, and Estates

STATE INTESTACY LAWS ─────────────────────────

WILLS ──────────────────────────────────

ESTATE ADMINISTRATION ───────────────────────

ESTATE PLANNING ────────────────────────────

I n this chapter we are concerned with the laws affecting the disposition of property when the owner of that property dies. The word estate means the interest a person has in property, both real property and personal property. Thus estate planning occurs during a person's life when he or she arranges for the future distribution of the estate. It is concerned with the distribution of a person's property not only after death but also during a person's lifetime.

This chapter first focuses on the state laws that govern the descent and distribution of a decedent's property. Those laws determine the persons who are entitled to receive that property if the decedent did not make a valid will. However, since a person can specify, with certain limitations, who shall inherit his or her property by making a valid will, the laws governing the making of a valid will are also examined. The chapter then briefly describes the process, known as estate administration, by which property is transferred from the decedent to those entitled to receive that property. Finally, some of the techniques used in estate planning—such as the creating of a trust

or the transfer of property to children, parents, or a charity during a person's lifetime—are discussed.

STATE INTESTACY LAWS

Two sets of state laws govern the inheritance of property. The first set come into effect if the person did not make a valid will and are referred to as the *intestacy* laws. When a person does make a valid "last will and testament," that person's property will be transferred according to the laws affecting the *testate* distribution of property.

There are significant differences in state inheritance laws, particularly as they relate to community property of married persons. While there are no federal laws governing the inheritance of property (although federal tax laws certainly affect estate planning), a uniform law governing the descent and distribution of property has been drafted and submitted to various state legislatures for approval. This law, the Uniform Probate Code, would provide much greater uniformity among the state laws. However, only a few states have as yet adopted the Uniform Probate Code. Thus our discussion of intestacy laws will focus on the general provisions found in most state statutes.

State intestacy laws govern the disposition of the decedent's real and personal property. Since real property descends to a person's heirs while personal property is distributed according to state statutes, these laws are generally referred to as statutes of descent and distribution.

The law of the state where the decedent's real estate is located determines the heirs to whom the real estate descends. Consequently, if an Indiana decedent owned a Michigan summer cottage, the statutory descent and distribution laws of Michigan will determine who inherits that real estate. But, since the decedent's personal property is distributed in accordance with the laws of the state where the decedent was domiciled, the furniture in that summer cottage will be distributed according to the Indiana descent and distribution statutes.

As a general rule, state intestacy laws provide that a decedent's estate, both real and personal property, shall be shared by the surviving spouse and children. The spouse's share will typically be from one-third to one-half if there are children or other descendants of the decedent, such as grandchildren. If no children or grandchildren have survived the decedent, the surviving spouse usually takes the entire estate.

If children and grandchildren have survived the decedent, the question arises as to how each of them will share in the decedent's estate. If there is no surviving spouse, the entire estate will usually be split among the lineal descendants (children and grandchildren) of the decedent. In determining the descendants' shares, it is generally provided that the children of a deceased child will take the share that that child would have been entitled to inherit. This method of dividing property is

known as *per stirpes* distribution. Consider the following example. John Adams is married to Jane Adams and they have three children, A, B, and C. Child C, who died before John Adams, is not a surviving child but his three children, G, H, and I, are descendants of John Adams. According to typical intestacy laws, John Adams's estate would be divided as follows:

1. A certain share to the surviving spouse, Jane Adams. Usually if there is more than one child who survives the decedent, the spouse will receive one-third of John Adams's estate.
2. The remaining two-thirds to be split in some way among the lineal descendants of Adams. According to the per stirpes distribution, each surviving child receives an equal share, and the children of the child who did not survive take the share that child would have taken.

In our example, then, the remaining two-thirds of John Adams's estate would be divided as follows:

1. One-third of the remaining two-thirds (two-ninths) to Child A
2. One-third of the remaining two-thirds (two-ninths) to Child B
3. The two-ninths share that would have gone to Child C instead is split equally among that child's children (Adams's grandchildren) so that G, H, and I each receive one-third of the two-ninths share or two twenty-sevenths of John Adams's estate.

Another method by which property may be distributed is on a *per capita* basis. This means that each person who is to receive a share of the estate as a descendant would receive a like amount. Usually, the per capita distribution system, if followed, is used for persons of the same generation rather than for persons of different generations. Thus it would probably not be used in dividing Adams's property among his two children and three grandchildren, but it might be used for dividing property among all grandchildren. Assume that neither Adams's spouse nor any children survived him and that there are six grandchildren. If the grandchildren shared according to a per stirpes distribution, their shares would be different than if they shared according to a per capita distribution, as the following chart indicates:

	Per Stirpes		Per Capita
Grandchild			
D	1/6 share	(1/2 of A's 1/3)	1/6 share
E	1/6 share	(1/2 of A's 1/3)	1/6 share
F	1/3 share	(all of B's 1/3)	1/6 share
G	1/9 share	(1/3 of C's 1/3)	1/6 share
H	1/9 share	(1/3 of C's 1/3)	1/6 share
I	1/9 share	(1/3 of C's 1/3)	1/6 share

In most states, if the decedent leaves neither a spouse nor descendants, the estate will be divided in some way among the decedent's parents, if living (known as ascendants), and surviving brothers and sisters, while in other states one or more parents may take the entire estate. If there are no people in these categories, the estate will usually be distributed to nephews and nieces since they are blood relatives of the decedent. It should also be noted that most statutes of descent and distribution make no provision for relatives by marriage. The spouse of a child, brother, or parent who is not a blood relative of the decedent usually takes no share of a decedent's estate. Similarly, stepchildren, unless they have been legally adopted, are usually excluded as heirs since they are not blood relatives. Adopted children are generally regarded as children and heirs of a decedent.

Finally, if there are no descendants, ascendants, or collateral relatives of the decedent, the intestacy laws provide that the property goes to the state. This provision, known as *escheat*, is rarely applied.

Interpretation of the intestacy laws is exemplified by the *Warpool* case.

Warpool v. Floyd

Supreme Court of Tennessee
524 S.W.2d 247 (1975)

This case presents for decision the issue of whether children of half-brothers and half-sisters of an intestate take equal shares of his personal property with children of brothers and sisters of the whole blood. The trial court held that they are entitled to equal shares, and the administrator of the estate appealed to the supreme court of Tennessee, seeking appropriate instructions as to the distribution of intestate personal property. The supreme court affirmed the decision granting the children of half-brothers and half-sisters equal shares with the children of brothers and sisters of the whole blood.

Harbinson, Judge

The decedent had one full brother and sister, both of whom predeceased him. The sister died without issue, but the brother left one child surviving. He is the administrator as well as the full nephew by blood of the decedent.

Decedent, who never married, was predeceased by both parents. His father, however, by a previous marriage had ten children, all of whom had predeceased the decedent. Eight of these, however, left surviving children, representatives of whom were named as defendants in the court below. There are some twenty-eight of these nephews and nieces of the half blood.

Under the law of intestate distribution in this state, there is no representation among collateral kindred, after the children of brothers and sisters. Children of brothers and sisters, however, do take by representation, and it has been held that they take the intestate's personal property *per stirpes,* rather than *per capita.*

The statutes governing distribution of intestate personal property give priority to the surviving spouse and/or children of a decedent. Where there are no persons in these categories, however, the parents are preferred. The statutes then provide as follows:

> "If no father or mother, to brothers and sisters, or the children of such brothers and sisters representing them, equally."

The statutes provide that if there are neither brothers, sisters, nieces nor nephews, then the personal estate is distributed "to every of the next of kin of the intestate who are in equal degree, equally."

In the case of Kyle v. Moore, 35 Tenn. 183 (1855), this Court expressly held that brothers and sisters of half blood shared equally in intestate personal property with brothers and sisters of the whole blood.

The Court noted that in the computation of the degrees of kinship, there was no distinction between the half blood and the whole blood. The Court said:

> "There is no law giving any preference to the half blood on the side of the transmitting ancestor, to the exclusion of the other line, in the distribution of personality." 35 Tenn. at 185.

The Court in that case took note of express provisions in the statutes governing the descent of real property, which had altered the feudal policy of earlier English law, excluding persons of the half blood entirely. Statutes in effect at the time of the decision of the *Kyle* case, and still in effect today, do make certain distinctions between acquired and inherited realty, insofar as inheritance by half-brothers or half-sisters are concerned.

These "ancestral property" provisions were not part of the law of distribution of personal property when the *Kyle* case was decided, nor have they since been included therein.

The *Kyle* case has not been overruled or modified by any subsequent decision of this Court, and appellant concedes that it would be controlling here except for certain changes in the statutes of distribution which occurred in the revision and codification of the state law, resulting in the Code of 1858. For the first time, in that code, there were included provisions for inheritance by brothers and sisters and their children, if the decedent did not leave a surviving spouse, child or parent.

It is insisted that because the words "brothers and sisters" were used in the Code of 1858, without qualification and without reference to relatives of the half blood, the

Legislature intended to prefer brothers and sisters of the whole blood to those of the half blood.

This Court is unable to find such a legislative intent in the Code of 1858. It is true that the "ancestral property" statutes governing real estate were then in force, and that they contained explicit reference to half-brothers and half-sisters. The argument before us is that if the legislature had intended for siblings of the half blood to share fully with those of the whole blood, the legislature would have so provided.

It is equally plausible to assume, however, that if the legislature had intended to exclude half-brothers and half-sisters or to put them in a less-preferred category than full siblings, it could easily have so provided. Since it did not do so, it is the opinion of the Court that the legislature did not so intend, and that the holdings in the *Kyle* and *Deadrick* cases, *supra,* were not intended to be modified.

Finding no legislative history which would lead us to believe that the General Assembly intended to prefer siblings of the whole blood over those of the half blood, we hold that half-brothers and half-sisters share equally with full brothers and sisters in the distribution of intestate personalty, and that their children, taking by representation, take equally with the children of full brothers and sisters.

The decree of the chancellor is affirmed.

WILLS

As we have seen, if a person does not make a will expressing his or her own desires regarding the distribution of property at death, the state intestacy laws will determine who inherits the property and how it will be divided. Thus the basic reason for preparing a will is to establish one's own plan rather than accept distribution by the state. A will is also used to ensure that persons of one's choice will care for and look after one's children and estate. The naming of a guardian for minor children and of a personal representative for one's property accomplish this purpose. Gifts to charities or the creation of trusts to split the use of property among several people can also be accomplished by a will. Finally, a will usually makes possible the settlement of an estate with a minimum of delay and expense. Accordingly, it is sound business practice for a person to prepare a will and to review its provisions periodically throughout his or her lifetime.

Requirements for a Valid Will

The requirements for a valid will are established by statute. The statutory requirements of the state where a person resides or is domiciled at the time of death must be met in order to dispose of personal property by a will. The statutes of the state where a person's real property is located must be complied with to dispose of it by a will. Since statutes vary from state to state, the person who drafts a will must be familiar with the law of the state where the will is to be effective. If the statutory requirements are not complied with, the will is usually not valid and the person's property then passes according to the intestacy laws.

Terminology. A *will* is a written declaration stating its maker's desires as to the disposition of his or her property or estate after death. The person making a will is called a *testator* if male and a *testatrix* if female; in this chapter, the term testator refers to both a testator and a testatrix. The person named by the testator to look after and administer the estate of the decedent is referred to as the *executor, administrator,* or *personal representative;* this chapter uses the term personal representative. Finally, the term *probate* refers to the process by which the will is legally approved as valid and through which the estate is administered until all its property is distributed. If a will is found to be invalid, it will be denied probate; in that case, it has no legal effect and does not control the distribution of the testator's estate. Review the effect of the court's decision in the *Kenney* case as it relates to the determination of the validity of a will.

Kenney v. Pasieka

Appellate Court of Illinois

260 N.E.2d 766 (1970)

This case involves the interpretation of an "ambiguous phrase" in a will. The testator left a share of his estate to the children of "Frank Pasieka." The decedent and two of his relatives had that name. The trial court determined that the testator meant himself when that name was used in his will. The appellate court found the phrase so ambiguous as to be without effect. Accordingly, since the decedent's property thus was to pass by the laws of intestacy, it reversed the trial court's decision.

Thomas J. Moran, Justice

This case involves three men with the same name—Frank Pasieka. The first is the deceased testator who lived at Tonica, Illinois and was, in the argument before this Court, called "Tonica Frank"; the second, a nephew of the testator, who resided in Peoria and was called "Peoria Frank"; and the third, a cousin of the testator, who resided in Chicago and was called "Chicago Frank".

Tonica Frank died on October 5, 1966, leaving a last will which was executed November 24, 1962. Tonica Frank was twice married and left surviving him his second wife. He had one child by his first marriage, Theodore Pasieka, and none by his second marriage. Theodore died on October 11, 1964, after the making of the will in question but before the death of his father.

During his lifetime, Tonica Frank took into his home two boys, Walter and Joseph, both of whom changed their last name to his and lived with him as his sons. Walter never married and has no children. Joseph, on the other hand, is married and is the father of three children.

Tonica Frank's will is relatively simple but the problems it creates are substantial. After providing for the payment of his debts and funeral expenses, he bequeathed all of his personal property to his second wife. He then devised all of his real estate to his son, Theodore, for life and provided that, upon the death of Theodore, the real estate would become part of the residue of his estate. The residue was then devised "one-third thereof to the children of Walter Pasieka, share and share alike; one-third thereof to the children of Joseph Pasieka, share and share alike; and one-third thereof to the children of Frank Pasieka, share and share alike". The will then provided, "In the event any child shall not be living at the time of the death of my son, Theodore

Pasieka, but shall leave brothers and sisters him surviving, said brothers and sisters shall take the share of such deceased child.''

The second wife renounced the will and the executor filed suit for a proper construction. There is no dispute as to the one-third share to the children of Joseph Pasieka. They do exist and are entitled to that portion. The difficulty, however, arises in determining which ''Frank Pasieka'' the testator intended, since there were three, and what happens to the share devised to the children of Walter Pasieka, since he has no children.

The trial court, after considerable deliberation and effort, wrote a memorandum of decision which concluded that the testator meant himself when he devised a one-third share to the children of ''Frank Pasieka'' and, therefore, this share was to be divided equally between Joseph and Walter, and finally that the one-third share to the children of Walter did not fail but passed one-half to the children of Joseph and one-fourth each to Joseph and to Walter.

This appeal followed raising the issues that the trial court erred in ruling that the testator meant himself and that the disposition of the one-third interest to the children of Walter was erroneous since there were no such children.

Both the plaintiffs and the trial court agree that the will before us presents latent ambiguities. Even though the language is clear and suggests a single meaning, extrinsic facts show the clear necessity for an interpretation,

In construing a will the guiding principle is the intention of the testator, and the question for our determination is not what the testator meant to say by the language employed, but rather what he meant by what he did say.

Therefore, in construing this will it was proper for the trial court, and it is proper for us, to consider the surrounding circumstances. The evidence presented clearly indicates that the decedent treated his own son, Theodore, and Joseph and Walter exactly the same. Joseph and Walter were never legally adopted but they were brought into the decedent's home, they took his name and he treated them as his sons. He never indicated any desire to have one receive more than another. It was really on this basis that the trial court reached its conclusion.

While that evidence is clear, it is not very helpful in construing the decedent's will. There, he did not treat the three boys alike because he gave his son, Theodore, all of his property for life and he gave nothing to Walter or Joseph, since the devise is to their children and not to them.

In determining who is the right ''Frank Pasieka'' it appears clear to us that it cannot be Peoria Frank. Peoria Frank had not seen the decedent for twenty-eight years before his death and they had no communication.

Similarly, it would seem clear that the Frank in question cannot be Chicago Frank because they were not close and saw each other only about once each year.

We are hard pressed to find that the decedent referred to himself because the gift, of course, is not to himself but to his children and he had already provided for his only natural child by giving him a life estate in all of his property.

Likewise, we cannot determine what the decedent meant by the gift to the ''children'' of Walter, since Walter never had and does not now have any children.

The sad thing about this case is that the decedent went to an attorney and made an attempt to write a will. Unfortunately, he did not make a will which completely disposed of his property and the only way there can be a complete disposition is for this Court to write his will for him or for the property to be administered as though the decedent had no will. While there is a presumption against intestacy and the court should make an effort to construe the will if that is possible, this Court has no power to write a new will for a decedent if it cannot determine his intention. As our Supreme Court said in Hampton v. Dill, 354 Ill. 415, 420, 188 N.E. 419, 421 (1933), the testator's "intention must be determined by the language of the will itself and not from any surmise that he used the language to express an intention or meaning he had in his mind which he failed to express. If he has overlooked a condition which he probably would have provided against had he thought of it, the court cannot guess which provision he would have made and read it into his will on the presumption that he would naturally have made such a provision if he had thought of it." Where a testator in disposing of his property overlooks a particular event, which, had it occurred to him, he would have in all probability provided against, the court will not supply a provision by intendment, on a presumption of what the testator would naturally have done.

While it is true that the presumption is always against intestacy, either in whole or in part, where a party has attempted to dispose of property by will, this is only a presumption and does not warrant this court, under the guise of construing a will, to add provisions which are offered in place of those omitted. Such presumptions cannot be indulged in either to overcome express language in a will or to supply an omission made by oversight, where no language is used to show an intention on the part of testator to dispose of the property.

We conclude that the two-thirds of the residue of the decedent's estate which were devised to the children of "Frank Pasieka" and to the children of Walter Pasieka, go as intestate under the statute.

The case is, therefore, reversed and remanded to the trial court with instructions to enter an order consistent with this opinion.

Reversed and remanded with instructions.

General Requirements. There are three different kinds of requirements that must be met according to the statutes in most states for a will to be valid. First, the person making the will must have proper testamentary capacity. A person's capacity to make valid contracts was discussed in Chapter 10. The testamentary capacity required by inheritance laws, while similar to the contractual capacity referred to, differs from it in several important respects. Second, testamentary intent is required to make a valid will. The testator must clearly intend that the document offered as his will be effective to transfer his property at his death. Thus, if a person intends to transfer property during his lifetime and writes a statement giving stock, jewelry, or personal property to another, that statement cannot be a will; it does not indicate the intent to transfer the property effective only with the testator's death. Third, the testator must comply with the statutory requirements relating to the execution or signing of the will. Certain formalities in writing, signing, and witnessing a will must be complied with in order for the will to be valid. If these requirements are not strictly adhered to, the proposed will is not valid and legally effective.

Testamentary Capacity. There are two elements of the requirement of testamentary capacity. The statutes require that the person making a will have attained a certain age (usually eighteen) before signing the will. A person who has not attained that age cannot leave his or her property to another by a will. A will executed or signed by a person who is under the statutory age is invalid for lack of testamentary capacity.

The second element of testamentary capacity is the testator's being of "sound mind." The test of a "sound mind" is expressed by courts in different terms, but usually it requires that the testator be aware of three different matters. The testator must know who are the "natural objects of his or her bounty." Usually this means the testator's family members, but it could also include close friends for whom the testator has special concerns. Second, the testator must realize the kind and extent of property that he is proposing to distribute by the will. Finally, the testator must be able to plan for the disposition of that property.

Each of these requirements is generally reviewed in a case where the testator's testamentary capacity is questioned. Usually, less mental capacity is required to make a valid will than is necessary to manage business affairs or enter into contracts. A person may be feeble, aged, or of low intelligence and still have the required testamentary capacity. In the *Lockwood* case, the court is asked to determine whether a codicil (an addition to or alteration of an existing will) is valid. The claim is that it is not valid because the testatrix, Mrs. Lockwood, lacked testamentary capacity at the time she signed the codicil.

In re Estate of Lockwood

California Court of Appeals
62 Cal. Rptr. 230 (1967)

The decedent executed a will in 1958; there is no question as to its validity. Four days before her death in 1964 at age eighty-nine, a codicil was executed. At that time, the decedent was very ill. The jury of the probate court denied probate to the codicil, and that decision was appealed. The court of appeals agreed with the probate court's decision that the decedent did not have testamentary capacity at the time the codicil was executed. Accordingly, it affirmed the trial court's decision.

Salsman, Associate Justice

This is an appeal from a judgment entered on a jury verdict denying probate of a codicil to the will of Annie L. Lockwood on the ground that the testatrix lacked testamentary capacity on February 28, 1964 when the codicil was executed, four days before her death. The will itself was admitted to probate, there being no question of Mrs. Lockwood's testamentary capacity on July 28, 1958 when it was executed.

The codicil revoked the testatrix's gift of her entire estate to William and Irene Rolfe, close friends for many years, who had rendered personal services to her at various times, and substituted a gift of $5,000 to May Delaney and gave the remainder of her estate to her heirs at law, Alan, Audrie and Sharon Swanson, who are appellants here.

The sole issue on appeal is whether there is any substantial evidence to support the verdict of the jury, which found, answering a special interrogatory of the court, that the testatrix was not mentally competent at the time she executed the codicil. In order to resolve this issue it is necessary to set forth the facts in detail.

The testatrix was 89 years of age at the time of her death on March 3, 1964. An autopsy report gave the cause of death as cardiac failure due to arteriosclerotic heart disease, but the report also catalogued the many physical miseries from which the testatrix suffered at the end of her life. Among the findings were: (1) arteriosclerotic heart disease, (a) coronary atherosclerosis, severe, with calcification, (b) myocardial fibrosis; (2) bronchopneumonia; (3) rectal abscess with fistula to perineum; (4) cirrhosis of liver with central hemorrhagic necrosis; (5) cholecystitis with choledocholithiasis; (6) esophageal ulceration, focal; (7) enteritis, acute, secondary; (8) adenomyosis; (9) nephroateriolarsclerosis; (10) rib fracture, old.

The testatrix was brought to the hospital on February 20, 1964, eight days before the execution of the codicil. Up to that date there was no serious question as to her mental competency. Her condition while in the hospital, that is, from February 20th to the date of her death on March 3rd, is described by numerous witnesses, and as will appear, their testimony is in conflict as to the mental competency of the testatrix during that interval.

Dr. Challen examined the testatrix on the 27th and again on the 28th and found her alert. Dr. Sharp saw her on the 21st, 25th and 29th and also found her alert. This witness also stated that the testatrix remained alert until the day of her death. The subscribing witnesses to the codicil, who of course were with the testatrix on the 28th when the codicil was executed, also testified that the testatrix was mentally alert, knew what she was doing, and answered questions logically and understandably at that time.

Nurse Ludwig, who attended the testatrix as her day nurse from February 20th to the 26th, testified that the testatrix was a very sick person. She described her many and grave physical ailments. As to her mental condition the witness said the testatrix was at times in a stupor or coma, and would be coherent for a few moments and then become incoherent for a period of three or four hours.

Frank Crouse, an intimate friend of the testatrix, visited her at the hospital on the 25th. He found her in a semi-coma, hardly able to communicate with him. She asked his name, was told, and a few minutes later repeated the inquiry. He visited her again on March 1st, and on this date the testatrix could not communicate at all.

Annie L. Crouse, also a close friend of the testatrix, visited her daily from the 20th to the 27th, and March 1st. She testified that on the 23rd the testatrix became progressively worse and less communicative, giving only momentary recognition to her friend, then saying, "Who are you?" On the 27th she found the testatrix in a deep coma, eyes and mouth open, unable to recognize her visitor.

Nurse Madeiros attended the testatrix from the 22nd to the 27th. She testified that the testatrix was noisy and confused. Asked her opinion of the mental competency of the testatrix she replied: "At no time did I ever see any evidence that Mrs. Lockwood was—mentally clear. She always—appeared confused and disorientated. At no time was I ever able to carry on a conversation with Mrs. Lockwood. I don't remember there was ever anything understandable from her."

Mrs. Rosalie King also attended Mrs. Lockwood as a nurse from February 25th through February 29th. She testified that the testatrix showed no acknowledgment or understanding. Although awake, she did not seem to be aware of her surroundings. She showed no recognition, and gradually slept more. Her condition became progressively worse, physically as well as mentally.

Fred Cline's mother was a patient at the hospital and occupied the same room with the testatrix. He visited his mother frequently, and at such times observed Mrs. Lockwood. According to his testimony, Mrs. Lockwood appeared to get worse, and merely lay in bed, moaning and groaning. His mother was released from the hospital on March 3rd, and on his visit a day or two before that date, Mrs. Lockwood was ". . . breathing hard and gasping, as a person in a terminal case. . . ."

Dr. Burton W. Adams, a psychiatrist, testified from medical records, including the autopsy report. His opinion was that on February 28th, when the codicil was executed, the testatrix was suffering from a hardening of the arteries, in the brain as well as the body, and that she was also suffering a severe impairment of her mental faculties as well as her physical health. Although the doctor admitted the possibility of periods of lucidity on February 28th he felt such an event unlikely because of her arteriosclerosis, infection and fever that prevailed throughout her hospital stay.

The trial court gave accurate, full and complete instructions to the jury.

They were instructed that the contestants had the burden of proving that the testatrix was not mentally competent to execute her codicil on the 28th of February, and that proof had to be by a preponderance of the evidence. A special interrogatory was given to the jury, with instructions to find whether the testatrix was mentally competent to execute said codicil to her will on the 28th day of February, 1964. The court then gave the jury the test by which it was to measure mental competency.

The instruction declared that: "The determinants of testamentary capacity are whether or not the decedent had sufficient mental capacity to be able to understand the nature of the act she was doing, and to understand and recollect the nature and situation of her property, and to remember and understand her relations to the persons who have claim upon her bounty and whose interests are affected by the provisions of the instrument." The jury was further instructed that the contestants were required to prove testamentary incapacity at the very moment of the execution of the will, and that a contestant must prove that the will was not made at a lucid interval. The court also instructed that: "Not every weakness and impairment of the faculties of a testatrix will invalidate a will or codicil. Even where a testatrix is feeble in health, suffering from disease and aged and infirm, yet if she was sufficiently of sound mind to be capable of understanding the nature and situation of her property, and disposing thereof intelligently, without any delusions affecting her actions, she had sufficient capacity to make a will or codicil." . . .

Upon submission, as we have related, the jury found the testatrix mentally incompetent to execute the codicil to her will. The superior court denied appellants' motion for judgment notwithstanding the verdict, and also denied their motion for a new trial.

In contending that the judgment is not supported by the evidence, appellants first emphasize the well established rule that testamentary capacity is presumed. . . .

The proponents of the codicil did produce evidence through the testimony of the subscribing witnesses to the instrument to show that at the time it was executed the testatrix was of sound mind. But there was contrary evidence. Thus Mrs. King, one of the hospital nurses who cared for the testatrix from the 25th of February to the 29th, including the day upon which the codicil was executed, testified that Mrs. Lockwood showed no recognition or understanding during that period of time, and did not realize or understand her surroundings. Other witnesses, however, were able only to testify as to Mrs. Lockwood's testamentary capacity before and after the date the codicil was executed. There was testimony that both before and after February 28th the testatrix was often in deep coma, unable to be aroused, unable to recognize old friends or to remember who such friends were even for brief moments after being told. Several witnesses testified that conversation and communication with the testatrix while she was in the hospital was virtually impossible. Thus the evidence shows that both before and after the 28th the testatrix, overcome both physically and mentally by the extremities of age and her many physical ailments, was unable to communicate with her nurses and old friends and was often, if not continuously, in a semi-coma from which she could not be aroused. It may be inferred from this evidence that, before the codicil was executed, and afterwards to the time of her death a few days later, the condition of the testatrix remained the same.

It has been held that, once it is shown that testamentary incapacity exists, and that it is caused by a mental disorder of a general and continuous nature, the inference is reasonable that the incompetency continues to exist.

Whether a testator has testamentary capacity at the time of the making of his will depends upon the facts found by the trier of fact. Thus, in every case, the fact finder must weigh and evaluate all of the evidence, and from it find whether the testator had sufficient mental capacity to understand his act, to recollect the nature and situation of his property, to remember and understand his relationship to persons who have claims upon his bounty and whose interests may be affected by the instrument he is about to execute. This is a pure fact finding function, and once the facts are found by the trier of fact we must treat the findings with respect, and uphold them if they are supported by substantial evidence. In a will contest, as in any other case, the trier of fact is the sole judge of the credibility and weight of the evidence.

We think the jury by its verdict, and the trial judge by denying the motion for judgment notwithstanding the verdict, and also in denying appellants' motion for a new trial, were justified in concluding that the decedent, weakened by age, illness and disease, lacked testamentary capacity both before and after she executed the codicil to her will, and in inferring that such lack of capacity existed at the very moment the codicil was executed. . . .

. . . Accordingly, we affirm the judgment.

Testamentary Intent. The testator must (1) intend to transfer the property and (2) intend that the transfer occur only upon his or her death. Thus a document that does not clearly show the testator's intent to transfer property will be lacking in testamentary intent. Suppose I have a valuable diamond ring in an envelope and write on the envelope "This ring is for my sister Susan Sleaford." If the other requirements for a valid will are met, would this document indicate my intent to transfer the property and to have the property transferred at my death? Review the *Brown* case that follows as it relates to this question.

A second problem with finding proper testamentary intent relates to influences upon the testator that may replace his intent with that of another. Chapter 9 discussed several problems related to the *genuine assent* required for entering into valid contracts. Similar problems can occur with a testamentary document such as a will. Did fraud, duress, undue influence, or mistake distort the testator's true intent? While each of these enemies of genuine assent or of valid testamentary intent can invalidate a will, most problems with testamentary intent concern undue influence: Did someone so influence the testator that the testator made a disposition of property contrary to what he would have done had he followed his own judgment? The *Franco* case, following *Brown*, concerns this problem of testamentary intent.

In re Estate of Brown

Court of Civil Appeals of Texas
507 S.W.2d 801 (1974)

Ada Brown wrote a short note on an envelope containing a certificate of deposit. It was offered as a codicil to her will and admitted to probate. The court of civil appeals held that the note met the requirements for a holographic codicil and affirmed the judgment of the trial court.

Claude Williams, Chief Justice

This appeal is from a judgment admitting to probate a writing offered as a codicil to the will of Ada B. Brown, deceased. Miss Brown executed a formal and witnessed will in 1965. Following Miss Brown's death in 1970 this will was duly probated by the County Court of Collin County, Texas, without contest. Thereafter Josephine May Benton filed her application in the County Court of Collin County to probate a written instrument as a codicil to Miss Brown's will. The writing tendered as a codicil was a cryptic note written on a envelope. The envelope contained a certificate of deposit dated July 2, 1968, from the First Savings and Loan Association of McKinney, Texas, in the principal sum of $10,000 payable to Ada B. Brown and reciting that the holder thereof would be paid earnings at the rate of five and one-half percent interest per annum. The writing on the envelope was as follows:

> This certafice [sic] from
> Ada B. Brown—
> Goes to Josephine May Benton—

Josephine Brown, a beneficiary under the 1965 will, filed a contest to the probate of the alleged codicil. The County Court ordered the tendered codicil to be probated. Appeal from this judgment was timely made to the District Court.

Trial was had before the court, without a jury. The proponent of the codicil offered in evidence the writing on the envelope, together with its contents. Two witnesses testified that the writing was entirely in the handwriting of Ada B. Brown. Sally Lou Brown Benton, the mother of Josephine May Benton and the other beneficiary under the original will, testified that in July 1968 she took Ada B. Brown to the First Savings and Loan Association in McKinney where she transacted some business. Mrs. Benton testified that at that time she saw the envelope and that Ada B. Brown said to her: "This is for Josephine if anything happens to me, and I don't need it." The witness said that she did not see the envelope again until Miss Brown died in 1970. At that time she gathered up all of Miss Brown's papers which the deceased had given her to keep at the time the deceased went to the hospital, and took these instruments, including the envelope with the writing thereon, to the office of Miss Brown's attorney, Mr. Truett, who is executor under the original will. On cross-examination the witness testified that the envelope, together with its writing, was not attached to the original will in any way; that Mr. Truett had possession of the will in his office.

Based upon this evidence the District Judge decided that the writing tendered was a valid holographic codicil to the 1965 will and decreed that it be admitted to probate. It is from this order that appellant-contestant appeals.

The principal question to be resolved is whether the instrument in question is testamentary in character. Ancillary to this question is whether extrinsic evidence may be offered and received by the court in determining the question of testamentary intent.

The right of a person who owns property in this state to give, bequeath or device it to another at his death is purely statutory. Tex.Prob.Code Ann. § 59 (1956) V.A.T.S., provides that every last will and testament, except when otherwise provided by law, shall be in writing and signed by the testator in person or by another person for him by his direction and shall, if not wholly in the handwriting of the testator, be attested by two or more credible witnesses above the age of fourteen years. Section 63 of the Probate Code provides that no will in writing shall be revoked, except by a subsequent will, codicil, or declaration in writing, executed with like formalities, or by the testator destroying or canceling the same.

Our statutes do not define in so many words what form an instrument shall take before it becomes a will. A will is generally defined as an instrument by which a person makes a disposition of his property, to take effect after his death, and which by its own nature is ambulatory and revocable during his lifetime.

If a writing in substance embodies the factors above enumerated the particular phraseology adopted by the draftsman is of no consequence.

It is established law in Texas that whether there was testamentary intent on the part of the maker is a proper question in a proceeding to probate or in a contest of an application to probate. . . . While the actual words utilized by the maker of an instrument are the primary subject of inquiry to resolve the question of testamentary intent the rule concerning the admissibility of extrinsic evidence to resolve any doubt created by the actual words used seems to be well settled. This rule is but a refinement of the long-followed principle of Texas law that the extrinsic evidence is inadmissible to supply something necessary in, but totally missing from, the instrument itself. The principal case illustrating the applicability of the rule which allows a court to receive extrinsic evidence in determining the vital question of whether a tendered instrument is a will or a codicil is Adams v. Maris, 213 S.W. 622. That case involved the question of whether certain writings on an envelope, together with papers attached or contained therein, constituted the will of Eve Vanlaw. The court, in an exhaustive opinion on the subject of admissibility of the extrinsic evidence to aid in the determination of the intent of the writer of an instrument that would be testamentary, concluded that such document, totally in the handwriting of the writer, was a valid will subject to probate.

Applying the rule announced to the factual situation presented to the trial court we conclude that it was not error for the trial court to receive and consider extrinsic evidence relating to the circumstances which surrounded the preparation of the writing in question as well as declarations on the part of the writer of the instrument wherein she definitely clarified the meaning of the words "from" and "goes to." These words could possibly express the intent of the writer to make a gift *inter vivos* of the certificate. Clearly the statement of the decedent to the effect that she wanted Josephine to have the certificate "if anything happens to me and I don't need it" clearly negates any intention on the part of the writer to give the certificate to Josephine prior to the time that "anything happens to me." The words "if I don't need it" clearly indicate the revocability of the instrument during the lifetime of the writer. The words "goes to" have been held to indicate testamentary intent, i. e., to give property upon death, especially when there are no findings of fact and conclusions of law. These words of the writer, when taken in connection with the fact that the writer did not deliver the certificate to Josephine but kept the same in her private papers where it remained until after her death, constitute adequate evidence of testamentary intent to support the trial court's findings and judgment ordering probate of the instrument.

Appellant-contestant argues that the codicil does not meet the requirements of the law in that it was not executed with the same formality as the original will and that it was not signed by the writer. While it is true that Tex.Prob.Code Ann. § 63 (1956) provides that a prior will may be revoked or changed by the execution of a subsequent codicil "with like formalities" this does not mean that the subsequent codicil must be entirely as formal as the prior will. Rather, the statute requires that the latter instrument must *also be in accordance with legal requirements.*

An instrument which is totally in the handwriting of the deceased, which includes the signature somewhere in the writing, satisfies the statutory requirements for a holographic codicil. It is not necessary that the signature appear at the bottom or end of the instrument in question.

All of appellant-contestant's points of error are overruled. The judgment of the trial court is affirmed.

Affirmed.

In re Estate of Franco

California Court of Appeals
122 Cal. Rptr. 661 (1975)

The decedent's sister filed a petition alleging that the will was obtained by undue influence and fraud. Because there was only circumstantial evidence of undue influence, the trial court ordered the will admitted to probate. The court of appeals reversed the trial court's decision.

Gargano, Associate Justice

These appeals are concerned with a probate action contesting the last will and testament of Carlo Franco and a civil action seeking to set aside a transfer of stock and to have title in the stock restored to the plaintiff; both actions were instituted by the decedent's sister, Caterina Armario. . . . [The portion of the opinion discussing the transfer of stock has been omitted.] The defendant in the probate action was John Leroy Franco, the executor of decedent's estate and decedent's nephew. . . .

The decedent was born in Genoa, Italy; he migrated to this country in his youth and died in Tuolumne County on May 30, 1970, at the age of 76. He was survived by his brother John, his sister Caterina and his sister Rosetta Vassello, who was living in Italy. A second brother, Joseph Franco, had died about two years earlier in Calistoga, California.

After settling in California, Carlo worked for many years as a farm hand on a ranch owned by Sal Ferretis near Groveland.

On May 28, 1968, Joseph Franco died intestate, leaving an estate valued at $40,000; John Franco was appointed administrator of the estate. In the meanwhile, Caterina Armario went to Calistoga and made funeral arrangements for her deceased brother. She also took care of some other matters that needed attention, expending some of her own money in the process. Then, when Caterina's son asked John Franco about presenting a claim in Joseph's estate for reimbursement for his mother, John told the son to "pad" the claim; John Franco and his sister Rosetta Vassello had been feuding over the distribution of an estate in Italy, and John told Caterina's son to double Caterina's expenses so the "son-of-a-bitch in Italy [would] get as little as possible." Later, John Franco showed the padded claim to Carlo and told his brother that Caterina was trying to cheat them out of their share of Joseph Franco's estate; Carlo became very angry over the incident.

On November 29, 1969, John Franco and his wife, Mary C. Franco, took Carlo to John's attorney in Merced where Carlo executed his will; with the exception of a $300 gift to Caterina, the will bequeathed all of Carlo's estate to John Franco's two sons, John Leroy Franco and James Carlo Franco, to be divided equally between them; John Leroy was named executor of the estate. . . .

On May 10, 1970, Carlo died alone in his small cabin. Thereafter, his will was admitted to probate, and John Leroy Franco was appointed the executor of the estate.

On November 2, 1970, Caterina filed a petition for revocation of probate; the petition alleged that the will which was admitted to probate was obtained by undue influence and fraud.

At the trial, it was established that Carlo Franco was illiterate; that he could write his name but he could not read or write English or his native Italian; that he had the mental maturity of a 14 to 16-year-old boy, was very naive in business matters and trusted anyone who was friendly with him; and that he was bashful, honest and very frugal.

It also was established that Caterina Armario was illiterate in the English language and almost illiterate in the Italian language and that she had no understanding of business affairs. There was testimony that she would sign anything that was put before her, that she could be influenced easily and that she and her brother Carlo trusted each other implicitly.

At the conclusion of the trial, the jury, in the probate action, returned a special verdict finding that Carlo Franco's will was obtained by undue influence. . . .

On February 22, 1972, the Francos, in the probate matter, made a motion for judgment notwithstanding the verdict in relation to the issue of undue influence.

The motion was granted, and the court entered an order in the probate action refusing to revoke the probate of the will. . . .

THE WILL CONTEST

We turn to Caterina's appeal in the probate action; she contends that the court erred in granting the Francos' motion for judgment notwithstanding the verdict and thus holding as a matter of law that the will was not obtained by undue influence.

Undue influence consists of conduct which subjugates the will of the testator to the will of another and constrains the testator to make a disposition of his property contrary to and different from that he would have done had he been permitted to follow his own inclination or judgment.

In Estate of Lingenfelter, 38 Cal.2d 571, 585, 241 P.2d 990, 999, the California Supreme Court stated:

> The indicia of undue influence have been stated as follows: '(1) The provisions of the will were unnatural. . . . (2) the dispositions of the will were at variance with the intentions of the decedent, expressed both before and after its execution; (3) the relations existing between the chief beneficiaries and the decedent afforded to the former an opportunity to control the testamentary act; (4) the decedent's mental and physical condition was such as to permit a subversion of his freedom of will; and (5) the chief beneficiaries under the will were active in procuring the instrument to be executed.' These, coupled with a confidential relationship between at least one of the chief beneficiaries and the testator, altogether were held 'sufficient to shift the burden to the proponents of the will to establish an absence of undue influence and coercion and to require the issues to be determined by the jury.'

In the case at bench, there was sufficient evidence to support a jury finding that decedent's mental condition was such as to permit a subversion of his freedom of will; Carlo had the mental maturity of a 14 to 16-year-old boy, and there was testimony that he was bashful and trusted anyone who was friendly to him.

There was also sufficient evidence to support a jury finding that the testamentary dispositions of Carlo's will were at variance with his intentions expressed both before and after its execution; before Carlo made his will, he never expressed a desire to make one; at different times he told his sister that she would inherit all of his American Telephone and Telegraph stock if he predeceased her. After he made the will, he became disenchanted with his nephews and before his death expressed a desire to change the will.

Next, there was substantial evidence for the jury to find that the will was unnatural; decedent in 1969 suddenly left almost his entire estate to two nephews he had only seen on five or six occasions during his lifetime, even though he not only had an older brother, two sisters and other nieces and nephews living, but for many years had been in rapport with his sister Caterina, and had been visiting another relative almost daily. Clearly, a will in which the decedent has left his entire estate to two nephews he had hardly known and seldom seen, to the exclusion of a sister with whom he had a long, close relationship and other close relatives, is unnatural; and while the decedent's action in the instant case may have been explainable, the evidence on this point was conflicting; it was up to the jury to resolve the conflict.

The question narrows to whether the third and fifth factors mentioned in *Estate of Lingenfelter, supra,* are present in this case. More specifically, the crucial question is whether John Leroy Franco, a chief beneficiary in decedent's will, had the opportunity to control his uncle's testamentary act and, if so, whether he actually participated in the preparation and execution of the will.

We have concluded that the circumstantial evidence allows for the inference that John Franco schemed to have his brother Carlo leave the bulk of his estate to John's two sons and that John Leroy Franco and his wife Reva were aware of the scheme and actively participated in its execution. In other words, we believe that the circumstantial evidence, when viewed as a whole, shows that at the very minimum the Francos from Merced not only induced Carlo to make his will but that it was John, John Leroy and Reva who must have suggested its provisions.

In summary, the evidence presented by Caterina in this case raises more than a mere suspicion that Carlo Franco's will was the product of undue influence. It paints a vivid picture of connivance, scheming and the application of undue pressure on the part of clever relatives which culminated in their becoming the objects of a not so clever testator's bounty.

A confidential relationship between the testator and beneficiary is not an essential factor in the indicia of undue influence mentioned in the *Lingenfelter* opinion; all that is required once the other factors enumerated in the opinion are present is circumstantial evidence giving rise to the inference that the relationship existing between the chief beneficiary and decedent offered the former the opportunity to control the testamentary act and that the chief beneficiary was active in procuring the instrument to be executed, at least in the sense that he discussed the terms of the will with the testator and suggested some of its provisions.

The order of the Tuolumne County Superior Court in Probate Action Number A-3748, entered subsequent to the granting of the motion for judgment notwithstanding the verdict, which refused to revoke the probate of the will, is reversed

---

Execution of a Will. While the formalities that must be complied with to validly execute a will vary from state to state, most states require that a will be written, signed, and witnessed. A written document is usually required, although in some states there are by statute certain instances in which oral wills are valid. The writing usually need not be on a particular kind of material nor made by particular instruments. A will can be written on a paper bag, a scrap of paper, or a piece of wallpaper. It can be typed or written in ink or crayon. No particular language is required as long as the testator's intentions can be determined.

A will must be signed by the testator. In some states, statutes specify that the signature be at the end of the will in order to assure that no pages are later added to the document that was signed. In most states, the statute specifies only that the will be signed but does not state where the signature is to appear.

Similarly, each state by statute and court decision indicates the type of signature that will be effective. Use of nicknames ("Junior"), marks ("X"), or other designations ("Mom") will usually be acceptable. As long as the testator has indicated by some mark or sign on the document that he approves and intends it to dispose of property at his death, the signature will be valid. A person who is unable to sign his name or make a mark may by state statute usually have another person, at the testator's request and in his presence, place the testator's signature on the document.

Finally, a will must be witnessed in order to be valid. Most states require two witnesses, but a few states require three. Witnesses are there to verify that the testator actually signed the document and that, according to the witnesses, he or she had the required testamentary intent and capacity at that time. A witness does not have to read the will in order to witness it.

Some states require that the witnesses actually see the testator sign the document; others require only that the testator in some way acknowledge to the witnesses that the signature is his or her signature. Some states also require that the witnesses sign their names to the document in the presence of the testator and in the presence of the other witnesses. The statutes may also require that the will be published, which means that the witnesses must be told that the paper they are signing is a will.

The witnesses to a will usually need not be of a specific age as long as they can understand that they are witnessing a signature. If a witness is an interested person who will receive some property by the will (a beneficiary), some statutes require an additional witness to verify the testator's signature or limit the witness's legacy to the amount he or she would have received had there been no valid will.

While other requirements may be imposed by some statutes, the writing, signing, and witnessing of the will are usually the only formalities that must be met to make a valid will. The will does not have to be prepared by an attorney, although preparation of a simple will by an attorney is usually not very costly. The will does not usually have to be notarized, although a notary can be a witness. The will does not have to be filed in a specific place in the county of a person's residence or handed over to an attorney. Each of those alternatives exists by statute in some states but usually they are not requirements. Whoever has the will of a person at the time that person dies is required by law to file it with a court (usually the probate court). Once the will or wills of a person are on file, admission to probate and the validation of the document as the last will and testament of the decedent can be sought.

Revocation of a Will

Since a will is without legal effect until the testator dies, a testator may revoke a will at any time prior to death. A person usually revokes a will when he or she desires to make a different distribution of the estate. The new will generally includes a clause stating that all prior wills made by the testator are revoked. In other situations, the testator may simply tear up or burn an existing will, leaving property to be distributed under the intestacy laws. In addition to these methods of revoking a will by the act of the testator, the law specifies several circumstances under which revocation of an existing will occurs.

If a person subsequently executes a new will or a codicil (an addition or alteration to an existing will) but does not state that the new revokes the old, the law generally presumes there was the intent to revoke the old will if the new one is totally inconsistent with it. If the new will and the old will are not totally inconsistent, both are read together.

If a person who has written a will changes his or her marital status, some state statutes provide that the will is automatically revoked. Thus the marriage of a person who was single or the divorce of a person who was married can by law automatically revoke a valid will. In some states, a divorce does not revoke the entire will but only that portion providing for the former spouse. State statutes usually provide that a person cannot totally disinherit a spouse. Thus a marriage subsequent to a will may not totally revoke the will; instead the surviving spouse will be allowed to take a share of the testator's estate (often one-third) even if no provision for the spouse was made in the will.

The birth of a child usually does not revoke a will, but most states provide that a child born after a will has been executed will receive that portion of the estate of the testator that he or she would have received had no will been made. However, if it appears from the terms of a will that a person does not want that child (or other children who were born before exe-cution of the will) to inherit property, the testator's intentions will be honored. Statutes usually do not provide for a forced share for the children of a decedent in the same way they provide for the surviving spouse.

ESTATE ADMINISTRATION

Whether or not the decedent makes a valid will, there still must be some method by which the decedent's property can be collected, debts and taxes paid, and the estate distributed among those people who are entitled to receive it. The rules and procedures for administering a decedent's estate determine what happens to the property from the moment of the decedent's death until the property and title to it are distributed according to law.

Probate of an Estate

Estates are usually administered according to statutory law and rules of procedure developed and overseen by probate courts. Note the court's reliance on statutes in the *Plummer* case.

In re Estate of Plummer
Appellate Court of Indiana
219 N.E.2d 917 (1966)

This case concerns the probate of two joint wills. The will of the husband was admitted to probate in Oregon, and a copy of the wife's will was submitted for probate in Indiana. The Indiana trial court admitted the copy of the wife's will to probate; the heir of the wife objected to that decision and appealed. The appellate court affirmed the trial court's admission of the wife's will to probate.

Wickens, Presiding Justice.

In 1954 Joseph and Inez Plummer executed joint wills in the State of Oregon where they then resided. Joseph died a resident of that state in 1955 and the instrument was probated as his will there. In 1958 Inez Plummer died a resident of Allen County, Indiana. Thereafter steps were taken in this proceeding to establish the will probated in Oregon as her will.

On June 2, 1961 the Allen Superior Court of Indiana pursuant to a proper petition, entered its finding and order for probate of said will, the necessary part of which is as follows:

> "That said Will was duly executed in the manner and form as provided by law and complies with the laws of the State of Indiana, and which said Will was declared by said Testatrix to be her Last Will and Testament in the presence of Philip Hayter and Janet Lundy, the two subscribing witnesses to said Will; and that the said Testatrix signed said Will in the presence of said subscribing witnesses, and the said subscribing witnesses signed said Will as such subscribing witnesses at the request and in the presence of said Testatrix and in the presence of each other, and said testimony being duly recorded in the County Court of Polk County, Oregon, and the original of said Will being of record in said County and State, it is, therefore, ordered, adjudged, and decreed by the Court that said photostatic duly authenticated copy of said Will be duly admitted to probate as the Last Will and Testament of the said Inez V. Plummer, deceased, and that the same be duly recorded in the Record of Wills of Allen County, Indiana."

Appellee was then appointed and qualified as administrator with the will annexed.

This appeal raises the question of whether the trial court had jurisdiction to probate as the will of the decedent a document which was in the custody of an Oregon court and had already been probated in Oregon as the will of decedent's husband.

Lack of jurisdiction to probate the instrument in question seems to be asserted by appellant on the assumption that an order of probate is void if it is based on proceedings which do not literally comply with the statutes regarding the proof required to admit a will to probate. Without total agreement on that premise, we shall examine the proceedings here to determine their conformity with the Indiana Probate Code and what we understand may be the common law pertaining thereto.

The Probate Code, which has been in effect since 1953, is very specific on the mechanics of probate. It contains a section which describes who may file a petition for probate of will, which also provides that such petition may be combined with the request for issuance of letters testamentary. This section states that no notice that a will is to be offered for probate or that it has been probated shall be required. Significantly, this section permits the will to be probated "whether the same is written or is unwritten, is in his [petitioner's] possession or not, is lost, destroyed, or *without the state*. . . ." [Our insertion and emphasis.]

Finally the Probate Code summarizes the two vital findings required for probate of will as:

> "(a) When a will is offered for probate, if the court or the judge or the clerk in vacation *finds that the decedent is dead* and *that the will was executed in all respects according to law,* it shall be admitted to probate as the last

will of the deceased, unless objections are filed as provided in section 716 [§ 7-116]." [Our emphasis.]

We find no statement in the Code that the original document purporting to be the will must be produced at the hearing on petition to probate. Not only does the Code not contain such specific requirement, but as we have seen the legislature contemplated that the document may not be in petitioner's possession, and that it might even be "without the state * * *." This legislative use of words clearly leaves it to the judiciary to determine what kind of evidence may be required. Until probate practically no legal rights are established by the paper purporting to be a will.

Therefore, this instrument, which because it has been probated becomes the effective will of the testator, is prior to probate merely evidence of the existence of a will. Such fact can also be established without requiring the original document to be present in court. We hold it to be unessential that the original of a written instrument purporting to be a will be *presented* to obtain probate jurisdiction.

Also appellant urges that the trial court was without jurisdiction to entertain probate because the court's order does not show that "one [1] or more of the subscribing witnesses" proved the will as provided in Section 709 (Burns' § 7-109), supra. In fact appellant contends that the court order shows proof was not in accord with his interpretation of the statutory requirement. As we have heretofore indicated, the necessary parts of the court's order are set out verbatim in the early portion of this opinion. It is not essential that the court show in its order of probate who testified. It is only required to validate the will, that the order show two things, (1) that the testator is dead and (2) that the will was executed according to law. The order of June 2, 1961 as set out in this opinion, is sufficient to establish these two points.

Appellant waited two years and seven months to then file an objection to probate. No contest has yet been filed according to the record before us and appellant's statement. After a will has been probated in Indiana and thus is judicially declared to be duly executed, only a will contest can present any question of the validity of the instrument or of its execution. Such contests are purely statutory; they can only be brought within the time and upon the grounds prescribed by statute.

We accordingly find and hold that the trial court had jurisdiction to probate the will of Inez Plummer. It exercised that power and such action was not in excess of the court's jurisdiction. Its action became final before any proper attack was commenced.

The judgment is in all things affirmed.

The first step in the administration or probate of a decedent's estate is to determine if the decedent had a valid will. If there is a will, the will should contain the name of the person who the decedent desired to be responsible for administering the estate—the *personal representative*. If there is no will, one of the decedent's heirs, usually a surviving spouse or child, will petition the probate court to be named the personal representative. The court will usually appoint such a close heir as personal representative although in some states the person appointed to administer the estate must live within the state where the court being petitioned is located.

If there is a will, the will must be admitted

to probate before it is considered valid. Persons interested in the will or in the decedent's estate must be notified that there is a petition to admit the will to probate. At the court hearing, proof that the will was executed according to the statutory requirements will be given. If anyone questions the execution of the will or either the testamentary intent or the capacity of the decedent, a will contest may develop. In extraordinary cases such as occurred when billionaire Howard Hughes died, the will contests may take years to resolve. In the usual case, the hearing of the court to probate the will and appoint the personal representative (whether there is a will or not) will be simple, uncontested, and quick. If more than one person seeks to be the personal representative, statutory provisions giving preference to close relatives will have to be consulted and interpreted by the court.

Once the personal representative has been appointed, the actual administration of the estate begins. Creditors of the decedent are notified, usually by publication in a local newspaper, that they must present their claims against the estate of the decedent within a specified time period (generally six months or less). A monetary award for the support of a surviving spouse while the estate is being administered is then made; the temporary support or allowance paid to the spouse generally takes precedence over all other claims.

Next, the personal representative must inventory all the assets in the estate and establish the value of the property. If there are sufficient assets, the funeral and burial expenses, expenses of the decedent's last illness, estate administration costs, and debts of the decedent are then paid.

Taxes that may be due the state or the federal government must be determined and paid. Estate taxes due to the federal government are assessed against the estate based on its value. Sizable exemptions from the estate taxes, particularly for bequests from spouse to spouse, were recently incorporated in the estate tax laws. Accordingly, most estates today do not have significant estate tax liability.

Inheritance taxes due to the state government are assessed on the property received from the decedent. The amount of tax depends not only on the value of the property received but also on the relationship between the decedent and the inheritor; the closer the relationship, the lower the rate of inheritance tax. These taxes are then due not from the decedent giver but from the living recipient. However, since the testator may have provided by will that the estate was to pay the inheritance tax, it can become liable for this tax. In any event, the taxing authorities can ensure that their taxes are paid before the title to any property is transferred from the estate.

After all administration expenses, taxes, and valid claims or debts have been paid, the personal representative furnishes an accounting to the court and, once it is approved, distributes the remaining property and money to the beneficiaries.

Alternative Methods of Estate Administration

Statutes in a number of states provide several alternatives to administering an estate through the probate procedure. A very simple procedure can usually be used for small estates that do not contain unusual amounts or types of property. Often these estates are exempt from the normal probate procedures. Other statutes provide for a probate procedure that can be used if the persons interested in the estate have no objections to it. Usually, the beneficiaries and heirs of the decedent are allowed to independently administer the estate with only minimal review by probate court authorities.

Finally, there are a number of estate planning techniques that can be used to minimize the need for estate administration under the probate court. Trusts, life insurance policies, custodial accounts, and joint tenancy agreements are often used. These techniques are discussed in the concluding pages of this chapter. Not each method is suitable in every situation, but alternatives to the formalized probate method of estate administration exist and should be considered in formulating an estate plan.

ESTATE PLANNING

Estate planning is the process of planning for the future distribution of a person's estate. The distribution of property during a person's life as well as after death can be planned to achieve various objectives. An estate plan cannot be simply chosen and then put aside; it requires periodic review and revision as a person's assets increase, marital status changes, and expenses such as those related to rearing and educating children or caring for elderly parents fluctuate.

There are often numerous objectives around which the estate must be planned. Generally, the primary objective is to ensure that the testator's property is distributed to those persons he or she wants to provide for, at the time and in the portion and manner most desirable to the testator. The estate plan also seeks to minimize the taxes and fees that will have to be paid from the estate. The payment of substantial taxes not only would interfere with the primary objective but also could force the sale of valuable property, such as a business, that the testator may prefer to pass along intact to the chosen beneficiaries.

Estate Planning and Taxation

The desire to avoid or minimize taxes due at one's death should not be the primary purpose of estate planning. A person's estate plan should seek instead to meet objectives regarding the distribution of the estate and the care and support of those who are to benefit from it. Only after the objectives of the plan have been determined and the means for attaining them have been examined should attention be focused on the taxation of the estate.

There are several taxes that affect an estate plan. The two that are of central concern are usually the federal estate tax and the state inheritance tax. Both must be paid before the decedent's property can be transferred to heirs or named beneficiaries.

Income taxes also must be paid from the estate for income received by the decedent prior to death. If the estate receives income while it is being administered, further income taxes may be due. One other aspect of income taxation is usually of concern to the estate planner. Since the federal income tax is levied on a graduated scale with a higher rate being assessed at higher income levels, splitting income between two persons generally results in lower taxes being due. For example, a person in the 50-percent tax bracket who receives $5,000 annually in stock dividends would owe $2,500 in taxes on that income. However, if that stock were given to other persons (such as children or a trust) who were in a 20-percent tax bracket, the tax liability on that same property ($1,000) would be significantly less.

Estate Planning and Trusts

Under a trust, a person has legal title to property but must use that property for the benefit of other people (the beneficiaries). The person who is given legal title to the property (the trustee) is generally instructed how the property is to be used in a written document referred to as a trust agreement or trust deed. If a person enters into a trust agreement and transfers property to someone else while living, the trust is referred to as a living or *inter vivos* trust. If the trust is established by the terms of a person's will, it is referred to as a *testamentary trust.*

A person who creates a living trust (the settlor) may want to retain the power to change the trust agreement to name a new trustee or totally revoke the trust. This type of living trust is a revocable trust and, since the creator of the trust can change it, the property in trust will usually be taxed as part of the estate of its creator. On the other hand, since the property has been transferred during the settlor's lifetime, it would not be property that is transferred at the settlor's death. Accordingly, the assets in the trust will usually not be subject to probate on the settlor's death.

If a person creates an irrevocable trust during his lifetime, the property in the trust is legally owned by the trustee. The trust, not the person who created it, now must pay taxes on income earned by the trust property. If the creator of the trust dies after having transferred property to the trustee, generally no estate taxes are assessed against that property and no probate fees are due for its administration. The property is not in the estate of the decedent at his death since he earlier transferred it to another person (the trustee). However, since the trust property is managed and administered by the trustee from the date the trust is established, fees are usually charged for those services. Most major banks have trust departments staffed by a variety of people who provide professional service to the property that the bank holds as trustee.

A testamentary trust found in a will does not become effective until the death of the testator. This means of course that the testamentary trust can be revoked or modified at any time during its creator's lifetime. Since the trust assets are in the control of the testator until death, the trust is actually created by transfer from the executor or personal representative of the decedent's estate to the person named as trustee. In many cases, the creator of a testamentary trust will name a bank to act as both the personal representative of the estate and as trustee of the trust. Its powers and directions are those specified by the will creating the trust (as well as some statutory and common law provisions).

One of the benefits of a trust is that it provides for professional property management by the trustee instead of by the person for whom the property is to be used. Another benefit is that the income from property can be given to one person for a limited time (ten years, twenty years, or a lifetime) with instructions that after that time another person is to become owner of the property. In this way, a trust can "skip" a generation, and the person in the skipped generation, who never owned the property, would not have that property subject to estate taxes or property fees at his or her death.

In the following example, George's children, Alice and Bill, are the skipped generation:

George Smith has $500,000 that he wants to give to his children and grandchildren. Since George's children are adults and have good jobs and reasonable incomes, George, by means of a trust, will primarily provide for his grandchildren. Assume that George has two children, Alice and Bill, and that each of them has two children; George then has four grandchildren. His inter vivos trust agreement would:

1. Give $500,000 to the First National Bank as trustee of the George Smith Trust
2. Provide that the income from the trust be paid annually in equal amounts to his children, Alice and Bill
3. Provide that on the death of either Alice or Bill, their share of the trust (one-half for each) should be kept in trust for the benefit of their children (grandchildren 1, 2, 3, and 4) until the youngest grandchild attains age 30 and then given to the grandchildren as their own property. (If one of the grandchildren dies before attaining age 30, that share could go to that grandchild's brothers or sisters. If both grandchildren of the same parent die before reaching age 30, their

shares would go to the surviving grandchildren.)

Review the *Estate of Hart* case to see how one court interpreted an inter vivos irrevocable trust agreement.

Connecticut Bank & Trust Co. (Estate of Hart) v. Hills

Supreme Court of Connecticut

254 A.2d 453 (1969)

The trustee of a trust brought this action in superior court to have the trust language construed. The instrument used the term "descendant" and the trustee wanted to know if that term included an adopted son of one of the trust beneficiaries. The superior court held that it did not include the adopted son and an appeal was filed with the supreme court of Connecticut. The supreme court affirmed the trial court's judgment.

King, Chief Justice

The plaintiff bank is the trustee of an irrevocable, inter vivos trust established by Helen Hart, of Hartford, on January 27, 1949. The provisions of the trust which are material to a disposition of this proceeding may be stated in simplified form as follows: The trust, the validity and interpretation of which was to be governed by the laws of Connecticut, provided that the income be paid to Lotta J. Kirkpatrick during her lifetime; that at her death the income should be paid equally to Charles I. Hills and Thomas K. Hills, who were brothers; that, at the death of either, his share of the income should continue to be paid "per stirpes, to his descendants living at the time of each regular income payment * * * during the period of the Trust and, if all descendants of such deceased cousin should die during such period the Trustee shall pay over the entire net income from this Trust to the survivor of said two cousins during his life". The father of Charles and Thomas Hills was the brother of Miss Hart's mother, and thus Charles and Thomas were Miss Hart's cousins.

Lotta J. Kirkpatrick died on May 26, 1962, and thereafter the income was paid to Charles and Thomas Hills until January 26, 1966, when Charles Hills died.

Charles Hills had no children of his own, but his wife had a son, William, born May 22, 1922, of a prior marriage, whom Charles adopted on March 19, 1936, and who thereafter had the name of William S. Hills and continued to live with his mother and adoptive father until his own marriage in 1944.

The basic question in this proceeding is whether William S. Hills is entitled to receive his adoptive father's share of the income of the trust and this question in turn depends on whether, as an adopted son, he is embraced in the term "descendants" of Charles Hills as used in the trust.

The present action was instituted by the trustee seeking advice as to the proper interpretation of the trust with respect to William's rights, if any, under it.

The words "descendant" or "issue" in their ordinary and primary meaning connote lineal relationship by blood, and they will be so construed unless it clearly appears that they were used in a more extended sense.

The court concluded that it did not clearly appear that Miss Hart used the word "descendants" with other than its primary meaning, and, so, it refused to find that William was embraced in the term "descendants" and answered the questions accordingly. From that decision William took this appeal.

William claims that under our cases words such as "descendant" or "issue" include an adopted child where (1) the adoption occurred prior to the execution of the instrument to be construed, (2) the testator or settlor regarded the adopted person as the son or daughter of the adoptive parent, and (3) the testator or settlor never expressed opposition to the adoption.

Our cases do not support any such mechanical rule of construction.

Moreover, precedents in the construction of wills or trusts are seldom of persuasive force, since the surrounding circumstances in each case, as well as the precise words employed, usually differ significantly.

Second, the quest in each case is the expressed intent of the testator or settlor in the light of the circumstances surrounding him at the time the instrument was executed.

Miss Hart was an educated woman, and there was much justification for the conclusion of the court that, had she intended to include William, she would not have chosen, in expressing such an intention, an inapt word primarily signifying lineal blood relationship. William claims, on a number of grounds, that the language of the trust instrument, read in the light of all of the circumstances surrounding Miss Hart at the time of execution, clearly demonstrated an intention that the word "descendants" should include him as an adopted child of Charles.

It is true, as William claims, that the fact that the adoption took place about thirteen years prior to the execution of the trust is an important factor. This is because it is seldom that any clear expression of an intention to include an adopted child in the use of a word such as "descendant" can be found if the adoption took place subsequent to the execution of the instrument and if the settlor, when the instrument was executed, did not know that any adoption was even contemplated. But the converse of William's claim does not follow. Thus, neither the fact that the adoption preceded the execution of the trust instrument nor the fact that, as the court found from circumstantial evidence, Miss Hart probably knew of the adoption when she established the trust would, even together, suffice to require the court to conclude that, in using the term "descendants" of Charles, she intended to include his adopted son William.

William makes much of the fact that there is nothing to indicate that Miss Hart disapproved of his adoption and that this added element is sufficient to prove that she intended to include him. This argument has little weight. It would have been rather bad manners and rather bad taste if Miss Hart had taken it upon herself to express to William, to his parents, or to anyone else, her disapproval of the adoption. This is especially so because it does not appear that she knew of the adoption until it had taken place and because William was the son of Charles' own wife by a previous marriage. Whatever might have been the case had Miss Hart expressed disapproval of the adoption, we attach no controlling significance to her failure so to do.

William claims that, since Thomas and Charles were in their late forties when the trust was executed and since neither had had natural children, it is necessary to conclude that the word "descendants" included an adopted child since there was no natural child to which the term "descendants" could apply. This is a circumstance to be considered, but many men of fifty or over become fathers, and we do not find this claim of William of controlling weight. It must also be remembered that the inter vivos trust was irrevocable and could not have been subsequently altered by Miss Hart, even had she so desired, to the prejudice of nonconsenting beneficiaries.

William also claims that there is a presumption against the disinheritance of heirs at law and that, under our adoption statute William was given the rights of inheritance of a natural child and, so, became an heir at law of his adoptive father.

Obviously, under a broad type of adoption statute such as ours, the use of the word "child" or "children" as intentionally inclusive of an adopted child is not unlikely. If the testator or settlor is the adopting parent, the term "child" or "children" is ordinarily held inclusive of an adopted child. But the same cannot be said of the term "descendants", which was the term used here, since that word, much more than the word "child" or "children", distinctly and emphatically connotes a lineal blood relationship.

The trial court concluded that there was nothing clearly to indicate that Miss Hart used the word "descendants" in other than its primary sense and that when so used it would not include William. We find no justification for disturbing either conclusion.

Affirmed.

Estate Planning and Joint Property

Joint property is used in estate planning to transfer property from one person to another by an agreement made during a person's life. Thus joint property is usually not in the *probate* estate of the first of the two persons to die; that property has been transferred by agreement prior to that person's death to the second person. However, joint property is usually a part of the *taxable* estate of the first person to die.

There are several ways in which the ownership of property can be shared by two or more people. The first method is to establish the two or more persons as joint tenants with rights of survivorship; the second is to establish them as joint tenants in common. The first method is probably the most common; most states have statutes that provide that bank accounts or securities held in two names are usually held as joint tenants with the right of survivorship. For example, Tom and Jane have a $1,000 savings account in their joint names. If Tom dies before Jane, the $1,000 is owned by Jane. It is not transferred to her by Tom's will or by the intestacy laws but by the agreement they made while they were both alive.

If Tom and Jane instead hold the savings account as tenants in common, both of them own one-half or $500. When Tom dies, $500 is transferred by his will or by the intestacy laws to his heirs or beneficiaries. Thus Jane would still have her $500, but the $500 owned by Tom might be transferred to her or to someone else.

If Tom and Jane are husband and wife, their joint property is sometimes referred to as being owned by them as "tenants in the entirety." This is simply a special term for joint tenants who are spouses and who want the survivor by virtue of the agreement they made (or which the law assumes they made) to inherit all their jointly held property.

A husband and wife often hold title to property jointly. This allows each access to the property during his or her lifetime and automatically provides that the property passes to the survivor on the death of either. Property that is held by joint tenants with right of survivorship (or by tenants in the entirety) avoids probate fees but usually not estate taxes. Often, because of the size of the estate and the marital deduction that the estate tax laws allow for transfers at death to one's spouse, estate taxes are not a consideration in the estate plan. Thus, joint property is a viable estate planning device for many people.

Estate Planning and Insurance

Life insurance can be used in a variety of ways in estate planning. Ownership of an insurance policy may be established in such a way that the proceeds from the policy at the insured's death will not be subject to federal estate taxes. Life insurance is usually not subject to probate expenses since the benefits are due pursuant to the policy and not by virtue of any provision in a will or the intestacy laws. In many states, some of the proceeds from insurance policies on the decedent's life are also exempt from state inheritance taxes.

Life insurance is thus often used as a means of providing security for the average person. A variety of policies—whole life, term, endowment, annuity—are available to serve different needs and desires. Persons who have significant assets in a business often use insurance as a means for transferring those assets to the surviving business associates. The business owns the insurance policy on the partner or key employee, and on that person's death the proceeds from the policy are used by the surviving business associates to purchase the decedent's share and to compensate the estate of the deceased for the decedent's ownership interest in the business.

Estate Planning and Custodial Accounts

The estate tax laws allow one to transfer during one's lifetime a $10,000 gift each year to a single donee or recipient. Thus if George Smith has three children, he can give each of them $10,000 each year ($30,000 total) and the gift will not affect the estate tax or inheritance tax that might be due if that money were transferred at his death. Gifts in these amounts can be made during one's lifetime without the donor incurring any tax liability.

If the recipient or donee is a child (under the legal age of majority in his or her state of residence), the gift must be given to someone in trust for the child. One of the most common ways to give such gifts is to establish a "custodial account." The donor can be the custodian or may name another person as custodian. When the property is transferred from the donor to the custodian, usually the property is no longer in the donor's estate (there can be some tax problems with a transfer from the donor to himself as custodian). If the donor dies, that property is not subject to taxes, either estate or inheritance, or to fees assessed for probate administration. During the time the property is being held for the child, the income received from the property is subject to income tax assessed on the child and not on the donor or custodian. If the child has little other property, the income may not total enough to subject the child to income taxes.

A custodial account established for a minor child thus allows the donor to remove property from his estate, possibly saving estate and inheritance taxes. Furthermore, since the property is owned by the custodian for the child, the income tax liability has been shifted from the donor to the child, and that probably decreases or eliminates some income tax liability. Probate fees are also saved if the property otherwise would be a part of the donor's estate.

It must be realized, though, that the transfer

of property to a custodian for a child legally transfers the ownership of that property to the child. The custodian cannot use it for his or her own benefit; it must be used for the child. Further, once the child attains the age of majority, the balance of the account must be turned over to the child. The control of the property is then in the child's hands, not the donor's.

However, if the donor wishes to establish a fund for the child's expenses (such as for a college education) and is willing to use the fund for the child while the child is a minor and to transfer it to the child when he or she attains the age of majority, the custodial account can be a useful tool in the donor's estate plan.

REVIEW PROBLEMS

1. On January 12, 1962, Thomas Jackson, an attorney, wrote to several of his clients; "As I am rather ill, I am discontinuing my active practice." Four months later, Jackson signed a will that his attorney had prepared for him. The will left Jackson's property to his wife and nothing to his two sons by a prior marriage. The two sons contended that the letter and other evidence showed that, during the period just prior to the date on which their father signed the will, Jackson was forgetful, less talkative and communicative, unable to drive a car, and prone to sit and stare for long periods of time. The decedent was seventy-two when he died on July 9, 1962. Do you think the decedent lacked testamentary capacity to make a will? Jackson v. Jackson 238 A. 2d 852, Court of Appeals of Maryland (1968)

2. Charles Jones and Mary Jones entered into a separation agreement that stipulated, among other things, that Charles execute a will providing that Mary and their daughter Betty would each receive a portion of his property and that such will would not be revoked. Charles executed a will that conformed to the agreement; however, ten years later he executed another will. The second will expressly revoked the first and named Charles's second wife, Helen, as his sole beneficiary. Is the second will valid? Jones v. Jones 200 S.E. 2d 725, Supreme Court of Georgia (1973)

3. William Birkeland died in 1972. In 1970, he had a document stated to be a will drafted by an attorney. However, contrary to the attorney's instructions, he did not sign it in the attorney's office. He had it sent to him and he signed it alone. Then, on separate occasions, it was witnessed by two witnesses. Birkeland did not tell either witness that the document was a will, and neither saw him sign his name. One witness said Birkeland had already signed it, and the other said he didn't recall if there was any other signature on it. The state statute requires that a will (1) be signed by the testator (2) in the presence of two attesting witnesses and (3) be acknowledged by the testator to the witnesses as his will. Is this will validly executed? In re Estate of Birkeland 519 P 2d 154, Supreme Court of Montana (1974)

4. A father wrote a letter to his son containing the following language: "I want to inform you that I bequeathed to you by my last Will the farm in Converville, Virginia after my wife's death and my own death. I have the Will in my safe here and it nullifies the one which is in the bank. Be sure and keep this letter." The son says the letter is a valid holographic will. The state statute says a will totally in the handwriting of the testator and signed by him can be given effect even if it is not witnessed. Does the letter constitute a will? Can it revoke a prior will

(the one in the bank)? Mumaw v. Mumaw 203 S.E. 2d 136, Supreme Court of Virginia (1974)

5. The decedent executed a will approximately one year before death. In the will she expressly excluded her husband because "he is financially well off" and her daughter because "she is financially well off and has not visited me for many years." The decedent was eighty-two when she died. Toward the end of her life, she expressed hostility toward her husband and voiced delusions about his attempts to poison her (which the facts show he did not do). The husband claims the decedent was unduly influenced by her son, who: (1) took his mother to a lawyer's office to arrange for her to make a will; (2) asked the family doctor to witness his mother's will but, when the doctor refused unless the mother was examined by a psychiatrist, declined to take his mother to a psychiatrist; (3) was present with his mother in the lawyer's office when she conferred about the will and also when she signed it. Do you think these facts constitute undue influence sufficient to set aside the will? In re Estate of Goetz 61 Cal. Rptr. 181, California Court of Appeals (1967)

6. Decedent died intestate in Buffalo, New York. Surviving him were six brothers and sisters. Also surviving him was a person who claimed to be his daughter. She claimed that the decedent had lived with her mother in Florida, where she now resided, for fifteen years prior to the decedent's move to Buffalo three years before his death. The person who claimed to be his daughter said that under Florida law she could be considered the decedent's daughter and as such should be chosen to be the personal representative of his estate. Under New York law, she would not be considered his daughter and would not have a claim to be his personal representative. Should the laws of Florida be referred to in order to determine her legal status and claim to be his personal representative? In re Estate of Thomas 367 N.Y.S. 2d 182, Surrogate's Court, Erie County (1975)

7. The decedent executed a valid will. Subsequent to its execution, he remarried but did not execute any other will or codicil. By state statute, the decedent's remarriage after the execution of his will revoked that portion of the will that bequeathed property to his first wife. The decedent's wife at the time of his death (his second wife) claimed that, since the state statute revokes a portion of the decedent's will, it also revokes his choice in that will of his personal representative. She claimed that, as his wife, she should be appointed his personal representative. Do you agree? Estate of Shemin 136 Cal.Rptr. 668, California Court of Appeals (1977)

8. The decedent died intestate; his widow selected her brother to be the personal representative of the decedent's estate. By the intestacy laws, the decedent's estate is to be shared by his widow, children, and grandchildren. The decedent's only brother objects to the appointment of the widow's brother as the personal representative. Should the court review his objection? Wansley v. Tull 264 S.E. 2d 567, Georgia Court of Appeals (1980)

PART VI
GOVERNMENT REGULATION

CHAPTER 37

Government Regulation of Business and the Role of Administrative Agencies

Part VI of this text deals with the impact of government regulatory agencies on business decision making. It was noted in Chapter 2 that recent court decisions interpreting the commerce clause of the U.S. Constitution have extended federal government influence over business activities affecting interstate commerce. Parallel to this trend in court decisions, Congress has created numerous administrative agencies to regulate business activities. This trend has stimulated the present national debate over whether government regulates business too much or not enough. Those who argue that there is too much regulation say that the President and Congress should get government "off the back" of business and let the laws of supply and demand dictate prices and production. They urge deregulation of business and elimination of some federal and state regulatory agencies. Those who argue in favor of government regulation note that it is the role of Congress, and of the regulatory agencies it has established, to protect the wider public interest. Pointing out that corporations are created to serve only the narrow interests of their stockholders, they argue that without government regulation the public interest would not be served in many instances where business activity impacts upon a community, a state, or the nation as a whole. This debate should be kept in mind while reading the chapters in Part VI.

The present chapter discusses the historical background of government regulation, the reasons for the creation of administrative agencies, and their role in regulating the commerce of this nation. Chapter 38 considers the types of business behavior that administrative agencies and courts have traditionally scrutinized under the antitrust laws. Chapters 39 and 40 examine several agencies that have been at the center of the debate over government regulation: the Federal Trade Commission (FTC), the Equal Employment Opportunity Commission, and the Office of Contract Compliance in the U.S. Department of Labor.

HISTORY OF GOVERNMENT REGULATION

In the eighteenth century the royal governments of Europe regulated and sometimes monopolized all forms of commerce. Their fear of such centralized government and economic regulation led the founders of the United States to espouse private property concepts and a laissez-faire theory of government. Eventually, however, the need to preserve competition and prevent corporate bad conduct made regulation a government interest. The Interstate Commerce Act (1887) was passed in response to farmers' complaints that the railroads were charging discriminatory rates. The Sherman Antitrust Act (1890) was passed in response to the growth of combinations or trusts in oil, whisky, sugar, lead, and beef. Federal regulation grew with the passage of the Clayton Act (1914) and the Federal Trade Commission Act (1914). Despite the passage of new legislation, the courts generally accepted the arguments of lawyers representing business, resisting many attempts by federal agencies to regulate business activities.

This came to an end in the 1930s when a breakdown of the free enterprise system necessitated vastly increased government intervention in the nation's economic life. The creation of such agencies as the Federal Communications Commission (FCC), the National Labor Relations Board (NLRB), the Civil Aeronautics Board (CAB), and the Securities and Exchange Commission (SEC) initiated unprecedented federal regulation of business. The acceptance by the courts of regulation was based in large part on their interpretation of congressional authority under the Commerce Clause. With the advent of civil-rights and worker-safety legislation in the 1960s and 1970s, new areas of regulation, along with new administrative agencies, came into being. In the federal government today we have over 150 regulatory agencies that affect all aspects of individual and business activity.[1]

ADMINISTRATIVE AGENCIES

Definition and Nature

As previously noted, every type of business enterprise in the United States falls within the area of concern of one or more administrative agencies. Our political system operates so extensively through administrative agencies that they have been called a "fourth branch of government" and the United States has been described as an "administrative state." Administrative agencies can be defined as governmental bodies, other than the courts and legislatures, that carry out the administrative tasks of government and affect the rights of private parties through adjudication or rule making.[2]

Administrative agencies are found at every level of government. Often they are called boards, commissions, or agencies; but the terms department, bureau, division, office, or authority also frequently designate an administrative agency. A municipal health board, a county zoning commission, a state public utilities commission, and federal organizations such as the NLRB and the Internal Revenue Service are but a few of the many agencies that directly influence American life.

Administrative agencies differ considerably in size. In general, federal agencies are highly structured, staffed with hundreds or thousands of employees; state and local agencies tend to be smaller and more loosely organized. As a result, state and local agencies are more informal, and much important business is carried out behind the scenes by people who are personally acquainted with the problems and the parties or their representatives. People in state and local agencies are also usually acquainted with others in government and can interact with them informally. Frequently they work in the same office building, share other facilities, and have a background of common participation in state and local party politics.

Administrative agencies affect the rights of private parties in many ways. Some, such as parole boards or the Immigration and Naturalization Service of the U.S. Department of Justice, are concerned with matters involving rights as basic as liberty itself. Others, such as state worker's compensation boards, make determinations that involve substantial monetary claims. The Interstate Commerce Commission (ICC) and state public utility commissions fix rates that influence profits in sizable segments of the economy. A principal function of other agencies is to police certain types of activities, such as the sale of liquor, by granting licenses and permits. Many of these same agencies also attempt to protect the public by prohibiting certain actions under threat of fine or suspension of license.

Sometimes an agency has the power to bring criminal actions against those who violate a statute that the agency has been authorized to enforce. The fields in which agencies operate are extensive and their influence in our society is far-reaching.

Reasons For Growth

With the growth of federal legislation noted previously, Congress found it necessary to set up agencies to carry out the details of the statutes enacted. Congress is composed of 435 members of the House of Representatives and 100 Senators. Collectively they could not realistically regulate the radio and television industry, for example, on a daily basis. Thus, when passing the Federal Communication Act of 1933, they created the FCC. A second reason for creating the agencies was the need for expertise to deal with complex and technical details that demand attention. For example, imagine a new Senator or Representative attempting to deal with the daily regulation of satellite communications. Members of the FCC staff have the training and experience to perform that task. A third reason Congress created administrative agencies was to keep a large number of complex cases out of the already overcrowded federal courts. To the extent that the ICC can settle disputes over trucking routes, for example, it keeps trucking cases out of court. Fourth, as one legal scholar notes, the desire of Congress to make legislative changes that will not be interpreted or construed away by conservative courts may be one of "the prime reasons for the growth of the administrative process."[3] For example, when Congress enacted the 1964 and 1965 civil rights acts it also created the Equal Employment Opportunity Commission. Congress was changing social policy with these statutes, and it wanted an administrative agency that would implement the legislation as Congress intended.

ADMINISTRATIVE AGENCIES AND CONSTITUTIONAL SEPARATION OF POWERS

Historically our government has been viewed as composed of three independent branches:

the executive, the legislative, and the judicial. Each possesses certain powers that enable it to restrain, but not entirely control, the actions of the others. The relationships between administrative agencies and the traditional branches of government influence to a large degree what agencies can accomplish. A working knowledge of these relationships is important to business people, for they can use this knowledge to modify the impact of agency activity.

Before examining the relationships, an important difference in the lines of authority between certain agencies and the executive branch needs to be considered. Several of the largest and most influential federal agencies are not part of any department of the executive branch. The ICC, FTC, SEC, and NLRB are examples of independent agencies that are very important to the business community. In some states major administrative agencies are independent of the chief executive. Many state constitutions provide for the election of important administrative officers, such as the attorney general and the state treasurer, and deny the governor the right to remove even appointive department heads except for cause.

On the other hand, some well-known federal agencies are parts of executive departments. For example, both the Food and Drug Administration and the Social Security Administration are parts of the U.S. Department of Health and Human Services. The Federal Aviation Administration (FAA) is a part of the U.S. Department of Transportation. Most local agencies and a majority of state agencies are also organized within larger executive departments. On a day-to-day basis, this does not make much difference because the agencies operate without interference from the other components of the executive branch, but when agencies are organized within the executive branch, greater potential for direct control exists. Many major policy decisions within the jurisdictional power of the agencies may be influenced by the chief executive and his staff.

Executive Branch and Independent Agencies

Although many federal agencies are structurally independent of the executive branch, the President, with the advice and consent of the Senate, does appoint the chief agency officials. Once the appointment is confirmed, however, the President has no direct control over the appointee. He cannot remove the individual from office. In addition, the enabling act that creates a commission generally requires that the commission itself be politically balanced within practical limits. The Federal Trade Commission Act, for example, provides as follows:

[A] commission is hereby created and established, to be known as The Federal Trade Commission, which shall be composed of five commissioners, who shall be appointed by the President by and with the advice and consent of the Senate. Not more than three of the commissioners shall be members of the same political party.[4]

The terms of commissioners tend to be quite lengthy—seven years is typical—and thus considerable time may elapse before a newly elected President is able to put his personal "stamp" on one of the commissions. In addition, the length of the terms tends to make even a President's own appointees somewhat independent. But in spite of this and of their structural independence from the executive branch, the major regulatory agencies are in reality subject to considerable executive influence. A member of the presidential staff sometimes attempts to directly persuade a commissioner to adopt the President's position. Because the independent regulatory agencies presumably make their decisions without interference from the executive branch, this type of influence is generally viewed with disapproval. More frequently, a presidential memorandum or the report of a presidential task force studying the matter also being investigated by a commission may be released to the public in a manner designed to sway the commission. Finally, executive influence may be asserted through the budgetary process. Agency requests for funds go through the Office of Management and Budget and so are subject to executive surveillance.

Judicial Review and Administrative Agencies

Although the scope of judicial review of particular administrative agency decisions is limited, most state and federal administrative agency decisions are subject to review by the courts. The logic underlying the limitations on judicial review is that the agency, rather than the court, is the expert in those fields in which it has been empowered to act. Clearly the courts can reverse any action taken by an agency that is outside the scope of the agency's jurisdiction.

As will be discussed later, administrative agencies may perform two separate functions. They may issue rules and regulations, and they may adjudicate cases. The criteria used by the courts in reviewing the actions of an agency may vary according to the functions involved. When an agency acts in a legislative manner, the courts will review the agency action to make sure that

1. The congressional delegation of legislative authority to the agency is constitutional in that Congress sufficiently limited the area within which the agency can act
2. The action of the agency was within the powers granted it by Congress
3. The agency action did not violate another constitutional limitation or disregard a prohibitory provision of an applicable federal statute

When an administrative agency acts in an adjudicative context, the courts review its procedures to ensure that

1. They are constitutionally valid
2. The agency had proper jurisdiction
3. The statutory rules controlling procedures have been observed

They may also review the agency's interpretation of substantive law in its adjudication, but the courts exercise substantial restraint in this area and their powers are limited.

Generally courts have accepted agency determinations of fact as final, provided that substantial evidence supporting the findings is shown by the record. Substantial evidence has been described as "the kind of evidence on which responsible persons are accustomed to rely in serious affairs"[5] and as "more than a mere scintilla. It means such relevant evidence as a reasonable mind might accept to support a conclusion."[6] Courts also have refused to consider suits brought by those who question the wisdom of the agency's discretionary decisions. If an administrative agency decides to apply a greater portion of its resources, such as funds and personnel, to a particular segment of the industry over which it has jurisdiction than it has previously done, an individual adversely affected by this new policy is not entitled to judicial review. Business people should object, however, to those discretionary agency decisions that appear to be clearly arbitrary or capricious, for courts will not allow these to stand even though the agency is the expert.

In spite of its limitations, judicial review of administrative agency actions is important to the business community. It provides a safeguard against administrative excesses and the unfair or arbitrary actions of overzealous officials. A court will be most likely to set aside an agency ruling when the agency has erred in the interpretation of a statute, has acted outside the scope of its authority, or appears to have denied due process by unfair agency procedures. Below is a case that illustrates the significance of judicial review for the business community. It reveals how an overzealous administrative agency can sometimes act outside the scope of its authority and endanger a total industry's control over a service it provides.

Federal Communications Commission v. Midwest Video Corporation

U.S. Supreme Court
440 U.S. 689 (1979)

Midwest Video Corporation (respondent) petitioned the Court of Appeals to review certain rules promulgated by the Federal Communications Commission (appellant) affecting the development of access channels of cable television operations through the country. The FCC promulgated rules requiring cable television systems that had 3,500 or more subscribers and carried broadcast signals to develop, at a minimum, a 20-channel capacity by 1986, to make available certain channels for access by public, educational, local governmental, and leased-access users, and to furnish equipment and facilities for access purposes. Under the rules, cable operators were deprived of all discretion regarding who might exploit their access channels and what might be transmitted over such channels. During the rule-making proceedings, the FCC rejected a challenge to the rules on jurisdictional grounds, maintaining that the rules would promote "the achievement of long-standing communications regulatory objectives by increasing outlets for local self-expression and augmenting the public's choice of program." On petition for review, the Court of Appeals set aside the FCC's rules as beyond the agency's jurisdiction. The court was of the view that the rules amounted to an attempt to impose common-carrier obligations on cable operators and thus ran counter to the command of Section 3(h) of the Communications Act of 1934 that "a person engaged in . . . broadcasting shall not . . . be deemed a common carrier." The FCC was granted a petition for review.

Held: Affirmed for Midwest Video.

White, Justice

The Commission derives its regulatory authority from the Communications Act of 1934. The Act preceded the advent of cable television and understandably does not expressly provide for the regulation of that medium. But it is clear that Congress meant to confer "broad authority" on the Commission, so as "to maintain, through appropriate administrative control, a grip on the dynamic aspects of radio transmission." To that end, Congress subjected to regulation "all interstate and foreign communication by wire or radio." Communications Act of 1934, § 2(a), 47 U.S.C. § 152(a). In *United States* v. *Southwestern Cable Co.,* we construed § 2(a) as conferring on the Commission a circumscribed range of power to regulate cable television, and we reaffirmed that determination in *United States* v. *Midwest Video Corp.* The question now before us is whether the Act, as construed in these two cases, authorizes the capacity and access regulations that are here under challenge. [The Court then reviewed *U.S.* v. *Southwestern Cable* and *U.S.* v. *Midwest Video*. The *Midwest Video* case was ruled on in 1972 and should not be confused with the present case involving the same corporation.]

Because its access and capacity rules promote the long-established regulatory goals of maximization of outlets for local expression and diversification of programming—the objectives promoted by the rule sustained in *Midwest Video*—the Commission maintains that it plainly had jurisdiction to promulgate them. Respondents, in opposition, view the access regulations as an intrusion on cable system operations that is qualitatively different from the impact of the rule upheld in *Midwest Video*. Specifically, it is urged that by requiring the allocation of access channels to categories of users specified by the regulations and by depriving the cable operator of the power to select individual users or to control the programming on such channels, the regulations wrest a considerable degree of editorial control from the cable operator and in effect compel the cable system to provide a kind of common-carrier service. Respondents contend, therefore, that the regulations are not only qualitatively different from those heretofore approved by the courts but also contravene statutory limitations designed to safeguard the journalistic freedom of broadcasters, particularly the command of § 3(h) of the Act that "a person engaged in . . . broadcasting shall not . . . be deemed a common carrier."

We agree with respondents that recognition of agency jurisdiction to promulgate the access rules would require an extension of this Court's prior decisions. Our holding in Midwest Video sustained the Commission's authority to regulate cable television with a purpose affirmatively to promote goals pursued in the regulation of television broadcasting; and the plurality's analysis of the origination requirement stressed the requirement's nexus to such goals. But the origination rule did not abrogate the cable operators' control over the composition of their programming, as do the access rules. It compelled operators only to assume a more positive role in that regard, one comparable to that fulfilled by television broadcasters. Cable operators had become enmeshed in the field of television broadcasting, and, by requiring them to engage in the functional equivalent of broadcasting, the Commission had sought "only to ensure that [they] satisfactorily [met] community needs within the context of their undertaking."

With its access rule, however, the Commission has transferred control of the content of access cable channels from cable operators to members of the public who wish to communicate by the cable medium. Effectively, the Commission has relegated cable systems, pro tanto, to common-carrier status. The Commission is directed explicitly by § 3(h) of the Act not to treat persons engated in broadcasting as common carriers. In determining, then, whether the Commission's assertion of jurisdiction is "reasonably ancillary to the effective performance of [its] responsibilities for the regulation of television broadcasting," we are unable to ignore Congress' stern disapproval—evidenced in § 3(h)—of negation of the editorial discretion otherwise enjoyed by broadcasters and cable operators alike. Though the lack of congressional guidance has in the past led us to defer—albeit cautiously—to the Commission's judgment regarding the scope of its authority, here there are strong indications that agency flexibility was to be sharply delimited.

> In light of the hesitancy with which Congress approached the access issue in the broadcast area, and in view of its outright rejection of a broad right of public access on a common-carrier basis, we are constrained to hold that the Commission exceeded those limits in promulgating its access rules. The Commission may not regulate cable systems as common carriers, just as it may not impose such obligations on television broadcasters. We think authority to compel cable operators to provide common carriage of public-originated transmissions must come specifically from Congress.

Legislatures and Administrative Agencies

Agencies acquire their authority to act from the legislature. For a legislative grant of authority to be constitutional, it must set standards to guide the agency's actions because the legislature is either delegating some of its power to a nonelected body or authorizing it to perform a judicial function. The legislation creating an agency is called an enabling act. Since the 1930s, very few respondents have successfully challenged the action of either state or federal agencies on the constitutional grounds that the act creating the agency did not include sufficient standards. Most modern enabling acts that allow an agency considerable discretion to act have been approved by the courts. Thus very broad and general standards may be constitutional. The Federal Trade Commission Act authorized the FTC to commence an action in a deceptive practice or false advertising case "if it shall appear to the Commission that a proceeding . . . would be in the interest of the public." The only standard is the Commission's own belief that an action is in the public interest.

Administrative agencies that have been created by the legislature can also be terminated by the legislature; however, the threat of termination has not been taken seriously in the past. Most legislative influence on agencies is the result of the agencies' dependence on the legislature for financial support. For example, much of the early history of the FTC was dominated by congressional refusal to adequately finance the agency. This was especially true in the early 1920s when the Commission planned an aggressive attack against the structure of American industry. Adverse congressional reaction to the Commission's investigation of the meat-packing industry led to a reduction in funds for the agency. Agency personnel had to be discharged, and Congress transferred jurisdiction over meat packing to the U.S. Department of Agriculture. In addition, the agency was denied appropriations for other investigations that it had planned.[7] More recently, after receiving harsh criticism in the late 1960s and early 1970s for being a "do nothing" agency, the FTC became active on behalf of consumers in such areas as deceptive advertising and antitrust. By 1980, the FTC, with its aggressive investigations and rule making, had alienated a large number of businesses, which then lobbied Congress for a cutback in the authority of the agency as well as in its level of funding. In response to this lobbying effort, Congress enacted the FTC Improvement Act of 1980.[8] The act provided for some clear restraints on FTC operations and much closer scrutiny by Congress through the House and Senate commerce committees, which are responsible for overseeing the agency. For example, one provision forced the FTC to reconsider any order previously issued upon the request of the corporation or person involved if it can be shown that changed conditions of law or fact require an altering, modifying, or setting aside of the order. Additionally, the act subjected any new FTC rule to a veto by a concurrent resolution of the House and Senate.[9] The FTC was required to submit advance notice of rule making to the oversight committees in both the House and Senate thirty days prior to publishing the rule in the Federal Register. In its notice, the FTC had to provide an explanation of the need for the new rule and its potential benefits and adverse effects. The Commission was barred from using any funds to issue or propose a regulation affecting the funeral industry similar to ones it had previously drafted. The 1980 act forbade the use of funds for initiating or conducting an investigation of the insurance industry. It also put a three-year moratorium on existing FTC authority to promulgate rules for unfair commercial advertising. When one reviews the 1980 act, it is clear that Congress intended the FTC to be a less activist agency. It also explains why all administrative agencies tend to be solicitous of Congressmen's views before launching investigations or proposing new rules.

WORK OF ADMINISTRATIVE AGENCIES

Administrative agencies do much of the day-to-day work of government. As a consequence they make many significant policy decisions. Business people who fail to recognize this will lose an opportunity to influence governmental changes that might benefit them and society. Some business people find that the record-keeping requirements of the various agencies that directly affect their business operations add significantly to costs and even adversely affect their competitive positions. Nevertheless, regulatory agencies perform many needed services and assist business people by working to control potentially harmful market conditions.

The work done by a single administrative agency may encompass a broad range of activities. In addition, the general nature and scope of operations often vary significantly from agency to agency. Thus a broad generalization regarding the work of administrative agencies is almost impossible. Some agencies, such as draft boards, were created to accomplish very limited objectives; others have very extensive assignments. The FTC, for example, has a primary responsibility for enforcing the antitrust provisions of the Clayton Act and the unfair business practices sections of the Federal Trade Commission Act. The Commission also has responsibility for carrying out all or some of the provisions of several other federal statutes.[10] An additional complication exists because agencies operate at all levels of government. As a result, they focus on problems and needs that are very different. In fact, arms of government sometimes appear to be working in opposition to each other. For example, at a time when the FCC was attempting to limit the sale of cigarettes by restricting television advertising, the U.S. Department of Agriculture continued to encourage the production of tobacco by paying price-supporting subsidies to tobacco growers.

The powers of those agencies that have the greatest impact on the business community are broad. Those agencies, which include the ICC, FTC, SEC, NLRB, and FPC, generally have the authority to make rules that have the force of law. Many agencies also function like courts. They settle disputes, and they hear and decide upon violations of statutes or of their own rules. Finally, much of the work of agencies is administrative in nature. This covers a wide variety of duties: investigating firms in the regulated industry, determining if formal action should be brought, and negotiating settlements. A substantial number of agencies have administrative responsibilities but do not have adjudicatory or rule-making powers.

Adjudication

Probably the best-known function of administrative agencies is judicial in nature. In many instances both state and federal agencies find facts and apply rules and regulations to these facts just as a court would. In carrying out this adjudicatory function, the federal agencies generally employ procedures similar to those used by the courts. This is probably due to the influence of the large number of legally trained people who are involved in some way with agency adjudication. In addition, the Administrative Procedure Act requires almost all federal agencies to meet certain standards in their procedures. As a result of these factors, generally there is considerable similarity in the enforcement procedures of federal agencies, and state agencies frequently follow similar patterns. Thus we can examine the procedures of an agency such as the FTC and obtain an idea how the adjudicatory function is performed in agencies in general.

In adjudication proceedings, the FTC, like most administrative agencies, follows a procedure of "investigation-complaint-hearing-order." However, because of limited resources, the Commission makes a determined effort to prevent disputes from reaching the hearing stage; as a result, more than 90 percent of the investigations of violations do not result in hearings.

Many cases are administratively "closed" by the Commission because investigation fails to turn up sufficient evidence to substantiate a violation or because the public interest does not warrant the lengthy and costly investigation needed to develop the facts necessary to establish a prima facie case. In a substantial number of cases where evidence of a violation does exist, the Commission is able to dispose of the case before a hearing by a consent order procedure.

Both the Commission and the respondent (corporation, partnership, or individual) benefit from the consent order procedure. The Commission obtains a binding cease-and-desist order with minimal cost and without having to worry about appeal. Respondents benefit because the agreement is for settlement purposes only and does not constitute an admission of guilt. As a result the order cannot be used in a triple-damage action brought against them, and they avoid the cost of litigation and the possible public disclosures that would stem from a formal hearing.[11]

If settlement attempts are unsuccessful, an initial hearing is conducted by an administrative law judge.[12] The procedures used are similar to those used by the federal courts, although the rules of evidence are relaxed. The parties have the rights of due notice, cross-examination, presentation of evidence, objections, motions, argument, and any other right essential to a fair trial. This does not include, however, the right to a jury, and factual questions as well as legal issues are resolved by the administrative law judge. In most instances the respondent will be represented by an attorney who ordinarily will be a specialist in the law related to the particular agency.

Within ninety days after the completion of the hearing, the administrative law judge files an initial decision, which becomes the decision of the Commission unless appealed. Any party to the proceeding, but not everyone who might be interested, may appeal the administrative law judge's decision to the Commission; or the Commission may review the decision of its administrative law judge upon its own motion. In the event of appeal or review, briefs are generally submitted by the parties and oral arguments are heard unless the Commission feels they are not necessary. In rendering its decision, the Commission has broad power to modify the administrative law judge's decision, including his findings of fact.

As stated earlier in this chapter, limited judicial review of the Commission's order to cease and desist is permitted in the Court of

Appeals. The facts as found by the Commission are conclusive if supported by evidence. Most appeals are taken on questions of law, although the Administrative Procedure Act allows review of agency decisions that are arbitrary, capricious, or an abuse of the agency's discretion, as well as those decisions or procedures that violate the Constitution or exceed the agency's statutory authority.[13] A final review may be requested of the Supreme Court, but the Supreme Court does not have to consider the case.

The case that follows is an example of a typical adjudication proceeding within an administrative agency. This is an SEC proceeding, although we have described procedures in the FTC. There is no dearth of FTC cases. The SEC case was selected to indicate the similarity between the adjudication machinery in these two agencies.

In the Matter of Paine, Webber, Jackson & Curtis

The Federal Securities and Exchange Commission

Securities Exchange Act Release No. 8500. January 22, 1969

A charge was filed with the SEC against Ralph M. Klopp, a salesman for Paine, Webber, Jackson & Curtis, claiming that he had induced excessive trading by customers by using false representations concerning the trading activities of another customer. In addition, his employer and William P. Cowden, a former office manager, were charged with failure to reasonably supervise Klopp.

Following hearings, a hearing examiner for the SEC filed an initial decision, in which he concluded that Klopp should be suspended from association with any brokers or dealers for a period of four months but that proceedings against Paine, Webber, Jackson, & Curtis and William P. Cowden should be dismissed.

Klopp petitioned for review of the examiner's decision and the Commission ordered a reconsideration of all issues. Briefs were filed by both the respondents and the Commission's Division of Trading and Marketing before the full Commission. Held; Affirmed but modified.

By the Commission (Chairman Cohen, Commissioners Owens, Budge, and Smith. Commissioner Wheat, not participating.)

The examiner found that during the period from about May, 1962 through October, 1963, Klopp made certain false representations to two of his customers, J. and R. Those customers, who were close friends, opened accounts with Klopp in the spring of 1961 and effected a number of transactions through him during the ensuing year, relying largely on the recommendations of an investment service to which they had subscribed at his suggestion. The examiner found that in May and June, 1962, Klopp told those customers that another customer had made substantial trading profits and that he would inform them of the trading by that customer so that they could duplicate his transactions. The examiner further found that as a result of the customers' reliance on false information concerning such trading given them by Klopp, Klopp in effect obtained discretionary power over their accounts and induced them to engage in excessive trading.

The two customers testified as follows: On May 29, 1962, while R. was at registrant's office, Klopp told him that one of his customers had a "huge" account, used the services of an investment adviser and had made large profits by selling his portfolio and selling additional stock short just before a sharp market drop on the preceding day and covering the short sales and purchasing stock just prior to the market rally on May 29. R. told J. of this conversation and Klopp himself made essentially the same representations to J. He also advised both customers that the other customer was a doctor, although he did not identify him by name; and used the services of a "Chinese chartist." When Klopp and J., in June, 1962, reviewed the latter's portfolio, consisting mostly of low priced over-the-counter securities which had depreciated, Klopp stated that he would inform J. about the doctor's transactions after they were executed. In July, 1962, Klopp informed J. that the doctor had just sold stock of Cinerama, Inc. short, and J. instructed Klopp to effect a short sale of stock for his account. This was followed by a series of further transactions, extending to September, 1963, which were effected by J. on the basis of Klopp's statements regarding transactions by the doctor. R.'s first transaction, based on a transaction reported to have been effected by the doctor, took place in August, 1962. In about November, 1962, R., based on Klopp's statement that it "might be a good idea to follow the doctor," sold many of the securities in his portfolio in order to obtain additional funds to follow the doctor's transactions. He continued to follow those transactions until October, 1963, when he ceased dealing with Klopp.

Klopp denied making any representations concerning the nature of, and transactions in another account, and testifies that, far from inducing J. and R. to increase their trading activity, he advised them to reduce such activity and instead to buy and hold high quality stocks, but that they disregarded his advice.

CREDIBILITY ISSUE

The examiner, in resolving the credibility issue against Klopp, noted that the probative effect of the testimony of J. and R. was weakened by a lack of specificity and consistency and some contradictory evidence in the record, but concluded that "in sum their testimony on salient aspects of the issues involved remains credible and must be accepted." His conclusion, in this respect is entitled to considerable weight and is supported by various facts shown by the record which provide strong corroboration for the customers' testimony.

There is a significant correlation between certain of the information which they testified was given to them and the actual activity in the account of a Dr. R., which was also serviced by Klopp and was a large and active one. The record shows that Dr. R. effected a substantial number of sales and short sales shortly prior to May 28, 1962, and the day before Klopp told J. that the "doctor" had sold Cinerama stock short, Dr. R. had effected a short sale of that stock. In addition, in October, 1962, the last month in which there was substantial activity in Dr. R.'s account, J. had eight transactions in stock of International Business Machines, Inc. ("IBM") which were identical in nature and date with transactions effected by Dr. R. These circumstances suggest that Klopp's representations had their genesis in Dr. R.'s account. Klopp testified, however, that as far as he knew Dr. R. did not have an investment adviser or a chartist. Further corroboration of the customers' testimony is provided by the fact that in November, 1962, J. had four transactions and R. three transactions in IBM stock which were identical as to nature and date with transactions in the account of Klopp's wife.

EXAMINER'S CONCLUSION ACCEPTED

We accordingly accept the examiner's conclusion on the credibility issue and concur with his findings as to the misrepresentations made by Klopp. We also agree with his finding that Klopp induced excessive trading in the accounts of the two customers.

In view of the foregoing, we find, as did the examiner, that Klopp willfully violated Section 10(b) of the Act and Rule 10b–5 thereunder, and Section 17(a) of the Securities Act of 1933.

PUBLIC INTEREST

We cannot agree with the conclusion of the examiner that, despite the serious nature of Klopp's violations, a four-month suspension is appropriate in the public interest. We conclude that notwithstanding the mitigating factors noted by the examiner, including Klopp's previously good record and his public service in civilian life and with the armed forces, his misconduct was such as to require in the public interest that a more substantial sanction be imposed. In our opinion, it is appropriate that he be barred from association with any broker or dealer, with the proviso that such bar shall not preclude his association, after a period of one year, with a broker or dealer in a nonsupervisory capacity upon a showing that he will be adequately supervised . . .

An appropriate order will issue.

Rule Making

When a pronouncement affecting the rights and duties of a number of people is made by an agency, the agency acts in the same manner as a legislature. The power to make rules and regulations of this kind, which may be as binding as laws passed by legislative bodies, has been delegated to the agency by the legislature. The only important difference between an agency rule and a "law" enacted by a legislative body is that the former may be slightly more susceptible to attack in the courts because the rule was not made by elected officials. Let us consider examples of the rule-making authority that some administrative agencies possess.

As a result of the collapse of the securities market in 1929, Congress passed legislation in 1934 designed to protect the public buying and selling of securities on national exchanges. The act, the Securities Exchange Act of 1934, created the SEC, which was given the job of enforcing and administering the act.[14] Over the five decades of its existence, the SEC has adopted many rules designed to protect buyers of securities. One of these rules requires broker-dealers who extend credit to customers buying on margin to furnish information about the credit charges. Both initial and periodic disclosures are necessary. As a result, Congress decided that it would be unnecessary to make the 1968 Truth-in-Lending Act applicable to loans made by brokers to customers buying securities on credit, because the SEC regulation already provided ample legal protection. In 1973 the CAB adopted a rule requiring specific sections aboard commercial aircraft to be designated as "smoking areas" and limiting smoking to those sections.[15] The SEC and CAB rules have the same legal effect as if these actions had been taken by Congress. Both, like rules promulgated by many other agencies, are the law of the land.

Administrative Activities

The acts of administrative agencies of most interest from the legal standpoint are those that involve rule making or adjudication. Agencies, however, act in many ways that are neither judicial nor legislative in nature. They carry out a myriad of statutory directives and have countless functions that defy classification. Many of these acts are purely administrative, although they may involve the rights and duties of many citizens, thousands of transactions, and millions of dollars. In many cases these acts are informal in nature and are usually not reviewed by a court.

Even when the possibility of judicial review of intra-agency actions exists, the person affected often does not, for many reasons, believe that review is practical, and the agency's action is accepted without formal protest.

Many examples of administrative acts of this nature can readily be cited. Agencies are often responsible for the allocation of funds and the granting of licenses; they make tests, manage government property, and supervise inmates in institutions. Different agencies carry out tasks as varied as clearing vessels to leave port and classifying grain. Agencies grant patents, collect taxes, and oversee educational institutions. Agencies frequently conduct investigations. Sometimes this is done at the request of the executive or the legislature, but many agencies have the power to initiate their own investigations. Some agencies are responsible for the business of law enforcement and prosecution. The principal function of others is to plan or to approve or disapprove the plans of others. Most of the countless jobs that are necessary in the administration of government are done by people in administrative agencies.

Many of these administrative acts are politically, economically, and socially significant and clearly relate to important issues of public policy. The SEC decision in the late 1960s to investigate the selling of mutual funds was an administrative act of this type. As a result of this investigation, the Commission proposed sweeping legislation curtailing certain practices in the industry. When the FTC decided in 1972 to bring a legal action against the major sellers of ready-to-eat cereals, alleging that they were involved in an illegal "shared monopoly," the decision to file suit, although administrative in nature, had a potentially substantial impact on many other areas of the economy. This suit was dropped by the Commission in 1981, ostensibly for failure to find anticompetitive conduct. Many believe it was a political decision made by appointees of a new administration that favored less regulation.

GOVERNMENT REGULATION AND ADMINISTRATIVE AGENCIES: AN EVALUATION

As stated at the beginning of this chapter, there exists a debate between those who advocate deregulation and the abolition of administrative agencies and those who argue that the wider public interest would suffer if there were no regulation. The work of administrative agencies in carrying out the statutory responsibilities that Congress and the President have given them is subject to criticism by industry, consumer, environmentalist, and other groups. Over the past fifty years, administrative agencies have probably been subject to more criticism than praise. One frequently expressed charge is that there is just too much regulation. The result is that the individual, the economy, in fact society as a whole, is stifled. Often this general condemnation is given added weight because critics are able to point to specific instances in which agencies have not performed well. Many times agencies, which supposedly are the experts, have erred in major decisions that have hurt both the regulated business and the general public. For example, long after it became clear in the 1930s that the nineteenth-century concept of the common-carrier responsibility of the railroads to provide a complete transportation service to every locality along every mile of track had become obsolete, the ICC only reluctantly allowed railroads to abandon unprofitable passenger service. This policy forced the railroads to continue passenger service, often when losing money, to the detriment of their competitive position. This eventually led to a deterioration in the ability of the railroads to provide the type of transportation that the economy actually needed.

Although some critics charge that agencies regulate too much, others claim that regulation is either insufficient or frequently oriented to the needs of the industry rather than to the needs of the public. Because most agencies operate in only one field, their members often acquire a sympathetic knowledge of the industry they are supposed to regulate. As a result, they forget their duty to regulate for the public welfare. This condemnation has been made by groups initiated by consumer advocate Ralph Nader that have reviewed the operations of the ICC and the FTC.

Industry Influence

The close ties that develop between the agencies and industry stem from a natural tend-ency of people to be interested in the problems of others with whom they share a common background. Few deliberate instances of industry-agency collusion can be supported. Commissioners and other agency executives frequently receive their appointments because they have employment backgrounds in the industry regulated by their agency. Often they intend to return to the industry after government service. Personnel who have not been hired from the industry may regard the industry as a potential employer; agency lawyers may think of it as a source of future fees. As a result of these and other considerations, regulators perhaps unconsciously curtail their activities.

Legislative Influence

Administrative agencies have also been accused of being overly susceptible to legislative as well as executive influence. Pressures that would never be countenanced by the courts are part of the everyday experience of many federal and state regulatory authorities. Pressures from legislative sources are highly effective because the legislatures control agency funds. Almost every state can point to at least one scandal in which legislative leverage has influenced a state agency. At the federal level, Congressmen and members of their immediate staffs have been exposed as sources of influence peddling. The power that some agencies have to grant the right to engage in certain types of highly profitable business makes them particularly susceptible to attempts to influence them. The allocation of scheduled air routes between cities by the CAB, for example, is a critically important factor in the competitive positions of the major airlines. For a long time the right to operate a television station was so valuable that the granting of such licenses by the FCC was thought to be similar to the granting of licenses to print money.

Other criticisms of a more esoteric nature have been directed against agencies. In several agencies rule making and adjudicatory functions are not separated. In other instances not only do agency personnel establish the rules and serve as the judges, but the decision to bring an action is also made within the agency. One of the highly esteemed American political traditions is the separation of legislative, judicial, and executive powers; this tradition would seem to be violated when the decision to bring an action is not separated from adjudication. During the 1940s, the NLRB was subjected to considerable criticism because its general counsel was controlled by the Board. Eventually, as a result of public pressure, Congress adopted legislation separating the office of the general counsel for the NLRB from the Board, which was responsible for deciding cases initiated by the general counsel. At the present time, staff personnel of the FTC adjudicate cases that are brought by the agency and that involve, in many instances, purported violations of agency rules.

Another charge against some agencies, including several of the most important federal agencies, is that the commissioners, who make the ultimate decisions in many cases, are removed from the actual fact finding. Thus, the critics argue, the commissioners never really know what is going on because they see only a record when they make their decisions. They act on the basis of facts found by an administrative law judge, and they do not hear the actual testimony themselves.

Many of these criticisms are partially valid, and most authorities agree that steps should be taken to improve the performance of the administrative agencies. In spite of their problems, they have performed an important function in our system of government, and they have unquestionably taken much of the burden from courts and legislatures, as noted earlier in this chapter. Without them in this age of rapidly increasing population, expanding technology, and specialization, the traditional branches of government would long ago have come to a standstill. Agencies appear to be the

most practical method of administering the complex statutes necessary to effectively regulate activities in our society. If some form of government regulation is desired by society, institutions of this type are inevitable. They have developed in all the heavily industrialized nations of the West and will continue to be important as technology expands and our economy becomes more complex.

Administrative Agency Reform

Recently a number of proposals have been made to improve the effectiveness of administrative agencies. These proposals range widely in nature and in the extent to which they advocate change. The modifications suggested include changes in the alignment of responsibilities of several agencies as well as in their internal structures and processes.

During recent administrations, a number of proposals to reorganize major federal agencies responsible to the President were carried out. These changes were the outcome of broad authority granted by Congress to the President to reorganize the executive branch. This authority allows the Chief Executive to submit proposals for reorganization of executive agencies to Congress. If Congress does not veto a proposal within sixty days, it automatically goes into effect (see footnote 9, p. 950). The presidential authority to modify agency organization and responsibility does not apply to the independent federal regulatory agencies.

Over the years numerous presidential, congressional, and private committees have studied the federal regulatory agencies and made suggestions for change. The most recent detailed proposal was submitted in 1971 by the President's Advisory Council on Executive Reorganization. This Council recommended major realignment of responsibility within the independent agencies. One proposal would have combined the ICC, the CAB, and the Federal Maritime Commission into a single transportation agency. The chief argument for this proposal was that the nation's transportation systems increasingly are becoming an integrated network, and overall regulation of all elements of the system is necessary for effective control.

A second proposal recommended dividing the FTC into two agencies. One would concentrate on antitrust matters, the other on consumer protection. The Council also considered combining the Justice Department's antitrust function with those recommended for separation from the present FTC. Antitrust activities would then be carried out either within the Justice Department or a new separate agency. A Reagan Administration proposal to do away with FTC antitrust authority met with opposition from Congress.

In addition to proposals realigning agency responsibility, the Council recommended modifications in internal organization and functions for some agencies. The most far-reaching proposal suggested replacing boards or commissions with single administrators. The rationale struck at the heart of the concept of having several governmental functions included in a single organization. Council members felt that a number of agencies would operate more effectively if policy or rule making were separated from adjudication. A single administrator would have final responsibility in these agencies as in the vast majority of executive department agencies. This person would be more accountable to Congress than the board or commission. Administrative courts would be created to carry out the current adjudicatory functions of the agency.

Opinions vary as to what is necessary to improve the regulatory system. On the one hand are numerous authorities who propose the creation of new, powerful independent agencies to solve society's problems. Congress has considered bills creating an independent Consumer Protection Agency, an independent Federal Elections Committee, an independent public prosecutor, and even an independent commission to review classified material. On the other hand, both in Congress and in many of the states, proposed legislation calls for the automatic termination of agencies after they have been in operation for a number of years. In some industries deregulation will lighten the work load of agencies.

A different approach to agency reform has been "sunshine" or "open government" legislation. Several states have adopted laws requiring governmental bodies to meet regularly in announced sessions open to the public. Bills introduced in Congress would require all agencies headed by two or more persons, a majority of whom were appointed by the President and confirmed by the Senate, to open all meetings to the public unless a majority voted to close. These bills also specifically set the types of meetings that could be closed by vote. These include meetings dealing with national defense, foreign policy, company trade secrets, and reviews of agency personnel rules and practices. This type of legislation may force administrative agencies to be more aware of the needs of the public.

Most recently Congress enacted the Regulatory Flexibility Act of 1980,[16] which seeks to force all agencies to fit regulations and information requirements made by the agency to the size of the business. This act was a result of agencies' making regulations for an industry that burdened small businesses with high costs. Whereas large businesses were able to pass on the costs of regulation to consumers, small businesses often could not. Under the act, an agency must show each October and April the areas of regulation it will be concerned with. The agency must present its agenda to the Small Business Administration, which will publish it for small businesses. Each agency must solicit comments from small businesses and periodically review all rules in order to assess their impact on small companies.

Additional reforms of administrative agencies have been making their way through both houses of Congress. In March 1982, the Senate passed a bill that would have given Congress a legislative veto over agencies' rule making. If both houses of Congress disapproved by a majority vote, a proposed rule would have had to be dropped by the agency (see footnote 9). The bill would also have required that an agency accompany each proposed new rule published for comment with a cost-benefit analysis. Finally, the bill would have denied any presumption of validity or expertise to administrative agency decisions. Judicial review of agency decisions would thus have been truly independent of the agency's determination. This bill reflected a growing disenchantment with government regulation.

REVIEW PROBLEMS

1. In September 1969, the State of Tennessee, following agreement with local Memphis city officials, acquired a right-of-way inside Overton Park. The right-of-way was to be used to extend Interstate 40 into Memphis. If so done, the park would have been cut in two, with the zoo on one side of the highway and all other facilities on the other. The U.S. Secretary of Transportation (Volpe), after consulting with state and local officials, approved the plan without indicating whether a "feasible" alternative existed. A citizens' group sued to enjoin the U.S. Department of Transportation from financing this extension of Interstate 40, claiming that Congress, in creating the Department of Transportation, prohibited the use of funds for highway construction through a park if "feasible" alternatives existed. The Citizens to Preserve Overton Park claimed that the Secretary of Transportation had failed to show that he had investigated and considered "feasible" alternatives or design changes that might have brought less harm to the park, with the result that his order approving the new route was invalid. What standards would a court have used in determining whether Secretary Volpe had met the statutory requirement? Who would win? Citizens to Preserve Overton Park v. Volpe, 401 U.S. 402 (1971)

2. The Federal Communications Commission set forth rules prohibiting cable television systems from broadcasting first-run feature films (shown on over-the-air television) that were less than three but more than ten years old. Home Box Office (HBO) appealed this rule and other restrictions to the District of Columbia Circuit Court of Appeals, claiming that this exercise of the Commission's rule-making authority was arbitrary and capricious and that it restricted competition. The Commission claimed that the regulations were needed to prevent siphoning by cable companies of copyrighted material broadcast over the air. Were the regulations arbitrary and capricious? Who wins? HBO v. Federal Communications Commission, 567 F.2d. 9 (D.C. Cir., 1977)

3. The Endangered Species Act of 1973 invested the Secretary of the Interior with exclusive authority to determine whether a species is "endangered" or "threatened" and to ascertain the factors that have led to the problem. The Secretary is also commanded by Congress under the 1973 act to issue regulations to provide for the conservation of the endangered species. The Secretary of the Interior set forth regulations that declared the snail darter as an endangered species whose habitat would have been destroyed by the creation of the Tellico Reservoir on the Little Tennessee River. The dam creating the reservoir was almost completed ($100 million having been spent) when environmental groups

and others brought suit under the 1973 act to enjoin the Tennessee Valley Authority from completing the dam. Would the court be usurping the power of the Secretary of the Interior and Congress if it failed to enforce the 1973 act? What about the $100 million spent on the dam? Is it significant in terms of the court's decision? Who wins? Tennessee Valley Authority v. Hill, 437 U.S. 153 (1978)

4. The Emergency Price Control Act established an Office of Price Administration with authority to promulgate rules and orders fixing maximum prices of commodities and rents during World War II. The Administrator of the OPA was given two standards by Congress to fix prices: (a) he had to consult with the industries and promulgate regulations that were "fair and equitable" and (b) due consideration had to be given to prices prevailing between October 1 and October 15, 1941. When Yakus and other defendants sold beef in excess of the wholesale price set by the regulations, they were prosecuted under a criminal section of the act and sentenced to six months in jail and fined $1,000 each. The defendants argued that the standards set by Congress for the Administrator were so broad that they failed to give adequate notice and thus violated the Fifth Amendment's due process requirements. Were they too broad? Who wins? Yakus v. United States, 321 U.S. 414 (1941)

5. The National Highway Traffic Safety Administration in 1972 issued a standard requiring that all pneumatic passenger tires retreaded after February 1974 contain information (permanently molded into one side of the tire) as to size, inflation pressure, load, and whether they were bias/-belted or radial. This rule was promulgated pursuant to the National Traffic and Motor Safety Vehicle Act of 1966, which required that rules be "practical" and "meet the need for motor vehicle safety." The National Tire Dealers and Retreaders Association opposed the rule, claiming that it was arbitrary and capricious in that it was not "practicable" and that the Administrator had failed to show that the information required by the rule met "the need for vehicle safety" only if it was permanently molded onto a tire. The Administrator of Traffic Safety argued that safety could be provided only through permanent labeling because tires are often transferred from wheel to wheel or car to car. Was the rule economically "feasible" and did it "meet the need for vehicle safety"? Who wins? National Tire Dealer & Retreaders Association v. Brinegar, 491 F.2d 21 (D.C. Cir., 1974)

6. An association of fisherman represented by the National Resources Defense Council sued U.S. Secretary of the Interior Morton, challenging the Secretary's decision to open a large part of the outer continental shelf off the Louisiana Coast to oil and gas exploration. Under the National Environmental Policy Act of 1969, Congress directed all governmental agencies to file environmental impact statements (EISs) noting "any adverse environmental effects of the proposed action" and "alternatives to the proposed action." The Secretary filed an EIS but failed to consider in any detailed way alternative methods for meeting the energy needs of the nation. The Secretary argued that he failed to consider alternatives (e.g., removal of oil import quotas, development of oil shale, coal liquification) because they were outside his statutory duty or had no prospect for increasing energy in 1970. The fishermen argued that the Secretary had failed to meet the statutory mandate and that his decision should be overturned. Who wins? National Resources Defense Council v. Morton, 458 F.2d 827 (D.C. Cir., 1972)

FOOTNOTES

[1] General Index, Code of Federal Regulations, Office of the Register, Revised Jan. 1, 1982 (Washington: National Archives and Record Service, General Services Administration).

[2] Kenneth Culp Davis, *Administrative Law Text* (St. Paul, Minn: West Publishing, 1959), p. 1.

[3] Id., p. 15.

[4] 15 United States Code Annotated, Section 41.

[5] National Labor Relations Board (NLRB) v. Remington Rand, Inc., 92 F.2d 862 (1938).

[6] Consolidated Edison v. NLRB, 305 U.S. 197 (1938).

[7] Susan Wagner, *The Federal Trade Commission* (N.Y.: Praeger, 1971), p. 24.

[8] 15 United States Code Annotated, Section 41 *et seq.* as amended by Publ L. 96–239.

[9] The constitutionality of a legislative veto of a specific Rule was called into question by a 1983 Supreme Court Decision: Immigration and Naturalization Service v. Chadha, 462 U.S. ———(1983).

[10] See S. Wagner, *The Federal Trade Commission* (N.Y.: Praeger, 1971), p. 233.

[11] See O.L. Reid, "Advertising and the FTC," in *Business Law: Key Issues and Concepts,* eds., T. Dunfee and J.D. Reitzel, p. 104.

[12] In 1972 the Civil Service Commission approved the title of "administrative law judge" for hearing examiners throughout the federal government.

[13] Administrative Procedure Act–5, United States Code 701–706.

[14] The Securities Exchange Commission is also charged with the enforcement and administration of the Securities Act of 1933.

[15] 16 C.F.R. Section 433 (1973).

[16] See Regulatory Flexibility Act Pub. L. 96–354.

CHAPTER 38

Regulation of Business Behavior

ENFORCEMENT OF THE ANTITRUST LAWS _____

EXEMPTIONS FROM THE ANTITRUST LAWS _____

BUSINESS BEHAVIOR REGULATED BY THE ANTITRUST LAWS _____

T his chapter addresses forms of business behavior that are considered to be anticompetitive and thus regulated by federal and state governments under the antitrust laws.

Historically, this nation's economy was founded on the concept of laissez faire—that is, government would not interfere in the activities of individual sellers freely competing in the marketplace. Underlying this classical economic theory was the assumption that there would be many sellers in the marketplace and a free flow of information between sellers and buyers. In the latter half of the nineteenth and the early twentieth century, business power in several industries (particularly oil) became concentrated in one or two companies. Public demand to break up of these "trusts" resulted in the passage of federal antitrust laws and some state statutes. (See Table 38–1 for a summary of these statutes and the business behavior they regulate. They will frequently be referred to throughout the chapter.) While concentrating on such business conduct as price fixing, conspiracies to restrain trade, and other anticompetitive behavior, this chapter will also look at how industry structure affects competition. When industry structure is mentioned, the reader should know that the concern of antitrust enforcement agencies will generally be with the number and size of sellers. If the industry has only four domestic sellers, like the auto industry, is it more or less competitive? Should we look further and include Volkswagen and Datsun when we talk about the number of sellers and how competitive the industry may be?

In some industries (including many of our most important national industries) a few firms account for all or sizable portions of production. A presidential task force reported in 1969 that

industries in which four or fewer firms account for more than 70 percent of output produce nearly ten percent of the total value of [all American] manufactured products; industries in which four or fewer firms account for more than 50 percent of output produce nearly 24 percent.[1]

Other industries are composed of a large number of relatively small firms with no single firm having a significant share of the market.

Table 38–1 IMPORTANT STATUTES REGULATING BUSINESS BEHAVIOR

Note: Statutes Are Federal Unless Indicated Otherwise

Structurally Oriented	Behaviorally Oriented
SHERMAN ACT (1890). Sec. 2 prohibits monopolies and attempts or conspiracies to monopolize.	SHERMAN ACT (1890). Sec. 1 condemns combinations and conspiracies in restraint of trade including vertical and horizontal price fixing, group boycotts, division of markets.
CLAYTON ACT (1914). Sec. 7 prohibits mergers, the effect of which may be substantially to lessen competition or to tend to create a monopoly. *Amended (1950). Celler-Kefauver Act* clarified application of Sec. 7 to acquistions of assets.	CLAYTON ACT (1914). Sec 2 prohibits price discriminations, substantially lessening sellers' level competition (primary line violations). *Amended (1936). Robinson-Patman Act* prohibits price discriminations, substantially lessening buyer's (and below) level competition (secondary line violations).
	CLAYTON ACT (1914). Sec. 3 prohibits exclusive dealing and tying arrangements, the effect of which may be to substantially lessen competition.
	FEDERAL TRADE COMMISSION ACT (1914). Sec. 5 prohibits unfair methods of competition, established and defined powers of FTC. *Amended (1938), Wheeler-Lea Act* prohibits unfair trade practices, false advertising.
	(STATE) MISCELLANEOUS PRICING STATUTES prohibit sales below cost, predatory pricing, sales insufficiently marked up, price fixing, etc., generally not successfully enforced.

A matter of concern to those charged with enforcing the antitrust laws is the relationship between differing industry structures and specific business behaviors, particularly pricing. For example, is there less competitive pricing (resulting in higher prices for consumers) in industries with just a few sizable firms? The importance of this question stems from the widespread belief that the pricing mechanism is a central component of viable competition. Thus, if proof exists that certain types of industry structure hamper the operation of the price mechanism, there is strong justification for government restriction of the formation of such structures and for affirmative action to break up firms. The reader will constantly be made aware of the relationship between industry structure (monopolistic, oligopolistic, and competitive) and company behavior (price fixing, customer and territorial restrictions).

This chapter identifies the important federal antitrust statutes, describes their enforcement, and explains certain exemptions. It then discusses a number of business behaviors that are regulated under these acts, with particular emphasis on monopolies and mergers.

ENFORCEMENT OF THE ANTITRUST LAWS

The major antitrust statutes are set forth in Table 38–1, along with the particular business behaviors they prohibit. As we examine several forms of business conduct prohibited by these laws, it should be remembered that their major purpose is to preserve a competitive industry structure and economy.

Actions under the antitrust laws may be initiated in one of the following three ways:

1. By the Department of Justice in the regular court system
2. By administrative agencies through specially established procedures
3. By private citizens to obtain compensation for injuries they have suffered as a result of violations of the antitrust laws

The Department of Justice has a special Antitrust Division, headed by an Assistant Attorney General, responsible for enforcing the Sherman Act and, together with the Federal Trade Commission (FTC), for enforcing the Clayton Act. In addition, the Antitrust Division has special powers relating to the antitrust actions of federal administrative agencies. The FTC is the most important agency in this field. It has exclusive jurisdiction to enforce the Federal Trade Commission Act and has concurrent jurisdiction with the Department of Justice to enforce the Clayton Act. In addition, the FTC has authority to enforce a number of other statutes relating to labeling and export trade. In jointly enforcing the Clayton Act, the Department of Justice and the FTC attempt to coordinate their efforts to prevent wasteful duplication. For example, the FTC has taken primary responsibility for enforcing the Robinson-Patman Act; the Department of Justice rarely litigates under that statute.

These public agencies make use of three basic remedies:

1. Injunctions
2. Criminal sanctions
3. Fines

An injunction is a court order prohibiting a specified action (for example, dissemination of pricing information by a trade association) or requiring affirmative action on the part of the party against whom the order applies (for example, the divestiture of certain designated assets).

Violation of the Sherman Act is a felony and may result in imprisonment for up to three years. Although the imposition of jail terms in Sherman Act proceedings has received considerable publicity when it has occurred, the number of instances in which jail terms have actually been imposed on defendant business people is relatively small. The Sherman Act also provides for fines of $100,000 per count for an individual and $1 million per count for a corporation.

Both the Clayton and Sherman acts provide for civil treble-damage suits by private citizens. Although victims of an electrical-equipment price-fixing conspiracy in the 1950s were able to recover hundreds of millions of dollars, private plaintiffs found that antitrust litigation was costly and time consuming. In addition, there is often an imbalance of economic interest in the law suit. An extreme example will emphasize the latter point. Suppose that the manufacturers of a mass-distributed product such as legal pads were to engage in a price-fixing conspiracy unlawfully raising the price five cents per pad. Even the most prolific purchasers of legal pads would find it hardly worth their while to bring suit. If they were to bring suit, they would find that the outcome of the case would be substantially more important to the manufacturers than it would be to them. There are two possible solutions to this dilemma. A state government might bring suit on behalf of all of its citizens and then spend whatever monies it obtained in the public interest. Or a *class action* might be allowed, whereby a sufficiently homogeneous group, having substantially the same claim, would bring action as though it were a single person. The courts may allow a class action in an antitrust suit if they are convinced that it is practicable and that there are no other realistic alternatives available to the plaintiffs comprising the class. The courts determine whether class actions will be allowed on a case-by-case basis.

The decision of the U.S. Supreme Court in Eisen v. Carlisle & Jacquelin, 417 U.S. 156 (1974), has had the effect of limiting the use of large class actions under the federal antitrust laws. In *Eisen,* the Court held that the plaintiff must bear the costs of notifying all the members of the class of their rights during the progress of the suit. The costs of notifying a large class that may involve tens of thousands (or, in some cases, even millions) are prohibitively high (postage alone would be staggering) and operate as a practical matter to discourage the very large class action.

In 1972, the Supreme Court had held in *Hawaii* v. *Standard Oil of California* that a state could not bring a civil antitrust action for damages against a defendant on behalf of all the citizens of the state. Ironically, in the *Hawaii* decision the Supreme Court suggested that a class action was the better way to deal with this problem. Hawaii had tried to bring an action as *parens patriae* (legal guardian) on behalf of its citizens.

In reaction to the *Eisen* and *Hawaii* decisions, Congress passed the Antitrust Improvements Act (1976), which established a statutory parens patriae right of action that would allow state attorneys general to bring civil treble-damage suits on behalf of all natural persons within the state against defendants who had committed violations of the antitrust laws. At the direction of the federal court, the proceeds of a successful suit would either be distributed to injured citizens or added to the state's general revenues. Damages would be calculated from the losses suffered by the natural citizens of the state. Sampling and aggregation techniques could be used to make the calculation if price fixing was involved.

In *Illinois Brick* v. *Illinois* (1977), the Supreme Court refused to allow Illinois and some 700 Illinois government entities to recover treble damages as indirect purchasers. The state had alleged that it and others had been overcharged $3 million for concrete blocks sold by Illinois Brick and other manufacturers who had engaged in price fixing. The manufacturers sold blocks to masonry contractors who in turn passed on the extra costs to general contractors who passed them on to the state when building office buildings. Illinois taxpayers were the injured citizens. To support its refusal, the Court cited the evidentiary complexity involved in analyzing price and output decisions based on economic models; it also pointed to problems associated with apportionment of damages. This decision has been criticized by Congress, the federal courts, and legal scholars.

Historically, a high percentage of the antitrust cases initiated by the Department of Justice have been settled by agreement between the government and the defendants. This is an impressive fact because it is more difficult for the government to settle a case than for a private litigant. Before a settlement may be judicially approved, the government must publish the terms of the proposed agreement along with a Competitive Impact Statement that details its likely economic effect. This is done to ensure that the interests of the public are served by the settlement. If the judge approves, a consent decree is filed with the court. Violation of the terms of the decree puts the violating party in contempt of court. If a criminal action has been filed, the same basic process is followed to obtain a decree of nolo contendere.

Settling of cases saves the government time

and money and allows the Department of Justice to deal with more antitrust violations. Nevertheless, the settlement of antitrust cases has several drawbacks. For example, if the government litigates and wins, that victory constitutes prima facie evidence of the antitrust violation and may be used by a private plaintiff in a civil treble-damages suit. It is then only necessary for the private plaintiff to prove the injuries that he or she suffered and that they resulted from the proven antitrust violation. On the other hand, a consent settlement entered into and accepted prior to the taking of any testimony carries no implications for a private suit. The private litigant will have to prove both the fact of the antitrust violation and his or her injuries resulting therefrom. In addition, it may be questioned whether an "I'll promise not to do it again if you won't prosecute" approach effectively deters others from engaging in similar practices.

EXEMPTIONS FROM THE ANTITRUST LAWS

Certain types of businesses and certain business and labor-union activities are specifically exempted from the antitrust laws. In some instances, exemptions are based on recognition of the fact that competition is not desirable in all market situations. Other exemptions, like the exempt status of professional baseball, are based on nothing more than historical legal quirks. Two of the most important exemptions —regulated industries and labor unions—are briefly discussed here. In addition to these two, there are other important exemptions, including the insurance industry and several types of agricultural marketing arrangements. In spite of the number of exemptions, the percentage of total goods produced by both *unregulated* and *exempted* industries is quite small.[2]

Regulated Industries

A number of important industries are closely regulated by federal and state agencies to protect the public interest. These include transportation, electricity, gas, telephone service, and broadcasting. Because intervention by antitrust enforcement agencies would be redundant, these industries enjoy a qualified exemption from direct application of the antitrust laws. In addition, some of these industries are thought to involve so-called natural monopolies, thus making competitive considerations irrelevant. The exemptions, however, are not absolute, and the Justice Department has the authority to review antitrust-related decisions by federal regulatory agencies.

Labor Unions

Over the years, Congress has exempted the organizational and operational activities of labor unions from the antitrust laws. Today labor unions retain their exempt status so long as they do not combine with nonlabor groups to effect restraints of trade. Thus, if a firm enters into a conspiracy with a labor union for the purpose of economically handicapping a competing firm, the antitrust laws will apply. There have been few examples of such outright labor-nonlabor conspiracies. Instead, the courts have had to deal with the question of the applicability of the antitrust laws to more ordinary and more subtle labor-management relationships. For example, labor in a sense combines with a nonlabor group every time a collective-bargaining agreement is signed. Yet the peaceful resolution of labor disputes through collective bargaining is encouraged by federal labor law. In view of these countervailing policies, can an anticompetitive provision contained in a collective-bargaining agreement in and of itself be considered a conspiracy in restraint of trade? The courts have yet to effectively resolve this difficult question.

BUSINESS BEHAVIOR REGULATED BY THE ANTITRUST LAWS

Price Fixing and Conspiracies in Restraint of Trade

Section 1 of the Sherman Act (summarized in Table 38–1) prohibits contracts, combinations, or conspiracies that restrain interstate trade. The U.S. Supreme Court has used two standards to determine what acts violate Section 1. In a landmark case, *Chicago Board of Trade v. U.S.* (1918)[3] the Court set out a *rule of reason* standard, noting that only *unreasonable* restraints of trade are illegal. The Court instructed lower courts and regulatory agencies to weigh the procompetitive effects of a particular business restraint against the anticompetitive effects to determine its reasonableness. Such factors as the nature of the business, the history of the restraint, the reason why businesses adopted it, and other factors peculiar to the business were to be considered.[4] Certain other business activities or restraints are treated as *per se* (in and of themselves) illegal. Once shown to exist, they are illegal, and no balancing of the pro- and anticompetitive effects will be allowed into evidence to prove their reasonableness. In *Northern Pacific Railway Co. v. United States* (1958), the Supreme Court defined a per se standard, noting that there are certain business practices or agreements "which because of their pernicious effect on competition . . . lack any redeeming virtue and are conclusively presumed to be unreasonable and therefore illegal without elaborate inquiry as to the precise harm they have caused or the business excuse for their use."[5]

The courts with few exceptions have applied a per se standard to price fixing. Agreements fixing prices have always appealed to business people because they reduce, even eliminate, the risks of economic loss. Suppose that competitors A, B, and C, the major manufacturers of generators, agree to take turns offering low bids. Each is assured a portion of the available market, and each knows that price competition with its attendant potential for monetary losses will be eliminated. Artificially high prices can safely be charged and greater profits made. Of course, those who buy generators will pay more than they would in a competitive market. Similar results would follow in a broader-based industry if the majority of firms were to agree to charge the same price, or at least that no one would charge less than a specified price. Price fixing of this kind—among competitors operating on the same level of the marketing structure—is referred to as *horizontal price fixing*.

Price fixing also occurs—in fact, it is probably more easily achieved—between firms at different levels of the distribution system for particular goods. Price agreements between wholesalers and retailers, manufacturers and dealers, franchisors and franchisees are examples of *vertical price fixing*. The parties to price-fixing agreements of this type are not competitors, but what they do affects competition.

The judicial rationalization for treating price fixing as a per se violation of the antitrust laws is provided by the following quotation from a 1927 case:

The aim and result of every price-fixing agreement, if effective, is the elimination of one form of competition. The power to fix prices, whether reasonably exercised or not, involves power to control the market and to fix arbitrary and unreasonable prices. The reasonable price fixed today may through economic and business changes become the unreasonable price of tomorrow. Once established, it may be maintained unchanged because of the absence of competition secured by the agreement for a price reasonable when fixed.[6]

In the important case that follows, the Supreme Court emphasized the significance it continues to attach to the per se rule as it is applied to price-fixing arrangements whether entered into by individuals or by corporations.

Arizona v. Maricopa County Medical Society
U.S. Supreme Court
457 U.S. 332 (1982)

Respondent foundations for medical care were organized by respondent, Maricopa County Medical Society, and another medical society to promote fee-for-service medicine and to provide the community with a competitive alternative to existing health insurance plans. The foundations, by agreement of their member doctors, established the maximum fees the doctors could claim in full payment for health services provided to policyholders of specified insurance plans. Petitioner State of Arizona filed a complaint against respondents in federal District Court, alleging that they were engaged in an illegal price-fixing conspiracy in violation of Section 1 of the Sherman Act. The Court of Appeals affirmed the lower court's denial of the motion for partial summary judgment and held that the certified question could not be answered without evaluating the purpose and effect of the agreements at a full trial.

Held. Reversed for State of Arizona.

Stevens, Justice

The question presented is whether §1 of the Sherman Act has been violated by an agreement among competing physicians setting, by majority vote, the maximum fees that they may claim in full payment for health services provided to policyholders of specified insurance plans.

The respondents recognize that our decisions establish that price fixing agreements are unlawful on their face. But they argue that the *per se* rule does not govern this case because the agreements at issue are horizontal and fix maximum prices, are among members of a profession, are in an industry with which the judiciary has little antitrust experience, and are alleged to have procompetitive justifications.

Our decisions foreclose the argument that the agreements at issue escape *per se* condemnation because they are horizontal and fix maximum prices. *Keifer-Stewart* and *Albrecht* place horizontal agreements to fix maximum prices on the same legal —even if not economic—footing as agreements to fix minimum or uniform prices. The *per se* rule "is grounded on faith in price competition as a market force [and not] on a policy of low selling prices at the price of eliminating competition." Rahl, Price Competition and the Price Fixing Rule—Preface and Perspective, 57 Nw. U. L. Rev. 137, 142 (1962). In this case the rule is violated by a price restraint that tends to provide the same economic rewards to all practitioners regardless of their skill, their experience, their training, or their willingness to employ innovative and difficult procedures in individual cases. Such a restraint also may discourage entry into the market and may deter experimentation and new developments by individual entrepreneurs. It may be a masquerade for an agreement to fix uniform prices, or it may in the future take on that character.

Nor does the fact that doctors—rather than nonprofessionals—are the parties to the price fixing agreements support the respondents' position. In *Goldfarb* v. *Virginia State Bar,* we stated that the "public service aspect, and other features of the professions, may require that a particular practice, which could properly be viewed as a violation of the Sherman Act in another context, be treated differently." See *National Society of Professional Engineers* v. *United States.* The price fixing agreements in this case, however, are not premised on public service or ethical norms. The respondents do not argue, as did the defendants in *Goldfarb* and *Professional Engineers,* that the quality of the professional service that their members provide is enhanced by the price restraint. The respondents' claim for relief from the *per se* rule is simply that the doctors' agreement not to charge certain insureds more than a fixed price facilitates the successful marketing of an attractive insurance plan. But the claim that the price restraint will make it easier for customers to pay does not distinguish the medical profession from any other provider of goods or services.

We are equally unpersuaded by the argument that we should not apply the *per se* rule in this case because the judiciary has little antitrust experience in the health care industry. The argument quite obviously is inconsistent with *Socony-Vacuum.* In unequivocal terms, we stated that, "[w]hatever may be its peculiar problems and characteristics, the Sherman Act, so far as price-fixing agreements are concerned, establishes one uniform rule applicable to all industries alike." We also stated that "[t]he elimination of so-called competitive evils [in an industry] is no legal justification" for price fixing agreements, yet the Court of Appeals refused to apply the *per se* rule in this case in part because the health care industry was so far removed from the competitive model. Consistent with our prediction in *Socony-Vacuum,* the result of this reasoning was the adoption by the Court of Appeals of a legal standard based on the reasonableness of the fixed prices, an inquiry we have so often condemned. Finally, the argument that the *per se* rule must be rejustified for every industry that has not been subject to significant antitrust litigation ignores the rationale for *per se* rules, which in part is to avoid the "necessity for an incredibly complicated and prolonged economic investigation into the entire history of the industry involved, as well as related industries, in an effort to determine at large whether a particular restraint has been unreasonable —an inquiry so often wholly fruitless when undertaken."

The respondents' principal argument is that the *per se* rule is inapplicable because their agreements are alleged to have procompetitive justifications. The argument indicates a misunderstanding of the *per se* concept. The anticompetitive potential inherent in all price fixing agreements justifies their facial invalidation even if procompetitive justifications are offered for some. Those claims of enhanced competition are so unlikely to prove significant in any particular case that we adhere to the rule of law that is justified in its general application. Even when the respondents are given every benefit of the doubt, the limited record in this case is not inconsistent with the presumption that the respondents' agreements will not significantly enhance competition.

The respondents contend that their fee schedules are procompetitive because they make it possible to provide consumers of health care with a uniquely desirable form of insurance coverage that could not otherwise exist. The features of the foundation-endorsed insurance plans that they stress are a choice of doctors, complete insurance coverage, and lower premiums. The first two characteristics, however, are hardly unique to these plans. Since only about 70% of the doctors in the relevant market are members of either foundation, the guarantee of complete coverage only applies when an insured chooses a physician in that 70%. If he elects to go to a non-foundation doctor, he may be required to pay a portion of the doctor's fee. It is fair to presume, however, that at least 70% of the doctors in other markets charge no more than the "usual, customary, and reasonable" fee that typical insurers are willing to reimburse in full. Thus, in Maricopa and Pima Counties as well as in most parts of the country, if an insured asks his doctor if the insurance coverage is complete, presumably in about 70% of the cases the doctor will say yes and in about 30% of the cases he will say no.

It is true that a binding assurance of complete insurance coverage—as well as most of the respondents' potential for lower insurance premiums—can be obtained only if the insurer and the doctor agree in advance on the maximum fee that the doctor will accept as full payment for a particular service. Even if a fee schedule is therefore desirable, it is not necessary that the doctors do the price fixing. The record indicates that the Arizona Comprehensive Medical/Dental Program for Foster Children is administered by the Maricopa foundation pursuant to a contract under which the maximum fee schedule is prescribed by a state agency rather than by the doctors. This program and the Blue Shield plan challenged in *Group Life & Health Insurance Co. v. Royal Drug Co.* indicate that insurers are capable not only of fixing maximum reimbursable prices but also of obtaining binding agreements with providers guaranteeing the insured full reimbursement of a participating provider's fee. In light of these examples, it is not surprising that nothing in the record even arguably supports the conclusion that this type of insurance program could not function if the fee schedules were set in a different way.

The most that can be said for having doctors fix the maximum prices is that doctors may be able to do it more efficiently than insurers. The validity of that assumption is far from obvious, but in any event there is no reason to believe that any savings that might accrue from this arrangement would be sufficiently great to affect the competitiveness of these kinds of insurance plans. It is entirely possible that the potential or actual power of the foundations to dictate the terms of such insurance plans may more than offset the theoretical efficiencies upon which the respondents' defense ultimately rests.

Our adherence to the *per se* rule is grounded not only on economic prediction, judicial convenience, and business certainty, but also on a recognition of the respective roles of the Judiciary and the Congress in regulating the economy. Given its generality, our enforcement of the Sherman Act has required the Court to provide much of its substantive content. By articulating the rules of law with some clarity and by adhering to rules that are justified in their general application, however, we enhance the legislative prerogative to amend the law. The respondents' arguments against application of the *per se* rule in this case therefore are better directed to the legislature. Congress may consider the exception that we are not free to read into the statute.

Horizontal Territorial Limitation and Customer Allocation

One device for reducing competition is an agreement between business rivals to divide markets on a geographic basis. Each of two or more competitors agrees not to sell in a designated territory. Courts have frequently referred to these agreements as *horizontal territorial limitations.* Similarly, business competitors sometimes agree to allocate customers. Where horizontal territorial limitations and/or customer allocations are carried out, the seller who is left in the market can generally obtain higher prices and provide less service because of its monopoly position. As territorial sales restrictions and customer allocation have few redeeming features, they have consistently been held to be per se violations of antitrust laws. In *United States* v. *Topco Associates, Inc.* (1972), the Supreme Court ruled that market allocations were per se illegal even when a group of small- and medium-sized grocery chains with 6 percent of the market created a joint subsidiary to market private-label products in competition with large supermarket chains such as A&P and Safeway. The Topco participants divided markets for the sale of Topco brand products so they could compete more efficiently with large rival chains. Competition among sellers of Topco private-label products in the same market was eliminated following the market division. This decision has been criticized in light of the *Sylvania* case to be read further on in this chapter. The critics argue that Topco had so little market power (6 percent) that it could not adversely affect interbrand competition—that is, between A&P and Topco or Safeway and Topco. Second, it is often argued that if Topco did not allocate exclusive territories to the participants they would have no incentive to compete with A&P or Safeway. Sellers of Topco labels in adjoining areas would undercut a participant's prices and also have a "free ride" on their promotions or advertising. Critics suggest that some joint ventures may be procompetitive and thus horizontal/vertical restraints might be best judged by a rule of reason.

Vertical Territorial Limitation and Customer Allocation

Agreements that limit territories in which sales can be made are frequently entered into by manufacturers and dealers or by distributors who sell the manufacturer's product. These *vertical territorial limitations* generally provide an exclusive territory for a single or small number of dealers in a particular product. Both the manufacturer and the dealer-distributor benefit from these territorial restraints. Many argue that limitations of this kind benefit society as well because they increase *interbrand* competition even though they clearly curtail *intrabrand* competition. For example, franchises frequently contain provisions limiting the territory in which the franchisee can operate.

Because under certain circumstances benefits can be shown as a result of market divisions of this nature, the Supreme Court has generally examined each case individually and weighed the reasons for the restrictions against the value of the general policy of fostering competition. Territorial restraints are important to successful quality merchandising. A manufacturer who wishes to keep dealers who are financially sound and able to provide high-grade distribution and service facilities frequently has to guarantee that the dealer will enjoy an exclusive right to market the product in a particular territory. Without such assurances some dealers might be reluctant to invest the capital necessary to develop and maintain quality facilities.

Another argument used to support the imposition of territorial restraints by a manufacturer on a distributor is that these restraints facilitate the distributor's ability to compete with other brands because he is not forced to spend his resources competing with others who sell the same brand. This, the argument goes, is one reason that small businesses sometimes survive in highly competitive markets. Preventing intrabrand competition also has social utility in a market in which a company competes with a much stronger rival as well as for enterprises that depend for their success on personal relationships between buyer and seller.

Territorial restraints that eliminate intrabrand competition, however, are not always in the best interests of the public. Many generically similar products sold under different brand names may be highly differentiated in the buyer's mind. Thus the buyer might consider purchasing only one brand and would look for price competition among different dealers in that brand. Much competition in the automobile industry is actually intrabrand. Were the antitrust laws to permit territorial arrangements that allocated exclusive territories to dealers in a particular brand, the ability of automobile buyers to compare prices among different dealers in that brand would be eliminated and a substantial reduction in competition would result. Another argument against intrabrand territorial restrictions is that the elimination of competitors often increases concentration in markets in which far too little competition already exists.

A corollary of the agreement that allots a specific territory to a seller is the agreement allocating customers. These two often go hand in hand because a territorial restriction prohibiting sales outside a specified area limits the customers with whom the seller may deal. Sometimes, however, customer restrictions go beyond territorial allocations. It is not unusual for a manufacturer to reserve a particular buyer for direct sales, prohibiting distributors and dealers from selling to that buyer. Most of the arguments for and against vertical territorial restrictions apply to vertical agreements dividing customers. In the case that follows, the manufacturer attempted to maintain control over territory by limiting locations from which retailers sold. Here the U.S. Supreme Court overrules a previous case where it had used a per se standard to judge nonprice vertical restrictions illegal. Using a rule of reason standard, it comes to a different conclusion as to the legality of vertical territorial restraints.

Continental T.V., Inc. v. GTE Sylvania

U.S. Supreme Court
433 U.S. 36 (1977)

GTE Sylvania (Sylvania) manufactures and sells television sets. Prior to 1962, Sylvania sold its televisions to independent or company-owned distributors, who resold to a large and diverse group of retailers. Prompted by a decline in its market share to 1–2 percent of the national market, Sylvania adopted a franchise plan.

Sylvania phased out its wholesale distributors and sold directly to a smaller and more select group of franchised retailers. In order to attract aggressive, competent retailers, Sylvania limited the number of franchises in any area and required each franchisee to sell only from the location at which he was franchised. A franchise did not constitute an exclusive territory. Sylvania retained the right to modify the number of franchises in an area.

The revised marketing strategy was successful, and by 1965 Sylvania's share of national television set sales had increased to approximately 5 percent. Dissatisfied with its sales in the city of San Francisco, Sylvania decided to establish an additional San Francisco retailer (Young Brothers), who would be in competition with Continental (defendant and petitioner-appellant in this case) since the proposed new franchisee would be only one mile away. Continental protested that the location of the new franchise violated Sylvania's marketing policy, but Sylvania persisted in its plan. Continental then canceled a large Sylvania order and placed an order with Phillips, one of Sylvania's competitors.

During this same period, Continental expressed a desire to open a store in Sacramento, a desire Sylvania attributed at least in part to Continental's displeasure over the Young Brothers decision. Sylvania believed that the Sacramento market was adequately served by existing Sylvania retailers and denied the request. In the face of this denial, Continental advised Sylvania in September 1965 that it was moving Sylvania merchandise from its San Jose warehouse to a new retail location that it had leased in Sacramento. Two weeks later, allegedly for unrelated reasons, Sylvania's credit department reduced Continental's credit line from $300,000 to $50,000. In response to the reduction in credit and the generally deteriorating relations with Sylvania, Continental withheld all payments owed to John P. Maguire & Co., Inc. (Maguire), the finance company that handled the credit arrangements between Sylvania and its retailers. Shortly thereafter, Sylvania terminated Continental's franchise, and Maguire filed this diversity action in the U.S. District Court seeking recovery of money owed and of secured merchandise held by Continental. Continental filed cross claims against Sylvania and Maguire, claiming that Sylvania had violated Section 1 of the Sherman Act by entering into and enforcing franchise agreements that prohibited sale of Sylvania products by Continental and other franchises except from specific locations. At the District Court level the jury found in favor of Continental, awarding treble (triple) damages totaling $1,774,515 for violations of Section 1 of the Sherman Act. The Court of Appeals reversed in favor of Sylvania.

Held: Affirmed for Sylvania.

Powell, Justice

We turn first to Continental's contention that Sylvania's restriction on retail locations is a *per se* violation of § 1 of the Sherman Act as interpreted in *Schwinn*. (United States v. Arnold Schwinn, 338 U.S. 365(1967)).

Schwinn came to this Court on appeal by the United States from the District Court's decision . . . . [T]he Court (in Schwinn) proceeded to articulate the following "bright line" *per se* rule of illegality for vertical restrictions: "Under the Sherman Act, it is unreasonable without more for a manufacturer to seek to restrict and confine areas or persons with whom an article may be traded after the manufacturer has parted with dominion over it." But the Court expressly stated that the rule of reason governs when "the manufacturer retains title, dominion, and risk with respect to the product and the position and function of the dealer in question are, in fact, indistinguishable from those of an agent or salesman of the manufacturer."

In the present case, it is undisputed that title to the televisions passed from Sylvania to Continental. Thus, the *Schwinn per se* rule applies unless Sylvania's restriction on locations falls outside *Schwinn's* prohibition against a manufacturer attempting to restrict a "retailer's freedom as to where and to whom it will resell the products."

Sylvania argues that if *Schwinn* cannot be distinguished, it should be reconsidered. Although *Schwinn* is supported by the principle of *stare decisis,* we are convinced that the need for clarification of the law in this area justifies reconsideration. *Schwinn* itself was an abrupt and largely unexplained departure from *White Motor Co.* v. *United States,* where only four years earlier the Court had refused to endorse a *per se* rule for vertical restrictions. Since its announcement, *Schwinn* has been the subject of continuing controversy and confusion, both in the scholarly journals and in the federal courts. The great weight of scholarly opinion has been critical of the decision, and a number of the federal courts confronted with analogous vertical restrictions have sought to limit its reach. In our view, the experience of the past 10 years should be brought to bear on this subject of considerable commercial importance.

In essence, the issue before us is whether *Schwinn's per se* rule can be justified under the demanding standards of *Northern Pac. R. Co.* The Court's refusal to endorse a *per se* rule in *White Motor Co.* was based on its uncertainty as to whether vertical restrictions satisfied those standards. Addressing this question for the first time, the Court stated:

> "We need to know more than we do about the actual impact of these arrangements on competition to decide whether they have such a 'pernicious effect on competition and lack . . . any redeeming virtue' and therefore should be classified as *per se* violations of the Sherman Act."

Only four years later the Court in *Schwinn* announced its sweeping *per se* rule without even a reference to *Northern Pac. R. Co.* and with no explanation of its sudden change in position. We turn now to consider *Schwinn* in light of *Northern Pac. R. Co.*

The question remains whether the *per se* rule stated in *Schwinn* should be expanded to include nonsale transactions or abandoned in favor of a return to the rule of reason. We have found no persuasive support for expanding the rule. As noted above, the *Schwinn* Court recognized the undesirability of "prohibit[ing] all vertical restrictions of territory and all franchising. . . ." And even Continental does not urge us to hold that all such restrictions are *per se* illegal.

We revert to the standard articulated in *Northern Pac. R. Co.,* and reiterated in *White Motor,* for determining whether vertical restriction must be "conclusively presumed to be unreasonable and therefore illegal without elaborate inquiry as to the precise harm they have caused or the business excuse for their use." Such restrictions, in varying forms, are widely used in our free market economy. As indicated above, there is substantial scholarly and judicial authority supporting their economic utility. There is relatively little authority to the contrary. Certainly, there has been no showing in this case, either generally or with respect to Sylvania's agreements, that vertical restrictions have or are likely to have a "pernicious effect on competition" or that they "lack . . . any redeeming virtue." Accordingly, we conclude that the *per se* rule stated in *Schwinn* must be overruled. In so holding we do not foreclose the possibility that particular applications of vertical restrictions might justify *per se* prohibition under *Northern Pac. R. Co.* But we do make clear that departure from the rule of reason standard must be based upon demonstrable economic effect rather than—as in *Schwinn*—upon formalistic line drawing.

In sum, we conclude that the appropriate decision is to return to the rule of reason that governed vertical restrictions prior to *Schwinn.* When competitive effects are shown to result from particular vertical restrictions they can be adequately policed under the rule of reason, the standard traditionally applied for the majority of anticompetitive practices challenged under § 1 of the Act.

Trade Associations

A trade association is a loosely knit combination of business firms operating in the same industry. Frequently the members are either competitors or potential competitors. Most associations are supported by dues and governed by directors elected by members. The relationship is often an informal one, and members can usually resign at will. Daily operations of the association generally are the responsibility of a paid executive director and his staff. In most instances the purpose of the association is to promote the common interests of the members by providing services, supplying information, and engaging in promotional activities such as institutional advertising. Many activities of trade associations are beneficial not only to the members but also to the economic system.

Trade associations sometimes promote more effective competition. When participants in a particular industry have some idea of industrywide inventories, sales, and costs of production, they can plan more efficiently. This reduces costs, prevents waste, and improves services to the public. Trade associations have often been leaders in the standardization and development of products. In addition, they may establish general rules for the industry, carry out market surveys, provide a means for exchanging credit information, and supply arbitrators to aid in settling disputes. Some trade associations have also been instrumental in developing and improving ethical standards within their industry.

The opportunity provided competitors by trade-association contacts, however, sometimes leads to activities that may violate the antitrust statutes. Activities that have resulted in antitrust prosecutions usually have involved some covert effort to control prices. When members report prices to their association, pressures can be used to force those firms charging lower prices (who are now clearly identified) to get into line with the industry. In several cases, trade associations have been used by dominant members to enforce desired price levels by denying certain benefits of the association to recalcitrants. These activities have reduced competition and increased profit levels for association members at the expense of the buying public.

In general, the courts attempt to distinguish between legitimate and illegitimate activities of trade associations. Price reports by members for the use of the membership are usually permitted if the association does not identify the prices with the names of the reporting firms and if the information is also available to nonmembers, customers, and the government. Just as knowledge of prices charged by competitors can be used to attain common industrywide prices, so other types of data sometimes supplied by members of a trade association may be used to restrict competition. Nevertheless, the compilation of cost data and the circulation of information about inventories, unused production capacity, unfilled orders, and sales can also encourage more realistic competition. As long as this type of information is disclosed in general terms, it is not subject to government restraints. If, however, such information is used solely by the membership and is not available to the public, the courts will closely scrutinize those activities.

Boycotts

Another business practice that is permissible if done individually but illegal if done in collusion is the boycott. A single business firm may withhold its patronage or refuse to sell in order to accomplish some self-serving end, but a concerted group refusal to deal has been held to violate Section 1 of the Sherman Act. Courts have generally applied a per se prohibition to this type of activity when carried out in a commercial context. Boycotts unrelated to the profits of the group refusing to deal have generally not been held violations of Section 1 of the Sherman Act. For example, when the National Organization of Women (NOW) organized a boycott of states that refused to endorse the proposed Equal Rights Amendment, Missouri sued NOW, claiming a violation of Section 1 of the Sherman Act. The Eighth Circuit Court of Appeals termed the Sherman Act inapplicable to this situation, and the Supreme Court denied Missouri's petition for review.[7]

Tying Agreements

Business managers who control the sale of a product in limited supply because of some natural advantage, or possibly because of a patent, have sometimes tried to increase the sale of another product by tying purchase of the two together. The buyer is not permitted to purchase one item without also purchasing the other. Arrangements of this kind are called tie-in or tying agreements. In one well-known case, the International Salt Company, which had patents on two salt-dispensing machines, leased the machines (the *tying* product) only if the lessee would agree to buy all the salt (the *tied* product) to be used in the machines from International Salt. The Supreme Court held this to be an unlawful restraint of trade.[8] Tying agreements have also been used by sellers who, for one reason or another, are convinced that the "leverage" of one of their products will enable them to sell another, less marketable product.

Tying agreements have been used extensively in sales to consumers, but most litigation has arisen out of transactions at the producer level. Economically the device is objectionable because it limits other sellers of the tied product (the second good or service) from competing in that particular market. This is considered an artificial barrier to competition and has been the subject of considerable judicial censure.

At one time the Supreme Court argued that the effects of a tie-in were so pernicious that mere proof of the agreement established a violation of the antitrust laws (Section 1 of the Sherman Act, Section 3 of the Clayton Act). That is, such agreements were to be condemned per se. This, however, does not appear to be the present state of the law. Tie-in agreements will almost invariably be struck down if the tying product is either a natural or a legal monopoly, such as a patented product. Even when the seller of the tying product does not have monopoly control, tying contracts will be unenforceable (1) if control of the tying product has given the seller sufficient economic power to lessen competition in the market where the tied product is sold and (2) if a substantial amount of interstate commerce is affected. This is true even if no actual injury to competition can be proved.

On the other hand, tying agreements have been allowed where the seller was able to prove that the tied product or service was necessary to maintain the utility and reputation of the desired product. Sellers have successfully defended also by showing that the tying product is only of minor importance in the market and that the buyer was not forced by economic pressures to accept the tied product. In addition, tie-ins are economically beneficial when used by new competitors to facilitate entry into markets dominated by established sellers.

Monopoly Behavior

Monopoly in its purest economic sense involves a single firm without any effective competition. This means that not only is no other firm producing the same product but that no other firm produces a product that consumers could switch to if the monopolist's prices are too high. The foregoing definition is far too restrictive for an antimonopoly statute because a firm could have the ability to act unilaterally and create market restraints without falling within the economic definition of a monopoly. Consequently, a legal definition of monopoly has been developed by the courts as they have interpreted the language of Section 2 of the Sherman Act. Section 2, summarized in Table 38–1 (p. 952), reads as follows:

Every person who shall monopolize, or attempt to monopolize, or combine or conspire with any other person or persons, to monopolize any part of the trade or commerce among the several States, or with foreign nations, shall be deemed guilty of a felony, and, on conviction thereof, shall be punished by fine not exceeding one-million dollars, if a corporation, or, if any other person, one-hundred thousand dollars, or by imprisonment not exceeding three years. . . .

As its language clearly indicates, Section 2 prohibits three types of activities: (1) monopolization, (2) attempts to monopolize, and (3) combinations or conspiracies to monopolize. Most actions under Section 2 have been against single firms charged with monopolization. Suits based on attempts or conspiracies to monopolize are much more difficult to win because they require proof of a specific intent to achieve the unlawful result of monopoly power.

The most difficult problem arising from the language of Section 2 is how the term *monopolize* should be legally defined. A variety of definitions is available to the courts. The courts could determine, for example, that only firms in single-firm industries are monopolies. They might alternatively decide that any firm capable of realizing specified "excess" profits by its pricing ability is a monopoly. They could take yet another approach and conclude that any firm controlling a certain percentage of an industry's total sales or assets is a monopoly. Unfortunately, the actual words of the statute provide little guidance in choosing among alternative definitions.

In analyzing monopoly cases, the courts have set out the guidelines discussed below as a basis for decision making. They can be helpful to business managers in making decisions also, especially in light of the harsh penalties for violations of Section 2 of the Sherman Act.

Relevant Product Market

To accurately judge whether a particular firm has overwhelming market power, it is necessary to determine the specific industry (market) in respect to which the firm's market power is to be judged. Thus a relevant competitive market must be delineated in terms of geography and product-line. First it is generally necessary to determine the relevant product market, because the relevant geographic market will ordinarily be defined in terms of the product. The following well-known case established the basic test of cross-elasticity or interchangeability that the courts use in defining relevant markets.

United States v. Du Pont & Co.
Supreme Court of the United States
351 U.S. 377(1956)

The government instituted suit under Section 2 of the Sherman Act alleging that Du Pont had monopolized and had attempted and conspired to monopolize the cellophane market. The government asked the court to issue an injunction to prevent further monopolization and to order the divestiture of plants and assets, if necessary. At the time of the suit, Du Pont produced approximately 75 percent of all cellophane sold in the United States. This in turn represented 17.9 percent of all flexible wrapping material. The District Court found that the relevant product market was all flexible wrapping materials and entered a judgment for Du Pont on all counts. The government appealed directly to the Supreme Court.

Held: Affirmed for Du Pont.

Reed, Justice

During the period that is relevant to this action, du Pont produced almost 75 percent of the cellophane sold in the United States, and cellophane constituted less than 20 percent of all "flexible packaging materials" sales. Du Pont . . . contends that the prohibition of § 2 against monopolization is not violated because it does not have the power to control the price of cellophane or to exclude competitors from the market in which cellophane is sold. The court below found that the "relevant market for determining the extent of du Pont's market control is the market for flexible packaging materials," and that competition from those other materials prevented du Pont from possessing monopoly powers in its sales of cellophane.

The Government asserts that cellophane and other wrapping materials are neither substantially fungible nor like priced. For these reasons, it argues that the market for other wrappings is distinct from the market for cellophane and that the competition afforded cellophane by other wrappings is not strong enough to be considered in determining whether du Pont has monopoly powers. . . . Every manufacturer is the sole producer of the particular commodity it makes, but its control, in the above sense of the relevant market, depends upon the availability of alternative commodities for buyers: i.e., whether there is a cross-elasticity of demand between cellophane and the other wrappings. This interchangeability is largely gauged by the purchase of competing products for similar uses considering the price, characteristics and adaptability of the competing commodities. The court below found that the flexible wrappings afforded such alternatives.

If cellophane is the "market" that du Pont is found to dominate, it may be assumed it does have monopoly power over that "market." Monopoly power is the power to control prices or exclude competition. It seems apparent that du Pont's power to set the price of cellophane has been limited only by the competition afforded by other flexible packaging materials. Moreover, it may be practically impossible for anyone to commence manufacturing cellophane without full access to du Pont's technique.

However, du Pont has no power to prevent competition from other wrapping materials. It is inconceivable that price could be controlled without power over competition or vice versa. . . .

Determination of the competitive market for commodities depends on how different from one another are the offered commodities in character or use, how far buyers will go to substitute one commodity for another. For example, one can think of building materials as in commodity competition, but one could hardly say that brick competed with steel or wood or cement or stone in the meaning of Sherman Act litigation; the products are too different . . . [T]here are certain differences in the formulae for soft drinks but one can hardly say that each one is an illegal monopoly.

Cellophane costs more than many competing products and less than a few.

Cellophane differs from other flexible packaging materials. From some, it differs more than from others.

It may be admitted that cellophane combines the desirable elements of transparency, strength and cheapness more definitely than any of the others. . . .

But, despite cellophane's advantages, it has to meet competition from other materials in every one of its uses. The Government makes no challenge to Finding 283 that cellophane furnishes less than seven percent of wrappings for bakery products, 25 percent for candy, 32 percent for snacks, 35 percent for meats and poultry, 27 percent for crackers and biscuits, 47 percent for fresh produce, and 34 percent for frozen foods. 75 to 80 percent of cigarettes are wrapped in cellophane. Finding 292. Thus, cellophane shares the packaging market with others. The overall result is that cellophane accounts for 17.9 percent of flexible wrapping materials, measured by the wrapping surface.

An element for consideration as to cross-elasticity of demand between products is the responsiveness of the sales of one product to price changes of the other . . . The court below held that the "[g]reat sensitivity of customers in the flexible packaging markets to price or quality changes" prevented du Pont from possessing monopoly control over price. . . .

We conclude that cellophane's interchangeability with the other materials mentioned suffices to make it a part of this flexible packaging material market.

Geographic Market. Once the relevant product market has been defined, it is necessary to determine the relevant geographic market. Basically, the courts define the relevant geographic market in terms of the area of the defendant firm's effective competitive presence in regard to sales of the relevant product. This determination has not represented an important issue in Section 2 proceedings because generally only national producers have been challenged as monopolies. However, the *Grinnell* case, appearing later in this chapter, did involve the issue of whether the national relevant geographic market found to exist by a lower court should be broken down into local markets.

Overwhelming Market Power. The development of a legally practical and economically meaningful test of monopoly power within a particular relevant competitive market has been a major task of the federal judiciary. The difficulties encountered by the federal courts in their search for an appropriate test have been due, in part, to the fact that a variety of tests could be considered consistent with the very general language of Section 2. Reasonable alternative approaches might include basing the determination of illegality on

1. The achievement of a particular absolute or relative size
2. The existence of a specified "monopolistic" intent
3. The actual commission of specified anticompetitive acts

The question of the competitive effect of sheer physical size is central to determining which alternative test is most appropriate for application by the courts in Section 2 cases. We often hear the term "big business" used in a derogatory sense. Noted judges have written that "bigness is bad." Unfortunately, economic theorists have yet to definitively answer, by empirical findings, the question of whether large firm size is necessary to realize productive efficiencies from the viewpoint of the economy as a whole.

Proponents of large firm size argue that large firms are more efficient by virtue of their ability to realize economies of scale in production and promotion, attract top talent, obtain capital market advantages, effectively conduct research, and introduce advanced technology. Opponents of large firm size argue that many firms become unmanageable beyond an optimum size, economies of scale are often not effectively realized, large size (which is likely to result in just a few firms in a particular industry) encourages collusive pricing and other harmful market practices, and the resulting lack of competition deters research. Opponents further argue that the promotion economies and capital-market power of large firms permit these less efficient firms to survive and even dominate their industries.

In applying Section 2 of the Sherman Act, the courts have been unable to rely directly on the economic model of monopoly, which posits a single firm in its market protected from entry of new firms and from the competition of substitute products. Because this is an exceedingly rare phenomenon in our modern economy, it does not afford a practical *legal* standard. The *Grinnell* case that follows dramatizes the generally analytical, nontechnical approach that the courts have used in determining the presence of the overwhelming market power necessary to violate the statute.

The first major monopoly case was the famous *Standard Oil of New Jersey* v. *United States* (1911).[9] That decision, which broke up the Standard Oil of New Jersey holding company, established a rule of reason approach—the Court looked for an intent to monopolize and actual instances of conduct manifesting that intent. Thus, if such elements were present, an illegal monopoly would be found to exist. That case was quickly followed by the *United States Steel Corporation* case in 1920, in which the Supreme Court stated that "the law does not make mere size an offense, or the existence of unexerted power an offense."[10] The Court found that United States Steel did not have the power to control prices, even though at times it had controlled 50 percent of the market, and refused to break up the company. This resulted in the so-called abuse theory under which the courts for the next twenty years looked for specific abuses and analyzed the actions of alleged monopolists to determine whether they were "good" or "bad" trusts. During this period, the courts applied essentially behavioral criteria to determine whether Section 2 had been violated.

The case establishing the modern interpretation of Section 2, and perhaps the most important monopoly case decided to date, is the circuit court opinion of Judge Learned Hand in *United States* v. *Aluminum Co. of America* (Alcoa) (1945). In *Alcoa* the court used a structuralist approach and focused mainly on the percentage of the market controlled by Alcoa. Judge Hand found that Alcoa had 90 percent of the relevant competitive market and concluded that "that percentage is enough to constitute a monopoly; it is doubtful whether 60 or 64 percent would be enough; and certainly 33 percent is not." On the basis of the monopolization cases decided to date, it can be said that when a firm controls more than 80 percent of a relevant competitive market it is likely to be found in violation of Section 2 of the Sherman Act. This "big is bad" approach by Judge Hand has been severely criticized because the monopoly position of a firm could have been gained by patents or internal efficiencies. Are innovative and efficient firms to be punished because they have obtained more than 80 percent of their market? Will a firm fail to expand and meet buyer demand for fear of obtaining too large a share of its market and becoming a "monopoly"? What effect does

this have on production, output, and employment? An equity standard that opposes "bigness" seems to be in conflict with an efficiency standard that is concerned with consumer welfare. The meaning of *Alcoa* is still debated.

Intent to Monopolize. The existence of market power by itself does not constitute monopolization. The defendant must be shown to have a *general intent* to exercise that power. General intent exists if acts are performed leading to the prohibited result regardless of whether that particular result was actually desired. It is not necessary to show specific intent—that is, that the defendant wanted to monopolize. Often, general intent to monopolize can be inferred from common and usual methods of doing business.

The case that follows is the last significant Supreme Court decision dealing with monopoly under Section 2 of the Sherman Act. It outlines the elements of monopoly and identifies conduct that may show an intent to monopolize. Additionally, the Court defines what constitutes a relevant product market.

United States v. Grinnell Corp.

Supreme Court of the United States
384 U.S. 563 (1966)

The United States charged Grinnell with monopolizing the accredited central-station protection business by using its subsidiaries (identified in the opinion) to obtain a dominant market position. Grinnell manufactured plumbing supplies and fire-sprinkler systems. It also owned 76 percent of the stock of ADT, 89 percent of the stock of AFA, and 100 percent of the stock of Holmes. ADT provided both burglary and fire-protection services; Holmes provided burglary services alone; AFA supplied only fire-protection service. Each offered a central-station service under which hazard-detecting devices installed on the protected premises automatically transmitted an electric signal to a central station. The three companies that Grinnell controlled had over 87 percent of the business. The District Court found for the government and ordered Grinnell to prepare a plan for divestiture of certain of its subsidiaries. The government felt that the relief granted was inadequate, and both parties appealed to the Supreme Court.

Held. Affirmed for the United States.

Douglas, Justice.

The offense of monopoly under § 2 of the Sherman Act has two elements: (1) the possession of monopoly power in the relevant market and (2) the willful acquisition or maintenance of that power as distinguished from growth or development as a consequence of a superior product, business acumen, or historic accident. In the present case, 87 percent of the accredited central station service business leaves no doubt that the congeries of these defendants have monopoly power—power which, as our discussion of the record indicates, they did not hesitate to wield—if that business is the relevant market. The only remaining question therefore is, what is the relevant market?

In case of a product, it may be of such a character that substitute products must also be considered, as customers may turn to them if there is a slight increase in the price of the main product. That is the teaching of the *du Pont* case . . . viz., that commodities reasonably interchangeable make up that "part" of trade or commerce which § 2 protects against monopoly power.

The District Court treated the entire accredited central station service business as a single market and we think it was justified in so doing. Defendants argue that the different central station services offered are so diverse that they cannot, under *du Pont,* be lumped together to make up the relevant market. For example, burglar alarm services are not interchangeable with fire alarm services. They further urge that *du Pont* requires that protective services other than those of the central station variety be included in the market definition.

But there is here a single use, *i.e.,* the protection of property, through a central station that receives signals. It is that service, accredited, that it unique and that competes with all the other forms of property protection. . . .

[W]e deal with services, not with products; and . . . we conclude that the accredited central station is a type of service that makes up a relevant market and that domination or control of it makes out a monopoly and a "part" of trade or commerce within the meaning of § 2 of the Sherman Act. The defendants have not made out a case for fragmentizing the types of services into lesser units.

There are, to be sure, substitutes for the accredited central station service. But none of them appears to operate on the same level as the central station service so as to meet the interchangeability test of the *du Pont* case.

Watchman service is far more costly and less reliable. Systems that set off an audible alarm at the site of a fire or burglary are cheaper but often less reliable. They may be inoperable without anyone's knowing it. Moreover, there is a risk that the local ringing of an alarm will not attract the needed attention and help. Proprietary systems that a customer purchases and operates are available; but they can be used only by a very large business or by government and are not realistic alternatives for most concerns.

The accredited, as distinguished from nonaccredited service, is a relevant part of commerce. Virtually, the only central station companies in the status of the nonaccredited are those that have not yet been able to meet the standards of the rating bureau. The accredited ones are indeed those that have achieved, in the eyes of underwriters, superiorities that other central stations do not have. These standards are important, as insurance carriers often require accredited central station service as a condition to writing insurance. There is indeed evidence that customers consider the unaccredited service as inferior.

As the District Court found, the relevant market for determining whether the defendants have monopoly power is not the several local areas which the individual stations serve, but the broader national market that reflects the reality of the way in which they build and conduct their businesses.

Grinnell was ordered to file, not later than April 1, 1966, a plan of divestiture of its stock in each of the other defendant companies. It was given the option either to sell the stock or distribute it to its stockholders or combine or vary those methods.

The defendants object to the requirements that Grinnell divest itself of its holdings in the three alarm company defendants, but we think that provision is wholly justified. Dissolution of the combination is essential as indicated by many of our cases, starting with *Standard Oil Co. v. United States.*

The few large American firms that control 40 to 60 percent of their identifiable relevant competitive markets react with extreme caution to changes in their market shares to make sure they will not be charged with monopolization. The restraint exercised by such firms directly affects their marketing and advertising strategies. These strategies often emphasize maintaining rather than increasing *relative* market shares, and steps are taken to make sure that the company does not have even the appearance of engaging in anticompetitive activities. Following the Grinnell case, one can imagine the reaction of the board of directors and top officers at General Motors to a proposal by a young marketing vice president for an aggressive long-run marketing strategy whose aim would be to obtain an 85 percent share of domestic auto sales within ten years. On occasion, the dominant firm in an industry has even provided marketing and research assistance to weak or marginal competitors to keep them in business.

Two important monopolization cases were settled in January 1982. If one or the other had been carried to the U.S. Supreme Court, we might have had a redefinition of the law of monopolization. The Justice Department suits against American Telephone and Telegraph (AT&T) and International Business Machines (IBM) charged both firms with monopolizing and attempting to monopolize services and equipment in the telecommunications and computer industries. After the cases were filed (in the early 1970s), more competitors entered both fields, domestically and abroad, and technology revolutionized the two industries. Also, congressional pressure, in the form of proposed legislation, was brought to bear on the companies and the Justice Department. All these factors led to an agreed modification of a 1956 consent decree (AT&T case) and a stipulated dismissal (IBM case).

From these cases and several cases reaching federal courts of appeal,[11] it has become clear that some monopolistic conduct will be considered permissible. When a monopolist seeks to protect its position against rivals entering the market with new products, aggressive pricing policies and innovative products, these actions will be considered legitimate as long as the monopolist does not subsidize one product with revenue from others. In addition to the intent to monopolize, it now appears that efficiency and consumer-welfare criteria will be considered by some federal courts in examining Section 2 monopoly charges against firms that have large shares of a market.

Attempt to Monopolize. Section 2 of the Sherman Act forbids *attempts* to monopolize as well as monopolization. In other words, a company does not have to be successful in monopolizing a market. Conduct that brought a corporation close to monopolization and showed an intent to monopolize was all that was required by the Supreme Court in early cases. Today, most authorities agree that an attempt to monopolize requires

1. Specific intent
2. Predatory or anticompetitive conduct to attain the purpose
3. A dangerous probability of success

A "dangerous probability of success" is usually shown through direct proof of the market power that the firm has attained. "Predatory pricing" has been the focus of much academic and case analysis of monopoly and price-discrimination situations. Courts have generally agreed that pricing above marginal or variable costs will obviously not be predatory and thus no specific intent can be shown to support charges that a firm attempted to monopolize. The question is at what point in a firm's pricing policy do prices become predatory? In light of the fact that an attempt to monopolize is punishable as a felony, with heavy criminal penalties, the answer to this question has some significance for businessmen. The Areeda-Turner standard[12] (most popular with the courts) states that when a firm sets its price below marginal cost (or average variable cost used as a substitute) it is engaged in predatory pricing because it no longer seeks to maximize profits but to eliminate an economically viable competitor. Critics of this standard argue that those not trained in economic analysis have a difficult time understanding terms such as marginal, variable, and fixed costs. They point out that accountants and economists who regularly use these terms define them differently. Because of the imprecision of economic analysis (particularly in a litigation context), critics argue that definitions of predatory pricing that include economic-cost terminology should be received with some skepticism by the courts.

Mergers

A *merger* is the acquisition by one corporation of the assets or stock of another independent corporation wherein the acquired corporation comes to be controlled by the acquirer. Mergers have had an important effect on the nature of industrial organization. They have accounted for a substantial degree of the current concentration in many industries. Many mergers take place in the United States each year. In the fiscal year 1981, 2,314 mergers took place in the United States, up 53 percent over the previous year. Du Pont's acquisition of Conoco and Sohio's of Kennecott Copper were the most prominent.[13] The increase in mergers in 1981 was largely due to the Reagan Administration's more relaxed approach to enforcement of Section 7 of the Clayton Act. Also, undervalued stocks, particularly in the oil industry, led companies to believe that it was cheaper to acquire a company than to finance internal expansion, especially at high interest rates. Finally, a number of companies divested themselves of subsidiaries purchased in the late 1950s and early 1960s that were no longer viable profit centers.

On the basis of the economic interrelationships between the firms involved, mergers may be classified into three basic types—horizontal, vertical, and conglomerate. A *horizontal merger* involves two competing firms at the same level of the distribution structure. A *vertical merger* involves two firms at different levels of the distribution structure that deal with the same basic product or process. A *conglomerate merger* results when noncompeting, nonrelated firms merge. The acquisition by RCA of the Hertz Rental Car Company is an example of a conglomerate merger.

Relevant Competitive Market. To evaluate the effect of a merger for regulatory purposes, it is necessary to define the product and geographic dimensions of a relevant competitive market. This is mandated by amended Section 7 of the Clayton Act, which provides:

No person engaged in commerce or in any activity affecting commerce shall acquire, directly or indirectly, the whole or any part of the stock or other share capital and no person subject to the jurisdiction of the Federal Trade Commission shall acquire the whole or any part of the assets of another person engaged also in commerce or in any activity affecting commerce, where in any line of commerce or in any activity affecting commerce in any section of the country, the effect of such acquisition may be substantially to lessen competition, or to tend to create a monopoly.

The determination of the relevant competitive market in a merger case often establishes whether the postmerger firm is relatively a whale or a minnow. It often is *the* critical factor in the lawsuit's ultimate outcome.

In defining "line of commerce"—that is, the relevant product market—the courts have used the same basic standards of cross-elasticity of demand and marketplace treatment discussed earlier in reference to monopoly. When considering mergers, the courts are concerned with the treatment accorded products by consumers and industry representatives. They have shown a willingness to break product lines into submarkets or to combine product lines into aggregate markets whenever the circumstances in a particular case justified either approach.

After having defined the relevant product market, the court must determine the relevant geographic market. Section 7 condemns mergers whose effects may be to substantially lessen competition "in any section of the country." On its face that language raises an important question. If a lessening of competition can be found to exist in any single market area, is it then necessary to define a relevant geographic market? For example, could an acquisition by American Motors of a small custom-car manufacturer in Maine (who sells interstate) be found to violate Section 7 because of its combined market share in Bangor? The implications of this question are particularly bothersome if we assume that in no other city of the United States would its combined market share represent a violative figure. To date, with one confusing exception, all the cases have involved delineation of a relevant geographic market even if that were only a single metropolitan or commercial area.

As should be apparent, the determination of the boundaries of the relevant geographic market may significantly influence the final outcome of a particular case. For example, assume that a twenty-five-store discount chain selling throughout Ohio were to acquire an even smaller discount chain selling only in southern Ohio. For jurisdictional purposes, further assume that both are interstate firms. If the relevant geographic market were found to be the nation as a whole, there would be little chance that the merger would be in violation of Section 7. If, on the other hand, the state of Ohio were found to comprise the relevant geographic market, the chances of the merger's being set aside would be substantially increased. In general, the smaller the relevant geographic market, the more likely the government will prevail. The larger the geographic market, the more likely the defendant firm will prevail.

In defining a relevant geographic market, the courts have sought to determine the boundaries of the geographic area of effective competition of the business involved in terms of the relevant product(s). When mergers at the manufacturing level are involved, the relevant geographic market is likely to be the nation as a whole, or at least several contiguous states. Retailing presents more complex questions, and a single large city (for supermarket retailing) or a contiguous four-county area (for commercial banking) may constitute the relevant geographic market. In the *Brown Shoe* case, excerpted later in this chapter, the court found the relevant geographic market to consist of those cities with populations of 10,000 or more in which both merging firms (Brown Shoe and Kinney Shoe) had outlets. Thus the courts have not required that the geographic market be defined as one unitary, contiguous area.

The Department of Justice has issued merger guidelines outlining the standards the department will apply in defining relevant competitive markets and in evaluating the legality of acquisitions. The guidelines do not have the force of a court decision and do not represent a legally binding interpretation of Section 7. In fact, each new administration of the Department of Justice is free to ignore or change the guidelines. In spite of this, the guidelines are of considerable value to businessmen because they give them and their attorneys a basis for estimating whether a proposed acquisition is likely to be challenged by the government. The merger guidelines indicate that a relevant geographic market will be determined for each product market of each merging firm. Depending on the nature of the product, the geographic market may be a city, a state, or the country. Taking the location of the merging firm (or of each plant for a multiplant firm) as a starting point, the Department of Justice first establishes a provisional geographic market based on the shipment patterns of the merging firm and its closest competitors. As a first approximation, the department tests the market by hypothesizing a small price increase (5 percent) and asks how many sellers could sell the product to customers included in the provisional market. If the relevant product can be obtained from sellers outside the provisional market in sufficient quantity at a comparable price, the relevant geographic market is expanded to include those firms that can make "significant sales" to customers within the new market boundaries. This expanded area is then defined as the relevant geographic market.

Potential Effect on Competition. Once a court has defined the boundaries of the relevant competitive market and has thereby implicitly determined the type of merger involved, it must then evaluate the potential effect of the proposed merger on competition within that market. Section 7 indicates, in general terms, the anticompetitive effect necessary in order to condemn a merger. The language "effect of such acquisition *may be* substantially to lessen competition" and "tend to create a monopoly" seems to indicate that it is not necessary for the government to prove an actual, existing competitive restraint. Instead, the language is concerned with future probabilities. Thus in the past the government was required to demonstrate only that a proposed merger would probably result in prohibited anticompetitive effects in order to obtain a judgment striking down the merger. More recently (as discussed at the end of this section) the courts have required stricter proof of anticompetitive effects by the government.

In developing the criteria by which to apply the general language of Section 7 to actual mergers, the courts have found it necessary to distinguish between the different types of mergers. Such distinctions are proper and logical because horizontal, vertical, and conglomerate mergers may have significantly different economic effects. Thus, even though the same language of the same statute is applied to each type of merger, the specific questions to be answered in applying the statute will vary. These distinctions will become evident in the following discussion.

HORIZONTAL MERGERS. Of the three types of mergers, a horizontal merger involves the most direct and immediate competitive effect. Unless a firm's acquisition of a competitor is offset by a new entry into the industry, an immediate result of the merger will be increased concentration. Because horizontally merging firms already have identifiable market shares in their industry, the courts have specific, objective criteria from which to draw initial conclusions concerning the competitive effect of the merger. Consequently, the courts have had to resolve the following two questions concerning the use of market-share information:

1. What postacquisition market shares, if any, are so insignificant that the merger may be found to be clearly legal without further questions?
2. What market shares, if any, are so probably anticompetitive that the merger may be found to be illegal without further investigation?

In *United States* v. *Philadelphia National Bank* (1963), the Supreme Court determined that a postacquisition market share of 30 percent or more was prima facie illegal and thus resolved the second question. Note that the *Philadelphia Bank* opinion indicated that a share smaller than 30 percent could be prima facie illegal, but no lower limit has yet been established by the Supreme Court.

The question of whether an identifiable minimum postacquisition market share could be clearly legal was faced by the Supreme Court in the first important merger case reaching it under Section 7. *Brown Shoe* v. *United States*, set out below, is particularly instructive because it clearly outlines the relevant product and geographic markets as well as the merger's potential effect on competition.

VERTICAL MERGERS. Vertical mergers are more difficult to evaluate because they do not involve combinations of direct competitors. Thus the courts cannot avail themselves of easily applied criteria such as market share or percentage of total productive assets controlled. Instead, the courts must analyze the resulting market structure and the probable market behavior of the postacquisition firm to determine if an actual or potential competitor is likely to be foreclosed from important markets. Ordinarily, the exclusion is of a direct competitor of one of the merging firms. For example, in *Brown Shoe* the reader will see the Supreme Court's concern that independent shoe manufacturers not be denied access to retail outlets because of the number of retail stores that Brown-Kinney would control after the acquisition; and because of the established tendency of retail stores acquired by Brown to sell a much higher percentage of Brown's shoes after acquisition. Typically, the foreclosure is of a manufacturer from retail outlets or from a needed source of supply. As in this case, it is most likely to occur in an industry in which a few large firms are vertically integrated and a large number of smaller competitors are not.

Brown Shoe Co. v. United States

Supreme Court of the United States

370 U.S. 294 (1962)

The government challenged the acquisition of the G. R. Kinney Company by Brown Shoe on the grounds that the merger violated Section 7 of the Clayton Act. Brown was the third-largest retail shoe seller (over 1,230 outlets) and the fourth-largest shoe manufacturer, while Kinney was the eighth-largest seller (over 350 outlets) and the twelfth-largest manufacturer. The District Court found for the government and Brown appealed to the Supreme Court.

Held: Affirmed for the United States.

Warren, Chief Justice.

This case is one of the first to come before us in which the Government's complaint is based upon allegations that the applicants have violated Section 7 of the Clayton Act, as that section was amended in 1950.

The dominant theme pervading congressional consideration of the 1950 amendments was a fear of what was considered to be a rising tide of economic concentration in the American economy. Other considerations cited in support of the bill were the desirability of retaining "local control" over industry and the protection of small businesses. Throughout the recorded discussion may be found examples of Congress' fear, not only of accelerated concentration of economic power on economic grounds, but also of the threat to other values a trend toward concentration was thought to pose.

Congress neither adopted nor rejected specifically any particular tests for measuring the relevant markets, either as defined in terms of product or in terms of geographic locus of competition, within which the anticompetitive effects of a merger were to be judged. Nor did it adopt a definition of the word "substantially," whether in quantitative terms of sales or assets or market shares or in designated qualitative terms, by which a merger's effects on competition were to be measured.

Congress used the words *"may tend substantially to lessen competition"* (emphasis supplied), to indicate that its common concern was with probabilities, not certainties. Statutes existed for dealing with clear-cut menaces to competition; no statute was sought for dealing with ephemeral possibilities. Mergers with a probable anticompetitive effect were to be proscribed by this Act.

THE VERTICAL ASPECTS OF THE MERGER

Economic arrangements between companies standing in a supplier-customer relationship are characterized as "vertical." The primary vice of a vertical merger or other arrangement tying a customer to a supplier is that, by foreclosing the competitors of either party from a segment of the market otherwise open to them, the arrangement may act as a "clog on competition," . . . which "deprive(s) . . . rivals of a fair opportunity to compete."

The "area of effective competition" must be determined by reference to a product market (the "line of commerce") and a geographic market (the "section of the country").

The Product Market

The outer boundaries of a product market are determined by the reasonable interchangeability of use or the cross-elasticity of demand between the product itself and substitutes for it. However, within this broad market, well-defined submarkets may exist which, in themselves, constitute product markets for antitrust purposes. The boundaries of such a submarket may be determined by examining such practical indicia as industry or public recognition of the submarket as a separate economic entity, the product's peculiar characteristics and uses, unique production facilities, distinct customers, distinct prices, sensitivity to price changes, and specialized vendors.

Applying these considerations to the present case, we conclude that the record supports the District Court's finding that the relevant lines of commerce are men's, women's, and children's shoes. The product lines are recognized by the public; each line is manufactured in separate plants; each has characteristics peculiar to itself rendering it generally noncompetitive with the others; and each is, of course, directed toward a distinct class of customers.

Appellant, however, contends that the District Court's definitions fail to recognize sufficiently "price/quality" distinctions in shoes. Brown argues that the predominantly medium-priced shoes which it manufactures occupy a product market different from the predominantly low-priced shoes which Kinney sells. But agreement with that argument would be equivalent to holding that medium-priced shoes do not compete with low-priced shoes. We think the District Court properly found the facts to be otherwise.

The Geographic Market

We agree with the parties and District Court that insofar as the vertical aspect of this merger is concerned, the relevant geographic market is the entire Nation.

The Probable Effect of the Merger

. . . (I)t is apparent from both past behavior of Brown and from testimony of Brown's president, that Brown would see its ownership of Kinney to force Brown shoes into Kinney stores.

Another important factor to consider is the trend toward concentration in the industry.

. . . The necessary corollary of these trends is the foreclosure of independent manufacturers from markets otherwise open to them. And because these trends are not the product of accident but are rather the result of deliberate policies of Brown and other leading shoe manufacturers, account must be taken of these facts in order to predict the probable future consequences of this merger.

THE HORIZONTAL ASPECTS OF THE MERGER

An economic arrangement between companies performing similar functions in the production or sale of comparable goods or services is characterized as "horizontal." Where the arrangement effects a horizontal merger between companies occupying the same product and geographic market, whatever competition previously may have existed in that market between the parties to the merger is eliminated. The 1950 amendments made plain Congress' intent that the validity of such combinations was to be gauged on a broader scale: Their effect on competition generally in an economically significant market.

Thus, again, the proper definition of the market is a "necessary predicate" to an examination of the competition that may be affected by the horizontal aspects of the merger. The acquisition of Kinney by Brown resulted in a horizontal combination at both the manufacturing and retailing levels of their businesses. (T)he District Court found that the merger of Brown's and Kinney's *manufacturing* facilities was economically too insignificant to come within the prohibition of the Clayton Act.

The Product Market

Shoes are sold in the United States in retail shoe stores and in shoe departments of general stores. These outlets sell: (1) Men's shoes, (2) women's shoes, (3) women's or children's shoes, or (4) men's, women's and children's shoes.

The Geographic Market

The criteria to be used in determining the appropriate geographic market are essentially similar to those used to determine the relevant product market. Moreover, just as a product submarket may have Section 7 significance as the proper "line of commerce," so may a geographic submarket be considered the appropriate "section of the country." . . . Congress prescribed a pragmatic, factual approach to the definition of the relevant market and not a formal, legalistic one. The geographic market selected must, therefore, both "correspond to the commercial realities" of the industry and be economically significant. Thus, although the geographic market in some instances may encompass the entire Nation under other circumstances, it may be as small as a single metropolitan area.

We believe, however, that the record fully supports the District Court's findings that shoe stores in the outskirts of cities compete effectively with stores in central downtown areas, and that while there is undoubtedly some commercial intercourse between smaller communities within a single "standard metropolitan area," the most intense and important competition in retail sales will be confined to stores within the particular communities in such an area and their immediate environs.

We therefore agree that the District Court properly defined the relevant geographic markets in which to analyze this merger as those cities with a population exceeding 10,000 and their environs in which both Brown and Kinney retailed shoes through their own outlets.

The Probable Effect of the Merger

Having delineated the product and geographic markets within which the effects of this merger are to be measured, we turn to an examination of the District Court's finding that, as a result of the merger, competition in the retailing of men's, women's, and children's shoes may be lessened substantially in those cities in which both Brown and Kinney stores are located.

In 118 separate cities, the combined shares of the market of Brown and Kinney in the sale of one of the relevant lines of commerce exceeded 5%. In 47 cities, their share exceeded 5% in all three lines.

The market share which companies may control by merging is one of the most important factors to be considered when determining the probable effects of the combination on effective competition in the relevant market. In an industry as fragmented as shoe retailing, the control of substantial shares of the trade in a city may have important effects on competition. If a merger achieving 5% control were now approved, we might be required to approve future merger efforts by Brown's competitors seeking similar market shares. The oligopoly Congress sought to avoid would then be furthered and it would be difficult to dissolve the combinations previously approved. Furthermore, in this fragmented industry, even if the combination controls but a small share of a particular market, the fact that this share is held by a large national chain can adversely affect competition. It is competition, not competitors, which the Act protects. But we cannot fail to recognize Congress' desire to promote competition through the protection of viable, small, locally owned businesses. Congress appreciated that occasional higher costs and prices might result from the maintenance of fragmented industries and markets. It resolved these competing considerations in favor of decentralization. We must give effect to that decision.

Other factors to be considered in evaluating the probable effects of a merger in the relevant market lend additional support to the District Court's conclusion that this merger may substantially lessen competition. One such factor is the history of tendency toward concentration in the industry. As we have previously pointed out, the shoe industry has, in recent years, been a prime example of such a trend.

On the basis of the record before us, we believe the Government sustained its burden of proof. We hold that the District Court was correct in concluding that this merger may tend to lessen competition substantially in the retail sale of men's, women's, and children's shoes in the overwhelming majority of those cities and their environs in which both Brown and Kinney sell through owned or controlled outlets.

Trends in Horizontal and Vertical Mergers

Since *United States* v. *General Dynamics* (1974), the Supreme Court has moved away from the aggregate numbers/relative percentage approach and begun to evidence a willingness to consider the competitive consequences or the specific economic characteristics of the market involved. The Court has looked not only at the conduct of the merging firms and the structure of their market but at the economic consequences of the merger for their industry. For example, the Court refused to allow the Justice Department to claim that the potential effect of a merger of one national bank and a bank in the Seattle area would be to decrease competition because the acquired bank would have expanded internally or merged with smaller banks if it were not acquired. The Court also rejected the claim that the acquiring bank was seeking to eliminate a "potential competitor." After examining the regulated nature of the banking industry and its effect on ease of entry into the Seattle banking market, the Court approved the merger.[14] Following this decision, the federal courts have required the Justice Department and FTC to show the actual anticompetitive effects of a merger they oppose. The government must demonstrate by objective facts that the acquiring firm would enter the market via internal expansion if the merger were disallowed. How near the firm was to entering the market on its own prior to the merger is a question that must be answered by the plaintiffs. Contentions based on subjective intent, or looking into the company's mind, are not acceptable.[15]

Price Discrimination

In an economy based on freedom and competition, neophyte business managers, not unnaturally, might expect that they would be permitted to price their products as the economics of production, distribution, and profit dictate. This, however, is not the case. Management responsible for determining prices must make its decisions within the framework of extensive federal and state regulations that restrict choices.

One of the most important statutory provisions influencing pricing decisions is Section 2 of the Clayton Act as amended by the Robinson-Patman Act. This legislation attempts to foster competition by prohibiting price discrimination in certain instances. Selling physically identical products at different prices can be anticompetitive in many situations. To be found illegal, price discrimination must occur in *interstate commerce* between a seller and different purchasers of commodities of like grade and quality, and the effect of such discrimination by the seller must be to substantially lessen competition or tend to create a monopoly. Congress enacted the law in 1936 to protect small businesses from huge sellers coming into a market and cutting prices on a product below cost for the sole purpose of driving out small sellers.

One situation, frequently referred to as "primary" or "seller's level" competition, involves competition between sellers and their rivals. The primary-seller's-level competitive strategy that is likely to violate Section 2 of the Clayton Act is *whip-sawing*. When, for example, the price-cutting seller operates in several geographic markets, it can cut prices in one while maintaining its prices in another. This gives it an unfair advantage when competing with a seller that operates only in a single geographic market. Unable to maintain its price, the latter has no way of keeping up its profits; the former, however, can make up at least a portion of its losses by profits earned in other areas. After eliminating one regional competitor by selective price-cutting, the firm functioning in several regions can then turn its attention to another and so on until all regional competitors have been eliminated.

Cases of blatant whip-sawing are rare, and selective price cutting can be done for legitimate economic motives—for example, when a firm wishes to secure a market share in a new geographic market area. The courts have had some difficulty balancing legitimate economic interests with the price-discrimination laws in the situation where a national firm invades a market area that is dominated by a regional firm.

The major defense of large sellers for their selective price cutting or discrimination among purchasers is a "meeting the competition" argument. It is the breadth of this defense, which is provided by Section 2 of the Robinson-Patman Act, that is a matter of controversy. Those who view the act as being noncompetitive in nature argue that this defense should be widened by the courts to allow the marketplace to dictate price. They argue that many inefficient, small businesses are kept in existence if this defense is narrowed, and consumers lose in the form of higher prices.

The case below illustrates the Supreme Court's most recent attempt to widen the "meeting-the-competition" defense.

Falls City Industries, Inc. v. Vanco Beverage, Inc.

Supreme Court of the United States

460 U.S. _____ (1983)

During a certain period of time from 1972 through 1978, petitioner (Falls City Industries, Inc.) sold its beer to respondent, the sole wholesale distributor for petitioner's beer in Vanderburgh County, Indiana, at a higher price than petitioner charged its only wholesale distributor in Henderson County, Kentucky. The two counties form a single metropolitan area extending across the state line. Under Indiana law, brewers were required to sell to all Indiana wholesalers at a single price, Indiana wholesalers were prohibited from selling to out-of-state retailers, and Indiana retailers were not permitted to purchase beer from out-of-state wholesalers. Respondent filed suit in Federal District Court, alleging that petitioner's price discrimination violated Section 2(a) of the Clayton Act, as amended by the Robinson-Patman Act. After trial, the court held that respondent had established a prima facie case of price discrimination, finding that although respondent and petitioner's Kentucky wholesaler did not sell to the same retailers, they competed for sale of petitioner's beer to consumers of beer from retailers in the market area; that petitioner's pricing policy resulted in lower retail prices for its beer in Kentucky than in Indiana; that many customers living in the Indiana portion of the market ignored Indiana law to purchase petitioner's beer more cheaply from Kentucky retailers; and that petitioner's pricing policy thus prevented respondent from competing effectively with petitioner's Kentucky wholesaler and caused respondent to sell less beer to Indiana retailers. The court rejected petitioner's "meeting-competition" defense under Section 2(b) of the Clayton Act, which provides that a defendant may rebut a prima facie showing of illegal price discrimination by establishing that its lower price to any purchaser or purchasers "was made in good faith to meet an equally low price of a competitor." The court reasoned that instead of reducing its prices to meet those of a competitor, petitioner had created the price disparity by raising its prices to Indiana wholesalers more than it had raised its Kentucky prices; that instead of adjusting prices on a customer-by-customer basis to meet competition from other brewers, petitioner charged a single price throughout each state; and that the higher Indiana price was not set in good faith but instead was raised solely to allow petitioner to follow other brewers to enhance its profits. The Court of Appeals affirmed. Falls City Industries appealed.

Blackmun, Justice

Section 2(b) of the Clayton Act, as amended by the Robinson-Patman Act, provides that a defendant may rebut a prima facie showing of illegal price discrimination by establishing that its lower price to any purchaser or purchasers "was made in good faith to meet an equally low price of a competitor." The United States Court of Appeals for the Seventh Circuit has concluded that the "meeting-competition" defense of §2(b) is available only if the defendant sets its lower price on a customer-by-customer basis and creates the price discrimination by lowering rather than by raising prices. We conclude that §2(b) is not so inflexible.

When proved, the meeting-competition defense of §2(b) exonerates a seller from Robinson-Patman Act liability. This Court consistently has held that the meeting-competition defense at least requires the seller, who has knowingly discriminated in price, to show the existence of facts which would lead a reasonable and prudent person to believe that the granting of a lower price would in fact meet the equally low price of a competitor. The seller must show that under the circumstances it was reasonable to believe that the quoted price or a lower one was available to the favored purchaser or purchasers from the seller's competitors. Neither the District Court nor the Court of Appeals addressed the question whether Falls City had shown information that would have led a reasonable and prudent person to believe that its lower Kentucky price would meet competitors' equally low prices there; indeed, no findings whatever were made regarding competitors' Kentucky prices, or the information available to Falls City about its competitors' Kentucky prices.

On its face, §2(b) requires more than a showing of facts that would have led a reasonable person to believe that a lower price was available to the favored purchaser from a competitor. The showing required is that the "lower price . . . was made in good faith to meet" the competitor's low price. Thus, the defense requires that the seller offer the lower price in good faith for the purpose of meeting the competitor's price, that is, the lower price must actually have been a good faith response to that competing low price. In most situations, a showing of facts giving rise to a reasonable belief that equally low prices were available to the favored purchaser from a competitor will be sufficient to establish that price. In others, however, despite the availability from other sellers of a low price, it may be apparent that the defendant's low offer was not a good faith response.

Almost 20 years ago, the FTC set forth the standard that governs the requirement of a "good faith response":

> "At the heart of Section 2(b) is the concept of 'good faith'. This is a flexible and pragmatic, not a technical or doctrinaire, concept. The standard of the prudent businessman responding fairly to what he reasonably believes is a situation of competitive necessity." Continental Baking Co., 63 FTC. 2071, 2163 (1963).

Although the District Court characterized the Indiana prices charged by Falls City and its competitors as "artificially high," there is no evidence that Falls City's lower prices in Kentucky were set as part of a plan to obtain artificially high profits in Indiana rather than in response to competitive conditions in Kentucky. Falls City did not adopt an illegal system of prices maintained by its competitors. The District Court found that Falls City's prices rose in Indiana in response to competitors' price increases there; it did not address the crucial question whether Falls City's Kentucky prices remained lower in response to competitors' prices in that State.

Vanco attempts to argue that the existence of industry-wide price discrimination within the single geographic retail market itself indicates "tacit or explicit collusion, or . . . market power" inconsistent with a good faith response.

The collusion argument founders on a complete lack of proof. Persistent, industry-wide price discrimination within a geographic market should certainly alert a court to a substantial possibility of collusion. Here, however, the persistent interstate price difference could well have been attributable, not to Falls City, but to extensive state regulation of the sale of beer. Indiana required each brewer to charge a single price for its beer throughout the State, and barred direct competition between Indiana and Kentucky distributors for sales to retailers. In these unusual circumstances, the prices charged to Vanco and other wholesalers in Vanderburgh County may have been influenced more by market conditions in distant Gary and Fort Wayne than by conditions in nearby Henderson County, Kentucky. Moreover, wholesalers in Henderson County competed directly, and attempted to price competitively, with wholesalers in neighboring Kentucky counties. A separate pricing structure might well have evolved in the two States without collusion, notwithstanding the existence of a common retail market along the border. Thus, the sustained price discrimination does not itself demonstrate that Falls City's Kentucky prices were not a good faith response to competitors' prices there.

The Court of Appeals explicitly relied on two other factors in rejecting Falls City's meeting-competition defense: the price discrimination was created by raising rather than lowering prices, and Falls City raised its prices in order to increase its profits. Neither of these factors is controlling. Nothing in §2(b) requires a seller to lower its price in order to meet competition. On the contrary, §2(b) requires the defendant to show only that its "lower price . . . was made in good faith to meet an equally low price of a competitor." A seller is required to justify a price difference by showing that it reasonably believed that an equally low price was available to the purchaser and that it offered the lower price for that reason; the seller is not required to show that the difference resulted from subtraction rather than addition.

A different rule would not only be contrary to the language of the statute, but also might stifle the only kind of legitimate price competition reasonably available in particular industries. In a period of generally rising prices, vigorous price competition for a particular customer or customers may take the form of smaller price increases rather than price cuts. Thus, a price discrimination created by selective price increases can result from a good faith effort to meet a competitor's low price.

Nor is the good faith with which the lower price is offered impugned if the prices raised, like those kept lower, respond to competitors' prices and are set with the goal of increasing the seller's profits. A seller need not choose between ruinously cutting its prices to all its customers to match the price offered to one, [and] refusing to meet the competition and then ruinously raising its prices to its remaining customers to cover increased unit costs. Nor need a seller choose between keeping all its prices ruinously low to meet the price offered to one, and ruinously raising its prices to all customers to a level significantly above that charged by its competitors. A seller is permitted "to retain a customer by realistically meeting in good faith the price offered to that customer, without necessarily changing the seller's price to its other customers." The plain language of §2(b) also permits a seller to retain a customer by realistically meeting in good faith the price offered to that customer, without necessarily freezing his price to his other customers.

Section 2(b) does not require a seller, meeting in good faith a competitor's lower price to certain customers, to forgo the profits that otherwise would be available in sales to its remaining customers. The very purpose of the defense is to permit a seller to treat different competitive situations differently. The prudent businessman responding fairly to what he believes in good faith is a situation of competitive necessity might well raise his prices to some customers to increase his profits, while meeting competitors' prices by keeping his prices to other customers low.

Vanco also contends that Falls City did not satisfy §2(b) because its price discrimination "was not a defensive response to competition." According to Vanco, the Robinson-Patman Act permits price discrimination only if its purpose is to retain a customer. We agree that a seller's response must be defensive, in the sense that the lower price must be calculated and offered in good faith to "meet not beat" the competitor's low price. Section 2(b), however, does not distinguish between one who meets a competitor's lower price to retain an old customer and one who meets a competitor's lower price in an attempt to gain new customers. Such a distinction would be inconsistent with that section's language and logic.

The Court of Appeals relied on *FTC* v. *Staley* for the proposition that the meeting-competition defense "places emphasis on individual [competitive] situations, rather than upon a general system of competition,' " 654 F.2d, at 1230 (quoting Staley, 324 U.S., at 753), and "does not justify the maintenance of discriminatory pricing among classes of customers that results merely from the adoption of a competitor's discriminatory pricing structure." The Court of Appeals was apparently invoking the District Court's findings that Falls City set prices statewide rather than on a "customer to customer basis," and the District Court's conclusion that this practice disqualified Falls City from asserting the meeting-competition defense.

There is no evidence that Congress intended to limit the availability of §2(b) to customer-specific responses. Section 2(b)'s predecessor, §2(b) of the original Clayton Act, stated that "nothing herein contained shall prevent . . . discrimination in price in the same or different communities made in good faith to meet competition."

Section 2(b) specifically allows a "lower price . . . to any purchaser or purchasers" made in good faith to meet a competitor's equally low price. A single low price surely may be extended to numerous purchasers if the seller has a reasonable basis for believing that the competitor's lower price is available to them. Beyond the requirement that the lower price be reasonably calculated to "meet not beat" the competition, Congress intended to leave it a "question of fact . . . whether the way in which the competition was met lies within the latitude allowed." 80 Cong. Rec. 9418 (1936) (remarks of Rep. Utterback). Once again, this inquiry is guided by the standard of the prudent businessman responding fairly to what he reasonably believes are the competitive necessities.

A seller may have good reason to believe that a competitor or competitors are charging lower prices throughout a particular region. In such circumstances, customer-by-customer negotiations would be unlikely to result in prices different from those set according to information relating to competitors' territorial prices. A customer-by-customer requirement might also make meaningful price competition unrealistically expensive for smaller firms such as Falls City, which was attempting to compete with larger national breweries in 13 separate States. Territorial pricing can be a perfectly reasonable method—sometimes the most reasonable method—of responding to rivals' low prices. We choose not to read into §2(b) a restriction that would deny the meeting-competition defense to one whose area-wide price is a well tailored response to competitors' low prices.

In summary, the meeting-competition defense requires the seller at least to show the existence of facts that would lead a reasonable and prudent person to believe that the seller's lower price would meet the equally low price of a competitor; it also requires the seller to demonstrate that its lower price was a good faith response to a competitor's lower price.

Falls City contends that it has established its meeting-competition defense as a matter of law. In the absence of further findings, we do not agree. The District Court and the Court of Appeals did not decide whether Falls City had shown facts that would have led a reasonable and prudent person to conclude that its lower price would meet the equally low price of its competitors in Kentucky throughout the period at issue in this suit. Nor did they apply the proper standards to the question whether Falls City's decision to set a single statewide price in Kentucky was a good faith, well-tailored response to the competitive circumstances prevailing there. The absence of allegations to the contrary is not controlling; the statute places the burden of establishing the defense on Falls City, not Vanco. There is evidence in the record that might support an inference that these requirements were met, but whether to draw that inference is a question for the trier of fact, not this Court.

REVIEW PROBLEMS

1. Beginning in 1959, four major distributors of stainless steel pipe and tubing who sold in Washington, Oregon, California, Idaho, and Utah began to experience substantial price competition from eastern mills and from small local jobbers, who sold but did not stock pipe and tubing. Upon the invitation of Tubesales Corporation, the dominant and largest distributor, a series of meetings was held to discuss mutual problems.

   The government claimed that at these meetings the parties agreed to reduce discounts to nonstocking jobbers from 10 percent to 5 percent and to reduce the freight factor in their prices; as a result, new price lists embracing lower freight rates were drawn up by Tubesales and hand delivered to the others. All four distributors were charged with violations of Section 1 of the Sherman Act. What result? Esco Corporation v. United States, 340 F.2d 1000 (1965)

2. In 1864 and 1870 Congress granted the Northern Pacific Railway Company approximately 40 million acres of land to facilitate financing and constructing a railroad to the northwest. The grant consisted of alternate sections of land in a belt twenty miles wide on each side of the track. The granted lands were of various kinds.

   By 1949, the railroad had sold about 37 million acres of its holdings and leased most of the rest. In a large number of sales and leases, the railroad had inserted "preferential routing" clauses that compelled the owner or lessee to ship over Northern Pacific lines all commodities produced on the land. The preferential routing clause applied only if Northern Pacific's rates were equal to those of competing carriers.

   In 1949, the government sued under Section 1 of the Sherman Act seeking a declaration that the preferential routing clauses were unlawful as unreasonable restraints of trade because they constituted tying arrangements. What result? Northern Pacific Railway Company v. United States, 356 U.S. 1(1957)

3. A group of Carvel franchisees operating stores selling soft ice cream products sued Carvel Corporation for treble damages. They alleged that Carvel engaged in illegal exclusive dealing and tying arrangements by requiring the franchisees (1) to refrain from selling non-Carvel products, (2) to purchase from Carvel or its designatees certain supplies that ultimately would be part of the final product sold (the franchisees were allowed to purchase equipment and paper goods from other sources subject to quality-control specifications), and (3) to follow "suggested" resale prices. What result? Susser v. Carvel Corporation, 322 F.2d 505 (1964)

4. From 1958 until 1961 Utah Pie Co., a local producer, was the leading seller of frozen pies in the Salt Lake City market. Because of the advantage of its location, the company usually was able to maintain the lowest prices in a market in which the major competitive weapon was price. During a four-year period, Utah Pie was challenged at one time or another by each of three major competitors, all of whom operated in several other markets. Evidence showed that each of these competitors sold frozen pies in the Salt Lake market at prices lower than they charged for pies of like grade and quality in other markets considerably closer to their plants. Evidence also indicated that in several instances one or more of them had sold at prices below actual cost and that one of the competitors had sent an industrial spy into Utah's plant.

During the period, price levels deteriorated substantially. In 1958 Utah had been selling pies for $4.15 per dozen. Some forty-four months later, Utah was selling similar pies for $2.75 per dozen. As a result of the actions of Pet Milk, Carnation, and Continental, the three major competitors, Utah Pie brought an action for treble damages charging each with a violation of Section 2 (a) of the Clayton Act as amended by the Robinson-Patman Act. What result? Utah Pie Company v. Continental Baking Co., 386 U.S. 685 (1967)

5. The Philadelphia National Bank and Girard Trust Bank were the second and third largest of the forty-two commercial banks with head offices in the metropolitan area consisting of the city of Philadelphia and three adjoining counties. Philadelphia National had assets over $1 billion, Girard had assets of over $750 million. The boards of directors of the banks approved a merger. If they merged, the resulting bank would be the largest in the four-county Philadelphia area. The two banks viewed the merger as strengthening their hand in competing with other large banks in the northeastern United States. The government filed suit alleging that the proposed merger was in violation of Section 7 of the Clayton Act and asking that the court enjoin it. What result? United States v. Philadelphia National Bank, 374 U.S. 321 (1963)

6. Reynolds Metal Company was the largest producer of aluminum foil in the world. In 1956 it acquired Arrow Brands, Inc., then engaged in converting aluminum and selling it nationally to wholesale florist-supply houses. Arrow purchased its "raw" aluminum from Reynolds, converted it, and, prior to its acquisition by Reynolds, accounted for 33 percent of the converted foil sold to the florist industry. Eight other firms also supplied converted aluminum to the florist industry, and some bought from Reynolds. The FTC sued under Section 7, claiming that aluminum foil in the florist trade was the relevant market. Reynolds argued that all trades that require specialized use of aluminum are the relevant product market. What result? Reynolds Metal Company v. Federal Trade Commission, 309 F. 2d. 223, (1962)

FOOTNOTES

1 *The White House Task Force Report on Antitrust Policy* (Washington, D.C.: Bureau of National Affairs, 1969), p. 3.

2 Clair Wilcox, *Public Policies Toward Business,* 4th Ed. (Homewood, Il: Richard D. Irwin, 1971), p. 690.

[3]246 U.S. 231 (1918).

[4]Id., at p. 237.

[5]Northern Pacific Railway Co. v. United States, 345 U.S. 1 (1958).

[6]United States v. Trenton Potteries Co., 273 U.S. 392 (1972).

[7]Missouri v. National Organization of Women, 620 F.2d. 1301 (8th Cir., 1980), cert. denied (101 S. Ct. 122).

[8]International Salt Co. v. United States, 332 U.S. 392 (1947).

[9]221 U.S. 1 (1911).

[10]251 U.S. 417 (1920).

[11]See Telex v. IBM, 510 F.2d 894 (10th Cir., 1975), Berkey Photo Inc. v. Eastman Kodak (2d Cir., 1979).

[12]See Phillip Areeda and Donald Turner, "Predatory Pricing and Related Practices Under Section 2 of the Sherman Act," 88 *Harv. L. Rev.* 697 (1975).

[13]*Merger and Acquisitions Quarterly,* Vol. 16 (4), Fall-Winter, 1981, p. 60.

[14]United States v. Marine Bancorporation, Inc., 418 U.S. 602 (1974).

[15]See FTC v. Atlantic Richfield Co., 549 F.2d 289 (4th Cir., 1977) and United States v. Siemens Corp., 621 F.2d 499 (2d. Cir., 1980).

CHAPTER 39

The Federal Trade Commission and Consumer Protection

THE FEDERAL TRADE COMMISSION AS AN ADMINISTRATIVE

AGENCY ————————————————————————————

THE FEDERAL TRADE COMMISSION AND UNFAIR TRADE

PRACTICES ————————————————————————————

THE FEDERAL TRADE COMMISSION AND CONSUMER-PROTECTION

LAWS ————————————————————————————

As previously discussed in Chapter 37, a national debate exists between those who favor increased government regulation of the private sector as a means of protecting the public interest and those who wish to get government agencies "off the back" of business. This debate has nowhere been more vigorously pursued by politicians, business people, consumerists, and scholars than in their discussion of the role of the Federal Trade Commission (FTC or Commission) as an enforcer of consumer-protection laws.

In the late 1960s, such diverse parties as the American Bar Association[1] and a Ralph Nader study group[2] accused the FTC of being a "do nothing" agency and called for its reorganization and a more activist stance in carrying out its duties under the antitrust statutes and the Federal Trade Commission Act of 1914. The Commission responded to these criticisms by upgrading its staff and organizing its bureaus by functions. Major procedural changes, granting the Commission specific authority to prescribe enforceable rules for the first time, were initiated by Congress with passage of the Magnuson-Moss Warranty–Federal Trade Commission Improvement Act of 1975[3] (Magnuson-Moss Act). Subsequent to the passage of this legislation, the Commission, using its rule-making authority, eliminated the "holder-in-due course" doctrine in consumer transactions and issued rules governing the advertisement of eyeglasses. It also proposed rules to regulate such diverse areas as the funeral industry, vocational schools, and children's advertising.

Additionally, a proconsumerist environment in the 1970s led Congress to pass numerous consumer-oriented statutes delegating regulatory authority and enforcement duties to the FTC. This increased authority and responsibility ultimately led to calls from affected private-sector interests for limits on the FTC. After being criticized for being a "do nothing" agency in the late 1960s, an activist Commission, ten years later, was "reined in" by Congress with passage of the 1980 Federal Trade Commission Improvement Act, which limited the FTC's rule-making authority and made it more accountable to Congress.

This chapter focuses on the role of the FTC in protecting consumers. First, the FTC's structure, membership, jurisdiction, and operations are examined. Second, Section 5 of the Federal Trade Commission Act of 1914, which prohibits unfair and deceptive practices, is discussed, particularly as it relates to commercial advertising. The chapter concludes with a discussion of the FTC's role in regulating consumer credit and debt collection.[4]

THE FEDERAL TRADE COMMISSION AS AN ADMINISTRATIVE AGENCY

History, Purpose, Jurisdiction

The Federal Trade Commission Act of 1914[5] created a five-member bipartisan Commission to enforce the antitrust laws discussed in Chapter 38. The Commission was particularly charged with enforcement of Sections 2, 3, 7, and 8 of the Clayton Act and Section 5 of the Federal Trade Commission Act. Section 5 forbids "unfair methods of competition." Congress sought to use this broad language to reach anticompetitive practices not covered by the Sherman and Clayton acts. Only civil remedies may be sought and no private treble-damage suits can be brought under Section 5 of the Federal Trade Commission Act. In

1938, the Wheeler-Lea amendment to Section 5 added the words "unfair or deceptive acts or practices," providing the Commission with broad authority to regulate business practices that may not violate the antitrust statutes but that are considered "unfair" or "deceptive." With this statutory language and a congressional mandate, the FTC ventured into the marketplace as a consumer protector.

Following the growth of a proconsumerist environment in the late 1960s and 1970s, Congress passed additional statutes delegating administrative and enforcement authority to the FTC beyond the original antitrust laws and the Federal Trade Commission Act of 1914. Some of these statutes are: the Export Trade Act, Packers and Stockyard Act, Wool Products Labeling Act, Lanham Trade Mark Act, Fur Products Labeling Act, Textile Fiber Product Identification Act, Federal Cigarette and Advertising Act, Fair Packaging and Labeling Act, Truth-in-Lending Act, Fair Credit Reporting Act, Fair Credit Billing Act, Equal Credit Opportunity Act, Hobby Protection Act, Magnuson-Moss Warranty–Federal Trade Improvement Act, Energy Policy and Conservation Act, Hart-Scott-Rodino Antitrust Improvement Act, and the Federal Drug and Cosmetic Act. It should be noted that Congress has given the FTC exclusive authority under some statutes, while in other instances the Commission shares authority with other agencies. For example, it shares enforcement authority with the Food and Drug Administration under the Federal Drug and Cosmetic Act.

Structure and Functions

The structure of the FTC is diagrammed in Figure 39-1. The chairman and four commissioners are appointed for five-year terms by the President of the United States with the advice and consent of the Senate. No more than three of the five may be from a single political party. The chairman is the executive and administrative head of the agency. He or

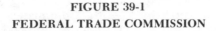

FIGURE 39-1
FEDERAL TRADE COMMISSION

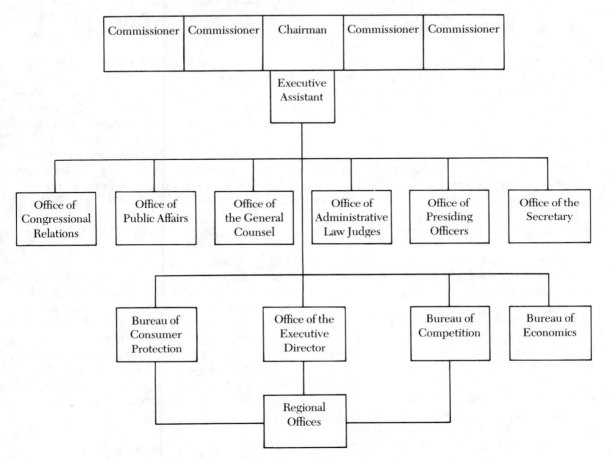

she presides at Commission meetings and hearings conducted by the Commission.

Other officers of the Commission include the executive director, who supervises regional offices and coordinates bureaus, and the general counsel, who is the chief law officer and adviser to the Commission, and who represents the Commission in federal and state courts. An important role played by the general counsel is to assist businessmen in obtaining advice from the Commission as to the legal propriety of a proposed course of action.

Three bureaus carry out the FTC's mandated functions. The Bureau of Competition investigates potentially unfair or deceptive acts or practices under Section 5 of FTCA and prosecutes cases before administrative-law judges after issuance of a formal complaint. These adjudication proceedings are described in Chapter 37. As an alternative to adjudication, it may obtain negotiated consent orders, which must be approved by the full Commission. The Bureau also conducts rule-making proceedings in order to define specific acts that may be violations of statutes enforced by the FTC. The Bureau of Consumer Protection is significant to the business community and consumers because it is the initiator of litigation in specific cases as well as the source of proposed rules that may affect an entire industry. Also, it makes public efforts to educate all parties as to the laws that it is charged with enforcing. The Bureau of Economics advises the Commission on the economic aspects of all its functions. Its work has become more important as the Commission has begun to rely on cost-benefit analyses in proposing new rules and evaluating present regulations.

Operations

The FTC has used its authority under Section 5 to investigate various types of unfair or deceptive business practices. The FTC staff seeks to bring about a voluntary admission of wrongdoing or a consent order from the firm involved in a questionable practice before issuing a formal complaint. If this negotiating procedure fails, the FTC initiates litigation before an administrative-law judge. Following a hearing and initial decision of the judge, either the staff of the FTC or the corporation may appeal. On appeal the case is heard by the full Commission. The Commission's decision becomes final if not appealed to a federal court of appeals within sixty days. The Commission issues cease-and-desist orders.

Additionally, the Commission, when asked, issues advisory opinions on the legality of a firm's proposed activity, assuming that such activity falls under one of the statutes enforced by the FTC. Advisory opinions are *not* binding on the Commission.

As discussed above, the FTC can also issue rules for an entire industry. For example, the FTC has proposed rules that would require the funeral industry to publish its rates. If proposed rules become final, they can be enforced against a violator by fines on individuals or firms of up to $10,000 per day per violation. The FTC can also obtain temporary restraining orders or preliminary injunctions from courts in order to prevent violations or threatened violations of Commission-administered

laws. The Magnuson-Moss Act provides that the Commission may bring civil actions in federal or state courts upon behalf of consumers if they have been injured by unfair or deceptive practices that violate Commission regulations.

The FTC's rule-making authority has come under closer scrutiny by Congress since passage of the 1980 Federal Trade Commission Improvement Act.[6] The act provided Congress with the power to override an FTC rule by majority votes of the Senate and the House. This "legislative veto" was applied in 1982 to an FTC regulation that required used-car dealers to list a car's major defects on the car before it was sold. Of the 286 House members who voted to kill the FTC regulation, 242 had received contributions to their 1980 campaigns totaling $675,000 from the Used Car Dealers Association's political action committees.[7] A federal Court of Appeals in October 1982 unanimously overturned the "legislative veto" of the FTC used-car regulation, claiming that such a veto of regulatory action violated the constitutional principle of separation of powers. As stated in Chapter 38, the United States Supreme Court in June 1983 declared legislative veto provisions within all federal acts to be unconstitutional.

THE FEDERAL TRADE COMMISSION AND UNFAIR TRADE PRACTICES

Section 5 of the Federal Trade Commission Act

As previously noted, Section 5 of the Federal Trade Commission Act allocates broad consumer-protection powers to the FTC because it forbids "unfair or deceptive acts or practices." While deceptive practices have a long history of common law definition, court and FTC interpretations of the word "unfair" now permit the FTC to investigate a practice that is neither deceptive nor a violation of the antitrust statutes under Section 5 if it (1) offends public policy, (2) is immoral, unethical, or unscrupulous, and (3) causes material or substantial harm to the consumer. The Commission has investigated false or misleading labeling, palming off, misleading product names, disparagement of competition, violations of warranties (see Chapter 17 for the FTC role), and many other practices using these standards; however, few practices affecting the consuming public have been so closely monitored by the FTC as deceptive and unfair advertising and product labeling.

The FTC and Deceptive Advertising

As previously stated, the Wheeler-Lea Act amended Section 5 of the Federal Trade Commission Act to include "unfair or deceptive trade practices." In passing the amendment, Congress made it clear that the FTC had broad power to "cover every form of advertisement deception over which it would be humanly practical to exercise governmental control." It was to reach every case, from inadvertent or uninformed to the most subtle or vicious advertising. Through a case approach to enforcement, the FTC evolved a standard by which the advertiser does not have to *intend* deception as in the common-law definition of deceit to be guilty of unfair or deceptive practices. All that is required is a misrepresentation and a tendency to deceive an ordinary purchaser at whom the advertisement is directed or by whom it is expected to be read or viewed.[8] The FTC does not have to demonstrate that specific consumers relied on or believed the advertisement. The FTC has generally concerned itself with advertising relating to price, product quality and quantity, and testimonials.

Deceptive-Price Advertising. Some examples of deceptive advertising are: false price comparisons (if the advertisement claims a price is reduced, it must be reduced from the regular price), bait and switch, and offers of a free good or service to a customer who buys one. The case below illustrates the "free good" type of deceptive price advertising.

Federal Trade Commission v. Mary Carter Paint Co., et al.

Supreme Court of the United States

382 U.S. 46 (1965)

Mary Carter Paint Company (respondent) manufactured and sold paint and related products. The FTC ordered respondent to cease and desist from the use of certain representations found by the Commission to be deceptive and in violation of Section 5 of the Federal Trade Commission Act. The representations appeared in advertisements that stated in various ways that, for every can of respondent's paint purchased by a buyer, the respondent would give the buyer a "free" can of equal quality and quantity. The Court of Appeals for the Fifth Circuit set aside the Commission's order.

Held: Reversed for Federal Trade Commission.

Brennan, Justice

Although there is some ambiguity in the Commission's opinion, we cannot say that its holding constituted a departure from Commission policy regarding the use of the commercially exploitable word "free." Initial efforts to define the term in decisions were followed by "Guides Against Deceptive Pricing." These informed businessmen that they might advertise an article as "free," even though purchase of another article was required, so long as the terms of the offer were clearly stated, the price of the article required to be purchased was not increased, and its quality and quantity were not diminished. With specific reference to two-for-the-price-of-one offers, the Guides required that either the sales price for the two be "the advertiser's usual and customary retail price for the single article in the recent, regular course of his business," or where the advertiser has not previously sold the article, the price for the two be the "usual and customary" price for one in the relevant trade areas. These, of course, were guides, not fixed rules as such, and were designed to inform businessmen of the factors which would guide Commission decisions. Although Mary Carter seems to have attempted to tailor its offer to come within these terms, the Commission found that it failed; the offer complied in appearance only.

The gist of the Commission's reasoning is in the hearing examiner's finding, which it adopted, that "the usual and customary retail price of each can of Mary Carter paint was not, and is not now, the price designated in the advertisement [$6.98] but was, and is now, substantially less than such price. The second can of paint was not, and is not now, 'free,' that is, was not, and is not now, given as a gift or gratuity. The offer is, on the contrary, an offer of two cans of paint for the price advertised as or purporting to be the list price or customary and usual price of one can." In sum, the Commission found that Mary Carter had no history of selling single cans of paint; it was marketing twins, and in allocating what is in fact the price of two cans to one can, yet calling one "free," Mary Carter misrepresented. It is true that respondent was not permitted to show that the quality of its paint matched those paints which usually and customarily sell in the $6.98 range, or that purchasers of paint estimate quality by the price they are charged. If both claims were established, it is arguable that any deception was limited to a representation that Mary Carter has a usual and customary price for single cans of paint, when it has no such price. However, it is not for courts to say whether this violates the Act. "[T]he Commission is often in a better position than are courts to determine when a practice is 'deceptive' within the meaning of the Act."

The Commission advises us in its brief that it believes it would be appropriate here "to remand the case to it for clarification of its order." The judgment of the Court of Appeals is therefore reversed and the case is remanded to that court with directions to remand to the Commission for clarification of its order.

Advertising and Product Quality and Quantity. There is often a fine line between "puffing" and deception. The FTC and the courts have recognized that certain types of claims by advertisers do not violate Section 5 of the Federal Trade Commission Act. A car salesman's claim that "this car is the best that ever came out of Detroit" is an example of "puffing," but when an advertisement claims that "this car will run for 50,000 miles without a mechanical breakdown" it goes beyond puffing and approaches deception. A famous example of deception arose in the case of a Firestone Tire and Rubber Company ad that stated: "When you buy a Firestone tire—no matter how much or little you pay—you get a safe tire."[9] It should be noted that a claim does not have to be expressly deceptive; it may deceive by implication. The FTC must also show that there was no basis for the claim. The Commission argued that the Firestone ad could have been interpreted to mean that, regardless of road conditions or usage, the tire was absolutely safe. This would obviously be false. In this case, the FTC was found to be correct in its position. The Commission requires that an advertiser keep data on file to support its claims as to quality, performance, and comparative price. During the Reagan Administration, the FTC chairman and the head of its Consumer Protection Bureau have argued that requirements of immense amount of data to support advertising claims are an unjustified burden on advertisers and hurtful to consumers because the cost of such substantiation is passed on to the consumer in the form of higher prices. The chief of the FTC Consumer Protection Bureau believes that criteria should be developed for the amount of substantiation of ads that is required. He argues that consumers who act reasonably "do not expect subjective claims to be backed up by substantiation." Consumer advocates do not agree; they argue that a loosening of FTC requirements established in the early 1970s would lead to increased unsubstantiated claims in advertising.

Sometimes advertisers are accused of deception by their competitors. Seven-Up, for example, accused Pepsi-Cola of false, misleading, and deceptive ads because Pepsi did not say clearly in its television ads that regular, sugared Pepsi Free wasn't completely caffeine free—only 99 percent. In two cases brought under the Lanham Act, Section 43(a), which forbids "false description or representation," McDonald's and Wendy's accused Burger King of falsely portraying its hamburger as superior on the basis of an alleged "taste test." Both plaintiffs challenged the method and results of the taste test and sought injunctions and corrective advertising.[10] The cases were settled out of court. The FTC can receive complaints from competitors as well as consumers, but it is not required to act on the complaints. The FTC generally takes the position that the government should not be involved when two or more private parties want to fight it out as to comparative advertising claims dealing with quality and quantity.

Deceptive Advertising and Testimonials. The FTC forbids endorsement of products by well-known personalities who either don't use the product or don't actually prefer it over another product. The Bureau of Consumer Protection also monitors claims by well-known personalities that they have superior knowledge of a product. In a negotiated consent order, entertainer Pat Boone agreed to pay damages to purchasers of Acne Stain. Boone represented the product as a cure for acne when in fact there was no scientific basis for such a claim. Boone also failed to reveal that he had a commercial interest in Acne Stain.

The FTC and Unfair Advertising

Section 5 forbids "unfair" as well as deceptive advertising. As discussed earlier in this chapter, advertising is considered "unfair" if it (1) offends public policy, (2) is immoral, unethical, or unscrupulous, and (3) causes material or substantial harm to the consumer.

The basis of FTC-proposed rules banning certain types of advertising for children is not that the ads are deceptive but that the particular group they are addressed to is incapable of judging their truthfulness. The ads are unfair also, according to the FTC, because the group they are addressed to is susceptible to a type of "brainwashing."

The failure of the Commission to provide a precise definition of the word "unfair" has led to calls by some at the FTC for more specificity from Congress. As an alternative others have argued that "unfair and deceptive practices" should be deleted from Section 5 of the Federal Trade Commission Act. Others have used the vagueness of definition as grounds for requesting an exemption from FTC authority under Section 5.

Remedies for Deceptive and Unfair Advertising

In adjudicative proceedings, the FTC has the power to issue cease-and-desist orders. It has also ordered firms to disclose their deceptive or unfair advertising to the public through corrective advertising. The firm is usually ordered to allocate a portion of its advertising budget under this remedy to correct the long-held impression it has created in the public mind. In the case below, corrective advertising was approved by a federal appeals court.

Warner Lambert v. Federal Trade Commission

U.S. Court of Appeals, D.C. Circuit

562 F.2d. 49 (1977)

Warner Lambert (petitioner) advertised that the product Listerine prevented, cured, or alleviated the common cold. Listerine had been on the market since 1879, and its formula and advertising (begun in 1921) had never changed. The FTC ordered the company to cease and desist advertising this claim and to devote $10 million to corrective advertising that included the following: "Contrary to prior advertising Listerine will not help prevent colds or sore throats or lessen their severity." Petitioner challenged this order. The administrative-law judge (ALJ) ruled in favor of the FTC staff. Petitioner appealed to the full Commission. The Commission affirmed essentially all the findings of the ALJ. Petitioner appealed to the Court of Appeals.

Held: Affirmed for FTC with modification.

Wright, Judge

The first issue on appeal is whether the Commission's conclusion that Listerine is not beneficial for colds or sore throats is supported by the evidence. The Commission's findings must be sustained if they are supported by substantial evidence on the record viewed as a whole. We conclude that they are.

Both the ALJ and the Commission carefully analyzed the evidence. They gave full consideration to the studies submitted by petitioner. The ultimate conclusion that Listerine is not an effective cold remedy was based on six specific findings of fact.

First, the Commission found that the ingredients of Listerine are not present in sufficient quantities to have any therapeutic effect. This was the testimony of two leading pharmacologists called by Commission counsel. The Commission was justified in concluding that the testimony of Listerine's experts was not sufficiently persuasive to counter this testimony.

Second, the Commission found that in the process of gargling it is impossible for Listerine to reach the critical areas of the body in medically significant concentration. The liquid is confined to the mouth chamber. Such vapors as might reach the nasal passage would not be in therapeutic concentration. Petitioner did not offer any evidence that vapors reached the affected areas in significant concentration.

Third, the Commission found that even if significant quantities of the active ingredients of Listerine were to reach the critical sites where cold viruses enter and infect the body, they could not interfere with the activities of the virus because they could not penetrate the tissue cells.

Fourth, the Commission discounted the results of a clinical study conducted by petitioner on which petitioner heavily relies. Petitioner contends that in a four-year study school children who gargled with Listerine had fewer colds and cold symptoms than those who did not gargle with Listerine. The Commission found that the design and execution of the "St. Barnabas study" made its results unreliable. For the first two years of the four-year test no placebo was given to the control group. For the last two years the placebo was inadequate: the control group was given colored water which did not resemble Listerine in smell or taste. There was also evidence that the physician who examined the test subjects was not blinded from knowing which children were using Listerine and which were not, that his evaluation of the cold symptoms of each child each day may have been imprecise, and that he necessarily relied on the non-blinded child's subjective reporting. Both the ALJ and the Commission analyzed the St. Barnabas study and the expert testimony about it in depth and were justified in concluding that its results are unreliable.

Fifth, the Commission found that the ability of Listerine to kill germs by millions on contact is of no medical significance in the treatment of colds or sore throats. Expert testimony showed that bacteria in the oral cavity, the "germs" which Listerine purports to kill, do not cause colds and play no role in cold symptoms. Colds are caused by viruses. Further, "while Listerine kills millions of bacteria in the mouth, it also leaves millions. It is impossible to sterilize any area of the mouth, let alone the entire mouth."

Sixth, the Commission found that Listerine has no significant beneficial effect on the symptoms of sore throat. The Commission recognized that gargling with Listerine could provide temporary relief from a sore throat by removing accumulated debris irritating the throat. But this type of relief can also be obtained by gargling with salt water or even warm water. The Commission found that this is not the significant relief promised by petitioner's advertisements. It was reasonable to conclude that "such temporary relief does not 'lessen the severity' of a sore throat any more than expectorating or blowing one's nose 'lessens the severity' of a cold."

Petitioner contends that even if its advertising claims in the past were false, the portion of the Commission's order requiring "corrective advertising" exceeds the Commission's statutory power. The argument is based upon a literal reading of Section 5 of the Federal Trade Commission Act, which authorizes the Commission to issue "cease and desist" orders against violators and does not expressly mention any other remedies. The Commission's position, on the other hand, is that the affirmative disclosure that Listerine will not prevent colds or lessen their severity is absolutely necessary to give effect to the prospective cease and desist order; a hundred years of false cold claims have built up a large reservoir of erroneous consumer belief which would persist, unless corrected, long after petitioner ceased making the claims.

The need for the corrective advertising remedy and its appropriateness in this case are important issues. But the threshold question is whether the Commission has the authority to issue such an order. We hold that it does [based on the legislative history of the Federal Trade Commission Act of 1914, the Wheeler-Lea Act Amendments of 1938, and the 1975 amendments, along with case precedents interpreting the Act].

Having established that the Commission does have the power to order corrective advertising in appropriate cases, it remains to consider whether use of the remedy against Listerine is warranted and equitable. We have concluded that part 3 of the order should be modified to delete the phrase "Contrary to prior advertising." With that modification, we approve the order.

Our role in reviewing the remedy is limited. The Supreme Court has set forth the standard:

> The Commission is the expert body to determine what remedy is necessary to eliminate the unfair or deceptive trade practices which have been disclosed. It has wide latitude for judgment and the courts will not interfere except where the remedy selected has no reasonable relation to the unlawful practices found to exist.

The Commission has adopted the following standard for the imposition of corrective advertising:

> [I]f a deceptive advertisement has played a substantial role in creating or reinforcing in the public's mind a false and material belief which lives on after the false advertising ceases, there is clear and continuing injury to competition and to the consuming public as consumers continue to make purchasing decisions based on the false belief. Since this injury cannot be averted by merely requiring respondent to cease disseminating the advertisement, we may appropriately order respondent to take affirmative action designed to terminate the otherwise continuing ill effects of the advertisement.

We think this standard is entirely reasonable. It dictates two factual inquiries: (1) Did Listerine's advertisements play a substantial role in creating or reinforcing in the public's mind a false belief about the product? and (2) Would this belief linger on after the false advertising ceases? It strikes us that if the answer to both questions is not yes, companies everywhere may be wasting their massive advertising budgets. Indeed, it is more than a little peculiar to hear petitioner assert that its commercials really have no effect on consumer belief.

The FTC and Deceptive Packaging and Labeling

Closely related to the problems associated with advertising are questions involved in packaging and labeling. Studies have indicated that consumers tend to rely more heavily on labeling than other forms of advertising. Labeling and packaging came under fire when a study by the Food and Drug Administration (1965) indicated that it was not uncommon to find packages with as little as 20 percent of the inner container filled with a food product.

Against this background Congress in 1966 passed the Fair Packaging and Labeling Act.[11] Congress ordered the Secretary of Health, Education and Welfare (HEW, now Health and Human Services) and the FTC to develop mandatory and discretionary rules governing the labeling and packaging of products. HEW was authorized to regulate packaging of foods, drugs, and cosmetics, while the FTC was given jurisdiction over other consumer commodities.

The rules require that a packaged or labeled consumer commodity must bear the following information:

1. The name and address of the manufacturer, packer, or distributor of the product
2. The net quantity, which must be conspicuously placed on the package front
3. An accurate description of the contents

These requirements were intended to enable consumers to compare prices of competing products on the basis of uniform measures. This seemed necessary because of the wide variety of package weights and volumes used by manufacturers.

In passing the Fair Packaging and Labeling Act, Congress authorized discretionary regulations to

1. Set up standards for size characterization (e.g. "small," "medium," "large")
2. Control "cents off" promotions
3. Regulate additional ingredient information on containers of drugs and cosmetics
4. Prevent nonfunctional slack fill of packages

The Fair Packaging and Labeling Act provides that any violation of the act is also a violation of Section 5 of the Federal Trade Commission Act. Thus the FTC has used the same enforcement measures for violations of both acts.

Criticisms of the Fair Packaging and Labeling Act have focused on the amount of disclosure required, the cost involved for companies, and the failure of Congress to define what products constitute "consumer commodities" under the act. There are several statutory omissions, such as uniform pricing per unit, that still make it difficult for consumers to compare prices. Some argue that the Act is unwieldy and should be scrapped. Others argue that it provides some benefits for consumers in terms of their ability to do comparison shopping and should be retained.

THE FEDERAL TRADE COMMISSION AND CONSUMER-PROTECTION LAWS

In 1968, Congress passed the Consumer Credit Protection Act,[12] which addresses problems associated with consumer buying on credit. This comprehensive act comprises the Truth-in-Lending Act (Title I), the Fair Credit Reporting Act (Title IV), the Equal Credit Opportunity Act (Title VI), and the Fair Debt Collection Practices Act. Basically, the act requires disclosure of information concerning the cost of credit transactions and prohibits unfair treatment of consumers in credit applications and debt collections.

Those who support consumer protection in the area of credit point to the fact that consumers owe over $1.5 trillion in debts and use credit cards frequently. They argue that prior to 1969 many abuses existed in the issuance and reporting of credit terms by the consumer-finance industry. Often a consumer-debtor did not know the dollar amount or the percentage rate that he or she was being charged for credit. A consumer might be paying 25 percent rather than the 8 percent he or she thought because the industry had no uniform way of quoting rates. Because the consumer was not able to compare rates, there was little competition among lenders. Also, there were abuses in the use of credit information. A consumer would be denied credit on the basis of outdated or inaccurate credit bureau files. Another common abuse was discrimination against women and nonwhites. Moreover, collection agencies sometimes harassed debtors by telephone at all hours of the night.

Those who oppose the Consumer Credit Protection Act argue that complete disclosure of credit information and attempts to impose honest conduct in the consumer-finance marketplace fail to pass a cost-benefit analysis. For example, it is argued that the Truth-in-Lending Act, which requires uniform disclosure of credit terms and conditions (interest rates or finance charges) to consumers, does little to help the lower-income and uneducated people for whose protection it was passed. Lower-income people, it is argued, do not buy on installments or borrow from a bank because they cannot meet credit standards. They do not need uniform guidelines as to interest rates and finance charges because they do not compare the credit charges. It is the rich and educated who benefit from such legislation, and presumably they can protect themselves or hire lawyers to speak for them. The un-regulated consumer-finance industry would normally supply most information now mandated by statute. Over the long run, it is argued, those in the consumer-finance industry who engage in unfair or deceptive practices will be exposed by the free-market mechanism. Traditional statutory-law punishments should be imposed at the state and local levels, where most illegal practices take place.[13] Opponents argue that consumers in fact "pay" twice for consumer-protection legislation: once through higher taxes and again through higher prices for credit. Initially, they pay taxes to cover the operating costs of the FTC and other agencies who implement the consumer protection statutes by passing regulations. Then consumer-finance and other private sector companies pass on their compliance costs to the consumer in the form of higher finance charges, interest rates or additional annual fees. For example, the applicant for a VISA or Mastercharge card pays the cost of his or her own consumer protection in increased annual fees. These fees in large part cover the administrative costs associated with doing the paperwork to comply with federal regulations.

Opponents of consumer legislation argue further that the FTC and other agencies would be more effective in combating misinformation and fraud in the consumer-credit markets if they could award reparations to injured consumers, invoke criminal sanctions against "bad actors" and force convicted companies to pay the costs of prosecution.

These arguments for and against consumer-protection legislation should be weighed carefully by readers as they examine the four consumer-protection statutes set out here.

The Truth-in-Lending Act

Title I of the Consumer Credit Protection Act is commonly known as the Truth-in-Lending Act. It was amended by the Truth-in-Lending Simplification and Reform Act, which became effective April 1, 1982.

The main thrust of the Truth-in-Lending Act is to require disclosure by creditors of the terms and conditions of consumer credit before extending such credit to consumer-debtors. In theory, as a result of these disclosures, the creditor and the consumer-debtor should have equal knowledge of the terms of the transaction, and the consumer should be able to shop for the cheapest price (interest rate or finance charge) in the credit marketplace. Competition in the consumer-credit markets should thus be enhanced.

Under the Truth-in-Lending Act the board of governors of the Federal Reserve Board is given the power to prescribe regulations. Regulation Z and its interpretations are given deference by the courts and thus are important in daily business transactions. The eight agencies responsible for enforcing the law and the bodies they regulate are: the Comptroller of the Currency (national banks), the Federal Reserve Board (member banks that are not national banks), the Federal Deposit Insurance Corporation (insured banks, not members of the Federal Reserve system), the Federal Home Loan Board (savings institutions not insured by the FDIC), the Bureau of Federal Credit Unions (federal credit unions), the Civil Aeronautics Board (creditors subject to the CAB), the Interstate Commerce Commission (creditors subject to the ICC), and the Packers and Stockyards Administration (creditors subject to the Packers and Stockyards Act). All truth-in-lending activities not regulated by these agencies are administered by the FTC. Thus the largest amount of enforcement activity against commercial lenders, other than banks and retailers who sell on credit, is left to the Commission. It is estimated that the number of creditors subject to FTC truth-in-lending enforcement exceeds 1.5 million. A violation of the Truth-in-Lending Act is also a violation of Regulation Z. Uniformity of enforcement was enhanced through adoption of the Uniform Guidelines for Enforcement of Regulation Z in 1978. Aimed primarily at violations resulting in overcharges to consumer-debtors, they require uniform corrective actions by all agencies enforcing the Truth-in-Lending Act. Most important, they allow a consumer to be reimbursed for disclosure errors with regard to finance or other charges by creditors, when these result from a clear and consistent pattern of negligence or a willful violation intended to mislead. Additionally, the Department of Justice, upon referral from an enforcement agency, can bring criminal actions under the Truth-in-Lending Act against creditors who "willfully and knowingly" give false information or fail to make proper disclosures as required by the act. If convicted, a creditor is subject to a fine of not more than $5,000 or imprisonment for not more than one year or both.

A consumer has a right to bring an individual action for damages if he or she can show that the transaction comes within the Truth-in-Lending Act and that the creditor failed to comply with the requirements of Regulation Z. It is *not* necessary for the consumer to show that the creditor's noncompliance was substantial, that it was relied on, or that any injury resulted. The measure of damages is actual damages plus a statutory penalty, usually twice the amount of the finance charges imposed when dealing with open-end transactions (e.g., installment credit where one can pay in full or partially, as in the case of VISA

or department-store accounts). The statutory penalty cannot exceed $1,000. Closed-end transactions (e.g., mortgages) limit creditors' liability for a statutory penalty to certain types of nondisclosure.

Scope of the Truth-in-Lending Act. The Truth-in-Lending Act affects a substantial number of credit transactions. Under the act, those who in the ordinary course of business regularly extend consumer credit must make proper disclosures. Basically, consumer-credit transactions are those in which credit of less than $25,000 is extended to a natural person for personal, family, or household use. Natural persons borrowing for business or commercial purposes, or those borrowing over $25,000 for any purpose, are not entitled to the Truth-in-Lending disclosures. Congress reasoned that people in these categories should be able to protect themselves. Disclosures also do not have to be made to organizations such as corporations, partnerships, trusts, estates, and associations, nor do the required disclosures have to be made to governments or units of government. Institutional debtors are not protected because they, like the business person and the wealthy individual, are assumed to be sophisticated borrowers with sufficient economic and legal resources to protect their interests. Transactions in real property exceeding $25,000 in which security interests are acquired are also exempt. Items of personal property used or expected to be used at the principal dwelling place of a consumer to which a security interest attaches are also excluded if their value exceeds $25,000. Finally, the consumer credit granted must involve a finance charge or be payable in four or more installments.

Finance Charges. For disclosure of the costs of credit to be meaningful each offer or extension of credit to a consumer should include all of the charges to be paid for the credit. If one potential lender includes in the cost of credit the premium on credit life insurance and a second does not (even though the latter also requires credit life insurance), the quoted costs to the consumer in the second instance will be misleading. The Truth-in-Lending Act and Regulation Z require all who extend credit to include certain costs if they are charged the consumer.

The Truth-in-Lending Act and Regulation Z use the term "finance charge" when referring to dollar charges that make up the cost of credit. Basically, any charge paid by a debtor that he or she would not have had to pay except for the grant of credit is to be included in the finance charge. Many of these charges are obvious, but in some instances the creditor must look to both Regulation Z and the Federal Reserve Board's interpretations to determine if a particular amount must be included in the finance charge.

Annual Percentage Rate. The "annual percentage rate" (APR) is similar to "simple annual interest." The requirement that the APR be disclosed allows consumers to compare finance charges on a common basis. The importance of this is illustrated by the following example.

Suppose that a consumer is interested in buying a combination stereo and color television unit that costs $500. The consumer's account with a large retail store allows him or her to pay all the bill or a specified minimum portion of it based upon the size of the balance. He or she may also pay any sum in between and may have a number of days within which to pay without incurring a finance charge. If the consumer does not pay the entire account,

monthly carrying charges are 1-½ percent on the average daily balance. The APR that the retailer must disclose is 18 percent.

A second alternative open to this consumer is to borrow the $500 from a bank, which may charge 7 percent if the loan is repaid in twenty-four monthly installments. The consumer is also required to pay $6, which includes charges for a credit report and credit life insurance. The bank would have to show finance charges of $76 and an APR of 14 percent. Without knowing the APR, this consumer would have difficulty comparing the two sources of credit.

General Disclosure Provisions. It should be emphasized that the Truth-in-Lending Act is solely a disclosure statute. It does not prescribe interest rates or finance charges. What must be disclosed will depend on whether the consumer-credit transaction is classified as open-end or closed-end. However, there are some general requirements imposed by the Act and Regulation Z, including the following:

1. All disclosure of terms and conditions of credit must be made "clearly and conspicuously in meaningful sequence."
2. Additional nonrequired information may be disclosed if it does not confuse customers.
3. A creditor must furnish the consumer with a copy of the disclosure requirements at the time of disclosure.

The case that follows addresses the "meaningful disclosure" requirement.

Bussey v. Georgia Bank Americard

U.S. Court of Appeals
516 F.2d 452 (1975)

Plaintiff was a credit-card customer of Georgia Bank Americard, which was a trade style of the First National Bank of Atlanta. Plaintiff claims that the terms "annual percentage rate" and "finance charge" were not disclosed as conspicuously as required by law on her periodic statement, that the disclosures relating to the finance charge were not made in terminology required by the Act, and the information disclosed on the statement was not in meaningful sequence. The open-end credit arrangement provided an account by which the First National Bank of Atlanta, doing business as its trade style, Georgia Bank Americard, made advances on behalf of plaintiff upon presentation to the bank of appropriate merchants sales drafts or made cash advances to plaintiff upon his application. The bank charged a monthly finance charge respecting the account and a fixed percentage on cash advances at the time of an advance. The plaintiff and defendant filed opposing motions for summary judgment in the U.S. District Court. The court assigned the case to a special master for findings and a recommendation. The special master recommended that summary judgment be granted in favor of the defendant. The District Court adopted the master recommendation and granted the defendant's motion for summary judgment.

Held: Affirmed for Defendant.

Before Justices Coleman, Hinsworth and Simpson: Per Curiam

Rather than rephrase that which has already been decided and with which we agree, we incorporate, as our opinion, the applicable portions of the special master's report and the District Court Order "RECOMMENDATION OF BANKRUPTCY JUDGE W. HOMER DRAKE, JR. SITTING AS SPECIAL MASTER."

The plaintiff contends that the periodic statement which the defendant utilized with respect to plaintiff was deficient in that the terms 'annual percentage rate' and 'finance charge' were not disclosed more conspicuously than other disclosures required by the Act and Regulation; that the disclosures relating to the finance charge were not made in the terminology required by the Act and Regulation; that the 'periodic rate' was not disclosed; and that the information disclosed on the periodic statement was not in a meaningful sequence.

The defendant filed a motion for summary judgment on August 6, 1974, and the plaintiff thereafter also filed a motion for summary judgment, and opposed defendant's motion for summary judgment.

The periodic statement of defendant utilizes a color-coordinated scheme to emphasize the disclosures required by the Regulation and the Act to be more 'conspicuous.' Attached to the motion for summary judgment of defendant and in support thereof is an affidavit which includes a periodic statement in its original form showing the colors as they appear on the statement as sent to customers of Bank Americard. The disclosures required to be 'more conspicuous,' that is, disclosures of 'annual percentage rate' and 'finance charge' are offset on a yellow background, which contrasts with the blue background, for all the remaining disclosures required by the Act and Regulation. This Court finds that such color offset system of disclosure does cause these disclosures to be 'more conspicuous' than the other disclosures required by the Act and Regulation. Plaintiff contends further, however, that even though this color contrast exists that, since not only is the total finance charge disclosed in this manner, but also the itemized portions of the finance charge are so disclosed, a violation of the Act and Regulation results. This Court finds this contention to be without merit.

The controlling regulation is Regulation 'Z,' which requires a periodic statement setting forth:

> (4) The amount of any finance charge, using the term "finance charge," debited to the account during the billing cycle, itemized and identified to show the amounts, if any, due to the application of periodic rates and the amount of any other charge included in the finance charge, such as a minimum fixed, check service, transaction, activity, or similar charge, using appropriate descriptive terminology.

This Court finds that the periodic statement used by defendant complies with this Regulation. The statement applies the appropriate descriptive terminology to the finance charge disclosure in all its aspects. It does so with respect to the required itemization of the components of the finance charge by using appropriate descriptive terminology of 'periodic finance charge at 1-½%' and 'cash advance finance charge at 4%', and it does so with respect to the entire finance charge with the appropriate descriptive terminology of 'total' finance charge.

This is in accord with the purpose of the Act and Regulation to assure 'meaningful information' to consumers. The method used by defendant provides the consumer in a meaningful way, information concerning those items which make up the entire finance charge, and the entire finance charge as a 'total.'

The periodic statement, therefore, complies with both the 'conspicuity' requirements of Regulation Z, and the finance charge disclosure requirements respecting periodic statements of Regulation Z.

Plaintiff also contends that defendant failed to disclose the 'periodic rate' pursuant to Regulation Z. This Court finds that defendant has complied with this Regulation by the statement at the lower, left-hand corner on the face of the periodic statement, describing that "the monthly periodic rate of 1-½% results in a corresponding nominal annual percentage rate of 18%.

Plaintiff has contended that the disclosures made by defendant are not in 'meaningful sequence' as required by Regulation Z. This contention is without merit. The disclosures of defendant are itemized in an arithmetical sequence which this Court finds to be understandable, clear, and in accordance with the requirements of the Act and Regulation.

In accordance with the foregoing, this Court does hereby:

. . . . . .

2) deny the motion for summary judgment of plaintiff; and

3) grant the motion for summary judgment of defendant.

This 23 day of September, 1974.

Closed-End Credit. Closed-end credit includes both loans to consumers and sales made on credit, where the credit is for a specific period of time and the total amount, number of payments, and due dates are agreed upon by buyer and seller. Typically, closed-end credit is used in buying or financing "big ticket" items like an automobile, washing machine, television set, or other major appliance. Closed-end credit also includes a single-payment loan.

If the credit is closed-end, in addition to an explanation of the "finance charge" and the "APR" the consumer is entitled upon written request to an itemization of the "amount financed." The creditor must affirmatively disclose this right to the consumer. Also, such terms as "total of payments" and "total sale price" must be described by the creditor. The Federal Reserve Board has prepared forms for creditors' use.

Open-End Credit. Regulation Z defines open-end credit as credit extended on an account pursuant to a plan under which

1. The creditor may permit the customer to make purchases or obtain loans from time to time
2. The customer has the privilege of paying the balance in full or in installments
3. A finance charge may be computed from time to time on an outstanding unpaid balance

An open-end credit plan as defined by the Reform Act includes a requirement that the creditor "reasonably contemplated repeated transactions." Common examples of this type of consumer credit are revolving charge accounts of retail stores, oil company and bank credit cards, and bank plans that permit limited overdrafts with finance charges periodically imposed on any unpaid balances.

For consumer credit of this type an initial statement by the creditor must be given at the time the account is opened. It must indicate the conditions under which the finance charge may be imposed, the method of computing it, and the means of determining the balance subject to the finance charge. The periodic rates as well as the corresponding annual percentage rates must also be disclosed in the initial statement.

At the end of each billing period the creditor must provide the customer with a statement if the customer's account has an outstanding balance of over $1. Regulation Z requires certain disclosures to appear on the face of the periodic statement.

Credit Advertising. The Truth-in-Lending Act requires that terms be disclosed before credit is granted. This provides some protection for the consumer. However, because the act does not require any specific time interval between the disclosures and the consummation of the credit transaction, the benefits of disclosure are frequently illusory in practice.

The act and Regulation Z impose restrictions on advertising as it relates to credit terms. The definition of advertising in Regulation Z is very broad. All of the usual channels —newspapers, radio, television, and direct mail—are specifically mentioned. The provisions also cover almost any "commercial message" made available to the public if the message "aids, promotes, or assists" an extension of consumer credit. Although a statement made by a salesman to a particular client is not considered to be an advertisement, a similar statement promoting a sale or loan posted in writing at the store or delivered over a store's public-address system would be an advertisement.

Both the act and Regulation Z prohibit lenders and sellers from advertising terms of credit that are not usually or regularly extended to customers. For example, a creditor who advertises "No down payment" or a seller who advertises "$5 down, $5 per month" must regularly extend credit on those terms. This provision helps to eliminate the practice of enticing customers by advertising generous credit terms that are seldom, if ever, granted. It does not require that every customer be offered the advertised terms, only that the terms be "usually and customarily" those upon which credit is granted.

The basic philosophy of the credit-advertising section of the Truth-in-Lending Act is *if* creditors advertise credit terms they must make disclosures. Following the 1982 amendments to the act, disclosures were limited to: (1) downpayment, if any, (2) terms of repayment, and (3) finance charges expressed as an annual percentage rate. Additionally, the act requires that an advertisement of consumer credit payable in four installments without a finance charge must clearly and conspicuously state: "THE COST OF CREDIT IS INCLUDED IN THE PRICE QUOTED FOR THE GOODS AND SERVICES."

Although credit advertising may merit regulation, the provisions of Truth-in-Lending do not effectively deal with the problems. First, the act provides only for criminal prosecution; civil suits are not authorized. Unfortunately, white-collar crime of this type traditionally has not been given a high priority by law-enforcement authorities. In addition, the prosecution has difficulty establishing a case because it must prove that the act was willfully and knowingly violated. "Intent" has been almost impossible to prove under other consumer protection statutes. Finally, the philosophy of requiring disclosure of *all* information if *any* specific information is given might, as a practical matter, result in less information. Creditors might decide to say nothing or to use very vague and general terms to avoid the necessity of making full disclosure. If this happens, consumers have less information than they had prior to Truth-in-Lending. The case that follows includes an FTC and federal court of appeals interpretation of Truth-in-Lending's provisions relating to credit disclosures and credit advertising.

Leon A. Tashoff v. Federal Trade Commission

U.S. Court of Appeals (D.C. Circuit)

473 F.2d 707 (1970)

Tashoff (Appellant) was the owner of New York Jewelry Company (NYJC) which advertised and sold jewelry in a low-income area of New York City. Not many NYJC customers had bank or charge accounts; thus 85 percent of all sales were made on credit. The staff of the FTC filed a complaint charging NYJC with engaging in deceptive credit practices and misrepresenting easy credit terms in its advertising (in addition to other unfair trade practices). The hearing examiner dismissed the staff's charges. The full Commission found in favor of the FTC staff. The appellant claimed the evidence was insufficient to support the Commission's findings, and in any event the order was not justified.

Held: Affirmed for the Commission.

Bazelon, Judge:

FAILURE TO DISCLOSE CREDIT CHARGES

Nearly all the evidence regarding NYJC's failure to inform its customers fully and adequately of all credit charges was documentary. It showed that NYJC used three different contract forms during the time in question. All three were materially deficient in one respect or another. The first form failed to disclose the annual percentage charge on the unpaid balance, the dollar amount of the credit charge, and the cash price of the item. The second form failed to show either a monthly or annual percentage interest rate. The third form failed to reveal the total obligation, the finance charge in dollars, and the annual percentage interest rate. Moreover, there was substantial evidence that NYJC often failed even to provide all the information contemplated by the contract form. Also, the evidence revealed unexplained discrepancies among NYJC's contract forms, its own internal records, and the "customer cards" it handed to credit clients.

We think the record amply supports the Commission's finding that NYJC's credit practices were deceptive. The offer of credit without disclosure of the charges therefore in an understandable fashion is, of course, likely to prevent the customer from learning about the cost of credit. This is particularly true for NYJC's customers, many of whom both lack the sophistication to make the complex calculation of credit costs for themselves, and must depend to a large extent on credit for their purchases.

FALSE REPRESENTATION OF "EASY CREDIT"

NYJC's advertising was permeated with references to "easy credit." The complaint charged that the credit was not easy for two reasons: first, because NYJC sought "often with success, to obtain garnishments against (customer's) wages," after having extended credit "without determining (the customer's) credit rating or financial ability to meet payments;" and second, because NYJC sold goods "at unconscionably high prices that greatly exceeded the prices charged for like or similar merchandise by other retail establishments." We hold that the record supports the Commission's finding that NYJC's representations of easy credit were misleading because of its rigorous collection policy. Consequently, there is no need to decide whether the Commission's finding that the representations were misleading because of the store's "greatly excessive prices" is adequately supported.

1. *Rigorous Collection Policy*—The Commission found that NYJC's collection policies were rigorous indeed, and therefore its representation of easy credit was misleading. The record supports this finding.

We have no doubt that the Commission was within its discretion in interpreting "easy credit" to refer not only to easy availability but also to easy terms and leniency with respect to repayment and collection. The Commission noted the oppressive effect of wage garnishments on persons who, like many of NYJC's customers, have low-paying jobs, and found that NYJC regularly garnished its customers' wages. In one year, for example, it sued some 1600 customers—about one out of every three. Firms with many more customers than NYJC used the garnishment process much less often. NYJC, which possessed all the relevant facts, offered nothing to negate the Commission's finding that it pursued a rigorous collection program, and, indeed, in this court did not challenge the Commission's opinion on this point.

NYJC does claim, however, that the complaint did not fairly apprise it of the charge that its easy credit representations might be found misleading on the basis of its collection policy. Although the complaint is hardly a model of clarity, we think that a fair reading provides sufficient notice. It is clear that the main charge is misrepresentation by use of the term "easy credit," not, as NYJC has urged throughout the course of proceedings, unconscionably high prices *per se*. High prices were but one of the two independent grounds said to make the representation deceptive. The other was NYJC's collection policies. Moreover, NYJC has claimed no prejudice from the alleged vagueness of the complaint. It has pointed to no evidence it might have introduced if it had been given clearer notice of the charge. And by the time of the hearing it must have known that its collection policies were under attack, for it agreed to a stipulation about the number of garnishments it, and other stores, filed each year.

2. *Greatly Excessive Prices*—The other ground for the Commission's ultimate conclusion that NYJC's representations of "easy credit" were misleading was its finding that NYJC charged "greatly excessive prices." We need not decide whether this finding is adequately supported, however, for, even if it is not, we have no "substantial doubt [that] the administrative agency would have made the same ultimate finding [i.e., that NYJC's representations of "easy credit" were misleading] with the erroneous findings or inferences out of the picture." In this case it is clear from the structure of the Commission's opinion and the reasons it gave in support of its order that NYJC's representations of "easy credit" were considered misleading on two separate grounds, to wit, the store's rigorous collection practices and its greatly excessive prices.

ENFORCEMENT

To combat NYJC's failure to reveal its credit terms, the Commission ordered it to disclose, both orally and in writing, a variety of factors relating to credit charges in its installment contracts. NYJC argues that the enactment of the new Truth-in-Lending Act shows that the Commission had theretofore lacked the power to order affirmative disclosures of credit information. The argument is without merit. The Act establishes minimum standards of disclosure which the Commission may enforce without proving unfairness and deception on a case-by-case basis. It was not intended to cure a previous deficiency in Commission power to deal with individual cases, and to shape its remedies to the facts of these cases.

Equally unpersuasive is NYJC's contention that the Truth-in-Lending Act sets the bounds of an affirmative disclosure order. NYJC has pointed to nothing in the terms of the Act or its legislative history which supports this view. The sole question for us is whether the remedy chosen by the Commission bears a reasonable relationship to the violations uncovered. Viewed in this light, NYJC's attacks on the disclosure order are unavailing. The Commission's demand that NYJC disclose credit terms in all transactions, for example, is reasonably related to its finding that many of NYJC's sales involved a small dollar credit charge, but a high percentage rate, and that credit information is crucial to NYJC's low income customers. Thus, the fact that the Truth-in-Lending Act exempts sales involving minimal dollar charges is not controlling. Similarly, the Commission's order that NYJC disclose its credit terms orally is reasonably related to the finding that many of NYJC's customers are unsophisticated consumers who would not benefit from written disclosure alone. That the Truth-in-Lending Act has no such requirement does not invalidate this portion of the order.

The Fair Credit Reporting Act

Purpose. The Fair Credit Reporting Act of 1970[14] was enacted by Congress to require consumer-credit-reporting agencies to adopt reasonable procedures for meeting the needs of lenders while maintaining the confidentiality, accuracy, and relevancy of their records. This legislation was aimed at several problems:

1. Inaccurate and sometimes misleading information in the files of credit-reporting agencies
2. Irrelevant information in such files (e.g., the name of a credit applicant's dog)
3. Lack of standards to maintain the confidentiality of credit files

Scope. The Fair Credit Reporting Act regulates the "consumer reporting agency," which is defined as any entity that "regularly" engages in the practice of assembling or evaluating consumer credit or other information on consumers for the purpose of furnishing "consumer reports to third parties." A business can escape the coverage of the act if it disseminates information *infrequently* or if it collects it solely for its own use and does not transmit it to third parties. The act's provisions contain:

1. Requirements for consumer reporting agencies
2. Requirements for users of consumer reports
3. Rights of consumers
4. Remedies for violations

The requirements for consumer-reporting agencies include a directive that all agencies must maintain "reasonable procedures" to avoid making a consumer report that contains obsolete information. Such information is "obsolete" under the act if it is older than seven years (ten years in the case of information relating to bankruptcy). These time limitations are inapplicable if the report is to be used in conjunction with a credit or life-insurance transaction involving $50,000 or more. If the consumer-reporting agency is reporting to a prospective employer, it cannot use materials that are not up-to-date. Further, the act requires that consumer-reporting agencies maintain "reasonable" procedures to assure that its reports will be furnished only to those designated or qualified under the act. They include:

1. A consumer who requests the reporting agency to furnish information
2. A court of law, or someone authorized by a valid court order
3. A person or entity whom the credit-reporting agency has "reason to believe" intends to use such information to determine if a consumer is eligible for credit, employment, government license, or other business purposes

The Fair Credit Reporting Act also prescribes certain regulations for users of reports received from credit-reporting agencies. Among the obligations users have is to notify a consumer in advance if they intend to order an investigative report from a reporting agency. They must also notify the consumer of the probable content of the report. If the user relies "wholly or partly" on the report in rejecting a consumer for credit, insurance, or employment, it must notify the consumer and provide the name and address of the reporting agency. If a consumer-reporting agency as defined by the act is *not* involved, the user of a report that is the basis for the denial of credit must make all such information available upon request and must advise the consumer of his or her right to make that request.

Consumers have rights under the act as noted above. Inaccurate and obsolete information cannot be used in their credit reports. They have a right to be notified of a reporting agency's reliance on adverse information when denied credit. The act gives the consumer a right of disclosure upon request. The reporting agency must disclose:

1. Nature and substance of all information (except medical)
2. Source of all information (except when it is used solely in preparing "investigative reports")
3. Names of any users of the report who have received the consumer's file in the last two years when employment was involved, the last six months for all other reasons

The consumer has a right to correct information in his or her file once it is received. Following notification of errors, the reporting agency must investigate the matter in the file that the consumer disputes, assuming that the correction is not frivolous or irrelevant. The agency must note the dispute and provide a consumer statement for the file or a summary of the consumer's views. Upon request, the reporting agency must notify any users of the file of the disputed information.

Remedies. The FTC has the principal responsibility for administering the act, and does so through cease-and-desist orders. Other agencies share enforcement authority when applicable to matters subject to their regulatory jurisdictions. Some of the same agencies are involved in enforcement of both the Fair Credit Reporting Act and the Truth-in-Lending Act. Criminal liability is involved if a user obtains information from a consumer-reporting agency "knowingly and willfully" under false pretenses. Officers and employees of an agency are also subject to a penalty of up to $5,000 and one year imprisonment for willfully providing information from an agency file to unauthorized persons. Civil liability is also provided for if there is a *willful* violation of the act by the reporting agency or user. Compensatory (actual) and punitive damages can be awarded to a consumer, along with attorney's fees and court costs. In case of *negligence* by a reporting agency or user, only compensatory damages are available. The major defense for a reporting agency in a civil suit is that "reasonable procedures" were used as required by the act.

The Equal Credit Opportunity Act

Purpose. Following a study by the National Commission on Consumer Finance, which showed blatant discrimination against women in the granting of credit, Congress in 1974 enacted the Equal Credit Opportunity Act[15] to prohibit discrimination against a person applying for credit based on sex or marital status. In 1976 Congress amended the act to include age, race, color, national origin, recipients of public-assistance, and those who exercise their rights under any section of the Consumer Credit Protection Act. The act empowers the Federal Reserve Board to prescribe regulations and allows the board to exempt "any classes of transaction not primarily for personal, family or household purposes." Regulation B has been issued by the board as a basis for interpreting and enforcing the act. Several administrative agencies share enforcement authority depending on the type of credit involved. Overall enforcement is entrusted to the FTC.

Scope. The Equal Credit Opportunity Act covers all phases of a credit transaction and all groups noted above. A creditor may not ask for information about race, age, sex, religion, or national origin. The act prohibits asking for information about marital status, alimony, child support, use of birth-control pills, and former spouses. A model application form has been issued by the Federal Reserve Board. Use of this form by the creditor offers a presumption of compliance with these provisions.

The act requires that a creditor give an applicant notification of action it has taken on his or her completed application for credit within thirty days. If the application is incomplete, a ninety-day notice period is required if the application is denied. The notification must include:

1. A statement of the action taken
2. Basic provisions of ECOA
3. Name and address of compliance agency
4. A statement of the specific reasons for the action taken, or a disclosure of the applicant's right to receive a statement of reason

Remedies. The FTC, as well as individuals, may sue to enforce the act. A person injured may recover actual and punitive damages. In individual actions such punitive damages may not exceed $10,000, while in class actions $500,000 or 1 percent of the net worth of the creditors (whichever is less) is the maximum.

The Fair Debt Collection Practices Act

Purpose. Up to this point, discussion has centered on federal laws that seek to protect consumers in obtaining credit. A consumer-debtor may be financially unable to pay his or her bills or may simply not pay them. Approximately 5,000 debt-collection agencies seek collection of approximately $5 billion in debts from 8 million consumers each year. These figures grow during times of recession. Collection agencies use computer calls and sophisticated WATS telephone lines to make 25–50 percent commissions on what they collect. Because of abusive practices, including threats of violence, obscene language, and anonymous phone calls in the middle of the night, Congress in 1977 passed the Fair Debt Collection Practices Act.[16] As noted previously, this and other pieces of consumer-protection legislation are included as separate titles under the Consumer Credit Protection Act. The FTC is charged with its administration and enforcement. A violation of this Act is considered to be an unfair or deceptive practice under Section 5 of the Federal Trade Commission Act.

Scope. Because laws preventing abuses in debt collection have been passed in many states, the Fair Debt Collection Practices Act allows exemptions for states that meet federal standards. Also, the Act covers only those debt collectors who collect for someone other than themselves. Large companies that do their own debt collecting are not covered by the Act but may be covered by state legislation. The act forbids the following practices:

1. A debt collector may contact someone other than the consumer debtor, his or her family, or his or her attorney only for purposes of finding the debtor. This section seeks to prevent a collector from ruining the good name of a debtor with his employer or neighbors.
2. Debt collectors may not contact a debtor at inconvenient times (9 P.M.–8 A.M.), or at all if the collector is aware that the consumer is represented by an attorney.
3. Any conduct by debt collectors that is abusive, deceptive, misleading, or unfair is forbidden. Posing as lawyers or police officers to collect debts, for example, is forbidden.
4. Collections that require liens on real property may be brought only where the property is located. Other collection actions must be brought where the debtor resides.

Remedies. Action can be brought by the FTC and individuals. Any violator of the Act is liable for actual damages and "additional damages" up to $1,000. Attorneys' fees and court costs also may be assessed.

REVIEW PROBLEMS

1. The Campbell Soup Company ran ads showing pictures of a bowl of soup in a ready-to-eat situation. Solid ingredients were shown at the top of the bowl. The Federal Trade Commission charged that this picture was a misrepresentation be-

cause the bowl of soup as shown was a "mock up" display. The company had placed marbles in the bottom of the soup bowl. The FTC charged that the marbles forced the solid ingredients to the top, making them visible to the viewer. The Commission argued that the solids would not have been visible at the top of the bowl but for the marbles and that therefore the picture was misleading. Is Campbell Soup in violation of Section 5 of the Federal Trade Commission Act? FTC v. Campbell Soup Company, Inc., FTC–DKT C–1741, May 25, 1970

2. *Readers Digest* magazine tested seven leading cigarettes in order to find out which was lowest in tar and nicotine. It published the results, stating that the cigarette "whose smoke was lowest in nicotine" was Old Gold. The report went on to say that the differences between the brands was small and that no single brand was so superior to its competitors as to justify its selection as less harmful. Lorrilard Company, manufacturer of Old Gold cigarettes, advertised: "Old Golds Found Lowest in Nicotine. Old Golds Found Lowest in Throat Irritating Tars and Resins. See Impartial Test by Readers Digest, July issue." Was this deceptive advertising under Section 5 of the Federal Trade Commission Act? P. Lorrilard Company v. Federal Trade Commission, 186 F.2d 52 (1970)

3. The Colgate Palmolive Company, manufacturer of a shaving cream, "Rapid Shave," sought to test the effectiveness of its cream on men's beards. In an advertising broadcast on television, Colgate sought to show that its product could soften even sandpaper. However, when the advertisement was run, a sheet of plexiglass with sand sprinkled on it was used in place of sandpaper. The FTC claimed that the commercial was deceptive and violated Section 5 of the FTC Act. Colgate claimed there was no deception because the viewer was simply being given a visual presentation of the test on sandpaper that had actually been made. Was there a violation of Section 5? FTC v. Colgate Palmolive Company, 380 U.S. 374 (1965)

4. Kathleen Carroll, a single working woman, applied for an Exxon credit card in August 1976 and was advised by mail shortly thereafter that her application for credit was denied. No reason for the denial was given. Fourteen days after the denial she asked to be advised of the specific reasons. In an undated letter she was told by Exxon that a local reporting agency had not been able to supply sufficient information. The name of the credit bureau used by Exxon was not included in any of their communications. Upon filing the present lawsuit, Carroll was given the name and address of the credit bureau. Carroll did not have a major credit card, nor a savings account, and had been employed for one year. Would Carroll win the suit? If so, based on what consumer protection statute(s)? Carroll v. Exxon, 434 F. Supp. 557 E. D. La. (1977)

5. For the price of $408 Linda Glaire obtained a seven-year membership in a health club owned and operated by LaLanne. The $408 was paid by Glaire over a two-year period at the rate of $17 monthly. The installment contract stated that there were no finance charges. The contract was sold to Universal Guidance Acceptance Corporation. LaLanne and Universal are in reality owned by the same shareholders, with Universal assisting LaLanne in financing. Glaire filed suit against LaLanne alleging violation of the Truth-in-Lending Act. Is there a violation of the Truth-in-Lending Act? Glaire v. LaLanne–Paris Health Spa, Inc., 528 P. 2d 357 (1974)

6. Rutyna was a 60-year-old widow and Social Security retiree, suffering from high blood pressure and epilepsy. In late December 1976 and early 1977 she incurred a debt for services performed by a doctor that were

not covered by Medicare or private insurance. Rutyna assumed it had been paid or would be paid by her insurance. When the defendant, a collection agency, notified her of $56 that remained unpaid to a medical group, she denied the existence of the debt. Rutyna claimed that she received telephone calls and a letter from the collection agency (defendant) notifying her of a neighborhood investigation that was to be undertaken. The letter, with the defendant's return address on it, required immediate payment or a visit by her to the defendant's office to prevent any further embarrassment. Upon receipt of this communication, Rutyna claimed she became very nervous and upset because of the embarrassment that might be caused by the defendant. Defendant claimed a lack of knowledge concerning Rutyna's reaction to their letter, denied the phone calls, and insisted that the plaintiff called many times. What consumer protection statute is the basis for Rutyna's claim? Will she win? Rutyna v. Collection Accounts Terminal, Inc., 478 F. Supp. 980 (N.D. Ill. 1979)

FOOTNOTES

[1]American Bar Association, *Report of the Commission to Study the Federal Trade Commission.*

[2]R. Fellmet & E. Cox, *Nader Report on the Federal Trade Commission* (1969).

[3]Pub.L. 96–637 (codified in various sections of 15 U.S.C.). This Act and the role of the FTC in enforcing warranties is discussed in Chapter 17 of this text.

[4]This chapter deals with consumer protection statutes enforced by the FTC. However, the reader should know that each of the 50 states, the District of Columbia, and Puerto Rico have state consumer protection statutes, and local ordinances dealing with consumer problems. Additionally, the Uniform Consumer Credit Code, a model piece of legislation, has been adopted by some states.

[5]15 U.S.C. 41–58.

[6]15 U.S.C. 45 *et seq.*

[7]See E. Drew, "Politics and Money," *New Yorker Magazine,* December 6, 1982, pp. 54–149, for an in-depth analysis of the impact of political action committees on the legislative and regulating process. See p. 131 for reference to their impact on the FTC.

[8]Rosen, George and Peter, *The Law of Advertising,* Vol. 2, Ch. 18, p. 46 (1982).

[9]Firestone Tire & Rubber Co. v. FTC, 481 F.2d. 246 (6th Cir. 1973).

[10]McDonald's v. Burger King, 82–2005 (S.D. Fla, 1982); Wendy's International, Inc. v. Burger King, C–2–82–1175 (S.D., Ohio).

[11]15 U.S.C. 1451.

[12]15 U.S.C. 1601 *et seq.*

[13]See R. Posner, *Economic Analysis of Law,* 2nd Ed. (1977), pp. 272–275, for additional thoughts on the value of mandated disclosure of credit terms.

[14]15 U.S.C. 1681, *et seq.*

[15]15 U.S.C. 1691, *et seq.*

[16]15 U.S.C. 1692, *et seq.*

Fair Employment Practices

S ince passage of the Civil Rights Act of 1964, employment discrimination has been one of the major policy concerns of business and industry. This federal statute, coupled with related federal and state regulations, affects the daily operation of business firms of all types. It is important not only to business executives but to employees, union leaders, and, because it deals with questions of fundamental fairness and economic opportunity, to all citizens. This chapter examines the boundaries and prohibitions of discrimination in employment on the basis of race, sex, national origin, and religion. It also explores the requirements and legal bases of affirmative-action programs.

STATUTES AND REGULATIONS

Fair-employment-practices law is primarily statutory. Although a body of case law is developing, the cases have been generally concerned with interpreting statutes that provide the framework for preventing discrimination in employment.

Title VII of the 1964 Civil Rights Act

Basic to an understanding of fair-employment-practices law is Title VII of the 1964 Civil Rights Act, which was strengthened by the Equal Employment Opportunity Act of 1972. Title VII was enacted as part of a broad civil rights program dealing with discrimination in restaurants and hotels (public accommodations), educational institutions, and federal programs as well as employment. It was one congressional response to the civil rights movement and resulting strife of the 1950s and 1960s.[1]

Title VII makes it unlawful for employers, unions, or employment agencies to make any decision concerning the employment or work status of an individual on the basis of race, sex, religion, or national origin. This prohibition covers private and public employers who have at least fifteen employees. One of the few defenses available under Title VII is the bona fide occupational qualification (bfoq). This provision allows an employer to hire and employ (or a union and employment agency to classify) on the basis of sex, religion, or national origin in limited circumstances where the sex, religion, or national origin of the individual is reasonably relevant to the employment. This defense or exception has been narrowly construed by the courts and is discussed more fully later. The bfoq provision does not mention race; discrimination on the basis of race, if proven, cannot be justified by this exception.

Executive Order 11246

In 1965 President Johnson issued Executive Order 11246, and in 1968 President Nixon issued another executive order to amend and strengthen it. Order 11246 prohibits federal contractors who receive more than $10,000 from the federal government from discriminating against any employee or applicant on the basis of race, sex, religion, or national origin. The executive order also requires employers to take "affirmative action" to ensure that applicants are employed, and that employees are treated during employment, without regard to their race, sex, religion, or national origin. Specifics of affirmative-action requirements are discussed later in the chapter.

Other Statutes

The Equal Pay Act. The Equal Pay Act of 1963 is an amendment to the Fair Labor Standards Act of 1938, the federal minimum-wage and maximum-hour law. Amendments to the Equal Pay Act in 1972 and 1974 broadened its coverage so that it mandates equal pay for equal work regardless of sex at professional and managerial levels, in state and local government, as well as in most private industries. The most difficult questions raised under the Equal Pay Act are determining whether male and female workers are actually doing substantially the same work and, if so, whether the pay differential is based on a factor other than sex. In most instances the nature of this inquiry demands a case-by-case analysis.

The National Labor Relations Act. The National Labor Relations Act of 1936 deals specifically with the right of employees to engage in or to refrain from collective-bargaining activities. Because once selected a union becomes the exclusive bargaining representative of the employees, the union has a duty of fair representation. To enforce this duty, the National Labor Relations Board has held that failures of fair representation, including acts of racial and gender-based discrimination, are unfair labor practices and subject to the usual remedies.[2] Since passage of the 1964 Civil Rights Act (Title VII), the use of this theory has been limited.

State and Local Law. Most states and many communities have their own fair-employment-practices laws and enforcement agencies that parallel the Title VII provisions. Title VII allows for, and in some instances mandates, deferral to these local agencies where the procedures are adequate and the responsibilities are similar.

Statutory Purpose and Constitutionality

The policies expressed by these statutes and regulations are both general and specific. Primarily, they reflect the judgment that the most effective way to end physical or economic segregation of women and minority-group members is to bring them fully into the business environment. Specifically, the statutes reject employment decisions based on group stereotypes. An applicant's or an employee's race, sex, religion, or national origin is irrelevant except in a few narrowly defined situations. Moreover, employment standards must be job-related or justified by business necessity if they have an unequal impact on any protected group. Implicitly, the fair-employment-practices laws pursue the traditional "work ethic" principle—that is, artificial barriers should not keep men or women from jobs they can perform.

The policies of the regulations as well as their specific mandates are constitutionally based. For example, the federal statutes are enacted under Congress's power to regulate interstate commerce and under Section 5 of the Fourteenth Amendment; state statutes are enacted under each state's police powers. The authority for the Executive Order is found in the constitutional command that the President "take care that the laws be faithfully executed"[3] and the Fifth Amendment's due-process clause, which requires equal protection of citizens by the federal government.

Administration and Enforcement

Each statute typically creates an administrative agency for enforcement. Most also encourage and rely on informal means of settling disputes. Title VII created the Equal Employment Opportunity Commission (EEOC), which presently is empowered to receive and investigate complaints, pursue informal conciliation, and bring suit in its own name against a respondent. The complainant also has the right to sue in federal district court after exhausting his or her administrative remedies. Additionally, the EEOC has the power to issue and to publish interpretations of Title VII. Although these guidelines do not have the force of law, they indicate the legal position of the EEOC, which is also likely to be its position in any future litigation. Statutory remedies include reinstatement, back-pay awards, injuctions, and other appropriate equitable relief.

A parallel structure has evolved to effectuate the mandates of the Executive Order. Primary responsibility is assigned to the Secretary of Labor and the Office of Federal Contract Compliance Programs (OFCCP). However, the secretary may delegate this authority to other agencies and has done so in such cases as schools and hospitals (Health and Human Services) and banks (Treasury). The OFCCP also publishes regulations and interpretive guidelines and seeks informal resolutions of disputes. The typical enforcement technique is an administrative compliance hearing resulting in the withdrawal of federal monies by the government.

State agencies often possess the above powers with the further authority to issue cease-and-desist orders enforceable through appropriate court action.

RACE DISCRIMINATION

The U.S. Constitution protects individual rights and sets the outer limits of permissible government activity. It is also the basis for suits by individuals against the government (or others if they are closely connected with the government). Specifically, individuals alleging unlawful discrimination challenge a particular action as a violation of the Fourteenth Amendment's equal protection clause, applicable to the states, or the Fifth Amendment's due-process clause, applicable to the federal government. Unlike the statutes discussed above, the equal protection clause is not limited to race or sex discrimination but applies to any sort of irrational discrimination. However, race and sex discrimination issues are tested by different standards. While in general discriminations are valid if they rest on any rational ground, distinctions on the basis of race or sex are not valid unless they rest on "compelling" grounds, in the case of race, or on "substantial" grounds, in the case of sex.

Neutral Standards

Since 1965, the effective date of Title VII, overt disparate treatment on the basis of race, sex, religion, or national origin has been increasingly rare. On the other hand, covert and unintentional discrimination remain problems often difficult to detect or to remedy. Much of the litigation following the enactment of Title VII has been in the area of apparently neutral standards for hiring, promotion, and other conditions of employment that, when applied, have disproportionately adverse effects on protected groups. In such cases, the burden of proof is on the plaintiff to show the disparate impact of applying the standard. When that has been established, the burden then shifts to the defendant to show that the standard in question is job-related or justified by business necessity. For example, suppose a state requires all its police officers to meet a 5'9" minimum height requirement. A woman presents evidence that approximately 95 percent of the female labor pool are disqualified by the standard. It is then the duty of the defendant to prove that the standard is job-related. That is, given the specific duties of a police officer, is the job performed more effectively by someone at least 5'9" tall? In the case of guards at maximum-security prisons in Alabama, the U.S. Supreme Court answered no.[4]

Particular problems are raised by testing and educational requirements. In an era when many people seek legitimation through objective measures, more employers are using the results of tests to make employment decisions, either in initial hiring, in promotion decisions, or in terminations. Title VII, Section 703 (h), provides that it is not unlawful for an employer

to give and to act upon the result of any professionally developed ability test, provided that such test, its administration or action upon the results is not designed, intended or used to discriminate because of race, color, religion, sex or national origin.

However, in many instances minority-group members score disproportionately lower in often-used standardized tests. Some experts argue that these tests are culturally biased.[5] Thus even a "professionally developed test" may have a discriminatory impact, inconsistent with the primary policies of the equal-employment-opportunity statute. In the courts' view, if the complainant can prove that a test has a disparate impact on a protected group, it is then the responsibility of the employer to show that the test is valid in both a legal and a psychological sense. For a test to be valid, it must be able to predict with some degree of accuracy whether an applicant will be successful on the particular job for which the test was used. To measure the chances of success on a particular job, one must know what the job requires, what "success" is for the job, and what qualities need to be examined.

Similar issues are raised concerning educational requirements for employment. On the one hand, Americans have great faith in their educational system. Education is mandatory for a certain number of years and involves a sizeable percentage of governmental expenditures. On the other hand, significant segments of the population get less education, either in quality or quantity, than the majority. Therefore the requirement of a diploma for employment may have a disparate impact on members of a protected group. If such an effect is shown, the employer must establish the job-relatedness of the requirement. Often the defendant's burden is not as great when the requirement is for a college degree, postgraduate education, or professional training as it is when the requirement is for passing grades on scored tests.

The dimensions of the job-relatedness standard are presently unclear. It appears to be a test of specificity, since notions of simply a "more intelligent" work force have been rejected by the courts. Job-relatedness also has been used to invalidate consideration of arrest records in an employment decision. On the other hand, the defendant's burden of proof is difficult to assess since there have been few cases where the attempt has even been made. Moreover, the distinction between the concepts of job-relatedness and business necessity remains unclear. At least one court[6] has held that an employment criterion having a disparate impact can be justified only by a showing that the criterion relates to job performance and not by a broader notion of business necessity. Other courts have said that similar criteria may be justified with reference to such business-related factors as employee morale and efficiency or the integrity and security of the business.

The inquiry does not necessarily end when the employer proves job-relatedness or business necessity. The court must still determine whether other tests or selection criteria would serve the employer's interest without the undesirable impact. The EEOC places this burden on the employer; the U.S. Supreme Court indicated, in a case it remanded for further proceedings, that the burden falls on the plaintiff.

Griggs v. Duke Power Co.

Supreme Court of the United States
401 U.S. 424 (1971)

A group of black employees (plaintiffs) brought a suit against Duke Power Co. (defendant) alleging violations of Title VII, Section 703(a), in requiring a high-school diploma and a passing score on a standardized general-intelligence test for employment or transfer. The District Court found for Duke Power Co. and the Court of Appeals affirmed. Held: Reversed.

Burger, Chief Justice

The District Court found that prior to July 2, 1965, the effective date of the Civil Rights Act of 1964, the Company openly discriminated on the basis of race in the hiring and assigning of employees at its Dan River plant. The plant was organized into five operating departments: (1) Labor, (2) Coal Handling, (3) Operations, (4) Maintenance, and (5) Laboratory and Test. Negroes were employed only in the Labor Department where the highest paying jobs paid less than the lowest paying jobs in the other four "operating" departments in which only whites were employed. Promotions were normally made within each department on the basis of job seniority. Transferees into a department usually began in the lowest position.

In 1955 the Company instituted a policy of requiring a high school education for initial assignment to any department except Labor, and for transfer from the Coal Handling to any "inside" department (Operations, Maintenance, or Laboratory). When the Company abandoned its policy of restricting Negroes to the Labor Department in 1965, completion of high school also was made a prerequisite to transfer from Labor to any other department. . . .

The Company added a further requirement for new employees on July 2, 1965, the date on which Title VII became effective. To qualify for placement in any but the Labor Department it became necessary to register satisfactory scores on two professionally prepared aptitude tests, as well as to have a high school education. Completion of high school alone continued to render employees eligible for transfer to the four desirable departments from which Negroes had been excluded if the incumbent had been employed prior to the time of the new requirement. In September 1965 the company began to permit incumbent employees who lacked a high school education to qualify for transfer from Labor or Coal Handling to an "inside" job by passing two tests—the Wonderlic Personnel Test, which purports to measure general intelligence, and the Bennett Mechanical Comprehension Test. Neither was directed or intended to measure the ability to learn to perform a particular job or category of jobs. The requisite scores used for both initial hiring and transfer approximated the national median for high school graduates.

The objective of Congress in the enactment of Title VII is plain from the language of the statute. It was to achieve equality of employment opportunities and remove barriers that have operated in the past to favor an identifiable group of white employees over other employees. Under the Act, practices, procedures, or tests neutral on their face, and even neutral in terms of intent, cannot be maintained if they operate to "freeze" the status quo of prior discriminatory employment practices. . . .

The Act describes not only overt discrimination but also practices that are fair in form, but discriminatory in operation. The touchstone is business necessity. If an employment practice which operates to exclude Negroes cannot be shown to be related to job performance, the practice is prohibited.

On the record before us, neither the high school completion requirement nor the general intelligence test is shown to bear a demonstrable relationship to successful performance of the jobs for which it was used. Both were adopted, as the Court of Appeals noted, without meaningful study of their relationship to job-performance ability. Rather, a vice president of the Company testified, the requirements were instituted on the Company's judgment that they generally would improve the overall quality of the work force.

The evidence, however, shows that employees who have not completed high school or taken the tests have continued to perform satisfactorily and make progress in departments for which the high school and test criteria are now used. . . .

The Company's lack of discriminatory intent is suggested by special efforts to help the undereducated employees through Company financing of two-thirds the cost of tuition for high school training. But Congress directed the thrust of the Act to the *consequences* of employment practices, not simply the motivation. More than that, Congress has placed on the employer the burden of showing that any given requirement must have a manifest relationship to the employment in question.

Held: Reversed.

Present Effects of Past Discrimination

Another form of discrimination that fair-employment-practices laws attempt to rectify is exclusion resulting from past discriminatory treatment or the continuing effects of prior exclusion. For example, previous experience on particular jobs is often a selection criterion. If blacks have been excluded from these particular jobs so that they were denied the opportunity to gain the requisite experience, the apparently neutral criterion has a disparate impact. Such criteria are difficult to justify in the face of the additional burden of showing that there is no less onerous alternative. An example of this perpetuation of past discrimination is provided in *Griggs*, discussed previously.

The issue of present effects of past discrimination is particularly important in connection with seniority systems, which affect, among other things, promotions and layoffs. Past exclusions were, according to the standards of the day, often legal. However, the present effects of these systems operate adversely on at least a generation of "locked-in" employees.

Seniority systems are among the major achievements of the labor movement in the United States. For the unions, there are several advantages to using seniority to determine issues of promotion and layoff. First, it prevents total domination and favoritism on the part of the employer. Second, seniority adds order and objectivity to dispute resolution. Third, seniority discourages rapid turnover both internally and externally and protects the employee's expectations. There are, however, important disadvantages to seniority systems in direct conflict with Title VII principles. Seniority as a determinant of promotions may or may not be job- or ability-related. More important, a seniority system may have serious present-day consequences for those who were treated unfairly before the enactment of Title VII.

For example, one problem under seniority systems is promotional opportunities for minority-group members hired in limited and segregated positions. Typically, minorities were limited in the past to jobs in only one department segregated from white employees. Seniority was department-based, and transfer to other departments was restricted, if not entirely prohibited. Under Title VII, transfer to other departments may still be limited or prohibited, but all departments are open to new employees. Complaints of discrimination come primarily from the minority-group members who were hired before enactment of Title VII or implementation of the company's nondiscrimination policy and who are now frozen into their department. Although the seniority system is neutral on its face, it has a disparate impact on such a group.

Congress's compromise solution to the problems presented by the present operation of seniority systems is another special section, 703(h), which allows

> different terms, conditions, or privileges of employment pursuant to a bona fide seniority system . . . provided that such differences are not the result of an intention to discriminate because of race, color, religion, sex or national origin. . . .

Lower federal courts have interpreted this section to require a balance between the protection of existing seniority rights and the need for a realistic remedy for past discrimination. The courts used "bona fide" and "the result of an intention to discriminate" to invalidate seniority systems that perpetuated pre-act discrimination. As a remedy, courts granted blacks artificial seniority, called constructive seniority, so that they would be able to obtain future positions that would have been open to them but for the previous discrimination.

In 1977 the U.S. Supreme Court in *International Brotherhood of Teamsters* v. *United States*, excerpted below, rejected previous interpretations of Section 703(h) and held that the section immunized seniority systems that did not originate in racial discrimination even if such systems perpetuated previous discrimination. At the same time the Court reaffirmed the validity of a 1976 decision holding that Section 703(h) allows the award of constructive seniority as a remedy for unlawful employment practices unrelated to the seniority system.

Another problem, critical in times of economic decline, is layoffs. The traditional rule of seniority systems is that the last person hired is the first person fired. In companies where minorities and women were previously excluded but are hired today, the effect of the "last hired–first fired" rule falls heavily on the recently employed minority and female employees. Here again a neutral rule has an adverse impact on protected groups, but the solution is not clear. Minor adjust-

ments in the seniority system do not effect a remedy. While deferring the promotion of a white male may be less onerous than a layoff, to lay off more senior white males in order not to lay off a woman or minority-group member would seem to violate the antipreference clause of Title VII, Section 703(j), and to be another form of discrimination in violation of the basic Title VII provision, Section 703(a). No adequate remedy has been found.

Teamsters v. United States
Supreme Court of the United States
431 U.S. 324 (1977)

The United States (plaintiff-respondent) brought suit against T.I.M.E.D.C. Inc. (company) and the International Brotherhood of Teamsters (defendant petitioner), alleging that the company and the union had engaged in a pattern or practice of discriminating against minorities in hiring line drivers. The District Court and the Court of Appeals found for the plaintiff. The Supreme Court affirmed on most issues but reversed the finding of discrimination because the seniority system perpetuated past discrimination.

Stewart, Justice

The District Court and the Court of Appeals also found that the seniority system contained in the collective-bargaining agreements between the company and the union operated to violate Title VII of the Act.

For purposes of calculating benefits, such as vacations, pensions, and other fringe benefits, an employee's seniority under this system runs from the date he joins the company and takes into account his total service in all jobs and bargaining units. For competitive purposes, however, such as determining the order in which employees may bid for particular jobs, are laid off, or are recalled from layoff, it is bargaining-unit seniority that controls. Thus, a line driver's seniority, for purposes of bidding for particular runs and protection against layoff, takes into account only the length of time he has been a line driver at a particular terminal. The practical effect is that a city driver or serviceman who transfers to a line-drive job must forfeit all the competitive seniority he has accumulated in his previous bargaining unit and start at the bottom of the line drivers' "board."

The vice of this arrangement, as found by the District Court and the Court of Appeals, was that it "locked" minority workers into inferior jobs and perpetuated prior discrimination by discouraging transfers to jobs as line drivers. While the disincentive applied to all workers, including whites, it was Negroes and Spanish-surnamed persons who, those courts found, suffered the most because many of them had been denied the equal opportunity to become line drivers when they were initially hired, whereas whites either had not sought or were refused line-driver positions for reasons unrelated to their race or national origin.

The linchpin of the theory embraced by the District Court and the Court of Appeals was that a discriminatee who must forfeit his competitive seniority in order finally to obtain a line-driver job will never be able to "catch up" to the seniority level of his contemporary who was not subject to discrimination. Accordingly, this continued, built-in disadvantage to the prior discriminatee who transfers to a line-driver job was held to constitute a continuing violation of Title VII, for which both the employer and the union who jointly create and maintain the seniority system were liable.

The union, while acknowledging that the seniority system may in some sense perpetuate the effects of prior discrimination, asserts that the system is immunized from a finding of illegality by reason of § 703(h) of Title VII, 42 U.S.C. § 2000e-2(h).

It argues that the seniority system in this case is "bona fide" within the meaning of § 703(h) when judged in light of its history, intent, application, and all of the circumstances under which it was created and is maintained. More specifically, the union claims that the central purpose of § 703(h) is to ensure that mere perpetuation of *pre-Act* discrimination is not unlawful under Title VII. And, whether or not § 703(h) immunizes the perpetuation of *post-Act* discrimination, the union claims that the seniority system in this litigation has no such effect. Its position in this Court, as has been its position throughout this litigation, is that the seniority system presents no hurdle to post-Act discriminatees who seek retroactive seniority to the date they would have become line drivers but for the company's discrimination. Indeed, the union asserts that under its collective-bargaining agreements the union will itself take up the cause of the post-Act victim and attempt, through grievance procedures, to gain for him full "make whole" relief, including appropriate seniority.

The Government responds that a seniority system that perpetuates the effects of prior discrimination—pre-Act or post-Act—can never be "bona fide" under § 703(h); at a minimum Title VII prohibits those applications of a seniority system that perpetuate the effects on incumbent employees of prior discriminatory job assignments.

The issues thus joined are open ones in this Court. We considered § 703(h) in Franks v. Bowman Transportation Co., 424 U.S. 747, but there decided only that § 703(h) does not bar the award of retroactive seniority to job applicants who seek relief from an employer's post-Act hiring discrimination.

Because the company discriminated both before and after the enactment of Title VII, the seniority system is said to have operated to perpetuate the effects of both pre- and post-Act discrimination. Post-Act discriminatees, however, may obtain full "make whole" relief, including retroactive seniority under *Franks* v. *Bowman, supra,* without attacking the legality of the seniority system as applied to them. *Franks* made clear and the union acknowledges that retroactive seniority may be awarded as relief from an employer's discriminatory hiring and assignment policies even if the seniority system agreement itself makes no provision for such relief. Here the Government has proved that the company engaged in a post-Act pattern of discriminatory hiring, assignment, transfer and promotion policies. Any Negro or Spanish-surnamed American injured by those policies may receive all appropriate relief as a direct remedy for this discrimination.[30]

(2)

What remains for review is the judgment that the seniority system unlawfully perpetuated the effects of *pre-Act* discrimination. We must decide, in short, whether § 703(h) validates otherwise bona fide seniority systems that afford no constructive seniority to victims discriminated against prior to the effective date of Title VII, and it is to that issue that we now turn.

Were it not for § 703(h), the seniority system in this case would seem to fall under the *Griggs* rationale. The heart of the system is its allocation of the choicest jobs, the greatest protection against layoffs, and other advantages to those employees who have been line drivers for the longest time. Where, because of the employer's prior intentional discrimination, the line drivers with the longest tenure are without exception white, the advantages of the seniority system flow disproportionately to them and away from Negro and Spanish-surnamed employees who might by now have enjoyed these advantages had not the employer discriminated before the passage of the Act. This disproportionate distribution of advantages does in a very real sense "operate to 'freeze' the status quo of prior discriminatory employment practices." Both the literal terms of § 703(h) and the legislative history of Title VII demonstrate that Congress considered this very effect of many seniority systems and extended a measure of immunity to them.

Throughout the initial consideration of H.R. 7152, later enacted as the Civil Rights Act of 1964, critics of the bill charged that it would destroy existing seniority rights. The consistent response of Title VII's congressional proponents and of the Justice Department was that seniority rights would not be affected even where the employer had discriminated prior to the Act.

In sum, the unmistakable purpose of § 703(h) was to make clear that the routine application of a bona fide seniority system would not be unlawful under Title VII. As the legislative history shows, this was the intended result even where the employer's pre-Act discrimination resulted in whites having greater seniority rights than Negroes. Although a seniority system inevitably tends to perpetuate the effects of pre-Act discrimination in such cases, the congressional judgment was that Title VII should not outlaw the use of existing seniority lists and thereby destroy or water down the vested seniority rights of employees simply because their employer had engaged in discrimination prior to the passage of the Act.

---

[30]The legality of the seniority system insofar as it perpetuates post-Act discrimination nonetheless remains at issue in this case, in light of the injunction entered against the union. See *supra,* at 331. Our decision today in *United Air Lines* v. *Evans, post,* p. 553, is largely depositive of this issue. *Evans* holds that the operation of a seniority system is not unlawful under Title VII even though it perpetuates post-Act discrimination that has not been the subject of a timely charge by the discriminatee. Here, of course, the Government has sued to remedy the post-Act discrimination directly, and there is no claim that any relief would be time barred. But this is simply an additional reason not to hold the seniority system unlawful, since such a holding would in no way enlarge the relief to be awarded. *See Franks* v. *Bowman Transportation Co.,* 424 U.S. 747, 778–779. Section 703(h) on its face immunizes all bona fide seniority systems, and does not distinguish between the perpetuation of pre- and post-Act discrimination.

To be sure, § 703(h) does not immunize all seniority systems. It refers only to "bona fide" systems, and a proviso requires that any differences in treatment not be "the result of an intention to discriminate because of race . . . or national origin. . . ." But our reading of the legislative history compels us to reject the Government's broad argument that no seniority system that tends to perpetuate pre-Act discrimination can be "bona fide." To accept the argument would require us to hold that a seniority system becomes illegal simply because it allows the full exercise of the pre-Act seniority rights of employees of a company that discriminated before Title VII was enacted. It would place an affirmative obligation on the parties to the seniority agreement to subordinate those rights in favor of the claims of pre-Act discriminates without seniority. The consequence would be a perversion of the congressional purpose. We cannot accept the invitation to disembowel § 703(h) by reading the words "bona fide" as the Government would have us do. Accordingly, we hold that an otherwise neutral, legitimate seniority system does not become unlawful under Title VII simply because it may perpetuate pre-Act discrimination. Congress did not intend to make it illegal for employees with vested seniority rights to continue to exercise those rights, even at the expense of pre-Act discriminatees.

Because the seniority system was protected by § 703(h), the union's conduct in agreeing to and maintaining the system did not violate Title VII. On remand, the District Court's injunction against the union must be vacated.

SEX DISCRIMINATION

Although sex discrimination is prohibited by the same statutes that prohibit racial, religious, and national-origin discrimination, there are some fundamental differences in the problems women face. Women constitute 40 percent of the labor force and more than 40 percent of white-collar workers. Women accounted for nearly three-fifths of the increase in the labor force in the last decade. Some legislation that is today considered discriminatory against women was actually enacted, in the belief of the legislators, for their protection. And all of us can recite basic cultural and biological distinctions between men and women. However, many of these protective laws and cultural and biological distinctions are used to deny women equal employment opportunity even though the distinctions are irrelevant or the laws unduly restrictive.

In 1978 the median salary for full-time, year-round work was $16,360 for white men; $12,530 for black men; $9,732 for white women; and $9,020 for black women.[7] The unemployment rates for persons aged 20 and over for 1979 are also significant: white men, 3.6 percent; black men, 8.4 percent; white women, 5.2 percent; and black women, 10.1 percent.[8] Moreover, even though women constitute more than 40 percent of all white-collar workers, only one-fifth of managers and administrators are women. Women constitute two-fifths of all professional and technical workers, but most of these women are teachers; in fact, women account for 72 percent of all teachers.

One purpose of fair-employment-practices legislation is to change this statistical picture by questioning widely accepted myths about women workers. One myth is that women as a group are too emotional for leadership positions. Another is that women are physically weak and morally delicate. Women, furthermore, are believed to be less committed than men to careers and therefore unreliable. Finally, there is a belief that women do not need to work, although the evidence contradicts this. In 1972 two-thirds of all women workers were single, widowed, divorced, separated, or married to men who made less than $7,000 a year. In 1974 46 percent of all families with incomes below the poverty level were headed by women. Moreover, the "need" standard is not applied universally to disqualify other workers. Psychological fulfillment, ego-gratification, and the desire to succeed are generally acceptable reasons for working.

To counter these myths, fair-employment-practices legislation encourages employment decisions to be made on an individual basis, not according to perceived group characteristics. Too, the bona-fide-occupational-qualification provision of Title VII and parallel laws provide an opportunity to test the validity of these myths.

Bona Fide Occupational Qualification (bfoq)

Section 703(e) of Title VII states:

Notwithstanding any other provision of this title, (1) it shall not be an unlawful employment practice for an employer to hire and employ employees . . . on the basis of his . . . sex . . . in those certain instances where . . . sex . . . is a bona fide occupational qualification reasonably necessary to the normal operation of that particular business. . . .

The bfoq exception also applies to discrimination on the basis of religion and national origin but not to discrimination based on race. This section reflects Congress's belief that in certain situations the sex of an applicant is relevant to job performance. Through its guidelines, the EEOC has narrowly defined these exceptions to include authenticity (model or actor) and sex-function (sperm donor or wet nurse).

Much sex-discrimination litigation has involved testing the scope of these exceptions. For example, many states have laws dealing with employment conditions for women. These laws restrict the number of hours per day or per week women can work, limit by weight the number of pounds women can lift or carry, exclude women from certain occupations, and provide certain minimal benefits (pay, rest periods, seats) that women must have. Under the supremacy clause of the U.S. Constitution, if these state statutes are in conflict with Title VII the federal law prevails. Consequently, courts first must decide whether a state law conflicts with Title VII and then determine the effect on state laws.

The EEOC's guidelines take the position that benefits provided to women by state laws should be extended to men in order to eliminate discriminatory treatment. Arguably, such action by a court is proper since it avoids holding a statute unconstitutional and is consistent with the legislative intent to protect workers from various hazards. Other state laws that limit or foreclose opportunities should be considered superseded by Title VII, according to the guidelines. In these cases, extension of the law's application to both sexes would be unworkable, leaving no one legally allowed to do certain work. Here new laws could be passed providing necessary protections for all workers but no outright prohibitions by sex. A more difficult problem is a third group of laws whose protections may not be perceived as beneficial —for example, maximum-hours laws. On the one hand, maximum-hours laws protect workers from compulsory overtime. On the other, such laws limit workers' opportunities to take advantage of the premium pay offered for overtime. It is clear, however, that the mere existence of a relevant state law does not provide an automatic basis for the bfoq exception.

A second issue raised by the bfoq provision is its relevance to customer preference. For example, can the fact that a particular business caters to male clients be the basis for hiring only men (or only women) to deal with these clients? What of the accounting firm that believes its clients will not take advice from a woman? Whether founded on fact or supposition, these beliefs, according to the EEOC's guidelines, should not be the basis for a bfoq exception. There are still unanswered questions concerning advertising tactics, maintenance of atmosphere and propriety, privacy, and the need for role models, as well as the practical implications of dictating this standard to employers. In one sense, the role of the EEOC can best be understood as educational as well as remedial. In another sense, a narrow functional definition of the bfoq provision would indicate that customer or co-worker preference as to the sex of an employee is irrelevant.

The burden of proof in establishing a bfoq exception falls on the employer. In *Weeks* v. *Southern Bell Telephone* (1969)[9] a federal court of appeals held that the defendant-employer could not exclude women as a class from a particularly strenuous job without establishing that "all or substantially all women" could not perform it. However, even this standard may be objectionable, since the "substantially all" language allows decisions to be based on group rather than individual characteristics. In *Diaz* v. *Pan American World Airways, Inc.* (1971)[10] the court held that the employer must prove that gender was essential to the job or business before establishing that all or substantially all men could not perform. Other courts have imposed a more stringent burden of proof, imposing a functional definition on bfoqs.

Rosenfeld v. Southern Pacific Co.

U.S. Court of Appeals
444 F. 2d 1219 (1971)

Leah Rosenfeld (plaintiff) brought an action against Southern Pacific Co. (defendant) under Title VII, Section 703(a), alleging that, in filling the position of agent-telegrapher, Southern Pacific discriminated against her solely because of her sex by assigning the position to a junior male employee. The District Court entered a summary judgment in favor of the plaintiff. Southern Pacific and the State of California (intervenor to defend validity of the state's labor laws) appealed. Held: Affirmed.

Hamley, Circuit Judge

On the merits, Southern Pacific argues that it is the company's policy to exclude women, generically, from certain positions. The company restricts these job opportunities to men for two basic reasons: (1) the arduous nature of the work-related activity renders women physically unsuited for the jobs; (2) appointing a woman to the position would result in a violation of California labor laws and regulations which limit hours of work for women and restrict the weight they are permitted to lift. Positions such as that of agent-telegrapher at Thermal fall within the ambit of this policy. The company concludes that effectuation of this policy is not proscribed by Title VII of the Civil Rights Act due to the exception created by the Act for those situations where sex is a "bona fide occupational qualification."

While the agent-telegrapher position at Thermal is no longer in existence, the work requirements which that position entailed are illustrative of the kind of positions which are denied to female employees under the company's labor policy described above. During the harvesting season, the position may require work in excess of ten hours a day and eighty hours a week. The position requires the heavy physical effort involved in climbing over and around boxcars to adjust their vents, collapse their bunkers and close and seal their doors. In addition, the employee must lift various objects weighing more than twenty-five pounds and, in some instances, more than fifty pounds. . . .

In the case before us, there is no contention that the sexual characteristics of the employee are crucial to the successful performance of the job, as they would be for the position of a wet-nurse, nor is there a need for authenticity or genuineness, as in the case of an actor or actress, 29 C.F.R. § 1604.1(a)(2). Rather, on the basis of a general assumption regarding the physical capabilities of female employees, the company attempts to raise a commonly accepted characterization of women as the "weaker sex" to the level of a BFOQ. The personnel policy of Southern Pacific here in question is based on "characteristics generally attributed to the group" of exactly the same type that the Commission has announced should not be the basis of an employment decision. 29 C.F.R. §1604.1(a)(1)(ii). Based on the legislative intent and on the Commission's interpretation, sexual characteristics, rather than characteristics that might, to one degree or another, correlate with a particular sex, must be the basis for the application of the BFOQ exception. *See* Developments in the Law—Title VII, 84 Harv. L. Rev. 1109, 1178–1179 (1971). Southern Pacific has not, and could not allege such a basis here, and section 703(e) thus could not exempt its policy from the impact of Title VII. There was no error in the granting of summary judgment on this issue. . . .

But the company points out that, apart from its intrinsic merit, its policy is compelled by California labor laws. One of the reasons Mrs. Rosenfeld was refused assignment to the Thermal position, and would presumably be refused assignment to like positions, is that she could not perform the tasks of such a position without placing the company in violation of California laws. Not only would the repeated lifting of weights in excess of twenty-five pounds violate the state's Industrial Welfare Order No. 9–63, but for her to lift more than fifty pounds as required by the job would violate section 1251 of the California Labor Code. Likewise, the peak-season days of over ten hours would violate section 1350 of the California Labor Code.

It would appear that these state law limitations upon female labor run contrary to the general objectives of Title VII of the Civil Rights Act of 1964, as reviewed above, and are therefore, by virtue of the Supremacy Clause, supplanted by Title VII. However, appellants again rely on section 703(e) and argue that since positions such as the Thermal agent-telegrapher required weight-lifting and maximum hours in excess of those permitted under the California statutes, being a man was indeed a bona fide occupational qualification. This argument assumes that Congress, having established by Title VII the policy that individuals must be judged as individuals, and not on the basis of characteristics generally attributed to racial, religious, or sex groups, was willing for this policy to be thwarted by state legislation to the contrary.

We find no basis in the statute or its legislative history for such an assumption. . . .

We have considered the meaning which appellants would ascribe to BFOQ, as provided for in the Act. We conclude, however, that the Commission is correct in determining that BFOQ establishes a narrow exception inapplicable where, as here, employment opportunities are denied on the basis of characterizations of the physical capabilities and endurance of women, even when those characteristics are recognized in state legislation.

Affirmed.

DISCRIMINATION BASED ON RELIGION AND NATIONAL ORIGIN

Fair-employment-practices law specifically prohibits discrimination on the basis of religion or national origin. Under Title VII these prohibitions are subject to the bfoq exceptions. In the area of religion or national origin, race or sex discrimination, though, a case raising racial discrimination often includes national origin issues or complaints. There are, however, several crucial problems in this area of fair employment.

Religious Discrimination

Overt discrimination on the basis of an applicant's or an employer's religion is illegal unless a bfoq exception is established by the employer. As with sex as a bfoq, group stereotypes or characteristics commonly associated with a particular religion cannot be the basis of a bfoq exception unless factually established by the employer.

Typically the issue of religious discrimination is raised because the religious beliefs of applicants or employees prohibit them from working on a particular day or during a particular time. Thus an employer might refuse to hire an applicant not because he or she was a Seventh Day Adventist but because that religion forbids its members to work from sundown Friday to sundown Saturday. Until 1972 the cases dealing with this issue were divided as to whether such a refusal to hire was discrimination on the basis of religion and, if so, what kind of accommodation must be made

by the employer. The position of the EEOC, through its guidelines, was that a refusal to hire and to accommodate was religious discrimination and that the duty not to discriminate included the obligation to make reasonable accommodations to the religious needs of the employee or applicant. Courts with contrary views held that such a denial was not based on religion but on the nonavailability of the employee or applicant at a particular time. Further, these courts held that employers had no obligation to accommodate religious beliefs, usually on the theory that such an accommodation would discriminate against other applicants or employees.

When Congress amended Title VII in 1972, it added to Section 701 subsection (j), which states:

The term "religion" includes all aspects of religious observances and practices, as well as belief, unless an employer demonstrates that he is unable to reasonably accommodate to an employee's or prospective employee's religious observance or practice without undue hardship on the conduct of the employer's business.

The extent to which an employer must reasonably accommodate and what constitutes undue hardship are not defined by the statute. In 1977 the Supreme Court took up these issues in *Trans World Airlines, Inc. v. Hardison.* The case has been criticized for its failure to address the constitutionality of Section 701(j) and its extremely narrow reading of Congress's intent in enacting the 1972 amendment.

Religious discrimination may be an issue in

other situations. For example, an employer may require all employees to attend weekly sermonettes, to donate blood, or to contribute money to a union in violation of an employee's religious convictions. It is unclear whether or in what way *Hardison* is applicable to these situations.

The implications of the other 1972 action by Congress relating to religious discrimination are also not straightforward. The 1972 amendment broadened the exemption for religious institutions (Section 702) by exempting them from the religious-discrimination prohibitions of Title VII with respect to all employees. Previously Section 702 had exempted only those positions that involved participating in the religious activities of the institution. The impetus for the more pervasive exclusion probably resulted from another Title VII amendment—one that removed the exemption of educational institutions. However, Section 702 raises a significant constitutional question because the exemption treats religious institutions differently from nonreligious institutions and thus may violate the First Amendment's clause prohibiting governmental establishment of religion.

Transworld Airlines, Inc. v. Hardison

Supreme Court of the United States
432 U.S. 63 (1977)

Hardison (plaintiff-respondent) brought suit against Transworld Airlines and the International Association of Machinists (defendants-petitioners) alleging that the defendants' failure to accommodate his religious practices and his subsequent discharge constituted religious discrimination in violation of Title VII. The District Court found for the defendants; the Court of Appeals reversed. The U.S. Supreme Court reversed, holding the defendants' conduct adequate to fulfill their duties under Title VII.

White, Justice

The issue in this case is the extent of the employer's obligation under Title VII to accommodate an employee whose religious beliefs prohibit him from working on Saturdays.

Petitioner Trans World Airlines (TWA) operates a large maintenance and overhaul base in Kansas City, Mo. On June 5, 1967, respondent Larry G. Hardison was hired by TWA to work as a clerk in the Stores Department at its Kansas City base. Because of its essential role in the Kansas City operation, the Stores Department must operate 24 hours per day, 365 days per year, and whenever an employee's job in that department is not filled, an employee must be shifted from another department, or a supervisor must cover the job, even if the work in other areas may suffer.

Hardison, like other employees at the Kansas City base, was subject to a seniority system contained in a collective-bargaining agreement that TWA maintains with petitioner International Association of Machinists and Aerospace Workers (IAM). The seniority system is implemented by the union steward through a system of bidding by employees for particular shift assignments, and the most junior employees are required to work when the union steward is unable to find enough people willing to work at a particular time or in a particular job to fill TWA's needs.

In the spring of 1968 Hardison began to study the religion known as the Worldwide Church of God. One of the tenets of that religion is that one must observe the Sabbath by refraining from performing any work from sunset on Friday until sunset on Saturday. The religion also prohibits work on certain specified religious holidays.

When Hardison informed Everett Kussman, the manager of the Stores Department, of his religious conviction regarding observance of the Sabbath, Kussman agreed that the union steward should seek a job swap for Hardison or a change of days off; that Hardison would have his religious holidays off whenever possible if Hardison agreed to work the traditional holidays when asked; and that Kussman would try to find Hardison another job that would be more compatible with his religious beliefs. The problem was temporarily solved when Hardison transferred to the 11 P.M.–7 A.M. shift. Working this shift permitted Hardison to observe his Sabbath.

The problem soon reappeared when Hardison bid for and received a transfer from Building 1, where he had been employed, to Building 2, where he would work the day shift. The two buildings had entirely separate seniority lists; and while in Building 1 Hardison had sufficient seniority to observe the Sabbath regularly, he was second from the bottom on the Building 2 seniority list.

In Building 2 Hardison was asked to work Saturdays when a fellow employee went on vacation. TWA agreed to permit the union to seek a change of work assignments for Hardison, but the union was not willing to violate the seniority provisions set out in the collective-bargaining contract, and Hardison had insufficient seniority to bid for a shift having Saturdays off.

A proposal that Hardison work only four days a week was rejected by the company. Hardison's job was essential and on weekends he was the only available person on his shift to perform it. To leave the position empty would have impaired Supply Shop functions, which were critical to airline operations; to fill Hardison's position with a supervisor or an employee from another area would simply have undermanned another operation; and to employ someone not regularly assigned to work Saturdays would have required TWA to pay premium wages.

When an accommodation was not reached, Hardison refused to report for work on Saturdays. A transfer to the twilight shift proved unavailing since that schedule still required Hardison to work past sundown on Fridays. After a hearing, Hardison was discharged on grounds of insubordination for refusing to work during his designated shift.

The Court of Appeals held that TWA had not made reasonable efforts to accommodate Hardison's religious needs under the 1967 EEOC guidelines in effect at the time the relevant events occurred. In its view, TWA had rejected three reasonable alternatives, any one of which would have satisfied its obligation without undue hardship. First, within the framework of the seniority system, TWA could have permitted Hardison to work a four-day week, utilizing in his place a supervisor or another worker on duty elsewhere. That this would have caused other shop functions to suffer was insufficient to amount to undue hardship in the opinion of the Court of Appeals. Second—according to the Court of Appeals, also within the bounds of the collective-bargaining contract—the company could have filled Hardison's Saturday shift from other available personnel competent to do the job, of which the court said there were at least 200. That this would have involved premium overtime pay was not deemed an undue hardship. Third, TWA could have arranged a "swap between Hardison and another employee either for another shift or for the Sabbath days." In response to the assertion that this would have involved a breach of the seniority provisions of the contract, the court noted that it had not been settled in the courts whether the required statutory accommodation to religious needs stopped short of transgressing seniority rules, but found it unnecessary to decide the issue because, as the Court of Appeals saw the record, TWA had not sought, and the union had therefore not declined to entertain, a possible variable from the seniority provisions of the collective-bargaining agreement. The company had simply left the entire matter to the union steward who the Court of Appeals said "likewise did nothing."

We disagree with the Court of Appeals in all relevant respects. It is our view that TWA made reasonable efforts to accommodate and that each of the Court of Appeals' suggested alternatives would have been an undue hardship within the meaning of the statute as construed by the EEOC guidelines.

A

It might be inferred from the Court of Appeals' opinion and from the brief of the EEOC in this Court that TWA's efforts to accommodate were no more than negligible. The findings of the District Court, supported by the record, are to the contrary. In summarizing its more detailed findings, the District Court observed:

> "TWA established as a matter of fact that it did take appropriate action to accommodate as required by Title VII. It held several meetings with plaintiff at which it attempted to find a solution to plaintiff's problems. It did accommodate plaintiff's observance of his special religious holidays. It authorized the union steward to search for someone who would swap shifts, which apparently was normal procedure." 375 F. Supp. at 890–891.

It is also true that TWA itself attempted without success to find Hardison another job. The District Court's view was that TWA had done all that could reasonably be expected within the bounds of the seniority system.

The Court of Appeals observed, however, that the possibility of a variance from the seniority system was never really posed to the union. This is contrary to the District Court's findings and to the record. As the record shows, Hardison himself testified that Kussman was willing, but the union was not, to work out a shift or job trade with another employee.

As will become apparent, the seniority system represents a neutral way of minimizing the number of occasions when an employee must work on a day that he would prefer to have off. Additionally, recognizing that weekend work schedules are the least popular, the company made further accommodation by reducing its work force to bare minimum on those days.

B

We are also convinced, contrary to the Court of Appeals, that TWA cannot be faulted for having failed itself to work out a shift or job swap for Hardison. Both the union and TWA had agreed to the seniority system; the union was unwilling to entertain a variance over the objections of men senior to Hardison; and for TWA to have arranged unilaterally for a swap would have amounted to a breach of the collective-bargaining agreement.

(1)

Hardison and the EEOC insist that the statutory obligation to accommodate religious needs take precedence over both the collective-bargaining contract and the seniority rights of TWA's other employees. We agree that neither a collective-bargaining contract nor a seniority system may be employed to violate the statute, but we do not believe that the duty to accommodate requires TWA to take steps inconsistent with the otherwise valid agreement. Collective bargaining, aimed at effecting workable and enforceable agreements between management and labor, lies at the core of our national labor policy, and seniority provisions are universally included in these contracts. Without a clear and express indication from Congress, we cannot agree with Hardison and EEOC that an agreed-upon seniority system must give way when necessary to accommodate religious observances. The issue is important and warrants some discussion.

It was essential to TWA's business to require Saturday and Sunday work from at least a few employees even though most employees preferred those days off. Allocating the burdens of weekend work was a matter for collective bargaining. In considering criteria to govern this allocation, TWA and the union had two alternatives: adopt a neutral system, such as seniority, a lottery, or rotating shifts; or allocate days off in accordance with the religious needs of its employees. TWA would have had to adopt the latter in order to assure Hardison and others like him of getting the days off necessary for strict observance of their religion, but it could have done so only at the expense of others who had strong, but perhaps nonreligious reasons for not working on weekends. There were no volunteers to relieve Hardison on Saturdays, and to give Hardison Saturdays off, TWA would have had to deprive another employee of his shift preference at least in part because he did not adhere to a religion that observed the Saturday Sabbath.

(2)

Our conclusion is supported by the fact that seniority systems are afforded special treatment under Title VII itself. [Discussion of *Teamsters* omitted.]

C

The Court of Appeals also suggested that TWA could have permitted Hardison to work a four-day week if necessary in order to avoid working on his Sabbath. Recognizing that this might have left TWA shorthanded on the one shift each week that Hardison did not work, the court still concluded that TWA would suffer no undue hardship if it were required to replace Hardison, either with supervisory personnel or with qualified personnel from other departments. Alternatively, the Court of Appeals suggested that TWA could have replaced Hardison on his Saturday shift with other available employees through the payment of premium wages. Both of these alternatives would involve costs to TWA, either in the form of lost efficiency in other jobs or as higher wages.

To require TWA to bear more than a *de minimus* cost in order to give Hardison

Saturdays off is an undue hardship. Like abandonment of the seniority system, to require TWA to bear additional costs when no such costs are incurred to give other employees the days off that they want would involve unequal treatment of employees on the basis of their religion. By suggesting that TWA should incur certain costs in order to give Hardison Saturdays off the Court of Appeals would in effect require TWA to finance an additional Saturday off and then to choose the employee who will enjoy it on the basis of his religious beliefs. While incurring extra costs to secure a replacement for Hardison might remove the necessity of compelling another employee to work involuntarily in Hardison's place, it would not change the fact that the privilege of having Saturdays off would be allocated according to religious beliefs. Reversed.

National Origin Discrimination

Issues of discrimination on the basis of national origin are often combined with cases involving racial discrimination. Similar problems arise as to the validity of tests and educational requirements. Specifically, national origin discrimination cases often raise such questions as the validity of an English-language test or of height and weight standards.

The particular problem raised in national-origin cases is whether discrimination on the basis of citizenship is in fact discrimination on the basis of national origin and, thus, in violation of the fair employment practices laws. In 1973 the U.S. Supreme Court, in *Espinoza* v. *Farah Manufacturing*,[11] held that, although Congress may have the power to prohibit discrimination on the basis of citizenship, it had not exercised such power in prohibiting discrimination on the basis of national origin. Specifically, the Court stated that a resident alien who was denied employment because she was not a U.S. citizen was not discriminated against on the basis of national origin (which the Court interpreted as ancestry) but rather on the basis of citizenship. However, the dissenting opinion by Justice Douglas in *Espinoza* argued that U.S. citizenship is directly related to ancestry. The dissenting opinion also urged the Court to examine this

charge in terms of the disparate-effect analysis used effectively in other areas.

EEOC's guidelines were amended in response to the *Espinoza* decision. At present they state:

[W]here discrimination on the basis of citizenship has the purpose or effect of discrimination on the basis of national origin, a lawfully immigrated alien who is domiciled or residing in this country may not be discriminated against on the basis of his (her) citizenship. . . .

Thus these guidelines may be the compromise necessary between the majority and dissenting opinions in *Espinoza*.

The *Espinoza* decision has been criticized on two other grounds. First, the majority opinion found significance in the fact that approximately 95 percent of the relevant work force consisted of people of Mexican ancestry. However, that fact relates to the employer's purpose or overall intention and does not deal with the specific allegations of the particular complainant. Second, the Court relied on the analogy with federal and state governments' requirements of citizenship to compete for civil-service jobs. There have been several recent cases that have held that such an employment rule if imposed by the states violates the Fourteenth Amendment's due-process and equal-protection clauses.[12] Since alienage is considered a "suspect classification," the courts have stated that the state must have a "compelling" reason to treat aliens differently from others in order to meet the courts' "strict scrutiny" standard of review. In these cases the state did not sustain that burden.

Further, it can be argued that the citizenship rule is unconstitutional because it is overbroad in that it may be sensible and permissible to limit some civil-service jobs to citizens but not to limit all jobs. On the other hand, it is possible that the constitutional citizenship cases and the *Espinoza* decision are consistent if the relevant distinction is the difference between treatment of public and private employees.

AGE DISCRIMINATION

In 1967 Congress enacted the Age Discrimination in Employment Act outlawing employment discrimination on the basis of age between ages 40 and 65. A recent amendment raised the upper limit to 70. The act is administered by the EEOC, and its scope, coverage, and procedures are similar to those of the Equal Pay Act. The purpose of the statute is to encourage the making of employment decisions on individual characteristics rather than on stereotypic notions of the effect of age on ability. The statute provides four defenses:

1. Age is a bona fide occupational qualification (bfoq) reasonably necessary to the normal operation of the particular business
2. The differentiation is based on reasonable factors other than age
3. The terms of a bona fide seniority system or any bona fide employee benefit plan (retirement, pension, or insurance) that is not a subterfuge

4. Discharge or discipline for good cause

Although the substantive and procedural provisions of the act are nearly identical to those of Title VII, the federal courts appear to apply different standards of proof and liability. The courts have found age discrimination justified by one of the defenses on the basis of less evidence than would satisfy the burden in a Title VII case. Probably the reasons for the distinction lie in the fact that age, at some point, is related to individual ability and that the basis for age discrimination is not hostility but inaccurate perceptions or miscalculated costs. Thus the test formulated by many courts is whether there is a generalization other than age that more accurately predicts ability or whether the employer can adequately test individually without a substantial increase in cost.

DISCRIMINATION IN PUBLIC EMPLOYMENT

Today most public employees are protected from discrimination on the basis of race, sex, religion, or national origin by fair-employment-practices laws, particularly Title VII of the Civil Rights Act of 1964. Before 1972, public employees' rights were protected, if at all, by separate legislation and constitutional doctrines. The Constitution remains an important source of law in employment decisions, although its protections are broader in some respects and narrower in others than Title VII or other fair-employment-practices laws.

It is essential to understand that the Constitution and its protections apply to public employees, although the precise effect of its applicability changes from case to case. Therefore, it is impossible to list in detail what the Constitution prohibits or allows in the employment field. What an individual may do, however, is to acquaint himself or herself with basic constitutional principles and study cases to discover the ways in which courts modify the principles in order to deal with the unique employer-employee relationship. A full discussion of these principles is not included in this chapter but is left to other courses where the underlying theories of the Constitution are studied.

AFFIRMATIVE ACTION PROGRAMS

Affirmative action programs are designed to effectuate equal employment opportunity laws. Such programs reduce reliance on case-by-case enforcement, provide faster, more effective relief, and generally tend to make equal employment opportunity a reality, not merely rhetoric. The key to affirmative action programs is the employers' mandatory self-evaluation as to all terms and conditions of employment.

Affirmative action obligations are twofold. First, employers must eliminate all present discriminatory practices and conditions—that is, they must comply with equal opportunity laws. More specifically, employers must eliminate discriminatory tests, non-job-related employment requirements, and other apparently neutral standards that, although nondiscriminatory on their face, have discriminatory effects when applied. Second, employers must take further affirmative steps to increase female and minority-group participation in their work forces. This latter obligation is a remedy for the present effects of past discrimination.

Authority for affirmative action programs derives from two primary sources—Executive Order 11246 as amended and Title VII of the 1964 Civil Rights Act as amended. The executive order is administered by the Secretary of Labor, who may (and does) delegate the authority to require and review affirmative-action plans to other federal agencies. Title VII (like similar state laws) gives the courts broad equitable powers to remedy discrimination, with the result that a court may order a particular defendant to engage in affirmative action. Additionally the EEOC often requires an affirmative-action plan as part of its conciliation efforts.

The constitutionality of present-day affirmative action plans has not been specifically decided by the Supreme Court. Lower courts have upheld more dubious plans (where the government imposed goals), and the various opinions in *Regents of the University of California* v. *Bakke* (1979)[13] provide some indication of the acceptable boundaries of such plans. *Bakke*, decided by an extremely divided court, dealt specifically with the legality of a special minority admissions program for medical school. The Court did not rule on affirmative-action plans under the executive order or on the legality of preferential treatment as a remedy following a judicially determined violation of Title VII.

When applied to specific situations, affirmative-action rules and regulations can be quite complex. Basically, affirmative-action programs require employers to evaluate their present work force to see if women and minority-group members are present in all positions in appropriate numbers. Appropriateness is determined by the number of women and minorities available and seeking work within the recruitment area. Specifically, there must be:

1. An evaluation of the employer's present work force—how many women, men, whites, and minority-group members at all levels
2. An analysis of all recruitment and selection procedures
3. An analysis of those people applying for employment, accepting employment, applying for promotion, receiving promotion, and terminating

4. Data to determine the hiring community's labor-force characteristics—total population, work-force population, training, unemployment

Once collected, these data can detail areas of disproportionate employment. It is then the obligation of the employer to examine these areas to determine if the employment of women or minorities is inhibited by any internal or external factor and, if so, to remedy the situation. With these data, goals and timetables can be set by the employer. Goals reflect employers' decisions concerning how many women and minority-group members are necessary for adequate balance, and timetables reflect employers' predictions of when these goals will be attained. An essential characteristic of affirmative action plans is the employers' determination of goals and timetables and relativeness of these goals and timetables to local work forces.

There are several common criticisms of affirmative action programs. Some argue that "goal" is a euphemism for "quota," and some employers act as if the distinction were only a semantic one. However, legally there is a difference in that a good-faith effort to meet affirmative action responsibility is a defense to nonattainment of a goal. Additionally, "goal" takes into account the availability of qualified workers.

A second criticism is that affirmative action results in lower quality among employees. However, if an employer takes into account valid qualifications, such a prediction is not true. Affirmative action may actually raise the quality of a particular work force since there is an expanded application pool and expanded perceptions of women and minorities.

A third criticism is that affirmation action is in fact unfair to white males, dictating reverse discrimination. This is the question that divided the Court in *Bakke.* In that case the Court held the particular program unlawful because it was unfair but was careful to reserve judgment as to other, less restrictive programs.

The sanctions for either not having an affirmative-action plan when required or not putting into effect an existing program can be quite severe; they may include withdrawal of all federal funds. Such a sanction can be imposed only after an administrative hearing on the merits. Arguably, fund termination is necessary since at least one line of thought reasons that it would be a violation of the Fifth Amendment's due-process clause for the federal government to continue financial assistance to a person or an organization that discriminates.

In reviewing the materials in this chapter, note that the basic aim of the regulations is to require employers to review their employment policies and to ensure that decisions are made on the basis of individual capacities rather than on stereotyped images or artificial standards.

REVIEW PROBLEMS

1. Marie Fernandez was employed by the Wynn Oil Co. from February 1968 to February 4, 1977. During that time, she held various positions, including that of administrative assistant to the executive vice-president reporting directly to Wynn's director of worldwide marketing. Wynn has extensive operations outside the United States. Much of its business, in fact, takes place in Latin America and Southeast Asia. Fernandez applied for and was denied a promotion to the position of director of inter-

national marketing. She sued Wynn, alleging that it discriminated against her on the basis of sex in violation of Title VII. Wynn defended by claiming that it was legally entitled to discriminate on the basis of sex in hiring for the position of director of international marketing because sex is a bona fide occupational qualification for the position. It argued that it would not consider any woman for the position because of the feeling among Wynn's customers and distributors that it would be less desirable to deal with a woman in a high-level management position. It contended that many of Wynn's South American distributors and customers, for instance, would be offended by a woman conducting business meetings in her hotel room. The offensive nature of this conduct stems from prevailing cultural customs and mores in Latin America. Will Wynn be successful in establishing sex as a bfoq for the position of director of international marketing? Fernandez v. Wynn Oil Co. 20 F.E.P. Cases 1162 (C.D. Calif. 1979)

2. Buck Green, who is black, applied for employment as a clerk at the Missouri Pacific Railroad Company's personnel office in the corporate headquarters in St. Louis, Missouri. In response to a question on the application form, Green disclosed that he had been convicted in December 1967 for refusing military induction. He stated that he had served twenty-one months in prison until paroled in 1970. After reviewing the application form, Missouri Pacific's personnel officer informed Green that he was not qualified for employment at Missouri Pacific because of his conviction and prison record. Missouri Pacific followed an absolute policy of refusing consideration to any person convicted of a crime other than a minor traffic offense. Green sued Missouri Pacific, seeking relief under Title VII. At trial, Green introduced statistical evidence showing that Missouri Pacific's policy operated automatically to exclude from employment 53 of every 1,000 black applicants but only 22 of every 1,000 white applicants. The rejection rate for blacks was two and one-half times that of whites under Missouri Pacific's policy. At trial, Missouri Pacific proffered the following reasons for following its policy: (1) fear of cargo theft; (2) handling company funds; (3) bonding qualifications; (4) possible impeachment of an employee as a witness; (5) possible liability for hiring persons with known violent tendencies; (6) employment disruption caused by recidivism; and (7) a lack of moral character of persons with convictions. Will Green be successful in his suit against Missouri Pacific? Green v. Missouri Pacific R.R. Co., 523 F. 2d 1290 (8th Cir. 1975)

3. Handy Dan's Barber Shop employed fifteen barbers at 30 Odd St., Anycity, Texas, of whom eleven were Spanish-surnamed Americans, two were black, and two were Caucasian. Handy Dan's maintained a long-standing rule forbidding its Spanish-surnamed American barbers from speaking Spanish to each other in the presence of English-speaking patrons. José Lopez and two other Spanish-surnamed American barbers were discharged pursuant to this policy. Did Handy Dan's violate Title VII? What additional information would be helpful in determining whether a violation exists? If Handy Dan's employed only fourteen barbers, would it be in violation of Title VII?

4. Jelleff Associates is a woman's specialty store that has traditionally catered to a clientele of mature women. It embarked on a program designed to reduce its personnel. This was necessitated by poor business conditions and excessive payroll expenses. By discharging its older employees (those over 40) and expanding its product line, the company hoped to appeal to a younger market. In terminating one employee, the company gave as its reason the fact that "business was falling off," another was terminated after

being advised that "business was slow." The terminated employees sued Jelleff Associates, claiming that it had violated the Age Discrimination in Employment Act. Who wins? Explain. Bishop v. Jelleff Associates, 398 F. Supp. 579 (D.D.C. 1974)

5. Joe Weiner, a disgruntled taxpayer, filed suit to set aside the award of a contract to the second-lowest bidder. The contract was for the installation of heating and air conditioning equipment in classrooms being constructed by the Cuyahoga Community College with federal funding. The college contended that the lowest bid was not acceptable because the contractor would not promise to refrain from discriminatory hiring practices. The lowest bid had been submitted by a contractor who would promise only that it would make a reasonable effort to hire blacks. The bidder who was awarded the contract promised the college that blacks would be represented in all crafts employed on the project. It was the taxpayer's contention that the promise made by the lowest bidder was consistent with state and federal law and that it was unlawful and unconstitutional abuse of discretion for the college to reject the bid. Who wins? Explain. Weiner v. Cuyahoga Community College 249 N.E. 2d 907 (Ohio 1969)

6. Ida Phillips applied for a job as assembly trainee with Martin Marietta Corp. She was denied the position because the company was not hiring women with preschool children. At the time that she applied, 70–75 percent of those applying were women; 75–80 percent of those hired were women. The company employed men with preschool children. Has Martin violated Title VII? Discuss. Phillips v. Martin Marietta Corp. 400 U.S. 542 (1971)

7. Maria Sanchez is a fifty-year-old black female worker in a large department store in Columbus, Ohio. Maria's job is fitter in the women's wear department. She is paid $150 per week. Harold Cranchford, a white male, worked as a fitter in the men's wear department, receiving a salary of $200 per week. Both Sanchez and Cranchford joined the company on the same day. Cranchford was fired for refusing to work on Saturdays because his church maintained that Saturday was a holy day of rest. Sanchez requested a transfer to Harold's vacant position. She was the worker with the most experience, which under company rules normally governed who received a transfer. Discuss the legal issues involved in the above facts.

FOOTNOTES

[1]Other congressional responses include the Voting Rights Act of 1965, the Fair Housing Act of 1968, and other educational amendments (for example, Title 9) in 1972.

[2]Local Union No. 12, United Rubber, Cork, Linoleum and Plastic Workers of America v. NLRB, 368 F. 2d 12 (5th Cir. 1966); United Packinghouse Food and Allied Workers International Union v. NLRB, 416 F. 2d 1126 (D.C. Cir. 1969).

[3]U.S. Constitution Art. 2, §3.

[4]Dothard v. Rawlinson, 433 U.S. 321 (1977).

[5]In Plaintiff's Memorandum of Law, Hicks v. Crown Zellerbach, reprinted in *Sovern, Racial Discrimination in Employment,* pp. 439–440 (1969); Note, *Legal Implications of the Use of Standardized Ability Tests in Employment and Education,* 68 *Coumm. L. Rev.* 691, pp. 701–703 (1968).

[6]Johnson v. Pike Corporation of America, 332 F. Supp. 490 (C.D. Cal 1971).

[7]1981 World Almanac and Book of Facts 271 (Newspaper Enterprise Assoc., Inc.).

[8]Id. at 177.

[9]408 F. 2d 228 (5th Cir. 1969).

[10]442 F. 2d 385 (5th Cir. 1971).

[11]414 U.S. 86 (1973)

[12]See Sugarman v. Dougall, 414 U.S. 86 (1973); Graham v. Richardson, 403 U.S. 365 (1971). In *Sugarman* the Court held unconstitutional a New York statute that provided that only United States citizens may hold permanent positions in the competitive class of the state civil service. The Court stated that the statute swept indiscriminately and was not narrowly limited to the accomplishment of substantial state interests.

In *Graham* the Court held unconsititional Arizona and Pennsylvania statutes that denied welfare benefits to resident aliens and to aliens who had not resided in the United States for a specified number of years. The Court rejected the states' justification that they could prefer their own citizens over aliens in the distribution of limited resources. 13.98 5. Ct. 2733 (1978).

[13]438 U.S. 265 (1979).

APPENDIX A
UNIFORM COMMERCIAL CODE
Selected Sections
[1972 Amendments]

ARTICLE ONE — GENERAL PROVISIONS

PART 1

Short Title, Construction, Application and Subject Matter of the Act

§ 1-101.   Short Title.—This Act shall be known and may be cited as Uniform Commercial Code.

§ 1-102.   Purposes; Rules of Construction; Variation by Agreement.—
(1) This Act shall be liberally construed and applied to promote its underlying purposes and policies.
(2) Underlying purposes and policies of this Act are
  (a) to simplify, clarify and modernize the law governing commercial transactions;
  (b) to permit the continued expansion of commercial practices through custom, usage and agreement of the parties;
  (c) to make uniform the law among the various jurisdictions.
(3) The effect of provisions of this Act may be varied by agreement, except as otherwise provided in this Act and except that the obligations of good faith, diligence, reasonableness and care prescribed by this Act may not be disclaimed by agreement but the parties may by agreement determine the standards by which the performance of such obligations is to be measured if such standards are not manifestly unreasonable.
(4) The presence in certain provisions of this Act of the words "unless otherwise agreed" or words of similar import does not imply that the effect of other provisions may not be varied by agreement under subsection (3).
(5) In this Act unless the context otherwise requires
  (a) words in the singular number include the plural, and in the plural include the singular.
  (b) words of the masculine gender include the feminine and the neuter, and when the sense so indicates words of the neuter gender may refer to any gender.

§ 1-103.   Supplementary General Principles of Law Applicable.—Unless displaced by the particular provisions of this Act, the principles of law and equity, including the law merchant and the law relative to capacity to contract, principal and agent, estoppel, fraud, misrepresentation, duress, coercion, mistake, bankruptcy, or other validating or invalidating cause shall supplement its provisions.

§ 1-104.   Construction Against Implicit Repeal.—This Act being a general act intended as a unified coverage of its subject matter, no part of it shall be deemed to be impliedly repealed by subsequent legislation if such construction can reasonably be avoided.

§ 1-105.   Territorial Application of the Act; Parties' Power to Choose Applicable Law.—
(1) Except as provided hereafter in this section, when a transaction bears a reasonable relation to this state and also to another state or nation the parties may agree that the law either of this state or of such other state or nation shall govern their rights and duties. Failing such agreement this Act applies to transactions bearing an appropriate relation to this state.
(2) Where one of the following provisions of this Act specifies the applicable law, that provision governs and a contrary agreement is effective only to the extent permitted by the law (including the conflict of laws rules) so specified:
  Rights of creditors against sold goods. Section 2-402.
  Applicability of the Article on Bank Deposits and Collections. Section 4-102.
  Bulk transfers subject to the Article on Bulk Transfers. Section 6-102.
  Applicability of the Article on Investment Securities. Section 8-106.
  Perfection provisions of the Article on Secured Transactions. Section 9-103.

§ 1-106.   Remedies to Be Liberally Administered.—
(1) The remedies provided by this Act shall be liberally administered to the end that the aggrieved party may be put in as good a position as if the other party had fully performed but neither consequential or special nor penal damages may be had except as specifically provided in this Act or by other rule of law.
(2) Any right or obligation declared by this Act is enforceable by action unless the provision declaring it specifies a different and limited effect.

§ 1-107.   Waiver or Renunciation of Claim or Right After Breach.—Any claim or right arising out of an alleged breach can be discharged in whole or in part without consideration by a written waiver or renunciation signed and delivered by the aggrieved party.

§ 1-108. **Severability.**—If any provision or clause of this Act or application thereof to any person or circumstances is held invalid, such invalidity shall not affect other provisions or applications of the Act which can be given effect without the invalid provision or application, and to this end the provisions of this Act are declared to be severable.

§ 1-109. **Section Captions.**—Section captions are parts of this Act.

PART 2

General Definitions and Principles of Interpretation

§ 1-201. **General Definitions.**—Subject to additional definitions contained in the subsequent Articles of this Act which are applicable to specific Articles or Parts thereof, and unless the context otherwise requires, in this Act:

(1) "Action" in the sense of a judicial proceeding includes recoupment, counter-claim, set-off, suit in equity and any other proceedings in which rights are determined.

(2) "Aggrieved party" means a party entitled to resort to a remedy.

(3) "Agreement" means the bargain of the parties in fact as found in their language or by implication from other circumstances including course of dealing or usage of trade or course of performance as provided in this Act (Sections 1-205 and 2-208). Whether an agreement has legal consequences is determined by the provisions of this Act, if applicable; otherwise by the law of contracts (Section 1-103). (Compare "Contract".)

(4) "Bank" means any person engaged in the business of banking.

(5) "Bearer" means the person in possession of an instrument, document of title, or certificated security payable to bearer or indorsed in blank.

(6) "Bill of lading" means a document evidencing the receipt of goods for shipment issued by a person engaged in the business of transporting or forwarding goods, and includes an airbill. "Airbill" means a document serving for air transportation as a bill of lading does for marine or rail transportation, and includes an air consignment note or air waybill.

(7) "Branch" includes a separately incorporated foreign branch of a bank.

(8) "Burden of establishing" a fact means the burden of persuading the triers of fact that the existence of the fact is more probable than its non-existence.

(9) "Buyer in ordinary course of business" means a person who in good faith and without knowledge that the sale to him is in violation of the ownership rights or security interest of a third party in the goods buys in ordinary course from a person in the business of selling goods of that kind but does not include a pawnbroker. [All persons who sell minerals or the like (including oil and gas) at wellhead or minehead shall be deemed to be persons in the business of selling goods of that kind.] "Buying" may be for cash or by exchange of other property or on secured or unsecured credit and includes receiving goods or documents of title under a pre-existing contract for sale but does not include a transfer in bulk or as security for or in total or partial satisfaction of a money debt.

(10) "Conspicuous": A term or clause is conspicuous when it is so written that a reasonable person against whom it is to operate ought to have noticed it. A printed heading in capitals (as NON-NEGOTIABLE BILL OF LADING) is conspicuous. Language in the body of a form is "conspicuous" if it is in larger or other contrasting type or color. But in a telegram any stated term is "conspicuous". Whether a term or clause is "conspicuous" or not is for decision by the court.

(11) "Contract" means the total legal obligation which results from the parties' agreement as affected by this Act and any other applicable rules or law. (Compare "Agreement".)

(12) "Creditor" includes a general creditor, a secured creditor, a lien creditor and any representative of creditors, including an assignee for the benefit of creditors, a trustee in bankruptcy, a receiver in equity and an executor or administrator of an insolvent debtor's or assignor's estate.

(13) "Defendant" includes a person in the position of defendant in a cross-action or counterclaim.

(14) "Delivery" with respect to instruments, documents of title, chattel paper, or certificated securities means voluntary transfer of possession.

(15) "Document of title" includes a bill of lading, dock warrant, dock receipt, warehouse receipt or order for the delivery of goods, and also any other document which in the regular course of business or financing is treated as adequately evidencing that the person in possession of it is entitled to receive, hold and dispose of the document and the goods it covers. To be a document of title a document must purport to be issued by or addressed to a bailee and purport to cover goods in the bailee's possession which are either identified or are fungible portions of an identified mass.

(16) "Fault" means wrongful act, omission or breach.

(17) "Fungible" with respect to goods or securities means goods or securities of which any unit is, by nature or usage of trade, the equivalent of any other like unit. Goods which are not fungible shall be deemed fungible for the purposes of this Act to the extent that under a particular agreement or document unlike units are treated as equivalents.

(18) "Genuine" means free of forgery or counterfeiting.

(19) "Good faith" means honesty in fact in the conduct or transaction concerned.

(20) "Holder" means a person who is in possession of a document of title or an instrument or a certificated investment security drawn, issued, or indorsed to him or his order or to bearer or in blank.

(21) To "honor" is to pay or to accept and pay, or where a credit so engages to purchase or discount a draft complying with the terms of the credit.

(22) "Insolvency proceedings" includes any assignment for the benefit of creditors or other proceedings intended to liquidate or rehabilitate the estate of the person involved.

(23) A person is "insolvent" who either has ceased to pay his debts in the ordinary course of business or cannot pay his debts as they become due or is insolvent within the meaning of the federal bankruptcy law.

(24) "Money" means a medium of exchange authorized or adopted by a domestic or foreign government as a part of its currency.

(25) A person has "notice" of a fact when

(a) he has actual knowledge of it; or

(b) he has received a notice of notification of it; or

(c) from all the facts and circumstances known to him at the time in question he has reason to know that it exists.

A person "knows" or has "knowledge" of a fact when he has actual knowledge of it. "Discover" or "learn" or a word or phrase of similar import refers to knowledge rather than to reason to know. The time and circumstances under which a notice or notification may cease to be effective are not determined by this Act.

(26) A person "notifies" or "gives" a notice or notification to another by taking such steps as may be reasonably required to inform the other in ordinary course whether or not such other actually comes to know of it. A person "receives" a notice or notification when

(a) it comes to his attention; or

(b) it is duly delivered at the place of business through which the contract was made or at any other place held out by him as the place for receipt of such communications.

(27) Notice, knowledge or a notice or notification received by an organization is effective for a particular transaction from the time when it is brought to the attention of the individual conducting that transaction, and in any event from the time when it would have been brought to his attention if the organization had exercised due diligence.

(28) "Organization" includes a corporation, government or governmental subdivision or agency, business trust, estate, trust, partnership or association, two or more persons having a joint or common interest, or any other legal or commercial entity.

(29) "Party", as distinct from "third party", means a person who has engaged in a transaction or made an agreement within this Act.

(30) "Person" includes an individual or an organization (See Section 1-102).

(31) "Presumption" or "presumed" means that the trier of fact must find the existence of the fact presumed unless and until evidence is introduced which would support a finding of its nonexistence.

(32) "Purchase" includes taking by sale, discount, negotiation, mortgage, pledge, lien, issue or re-issue, gift or any other voluntary transaction creating an interest in property.

(33) "Purchaser" means a person who takes by purchase.

(34) "Remedy" means any remedial right to which an aggrieved party is entitled with or without resort to a tribunal.

(35) "Representative" includes an agent, an officer of a corporation or association, and a trustee, executor or administrator of an estate, or any other person empowered to act for another.

(36) "Rights" includes remedies.

(37) "Security interest" means an interest in personal property or fixtures which secures payment or performance of an obligation. The retention or reservation of title by a seller of goods notwithstanding shipment or delivery to the buyer (Section 2-401) is limited in effect to a reservation of a "security interest". The term also includes any interest of a buyer of accounts [or] chattel paper which is subject to Article 9. The special property interest of a buyer of goods on identification of such goods to a contract for sale under Section 2-401 is not a "security interest", but a buyer may also acquire a "security interest" by complying with Article 9. Unless a lease or consignment is intended as security, reservation of title thereunder is not a "security interest" but a consignment is in any event subject to the provisions on consignment sales (Section 2-326). Whether a lease is intended as security is to be determined by the facts of each case; however,

(a) the inclusion of an option to purchase does not of itself make the lease one intended for security, and

(b) an agreement that upon compliance with the terms of the lease the lessee shall become or has the option to become the owner of the property for no additional consideration or for a nominal consideration does make the lease one intended for security.

(38) "Send" in connection with any writing or notice means to deposit in the mail or deliver for transmission by any other usual means of communication with postage or cost of transmission provided for and properly addressed and in the case of an instrument to an address specified thereon or otherwise agreed, or if there be none to any address specified thereon or otherwise agreed, or if there be none to any address reasonable under the circumstances. The receipt of any writing or notice within the time at which it would have arrived if properly sent has the effect of a proper sending.

(39) "Signed" includes any symbol executed or adopted by a party with present intention to authenticate a writing.

(40) "Surety" includes guarantor.

(41) "Telegram" includes a message transmitted by radio, teletype, cable, any mechanical method of transmission, or the like.

(42) "Term" means that portion of an agreement which relates to a particular matter.

(43) "Unauthorized" signature or indorsement means one made without actual implied or apparent authority and includes a forgery.

(44) "Value". Except as otherwise provided with respect to negotiable instruments and bank collections (Sections 3-303, 4-208 and 4-209) a person gives "value" for rights if he acquires them

(a) in return for a binding commitment to extend credit or for the extension of immediately available credit whether or not drawn upon and whether or not a charge-back is provided for in the event of difficulties in collection; or

    (b) as security for or in total or partial satisfaction of a pre-existing claim; or

    (c) by accepting delivery pursuant to a pre-existing claim; or

    (d) generally, in return for any consideration sufficient to support a simple contract.

(45) "Warehouse receipt" means a receipt issued by a person engaged in the business of storing goods for hire.

(46) "Written" or "writing" includes printing, typewriting or any other intentional reduction to tangible form.

§ 1-202. Prima Facie Evidence by Third Party Documents.—A document in due form purporting to be a bill of lading, policy or certificate of insurance, official weigher's or inspector's certificate, consular invoice, or any other document authorized or required by the contract to be issued by a third party shall be prima facie evidence of its own authenticity and genuineness and of the facts stated in the document by the third party.

§ 1-203. Obligation of Good Faith—Every contract or duty within this Act imposes an obligation of good faith in its performance or enforcement.

§ 1-204. Time; Reasonable Time; "Seasonably".—

(1) Whenever this Act requires any action to be taken within a reasonable time, any time which is not manifestly unreasonable may be fixed by agreement.

(2) What is a reasonable time for taking any action depends on the nature, purpose and circumstances of such action.

(3) An action is taken "seasonably" when it is taken at or within the time agreed or no time agreed at or within a reasonable time.

§ 1-205. Course of Dealing and Usage of Trade.—

(1) A course of dealing is a sequence of previous conduct between the parties to a particular transaction which is fairly to be regarded as establishing a common basis of understanding for interpreting their expressions and other conduct.

(2) A usage of trade is any practice or method of dealing having such regularity of observance in a place, vocation or trade as to justify an expectation that it will be observed with respect to the transaction in question. If it is established that such usage is embodied in a written trade code or similar writing the interpretation of the writing is for the court.

(3) A course of dealing between parties and any usage of trade in the vocation of trade in which they are engaged or of which they are or should be aware give particular meaning to and supplement or qualify terms of an agreement.

(4) The express terms of an agreement and an applicable course of dealing or usage of trade shall be construed wherever reasonable as consistent with each other; but when such construction is unreasonable express terms control both course of dealing and usage of trade and course of dealing controls usage of trade.

(5) An applicable usage of trade in the place where any part of performance is to occur shall be used in interpreting the agreement as to that part of the performance.

(6) Evidence of a relevant usage of trade offered by one party is not admissible unless and until he has given the other party such notice as the court finds sufficient to prevent unfair surprise to the latter.

§ 1-206. Statute of Frauds for Kinds of Personal Property Not Otherwise Covered.—

(1) Except in the cases described in subsection (2) of this section a contract for the sale of personal property is not enforceable by way of action or defense beyond five thousand dollars in amount or value of remedy unless there is some writing which indicates that a contract for sale has been made between the parties at a defined or stated price, reasonably identifies the subject matter, and is signed by the party against whom enforcement is sought or by his authorized agent.

(2) Subsection (1) of this section does not apply to contracts for the sale of goods (Section 2-201) nor of securities (Section 8-319) nor to security agreements (Section 9-203).

§ 1-207. Performance or Acceptance Under Reservation of Rights.—A party who with explicit reservation of rights performs or promises performance or assents to performance in a manner demanded or offered by the other party does not thereby prejudice the rights reserved. Such words as "without prejudice", "under protest" or the like are sufficient.

§ 1-208. Option to Accelerate at Will.—A term providing that one party or his successor in interest may accelerate payment or performance or require collateral or additional collateral "at will" or "when he deems himself insecure" or in words of similar import shall be construed to mean that he shall have power to do so only if he in good faith believes that the prospect of payment or performance is impaired. The burden of establishing lack of good faith is on the party against whom the power has been exercised.

ARTICLE TWO — SALES

PART 1

Short Title, General Construction and Subject Matter

§ 2-101. Short Title.—This Article shall be known and may be cited as Uniform Commercial Code—Sales.

§ **2-102. Scope; Certain Security and Other Transactions Excluded From This Article.**—Unless the context otherwise requires, this Article applies to transactions in goods; it does not apply to any transaction which although in the form of an unconditional contract to sell or present sale is intended to operate only as a security transaction nor does this Article impair or repeal any statute regulating sales to consumers, farmers or other specified classes of buyers.

§ **2-103. Definitions and Index of Definitions.**—

(1) In this Article unless the context otherwise requires

    (a) "Buyer" means a person who buys or contracts to buy goods.

    (b) "Good faith" in the case of a merchant means honesty in fact and the observance of reasonable commercial standards of fair dealing in the trade.

    (c) "Receipt" of goods means taking physical possession of them.

    (d) "Seller" means a person who sells or contracts to sell goods. . . .

§ **2-104. Definitions: "Merchant"; "Between Merchants"; "Financing Agency."**—

(1) "Merchant" means a person who deals in goods of the kind or otherwise by his occupation holds himself out as having knowledge or skill peculiar to the practices or goods involved in the transaction or to whom such knowledge or skill may be attributed by his employment of an agent or broker or other intermediary who by his occupation holds himself out as having such knowledge or skill.

(2) "Financing agency" means a bank, finance company or other person who in the ordinary course of business makes advances against goods or documents of title or who by arrangement with either the seller or the buyer intervenes in ordinary course to make or collect payment due or claimed under the contract for sale, as by purchasing or paying the seller's draft or making advances against it or by merely taking it for collection whether or not documents of title accompany the draft. "Financing agency" includes also a bank or other person who similarly intervenes between persons who are in the position of seller and buyer in respect to the goods (Section 2-707).

(3) "Between merchants" means in any transaction with respect to which both parties are chargeable with the knowledge or skill of merchants.

§ **2-105. Definitions: Transferability; "Goods"; "Future" Goods; "Lot"; "Commercial Unit".**—

(1) "Goods means all things (including specially manufactured goods) which are movable at the time of identification to the contract for sale other than the money in which the price is to be paid, investment securities (Article 8) and things in action. "Goods" also includes the unborn young of animals and growing crops and other identified things attached to realty as described in the section on goods to be severed from realty (Section 2-107.)

(2) Goods must be both existing and identified before any interest in them can pass. Goods which are not both existing and identified are "future" goods. A purported present sale of future goods or of any interest therein operates as a contract to sell.

(3) There may be a sale of a part interest in existing identified goods.

(4) An undivided share in an identified bulk of fungible goods is sufficiently identified to be sold although the quantity of the bulk is not determined. Any agreed proportion of such a bulk or any quantity thereof agreed upon by number, weight or other measure may to the extent of the seller's interest in the bulk be sold to the buyer who then becomes an owner in common.

(5) "Lot" means a parcel or a single article which is the subject matter of a separate sale or delivery, whether or not it is sufficient to perform the contract.

(6) "Commercial unit" means such a unit of goods as by commercial usage is a single whole for purposes of sale and division of which materially impairs its character or value on the market or in use. A commercial unit may be a single article (as a machine) or a set of articles (as a suite of furniture or an assortment of sizes) or a quantity (as a bale, gross, or carload) or any other unit treated in use of in the relevant market as a single whole.

§ **2-106. Definitions: "Contract"; "Agreement"; "Contract for Sale"; "Sale"; "Present Sale"; "Conforming" to Contract; "Termination"; "Cancellation".**—

(1) In This Article unless the context otherwise requires "contract" and "agreement" are limited to those relating to the present or future sale of goods. "Contract for sale" includes both a present sale of goods and a contract to sell goods at a future time. A "sale" consists in the passing of title from the seller to the buyer for a price (Section 2-401). A "present sale" means a sale which is accomplished by the marking of the contract.

(2) Goods or conduct including any part of a performance are "conforming" or conform to the contract when they are in accordance with the obligations under the contract.

(3) "Termination" occurs when either party pursuant to a power created by agreement or law puts an end to the contract otherwise than for its breach. On "termination" all obligations which are still executory on both sides are discharged but any right based on prior breach or performance survives.

(4) "Cancellation" occurs when either party puts an end to the contract for breach by the other and its effect is the same as that of "termination" except that the cancelling party also retains any remedy for breach of the whole contract or any unperformed balance.

§ **2-107. Goods to Be Severed From Realty: Recording.**—

(1) A contract for the sale of minerals or the like [(including oil and gas)] or a structure or its materials to be removed from realty is a contract for the sale of goods within this Article if they are to be severed by the seller but until severance a purported present sale thereof which is not effective as a transfer of an interest in land is effective only as a contract to sell.

(2) A contract for the sale apart from the land of growing crops or other things attached to realty and capable of severance without material harm thereto but not described in subsection (1) [or of timber to be

cut] is a contract for the sale of goods within this Article whether the subject matter is to be severed by the buyer or by the seller even though it forms part of the realty at the time of contracting, and the parties can by identification effect a present sale before severance.

(3) The provision of this section are subject to any third party rights provided by the law relating to realty records, and the contract for sale may be executed and recorded as a document transferring an interest in land and shall then constitute notice to third parties of the buyer's rights under the contract for sale.

PART 2

Form, Formation and Readjustment of Contract

§ 2-201. **Formal Requirements; Statute of Frauds.**—
(1) Except as otherwise provided in this section a contract for the sale of goods for the price of $500 or more is not enforceable by way of action or defense unless there is some writing sufficient to indicate that a contract for sale has been made between the parties and signed by the party against whom enforcement is sought or by his authorized agent or broker. A writing is not insufficient because it omits or incorrectly states a term agreed upon but the contract is not enforceable under this paragraph beyond the quantity of goods shown in such writing.

(2) Between merchants if within a reasonable time a writing in confirmation of the contract and sufficient against the sender is received and the party receiving it has reason to know its contents, it satisfies the requirements of subsection (1) against such party unless written notice of objection to its contents is given within ten days after it is received.

(3) A contract which does not satisfy the requirements of subsection (1) but which is valid in other respects is enforceable

(a) if the goods are to be specially manufactured for the buyer and are not suitable for sale to others in the ordinary course of the seller's business and the seller, before notice of repudiation is received and under circumstances which reasonably indicate that the goods are for the buyer, has made either a substantial beginning of their manufacture or commitments for their procurement; or

(b) if the party against whom enforcement is sought admits in his pleading, testimony or otherwise in court that a contract for sale was made, but the contract is not enforceable under this provision beyond the quantity of goods admitted; or

(c) with respect to goods for which payment has been made and accepted or which have been received and accepted (Sec. 2-606).

§ 2-202. **Final Written Expression: Part or Extrinsic Evidence.**—Terms with respect to which the confirmatory memoranda of the parties agree or which are otherwise set forth in a writing intended by the parties as a final expression of their agreement with respect to such terms as are included therein may not be contradicted by evidence of any prior agreement or of a contemporaneous oral agreement but may be explained or supplemented

(a) by course of dealing or usage of trade (Section 1-205) or by course of performance (Section 2-208); and

(b) by evidence of consistent additional terms unless the court finds the writing to have been intended also as a complete and exclusive statement of the terms of the agreement.

§ 2-203. **Seals Inoperative.**—The affixing of a seal to a writing evidencing a contract for sale or an offer to buy or sell goods does not constitute the writing a sealed instrument and the law with respect to sealed instruments does not apply to such a contract or offer.

§ 2-204. **Formation in General.**—
(1) A contract for sale of goods may be made in any manner sufficient to show agreement, including conduct by both parties which recognizes the existence of such a contract.

(2) An agreement sufficient to constitute a contract for sale may be found even though the moment of its making is undetermined.

(3) Even though one or more terms are left open a contract for sale does not fail for indefiniteness if the parties have intended to make a contract and there is a reasonably certain basis for giving an appropriate remedy.

§ 2-205. **Firm Offers.**—An offer by a merchant to buy or sell goods in a signed writing which by its terms gives assurance that it will be held open is not revocable, for lack of consideration, during the time stated or if no time is stated for a reasonable time, but in no event may such period of irrevocability exceed three months; but any such term of assurance on a form supplied by the offeree must be separately signed by the offeror.

§ 2-206. **Offer and Acceptance in Formation of Contract.**—
(1) Unless otherwise unambiguously indicated by the language or circumstances

(a) an offer to make a contract shall be construed as inviting acceptance in any manner and by any medium reasonable in the circumstances.

(b) an order or other offer to buy goods for prompt or current shipment shall be construed as inviting acceptance either by a prompt promise to ship or by the prompt or current shipment of conforming or non-conforming goods, but such a shipment of non-conforming goods does not constitute an acceptance if the seller seasonably notifies the buyer that the shipment is offered only as an accommodation to the buyer.

(2) Where the beginning of a requested performance is a reasonable mode of acceptance an offeror who is not notified of acceptance within a reasonable time may treat the offer as having lapsed before acceptance.

§ 2-207. Additional Terms in Acceptance or Confirmation.—

(1) A definite and seasonable expression of acceptance or a written confirmation which is sent within a reasonable time operates as an acceptance even though it states terms additional to or different from those offered or agreed upon, unless acceptance is expressly made conditional on assent to the additional or different terms.

(2) The additional terms are to be construed as proposals for addition to the contract. Between merchants such terms become part of the contract unless:

    (a) the offer expressly limits acceptance to the terms of the offer;

    (b) they materially alter it; or

    (c) notification of objection to them has already been given or is given within a reasonable time after notice of them is received.

(3) Conduct by both parties which recognizes the existence of a contract is sufficient to establish a contract for sale although the writings of the parties do not otherwise establish a contract. In such case the terms of the particular contract consist of those terms on which the writings of the parties agree, together with any supplementary terms incorporated under any other provisions of this Act.

§ 2-208. Course of Performance or Practical Construction.—

(1) Where the contract for sale involves repeated occasions for performance by either party with knowledge of the nature of the performance and opportunity for objection to it by the other, any course of performance accepted or acquiesced in without objection shall be relevant to determine the meaning of the agreement.

(2) The express terms of the agreement and any such course of performance, as well as any course of dealing and usage of trade, shall be construed whenever reasonable as consistent with each other; but when such construction is unreasonable, express terms shall control course of performance and course of performance shall control both course of dealing and usage of trade (Section 1-205).

(3) Subject to the provisions of the next section on modification and waiver, such course of performance shall be relevant to show a waiver or modification of any term inconsistent with such course of performance.

§ 2-209. Modification, Rescission and Waiver.—

(1) An agreement modifying a contract within this Article needs no consideration to be binding.

(2) A signed agreement which excludes modification or rescission except by a signed writing cannot be otherwise modified or rescinded, but except as between merchants such a requirement on a form supplied by the merchant must be separately signed by the other party.

(3) The requirements of the statute of frauds section of this Article (Section 2-201) must be satisfied if the contract as modified is within its provisions.

(4) Although an attempt at modification or rescission does not satisfy the requirements of subsection (2) or (3) it can operate as a waiver.

(5) A party who has made a waiver affecting an executory portion of the contract may retract the waiver by reasonable notification received by the other party that strict performance will be required of any term waived, unless the retraction would be unjust in view of a material change of position in reliance on the waiver.

§ 2-210. Delegation of Performance; Assignment of Rights.—

(1) A party may perform his duty through a delegate unless otherwise agreed or unless the other party has a substantial interest in having his original promisor perform or control the acts required by the contract. No delegation of performance relieves the party delegating of any duty to perform or any liability for breach.

(2) Unless otherwise agreed all rights of either seller or buyer can be assigned except where the assignment would materially change the duty of the other party, or increase materially the burden or risk imposed on him by his contract, or impair materially his chance of obtaining return performance. A right to damages for breach of the whole contract or a right arising out of the assignor's due performance of his entire obligation can be assigned despite agreement otherwise.

(3) Unless the circumstances indicate the contrary a prohibition of assignment of "the contract" is to be construed as barring only the delegation to the assignee of the assignor's performance.

(4) An assignment of "the contract" or of "all my rights under the contract" or an assignment in similar general terms is an assignment of rights and unless the language or the circumstances (as in an assignment for security) indicate the contrary, it is a delegation of performance of the duties of the assignor and its acceptance by the assignee constitutes a promise by him to perform those duties. This promise is enforceable by either the assignor or the other party to the original contract.

(5) The other party may treat any assignment which delegates performance as creating reasonable grounds for insecurity and may without prejudice to his rights against the assignor demand assurances from the assignee (Section 2-609).

PART 3

General Obligation and Construction of Contract

§ 2-301. General Obligations of Parties.—

The obligation of the seller is to transfer and deliver and that of the buyer is to accept and pay in accordance with the contract.

§ 2-302. Unconscionable Contract or Clause.—

(1) If the court as a matter of law finds the contract or any clause of the contract to have been unconscionable at the time it was made the court may refuse to enforce the contract, or it may enforce the remainder of the contract without the unconscionable clause, or it may so limit the application of any unconscionable clause as to avoid any unconscionable result.

(2) When it is claimed or appears to the court that the contract or any clause thereof may be unconscionable the parties shall be afforded a reasonable opportunity to present evidence as to its commercial setting, purpose and effect to aid the court in making the determination.

§ 2-303. Allocation or Division of Risks.—Where this Article allocates a risk or a burden as between the parties ''unless otherwise agreed,'' the agreement may not only shift the allocation but may also divide the risk or burden.

§ 2-304. Price Payable in Money, Goods, Realty, or Otherwise.—

(1) The price can be made payable in money or otherwise. If it is payable in whole or in part in goods each party is a seller of the goods which he is to transfer.

(2) Even though all or part of the price is payable in an interest in realty the transfer of the goods and the seller's obligations with reference to them are subject to this Article, but not the transfer of the interest in realty or the transferor's obligations in connection therewith.

§ 2-305. Open Price Term.—

(1) The parties if they so intend can conclude a contract for sale even though the price is not settled. In such a case the price is a reasonable price at the time for delivery if:

(a) nothing is said as to price; or

(b) the price is left to be agreed by the parties and they fail to agree; or

(c) the price is to be fixed in terms of some agreed market or other standard as set or recorded by a third person or agency and it is not so set or recorded.

(2) A price to be fixed by the seller or by the buyer means a price for him to fix in good faith.

(3) When a price left to be fixed otherwise than by agreement of the parties fails to be fixed through fault of one party the other may at his option treat the contract as cancelled or himself fix a reasonable price.

(4) Where, however, the parties intend not to be bound unless the price be fixed or agreed and it is not fixed or agreed there is no contract. In such a case the buyer must return any goods already received or if unable so to do must pay their reasonable value at the time of delivery and the seller must return any portion of the price paid on account.

§ 2-306. Output, Requirements and Exclusive Dealings.—

(1) A term which measures the quantity by the output of the seller or the requirements of the buyer means such actual output or requirements as may occur in good faith, except that no quantity unreasonably disproportionate to any stated estimate or in the absence of a stated estimate to any normal or otherwise comparable prior output or requirements may be tendered or demanded.

(2) A lawful agreement by either the seller or the buyer for exclusive dealing in the kind of goods concerned imposes unless otherwise agreed an obligation by the seller to use best efforts to supply the goods and by the buyer to use best efforts to promote their sale.

§ 2-307. Delivery in Single Lot or Several Lots.—Unless otherwise agreed all goods called for by a contract for sale must be tendered in a single delivery and payment is due only on such tender but where the circumstances give either party the right to make or demand delivery in lots the price if it can be apportioned may be demanded for each lot.

§ 2-308. Absence of Specified Place for Delivery.—Unless otherwise agreed

(a) the place for delivery of goods is the seller's place of business or if he has none his residence; but

(b) in a contract for sale of identified goods which to the knowledge of the parties at the time of contracting are in some other place, that place is the place for their delivery; and

(c) documents of title may be delivered through customary banking channels.

§ 2-309. Absence of Specific Time Provisions; Notice of Termination.—

(1) The time for shipment or delivery of any other action under a contract if not provided in this Article or agreed upon shall be a reasonable time.

(2) Where the contract provides for successive performances but is indefinite in duration it is valid for a reasonable time but unless otherwise agreed may be terminated at any time by either party.

(3) Termination of a contract by one party except on the happening of an agreed event requires that reasonable notification be received by the other party and an agreement dispensing with notification is invalid if its operation would be unconscionable.

§ 2-310. Open Time for Payment or Running of Credit; Authority to Ship Under Reservation.—Unless otherwise agreed

(a) payment is due at the time and place at which the buyer is to receive the goods even though the place of shipment is the place of delivery; and

(b) if the seller is authorized to send the goods he may ship them under reservation, and may tender the documents of title, but the buyer may inspect the goods after their arrival before payment is due unless such inspection is inconsistent with the terms of the contract (Section 2-513); and

(c) if delivery is authorized and made by way of documents of title otherwise than by subsection (b) then payment is due at the time and place at which the buyer is to receive the documents regardless of where the goods are to be received; and

(d) where the seller is required or authorized to ship the goods on credit the credit period runs from the time of shipment but post-dating the invoice or delaying its dispatch will correspondingly delay the starting of the credit period.

§ 2-311. Options and Cooperation Respecting Performance.—

(1) An agreement for sale which is otherwise sufficiently definite (subsection (3) of Section 2-204) to be a contract is not made invalid by the fact that it leaves particulars of performance to be specified by one of the parties. Any such specification must be made in good faith and within limits set by commercial reasonableness.

(2) Unless otherwise agreed specifications relating to assortment of the goods are at the buyer's option and except as otherwise provided in subsections (1) (c) and (3) of Section 2-319 specifications or arrangements relating to shipment are at the seller's option.

(3) Where such specification would materially affect the other party's performance but is not seasonably made or where one party's cooperation is necessary to the agreed performance of the other but is not seasonably forthcoming, the other party in addition to all other remedies

(a) is excused for any resulting delay in his own performance; and

(b) may also either proceed to perform in any reasonable manner or after the time for a material part of his own performance treat the failure to specify or to cooperate as a breach by failure to deliver or accept the goods.

§ 2-312. Warranty of Title and Against Infringement; Buyer's Obligation Against Infringement.—

(1) Subject to subsection (2) there is in a contract for sale a warranty by the seller that

(a) the title conveyed shall be good, and its transfer rightful; and

(b) the goods shall be delivered free from any security interest or other lien or encumbrance of which the buyer at the time of contracting has no knowledge.

(2) A warranty under subsection (1) will be excluded or modified only by specific language or by circumstances which give the buyer reason to know that the person selling does not claim title in himself or that he is purporting to sell only such right or title as he or a third person may have.

(3) Unless otherwise agreed a seller who is a merchant regularly dealing in goods of the kind warrants that the goods shall be delivered free of the rightful claim of any third person by way of infringement or the like but a buyer who furnishes specifications to the seller must hold the seller harmless against any such claim which arises out of compliance with the specifications.

§ 2-313. Express Warranties by Affirmation, Promise, Description, Sample.—

(1) Express warranties by the seller are created as follows:

(a) Any affirmation of fact or promise made by the seller to the buyer which relates to the goods and becomes part of the basis of the bargain creates an express warranty that the goods shall conform to the affirmation or promise.

(b) Any description of the goods which is made part of the basis of the bargain creates an express warranty that the goods shall conform to the description.

(c) Any sample or model which is made part of the basis of the bargain creates an express warranty that the whole of the goods shall conform to the sample or model.

(2) It is not necessary to the creation of an express warranty that the seller use formal words such as "warrant" or "guarantee" or that he have a specific intention to make a warranty, but an affirmation merely of the value of the goods or a statement purporting to be merely the seller's opinion or commendation of the goods does not create a warranty.

§ 2-314. Implied Warranty: Merchantability; Usage of Trade.—

(1) Unless excluded or modified (Section 2-316), a warranty that the goods shall be merchantable is implied in a contract for their sale if the seller is a merchant with respect to goods of that kind. Under this section the serving for value of food or drink to be consumed either on the premises or elsewhere is a sale.

(2) Goods to be merchantable must be at least such as

(a) pass without objection in the trade under the contract description; and

(b) in the case of fungible goods, are of fair average quality within the description; and

(c) are fit for the ordinary purposes for which such goods are used; and

(d) run, within the variations permitted by the agreement, of even kind, quality and quantity within each unit and among all units involved; and

(e) are adequately contained, packaged, and labeled as the agreement may require; and

(f) conform to the promises or affirmations of fact made on the container or label if any.

(3) Unless excluded or modified (Section 2-316) other implied warranties may arise from course of dealing or usage of trade.

§ 2-315. Implied Warranty: Fitness for Particular Purpose.—Where the seller at the time of contracting has reason to know any particular purpose for which the goods are required and that the buyer is relying on the seller's skill or judgment to select or furnish suitable goods, there is unless excluded or modified under the next section an implied warranty that the goods shall be fit for such purpose.

§ 2-316. Exclusion or Modification of Warranties.—

(1) Words or conduct relevant to the creation of an express warranty and words or conduct tending to negate or limit warranty shall be construed wherever reasonable as consistent with each other; but subject to the provisions of this Article on parol or extrinsic evidence (Section 2-202) negation or limitation is inoperative to the extent that such construction is unreasonable.

(2) Subject to subsection (3), to exclude or modify the implied warranty of merchantability or any part of it the language must mention merchantability and in case of a writing must be conspicuous, and to exclude or modify any implied warranty of fitness the exclusion must be by a writing and conspicuous. Language to exclude all implied warranties of fitness is sufficient if it states, for example, that "There are no warranties which extend beyond the description on the face hereof."

(3) Notwithstanding subsection (2)

(a) unless the circumstances indicate otherwise, all implied warranties are excluded by expressions like "as is," "with all faults" or other language which in common understanding calls the buyer's attention to the exclusion of warranties and makes plain that there is no implied warranty; and

(b) when the buyer before entering into the contract has examined the goods or the sample or model as fully as he desired or has refused to examine the goods there is no implied warranty with regard to defects which an examination ought in the circumstances to have revealed to him; and

(c) an implied warranty can also be excluded or modified by course of dealing or course of performance or usage of trade.

(4) Remedies for breach of warranty can be limited in accordance with the provisions of this Article on liquidation or limitation of damages and on contractual modification of remedy (Sections 2-718 and 2-719).

§ 2-317. Cumulation and Conflict of Warranties Express or Implied.—Warranties whether express or implied shall be construed as consistent with each other and as cumulative, but if such construction is unreasonable the intention of the parties shall determine which warranty is dominant. In ascertaining that intention the following rules apply:

(a) Exact or technical specifications displace an inconsistent sample or model or general language of description.

(b) A sample from an existing bulk displaces inconsistent general language of description.

(c) Express warranties displace inconsistent implied warranties other than an implied warranty of fitness for a particular purpose.

§ 2-318. Third Party Beneficiaries of Warranties Express or Implied.—A seller's warranty whether express or implied extends to any natural person who is in the family or household of his buyer or who is a guest in his home if it is reasonable to expect that such person may use, consume or be affected by the goods and who is injured in person by breach of the warranty. A seller may not exclude or limit the operation of this section.

§ 2-319. F.O.B. and F.A.S. Terms.—

(1) Unless otherwise agreed the term F.O.B. (which means "free on board") at a named place, even though used only in connection with the stated price, is a delivery term under which

(a) when the term is F.O.B. the place of shipment, the seller must at that place ship the goods in the manner provided in this Article (Section 2-504; and bear the expense and risk of putting them into the possession of the carrier; or

(b) when the term is F.O.B. the place of destination, the seller must at his own expense and risk transport the goods to that place and there tender delivery of them in the manner provided in this Article (Section 2-503);

(c) when under either (a) or (b) the term is also F.O.B. vessel, car or other vehicle, the seller must in addition at his own expense and risk load the goods on board. If the term is F.O.B. vessel the buyer must name the vessel and in an appropriate case the seller must comply with the provisions of this Article on the form of bill of lading (Section 2-323).

(2) Unless otherwise agreed the term F.A.S. vessel (which means "free alongside") at a named port, even though used only in connection with the stated price, is a delivery term under which the seller must

(a) at his own expense and risk deliver the goods alongside the vessel in the manner usual in that port or on a dock designated and provided by the buyer; and

(b) obtain and tender a receipt for the goods in exchange for which the carrier is under a duty to issue a bill of lading.

(3) Unless otherwise agreed in any case falling within subsection (1) (a) or (c) or subsection (2) the buyer must seasonably give any needed instructions for making delivery, including when the term is F.A.S. or F.O.B. the loading berth of the vessel and in an appropriate case its name and sailing date. The seller may treat the failure of needed instructions as a failure of cooperation under this Article (Section 2-311). He may also at his option move the goods in any reasonable manner preparatory to delivery or shipment.

(4) Under the term F.O.B. vessel or F.A.S. unless otherwise agreed the buyer must make payment against tender of the required documents and the seller may not tender nor the buyer demand delivery, of the goods in substitution for the documents.

§ 2-320. C.I.F. and C. & F. Terms.—

(1) The term C.I.F. means that the price includes in a lump sum the cost of the goods and the insurance and freight to the named destination.

(2) Unless otherwise agreed and even though used only in connection with the stated price and destination, the term C.I.F. destination or its equivalent requires the seller at his own expense and risk to

(a) put the goods into the possession of a carrier at the port for shipment and obtain a negotiable bill or bills of lading covering the entire transportation to the named destination; and

(b) load the goods and obtain a receipt from the carrier (which may be contained in the bill of lading) showing that the freight has been paid or provided for; and

(c) obtain a policy or certificate of insurance, including any war risk insurance, of a kind and on terms then current at the port of shipment in the usual amount, in the currency of the contract, shown to cover the same goods covered by the bill of lading and providing for payment of loss to the order of the buyer or for the account of whom it may concern; but the seller may add to the price the amount of the premium for any such war risk insurance; and

(d) prepare an invoice of the goods and procure any other documents required to effect shipment or to comply with the contract; and

(e) forward and tender with commercial promptness all the documents in due form and with any indorsement necessary to perfect the buyer's rights.

(3) Unless otherwise agreed the term C. & F. or its equivalent has the same effect and imposes upon the seller the same obligations and risks as a C.I.F. term except the obligation as to insurance.

(4) Under the term C.I.F. or C. & F. unless otherwise agreed the buyer must make payment against tender of the required documents and the seller may not tender nor the buyer demand delivery of the goods in substitution for the documents.

§ 2-321. C.I.F. or C. & F.: "Net Landed Weights"; "Payment on Arrival"; Warranty of Condition on Arrival.—Under a contract containing a term C.I.F. or C. & F.

(1) Where the price is based on or is to be adjusted according to "net landed weights," "delivered weights," "out turn" quantity or quality or the like, unless otherwise agreed the seller must reasonably estimate the price. The payment due on tender of the documents called for by the contract is the amount so estimated but after final adjustment of the price a settlement must be made with commercial promptness.

(2) An agreement described in subsection (1) or any warranty of quality or condition of the goods on arrival places upon the seller the risk of ordinary deterioration, shrinkage and the like in transportation but has no effect on the place or time of identification to the contract for sale or delivery or on the passing of the risk of loss.

(3) Unless otherwise agreed where the contract provides for payment on or after arrival of the goods the seller must before payment allow such preliminary inspection as is feasible; but if the goods are lost delivery of the documents and payment are due when the goods should have arrived.

§ 2-322. Delivery "Ex-Ship".—

(1) Unless otherwise agreed a term for delivery of goods "ex-ship" (which means from the carrying vessel) or in equivalent language is not restricted to a particular ship and requires delivery from a ship which has reached a place at the named port of destination where goods of the kind are usually discharged.

(2) Under such a term unless otherwise agreed

(a) the seller must discharge all liens arising out of the carriage and furnish the buyer with a direction which puts the carrier under a duty to deliver the goods; and

(b) the risk of loss does not pass to the buyer until the goods leave the ship's tackle or are otherwise properly unloaded.

§ 2-323. Form of Bill of Lading Required in Overseas Shipments; "Overseas."—

(1) Where the contract contemplates overseas shipment and contains a term C.I.F. or C. & F. or F.O.B. vessel, the seller unless otherwise agreed must obtain a negotiable bill of lading stating that the goods have been loaded on board or, in the case of a term C.I.F. or C. & F., received for shipment.

(2) Where in a case within subsection (1) a bill of lading has been issued in a set of parts, unless otherwise agreed if the documents are not to be sent from abroad the buyer may demand tender of the full set; otherwise only one part of the bill of lading need be tendered. Even if the agreement expressly requires a full set

(a) due tender of a single part is acceptable within the provisions of this Article on cure of improper delivery (subsection (1) of Section 2-508); and

(b) even though the full set is demanded, if the documents are sent from abroad the person tendering an incomplete set may nevertheless require payment upon furnishing an indemnity which the buyer in good faith deems adequate.

(3) A shipment by water or by air or a contrct contemplating such shipment is "overseas" insofar as by usage of trade or agreement it is subject to the commercial, financing or shipping practices characteristic of international deep water commerce.

§ 2-324. "No Arrival, No Sale" Term.—Under a term "no arrival, no sale" or terms of the like meaning, unless otherwise agreed

(a) the seller must properly ship conforming goods and if they arrive by any means he must tender them on arrival but he assures no obligation that the goods will arrive unless he has caused the non-arrival; and

(b) where without fault of the seller the goods are in part lost or have so deteriorated as no longer to conform to the contract or arrive after the contract time, the buyer may proceed as if there had been casualty to identified goods (Section 2-613).

§ 2-325. "Letter of Credit" Term; "Confirmed Credit."—

(1) Failure of the buyer seasonably to furnish an agreed letter of credit is a breach of the contract for sale.

(2) The delivery to seller of a proper letter of credit suspends the buyer's obligation to pay. If the letter of credit is dishonored, the seller may on seasonable notification to the buyer require payment directly from him.

(3) Unless otherwise agreed the term "letter of credit" or "banker's credit" in a contract for sale means an irrevocable credit issued by a financing agency of good repute and, where the shipment is overseas, of good international repute. The term "confirmed credit" means that the credit must also carry the direct obligation of such an agency which does business in the seller's financial market.

§ 2-326. Sale on Approval and Sale or Return; Consignment Sales and Rights of Creditors.—

(1) Unless otherwise agreed, if delivered goods may be returned by the buyer even though they conform to the contract, the transaction is

(a) a "sale on approval" if the goods are delivered primarily for use, and

(b) a "sale or return" if the goods are delivered primarily for resale.

(2) Except as provided in subsection (3), goods held on approval are not subject to the claims of the

buyer's creditors until acceptance; goods held on sale or return are subject to such claims while in the buyer's possession.

(3) Where goods are delivered to a person for sale and such person maintains a place of business at which he deals in goods of the kind involved, under a name other than the name of the person making delivery, then with respect to claims of creditors of the person conducting the business the goods are deemed to be on sale or return. The provisions of this subsection are applicable even though an agreement purports to reserve title to the person making delivery until payment or resale or uses such words as "on consignment" or "on memorandum." However, this subsection is not applicable if the person making delivery

    (a) complies with an applicable law providing for a consignor's interest or the like to be evidenced by a sign, or

    (b) establishes that the person conducting the business is generally known by his creditors to be substantially engaged in selling the goods of others, or

    (c) complies with the filing provisions of the Article on Secured Transactions (Article 9).

(4) Any "or return" term of a contract for sale is to be treated as a separate contract for sale within the statute of frauds section of this Article (Section 2-201) and as contradicting the sale aspect of the contract within the provisions of this Article on parol or extrinsic evidence (Section 2-202).

§ 2-327. Special Incidents of Sale on Approval and Sale or Return.—

(1) Under a sale on approval unless otherwise agreed

    (a) although the goods are identified to the contract the risk of loss and the title do not pass to the buyer until acceptance; and

    (b) use of goods consistent with the purpose of trial is not acceptance but failure seasonably to notify the seller of election to return the goods is acceptance, and if the goods conform to the contract acceptance of any part is acceptance of the whole; and

    (c) after due notification of election to return, the return is at the seller's risk and expense but a merchant buyer must follow any reasonable instructions.

(2) Under a sale or return unless otherwise agreed

    (a) the option to return extends to the whole or any commercial unit of the goods while in substantially their original condition, but must be exercised seasonably; and

    (b) the return is at the buyer's risk and expense.

§ 2-328. Sale by Auction.—

(1) In a sale by auction if goods are put up in lots each lot is the subject of a separate sale.

(2) A sale by auction is complete when the auctioneer so announces by the fall of the hammer or in other customary manner. Where a bid is made while the hammer is falling in acceptance of a prior bid the auctioneer may in his discretion reopen the bidding or declare the goods sold under the bid on which the hammer was falling.

(3) Such a sale is with reserve unless the goods are in explicit terms put up without reserve. In an auction with reserve the auctioneer may withdraw the goods at any time until he announces completion of the sale. In an auction without reserve, after the auctioneer calls for bids on an article or lot, that article or lot cannot be withdrawn unless no bid is made within a reasonable time. In either case a bidder may retract his bid until the auctioneer's announcement of completion of the sale, but a bidder's retraction does not revive any previous bid.

(4) If the auctioneer knowingly receives a bid on the seller's behalf or the seller makes or procures such a bid, and notice has not been given that liberty for such bidding is reserved, the buyer may at his option avoid the sale or take the goods at the price of the last good faith bid prior to the completion of the sale. This subsection shall not apply to any bid at a forced sale.

PART 4

Title, Creditors and Good Faith Purchasers

§ 2-401. Passing of Title; Reservation for Security; Limited Application of This Section.—Each provision of this Article with regard to the rights, obligations and remedies of the seller, the buyer, purchasers or other third parties applies irrespective of title to the goods except where the provision refers to such title. Insofar as situations are not covered by the other provisions of this Article and matters concerning title become material the following rules apply:

(1) Title to goods cannot pass under a contract for sale prior to their identification to the contract (Section 2-501), and unless otherwise explicitly agreed the buyer acquires by their identification a special property as limited by this Act. Any retention or reservation by the seller of the title (property) in goods shipped or delivered to the buyer is limited in effect to a reservation of a security interest. Subject to these provisions and to the provisions of the Article on Secured Transactions (Article 9), title to goods passes from the seller to the buyer in any manner and on any conditions explicitly agreed on by the parties.

(2) Unless otherwise explicitly agreed title passes to the buyer at the time and place at which the seller completes his performance with reference to the physical delivery of the goods, despite any reservation of a security interest and even though a document of title is to be delivered at a different time or place; and in particular and despite any reservation of a security interest by the bill of lading.

    (a) if the contract requires or authorizes the seller to send the goods to the buyer but does not require him to deliver them at destination, title passes to the buyer at the time and place of shipment; but

    (b) if the contract requires delivery at destination, title passes on tender there.

(3) Unless otherwise explicitly agreed where delivery is to be made without moving the goods,

(a) if the seller is to deliver a document of title, title passes at the time when and the place where he delivers such documents; or

(b) if the goods are at the time of contracting already identified and no documents are to be delivered, title passes at the time and place of contracting.

(4) A rejection or other refusal by the buyer to receive or retain the goods, whether or not justified, or a justified revocation of acceptance revests title to the goods in the seller. Such revesting occurs by operation of law and is not a "sale."

§ 2-402.   Rights of Seller's Creditors Against Sold Goods.—

(1) Except as provided in subsections (2) and (3), rights of unsecured creditors of the seller with respect to goods which have been identified to a contract for sale are subject to the buyer's rights to recover the goods under this Article (Sections 2-502 and 2-716).

(2) A creditor of the seller may treat a sale or an identification of goods to a contract for sale as void if as against him a retention of possession by the seller is fraudulent under any rule of law of the state where the goods are situated, except that retention of possession in good faith and current course of trade by a merchant-seller for a commercially reasonable time after a sale or identification is not fraudulent.

(3) Nothing in this Article shall be deemed to impair the rights of creditors of the seller

(a) under the provisions of the Article on Secured Transactions (Article 9); or

(b) where identification to the contract or delivery is made not in current course of trade but in satisfaction of or as security for a preexisting claim for money, security or the like and is made under circumstances which under any rule of law of the state where the goods are situated would apart from this Article constitute the transaction a fraudulent transfer or voidable preference.

§ 2-403.   Power to Transfer; Good Faith Purchase of Goods; "Entrusting."—

(1) A purchaser of goods acquires all title which his transferor had or had power to transfer except that a purchaser of a limited interest acquires rights only to the extent of the interest purchased. A person with voidable title has power to transfer a good title to a good faith purchaser for value. When goods have been delivered under a transaction of purchase the purchaser has such power even though

(a) the transferor was deceived as to the identity of the purchaser, or

(b) the delivery was in exchange for a check which is later dishonored, or

(c) it was agreed that the transaction was to be a "cash sale," or

(d) the delivery was procured through fraud punishable as larcenous under the criminal law.

(2) Any entrusting of possession of goods to a merchant who deals in goods of that kind gives him power to transfer all rights of the entruster to a buyer in ordinary course of business.

(3) "Entrusting" includes any delivery and any acquiescence in retention of possession regardless of any condition expressed between the parties to the delivery or acquiescence and regardless of whether the procurement of the entrusting or the possessor's disposition of the goods have been such as to be larcenous under the criminal law.

(4) The rights of other purchasers of goods and of lien creditors are governed by the Articles on Secured Transactions (Article 9), Bulk Transfers (Article 6) and Documents of Title (Article 7).

PART 5

Performance

§ 2-501.   Insurable Interest in Goods; Manner of Identification of Goods.—

(1) The buyer obtains a special property and an insurable interest in goods by identification of existing goods as goods to which the contract refers even though the goods so identified are non-conforming and he has an option to return or reject them. Such identification can be made at any time and in any manner explicitly agreed to by the parties. In the absence of explicit agreement identification occurs

(a) when the contract is made if it is for the sale of goods already existing and identified;

(b) if the contract is for the sale of future goods other than those described in paragraph (c), when goods are shipped, marked or otherwise designated by the seller as goods to which the contract refers;

(c) when the crops are planted or otherwise become growing crops or the young are conceived if the contract is for the sale of unborn young to be born within twelve months after contracting or for the sale of crops to be harvested within twelve months or the next normal harvest season after contracting whichever is longer.

(2) The seller retains an insurable interest in goods so long as title to or any security interest in the goods remains in him and where the identification is by the seller alone he may until default or insolvency or notification to the buyer that the identification is final substitute other goods for those identified.

(3) Nothing in this section impairs any insurable interest recognized under any other statute or rule of law.

§ 2-502.   Buyer's Right to Goods on Seller's Insolvency.—

(1) Subject to subsection (2) and even though the goods have not been shipped a buyer who has paid a part or all of the price of goods in which he has a special property under the provisions of the immediately preceding section may on making and keeping good a tender of any unpaid portion of their price recover them from the seller if the seller becomes insolvent within ten days after receipt of the first installment on their price.

(2) If the identification creating his special property has been made by the buyer he acquires the right to recover the goods only if they conform to the contract for sale.

§ 2-503. Manner of Seller's Tender of Delivery.—

(1) Tender of delivery requires that the seller put and hold conforming goods at the buyer's disposition and give the buyer any notification reasonably necessary to enable him to take delivery. The manner, time and place for tender are determined by the agreement and this Article, and in particular

    (a) tender must be at a reasonable hour, and if it is of goods they must be kept available for the period reasonably necessary to enable the buyer to take possession; but

    (b) unless otherwise agreed the buyer must furnish facilities reasonably suited to the receipt of the goods.

(2) Where the case is within the next section respecting shipment tender requires that the seller comply with its provisions.

(3) Where the seller is required to deliver at a particular destination tender requires that he comply with subsection (1) and also in any appropriate case tender documents as described in subsections (4) and (5) of this section.

(4) Where goods are in the possession of a bailee and are to be delivered without being moved

    (a) tender requires that the seller either tender a negotiable document of title covering such goods or procure acknowledgment by the bailee of the buyer's right to possession of the goods; but

    (b) tender to the buyer of a nonnegotiable document of title or of a written direction to the bailee to deliver is sufficient tender unless the buyer seasonably objects, and receipt by the bailee of notification of the buyer's rights fixes those rights as against the bailee to honor the non-negotiable document of title or to obey the direction remains on the seller until the buyer has had a reasonable time to present the document or direction, and a refusal by the bailee to honor the document or to obey the direction defeats the tender.

(5) Where the contract requires the seller to deliver documents

    (a) he must tender all such documents in correct form, except as provided in this Article with respect to bills of lading in a set (subsection (2) of Section 2-323); and

    (b) tender through customary banking channels is sufficient and dishonor of a draft accompanying the documents constitutes non-acceptance or rejection.

§ 2-504. Shipment by Seller.—

Where the seller is required or authorized to send the goods to the buyer and the contract does not require him to deliver them at a particular destination, then unless otherwise agreed he must

    (a) put the goods in the possession of such a carrier and make such a contract for their transportation as may be reasonable having regard to the nature of the goods and other circumstances of the case; and

    (b) obtain and promptly deliver or tender in due form any document necessary to enable the buyer to obtain possession of the goods or otherwise required by the agreement or by usage of trade; and

(c) promptly notify the buyer of the shipment.

Failure to notify the buyer under paragraph (c) or to make a proper contract under paragraph (a) is a ground for rejection only if material delay or loss ensues.

§ 2-505. Seller's Shipment Under Reservation.—

(1) Where the seller has identified goods to the contract by or before shipment:

    (a) his procurement of a negotiable bill of lading to his own order or otherwise reserves in him a security interest in the goods. His procurement of the bill to the order of a financing agency or of the buyer indicates in addition only the seller's expectation of transferring that interest to the person named.

    (b) a non-negotiable bill of lading to himself or his nominee reserves possession of the goods as security but except in a case of conditional delivery (subsection (2) of Section 2-507) a non-negotiable bill of lading naming the buyer as consignee reserves no security interest even though the seller retains possession of the bill of lading.

(2) When shipment by the seller with reservation of a security interest is in violation of the contract for sale it constitutes an improper contract for transportation within the preceding section but impairs neither the rights given to the buyer by shipment and identification of the goods to the contract nor the seller's powers as a holder of a negotiable document.

§ 2-506. Rights of Financing Agency.—

(1) A financing agency by paying or purchasing for value a draft which relates to a shipment of goods acquires to the extent of the payment or purchase and in addition to its own rights under the draft and any document of title securing it any rights of the shipper in the goods including the right to stop delivery and the shipper's right to have the draft honored by the buyer.

(2) The right to reimbursement of a financing agency which has in good faith honored or purchased the draft under commitment to or authority from the buyer is not impaired by subsequent discovery of defects with reference to any relevant document which was apparently regular on its face.

§ 2-507. Effect of Seller's Tender; Delivery on Condition.—

(1) Tender of delivery is a condition to the buyer's duty to accept the goods and, unless otherwise agreed, to his duty to pay for them. Tender entitles the seller to acceptance of the goods and to payment according to the contract.

(2) Where payment is due and demanded on the delivery to the buyer of goods or documents of title, his right as against the seller to retain or dispose of them is conditional upon his making the payment due.

§ 2-508. Cure by Seller of Improper Tender or Delivery; Replacement.—

(1) Where any tender or delivery by the seller is rejected because non-conforming and the time for performance has not yet expired, the seller may seasonally notify the buyer of his intention to cure and may then within the contract time make a conforming delivery.

(2) Where the buyer rejects a non-conforming tender which the seller had reasonable grounds to believe would be acceptable with or without money allowance the seller may if he seasonably notifies the buyer have a further reasonable time to substitute a conforming tender.

§ 2-509. Risk of Loss in the Absence of Breach.—

(1) Where the contract requires or authorizes the seller to ship the goods by carrier

(a) if it does not require him to deliver them at a particular destination, the risk of loss passes to the buyer when the goods are duly delivered to the carrier even though the shipment is under reservation (Section 2-505); but

(b) if it does require him to deliver them at a particular destination and the goods are there duly tendered while in the possession of the carrier, the risk of loss passes to the buyer when the goods are there duly so tendered as to enable the buyer to take delivery.

(2) Where the goods are held by a bailee to be delivered without being moved, the risk of loss passes to the buyer

(a) on his receipt of a negotiable document of title covering the goods; or

(b) on acknowledgment by the bailee of the buyer's right to possession of the goods; or

(c) after his receipt of a non-negotiable document of title or other written direction to deliver, as provided in subsection (4) (b) of Section 2-503.

(3) In any case not within subsection (1) or (2), the risk of loss passes to the buyer on his receipt of the goods if the seller is a merchant; otherwise the risk passes to the buyer on tender of delivery.

(4) The provisions of this section are subject to contrary agreement of the parties and to the provisions of this Article on sale on approval (Section 2-327) and on effect of breach on risk of loss (Section 2-510).

§ 2-510. Effect of Breach on Risk of Loss.—

(1) Where a tender or delivery of goods so fails to conform to the contract as to give a right of rejection the risk of their loss remains on the seller until cure or acceptance.

(2) Where the buyer rightfully revokes acceptance he may to the extent of any deficiency in his effective insurance coverage treat the risk of loss as having rested on the seller from the beginning.

(3) Where the buyer as to conforming goods already identified to the contract for sale repudiates or is otherwise in breach before risk of their loss has passed to him, the seller may to the extent of any deficiency in his effective insurance coverage treat the risk of loss as resting on the buyer for a commercially reasonable time.

§ 2-511. Tender of Payment by Buyer; Payment by Check.—

(1) Unless otherwise agreed tender of payment is a condition to the seller's duty to tender and complete any delivery.

(2) Tender of payment is sufficient when made by any means or in any manner current in the ordinary course of business unless the seller demands payment in legal tender and gives any extension of time reasonably necessary to procure it.

(3) Subject to the provisions of this Act on the effect of an instrument on an obligation (Section 3-802), payment by check is conditional and is defeated as between the parties by dishonor of the check on due presentment.

§ 2-512. Payment by Buyer Before Inspection.—

(1) Where the contract requires payment before inspection non-conformity of the goods does not excuse the buyer from so making payment unless

(a) the non-conformity appears without inspection; or

(b) despite tender of the required documents the circumstances would justify injunction against honor under the provisions of this Act (Section 5-114).

(2) Payment pursuant to subsection (1) does not constitute an acceptance of goods or impair the buyer's right to inspect or any of his remedies.

§ 2-513. Buyer's Right to Inspection of Goods.—

(1) Unless otherwise agreed and subject to subsection (3), where goods are tendered or delivered or identified to the contract for sale, the buyer has a right before payment or acceptance to inspect them at any reasonable place and time and in any reasonable manner. When the seller is required or authorized to send the goods to the buyer, the inspection may be after their arrival.

(2) Expenses of inspection must be borne by the buyer but may be recovered from the seller if the goods do not conform and are rejected.

(3) Unless otherwise agreed and subject to the provisions of this Article on C.I.F. contracts (subsection (3) of Section 2-321), the buyer is not entitled to inspect the goods before payment of the price when the contract provides

(a) for delivery "C.O.D." or on other like terms; or

(b) for payment against documents of title, except where such payment is due only after the goods are to become available for inspection.

(4) A place or method of inpspection fixed by the parties is presumed to be exclusive but unless otherwise expressly agreed it does not postpone identification or shift the place for delivery or for passing the risk of loss. If compliance becomes impossible, inspection shall be as provided in this section unless the place or method fixed was clearly intended as an indispensable condition failure of which avoids the contract.

§ **2-514. When Documents Deliverable on Acceptance; When on Payment.**—Unless otherwise agreed documents against which a draft is drawn are to be delivered to the drawee on acceptance of the draft if it is payable more than three days after presentment; otherwise, only on payment.

§ **2-515. Preserving Evidence of Goods in Dispute.**—In furtherance of the adjustment of any claim or dispute

(a) either party on reasonable notification to the other and for the purpose of ascertaining the facts and preserving evidence has the right to inspect, test and sample the goods including such of them as may be in the possession or control of the other; and

(b) the parties may agree to a third party inspection or survey to determine the conformity or condition of the goods and may agree that the findings shall be binding upon them in any subsequent litigation or adjustment.

PART 6

Breach, Repudiation and Excuse

§ **2-601. Buyer's Rights on Improper Delivery.**—Subject to the provisions of this Article on breach in installment contract (Section 2-612) and unless otherwise agreed under the sections on contractual limitations of remedy (Sections 2-718 and 2-719), if the goods or the tender of delivery fail in any respect to conform to the contract, the buyer may

(a) reject the whole; or

(b) accept the whole; or

(c) accept any commercial unit or units and reject the rest.

§ **2-602. Manner and Effect of Rightful Rejection.**—

(1) Rejection of goods must be within a reasonable time after their delivery or tender. It is ineffective unless the buyer seasonably notifies the seller.

(2) Subject to the provisions of the two following sections on rejected goods (Sections 2-603 and 2-604)

(a) after rejection any exercise of ownership by the buyer with respect to any commercial unit is wrongful as against the seller; and

(b) if the buyer has before rejection taken physical possession of goods in which he does not have a security interest under the provisions of this Article (subsection (3) of Section 2-711), he is under a duty after rejection to hold them with reasonable care at the seller's disposition for a time sufficient to permit the seller to remove them; but

(c) the buyer has no further obligations with regard to goods rightfully rejected.

(3) The seller's rights with respect to goods wrongfully rejected are governed by the provisions of this Article on Seller's remedies in general (Section 2-703).

§ **2-603. Merchant Buyer's Duties as to Rightfully Rejected Goods.**—

(1) Subject to any security interest in the buyer (subsection (3) of Section 2-711), when the seller has no agent or place of business at the market or rejection a merchant buyer is under a duty after rejection of goods in his possession or control to follow any reasonable instructions received from the seller with respect to the goods and in the absence of such instructions to make reasonable efforts to sell them for the seller's account if they are perishable or threaten to decline in value speedily. Instructions are not reasonable if on demand indemnity for expenses is not forthcoming.

(2) When the buyer sells goods under subsection (1), he is entitled to reimbursement from the seller or out of the proceeds for reasonable expenses of caring for and selling them, and if the expenses include no selling commission then to such commission as is usual in the trade or if there is none to a reasonable sum not exceeding ten per cent on the gross proceeds.

(3) In complying with this section the buyer is held only to good faith and good faith conduct hereunder is neither acceptance nor conversion nor the basis of an action for damages.

§ **2-604. Buyer's Options as to Salvage of Rightfully Rejected Goods.**—Subject to the provisions of the immediately preceding section on perishables if the seller gives no instructions within a reasonable time after notification of rejection the buyer may store the rejected goods for the seller's account or reship them to him or resell them for the seller's account with reimbursement as provided in the preceding section. Such action is not acceptance or conversion.

§ **2-605. Waiver of Buyer's Objections by Failure to Particularize.**—

(1) The buyer's failure to state in connection with rejection a particular defect which is ascertainable by reasonable inspection precludes him from relying on the unstated defect to justify rejection or to establish breach

(a) where the seller could have cured it if stated seasonably; or

(b) between merchants when the seller has after rejection made a request in writing for a full and final written statement of all defects on which the buyer proposes to rely.

(2) Payment against documents made without reservation of rights precludes recovery of the payment for defects apparent on the face of the documents.

§ **2-606. What Constitutes Acceptance of Goods.**—

(1) Acceptance of goods occurs when the buyer

(a) after a reasonable opportunity to inspect the goods signifies to the seller that the goods are conforming or that he will take or retain them in spite of their non-conformity; or

(b) fails to make an effective rejection (subsection (1) of Section 2-602), but such acceptance does not occur until the buyer has had a reasonable opportunity to inspect them; or

(c) does any act inconsistent with the seller's ownership; but if such act is wrongful as against the seller it is an acceptance only if ratified by him.

(2) Acceptance of a part of any commercial unit is acceptance of that entire unit.

§ 2-607. Effect of Acceptance; Notice of Breach; Burden of Establishing Breach After Acceptance; Notice of Claim or Litigation to Person Answerable Over.—

(1) The buyer must pay at the contract rate for any goods accepted.

(2) Acceptance of goods by the buyer precludes rejection of the goods accepted and if made with knowledge of a nonconformity cannot be revoked because of it unless the acceptance was on the reasonable assumption that the non-conformity would be seasonably cured but acceptance does not of itself impair any other remedy provided by this Article for non-conformity.

(3) Where a tender has been accepted

(a) the buyer must within a reasonable time after he discovers or should have discovered any breach notify the seller of breach or be barred from any remedy; and

(b) if the claim is one for infringement or the like (subsection (3) of Section 2-312) and the buyer is sued as a result of such a breach he must so notify the seller within a reasonable time after he receives notice of the litigation or be barred from any remedy over for liability established by the litigation.

(4) The burden is on the buyer to establish any breach with respect to the goods accepted.

(5) Where the buyer is sued for breach of a warranty or other obligation for which his seller is answerable over

(a) he may give his seller written notice of the litigation. If the notice states that the seller may come in and defend and that if the seller does not do so he will be bound in any action against him by his buyer by any determination of fact common to the two litigations, then unless the seller after seasonable receipt of the notice does come in and defend he is so bound.

(b) if the claim is one for infringement or the like (subsection (3) of Section 2-312) the original seller may demand in writing that his buyer turn over to him control of the litigation including settlement or else be barred from any remedy over and if he also agrees to bear all expense and to satisfy any adverse judgment, then unless the buyer after seasonable receipt of the demand does turn over control the buyer is so barred.

(6) The provisions of subsections (3), (4) and (5) apply to any obligation of a buyer to hold the seller harmless against infringement or the like (subsection (3) of Section 2-312).

§ 2-608. Revocation of Acceptance in Whole or in Part.—

(1) The buyer may revoke his acceptance of a lot or commercial unit whose non-conformity substantially impairs its value to him if he has accepted it

(a) on the reasonable assumption that its non-conformity would be cured and it has not been seasonably cured; or

(b) without discovery of such nonconformity if his acceptance was reasonably induced either by the difficulty of discovery before acceptance or by the seller's assurances.

(2) Revocation of acceptance must occur within a reasonable time after the buyer discovers or should have discovered the ground for it and before any substantial change in condition of the goods which is not caused by their own defects. It is not effective until the buyer notifies the seller of it.

(3) A buyer who so revokes has the same rights and duties with regard to the goods involved as if he had rejected them.

§ 2-609. Right to Adequate Assurance of Performance.—

(1) A contract for sale imposes an obligation on each party that the other's expectation of receiving due performance will not be impaired. When reasonable grounds for insecurity arise with respect to the performance of either party the other may in writing demand adequate assurance of due performance and until he receives such assurance may if commercially reasonable suspend any performance for which he has not already received the agreed return.

(2) Between merchants the reasonableness of grounds for insecurity and the adequacy of any assurance offered shall be determined according to commercial standards.

(3) Acceptance of any improper delivery or payment does not prejudice the aggrieved party's right to demand adequate assurance of future performance.

(4) After receipt of a justified demand failure to provide within a reasonable time not exceeding thirty days such assurance of due performance as is adequate under the circumstances of the particular case is a repudiation of the contract.

§ 2-610. Anticipatory Repudiation.—When either party repudiates the contract with respect to a performance not yet due the loss of which will substantially impair the value of the contract to the other, the aggrieved party may

(a) for a commercially reasonable time await performance by the repudiating party; or

(b) resort to any remedy for breach (Section 2-703 or Section 2-711), even though he has notified the repudiating party that he would await the latter's performance and has urged retraction; and

(c) in either case suspend his own performance or proceed in accordance with the provisions of this Article on the seller's right to identify goods to the contract notwithstanding breach or to salvage unfinished goods (Section 2-704).

§ 2-611. Retraction of Anticipatory Repudiation.—

(1) Until the repudiating party's next performance is due he can retract his repudiation unless the aggrieved party has since the repudiation cancelled or materially changed his position or otherwise indicated that he considers the repudiation final.

(2) Retraction may be by any method which clearly indicates to the aggrieved party that the repudiating party intends to perform, but must include any assurance justifiably demanded under the provisions of this Article (Section 2-609).

(3) Retraction reinstates the repudiating party's rights under the contract with due excuse and allowance to the aggrieved party for any delay occasioned by the repudiation.

§ 2-612. "Installment Contract"; Breach.—

(1) An "installment contract" is one which requires or authorizes the delivery of goods in separate lots to be separately accepted, even though the contract contains a clause "each delivery is a separate contract" or its equivalent.

(2) The buyer may reject any installment which is non-conforming if the nonconformity substantially impairs the value of that installment and cannot be cured or if the non-conformity is a defect in the required documents; but if the non-conformity does not fall within subsection (3) and the seller gives adequate assurance of its cure the buyer must accept that installment.

(3) Whenever non-conformity or default with respect to one or more installments substantially impairs the value of the whole contract there is a breach of the whole. But the aggrieved party reinstates the contract if he accepts a non-conforming installment without seasonably notifying of cancellation or if he brings an action with respect only to past installments or demands performance as to future installments.

§ 2-613. Casualty to Identified Goods.—

Where the contract requires for its performance goods identified when the contract is made, and the goods suffer casualty without fault of either party before the risk of loss passes to the buyer, or in a proper case under a "no arrival, no sale" term (Section 2-324) then

(a) if the loss is total the contract is avoided; and

(b) if the loss is partial or the goods have so deteriorated as no longer to conform to the contract the buyer may nevertheless demand inspection and at his option either treat the contract as avoided or accept the goods with due allowance from the contract price for the deterioration or the deficiency in quantity but without further right against the seller.

§ 2-614. Substituted Performance.—

(1) Where without fault of either party the agreed berthing, loading, or unloading facilities fail or an agreed type of carrier becomes unavailable or the agreed manner of delivery otherwise becomes commercially impracticable but a commercially reasonable substitute is available, such substitute performance must be tendered and accepted.

(2) If the agreed means or manner of payment fails because of domestic or foreign governmental regulation, the seller may withhold or stop delivery unless the buyer provides a means or manner of payment which is commercially a substantial equivalent. If delivery has already been taken, payment by the means or in the manner provided by the regulation discharges the buyer's obligation unless the regulation is discriminatory, oppressive or predatory.

§ 2-615. Excuse by Failure of Presupposed Conditions.—

Except so far as a seller may have assumed a greater obligation and subject to the preceeding section on substituted performance:

(a) Delay in delivery or non-delivery in whole or in part by a seller who complies with paragraphs (b) and (c) is not a breach of his duty under a contract for sale if performance as agreed has been made impracticable by the occurrence of a contingency the non-occurrence of which was a basic assumption on which the contract was made or by compliance in good faith with any applicable foreign or domestic governmental regulation or order whether or not it later proves to be invalid.

(b) Where the causes mentioned in paragraph (a) affect only a part of the seller's capacity to perform, he must allocate production and deliveries among his customers but may at his option include regular customers not then under contract as well as his own requirements for further manufacture. He may so allocate in any manner which is fair and reasonable.

(c) The seller must notify the buyer seasonably that there will be delay or non-delivery and, when allocation is required under paragraph (b), of the estimated quota this made available for the buyer.

§ 2-616. Procedure on Notice Claiming Excuse.—

(1) Where the buyer receives notification of a material or indefinite delay or an allocation justified under the preceding section he may by written notification to the seller as to any delivery concerned, and where the prospective deficiency substantially impairs the value of the whole contract under the provisions of this Article relating to breach of installment contracts (Section 2-612), then also as to the whole,

(a) terminate and thereby discharge any unexecuted portion of the contract; or

(b) modify the contract by agreeing to take his available quota in substitution.

(2) If after receipt of such notification from the seller the buyer fails so to modify the contract within a reasonable time not exceeding thirty days the contract lapses with respect to any deliveries affected.

(3) The provisions of this section may not be negated by agreement except in so far as the seller has assumed a greater obligation under the preceding section.

PART 7

Remedies

§ 2-701. Remedies for Breach of Collateral Contracts Not Impaired.—

Remedies for breach of any obligation or promise collateral or ancillary to a contract for sale are not impaired by the provisions of this Article.

§ 2-702. Seller's Remedies on Discovery of Buyer's Insolvency.—

(1) Where the seller discovers the buyer to be insolvent he may refuse delivery except for cash including payment for all goods theretofore delivered under the contract, and stop delivery under this Article (Section 2-705).

(2) Where the seller discovers that the buyer has received goods on credit while insolvent he may reclaim the goods upon demand made within ten days after the receipt, but if misrepresentation of solvency has been made to the particular seller in writing within three months before delivery the ten day limitation does not apply. Except as provided in this subsection the seller may not base a right to reclaim goods on the buyer's fraudulent or innocent misrepresentation of solvency or of intent to pay.

(3) The seller's right to reclaim under subsection (2) is subject to the rights of a buyer in ordinary course or other good faith purchaser or lien creditor under this Article (Section 2-403). Successful reclamation of goods excludes all other remedies with respect to them.

§ 2-703. Seller's Remedies in General.—Where the buyer wrongfully rejects or revokes acceptance of goods or fails to make a payment due on or before delivery or repudiates with respect to a part or the whole, then with respect to any goods directly affected and, if the breach is of the whole contract (Section 2-612), then also with respect to the whole undelivered balance, the aggrieved seller may

(a) withhold delivery of such goods;

(b) stop delivery by any bailee as hereafter provided (Section 2-705);

(c) proceed under the next section respecting goods still unidentified to the contract;

(d) resell and recover damages as hereafter provided (Section 2-706);

(e) recover damages for non-acceptance (Section 2-708) or in a proper case the price (Section 2-709);

(f) cancel.

§ 2-704. Seller's Right to Identify Goods to the Contract Notwithstanding Breach or to Salvage Unfinished Goods.—

(1) An aggrieved seller under the preceding section may

(a) identify to the contract conforming goods not already identified if at the time he learned of the breach they are in his possession or control;

(b) treat as the subject of resale goods which have demonstrably been intended for the particular contract even though those goods are unfinished.

(2) Where the goods are unfinished an aggrieved seller may in the exercise of reasonable commercial judgment for the purposes of avoiding loss and of effective realization either complete the manufacture and wholly identify the goods to the contract or cease manufacture and resell for scrap or salvage value or proceed in any other reasonable manner.

§ 2-705. Seller's Stoppage of Delivery in Transit or Otherwise.—

(1) The seller may stop delivery of goods in the possession of a carrier or other bailee when he discovers the buyer to be insolvent (Section 2-702) and may stop delivery of carload, truckload, planeload or larger shipments of express or freight when the buyer repudiates or fails to make a payment due before delivery or if for any other reason the seller has a right to withhold or reclaim the goods.

(2) As against such buyer the seller may stop delivery until

(a) receipt of the goods by the buyer; or

(b) acknowledgment to the buyer by any bailee of the goods except a carrier that the bailee holds the goods by the buyer; or

(c) such acknowledgment to the buyer by a carrier by reshipment or as warehouseman; or

(d) negotiation to the buyer of any negotiable document of title covering the goods.

(3) (a) To stop delivery the seller must so notify as to enable the bailee by reasonable diligence to prevent delivery of the goods.

(b) After such notification the bailee must hold and deliver the goods according to the directions of the seller but the seller is liable to the bailee for any ensuing charges or damages.

(c) If a negotiable document of title has been issued for goods the bailee is not obliged to obey a notification to stop until surrender of the document.

(d) A carrier who has issued a non-negotiable bill of lading is not obliged to obey a notification to stop received from a person other than the consignor.

§ 2-706. Seller's Resale Including Contract for Resale.—

(1) Under the conditions stated in Section 2-703 on seller's remedies, the seller may resell the goods concerned or the undelivered balance thereof. Where the resale is made in good faith and in a commercially reasonable manner the seller may recover the difference between the resale price and the contract price together with any incidental damages allowed under the provisions of this Article (Section 2-710), but less expenses saved in consequence of the buyer's breach.

(2) Except as otherwise provided in subsection (3) or unless otherwise agreed resale may be at public or private sale including sale by way of one or more contracts to sell or of identification to an existing contract of the seller. Sale may be as a unit or in parcels and at any time and place and on any terms but every aspect of the sale including the method, manner, time, place and terms must be commercially reasonable. The resale must be reasonably identified as referring to the broken contract, but it is not necessary that the goods be in existence or that any or all of them have been identified to the contract before the breach.

(3) Where the resale is at private sale the seller must give the buyer reasonable notification of his intention to resell.

(4) Where the resale is at public sale

(a) only identified goods can be sold except where there is a recognized market for a public sale of futures in goods of the kind; and

(b) it must be made at a usual place or market for public sale if one is reasonably available and except in the case of goods which are perishable or threaten to decline in value speedily the seller must give the buyer reasonable notice of the time and place of the resale; and

(c) if the goods are not to be within the view of those attending the sale the notification of sale must state the place where the goods are located and provide for their reasonable inspection by prospective bidders; and

(d) the seller may buy.

(5) A purchaser who buys in good faith at a resale takes the goods free of any rights of the original buyer even though the seller fails to comply with one or more of the requirements of this section.

(6) The seller is not accountable to the buyer for any profit made on any resale. A person in the position of a seller (Section 2-707) or a buyer who has rightfully rejected or justifiably revoked acceptance must account for any excess over the amount of his security interest, as hereinafter defined (subsection (3) of Section 2-711).

§ 2-707. "Person in the Position of a Seller."—

(1) A "person in the position of a seller" includes as against a principal an agent who has paid or become responsible for the price of goods on behalf of his principal or anyone who otherwise holds a security interest or other right in goods similar to that of a seller.

(2) A person in the position of a seller may as provided in this Article withhold or stop delivery (Section 2-705) and resell (Section 2-706) and recover incidental damages (Section 2-710).

§ 2-708. Seller's Damages for Nonacceptance or Repudiation.—

(1) Subject to subsection (2) and to the provisions of this Article with respect to proof of market price (Section 2-723), the measure of damages for non-acceptance or repudiation by the buyer is the difference between the market price at the time and place for tender and the unpaid contract price together with any incidental damages provided in this Article (Section 2-710), but less expenses saved in consequence of the buyer's breach.

(2) If the measure of damages provided in subsection (1) is inadequate to put the seller in as good a position as performance would have done then the measure of damages is the profit (including reasonable overhead) which the seller would have made from full performance by the buyer, together with any incidental damages provided in this Article (Section 2-710), due allowance for costs reasonably incurred and due credit for payments or proceeds of resale.

§ 2-709. Action for the Price.—

(1) When the buyer fails to pay the price as it becomes due the seller may recover, together with any incidental damages under the next section, the price

(a) of goods accepted or of conforming goods lost or damaged within a commercially reasonable time after risk of their loss has passed to the buyer; and

(b) of goods identified to the contract if the seller is unable after reasonable effort to resell them at a reasonable price or the circumstances reasonably indicate that such effort will be unavailing.

(2) Where the seller sues for the price he must hold for the buyer any goods which have been identified to the contract and are still in his control except that if resale becomes possible he may resell them at any time prior to the collection of the judgment. The net proceeds of any such resale must be credited to the buyer and payment of the judgment entitles him to any goods not resold.

(3) After the buyer has wrongfully rejected or revoked acceptance of the goods or has failed to make a payment due or has repudiated (Section 2-610), a seller who is held and entitled to the price under this section shall nevertheless be awarded damages for non-acceptance under the preceding section.

§ 2-710. Seller's Incidental Damages.—

Incidental damages to an aggrieved seller include any commercially reasonable charges, expenses or commissions incurred in stopping delivery, in the transportation, care and custody of goods after the buyer's breach, in connection with return or resale of the goods or otherwise resulting from the breach.

§ 2-711. Buyer's Remedies in General, Buyer's Security Interest in Rejected Goods.—

(1) Where the seller fails to make delivery or repudiates or the buyer rightfully rejects or justifiably revokes acceptance then with respect to any goods involved, and with respect to the whole if the breach goes to the whole contract (Section 2-612), the buyer may cancel and whether or not he has done so may in addition to recovering so much of the price as has been paid

(a) "cover" and have damages under the next section as to all the goods affected whether or not they have been identified to the contract; or

(b) recover damages for non-delivery as provided in this Article (Section 2-713).

(2) Where the seller fails to deliver or repudiates the buyer may also

(a) if the goods have been identified recover them as provided in this Article (Section 2-502); or

(b) in a proper case obtain specific performance or replevy the goods as provided in this Article (Section 2-716).

(3) On rightful rejection or justifiable revocation of acceptance a buyer has a security interest in goods in his possession or control for any payments made on their price and any expenses reasonably incurred in their inspection, receipt, transportation, care and custody and may hold such goods and resell them in like manner as an aggrieved seller (Section 2-706).

§ 2-712. "Cover"; Buyer's Procurement of Substitute Goods.—

(1) After a breach within the preceding section the buyer may "cover" by making in good faith and without unreasonable delay any reasonable purchase of or contract to purchase goods in substitution for those due from the seller.

(2) The buyer may recover from the seller as damages the difference between the cost of cover and the contract price together with any incidental or consequential damages as hereinafter defined (Section 2-715), but less expenses saved in consequence of the seller's breach.

(3) Failure of the buyer to effect cover within this section does not bar him from any other remedy.

§ 2-713. Buyer's Damages for Non-Delivery or Repudiation.—

(1) Subject to the provisions of this Article with respect to proof of market price (Section 2-723), the measure of damages for non-delivery or repudiation by the seller is the difference between the market price at the time when the buyer learned of the breach and the contract price together with any incidental and consequential damages provided in this Article (Section 2-715), but less expenses saved in consequence of the seller's breach.

(2) Market price is to be determined as of the place for tender or, in cases of rejection after arrival or revocation of acceptance, as of the place of arrival.

§ 2-714. Buyer's Damages for Breach in Regard to Accepted Goods.—

(1) Where the buyer has accepted goods and given notification (subsection (3) of Section 2-607) he may recover as damages for any non-conformity of tender the loss resulting in the ordinary course of events from the seller's breach as determined in any manner which is reasonable.

(2) The measure of damages for breach of warranty is the difference at the time and place of acceptance between the value of the goods accepted and the value they would have had if they had been as warranted, unless special circumstances show proximate damages of a different amount.

(3) In a proper case any incidental and consequential damages under the next section may also be recovered.

§ 2-715. Buyer's Incidental and Consequential Damages.—

(1) Incidental damages resulting from the seller's breach include expenses reasonably incurred in inspection, receipt, transportation and care and custody of goods rightfully rejected, and any commercially reasonable charges, expenses or commissions in connection with effecting cover and any other reasonable expense incident to the delay or other breach.

(2) Consequential damages resulting from the seller's breach include

(a) any loss resulting from general or particular requirements and needs of which the seller at the time of contracting had reason to know and which could not reasonably be prevented by cover or otherwise; and

(b) injury to person or property proximately resulting from any breach of warranty.

§ 2-716. Buyer's Right to Specific Performance or Replevin.—

(1) Specific performance may be decreed where the goods are unique or in other proper circumstances.

(2) The decree for specific performance may include such terms and conditions as to payment of the price, damages, or other relief as the court may deem just.

§ 2-717. Deduction of Damages From the Price.—

The buyer on notifying the seller of his intention to do so may deduct all or any part of the damages resulting from any breach of the contract from any part of the price still due under the same contract.

§ 2-718. Liquidation or Limitation of Damages; Deposits.—

(1) Damages for breach by either party may be liquidated in the agreement but only at an amount which is reasonable in the light of the anticipated or actual harm caused by the breach, the difficulties of proof of loss, and the inconvenience or nonfeasibility of otherwise obtaining an adequate remedy. A term fixing unreasonably large liquidated damages is void as a penalty.

(2) Where the seller justifiably withholds delivery of goods because of the buyer's breach, the buyer is entitled to restitution of any amount by which the sum of his payments exceeds

(a) The amount to which the seller is entitled by virtue of terms liquidating the seller's damages in accordance with subsection (1), or

(b) in the absence of such terms, twenty per cent of the value of the total performance for which the buyer is obligated under the contract or $500, whichever is smaller.

(3) The buyer's right to restitution under subsection (2) is subject to offset to the extent that the seller establishes

(a) a right to recover damages under the provisions of this Article other than subsection (1), and

(b) the amount or value of any benefits received by the buyer directly or indirectly by reason of the contract.

(4) Where a seller has received payment in goods their reasonable value or the proceeds of their resale shall be treated as payments for the purposes of subsection (2); but if the seller has notice of the buyer's breach before reselling goods received in part performance, his resale is subject to the conditions laid down in this Article on resale by an aggrieved seller (Section 2-706).

§ 2-719. Contractual Modification or Limitation of Remedy.—

(1) Subject to the provisions of subsections (2) and (3) of this section and of the preceding section on liquidation and limitation of damages,

(a) the agreement may provide for remedies in addition to or in substitution for those provided in this Article and may limit or alter the measure of damages recoverable under this Article, as by limiting the buyer's remedies to return of the goods and repayment of the price or to repair and replacement of non-conforming goods or parts; and

(b) resort to a remedy as provided is optional unless the remedy is expressly agreed to be exclusive, in which case it is the sole remedy.

(2) Where circumstances cause an exclusive or limited remedy to fail of its essential purpose, remedy may be had as provided in this Act.

(3) Consequential damages may be limited or excluded unless the limitation or exclusion is unconscionable. Limitation of consequential damages for injury to the person in the case of consumer goods is prima facie unconscionable but limitation of damages where the loss is commercial is not.

§ **2-720. Effect of "Cancellation" or "Rescission" on Claims for Antecedent Breach.**—Unless the contrary intention clearly appears, expressions of "cancellation" or "rescission" of the contract or the like shall not be construed as a renunciation or discharge of any claim in damages for an antecedent breach.

§ **2-721. Remedies for Fraud.**—Remedies for material misrepresentation or fraud include all remedies available under this Article for non-fraudulent breach. Neither rescission or a claim for rescission of the contract for sale nor rejection or return of the goods shall bar or be deemed inconsistent with a claim for damages or other remedy.

§ **2-722. Who Can Sue Third Parties for Injury to Goods.**—Where a third party so deals with goods which have been identified to a contract for sale as to cause actionable injury to a party to that contract

(a) a right of action against the third party is in either party to the contract for sale who has title to or a security interest or a special property or an insurable interest in the goods; and if the goods have been destroyed or converted a right of action is also in the party who either bore the risk of loss under the contract for sale or has since the injury assumed that risk as against the other;

(b) if at the time of the injury the party plaintiff did not bear the risk of loss as against the other party to the contract for sale and there is no arrangement between them for disposition of the recovery, his suit or settlement is, subject to his own interest, as a fiduciary for the other party to the contract;

(c) either party may with the consent of the other sue for the benefit of whom it may concern.

§ **2-723. Proof of Market Price: Time and Place.**—

(1) If an action based on anticipatory repudiation comes to trial before the time for performance with respect to some or all of the goods, any damages based on market price (Section 2-708 or Section 2-713) shall be determined according to the price of such goods prevailing at the time when the aggrieved party learned of the repudiation.

(2) If evidence of a price prevailing at the times or places described in this Article is not readily available the price prevailing within any reasonable time before or after the time described or at any other place which in commercial judgment or under usage of trade would serve as a reasonable substitute for the one described may be used, making any proper allowance for the cost of transporting the goods to or from such other place.

(3) Evidence of a relevant price prevailing at a time or place other than the one described in this Article offered by one party is not admissible unless and until he has given the other party such notice as the court finds sufficient to prevent unfair surprise.

§ **2-724. Admissibility of Market Quotations.**—Whenever the prevailing price or value of any goods regularly bought and sold in any established commodity market is in issue, reports in official publications or trade journals or in newspapers or periodicals of general circulation published as the reports of such market shall be admissible in evidence. The circumstances of the preparation of such a report may be shown to affect its weight but not its admissibility.

§ **2-725. Statute of Limitations in Contracts for Sale.**—

(1) An action for breach of any contract for sale must be commenced within four years after the cause of action has accrued. By the original agreement the parties may reduce the period of limitation to not less than one year but may not extend it.

(2) A cause of action accrues when the breach occurs, regardless of the aggrieved party's lack of knowledge of the breach. A breach of warranty occurs when tender of delivery is made, except that where a warranty explicitly extends to future performance of the goods and discovery of the breach must await the time of such performance the cause of action accrues when the breach is or should have been discovered.

(3) Where an action commenced within the time limited by subsection (1) is so terminated as to leave available a remedy by another action for the same breach such other action may be commenced after the expiration of the time limited and within six months after the termination of the first action unless the termination resulted from voluntary discontinuance or from dismissal for failure or neglect to prosecute.

(4) This section does not alter the law on tolling of the statute of limitations nor does it apply to causes of action which have accrued before this Act becomes effective.

ARTICLE THREE—COMMERCIAL PAPER

PART 1

Short Title, Form and Interpretation

§ **3-101. Short Title.**—This Article shall be known and may be cited as Uniform Commercial Code—Commercial Paper.

§ **3-102. Definitions and Index of Definitions.**—

(1) In this Article unless the context otherwise requires

(a) "Issue" means the first delivery of an instrument to a holder or a remitter.

(b) An "order" is a direction to pay and must be more than an authorization or request. It must identify the person to pay with reasonable certainty. It may be addressed to one or more such persons jointly or in the alternative but not in succession.

(c) A "promise" is an undertaking to pay and must be more than an acknowledgment of an obligation.

(d) "Secondary party" means a drawer or endorser.

(e) "Instrument" means a negotiable instrument. . . .

§ 3-103. Limitations on Scope of Article.—

(1) This Article does not apply to money, documents of title or investment securities.

(2) The provisions of this Article are subject to the provisions of the Article on Bank Deposits and Collections (Article 4) and Secured Transactions (Article 9).

§ 3-104. Form of Negotiable Instruments; "Draft"; "Check"; "Certificate of Deposit"; "Note."—

(1) Any writing to be a negotiable instrument within this Article must

(a) be signed by the maker or drawer; and

(b) contain an unconditional promise or order to pay a sum certain in money and no other promise, order, obligation or power given by the maker or drawer except as authorized by this Article; and

(c) be payable on demand or at a definite time; and

(d) be payable to order or to bearer.

(2) A writing which complies with the requirements of this section is

(a) a "draft" ("bill of exchange") if it is an order;

(b) a "check" if it is a draft drawn on a bank and payable on demand;

(c) a "certificate of deposit" if it is an acknowledgment by a bank of receipt of money with an engagement to repay it;

(d) a "note" if it is a promise other than a certificate of deposit.

(3) As used in other Articles of this Act, and as the context may require, the terms "draft", "check", "certificate of deposit" and "note" may refer to instruments which are not negotiable within this Article as well as to instruments which are so negotiable.

§ 3-105. When Promise or Order Unconditional.—

(1) A promise or order otherwise unconditional is not made conditional by the fact that the instrument

(a) is subject to implied or constructive conditions; or

(b) states its consideration, whether performed or promised, or the transaction which gave rise to the instrument, or that the promise or order is made or the instrument matures in accordance with or "as per" such transaction; or

(c) refers to or states that it arises out of a separate agreement; or

(d) states that it is drawn under a letter of credit; or

(e) states that it is secured, whether by mortgage, reservation of title or otherwise; or

(f) indicates a particular account to be debited or any other fund or source from which reimbursement is expected; or

(g) is limited to payment out of a particular fund or the proceeds of a particular source, if the instrument is issued by a government or governmental agency or unit; or

(h) is limited to payment out of the entire assets of a partnership, unincorporated association, trust or estate by or on behalf of which the instrument is issued.

(2) A promise or order is not unconditional if the instrument

(a) states that it is subject to or governed by any other agreement; or

(b) states that it is to be paid only out of a particular fund or source except as provided in this Section.

§ 3-106. Sum Certain.—

(1) The sum payable is a sum certain even though it is to be paid

(a) with stated interest or by stated installments; or

(b) with stated different rates of interest before and after default or a specified date; or

(c) with a stated discount or addition if paid before or after the date fixed for payment; or

(d) with exchange or less exchange, whether at a fixed rate or at the current rate; or

(e) with costs of collection or an attorney's fee or both upon default.

(2) Nothing in this Section shall validate any term which is otherwise illegal.

§ 3-107. Money.—

(1) An instrument is payable in money if the medium of exchange in which it is payable is money at the time the instrument is made. An instrument payable in "currency" or "current funds" is payable in money.

(2) A promise or order to pay a sum stated in a foreign currency is for a sum certain in money and, unless a different medium of payment is specified in the instrument, may be satisfied by payment of that number of dollars which the stated foreign currency will purchase at the buying sight rate for that currency on the day on which the instrument is payable or, if payable on demand, on the date of demand. If such an instrument specifies a foreign currency as the medium of payment the instrument is payable in that currency.

§ 3-108. Payable on Demand.—Instruments payable on demand include those payable at sight or on presentation and those in which no time for payment is stated.

§ 3-109. Definite Time.—

(1) An instrument is payable at a definite time if by its terms it is payable

(a) on or before a stated date or at a fixed period after a stated date; or

(b) at a fixed period after sight; or

(c) at a definite time subject to any acceleration; or

(d) at a definite time subject to extension at the option of the holder, or to extension to a further definite time at the option of the maker or acceptor or automatically upon or after a specified act or event.

(2) An instrument which by its terms is otherwise payable only upon an act or event uncertain as to time of occurrence is not payable at a definite time even though the act or event has occurred.

§ 3-110.   Payable to Order.—

(1) An instrument is payable to order when by its terms it is payable to the order or assigns of any person therein specified with reasonable certainty, or to him or his order, or when it is conspicuously designated on its face as "exchange" or the like and names a payee. It may be payable to the order of

(a) the maker or drawer; or

(b) the drawee; or

(c) A payee who is not maker, drawer or drawee; or

(d) two or more payees together or in the alternative; or

(e) an estate, trust or fund, in which case it is payable to the order of the representative of such estate, trust or fund or his successors; or

(f) an office, or an officer by his title as such in which case it is payable to the principal but the incumbent of the office or his successors may act as if he or they were the holder; or

(g) a partnership or unincorporated association, in which case it is payable to the partnership or association and may be indorsed or transferred by any person thereto authorized.

(2) An instrument not payable to order is not made so payable by such words as "payable upon return of this instrument properly indorsed."

(3) An instrument made payable both to order and to bearer is payable to order unless the bearer words are handwritten or typewritten.

§ 3-111.   Payable to Bearer.—An instrument is payable to bearer when by its terms it is payable to

(a) bearer or the order of bearer; or

(b) a specified person or bearer; or

(c) "cash" or the order of "cash", or any other indication which does not purport to designate a specific payee.

§ 3-112.   Terms and Omissions Not Affecting Negotiability.—

(1) The negotiability of an instrument is not affected by

(a) the omission of a statement of any consideration or of the place where the instrument is drawn or payable; or

(b) a statement that collateral has been given for the instrument or in case of default on the instrument the collateral may be sold; or

(c) a promise or power to maintain or protect collateral or to give additional collateral; or

(d) a term authorizing a confession of judgment on the instrument if it is not paid when due; or

(e) a term purporting to waive the benefit of any law intended for the advantage or protection of any obligor; or

(f) a term in a draft providing that the payee by indorsing or cashing it acknowledges full satisfaction of an obligation of the drawer; or

(g) a statement in a draft drawn in a set of parts (Section 3-801) to the effect that the order is effective only if no other part has been honored.

(2) Nothing in this Section shall validate any term which is otherwise illegal.

§ 3-113.   Seal.—An instrument otherwise negotiable is within this Article even though it is under a seal.

§ 3-114.   Date, Antedating, Postdating.—

(1) The negotiability of an instrument is not affected by the fact that it is undated, antedated or post-dated.

(2) Where an instrument is antedated or postdated the time when it is payable is determined by the stated date if the instrument is payable on demand or at a fixed period after date.

(3) Where the instrument or any signature thereon is dated, the date is presumed to be correct.

§ 3-115.   Incomplete Instruments.—

(1) When a paper whose contents at the time of signing show that it is intended to become an instrument is signed while still incomplete in any necessary respect it cannot be enforced until completed, but when it is completed in accordance with authority given it is effective as completed.

(2) If the completion is unauthorized the rules as to material alteration apply (Section 3-407), even though the paper was not delivered by the maker or drawer; but the burden of establishing that any completion is unauthorized is on the party so asserting.

§ 3-116.   Instruments Payable to Two or More Persons.—An instrument payable to the order of two or more persons

(a) if in the alternative is payable to any one of them and may be negotiated, discharged or enforced by any of them who has possession of it;

(b) if not in the alternative is payable to all of them and may be negotiated, discharged or enforced only by all of them.

§ 3-117.   Instruments Payable With Words of Description.—An instrument made payable to a named person with the addition of words describing him

(a) as agent or officer of a specified person is payable to his principal but the agent or officer may act as if he were the holder;

(b) as any other fiduciary for a specified person or purpose is payable to the payee and may be negotiated, discharged or enforced by him;

(c) in any other manner is payable to the payee unconditionally and the additional words are without effect on subsequent parties.

§ 3-118. Ambiguous Terms and Rules of Construction.—The following rules apply to every instrument:

(a) Where there is doubt whether the instrument is a draft or a note the holder may treat it as either. A draft drawn on the drawer is effective as a note.

(b) Handwritten terms control typewritten and printed terms, and typewritten control printed.

(c) Words control figures except that if the words are ambiguous figures control.

(d) Unless otherwise specified a provision for interest means interest at the judgment rate at the place of payment from the date of the instrument, or if it is undated from the date of issue.

(e) Unless the instrument otherwise specifies two or more persons who sign as maker, acceptor or drawer or indorser and as a part of the same transaction are jointly and severally liable even though the instrument contains such words as "I promise to pay."

(f) Unless otherwise specified consent to extension authorizes a single extension for not longer than the original period. A consent to extension, expressed in the instrument, is binding on secondary parties and accommodation makers. A holder may not exercise his option to extend an instrument over the objection of a maker or acceptor or other party who in accordance with Section 3-604 tenders full payment when the instrument is due.

§ 3-119. Other Writings Affecting Instrument.—

(1) As between the obligor and his immediate obligee or any transferee the terms of an instrument may be modified or affected by any other written agreement executed as a part of the same transaction, except that a holder in due course is not affected by any limitation of his rights arising out of the separate written agreement if he had no notice of the limitation when he took the instrument.

(2) A separate agreement does not affect the negotiability of an instrument.

§ 3-120. Instruments "Payable Through" Bank.—An instrument which states that it is "payable through" a bank or the like designates that bank as a collecting bank to make presentment but does not of itself authorize the bank to pay the instrument.

§ 3-121. Instruments Payable at Bank.—A note or acceptance which states that it is payable at a bank is not of itself an order or authorization to the bank to pay it.

§ 3-122. Accrual of Cause of Action.—

(1) A cause of action against a maker or an acceptor accrues

(a) in the case of a time instrument on the day after maturity;

(b) in the case of a demand instrument upon its date or, if no date is stated, on the date of issue.

(2) A cause of action against the obligor of a demand or time certificate of deposit accrues upon demand, but demand on a time certificate may not be made until on or after the date of maturity.

(3) A cause of action against a drawer of a draft or an indorser of any instrument accrues upon demand following dishonor of the instrument. Notice of dishonor is a demand.

(4) Unless an instrument provides otherwise, interest runs at the rate provided by law for a judgment

(a) in the case of a maker acceptor or other primary obligor of a demand instrument, from the date of demand;

(b) in all other cases from the date of accrual of the cause of action.

PART 2

Transfer and Negotiation

§ 3-201. Transfer: Right to Indorsement.—

(1) Transfer of an instrument vests in the transferee such rights as the transferor has therein, except that a transferee who has himself been a party to any fraud or illegality affecting the instrument or who as a prior holder had notice of a defense or claim against it cannot improve his position by taking from a later holder in due course.

(2) A transfer of a security interest in an instrument vests the foregoing rights in the transferee to the extent of the interest transferred.

(3) Unless otherwise agreed any transfer for value of an instrument not then payable to bearer gives the transferee the specifically enforceable right to have the unqualified indorsement of the transferor. Negotiation takes effect only when the indorsement is made and until that time there is no presumption that the transferee is the owner.

§ 3-202. Negotiation.—

(1) Negotiation is the transfer of an instrument in such form that the transferee becomes a holder. If the instrument is payable to order it is negotiated by delivery with any necessary indorsement; if payable to bearer it is negotiated by delivery.

(2) An indorsement must be written by or on behalf of the holder and on the instrument or on a paper so firmly affixed thereto as to become a part thereof.

(3) An indorsement is effective for negotiation only when it conveys the entire instrument or any unpaid residue. If it purports to be of less it operates only as a partial assignment.

(4) Words of assignment, condition, waiver, guaranty, limitation or disclaimer of liability and the like accompanying an indorsement do not affect its character as an indorsement.

§ **3-203. Wrong or Misspelled Name.**—Where an instrument is made payable to a person under a misspelled name or one other than his own he may indorse in that name or his own or both; but signature in both names may be required by a person paying or giving value for the instrument.

§ **3-204. Special Indorsement; Blank Indorsement.**—

(1) A special indorsement specifies the person to whom or to whose order it makes the instrument payable. Any instrument specially indorsed becomes payable to the order of the special indorsee and may be further negotiated only by his indorsement.

(2) An indorsement in blank specifies no particular indorsee and may consist of a mere signature. An instrument payable to order and indorsed in blank becomes payable to bearer and may be negotiated by delivery alone until specially indorsed.

(3) The holder may convert a blank indorsement into a special indorsement by writing over the signature of the indorser in blank any contract consistent with the character of the indorsement.

§ **3-205. Restrictive Indorsements.**—an indorsement is restrictive which either
    (a) is conditional; or
    (b) purports to prohibit further transfer of the instrument; or
    (c) includes the words "for collection", "for deposit", "pay any bank", or like terms signifying a purpose of deposit or collection; or
    (d) otherwise states that it is for the benefit or use of the indorser or of another person.

§ **3-206. Effect of Restrictive Indorsement.**—

(1) No restrictive indorsement prevents further transfer or negotiation of the instrument.

(2) An intermediary bank, or a payor bank which is not the depositary bank, is neither given notice nor otherwise affected by a restrictive indorsement of any person except the bank's immediate transferor or the person presenting for payment.

(3) Except for an intermediary bank, any transferee under an indorsement which is conditional or includes the words "for collection", "for deposit", "pay any bank", or like terms (subparagraphs (a) and (c) of Section 3-205) must pay or apply any value given by him for or on the security of the instrument consistently with the indorsement and to the extent that he does so he becomes a holder for value. In addition such transferee is a holder in due course if he otherwise complies with the requirements of Section 3-302 on what constitutes a holder in due course.

(4) The first taker under an indorsement for the benefit of the indorser or another person (subparagraph (d) of Section 3-205) must pay or apply any value given by him for or on the security of the instrument consistently with the indorsement and to the extent that he does so he becomes a holder for value. In addition such taker is a holder in due course if he otherwise complies with the requirements of Section 3-302 on what constitutes a holder in due course. A later holder for value is neither given notice nor otherwise affected by such restrictive indorsement unless he has knowledge that a fiduciary or other person has negotiated the instrument in any transaction for his own benefit or otherwise in breach of duty (subsection (2) of Section 3-304).

§ **3-207. Negotiation Effective Although It May Be Rescinded.**—

(1) Negotiation is effective to transfer the instrument although the negotiation is
    (a) made by an infant, a corporation exceeding its powers, or any other person without capacity; or
    (b) obtained by fraud, duress or mistake of any kind; or
    (c) part of an illegal transaction; or
    (d) made in breach of duty.

(2) Except as against a subsequent holder in due course such negotiation is in an appropriate case subject to rescission, the declaration of a constructive trust or any other remedy permitted by law.

§ **3-208. Reacquisition.**—Where an instrument is returned to or required by a prior party he may cancel any indorsement which is not necessary to his title and reissue or further negotiate the instrument, but any intervening party is discharged as against the reacquiring party and subsequent holders not in due course and if his indorsement has been cancelled is discharged as against subsequent holders in due course as well.

PART 3

Rights of a Holder

§ **3-301. Rights of a Holder.**—The holder of an instrument whether or not he is the owner may transfer or negotiate it and, except as otherwise provided in Section 3-603 on payment or satisfaction, discharge it or enforce payment in his own name.

§ **3-302. Holder in Due Course.**—

(1) A holder in due course is a holder who takes the instrument
    (a) for value; and
    (b) in good faith; and
    (c) without notice that it is overdue or has been dishonored or of any defense against or claim to it on the part of any person.

(2) A payee may be a holder in due course.

(3) A holder does not become a holder in due course of an instrument:

    (a) by purchase of it at judicial sale or by taking it under legal process; or

    (b) by acquiring it in taking over an estate; or

    (c) by purchasing it as part of a bulk transaction not in regular course of business of the transferor.

(4) A purchaser of a limited interest can be a holder in due course only to the extent of the interest purchased.

§ 3-303. Taking for Value.—A holder takes the instrument for value

    (a) to the extent that the agreed consideration has been performed or that he acquires a security interest in or a lien on the instrument otherwise than by legal process; or

    (b) when he takes the instrument in payment of or as security for an antecedent claim against any person whether or not the claim is due; or

    (c) when he gives a negotiable instrument for it or makes an irrevocable commitment to a third person.

§ 3-304. Notice to Purchaser.—

(1) The purchaser has notice of a claim or defense if

    (a) the instrument is so incomplete, bears such visible evidence of forgery or alteration, or is otherwise so irregular as to call into question its validity, terms or ownership or to create an ambiguity as to the party to pay; or

    (b) the purchaser has notice that the obligation of any party is voidable in whole or in part, or that all parties have been discharged.

(2) The purchaser has notice of a claim against the instrument when he has knowledge that a fiduciary has negotiated the instrument in payment of or as security for his own debt or in any transaction for his own benefit or otherwise in breach of duty.

(3) The purchaser has notice that an instrument is overdue if he has reason to know

    (a) that any part of the principal amount is overdue or that there is an uncured default in payment of another instrument of the same series; or

    (b) that acceleration of the instrument has been made; or

    (c) that he is taking a demand instrument after demand has been made or more than a reasonable length of time after its issue. A reasonable time for a check drawn and payable within the states and territories of the United States and the District of Columbia is presumed to be thirty days.

(4) Knowledge of the following facts does not of itself give the purchaser notice of a defense or claim

    (a) That the instrument is antedated or postdated;

    (b) that it was issued or negotiated in return for an executory promise or accompanied by a separate agreement, unless the purchaser has notice that a defense or claim has arisen from the terms thereof;

    (c) that any party has signed for accommodation;

    (d) that an incomplete instrument has been completed, unless the purchaser has notice of any improper completion;

    (e) that any person negotiating the instrument is or was a fiduciary;

    (f) that there has been default in payment of interest on the instrument or in payment of any other instrument, except one of the same series.

(5) The filing or recording of a document does not of itself constitute notice within the provisions of this Article to a person who would otherwise be a holder in due course.

(6) To be effective notice must be received at such time and in such manner as to give a reasonable opportunity to act on it.

§ 3-305. Rights of Holder in Due Course.—To the extent that a holder is a holder in due course he takes the instrument free from

(1) all claims to it on the part of any person; and

(2) all defenses of any party to the instrument with whom the holder has not dealt except

    (a) infancy, to the extent that it is a defense to a simple contract; and

    (b) such other incapacity, or duress, or illegality of the transaction, as renders the obligation of the party a nullity; and

    (c) such misrepresentation as has induced the party to sign the instrument with neither knowledge nor reasonable opportunity to obtain knowledge of its character or its essential terms; and

    (d) discharge in insolvency proceedings; and

    (e) any other discharge of which the holder has notice when he takes the instrument.

§ 3-306. Rights of One Not Holder in Due Course.—Unless he has the rights of a holder in due course any person takes the instrument subject to

    (a) all valid claims to it on the part of any person; and

    (b) all defenses of any party which would be available in an action on a simple contract; and

    (c) the defenses of want or failure of consideration, non-performance of any condition precedent, non-delivery, or delivery for a special purpose (Section 3-408); and

    (d) the defense that he or a person through whom he holds the instrument acquired it by theft, or that payment or satisfaction to such holder would be inconsistent with the terms of a restrictive indorsement. The claim of any third person to the instrument is not otherwise available as a defense to any party liable thereon unless the third person himself defends the action for such party.

§ 3-307. Burden of Establishing Signatures, Defenses and Due Course.—

(1) Unless specifically denied in the pleadings each signature on an instrument is admitted. When the

effectiveness of a signature is put in issue

(a) the burden of establishing it is on the party claiming under the signature; and

(b) the signature is presumed to be genuine or authorized except where the action is to enforce the obligation of a purported signer who has died or become incompetent before proof is required.

(2) When signatures are admitted or established, production of the instrument entitles a holder to recover on it unless the defendant establishes a defense.

(3) After it is shown that a defense exists a person claiming the rights of a holder in due course has the burden of establishing that he or some person under whom he claims is in all respects a holder in due course.

PART 4

Liability of Parties

§ **3-401. Signature.**—

(1) No person is liable on an instrument unless his signature appears thereon.

(2) A signature is made by use of any name, including any trade or assumed name, upon an instrument, or by any word or mark used in lieu of a written signature.

§ **3-402. Signature in Ambiguous Capacity.**—Unless the instrument clearly indicates that a signature is made in some other capacity it is an indorsement.

§ **3-403. Signature by Authorized Representative.**—

(1) A signature may be made by an agent or other representative, and his authority to make it may be established as in other cases of representation. No particular form of appointment is necessary to establish such authority.

(2) An authorized representative who signs his own name to an instrument

(a) is personally obligated if the instrument neither names the person represented nor shows that the representative signed in a representative capacity;

(b) except as otherwise established between the immediate parties, is personally obligated if instrument names the person represented but does not show that the representative signed in a representative capacity, or if the instrument does not name the person represented but does show that the representative signed in a representative capacity.

(3) Except as otherwise established the name of an organization preceded or followed by the name and office of an authorized individual is a signature made in a representative capacity.

§ **3-404. Unauthorized Signatures.**—

(1) Any unauthorized signature is wholly inoperative as that of the person whose name is signed unless he ratifies it or is precluded from denying it; but it operates as the signature of the unauthorized signer in favor of any person who in good faith pays the instrument or takes it for value.

(2) Any unauthorized signature may be ratified for all purposes of this Article. Such ratification does not of itself affect any rights of the person ratifying against the actual signer.

§ **3-405. Imposters; Signature in Name of Payee.**—

(1) An indorsement by any person in the name of a named payee is effective if

(a) an imposter by use of the mails or otherwise has induced the maker or drawer to issue the instrument to him or his confederate in the name of the payee; or

(b) a person signing as or on behalf of a maker or drawer intends the payee to have no interest in the instrument; or

(c) an agent or employee of the maker or drawer has supplied him with the name of the payee intending the latter to have no such interest.

(2) Nothing in this Section shall affect the criminal or civil liability of the person to indorsing.

§ **3-406. Negligence Contributing to Alteration or Unauthorized Signature.**—Any person who by his negligence substantially contributes to a material alteration of the instrument or to the making of an unauthorized signature is precluded from asserting the alteration or lack of authority against a holder in due course or against a drawee or other payor who pays the instrument in good faith and in accordance with the reasonable commercial standards of the drawee's or payor's business.

§ **3-407. Alteration.**—

(1) Any alteration of an instrument is material which changes the contract of any party thereto in any respect, including any such change in

(a) the number of relations of the parties; or

(b) an incomplete instrument, by completing it otherwise than as authorized; or

(c) the writing as signed, by adding to it or by removing any part of it.

(2) As against any person other than a subsequent holder in due course

(a) alteration by the holder which is both fraudulent and material discharges any party whose contract is thereby changed unless that party assents or is precluded from asserting the defense;

(b) no other alteration discharges any party and the instrument may be enforced according to its original tenor, or as to incomplete instruments according to the authority given.

(3) A subsequent holder in due course may in all cases enforce the instrument according to its original tenor, and when an incomplete instrument has been completed, he may enforce it as completed.

§ 3-408. Consideration.—Want or failure of consideration is a defense as against any person not having the rights of a holder in due course (Section 3-305), except that no consideration is necessary for an instrument or obligation thereon given in payment of or as security for an antecedent obligation of any kind. Nothing in this Section shall be taken to displace any statute outside this Act under which a promise is enforceable notwithstanding lack or failure of consideration. Partial failure of consideration is a defense pro tanto whether or not the failure is in an ascertained or liquidated amount.

§ 3-409. Draft Not an Assignment.—

(1) A check or other draft does not of itself operate as an assignment of any funds in the hands of the drawee available for its payment, and the drawee is not liable on the instrument until he accepts it.

(2) Nothing in this Section shall affect any liability in contract, tort or otherwise arising from any letter of credit or other obligation or representation which is not an acceptance.

§ 3-410. Definition and Operation of Acceptance.—

(1) Acceptance is the drawee's signed engagement to honor the draft as presented. It must be written on the draft, and may consist of his signature alone. It becomes operative when completed by delivery or notification.

(2) A draft may be accepted although it has not been signed by the drawer or is otherwise incomplete or is overdue or has been dishonored.

(3) Where the draft is payable at a fixed period after sight and the acceptor fails to date his acceptance the holder may complete it by supplying a date in good faith.

§ 3-411. Certification of a Check.—

(1) Certification of a check is acceptance. Where a holder procures certification the drawer and all prior indorsers are discharged.

(2) Unless otherwise agreed a bank has no obligation to certify a check.

(3) A bank may certify a check before returning it for lack of proper indorsement. If it does so the drawer is discharged.

§ 3-412. Acceptance Varying Draft.—

(1) Where the drawee's proffered acceptance in any manner varies the draft as presented the holder may refuse the acceptance and treat the draft as dishonored in which case the drawee is entitled to have his acceptance cancelled.

(2) The terms of the draft are not varied by an acceptance to pay at any particular bank or place in the continental United States, unless the acceptance states that the draft is to be paid only at such bank or place.

(3) Where the holder assents to an acceptance varying the terms of the draft each drawer and indorser who does not affirmatively assent is discharged.

§ 3-413. Contract of Maker, Drawer and Acceptor.—

(1) The maker or acceptor engages that he will pay the instrument according to its tenor at the time of his engagement or as completed pursuant to Section 3-115 on incomplete instruments.

(2) The drawer engages that upon dishonor of the draft and any necessary notice of dishonor or protest he will pay the amount of the draft to the holder or to any indorser who takes it up. The drawer may disclaim this liability by drawing without recourse.

(3) By making, drawing or accepting the party admits as against all subsequent parties including the drawee the existence of the payee and his then capacity to indorse.

§ 3-414. Contract of Indorser; Order of Liability.—

(1) Unless the indorsement otherwise specifies (as by such words as "without recourse") every indorser engages that upon dishonor and any necessary notice of dishonor and protest he will pay the instrument according to its tenor at the time of his indorsement to the holder or to any subsequent indorser who takes it up, even though the indorser who takes it up was not obligated to do so.

(2) Unless they otherwise agree indorsers are liable to one another in the order in which they indorse, which is presumed to be the order in which their signatures appear on the instrument.

§ 3-415. Contract of Accommodation Party.—

(1) An accommodation party is one who signs the instrument in any capacity for the purpose of lending his name to another party to it.

(2) When the instrument has been taken for value before it is due the accommodation party is liable in the capacity in which he has signed even though the taker knows of the accommodation.

(3) As against a holder in due course and without notice of the accommodation oral proof of the accommodation is not admissible to give the accommodation party the benefit of discharges dependent on his character as such. In other cases the accommodation character may be shown by oral proof.

(4) An indorsement which shows that it is not in the chain of title is notice of its accommodation character.

(5) An accommodation party is not liable to the party accommodated, and if he pays the instrument has a right of recourse on the instrument against such party.

§ 3-416. Contract of Guarantor.—

(1) "Payment guaranteed" or equivalent words added to a signature mean that the signer engages that if the instrument is not paid when due he will pay it according to its tenor without resort by the holder to any other party.

(2) "Collection guaranteed" or equivalent words added to a signature mean that the signer engages that if the instrument is not paid when due he will pay it according to its tenor, but only after the holder has reduced his claim against the maker or acceptor to judgment and execution has been returned unsatisfied, or

after the maker or acceptor has become insolvent or it is otherwise apparent that it is useless to proceed against him.

(3) Words of guaranty which do not otherwise specify guarantee payment.

(4) No words of guaranty added to the signature of a sole maker or acceptor affect his liability on the instrument. Such words added to the signature of one of two or more makers or acceptors create a presumption that the signature is for the accommodation of the others.

(5) When words of guaranty are used presentment, notice of dishonor and protest are not necessary to charge the user.

(6) Any guaranty written on the instrument is enforceable notwithstanding any statute of frauds.

§ 3-417.   Warranties on Presentment and Transfer.—

(1) Any person who obtains payment or acceptance and any prior transferor warrants to a person who in good faith pays or accepts that

(a) he has a good title to the instrument or is authorized to obtain payment of acceptance on behalf of one who has a good title; and

(b) he has no knowledge that the signature of the maker or drawer is unauthorized, except that this warranty is not given by a holder in due course acting in good faith

(i) To a maker with respect to the maker's own signature; or

(ii) To a drawer with respect to the drawer's own signature, whether or not the drawer is also the drawee; or

(iii) to an acceptor of a draft if the holder in due course took the draft after the acceptance or obtained the acceptance without knowledge that the drawer's signature was unauthorized; and

(c) the instrument has not been materially altered, except that this warranty is not given by a holder in due course acting in good faith

(i) to the maker of a note; or

(ii) To the drawer of a draft whether or not the drawer is also the drawee; or

(iii) to the acceptor of a draft with respect to an alteration made prior to the acceptance if the holder in due course took the draft after the acceptance, even though the acceptance provided "payable as originally drawn" or equivalent terms; or

(iv) to the acceptor of a draft with respect to an alteration made after the acceptance.

(2) Any person who transfers an instrument and receives consideration warrants to his transferee and if the transfer is by indorsement to any subsequent holder who takes the instrument in good faith that

(a) he has a good title to the instrument or is authorized to obtain payment or acceptance on behalf of one who has a good title and the transfer is otherwise rightful; and

(b) all signatures are genuine or authorized; and

(c) the instrument has not been materially altered; and

(d) no defense of any party is good against him; and

(e) he has no knowledge of any insolvency proceeding instituted with respect to the maker or acceptor or the drawer of an unaccepted instrument.

(3) By transferring "without recourse" the transferor limits the obligation stated in subsection (2) (d) to a warranty that he has no knowledge of such a defense.

(4) A selling agent or broker who does not disclose the fact that he is acting only as such gives the warranties provided in this Section, but if he makes such disclosure warrants only his good faith and authority.

§ 3-418.   Finality of Payment or Acceptance.—

Except for recovery of bank payments as provided in the Article on Bank Deposits and Collections (Article 4) and except for liability for breach of warranty on presentment under the preceding section, payment or acceptance of any instrument is final in favor of a holder in due course, or a person who has in good faith changed his position in reliance on the payment.

§ 3-419.   Conversion of Instrument; Innocent Representative.—

(1) An instrument is converted when

(a) a drawee to whom it is delivered for acceptance refuses to return it on demand; or

(b) any person to whom it is delivered for payment refuses on demand either to pay or to return it; or

(c) it is paid on a forged indorsement.

(2) In an action against a drawee under subsection (1) the measure of the drawee's liability is the face amount of the instrument. In any other action under subsection (1) the measure of liability is presumed to be the face amount of the instrument.

(3) Subject to the provisions of this Act concerning restrictive indorsements a representative, including a depositary or collecting bank, who has in good faith and in accordance with the reasonable commercial standards applicable to the business of such representative dealt with an instrument or its proceeds on behalf of one who was not the true owner is not liable in conversion or otherwise to the true owner beyond the amount of any proceeds remaining in his hands.

(4) An intermediary bank or payor bank which is not a depositary bank is not liable in conversion solely by reason of the fact that proceeds of an item indorsed restrictively (Section 3-205 and 3-206) are not paid or applied consistently with the restrictive indorsement of an indorser other than its immediate transferor.

PART 5

Presentment, Notice of Dishonor and Protest

§ 3-501.   When Presentment, Notice of Dishonor, and Protest Necessary or Permissible.—

(1) Unless excused (Section 3-511) presentment is necessary to charge secondary parties as follows:

(a) presentment for acceptance is necessary to charge the drawer and indorsers of a draft where the draft so provides, or is payable elsewhere than at the residence or place of business of the drawee, or its date of payment depends upon such presentment. The holder may at his option present for acceptance any other draft payable at a stated date;

(b) presentment for payment is necessary to charge any indorser;

(c) in the case of any drawer, the acceptor of a draft payable at a bank or the maker of a note payable at a bank, presentment for payment is necessary, but failure to make presentment discharges such drawer, acceptor or maker only as stated in Section 3-502 (1) (b).

(2) Unless excused (Section 3-511)

(a) notice of any dishonor is necessary to charge any indorser;

(b) in the case of any drawer, the acceptor of a draft payable at a bank or the maker of a note payable at a bank notice of any dishonor is necessary, but failure to give such notice discharges such drawer, acceptor or maker only as stated in Section 3-502 (1) (b).

(3) Unless excused (Section 3-511) protest of any dishonor is necessary to charge the drawer and indorsers of any draft which on its face appears to be drawn or payable outside of the states and territories of the United States and the District of Columbia. The holder may at his option make protest of any dishonor of any other instrument and in the case of a foreign draft may on insolvency of the acceptor before maturity make protest for better security.

(4) Notwithstanding any provision of this Section, neither presentment nor notice of dishonor nor protest is necessary to charge an indorser who has indorsed an instrument after maturity.

§ 3-502.   Unexcused Delay; Discharge.—

(1) Where without excuse any necessary presentment or notice of dishonor is delayed beyond the time when it is due

(a) Any indorser is discharged; and

(b) any drawer or the acceptor of a draft payable at a bank or the maker of a note payable at a bank who because the drawee or payor bank becomes insolvent during the delay is deprived of funds maintained with the drawee or payor bank to cover the instrument may discharge his liability by written assignment to the holder of his rights against the drawee or payor bank in respect of such funds, but such drawer, acceptor or maker is not otherwise discharged.

(2) Where without excuse a necessary protest is delayed beyond the time when it is due any drawer or indorser is discharged.

§ 3-503.   Time of Presentment.—

(1) Unless a different time is expressed in the instrument the time for any presentment is determined as follows:

(a) where an instrument is payable at or a fixed period after a stated date any presentment for acceptance must be made on or before the date it is payable;

(b) where an instrument is payable after sight it must either be presented for acceptance or negotiated within a reasonable time after date or issue whichever is later;

(c) where an instrument shows the date on which it is payable presentment for payment is due on that date;

(d) where an instrument is accelerated presentment for payment is due within a reasonable time after the acceleration;

(e) with respect to the liability of any secondary party presentment for acceptance or payment of any other instrument is due within a reasonable time after such party becomes liable thereon.

(2) A reasonable time for presentment is determined by the nature of the instrument, any usage of banking or trade and the facts of the particular case. In the case of an uncertified check which is drawn and payable within the United States and which is not a draft drawn by a bank the following are presumed to be reasonable periods within which to present for payment or to initiate bank collection:

(a) with respect to the liability of the drawer, thirty days after date or issue whichever is later; and

(b) with respect to the liability of an endorser, seven days after his indorsement.

(3) Where any presentment is due on a day which is not a full business day for either the person making presentment or the party to pay or accept, presentment is due on the next following day which is a full business day for both parties.

(4) Presentment to be sufficient must be made at a reasonable hour, and if at a bank during its banking day.

§ 3-504.   How Presentment Made.—

(1) Presentment is a demand for acceptance or payment made upon the maker, acceptor, drawee or other payor by or on behalf of the holder.

(2) Presentment may be made

(a) by mail, in which event the time of presentment is determined by the time of receipt of the mail; or

(b) through a clearing house; or

(c) at the place of acceptance or payment specified in the instrument or if there be none at the place of business or residence of the party to accept or pay. If neither the party to accept or pay nor anyone authorized to act for him is present or accessible at such place presentment is excused.

(3) It may be made

(a) to any one of two or more makers, acceptors, drawees or other payors; or

(b) to any person who has authority to make or refuse the acceptance or payment.

(4) A draft accepted or a note made payable at a bank in the continental United States must be presented at such bank.

(5) In the cases described in Section 4-210 presentment may be made in the manner and with the result stated in that section.

§ 3-505. Rights of Party to Whom Presentment is Made.—

(1) The party to whom presentment is made may without dishonor require

    (a) exhibition of the instrument; and

    (b) reasonable identification of the person making presentment and evidence of his authority to make it if made for another; and

    (c) that the instrument be produced for acceptance or payment at a place specified in it, or if there be none at any place reasonable in the circumstances; and

    (d) a signed receipt on the instrument for any partial or full payment and its surrender upon full payment.

(2) Failure to comply with any such requirements invalidates the presentment but the person presenting has a reasonable time in which to comply and the time for acceptance or payment runs from the time of compliance.

§ 3-506. Time Allowed for Acceptance or Payment.—

(1) Acceptance may be deferred without dishonor until the close of the next business day following presentment. The holder may also in a good faith effort to obtain acceptance and without either dishonor of the instrument or discharge of secondary parties allow postponement of acceptance for an additional business day.

(2) Except as longer time is allowed in the case of documentary drafts drawn under a letter of credit, and unless an earlier time is agreed to by the party to pay, payment of an instrument may be deferred without dishonor pending reasonable examination to determine whether it is properly payable, but payment must be made in any event before the close of business on the day of presentment.

§ 3-507. Dishonor; Holder's Right of Recourse; Term Allowing Re-Presentment.—

(1) An instrument is dishonored when

    (a) a necessary or optional presentment is duly made and due acceptance or payment is refused or cannot be obtained within the prescribed time or in case of bank collections the instrument is seasonably returned by the midnight deadline (Section 4-301); or

    (b) presentment is excused and the instrument is not duly accepted or paid.

(2) Subject to any necessary notice of dishonor and protest, the holder has upon dishonor an immediate right of recourse against the drawers and indorsers.

(3) Return of an instrument for lack of proper indorsement is not dishonor.

(4) A term in a draft or an indorsement thereof allowing a stated time for representment in the event of any dishonor of the draft by nonacceptance if a time draft or by nonpayment if a sight draft gives the holder as against any secondary party bound by the term an option to waive the dishonor without affecting the liability of the secondary party and he may present again up to the end of the stated time.

§ 3-508. Notice of Dishonor.—

(1) Notice of dishonor may be given to any person who may be liable on the instrument by or on behalf of the holder or any party who has himself received notice, or any other party who can be compelled to pay the instrument. In addition an agent or bank in whose hands the instrument is dishonored may give notice to his principal or customer or to another agent or bank from which the instrument was received.

(2) Any necessary notice must be given by a bank before its midnight deadline and by any other person before midnight of the third business day after dishonor or receipt of notice of dishonor.

(3) Notice may be given in any reasonable manner. It may be oral or written and in any terms which identify the instrument and state that it has been dishonored. A misdescription which does not mislead the party notified does not vitiate the notice. Sending the instrument bearing a stamp, ticket or writing stating that acceptance or payment has been refused or sending a notice of debit with respect to the instrument is sufficient.

(4) Written notice is given when sent although it is not received.

(5) Notice to one partner is notice to each although the firm has been dissolved.

(6) When any party is in insolvency proceedings instituted after the issue of the instrument notice may be given either to the party or to the representative of his estate.

(7) When any party is dead or incompetent notice may be sent to his last known address or given to his personal representative.

(8) Notice operates for the benefit of all parties who have rights on the instrument against the party notified.

§ 3-509. Protest; Noting for Protest.—

(1) A protest is a certificate of dishonor made under the hand and seal of a United States consul or vice consul or a notary public or other person authorized to certify dishonor by the law of the place where dishonor occurs. It may be made upon information satisfactory to such person.

(2) The protest must identify the instrument and certify either that due presentment has been made or the reason why it is excused and that the instrument has been dishonored by non-acceptance or nonpayment.

(3) The protest may also certify that notice of dishonor has been given to all parties or to specified parties.

(4) Subject to subsection (5) any necessary protest is due by the time that notice of dishonor is due.

(5) If, before protest is due, an instrument has been noted for protest by the officer to make protest, the protest may be made at any time thereafter as of the date of the noting.

§ 3-510. Evidence of Dishonor and Notice of Dishonor.—The following are admissable as evidence and create a presumption of dishonor and of any notice of dishonor therein shown:

    (a) a document regular in form as provided in the preceding section which purports to be a protest;

(b) the purported stamp or writing of the drawee, payor bank or presenting bank on the instrument or accompanying it stating that acceptance or payment has been refused for reasons consistent with dishonor;

(c) any book or record of the drawee, payor bank, or any collecting bank kept in the usual course of business which shows dishonor, even though there is no evidence of who made the entry.

§ 3-511.   Waived or Excused Presentment, Protest or Notice of Dishonor or Delay Therein.—

(1) Delay in presentment, protest or notice of dishonor is excused when the party is without notice that it is due or when the delay is caused by circumstances beyond his control and he exercises reasonable diligence after the cause of the delay ceases to operate.

(2) Presentment or notice or protest as the case may be is entirely excused when

(a) the party to be charged has waived it expressly or by implication either before or after it is due; or

(b) such party has himself dishonored the instrument or has countermanded payment or otherwise has no reason to expect or right to require that the instrument be accepted or paid; or

(c) by reasonable diligence the presentment or protest cannot be made of the notice given.

(3) Presentment is also entirely excused when

(a) the maker, acceptor or drawee of any instrument except a documentary draft is dead or in insolvency proceedings instituted after the issue of the instrument; or

(b) acceptance or payment is refused but not for want of proper presentment

(4) Where a draft has been dishonored by nonacceptance a later presentment for payment and any notice of dishonor and protest for nonpayment are excused unless in the meantime the instrument has been accepted.

(5) A waiver of protest is also a waiver of presentment and of notice of dishonor even though protest is not required.

(6) Where a waiver of presentment or notice of protest is embodied in the instrument itself it is binding upon all parties; but where it is written above the signature of an indorser it binds him only.

PART 6

Discharge

§ 3-601.   Discharge of Parties.—

The extent of the discharge of any party from liability on an instrument is governed by the sections on

(a) payment or satisfaction (Section 3-603); or

(b) tender of payment (Section 3-604); or

(c) cancellation or renunciation (Section 3-605); or

(d) impairment of right of recourse or of collateral (Section 3-606); or

(e) reacquisition of the instrument by a prior party (Seciton 3-208); or

(f) fraudulent and material alteration (Section 3-407); or

(g) certification of a check (Section 3-411); or

(h) acceptance varying a draft (Section 3-412); or

(i) unexcused delay in presentment or notice of dishonor or protest (Section 3-502).

(2) Any party is also discharged from his liability on an instrument to another party by any other act or agreement with such a party which would discharge his simple contract for the payment of money.

(3) The liability of all parties is discharged when any party who has himself no right of action or recourse on the instrument

(a) reacquires the instrument in his own right; or

(b) is discharged under any provisions of this Article, except as otherwise provided with respect to discharge for impairment of recourse or of collateral (Section 3-606).

§ 3-602.   Effects of Discharge Against Holder in Due Course.—No discharge of any party provided by this Article is effective against a subsequent holder in due course unless he has notice thereof when he takes the instrument.

§ 3-603.   Payment or Satisfaction.—

(1) The liability of any party is discharged to the extent of his payment or satisfaction to the holder even though it is made with knowledge of a claim of another person to the instrument unless prior to such payment or satisfaction the person making the claim either supplies indemnity deemed adequate by the party seeking the discharge or enjoins payment or satisfaction by order of a court of competent jurisdiction in an action in which the adverse claimant and the holder are parties. This subsection does not, however, result in the discharge of the liability

(a) of a party who in bad faith pays or satisfies a holder who acquired the instrument by theft or who (unless having the rights of a holder in due course) holds through one who so acquired it; or

(b) of a party (other than an intermediary bank or a payor bank which is not a depositary bank) who pays or satisfies the holder of an instrument which has been restrictively indorsed in a manner not consistent with the terms of such restrictive indorsement.

(2) Payment of satisfaction may be made with the consent of the holder by any person including a stranger to the instrument. Surrender of the instrument to such a person gives him the rights of a transferee (Section 3-201).

§ 3-604.   Tender of Payment.—

(1) Any party making tender of full payment to a holder when or after it is due is discharged to the extent

of all subsequent liability for interest, costs and attorney's fees.

(2) The holder's refusal of such tender wholly discharges any party who has a right of recourse against the party making the tender.

(3) Where the maker or acceptor of an instrument payable otherwise than on demand is able and ready to pay at every place of payment specified in the instrument when it is due, it is equivalent to tender.

§ 3-605. Cancellation and Renunciation.—

The holder of an instrument may even without consideration discharge any party

(a) in any manner apparent on the face of the instrument or the indorsement, as by intentially cancelling the instrument or the party's signature by destruction or mutilation, or by striking out the party's signature; or

(b) by renouncing his rights by a writing signed and delivered or by surrender of the instrument to the party to be discharged.

(2) Neither cancellation nor renunciation without surrender of the instrument affects the title thereto.

§ 3-606. Impairment of Recourse or of Collateral.—

(1) The holder discharges any party to the instrument to the extent that without such party's consent the holder

(a) without express reservation of rights releases or agrees not to sue any person against whom the party has to the knowledge of the holder a right of recourse or agrees to suspend the right to enforce against such person the instrument or collateral or otherwise discharges such person, except that failure or delay in effecting any required presentment, protest or notice of dishonor with respect to any such person does not discharge any party as to whom presentment, protest or notice of dishonor is effective or unnecessary; or

(b) unjustifiably impairs any collateral for the instrument given by or on behalf of the party or any person against whom he has a right of recourse.

(2) By express reservation of rights against a party with a right of recourse the holder preserves

(a) all his rights against such party as of the time when the instrument was originally due; and

(b) the right of the party to pay the instrument as of that time; and

(c) all rights of such party to recourse against others.

PART 7

Advice of International Sight Draft
(omitted)

PART 8

Miscellaneous

§ 3-801. omitted.

§ 3-802. Effect of Instrument on Obligation for Which It Is Given.—

(1) Unless otherwise agreed where an instrument is taken for an underlying obligation

(a) the obligation is pro tanto discharged if a bank is drawer, maker or acceptor of an instrument and there is no recourse on the instrument against the underlying obligor; and

(b) in any other case the obligation is suspended pro tanto until the instrument is due or if it is payable on demand until its presentment. If the instrument is dishonored action may be maintained on either the instrument or the obligation; discharge of the underlying obligor on the instrument also discharges him on the obligation.

(2) The taking in good faith of a check which is not postdated does not of itself so extend the time on the original obligation as to discharge a surety.

§ 3-803. Notice to Third Party.—Where a defendant is sued for breach of an obligation for which a third person is answerable over under this Article he may give the third person written notice of the litigation, and the person notified may then give similar notice to any other person who is answerable over to him under this Article. If the notice states that the person notified may come in and defend and that if the person notified does not do so he will in any action against him by the person giving the notice be bound by any determination of fact common to the two litigations, then unless after seasonable receipt of the notice the person notified does come in and defend he is so bound.

§ 3-804. Lost, Destroyed or Stolen Investments.—The owner of an instrument which is lost, whether by destruction, theft or otherwise, may maintain an action in his own name and recover from any party liable thereon upon due proof of his ownership, the facts which prevent his production of the instrument and its terms. The court may require security indemnifying defendant against loss by reason of further claims on the instrument.

§ 3-805. Instruments Not Payable to Order or to Bearer.—This Article applies to any instrument whose terms do not preclude transfer and which is otherwise negotiable within this Article but which is not payable to order or to bearer, except that there can be no holder in due course of such an instrument.

ARTICLE FOUR — BANK DEPOSITS AND COLLECTIONS

PART I

General Provisions and Definitions

§ 4-101.   Short Title.—This Article shall be known and may be cited as Uniform Commercial Code— Bank Deposits and Collections.

§ 4-102.   Applicability.—

(1) To the extent that items within this Article are also within the scope of Articles 3 and 8, they are subject to the provisions of those Articles. In the event of conflict the provisions of this Article govern those of Article 3 but the provisions of Article 8 govern those of this Article.

(2) The liability of a bank for action or non-action with respect to any item handled by it for purposes of presentment, payment or collection is governed by the law of the place where the bank is located. In the case of action or non-action by or at a branch or separate office of a bank, its liability is governed by the law of the place where the branch or separate office is located.

§ 4-103.   Variation by Agreement; Measure of Damages; Certain Action Constituting Ordinary Care.—

(1) the effect of the provisions of this Article may be varied by agreement except that no agreement can disclaim a bank's responsibility for its own lack of good faith or failure to exercise ordinary care or can limit the measure of damages for such lack or failure; but the parties may by agreement determine the standards by which such responsibility is to be measured if such standards are not manifestly unreasonable.

(2) Federal reserve regulations and operating letters, clearing house rules, and the like, have the effect of agreements under subsection (1), whether or not specifically assented to by all parties interested in items handled.

(3) Action or non-action approved by this Article or pursuant to Federal Reserve regulations or operating letters constitutes the exercise of ordinary care and, in the absence of special instructions, action or non-action consistent with clearing house rules and the like or with a general banking usage not disapproved by this Article, prima facie constitutes the exercise of ordinary care.

(4) The specification or approval of certain procedures by this Article does not constitute disapproval of other procedures which may be reasonable under the circumstances.

(5) The measure of damages for failure to exercise ordinary care in handling an item is the amount of the item reduced by an amount which could not have been realized by the use of ordinary care, and where there is bad faith it includes other damages, if any, suffered by the party as a proximate consequence.

§ 4-104.   Definitions and Index of Definitions.—

(1) In this Article unless the context otherwise requires

(a) "Account" means any account with a bank and includes a checking, time, interest or savings account;

(b) "Afternoon" means the period of a day between noon and midnight.

(c) "Banking day" means that part of any day on which a bank is open to the public for carrying on substantially all of its banking functions;

(d) "Clearing house" means any association of banks or other payors regularly clearing items;

(e) "Customer" means any person having an account with a bank or for whom a bank has agreed to collect items and includes a bank carrying an account with another bank;

(f) "Documentary draft" means any negotiable or non-negotiable draft with accompanying documents, securities or other papers to be delivered against honor of the draft;

(g) "Item" means any instrument for the payment of money even though it is not negotiable but does not include money;

(h) "Midnight deadline" with respect to a bank is midnight on its next banking day following the banking day on which it receives the relevant item or notice or from which the time for taking action commences to run, whichever is later;

(i) "Property payable" includes the availability of funds for payment at the time of decision to pay or dishonor;

(j) "Settle" means to pay in cash, by clearing house settlement, in a charge or credit or by remittance, or otherwise as instructed. A settlement may be either provisional or final;

(k) "Suspends payments" with respect to bank means that it has been closed by order of the supervisory authorities, that a public officer has been appointed to take it over or that it ceases or refuses to make payments in the ordinary course of business.

(2) Other definitions applying to this Article and the sections in which they appear are:

"Collecting bank"	Section 4-105.
"Depositary bank"	Section 4-105.
"Intermediary bank"	Section 4-105.
"Payor bank"	Section 4-105.
"Presenting bank"	Section 4-105.
"Remitting bank"	Section 4-105.

(3) The following definitions in other Articles apply to this Article:

"Acceptance"	Section 3-410.
"Certificate of deposit"	Section 3-104.

"Certification"	Section 3-411.
"Check"	Section 3-104.
"Draft"	Section 3-104.
"Holder in due course"	Section 3-302.
"Notice of dishonor"	Section 3-508.
"Presentment"	Section 3-504.
"Protest"	Section 3-509.
"Secondary party"	Section 3-102.

(4) In addition Article 1 contains general definitions and principles of construction and interpretation applicable throughout this Article.

§ 4-105. "Depository Bank"; "Intermediary Bank"; "Collecting Bank"; "Payor Bank"; "Presenting Bank"; "Remitting Bank"—In this Article unless the context otherwise requires:

(a) "Depository bank" means the first bank to which an item is transferred for collection even though it is also the payor bank.

(b) "Payor bank" means a bank by which an item is payable as drawn or accepted;

(c) "Intermediary bank" means any bank to which an item is transferred in course of collection except the depositary or payor bank;

(d) "Collecting bank" means any bank handling the item for collection except the payor bank;

(e) "Presenting bank" means any bank presenting an item except a payor bank;

(f) "Remitting bank" means any payor or intermediary bank remitting for an item.

§ 4-106. Separate Office of a Bank.—A branch or separate office of a bank [maintaining its own deposit ledgers] is a separate bank for the purpose of computing the time within which and the place at or to which action may be taken or notices or orders shall be given under this Article.

Note: The brackets are to make it optional with the several states whether to require a branch to maintain its own deposit ledgers in order to be considered to be a separate bank for certain purposes under Article 4. In some states "maintaining its own deposit ledgers" is a satisfactory test. In others branch banking practices are such that this test would not be suitable.

§ 4-107. Time of Receipt of Items.—

(1) For the purpose of allowing time to process items, prove balances and make the necessary entries on its books to determine its position for the day, a bank may fix an afternoon hour of two P.M. or later as a cut-off hour for the handling of money and items and the making of entries on its books.

(2) Any item or deposit of money received on any day after a cut-off hour so fixed or after the close of the banking day may be treated as being received at the opening of the next banking day.

§ 4-108. Delays.—

(1) Unless otherwise instructed, a collecting bank in a good faith effort to secure payment may, in the case of specific items and with or without the approval of any person involved, waive, modify or extend time limits imposed or permitted by this Act for a period not in excess of an additional banking day without discharge of secondary parties and without liability to its transferor or any prior party.

(2) Delay by a collecting bank or payor bank beyond time limits prescribed or permitted by this Act or by instructions is excused if caused by interruption of communication facilities, suspension of payments by another bank, war, emergency conditions or other circumstances beyond the control of the bank provided it exercises such diligence as the circumstances require.

PART 2

Collection of Items: Depositary and Collecting Banks

§ 4-201. Presumption and Duration of Agency Status of Collecting Banks and Provisional Status of Credits; Applicability of Article; Item Indorsed "Pay Any Bank".—

(1) Unless a contrary intent clearly appears and prior to the time that a settlement given by a collecting bank for an item is or becomes final (subsection (3) of Section 4-211 and Section 4-212 and 4-213) the bank is an agent or sub-agent of the owner of the item and any settlement given for the item is provisional. This provision applies regardless of the form of indorsement or lack of indorsement and even though credit given for the item is subject to immediate withdrawal as of right or is in fact withdrawn; but the continuance of ownership of an item by its owner and any rights of the owner to proceeds of the item are subject to rights of a collecting bank such as those resulting from outstanding advances on the item and valid rights of setoff. When an item is handled by banks for purposes of presentment, payment and collection, the relevant provisions of this Article apply even though action of parties clearly establishes that a particular bank has purchased the item and is the owner of it.

(2) After an item has been indorsed with the words "pay any bank" or the like, only a bank may acquire the rights of a holder

(a) until the item has been returned to the customer initiating collection; or

(b) until the item has been specially endorsed by a bank to a person who is not a bank.

§ 4-202. Responsibility for Collection; When Action Seasonable.—

(1) A collecting bank must use ordinary care in

(a) presenting an item or sending it for presentment; and

(b) sending notice of dishonor or non-payment or returning an item other than a documentary draft to the bank's transferor [or directly to the depositary bank under subsection (2) of Section 4-212] *(see note to Section 4-212)* after learning that the item has not been paid or accepted, as the case may be; and

(c) settling for an item when the bank receives final settlement; and

(d) making or providing for any necessary protest; and

(e) notifying its transferor of any loss or delay in transit within a reasonable time after discovery thereof.

(2) A collecting bank taking proper action before its midnight deadline following receipt of an item, notice or payment acts seasonably; taking proper action within a reasonably longer time may be seasonable but the bank has the burden of so establishing.

(3) Subject to subjection (1) (a), a bank is not liable for the insolvency, neglect, misconduct, mistake or default of another bank or person or for loss or destruction of an item in transit or in the possession of others.

§ 4-203. Effect of Instructions.—Subject to the provisions of Article 3 concerning conversion of instruments (Section 3-419) and the provisions of both Article 3 and this Article concerning restrictive indorsements only a collecting bank's transferor can give instructions which affect the bank or constitute notice to it and a collecting bank is not liable to prior parties for any action taken pursuant to such instructions or in accordance with any agreement with its transferor.

§ 4-204. Methods of Sending and Presenting; Sending Direct to Payor Bank—

(1) A collecting bank must send items by reasonably prompt method taking into consideration any relevant instructions, the nature of the item, the number of such items on hand, and the cost of collection involved and the method generally used by it or others to present such items.

(2) A collecting bank may send

(a) any item direct to the payor bank;

(b) any item to any non-bank payor if authorized by its transferor; and

(c) any item other than documentary drafts to any non-bank payor, if authorized by Federal Reserve regulation or operating letter, clearing house rule or the like.

§ 4-205. Supplying Missing Indorsement; No Notice From Prior Indorsement.—

(1) A depositary bank which has taken an item for collection may supply any indorsement of the customer which is necessary to title unless the item contains the words "payee's indorsement required" or the like. In the absence of such a requirement a statement placed on the item by the depositary bank to the effect that the item was deposited by a customer or credited to his account is effective as the customer's indorsement.

(2) An intermediary bank, or payor bank which is not a depositary bank, is neither given notice nor otherwise affected by a restrictive indorsement of any person except the bank's immediate transferor.

§ 4-206. Transfer Between Banks—Any agreed method which identifies the transferor bank is sufficient for the item's further transfer to another bank.

§ 4-207. Warranties of Customer and Collecting Bank on Transfer or Presentment of Items; Time for Claims.—

(1) Each customer or collecting bank who obtains payment or acceptance of an item and each prior customer and collecting bank warrants to the payor bank or other payor who in good faith pays or accepts the item that

(a) he has a good title to the item or is authorized to obtain payment or acceptance on behalf of one who has a good title; and

(b) he has no knowledge that the signature of the maker or drawer is unauthorized, except that this warranty is not given by any customer or collecting bank that is a holder in due course and acts in good faith

(i) to a maker with respect to the maker's own signature; or

(ii) to a drawer with respect to the drawer's own signature, whether or not the drawer is also the drawee; or

(iii) to an acceptor of an item if the holder in due course took the item after the acceptance or obtained the acceptance without knowledge that the drawer's signature was unauthorized; and

(c) the item has not been materially altered, except that this warranty is not given by any customer or collecting bank that is a holder in due course and acts in good faith

(i) to the maker of a note; or

(ii) to the drawer of a draft whether or not the drawer is also the drawee; or

(iii) to the acceptor of an item with respect to an alteration made prior to the acceptance if the holder in due course took the item after the acceptance, even though the acceptance provided "payable as originally drawn" equivalent terms; or

(iv) to the acceptor of an item with respect to an alteration made after the acceptance.

(2) Each customer and collecting bank who transfers an item and receives a settlement or other consideration for it warrants to his transferee and to any subsequent collecting bank who takes the item in good faith and

(a) he has a good title to the item or is authorized to obtain payment or acceptance on behalf of one who has a good title and the transfer is otherwise rightful; and

(b) all signatures are genuine or authorized; and

(c) the item has not been materially altered; and

(d) no defense of any party is good against him; and

(e) he has no knowledge of any insolvency proceeding instituted with respect to the maker or acceptor or the drawer of an unaccepted item.

In addition each customer and collecting bank so transferring an item and receiving a settlement or other consideration engages that upon dishonor and any necessary notice of dishonor and protest he will take up the item.

(3) The warranties and the engagement to honor set forth in the two preceding subsections arise notwithstanding the absence of endorsement or words of guaranty or warranty in the transfer or presentment and a collecting bank remains liable for their breach despite remittance to its transferor. Damages for breach of such warranties or engagement to honor shall not exceed the consideration received by the customer or collecting bank responsible plus finance changes and expenses related to the item, if any.

(4) Unless a claim for breach of warranty under this section is made within a reasonable time after the person claiming learns of the breach, the person liable is discharged to the extent of any loss caused by the delay in making claim.

§ 4-208. Security Interest of Collecting Bank in Items, Accompanying Documents and Proceeds.—

(1) A bank has a security interest in an item and any accompanying documents or the proceeds of either
  (a) in case of an item deposited in an account to the extent to which credit given for the item has been withdrawn or applied;
  (b) in case of an item for which it has given credit available for withdrawal as of right, to the extent of the credit given whether or not the credit is drawn upon and whether or not there is a right of charge-back; or
  (c) if it makes an advance on or against the item.

(2) When credit which has been given for several items received at one time or pursuant to a single agreement is withdrawn or applied in part the security interest remains upon all the items, any accompanying documents or the proceeds of either. For the purpose of this section, credits first given are first withdrawn.

(3) Receipt by a collecting bank of a final settlement for an item is a realization on its security interest in the item, accompanying documents and proceeds. To the extent and so long as the bank does not receive final settlement for the item or give up possession of the item or accompanying documents for purposes other than collection, the security interest continues and is subject to provisions of Article 9 except that

  (a) no security agreement is necessary to make the security interest enforceable (subsection (1)(b) of Section 9-203); and
  (b) no filing is required to perfect the security interest; and
  (c) the security interest has priority over conflicting perfected security interests in the item, accompanying documents or proceeds.

§ 4-209. When Bank Gives Value for Purposes of Holder in Due Course.—For purposes of determining its status as a holder in due course, the bank has given value to the extent that it has a security interest in an item provided that the bank otherwise complies with the requirements of Section 3-302 on what constitutes a holder in due course.

§ 4-210. Presentment by Notice of Item Not Payable by, Through or at a Bank; Liability of Secondary Parties.—

(1) Unless otherwise instructed, a collecting bank may present an item not payable by, through or at a bank by sending to the party to accept or pay a written notice that the bank holds the item for acceptance or payment. The notice must be sent in time to be received on or before the day when presentment is due and the bank must meet any requirement of the party to accept or pay under Section 3-505 by the close of the bank's next banking day after it knows of the requirement.

(2) Where presentment is made by notice and neither honor nor request for compliance with a requirement under Section 3-505 is received by the close of business on the day after maturity or in the case of demand items by the close of business on the third banking day after notice was sent, the presenting bank may treat the item as dishonored and charge any secondary party by sending him notice of the facts.

§ 4-211. Media of Remittance; Provisional and Final Settlement in Remittance Cases.—

(1) A collecting bank may take in settlement of an item
  (a) a check of the remitting bank or of another bank on any bank except the remitting bank; or
  (b) a cashier's check or similar primary obligation of a remitting bank which is a member of or clears through a member of the same clearing house or group as the collecting bank; or
  (c) appropriate authority to charge an account of the remitting bank or of another bank with the collecting bank; or
  (d) if the item is drawn upon or payable by a person other than a bank, a cashier's check, certified check or other bank check or obligation.

(2) If before its midnight deadline the collecting bank properly dishonors a remittance check or authorization to charge on itself or presents or forwards for collection a remittance instrument of or on another bank which is of a kind approved by subsection (1) or has not been authorized by it, the collecting bank is not liable to prior parties in the event of the dishonor of such check, instrument or authorization.

(3) A settlement for an item by means of a remittance instrument or authorization to charge is or becomes a final settlement as to both the person making and the person receiving the settlement

  (a) if the remittance instrument or authorization to charge is of a kind approved by subsection (1) or has not been authorized by the person receiving the settlement and in either case the person receiving the settlement acts seasonably before its midnight deadline in presenting, forwarding for collection or paying the instrument or authorization,—at the time the remittance instrument or authorization is finally paid by the payor by which it is payable;
  (b) if the person receiving the settlement has authorized remittance by a non-bank check or obligation or by a cashier's check or similar primary obligation of or a check upon the payor or other remitting

Bank which is not of a kind approved by subsection (1)(b),—at the time of the receipt of such remittance check or obligation; or

(c) if in a case not covered by subparagraphs (a) or (b) the person receiving the settlement fails to seasonally present, forward for collection, pay or return a remittance instrument or authorization to it to charge before its midnight deadline,—at such midnight deadline.

§ 4-212.   Right of Charge-Back or Refund.—

(1) If a collecting bank has made provisional settlement with its customer for an item and itself fails by reason of dishonor, suspension of payments by a bank or otherwise to receive a settlement for the item which is or becomes final, the bank may revoke the settlement given by it, charge back the amount of any credit given for the item to its customer's account or obtain refund from its customer whether or not it is able to return the items if by its midnight deadline or within a longer reasonable time after it learns the facts it returns the item or sends notification of the facts. These rights to revoke, chargeback and obtain refund terminate if and when a settlement for the item received by the bank is or becomes final (subsection (3) of Section 4-211 and subsections (2) and (3) of Section 4-213).

[(2) Within the time and manner prescribed by this section and Section 4-301, an intermediary or payor bank, as the case may be, may return an unpaid item directly to the depositary bank and may send for collection a draft on the depositary bank and obtain reimbursement. In such case, if the depositary bank has received provisional settlement for the item, it must reimburse the bank drawing the draft and any provisional credits for the item between banks shall become and remain final.]

Note: *Direct return is recognized as an innovation that is not yet established bank practice, and therefore, Paragraph 2 has been bracketed. Some lawyers have doubts whether it should be included in legislation or left to development by agreement.*

(3) A depositary bank which is also the payor may charge-back the amount of an item to its customer's account or obtain refund in accordance with the section governing return of an item received by a payor bank for credit on its books (Section 4-301).

(4) The right to charge-back is not affected by

(a) prior use of the credit given for the item; or

(b) failure by any bank to exercise ordinary care with respect to the item but any bank so failing remains liable.

(5) A failure to charge-back or claim refund does not affect other rights of the bank against the customer or any other party.

(6) If credit is given in dollars as the equivalent of the value of an item payable in a foreign currency the dollar amount of any charge-back or refund shall be calculated on the basis of the buying sight rate for the foreign currency prevailing on the day when the person entitled to the charge-back or refund learns that it will not receive payment in ordinary course.

§ 4-213.   Final Payment of Item by Payor Bank; When Provisional Debits and Credits Become Final; When Certain Credits Become Available for Withdrawal.—

(1) An item is finally paid by a payor bank when the bank has done any of the following, whichever happens first:

(a) paid the item in cash; or

(b) settled for the item without reserving a right to revoke the settlement and without having such right under statute, clearing house rule or agreement; or

(c) completed the process of posting the item to the indicated account of the drawer, maker or other person to be charged therewith; or

(d) made a provisional settlement for the item and failed to revoke the settlement in the time and manner permitted by statute, clearing house rule or agreement.

Upon a final payment under subparagraphs (b), (c) or (d) the payor bank shall be accountable for the amount of the item.

(2) If provisional settlement for an item between the presenting and payor banks is made through a clearing house or by debits or credits in an account between them, then to the extent that provisional debits or credits for the item are entered in accounts between the presenting and payor banks or between the presenting and successive prior collecting banks seriatim, they become final upon final payment of the item by the payor bank.

(3) If a collecting bank receives a settlement for an item which is or becomes final (subsection (3) of Section 4-211, subsection (2) of Section 4-213) the bank is accountable to its customer for the amount of the item and any provisional credit given for the item in an account with its customer becomes final.

(4) Subject to any right of the bank to apply the credit to an obligation of the customer, credit given by a bank for an item in an account with its customer becomes available for withdrawal as of right.

(a) in any case where the bank has received a provisional settlement for the item,—when such settlement becomes final and the bank has had a reasonable time to learn that the settlement is final;

(b) in any case where the bank is both a depositary bank and a payor bank and the item is finally paid,—at the opening of the bank's second banking day following receipt of the item.

(5) A deposit of money in a bank is final when made but, subject to any right of the bank to apply the deposit to an obligation of the customer, the deposit becomes available for withdrawal as of right at the opening of the bank's next banking day following receipt of the deposit.

§ 4-214.   Insolvency and Preference.—

(1) Any item in or coming into the possession of a payor or collecting bank which suspends payment and which item is not finally paid shall be returned by the receiver, trustee or agent in charge of the closed bank to the presenting bank or the closed bank's customer.

(2) If a payor bank finally pays an item and suspends payments without making a settlement for the item with its customer or the presenting bank which settlement is or becomes final, the owner of the item has a preferred claim against the payor bank.

(3) If a payor bank gives or a collecting bank gives or receives a provisional settlement for an item and thereafter suspends payments, the suspension does not prevent or interfere with the settlement becoming final if such finality occurs automatically upon the lapse of certain time or the happening of certain events (subsection (3) of Section 4-211, subsections (1) (d), (2) and (3) of Section 4-213).

(4) If a collecting bank receives from subsequent parties settlement for an item which settlement is or becomes final and suspends payments without making a settlement for the item with its customer which is or becomes final, the owner of the item has a preferred claim against such collecting bank.

PART 3

Collection of Items: Payor Banks

§ 4-301.   Deferred Posting; Recovery of Payment by Return of Items; Time of Dishonor.—

(1) Where an authorized settlement for a demand item (other than a documentary draft) received by a payor bank otherwise than for immediate payment over the counter has been made before midnight of the banking day of receipt the payor bank may revoke the settlement and recover any payment if before it has made final payment (subsection (1) of Section 4-213) and before its midnight deadline it

    (a) returns the item; or

    (b) sends written notice of dishonor or nonpayment if the item is held for protest or is otherwise unavailable for return.

(2) If a demand item is received by a payor bank for credit on its books it may return such item or send notice of dishonor and may revoke any credit given or recover the amount thereof withdrawn by its customer, if it acts within the time limit and in the manner specified in the preceding subsection.

(3) Unless previous notice of dishonor has been sent an item is dishonored at the time when for purposes of dishonor it is returned or notice sent in accordance with this section.

(4) An item is returned:

    (a) as to an item received through a clearing house, when it is delivered to the presenting or last collecting bank or the clearing house or is sent or delivered in accordance with its rules; or

    (b) in all other cases, when it is sent or delivered to the bank's customer or transferor or pursuant to his instructions.

§ 4-302.   Payor Bank's Responsibility for Late Return of Item.—

In the absence of a valid defense such as breach of a presentment warranty (subsection (1) of Section 4-207), settlement effected or the like, if an item is presented on and received by a payor bank the bank is accountable for the amount of

    (a) a demand item other than a documentary draft whether properly payable or not if the bank, in any case where it is not also the depositary bank, retains the item beyond midnight of the banking day of receipt without settling for it or, regardless of whether it is also the depositary bank, does not pay or return the item or send notice of dishonor until after its midnight deadline; or

    (b) any other properly payable item unless within the time allowed for acceptance or payment of that item the bank either accepts or pays the item or returns it and accompanying documents.

§ 4-303.   When Item Subject to Notice, Stop-Order, Legal Process or Setoff; Order in Which Items May Be Charged or Certified.—

(1) Any knowledge, notice or stop-order received by, legal process served upon or setoff exercised by a payor bank, whether or not effective under other rules of law to terminate, suspend or modify the bank's right or duty to pay an item or to charge its customer's account for the item, comes too late to so terminate, suspend or modify such right or duty if the knowledge, notice, stop-order or legal process is received or served and a reasonable time for the bank to act thereon expires or the setoff is exercised after the bank has done any of the following;

    (a) accepted or certified the item;

    (b) paid the item in cash;

    (c) settled for the item without reserving a right to revoke the settlement and without having such right under statute, clearing house rule or agreement;

    (d) completed the process of posting the item to the indicated account of the drawer, maker or other person to be charged therewith or otherwise has evidenced by examination of such indicated account and by action its decision to pay the item; or

    (e) become accountable for the amount of the item under subsection (1) (d) of Section 4-213 and Section 4-302 dealing with the payor bank's responsibility for late return of items.

(2) Subject to the provisions of subsection (1) items may be accepted, paid, certified or charged to the indicated account of its customer in any order convenient to the bank.

PART 4

Relationship Between Payor Bank and Its Customer

§ 4-401.   When Bank May Charge Customer's Account.—

(1) As against its customer, a bank may charge against his account any item which is otherwise properly payable from that account even though the charge creates an overdraft.

(2) A bank which in good faith makes payment to a holder may charge the indicated account of its customer according to

  (a) the original tenor of his altered item; or

  (b) the tenor of his completed item, even though the bank knows the item has been completed unless the bank has notice that the completion was improper.

§ 4-402. **Bank's Liability to Customer for Wrongful Dishonor.**—A payor bank is liable to its customer for damages proximately caused by the wrongful dishonor of an item. When the dishonor occurs through mistake liability is limited to actual damages proved. If so proximately caused and proved damages may include damages for an arrest or prosecution of the customer or other consequential damages. Whether any consequential damages are proximately caused by the wrongful dishonor is a question of fact to be determined in each case.

§ 4-403. **Customer's Right to Stop Payment; Burden of Proof of Loss.**—

(1) A customer may by order to his bank stop payment of any item payable for his account but the order must be received at such time and in such manner as to afford the bank a reasonable opportunity to act on it prior to any action by the bank with respect to the item described in Section 4-303.

(2) An oral order is binding upon the bank only for fourteen calendar days unless confirmed in writing within that period. A written order is effective for only six months unless renewed in writing.

(3) The burden of establishing the fact and amount of loss resulting from the payment of an item contrary to a binding stop payment order is on the customer.

§ 4-404. **Bank Not Obligated to Pay Check More Than Six Months Old.**—A bank is under no obligation to a customer having a checking account to pay a check, other than a certified check, which is presented more than six months after its date, but it may charge its customer's account for a payment made thereafter in good faith.

§ 4-405. **Death or Incompetence of Customer.**—

(1) A payor or collecting bank's authority to accept, pay or collect an item or to account for proceeds of its collection if otherwise effective is not rendered ineffective by incompetence of a customer of either bank existing at the time the item is issued or its collection undertaken if the bank does not know of an adjudication of incompetence. Neither death nor incompetence of a customer revokes such authority to accept, pay, collect or account until the bank knows of the fact of death or of an adjudication of incompetence and has reasonable opportunity to act on it.

(2) Even with knowledge a bank may for ten days after the date of death pay or certify checks drawn on or prior to that date unless ordered to stop payment by a person claiming an interest in the account.

§ 4-406. **Customer's Duty to Discover and Report Unauthorized Signature or Alteration.**—

(1) When a bank sends to its customer a statement of account accompanied by items paid in good faith in support of the debit entries or holds the statement and items pursuant to a request or instructions of its customer or otherwise in a reasonable manner makes the statement and items available to the customer, the customer must exercise reasonable care and promptness to examine the statement and items to discover his unauthorized signature or any alteration on an item and must notify the bank promptly after discovery thereof.

(2) If the bank establishes that the customer failed with respect to an item to comply with the duties imposed on the customer by subsection (1) the customer is precluded from asserting against the bank

  (a) his unauthorized signature or any alteration on the item if the bank also establishes that it suffered a loss by reason of such failure; and

  (b) an unauthorized signature or alteration by the same wrongdoer on any other item paid in good faith by the bank after the first item and statement was available to the customer for a reasonable period not exceeding fourteen calendar days and before the bank receives notification from the customer of any such unauthorized signature or alteration.

(3) The preclusion under subsection (2) does not apply if the customer establishes lack of ordinary care on the part of the bank in paying the item(s).

(4) Without regard to care or lack of care of either the customer or the bank a customer who does not within one year from the time the statement and items are made available to the customer (subsection (1)) discover and report his unauthorized signature or any alteration on the face or back of the item or does not within three years from that time discover and report any unauthorized indorsement is precluded from asserting against the bank such unauthorized signature or endorsement or such alteration.

(5) If under this section a payor bank has a valid defense against a claim of a customer upon or resulting from payment of an item and waives or fails upon request to assert the defense the bank may not assert against any collecting bank or other prior party presenting or transferring the item a claim based upon the unauthorized signature or alteration giving rise to the customer's claim.

§ 4-407. **Payor Bank's Right to Subrogation on Improper Payment.**—If a payor bank has paid an item over the stop payment order of the drawer or maker or otherwise under circumstances giving a basis for objection by the drawer or maker, to prevent unjust enrichment and only to the extent necessary to prevent loss to the bank by reason of its payment of the item, the payor bank shall be subrogated to the rights

  (a) of any holder in due course on the item against the drawer or maker; and

  (b) of the payee or any other holder of the item against the drawer or maker either on the item or under the transaction out of which the item arose; and

  (c) of the drawer or maker against the payee or any other holder of the item with respect to the transaction out of which the item arose.

PART 5

Collection of Documentary Drafts

§ **4-501.   Handling of Documentary Drafts; Duty to Send for Presentment and to Notify Customer of Dishonor.**—A bank which takes a documentary draft for collection must present or send the draft and accompanying documents for presentment and upon learning that the draft has not been paid or accepted in due course must seasonably notify its customer of such fact even though it may have discounted or bought the draft or extended credit available for withdrawal as of right.

§ **4-502.   Presentment of "On Arrival" Drafts.**—When a draft or the relevant instructions require presentment "on arrival", "when goods arrive" or the like, the collection bank need not present until in its judgment a reasonable time for arrival of the goods has expired. Refusal to pay or accept because the goods have not arrived is not dishonor; the bank must notify its transferor of such refusal but need not present the draft again until it is instructed to do so or learns of the arrival of the goods.

§ **4-503.   Responsibility of Presenting Bank for Documents and Goods; Report of Reasons for Dishonor; Referee in Case of Need.**—Unless otherwise instructed and except as provided in Article 5 a bank presenting a documentary draft

(a) must deliver the documents to the drawee on acceptance of the draft if it is payable more than three days after presentment; otherwise, only on payment; and

(b) upon dishonor, either in the case of presentment for acceptance or presentment for payment, may seek and follow instructions from any referee in case of need designated in the draft or if the presenting bank does not choose to utilize his services it must use diligence and good faith to ascertain the reason for dishonor, must notify its transferor of the dishonor and of the results of its effort to ascertain the reasons therefor and must request instructions.

But the presenting bank is under no obligation with respect to goods represented by the documents except to follow any reasonable instructions seasonably received; it has a right to reimbursement for any expense incurred in following instructions and to prepayment of or indemnity for such expenses.

§ **4-504.   Privilege of Presenting Bank to Deal With Goods; Security Interest for Expenses.**—

(1) A presenting bank which, following the dishonor of a documentary draft, has seasonably requested instructions but does not receive them within a reasonable time may store, sell, or otherwise deal with the goods in any reasonable manner.

(2) For its reasonable expenses incurred by action under subsection (1) the presenting bank has a lien upon the goods or their proceeds, which may be forclosed in the same manner as an unpaid seller's lien.

ARTICLE FIVE—LETTERS OF CREDIT

§ **5-101.   Short Title.**—This Article shall be known and may be cited as Uniform Commercial Code— Letters of Credit.

§ **5-102.   Scope.**—

(1) This Article applies

(a) to a credit issued by a bank if the credit requires a documentary draft or a documentary demand for payment; and

(b) to a credit issued by a person other than a bank if the credit requires that the draft or demand for payment be accompanied by a document of title; and

(c) to a credit issued by a bank or other person if the credit is not within subparagraphs (a) or (b) but conspicuously states that it is a letter of credit or is conspicuously so entitled.

. . . [The remaining portion of this article omitted as it contains materials not usually covered in Business Law.]

ARTICLE SIX—BULK TRANSFERS

§ **6-101.   Short Title.**—This Article shall be known and may be cited as Uniform Commercial Code— Bulk Transfers.

§ **6-102.   "Bulk Transfer"; Transfers of Equipment; Enterprises Subject to This Article; Bulk Transfers Subject to This Article.**—

(1) A "bulk transfer" is any transfer in bulk and not in the ordinary course of the transferor's business of a major part of the materials, supplies, merchandise or other inventory (Section 9-109) of an enterprise subject to this Article.

(2) A transfer of a substantial part of the equipment (Section 9-109) of such an enterprise is a bulk transfer if it is made in connection with a bulk transfer of inventory, but not otherwise.

(3) The enterprises subject to this Article are all those whose principal business is the sale of merchandise from stock, including those who manufacture what they sell.

(4) Except as limited by the following section all bulk transfers of goods located within this State are subject to this Article.

§ 6-103.   Transfers Excepted From This Article.—The following transfers are not subject to this Article:

(1) Those made to give security for the performance of an obligation;

(2) General assignments for the benefit of all the creditors of the transferor, and subsequent transfers by the assignee thereunder;

(3) Transfers in settlement or realization of alien or other security interests;

(4) Sales by executors, administrators, receivers, trustees in bankruptcy, or any public offer under judicial process;

(5) Sales made in the course of judicial or administrative proceedings for the dissolution or reorganization of a corporation and of which notice is sent to the creditors of the corporation pursuant to order of the court or administrative agency;

(6) Transfers to a person maintaining a known place of business in this State who becomes bound to pay the debts of the transferor in full and gives public notice of that fact, and who is solvent after becoming so bound;

(7) A transfer to a new business enterprise organized to take over and continue the business, if public notice of the transaction is given and the new enterprise assumes the debts of the transferor and he receives nothing from the transaction except an interest in the new enterprise junior to the claims of creditors;

(8) Transfers of property which is exempt from execution.

§ 6-104.   Schedule of Property, List of Creditors.—

(1) Except as provided with respect to auction sales (Section 6-108), a bulk transfer subject to this Article is ineffective against any creditor of the transferor unless:

(a) The transferee requires the transferor to furnish a list of his existing creditors prepared as stated in this section; and

(b) The parties prepare a schedule of the property transferred sufficient to identify it; and

(c) The transferee preserves the list and schedule for six months next following the transfer and permits inspection of either or both and copying therefrom at all reasonable hours by any creditor of the transferor, or files the list and schedule in *(a public office to be here identified)*.

(2) The list of creditors must be signed and sworn to or affirmed by the transferor or his agent. It must contain the names and business addresses of all creditors of the transferor, with the amounts when known, and also the names of all persons who are known to the transferor to assert claims against him even though such claims are disputed.

(3) Responsibility for the completeness and accuracy of the list of creditors rests on the transferor, and the transfer is not rendered ineffective by errors or omissions therein unless the transferee is shown to have had knowledge.

§ 6-105.   Notice to Creditors.—In addition to the requirements of the preceding section, any bulk transfer subject to this Article except one made by auction sale (Section 6-108) is ineffective against any creditor of the transferor unless at least ten days before he takes possession of the goods or pays for them, whichever happens first, the transferee gives notice of the transfer in the manner and to the persons hereafter provided (Section 6-107).

[§ 6-106.   Application of the Proceeds.—In addition to the requirements of the two preceding sections:

(1) Upon every bulk transfer subject to this Article for which new consideration becomes payable except those made by sale at auction it is the duty of the transferee to assure that such consideration is applied so far as necessary to pay those debts of the transferor which are either shown on the list furnished by the transferor (Section 6-104) or filed in writing in the place stated in the notice (Section 6-107) within thirty days after the mailing of such notice. This duty of the transferee runs to all the holders of such debts, and may be enforced by any of them for the benefit of all.

(2) If any of said debts are in dispute the necessary sum may be withheld from distribution until the dispute is settled or adjudicated.

(3) If the consideration payable is not enough to pay all of the said debts in full distribution shall be made pro rata.]

Note: *This section is bracketed to indicate division of opinion as to whether or not it is a wise provision, and to suggest that this is a point on which State enactments may differ without serious damage to the principle of uniformity.*

In any State where this section is omitted, the following parts of sections, also bracketed in the text, should also be omitted, namely:

> *Section 6-107(2)(e).*
> *6-108(3)(c).*
> *6-109(2).*

In any State where this section is enacted, these other provisions should be also.

§ 6-107.   The Notice.—

(1) The notice to creditors (Section 6-105) shall state:

(a) that a bulk transfer is about to be made; and

(b) the names and business addresses of the transferor and transferee, and all other business names and addresses used by the transferor within three years last past so far as known to the transferee; and

(c) whether or not all the debts of the transferor are to be paid in full as they fall due as a result of the transaction, and if so, the address to which creditors should send their bills.

(2) If the debts of the transferor are not to be paid in full as they fall due or if the transferee is in doubt on that point then the notice shall state further:

(a) the location and general description of the property to be transferred and the estimated total of the transferor's debts;

(b) the address where the schedule of property and list of creditors (Section 6-104) may be inspected;

(c) whether the transfer is to pay existing debts and if so the amount of such debts and to whom owing;

(d) whether the transfer is for new consideration and if so the amount of such consideration and the time and place of payment; and

[(e) if for new consideration the time and place where creditors of the transferor are to file their claims.]

(3) The notice in any case shall be delivered personally or sent by registered mail to all the persons shown on the list of creditors furnished by the transferor (Section 6-104) and to all other persons who are known to the transferee to hold or assert claims against the transferor.

§ 6-108.   Auction Sales; "Auctioneer".—

(1) A bulk transfer is subject to this Article even though it is by sale at auction, but only in the manner and with the results stated in this section.

(2) The transferor shall furnish a list of his creditors and assist in the preparation of a schedule of the property to be sold, both prepared as before stated (Section 6-104).

(3) The person or persons other than the transferor who direct, control or are responsible for the auction are collectively called the "auctioneer". The auctioneer shall:

(a) receive and retain the list of creditors and prepare and retain the schedule of property for the period stated in this Article (Section 6-104);

(b) give notice of the auction personally or by registered mail at least ten days before it occurs to all persons shown on the list of creditors and to all other persons who are known to him to hold or assert claims against the transferor; [and]

[(c) assure that the net proceeds of the auction are applied as provided in this Article (Section 6-106).]

(4) Failure of the auctioneer to perform any of these duties does not affect the validity of the sale or the title of the purchasers, but if the auctioneer knows that the auction constitutes a bulk transfer such failure renders the auctioneer liable to the creditors of the transferor as a class for the sums owing to them from the transferor up to but not exceeding the net proceeds of the auction. If the auctioneer consists of several persons their liability is joint and several.

§ 6-109.   What Creditors Protected.—

(1) The creditors of the transferor mentioned in this Article are those holding claims based on transactions occurring before the bulk transfer, but creditors who become such after notice to creditors is given (Sections 6-105 and 6-107) are not entitled to notice.

[(2) Against the aggregate obligation imposed by the provisions of this Article concerning the application of the proceeds (Section 6-106 and subsection (3)(c) of 6-108) the transferee or auctioneer is entitled to credit for sums paid to particular creditors of the transferor, not exceeding the sums believed in good faith at the time of the payment to be properly payable to such creditors.]

§ 6-110.   Subsequent Transfers.—When the title of a transferee to property is subject to a defect by reason of his noncompliance with the requirements of this Article, then:

(1) a purchaser of any such property from such transferee who pays no value or who takes with notice of such noncompliance takes subject to such defect, but

(2) a purchaser for value in good faith and without such notice takes free of such defect.

§ 6-111.   Limitation of Actions and Levies.—No action under this article shall be brought nor levy made more than six months after the date on which the transferee took possession of the goods unless the transfer has been concealed. If the transfer has been concealed, actions may be brought or levies made within six months after its discovery.

Note to Article 6: *Section 6-106 is bracketed to indicate division of opinion as to whether or not it is a wise provision and to suggest that this is a point on which State enactments may differ without serious damage to the principal of uniformity.*

In any State where Section 6-106 is not enacted, the following parts of sections, also bracketed in the text, should also be omitted, namely:

Sec. 6-107(2)(e)
6-108(3)(c)
6-109(2).

In any State where Section 6-106 is enacted, these other provisions should be also.

ARTICLE SEVEN—WAREHOUSE RECEIPTS, BILLS OF LADING AND OTHER DOCUMENTS OF TITLE

PART 1

General

§ 7-101. **Short Title.**—This Article shall be known and may be cited as Uniform Commercial Code—Documents of Title.

. . . [The remaining portion of this article omitted as it contains material not usually covered in Business Law.]

ARTICLE EIGHT—INVESTMENT SECURITIES

PART 1

Short Title and General Matters

§ 8—101. **Short Title.**—This Article shall be known and may be cited as Uniform Commercial Code—Investment Securities.

§ 8—102. **Definitions and Index of Definitions.**

(1) In this Article, unless the context otherwise requires:

(a) A "certificated security" is a share, participation, or other interest in property of or an enterprise of the issuer or an obligation of the issuer which is

(i) represented by an instrument issued in bearer or registered form;

(ii) of a type commonly dealt in on securities exchanges or markets or commonly recognized in any area in which it is issued or dealt in as a medium for investment; and

(iii) either one of a class or series or by its terms divisible into a class or series of shares, participations, interests, or obligations.

(b) An "uncertificated security" is a share, participation, or other interest in property or an enterprise of the issuer or an obligation of the issuer which is

(i) not represented by an instrument and the transfer of which is registered upon books maintained for that purpose by or on behalf of the issuer;

(ii) of a type commonly dealt in on securities exchanges or markets; and

(iii) either one of a class or series or by its terms divisible into a class or series of shares, participations, interests, or obligations.

(c) A "security" is either a certificated or an uncertificated security. If a security is certificated, the terms "security" and "certificated security" may mean either the intangible interest, the instrument representing that interest, or both, as the context requires. A writing that is a certificated security is governed by this Article and not by Article 3, even though it also meets the requirements of that Article. This Article does not apply to money. If a certificated security has been retained by or surrendered to the issuer or its transfer agent for reasons other than registration of transfer, other temporary purpose, payment, exchange, or acquisition by the issuer, that security shall be treated as an uncertificated security for purposes of this Article.

(d) A certificated security is in "registered form" if

(i) it specifies a person entitled to the security or the rights it represents; and

(ii) its transfer may be registered upon books maintained for that purpose by or on behalf of the issuer, or the security so states.

(e) A certificated security is in "bearer form" if it runs to bearer according to its terms and not by reason of any indorsement.

(2) A "subsequent purchaser" is a person who takes other than by original issue.

(3) A "clearing corporation" is a corporation registered as a "clearing agency" under the federal securities laws or a corporation:

(a) at least 90 percent of whose capital stock is held by or for one or more organizations, none of which, other than a national securities exchange or association, holds in excess of 20 percent of the capital stock of the corporation, and each of which is

(i) subject to supervision or regulation pursuant to the provisions of federal or state banking laws or state insurance laws,

(ii) a broker or dealer or investment company registered under the federal securities laws, or

(iii) a national securities exchange or association registered under the federal securities laws; and

(b) any remaining capital stock of which is held by individuals who have purchased it at or prior to the time of their taking office as directors of the corporation and who have purchased only so much of the capital stock as is necessary to permit them to qualify as directors.

(4) A "custodian bank" is a bank or trust company that is supervised and examined by state or federal authority having supervision over banks and is acting as custodian for a clearing corporation.

(5) Other definitions applying to this Article or to specified Parts thereof and the sections in which they appear are:

"Adverse claim". Section 8—302.

"Bona fide purchaser". Section 8—302.

"Broker". Section 8—303.

"Debtor". Section 9—105.

"Financial intermediary". Section 8—313.

"Guarantee of the signature". Section 8—402.

"Initial transaction statement". Section 8—408.

"Instruction". Section 8—308.

"Intermediary bank". Section 4—105.

"Issuer". Section 8—201.

"Overissue". Section 8—104.

"Secured Party". Section 9—105.

"Security Agreement". Section 9—105.

(6) In addition, Article 1 contains general definitions and principles of construction and interpretation applicable throughout this Article.

§ 8—103. Issuer's Lien.—A lien upon a security in favor of an issuer thereof is valid against a purchaser only if:

(a) the security is certificated and the right of the issuer to the lien is noted conspicuously thereon; or

(b) the security is uncertificated and a notation of the right of the issuer to the lien is contained in the initial transaction statement sent to the purchaser or, if his interest is transferred to him other than by registration of transfer, pledge, or release, the initial transaction statement sent to the registered owner or the registered pledgee.

§ 8—104. Effect of Overissue; "Overissue".

(1) The provisions of this Article which validate a security or compel its issue or reissue do not apply to the extent that validation, issue, or reissue would result in overissue; but if:

(a) an identical security which does not constitute an overissue is reasonably available for purchase, the person entitled to issue or validation may compel the issuer to purchase the security for him and either to deliver a certificated security or to register the transfer of an uncertificated security to him, against surrender of any certificated security he holds; or

(b) a security is not so available for purchase, the person entitled to issue or validation may recover from the issuer the price he or the last purchaser for value paid for it with interest from the date of his demand.

(2) "Overissue" means the issue of securities in excess of the amount the issuer has corporate power to issue.

§ 8—105. Certificated Securities Negotiable; Statements and Instructions Not Negotiable; Presumptions.

(1) Certificated securities governed by this Article are negotiable instruments.

(2) Statements (Section 8—408), notices, or the like, sent by the issuer of uncertificated securities and instructions (Section 8—308) are neither negotiable instruments nor certificated securities.

(3) In any action on a security:

(a) unless specifically denied in the pleadings, each signature on a certificated security, in a necessary indorsement, on an initial transaction statement, or on an instruction, is admitted;

(b) if the effectiveness of a signature is put in issue, the burden of establishing it is on the party claiming under the signature, but the signature is presumed to be genuine or authorized;

(c) if signatures on a certificated security are admitted or established, production of the security entitles a holder to recover on it unless the defendant establishes a defense or a defect going to the validity of the security;

(d) if signatures on an initial transaction statement are admitted or established, the facts stated in the statement are presumed to be true as of the time of its issuance; and

(e) after it is shown that a defense or defect exists, the plaintiff has the burden of establishing that he or some person under whom he claims is a person against whom the defense or defect is ineffective (Section 8—202).

§ 8—106. Applicability.—The law (including the conflict of laws rules) of the jurisdiction of organization of the issuer governs the validity of a security, the effectiveness of registration by the issuer, and the rights and duties of the issuer with respect to:

(a) registration of transfer of a certificated security;

(b) registration of transfer, pledge, or release of an uncertificated security; and

(c) sending of statements of uncertificated securities.

§ 8—107. Securities Transferable; Action for Price.

(1) Unless otherwise agreed and subject to any applicable law or regulation respecting short sales, a person obligated to transfer securities may transfer any certificated security of the specified issue in bearer form or registered in the name of the transferee, or indorsed to him or in blank, or he may transfer an equivalent uncertificated security to the transferee or a person designated by the transferee.

(2) If the buyer fails to pay the price as it comes due under a contract of sale, the seller may recover the price of:

(a) certificated securities accepted by the buyer;

(b) uncertificated securities that have been transferred to the buyer or a person designated by the buyer; and

(c) other securities if efforts at their resale would be unduly burdensome or if there is no readily available market for their resale.

§ 8—108. Registration of Pledge and Release of Uncertificated Securities.—A security interest in an uncertificated security may be evidenced by the registration of pledge to the secured party or a person designated by him. There can be no more than one registered pledge of an uncertificated security at any time. The registered owner of an uncertificated security is the person in whose name the security is registered, even if the security is subject to a registered pledge. The rights of a registered pledgee of an uncertificated security under this Article are terminated by the registration of release.

PART 2

Issue—Issuer

§ 8—201. "Issuer."

(1) With respect to obligations on or defenses to a security, "issuer" includes a person who:

(a) places or authorizes the placing of his name on a certificated security (otherwise than as authenticating trustee, registrar, transfer agent, or the like) to evidence that it represents a share, participation, or other interest in his property or in an enterprise, or to evidence his duty to perform an obligation represented by the certificated security;

(b) creates shares, participations, or other interests in his property or in an enterprise or undertakes obligations, which shares, participations, interests, or obligations are uncertificated securities;

(c) directly or indirectly creates fractional interests in his rights or property, which fractional interests are represented by certificated securities; or

(d) becomes responsible for or in place of any other person described as an issuer in this section.

(2) With respect to obligations on or defenses to a security, a guarantor is an issuer to the extent of his guaranty, whether or not his obligation is noted on a certificated security or on statements of uncertificated securities sent pursuant to Section 8—408.

(3) With respect to registration of transfer, pledge, or release (Part 4 of this Article), "issuer" means a person on whose behalf transfer books are maintained.

§ 8—202. Issuer's Responsibility and Defenses; Notice of Defect or Defense.

(1) Even against a purchaser for value and without notice, the terms of a security include:

(a) if the security is certificated, those stated on the security;

(b) if the security is uncertificated, those contained in the initial transaction statement sent to such purchaser or, if his interest is transferred to him other than by registration of transfer, pledge, or release, the initial transaction statement sent to the registered owner or registered pledgee; and

(c) those made part of the security by reference, on the certificated security or in the initial transaction statement, to another instrument, indenture, or document or to a constitution, statute, ordinance, rule, regulation, order or the like, to the extent that the terms referred to do not conflict with the terms stated on the certificated security or contained in the statement. A reference under this paragraph does not of itself charge a purchaser for value with notice of a defect going to the validity of the security, even though the certificated security or statement expressly states that a person accepting it admits notice.

(2) A certificated security in the hands of a purchaser for value or an uncertificated security as to which an initial transaction statement has been sent to a purchaser for value, other than a security issued by a government or governmental agency or unit, even though issued with a defect going to its validity, is valid with respect to the purchaser if he is without notice of the particular defect unless the defect involves a violation of constitutional provisions, in which case the security is valid with respect to a subsequent purchaser for value and without notice of the defect. This subsection applies to an issuer that is a government or governmental agency or unit only if either there has been substantial compliance with the legal requirements governing the issue or the issuer has received a substantial consideration for the issue as a whole or for the particular security and a stated purpose of the issue is one for which the issuer has power to borrow money or issue the security.

(3) Except as provided in the case of certain unauthorized signatures (Section 8—205), lack of genuineness of a certificated security or an initial transaction statement is a complete defense, even against a purchaser for value and without notice.

(4) All other defenses of the issuer of a certificated or uncertificated security, including nondelivery and conditional delivery of a certificated security, are ineffective against a purchaser for value who has taken without notice of the particular defense.

(5) Nothing in this section shall be construed to affect the right of a party to a "when, as and if issued" or a "when distributed" contract to cancel the contract in the event of a material change in the character of the security that is the subject of the contract or in the plan or arrangement pursuant to which the security is to be issued or distributed.

§ 8—203. Staleness as Notice of Defects or Defenses.

(1) After an act or event creating a right to immediate performance of the principal obligation represented by a certificated security or that sets a date on or after which the security is to be presented or surrendered for redemption or exchange, a purchaser is charged with notice of any defect in its issue or defense of the issuer if:

(a) the act or event is one requiring the payment of money, the delivery of certificated securities, the registration of transfer of uncertificated securities, or any of these on presentation or surrender of the certificated security, the funds or securities are available on the date set for payment or exchange, and he takes the security more than one year after that date; and

(b) the act or event is not covered by paragraph (a) and he takes the security more than 2 years after the date set for surrender or presentation or the date on which performance became due.

(2) A call that has been revoked is not within subsection (1).

§ 8—204. Effect of Issuer's Restrictions on Transfer.—A restriction on transfer of a security imposed by the issuer, even if otherwise lawful, is ineffective against any person without actual knowledge of it unless:

(a) the security is certificated and the restriction is noted conspicuously thereon; or

(b) the security is uncertificated and a notation of the restriction is contained in the initial transaction statement sent to the person or, if his interest is transferred to him other than by registration of transfer, pledge, or release, the initial transaction statement sent to the registered owner or the registered pledgee.

§ 8—205. Effect of Unauthorized Signature on Certificated Security or Initial Transaction Statement.—An unauthorized signature placed on a certificated security prior to or in the course of issue or placed on an initial transaction statement is ineffective, but the signature is effective in favor of a purchaser for value of the certificated security or a purchaser for value of an uncertificated security to whom the initial transaction statement has been sent, if the purchaser is without notice of the lack of authority and the signing has been done by:

(a) an authenticating trustee, registrar, transfer agent, or other person entrusted by the issuer with the signing of the security, of similar securities, or of initial transaction statements or the immediate preparation for signing of any of them; or

(b) an employee of the issuer, or of any of the foregoing, entrusted with responsible handling of the security or initial transaction statement.

§ 8—206. Completion or Alteration of Certificated Security or Initial Transaction Statement.

(1) If a certificated security contains the signatures necessary to its issue or transfer but is incomplete in any other respect:

(a) any person may complete it by filling in the blanks as authorized; and

(b) even though the blanks are incorrectly filled in, the security as completed is enforceable by a purchaser who took it for value and without notice of the incorrectness.

(2) A complete certificated security that has been improperly altered, even though fraudulently, remains enforceable, but only according to its original terms.

(3) If an initial transaction statement contains the signatures necessary to its validity, but is incomplete in any other respect:

(a) any person may complete it by filling in the blanks as authorized; and

(b) even though the blanks are incorrectly filled in, the statement as completed is effective in favor of the person to whom it is sent if he purchased the security referred to therein for value and without notice of the incorrectness.

(4) A complete initial transaction statement that has been improperly altered, even though fraudulently, is effective in favor of a purchaser to whom it has been sent, but only according to its original terms.

§ 8—207. Rights and Duties of Issuer With Respect to Registered Owners and Registered Pledgees.

(1) Prior to due presentment for registration of transfer of a certificated security in registered form, the issuer or indenture trustee may treat the registered owner as the person exclusively entitled to vote, to receive notifications, and otherwise to exercise all the rights and powers of an owner.

(2) Subject to the provisions of subsections (3), (4), and (6), the issuer or indenture trustee may treat the registered owner of an uncertificated security as the person exclusively entitled to vote, to receive notifications, and otherwise to exercise all the rights and powers of an owner.

(3) The registered owner of an uncertificated security that is subject to a registered pledge is not entitled to registration of transfer prior to the due presentment to the issuer of a release instruction. The exercise of conversion rights with respect to a convertible uncertificated security is a transfer within the meaning of this section.

(4) Upon due presentment of a transfer instruction from the registered pledgee of an uncertificated security, the issuer shall:

(a) register the transfer of the security to the new owner free of pledge, if the instruction specifies a new owner (who may be the registered pledgee) and does not specify a pledgee;

(b) register the transfer of the security to the new owner subject to the interest of the existing pledgee, if the instruction specifies a new owner and the existing pledgee; or

(c) register the release of the security from the existing pledge and register the pledge of the security to the other pledgee, if the instruction specifies the existing owner and another pledgee.

(5) Continuity of perfection of a security interest is not broken by registration of transfer under subsection (4)(b) or by registration of release and pledge under subsection (4)(c), if the security interest is assigned.

(6) If an uncertificated security is subject to a registered pledge:

(a) any uncertificated securities issued in exchange for or distributed with respect to the pledged security shall be registered subject to the pledge;

(b) any certificated securities issued in exchange for or distributed with respect to the pledged security shall be delivered to the registered pledgee; and

(c) any money paid in exchange for or in redemption of part or all of the security shall be paid to the registered pledgee.

(7) Nothing in this Article shall be construed to affect the liability of the registered owner of a security for calls, assessments, or the like.

§ 8—208. Effect of Signature of Authenticating Trustee, Registrar, or Transfer Agent.

(1) A person placing his signature upon a certificated security or an initial transaction statement as authenticating trustee, registrar, transfer agent, or the like, warrants to a purchaser for value of the certificated security or a purchaser for value of an uncertificated security to whom the initial transaction statement has been sent, if the purchaser is without notice of the particular defect, that:

(a) the certificated security or initial transaction statement is genuine;

(b) his own participation in the issue or registration of the transfer, pledge, or release of the security is within his capacity and within the scope of the authority received by him from the issuer; and

(c) he has reasonable grounds to believe the security is in the form and within the amount the issuer is authorized to issue.

(2) Unless otherwise agreed, a person by so placing his signature does not assume responsibility for the validity of the security in other respects.

PART 3

Transfer

§ 8—301. Rights Acquired by Purchaser.

(1) Upon transfer of a security to a purchaser (Section 8—313), the purchaser acquires the rights in the security which his transferor had or had actual authority to convey unless the purchaser's rights are limited by Section 8—302(4).

(2) A transferee of a limited interest acquires rights only to the extent of the interest transferred. The creation or release of a security interest in a security is the transfer of a limited interest in that security.

§ 8—302. "Bona Fide Purchaser"; "Adverse Claim"; Title Acquired by Bona Fide Purchaser.

(1) A "bona fide purchaser" is a purchaser for value in good faith and without notice of any adverse claim:

(a) who takes delivery of a certificated security in bearer form or in registered form, issued or indorsed to him or in blank;

(b) to whom the transfer, pledge, or release of an uncertificated security is registered on the books of the issuer; or

(c) to whom a security is transferred under the provisions of paragraph (c), (d)(i), or (g) of Section 8—313(1).

§ 8—303. "Broker".—"Broker" means a person engaged for all or part of his time in the business of buying and selling securities, who in the transaction concerned acts for, buys a security from, or sells a security to, a customer. Nothing in this Article determines the capacity in which a person acts for purposes of any other statute or rule to which the person is subject.

§ 8—304. Notice to Purchaser of Adverse Claims.

(1) A purchaser (including a broker for the seller or buyer, but excluding an intermediary bank) of a certificated security is charged with notice of adverse claims if:

(a) the security, whether in bearer or registered form, has been indorsed "for collection" or "for surrender" or for some other purpose not involving transfer; or

(b) the security is in bearer form and has on it an unambiguous statement that it is the property of a person other than the transferor. The mere writing of a name on a security is not such a statement.

(2) A purchaser (including a broker for the seller or buyer, but excluding an intermediary bank) to whom the transfer, pledge, or release of an uncertificated security is registered is charged with notice of adverse claims as to which the issuer has a duty under Section 8—403(4) at the time of registration and which are noted in the initial transaction statement sent to the purchaser or, if his interest is transferred to him other than by registration of transfer, pledge, or release, the initial transaction statement sent to the registered owner or the registered pledgee.

(3) The fact that the purchaser (including a broker for the seller or buyer) of a certificated or uncertificated security has notice that the security is held for a third person or is registered in the name of or indorsed by a fiduciary does not create a duty of inquiry into the rightfulness of the transfer or constitute constructive notice of adverse claims. However, if the purchaser (excluding an intermediary bank) has knowledge that the proceeds are being used or the transaction is for the individual benefit of the fiduciary or otherwise in breach of duty, the purchaser is charged with notice of adverse claims.

§ 8—305. Staleness as Notice of Adverse Claims.—An act or event that creates a right to immediate performance of the principal obligation represented by a certificated security or sets a date on or after which a certificated security is to be presented or surrendered for redemption or exchange does not itself constitute any notice of adverse claims except in the case of a transfer:

(a) after one year from any date set for presentment or surrender for redemption or exchange; or

(b) after 6 months from any date set for payment of money against presentation or surrender of the security if funds are available for payment on that date.

§ 8—306. Warranties on Presentment and Transfer of Certificated Securities; Warranties of Originators of Instructions.

(1) A person who presents a certificated security for registration of transfer or for payment or exchange warrants to the issuer that he is entitled to the registration, payment, or exchange. But, a purchaser for value and without notice of adverse claims who receives a new, reissued, or re-registered certificated security on registration of transfer or receives an initial transaction statement confirming the registration of transfer of an equivalent uncertificated security to him warrants only that he has no knowledge of any unauthorized signature (Section 8—311) in a necessary indorsement.

(2) A person by transferring a certificated security to a purchaser for value warrants only that:

(a) his transfer is effective and rightful;

(b) the security is genuine and has not been materially altered; and

(c) he knows of no fact which might impair the validity of the security.

(3) If a certificated security is delivered by an intermediary known to be entrusted with delivery of the security on behalf of another or with collection of a draft or other claim against delivery, the intermediary by delivery warrants only his own good faith and authority, even though he has purchased or made advances against the claim to be collected against the delivery.

(4) A pledgee or other holder for security who redelivers a certificated security received, or after payment and on order of the debtor delivers that security to a third person, makes only the warranties of an intermediary under subsection (3).

(5) A person who originates an instruction warrants to the issuer that:

(a) he is an appropriate person to originate the instruction; and

(b) at the time the instruction is presented to the issuer he will be entitled to the registration of transfer, pledge, or release.

(6) A person who originates an instruction warrants to any person specially guaranteeing his signature (subsection 8—312(3)) that:

(a) he is an appropriate person to originate the instruction; and

(b) at the time the instruction is presented to the issuer

(i) he will be entitled to the registration of transfer, pledge, or release; and

(ii) the transfer, pledge, or release requested in the instruction will be registered by the issuer free from all liens, security interests, restrictions, and claims other than those specified in the instruction.

(7) A person who originates an instruction warrants to a purchaser for value and to any person guaranteeing the instruction (Section 8—312(6)) that:

(a) he is an appropriate person to originate the instruction;

(b) the uncertificated security referred to therein is valid; and

(c) at the time the instruction is presented to the issuer

(i) the transferor will be entitled to the registration of transfer, pledge, or release;

(ii) the transfer, pledge, or release requested in the instruction will be registered by the issuer free from all liens, security interests, restrictions, and claims other than those specified in the instruction; and

(iii) the requested transfer, pledge, or release will be rightful.

(8) If a secured party is the registered pledgee or the registered owner of an uncertificated security, a person who originates an instruction of release or transfer to the debtor or, after payment and on order of the debtor, a transfer instruction to a third person, warrants to the debtor or the third person only that he is an appropriate person to originate the instruction and, at the time the instruction is presented to the issuer, the transferor will be entitled to the registration of release or transfer. If a transfer instruction to a third person who is a purchaser for value is originated on order of the debtor, the debtor makes to the purchaser the warranties of paragraphs (b), (c)(ii) and (c)(iii) of subsection (7).

(9) A person who transfers an uncertificated security to a purchaser for value and does not originate an instruction in connection with the transfer warrants only that:

(a) his transfer is effective and rightful; and

(b) the uncertificated security is valid.

(10) A broker gives to his customer and to the issuer and a purchaser the applicable warranties provided in this section and has the rights and privileges of a purchaser under this section. The warranties of and in favor of the broker, acting as an agent are in addition to applicable warranties given by and in favor of his customer.

§ 8—307. Effect of Delivery Without Indorsement; Right to Compel Indorsement.—If a certificated security in registered form has been delivered to a purchaser without a necessary indorsement he may become a bona fide purchaser only as of the time the indorsement is supplied; but against the transferor, the transfer is complete upon delivery and the purchaser has a specifically enforceable right to have any necessary indorsement supplied.

§ 8—308. Indorsements; Instructions.

(1) An indorsement of a certificated security in registered form is made when an appropriate person signs on it or on a separate document an assignment or transfer of the security or a power to assign or transfer it or his signature is written without more upon the back of the security.

(2) An indorsement may be in blank or special. An indorsement in blank includes an indorsement to bearer. A special indorsement specifies to whom the security is to be transferred, or who has power to transfer it. A holder may convert a blank indorsement into a special indorsement.

(3) An indorsement purporting to be only of part of a certificated security representing units intended by the issuer to be separately transferable is effective to the extent of the indorsement.

(4) An "instruction" is an order to the issuer of an uncertificated security requesting that the transfer, pledge, or release from pledge of the uncertificated security specified therein be registered.

(5) An instruction originated by an appropriate person is:

(a) a writing signed by an appropriate person; or

(b) a communication to the issuer in any form agreed upon in a writing signed by the issuer and an appropriate person.

If an instruction has been originated by an appropriate person but is incomplete in any other respect, any person may complete it as authorized and the issuer may rely on it as completed even though it has been completed incorrectly.

(6) "An appropriate person" in subsection (1) means the person specified by the certificated security or by special indorsement to be entitled to the security.

(7) "An appropriate person" in subsection (5) means:

(a) for an instruction to transfer or pledge an uncertificated security which is then not subject to a registered pledge, the registered owner; or

(b) for an instruction to transfer or release an uncertificated security which is then subject to a registered pledge, the registered pledgee.

(8) In addition to the persons designated in subsections (6) and (7), "an appropriate person" in subsections (1) and (5) includes:

(a) if the person designated is described as a fiduciary but is no longer serving in the described capacity, either that person or his successor;

(b) if the persons designated are described as more than one person as fiduciaries and one or more are no longer serving in the described capacity, the remaining fiduciary or fiduciaries, whether or not a successor has been appointed or qualified;

(c) if the person designated is an individual and is without capacity to act by virtue of death, incompetence, infancy, or otherwise, his executor, administrator, guardian, or like fiduciary;

(d) if the persons designated are described as more than one person as tenants by the entirety or with right of survivorship and by reason of death all cannot sign, the survivor or survivors;

(e) a person having power to sign under applicable law or controlling instrument; and

(f) to the extent that the person designated or any of the foregoing persons may act through an agent, his authorized agent.

(9) Unless otherwise agreed, the indorser of a certificated security by his indorsement or the originator of an instruction by his origination assumes no obligation that the security will be honored by the issuer but only the obligations provided in Section 8—306.

(10) Whether the person signing is appropriate is determined as of the date of signing and an indorsement made by or an instruction originated by him does not become unauthorized for the purposes of this Article by virtue of any subsequent change of circumstances.

(11) Failure of a fiduciary to comply with a controlling instrument or with the law of the state having jurisdiction of the fiduciary relationship, including any law requiring the fiduciary to obtain court approval of the transfer, pledge, or release, does not render his indorsement or an instruction originated by him unauthorized for the purposes of this Article.

§ 8—309. Effect of Indorsement Without Delivery.—An indorsement of a certificated security, whether special or in blank, does not constitute a transfer until delivery of the certificated security on which it appears or, if the indorsement is on a separate document, until delivery of both the document and the certificated security.

§ 8—310. Indorsement of Certificated Security in Bearer Form.—An indorsement of a certificated security in bearer form may give notice of adverse claims (Section 8—304) but does not otherwise affect any right to registration the holder possesses.

§ 8—311. Effect of Unauthorized Indorsement or Instruction.—Unless the owner or pledgee has ratified an unauthorized indorsement or instruction or is otherwise precluded from asserting its ineffectiveness:

(a) he may assert its ineffectiveness against the issuer or any purchaser, other than a purchaser for value and without notice of adverse claims, who has in good faith received a new, reissued, or re-registered certificated security on registration of transfer or received an initial transaction statement confirming the registration of transfer, pledge, or release of an equivalent uncertificated security to him; and

(b) an issuer who registers the transfer of a certificated security upon the unauthorized indorsement or who registers the transfer, pledge, or release of an uncertificated security upon the unauthorized instruction is subject to liability for improper registration (Section 8—404).

§ 8—312. Effect of Guaranteeing Signature, Indorsement or Instruction.
(1) Any person guaranteeing a signature of an indorser of a certificated security warrants that at the time of signing:

(a) the signature was genuine;

(b) the signer was an appropriate person to indorse (Section 8—308); and

(c) the signer had legal capacity to sign.

(2) Any person guaranteeing a signature of the originator of an instruction warrants that at the time of signing:

(a) the signature was genuine;

(b) the signer was an appropriate person to originate the instruction (Section 8—308) if the person specified in the instruction as the registered owner or registered pledgee of the uncertificated security was, in fact, the registered owner or registered pledgee of the security, as to which fact the signature guarantor makes no warranty;

(c) the signer had legal capacity to sign; and

(d) the taxpayer identification number, if any, appearing on the instruction as that of the registered owner or registered pledgee was the taxpayer identification number of the signer or of the owner or pledgee for whom the signer was acting.

(3) Any person specially guaranteeing the signature of the originator of an instruction makes not only the warranties of a signature guarantor (subsection (2)) but also warrants that at the time the instruction is presented to the issuer:

(a) the person specified in the instruction as the registered owner or registered pledgee of the uncertificated security will be the registered owner or registered pledgee; and

(b) the transfer, pledge, or release of the uncertificated security requested in the instruction will be registered by the issuer free from all liens, security interests, restrictions, and claims other than those specified in the instruction.

(4) The guarantor under subsections (1) and (2) or the special guarantor under subsection (3) does not otherwise warrant the rightfulness of the particular transfer, pledge, or release.

(5) Any person guaranteeing an indorsement of a certificated security makes not only the warranties of a signature guarantor under subsection (1) but also warrants the rightfulness of the particular transfer in all respects.

(6) Any person guaranteeing an instruction requesting the transfer, pledge, or release of an uncertificated security makes not only the warranties of a special signature guarantor under subsection (3) but also warrants the rightfulness of the particular transfer, pledge, or release in all respects.

(7) No issuer may require a special guarantee of signature (subsection (3)), a guarantee of indorsement (subsection (5)), or a guarantee of instruction (subsection (6)) as a condition to registration of transfer, pledge, or release.

(8) The foregoing warranties are made to any person taking or dealing with the security in reliance on the guarantee, and the guarantor is liable to the person for any loss resulting from breach of the warranties.

§ 8—313. When Transfer to Purchaser Occurs; Financial Intermediary as Bona Fide Purchaser; "Financial Intermediary".
(1) Transfer of a security or a limited interest (including a security interest) therein to a purchaser occurs only:

(a) at the time he or a person designated by him acquires possession of a certificated security;

(b) at the time the transfer, pledge, or release of an uncertificated security is registered to him or a person designated by him;

(c) at the time his financial intermediary acquires possession of a certificated security specially indorsed to or issued in the name of the purchaser;

(d) at the time a financial intermediary, not a clearing corporation, sends him confirmation of the purchase and also by book entry or otherwise identifies as belonging to the purchaser

(i) a specific certificated security in the financial intermediary's possession;

(ii) a quantity of securities that constitute or are part of a fungible bulk of certificated securities in the financial intermediary's possession or of uncertificated securities registered in the name of the financial intermediary; or

(iii) a quantity of securities that constitute or are part of a fungible bulk of securities shown on the account of the financial intermediary on the books of another financial intermediary;

(e) with respect to an identified certificated security to be delivered while still in the possession of a third person, not a financial intermediary, at the time that person acknowledges that he holds for the purchaser;

(f) with respect to a specific uncertificated security the pledge or transfer of which has been registered to a third person, not a financial intermediary, at the time that person acknowledges that he holds for the purchaser;

(g) at the time appropriate entries to the account of the purchaser or a person designated by him on the books of a clearing corporation are made under Section 8—320;

(h) with respect to the transfer of a security interest where the debtor has signed a security agreement containing a description of the security, at the time a written notification, which, in the case of the creation of the security interest, is signed by the debtor (which may be a copy of the security agreement) or which, in the case of the release or assignment of the security interest created pursuant to this paragraph, is signed by the secured party, is received by

(i) a financial intermediary on whose books the interest of the transferor in the security appears;

(ii) a third person, not a financial intermediary, in possession of the security, if it is certificated;

(iii) a third person, not a financial intermediary, who is the registered owner of the security, if it is uncertificated and not subject to a registered pledge; or

(iv) a third person, not a financial intermediary, who is the registered pledgee of the security, if it is uncertificated and subject to a registered pledge;

(i) with respect to the transfer of a security interest where the transferor has signed a security agreement containing a description of the security, at the time new value is given by the secured party; or

(j) with respect to the transfer of a security interest where the secured party is a financial intermediary and the security has already been transferred to the financial intermediary under paragraphs (a), (b), (c), (d), or (g), at the time the transferor has signed a security agreement containing a description of the security and value is given by the secured party.

(2) The purchaser is the owner of a security held for him by a financial intermediary, but cannot be a bona fide purchaser of a security so held except in the circumstances specified in paragraphs (c), (d)(i), and (g) of subsection (1). If a security so held is part of a fungible bulk, as in the circumstances specified in paragraphs (d)(ii) and (d)(iii) of subsection (1), the purchaser is the owner of a proportionate property interest in the fungible bulk.

(3) Notice of an adverse claim received by the financial intermediary or by the purchaser after the financial intermediary takes delivery of a certificated security as a holder for value or after the transfer, pledge, or release of an uncertificated security has been registered free of the claim to a financial intermediary who has given value is not effective either as to the financial intermediary or as to the purchaser. However, as between the financial intermediary and the purchaser the purchaser may demand transfer of an equivalent security as to which no notice of adverse claim has been received.

(4) A "financial intermediary" is a bank, broker, clearing corporation, or other person (or the nominee of any of them) which in the ordinary course of its business maintains security accounts for its customers and is acting in that capacity. A financial intermediary may have a security interest in securities held in account for its customer.

§ 8—314. Duty to Transfer, When Completed.

(1) Unless otherwise agreed, if a sale of a security is made on an exchange or otherwise through brokers:

(a) the selling customer fulfills his duty to transfer at the time he:

(i) places a certificated security in the possession of the selling broker cr a person designated by the broker;

(ii) causes an uncertificated security to be registered in the name of the selling broker or a person designated by the broker;

(iii) if requested, causes an acknowledgment to be made to the selling broker that a certificated or uncertificated security is held for the broker; or

(iv) places in the possession of the selling broker or of a person designated by the broker a transfer instruction for an uncertificated security, providing the issuer does not refuse to register the requested transfer if the instruction is presented to the issuer for registration within 30 days thereafter; and

(b) the selling broker, including a correspondent broker acting for a selling customer, fulfills his duty to transfer at the time he:

(i) places a certificated security in the possession of the buying broker or a person designated by the buying broker;

(ii) causes an uncertificated security to be registered in the name of the buying broker or a person designated by the buying broker;

(iii) places in the possession of the buying broker or of a person designated by the buying broker a transfer instruction for an uncertificated security, providing the issuer does not refuse to register the requested transfer if the instruction is presented to the issuer for registration within 30 days thereafter; or

(iv) effects clearance of the sale in accordance with the rules of the exchange on which the transaction took place.

(2) Except as provided in this section or unless otherwise agreed, a transferor's duty to transfer a security under a contract of purchase is not fulfilled until he:

(a) places a certificated security in form to be negotiated by the purchaser in the possession of the purchaser or of a person designated by the purchaser;

(b) causes an uncertificated security to be registered in the name of the purchaser or a person designated by the purchaser; or

(c) if the purchaser requests, causes an acknowledgment to be made to the purchaser that a certificated or uncertificated security is held for the purchaser.

(3) Unless made on an exchange, a sale to a broker purchasing for his own account is within subsection (2) and not within subsection (1).

§ 8—315. Action Against Transferee Based Upon Wrongful Transfer

(1) Any person against whom the transfer of a security is wrongful for any reason, including his incapacity, as against anyone except a bona fide purchaser, may:

(a) reclaim possession of the certificated security wrongfully transferred;

(b) obtain possession of any new certificated security representing all or part of the same rights;

(c) compel the origination of an instruction to transfer to him or a person designated by him an uncertificated security constituting all or part of the same rights; or

(d) have damages.

(2) If the transfer is wrongful because of an unauthorized indorsement of a certificated security, the owner may also reclaim or obtain possession of the security or a new certificated security, even from a bona fide purchaser, if the ineffectiveness of the purported indorsement can be asserted against him under the provisions of this Article on unauthorized indorsements (Section 8—311).

(3) The right to obtain or reclaim possession of a certificated security or to compel the origination of a transfer instruction may be specifically enforced and the transfer of a certificated or uncertificated security enjoined and a certificated security impounded pending the litigation.

§ 8—316. Purchaser's Right to Requisites for Registration of Transfer, Pledge, or Release on Books—Unless otherwise agreed, the transferor of a certificated security or the transferor, pledgor, or pledgee of an uncertificated security on due demand must supply his purchaser with any proof of his authority to transfer, pledge, or release or with any other requisite necessary to obtain registration of the transfer, pledge, or release of the security; but if the transfer, pledge, or release is not for value, a transferor, pledgor, or pledgee need not do so unless the purchaser furnishes the necessary expenses. Failure within a reasonable time to comply with a demand made gives the purchaser the right to reject or rescind the transfer, pledge, or release.

§ 8—317. Creditors' Rights

(1) Subject to the exceptions in subsections (3) and (4), no attachment or levy upon a certificated security or any share or other interest represented thereby which is outstanding is valid until the security is actually seized by the officer making the attachment or levy, but a certificated security which has been surrendered to the issuer may be reached by a creditor by legal process at the issuer's chief executive office in the United States.

(2) An uncertificated security registered in the name of the debtor may not be reached by a creditor except by legal process at the issuer's chief executive office in the United States.

(3) The interest of a debtor in a certificated security that is in the possession of a secured party not a financial intermediary or in an uncertificated security registered in the name of a secured party not a financial intermediary (or in the name of a nominee of the secured party) may be reached by a creditor by legal process upon the secured party.

(4) The interest of a debtor in a certificated security that is in the possession of or registered in the name of a financial intermediary or in an uncertificated security registered in the name of a financial intermediary may be reached by a creditor by legal process upon the financial intermediary on whose books the interest of the debtor appears.

(5) Unless otherwise provided by law, a creditor's lien upon the interest of a debtor in a security obtained pursuant to subsection (3) or (4) is not a restraint on the transfer of the security, free of the lien, to a third party for new value; but in the event of a transfer, the lien applies to the proceeds of the transfer in the hands of the secured party or financial intermediary, subject to any claims having priority.

(6) A creditor whose debtor is the owner of a security is entitled to aid from courts of appropriate jurisdiction, by injunction or otherwise, in reaching the security or in satisfying the claim by means allowed at law or in equity in regard to property that cannot readily be reached by ordinary legal process.

§ 8—318. No Conversion by Good Faith Conduct—An agent or bailee who in good faith (including observance of reasonable commercial standards if he is in the business of buying, selling, or otherwise dealing with securities) has received certificated securities and sold, pledged, or delivered them or has sold or caused the transfer or pledge of uncertificated securities over which he had control according to the instructions of his principal, is not liable for conversion or for participation in breach of fiduciary duty although the principal had no right so to deal with the securities.

§ 8—319. Statute of Frauds—A contract for the sale of securities is not enforceable by way of action or defense unless:

(a) there is some writing signed by the party against whom enforcement is sought or by his authorized agent or broker, sufficient to indicate that a contract has been made for sale of a stated quantity of described securities at a defined or stated price;

(b) delivery of a certificated security or transfer instruction has been accepted, or transfer of an uncertificated security has been registered and the transferee has failed to send written objection to the issuer within 10 days after receipt of the initial transaction statement confirming the registration, or payment has been made, but the contract is enforceable under this provision only to the extent of the delivery, registration, or payment;

(c) within a reasonable time a writing in confirmation of the sale or purchase and sufficient against the sender under paragraph (a) has been received by the party against whom enforcement is sought and he has failed to send written objection to its contents within 10 days after its receipt; or

(d) the party against whom enforcement is sought admits in his pleading, testimony, or otherwise in court that a contract was made for the sale of a stated quantity of described securities at a defined or stated price.

§ 8—320. Transfer or Pledge Within Central Depository System

(1) In addition to other methods, a transfer, pledge, or release of a security or any interest therein may be effected by the making of appropriate entries on the books of a clearing corporation reducing the account of the transferor, pledgor, or pledgee and increasing the account of the transferee, pledgee, or pledgor by the amount of the obligation or the number of shares or rights transferred, pledged, or released, if the security is shown on the account of a transferor, pledgor, or pledgee on the books of the clearing corporation; is subject to the control of the clearing corporation; and

(a) if certificated,

(i) is in the custody of the clearing corporation, another clearing corporation, a custodian bank, or a nominee of any of them; and

(ii) is in bearer form or indorsed in blank by an appropriate person or registered in the name of the clearing corporation, a custodian bank, or a nominee of any of them; or

(b) if uncertificated, is registered in the name of the clearing corporation, another clearing corporation, a custodian bank, or a nominee of any of them.

(2) Under this section entries may be made with respect to like securities or interests therein as a part of a fungible bulk and may refer merely to a quantity of a particular security without reference to the name of the registered owner, certificate or bond number, or the like, and, in appropriate cases, may be on a net basis taking into account other transfers, pledges, or releases of the same security.

(3) A transfer under this section is effective (Section 8—313) and the purchaser acquires the rights of the transferor (Section 8—301). A pledge or release under this section is the transfer of a limited interest. If a pledge or the creation of a security interest is intended, the security interest is perfected at the time when both value is given by the pledgee and the appropriate entries are made (Section 8—321). A transferee or pledgee under this section may be a bona fide purchaser (Section 8—302).

(4) A transfer or pledge under this section is not a registration of transfer under Part 4.

(5) That entries made on the books of the clearing corporation as provided in subsection (1) are not appropriate does not affect the validity or effect of the entries or the liabilities or obligations of the clearing corporation to any person adversely affected thereby.

§ 8—321. Enforceability, Attachment, Perfection and Termination of Security Interests

(1) A security interest in a security is enforceable and can attach only if it is transferred to the secured party or a person designated by him pursuant to a provision of Section 8—313(1).

(2) A security interest so transferred pursuant to agreement by a transferor who has rights in the security to a transferee who has given value is a perfected security interest, but a security interest that has been transferred solely under paragraph (i) of Section 8—313(1) becomes unperfected after 21 days unless, within that time, the requirements for transfer under any other provision of Section 8—313(1) are satisfied.

(3) A security interest in a security is subject to the provisions of Article 9, but:

(a) no filing is required to perfect the security interest; and

(b) no written security agreement signed by the debtor is necessary to make the security interest enforceable, except as provided in paragraph (h), (i), or (j) of Section 8—313(1). The secured party has the rights and duties provided under Section 9—207, to the extent they are applicable, whether or not the security is certificated, and, if certificated, whether or not it is in his possession.

(4) Unless otherwise agreed, a security interest in a security is terminated by transfer to the debtor or a person designated by him pursuant to a provision of Section 8—313(1). If a security is thus transferred, the security interest, if not terminated, becomes unperfected unless the security is certificated and is delivered to the debtor for the purpose of ultimate sale or exchange or presentation, collection, renewal, or registration of transfer. In that case, the security interest becomes unperfected after 21 days unless, within that time, the security (or securities for which it has been exchanged) is transferred to the secured party or a person designated by him pursuant to a provision of Section 8—313(1).

PART 4

Registration

§ 8—401. Duty of Issuer to Register Transfer, Pledge, or Release

(1) If a certificated security in registered form is presented to the issuer with a request to register transfer or an instruction is presented to the issuer with a request to register transfer, pledge, or release, the issuer shall register the transfer, pledge, or release as requested if:

(a) the security is indorsed or the instruction was originated by the appropriate person or persons (Section 8—308);

(b) reasonable assurance is given that those indorsements or instructions are genuine and effective (Section 8—402);

(c) the issuer has no duty as to adverse claims or has discharged the duty (Section 8—403);

(d) any applicable law relating to the collection of taxes has been complied with; and

(e) the transfer, pledge, or release is in fact rightful or is to a bona fide purchaser.

(2) If an issuer is under a duty to register a transfer, pledge, or release of a security, the issuer is also liable to the person presenting a certificated security or an instruction for registration or his principal for loss resulting from any unreasonable delay in registration or from failure or refusal to register the transfer, pledge, or release.

§ 8—402. Assurance that Indorsements and Instructions Are Effective

(1) The issuer may require the following assurance that each necessary indorsement of a certificated security or each instruction (Section 8—308) is genuine and effective:

(a) in all cases, a guarantee of the signature (Section 8—312(1) or (2)) of the person indorsing a certificated security or originating an instruction including, in the case of an instruction, a warranty of the taxpayer identification number or, in the absence thereof, other reasonable assurance of identity;

(b) if the indorsement is made or the instruction is originated by an agent, appropriate assurance of authority to sign;

(c) if the indorsement is made or the instruction is originated by a fiduciary, appropriate evidence of appointment or incumbency;

(d) if there is more than one fiduciary, reasonable assurance that all who are required to sign have done so; and

(e) if the indorsement is made or the instruction is originated by a person not covered by any of the foregoing, assurance appropriate to the case corresponding as nearly as may be to the foregoing.

(2) A "guarantee of the signature" in subsection (1) means a guarantee signed by or on behalf of a person reasonably believed by the issuer to be responsible. The issuer may adopt standards with respect to responsibility if they are not manifestly unreasonable.

(3) "Appropriate evidence of appointment or incumbency" in subsection (1) means:

(a) in the case of a fiduciary appointed or qualified by a court, a certificate issued by or under the direction or supervision of that court or an officer thereof and dated within 60 days before the date of presentation for transfer, pledge, or release; or

(b) in any other case, a copy of a document showing the appointment or a certificate issued by or on behalf of a person reasonably believed by the issuer to be responsible or, in the absence of that document or certificate, other evidence reasonably deemed by the issuer to be appropriate. The issuer may adopt standards with respect to the evidence if they are not manifestly unreasonable. The issuer is not charged with notice of the contents of any document obtained pursuant to this paragraph (b) except to the extent that the contents relate directly to the appointment or incumbency.

(4) The issuer may elect to require reasonable assurance beyond that specified in this section, but if it does so and, for a purpose other than that specified in subsection (3)(b), both requires and obtains a copy of a will, trust, indenture, articles of co-partnership, by-laws, or other controlling instrument, it is charged with notice of all matters contained therein affecting the transfer, pledge, or release.

§ 8—403. Issuer's Duty as to Adverse Claims

(1) An issuer to whom a certificated security is presented for registration shall inquire into adverse claims if:

(a) a written notification of an adverse claim is received at a time and in a manner affording the issuer a reasonable opportunity to act on it prior to the issuance of a new, reissued, or re-registered certificated security, and the notification identifies the claimant, the registered owner, and the issue of which the security is a part, and provides an address for communications directed to the claimant; or

(b) the issuer is charged with notice of an adverse claim from a controlling instrument it has elected to require under Section 8—402(4).

(2) The issuer may discharge any duty of inquiry by any reasonable means, including notifying an adverse claimant by registered or certified mail at the address furnished by him or, if there be no such address, at his residence or regular place of business that the certificated security has been presented for registration of transfer by a named person, and that the transfer will be registered unless within 30 days from the date of mailing the notification, either:

(a) an appropriate restraining order, injunction, or other process issues from a court of competent jurisdiction; or

(b) there is filed with the issuer an indemnity bond, sufficient in the issuer's judgment to protect the issuer and any transfer agent, registrar, or other agent of the issuer involved from any loss it or they may suffer by complying with the adverse claim.

(3) Unless an issuer is charged with notice of an adverse claim from a controlling instrument which it has elected to require under Section 8—402(4) or receives notification of an adverse claim under subsection (1), if a certificated security presented for registration is indorsed by the appropriate person or persons the issuer is under no duty to inquire into adverse claims. In particular:

(a) an issuer registering a certificated security in the name of a person who is a fiduciary or who is described as a fiduciary is not bound to inquire into the existence, extent, or correct description of the fiduciary relationship; and thereafter the issuer may assume without inquiry that the newly registered owner continues to be the fiduciary until the issuer receives written notice that the fiduciary is no longer acting as such with respect to the particular security;

(b) an issuer registering transfer on an indorsement by a fiduciary is not bound to inquire whether the transfer is made in compliance with a controlling instrument or with the law of the state having jurisdiction of the fiduciary relationship, including any law requiring the fiduciary to obtain court approval of the transfer; and

(c) the issuer is not charged with notice of the contents of any court record or file or other recorded or unrecorded document even though the document is in its possession and even though the transfer is made on the indorsement of a fiduciary to the fiduciary himself or to his nominee.

(4) An issuer is under no duty as to adverse claims with respect to an uncertificated security except:

(a) claims embodied in a restraining order, injunction, or other legal process served upon the issuer if the process was served at a time and in a manner affording the issuer a reasonable opportunity to act on it in accordance with the requirements of subsection (5);

(b) claims of which the issuer has received a written notification from the registered owner or the registered pledgee if the notification was received at a time and in a manner affording the issuer a reasonable opportunity to act on it in accordance with the requirements of subsection (5);

(c) claims (including restrictions on transfer not imposed by the issuer) to which the registration of transfer to the present registered owner was subject and were so noted in the initial transaction statement sent to him; and

(d) claims as to which an issuer is charged with notice from a controlling instrument it has elected to require under Section 8—402(4).

(5) If the issuer of an uncertificated security is under a duty as to an adverse claim, he discharges that duty by:

(a) including a notation of the claim in any statements sent with respect to the security under Sections 8—408(3), (6), and (7); and

(b) refusing to register the transfer or pledge of the security unless the nature of the claim does not preclude transfer or pledge subject thereto.

(6) If the transfer or pledge of the security is registered subject to an adverse claim, a notation of the claim must be included in the initial transaction statement and all subsequent statements sent to the transferee and pledgee under Section 8—408.

(7) Notwithstanding subsections (4) and (5), if an uncertificated security was subject to a registered pledge at the time the issuer first came under a duty as to a particular adverse claim, the issuer has no duty as to that claim if transfer of the security is requested by the registered pledgee or an appropriate person acting for the registered pledgee unless:

(a) the claim was embodied in legal process which expressly provides otherwise;

(b) the claim was asserted in a written notification from the registered pledgee;

(c) the claim was one as to which the issuer was charged with notice from a controlling instrument it required under Section 8—402(4) in connection with the pledgee's request for transfer; or

(d) the transfer requested is to the registered owner.

§ 8—404. Liability and Non-Liability for Registration

(1) Except as provided in any law relating to the collection of taxes, the issuer is not liable to the owner, pledgee, or any other person suffering loss as a result of the registration of a transfer, pledge, or release of a security if:

(a) there were on or with a certificated security the necessary indorsements or the issuer had received an instruction originated by an appropriate person (Section 8—308); and

(b) the issuer had no duty as to adverse claims or has discharged the duty (Section 8—403).

(2) If an issuer has registered a transfer of a certificated security to a person not entitled to it, the issuer on demand shall deliver a like security to the true owner unless:

(a) the registration was pursuant to subsection (1);

(b) the owner is precluded from asserting any claim for registering the transfer under Section 8—405(1); or

(c) the delivery would result in overissue, in which case the issuer's liability is governed by Section 8—104.

(3) If an issuer has improperly registered a transfer, pledge, or release of an uncertificated security, the issuer on demand from the injured party shall restore the records as to the injured party to the condition that would have obtained if the improper registration had not been made unless:

(a) the registration was pursuant to subsection (1); or

(b) the registration would result in overissue, in which case the issuer's liability is governed by Section 8—104.

§ 8—405. Lost, Destroyed, and Stolen Certificated Securities

(1) If a certificated security has been lost, apparently destroyed, or wrongfully taken, and the owner fails to notify the issuer of that fact within a reasonable time after he has notice of it and the issuer registers a transfer of the security before receiving notification, the owner is precluded from asserting against the issuer any claim for registering the transfer under Section 8—404 or any claim to a new security under this section.

(2) If the owner of a certificated security claims that the security has been lost, destroyed, or wrongfully taken, the issuer shall issue a new certificated security or, at the option of the issuer, an equivalent uncertificated security in place of the original security if the owner:

(a) so requests before the issuer has notice that the security has been acquired by a bona fide purchaser;

(b) files with the issuer a sufficient indemnity bond; and

(c) satisfies any other reasonable requirements imposed by the issuer.

(3) If, after the issue of a new certificated or uncertificated security, a bona fide purchaser of the original certificated security presents it for registration of transfer, the issuer shall register the transfer unless registration would result in overissue, in which event the issuer's liability is governed by Section 8—104. In addition to any rights on the indemnity bond, the issuer may recover the new certificated security from the person to whom it was issued or any person taking under him except a bona fide purchaser or may cancel the uncertificated security unless a bona fide purchaser or any person taking under a bona fide purchaser is then the registered owner or registered pledgee thereof.

§ 8—406. Duty of Authenticating Trustee, Transfer Agent, or Registrar

(1) If a person acts as authenticating trustee, transfer agent, registrar, or other agent for an issuer in the registration of transfers of its certificated securities or in the registration of transfers, pledges, and releases of its uncertificated securities, in the issue of new securities, or in the cancellation of surrendered securities:

(a) he is under a duty to the issuer to exercise good faith and due diligence in performing his functions; and

(b) with regard to the particular functions he performs, he has the same obligation to the holder or owner of a certificated security or to the owner or pledgee of an uncertificated security and has the same rights and privileges as the issuer has in regard to those functions.

(2) Notice to an authenticating trustee, transfer agent, registrar or other agent is notice to the issuer with respect to the functions performed by the agent.

§ 8—407. Exchangeability of Securities

(1) No issuer is subject to the requirements of this section unless it regularly maintains a system for issuing the class of securities involved under which both certificated and uncertificated securities are regularly issued to the category of owners, which includes the person in whose name the new security is to be registered.

(2) Upon surrender of a certificated security with all necessary indorsements and presentation of a written request by the person surrendering the security, the issuer, if he has no duty as to adverse claims or has discharged the duty

(Section 8—403), shall issue to the person or a person designated by him an equivalent uncertificated security subject to all liens, restrictions, and claims that were noted on the certificated security.

(3) Upon receipt of a transfer instruction originated by an appropriate person who so requests, the issuer of an uncertificated security shall cancel the uncertificated security and issue an equivalent certificated security on which must be noted conspicuously any liens and restrictions of the issuer and any adverse claims (as to which the issuer has a duty under Section 8—403(4)) to which the uncertificated security was subject. The certificated security shall be registered in the name of and delivered to:

(a) the registered owner, if the uncertificated security was not subject to a registered pledge; or

(b) the registered pledgee, if the uncertificated security was subject to a registered pledge.

§ 8—408. Statements of Uncertificated Securities

(1) Within 2 business days after the transfer of an uncertificated security has been registered, the issuer shall send to the new registered owner and, if the security has been transferred subject to a registered pledge, to the registered pledgee a written statement containing:

(a) a description of the issue of which the uncertificated security is a part;

(b) the number of shares or units transferred;

(c) the name and address and any taxpayer identification number of the new registered owner and, if the security has been transferred subject to a registered pledge, the name and address and any taxpayer identification number of the registered pledgee;

(d) a notation of any liens and restrictions of the issuer and any adverse claims (as to which the issuer has a duty under Section 8—403(4)) to which the uncertificated security is or may be subject at the time of registration or a statement that there are none of those liens, restrictions, or adverse claims; and

(e) the date the transfer was registered.

(2) Within 2 business days after the pledge of an uncertificated security has been registered, the issuer shall send to the registered owner and the registered pledgee a written statement containing:

(a) a description of the issue of which the uncertificated security is a part;

(b) the number of shares or units pledged;

(c) the name and address and any taxpayer identification number of the registered owner and the registered pledgee;

(d) a notation of any liens and restrictions of the issuer and any adverse claims (as to which the issuer has a duty under Section 8—403(4)) to which the uncertificated security is or may be subject at the time of registration or a statement that there are none of those liens, restrictions, or adverse claims; and

(e) the date the pledge was registered.

(3) Within 2 business days after the release from pledge of an uncertificated security has been registered, the issuer shall send to the registered owner and the pledgee whose interest was released a written statement containing:

(a) a description of the issue of which the uncertificated security is a part;

(b) the number of shares or units released from pledge;

(c) the name and address and any taxpayer identification number of the registered owner and the pledgee whose interest was released;

(d) a notation of any liens and restrictions of the issuer and any adverse claims (as to which the issuer has a duty under Section 8—403(4)) to which the uncertificated security is or may be subject at the time of registration or a statement that there are none of those liens, restrictions, or adverse claims; and

(e) the date the release was registered.

(4) An "initial transaction statement" is the statement sent to:

(a) the new registered owner and, if applicable, to the registered pledgee pursuant to subsection (1);

(b) the registered pledgee pursuant to subsection (2); or

(c) the registered owner pursuant to subsection (3).

Each initial transaction statement shall be signed by or on behalf of the issuer and must be identified as "Initial Transaction Statement".

(5) Within 2 business days after the transfer of an uncertificated security has been registered, the issuer shall send to the former registered owner and the former registered pledgee, if any, a written statement containing:

(a) a description of the issue of which the uncertificated security is a part;

(b) the number of shares or units transferred;

(c) the name and address and any taxpayer identification number of the former registered owner and of any former registered pledgee; and

(d) the date the transfer was registered.

(6) At periodic intervals no less frequent than annually and at any time upon the reasonable written request of the registered owner, the issuer shall send to the registered owner of each uncertificated security a dated written statement containing:

(a) a description of the issue of which the uncertificated security is a part;

(b) the name and address and any taxpayer identification number of the registered owner;

(c) the number of shares or units of the uncertificated security registered in the name of the registered owner on the date of the statement;

(d) the name and address and any taxpayer identification number of any registered pledgee and the number of shares or units subject to the pledge; and

(e) a notation of any liens and restrictions of the issuer and any adverse claims (as to which the issuer has a duty under Section 8—403(4)) to which the uncertificated security is or may be subject or a statement that there are none of those liens, restrictions, or adverse claims.

(7) At periodic intervals no less frequent than annually and at any time upon the reasonable written request of the registered pledgee, the issuer shall send to the registered pledgee of each uncertificated security a dated written statement containing:

(a) a description of the issue of which the uncertificated security is a part;

(b) the name and address and any taxpayer identification number of the registered owner;

(c) the name and address and any taxpayer identification number of the registered pledgee;

(d) the number of shares or units subject to the pledge; and

(e) a notation of any liens and restrictions of the issuer and any adverse claims (as to which the issuer has a duty under Section 8—403(4)) to which the uncertificated security is or may be subject or a statement that there are none of those liens, restrictions, or adverse claims.

(8) If the issuer sends the statements described in subsections (6) and (7) at periodic intervals no less frequent than quarterly, the issuer is not obliged to send additional statements upon request unless the owner or pledgee requesting them pays to the issuer the reasonable cost of furnishing them.

(9) Each statement sent pursuant to this section must bear a conspicuous legend reading substantially as follows: "This statement is merely a record of the rights of the addressee as of the time of its issuance. Delivery of this statement, of itself, confers no rights on the recipient. This statement is neither a negotiable instrument nor a security."

ARTICLE NINE—SECURED TRANSACTIONS

PART 1

Short Title, Applicability and Definitions

§ 9-101. Short Title.—This Article shall be known and may be cited as Uniform Commercial Code—Secured Transactions.

§ 9-102. Policy and [Subject Matter] of Article.—

(1) Except as otherwise provided in Section 9-103 on multiple state transactions and in Section 9-104 on excluded transactions, this Article applies so far as concerns any personal property and fixtures within the jurisdiction of this State

(a) to any transaction (regardless of its form) which is intended to create a security interest in personal property or fixtures including goods, documents, instruments, general intangibles, chattel paper of accounts and also

(b) to any sale [or] accounts or chattel paper.

(2) This Article applies to security interests created by contract including pledge, assignment, chattel mortgage, chattel trust, trust deed, factor's lien, equipment trust, conditional sale, trust receipt, other lien or title retention contract and lease or consignment intended as security. This Article does not apply to statutory liens except as provided in Section 9-310.

(3) The application of this Article to a security interest in a secured obligation is not affected by the fact that the obligation is itself secured by a transaction or interest to which this Article does not apply.

§ 9-103* [Perfection of Security Interests in Multiple State Transactions—

(1) Documents, instruments and ordinary goods.

(a) This subsection applies to documents and instruments and to goods other than those covered by a certificate of title described in subsection (2), mobile goods described in subsection (3), and minerals described in subsection (5).

(b) Except as otherwise provided in this subsection, perfection and the effect of perfection or nonperfection of a security interest in collateral are governed by the law of the jurisdiction where the collateral is when the last event occurs on which is based the assertion that the security interest is perfected or unperfected.

(c) If the parties to a transaction creating a purchase money security interest in goods in one jurisdiction understand at the time that the security interest attaches that the goods will be kept in another jurisdiction, then the law of the other jurisdiction governs the perfection and the effect of perfection or non-perfection of the security interest from the time it attaches until thirty days after the debtor receives possession of the goods and thereafter if the goods are taken to the other jurisdiction before the end of the thirty-day period.

(d) When collateral is brought into and kept in this state while subject to a security interest perfected under the law of the jurisdiction from which the collateral was removed, the security interest remains perfected, but if action is required by Part 3 of this Article to perfect the security interest,

(i) if the action is not taken before the expiration of the period of perfection in the other jurisdiction or the end of four months after the collateral is brought into this state, whichever period first expires, the security interest becomes unperfected at the end of that period and is thereafter deemed to have been unperfected as against a person who became a purchaser after removal;

(ii) if the action is taken before the expiration of the period specified in sub-paragraph (i), the security interest continues perfected thereafter;

(iii) for the purpose of priority over a buyer of consumer goods (subsection (2) of Section 9-307), the period of the effectiveness of a filing in the jurisdiction from which the collateral is removed is governed by the rules with respect to perfection in subparagraphs (i) and (ii).

(2) Certificate of title.

(a) This subsection applies to goods covered by a certificate of title issued under a statute of this state or of another jurisdiction under the law of which indication of a security interest on the certificate is required as a condition of perfection.

(b) Except as otherwise provided in this subsection, perfection and the effect of perfection or nonperfection of the security interest are governed by the law (including the conflict of laws rules) of the jurisdiction issuing the certificate until four months after the goods are removed from that jurisdiction and thereafter until the goods are registered in another jurisdiction, but in any event not beyond surrender of the certificate. After the expiration of that period, the goods are not covered by the certificate of title within the meaning of this section.

(c) Except with respect to the rights of a buyer described in the next paragraph, a security interest, perfected in another jurisdiction otherwise than by notation on a certificate of title, in goods brought into this state and thereafter covered by a certificate of title issued by this state is subject to the rules stated in paragraph (d) of subsection (1).

(d) If goods are brought into this state while a security interest therein is perfected in any manner under the law of the jurisdiction from which the goods are removed and a certificate of title is issued by this state and the certificate does not show that the goods are subject to the security interest or that they may be subject to security interests not shown on the certificate, the security interest is subordinate to the rights of a buyer of the goods who is not in the business of selling goods of that kind to the extent that he gives value and receives delivery of the goods after issuance of the certificate and without knowledge of the security interest.

(3) Accounts, general intangibles and mobile goods.

(a) This subsection applies to accounts (other than an account described in subsection (5) on minerals) and general intangibles and to goods which are mobile and which are of a type normally used in more than one jurisdiction, such as motor vehicles, trailers, rolling stock, airplanes, shipping containers, road building and construction machinery and commercial harvesting machinery and the like, if the goods are equipment or are inventory leased or held for lease by the debtor to others, and are not covered by a certificate of title described in subsection (2).

(b) The law (including the conflict of laws rules) of the jurisdiction in which the debtor is located governs the perfection and the effect of perfection or non-perfection of the security interest.

(c) If, however, the debtor is located in a jurisdiction which is not a part of the United States, and which does not provide for perfection of the security interest by filing or recording in that jurisdiction, the law of the jurisdiction in the United States in which the debtor has its major executive office in the United States governs the perfection and the effect of perfection or non-perfection of the security interest through filing. In the alternative, if the debtor is located in a jurisdiction which is not a part of the United States or Canada and the collateral is accounts or general intangibles for money due or to become due, the security interest may be perfected by notification to the account debtor. As used in this paragraph, "United States" includes its territories and possessions and the Commonwealth of Puerto Rico.

(d) A debtor shall be deemed located at his place of business if he has one, at his chief executive office if he has more than one place of business, otherwise at his residence. If, however, the debtor is a foreign air carrier under the Federal Aviation Act of 1958, as amended, it shall be deemed located at the designated office of the agent upon whom service of process may be made on behalf of the foreign air carrier.

(e) A security interest perfected under the law of the jurisdiction of the location of the debtor is perfected until the expiration of four months after a change of the debtor's location to another jurisdiction, or until perfection would have ceased by the law of the first jurisdiction, whichever period first expires. Unless perfected in the new jurisdiction before the end of that period, it becomes unperfected thereafter and is deemed to have been unperfected as against a person who became a purchaser after the change.

(4) Chattel paper. The rules stated for goods in subsection (1) apply to a possessory security interest in chattel paper. The rules stated for accounts in subsection (3) apply to a non-possessory security interest in chattel paper, but the security interest may not be perfected by notification to the account debtor.

(5) Minerals. Perfection and the effect of perfection or non-perfection of a security interest which is created by a debtor who has an interest in minerals or the like (including oil and gas) before extraction and which attaches thereto as extracted, or which attaches to an account resulting from the sale thereof at the wellhead or minehead are governed by the law (including the conflict of laws rules) of the jurisdiction where in the well head or minehead is located.

(6) Uncertificated securities. The law (including the conflict of laws rules) of the jurisdiction of organization of the issuer governs the perfection and the effect of perfection or nonperfection of a security interest in uncertificated securities.

*[This section 9-103 has been completely rewritten]

§ 9-104. **Transactions Excluded From Article.**—This Article does not apply

(a) to a security interest subject to any statute of the United States such as the Ship Mortgage Act, 1920, to the extent that such statute governs the rights of parties to and third parties affected by transactions in particular types of property; or

(b) to a landlord's lien; or

(c) to a lien given by statute or other rule of law for services or materials except as provided in Section 9-310 on priority of such liens; or

(d) to a transfer of a claim for wages, salary or other compensation of an employee, or

(e) to a transfer by a government or governmental subdivision or agency; or

(f) to a sale of accounts or chattel paper as part of a sale of the business out of which they arose, or an assignment of accounts or chattel paper which is for the purpose of a collection only, or a transfer of a right to payment under a contract to an assignee who is also to do the performance under the contract or a transfer of a single account to an assignee in whole or partial satisfaction of a preexisting indebtedness; or

(g) to a transfer of an interest or claim in or under any policy of insurance, except as provided with respect to proceeds (Section 9-306) and priorities in proceeds (Section 9-312); or

(h) to a right represented by a judgment; (other than a judgment taken on a right to payment which was collateral); or

(i) to any right of set-off; or

(j) except to the extent that provision is made for fixtures in Section 9-313, to the creation or transfer of an interest in or lien on real estate, including a lease or rents thereunder; or

(k) to a transfer in whole or in part of any claim arising out of tort; or

(l) to a transfer in any deposit account (Subsection (1) of Section 9-105), except as provided with respect to proceeds (Section 9-106) and priorities in proceeds (Section 9-312).

§ 9-105. Definitions and Index of Definitions.—

(1) In this Article unless the context otherwise requires:

(a) "Account debtor" means the person who is obligated on an account, chattel paper, contract right or general intangible;

(b) "Chattel paper" means a writing or writings which evidence both a monetary obligation and a security interest in or a lease of specific goods. When a transaction is evidenced both by such a security agreement or a lease and by an instrument or a series of instruments, the group of writings taken together constitutes chattel paper;

(c) "Collateral" means the property subject to a security interest, and includes accounts, contract rights and chattel paper which have been sold;

(d) "Debtor" means the person who owes payment or other performance of the obligation secured, whether or not he owns or has rights in the collateral, and includes the seller of accounts, contract rights or chattel paper. Where the debtor and the owner of the collateral are not the same person, the term "debtor" means the owner of the collateral in any provision of the Article dealing with the collateral, the obligor in any provision dealing with the obligation, and may include both where the context so requires;

[(e) "Deposit account" means a demand, time, savings, passbook or like account maintained with a bank, savings and loan association, credit union or like organization, other than an account evidenced by a certificate of deposit;]

[(f)] "Document" means document of title as defined in the general definitions of Article 1 (Section 1-201), [and a receipt of the kind described in subsection (2) of Section 7-201;]

[(g) "Encumbrance" includes real estate mortgages and other liens on real estate and all other rights in real estate that are not ownership interests.]

[(h)] "Goods" includes all things which are movable at the time the security interest attaches or which are fixtures (Section 9-313), but does not include money, documents, instruments, accounts, chattel paper, general intangibles, or minerals or the like (including oil and gas) before extraction. "Goods" also includes standing timber which is to be cut and removed under a conveyance or contract for sale, the unborn young of animals, and growing crops.

[(i)] "Instrument" means a negotiable instrument (defined in Section 3-104), or a certificated security (defined in Section 8-102) or any other writing which evidences a right to the payment of money and is not itself a security agreement or lease and is of a type which is in ordinary course of business transferred by delivery with any necessary indorsement or assignment;

[(j) "Mortgage" means a consensual interest created by a real estate mortgage, a trust deed on real estate, or the like;]

[(k) An advance is made "pursuant to commitment" if the secured party has bound himself to make it, whether or not a subsequent event of default or other event not within his control has relieved or may relieve him from his obligation.]

[(l)] ["Security agreement" means an agreement which] creates or provides for a security interest;

[(m)] "Secured party" means a lender, seller or other person in whose favor there is a security interest, including a person to whom accounts, (contract rights) or chattel paper have been sold. When the holders of obligations issued under an indenture of trust, equipment trust agreement or the like are represented by a trustee or other person, the representative is the secured party;

[(n) "Transmitting utility" means any person primarily engaged in the railroad, street railway or trolley bus business, the electric or electronics communications transmission business, the transmission of goods by pipeline, or the transmission or the production and transmission of electricity, steam, gas or water, or the provision of sewer service.]

(2) Other definitions applying to this Article and the sections in which they appear are: . . .

§ 9-106. Definitions: "Account"; "Contract Right"; "General Intangibles."—

"Account" means any right to payment for goods sold or leased or for services rendered which is not evidenced by an instrument or chattel paper [whether or not it has been earned by performance.] "General intangibles" means any personal property (including things in action) other than goods, accounts, chattel paper, documents, instruments [and money] . . .

§ 9-107. Definitions: "Purchase Money Security Interest."—

A security interest is a "purchase money security interest" to the extent that it is

(a) taken or retained by the seller of the collateral to secure all or part of its price; or

(b) taken by a person who by making advances or incurring an obligation gives value to enable the debtor to acquire rights in or the use of collateral if such value is in fact so used.

§ 9-108. When After-Acquired Collateral Not Security for Antecedent Debt.—

Where a secured party makes an advance, incurs an obligation, releases a perfected security interest, or otherwise gives new value which is to be secured in whole or in part by after-acquired property his security interest in the after-acquired collateral shall be deemed to be taken for new value and not as security for an antecedent debt if the debtor acquires his rights in such collateral either in the ordinary course of his business or under a contract of purchase made pursuant to the security agreement within a reasonable time after new value is given.

§ 9-109. Classification of Goods; "Consumer Goods"; "Equipment"; "Farm Products"; "Inventory."—Goods are

(1) "consumer goods" if they are used or brought for use primarily for personal, family or household purposes;

(2) "equipment" if they are used or bought for use primarily in business (including farming or a profession) or by a debtor who is a non-profit organization or a governmental subdivision or agency or if the goods are not included in the definitions of inventory, farm products or consumer goods;

(3) "farm products" if they are crops or livestock or supplies used or produced in farming operations or if they are products of crops or livestock in their unmanufactured states (such as ginned cotton, woolclip, maple syrup, milk and eggs), and if they are in the possession of a debtor engaged in raising, fattening, grazing or other farming operations. If goods are farm products they are neither equipment nor inventory;

(4) "inventory" if they are held by a person who holds them for sale or lease or to be furnished under contracts of service or if he has so furnished them, or if they are raw materials, work in process or materials used or consumed in a business. Inventory of a person is not to be classified as his equipment.

§ 9-110. Sufficiency of Description.—For the purposes of this Article any description of personal property or real estate is sufficient whether or not it is specific if it reasonably identifies what is described.

§ 9-111. Applicability of Bulk Transfer Laws.—The creation of a security interest is not a bulk transfer under Article 6 (see Section 6-103).

§ 9-112. Where Collateral Is Not Owned by Debtor.—Unless otherwise agreed, when a secured party knows that collateral is owned by a person who is not the debtor, the owner of the collateral is entitled to receive from the secured party any surplus under Section 9-502(2) or under Section 9-504(1), and is not liable for the debt or for any deficiency after resale, and he has the same right as the debtor

(a) to receive statements under Section 9-208;

(b) to receive notice of and to object to a secured party's proposal to retain the collateral in satisfaction of the indebtedness under Secton 9-505;

(c) to redeem the collateral under Section 9-506;

(d) to obtain injunctive or other relief under Section 9-507(1) Section 9-507 (1); and

(e) to recover losses caused to him under Section 9-208(2).

§ 9-113. Security Interests Arising Under Article on Sales.—A security interest arising solely under the Article on Sales (Article 2) is subject to the provisions of this Article except that to the extent that and so long as the debtor does not have or does not lawfully obtain possession of the goods

(a) no security agreement is necessary to make the security interest enforceable; and

(b) no filing is required to perfect the security interest; and

(c) the rights of the secured party on default by the debtor are governed by the Article on Sales (Article 2).

§ 9-114. Consignment—

(1) A person who delivers goods under a consignment which is not a security interest and who would be required to file under this Article by paragraph (3) (c) of Section 2-326 has priority over a secured party who is or becomes a creditor of the consignee and who would have a perfected security interest in the goods if they were the property of the consignee, and also has priority with respect to identifiable cash proceeds received on or before delivery of the goods to a buyer, if

(a) the consignor complies with the filing provision of the Article on Sales with respect to consignments (paragraph (3) (c) of Section 2-326) before the consignee receives possession of the goods; and

(b) the consignor gives notification in writing to the holder of the security interest if the holder has filed a financing statement covering the same types of goods before the date of the filing made by the consignor; and

(c) the holder of the security interest receives the notification within five years before the consignee receives possession of the goods; and

(d) the notification states that the consignor expects to deliver goods on consignment to the consignee, describing the goods by item or type.

(2) In the case of a consignment which is not a security interest and in which the requirements of the preceding subsection have not been met, a person who delivers goods to another is subordinate to a person who would have a perfected security interest in the goods if they were the property of the debtor.]*

*This section new in 1972.

PART 2

Validity of Security Agreement and Rights of Parties Thereto

§ 9-201. General Validity of Security Agreement.—Except as otherwise provided by this Act a security agreement is effective according to its terms between the parties, against purchasers of the collateral and against creditors. Nothing in this Article validates any charge or practice illegal under any statute or regulation thereunder governing usury, small loans, retail installment sales, or the like or extends the application of any such statute or regulation to any transaction not otherwise subject thereto.

§ 9-202. Title to Collateral Immaterial.—Each provision of this Article with regard to rights, obligations and remedies applies whether title to collateral is in the secured party or in the debtor.

§ 9-203. [Attachment and] Enforceability of Security Interest; Proceeds; Formal Requisites.—

[(1) Subject to the provisions of Section 4-208 on the security interest of a collecting bank, Section 8-321 on security interests in securities and Section 9-113 on a security interest arising under the Article on Sales, a security interest is not enforceable against the debtor or third parties with respect to the collateral and does not attach unless

(a) the collateral is in the possession of the secured party pursuant to agreement, or the debtor has signed a security agreement which contains a description of the collateral and in addition, when the security interest covers crops growing or to be grown or timber to be cut, a description of the land concerned; and

(b) value has been given; and

(c) the debtor has rights in the collateral.

(2) A security interest attaches when it becomes enforceable against the debtor with respect to the collateral. Attachment occurs as soon as all of the events specified in subsection (1) have taken place unless explicit agreement postpones the time of attaching.

(3) Unless otherwise agreed a security agreement gives the secured party the rights to proceeds provided by Section 9-306.]

[(4)] A transaction, although subject to this Article, is also subject to the "Consumer Finance Act" . . . "The Retail Installment Sales Act" . . . and in the case of conflict between the provisions of this Article and any such statute, the provisions of such statute control. Failure to comply with any applicable statute has only the effect which is specified therein.

§ 9-204. When Security Attaches; After-Acquired Property; Future Advances.—

[(1) Except as provided in subsection (2), a security agreement may provide that any or all obligations covered by the security agreement are to be secured by after-acquired collateral.

(2) No security interest attaches under an after-acquired property clause to consumer goods other than accessions (Section 9-314) when given as additional security unless the debtor acquires rights in them within ten days after the secured party gives value.]

[(3)] Obligations covered by a security agreement may include future advances or other value whether or not the advances or value are given pursuant to commitment [subsection (k) of Section (1) of Section 9-105).]

§ 9-205. Use or Disposition of Collateral Without Accounting Permissible.—A security interest is not invalid or fraudulent against creditors by reason of liberty in the debtor to use, commingle or dispose of all or part of the collateral (including returned or repossessed goods) or to collect or compromise accounts, contract rights or chattel paper, or to accept the return of goods or make repossessions, or to use, commingle or dispose of proceeds, or by reason of the failure of the secured party to require the debtor to account for proceeds or replace collateral. This Section does not relax the requirements of possession where perfection of a security interest depends upon possession of the collateral by the secured party or by a bailee.

§ 9-206. Agreement Not to Assert Defenses Against Assignee; Modification of Sales Warranties Where Security Agreement Exists.—

(1) Subject to any statute or decision which establishes a different rule for buyers of consumer goods, an agreement by a buyer that he will not assert against an assignee any claim or defense which he may have against the seller is enforceable by an assignee who takes his assignment for value, in good faith and without notice of a claim or defense, except as to defenses of a type which may be asserted against a holder in due course of a negotiable instrument under the Article on Commercial Paper (Article 3). A buyer who as part of one transaction signs both a negotiable instrument and a security agreement makes such an agreement.

(2) When a seller retains a purchase money security interest in goods the Article on Sales (Article 2) governs the sale and any disclaimer, limitation or modification of the seller's warranties.

§ 9-207. Rights and Duties When Collateral Is in Secured Party's Possession.—

(1) A secured party must use reasonable care in the custody and preservation of collateral in his possession. In the case of an instrument or chattel paper reasonable care includes taking necessary steps to preserve rights against prior parties unless otherwise agreed.

(2) Unless otherwise agreed, when collateral is in the secured party's possession

(a) reasonable expenses (including the cost of any insurance and payment of taxes or other charges) incurred in the custody, preservation, use or operation of the collateral are chargeable to the debtor and are secured by the collateral;

(b) the risk of accidental loss or damage is on the debtor to the extent of any deficiency in any effective insurance coverage;

(c) the secured party may hold as additional security any increase or profits (except money) received from the collateral, but money so received, unless remitted to the debtor, shall be applied in reduction of the secured obligation;

(d) the secured party must keep the collateral identifiable but fungible collateral may be commingled;

(e) the secured party may repledge the collateral upon terms which do not impair the debtor's right to redeem it.

(3) A secured party is liable for any loss caused by his failure to meet any obligation imposed by the preceding subsections but does not lose his security interest.

(4) A secured party may use or operate the collateral for the purpose of preserving the collateral or its value or pursuant to the order of a court of appropriate jurisdiction or, except in the case of consumer goods, in the manner and to the extent provided in the security agreement.

§ 9-208. Request for Statement of Account or List of Collateral.—

(1) A debtor may sign a statement indicating what he believes to be the aggregate amount of unpaid indebtedness as of a specified date and may send it to the secured party with a request that the statement be approved or corrected and returned to the debtor. When the security agreement or any other record kept by the secured party identifies the collateral a debtor may similarly request the secured party to approve or correct a list of the collateral.

(2) The secured party must comply with such a request within two weeks after receipt by sending a written correction or approval. If the secured party claims a security interest in all of a particular type of collateral owned by the debtor he may indicate that fact in his reply and need not approve or correct an itemized list of such collateral. If the secured party without reasonable excuse fails to comply he is liable for any loss caused to the debtor thereby; and if the debtor has properly included in his request a good faith statement of the obligation or a list of the collateral or both, the secured party may claim a security interest only as shown in the statement against persons misled by his failure to comply. If he no longer has an interest in the obligation or collateral at the time the request is received he must disclose the name and address of any successor in interest known to him and he is liable for any loss caused to the debtor as a result or failure to disclose. A successor in interest is not subject to this Section until a request is received by him.

(3) A debtor is entitled to such a statement once every 6 months without charge. The secured party may require payment of a charge not exceeding $10 for each additional statement furnished.

PART 3

Rights of Third Parties; Perfected and Unperfected
Security Interests; Rules of Priority

§ 9-301. Persons Who Take Priority Over Unperfected Security Interests; [Rights of] "Lien Creditor".—

(1) Except as otherwise provided in subsection (2), an unperfected security interest is subordinate to the rights of

    (a) persons entitled to priority under Section 9-312;

    (b) a person who becomes a lien creditor before [the security interest] is perfected;

    (c) in the case of goods, instruments, documents, and chattel paper, a person who is not a secured party and who is a transferee in bulk or other buyer not in ordinary course of business, [or is a buyer of farm products in the ordinary course of business] to the extent that he gives value and receives delivery of the collateral without knowledge of the security interest and before it is perfected;

    (d) in the case of accounts, contract rights, and general intangibles, a person who is not a secured party and who is a transferee to the extent that he gives value without knowledge of the security interest and before it is perfected.

(2) If the secured party files with respect to a purchase money security interest before or within ten days after the [debtor receives possession of the] collateral, he takes priority over the rights of a transferee in bulk or of a lien creditor which arise between the time the security interest attaches and the time of filing.

(3) A "lien creditor" means a creditor who has acquired a lien on the property involved by attachment, levy or the like and includes as assignee for benefit of creditors from the time of assignment, and a trustee in bankruptcy from the date of the filing of the petition or a receiver in equity from the time of appointment. Unless all the creditors represented had knowledge of the security interests such a representative of creditors is a lien creditor without knowledge even though he personally has knowledge of the security interest.

[(4) A person who becomes a lien creditor while a security interest is perfected takes subject to the security interest only to the extent that it secures advances made before he becomes a lien creditor or within 45 days thereafter or made without knowledge of the lien or pursuant to a commitment entered into without knowledge of the lien.]

§ 9-302. When Filing is Required to Perfect Security Interest; Security Interests to Which Filing Provisions of This Article Do Not Apply.—

(1) A financing statement must be filed to perfect all security interests except the following:

    (a) a security interest in collateral in possession of the secured party under Section 9-305;

    (b) a security interest temporarily perfected in instruments or documents without delivery under Section 9-034 or in proceeds for a 10 day period under Section 9-306;

    [(c) a security interest created by an assignment of a beneficial interest in a trust of a decedent's estate;]

    (d) a purchase money security interest in consumer goods; but filing is required [for a motor vehicle required to be registered; and fixture filing is required for priority over conflicting interests in fixtures to the extent provided in Section 9-313;]

    (e) an assignment of accounts or contract rights which does not alone or in conjunction with other assignments to the same assignee transfer a significant part of the outstanding accounts or contract rights of the assignor;

(f) a security interest of a collecting bank (Section 4-208) or in securities (Section 8-321) or arising under the Article on Sales (see Section 9-113) or covered in subsection (3) of this section;

[(g) an assignment for the benefit of all the creditors of the transferor, and subsequent transfers by the assignee thereunder.]

(2) If a secured party assigns a perfected security interest, no filing under this Article is required in order to continue the perfected status of the security interest against creditors of and transferees from the original debtor.

[(3) The filing of a financing statement otherwise required by this Article is not necessary or effective to perfect a security interest in property subject to

(a) a statute or treaty of the United States which provides for a national or international registration or a national or international certificate of title or which specifies a place of filing different from that specified in this Article for filing of the security interest; or

(b) the following statutes of this state; [[list any certificate of title statute covering automobiles, trailers, mobile homes, boats, farm tractors, or the like, and any central filing statute*.]]; but during any period in which collateral is inventory held for sale by a person who is in the business of selling goods of that kind, the filing provisions of this Article (Part 4) apply to a security interest in that collateral created by him as debtor; or

(c) a certificate of title statute of another jurisdiction under the law of which indication of a security interest on the certificate is required as a condition of perfection (subsection (2) of Section 9-103).

(4) Compliance with a statute or treaty described in subsection (3) is equivalent to the filing of a financing statement under this Article, and a security interest in property subject to the statute or treaty can be perfected only by compliance therewith except as provided in Section 9-103 on multiple state transactions. Duration and renewal of perfection of a security interest perfected by compliance with the statute or treaty are governed by the provisions of the statute or treaty; in other respects the security interest is subject to this Article.

*Note: *It is recommended that the provisions of certificate of title acts for perfection of security interests by notation on the certificates should be amended to exclude coverage of inventory held for sale.*]

§ 9-303. When Security Interest Is Perfected; Continuity of Perfection.—

(1) A security interest is perfected when it has attached and when all of the applicable steps required for perfection have been taken. Such steps are specified in Sections 9-302, 9-304, 9-306. If such steps are taken before the security interest attaches, it is perfected at the time when it attaches.

(2) If a security interest is originally perfected in any way permitted under this Article and is subsequently perfected in some other way under this Article, without an intermediate period when it was unperfected, the security interest shall be deemed to be perfected continuously for the purposes of this Article.

§ 9-304. Perfection of Security Interest in Instruments, Documents and Goods Covered by Documents; Perfection by Permissive Filing; Temporary Perfection Without Filing or Transfer of Possession.—

(1) A security interest in chattel paper or negotiable documents may be perfected by filing. A security interest in money or instruments (other than certificated securities or instruments which constitute part of chattel paper) can be perfected only by the secured party's taking possession, except as provided in subsections (4) and (5) of this section and subsections (2) and (3) of Section 9—306 on proceeds.

(2) During the period that goods are in the possession of the issuer of a negotiable document therefor, a security interest in the goods is perfected by perfecting a security interest in the document, and any security interest in the goods otherwise perfected during such period is subject thereto.

(3) A security interest in goods in the possession of a bailee other than one who has issued a negotiable document therefor is perfected by issuance of a document in the name of the secured party or by the bailee's receipt of notification of the secured party's interest or by filing as to the goods.

(4) A security interest in instruments (other than certificated securities) or negotiable documents is perfected without filing or the taking of possession for a period of 21 days from the time it attaches to the extent that it arises for new value given under a written security agreement.

(5) A security interest remains perfected for a period of 21 days without filing where a secured party having a perfected security interest in an instrument (other than a certificated security), a negotiable document or goods in possession of a bailee other than one who has issued a negotiable document therefor

(a) makes available to the debtor the goods or documents representing the goods for the purpose of ultimate sale or exchange or for the purpose of loading, unloading, storing, shipping, transshipping, manufacturing, processing or otherwise dealing with them in a manner preliminary to their sale or exchange, but priority between conflicting security interests in the goods is subject to subsection (3) of Section 9—312; or

(b) delivers the instrument to the debtor for the purpose of ultimate sale or exchange or of presentation, collection, renewal or registration of transfer.

(6) After the 21 day period in subsections (4) and (5) perfection depends upon compliance with applicable provisions of this Article.

§ 9—305. When Possession by Secured Party Perfects Security Interest Without Filing—

A security interest in letters of credit and advices of credit (subsection (2)(a) of Section 5—116), goods, instruments (other than certificated securities), money, negotiable documents, or chattel paper may be perfected by the secured party's taking possession of the collateral. If such collateral other than goods covered by a negotiable document is held by a bailee, the secured party is deemed to have possession from the time the bailee receives notification of the secured party's interest. A security interest is perfected by possession from the time possession is taken without a relation back and continues only so long as possession is retained, unless otherwise specified in this Article. The security interest may be otherwise perfected as provided in this Article before or after the period of possession by the secured party.

§ 9-306. "Proceeds"; Secured Party's Rights on Disposition of Collateral

(1) ["Proceeds" includes whatever is received upon the sale, exchange, collection or other disposition of collateral or proceeds. Insurance payable by reason of loss or damage to the collateral is proceeds, except to the extent that it is payable to a person other than a party to the security agreement.] Money, checks, [deposit accounts,] and the like are "cash proceeds". All other proceeds are "non-cash proceeds".

(2) Except where this Article otherwise provides, a security interest continues in collateral notwithstanding sale, exchange or other disposition thereof unless [the disposition was] authorized by the secured party in the security agreement or otherwise, and also continues in any identifiable proceeds including collections received by the debtor.

(3) The security interest in proceeds is a continuously perfected security interest if the interest in the original collateral was perfected but it ceases to be a perfected security interest and becomes unperfected ten days after receipt of the proceeds by the debtor unless

[(a) a filed financing statement covers the original collateral and the proceeds are collateral in which a security interest may be perfected by filing in the office or offices where the financing statement has been filed and, if the proceeds are acquired with cash proceeds, the description of collateral in the financing statement indicates the types of property constituting the proceeds; or]

[(b) a filed financing statement covers the original collateral and the proceeds are identifiable cash proceeds; or]

[(c)] the security interest in the proceeds is perfected before the expiration of the ten day period. [Except as provided in this section, a security interest in proceeds can be perfected only by the methods or under the circumstances permitted in this Article for original collateral of the same type.]

(4) In the event of insolvency proceeding instituted by or against a debtor, a secured party with a perfected security interest in proceeds has a perfected security interest [only in the following proceeds:]

(a) in identifiable non-cash proceeds[,] [and in separate deposit accounts containing only proceeds;]

(b) in identifiable cash proceeds in the form of money which is [neither] commingled with other money [nor] deposited in a [deposit] account prior to the insolvency proceedings;

(c) in identifiable cash proceeds in the form of checks and the like which are not deposited in a [deposit] account prior to the insolvency proceedings; and

(d) in all cash and [deposit] accounts of the debtor [in which] proceeds have been commingled [with other funds,] but the perfected security interest under this paragraph (d) is

(i) subject to any right of set-off; and

(ii) limited to an amount not greater than the amount of any cash proceeds received by the debtor within ten days before the institution of the insolvency proceedings [less the sum of (I) the payments to the secured party on account of cash proceeds received by the debtor during such period and (II) the cash proceeds received by the debtor during such period to which the secured party is entitled under paragraphs (a) through (c) of this subsection (4).]

(5) If a sale of goods results in an account or chattel paper which is transferred by the seller to a secured party, and if the goods are returned to or are repossessed by the seller or the secured party, the following rules determine priorities:

(a) If the goods were collateral at the time of sale for an indebtedness of the seller which is still unpaid, the original security interest attaches again to the goods and continues as a perfected security interest if it was perfected at the time when the goods were sold. If the security interest was originally perfected by a filing which is still effective, nothing further is required to continue the perfected status; in any other case, the secured party must take possession of the returned or repossessed goods or must file.

(b) An unpaid transferee of the chattel paper has a security interest in the goods against the transferor. Such security interest is prior to a security interest asserted under paragraph (a) to the extent that the transferee of the chattel paper was entitled to priority under Section 9-308.

(c) An unpaid transferee of the account has a security interest in the goods against the transferor. Such security interest is subordinate to a security interest asserted under paragraph (a).

(d) A security interest of an unpaid transferee asserted under paragraph (b) or (c) must be perfected for protection against creditors of the transferor and purchasers of the returned or repossessed goods.

§ 9-306.01. Debtor Disposing of Collateral and Failing to Pay Secured Party Amount Due under Security Agreement; Penalties for Violation.—

(1) It is unlawful for a debtor under the terms of a security agreement (a) who has no right of sale or other disposition of the collateral or (b) who has a right of sale or other disposition of the collateral and is to account to the secured party for the proceeds of any sale or other disposition of the collateral, to sell or otherwise dispose of the collateral and willfully and wrongfully to fail to pay the secured party the amount of said proceeds due under the security agreement.

(2) An individual convicted of a violation of this Section shall be punished by imprisonment in the penitentiary for not less than one year nor more than ten years.

(3) A corporation convicted of a violation of this Section shall be punished by a fine of not less than two thousand dollars nor more than ten thousand dollars.

(4) In the event the debtor under the terms of a security agreement is a corporation or a partnership, any officer, director, manager, or managerial agent of the debtor who violates this Section or causes the debtor to violate this Section shall, upon conviction thereof, be punished by imprisonment in the penitentiary for not less than one year nor more than ten years.

§ 9-307. Protection of Buyers of Goods.—

(1) A buyer in ordinary course of business (subsection (9) of Section 1-201) other than a person buying farm products from a person engaged in farming operations takes free of a security interest created by his seller even though the security interest is perfected and even though the buyer knows of its existence.

(2) In the case of consumer goods, a buyer takes free of a security interest even though perfected if he buys without knowledge of the security interest, for value and for his own personal, family or household purposes or his own farming operations unless prior to the purchase the secured party has filed a financing statement covering such goods.

[(3) A buyer other than a buyer in ordinary course of business (subsection (1) of this section) takes free of a security interest to the extent that it secures future advances made after the secured party acquires knowledge of the purchase, or more than 45 days after the purchase, whichever first occurs, unless made pursuant to a commitment entered into without knowledge of the purchase and before the expiration of the 45 day period.]

§ 9-308.* Purchase of Chattel Paper and Instruments—[A purchaser of chattel paper or an instrument who gives new value and takes possession of it in the ordinary course of his business has priority over a security interest in the chattel paper or instrument

(a) which is perfected under Section 9-304 (permissive filing and temporary perfection) or under Section 9-306 (perfection as to proceeds) if he acts without knowledge that the specific paper or instrument is subject to a security interest; or

(b) which is claimed merely as proceeds of inventory subject to a security interest (Section 9-306) even though he knows that the specific paper or instrument is subject to the security interest.]

*This section was redrafted in 1972.

§ 9—309. Protection of Purchasers of Instruments, Documents and Securities—Nothing in this Article limits the rights of a holder in due course of a negotiable instrument (Section 3-302) or a holder to whom a negotiable document of title has been duly negotiated (Section 7—501) or a bona fide purchaser of a security (Section 8—302) and the holders or purchasers take priority over an earlier security interest even though perfected. Filing under this Article does not constitute notice of the security interest to such holders or purchasers.

§ 9-310. Priority of Certain Liens Arising by Operation of Law.—When a person in the ordinary course of his business furnishes services or materials with respect to goods subject to a security interest, a lien upon goods in the possession of such person given by statute or rule of law for such materials or services takes priority over a perfected security interest unless the lien is statutory and the statute expressly provides otherwise.

§ 9-311. Alienability of Debtor's Rights: Judicial Process.—The debtor's rights in collateral may be voluntarily or involuntarily transferred (by way of sale, creation of a security interest, attachment, levy, garnishment or other judicial process) notwithstanding a provision in the security agreement prohibiting any transfer or making the transfer constitute a default.

§ 9-312. Priorities Among Conflicting Security Interests in the Same Collateral.—

[(1) The rules of priority stated in other sections of this Part and in the following sections shall govern when applicable: Section 4-208 with respect to the security interests of collecting banks in items being collected, accompanying documents and proceeds; Section 9-103 on security interests related to other jurisdictions; Section 9-114 on consignments.]

(2) A perfected security interest in crops for new value given to enable the debtor to produce the crops during the production season and given not more than three months before the crops become growing crops by planting or otherwise takes priority over an earlier perfected security interest to the extent that such earlier interest secures obligations due more than six months before the crops become growing crops by planting or otherwise, even though the person giving new value had knowledge of the earlier security interest.

[(3) A perfected purchase money security interest in inventory has priority over a conflicting security interest in the same inventory and also has priority in identifiable cash proceeds received on or before the delivery of the inventory to a buyer if

(a) the purchase money security interest is perfected at the time the debtor receives possession of the inventory; and

(b) the purchase money secured party gives notification in writing to the holder of the conflicting security interest if the holder had filed a financing statement covering the same types of inventory (i) before the date of the filing made by the purchase money secured party, or (ii) before the beginning of the 21 day period where the purchase money security interest is temporarily perfected without filing or possession (subsection (5) of Section 9-304); and

(c) the holder of the conflicting security interest receives the notification within five years before the debtor receives possession of the inventory; and

(d) the notification states that the person giving the notice has or expects to acquire a purchase money security interest in inventory of the debtor, describing such inventory by item or type.]

(4) A purchase money security interest in collateral other than inventory has priority over a conflicting security interest in the same collateral [or its proceeds] if the purchase money security interest is perfected at the time the debtor receives possession of the collateral or within 10 days thereafter.

(5) In all cases not governed by other rules stated in this section (including cases of purchase money security interests which do not qualify for the special priorities set forth in subsections (3) and (4) of this section), priority between conflicting security interests in the same collateral shall be determined [according to the following rules:

(a) Conflicting security interests rank according to priority in time of filing or perfection. Priority dates from the time a filing is first made covering the collateral or the time the security interest is first perfected, whichever is earlier, provided that there is no period thereafter when there is neither filing nor perfection.

(b) So long as conflicting security interests are unperfected, the first to attach has priority.]

[(6) For the purposes of subsection (5) a date of filing or perfection as to collateral is also a date of filing or perfection as to proceeds.

(7) If future advances are made while a security interest is perfected by filing, the taking of possession, or under Section 8—321 on securities, the security interest has the same priority for the purposes of subsection (5) with respect to the future advances as it does with respect to the first advance. If a commitment is made before or while the security interest is so perfected, the security interest has the same priority with respect to advances made pursuant thereto. In other cases a perfected security interest has priority from the date the advance is made.

§ 9-313. Priority of Security Interests in Fixtures.—

[(1) In this section and in the provisions of Part 4 of this Article referring to fixture filing, unless the context otherwise requires

(a) goods are "fixtures" when they become so related to particular real estate that an interest in them arises under real estate law

(b) a "fixture filing" is the filing in the office where a mortgage on the real estate would be filed or a recorded of a financing statement covering goods which are or are to become fixtures and conforming to the requirements of subsection (5) of Section 9-402

(c) a mortgage is a "construction mortgage" to the extent that it secures an obligation incurred for the construction of an improvement on land including the acquisition cost of the land, if the recorded writing so indicates.

(2) A security interest under this Article may be created in goods which are fixtures or may continue in goods which become fixtures, but no security interest exists under this Article in ordinary building materials incorporated into an improvement on land.

(3) This Article does not prevent creation of an encumbrance upon fixtures pursuant to real estate law.

(4) A perfected security interest in fixtures has priority over the conflicting interest of an encumbrancer or owner of the real estate where

(a) the security interest is a purchase money security interest, the interest of the encumbrancer or owner arises before the goods become fixtures, the security interest is perfected by a fixture filing before the goods become fixtures or within ten days thereafter, and the debtor has an interest of record in the real estate or is in possession of the real estate; or

(b) the security interest is perfected by a fixture filing before the interest of the encumbrancer or owner is of record, the security interest has priority over any conflicting interest of a predecessor in title of the encumbrancer or owner, and the debtor has an interest of record in the real estate or is in possession of the real estate; or

(c) the fixtures are readily removable factory or office machines or readily removable replacements of domestic appliances which are consumer goods, and before the goods become fixtures the security interest is perfected by any method permitted by this Article; or

(d) the conflicting interest is a lien on the real estate obtained by legal or equitable proceedings after the security interest was perfected by any method permitted by this Article.

(5) A security interest in fixtures, whether or not perfected, has priority over the conflicting interest of an encumbrancer or owner of the real estate where

(a) the encumbrancer or owner has consented in writing to the security interest or has disclaimed an interest in the goods as fixtures; or

(b) the debtor has a right to remove the goods as against the encumbrancer or owner. If the debtor's right terminates, the priority of the security interest continues for a reasonable time.

(6) Notwithstanding paragraph (a) of subsection (4) but otherwise subject to subsections (4) and (5), a security interest in fixtures is subordinate to a construction mortgage recorded before the goods become fixtures if the goods become fixtures before the completion of the construction. To the extent that it is given to refinance a construction mortgage, a mortgage has this priority to the same extent as the construction mortgage.

(7) In cases not within the preceding subsections, a security interest in fixtures is subordinate to the conflicting interest of an encumbrancer or owner of the related real estate who is not the debtor.]

[(8)] When the secured party has priority over all owners and encumbrancers of the real estate, he may, on default, subject to the provisions of Part 5, remove his collateral from the real estate but he must reimburse any encumbrancer or owner of the real estate who is not the debtor and who has not otherwise agreed for the cost of repair of any physical injury, but not for any diminution in value of the real estate caused by the absence of the goods removed or by any necessity for replacing them. A person entitled to reimbursement may refuse permission to remove until the secured party gives adequate security for the performance of this obligation.

§ 9-314. Accessions.—

(1) A security interest in goods which attaches before they are installed in or affixed to other goods takes priority as to the goods installed or affixed (called in this section "accessions") over the claims of all persons to the whole except as stated in subsection (3) and subject to Section 9-315(1).

(2) A security interest which attaches to goods after they become part of a whole is valid against all persons subsequently acquiring interests in the whole except as stated in subsection (3) but is invalid against any person with an interest in the whole at the time the security interest attaches to the goods who has not in writing consented to the security interest or disclaimed an interest in the goods as part of the whole.

(3) The security interests described in subsections (1) and (2) do not take priority over

    (a) a subsequent purchaser for value of any interest in the whole; or

    (b) a creditor with a lien on the whole subsequently obtained by judicial proceedings; or

    (c) a creditor with a prior perfected security interest in the whole to the extent that he makes subsequent advances

if the subsequent purchase is made, the lien by judicial proceedings obtained or the subsequent advance under the prior perfected security interest is made or contracted for without knowledge of the security interest and before it is perfected. A purchaser of the whole at a foreclosure sale other than the holder of a perfected security interest purchasing at his own foreclosure sale is a subsequent purchaser within this Section.

(4) When under subsections (1) or (2) and (3) a secured party has an interest in accessions which has priority over the claims of all persons who have interests in the whole, he may on default subject to the provisions of Part 5 remove his collateral from the whole but he must reimburse any encumbrancer or owner of the whole who is not the debtor and who has not otherwise agreed for the cost of repair of any physical injury but not for any diminution in value of the whole caused by the absence of the goods removed or by any necessity for replacing them. A person entitled to reimbursement may refuse permission to remove until the secured party gives adequate security for the performance of this obligation.

§ 9-315. Priority When Goods Are Commingled or Processed.—

(1) If a security interest in goods was perfected and subsequently the goods or a part thereof have become part of a product or mass, the security interest continues in the product or mass if

    (a) the goods are so manufactured, processed, assembled or commingled that their identity is lost in the product or mass; or

    (b) a financing statement covering the original goods also covers the product into which the goods have been manufactured, processed or assembled.

In a case to which paragraph (b) applies, no separate security interest in that part of the original goods which has been manufactured, processed or assembled into the product may be claimed under Section 9-314.

(2) When under subsection (1) more than one security interest attaches to the product or mass, they rank equally according to the ratio that the cost of the goods to which each interest originally attached bears to the cost of the total product or mass.

§ 9-316. Priority Subject to Subordination.—Nothing in this Article prevents subordination by agreement by any person entitled to priority.

§ 9-317. Secured Party Not Obligated on Contract of Debtor.—The mere existence of a security interest or authority given to the debtor to dispose of or use collateral does not impose contract or tort liability upon the secured party for the debtor's acts or omissions.

§ 9-318. Defenses Against Assignee; Modification of Contract After Notification of Assignment; Term Prohibiting Assignment Ineffective; Identification and Proof of Assignment.—

(1) Unless an account debtor has made an enforceable agreement not to assert defenses or claims arising out of a sale as provided in Section 9-206 the rights of an assignee are subject to

    (a) all the terms of the contract between the account debtor and assignor and any defense or claim arising therefrom; and

    (b) any other defense or claim of the account debtor against the assignor which accrues before the account debtor receives notification of the assignment.

(2) So far as the right to payment [or a part thereof] under an assigned contract [has not been fully earned by performance,] and notwithstanding notification of the assignment, any modification of or substitution for the contract made in good faith and in accordance with reasonable commercial standards is effective against an assignee unless the account debtor has otherwise agreed but the assignee acquires corresponding rights under the modified or substituted contract. The assignment may provide that such modification or substitution is a breach by the assignor.

(3) The account debtor is authorized to pay the assignor until the account debtor receives notification that the [amount due or to become due] has been assigned and that payment is to be made to the assignee. A notification which does not reasonably identify the rights assigned is ineffective. If requested by the account debtor, the assignee must seasonably furnish reasonable proof that the assignment has been made and unless he does so the account debtor may pay the assignor.

(4) A term in any contract between an account debtor and an assignor [is ineffective if it] prohibits assignment of an account [or prohibits creation of a security interest in a general intangible for money due or to become due or requires the account debtor's consent to such assignment or security interest.]

PART 4

FILING

§ 9-401. Place of Filing; Erroneous Filing; Removal of Collateral

First Alternative Subsection (1)

(1) The proper place to file in order to perfect a security interest is as follows:

    [(a) when the collateral is timber to be cut or is minerals or the like (including oil and gas) or accounts subject to subsection (5) of Section 9-103, or when the financing statement is filed as a fixture filing

(Section 9-313) and] the collateral is goods which are or are to become fixtures, then in the office where a mortgage on the real estate would be filed or recorded;

(b) in all other cases, in the office of the Secretary of State.

Second Alternative Subsection (1)

(1) The proper place to file in order to perfect a security interest is as follows:

(a) when the collateral is equipment used in farming operations, or farm products, or accounts, [contract rights] or general intangibles arising from or relating to the sale of farm products by a farmer, or consumer goods, then in the office of the........in the county of the debtor's residence or if the debtor is not a resident of this state then in the office of the........in the county where the goods are kept, and in addition when the collateral is crops [growing or to be grown] in the office of the........in the county where the land [on which the crops are growing or to be grown] is located;

(b) when the collateral is [timber to be cut or is minerals or the like (including oil and gas) or accounts subject to subsection (5) of Section 9-103, or when the financing statement is filed as a fixture filing (Section 9-313) and the collateral is goods which are or are to become fixtures,] then in the office where a mortgage on the real estate would be filed or recorded;

(c) in all other cases, in the office of the Secretary of State.

Third Alternative Subsection (1)

(1) The proper place to file in order to perfect a security interest is as follows:

(a) when the collateral is equipment used in farming operations, or farm products, or accounts, [contract rights] or general intangibles arising from or relating to the sale of farm products by a farmer, or consumer goods, then in the office of the........in the county of the debtor's residence or if the debtor is not a resident of this state then in the office of the........in the county where the goods are kept, and in addition when the collateral is crops growing or to be grown in the office of the........in the county where the land [on which the crops are growing or to be grown] is located;

(b) when the collateral is [goods which at the time the security interest attaches are or are to become fixtures] timber to be cut or is minerals or the like (including oil and gas) or accounts subject to subsection (5) of Section 9-103, or when the financing statement is filed as a fixture filing (Section 9-313) and the collateral is goods which are or are to become fixtures, then in the office where a mortgage on the real estate [concerned] would be filed or recorded;

(c) in all other cases, in the office of the Secretary of State and in addition, if the debtor has a place of business in only one county of this state, also in the office of........of such county, or, if the debtor has no place of business in this state, but resides in the state, also in the office of........of the county in which he resides.

Note: *One of the three alternatives should be selected as subsection (1).*

(2) A filing which is made in good faith in an improper place or not in all of the places required by this section is nevertheless effective with regard to any collateral as to which the filing complied with the requirements of this Article and is also effective with regard to collateral covered by the financing statement against any person who has knowledge of the contents of such financing statement.

(3) A filing which is made in the proper place in this State continues effective even though the debtor's residence or place of business or the location of the collateral or its use, whichever controlled the original filing, is thereafter changed.

(4) [The] rules stated in Section 9-103 determine whether filing is necessary in this State.

[(5) Notwithstanding the preceding subsections, and subject to subsection (3) of Section 9-302, the proper place to file in order to perfect a security interest in collateral, including fixtures, of a transmitting utility is the office of the Secretary of State. This filing constitutes a fixture filing (Section 9-313) as to the collateral described therein which is or is to become fixtures.

(6) For the purposes of this section, the residence of an organization is its place of business if it has one or its chief executive office if it has more than one place of business.]

Note: *Subsection (6) should be used only if the state chooses the Second or Third Alternative Subsection (1).*

§ 9-402. Formal Requisites of Financing Statement; Amendments; Mortgage as Financing Statement.—

(1) A financing statement is sufficient if it [gives the names of the debtor and the secured party,] is signed by the debtor, gives an address of the secured party from which information concerning the security interest may be obtained, gives a mailing address of the debtor and contains a statement indicating the types, or describing the items, of collateral. A financing statement may be filed before a security agreement is made or a security interest otherwise attaches. When the financing statement covers crops growing or to be grown [or goods which are or are to become fixtures,] the statement must also contain a description of the real estate concerned. [When the financing statement covers timber to be cut or covers minerals or the like (including oil and gas) or accounts subject to subsection (5) of Section 9-103, or when the financing statement is filed as a fixture filing (Section 9-313) and the collateral is goods which are or are to become fixtures, the statement must also comply with subsection (5).] A copy of the security agreement is sufficient as a financing statement if it contains the above information and is signed by [the debtor. A carbon, photographic or other reproduction of a security agreement or a financing statement is sufficient as a financing statement if the security agreement so provides or if the original has been filed in this state.]

(2) A financing statement which otherwise complies with subsection (1) is sufficient [when] it is signed by the secured party [instead of the debtor] if it is filed to perfect a security interest in

    (a) collateral already subject to a security interest in another jurisdiction when it is brought into this state, [or when the debtor's location is changed to this state.] Such a financing statement must state that the collateral was brought into this state [or that the debtor's location was changed to this state] under such circumstances; [or]

    (b) proceeds under Section 9-306 if the security interest in the original collateral was perfected. Such a financing statement must describe the original collateral; [or

    (c) collateral as to which the filing has lapsed; or

    (d) collateral acquired after a change of name, identity or corporate structure of the debtor (subsection (7).]

(3) A form substantially as follows is sufficient to comply with subsection (1):

Name of debtor (or assignor) ....

Address ....

Name of secured party or assignee) ....

Address ....

    1. This financing statement covers the following types (or items) of property:

        (Describe) ....

    2. (If collateral is crops) The above described crops are growing or are to be grown on:

        (Describe Real Estate) ....

    [3. (If applicable) The above goods are to become fixtures on*]

*Where appropriate substitute either "The above timber is standing on...." or "The above minerals or the like (including oil and gas) or accounts will be financed at the wellhead or minehead of the well or mine located on...."

    [(Describe Real Estate) ....
and this financing statement is to be filed [for record] in the real estate records. (If the debtor does not have an interest of record) The name of a record owner is] ....
    4. (If [proceeds or] products of collateral are claimed) Products of the collateral are also covered.

(use   ....
whichever   Signature of Debtor (or Assignor)
is   ....
applicable)   Signature of Secured Party (or Assignee)

(4) [A financing statement may be amended by filing a writing signed by both the debtor and the secured party. An amendment does not extend the period of effectiveness of a financing statement.] If any amendment adds collateral, it is effective as to the added collateral only from the filing date of the amendment. [In this Article, unless the context otherwise requires, the term "financing statement" means the original financing statement and any amendments.

(5) A financing statement covering timber to be cut or covering minerals or the like (including oil and gas) or accounts subject to subsection (5) of Section 9-103, or a financing statement filed as a fixture filing (Section 9-313) where the debtor is not a transmitting utility, must show that it covers this type of collateral, must recite that it is to be filed [for record] in the real estate records, and the financing statement must contain a description of the real estate [sufficient if it were contained in a mortgage of the real estate to give constructive notice of the mortgage under the law of this state.] If the debtor does not have an interest of record in the real estate, the financing statement must show the name of a record owner.

(6) A mortgage is effective as a financing statement filed as a fixture filing from the date of its recording if (a) the goods are described in the mortgage by item or type, (b) the goods are or are to become fixtures related to the real estate described in the mortgage, (c) the mortgage complies with the requirements for a financing statement in this section other than a recital that it is to be filed in the real estate records, and (d) the mortgage is duly recorded. No fee with reference to the financing statement is required other than the regular recording and satisfaction fees with respect to the mortgage.

(7) A financing statement sufficiently shows the name of the debtor if it gives the individual, partnership or corporate name of the debtor, whether or not it adds other trade names or the names of partners. Where the debtor so changes his name or in the case of an organization its name, identity or corporate structure that a filed financing statement becomes seriously misleading, the filing is not effective to perfect a security interest in collateral acquired by the debtor more than four months after the change; unless a new appropriate financing statement is filed before the expiration of that time. A filed financing statement remains effective with respect to collateral transferred by the debtor even though the secured party knows of or consents to the transfer.]

[(8)] A financing statement substantially complying with the requirements of this section is effective even though it contains minor errors which are not seriously misleading.

§ 9-403. **What Constitutes Filing; Duration of Filing; Effect of Lapsed Filing; Duties of Filing Officer.—**

(1) Presentation for filing of a financing statement and tender of the filing fee or acceptance of the statement by the filing officer constitutes filing under this Article.

[(2) Except as provided in Subsection (6)] a filed financing statement is effective for a period of five years from the date of filing. The effectiveness of a filed financing statement lapses on the expiration of [the five] year period unless a continuation statement is filed prior to the lapse. [If a security interest perfected by filing exists at the time insolvency proceedings are commenced by or against the debtor, the security interest remains perfected until termination of the insolvency proceedings and thereafter for a period of sixty days or until expiration of the five year period, whichever occurs later.] Upon lapse the security interest becomes unperfected, [unless it is perfected without filing. If the security interest becomes unperfected upon lapse, it is deemed to have been unperfected as against a person who became a purchaser or lien creditor before lapse.]

(3) A continuation statement may be filed by the secured party [(i) within six months before and sixty days after a stated maturity date of five years or less, and (ii) otherwise] within six months prior to the expiration of the five year period specified in subsection (2). Any such continuation statement must be signed by the secured party, identify the original statement by file number and state that the original statement is still effective. [A continuation statement signed by a person other than the secured party of record must be accompanied by a separate written statement of assignment signed by the secured party of record and complying with subsection (2) of Section 9-405, including payment of the required fee.] Upon timely filing of the continuation statement, the effectiveness of the original statement is continued for five years after the last date to which the filing was effective whereupon it lapses in the same manner as provided in subsection (2) unless another continuation statement is filed prior to such lapse. Succeeding continuation statements may be filed in the same manner to continue the effectiveness of the original statement. Unless a statute on disposition of public records provides otherwise, the filing officer may remove a lapsed statement from the files and destroy it [immediately if he has retained a microfilm or other photographic record, or in other cases after one year after the lapse. The filing officer shall so arrange matters by physical annexation of financing statements to continuation statements or other related filings, or by other means, that if he physically destroys the financing statements of a period more than five years past, those which have been continued by a continuation statement or which are still effective under subsection (6) shall be retained.]

[(4) Except as provided in subsection (7) a] filing officer shall mark each statement with a [consecutive] file number and with the date and hour of filing and shall hold the statement [or a microfilm or other photographic copy thereof] for public inspection. In addition the filing officer shall index the statements according to the name of the debtor and shall note in the index the file number and the address of the debtor given in the statement.

[(5) The uniform fee for filing and indexing and for stamping a copy furnished by the secured party to show the date and place of filing for an original financing statement or for a continuation statement shall be $........if the statement is in the standard form prescribed by the [Secretary of State] and otherwise shall be $........, plus in each case, if the financing statement is subject to subsection (5) of Section 9-402, $........The uniform fee for each name more than one required to be indexed shall be $........The secured party may at his option show a trade name for any person and an extra uniform indexing fee of $........shall be paid with respect thereto.

(6) If the debtor is a transmitting utility (subsection (5) of Section 9-401) and a filed financing statement so states, it is effective until a termination statement is filed. A real estate mortgage which is effective as a fixture filing under subsection (6) of Section 9-402 remains effective as a fixture filing until the mortgage is released or satisfied of record or its effectiveness otherwise terminates as to the real estate.

(7) When a financing statement covers timber to be cut or covers minerals or the like (including oil and gas) or accounts subject to subsection (5) of Section 9-103, or is filed as a fixture filing, [it shall be filed for record and] the filing officer shall index it under the names of the debtor and any owner of record shown on the financing statement in the same fashion as if they were the mortgagors in a mortgage of the real estate described, and, to the extent that the law of this state provides for indexing of mortgages under the name of the mortgagee, under the name of the secured party as if he were the mortgagee thereunder, or where indexing is by description in the same fashion as if the financing statement were a mortgage of the real estate described.]

§ 9-404. Termination Statement.—

[(1) If a financing statement covering consumer goods is filed on or after........, then within one month or within ten days following written demand by the debtor after there is no outstanding secured obligation and no commitment to make advances, incur obligations or otherwise give value, the secured party must file with each filing officer with whom the financing statement was filed, a termination statement to the effect that he no longer claims a security interest under the financing statement, which shall be identified by file number. In other cases whenever there is no outstanding] secured obligation and no commitment to make advances, incur obligations or otherwise give value, the secured party must on written demand by the debtor send the debtor, [for each filing officer with whom the financing statement was filed,] a [termination] statement [to the effect] that he no longer claims a security interest under the financing statement, which shall be identified by file number. A termination statement signed by a person other than the secured party of record must be accompanied by a [separate written] statement [of assignment signed] by the secured party of record [complying with subsection (2) of Section 9-405, including payment of the required fee.] If the affected secured party fails to [file such a termination statement as required by this subsection, or to] send such a termination statement within ten days after proper demand therefor he shall be liable to the debtor for one hundred dollars, and in addition for any loss caused to the debtor by such failure.

(2) On presentation to the filing officer of such a termination statement he must note it in the index. [If he has received the termination statement in duplicate, he shall return one copy of the termination statement to the secured party stamped to show the time of receipt thereof. If the filing officer has a microfilm or other photographic record of the financing statement, and of any related continuation statement, statement of assignment and statement of release, he may remove the originals from the files at any time after receipt of the termination statement, or if he has no such record, he may remove them from the files at any time after one year after receipt of the termination statement.]

[(3) If the termination statement is in the standard form prescribed by the Secretary of State,] the uniform fee for filing and indexing [the] termination statement shall be $........, [and otherwise shall be $........, plus in each case an additional fee of $........for each name more than one against which the termination statement is required to be indexed.]

Note: *The date to be inserted should be the effective date of the revised Article 9.*

§ **9-405. Assignment of Security Interest; Duties of Filing Officer; Fees.—**

(1) A financing statement may disclose an assignment of a security interest in the collateral described in the [financing] statement by indication in the [financing] statement of the name and address of the assignee or by an assignment itself or a copy thereof on the face or back of the statement. On presentation to the filing officer of such a financing statement the filing officer shall mark the same as provided in Section 9-403(4). The uniform fee for filing, indexing and furnishing filing data for a financing standard form prescribed by the Secretary of State and otherwise shall be $........, plus an additional fee of $........for each name more than one against which the financing statement is required to be indexed.]

(2) A secured party may assign of record all or a part of his rights under a financing statement by the filing [in the place where the original financing statement was filed] of a separate written statement of assignment signed by the secured party of record and setting forth the name of the secured party of record and the debtor, the file number and the date of filing of the financing statement and the name and address of the assignee and containing a description of the collateral assigned. A copy of the assignment is sufficient as a separate statement if it complies with the preceding sentence. On presentation to the filing officer of such a separate statement, the filing officer shall mark such separate statement with the date and hour of the filing. He shall note the assignment on the index of the financing statement [or in the case of a fixture filing, or a filing covering timber to be cut, or covering minerals or the like (including oil and gas) or accounts subject to subsection (5) of Section 9-103, he shall index the assignment under the name of the assignor as grantor and, to the extent that the law of this state provides for indexing the assignment of a mortgage under the name of the assignee. The uniform fee for filing, indexing and furnishing filing data about such a separate statement of assignment shall be $........if the statement is in the standard form prescribed by the Secretary of State and otherwise shall be $........, plus in each case an additional fee of $........for each name more than one against which the statement of assignment is required to be indexed. Notwithstanding the provisions of this subsection, an assignment of record of a security interest in a fixture contained in a mortgage effective as a fixture filing (subsection (6) of Section 9-402) may be made only by an assignment of the mortgage in the manner provided by the law of this state other than this Act.]

(3) After the disclosure or filing of an assignment under this section, the assignee is the secured party of record.

§ **9-406. Release of Collateral; Duties of Filing Officer; Fees.—**A secured party of record may by his signed statement release all or a part of a collateral described in a filed financing statement. The statement of release is sufficient if it contains a description of the collateral being released, the name and address of the debtor, the name and address of the secured party, and the file number of the financing statement. [A statement of release signed by a person other than the secured party of record must be accompanied by a separate written statement of assignment signed by the secured party of record and complying with subsection (2) of Section 9-405, including payment of the required fee.] Upon presentation of such a statement [of release] to the filing officer he shall mark the statement with the hour and date of filing and shall note the same upon the margin of the index of the filing of the financing statement. The uniform fee for filing and noting such a statement of release shall be $........[if the statement is in the standard form prescribed by the [Secretary of State] and otherwise shall be $........,plus in each case an additional fee of $........for each name more than one against which the statement of release is required to be indexed.

[§ **9-407. Information From Filing Officer.]***—

[(1) If the person filing any financing statement, termination statement, statement of assignment, or statement release, furnishes the filing officer a copy thereof, the filing officer shall upon request note upon the copy the file number and date and hour of the filing of the original and deliver or send the copy to such person.]

[(2) Upon request of any person, the filing officer shall issue his certificate showing whether there is on file on the date and hour stated therein, any presently effective financing statement naming a particular debtor and any statement of assignment thereof and if there is, giving the date and hour of filing of each such statement and the names and addresses of each secured party therein. The uniform fee for such a certificate shall be $........if the request for the certificate is in the standard form prescribed by the [Secretary of State] and otherwise shall be $........ Upon request the filing officer shall furnish a copy of any filed financing statement or statement of assignment for a uniform fee of $........per page.]

*This section optional.

§ **9-408. Financing Statements Covering Consigned or Leased Goods.—***A consignor or lessor of goods may file a financing statement using the terms "consignor," "consignee," "lessor," "lessee" or the like instead of the terms specified in Section 9-402. The provisions of this Part shall apply as appropriate to such a financing statement but its filing shall not of itself be a factor in determining whether or not the consignment or lease is intended as security (Section 1-201(37)). However, if it is determined for other reasons that the consignment or lease is so intended, a security interest of the consignor or lessor which attaches to the consigned or leased goods is perfected by such filing.

*This section new in 1972.

PART 5

Default

§ 9-501. Default; Procedure When Security Agreement Covers Both Real and Personal Property.—

(1) When a debtor is in default under a security agreement, a secured party has the rights and remedies provided in this Part and except as limited by subsection (3) those provided in the security agreement. He may reduce his claim to judgment, foreclose or otherwise enforce the security interest by any available judicial procedure. If the collateral is documents the secured party may proceed either as to the documents or as to the goods covered thereby. A secured party in possession has the rights, remedies and duties provided in Section 9-207. The rights and remedies referred to in this subsection are cumulative.

(2) After default, the debtor has the rights and remedies provided in this Part, those provided in the security agreement and those provided in Section 9-207.

(3) To the extent that they give rights to the debtor and impose duties on the secured party, the rules stated in the subsections referred to below may not be waived or varied except as provided with respect to compulsory disposition of collateral [(subsection (3) of Section 9-504 and] Section 9-505) and with respect to redemption of collateral (Section 9-506) but the parties may by agreement determine the standards by which the fulfillment of these rights and duties is to be measured if such standards are not manifestly unreasonable:

(a) subsection (2) of Section 9-502 and subsection (2) of Section 9-504 insofar as they require accounting for surplus proceeds of collateral;

(b) subsection (3) of Section 9-504 and subsection (1) of Section 9-505 which deal with disposition of collateral;

(c) subsection (2) of Section 9-505 which deals with acceptance of collateral as discharge of obligation;

(d) Section 9-506 which deals with redemption of collateral; and

(e) subsection (1) of Section 9-507 which deals with the secured party's liability for failure to comply with this Part.

(4) If the security agreement covers both real and personal property, the secured party may proceed under this Part as to the personal property or he may proceed as to both the real and the personal property in accordance with his rights and remedies in respect to the real property in which case the provisions of this Part do not apply.

(5) When a secured party has reduced his claim to judgment the lien of any levy which may be made upon his collateral by virtue of any execution based upon the judgment shall relate back to the date of the perfection of the security interest in such collateral. A judicial sale, pursuant to such execution, is a foreclosure of the security interest by judicial procedure within the meaning of this Section, and the secured party may purchase at the sale and thereafter hold the collateral free of any other requirements of this Article.

§ 9-502. Collection Rights of Secured Party.—

(1) When so agreed and in any event on default the secured party is entitled to notify an account debtor or the obligor on an instrument to make payment to him whether or not the assignor was theretofore making collections on the collateral, and also to take control of any proceeds to which he is entitled under Section 9-306.

(2) A secured party who by agreement is entitled to charge back uncollected collateral or otherwise to full or limited recourse against the debtor and who undertakes to collect from the account debtors or obligors must proceed in a commercially reasonable manner and may deduct his reasonable expenses of realization from the collections. If the security agreement secures an indebtedness, the secured party must account to the debtor for any surplus, and unless otherwise agreed, the debtor is liable for any deficiency. But, if the underlying transaction was a sale of accounts or chattel paper, the debtor is entitled to any surplus or is liable for any deficiency only if the security agreement so provides.

§ 9-503. Secured Party's Right to Take Possession After Default.—Unless otherwise agreed a secured party has on default the right to take possession of the collateral. In taking possession a secured party may proceed without judicial process if this can be done without breach of the peace or may proceed by action.

If the security agreement so provides the secured party may require the debtor to assemble the collateral and make it available to the secured party at a place to be designated by the secured party which is reasonably convenient to both parties. Without removal a secured party may render equipment unusable, and may dispose of collateral on the debtor's premises under Section 9-504.

§ 9-504. Secured Party's Right to Dispose of Collateral After Default; Effect of Disposition.—

(1) A secured party after default may sell, lease or otherwise dispose of any or all of the collateral in its then condition or following any commercially reasonable preparation or processing. Any sale of goods is subject to the Article on Sales (Article 2). The proceeds of disposition shall be applied in the order following to

(a) the reasonable expenses of retaking, holding, preparing for sale [or lease,] selling, [leasing] and the like and, to the extent provided for in the agreement and not prohibited by law, the reasonable attorneys' fees and legal expenses incurred by the secured party;

(b) the satisfaction of indebtedness secured by the security interest under which the disposition is made;

(c) the satisfaction of indebtedness secured by any subordinate security interest in the collateral if written notification of demand therefor is received before distribution of the proceeds is completed. If requested by the secured party, the holder of a subordinate security interest must seasonably furnish reasonable proof of his interest, and unless he does so, the secured party need not comply with his demand.

(2) If the security interest secures an indebtedness, the secured party must account to the debtor for any surplus, and, unless otherwise agreed, the debtor is liable for any deficiency. But if the underlying transaction was a sale of accounts or chattel paper, the debtor is entitled to any surplus or is liable for any deficiency only if the security agreement so provides.

(3) Disposition of the collateral may be by public or private proceedings and may be made by way of one or more contracts. Sale or other disposition may be as a unit or in parcels and at any time and place and on any terms but every aspect of the disposition including the method, manner, time, place and terms must be commercially reasonable. Unless collateral is perishable or threatens to decline speedily in value or is of a type customarily sold on a recognized market, reasonable notification of the time and place of any public sale or reasonable notification of the time after which any private sale or other intended disposition is to be made shall be sent by the secured party to the debtor, if he has not signed after default a statement renouncing or modifying his right to notification of sale. In the case of consumer goods no other notification need be sent. In other cases notification shall be sent to any other secured party from whom the secured party has received (before sending his notification to the debtor or before the debtor's renunciation of his rights) written notice of a claim of an interest in the collateral. The secured party may buy at any public sale and if the collateral is of a type customarily sold in a recognized market or is of a type which is the subject of widely distributed standard price quotations he may buy at private sale.

(4) When collateral is disposed of by a secured party after default, the disposition transfers to a purchaser for value all of the debtor's rights therein, discharges the security interest under which it is made and any security interest or lien subordinate thereto. The purchaser takes free of all such rights and interests even though the secured party fails to comply with the requirements of this Part or of any judicial proceedings

(a) in the case of a public sale, if the purchaser has no knowledge of any defects in the sale and if he does not buy in collusion with the secured party, other bidders or the person conducting the sale; or

(b) in any other case, if the purchaser acts in good faith.

(5) A person who is liable to a secured party under a guaranty, indorsement, repurchase agreement or the like and who receives a transfer of collateral from the secured party or is subrogated to his rights has thereafter the rights and duties of the secured party. Such a transfer of collateral is not a sale or disposition of the collateral under this Article.

§ 9-505. Compulsory Disposition of Collateral; Acceptance of the Collateral as Discharge of Obligation.—

(1) If the debtor has paid 60 percent of the cash price in the case of a purchase money security interest in consumer goods or 60 percent of the loan in the case of another security interest in consumer goods, and has not signed after default a statement renouncing or modifying his rights under this Part a secured party who has taken possession of collateral must dispose of it under Section 9-504 and if he fails to do so within ninety days after he takes possession the debtor at his option may recover in conversion or under Section 9-507(1) on secured party's liability.

(2) In any other case involving consumer goods or any other collateral a secured party in possession may, after default, propose to retain the collateral in satisfaction of the obligation. Written notice of such proposal shall be sent to the debtor [if he has not signed after default a statement renouncing or modifying his rights under this subsection. In the case of consumer goods no other notice need be given. In other cases notice shall be sent to any other secured party from whom the secured party has received (before sending his notice to the debtor or before the debtor's renunciation of his rights) written notice of a claim of an interest in the collateral. If the secured party receives objection in writing from a person entitled to receive notification within twenty-one days after the notice was sent, the secured party must dispose of the collateral under Section 9-504.] In the absence of such written objection the secured party may retain the collateral in satisfaction of the debtor's obligation.

§ 9-506. Debtor's Right to Redeem Collateral.—

At any time before the secured party has disposed of collateral or entered into a contract for its disposition under Section 9-504 or before the obligation has been discharged under Section 9-505(2) the debtor or any other secured party may unless otherwise agreed in writing after default redeem the collateral by tendering fulfillment of all obligations secured by the collateral as well as the expenses reasonably incurred by the secured party in retaking, holding, and preparing the collateral for disposition, in arranging for the sale, and to the extent provided in the agreement and not prohibited by law, his reasonable attorneys' fees and legal expenses.

§ 9-507. Secured Party's Liability for Failure to Comply With This Part.—

(1) If it is established that the secured party is not proceeding in accordance with the provisions of this Part disposition may be ordered or restrained on appropriate terms and conditions. If the disposition has occurred the debtor or any person entitled to notification or whose security interest has been made known to the secured party prior to the disposition has a right to recover from the secured party any loss caused by a failure to comply with the provisions of this Part. If the collateral is consumer goods, the debtor has a right to recover in any event an amount not less than the credit service charge plus 10 percent of the principal amount of the debt or the time price differential plus 10 percent of the cash price.

(2) The fact that a better price could have been obtained by a sale at a different time or in a different method from that selected by the secured party is not of itself sufficient to establish that the sale was not

made in a commercially reasonable manner. If the secured party either sells the collateral in the usual manner in any recognized market therefor or if he sells at the price current in such market at the time of his sale or if he has otherwise sold in conformity with reasonable commercial practices among dealers in the type of property sold he has sold in a commercially reasonable manner. The principles stated in the two preceding sentences with respect to sales also apply as may be appropriate to other types of disposition. A disposition which has been approved in any judicial proceeding or by any bona fide creditors' committee or representative of creditors shall conclusively be deemed to be commercially reasonable, but this sentence does not indicate that any such approval must be obtained in any case nor does it indicate that any disposition not so approved is not commercially reasonable.

Appendix B
UNIFORM PARTNERSHIP ACT

Part I

Preliminary Provisions

§ 1. **Name of Act.**—This Act may be cited as Uniform Partnership Act.

§ 2. **Definition of Terms.**—In this Act, "Court" includes every court and judge having jurisdiction in the case.

"Business" includes every trade, occupation, or profession.

"Person" includes individuals, partnerships, corporations, and other associations.

"Bankrupt" includes bankrupt under the Federal Bankruptcy Act or insolvent under any state insolvent act.

"Conveyance" includes every assignment, lease, mortgage, or encumbrance.

"Real property" includes land and any interest or estate in land.

§ 3. **Interpretation of Knowledge and Notice.**—(1) A person has "knowledge" of a fact within the meaning of this Act not only when he has actual knowledge thereof, but also when he has knowledge of such other facts as in the circumstances shows bad faith.

(2) A person has "notice" of a fact within the meaning of this Act when the person who claims the benefit of the notice:

(a) States the fact to such person, or

(b) Delivers through the mail, or by other means of communication, a written statement of the fact to such person or to a proper person at his place of business or residence.

§ 4. **Rules of Construction.**—(1) The rule that statutes in derogation of the common law are to be strictly construed shall have no application to this Act.

(2) The law of estoppel shall apply under this Act.

(3) The law of agency shall apply under this Act.

(4) This Act shall be so interpreted and construed as to effect its general purpose to make uniform the law of those states which enact it.

(5) This Act shall not be construed so as to impair the obligations of any contract existing when the Act goes into effect, nor to affect any action or proceedings begun or right accrued before this Act takes effect.

§ 5. **Rules for Cases not Provided for in this Act.**—In any case not provided for in this Act the rules of law and equity, including the law merchant, shall govern.

Part II

Nature of a Partnership

§ 6. **Partnership Defined.**—(1) A partnership is an association of two or more persons to carry on as co-owners a business for profit.

(2) But any association formed under any other statute of this state, or any statute adopted by authority, other than the authority of this state, is not a partnership under this act, unless such association would have been a partnership in this state prior to the adoption of this act; but this act shall apply to limited partnerships except in so far as the statutes relating to such partnerships are inconsistent herewith.

§ 7. **Rules for Determining the Existence of a Partnership.**—In determining whether a partnership exists, these rules shall apply:

(1) Except as provided by § 16 persons who are not partners as to each other are not partners as to third persons

(2) Joint tenancy, tenancy in common, tenancy by the entireties, joint property, common property, or part ownership does not of itself establish a partnership, whether such co-owners do or do not share any profits made by the use of the property.

(3) The sharing of gross returns does not of itself establish a partnership, whether or not the persons sharing them have a joint or common right or interest in any property from which the returns are derived.

(4) The receipt by a person of a share of the profits of a business is prima facie evidence that he is a partner in the business, but no such inference shall be drawn if such profits were received in payment:

(a) As a debt by installments or otherwise.

(b) As wages of an employee or rent to a landlord,

(c) As an annuity to a widow or representative of a deceased partner,

(d) As interest on a loan, though the amount of payment vary with the profits of the business.

(e) As the consideration for the sale of a good-will of a business or other property by installments or otherwise.

§ 8. **Partnership Property.**—(1) All property originally brought into the partnership stock or subsequently acquired by purchase or otherwise, on account of the partnership, is partnership property.

(2) Unless the contrary intention appears, property acquired with partnership funds is partnership property.

(3) Any estate in real property may be acquired in the partnership name. Title so acquired can be conveyed only in the partnership name.

(4) A conveyance to a partnership in the partnership name, though without words of inheritance, passes the entire estate of the grantor unless a contrary intent appears.

Part III

Relations of Partners to Persons Dealing With the Partnership

§ 9. **Partner Agent of Partnership as to Partnership Business.**—(1) Every partner is an agent of the partnership for the purpose of its business, and the act of every partner, including the execution in the partnership name of any instrument, for apparently carrying on in the usual way the business of the partnership of which he is a member binds the partnership, unless the partner so acting has in fact no authority to act for the partnership in the particular matter, and the person with whom he is dealing has knowledge of the fact that he has no such authority.

(2) An act of a partner which is not apparently for the carrying on of the business of the partnership in the usual way does not bind the partnership unless authorized by the other partners.

(3) Unless authorized by the other partners or unless they have abandoned the business, one or more but less than all the partners have no authority to:

(a) Assign the partnership property in trust for creditors or on the assignee's promise to pay the debts of the partnership,

(b) Dispose of the good-will of the business,

(c) Do any other act which would make it impossible to carry on the ordinary business of a partnership,

(d) Confess a judgment,

(e) Submit a partnership claim or liability in arbitration or reference.

(4) No act of a partner in contravention of a restriction on authority shall bind the partnership to persons having knowledge of the restriction.

§ 10. Conveyance of Real Property of the Partnership.—(1) Where title to real property is in the partnership name, any partner may convey title to such property by a conveyance executed in the partnership name; but the partnership may recover such property unless the partner's act binds the partnership under the provisions of paragraph (1) of §9 or unless such property has been conveyed by the grantee or a person claiming through such grantee to a holder for value without knowledge that the partner, in making the conveyance, has exceeded his authority.

(2) Where title to real property is in the name of the partnership, a conveyance executed by a partner, in his own name, passes the equitable interest of the partnership, provided the act is one within the authority of the partner under the provisions of paragraph (1) of §9.

(3) Where the title to real property is in the name of one or more but not all the partners, and the record does not disclose the right of the partnership, the partners in whose name the title stands may convey title to such property, but the partnership may recover such property if the partners' act does not bind the partnership under the provisions of paragraph (1) of §9, unless the purchaser or his assignee, is a holder for value, without knowledge.

(4) Where the title to real property is in the name of one or more or all the partners, or in a third person in trust for the partnership, a conveyance executed by a partner in the partnership name, or in his own name, passes the equitable interest of the partnership, provided the act is one within the authority of the partner under the provisions of paragraph (1) of §9.

(5) Where the title to real property is in the names of all the partners a conveyance executed by all the partners passes all their rights in such property.

§ 11. Partnership Bound by Admission of Partner.—An admission or representation made by any partner concerning partnership affairs within the scope of his authority as conferred by this Act is evidence against the partnership.

§ 12. Partnership Charged with Knowledge of or Notice to Partner.—Notice to any partner of any matter relating to partnership affairs, and the knowledge of the partner acting in the particular matter, acquired while a partner or then present to his mind, and the knowledge of any other partner who reasonably could and should have communicated it to the acting partner, operate as notice to or knowledge of the partnership, except in the case of a fraud on the partnership committed by or with the consent of that partner.

§ 13. Partnership Bound by Partner's Wrongful Act.—Where, by any wrongful act or omission of any partner acting in the ordinary course of the business of the partnership or with the authority of his co-partners, loss or injury is caused to any person, not being a partner in the partnership, or any penalty is incurred, the partnership is liable therefor to the same extent as the partner so acting or omitting to act.

§ 14. Partnership Bound by Partner's Breach of Trust.—The partnership is bound to make good the loss:

(a) Where one partner acting within the scope of his apparent authority receives money or property of a third person and misapplies it; and

(b) Where the partnership in the course of its business receives money or property of a third person and the money or property so received is misapplied by any partner while it is in the custody of the partnership.

§ 15. Nature of Partner's Liability.—All partners are liable:

(a) Jointly and severally for everything chargeable to the partnership under §§13 and 14.

(b) Jointly for all other debts and obligations of the partnership; but any partner may enter into a separate obligation to perform a partnership contract.

§ 16. Partner by Estoppel.—(1) When a person, by words spoken or written or by conduct, represents himself, or consents to another representing him to any one, as a partner in an existing partnership or with one or more persons not actual partners, he is liable to any such person to whom such representation has been made, who has, on the faith of such representation, given credit to the actual or apparent partnership, and if he has made such representation or consented to its being made in a public manner he is liable to such person, whether the representation has or has not been made or communicated to such person so giving credit by or with the knowledge of the apparent partner making the representation or consenting to its being made:

(a) When a partnership liability results, he is liable as though he were an actual member of the partnership.

(b) When no partnership liability results, he is liable jointly with the other persons, if any, so consenting to the contract or representation as to incur liability, otherwise separately.

(2) When a person has been thus represented to be a partner in an existing partnership, or with one or more persons not actual partners, he is an agent of the persons consenting to such representation to bind them to the same extent and in the same manner as though he were a partner in fact, with respect to persons who rely upon the representation. Where all the members of the existing partnership consent to the representation, a partnership act or obligation results; but in all other cases it is the joint act or obligation of the person acting and the persons consenting to the representation.

§ 17. Liability of Incoming Partner.—A person admitted as a partner into an existing partnership is liable for all the obligations of the partnership arising before his admission as though he had been a partner when such obligations were incurred, except that this liability shall be satisfied only out of partnership property.

Part IV

Relations of Partners to One Another

§ 18. Rules Determining Rights and Duties of Partners.—The rights and duties of the partners in relation to the partnership shall be determined, subject to any agreement between them, by the following rules:

(a) Each partner shall be repaid his contributions, whether by way of capital or advances to the partnership property and share equally in the profits and surplus remaining after all liabilities, including those to partners, are satisfied; and must contribute towards the losses, whether of capital or otherwise, sustained by the partnership according to his share in the profits.

(b) The partnership must indemnify every partner in respect of payments made and personal liabilities reasonably incurred by him in the ordinary and proper conduct of its business, or for the preservation of its business or property.

(c) A partner, who in aid of the partnership makes any

payment or advance beyond the amount of capital which he agreed to contribute, shall be paid interest from the date of the payment or advance.

(d) A partner shall receive interest on the capital contributed by him only from the date when repayment should be made.

(e) All partners have equal rights in the management and conduct of the partnership business.

(f) No partner is entitled to remuneration for acting in the partnership business, except that a surviving partner is entitled to reasonable compensation for his services in winding up the partnership affairs.

(g) No person can become a member of a partnership without the consent of all the partners.

(h) Any difference arising as to ordinary matters connected with the partnership business may be decided by a majority of the partners; but no act in contravention of any agreement between the partners may be done rightfully without the consent of all the partners.

§ 19. Partnership Books.—The partnership books shall be kept, subject to any agreement between the partners, at the principal place of business of the partnership, and every partner shall at all times have access to and may inspect and copy any of them.

§ 20. Duty of Partners to Render Information.—Partners shall render on demand true and full information of all things affecting the partnership to any partner or the legal representative of any deceased partner or partner under legal disability.

§ 21. Partner Accountable as a Fiduciary.—(1) Every partner must account to the partnership for any benefit, and hold as trustee for it any profits derived by him without the consent of the other partners from any transaction connected with the formation, conduct, or liquidation of the partnership or from any use by him of its property.

(2) This section applies also to the representatives of a deceased partner engaged in the liquidation of the affairs of the partnership as the personal representatives of the last surviving partner.

§ 22. Right to an Account.—Any partner shall have the right to a formal account as to partnership affairs:

(a) If he is wrongfully excluded from the partnership business or possession of its property by his co-partners.

(b) If the right exists under the terms of any agreement,

(c) As provided by §21,

(d) Whenever other circumstances render it just and reasonable.

§ 23. Continuation of Partnership Beyond Fixed Term.—(1) When a partnership for a fixed term or particular undertaking is continued after the termination of such term or particular undertaking without any express agreement, the rights and duties of the partners remain the same as they were at such termination, so far as is consistent with a partnership at will.

(2) A continuation of the business by the partners or such of them as habitually acted therein during the term, without any settlement or liquidation of the partnership affairs, is prima facie evidence of a continuation of the partnership.

Part V

Property Rights of a Partner

§ 24. Extent of Property Rights of a Partner.—The property rights of a partner are (1) his rights in specific partnership property, (2) his interest in the partnership, and (3) his right to participate in the management.

§ 25. Nature of a Partner's Right in Specific Partnership Property.—(1) A partner is co-owner with his partners of specific partnership property holding as a tenant in partnership.

(2) The incidents of this tenancy are such that:

(a) A partner, subject to the provisions of this Act and to any agreement between the partners, has an equal right with his partners to possess specific partnership property for partnership purposes; but he has no right to possess such property for any other purpose without the consent of his partners.

(b) A partner's right in specific partnership property is not assignable except in connection with the assignment of rights of all the partners in the same property.

(c) A partner's right in specific partnership property is not subject to attachment or execution, except on a claim against the partnership. When partnership property is attached for a partnership debt the partners, or any of them, or the representatives of a deceased partner, cannot claim any right under the homestead or exemption laws.

(d) On the death of a partner his right in specific partnership property vests in the surviving partner or partners, except where the deceased was the last surviving partner, when his right in such property vests in his legal representative. Such surviving partner or partners, or the legal representative of the last surviving partner, has no right to possess the partnership property for any but a partnership purpose.

(e) A partner's right in specific partnership property is not subject to dower, curtesy, or allowances to widows, heirs, or next of kin.

§ 26. Nature of Partner's Interest in the Partnership.—A partner's interest in the partnership is his share of the profits and surplus, and the same is personal property.

§ 27. Assignment of Partner's Interest.—(1) A conveyance by a partner of his interest in the partnership does not of itself dissolve the partnership, nor, as against the other partners in the absence of agreement, entitle the assignee, during the continuance of the partnership to interfere in the management or administration of the partnership business or affairs, or to require any information or account of partnership transactions, or to inspect the partnership books; but it merely entitles the assignee to receive in accordance with his contract the profits to which the assigning partner would otherwise be entitled.

(2) In case of a dissolution of the partnership, the assignee is entitled to receive his assignor's interest and may require an account from the date only of the last account agreed to by all the partners.

§ 28. Partner's Interest Subject to Charging Order.—(1) On due application to a competent court by any judgment creditor of a partner, the court which entered the judgment, order, or decree, or any other court, may charge the interest of the debtor partner with payment of the unsatisfied amount of such judgment debt with interest thereon; and may then or later appoint a receiver of his share of the profits, and of any other money due or to fall due to him in respect of the partnership, and make all other orders, directions, accounts and inquiries which the debtor partner might have made, or which the circumstances of the case may require.

(2) The interest charged may be redeemed at any time before foreclosure, or in case of a sale being directed by the court may be purchased without thereby causing a dissolution:

(a) With separate property, by any one or more of the partners, or

(b) With partnership property, by any one or more of the partners with the consent of all the partners whose interests are not so charged or sold.

(3) Nothing in this Act shall be held to deprive a partner of his right, if any, under the exemption laws, as regards his interest in the partnership.

Part VI

Dissolution and Winding Up

§ 29. Dissolution Defined.—The dissolution of a partnership is the change in the relation of the partners caused by any partner ceasing to be associated in the carrying on as distinguished from the winding up of the business.

§ 30. Partnership Not Terminated by Dissolution.—On dissolution the partnership is not terminated, but continues until the winding up of partnership affairs is completed.

§ 31. Causes of Dissolution.—Dissolution is caused:
(1) Without violation of the agreement between the partners:
  (a) By the termination of the definite term or particular undertaking specified in the agreement,
  (b) By the express will of any partner when no definite term or particular undertaking is specified,
  (c) By the express will of all the partners who have not assigned their interests or suffered them to be charged for their separate debts, either before or after the termination of any specified term or particular undertaking,
  (d) By the expulsion of any partner from the business bona fide in accordance with such a power conferred by the agreement between the partners;
(2) In contravention of the agreement between the partners, where the circumstances do not permit a dissolution under any other provision of this section, by the express will of any partner at any time;
(3) By any event which makes it unlawful for the business of the partnership to be carried on or for the members to carry it on in partnership;
(4) By the death of any partner;
(5) By the bankruptcy of any partner or the partnership;
(6) By decree of court under §32.

§ 32. Dissolution by Decree of Court.—(1) On application by or for a partner the court shall decree a dissolution whenever:
  (a) A partner has been declared a lunatic in any judicial proceeding or is shown to be of unsound mind,
  (b) A partner becomes in any other way incapable of performing his part of the partnership contract,
  (c) A partner has been guilty of such conduct as tends to affect prejudicially the carrying on of the business,
  (d) A partner wilfully or persistently commits a breach of the partnership agreement, or otherwise so conducts himself in matters relating to the partnership business that it is not reasonably practicable to carry on the business in partnership with him.
  (e) The business of the partnership can only be carried on at a loss,
  (f) Other circumstances render a dissolution equitable.
(2) On the application of the purchaser of a partner's interest under §§27 or 28:
  (a) After the termination of the specified term or particular undertaking,
  (b) At any time if the partnership was a partnership at will when the interest was assigned or when the charging order was issued.

§ 33. General Effect of Dissolution on Authority of Partner.—Except so far as may be necessary to wind up partnership affairs or to complete transactions begun but not then finished, dissolution terminates all authority of any partner to act for the partnership,
(1) With respect to the partners,
  (a) When the dissolution is not by the act, bankruptcy or death of a partner; or
  (b) When the dissolution is by such act, bankruptcy or death of a partner, in cases where §34 so requires.
(2) With respect to persons not partners, as declared in §35.

§ 34. Right of Partner to Contribution From Co-partners After Dissolution.—Where the dissolution is caused by the act, death or bankruptcy of a partner, each partner is liable to his co-partners for his share of any liability created by any partner acting for the partnership as if the partnership had not been dissolved unless:
  (a) The dissolution being by act of any partner, the partner acting for the partnership had knowledge of the dissolution, or
  (b) The dissolution being by the death or bankruptcy of a partner, the partner acting for the partnership had knowledge or notice of the death or bankruptcy.

§ 35. Power of Partner to Bind Partnership to Third Persons After Dissolution.—(1) After dissolution a partner can bind the partnership except as provided in Paragraph (3)
  (a) By any act appropriate for winding up partnership affairs or completing transactions unfinished at dissolution;
  (b) By any transaction which would bind the partnership if dissolution had not taken place, provided the other party to the transaction:
    (I) Had extended credit to the partnership prior to dissolution and had no knowledge or notice of the dissolution; or
    (II) Though he had not so extended credit, had nevertheless known of the partnership prior to dissolution, and, having no knowledge or notice of dissolution, the fact of dissolution had not been advertised in a newspaper of general circulation in the place (or in each place if more than one) at which the partnership business was regularly carried on.
(2) The liability of a partner under paragraph (1b) shall be satisfied out of partnership assets alone when such partner had been prior to dissolution:
  (a) Unknown as a partner to the person with whom the contract is made; and
  (b) So far unknown and inactive in partnership affairs that the business reputation of the partnership could not be said to have been in any degree due to his connection with it.
(3) The partnership is in no case bound by any act of a partner after dissolution:
  (a) Where the partnership is dissolved because it is unlawful to carry on the business, unless the act is appropriate for winding up partnership affairs; or
  (b) Where the partner has become bankrupt; or
  (c) Where the partner has no authority to wind up partnership affairs; except by a transaction with one who:
    (I) Had extended credit to the partnership prior to dissolution and had no knowledge or notice of his want of authority; or
    (II) Had not extended credit to the partnership prior to dissolution, and, having no knowledge or notice of his want of authority, the fact of his want of authority has not been advertised in the manner provided for advertising the fact of dissolution in paragraph (1bII).
(4) Nothing in this section shall affect the liability under §16 of any person who after dissolution represents himself or consents to another representing him as a partner in a partnership engaged in carrying on business.

§ 36. Effect of Dissolution on Partner's Existing Liability.—(1) The dissolution of the partnership does not of itself discharge the existing liability of any partner.
(2) A partner is discharged from any existing liability upon dissolution of the partnership by an agreement to that effect between himself, the partnership creditor and the person or partnership continuing the business; and such agreement may be inferred from the course of dealing between the creditor having knowledge of the dissolution and the person or partnership continuing the business.

(3) Where a person agrees to assume the existing obligations of a dissolved partnership, the partners whose obligations have been assumed shall be discharged from any liability to any creditor of the partnership who, knowing of the agreement, consents to a material alteration in the nature or time of payment of such obligations.

(4) The individual property of a deceased partner shall be liable for all obligations of the partnership incurred while he was a partner but subject to the prior payment of his separate debts.

§ 37. Right to Wind Up.—Unless otherwise agreed the partners who have not wrongfully dissolved the partnership or the legal representative of the last surviving partner, not bankrupt, has the right to wind up the partnership affairs; provided, however, that any partner, his legal representative or his assignee, upon cause shown, may obtain winding up by the court.

§ 38. Rights of Partners to Application of Partnership Property.—(1) When dissolution is caused in any way, except in contravention of the partnership agreement, each partner as against his co-partners and all persons claiming through them in respect of their interests in the partnership, unless otherwise agreed, may have the partnership property applied to discharge its liabilities, and the surplus applied to pay in cash the net amount owing to the respective partners. But if dissolution is caused by expulsion of a partner, bona fide under the partnership agreement and if the expelled partner is discharged from all partnership liabilities, either by payment or agreement under §36 (2), he shall receive in cash only the net amount due him from the partnership.

(2) When dissolution is caused in contravention of the partnership agreement the rights of the partners shall be as follows:

(a) Each partner who has not caused dissolution wrongfully shall have:

(I) All the rights specified in paragraph (1) of this section, and

(II) The right, as against each partner who has caused the dissolution wrongfully, to damages for breach of the agreement.

(b) The partners who have not caused the dissolution wrongfully, if they all desire to continue the business in the same name, either by themselves or jointly with others, may do so, during the agreed term for the partnership and for that purpose may possess the partnership property, provided they secure the payment by bond approved by the court, or pay to any partner who has caused the dissolution wrongfully, the value of his interest in the partnership at the dissolution, less any damages recoverable under clause (2aII) of the section, and in like manner indemnify him against all present or future partnership liabilities.

(c) A partner who has caused the dissolution wrongfully shall have:

(I) If the business is not continued under the provisions of paragraph (2b) all the rights of a partner under paragraph (1), subject to clause (2aII), of this section,

(II) If the business is continued under paragraph (2b) of this section the right as against his co-partners and all claiming through them in respect of their interests in the partnership, to have the value of his interest in the partnership, less any damages caused to his co-partners by the dissolution, ascertained and paid him in cash, or the payment secured by bond approved by the court, and to be released from all existing liabilities of the partnership; but in ascertaining the value of the partner's interest the value of the good-will of the business shall not be considered.

§ 39. Rights Where Partnership is Dissolved for Fraud or Misrepresentation.—Where a partnership contract is rescinded on the ground of the fraud or misrepresentation of one of the parties thereto, the party entitled to rescind is, without prejudice to any other right, entitled:

(a) To a lien on, or right of retention of, the surplus of the partnership property after satisfying the partnership liabilities to third persons for any sum of money paid by him for the purchase of an interest in the partnership and for any capital or advances contributed by him; and

(b) To stand, after all liabilities to third persons have been satisfied, in the place of the creditors of the partnership for any payments made by him in respect of the partnership liabilities; and

(c) To be indemnified by the person guilty of the fraud or making the representation against all debts and liabilities of the partnership.

§ 40. Rules for Distribution.—In settling accounts between the partners after dissolution, the following rules shall be observed, subject to any agreement to the contrary:

(a) The assets of the partnership are:

(I) The partnership property,

(II) The contributions of the partners necessary for the payment of all the liabilities specified in clause (b) of this paragraph.

(b) The liabilities of the partnership shall rank in order of payment, as follows:

(I) Those owing to creditors other than partners,

(II) Those owing to partners other than for capital and profits,

(III) Those owing to partners in respect of capital,

(IV) Those owing to partners in respect of profits.

(c) The assets shall be applied in the order of their declaration in clause (a) of this paragraph to the satisfaction of the liabilities.

(d) The partners shall contribute, as provided by §18 (a) the amount necessary to satisfy the liabilities; but if any, but not all, of the partners are insolvent, or, not being subject to process, refuse to contribute, the other partners shall contribute their share of the liabilities, and, in the relative proportions in which they share the profits, the additional amount necessary to pay the liabilities.

(e) An assignee for the benefit of creditors or any person appointed by the court shall have the right to enforce the contributions specified in clause (d) of this paragraph.

(f) Any partner or his legal representative shall have the right to enforce the contributions specified in clause (d) of this paragraph, to the extent of the amount which he has paid in excess of his share of the liability.

(g) The individual property of a deceased partner shall be liable for the contributions specified in clause (d) of this paragraph.

(h) When partnership property and the individual properties of the partners are in possession of a court for distribution, partnership creditors shall have priority on partnership property and separate creditors on individual property, saving the rights of lien or secured creditors as heretofore.

(i) Where a partner has become bankrupt or his estate is insolvent the claims against his separate property shall rank in the following order:

(I) Those owing to separate creditors,

(II) Those owing to partnership creditors,

(III) Those owing to partners by way of contribution.

§ 41. Liability of Persons Continuing the Business in Certain Cases.—(1) When any new partner is admitted into an existing partnership, or when any partner retires and assigns (or the representative of the deceased partner assigns) his rights in partnership property to two or more of the partners, or to one or more of the partners and one or more third persons, if the business is continued without liquidation of the partnership affairs, creditors of the first or dissolved partnership are also creditors of the partnership so continuing the business.

(2) When all but one partner retire and assign (or the representative of a deceased partner assigns) their rights in partnership property to the remaining partner, who continues the business without liquidation of partnership affairs, either alone or with others, creditors of the dissolved partnership are also creditors of the person or partnership so continuing the business.

(3) When any partner retires or dies and the business of the dissolved partnership is continued as set forth in paragraphs (1) and (2) of this section, with the consent of the retired partners or the representative of the deceased partner, but without any assignment of his right in partnership property, rights of creditors of the dissolved partnership and of the creditors of the person or partnership continuing the business shall be as if such assignment had been made.

(4) When all the partners or their representatives assign their rights in partnership property to one or more third persons who promise to pay the debts and who continue the business of the dissolved partnership, creditors of the dissolved partnership are also creditors of the person or partnership continuing the business.

(5) When any partner wrongfully causes a dissolution and the remaining partners continue the business under the provisions of §38 (2b), either alone or with others, and without liquidation of the partnership affairs, creditors of the dissolved partnership are also creditors of the person or partnership continuing the business.

(6) When a partner is expelled and the remaining partners continue the business either alone or with others, without liquidation of the partnership affairs, creditors of the dissolved partnership are also creditors of the person or partnership continuing the business.

(7) The liability of a third person becoming a partner in the partnership continuing the business, under this section, to the creditors of the dissolved partnership shall be satisfied out of partnership property only.

(8) When the business of a partnership after dissolution is continued under any conditions set forth in this section the creditors of the dissolved partnership, as against the separate creditors of the retiring or deceased partner or the representative of the deceased partner, have a prior right to any claim of the retired partner or the representative of the deceased partner against the person or partnership continuing the business, on account of the retired or deceased partner's interest in the dissolved partnership

or on account of any consideration promised for such interest or for his right in partnership property.

(9) Nothing in this section shall be held to modify any right of creditors to set aside any assignment on the ground of fraud.

(10) The use by the person or partnership continuing the business of the partnership name, or the name of a deceased partner as part thereof, shall not of itself make the individual property of the deceased partner liable for any debts contracted by such person or partnership.

§ 42. Rights of Retiring or Estate of Deceased Partner When the Business is Continued.—When any partner retires or dies, and the business is continued under any of the conditions set forth in §41 (1, 2, 3, 5, 6), or §38 (2b), without any settlement of accounts as between him or his estate and the person or partnership continuing the business, unless otherwise agreed, he or his legal representative as against such persons or partnership may have the value of his interest at the date of dissolution ascertained, and shall receive as an ordinary creditor an amount equal to the value of his interest in the dissolved partnership with interest, or, at his option or at the option of his legal representative, in lieu of interest, the profits attributable to the use of his right in the property of the dissolved partnership; provided that the creditors of the dissolved partnership as against the separate creditors, or the representative of the retired or deceased partner, shall have priority on any claim arising under this section, as provided by §41 (8) of this Act.

§ 43. Accrual of Actions.—The right to an account of his interest shall accrue to any partner, or his legal representative, as against the winding up partners or the surviving partners or the person or partnership continuing the business, at the date of dissolution, in the absence of any agreement to the contrary.

Part VII

Miscellaneous Provisions

§ 44. When Act Takes Effect.—This Act shall take effect on the . . . . . . day of . . . . . . one thousand nine hundred and . . . . .

§ 45. Legislation Repealed.—All Acts or parts of Acts inconsistent with this Act are hereby repealed.

Appendix C
UNIFORM LIMITED PARTNERSHIP ACT (1976)

Article 1

General Provisions

§ 101. **Definitions.**—As used in this Act, unless the context otherwise requires:

(1) "Certificate of limited partnership" means the certificate referred to in Section 201, and the certificate as amended.

(2) "Contribution" means any cash, property, services rendered, or a promissory note or other binding obligation to contribute cash or property or to perform services, which a partner contributes to a limited partnership in his capacity as a partner.

(3) "Event of withdrawal of a general partner" means an event that causes a person to cease to be a general partner as provided in Section 402.

(4) "Foreign limited partnership" means a partnership formed under the laws of any State other than this State and having as partners one or more general partners and one or more limited partners.

(5) "General partner" means a person who has been admitted to a limited partnership as a general partner in accordance with the partnership agreement and named in the certificate of limited partnership as a general partner.

(6) "Limited partner" means a person who has been admitted to a limited partnership as a limited partner in accordance with the partnership agreement and named in the certificate of limited partnership as a limited partner.

(7) "Limited partnership" and "domestic limited partnership" mean a partnership formed by 2 or more persons under the laws of this State and having one or more general partners and one or more limited partners.

(8) "Partner" means a limited or general partner.

(9) "Partnership agreement" means any valid agreement, written or oral, of the partners as to the affairs of a limited partnership and the conduct of its business.

(10) "Partnership interest" means a partner's share of the profits and losses of a limited partnership and the right to receive distributions of a partnership assets.

(11) "Person" means a natural person, partnership, limited partnership (domestic or foreign), trust, estate, association, or corporation.

(12) "State" means a state, territory, or possession of the United States, the District of Columbia, or the Commonwealth of Puerto Rico.

§ 102. **Name.**—The name of each limited partnership as set forth in its certificate of limited partnership:

(1) shall contain without abbreviation the words "limited partnership";

(2) may not contain the name of a limited partner unless (i) it is also the name of a general partner or the corporate name of a corporate general partner, or (ii) the business of the limited partnership had been carried on under that name before the admission of that limited partner;

(3) may not contain any word or phrase indicating or implying that it is organized other than for a purpose stated in its certificate of limited partnership;

(4) may not be the same as, or deceptively similar to, the name of any corporation or limited partnership organized under the laws of this State or licensed or registered as a foreign corporation or limited partnership in this State; and

(5) may not contain the following words [here insert prohibited words].

§ 103. **Reservation of Name.**—

(a) The exclusive right to the use of a name may be reserved by:

(1) any person intending to organize a limited partnership under this Act and to adopt that name;

(2) any domestic limited partnership or any foreign limited partnership registered in this State which, in either case, intends to adopt that name;

(3) any foreign limited partnership intending to register in this State and adopt that name; and

(4) any person intending to organize a foreign limited partnership and intending to have it register in this State and adopt that name.

(b) The reservation shall be made by filing with the Secretary of State an application, executed by the applicant, to reserve a specified name. If the Secretary of State finds that the name is available for use by a domestic or foreign limited partnership, he shall reserve the name for the exclusive use of the applicant for a period of 120 days. Once having so reserved a name, the same applicant may not again reserve the same name until more than 60 days after the expiration of the last 120-day period for which that applicant reserved that name. The right to the exclusive use of a reserved name may be transferred to any other person by filing in the office of the Secretary of State a notice of the transfer, executed by the applicant for whom the name was reserved and specifying the name and address of the transferee.

§ 104. **Specified Office and Agent.**—Each limited partnership shall continuously maintain in this State:

(1) an office, which may but need not be a place of its business in this State, at which shall be kept the records required by Section 105 to be maintained; and

(2) an agent for service of process on the limited partnership, which agent must be an individual resident of this State, a domestic corporation, or a foreign corporation authorized to do business in this State.

§ 105. **Records to be Kept.**—Each limited partnership shall keep at the office referred to in Section 104(1) the following: (1) a current list of the full name and last known business address of each partner set forth in alphabetical order, (2) a copy of the certificate of limited partnership and all certificates of amendment thereto, together with executed copies of any powers of attorney pursuant to which any certificate has been executed, (3) copies of the limited partnership's federal, state and local income tax returns and reports, if any, for the 3 most recent years, and (4) copies of any then effective written partnership agreements and of any financial statements of the limited partnership for the 3 most recent years. Those records are subject to inspection and copying at the reasonable request, and at the expense, of any partner during ordinary business hours.

§ 106. **Nature of Business.**—A limited partnership may carry on any business that a partnership without limited partners may carry on except [here designate prohibited activities].

§ 107. **Business Transactions of Partner with Partnership.**—Except as provided in the partnership agreement, a partner may lend money to and transact other business with the limited partnership and, subject to other applicable law, has the same rights and obligations with respect thereto as a person who is not a partner.

Article 2

Formation: Certificate of Limited Partnership

§ 201. Certificate of Limited Partnership.—

(a) In order to form a limited partnership two or more persons must execute a certificate of limited partnership. The certificate shall be filed in the office of the Secretary of State and set forth:

(1) the name of the limited partnership;

(2) the general character of its business;

(3) the address of the office and the name and address of the agent for service of process required to be maintained by Section 104;

(4) the name and the business address of each partner (specifying separately the general partners and limited partners);

(5) the amount of cash and a description and statement of the agreed value of the other property or services contributed by each partner and which each partner has agreed to contribute in the future;

(6) the times at which or events on the happening of which any additional contributions agreed to be made by each partner are to be made;

(7) any power of a limited partner to grant the right to become a limited partner to an assignee of any part of his partnership interest, and the terms and conditions of the power;

(8) if agreed upon, the time at which or the events on the happening of which a partner may terminate his membership in the limited partnership and the amount of, or the method of determining, the distribution to which he may be entitled respecting his partnership interest, and the terms and conditions of the termination and distribution;

(9) any right of a partner to receive distributions of property, including cash from the limited partnership;

(10) any right of a partner to receive, or of a general partner to make, distributions to a partner which include a return of all or any part of the partner's contribution;

(11) any time at which or events upon the happening of which the limited partnership is to be dissolved and its affairs wound up;

(12) any right of the remaining general partners to continue the business on the happening of an event of withdrawal of a general partner; and

(13) any other matters the partners determine to include therein.

(b) A limited partnership is formed at the time of the filing of the certificate of limited partnership in the office of the Secretary of State or at any later time specified in the certificate of limited partnership if, in either case, there has been substantial compliance with the requirements of this section.

§ 202. Amendment to Certificate.—

(a) A certificate of limited partnership is amended by filing a certificate of amendment thereto in the office of the Secretary of State. The certificate shall set forth:

(1) the name of the limited partnership;

(2) the date of filing the certificate; and

(3) the amendment to the certificate.

(b) Within 30 days after the happening of any of the following events, an amendment to a certificate of limited partnership reflecting the occurrence of the event or events shall be filed:

(1) a change in the amount or character of the contribution of any partner, or in any partner's obligation to make a contribution:

(2) the admission of a new partner;

(3) the withdrawal of a partner; or

(4) the continuation of the business under Section 801 after an event of withdrawal of a general partner.

(c) A general partner who becomes aware that any statement in a certificate of limited partnership was false when made or that any arrangements or other facts described have changed, making the certificate inaccurate in any respect, shall promptly amend the certificate, but an amendment to show a change of address of a limited partner need be filed only once every 12 months.

(d) A certificate of limited partnership may be amended at any time for any other proper purpose the general partners determine.

(e) No person has any liability because an amendment to a certificate of limited partnership has not been filed to reflect the occurrence of any event referred to in subsection (b) of this Section if the amendment is filed within the 30-day period specified in subsection (b).

§ 203. Cancellation of Certificate.—

A certificate of limited partnership shall be cancelled upon the dissolution and the commencement of winding up of the partnership or at any other time there are no limited partners. A certificate of cancellation shall be filed in the office of the Secretary of State and set forth:

(1) the name of the limited partnership;

(2) the date of filing of its certificate of limited partnership;

(3) the reason for filing the certificate of cancellation;

(4) the effective date (which shall be a date certain) of cancellation if it is not to be effective upon the filing of the certificate; and

(5) any other information the general partners filing the certificate determine.

§ 204. Execution of Certificates.—

(a) Each certificate required by this Article to be filed in the office of the Secretary of State shall be executed in the following manner:

(1) an original certificate of limited partnership must be signed by all partners named therein;

(2) a certificate of amendment must be signed by at least one general partner and by each other partner designated in the certificate as a new partner or whose contribution is described as having been increased; and

(3) a certificate of cancellation must be signed by all general partners;

(b) Any person may sign a certificate by an attorney-in-fact, but a power of attorney to sign a certificate relating to the admission, or increased contribution, of a partner must specifically describe the admission or increase.

(c) The execution of a certificate by a general partner constitutes an affirmation under the penalties of perjury that the facts stated therein are true.

§ 205. Amendment or Cancellation by Judicial Act.—

If a person required by Section 204 to execute a certificate of amendment or cancellation fails or refuses to do so, any other partner, and any assignee of a partnership interest, who is adversely affected by the failure or refusal, may petition the [here designate the proper court] to direct the amendment or cancellation. If the court finds that the amendment or cancellation is proper and that any person so designated has failed or refused to execute the certificate, it shall order the Secretary of State to record an appropriate certificate of amendment or cancellation.

§ 206. Filing in Office of Secretary of State.—

(a) Two signed copies of the certificate of limited partnership and of any certificates of amendment or cancellation (or of any judicial decree of amendment or cancellation) shall be delivered to the Secretary of State. A person who executes a certificate as an agent or fiduciary need not exhibit evidence of his authority as a prerequisite to filing. Unless the Secretary of State finds that any certificate does not conform to law, upon receipt of all filing fees required by law he shall:

(1) endorse on each duplicate original the word "Filed" and the day, month and year of the filing thereof;

(2) file one duplicate original in his office; and

(3) return the other duplicate original to the person who filed it or his representative.

(b) Upon the filing of a certificate of amendment (or judicial decree of amendment) in the office of the Secretary of State, the certificate of limited partnership shall be amended as set forth therein, and upon the effective date of a certificate of cancellation (or a judicial decree thereof), the certificate of limited partnership is cancelled.

§ 207. Liability for False Statement in Certificate.—If any certificate of limited partnership or certificate of amendment or cancellation contains a false statement, one who suffers loss by reliance on the statement may recover damages for the loss from:

(1) any person who executes the certificate, or causes another to execute it on his behalf, and knew, and any general partner who knew or should have known, the statement to be false at the time the certificate was executed; and

(2) any general partner who thereafter knows or should have known that any arrangement or other fact described in the certificate has changed, making the statement inaccurate in any respect within a sufficient time before the statement was relied upon reasonably to have enabled that general partner to cancel or amend the certificate, or to file a petition for its cancellation or amendment under Section 205.

§ 208. Notice.—The fact that a certificate of limited partnership is on file in the office of the Secretary of State is notice that the partnership is a limited partnership and the persons designated therein as limited partners are limited partners, but it is not notice of any other fact.

§ 209. Delivery of Certificates to Limited Partners.—Upon the return by the Secretary of State pursuant to Section 206 of a certificate marked "Filed", the general partners shall promptly deliver or mail a copy of the certificate of limited partnership and each certificate to each limited partner unless the partnership agreement provides otherwise.

Article 3

Limited Partners

§ 301. Admission of Additional Limited Partners.—(a) After the filing of a limited partnership's original certificate of limited partnership, a person may be admitted as an additional limited partner:

(1) in the case of a person acquiring a partnership interest directly from the limited partnership, upon the compliance with the partnership agreement or, if the partnership-agreement does not so provide, upon the written consent of all partners; and

(2) in the case of an assignee of a partnership interest of a partner who has the power, as provided in Section 704, to grant the assignee the right to become a limited partner, upon the exercise of that power and compliance with any conditions limiting the grant or exercise of the power.

(b) In each case under subsection (a), the person acquiring the partnership interest becomes a limited partner only upon amendment of the certificate of limited partnership reflecting that fact.

§ 302. Voting.—Subject to Section 303, the partnership agreement may grant to all or a specified group of the limited partners the right to vote (on a per capita or other basis) upon any matter.

§ 303. Liability to Third Parties.—(a) Except as provided in subsection (d), a limited partner is not liable for the obligations of a limited partnership unless he is also a general partner or, in addition to the exercise of his rights and powers as a limited partner, he takes part in the control of the business. However, if the limited partner's participation in the control of the business is not substantially the same as the exercise of the powers of a general partner, he is liable only to persons who transact business with the limited partnership with actual knowledge of his participation in control.

(b) A limited partner does not participate in the control of the

business within the meaning of subsection (a) solely by doing one or more of the following:

(1) being a contractor for or an agent or employee of the limited partnership or of a general partner;

(2) consulting with and advising a general partner with respect to the business of the limited partnership;

(3) acting as surety for the limited partnership;

(4) approving or disapproving an amendment to the partnership agreement; or

(5) voting on one or more of the following matters:

(i) the dissolution and winding up of the limited partnership;

(ii) the sale, exchange, lease, mortgage, pledge, or other transfer of all or substantially all of the assets of the limited partnership other than in the ordinary course of its business;

(iii) the incurrence of indebtedness by the limited partnership other than in the ordinary course of its business;

(iv) a change in the nature of the business; or

(v) the removal of a general partner.

(c) the enumeration in subsection (b) does not mean that the possession or exercise of any other powers by a limited partner constitutes participation by him in the business of the limited partnership.

(d) A limited partner who knowingly permits his name to be used in the name of the limited partnership, except under circumstances permitted by Section 102(2)(i), is liable to creditors who extend credit to the limited partnership without actual knowledge that the limited partner is not a general partner.

§ 304. Person Erroneously Believing Himself Limited Partner.—(a) Except as provided in subsection (b), a person who makes a contribution to a business enterprise and erroneously but in good faith believes that he has become a limited partner in the enterprise is not a general partner in the enterprise and is not bound by its obligations by reason of making the contribution, receiving distributions from the enterprise, or exercising any rights of a limited partner, if, on ascertaining the mistake, he:

(1) causes an appropriate certificate of limited partnership or a certificate of amendment to be executed and filed; or

(2) withdraws from future equity participation in the enterprise.

(b) A person who makes a contribution of the kind described in subsection (a) is liable as a general partner to any third party who transacts business with the enterprise (i) before the person withdraws and an appropriate certificate is filed to show withdrawal, or (ii) before an appropriate certificate is filed to show his status as a limited partner and, in the case of an amendment, after expiration of the 30-day period for filing an amendment relating to the person as a limited partner under Section 202, but in either case only if the third party actually believed in good faith that the person was a general partner at the time of the transaction.

§ 305. Information.—Each limited partner has the right to:

(1) inspect and copy any of the partnership records required to be maintained by Section 105; and

(2) obtain from the general partners from time to time upon reasonable demand (i) true and full information regarding the state of the business and financial condition of the limited partnership, (ii) promptly after becoming available, a copy of the limited partnership's federal, state and local income tax returns for each year, and (iii) other information regarding the affairs of the limited partnership as is just and reasonable.

Article 4

General Partners

§ 401. Admission of Additional General Partners.—After the filing of a limited partnership's original certificate of limited partnership, additional general partners may be admitted only with the specific written consent of each partner.

§ 402. Events of Withdrawal.—Except as approved by the specific written consent of all partners at the time, a person ceases to be a general partner of a limited partnership upon the happening of any of the following events:

(1) the general partner withdraws from the limited partnership as provided in Section 602;

(2) the general partner ceases to be a member of the limited partnership as provided in Section 702;

(3) the general partner is removed as a general partner in accordance with the partnership agreement;

(4) unless otherwise provided in the certificate of limited partnership, the general partner: (i) makes an assignment for the benefit of creditors; (ii) files a voluntary petition in bankruptcy; (iii) is adjudicated a bankrupt or insolvent; (iv) files a petition or answer seeking for himself any reorganization, arrangement, composition, readjustment, liquidation, dissolution or similar relief under any statute, law, or regulation; (v) files an answer or other pleading admitting or failing to contest the material allegations of a petition filed against him in any proceeding of this nature; or (vi) seeks, consents to, or acquiesces in the appointment of a trustee, receiver, or liquidator of the general partner or of all or any substantial part of his properties;

(5) unless otherwise provided in the certificate of limited partnership, [120] days after the commencement of any proceeding against the general partner seeking reorganization, arrangement, composition, readjustment, liquidation, dissolution or similar relief under any statute, law, or regulation, the proceeding has not been dismissed, or if within [90] days after the appointment without his consent or acquiescence of a trustee, receiver, or liquidator of the general partner or of all or any substantial part of his properties, the appointment is not vacated or stayed or within [90] days after the expiration of any such stay, the appointment is not vacated;

(6) in the case of a general partner who is a natural person,

(i) his death; or

(ii) the entry by a court of competent jurisdiction adjudicating him incompetent to manage his person or his estate;

(7) in the case of a general partner who is acting as a general partner by virtue of being a trustee of a trust, the termination of the trust (but not merely the substitution of a new trustee);

(8) in the case of a general partner that is a separate partnership, the dissolution and commencement of winding up of the separate partnership;

(9) in the case of a general partner that is a corporation, the filing of a certificate of dissolution, or its equivalent, for the corporation or the revocation of its charter; or

(10) in the case of an estate, the distribution by the fiduciary of the estate's entire interest in the partnership.

§ 403. General Powers and Liabilities.—Except as provided in this Act or in the partnership agreement, a general partner of a limited partnership has the rights andpowers and is subject to the restrictions and liabilities of a partner in a partnership without limited partners.

§ 404. Contributions by General Partner.—A general partner of a limited partnership may make contributions to the partnership and share in the profits and losses of, and in distributions from, the limited partnership as a general partner. A general partner also may make contributions to and share in profits, losses, and distributions as a limited partner. A person who is both a general partner and a limited partner has the rights and powers, and is subject to the restrictions and liabilities, of a general partner and, except as provided in the partnership agreement, also has the powers, and is subject to the restrictions, of a limited partner to the extent of his participation in the partnership as a limited partner.

§ 405. Voting.—The partnership agreement may grant to all or certain identified general partners the right to vote (on a per capita or any other basis), separately or with all or any class of the limited partners, on any matter.

Article 5

Finance

§ 501. Form of Contribution.—The contribution of a partner may be in cash, property, or services rendered, or a promissory note or other obligation to contribute cash or property or to perform services.

§ 502. Liability for Contribution.—(a) Except as provided in the certificate of limited partnership, a partner is obligated to the limited partnership to perform any promise to contribute cash or property or to perform services, even if he is unable to perform because of death, disability or any other reason. If a partner does not make the required contribution of property or services, he is obligated at the option of the limited partnership to contribute cash equal to that portion of the value (as stated in the certificate of limited partnership) of the stated contribution that has not been made.

(b) Unless otherwise provided in the partnership agreement, the obligation of a partner to make a contribution or return money or other property paid or distributed in violation of this Act may be compromised only by consent of all the partners. Notwithstanding the compromise, a creditor of a limited partnership who extends credit, or whose claim arises, after the filing of the certificate of limited partnership or an amendment thereto which, in either case, reflects the obligation, and before the amendment or cancellation thereof to reflect the compromise, may enforce the original obligation.

§ 503. Sharing of Profits and Losses.—The profits and losses of a limited partnership shall be allocated among the partners, and among classes of partners, in the manner provided in the partnership agreement. If the partnership agreement does not so provide, profits and losses shall be allocated on the basis of the value (as stated in the certificate of limited partnership) of the contributions made by each partner to the extent they have been received by the partnership and have not been returned.

§ 504. Sharing of Distributions.—Distributions of cash or other assets of a limited partnership shall be allocated among the partners, and among classes of partners, in the manner provided in the partnership agreement. If the partnership agreement does not so provide, distributions shall be made on the basis of the value (as stated in the certificate of limited partnership) of the contributions made by each partner to the extent they have been received by the partnership and have not been returned.

Article 6

Distribution and Withdrawal

§ 601. Interim Distributions.—Except as provided in this Article, a partner is entitled to receive distributions from a limited partnership before his withdrawal from the limited partnership and before the dissolution and winding up thereof:

(1) to the extent and at the times or upon the happening of the events specified in the partnership agreement; and

(2) if any distribution constitutes a return of any part of his contribution under Section 608(c), to the extent and at the times or upon the happening of the events specified in the certificate of limited partnership.

§ 602. Withdrawal of General Partner.—A general partner may withdraw from a limited partnership at any time by giving written notice to the other partners, but if the withdrawal violates the partnership agreement, the limited partnership may recover from the withdrawing general partner damages for breach of the partnership agreement and offset the damages against the amount otherwise distributable to him.

§ 603. Withdrawal of Limited Partner.—A limited partner may withdraw from a limited partnership at the time or upon the happening of events specified in the certificate of limited partnership and in accordance with the partnership agreement. If the certificate does not specify the time or the events upon the happening of which a limited partner may withdraw or a definite time for the dissolution and winding up of the limited partnership, a limited partner may withdraw upon not less than 6 months' prior written notice to each general partner at his address on the books of the limited partnership at its office in this State.

§ 604. Distribution Upon Withdrawal.—Except as provided in this Article, upon withdrawal any withdrawing partner is entitled to receive any distribution to which he is entitled under the partnership agreement and, if not otherwise provided in the agreement, he is entitled to receive, within a reasonable time after withdrawal, the fair value of his interest in the limited partnership as of the date of withdrawal based upon his right to share in distributions from the limited partnership.

§ 605. Distribution in Kind.—Except as provided in the certificate of limited partnership, a partner, regardless of the nature of his contribution, has no right to demand and receive any distribution from a limited partnership in any form other than cash. Except as provided in the partnership agreement, a partner may not be compelled to accept a distribution of any asset in kind from a limited partnership to the extent that the percentage of the asset distributed to him exceeds a percentage of that asset which is equal to the percentage in which he shares in distributions from the limited partnership.

§ 606. Right to Distribution.—At the time a partner becomes entitled to receive a distribution, he has the status of, and is entitled to all remedies available to, a creditor of the limited partnership with respect to the distribution.

§ 607. Limitations on Distribution.—A partner may not receive a distribution from a limited partnership to the extent that, after giving effect to the distribution, all liabilities of the limited partnership, other than liabilities to partners on account of their partnership interests, exceed the fair value of the partnership assets.

§ 608. Liability Upon Return of Contribution.—(a) If a partner has received the return of any part of his contribution without violation of the partnership agreement or this Act, he is liable to the limited partnership for a period of one year thereafter for the amount of the returned contribution, but only to the extent necessary to discharge the limited partnership's liabilities to creditors who extended credit to the limited partnership during the period the contribution was held by the partnership.

(b) If a partner has received the return of any part of his contribution in violation of the partnership agreement or this Act, he is liable to the limited partnership for a period of 6 years thereafter for the amount of the contribution wrongfully returned.

(c) A partner receives a return of his contribution to the extent that a distribution to him reduces his share of the fair value of the net assets of the limited partnership below the value (as set forth in the certificate of limited partnership) of his contribution which has not been distributed to him.

Article 7

Assignment of Partnership Interests

§ 701. Nature of Partnership Interest.—A partnership interest is personal property.

§ 702. Assignment of Partnership Interest.—Except as provided in the partnership agreement, a partnership interest is assignable in whole or in part. An assignment of a partnership interest does not dissolve a limited partnership or entitle the assignee to become or to exercise any rights of a partner. An assignment entitles the assignee to receive, to the extent assigned, only the distribution to which the assignor would be entitled. Except as provided in the partnership agreement, a partner ceases to be a partner upon assignment of all his partnership interest.

§ 703. Rights of Creditor.—On application to a court of competent jurisdiction by any judgment creditor of a partner, the court may charge the partnership interest of the partner with payment of the unsatisfied amount of the judgment with interest. To the extent so charged, the judgment creditor has only the rights of an assignee of the partnership interest. This Act does not deprive any partner of the benefit of any exemption laws applicable to his partnership interest.

§ 704. Right of Assignee to Become Limited Partner.—(a) An assignee of a partnership interest, including an assignee of a general partner, may become a limited partner if and to the extent that (1) the assignor gives the assignee that right in accordance with authority described in the certificate of limited partnership, or (2) all other partners consent.

(b) An assignee who has become a limited partner has, to the extent assigned, the rights and powers, and is subject to the restrictions and liabilities, of a limited partner under the partnership agreement and this Act. An assignee who becomes a limited partner also is liable for the obligations of his assignor to make and return contributions as provided in Article 6. However, the assignee is not obligated for liabilities unknown to the assignee at the time he became a limited partner and which could not be ascertained from the certificate of limited partnership.

(c) If an assignee of a partnership interest becomes a limited partner, the assignor is not released from his liability to the limited partnership under Sections 207 and 502.

§ 705. Power of Estate of Deceased or Incompetent Partner.— If a partner who is an individual dies or a court of competent jurisdiction adjudges him to be incompetent to manage his person or his property, the partner's executor, administrator guardian, conservator, or other legal representative may exercise all the partner's rights for the purpose of settling his estate or administering his property, including any power the partner had to give an assignee the right to become a limited partner. If a partner is a corporation, trust, or other entity and is dissolved or terminated, the powers of that partner may be exercised by its legal representative or successor.

Article 8

Dissolution

§ 801. Nonjudicial Dissolution.—A limited partnership is dissolved and its affairs shall be wound up upon the happening of the first to occur of the following:

(1) at the time or upon the happening of events specified in the certificate of limited partnership;

(2) written consent of all partners;

(3) an event of withdrawal of a general partner unless at the time there is at least one other general partner and the certificate of limited partnership permits the business of the limited partnership to be carried on by the remaining general partner and that partner does so, but the limited partnership is not dissolved and is not required to be wound up by reason of any event of withdrawal if, within 90 days after the withdrawal, all partners agree in writing to continue the business of the limited partnership and to the appointment of one or more additional partners if necessary or desired; or

(4) entry of a decree of judicial dissolution under Section 802.

§ 802. **Judicial Dissolution.**—On application by or for a partner the [here designate the proper court] court may decree dissolution of a limited partnership whenever it is not reasonably practicable to carry on the business in conformity with the partnership agreement.

§ 803. **Winding Up.**—Except as provided in the partnership agreement, the general partners who have not wrongfully dissolved a limited partnership or, if none, the limited partners, may wind up the limited partnership's affairs; but the [here designate the proper court] court may wind up the limited partnership's affairs upon application of any partner, his legal representative, or assignee.

§ 804. **Distribution of Assets.**—Upon the winding up of a limited partnership, the assets shall be distributed as follows:

(1) to creditors, including partners who are creditors, to the extent permitted by law, in satisfaction of liabilities of the limited partnership other than liabilities for distributions to partners under Section 601 or 604;

(2) except as provided in the partnership agreement, to partners and former partners in satisfaction of liabilities for distributions under Section 601 or 604; and

(3) except as provided in the partnership agreement, to partners *first* for the return of their contributions and *secondly* respecting their partnership interests, in the proportions in which the partners share in distributions.

Article 9

Foreign Limited Partnerships

§ 901. **Law Governing.**—Subject to the Constitution of this State, (1) the laws of the state under which a foreign limited partnership is organized govern its organization and internal affairs and the liability of its limited partners, and (2) a foreign limited partnership may not be denied registration by reason of any difference between those laws and the laws of this State.

§ 902. **Registration.**—Before transacting business in this State, a foreign limited partnership shall register with the Secretary of State. In order to register, a foreign limited partnership shall submit to the Secretary of State, in duplicate, an application for registration as a foreign limited partnership, signed and sworn to by a general partner and setting forth:

(1) the name of the foreign limited partnership and, if different, the name under which it proposes to register and transact business in this State;

(2) the state and date of its formation;

(3) the general character of the business it proposes to transact in this State;

(4) the name and address of any agent for service of process on the foreign limited partnership whom the foreign limited partnership elects to appoint; the agent must be an individual resident of this state, a domestic corporation, or a foreign corporation having a place of business in, and authorized to do business in, this State;

(5) a statement that the Secretary of State is appointed the agent of the foreign limited partnership for service of process if no agent has been appointed under paragraph (4) or, if appointed, the agent's authority has been revoked or if the agent cannot be found or served with the exercise of reasonable diligence;

(6) the address of the office required to be maintained in the State of its organization by the laws of that State or, if not so required, of the principal office of the foreign limited partnership; and

(7) if the certificate of limited partnership filed in the foreign limited partnership's state of organization is not required to include the names and business addresses of the partners, a list of the names and addresses.

§ 903. **Issuance of Registration.**—

(a) If the Secretary of State finds that an application for registration conforms to law and all requisite fees have been paid, he shall:

(1) endorse on the application the word "Filed", and the month, day and year of the filing thereof;

(2) file in his office a duplicate original of the application; and

(3) issue a certificate of registration to transact business in this State.

(b) The certificate of registration, together with a duplicate original of the application, shall be returned to the person who filed the application or his representative.

§ 904. **Name.**—A foreign limited partnership may register with the Secretary of State under any name (whether or not it is the name under which it is registered in its state of organization) that includes without abbreviation the words "limited partnership" and that could be registered by a domestic limited partnership.

§ 905. **Changes and Amendments.**—If any statement in the application for registration of a foreign limited partnership was false when made or any arrangements or other facts described have changed, making the application inaccurate in any respect, the foreign limited partnership shall promptly file in the office of the Secretary of State a certificate, signed and sworn to by a general partner, correcting such statement.

§ 906. **Cancellation of Registration.**—A foreign limited partnership may cancel its registration by filing with the Secretary of State a certificate of cancellation signed and sworn to by a general partner. A cancellation does not terminate the authority of the Secretary of State to accept service of process on the foreign limited partnership with respect to [claims for relief] [causes of action] arising out of the transactions of business in this State.

§ 907. **Transaction of Business Without Registration.**—(a) A foreign limited partnership transacting business in this State may not maintain any action, suit, or proceeding in any court of this State until it has registered in this State.

(b) The failure of a foreign limited partnership to register in this State does not impair the validity of any contract or act of the foreign limited partnership or prevent the foreign limited partnership from defending any action, suit, or proceeding in any court of this State.

(c) A limited partner of a foreign limited partnership is not liable as a general partner of the foreign limited partnership solely by reason of having transacted business in this State without registration.

(d) A foreign limited partnership, by transacting business in this State without registration, appoints the Secretary of State as its agent for service of process with respect to [claims for relief] [causes of action] arising out of the transaction of business in this State.

§ 908. **Action by [Appropriate Official.]**—The [appropriate official] may bring an action to restrain a foreign limited partnership from transacting business in this State in violation of the Article.

Article 10

Derivative Actions

§ 1001. **Right of Action.**—A limited partner may bring an action in the right of a limited partnership to recover a judgment in its favor if general partners with authority to do so have refused to bring the action or if an effort to cause those general partners to bring the action is not likely to succeed.

§ 1002. **Proper Plaintiff.**—In a derivative action, the plaintiff must be a partner at the time of bringing the action and (1) at the time of the transaction of which the complains or (2) his status as a partner had devolved upon him by operation of law or pursuant to the terms of the partnership agreement from a person who was a partner at the time of the transaction.

§ 1003. **Pleading.**—In a derivative action, the complaint shall set forth with particularity the effort of the plaintiff to secure initiation of the action by a general partner or the reasons for not making the effort.

§ 1004. **Expenses.**—If a derivative action is successful, in whole or in part, or if anything is received by the plaintiff as a result of a judgment, compromise or settlement of an action or claim, the court may award the plaintiff reasonable expenses, including reasonable attorney's fees, and shall direct him to remit to the limited partnership the remainder of those proceeds received by him.

Article 11

Miscellaneous

§ 1101. **Construction and Application.**—This Act shall be so applied and construed to effectuate its general purpose to make uniform the law with respect to the subject of this Act among states enacting it.

§ 1102. **Short Title.**—This Act may be cited as the Uniform Limited Partnership Act.

§ 1103. **Severability.**—If any provision of this Act or its application to any person or circumstance is held invalid, the invalidity does not affect other provisions or applications of the Act which can be given effect without the invalid provision or application, and to this end the provisions of this Act are severable.

§ 1104. **Effective Date, Extended Effective Date and Repeal.**— Except as set forth below, the effective date of this Act is   and the following Acts [list prior limited partnership acts] are hereby repealed:

(1) The existing provisions for execution and filing of certificates of limited partnerships and amendments thereunder and cancellations thereof continue in effect until [specify time required to create central filing system], the extended effective date, and Sections 102, 103, 104, 105, 201, 202, 203, 204 and 206 are not effective until the extended effective date.

(2) Section 402, specifying the conditions under which a general partner ceases to be a member of a limited partnership, is not effective until the extended effective date, and the applicable provisions of existing law continue to govern until the extended effective date.

(3) Sections 501, 502, and 608 apply only to contributions and distributions made after the effective date of this Act.

(4) Section 704 applies only to assignments made after the effective date of this Act.

(5) Article 9, dealing with registration of foreign limited partnerships, is not effective until the extended effective date.

§ 1105. **Rules for Cases Not Provided for in This Act.**—In any case not provided for in this Act the provisions of the Uniform Partnership Act govern.

APPENDIX D
1983 REVISED MODEL BUSINESS CORPORATION ACT
Contents of 1983 Revised Model Business Corporation Act Cross-Referenced to Contents of 1969 Model Business Corporation Act
(Sections marked with an * are not included in this appendix)

Section No. in 1983 Act	Section Title	Section No. in 1969 Act
	Chapter 1. General provisions	
	Subchapter A. Short title and reservation of power	
1.01	Short title	1
1.02*	Reservation of power to amend or repeal	149
	Subchapter B. Filing documents	
1.20*	Filing requirements	new
1.21*	Forms	142
1.22*	Filing, service, and copying fees	128, 129
1.23*	Effective date of filing	new
1.24*	Correcting filed document	new
1.25*	Filing duty of secretary of state	new
1.26*	Appeal from secretary of state's refusal to file document	140
1.27*	Evidentiary effect of copy of filed document	141
1.28*	Certificate of good standing	new
1.29*	Penalty for signing false document	136
	Subchapter C. Secretary of State	
1.30*	Powers	139
	Subchapter D. Definitions	
1.40*	Act definitions	2
1.41*	Notice	new
1.42*	Number of shareholders	new
	Chapter 2. Incorporation	
2.01	Incorporators	53
2.02	Articles of incorporation	54
2.03*	Incorporation	55, 56
2.04*	Liability for preincorporation transactions	146
2.05	Organization of corporation	57
2.06	Bylaws	27 sent. 1, 3
2.07	Emergency bylaws	27A part
	Chapter 3. Purposes and powers	
3.01	Purposes	3
3.02	General powers	4
3.03*	Emergency powers	27A part
3.04	Ulta vires	7
	Chapter 4. Name	
4.01	Corporate name	8
4.02	Reserved name	9
4.03*	Registered name	10, 11
	Chapter 5. Office and agent	
5.01*	Registered office and registered agent	12
5.02*	Change of registered office or registered agent	13 part
5.03*	Resignation of registered agent	13 part
5.04*	Service on corporation	14

Section No. in 1983 Act	Section Title	Section No. in 1969 Act
	Chapter 6. Shares and distributions	
	Subchapter A. Types of shares	
6.01	Authorization generally	15
6.02	Classes of preferred shares	15
6.03	Series within a class	16
6.04*	Fractional shares	24
	Subchapter B. Issuance of shares	
6.20	Subscription for shares	17
6.21	Issuance of shares	18(a), 19
6.22	Liability of subscribers and shareholders	25
6.23	Share exchanges, dividends, and splits	18(b)
6.24	Share rights and options	20
6.25*	Form and content of certificates	23
6.26*	Shares without certificates	23
6.27	Restriction on transfer or registration of shares or other securities	new
6.28*	Expense of issue	22
	Subchapter C. Acquisition of shares by shareholders and corporation	
6.30	Shareholders' preemptive rights	26, 26A
6.31	Corporation's power to acquire own shares	6
	Subchapter D. Distributions	
6.40	Distributions to shareholders	45
	Chapter 7. Shareholders	
	Subchapter A. Meetings	
7.01	Annual Meeting	28
7.02	Special Meeting	28
7.03*	Court-ordered meeting	new
7.04	Action without meeting	145
7.05	Notice of meeting	29
7.06	Waiver of notice	144
7.07	Record date	30
	Subchapter B. Voting	
7.20	Shareholders' list for meeting	31
7.21	Voting entitlement of shares	33
7.22	Proxies	33
7.23*	Shares held by nominees	2(f)
7.24	Corporation's acceptance of votes	33
7.25*	Normal quorum and voting requirements	32
7.26*	Class voting	new
7.27*	Greater quorum or voting requirements	143
7.28*	Cumulative voting for directors	33
	Subchapter C. Voting trusts and agreements	
7.30	Voting trusts	34
7.31	Voting agreements	34
	Subchapter D. Derivative proceedings	
7.40	Procedure in derivative proceedings	49
	Chapter 8. Directors and officers	
	Subchapter A. Board of directors	
8.01	Requirement for and duties of board	35
8.02	Qualifications of directors	35
8.03	Number and election of directors	36 part
8.04*	Election of directors by certain classes of shareholders	new

Section No. in 1983 Act	Section Title	Section No. in 1969 Act
8.05	Terms of directors generally	36 part, 38 part
8.06	Staggered terms for directors	37
8.07*	Resignation of directors	new
8.08	Removal of directors by shareholders	39
8.09*	Removal of directors by judicial proceeding	new
8.10	Vacancy on board	38 part
8.11*	Compensation of directors	35

Subchapter B. Meetings and action of board

8.20	Meetings	43
8.21	Action without meeting	44
8.22	Notice of meeting	43
8.23	Waiver of notice	144, 43
8.24	Quorum and voting	40
8.25	Committees	42

Subchapter C. Standards of conduct

8.30	General standards for directors	35
8.31	Director or officer conflict of interest	41
8.32	Loans to directors	47
8.33*	Liability for unlawful distributions	48

Subchapter D. Officers

8.40	Required officers	50
8.41	Duties of officers	50
8.42	Standards of conduct for officers	new
8.43	Resignation and removal of officers	51 part
8.44*	Contract rights of officers	51 part

Subchapter E. Indemnification

8.50	Subchapter definitions	5(a), (b)(3) part
8.51*	Authority to indemnify	5(b), (c), (h) part
8.52*	Mandatory indemnification	5 (d)(1)
8.53*	Advance for expenses	5(f)
8.54*	Court-ordered indemnification	5(d) (2)
8.55*	Determination and authorization of indemnification	5(e)
8.56*	Indemnification of officers, employees, and agents	5(i)
8.57*	Insurance	5(k)
8.58*	Application of subchapter	5(g)

Chapter 10. Amendment of articles of incorporation and bylaws

Subchapter A. Amendment of articles of incorporation

10.01*	Authority to amend	58
10.02	Amendment by directors	59(a) sent. 3
10.03	Amendment by directors and shareholders	59(a) sent. 1, (b)
10.04	Shareholder class voting on amendments	60
10.05*	Amendment before issuance of shares	59(a) sent. 2
10.06*	Articles of amendment	61, 62
10.07*	Restated articles of incorporation	64
10.08*	Amendment pursuant to reorganization	65
10.09*	Effect of amendment and restatement	63

Subchapter B. Amendment of bylaws

10.20	Amendment by directors or shareholders	27 sent. 2

Chapter 11. Merger and share exchange

11.01*	Merger	71
11.02*	Share exchange	72A
11.03	Action on plan by shareholders	73
11.04*	Merger of subsidiary	75
11.05*	Articles of merger or share exchange	74, 75

§ 1.01. Short Title

This Act shall be known and may be cited as the "[name of state] Business Corporation Act."

§ 2.01. Incorporators

One or more persons may act as the incorporator or incorporators of a corporation by delivering to the secretary of state articles of incorporation.

§ 2.02. Articles of Incorporation

(a) The articles of incorporation must set forth:

(1) a corporate name for the corporation that satisfies the requirements of section 4.01;

(2) the number of shares the corporation is authorized to issue;

(3) the address of the corporation's initial registered office and the name of its initial registered agent at that office; and

(4) the name and address of each incorporator.

(b) The articles of incorporation may set forth:

(1) the names and addresses of the individuals who are to serve as the initial directors;

(2) provisions not inconsistent with law regarding:

(i) the purpose or purposes for which the corporation is organized;

(ii) managing the business and regulating the affairs of the corporation;

(iii) defining, limiting, and regulating the powers of the corporation, its directors, and shareholders;

(iv) a par value for authorized shares or classes of shares; and

(3) any provision that under this Act is required or permitted to be set forth in the bylaws.

(c) The articles of incorporation need not set forth any of the corporate powers enumerated in this Act.

§ 2.05. Organization of Corporation

(a) After incorporation:

(1) if initial directors are named in the articles of incorporation, the initial directors shall hold an organizational meeting, at the call of a majority of the directors, to complete the organization of the corporation by appointing officers, adopting bylaws, and carrying on any other business brought before the meeting;

(2) if initial directors are not named in the articles, the incorporator or incorporators shall hold an organizational meeting at the call of a majority of the incorporators:

(i) to complete the organization of the corporation; or

(ii) to elect directors who shall complete the organization of the corporation.

(b) Action required or permitted by this Act to be taken by incorporators at an organizational meeting may be taken without a meeting if the action taken is evidenced by one or more written consents describing the action taken and signed by each incorporator.

(c) An organizational meeting may be held in or out of this state.

§ 2.06. Bylaws

(a) The incorporators or initial directors of a corporation shall adopt initial bylaws for the corporation.

(b) The bylaws of a corporation may contain any provision for managing the business and regulating the affairs of the corporation that is not inconsistent with law or the articles of incorporation.

§ 2.07. Emergency Bylaws

(a) Unless the articles of incorporation provide otherwise, the directors of a corporation may adopt bylaws to be effective only in an emergency defined in subsection (d). The emergency bylaws, which are subject to amendment or repeal by the shareholders, may make all provisions necessary for managing the corporation during the emergency, including:

(1) procedures for calling a meeting of the board;

(2) quorum requirements for the meeting; and

(3) designation of additional or substitute directors.

(b) All provisions of the regular bylaws consistent with the emergency bylaws remain effective during the emergency. The emergency bylaws are not effective after the emergency ends.

(c) Corporate action taken in good faith in accordance with the emergency bylaws:

(1) binds the corporation; and

(2) may not be used to impose liability on a corporate director, officer, employee, or agent.

(d) An emergency exists for purposes of this section if a quorum of the corporation's directors cannot readily be assembled:

(1) because of attack on the United States or on the location where the corporation conducts its business or where its directors or shareholders customarily meet;

(2) because of nuclear disaster; or

(3) because of some other catastrophic event.

§ 3.01. Purposes

(a) Every corporation incorporated under this Act has the purpose of engaging in any lawful business unless a narrower purpose is set forth in the articles of incorporation.

(b) A corporation engaging in a business that is subject to regulation under another statute of this state may incorporate under this Act only if permitted by, and subject to all limitations of, the other statute.

§ 3.02. General Powers

Unless its articles of incorporation provide otherwise, every corporation has the same powers as an individual to do all things necessary or convenient to carry out its business and affairs, including without limitation power:

(1) to have perpetual duration and succession in its corporate name;

(2) to sue and be sued, complain and defend in its corporate name;

(3) to have a corporate seal, which may be altered at will, and to use it, or a facsimile of it, by impressing or affixing it or in any other manner reproducing it;

(4) to make and amend bylaws, not inconsistent with its articles of incorporation or with the laws of this state, for managing the business and regulating the affairs of the corporation;

(5) to purchase, receive, lease, or otherwise acquire, and own, hold, improve, use, and otherwise deal with, real or personal property, or any legal or equitable interest in property, wherever located;

(6) to sell, convey, mortgage, pledge, lease, exchange, and otherwise dispose of all or any part of its property;

(7) to purchase, receive, subscribe for, or otherwise acquire; own, hold, vote, use, sell, mortgage, lend, pledge, or otherwise dispose of; and deal in and with shares or other interests in, or

obligations of, other domestic or foreign corporations, associations, partnerships (without regard to their purpose or purposes), and individuals, the United States, a state, or a foreign government;

(8) to make contracts and guarantees, incur liabilities, borrow money, issue its notes, bonds, and other obligations, and secure any of its obligations by mortgage or pledge of any of its property, franchises, or income;

(9) to lend money, invest and reinvest its funds, and receive and hold real and personal property as security for repayment;

(10) to be a promoter, partner, member, associate, or manager of any partnership, joint venture, trust, or other entity;

(11) to conduct its business, locate offices, and exercise the powers granted by this Act within or without this state;

(12) to elect directors and appoint officers, employees, and agents of the corporation, define their duties, fix their compensation, and lend them money and credit;

(13) to pay pensions and establish pension plans, pension trusts, profit sharing plans, share bonus plans, share option plans, and benefit and incentive plans for any or all of its current or former directors, officers, employees, and agents;

(14) to make donations for the public welfare or for charitable, scientific, or educational purposes;

(15) to transact any lawful business that will aid governmental policy;

(16) to make payments or donations, or do any other act, not inconsistent with law, that furthers the business and affairs of the corporation.

§ 3.04. Ultra Vires

(a) Except as provided in subsection (b), the validity of corporate action may not be challenged on the ground that the corporation lacks or lacked power to act.

(b) A corporation's lack of power to act may be challenged:

(1) in a proceeding by a shareholder against the corporation to enjoin the act;

(2) in a proceeding by the corporation, directly, derivatively, or through a receiver, trustee, or other legal representative, against an incumbent or former director, officer, employee, or agent of the corporation; or

(3) in a proceeding by the Attorney General under section 14.30.

(c) In a shareholder's proceeding under subsection (b)(1) to enjoin an unauthorized corporate act, the court may enjoin or set aside the act, if equitable and if all affected persons are parties to the proceeding, and may award damages for loss (other than anticipated profits) suffered by the corporation or another party because of enjoining the unauthorized act.

§ 4.01. Corporate Name

(a) A corporate name:

(1) must contain the word "corporation," "incorporated," "company," or "limited," or the abbreviation "corp.," "inc.," "co.," or "ltd."; and

(2) may not contain language stating or implying that the corporation is organized for a purpose other than that permitted by section 3.01 and its articles of incorporation.

(b) Except as authorized by subsections (c) and (d), a corporate name must be distinguishable upon the records of the secretary of state from:

(1) the corporate name of a corporation incorporated or authorized to transact business in this state;

(2) a corporate name reserved or registered under section 4.02 or 4.03; and

(3) the fictitious name adopted by a foreign corporation authorized to transact business in this state because its real name is unavailable.

(c) A corporation may apply to the secretary of state for authorization to use a name that is not distinguishable upon his records from one or more of the names described in subsection (b). The

Secretary of State shall authorize use of the name applied for if:

(1) the other corporation consents to the use in writing and submits an undertaking in form satisfactory to the secretary of state to change its name to a name that is distinguishable upon the records of the secretary of state from the name of the applying corporation; or

(2) the applicant delivers to the secretary of state a certified copy of the final judgment of a court of competent jurisdiction establishing the applicant's right to use the name applied for in this state.

(d) A corporation may use the name (including the fictitious name) of another domestic or foreign corporation that is used in this state if the other corporation is incorporated or authorized to transact business in this state and the proposed user corporation:

(1) has merged with the other corporation;

(2) has been formed by reorganization of the other corporation; or

(3) has acquired all or substantially all of the assets, including the corporate name, of the other corporation.

§ 4.02. Reserved Name

(a) A person may apply to the secretary of state to reserve the exclusive use of a corporate name, including a fictitious name for a foreign corporation whose corporate name is not available. If the secretary of state finds that the corporate name applied for is available, he shall reserve the name for the applicant's exclusive use for a nonrenewable 120-day period.

(b) The owner of a reserved corporate name may transfer the reservation to another person by delivering to the secretary of state a signed notice of the transfer that states the name and address of the transferee.

§ 6.01. Authorization Generally

(a) Each corporation may create and issue the number of shares of each class stated in its articles of incorporation.

(b) If classes of shares are authorized, the articles of incorporation must describe the designations, preferences, limitations, and relative rights of each class.

(c) The articles of incorporation may limit or deny the voting rights of or provide special voting rights for the shares of any class except to the extent prohibited by this Act.

(d) The articles of incorporation may authorize:

(1) the redemption at the option of the corporation or shareholder of:

(i) classes of preferred shares that have a preference over any other class of shares in the assets of the corporation upon liquidation; and

(ii) classes of common shares, whether or not they have a preference over other classes of common shares, if there exists at least one class of voting common shares not subject to redemption;

(2) the redemption at the option of the shareholder of shares of an investment corporation regulated under federal law; and

(3) the redemption at the option of the corporation of common shares issued by:

(i) a corporation that is subject to governmental regulation or regulation by a national securities exchange, if the regulation requires some or all of the shareholders to possess prescribed qualifications or limits the permissible holdings of shareholders and redemption is necessary to prevent loss or allow reinstatement of benefits or entitlements;

(ii) a professional corporation, if the redemption complies with [section 23 of the Model Professional Corporation Supplement].

§ 6.02. Classes of Preferred Shares

(a) If the articles of incorporation so provide, a corporation may issue classes of preferred shares:

(1) subject to the right or duty of the corporation to redeem the shares under section 6.01(d) at a price fixed in accordance with the articles of incorporation;

(2) entitling the holders of the shares to cumulative, non-cumulative, or partially cumulative dividends;

(3) having preference over any other class of shares in the payment of dividends;

(4) having preference over any other class of shares in the assets of the corporation upon liquidation;

(5) convertible into shares of any other class or into shares of any series of the same or any other class, except a class having a prior or superior right to the payment of dividends or in the assets upon liquidation.

(b) Subsection (a)'s description of the designations, preferences, limitations, and relative rights of share classes is not exhaustive.

§ 6.03. Series Within a Class

(a) If the articles of incorporation so provide, a corporation may issue the shares of any preferred class in series.

(b) The articles may authorize the board of directors to create one or more series within a preferred class of shares and determine the designation, relative rights, preferences, and limitations of each series in accordance with the requirements of this section and the articles of incorporation.

(c) Each series of a class must be given a unique designation.

(d) All shares of the same class must provide identical relative rights, preferences, and limitations except with respect to:

(1) dividend rates;

(2) redeemability, including the redemption price, terms, and conditions;

(3) repurchase obligations of the corporation for all or part of a series at the option of the holders of another class;

(4) the amount payable per share upon liquidation;

(5) sinking fund provisions for the redemption or repurchase of shares;

(6) convertibility, including the terms and conditions of conversion;

(7) voting rights.

(e) Before issuing any shares of a series created under subsection (b), the corporation must deliver to the secretary of state articles of amendment, which are effective without shareholder action, that set forth:

(1) the name of the corporation;

(2) a copy of the resolution creating the series showing the date it was adopted; and

(3) a statement that the resolution was duly adopted by the board.

§ 6.20. Subscription for Shares

(a) A subscription for shares entered into before incorporation is irrevocable for six months unless the subscription agreement provides a longer or shorter period or all the subscribers agree to revocation.

(b) A subscription agreement entered into after incorporation is a contract between the subscriber and corporation.

(c) The board of directors may determine the payment terms of subscriptions for shares, whether entered into before or after incorporation, unless the subscription agreement specifies them. The board's call for payment on subscriptions must be uniform as to all shares of the same class or series.

(d) If a subscriber defaults in payment under the agreement, the corporation may collect the amount owed as any other debt. The bylaws may prescribe other penalties for nonpayment but a subscription and the installments already paid on it may not be forfeited unless the corporation demands the amount due by written notice to the subscriber and it remains unpaid for at least 20 days after the effective date of the notice.

(e) If a subscription for unissued shares is forfeited for nonpayment, the corporation may sell the shares subscribed for. If the shares are sold for more than the amount due on the subscription, the corporation shall pay the excess, after deducting the expense of sale, to the subscriber or his representative.

§ 6.21. Issuance of Shares

(a) The powers granted in this section are subject to restriction by the articles of incorporation.

(b) Shares may be issued at a price determined by the board of directors, or the board may set a minimum price or establish a formula or method by which the price may be determined.

(c) Consideration for shares may consist of cash, promissory notes, services performed, contracts for services to be performed, or any other tangible or intangible property. If shares are issued for other than cash, the board of directors shall determine the value of the consideration received as of the time the shares are issued.

(d) Shares issued when the corporation receives the consideration determined by the board are validly issued, fully paid, and nonassessable.

(e) A good faith judgment of the board of directors as to the value of the consideration received for shares is conclusive.

(f) The corporation may place shares issued for a contract for future services or a promissory note in escrow, or make other arrangements to restrict the transfer of the shares, and may credit distributions in respect of the shares against their purchase price, until the services are performed or the note is paid. If the services are not performed or the note is not paid, the shares escrowed or restricted and the distributions credited may be cancelled in whole or part.

§ 6.22. Liability of Subscribers and Shareholders

(a) A subscriber for or holder of shares of a corporation is not liable to the corporation or its creditors with respect to the shares except to pay the subscription price or the consideration determined for them under section 6.21.

(b) If shares are issued for promissory notes, for contracts for services to be performed, or before subscriptions are fully paid, a transferee of the shares is not liable to the corporation or its creditors for the unpaid balance but the transferor remains liable.

§ 6.23. Share Exchanges, Dividends, and Splits

(a) The powers granted in this section are subject to restriction by the articles of incorporation.

(b) If authorized by its board of directors, and subject to the limitation of subsection (c), a corporation may, without requiring consideration:

(1) issue its own shares to its shareholders in exchange for or in conversion of its outstanding shares; or

(2) issue its own shares pro rata to its shareholders or to the shareholders of one or more classes or series to effectuate share dividends or splits.

(c) Shares of one class or series may not be issued to the shareholders of another class or series unless (1) the articles of incorporation so authorize, (2) the holders of at least a majority of the outstanding votes of the class or series to be issued consent in writing to or vote affirmatively for the issue, or (3) there are no holders of the class or series to be issued.

§ 6.24. Share Rights and Options

(a) The powers granted in this section are subject to restriction by the articles of incorporation.

(b) A corporation may create and issue rights or options entitling their holders to purchase shares of any class, or any series within a class, in forms, on terms, at times, and for prices prescribed by the corporation's board of directors. Rights or options may be issued together with or independently of the corporation's issue and sale of its shares or other securities and may be issued as incentives to directors, officers, or employees of the corporation or any of its subsidiaries.

(c) A good faith judgment of the board of directors as to the value of the consideration received for rights or options entitling their holders to purchase shares is conclusive.

§ 6.27. Restriction on Transfer or Registration of Shares and Other Securities

(a) The articles of incorporation, bylaws, an agreement among shareholders, or an agreement between shareholders and the corporation may impose restrictions on the transfer or registration of transfer of shares of the corporation. A restriction does not affect shares issued before the restriction was adopted unless the holders of the shares are parties to the restriction agreement or voted in favor of the restriction.

(b) A restriction on the transfer or registration of transfer of shares is valid and enforceable against the holder or a transferee of the holder if the restriction is authorized by this section and is noted conspicuously on the front or back of the certificate or is contained in the information statement required by section 6.26(b). Unless so noted, a restriction is not enforceable against a person without knowledge of the restriction.

(c) A restriction on the transfer or registration of transfer of shares is authorized:

(1) to maintain the corporation's status when it is dependent on the number or identity of its shareholders;

(2) to preserve exemptions under federal or state securities law;

(3) for any other reasonable purpose.

(d) A restriction on the transfer or registration of transfer of shares may:

(1) obligate the shareholder first to offer the corporation or other persons (separately, consecutively, or simultaneously) an opportunity to acquire the restricted shares;

(2) obligate the corporation or other persons (separately, consecutively, or simultaneously) to acquire the restricted shares;

(3) require the corporation, the holders of any class of its shares, or another person to approve the transfer of the restricted shares, if the requirement is not manifestly unreasonable;

(4) prohibit the transfer of the restricted shares to designated persons or classes of persons, if the prohibition is not manifestly unreasonable.

(e) For purposes of this section, "shares" includes a security convertible into or carrying a right to subscribe for or acquire shares.

§ 6.30. Shareholders' Preemptive Rights

(a) The shareholders of a corporation do not have a preemptive right to acquire the corporation's unissued shares except to the extent the articles of incorporation so provide.

(b) A statement included in the articles of incorporation that "the corporation elects to have preemptive rights" (or words of similar import) means that subsections (c) through (f) apply except to the extent the articles of incorporation expressly provide otherwise.

(c) If the articles of incorporation provide for preemptive rights, the shareholders of a corporation have a preemptive right, granted on uniform terms and conditions prescribed by the board of directors to provide a fair and reasonable opportunity to exercise the right, to acquire proportional amounts of the corporation's unissued shares upon the decision of the board of directors to issue them.

(d) A shareholder may waive his preemptive right. A waiver evidenced by a writing is irrevocable even though it is not supported by consideration.

(e) There is no preemptive right:

(1) to acquire shares issued as incentives to directors, officers, or employees under section 6.24;

(2) to acquire shares issued to satisfy conversion or option rights;

(3) to acquire shares authorized in articles of incorporation that are issued within six months from the effective date of incorporation;

(4) to acquire shares sold otherwise than for money;

(5) for holders of shares of any class preferred or limited as to entitlement to dividends or assets;

(6) for holders of common shares to acquire shares of any class preferred or limited as to obligations or entitlement to dividends or assets unless the shares are convertible into common shares or carry a right to subscribe for or acquire common shares.

(f) Shares subject to preemptive rights that are not acquired by shareholders may be issued to any person for a period of one year after being offered to shareholders at a consideration set by the board of directors that is not lower than the consideration set for the exercise of preemptive rights. An offer at a lower consideration or after the expiration of one year is subject to the shareholders' premptive rights.

§ 6.31. Corporation's Power to Acquire Own Shares

(a) A corporation may acquire its own shares.

(b) If a corporation acquires its own shares, they constitute authorized but unissued shares unless the articles of incorporation prevent reissue, in which event the acquired shares are cancelled and the number of authorized shares is reduced by the number of shares acquired.

(c) If the number of authorized shares is reduced by an acquisition, the corporation must deliver to the secretary of state, not later than the due date of its next annual report, articles of amendment, which are effective without shareholder action, that set forth:

(1) the name of the corporation;

(2) the number of acquired shares cancelled, itemized by class and series; and

(3) the total number of authorized shares, itemized by class and series, remaining after cancellation of the acquired shares.

§ 6.40. Distributions to Shareholders

(a) Subject to restriction by the articles of incorporation and the limitation in subsection (c), a board of directors may authorize and the corporation may make distributions to its shareholders.

(b) If the directors do not fix the record date for determining shareholders entitled to a distribution (other than one involving a repurchase or reacquisition of shares), it is the date the board authorizes the distribution.

(c) No distribution may be made if, after giving it effect:

(1) the corporation would not be able to pay its debts as they become due in the usual course of business; or

(2) the corporation's total assets would be less than the sum of its total liabilities plus (unless the articles of incorporation permit otherwise) the maximum amount payable at the time of distribution to shareholders having preferential rights in liquidation.

(d) A board may base a determination that a distribution may be made under subsection (c) either on financial statements prepared on the basis of accounting practices and principles that are reasonable in the circumstances or on a fair valuation or other method that is reasonable in the circumstances.

(e) The effect of a distribution under subsection (c) is measured:

(1) in the case of distribution by purchase, redemption, or other acquisition of the corporation's shares, as of the earlier of (i) the date money or other property is transferred or debt incurred by the corporation or (ii) the date the shareholder ceases to be a shareholder with respect to the acquired shares;

(2) in all other cases, as of (i) the date of its authorization if payment occurs within 120 days after the date of authorization or (ii) the date of payment if payment occurs more than 120 days after the date of authorization.

(f) A corporation's indebtedness to a shareholder incurred by reason of a distribution made in accordance with this section is at parity with the corporation's indebtedness to its general, unsecured creditors except to the extent subordinated by agreement.

§ 7.01. Annual Meeting

(a) A corporation shall hold a shareholders' meeting annually at a time stated in or fixed in accordance with the bylaws.

(b) Annual shareholders' meetings may be held in or out of this state at the place stated in or fixed in accordance with the bylaws. If no place is stated in or fixed in accordance with the bylaws, annual meetings shall be held at the corporation's principal office.

(c) The failure to hold an annual meeting at the time stated in or fixed in accordance with a corporation's bylaws does not affect the validity of any corporate action.

§ 7.02. Special Meeting

(a) A corporation shall hold a special shareholders' meeting:

(1) on call of its board of directors or the individual or individuals authorized to do so by the articles of incorporation or bylaws; or

(2) if the holders of at least five percent of all the votes entitled to be cast at a proposed special meeting sign and deliver to the corporation's secretary one or more written demands for the meeting describing the purpose or purposes for which it is to be held.

(b) If not otherwise fixed under section 7.07, the record date for determining shareholders entitled to demand a special meeting is the date the first shareholder signs the demand.

(c) Special shareholders' meetings may be held in or out of this state at the place stated in or fixed in accordance with the bylaws. If no place is stated or fixed in accordance with the bylaws, special meetings shall be held at the corporation's principal office.

(d) Only business within the purpose or purposes described in the meeting notice required by section 7.05 (c) may be conducted at a special shareholders' meeting.

§ 7.04. Action Without Meeting

(a) Action required or permitted by this Act to be taken at a shareholders' meeting may be taken without a meeting and without action by the directors if the action is taken by all the shareholders entitled to vote on the action. The action must be evidenced by one or more written consents describing the action taken, signed by all the shareholders entitled to vote on the action, and delivered to the secretary of the corporation for inclusion in the minutes or filing with the corporate records.

(b) If not otherwise determined under section 7.07, the record date for determining shareholders entitled to take action without a meeting is the date the first shareholder signs the consent under subsection (a).

(c) A consent signed under this section has the effect of a meeting vote and may be described as such in any document.

(d) If this Act requires that notice of proposed action be given to nonvoting shareholders and the action is to be taken by unanimous consent of the voting shareholders, the corporation must give its nonvoting shareholders written notice of the proposed action at least 10 days before it is to be taken. The written consent or consents must recite that this notice was given.

§ 7.05. Notice of Meeting

(a) An officer of the corporation shall notify its shareholders of the date, time, and place of each annual and special shareholders' meeting no fewer than 10 nor more than 50 days before the meeting date. Unless this Act or the articles of incorporation require otherwise, the corporation is required to give notice only to shareholders entitled to vote at the meeting.

(b) Unless this Act or the articles of incorporation require otherwise, notice of an annual meeting need not include a description of the purpose or purposes for which the meeting is called.

(c) Notice of a special meeting must include a description of the purpose or purposes for which the meeting is called.

(d) If not otherwise fixed under section 7.07, the record date for determining shareholders entitled to notice of and to vote at an annual or special shareholders' meeting is the close of business on the day before the notice is mailed to the shareholders.

(e) Unless the bylaws require otherwise, if an annual or special shareholders' meeting is adjourned to a different date, time, or place, notice need not be given of the new date, time, or place if the new date, time, or place is announced at the meeting before adjournment. If a new record date for the adjourned meeting is or must be fixed under section 7.07, however, notice of the adjourned meeting must be given under this section to the shareholders of record on the new record date.

§ 7.06. Waiver of Notice
(a) A shareholder may waive any notice required by this Act, the articles of incorporation, or bylaws before or after the date and time stated in the notice. The waiver must be in writing, be signed by the shareholder entitled to the notice, and be delivered to the secretary of the corporation for inclusion in the minutes or filing with the corporate records.

(b) A shareholder's attendance at a meeting:

(1) waives objection to lack of notice or defective notice of the meeting, unless the shareholder at the beginning of the meeting objects to holding the meeting or transacting business at the meeting;

(2) waives objection to consideration of a particular matter at the meeting that is not within the purpose or purposes described in the meeting notice, unless the shareholder objects to considering the matter when it is presented.

§ 7.07. Record Date
(a) The bylaws may fix or provide the manner of fixing the record date for determining the shareholders entitled to notice of a shareholders' meeting, to demand a special meeting, to vote, or to take any other action. If the bylaws do not fix or provide for fixing a record date, the directors of the corporation may fix a future date as the record date.

(b) A record date fixed under this section may not be more than 60 days before the meeting or action requiring a determination of shareholders.

(c) A determination of shareholders entitled to notice of or to vote at a shareholders' meeting is effective for any adjournment of the meeting unless the board fixes a new record date, which it must do if the meeting is adjourned to a date more than 120 days after the record date fixed for the original meeting.

(d) If a court orders a meeting adjourned to a date more than 120 days after the record date, it may provide that the original record date continues in effect or it may fix a new record date.

§ 7.20. Shareholders' List for Meeting
(a) After fixing a record date for a meeting, a corporation shall prepare an alphabetical list of the names of all its shareholders who are entitled to notice of a shareholders' meeting. The list must be arranged by class of shares and showing the address of and number of shares held by each shareholder.

(b) The shareholders' list must be available for inspection by any shareholder, beginning two business days after notice of the meeting for which the list was prepared is given and continuing through the meeting, at the corporation's principal office or at a place identified in the meeting notice in the city where the meeting will be held. A shareholder, his agent, or attorney is entitled on written demand to inspect and copy the list, during regular business hours and at his expense, during the period it is available for inspection.

(c) The corporation shall make the shareholders' list available at the meeting, and any shareholder, his agent, or attorney is entitled to inspect and copy the list at any time during the meeting or any adjournment.

(d) If the corporation refuses to allow a shareholder, his agent, or attorney to inspect and copy the shareholders' list before or at the meeting, the [name or describe] court in the county where the corporation's principal office (or if none in this state its registered office) is located, on application of the shareholder, may summarily order the inspection and copying at the corporation's expense and may postpone the meeting for which the list was prepared until the inspection and copying are complete.

(e) Refusal or failure to prepare or make available the shareholders' list does not affect the validity of action taken at the meeting.

§ 7.21. Voting Entitlement of Shares
(a) Except as provided in subsections (b) and (c) or unless the articles of incorporation provide otherwise, each outstanding share, regardless of class, is entitled to one vote on each matter voted on at a shareholders' meeting. Only shares are entitled to vote.

(b) Absent special circumstances, the shares of a corporation are not entitled to vote if they are owned, directly or indirectly, by a second corporation, domestic or foreign, and the first corporation owns, directly or indirectly, a majority of the shares entitled to vote for directors of the second corporation.

(c) Redeemable shares are not entitled to vote after notice of redemption is mailed to the holders and a sum sufficient to redeem the shares has been deposited with a bank, trust company, or other financial institution under an irrevocable obligation to pay the holders the redemption price on surrender of the shares.

§ 7.22. Proxies
(a) A shareholder may vote his shares in person or by proxy.

(b) A shareholder may appoint a proxy to vote or otherwise act for him by signing an appointment form, either personally or by his attorney-in-fact.

(c) An appointment of a proxy is effective when received by the secretary or other officer or agent authorized to tabulate votes. An appointment is valid for 11 months unless a longer period is expressly provided in the appointment form.

(d) An appointment of a proxy is revocable by the shareholder unless the appointment form conspicuously states that it is irrevocable and the appointment is coupled with an interest. Appointments coupled with an interest include the appointment of:

(1) a pledgee;

(2) a person who purchased or agreed to purchase the shares;

(3) a creditor of the corporation who extended it credit under terms requiring the appointment;

(4) an employee of the corporation whose employment contract requires the appointment; or

(5) a party to a voting agreement created under section 7.31.

(e) The death or incapacity of the shareholder appointing a proxy does not affect the right of the corporation to accept the proxy's authority unless notice of the death or incapacity is received by the secretary or other officer or agent authorized to tabulate proxy votes before the proxy exercises his authority under the appointment.

(f) An appointment made irrevocable under subsection (d) is revoked when the interest with which it is coupled is extinguished.

(g) A transferee for value of shares subject to an irrevocable appointment may revoke the appointment if he did not know of its existence when he acquired the shares and the existence of the irrevocable appointment was not noted conspicuously on the certificate representing the shares or on the information statement for shares without certificates.

(h) Subject to section 7.24 and to any express limitation on the proxy's authority appearing on the face of the appointment form, a corporation is entitled to accept the proxy's vote or other action as that of the shareholder making the appointment.

§ 7.24. Corporation's Acceptance of Votes
(a) If the name signed on a vote, consent, waiver, or proxy appointment corresponds to the name of a shareholder, the corporation if acting in good faith is entitled to accept the vote, consent, waiver, or proxy appointment and give it effect as the act of the shareholder.

(b) If the name signed on a vote, consent, waiver, or proxy appointment does not correspond to the name of its shareholder, the corporation if acting in good faith is nevertheless entitled to accept the vote, consent, waiver, or proxy appointment and give it effect as the act of the shareholder if:

(1) the shareholder is an entity and the name signed purports

to be that of an officer or agent of the entity;

(2) the name signed purports to be that of an administrator, executor, guardian, or conservator representing the shareholder and, if the corporation requests, evidence of fiduciary status acceptable to the corporation has been presented with respect to the vote, consent, waiver, or proxy appointment;

(3) the name signed purports to be that of a receiver or trustee in bankruptcy of the shareholder and, if the corporation requests, evidence of this status acceptable to the corporation has been presented with respect to the vote, consent, waiver, or proxy appointment;

(4) the name signed purports to be that of a pledgee, beneficial owner, or attorney-in-fact of the shareholder and, if the corporation requests, evidence acceptable to the corporation of the signatory's authority to sign for the shareholder has been presented with respect to the vote, consent, waiver, or proxy appointment;

(5) two or more persons are the shareholder as cotenants or fiduciaries and the name signed purports to be the name of at least one of the coowners and the person signing appears to be acting on behalf of all the coowners.

(c) The corporation is entitled to reject a vote, consent, waiver, or proxy appointment if the secretary or other officer or agent authorized to tabulate votes, acting in good faith, has reasonable basis for doubt about the validity of the signature on it or about the signatory's authority to sign for the shareholder.

(d) The corporation and its officer or agent who accepts or rejects a vote, consent, waiver, or proxy appointment in good faith and in accordance with the standards of this section are not liable in damages to the shareholder for the consequences of the acceptance or rejection.

(e) Corporate action based on the acceptance or rejection of a vote, consent, waiver, or proxy appointment under this section is valid unless a court of competent jurisdiction determines otherwise.

§ 7.30. Voting Trusts

(a) Shareholders may create a voting trust, conferring on a trustee the right to vote or otherwise act for them, by signing an agreement setting out the provisions of the trust (which may include anything consistent with its purpose) and transferring their shares to the trustee. When a voting trust agreement is signed, the trustee shall prepare a list of the names and addresses of all owners of beneficial interests in the trust, together with the number and class of shares each transferred to the trust, and deliver copies of the list and agreement to the corporation's principal office.

(b) A voting trust becomes effective on the date the shares subject to the trust are registered in the trustee's name. A voting trust is valid for not more than 10 years after its effective date unless extended under subsection (c).

(c) All or some of the parties to a voting trust may extend it for additional terms of not more than 10 years each by signing an extension agreement and obtaining the voting trustee's written consent to the extension. An extension agreement must be executed during the 12-month period immediately preceding expiration of the voting trust it is intended to extend. The voting trustee must deliver copies of the extension agreement and list of beneficial owners to the corporation's principal office. An extension agreement binds only those parties signing it.

§ 7.31. Voting Agreements

(a) Two or more shareholders may provide for the manner in which they will vote their shares by signing an agreement for that purpose. A voting agreement created under this section is not subject to the provisions of section 7.30.

(b) A voting agreement created under this section is specifically enforceable.

§ 7.40. Procedure in Derivative Proceedings

(a) A person may not commence a proceeding in the right of a domestic or foreign corporation unless he was a shareholder of the corporation when the transaction complained of occurred or unless he became a shareholder through transfer by operation of law from one who was a shareholder at that time.

(b) A complaint in a proceeding brought in the right of a corporation must be verified and allege with particularity the demand made, if any, to obtain action by the directors and either that the demand was refused or ignored or why he did not make the demand. Whether or not a demand for action was made, if the corporation commences an investigation of the changes made in the demand or complaint, the court may stay any proceeding until the investigation is completed.

(c) A proceeding commenced under this section may not be discontinued or settled without the court's approval. If the court determines that a proposed discontinuance or settlement will substantially affect the interest of the corporation's shareholders or a class of shareholders, the court shall direct that notice be given the shareholders affected.

(d) On termination of the proceeding the court may require the plaintiff to pay any defendant's reasonable expenses (including counsel fees) incurred in defending the proceeding if it finds that the proceeding was commenced without reasonable cause.

(e) For purposes of this section, "shareholder" includes a beneficial owner whose shares are held in a voting trust or held by a nominee on his behalf.

§ 8.01. Requirement for and Duties of Board

(a) Except as provided in subsection (c), each corporation must have a board of directors.

(b) All corporate powers shall be exercised by or under the authority of, and the business and affairs of the corporation managed under the direction of, its board.

(c) A corporation having 50 or fewer shareholders may dispense with or limit the authority of a board of directors by describing in its articles of incorporation who will perform some or all of the duties of a board.

§ 8.02. Qualifications of Directors

The articles of incorporation or bylaws may prescribe qualifications for directors. A director need not be a resident of this state or a shareholder of the corporation unless the articles of incorporation or bylaws so prescribe.

§ 8.03. Number and Election of Directors

(a) A board of directors must consist of one or more individuals, with the number specified in or fixed in accordance with the articles of incorporation or bylaws.

(b) If a board of directors has power to fix or change the number of directors, the board may increase or decrease by 30 percent or less the number of directors last approved by the shareholders, but only the shareholders may increase or decrease by more than 30 percent the number of directors last approved by the shareholders.

(c) The bylaws may establish a variable range for the size of the board by fixing a minimum and maximum number of directors. If a variable range is established, the number of directors may be fixed or changed from time to time, within the minimum and maximum, by the shareholders or the board. After shares are issued, only the shareholders may change a variable-range board size or change from a fixed to a variable-range board size or vice versa.

(d) Directors are elected at the first annual shareholders' meeting and at each annual meeting thereafter unless their terms are staggered under section 8.06.

§ 8.05. Terms of Directors Generally

(a) The terms of the initial directors of a corporation expire at the first annual shareholders' meeting.

(b) The terms of all other directors expire at the next annual shareholders' meeting following their election unless their terms are staggered under section 8.06.

(c) A decrease in the number of directors does not shorten an incumbent director's term.

(d) The term of a director elected to fill a vacancy expires at the next shareholders' meeting at which directors are elected.

(e) Despite the expiration of a director's term, he continues to serve until his successor is elected and qualifies or until there is a decrease in the number of directors.

§ 8.06. Staggered Terms for Directors

If there are nine or more directors, the articles of incorporation may provide for staggering their terms by dividing the total number of directors into two or three groups, with each group containing one-half or one-third of the total, as near as may be, and specifying that the terms of directors in the first group expire at the first annual shareholders' meeting after their election, that the terms of the second group expire at the second annual shareholders' meeting after their election, and that the terms of the third group, if any, expire at the third annual shareholders' meeting after their election.

§ 8.08. Removal of Directors by Shareholders

(a) The shareholders may remove a director with or without cause unless the articles of incorporation provide that directors may be removed only for cause.

(b) If a director is elected by a class of shareholders, he may be removed only by the shareholders of that class.

(c) If cumulative voting is authorized, a director may not be removed if the number of votes, or if he was elected by a class of shareholders the number of votes of that class, sufficient to elect him under cumulative voting is voted against his removal.

(d) A director may be removed by the shareholders only at a meeting called for the purpose of removing him and the meeting notice must state that the purpose, or one of the purposes, of the meeting is removal of the director. Except as provided in subsection (c), a director may be removed only if the number of votes cast to remove him would be sufficient to elect him at a meeting to elect directors.

(e) An entire board of directors may be removed under this section.

§ 8.10. Vacancy on Board

(a) Unless the articles of incorporation provide otherwise, if a vacancy occurs on a board of directors, including a vacancy resulting from an increase in the number of directors:

(1) the board of directors may fill the vacancy; or

(2) if the directors remaining in office constitute fewer than a quorum of the board, they may fill the vacancy by the affirmative vote of a majority of all the directors remaining in office.

(b) If the vacant office was held by a director elected by a class of shareholders, only the holders of that class of shares are entitled to vote to fill the vacancy if it is filled by the shareholders.

(c) A vacancy that will occur at a specific future date (by reason of a resignation effective at a future date under section 8.07(b) or otherwise) may be filled before the vacancy occurs if the new director does not take office until the vacancy occurs.

§ 8.20. Meetings

(a) A board of directors may hold regular or special meetings in or out of this state.

(b) Unless the articles of incorporation or bylaws provide otherwise, a board may permit one or more directors to participate in a regular or special meeting by, or conduct the meeting through the use of, any means of communication by which all directors participating may simultaneously hear each other during the meeting. A director participating in a meeting by this means is deemed to be present in person at the meeting.

§ 8.21 Action Without Meeting

(a) Unless the articles of incorporation or bylaws provide otherwise, action required or permitted by this Act to be taken at a board of directors' meeting may be taken without a meeting if the action is taken by all members of the board. The action must be evidenced by one or more written consents describing the action taken, signed by each director, and delivered to the secretary of the board for inclusion in the minutes or filing with the corporate records.

(b) Action taken under this section is effective when the last director signs the consent, unless the consent specifies a different effective date.

(c) A consent signed under this section has the effect of a meeting vote and may be described as such in any document.

§ 8.22. Notice of Meeting

(a) Unless the articles of incorporation or bylaws provide otherwise, regular meetings of the board may be held without notice of the date, time, place, or purpose of the meeting.

(b) Unless the articles of incorporation or bylaws provide for a longer or shorter period, special meetings of the board must be preceded by at least two days' notice of the date, time, and place of the meeting. The notice need not describe the purpose of the special meeting unless required by the articles of incorporation or bylaws.

§ 8.23. Waiver of Notice

(a) A director may waive any notice required by this Act, the articles of incorporation, or bylaws before or after the date and time stated in the notice. The waiver must be in writing, signed by the director entitled to the notice, and delivered to the secretary of the corporation for inclusion in the minutes or filing with the corporate records.

(b) A director's attendance at or participation in a regular or special meeting waives any required notice of the meeting unless the director at the beginning of the meeting objects to holding the meeting or transacting business at the meeting and does not thereafter vote for or assent to action taken at the meeting.

§ 8.24. Quorum and Voting

(a) Unless the articles of incorporation or bylaws require a greater number, a quorum of a board of directors consists of:

(1) a majority of the fixed number of directors if the corporation has a fixed board size; or

(2) a majority of the number of directors prescribed, or if no number is prescribed the number in office immediately before the meeting begins, if the corporation has a variable-range board size.

(b) The articles of incorporation may authorize a quorum of a board of directors to consist of no fewer than one-third of the fixed or prescribed number of directors determined under subsection (a).

(c) If a quorum is present when a vote is taken, the affirmative vote of a majority of directors present is the act of the board unless the articles of incorporation or bylaws require the vote of a greater number of directors.

(d) A director who is present at a meeting of the board or a committee of the board when corporate action is taken is deemed to have assented to the action taken unless: (1) he objects at the beginning of the meeting to holding it or transacting business at the meeting; (2) he requests that his dissent from the action taken be entered in the minutes of the meeting; or (3) he gives written notice of his dissent to the presiding officer of the meeting before its adjournment or to the secretary of the corporation immediately after adjournment of the meeting. The right of dissent is not available to a director who votes in favor of the action taken.

§ 8.25. Committees

(a) If the articles of incorporation or bylaws so provide, a board of directors may create one or more committees and appoint members of the board to serve on them. Each committee may have two or more members, who serve at the pleasure of the board.

(b) The creation of a committee and appointment of members to it must be approved by the greater of (1) a majority of all the directors in office when the action is taken or (2) the number of directors required by the articles of incorporation or bylaws to take action under section 8.24.

(c) Sections 8.20 through 8.24, which govern meetings, action without meetings, notice and waiver of notice, and quorum and voting requirements of the board of directors, apply to committees and their members as well.

(d) To the extent specified by the board of directors or in the articles of incorporation or bylaws, each committee may exercise the board's authority under section 8.01.

(e) A committee may not, however:

(1) authorize distributions;

(2) approve or recommend to shareholders action that this Act requires to be approved by shareholders;

(3) fill vacancies on the board or on any of its committees;

(4) adopt, amend, or repeal the bylaws;

(5) approve a plan of merger not requiring shareholder approval;

(6) authorize or approve reacquisition of shares, except according to a general formula or method prescribed by the board; or

(7) authorize or approve the issuance or sale or contract for sale of shares, or determine the designation and relative rights, preferences, and limitations of a series of shares, except that the board may direct a committee (or another person or persons) to fix the specific terms of the issuance or sale or contract for sale.

(f) The creation of, delegation of authority to, or action by a committee does not alone constitute compliance by a director with the standards of conduct described in section 8.30.

§ 8.30. General Standards for Directors

(a) A director shall discharge his duties as a director, including his duties as a member of a committee:

(1) in good faith;

(2) with the care an ordinarily prudent person in a like position would exercise under similar circumstances; and

(3) when exercising his business judgment, with the belief, premised on a rational basis, that his decision is in the best interests of the corporation.

(b) In discharging his duties a director is entitled to rely on information, opinions, reports, or statements, including financial statements and other financial data, if prepared or presented by:

(1) one or more officers or employees of the corporation whom the director reasonably believes to be reliable and competent in the matters presented;

(2) legal counsel, public accountants, or other persons as to matters the director reasonably believes are within the person's professional or expert competence; or

(3) a committee of the board of which he is not a member, as to matters within its jurisdiction, if the director reasonably believes the committee merits confidence.

(c) A director is not acting in good faith if he has knowledge concerning the matter in question that makes reliance otherwise permitted by subsection (b) unwarranted.

(d) Subject to compliance with section 8.31 if a director has an interest in a transaction:

(1) the director is not liable for the performance of the duties of his office if he acted in compliance with this section; and

(2) a person alleging a violation of this section has the burden of proving the violation.

(e) Subject to compliance with other provisions of this Act and other applicable law, a proceeding to enjoin, modify, rescind, or reverse a business decision, based on an alleged violation of this section, may not prevail if the directors who made the decision discharged their duties in compliance with this section.

§ 8.31. Director or Officer Conflict of Interest

(a) If a transaction is fair to a corporation at the time it is authorized, approved, or ratified, the fact that a director or officer of the corporation has a direct or indirect interest in the transaction is not a ground for invalidating the transaction or for imposing liability on that director or officer.

(b) In a proceeding contesting the validity of a transaction in which a director or officer has an interest, the person asserting validity has the burden of proving fairness unless:

(1) the material facts of the transaction and the director's or officer's interest were disclosed or known to the board of directors or a committee of the board and the board or committee authorized, approved, or ratified the transaction by the vote of a requisite quorum of directors who had no interest in the transaction; or

(2) the material facts of the transaction and the director's or officer's interest were disclosed to the shareholders entitled to vote and they authorized, approved, or ratified the transaction by the vote of a requisite quorum of shareholders who had no interest in the transaction.

(c) The presence of, or votes entitled to be cast by, the director or officer who has a direct or indirect interest in the transaction may be counted in determining whether a quorum is present but may not be counted when the board of directors, a committee of the board, or the shareholders vote on the transaction.

(d) For purposes of this section, a director or officer has an indirect interest in a transaction if an entity in which he has a material financial interest or in which he is an officer, director, or general partner is a party to the transaction. A vote or consent of that entity is deemed to be a vote or consent of the director or officer for purposes of subsection (c).

§ 8.32. Loans to Directors

(a) Except as provided by subsection (c), a corporation may not lend money to or guarantee the obligation of a director of the corporation unless:

(1) the particular loan or guarantee is approved by vote of the holders of at least a majority of the votes represented by the outstanding voting shares of all classes, except the votes of the benefited director; or

(2) the corporation's board of directors determines that the loan or guarantee benefits the corporation and either approves the specific loan or guarantee or a general plan authorizing loans and guarantees.

(b) The fact that a loan or guarantee is made in violation of this section does not affect the borrower's liability on the loan.

(c) This section does not apply to loans and guarantees authorized by statute regulating any special class of corporations.

§ 8.40. Required Officers

(a) A corporation has the officers described in its bylaws or appointed by the board of directors in accordance with the bylaws.

(b) A duly appointed officer may appoint one or more assistant officers if authorized by the board of directors.

(c) The board shall delegate to one of the officers responsibility for preparing minutes of the directors' and shareholders' meetings and for authenticating records of the corporation. The officer with this responsibility is deemed to be the secretary of the corporation for purposes of this Act.

(d) The same individual may simultaneously hold more than one office in a corporation.

§ 8.41. Duties of Officers

Each officer has the authority and shall perform the duties set forth in the bylaws or, to the extent consistent with the bylaws, the duties prescribed in a resolution of the board of directors or by direction of an officer authorized by the board to prescribe the duties of other officers.

§ 8.42. Standards of Conduct for Officers

(a) An officer with discretionary authority shall discharge his duties under that authority:

(1) in good faith;

(2) with the care an ordinarily prudent person in a like position would exercise under similar circumstances; and

(3) when exercising his business judgment, with the belief, premised on a rational basis, that his decision is in the best interests of the corporation.

(b) In discharging his duties an officer is entitled to rely on information, opinions, reports, or statements, including financial statements and other financial data, if prepared or presented by:

(1) one or more officers or employees of the corporation whom the officer reasonably believes to be reliable and competent in the matters presented; or

(2) legal counsel, public accountants, or other persons as to matters the officer reasonably believes are within the person's professional or expert competence.

(c) An officer is not acting in good faith if he has knowledge concerning the matter in question that makes reliance otherwise permitted by subsection (b) unwarranted.

(d) Subject to compliance with section 8.31 if an officer has an interest in a transaction:

(1) an officer is not liable for the performance of the duties of his office if he acted in compliance with this section; and

(2) a person alleging a violation of this section has the burden of proving the violation.

(e) Subject to compliance with other provisions of this Act and other applicable law, a proceeding to enjoin, modify, rescind, or reverse a business decision, based on an alleged violation of this section, may not prevail if the officer who made the decision discharged his duty in compliance with this section.

§ 8.43. Resignation and Removal of Officers

(a) An officer may resign at any time by giving written notice to the corporation. A resignation is effective when the notice is given unless the notice specifies a future effective date. If a resignation is made effective at a future date and the corporation accepts the future effective date, its board of directors may fill the pending vacancy before the effective date if the board provides that the successor does not take office until the effective date.

(b) A board of directors may remove any officer at any time with or without cause.

§ 8.50. Subchapter Definitions

In this subchapter:

(1) "Corporation" includes any domestic or foreign predecessor entity of a corporation in a merger or other transaction in which the predecessor's existence ceased upon consummation of the transaction.

(2) "Director" means an individual who is or was a director of a corporation or an individual who, while a director of a corporation, is or was serving at the corporation's request as a director, officer, partner, trustee, employee, or agent of another foreign or domestic corporation, partnership, joint venture, trust, employee benefit plan, or other enterprise. A director is considered to be serving an employee benefit plan at the corporation's request if his duties to the corporation also impose duties on, or otherwise involve services by, him to the plan or to participants in or beneficiaries of the plan.

(3) "Expenses" include counsel fees.

(4) "Liability" means the obligation to pay a judgment, settlement, penalty, fine (including an excise tax assessed with respect to an employee benefit plan), or reasonable expenses incurred with respect to a proceeding.

(5) "Official capacity" means: (i) when used with respect to a director, the office of director in a corporation; and (ii) when used with respect to an individual other than a director, as contemplated in section 8.56, the office in a corporation held by the officer or the employment or agency relationship undertaken by the employee or agent on behalf of the corporation. "Official capacity" does not include service for any other foreign or domestic corporation or any partnership, joint venture, trust, employee benefit plan, or other enterprise.

(6) "Party" includes an individual who was, is, or is threatened to be made a named defendant or respondent in a proceeding.

(7) "Proceeding" means any threatened, pending, or completed action, suit, or proceeding, whether civil, criminal, administrative, or investigative and whether formal or informal.

§ 10.02. Amendment by Directors

Unless the articles of incorporation provide otherwise, a corporation's board of directors may adopt one or more amendments to the corporation's articles of incorporation without shareholder action:

(1) to extend the duration of the corporation if it was incorporated at a time when limited duration was required by law;

(2) to delete the names and addresses of the initial directors;

(3) to delete the name and address of the initial registered agent or registered office, if a statement of change is on file with the secretary of state;

(4) to split the issued and unissued authorized shares if the corporation has only one class of shares and, if the shares have a par value, to reduce proportionately the par value;

(5) to change the corporate name by substituting the word "corporation," "incorporated," "company," "limited," or the abbreviation "corp.," "inc.," "co.," or "ltd.," for a similar word or abbreviation in the name, or by adding, deleting, or changing a geographical attribution for the name; or

(6) to make any other change expressly permitted by this Act to be made without shareholder action.

§ 10.03. Amendment by Directors and Shareholders

(a) A corporation's board of directors may propose one or more amendments to the articles of incorporation for action by the shareholders.

(b) To be adopted:

(1) the board must recommend the amendment to the shareholders unless the board determines that because of conflict of interest or other special circumstances it should make no recommendation and communicates the basis for its determination to the shareholders with the amendment; and

(2) the shareholders must approve the amendment.

(c) The board may condition its submission of the proposed amendment on any basis.

(d) The corporation shall notify each shareholder, whether or not entitled to vote, of the proposed shareholders' meeting in accordance with section 7.05. The notice must also state that the purpose, or one of the purposes, of the meeting is to consider the proposed amendment and contain or be accompanied by a copy or summary of the amendment.

(e) Unless this Act or the articles of incorporation require a greater vote:

(1) if the amendment would create dissenters' rights, the amendment to be adopted must be approved by a majority of all votes entitled to be cast on the amendment;

(2) all other amendments to be adopted must be approved by the holders of a majority of all votes cast on the amendment.

§ 10.04. Shareholder Class Voting on Amendments

(a) The holders of the outstanding shares of a class are entitled to vote as a class (if shareholder voting is otherwise required) on a proposed amendment if the amendment would:

(1) increase or decrease the aggregate number of authorized shares of the class;

(2) effect an exchange or reclassification of all or part of the shares of the class;

(3) effect an exchange, or create the right of exchange, of all or part of the shares of the class into the shares of another class;

(4) change the designation, relative rights, voting rights, preferences, or limitations of all or part of the shares of the class;

(5) change the shares of all or part of the class into the same or a different number of shares of the same class or another class;

(6) create a new class of shares having rights or preferences prior, superior, or substantially equal to the shares of the class, or increase the rights, preferences, or number of authorized shares of any class having rights or preferences prior, superior, or substantially equal to the shares of the class;

(7) in the case of a preferred class of shares, divide the shares

into a series, designate the series, and determine (or authorize the board of directors to determine) variations in the relative rights and preferences between the shares of the series;

(8) limit or deny an existing preemptive right of all or part of the shares of the class; or

(9) cancel or otherwise affect dividends on all or part of the shares of the class that have accumulated but not yet been declared.

(b) If a proposed amendment would affect a series of a class of shares in one or more of the ways described in subsection (a), the holders of that series are entitled to vote as a separate class on the proposed amendment.

(c) If a proposed amendment that entitles two or more series to vote as separate classes under subsection (b) would affect two or more series of a class of shares in the same or a substantially similar way, the holders of the shares of all the series so affected must vote as a single class on the proposed amendment.

(d) A class or series of shares is entitled to the voting rights granted by this section although the articles of incorporation provide that the shares are nonvoting shares.

§ 10.20. Amendment by Directors or Shareholders

(a) A corporation's board of directors may amend or repeal the corporation's bylaws unless:

(1) the articles of incorporation reserve this power exclusively to the shareholders in whole or part; or

(2) the shareholders in amending or repealing a particular bylaw provide expressly that the directors may not amend or repeal that bylaw.

(b) A corporation's shareholders may amend or repeal the corporation's bylaws even though the bylaws may also be amended or repealed by its board of directors.

11.03. Action on Plan by Shareholders

(a) After adopting a plan of merger or share exchange, the board of directors of each corporation party to the merger, and the board of directors of the corporation whose shares will be acquired in the share exchange, shall submit the plan of merger (except as provided in subsection (g)) or share exchange for action by its shareholders.

(b) To be authorized:

(1) the board must recommend the plan of merger or share exchange to the shareholders unless the board determines that because of conflict of interest or other special circumstances it should make no recommendation and communicates the basis for its determination to the shareholders with the plan; and

(2) the shareholders must approve the plan.

(c) The board may condition its submission of the proposed merger or share exchange on any basis.

(d) The corporation shall notify each shareholder, whether or not entitled to vote, of the proposed shareholders' meeting in accordance with section 7.05. The notice must also state that the purpose, or one of the purposes, of the meeting is to consider the plan of merger or share exchange and contain or be accompanied by a copy or summary of the plan.

(e) Unless this Act, the articles of incorporation, or the board require a greater vote, the plan of merger or share exchange to be authorized must be approved by the holders of a majority of all the votes entitled to be cast on the plan.

(f) Voting by a class or series of shares is required:

(1) on a plan of merger if the plan contains a provision that, if contained in a proposed amendment to articles of incorporation, would entitle the class or series to vote as a class or series on the proposed amendment under section 10.04;

(2) on a plan of share exchange if the class or series is included in the exchange.

(g) Action by the shareholders of the surviving corporation on a plan of merger is not required if:

(1) the articles of incorporation of the surviving corporation

will not differ (except in name) from its articles before the merger;

(2) each shareholder of the surviving corporation whose shares were outstanding immediately before the effective date of the merger will hold the same number of shares, with identical designations, preferences, limitations, and relative rights, immediately after;

(3) the number of voting shares outstanding immediately after the merger, plus the number of voting shares issuable on conversion of other securities or on exercise of rights and warrants issued pursuant to the merger, will not exceed by more than 20 percent the total number of voting shares of the surviving corporation outstanding immediately before the merger; and

(4) the number of participating shares outstanding immediately after the merger, plus the number of participating shares issuable on conversion of other securities or on exercise of rights and warrants issued pursuant to the merger, will not exceed by more than 20 percent the total number of participating shares outstanding immediately before the merger.

(h) As used in subsection (g):

(1) "Participating shares" means shares that entitle their holders to participate without limitation in distributions.

(2) "Voting shares" means shares that entitle their holders to vote unconditionally in elections of directors.

(i) After a merger or share exchange is authorized, and at any time before articles of merger or share exchange are filed, the planned merger or share exchange may be abandoned, subject to any contractual rights, without further shareholder action.

§ 12.01. Sale of Assets in Regular Course of Business and Mortgage of Assets

(a) A corporation may sell, lease, exchange, or otherwise dispose of all, or substantially all, of its property in the usual and regular course of business, or mortgage, pledge, or dedicate to the repayment of indebtedness (whether with or without recourse) any or all of its property whether or not in the usual and regular course of business, on the terms and conditions and for the consideration determined by the board of directors.

(b) Unless the articles of incorporation require it, approval by the shareholders of a transaction described in subsection (a) is not required.

§ 12.02. Sale of Assets Other Than in Regular Course of Business

(a) A corporation may sell, lease, exchange, or otherwise dispose of all, or substantially all, of its property (with or without the good will), otherwise than in the usual and regular course of business, on the terms and conditions and for the consideration determined by the corporation's board of directors, if the board adopts and its shareholders approve the proposed transaction.

(b) To be authorized:

(1) the board must recommend the proposed transaction to the shareholders unless the board determines that because of conflict of interest or other special circumstances it should make no recommendation and communicates the basis for its determination to the shareholders with the proposed transaction; and

(2) the shareholders must approve the transaction.

(c) The board may condition its submission of the proposed transaction on any basis.

(d) The corporation shall notify each shareholder, whether or not entitled to vote, of the proposed shareholders' meeting in accordance with section 7.05. The notice must also state that the purpose, or one of the purposes, of the meeting is to consider the sale, lease, exchange, or other disposition of all, or substantially all, the property of the corporation and contain or be accompanied by a description of the transaction.

(e) Unless the articles of incorporation or the board require a greater vote, the transaction to be authorized must be approved by the holders of a majority of all the votes entitled to be cast on the transaction.

(f) After a sale, lease, exchange, or other disposition of property is authorized, the transaction may be abandoned, subject to any contractual rights, without further shareholder action.

(g) A transaction that constitutes a distribution is governed by section 6.40 and not by this section.

§ 13.01. Definitions

In this chapter:

(1) "Corporation" means the issuer of the shares held by a dissenter before the corporate action, or the surviving or acquiring corporation by merger or share exchange of that issuer.

(2) "Dissenter" means a shareholder who is entitled to dissent from corporate action under section 13.02 and who exercises that right when and in the manner required by sections 13.20 through 13.28.

(3) "Fair value," with respect to a dissenter's shares, means the value of the shares immediately before the effectuation of the corporate action to which the dissenter objects, excluding any appreciation or depreciation in anticipation of the corporate action unless exclusion would be inequitable.

(4) "Interest" means interest from the effective date of the corporate action until the date of payment, at the average rate currently paid by the corporation on its principal bank loans or, if none, at a rate that is fair and equitable under all the circumstances.

(5) "Shareholder" includes a beneficial owner of shares held by a nominee.

§ 13.02. Right to Dissent

(a) A shareholder of a corporation is entitled to dissent from, and obtain payment for his shares in the event of, any of the following corporate actions:

(1) consummation of a plan of merger to which the corporation is a party if (i) shareholder approval is required for the merger by section 11.03 or the articles of incorporation or (ii) the corporation is a subsidiary that is merged with its parent under section 11.04;

(2) consummation of a plan of share exchange to which the corporation is a party as the corporation whose shares will be acquired;

(3) consummation of a sale or exchange of all, or substantially all, of the property of the corporation other than in the usual and regular course of business, including a sale in dissolution, but not including a sale pursuant to court order or a sale for cash pursuant to a plan by which all or substantially all of the net proceeds of the sale will be distributed to the shareholders within one year after the date of sale;

(4) an amendment of the articles of incorporation that materially and adversely affects rights in respect of a dissenter's shares because it:

(i) alters or abolishes a preferential right of the shares;

(ii) creates, alters, or abolishes a right in respect of redemption, including a provision respecting a sinking fund for the redemption or repurchase, of the shares;

(iii) alters or abolishes a preemptive right to acquire shares or other securities;

(iv) excludes or limits the right to vote on any matter, or to cumulate votes, other than a limitation by dilution through issuance of shares or other securities with similar voting rights; or

(5) any other corporate action taken pursuant to a shareholder vote if the articles of incorporation, bylaws, or a resolution of the board of directors provides that shareholders are entitled to dissent and obtain payment for their shares.

(b) A shareholder entitled to dissent and obtain payment for his shares under this chapter may not challenge the corporate action creating his entitlement unless the action is unlawful or fraudulent with respect to the shareholder or the corporation.

§ 13.20. Notice of Dissenters' Rights

(a) If proposed corporate action creating dissenters' rights under section 13.02 is submitted to a vote at a shareholders' meeting, the meeting notice must state that shareholders are or may be entitled to assert dissenters' rights under this chapter and be accompanied by a copy of this chapter.

(b) If proposed corporate action creating dissenters' rights under section 13.02 is taken without a vote of shareholders, the corporation shall notify in writing all shareholders entitled to assert dissenters' rights that the action was taken and send them the notice described in section 13.22.

§ 13.22. Notice of How to Demand Payment

(a) If proposed corporate action creating dissenters' rights under section 13.02 is authorized at a shareholders' meeting, the corporation shall notify in writing all shareholders who satisfied the requirements of section 13.21 how to demand payment for their shares.

(b) The subsection (a) notice must:

(1) state where the payment demand must be sent and where and when certificates for certificated shares must be deposited;

(2) inform holders of uncertificated shares to what extent transfer of the shares will be restricted after the payment demand is received;

(3) supply a form for demanding payment that includes the date of the first announcement to news media or to shareholders of the terms of the proposed corporate action and requires that the person asserting dissenters' rights certify whether he acquired beneficial ownership of the shares before or after that date;

(4) set a date by which the corporation must receive the payment demand, which date may not be fewer than 30 nor more than 60 days after the effective date of the subsection (a) notice; and

(5) be accompanied by a copy of this chapter.

§ 13.23. Duty to Demand Payment

(a) A shareholder notified of how to demand payment for his shares under section 13.22 must demand payment, certify that he acquired beneficial ownership of the shares either before or after the first announcement date, and deposit his certificates in accordance with the terms of the notice.

(b) A shareholder who does not demand payment or deposit his share certificates where required, each by the date set in the demand notice, is not entitled to payment for his shares under this chapter.

§ 13.24. Share Restrictions

(a) The corporation may restrict the transfer of uncertificated shares from the date the demand for their payment is received until the proposed corporate action is effectuated or the restrictions released under section 13.26.

(b) The person for whom dissenters' rights are asserted as to uncertificated shares retains all other rights of a shareholder until these rights are modified by effectuation of the proposed corporate action.

§ 13.25. Payment

(a) As soon as the proposed corporate action is effectuated, or upon receipt of a payment demand if the action has already been effectuated, the corporation shall pay each dissenter who complied with section 13.23 the amount the corporation estimates to be the fair value of his shares, plus accrued interest.

(b) The payment must be accompanied by:

(1) the corporation's balance sheet as of the end of a fiscal year ending not more than 16 months before the date of payment, an income statement for that year, a statement of changes in shareholders' equity for that year, and the latest available interim financial statements, if any;

(2) a statement of the corporation's estimate of the fair value of the shares;

(3) a statement of the dissenter's right to demand payment under section 13.28; and

(4) a copy of this chapter.

§ 13.28. Procedure if Shareholder Dissatisfied with Payment or Offer

(a) A dissenter may notify the corporation in writing of his own estimate of the fair value of his shares and amount of interest due, and demand payment of the difference between his estimate and the corporation's payment under section 13.25, or reject the corporation's offer under section 13.27 and demand payment of the fair value of his shares and interest due, if:

(1) the dissenter believes that the amount paid under section 13.25 or offered under section 13.27 is less than the fair value of his shares or that the interest due is incorrectly calculated; or

(2) the corporation does not make payment and does not return the deposited certificates or release the transfer restrictions imposed on uncertificated shares within 60 days after the date set for demanding payment.

(b) A dissenter waives his right to demand payment under this section unless he notifies the corporation of his demand in writing under subsection (a) within 30 days after the corporation made or offered payment for his shares.

§ 13.30. Court Action

(a) If a demand for payment under section 13.28 remains unsettled, the corporation shall commence a proceeding within 60 days after receiving the payment demand and petition the [name or describe] court to determine the fair value of the shares and accrued interest. If the corporation does not commence the proceeding within the 60-day period, it shall pay each dissenter whose demand remains unsettled the amount demanded.

(b) The corporation shall commence the proceeding in the county where its principal office, or if none in this state its registered office, is located. If the corporation is a foreign corporation without a registered office in this state, it shall commence the proceeding in the county in this state where the registered office of the domestic corporation merged with or whose shares were acquired by the foreign corporation was located.

(c) The corporation shall make all dissenters (whether or not residents of this state) whose demands remain unsettled parties to the proceeding as in an action against their shares and all parties must be served with a copy of the petition. Nonresidents may be served by registered or certified mail or by publication as provided by law.

(d) The jurisdiction of the court in which the proceeding is commenced under subsection (b) is plenary and exclusive. The court may appoint one or more persons as appraisers to receive evidence and recommend decision on the question of fair value. The appraisers have the powers described in the order appointing them, or in any amendment to it. The dissenters are entitled to the same discovery rights as parties in other civil proceedings.

(e) Each dissenter made a party to the proceeding is entitled to judgment (1) for the amount, if any, by which the court finds the fair value of his shares, plus interest, exceeds the amount paid by the corporation or (2) for the fair value, plus accured interest, of his after-acquired shares for which the corporation elected to withhold payment under section 13.27.

§ 13.31. Court Costs and Counsel Fees

(a) The court in an appraisal proceeding commenced under section 13.30 shall determine all costs of the proceeding, including the reasonable compensation and expenses of appraisers appointed by the court, and shall assess the costs against the corporation. The court may assess costs against all or some of the dissenters, in amounts the court finds equitable, to the extent the court finds the dissenters acted arbitrarily, vexatiously, or not in good faith in demanding payment under section 13.28.

(b) The court may also assess the fees and expenses of counsel and experts for the respective parties, in amounts the court finds equitable:

(1) against the corporation and in favor of any or all dissenters if the court finds the corporation did not substantially comply with the requirements of sections 13.20 through 13.28; or

(2) against either the corporation or a dissenter, in favor of any other party, if the court finds that the party against whom the fees and expenses are assessed acted arbitrarily, vexatiously, or not in good faith with respect to the rights provided by this chapter.

(c) If the court finds that the services of counsel for any dissenter were of substantial benefit to other dissenters similarly situated, and that the fees for those services should not be assessed against the corporation, the court may award to these counsel reasonable fees to be paid out of the amounts awarded to the dissenters who were benefited.

§ 14.02. Dissolution by Directors and Shareholders

(a) A corporation's board of directors may propose dissolution for action by the shareholders.

(b) To be authorized:

(1) the board must recommend dissolution to the shareholders unless the board determines that because of conflict of interest or other special circumstances it should make no recommendation and communicates the basis for its determination to the shareholders; and

(2) the shareholders must approve dissolution.

(c) The board may condition its submission of the proposal for dissolution on any basis.

(d) The corporation shall notify each shareholder, whether or not entitled to vote, of the proposed shareholders' meeting in accordance with section 7.05. The notice must also state that the purpose, or one of the purposes, of the meeting is to consider dissolving the corporation.

(e) Unless the articles of incorporation or the board require a greater vote, dissolution is authorized if approved by the holders of a majority of all votes entitled to be cast at the meeting.

§ 16.01. Corporate Records

(a) A corporation shall keep as permanent records minutes of all meetings of its shareholders and board of directors, a record of all actions taken by the shareholders or directors without a meeting, and a record of all actions taken by a committee of the board of directors in place of the board on behalf of the corporation.

(b) A corporation shall maintain appropriate accounting records.

(c) A corporation or its agent shall maintain a record of its shareholders, in a form that permits preparation of a list of the names and addresses of all shareholders, in alphabetical order by class of shares showing the number and class of shares held by each.

(d) A corporation shall maintain its records in written form or in another form capable of conversion into written form within a reasonable time.

(e) A corporation shall keep the following records at its principal office:

(1) its articles or restated articles of incorporation and all amendments to them currently in effect;

(2) its bylaws or restated bylaws and all amendments to them currently in effect;

(3) resolutions adopted by its board of directors creating one or more series of shares, and fixing their relative rights, preferences, and limitations, if shares issued pursuant to those resolutions are outstanding;

(4) the minutes of all shareholders' meetings, and records of all action taken by shareholders without a meeting, for the past three years;

(5) all written communications to shareholders generally within the past three years, including the financial statements furnished for the past three years under section 16.20;

(6) a list of the names and business addresses of its current directors and officers; and

(7) a copy of its most recent annual report supplied the secretary of state under section 16.22.

§ 16.02. Inspection of Records by Shareholders

(a) Subject to section 16.03 (c), a shareholder of a corporation is entitled to inspect and copy, during regular business hours at the corporation's principal office, any of the records of the corporation described in section 16.01 (e) if he gives the corporation written notice of his demand at least five business days before the date on which he wishes to inspect and copy.

(b) A shareholder of a corporation is entitled to inspect and copy, during regular business hours at a reasonable location specified by the corporation, any of the following records of the corporation if the shareholder meets the requirements of subsection (c) and gives the corporation written notice of his demand at least five business days before the date on which he wishes to inspect and copy:

(1) excerpts from minutes of any meeting of the board of directors, records of any action of a committee of the board while acting in place of the board on behalf of the corporation, minutes of any meeting of the shareholders, and records of action taken by the shareholders or directors without a meeting, to the extent not subject to inspection under section 16.02(a);

(2) accounting records of the corporation; and

(3) the record of shareholders.

(c) A shareholder may inspect and copy the records identified in subsection (b) only if:

(1) his demand is made in good faith and for a proper purpose;

(2) he describes with reasonable particularity his purpose and the records he desires to inspect; and

(3) the records are directly connected with his purpose.

(d) The right of inspection granted by this section may not be abolished or limited by a corporation's articles of incorporation or bylaws.

(e) This section does not affect:

(1) the right of a shareholder to inspect records under section 7.20 or, if the shareholder is in litigation with the corporation, to the same extent as any other litigant;

(2) the power of a court, independently of this Act, to compel the production of corporate records for examination.

§ 16.03. Scope of Inspection Right

(a) A shareholder's agent or attorney has the same inspection and copying rights as the shareholder he represents.

(b) The right to copy records includes, if reasonable, the right to receive copies made by photographic, xerographic, or other means.

(c) The corporation may impose a reasonable charge, covering the costs of labor and material, for providing copies of any documents the shareholder is entitled to inspect. The charge may not exceed the estimated cost of production or reproduction of the records.

(d) The corporation may comply with a shareholder's demand to inspect the record of shareholders under section 16.02 (b)(3) by providing him with a list of its shareholders that was compiled no earlier than the date of the shareholder's demand.

§ 16.04 Court-Ordered Inspection

(a) If a corporation does not allow a shareholder who complies with section 16.02 (a) to inspect and copy any records required by that subsection to be available for inspection, the [name or describe court] in the county where the corporation's principal office, or if none in this state its registered office, is located may summarily order inspection and copying of the records demanded at the corporation's expense upon application of the shareholder.

(b) If a corporation does not within a reasonable time allow a shareholder to inspect and copy any other record, the shareholder who complies with section 16.02(b) and (c) may apply to the [name or describe court] in the county where the corporation's principal office, or if none in this state its registered office, is located for an order to permit inspection and copying of the records demanded. The court shall dispose of an application under this subsection on an expedited basis.

(c) If the court orders inspection and copying of the records demanded, it shall also order the corporation to pay the shareholder's costs (including reasonable counsel fees) incurred to obtain the order unless the corporation proves that it refused inspection in good faith because it had a reasonable basis for doubt about the right of the shareholder to inspect the records demanded.

(d) If the court orders inspection and copying of the records demanded, it may impose reasonable restrictions on the use or distribution of the records by the demanding shareholder.

pose of authentication.

Automated teller machine—A machine that enables the user to withdraw cash, make deposits, transfer money from one account to another, and carry on other similar transactions with a bank.

Aver—To set out formally; assert; allege in a formal complaint before a court of law.

Bailee—The person to whom personal property is delivered by a bailor under a contract of bailment.

Bailment—Delivery of personal property by owner to bailee in trust for a specific purpose. Delivery takes place as a result of an expressed or implied agreement between the parties.

Bailor—The person who initiates a contract of bailment and delivers the personal property to the bailee.

Bait and switch—A manner of selling in which the seller advertises a product at a low price in order to bring a customer into the store (bait) and then directs the buyer to a higher-priced product (switch), claiming that the low-priced product is sold out or is of lower quality.

Banc—The full court (French). A court sits *en banc* or *in banc* when all judges making up a court (e.g., federal circuit court of appeals) sit for the purpose of hearing oral arguments on points of procedural or substantive law, as distinguished from the sitting of a single judge, or a portion of the court, in the case of an appellate court.

Bankruptcy—Process by which a person who is unable to pay his, her, or its (corporation) debts is declared a bankrupt, has its nonexempt debts distributed by a bankruptcy court, and thereafter is released from claims on any balance due to creditors. Bankruptcy is not *insolvency*.

Bar—1. A group of lawyers licensed to practice before a particular federal or state court. 2. An answer in defendant's pleadings that may lead to a court ruling dismis-

sing plaintiff's alleged cause of action.

Bargain and sale deed—A deed that conveys title but makes no warranties.

Battery—Intentional physical contact by one individual (or through a thing in the control of that person) with another individual. Can be a basis for criminal and/or tort action.

Bearer—Person possessing a negotiable instrument (e.g., a check) that is payable to any individual and does not specifically designate a payee. The instrument may be made "payable to bearer" or indorsed in blank.

Bearer paper—Instrument that is payable to bearer.

Beneficiary—Person who receives benefit from an insurance policy as a payee, who benefits from a trust, or who inherits under a will. *Creditor beneficiary* is one who is not a direct party to an agreement between a promisor and promisee but receives performance because the promisee wishes to discharge a debt to him or her. A *donee beneficiary* is one who is also not a party to the original agreement but receives benefit from the agreement as a gift (e.g., life insurance policy designated for a child upon the death of parents).

Bequeath—To give personal property to another by a will.

Bid—A legal offer for property at an auction.

Bilateral contract—An agreement in which the oral or written promises of the parties serve as consideration for each others' promises.

Bill of complaints—A formal written declaration of bases for a plaintiff's action against a defendant in a court proceeding.

Bill of lading—A document of title or acknowledgment evidencing receipt of particular goods on board a ship (or by whoever is transporting the goods); the bill of lading also serves to note that the goods were in good order and fit for shipment.

Bill of particulars—A specific statement of the charges by a plaintiff (civil) or prosecutor (criminal) upon the request of the person

against whom a complaint has been filed or who has been charged.

Blank indorsement—An indorsement that does not specify a particular payee.

"Blue Sky" laws—A common or popular term for state and federal statutes that regulate the sale of securities. These laws seek to protect investors from fraudulent or unethical promoters of investment schemes.

Boiler plate—A standard form contract, or clause in a contract, that is not drafted for the particular client but is generally issued (e.g., insurance contracts and clauses therein).

Bona fide—In good faith (Latin).

Boycott—A conspiracy on the part of individuals, unions, or firms to refuse to do business with someone else, or to prevent others from doing business with, or employing, others.

Brief—A written summary for an appellate court setting forth facts, issues, and points of law argued by counsel in a lower court. Also students use a *brief* of a case as a way of summarizing a long published case and thus preparing for class.

Broker—1. Person who carries on negotiations and makes contracts for a principal. 2. Person who buys and sells securities on behalf of a third party.

Bulk transfer—A sale or transfer of major inventory of a business at one particular time, such sale not ordinarily carried on in daily business.

Burden of proof—Process in a lawsuit by which one party has the duty of proving the facts in dispute.

Bylaws—The internal self-made regulations of a corporation adopted for the purpose of governing the company's internal management. Nonprofit organizations and other business associations also have bylaws.

C.O.D.—Cash on delivery. The buyer must pay for the goods upon receipt before opening goods.

Capacity—Ability or competency to do something at law. For example, a child is capable of entering a contract depending on his or her age; a person is capable of committing a crime depending on his or her state of mind at the time of commission.

Carte blanche—A paper or document given by one individual or institution to another with the former's signature and no terms designated. The receiver is thus given unlimited authority to fill in the terms.

Cash dispenser—A machine that dispenses cash.

Causa mortis gift—A gift given by a living person in contemplation of approaching death.

Cause of action—When a person's legal rights have been invaded, the facts showing that invasion constitute a *cause of action* and are usually set out in a complaint. The failure to set out these facts by the plaintiff will lead to a motion for dismissal of the case by the defendant, alleging that the plaintiff has failed to state a cause of action.

Caveat emptor—Let the buyer beware (Latin). This idea at common law expressed the view that the buyer could not depend on the seller for any warranties after sale and thus should be careful in making his or her purchase.

Caveat venditor—Let the seller beware (Latin). Present-day maxim that, considering the amount of consumer action legislation and the number of pro-consumer court decisions, it is the seller who should be careful to whom he, she, or it sells.

Cease and desist order—An order by a court or administrative agency requiring an individual or a corporation to stop carrying on a particular act.

Certificate of title—A written opinion by a lawyer that title to property is valid.

Certification—An acceptance by a bank of a check; it guarantees that the bank will pay the check when it is presented.

Chancery—A system of common law courts that had only equity jurisdiction.

Chattel mortgage—A transfer of a right in personal property or a

lien on such that serves as security for payment of a debt or performance of a promised act.

Chattels—Personal property.

Check—A bank draft that is payable on demand.

Chose in action—A personal right of an owner to recover in a legal action things owned by him or her but not in his or her possession.

Code of Professional Responsibility—Rules governing the practice of law; drafted by the American Bar Association and adopted by the chief governing authority of each state bar.

Codicil—An addition to a person's will modifying, altering, or revoking provisions.

Collateral action—An attempt to avoid or evade a judicial proceeding or order by instituting a proceeding in another court attacking such.

Common carrier—One who transports goods (e.g., train) or services (e.g., telephone) for hire to the public and is regulated by federal and/or state agencies who insure that the public convenience and necessity is served.

Compensatory damages—Term used to denote damages that compensate the injured party for the injury suffered and nothing more.

Competent—Describes one who is capable at law. *See* **capacity.**

Complainant—A person who asks a court of law for redress of an injury allegedly suffered.

Composition—A legal agreement made between a debtor and several creditors whereby the latter agree to accept less from the debtor on a *pro rata* basis in satisfaction of all debts.

Concentrated markets—Markets in which the four to six largest firms hold a significant composite share (usually in excess of 60 percent). *Concentration ratios*, a measure of the trend toward bigness, indicate the amount of total output produced by large firms in a market as compared to small businesses.

Concur—To agree. With reference to appellate court decisions a "concurring opinion" is often written by a judge who may agree with the majority opinion's con-

clusion, but for differing reasons; thus he or she writes a separate opinion.

Condition concurrent—A condition in a contract performed simultaneously by both parties. For example, *A* agrees to deliver a car to *B*, cash on delivery.

Condition precedent—A provision in an agreement that provides for the happening of some event or the performance of some act before the contract becomes binding. For example, *A* agrees to purchase all of *B*'s crop of wheat if *B* delivers by a specified date.

Condition subsequent—A clause in a contract that provides for the release or discharge of an obligation upon the happening of a certain event. For example, a clause in a car insurance contract that provides for termination of the agreement if the insured fails to pay the full amount of the premium within 30 days of entering into the agreement.

Conditional acceptance—A statement by the offeree to a bargain that he or she will enter into an agreement that differs from the original offer. In effect a *conditional acceptance* constitutes a counteroffer as to personal and real property. Often used to qualify or limit offeree's liability on bills of exchange.

Conditional sale—Sale of goods in which buyer obtains possession but seller retains title until the purchase price is paid.

Confession of judgment—Process by which a debtor agrees to submit to the jurisdiction of a court, and the judgment of such court, without extended legal proceedings, in the event that he or she breaches an agreement.

Conforming goods—Under the Uniform Commercial Code, such goods are those that conform to the description and quality as set out in a contract. *Conduct* inclusive of any part of performance is also included under this term.

Conglomerate—Large corporation that operates in an industry other than the one in which it is primarily engaged.

Conscious parallelism—A form of conduct in which a leading firm announces a price increase and other firms follow suit; such decisions are not part of a conspiracy but are made independently by each firm.

Consent order—Voluntary agreement entered into by a corporation and a government unit (e.g., Federal Trade Commission) in which the corporation agrees to stop and/or correct a certain practice that is allegedly in violation of law. The corporation admits of no guilt in this process.

Consequential damages—Damages that do not flow directly from the acts of a party (e.g., breach of contract) but only indirectly.

Conservator—A person appointed by a court to take over as a guardian, preserver, or protector of a mentally incompetent person.

Consign—Process by which a debtor delivers to a third person for delivery to a creditor. Often used in terms of shipping goods to merchants by common carrier.

Consignee—A person to whom goods are transported for sale.

Consignment—1. Delivery of goods to a seller to be sold for the owner's account. 2. Delivery of goods to a common carrier to be shipped as directed by the owner.

Conspiracy—An agreement among two or more individuals to commit an unlawful act or to use unlawful means to commit an act.

Constructive fraud—Acts or omissions that, though having no intent to deceive, by their nature mislead an individual, corporation, or the public at large.

Constructive notice—A legal presumption that a person has knowledge of certain facts.

Consummation—The completion of an agreement or the carrying out of such.

Contempt citation—An order issued by a judge holding a person for incarceration following the individual's affront to the judge or his or her attempts to obstruct the court processes.

Conversion—The taking and keeping of personal property or goods without an owner's consent.

Corporeal—Term pertaining to something that is tangible and has substance.

Cost-benefit analysis—A measurement technique by which one adds up the total cost of implementation of a regulation(s), then compares it to the benefits accrued to both private and public parties.

Counterclaim—A claim by the defendant in opposition to plaintiff's claim that, if proved true would tend to diminish, alter, or defeat plaintiff's action.

Counteroffer—An offer made by the offeree to the offeror that would materially alter the original offer and thus demand acceptance by the offeror.

Covenant—Term used commonly to mean any agreement. Also used to mean a restriction in a deed for real property. For example, a "covenant for title" binds the grantor of land as to the security of title transferred to the grantee.

Cover—Remedy for buyer under the Uniform Commercial Code that allows the buyer in good faith to purchase, or make a contract to purchase, goods in substitution for those seller has not been able to deliver.

Coverture—The legal state or condition of being a married woman. Originally used as a term showing that a woman at law is under the protection of her husband.

Cross-appeal—Term used to denote a situation where both parties appeal from a lower court decision. Their appeals are said to "cross" each other.

Cross-examination—The examination of a witness provided by the opposition in a civil or criminal trial.

Curtesy—The estate at common law which a husband has in the estate of his wife upon her death.

Custodial account—An account in which one person holds property and uses it for the benefit of another; the person for whom the property is to be used is generally regarded as its owner for tax purposes.

De facto—What has happened *in fact* as opposed to what was ordered or may be ordered at law (Latin).

De jure—An action is taken by *right* or by *law* (Latin).

De novo—To begin anew (Latin). Usually refers to the necessity of a new hearing on the same facts and law once litigated.

De minimus—Term used to denote a small or trivial matter of which the court refuses ordinarily to take notice. (Latin).

Debenture—Instrument issued as evidence of unsecured debt. A debenture is usually made payable to bearer with interest to be paid (e.g., a corporate bond).

Debtor—One who is under an obligation to pay a sum of money to another.

Decedent—A deceased person.

Deceit—A fraudulent mispresentation, or device by which one person tricks another who is ignorant of or does not have full knowledge of the facts.

Declaratory judgment—An order of the court that renders an opinion on a question of law but does not order the parties to do any specific act.

Decree—An order of a court in equity determining the rights of both parties.

Deed—An instrument that transfers title to real estate.

Deed of trust—An instrument that conveys title to real estate to a trustee, who holds title as security for a debt owed to a lender who is the beneficiary of the trust.

Default—A failure on the part of a party to perform a legal obligation. For example, the failure of a party to appear to defend against a claim brought against him may result in a *default judgment*.

Defeasible—Term that refers to the capability of title for real property being defeated or revoked.

Defendant—A party who is being sued in a civil action or accused of a crime in a criminal matter.

Defendant in error—Party who receives a favorable judgment in a lower court, which *plaintiff in error* now seeks to reverse.

Delegatee—A person to whom a *delegator* transfers rights and duties.

Delegation—The process of transferring or assigning authority from one person to another.

Delagator—The person who is responsible for transferring rights and duties.

Demurrer—Equivalent of a motion by defendant to dismiss, because even admitting the facts stated in plaintiff's complaint, they are insufficient for plaintiff to proceed on, and serve as no basis for defendant to form an answer.

Deposition—The process by which testimony of witnesses is taken in writing prior to a trial for use in the actual court action. The basis for this process may be by court order or statutory rules of procedure.

Depository bank—The bank in which an instrument is first deposited for purpose of collection.

Derivative action—A suit by shareholder(s) of a corporation to force the corporation to enforce shareholders' rights against a third party (often an officer of the company).

Descent—Term used to denote a receiving of real property by inheritance.

Detriment (legal)—Term used to show a loss or harm suffered to real or personal property or the giving up of a right to take action.

Dictum—Statement or observation (Latin). Commonly used to refer to *obiter dictum:* An observation by a judge in an opinion that is not particularly germane to the case being decided.

Directed verdict—A verdict that the court instructs the jury to bring back, such as a verdict in favor of one party because reasonable minds could not differ as to the facts. This verdict usually results from a motion on the part of counsel for either party in a trial but can be granted by the judge alone as well.

Disaffirm—To revoke or repudiate. For example, an infant may *disaffirm* a contract prior to reaching the age of majority, or within a reasonable time thereafter.

Discharge—To release a party from obligations set forth in a contract. Also, a term used in bankruptcy to denote a release from all obligations. Used after a person is adjudicated a bankrupt.

Disclaimer—A refusal or rejection. For example a *disclaimer* clause in a contract notes the promises or warranties that will be given and disclaims all other responsibilities or warranties.

Discount—A process by which the lender receives compensation (interest) on the loan in advance, usually at the time of making a loan.

Discovery—The pretrial process by which parties to a suit disclose to each other relevant facts that are necessary for framing the issues, correcting them, and expediting trial procedure.

Dishonor—The refusal to pay or accept a negotiable instrument upon presentation for acceptance.

Dismiss—Term used to show a discharge of a cause of action. A *motion* for *dismissal* can be made by either party and will be ruled on by the judge.

Disparagement—The act of discrediting. For example, the tort of *disparagement* is a basis for a claim for damages when a business can show that a competitor has with intent injured the reputation and product of the business.

Dissolution—Cancellation or breaking up by mutual agreement. For example, the dissolution of a marriage contract.

Distribution—The division of personal property of a person who dies without a will; often also applied to the division of real property of a person who dies without a will.

Diversion—Alteration or change. Often it refers to the changing of the course of a waterway by upper riparian owners to the detriment of those downstream.

Diversity of citizenship—One of the bases of jurisdiction for the federal courts; i.e., when parties to a suit are citizens from different states.

Divestiture—One of the remedies used by the federal government to force companies to get rid of certain assets when they are found by the courts to be involved in violation of antitrust statutes. For example, when two merging companies are found to have violated Section 7 of the Clayton

Act, the acquiring company may be required to divest itself of all or parts of the acquired company (e.g., IT&T).

Document of title to personal property—Any document that in the regular course of business financing is treated as adequately evidencing that the person in possession of it is entitled to receive, hold, and dispose of the document and the goods it covers. To be a document of title, the document must purport to be issued by or addressed to a bailee and purport to cover goods in the bailee's possession, which are either identified or are fungible portions of an identified mass.

Documentary draft—A draft used with an attached bill of lading.

Domain—The absolute and complete ownership of real property. For example, the right of *eminent domain* relates to the primary power of the legislature to control private property when it uses such for public purposes and compensates the owners.

Domicile—A legal permanent residence to which an individual intends to return.

Dominion—Perfect ownership or power over something.

Dormant—Term that refers to someone who is a silent or inactive partner in a business.

Double indemnity—Term used in a clause in an insurance policy that provides for a payoff of twice the amount to an insured upon the happening of a certain event in a certain manner. For example, a clause might state that if a person dies by accident, his or her beneficiaries will receive twice the amount obtained if the death had been by natural means.

Dower—Right of a wife to the real property of her husband as set forth by state statute.

Draft—A written order to pay money to another on demand or at a stated date.

Drawee—The individual to whom a bill of exchange is addressed and to whom a request for payment is made by a *drawer*.

Drawee bank—A bank that a check or draft is drawn on and that is ordered to pay the instrument when it is presented.

Drawer—The person who draws a bill of exchange.

Due-on-sale clause—A clause in a mortgage allowing the lender to treat sale of the property by the owner as a default.

Duress—An unlawful restraint placed on an individual by another. It does not have to be the use of physical force; it may be any form of coercion that leads an individual to an act contrary to his or her free will.

Easement—Right of an individual to use the land of another for a limited purpose without obtaining possession or title.

Ejectment—A legal action to recover possession of land at common law. In many states today *ejection* is a statutory action for the eviction of a tenant who is holding over after termination of a lease or in breach of terms.

Electronic fund transfer—Any transfer of funds, other than a transaction originated by check draft or similar paper instrument, that is initiated through an electronic terminal, telephonic instrument, computer, or magnetic tape so as to order, instruct, or authorize a financial institution to debit or credit an account.

Eleemosynary corporation—A private corporate entity created for charitable purposes.

Emancipation—The liberating at law of someone who formerly had been under the legal control of another. For example, *emancipation* generally refers to a parent's surrendering all control over care, custody, and earnings of a minor child.

Encumbrance—A right in land of a third person (neither buyer nor seller) that may lessen the value, despite passing of title between two other individuals.

Endorsement—*See Indorsement*

Equitable estoppel—Term which refers to the inability of an individual based on justice and fairness (equity) to assert legal rights, especially when another individual has been induced to act based on conduct or silence of the former's representation.

Equity—A legal system that developed in England. Today *equity* is used to denote fairness and justice as opposed to statutory or case law as a basis for decisions.

Error of law—Drawing incorrect conclusions of law from known and existing facts. Refers to the basis for appeals from lower courts to appellate courts.

Escheat—A reversion of property rights to the state when there is no individual competent to inherit.

Estate—The interest that anyone has in land. An *estate for life* denotes an interest in land that an individual has for his or her life or the life of another.

Estate planning—The process of planning for the future distribution of a person's property or estate.

Estate taxes—Taxes due to the government for the transfer of property at death; calculated on the value of the decedent's estate minus applicable exemptions.

Ethics—Standards of behavior based on personal values and external standards. Ethics are principles reflecting what is good or bad and what is acceptable to one's self and to others.

Ex contractu—Out of a contract (Latin). Refers to a legal action arising out of a breach of contract.

Ex delicto—From a tort or fault (Latin). Refers to a legal action arising out of fault, misconduct, or malfeasance.

Exculpatory—Clearing someone from guilt or excusing a party to a contract from doing something. For example an *exculpatory clause* may excuse the seller from some warranties on the product sold.

Executed—Denoting a form of contract that has been completely performed and is now in effect.

Execution—The process of completing or carrying out something.

Executor—A man appointed by the deceased to carry out his or her directions as set out in a will.

Executory—Not yet completed because acts are incomplete.

Executrix—A woman appointed by a testator to carry out the terms of his or her will.

Exemplary damages—Damages granted to an injured party to compensate her or him for mental anguish and shame when there is shown that wrong was done with malice or wanton conduct. Often called *punitive damages.*

Exhaustion of administrative remedies—A legal doctrine that requires a party to seek all remedies within an administrative agency or entity if provided for by statute before requesting assistance from a court of law.

Expressed authority—Authority given in writing or by words, as opposed to that given by implication from a principal to an agent.

Expropriation—The taking of another's property, by a private party or for public use by the right of eminent domain.

Extrinsic evidence—Those facts obtained from things outside an agreement. For example, the fact that an individual was or was not competent to sign an agreement is *extrinsic* to the terms of the agreement itself.

F.A.S.—Abbreviation for "free alongside ship." Denotes that seller must deliver goods to the correctly designated dock where ship is waiting to be loaded and must assume all expenses and risks up to that point.

F.O.B.—Abbreviation for "free on board." Denotes that seller must ship and bear expenses to the point designated for delivery.

Fair market value—Price at which a willing seller and buyer will trade.

Fee simple—An estate in real property that is limited to an individual and heirs and assigns forever without any limitations on title or ownership.

Felony—A crime that is of a graver nature than misdemeanor and is punishable by incarceration in a state or federal prison. A *felony* will always be set out by statute.

Fiduciary—A person holding a relationship of trust in which he or she acts primarily for the benefit of another in certain matters.

First instance—Trial court in which a case is first tried, as opposed to an appellate court.

Fixture—A chattel attached to real property. Generally refers to something attached to real property and intended to be permanent.

Forbearance—The giving up of a right by one party to a contract in exchange for a promise by the other.

Foreclosure—Termination of all interests or rights of the mortgagor in property covered by a mortgage.

Franchise—1. A special privilege conferred by governments on citizens. 2. A form of contract between a supplying corporation (franchisor) and an individual retailer (franchisee) to market goods or services.

Fraud—Intentional misrepresentation of facts relied on by another, leading to legal injury.

Freehold—An estate for one's lifetime; generally a property right for an unstated period.

Frolic—In agency law an act by an employee not within the scope of his or her authority.

Full faith and credit rule—Article IV, Section 1, in the United States Constitution, which requires that each state treat as valid and enforceable where appropriate the laws of other states.

Fungible—Describing goods that are equivalent to each other in general mercantile usage; for example, wines and liquors; used in the UCC.

Future interests—Present interest in real or personal property that gives the right to future use.

Futures contract—Contract for future delivery of goods.

Garnishee—A person holding money or property of a debtor that a creditor is trying to reach. A garnishee is served with a garnishment order.

Garnishment—Process by which a creditor obtains money or property of a debtor that is in the possession of another (garnishee).

General creditor—A creditor whose debt or claim is not secured by a lien on particular property; i.e., it must be paid from the debtor's assets or estate.

Good faith—In Uniform Commercial Code transactions, honesty in fact in the conduct or transaction concerned.

Grandfather clause—An exception to a contract or statute that allows certain individuals to continue doing an act even though the act is now forbidden.

Grantee—An individual to whom a grant is given. Usually refers to the deeding of land or the assignment of real property.

Grantor—An individual who is assigning or granting something.

Gratuitous promise—Promise made as part of an agreement without consideration for such promise being expected.

Guarantor—A person who signs an instrument agreeing to pay the instrument under certain circumstances.

Guaranty—A promise by an individual to answer for the debt of another in the event that the latter cannot pay.

Habeas corpus—Generally refers to any of the common law writs that bring a prisoner before a court (Latin). Used today to determine whether a prisoner was incarcerated in accordance with due process procedure.

Hearing examiner—An individual who is the chief fact finder in most federal administrative agency hearings.

Hearsay—Evidence coming not from a primary source but from an individual who has obtained such information from others, or a secondary source.

Hold harmless—A clause in an agreement in which an individual agrees to hold another party not liable and pay all claims against that party.

Holder—Anyone in possession of an instrument drawn, issued, or indorsed to him, to his order, to bearer, or in blank.

Holder in due course—An individual holder of a negotiable instrument who has taken it in good faith, for value, complete on its face, without knowledge of the instrument's being dishonored or overdue, and without notice of defect in the title.

Holding company—A corporation that owns other companies' stock but is not responsible for their day-to-day operations.

Illusory contract—An agreement that on its face appears to be binding but in reality lacks mutuality of obligation.

Implied agency rule—Rule in contract law that implies the proper form of communication by offeree in transmitting an acceptance to an offeror, though it may not be clear from words or writings.

Implied authority—Form of authority of an agent inferred from his or her position and conduct in representing a principal. The principal will be bound in contract to a third party based on this authority unless he or she renounces such authority and communicates such to the third party.

Impossibility—A doctrine in contract law that allows for a rescission when a contract becomes legally impossible to perform. For example, if the subject matter of an agreement is destroyed by an unforeseen tornado, the defendant will plead impossibility of performance.

Impracticability—Doctrine that may allow for rescission of a contract when it becomes commercially impracticable to perform. This excuse for performance has been adopted by the Uniform Commercial Code in the event that a contingency occurs that was not planned for and that affects the complete capacity of the seller to perform.

In camera—In chambers (Latin). A court hearing that is closed to public scrutiny. Often used in cases where matters under consideration affect the national security of the country.

In extremis—Last illness before dying (Latin).

In pari delicto—In equal fault (Latin). Often used as a basis in tort law for joining two parties as defendants in a legal action.

In personam—Against a person

(Latin). Basis for jurisdiction in a legal action to enforce rights against a specific person. For example, a suit brought against another person for injuries suffered in an automobile accident is *in personam* because it is against the driver or owner only.

In re—In the matter of (Latin). Often used in the heading of a case to denote that the suit is concerned with a thing rather than a lawsuit between two individuals directly. For example, "In re Brennan's Estate" refers to a title of a legal proceeding to dispose of property of a dead person.

In rem—Against a thing (Latin). Basis for jurisdiction in a legal action against the whole world, as opposed to in personam jurisdiction. For example, a suit to establish title to land. The winner has title against all other possible claimants, or the whole world.

Inalienable—Not transferable; used to denote the nontransferability of property or legal rights.

Inchoate—Started but not complete. For example, a contract not executed by all parties or a deed not properly registered or recorded.

Incontestability—Term used to denote the fact that for the life of an agreement or patent it is not open to any contesting claims.

Incorporate—To create a formal corporate entity.

Indemnify—To provide security for an individual in the event of an anticipated loss. Often used to denote the promise of a reimbursement.

Independent contractor—An individual who contracts with a principal to do work by his or her own methods, unsupervised, and not subject to any control of the principal. He or she is soley responsible for the finished work product.

Indictment—Charge by a group of sitting jurors that an individual has committed some crime punishable by incarceration in a prison.

Indorsement—The signing of the back of a negotiable instrument by a drawee, thus assigning such property to another.

Infringement—An encroachment

on others' rights in violation of law. For example, the unauthorized use for profit of a patented invention is a basis for a legal action for an *infringement of patent.*

Inheritance taxes—Taxes due a state government assessed on property received from a person who has died. The amount of the tax depends on the relationship between the decedent and the inheritor and on the value of the property inherited.

Injunction—An equitable writ or order directing the defendant to stop doing an act or preventing him or her from continuing a course of conduct.

Insolvency—Inability of an individual legal entity to pay its, his, or her debts at the time they become due.

Insurable interest—An interest in property protected that would lead to a benefit from property owned, or a loss in case of destruction. Such an interest is usually protected by an insurance policy covering a risk.

Integrated—Describing legal writings that are considered to be final and complete to all parties having a direct interest.

Inter alia—Among other things (Latin). Often used in pleadings and other legal documents to show that only a portion of a statute or a line of cases is cited.

Inter vivos gift—Gift given by a living person to another living person.

Inter vivos trust—A trust that is established by a person while he or she is alive and that transfers property to the trustee prior to the death of the person establishing it.

Interlocutory—Denoting decisions made by a court during a pending lawsuit; not final as to the substance of the litigation.

Intermediary bank—Any bank to which an instrument is transferred in the course of collection except the depository bank or payor bank.

Interpleader—Process by which a third party having no ownership in held property brings two adversary claimants into court and

asks the judge to decide which claimant is entitled to the property.

Interpretation—The process by which a statute or written document is given meaning.

Intestate—Legal state in which a person dies without a will.

Intrinsic evidence—Evidence gained directly from a document submitted to the court at trial and not from outside sources or testimony.

Ipso facto—By the fact itself (Latin).

Irreparable harm—An injury that cannot be measured and for which a court remedy would be insufficient or which a court would be incapable of redressing.

Issue—The voluntary delivery of an instrument by the maker or drawer to the payee.

Joint and several—Referring to a situation in which two parties having a related obligation can be sued jointly or individually.

Joint property—Property owned by two or more persons.

Joint tenancy—An estate in which two co-owners have undivided interests; upon death of one owner his or her interest passes to the other.

Judgment n.o.v.—Judgment notwithstanding a verdict. Refers to a situation in which a judge will grant a motion to enter a judgment contrary to a jury verdict.

Jurisdiction—The geographic area, persons, and subject matter over which a particular court has the power to make decisions.

Jurisprudence—The philosophy of law. Schools of jurisprudence include positivist, sociological, existential, and natural law.

Justiciable—Pertaining to a matter that a court can properly decide. For example, a *justiciable* controversy is one that is real, not one that requires merely a social argument or decision.

Laches—Term that refers to Equitable doctrine and defense that claims that the failure of a plaintiff to pursue a claim within a reasonable time has, in and of itself, hurt or prejudiced the defendant's case.

Legacy—A gift or bequest of personal property.

Legislative veto—Method by which Congress reserves to itself the right to prevent a proposed agency regulation from becoming law.

Letter of credit—An instrument issued by a bank that requests payment to bearer or guarantees payment of financial obligation for goods sold on credit.

Levy—To collect, or to seize goods by an officer of the law.

Lex loci contractus—The law of the place (Latin). Refers to the fact that courts will apply the law of the place where a crime was committed or a contract was signed.

Libel—Written defamation in which an individual is held up to public contempt and ridicule that injures his or her reputation.

Lien creditor—A creditor whose debt or claim is secured by a lien on particular property.

Life estate—An estate whose duration is measured by the life of the holder or some other person.

Liquidated damages—A form of damages fixed as part of a contractual relationship. For example, a general contractor agrees with an owner that for every day's delay in completion of a commercial building beyond an agreed date the contractor will pay the owner $1,000 a day.

Litigant—A party to a legal action.

Litigation—A lawsuit.

Magistrate—A public official who is often a lower court judge (e.g., justices of peace and police judges). Also, a *magistrate* may have executive, legislative, and judicial power based on a state or federal constitution.

Maker—Person who makes or first executes a negotiable instrument.

Mandamus—We command (Latin). Term that denotes a court order directing an officer of a private or public corporation to carry out a specified act that is within his or her power by virtue of the office held.

Material—Term describing something essential or significant. For example, a *material* alteration in a contract might be a six-month delay in delivery when the parties agree on a specific date that both knew was important to the buyer.

Material alteration—In commercial paper, any alteration of the instrument that changes the contract of any party to the instrument.

Mechanic's lien—A claim on real property that seeks to secure priority of payment on debts owed for value of work completed and materials supplied in constructing or making improvements on debtor-owned building.

Mens rea—A guilty mind (Latin). Term used to show criminal intent; an essential element of a crime.

Merchantability—Term used to show the goods sold are fit for the purpose for which they are sold.

Merger guidelines—Specific U.S. Justice Department guidelines for private sector corporate mergers set forth as a warning that the Department *may* challenge companies who violate or plan to violate them. The guidelines are *not* law.

Misappropriation—The act of taking something one does not own and using it for a wrongful purpose. For example, in some states a banker may be accused of *misappropriation* of funds if he or she deals fraudulently with money entrusted to him or her.

Misdemeanor—A crime considered less serious than a felony and punishable by a fine or incarceration in an institution other than a state penitentiary for less than one year.

Misrepresentation—Words or conduct that misleads others as to the material facts of a situation. If such acts or conduct are unintentional, *innocent misrepresentation* has taken place. If done with intent and relied on by a party, and injury can be proven, fraud has been committed.

Mistake—An unintentional act or omission of law or fact. A *bilateral* or *mutual mistake* is an error made by both parties; if material to a contract, it will be grounds for

rescission or reformation. A *unilateral mistake* is an error made by a single party and is not usually grounds for rescission.

Mistrial—A fundamental error in procedure that causes a trial judge to end and cancel out the proceedings of a trial. This is done usually without prejudice to a new trial's taking place. For example, an error in selection of jurors may be a basis for *mistrial.*

Mitigation of damages—A lowering or abatement of injury from a wrongful act.

Monopoly—A market structure in which a single seller (monopolist) has virtually complete control over the source of goods as well as the means of production. The monopolist is the sole influence on the price variable in this market.

Mortgage—A contract or conveyance of a lien on real property by a debtor to a creditor to secure the payment of an obligation by the debtor.

Mortgagee—An individual who receives or takes a mortgage, e.g., a financial institution.

Mortgagor—The debtor who gives a mortgage for purpose of securing a debt owed by mortgagee.

Movables—Personal property in general and specifically such property that an owner has personal control over and can carry with him or her.

Necessaries—Goods and services that are reasonably proper for the maintenance of a minor in light of his or her family's income and position in the community. For example, food, clothing, shelter, and education through high school.

Negligence—A theory of tort law where damages are awarded based on the failure of an individual to exercise reasonable care when there existed such a duty toward another individual. This failure must be the proximate cause of damage to that individual.

Negotiable instrument—A written instrument that is executed containing an unconditional promise to pay a certain amount of money on demand or at an agreed time to order or to bearer.

No-par value stock—Stock issued with no value amount on its certificate. A subscriber will pay that value as set by the board of directors of the corporation.

Nolo contendere—I will not contest it (Latin). A plea in a criminal action; it is treated by most courts as the equivalent of a guilty plea. It allows the defendant freedom from liability in a civil suit based on the same cause of action.

Nominal consideration—Consideration passing between parties may be *nominal*, thus inflating a portion of the exchange. For example, A deeds two acres of land to his son in exchange for one dollar.

Nominal damages—A small sum of money awarded to a plaintiff who is unable to prove substantial loss.

Nonfeasance—The failure of one party to attempt performance. Often referred to in agency law when an agent fails to begin performance of agreed upon duties.

Nonsuit—Term used for judgment entered by a court when a plaintiff fails to carry the burden of proof or proceed with a case.

Note—A written promise to pay money to another on demand or at a stated date.

Novation—An agreement to substitute one party for another in a contract.

Nuisance—A legal action in which plaintiff attempts to show that someone is interferring with the use and enjoyment of his or her property.

Obligee—A creditor or promisee.

Obligor—A debtor or promisor.

Offeree—One who accepts an offer or acts upon a legal offer in some manner.

Offeror—One who initiates or makes an offer.

Oligopoly—An industry structure where a few firms are able to control price, means of production, and a substantial share of the market.

Option contract—A contract in which one party has exchanged consideration for the sole purpose of having the right to buy certain real property or goods at a time of his or her choosing, at a price stated in the option agreement.

Order paper—An instrument that is payable to the order of a specific person.

Ostensible authority—Such authority in agency law that is allowed by a principal to his or her agent as seen from the perspective of a third party dealing with the agent.

Overdraft—Withdrawal of money by a depositor in excess of that which he or she has on account. Can also be used to mean a form of loan to depositor.

Parens patriae—"Father of his country" (Latin). Generally refers to a guardianship over an individual considered legally incompetent (e.g., minor, insane). A government may be able to bring an action on behalf of its subject.

Parol evidence—Evidence extrinsic or external to that set out in writing.

Partition—Proceedings by which a court divides lands usually held by joint tenants or tenants in common so that parties can hold such real property separately.

Passing off—Process by which one corporation will attempt to pass its product off as being that of a well-advertised manufacturer by making its product similar in appearance.

Payee—An individual who is paid, or to whom an instrument is made payable.

Payor bank—Bank on which an instrument is drawn.

Per capita distribution—Distribution of property among a person's descendants whereby each descendant's share is determined pro rata based on the number of beneficiaries.

Per curiam—By the court (Latin). Generally refers to a short statement of decision by the whole court as distinguished from a decision with reasoning written by an individual judge.

Per se—By himself or itself (Latin). Term referring to something forbidden in and of itself because of its pernicious nature, with the court not allowing an argument for the reasonableness of conduct. For example, price fixing in the antitrust area is *per se* illegal.

Per stirpes—The distribution of property among a person's descendants whereby equal shares are granted to the first generation of beneficiaries. If a beneficiary predeceases the testator, the beneficiary's descendants must share his or her portion.

Perfection—Priority given a secured party on the collateral of his or her debtor by virtue of giving notice to all interested parties who may also have claims.

Perjury—The giving of willful false statements under oath in a court of law or in depositions material to such proceeding. One can also *perjure* oneself before legislative bodies.

Personal representative—Person named by the testator to look after and administer his or her estate after death.

Petitioner—Party that files an appeal with a higher court after losing in a lower court.

Plaintiff-in-error—Generally, a party who is appealing from a lower court decision which has gone against him or her.

Planned unit development—A form of zoning that allows various uses of a site in order to provide maximum land for open space.

Pledge—A delivery of personal property by a debtor to a creditor to be held for security until a debt is discharged. Often held as a bailment by a creditor.

Pledgee—Party to whom goods are pledged.

Pledgor—Party pledging goods.

Point of sale terminal—A machine that permits the transfer of funds from an individual's account directly into an account maintained by the business in payment for goods or services.

Possession—Dominion or control over property.

Power of attorney—Executed instrument authorizing an agent to represent the individual signing in a general manner or only with reference to a particular transaction or proceeding.

Precedent—A previous decision relied upon by a court for authority in making a current decision.

Prescription—Method of obtaining a right to use another's land through wrongful use for a period of time established by statute.

Prima facie—"At first sight" (Latin). Denoting a fact that appears true and will stand as such in the eyes of the court until contradicted.

Principal—In agency law an individual who delegates authority to an agent to represent him or her either generally or only for a specific transaction.

Privileged communication—Term used to denote the right of counsel to refuse disclosure of any communication between the attorney and his or her client to any individual or court of law.

Privity—A contractual relation between parties to a contract as opposed to those affected by the agreement but not parties to it.

Pro rata—"Proportionately, or by share" (Latin).

Probate—Legal process by which a will is proven valid and conflicting claims on the estate are settled. This process takes place in a *probate* court.

Procure—To initiate a proceeding.

Promisee—An individual who receives a promise.

Promisor—An individual who initiates and makes a promise to promisee.

Promissory estoppel—An equitable doctrine often used as a substitute when consideration is not present in a contract and a grave injustice will result if the agreement is not enforced. The doctrine will be specifically invoked when a promise is made by one party which induces justifiable reliance by the other and causes a change in position on the part of the injured party.

Promissory note—A written promise to pay a certain sum to order or bearer within a specific period or at a stated time.

Prospectus—1. A written document in which a corporation or its agents explain the purpose of the issuance of shares and invite people to subscribe. 2. Sometimes refers to an introductory proposal (not a legal offer) in the process of negotiating a contract.

Proximate cause—Used in tort law and negligence theory to denote the direct and natural sequence between the breach of a duty and the injury to an individual.

Proxy—Process by which a shareholder gives another the right to vote his or her stock.

Punitive damages—Those nonquantifiable damages that do not flow directly from a cause of action but are awarded by the court because of the willful and malicious nature of conduct of the defendant. The court sees such damages as a deterrent to future wrongful conduct.

Putative—Term used to denote an "alleged" or "reputed" father of a child in a paternity proceeding.

Qualified indorsement—Indorsement that eliminates the secondary liability of an indorser on the instrument.

Qualified privilege—In tort actions, an exemption for a speaker from liability on a charge of libel or slander unless the defendant can be shown to have had actual malice and knowledge of the falsity of the statement.

Quantum meruit—"As much as he deserved" (Latin). An old common law pleading requesting recovery for materials and services rendered.

Quasi contract—A court-imposed agreement designed to provide equitable relief when one party has received a benefit at the expense of the other. The court imposes a legal relationship on the parties even though all the elements of a contract are not present.

Quit claim deed—An instrument of conveyance of the grantor. It passes rights and interest in real property but does not warrant title.

Ratification—The process by which one adopts the terms of an agreement by silence or affirmative conduct. For example, a minor ratifies agreements made in his or her minority by continuous adherence to the terms for a reasonable

period after reaching legal majority.

Rebate—A discount or deduction. For example, a discount or rebate on a premium for insurance may be received for prompt payment.

Rebuttal—Introduction of evidence in a trial that attempts to show that a previous witness's testimony is not credible.

Recoupment—A holding back of an amount of money by a defendant that is owed plaintiff for damages. Defendant may argue that, although he or she breached, plaintiff also failed to comply with obligations arising out of the same agreement.

Regulation Z—A group of rules set forth by the Federal Reserve Board that requires lenders to disclose a number of items to borrowers.

Release—The giving up of a claim or right on the part of one party in exchange for some consideration.

Remainderman—An individual who obtains the remnant of an estate after an estate carved out of it has expired. For example, Blackacre to wife for life, remainder to son.

Remand—An action by an appellate court in sending a case back to a lower court (usually a trial court) with instructions as to action that should be taken.

Renunciation—In the law of negotiable instruments, the act of a holder in giving up all rights and claims against a party to an instrument by surrendering it, usually without consideration.

Replevin—Common law term referring to the legal process of obtaining, or taking back, of personal property that is in the hands of another.

Res—thing or object (Latin).

Res ipsa loquitur—The thing speaks for itself (Latin). Presumption in tort law that defendant is negligent because instrument was in sole control of him or her, and accident would not have happened but for defendant's negligence.

Res judicata—A thing decided (Latin). A legal doctrine that a decision by a court in a suit is final as to future suits on the same cause of action and between the same parties.

Rescission—A remedy in contract law that cancels or abrogates an agreement.

Respondent—An appellee or a person who usually has won a verdict in a lower court, and against whom an appeal is being taken.

Restatement of agency—A scholarly work prepared by the American Law Institute summarizing the law of agency; the model the authors recommend be followed for the future.

Restatement of contracts—A scholarly work prepared by the American Law Institute summarizing present contract law; the model the authors recommend be followed for the future.

Restitution—A remedy for breach of a contract in which the court seeks to restore both parties to their original position following rescission of the agreement.

Restrictive indorsement—Indorsement that is conditional, or purports to prohibit the further transfer of the instrument, or includes words that signify a purpose of deposit or collection, or otherwise states that it is for the benefit or use of the indorsee or another person.

Reversion—The returning of an estate left to a grantor after the termination of an estate granted by him or her to another individual.

Revocation—Recall of an offer by an offeror prior to acceptance by offeree.

Riparian—Pertaining to land adjacent to a flowing stream or waterway.

Rule making—A function of most federal agencies; allows interested parties to comment on proposed binding rules prior to their enactment.

Satisfaction—Discharge of a debt by payment in full or in part, with agreement of the parties.

Scienter—"Knowingly" (Latin). Generally refers to need for knowledge as an essential element in a tort action for deceit or fraud.

Seasonable—Generally used to denote a reasonable period of time.

Security interest—A pledge by debtor of property or other matters of value, to make his or her promise of payment under a contract enforceable by creditor in the event of a breach.

Sequestration—1. Process in equity by which a defendant's personal and real property is taken into custody by the court when he or she is in contempt. 2. Process by which a jury is isolated from the outside world during a trial to prevent bias entering into their decision.

Set-off—Cross complaint by a defendant not directly related to the cause of action (usually a breach of contract situation) but related to the general subject matter being litigated.

Severable—Capable of being divided and existing independently. For example, a severable contract is one that can be enforced in part, since performance can be divided and apportioned.

Signature—In commercial paper, any symbol on an instrument executed or adopted by the party signing the instrument with the intent to authenticate the writing.

Sinking fund—Separate fund in which revenues are accumulated by a corporation or government entity to be used at intervals for the buying back of securities and the extinguishment of debt.

Situs—Situation or location (Latin). Generally, the location of a thing in terms of a court's jurisdiction over it. For example, the *situs* of land will be the county it is located in.

Special indorsement—An indorsement that specifies the person to whom or to whose order the instrument is payable.

Stale check—An uncertified check that is presented for payment more than six months after date of issue.

Stare decisis—A legal doctrine stating that decisions of a court should serve as precedent for future legal actions dealing with similar factual situations and points of law.

Stated capital—Revenues received by a corporation upon a stock issuance minus that assigned to capital surplus.

Statute of frauds—State laws that require certain forms of contracts to be in writing. For example, a promise in consideration of marriage in some states is required to be in writing.

Stay order—A court judgment that prevents a lower court order from being enforced pending an appeal by one of the parties.

Stop payment order—Order by a customer to the drawee not to pay a check when it is presented for payment.

Subpoena—Process by which a court orders an individual to appear and testify at a time stated.

Subpoena duces tecum—Process by which, at the request of a party to a suit, the court orders a witness to appear with a relevant document in his or her possession.

Substantial performance—In contract law, the term indicates that all material terms of an agreement have been met, and only insignificant matters remain.

Substantive—Pertaining to essential or basic law that sets out rights. Procedural law is concerned with the legal procedures necessary to obtain these rights in courts or administrative agencies.

Sui generis—One of a kind (Latin).

Supra—Above (Latin). Term refers the reader to a previous part of a book.

Surety—An individual who is originally bound on a debtor-creditor contract to assume primary liability for his or her principal (debtor) in case of a failure of the latter to perform.

Tacking—Adding periods of wrongful occupancy of real property to meet the statutory period necessary to establish title by adverse possession.

Takeover—Process by which an individual or a corporation seeks to obtain control of the management of a corporation by purchasing controlling shares of the stock.

Tenants in common—Method of holding title to property in which each person owns a certain amount of the property; on the death of one of the parties, that person's property goes to his or her heirs, not to the other tenant.

Tenants in the entirety—Joint tenants who are spouses and who provide that the survivor of them will automatically become the owner of the property held as joint tenants.

Tender—An offer to pay a sum of money without conditions attached.

Testamentary trust—A trust created by a person's will; comes into effect only on that person's death.

Testator—An individual who has died leaving a will.

Tipper—A person who receives inside information about a company not available to the average prudent investor and passes such on to another (tippee) who benefits by buying or selling shares based on this information.

Tort-feasor—In law of torts, a wrong-doer, or one guilty of a tort.

Trade acceptance—Time draft drawn by a seller naming the seller as payee and the purchaser of goods as drawee; obligates the buyer to pay the draft upon acceptance of the goods.

Trade fixtures—Articles a tenant attaches to land or buildings to be used in the tenant's trade or business.

Transferability—An instrument's assignability or negotiability.

Transferee—An individual to whom a transfer is made.

Transferor—A person who initiates or makes a transfer.

Treasury shares—Generally refers to stock issued by a corporation to shareholders and subsequently acquired by the issuing corporation.

Treble damages—Refers to triple the amount of damages awarded by a jury. The purpose of such is to discourage similar conduct in the future. Such statutory damages are usually awarded by the court on motion of the plaintiff following a jury award.

Trespass—Unlawful violation of another's person or property.

Trover—An action for damages against an individual who has unlawfully converted personal property of another.

Trust—1. An interest or right in real or personal property by one party for the benefit of another. 2. In

antitrust law an unlawful combination seeking to do an act in contravention of federal or state statute.

Trustee in bankruptcy—Individual who holds title to a bankrupt's property at the direction of the court. His or her function is to defend all assets in suits and to provide an accounting to the court of moneys for distribution to creditors.

Tying agreements—In antitrust law, a refusal by a manufacturer to sell a primary product (tying) unless the retailer or franchisee agrees to buy a secondary product (tied).

Ultra vires—"Beyond its power" (Latin). Pertaining to a corporation's acting beyond the scope of the power set out in its charter or articles of incorporation.

Unconscionable—Denoting a contract that is grossly unfair and shocking to the conscience. For example, the use of small print and technical language in a contract for necessaries with poor, illiterate people while charging prices that are far above normal market prices. The court will generally not enforce such agreement and will order a rescission.

Underwriter—Usually, a firm that markets securities for a corporate registrant. It sells corporate securities as an agent and receives a commission for such work.

Undue influence—Pressure exerted on an individual to sign an agreement. Generally it refers to the misuse of a position of confidential communication (e.g., doctor-patient) to influence an individual.

Unilateral—Pertaining to one side, or to only one party. For example, a *unilateral* mistake by a party to a contract is a misunderstanding of the terms of an agreement by one party but not the other.

Unliquidated debt—A debt the exact amount of which cannot be determined by the terms of the obligation.

Usage of trade—Well-known manner of conducting transactions in a particular industry or trade.

Usury—The loan of money at an in-

terest rate in excess of that allowed by law.

Valid—Containing all the elements of a contract and is thus operative at law.

Vendee—A purchaser of property.

Vendor—A seller of property.

Venue—County or other jurisdiction in which a complaint is made in civil litigation and prosecution takes place in criminal action.

Vest—To give an immediate fixed right of possession in an estate of real property.

Vicarious liability—Indirect liability. Used in agency law to describe a principal's liability to third party for the acts of an agent.

Void—Having no legal force in the eyes of the law at its inception. A *void* agreement can never be cured of its defect and will always be inoperative.

Voidable—Pertaining to an agreement that becomes inoperative when the parties treat it as effective and binding.

Waive—To relinquish intentionally a legal right that could be exercised.

Warehouse receipt—A receipt, issued by a warehouse supervisor, that enables the person in possession of it to pick up goods from the warehouse.

Warranty—An undertaking by a seller to guarantee a product against defects. The scope of such warranty as to goods is usually set out in writing. Implied warranties are those established from the nature of goods and their intended purpose.

Warranty deed—Deed that conveys title and warrants that the seller's title to the real estate is marketable.

Watered stock—Issued stock that is represented as fully paid but in fact is not paid up.

Whistle blowing—Reporting the wrongdoing of another person to someone in authority; a type of ethical problem that places one person in a position of telling his or her supervisors that the actions of someone else are illegal, wrongful or unethical.

Will—Written declaration stating its maker's desires as to the disposition of his or her property or estate after death.

Workable competition—Term used to denote industrial organization economists' yardstick for measuring the effect a merger will have on an industry's competitive framework. Conduct, structure and performance criteria are used to judge the effectiveness of competition in a market.

Writ of certiorari—Petition for review. Used to refer to the request made by an appellant to an appeals court to hear a case. The court will decide whether to grant or deny the *writ of certiorari*.

Subject Index

Case
Index

Italic type indicates cases that are excerpted in the text; roman type indicates cases otherwise cited.

1180

About the Authors

Thomas W. Dunfee is the Joseph Kolodny Professor of Social Responsibility at the Wharton School, University of Pennsylvania. He received the J.D. degree in 1966 and the LL.M. in 1969 from the New York University School of Law. He is Chairman of the Department of Legal Studies and also has an appointment in marketing at the Wharton School. He has served as Editor-in-Chief of *The American Business Law Journal* for three years. He is the author of many books on the subject of business law and has published widely in academic journals, including *The Northwestern Law Review* and *The American Business Law Journal.* He also has wide experience acting as consultant to corporations, government agencies, and trade associations.

Frank F. Gibson is a Professor of Business Law and Legal Environment in the College of Administrative Science of The Ohio State University, where he has taught since 1966. He also serves as Associate Director of the Center for Real Estate Education and Research. He was formerly Editor-in-Chief of *The American Business Law Journal,* and currently serves as Secretary-Treasurer of the American Business Law Association.

John D. Blackburn is an Associate Professor of business law at The Ohio State University. He received his B.S. degree from Indiana University and his J.D. degree from The University of Cincinnati. He has served on the faculties of The University of Cincinnati, Indiana State University, and The Wharton School, University of Pennsylvania. He has published articles and books in the field of labor law, including *The Legal Environment of Business; and Labor Relations: Law, Practice, and Policy.*

Douglas Whitman is an Associate Professor at the School of Business Administration of the University of Kansas. He received his B.A. from Knox College, his M.B.A. from the University of Kansas, J.D. from the University of Missouri, and LL.M. from the University of Missouri. He has written articles on advertising law and products liability, and has published in *St. John's Law Review; Southwestern Law Journal* (at Southern Methodist Law School); *The University of California, Davis Law Review; The University of Pittsburgh Law Review Journal of Product Liability;* and *American Business Law Journal.* His articles have also been reprinted in *The Advertising Law Anthology, The Personal Injury Desk Book, The Corporate Counsel's Annual,* and by The American Trial Lawyer's Association. He has also written articles for the Advertising Compliance Service.

F. William McCarty is Professor in the Department of Finance and Commercial Law at Western Michigan University. A specialist in international business law, administrative law, and estate planning, Professor McCarty received his J.D. degree from the University of Michigan. He is the author of numerous articles and books, including *Modern Business Law: Contracts, Modern Business Law: Legal Environment,* and *Legal Environment: An Introduction to the American Legal Environment.*

Bartley A. Brennan is a graduate of the School of Foreign Service, Georgetown University (B.S., International Economics) and The College of Law, State University of New York at Buffalo (J.D.). He was a Volunteer in the United States Peace Corps, was employed by the Office of Opinions and Review of the Federal Communications Commission, and worked in the General Counsel's office of a private corporation. He has received appointments as a visiting Associate Professor, The Wharton School, The University of Pennsylvania, and as a Research Fellow, Ethics Resource Center, Washington, D.C. He is author of articles dealing with government regulation.